MARKETING management

TEXT AND CASES

MARKETING management
TEXT AND CASES

SHH KAZMI

EXCEL BOOKS

ISBN: 81-7446-542-1

First Edition: New Delhi, 2007

EXCEL BOOKS
A-45, Naraina, Phase I,
New Delhi - 110 028

Published by Anurag Jain for Excel Books, A-45, Naraina, Phase-I, New Delhi -110 028
and printed by him at Excel Printers, C-206, Naraina, Phase-I, New Delhi -110 028

Dedicated to

My Wife Roshan Akhtar

and

Son, Sufee

BRIEF CONTENTS

DETAILED CONTENTS

PREFACE

Man as a negotiator has been a marketer of sorts from time immemorial. Marketing, therefore, has continued to be an evolving and a dynamic discipline. Consequently marketing *mantras* have also been changing from product-centric to customer-centric, and from customer satisfaction to customer delight. The three Cs – viz. control, convenience, and choice, are replacing the popular four Ps – product, price, placement, and promotion gradually.

Markets are said to be the basis of economic health of a country, and marketers in many ways help make markets more efficient and effective. Marketers are acquiring information and understanding of customers on an ongoing basis and have been a major driving force in making an ever increasing number of products and services available at lower prices that more effectively and efficiently satisfy consumer needs and wants. All this makes marketing not only relevant but also quite an exciting subject of study.

All students pursuing their MBA or PGDM programmes in management institutions have to study marketing as a core subject. Many highly acclaimed textbooks on the subject are available in our country. Within the last two decades, many Indian authors have written texts on the subject and many more are writing to meet the long-felt and increasing demand of Indian students looking for marketing texts with nearer home examples.

The present text has depth and relevance and is aimed at meeting the needs of students, thanks to its easy-to-read text. Most of the examples relate to Indian businesses. A few examples from other countries have also been included keeping in view the present context of open borders for multinational companies and rapid changes in marketing practices.

The subject of marketing cannot be neatly divided into watertight compartments. In the real world of marketing, it is not difficult to appreciate that even a subtle change in one aspect often precipitates visible consequences in other aspects. As such, the book has been divided in eight parts in order to provide a structure approach. These parts have been further divided into twenty-six chapters. At the end of each part, there are quite a few case studies. In all, there are forty-two cases. This not only provides a wide choice of cases suitable for discussion, but also furnishes detailed examples of business situations from a variety of industries. All the cases portray real life business situations and offer deep insight into the game of marketing warfare.

Over the years, as a teacher of marketing (core paper) and some specialisation courses in marketing, I have observed a wide range of student responses concerning what they want from a good text on marketing, including a rather strange response of a few students complaining that some texts to which they are asked to refer, are too voluminous and exhaustive—something that puts them off. This is totally contrary to my belief. I doubt if any meaningful text on marketing can be significantly condensed in just a few pages to meet the requirements of MBA students.

Much effort has been made to make the text student-friendly, easy-to-read and comprehend, and relevant to student needs in India and other neighbouring countries.

S. H. H. KAZMI

ACKNOWLEDGEMENTS

Over the years, I have found my students to be an interesting lot and a source of silent inspiration. I am indeed indebted to them for unintentionally providing both insight and inputs through their probing questions during classroom discussions.

I am also very grateful to all the authors both Indian and foreign of various texts and articles, who have been of great help; their impact can be read between the lines throughout the book. I admit it is difficult to mention their names individually, considering their number. Every effort has been made to trace the copyright holders but if any have been inadvertently overlooked, I will be pleased to make the necessary acknowledgements at the first opportunity.

A large number of my friends and colleagues in the teaching fraternity extended their help in the form of criticism, ideas, suggestions, and references. Dr. Satish K. Batra and Prof. Arvinder Singh deserve special mention for their considerable help with this book. Ashish and his wife Amita, helped me with access to articles and library resources in USA. I am lucky to have had access to the libraries of Bhavan's College of Communication and Management, Poddar Institute of Management, and ICFAI University, Jaipur for books and magazines. I would like to convey my gratitude to USP Age, Brand Reporter, and A & M.

Last but not least, I am particularly grateful to my wife Dr. R.A Kazmi, who despite her busy schedule at the University, kept me properly fed and always encouraged and took very good care of me. During all this period, I missed my son Sufee Kazmi, now studying abroad, who always solved my computer related problems.

My publishers, Excel Books deserve credit and are greatly responsible for motivating me to write this text. Without their consistent encouragement, this book would not have been possible. My special thanks to Mr. Anurag Jain, Publisher, Excel Books, Mr. Rajan Wadhwa, Ms.Sandhya, and other staff members, for their timely support and constructive suggestions.

ABOUT THE AUTHOR

S. H. H. Kazmi has worked in industry for nearly twenty-six years. He completed a three-year course in management from R. A. Poddar Institute of Management. For the last more than fifteen years, he has been associated as visiting faculty with a number of management institutions, including Bhavan's College of Communication and Management, Banasthali Vidyapith (Deemed University), Malviya National Institute of Technology, ICFAI, and Poddar Institute of Management. His areas of interest are marketing, advertising and sales promotion, and consumer behaviour. Earlier, he has written two books in collaboration with Dr. Satish K. Batra – 'Advertising and Sales Promotion' (now in its 3rd edition) and 'Consumer Behaviour' both published by Excel Books. His books are widely used in top business schools including the IIM's as core textbooks.

PART 1

Introduction to Marketing

CHAPTER 1

LEARNING OBJECTIVES

After going through this chapter, you will understand:

- Marketing definitions
- The difference between needs, wants, and demands
- The relevance of exchange
- Meaning of customer value and its impact on customer satisfaction
- Different marketing philosophies and marketing concepts
- The concept and importance of marketing mix variables

rocter & Gamble, the word's third largest beauty-care provider, has developed a technology to customise cosmetics and hair-care products to the needs and preferences of every individual woman who shops on the Internet.

And this is not about 'packed just for you' markings and other such 'personalised' gimmicks. This is a genuine attempt at 'mass customisation'. At one time, there were two big reasons behind large-scale production of products. One, a benefit: it allowed assembly line production, which increased volumes and lowered costs dramatically. Two, a constraint: It was impossible to capture perfect market information, person by person, of more than a handful of people.

The Internet has eased this constraint. When it comes to production method, however, there is no going back from the assembly line system. But if factory machines are computerised and connected to the same network that captures market information, it's possible to quasi-customise large volumes of the products without a significant drop in efficiency, or jump in production cost.

The point is, 'mass customisation' is neither an oxymoron nor a gimmicky term.

P&G's idea is to operate on full consumer information. This means that if a certain Kajol Mukherjee needs a uniquely constituted blush-on that both adds value to her smile and doesn't react on her skin, P&G would like to know about it. The general idea is to provide products so personalised that no two individuals would be found using the same regimen ('solution', 'prescription', whatever).

P&G has already created a prototype website for its new venture. It is called, appropriately, www.reflect.com.

P&G is a company that has always been known for its sincere attention to planning. Contrary to appearances, the Internet strategy evolved over quite some time – after due deliberation, which involved gruelling sessions with successful entrepreneurs and executives about their secrets of Internet success.

What was obvious to P&G was that the Net venture could not simply be an arm of the old business. It certainly couldn't succeed if treated like just another sales window or phone-in message cell. Or, even a TV shopping channel.

All those multitude layers of command-and-control management would do it no good either, and what was clearly required was a flat culture – one where ideas are bounced around and innovation is a daily affair.

Will it work? Depends on just how much extra the business gains by way of customer knowledge. The website has begun an interactive-question-and-answer process to capture consumer information.

(Source: A & M, October 15, 1999.)

The change by itself in the business and marketing scenario today is nothing new to the world, to be looked at as a cause of alarm. There have always been changes in every area of global societies. Some changes occur slowly and are almost unnoticeable in everyday life, while some others are so rapid that the affected parties face a lot of difficulty in adjusting to them in the short-run. Most of all, businesses have a powerful tendency to welcome and embrace changes in the market place. It is the change that throws up new opportunities and inspires businesses to take fresh paths –a welcome feature for marketers.

With the opening up of the Indian economy, we are beginning to taste the fruits of globalisation. As already stated above, the phenomenon of change is nothing new. Everything changes with the passage of time. There is a saying, "whatever fails to change, fails to survive." Therefore, with the opening up of our economy, and with globalisation as the reality, the marketing scenario in India has changed rapidly and businesses are becoming increasingly proactive in anticipating rapidly occurring changes in the larger environment. The most significant element that has influenced the vast global changes is the rapid advance in the fields of science and technology. Developments in the field of electronics, computer technology, and telecommunications are nothing if not stupendous. With messages being transmitted almost at the speed of light, the Internet has shrunk time and distance. These developments have led to the availability of high-tech products, higher product quality, shorter product life cycles, intensified competition, and businesses that are not in step with these changes are hard put to survive.

The scope of private sector in India has been broadened and out of the 17 reserved industries for public sector, nearly 75% have been handed over to the private sector. Foreign Direct Investment (FDI) in many sectors is open and is likely to be extended in other sectors gradually. The Indian businesses will be exposed increasingly to technological advances, globalisation, and deregulations. All these factors will affect the business prospects and practices of the individual companies and the life of individuals.

The advantage of technological superiority is disappearing fast and companies introducing superior products get very little time to enjoy this advantage before other competitors achieve parity or introduce even better products. Business Process Outsourcing (BPO) is wiping out the cost advantage due to the availability of cheap domestic labour for many Indian companies against their foreign competitors.

The digital developments have put at the disposal of consumers and marketers some important capabilities. Customers can quickly compare the features and prices of almost all the competing brands sitting in their homes and connected with Internet. Some sites, such as Priceline.com allow customers to specify the price they wish to pay for airline tickets, or hotel accommodation and find out if there are any willing sellers.

A customer can order almost anything in developed economies and some of the Indian companies too, have started accepting orders and payments online. Indian Railways have started the facility of ticket reservation online (IRCTC.co.in). Many online stores such as Amazon.com, Fabmart.com, and firstandsecond.com sell books and a large number of other items online.

The Internet has opened the doors to unlimited information about practically anything. This information can be accessed from anywhere in the world. An individual with an Internet connection can access online newspapers, dictionaries, encyclopaedias, medical information, business magazines, and any other information from countless information sources around the world.

Customers can access chat rooms according to their area of interest and can freely exchange bundles of information, evaluation, and opinions. An important feature of all these aspects discussed in these paragraphs is that these facilities are available seven days a week, eliminating any waiting time.

The management thinking and practices in India have undergone a desirable change and businesses are intelligently adjusting and changing their business practices and strategies to suit the current and emerging set of business needs and requirements according to the times.

Marketing practices have evolved gradually over an extremely long period of time. In the sense that marketing is defined, it has been around since ancient times. In those earliest days, human beings learned to exchange things they needed with others. It can be assumed that the outcome of such exchanges was satisfying for concerned parties. Marketing as a discipline of study is relatively quite new. However, the purpose of exchanges then and now is the same – to satisfy needs and wants.

Pre-industrial era economy was based on agriculture and handicrafts everywhere in the world. There was no need to have any elaborate systems of distribution because whatever was produced through agriculture or crafted by artisans would have been conceivably very meagre compared to modern standards and whatever surplus was produced was consumed within very limited neighbourhood areas. Before the money economy, barter was the only means to affect exchanges in which both parties were buyers and sellers at the same time. Not that there is no barter any longer, barter is still practiced, sometimes even between nations.

For example, a country might offer food products in exchange for petroleum crude or mineral ores. Or, there might be student exchange programmes and neither party makes any monetary payments.

One may imagine situations when someone needed something but had a product that was not needed by the other party. Perhaps, this situation stimulated the more imaginative persons to think of some common medium of exchange. In any case, the next major development after barter was introduction of money economy. The Greeks are known to be the first to use metal coins as a common medium of exchange. Everybody was comfortable because money could buy almost all the products and services that were needed, provided the producers made them available.

Market: A market can be viewed as any person, group, or organisation with which an individual, group, or organisation has an existing or potential exchange relationship. We can distinguish four broad markets:

1. Consumer markets.
2. Business markets.
3. Global or international markets.
4. Non-profit and governmental markets.

Defining Marketing

Marketing starts with customers and ends with customers. Creation of superior customer value and delivering high levels of customer satisfaction are at the heart of present day marketing. It is a matter of common sense to appreciate the key marketing success factors. In case a company really endeavours to understand customer needs, carefully studies competition, develops and offers superior value at a reasonable price, makes these products available at places convenient to customers, and communicates with them effectively and efficiently, such products have every reason to be in demand and will sell consistently.

Successful companies have one common trait. They are all very strongly customer-focused in their orientation. Many other factors contribute to achieving business success, such as developing great strategy, committed and skilled human resources, reliable and fast information systems, and excellent implementation and control. But in the final analysis, the focus and dedication of all these companies is to really understand customers' needs and wants as much as possible and create satisfied customers in their target markets.

In case someone asks several people what they think marketing is, the chances are these casually picked persons will reveal a variety of descriptions in their responses. Probably, the first two items describing marketing will be advertising and personal selling, as these two are the most visible aspects of marketing for most people. Marketing includes many more activities than what most people realise. The shortest definition of marketing is satisfying consumer needs in a socially responsible way at a profit. Authors of marketing books have defined marketing in different words. A few of these definitions are mentioned here.

The American Marketing Association defines marketing as:

"Marketing is an organisational function and a set of processes for creating, communicating, and delivering value to customers and for managing customer relationships in ways that benefit the organisation and its stakeholders."

Philip Kotler says, *"Marketing is a societal process by which individuals and groups obtain what they need and want through creating, offering, and freely exchanging products and services of value with others."*

Pride and Ferrel's definition says,

"We define marketing as the process of creating, distributing, promoting, and pricing goods, services, and ideas to facilitate exchange relationships in a dynamic environment."

"Marketing is a total system of business activities designed to plan, price, promote, and distribute want-satisfying products to target markets to achieve organisational objectives."

(William J. Stanton, Michael J. Etzel, and Bruce J. Walker, Fundamentals of Marketing, McGraw-Hill, 1994.)

"It (marketing) is the whole business seen from the point of view of its final result, that is, from the customer's point of view." (Peter F. Drucker, *Practice of Management* (1954).

The essence of all these definitions of marketing is satisfying customer needs and wants. Apparently, this core objective sounds simple, but it is not. Research shows that in many cases customers either have inhibitions about revealing their real needs or wants by intent or may not really know themselves. It is believed that the subconscious is the real storehouse of deep-rooted motives. To the extent possible, marketers undertake consumer research and try to learn about the target customers' needs and wants, and design appropriate marketing programmes to satisfy target customers.

Keeping in view the definitions of marketing, some important aspects of modern marketing can be distinguished:

1. Marketing is a societal process.
2. Marketing deals with customer needs, wants, products, pricing, distribution, and promotion.
3. Marketing focuses on delivering value and satisfaction to customers through products, services, ideas, etc.
4. Marketing facilitates satisfying exchange relationships.
5. Marketing takes place in a dynamic environment.
6. Marketing is used in both for-profit and not-for-profit organisations.
7. Marketing is extremely important to businesses and the economy of a country.

Needs, Wants, and Demand

The very existence of human beings spells the presence of needs, and marketing thinking starts with this very important realisation. It is wrong to believe that anyone can invent needs. Needs are part of the basic fabric of human life. *A need can be defined as a felt state of deprivation of some basic satisfaction.* This means that unless the individual feels deprived of some basic satisfaction, at least for this individual, the need does not exist. Humans have a long list of needs, some very basic and others complex. The basic needs are **physiological** or **biogenic** in nature, and individuals are born with them. These needs are essential to sustaining human life such as need for air, water, food, shelter, clothing, and sex. These basic needs are also referred to as **primary needs**. Other types of needs are those that individuals learn as a result of being brought up in a culture and society such as need to belong, acquire knowledge, self-expression, self-esteem, prestige, power, achievement, etc. These are considered as **secondary needs**, also called **acquired needs** and generally believed to be the result of an individual's subjective psychological make up and relationship with others.

To differentiate between need and want, let us assume four individuals are hungry; their need is food. Assuming they have the resources to get involved in acquiring food to satisfy hunger, they go to McDonald's.

One orders a vegetable burger; the second orders a puff, the third asks for a chicken burger, and the fourth buys a huge ice cream. All of them are eating some variation of food to satisfy hunger. *The specific satisfier that an individual looks for defines the want.* Therefore, wants are specific satisfiers of some needs. Individual wants are shaped by culture, life style, and personality. For example, an individual buys a Mercedes as a status symbol and a tribal chief in some remote area of Amazon rain forests sticks an eagle feather in his headgear as status symbol.

To satisfy any given need, different people may express a variety of wants and the total number of wants for all sorts of needs is apparently unlimited. Just because people have needs and wants is not enough to affect exchanges. The resources to acquire the products are limited for every individual and hence people want to buy products that they believe will provide the maximum value and satisfaction for their money. When the want is backed by purchasing power, it is called the **demand** and marketers are particularly interested in demand rather than just needs or wants. Marketing aims at identifying human and social needs and endeavours to satisfy them by creating, communicating, and delivering products and services. According to Kotler, marketers are involved in marketing 10 different entities: tangible products, services, events, information, ideas, places, persons, experiences, properties, and organisations to accomplish the objective of delivering satisfaction to customers.

People buy products only because these are seen as means to satisfy certain needs or wants. The concept of product is broad in its meaning and includes everything that is capable of satisfying a need and can be a physical product, service, idea, person, place, or organisation. Marketers make a sensible distinction between goods and services to place them in right perspective. Physical products are tangible and services are intangible. People acquire products or buy the services not so much for the sake of being the owner or consumer, but to derive the benefits they provide. Who would buy food just to look at it? No one presumably would buy a refrigerator to just own it but for the reason that it provides the benefit of protecting the food from becoming stale and keeping it fresh. A large family with more resources will probably buy a bigger two-door refrigerator, while a nuclear two or three member family with lesser resources may perhaps want a smaller capacity refrigerator.

The Concept of Exchange

The concept of exchange is the essence and central to marketing thinking. Unless there is actual or potential exchange, there is no marketing. People can acquire what they need or want by pursuing socially acceptable behaviours or the behaviours not approved by the society. Two socially acceptable approaches of acquiring things include self-producing or exchanging what a person needs or wants. The third method, begging is viewed in some societies as a somewhat less than dignified way of acquiring things. The fourth approach may include behaviours such as shoplifting, burglary, or using potentially threatening force, etc., to acquire things, and these means are totally unacceptable by all civilised societies and punishable by law. The highly regarded way to acquire what a person needs or wants is the concept of exchange in marketing context. Both parties in an exchange offer something of value, and freely acceptable to each other. It is understandable that parties involved in an exchange must first agree to terms and conditions laid-down by each party so that actual exchange takes place.

FIGURE 1.1

The Concept of Exchange

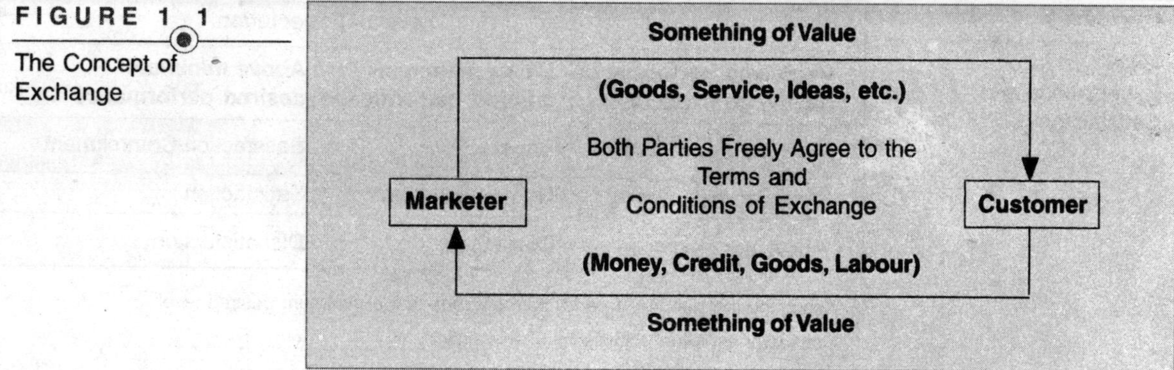

Customer Value and Satisfaction

In developed and developing economies, consumers have several products or brands to choose from to satisfy a given need or a group of needs. Much depends on what consumers' perceptions are about the value that different products or services are expected to deliver. The sources that build customer expectations include experience with products, friends, family members, neighbours, associates, consumer reports, and marketing communications. Customer value is the ratio of perceived benefits and costs that the customer has to incur in acquiring that product or service. The emphasis here is on customers' perceptions and not the accurate, objective evaluation of value and costs, as customers often do not judge values and costs accurately. **Value** indicates that a certain product or service is perceived as having the kinds and amounts of benefits (economic, functional, and emotional) that customers expect from that product or service at a certain cost (monetary costs, time costs, psychic, and energy costs). Thus, value is primarily determined by a combination of quality, service, and cost. The value to the customer can be made favourable either by increasing the total benefits at the same cost, maintaining the same benefit level and decreasing the cost, or increasing both the benefits and the costs, but the proportion of benefits is higher than the increase in costs.

FIGURE 1.2

Satisfaction Depends on Customer's Perceived Total Costs and Value

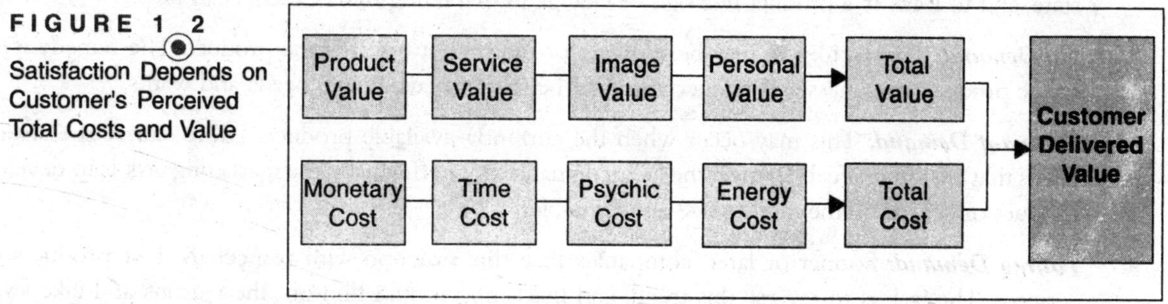

Customers generally experience satisfaction when the performance level meets or exceeds the minimum performance expectation levels. Similarly, when the performance level far exceeds the desired performance level, the customer will not only be satisfied but will also most likely be delighted. Therefore, rewarding experience with a given product or service encourages customers to repeat the same behaviour in future (buying the same brand). A delighted customer is likely to be committed and enthusiastic about a particular brand is usually unlikely to be influenced by a competitor's actions and is an asset to the marketer, being inclined to spread favourable word-of-mouth information or opinions. When a customer's perceived performance level is below expectations, it definitely causes dissatisfaction and the brand (product or service) will probably not be purchased on any future occasion. In extreme cases of dissatisfaction, the customer might even completely abandon the company and bad-mouth its products or services, a process over which a marketer has no control. In the true sense, marketing starts with the customer and ends with customer.

FIGURE 1.3

Relationship of Expectations and Satisfaction

Perceived performance relative to expectation	Level of Expectation: Below minimum desired performance	Level of Expectation: Above minimum desired performance
More than expected	Satisfaction*	Satisfaction/Commitment
Same as expected	Non-satisfaction**	Satisfaction
Worse than expected	Dissatisfaction	Dissatisfaction

* Assuming the perceived performance exceeds the minimum desired level.
** Consumer is neither satisfied nor dissatisfied.

The key to inducing brand **loyalty** among customers can only be achieved by delivering higher value to delight customers than competitors. Satisfaction is basically a feeling of pleasure, and marketers should be aware of satisfaction delivered by competitors and try surpass that level in an attempt to delight customers. Delivering higher value can lead to delighting customers which, in turn, seems to be the key factor in developing loyalty, more so if the brand generates emotional bonding. This emotional bonding is not just a preference based on rational content but is largely feeling based.

Marketing Tasks

In a nutshell, marketing is demand management and the demand for products and services often requires different approaches for a variety of reasons. There may also be other situations where demand management would require different types of handling. For example, demand for hotel accommodation at Mussoorie declines during a severe winter. Philip Kotler and Sidney J. Levy identified eight major demand states in two different articles:

1. ***Negative Demand:*** This situation is faced when a major part of the target market dislikes the product and may even pay a price to avoid it. The marketing task is to unearth and analyse the reasons for this state, and to learn if a product redesign or change in marketing mix elements can help.
2. ***No Demand:*** The customers may be unaware or indifferent towards the product. The remedy is to create product awareness and connect product benefits to customers' needs and wants.
3. ***Dormant Demand:*** This may occur when the currently available products fail to satisfy the strong needs that customers feel. To meet the latent demand more effectively, the marketing task is to develop product or service if the market size is favourable.
4. ***Falling Demand:*** Sooner or later, companies face this situation with respect to their products or services. The task is to reverse this trend, and marketing should find out the reasons and take swift remedial action. New markets, product feature modification, or more focused and effective promotion may hold the solution.
5. ***Fluctuating Demand:*** Many companies experience this pattern, the demand varying according to the season, or festivals, etc. The task is to synchronise marketing efforts to alter the demand pattern by adopting flexible pricing, and sales promotion techniques.
6. ***Full Demand:*** This is a situation all companies aspire and work for. The task is to maintain the level of demand and keep pace with the changing customer preferences and ever increasing competition and monitor customer satisfaction.
7. ***Excess Demand:*** At this demand level, the company is unable to meet the demand level. The only option usually available is to find ways to decrease demand temporarily or permanently. Generally,

marketing seeks to discourage overall demand through demarketing, either by increasing prices or reducing promotion and services. Selective demarketing involves reducing demand from those markets that are less profitable.

8. ***Unwholesome Demand:*** This concerns managing demand for harmful products. The marketing task is to make the public aware about the dangers and harmful effects caused through misuse or over use of such products by using appropriate degree of fear appeals, price hike, or reduced availability.

EVOLUTION OF MARKETING CONCEPT

Since the later part of the 19th century, marketing has gradually evolved through various marketing orientations. These stages in marketing evolution present a generalised picture and a sufficiently significant number of companies have adopted the most modern marketing concept or philosophy.

The Production Concept

This concept, viewed as one of the oldest of managerial orientations, typically aimed at achieving as high an output as possible. This philosophy assumed that customers would be more interested in acquiring conveniently available, reasonably priced, and well-made products. Keeping in view the market behaviour prevailing in times when customers did not have much choice, it was a sound approach. The focus of managers, generally having backgrounds in manufacturing and engineering, was to concentrate on achieving increasingly higher efficiency in production, lower production costs, and more intensive distribution. Even today, this approach seems to be quite sensible in relatively underdeveloped and developing economies because customers are more interested in owning a product and not overly concerned about finer features and aesthetic appeal. In general, one important condition seems to be favourable to adopt production orientation: when the masses look for a cheaper product and demand far exceeds production. In India, The National Textile Corporation (NTC) and all its subsidiaries are sticking to this philosophy while producing textiles for the huge, poverty-stricken population in this country. Their philosophy and positioning is reflected in their ad, "Clothiers of the nation with affordable prices." In the global scenario, for nearly three decades Intel Corporation focused on achieving increasingly high production output of its successive generations of processors so as to bring down the prices of each improved version. The production concept is unlikely to get discarded for a very long time to come, because there would always be products and populations of such a nature that some companies would feel comfortable with this philosophy.

The Selling Concept

Sales concept seems to be based on a lurking apprehension that customers will not buy the product in sufficient quantities unless aggressively pressurised. The selling concept was the major means of increasing sales and profits during 1920s to 1950s in the developed countries of that period. Companies believed that the most important marketing activities were personal selling, advertising, and distribution. Selling concept is geared towards converting existing product(s) into cash rather than first finding and then satisfying customer needs. Sales concept is often observed in practice when companies show heavy reliance on their promotional capabilities based on "hard sell" approach. It is obvious that if a company's products do not match the changing tastes and requirements of customers, with many alternative choices available, managers might be inclined to go for aggressive promotional efforts to sell enough quantities. In his book, *The End of Marketing as We Know It*, Sergio Zyman writes that the purpose of marketing is to sell more stuff to more people more often for more money in order to make more profit. Of late, this has been happening in case of some Credit Cards in our country. Generally, "hard sell" is often seen in case of products or services that people buy without giving much thought to the matter, such as non-essential goods, and tend to postpone such purchases. With ever intensifying competition, products becoming more standardised without any meaningful differentiation i.e., commoditization, heavy promotional efforts in all possible manners are bound to remain the practice, in order to grab more share of the customers' purse. The consequences of "hard sell" might harm the customer base to the extent that, in some cases, they might even bad-mouth the product if the product fails to match up to their expectations.

The Marketing Concept

After World War II, the variety of products increased, people had more discretionary income, and could afford to be selective and buy only those products that more precisely met their changing needs and wants. However, these needs were not immediately obvious. Sometime during the mid-1950s, there was growing recognition among American business people that merely efficient production and extensive promotion, including hard selling, did not guarantee that customers would buy products. With the passage of time, more knowledge, and experience, customers increasingly seemed unwilling to be persuaded. More and more companies found that determining what customers wanted was a must before making a product, rather than producing products first and then persuading them to buy. The key questions became:

1. What do customers really want?
2. Can we develop it while they still want?
3. How can we keep our customers satisfied?

Thus, the marketing concept era began. Marketing concept proposes that an organisation should focus on customer needs and wants, coordinate its efforts, and endeavour to accomplish organisational goals. Geraldine E Williams reported that the CEO of Nike said, "For years we thought of ourselves as a production-oriented company, meaning we put all our emphasis on designing and manufacturing the product. But now we understand that the most important thing we do is market the product." The major focus of all sets of organisational activities should be satisfying customer needs. This requires carefully listening to customers as a student listens to a teacher. Stanley F. Slater and John C. Narver reported that there is positive relationship between market orientation and performance.

Sometimes, philosophies that sound quite reasonable and appear attractive on paper, are difficult to put into practice. To embrace the marketing concept as the guiding philosophy, the concerned firm must accept certain general conditions and manage some problems. Alan Grant and Leonard Schlesinger are of the view that market-orientation requires organisation-wide generation of market intelligence across departments, and organisation wide responsiveness to it. It means establishing a reliable information system to learn about real needs of customers and design the right need satisfying solutions. Setting up an information system can usually be an expensive proposition and requires committing money and time to its development and maintenance. Company-wide coordination may require restructuring the internal operations and overall objectives in case of one or more departments. Appreciating the critical role of marketing, the head of marketing has to be part of the top management team. Acceptance and implementation of marketing concept demands support of top management and other managers and staff. To inculcate a customer-orientation culture, it is necessary that employees at all levels in the organisation should understand the value of the customer and the importance of the customer satisfaction. Obviously, the internal customers (company employees at all levels) themselves should be satisfied and motivated to promote an organisation-wide culture that puts high value on creating a satisfied customer. For this, the company has to ensure an appropriate work environment and take care of their legitimate needs. Benson P. Shapiro is of the opinion that a company is customer focused if the answers are "yes" to the four critical questions:

1. Are we easy for customers to do business with?
2. Do we keep our promises?
3. Do we meet the standards we set?
4. Are we responsive to customer needs?

The **marketing concept** emphasises three main principles.

Customer-oriented planning and implementations

It should be the sole aim of all employees, irrespective of their department or functional area, to satisfy customers' needs. It would require carefully segmenting the market on the basis of the right criteria, targeting suitable segment(s), learning about customer needs and wants, analysing and spotting the right opportunities and matching them with the company's strengths.

Coordination of all organisational activities

Mainly product planning, pricing, distribution, and promotion should be combined in a sensible and consistent manner, and the head of marketing should be a part of top-level management.

Coordinated marketing is critically important to achieve organisational goals

The reward of doing the job well will bring in sales and profits because without profits, the firm cannot survive, neither would it be in a position to improve its offers.

Marketing concept is significantly different from production concept and selling concept. Not long ago, Indian auto companies, Hindustan Motors, Premier Automobiles, and Bajaj Auto hardly showed any consideration for customers, producing obsolete models in large numbers (demand exceeded the supply). Though the prices kept on increasing, little was done to improve the models. Bajaj was the only manufacturer of scooters preferred by customers and to own one, customers had to deposit money in advance and wait for five to ten years before they could become proud owners. It is only after the entry of Maruti cars, with Japanese collaboration, that things started changing. Premier Auto, and Hindustan Motors experienced major setbacks, sales declined and ultimately there were hardly any willing buyers. In the beginning, Maruti found it difficult to meet the demand and buyers willingly booked the car and waited for delivery. Bajaj Auto faced a similar situation as customers had many choices of two-wheelers. The position now appears as if almost every auto manufacturer is desperately trying to please customers. Customers have strong preferences for certain features and price ranges. Maruti has even started selling second-hand, reconditioned, and reliable cars from its outlets to customers looking for such deals, is order to expand its hold on the market.

FIGURE 1.4
Typical Organisational Pyramid and Its Inverted Position

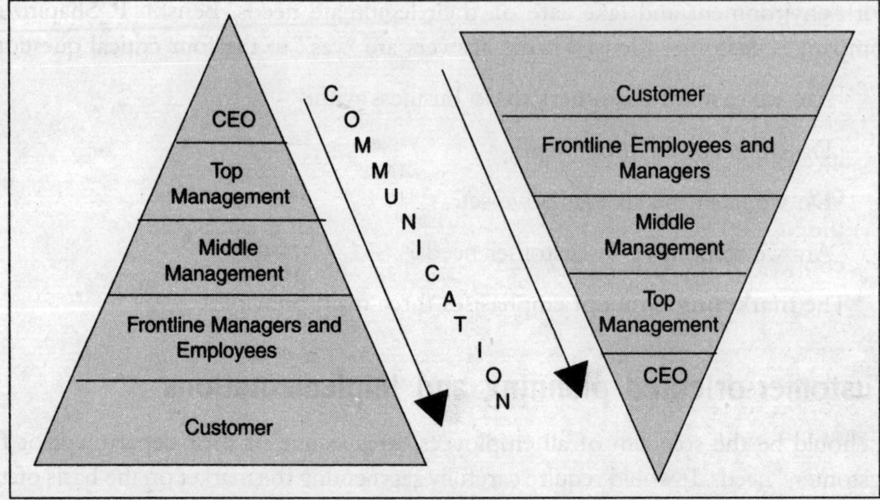

In line with the marketing concept, it is imperative that the typical pyramid depicting an organisation needs to be inverted to pursue marketing concept. In an inverted position, the customer will occupy the highest pedestal and top management will be at the bottom position. The communication flow will start from the customer, and the employees and executives will look up to learn what the customer wants and then respond to the inputs. This is the way to offer desired value, deliver more satisfaction, and help retain the customer.

Marketing concept is sometimes interpreted as a philosophy of attempting to satisfy all customers' needs with no concern for the cost. This would seem to be a sure way to financial disaster. The marketing concept is consistent with the idea of taking into consideration only those customer segments that the company can satisfy both effectively and profitably. The firm has to earn profits to survive, offer new and better products and services, and be a meaningful member of society. A company might therefore choose to offer less costly products and services to unprofitable customer segments, or even avoid them altogether. Being market-oriented pays dividends and has a significant effect on company performance.

Relationship Marketing

Companies in developed countries and many businesses in developing countries aim to satisfy customer needs and build lasting relationships. The issue focuses on reliability and trust between customer and organisation. As a result of this customer focus, a whole new subject, **customer relationship management** is now studied in marketing courses. According to Jagdish N. Sheth and Rajendra Sisodia, the term **relationship marketing** refers to long-term and mutually beneficial arrangements wherein both buyer and seller focus on value enhancement through the creation of more satisfying exchanges. This approach attempts to transcend the simple purchase exchange process with customers to make more meaningful and richer contacts by providing a more holistic, personalised purchase, and use or consumption experience to create stronger ties.

The new approaches to marketing such as experiential, permission, and one-to-one marketing can all be seen as means of creating stronger relationships with customers. The emphasis is on developing long-term bonds with customers by making them feel good about how the firm interacts or does business with them by giving them some kind of personal connection to the company. Real relationship-marketing programme is much more than the use of database marketing to target customers more precisely. Its purpose is that each customer must feel she/he has received something in return for being a member of the partnership. Firms have found that Internet is an inexpensive, efficient and more productive means to extend a firm's customer services. Internet permits firms to ask consumers if they permit the company to send them targeted e-mail ads, promotions, or messages, before actually doing so. Some airlines, hotel chains, credit card businesses, and big retailers, etc., use relationship marketing techniques by awarding points to committed customers that can be used to obtain additional goods or services from the concerned company. To put it differently, relationship marketing is all about building trust between the company and its customers and keeping promises. These factors increasingly strengthen the customer dependence on the organisation, as a result of which the customer's confidence grows, while the company better understands the customer and her/his needs and wants. Ultimately, this helps in cementing the relationship and encourages cooperative problem solving.

Relationship marketing is based on the principle that current customers are the key to long-term business success. According to Frederick F. Reichheld, the importance of customer retention can be judged by observing some of the following benefits it provides:

- Acquiring new customers can be five times more expensive than the costs involved in satisfying and retaining existing customers.
- The average company loses 10 per cent of its customers each year.
- A decrease of 5 per cent in the customer defection rate can increase profits by 25 per cent to 85 per cent, depending on the industry.
- The customer profit rate tends to increase over the life of retained customer.

Jagdish N. Sheth and Atul Parvatiyar are also of the opinion that it is to a company's advantage to develop long-term relationships with current customers because it is easier and costs less to make an additional sale to an existing customer than to make a new sale to a new customer. Neighbourhood grocery shop owners frequently reassure their frequent customers that if they are not satisfied with a consumable product, they can return it, even after some use and get the full replacement. They practice relationship marketing based on conventional marketing wisdom obtaining in India.

Acquiring New Customers vs. Retaining Old Customers

■ The telecom paradigm is perceptibly changing. As the focus shifts from increasing the customer base to growing the share of revenue, mobile phone service providers are focusing on a model where customer retention becomes the key focus area.

■ In India, significant changes in the telecom scenario have influenced the strategy shift. To start with, we had two operators in every circle. Now six or even seven operators compete in the same service area. Then, telecom costs have been consistently sliding, leading to the cheapest telecom rates in the world. All this has led to an explosion in subscriber numbers. But they also increased

■ customer churn.

Even acquisition costs per subscriber were going down (from between Rs 5,000 and Rs 10,000 in the late 1990s, it is now about Rs 1,000 per customer). But break-even on new customers still takes 18 to 24 months. Given these dynamics, it is more profitable to retain an existing customer than fighting for a new customer.

Today, non-portability of numbers in India acts as one of the biggest retention devices but this could be a temporary benefit. During the early stages of mobile telephony, customer retention typically meant providing basic customer services.

But when new entrants were actively wooing our customers, we recognised the need to focus on customer retention. We formed the Customer Asset Management (CAM) team, the business

Contd...

> division parallel to our sales business unit. This team has a single-minded focus on retention activities with a direct say in all aspects of the business.
>
> We also started to focus on attracting the right quality of customers. Towards this, we fine-tuned our acquisition strategy. We are exploring alternative channels for selling.
>
> It is important for a service brand to create differentiation, which is an experiential sum of all its interactions with the customer.
>
> The total experience is our ability to deliver advanced products first in the market, providing an impeccable network quality and rounding off the product experience with a memorable service experience every time the customer interacts with us.
>
> (Krishna Angara, Executive Vice President, BPL Mobiles, Business Standard, June 19, 2005).

According to Steve Schriver, research indicates that consumers are less loyal now than in the past due to the following reasons:

1. The abundance of choice.
2. Availability of information.
3. Customers ask, "What have you done for me lately?"
4. Most products/services appear to be similar – nothing stands out.
5. Customers' financial problems reduce loyalty.
6. Time scarcity (not enough time to be loyal).

These forces lead to consumer defections, complaints, cynicism, decreased affiliation, greater price sensitivity, and a tendency to carry on lawsuits.

The major differences between selling concept and marketing concept

1. The selling concept starts with the seller and its focus is on existing products, it being seller-oriented. The company believes in aggressive selling and other promotions. Customer value and satisfaction are no concern for the seller. The firm produces the products first and then figures out ways to sell and make profits. Different company departments operate without coordination.
2. Marketing orientation starts with the customer and the company strives to learn customer needs and wants, develops appropriate products or services to satisfy the customer. Business is viewed as a customer need satisfying activity. All departments coordinate their activities and the focus is on customer needs. Profits are an outcome of doing the job well by the company. It requires reliable company-wide information system and maintains it. All departments are responsive to informational inputs. Everybody understands the critical role played by marketing, a fact visibly demonstrable when the head of marketing is part of top management.

The Societal Marketing Concept

Marketing concept was accepted widely among companies in developed and some developing countries and continued to evolve and take on new meanings. Not long after this, criticism started about the nature of its social responsibility. The emphasis shifted to how marketing affected society as a whole in an age of depleting and increasingly scarce resources, environmental deterioration, etc. It was good enough to produce what customers needed or wanted, and for achieving organisational objectives, but in certain cases the concept could be in conflict with customers' and society's best long-run interests. *Societal marketing concept is a management philosophy that takes into account the welfare of society, the organisation, and its customers.*

Adoption of this concept requires that marketing decisions be made in an ethical and socially responsible manner. Companies must pay attention not only to the short-term needs of customers but also to their long-term well being. This includes, for instance, excess fat content in ready-to-eat foods, toxic wastes, and environmental issues.

The need is to strike a balance between the interest of customers, the company itself, and the society in which operations are conducted. Some responsible firms have started using recyclable packaging materials and products that do not harm the environment. Among the marketing tasks, demarketing is an approach that reflects the societal marketing philosophy.

Many companies encounter several hurdles in adopting the marketing concept. For some firms, it is simply too difficult to understand the underlying philosophy and they fail to implement it. Other companies face a conflict between short-term and long-term objectives and have no inclination to sacrifice short-term gains for the sake of customer satisfaction, simply because the customer is not the major priority of top management.

Holistic Marketing Approach

There have been major changes in almost every sphere of human activity over the last decade, like implication being that this requires fresh marketing thinking, a fresh approach to business, and this calls for a **holistic marketing** approach. This new thinking relies upon marketing research to define market segments, their size, and their needs. To more completely satisfy those needs, marketers need to have a more complete and cohesive approach to internal marketing, targeted marketing, relationship marketing, be visibly socially responsible, and make decisions about the controllable elements of the **marketing mix**.

Marketing Mix

Marketing mix is a major concept in modern marketing and involves practically everything that a marketing company can use to influence consumer perceptions favourably towards its products or services so that consumer and organisational objectives are attained. Marketing mix is a model of crafting and implementing marketing strategy. Prof. Neil H. Borden first used the term "marketing mix" in 1949 to include in the marketing process factors such as distribution, advertising, personal selling, and pricing. Borden claims that the phrase came to him while reading James Culliton's description of the activities of a business executive:

(An executive) *"a mixer of ingredients, who sometimes follows a recipe as he goes along, sometimes adapts a recipe to the ingredients immediately available, and sometimes experiments with or invents ingredients no one else has tried."* [Wikipedia: James Culliton, *The Management of Marketing Costs*, Research Division, Harvard University (1948)].

There are virtually dozens of marketing mix tools. However, Prof. E. Jerome McCarthy classified the "Marketing Mix Variables" in terms of **4 Ps: Product, Price, Place** (distribution) and **Promotion**. These 4 Ps represent the tactical controllable factors and vary in case of different products and target markets. This classification is believed to be quite popular in marketing circles across the world.

TABLE 1.1

Marketing Mix Elements (4Ps)

Product Decisions	Price Decisions	Place Decisions	Promotion Decisions
Brand name	Pricing strategy	Distribution	
Functionality	Suggested retail price	channels	(push, pull, etc.)
Styling	Wholesale price	Market coverage	Advertising
Quality	Various discounts	- intensive	Sales promotion
Safety	Seasonal pricing	- selective	Personal selling
Packaging	Bundling	- exclusive	PR / publicity
Repairs & support	Price flexibility	Inventory	Promotional budget
Warranty Accessories and Services	Price discrimination	Warehousing Order processing Transportation	

Three other marketing mix classifications by: (1) Albert Frey, (2) William Lazer and Eugene J. Kelly, and (3) Mary Bitner and Bernard Booms are worth noting. Frey's two-factor classification includes, (1) The Offering: product, packaging, brand, price, and service. (2) Methods and Tools includes distribution channels, personal selling, advertising, sales promotion, and publicity. The second classification proposed by Lazer and Kelly includes three factors: (1) Goods and Services Mix, (2) Distribution Mix, and (3) Communications Mix, and Bitner and Boom's includes 7 Ps. However, the 4Ps remain the most popular classification in terms of marketing mix.

A more recent marketing mix classification proposed by Robert Lauterborn focuses on customer's point of view and includes: (1) Customer Benefit, (2) Customer Cost, (3) Customer Convenience, and (4) Communication. Lauterborn's view is that 4Ps correspond to customer's 4Cs.

McCarthy's Classification (4Ps)	Lauterborn's Classification (4Cs)
1. Product.	Customer Benefit.
2. Promotion.	Communication.
3. Place (distribution).	Customer Convenience.
4. Price.	Customer Cost.

Marketing management strives to develop the most appropriate combination of marketing mix variables for each product to match the needs of the target market. Marketing mix elements are altered to accommodate the changing market conditions and changing marketing strategies adopted by competing companies.

Product (Customer Benefit)

In the marketing mix, the product or service is the most important element. There is an old saying in marketing: "Without a good product, you have nothing." Product is directly related to satisfying the customer needs and wants in the target market. Customers acquire products for the singular reason that they are perceived as the means to satisfying their needs and wants. According to Philip Kotler, *"A products anything that can be offered to a market for attention, acquisition, use, or consumption that might satisfy a need or want."* In effect, according to this definition products include physical products, services, persons, places, organisations and ideas. Various product attributes such as quality, variety, design, brand, packaging, services, and warranties, etc., can be manipulated depending on what the target market wants. This may ultimately affect the product quality that can be kept high or low. Marketers also develop other product aspects such as service, packaging, labelling, instruction manual, warranties, and after sales service. Customers always look for new and improved things, which is why marketers should improve existing products, develop new ones, and discontinue old ones that are no longer needed or wanted by customers.

Promotion (Marketing Communications)

Promotion is a key element of marketing programme and is concerned with effectively and efficiently communicating the decisions of marketing strategy, to favourably influence target customers' perceptions to facilitate exchange between the marketer and the customer that may satisfy the objectives of both customers and the company. In reality, everything that a company does has the potential to communicate something to the target customers. For instance, the price of a product has the potential to communicate to target customers a certain image of the product. For example, a low-priced designer dress is unlikely to attract high-profit, well-heeled target customers, while less affluent buyers may find the designs too avant garde for comfort. The major elements of promotion mix include advertising, personal selling, sales promotion, direct marketing, and publicity. A company's promotion efforts are the only controllable means to create awareness among publics about itself, the products and services it offers, their features, and influence their attitudes favourably. It is critically important for marketing managers to create a strong marketing mix, because any weak element not complementing others can adversely affect the chances of a product's success in the market-place. All the marketing mix elements should complement others to communicate effectively with target market. The best products and high class promotional efforts would not sell it, if their products are not available at distribution outlets.

Distribution (Customer Convenience)

Decisions with respect to distribution channel focus on making the product available in adequate quantities at places where customers are normally expected to shop for them to satisfy their needs. The aim of the management is also to keep the physical distribution costs (that would include inventory, transportation, and storage) as low as possible. Depending on the nature of the product, marketing management decides to put into place an exclusive, selective, or intensive network of distribution, while selecting the appropriate dealers or wholesalers. The right choice of these factors can give a company some competitive advantage. For example, a low-priced product consumed regularly on an ongoing basis should be available at as many outlets as possible (intensive distribution) otherwise consumers would buy any other substitutes that are more conveniently available. On the other hand, for purchasing products such as CTV, washing machine, computer, or other similar durable items, consumers don't mind visiting some selected dealers (selective distribution), and for high-end, very expensive items such as Mercedes Benz cars, expensive and exclusive jewelry status watches and accessories, etc., customers are quite willing to visit exclusive dealerships, even if there are just one or two in the city (exclusive distribution).

Price (Customer Cost)

Pricing decisions are almost always made in consultation with marketing management. Price is the only marketing mix variable that can be altered quickly. Price variable such as dealer price, retail price, discounts, allowances, credit terms, etc., directly influence the development of marketing strategy, as price is a major factor that influences the assessment of value obtained by customers. Price can be kept as high or low, or at any level in between these two extremes. Too high would be the point at which any meaningful sales are not possible because the target customers won't accept the product, and too low would be the point at which company would incur losses instead of profits. Price is said to be an important competitive tool, and intense price competition between rival companies often culminates in a price war and the contestants generally end up gaining nothing. The customers, however, enjoy the benefit of low prices till such time that good sense prevails between contestants and prices are brought back to normal. In case of certain products, price becomes the indicator of product quality and helps impart an image to the product.

The Marketing Mix Coherency

Refers to how well the different elements of the mix blend together to accomplish the desired impact. For example, to sell an expensive luxury item in discount or bargain stores would show poor coherency between distribution and product offering.

The Marketing Mix Dynamics

Focuses on how the mix must be adapted to suit the changing business environment, changes in company resources, and the changes in product life cycle stages.

Summary

Marketing started in ancient times since people got involved in exchanges. As an academic discipline, marketing is quite new. The present day marketing is all about satisfying customer needs and wants profitably in a socially responsible manner. This presupposes a process of planning and executing the concept, through pricing, promotion, and distribution of products, services, ideas to facilitate satisfying exchanges and achieving company objectives. Exchange may take place in an effective manner only when there are at least two participating parties, each of which has something of value desired by the other. These parties are capable of communicating with each other to offer available "value"; each party is free and willing to exchange "value," and each party believes that their deal is appropriate and likely to be satisfying.

Marketing has evolved through traversing three major eras of: production orientation, selling orientation, and marketing orientation. Marketing concept is a management philosophy where the customer is the pivotal point. This requires first finding out customer needs and wants and works to satisfy them through coordinated set of activities, thereby achieving company objectives. Customer satisfaction and retention is the most important task for companies adopting marketing concept. The societal marketing concept proposes that companies do not operate in a vacuum, but take into account the larger societal concerns of welfare and not just focus on the customer needs in the short-term.

Adoption of marketing concept requires taking a critical look at the organisational structure. Typically, the CEO is at the top and front line managers and other employees are at the bottom of the company pyramid. This perspective has to change to an inverted pyramid, where the frontline employees are at the top, as they are the ones who frequently interact with customers and are in a better position to know intimate details about customer needs, wants, and preferences. The flow of communication is from customers to frontline employees and subsequently to other managerial layers and ultimately to the CEO.

Marketing mix is a model of crafting and implementing marketing strategies. It represents controllable tactical elements. The most popular classification of marketing mix includes product, price, place (distribution), and promotion.

Questions for Discussion

1. How would you define marketing? Discuss the evolution of marketing.
2. Do you know any company in India that has adopted marketing concept? Give suitable examples to justify your opinion.

3. Discuss the concept of exchange. What conditions are necessary for exchange to take place? Mention an example that does not involve money in affecting exchange.
4. Are there companies still operating as production oriented and sales oriented, in your view?
5. Why has marketing concept acquired so much importance in modern day marketing?
6. Discuss in detail the important principles on which implementation of marketing concept rests.
7. Why should the marketing manager be a part of top management team, and why should the CEO be marketing oriented?
8. What is meant by the term 'coordinated marketing'? Why is it necessary?
9. What is the significance of customer satisfaction and customer retention?
10. Discuss the difference between sales orientation and marketing orientation. Give suitable examples.

Projects

1. If you were the marketing manager, develop a plan for your company to help it satisfy and retain its customers.
2. Study a company in your city and identify what practices it has adopted to meet the requirements of being customer-oriented.
3. Study a consumer durable marketing company. Discuss its important practices that you think appear to keep in view the long-term welfare of the society.

Bibliography

1. American Marketing Association, 2004.
2. Philip Kotler, *Marketing Management*, Prentice-Hall, 11th Ed. 2003.
3. William M. Pride and O. C. Ferrel, *Marketing: Concepts and Strategies*, Houghton Mifflin Company, 2000.
4. Philip Kotler, "The Major Tasks of Marketing Management," *Journal of Marketing*, October 1973.
5. Kotler and Sidney J. Levy, "Demarketing, Yes, Demarketing," *Harvard Business Review*, November-December 1971.
6. Neil H. Borden, "The Concept of the Marketing Mix," *Journal of Advertising Research*, vol. 4, June 1964.
7. E. Jerome McCarthy, Basic Marketing: A Managerial Approach, 1996.
8. R. Lauterborn, "New Marketing Litany: 4Ps Passe; C word take over," *Advertising Age*, October 1, 1990.
9. Albert Frey, *Advertising*, 3rd ed. 1961.
10. Mary Bitner and Bernard Booms, *Marketing Strategies and Organisational Structures for Service Firms*, in J. Donnelly and W. George, *Marketing of Services*, AMA, 1981.
11. Geraldine E. Williams, "High Performance Marketing: An Interview with Nike's Phil Knight," *Harvard Business Review*, July-August 1992.
12. Stanley F. Slater and John C. Narver, "Does Competitive Environment Moderate the Market Orientation – Performance Relationship" *Journal of Marketing*, January 1994.

13. Alan Grant and Leonard Schlesinger, "Realise Your Customers' Full Profit Potential," *Harvard Business Review*, September-October 1995.

14. Benson P. Shapiro, "What the Hell is 'Market-Oriented'?" *Harvard Business Review*, November-December 1988.

15. Jagdish N. Sheth and Rajendras Sisodia, "More Than Ever Before, Marketing is Under Fire to Account for What It Spends," *Marketing Management*, Fall 1995.

16. Fredrick F. Reichheld, The Loyalty Effect, as discussed by Kevin Lane Keller in *Strategic Brand Management.*

17. Jagdish N. Sheth and Atul Parvatiyar, "Relationship Marketing in Consumer Marketing: Antecedents and Consequences," *Journal of the Academy of Marketing Science*, Fall 1995.

18. Steve Schriver, "Customer Loyalty: Going, Going ..." *American Demographics*, September 1997.

Strategic Market Planning

CHAPTER 2

LEARNING OBJECTIVES

After going through this chapter, you will understand:

- Strategic market planning
- The meaning and importance of corporate mission
- Strategic business unit
- Various approaches to allocate resources to SBUs
- Porter's generic strategies
- Value chain analysis
- Different growth strategies
- The concept of marketing mix
- Important constituents of marketing plan

nce upon a time, the name Bata was synonymous with footwear. The Calcutta-based company was a popular family destination - the whole family would buy only Bata shoes. Then somewhere, somehow, Bata lost its way - and its sheen.

The slide started sometime before 1995, when Bata changed its positioning and decided to disengage itself from the traditional stronghold in the middle and lower-income segment. Wanting to woo the premium segment, Bata's entire strategy underwent a change. It backfired and the result: a huge loss of Rs. 42 crore in 1995. Then came the labour problems, which continue to haunt the company. One of few really successful players in the organised sector didn't really know what hit it.

Production of rubber and canvas footwear, its mainstay, stagnated at a level between 18,000 and 19,000 till 1998. Production of leather footwear fell from 14.6 million pairs in 1997 to 11.8 million pairs in 1999. Its stock has been performing miserably in recent times. From a high of Rs.257 in 1998, it is hovering at levels of Rs. 65 - 70 now.

In 1997, Bata decided to pull up its socks. The main focus was on controlling expenditure. Led by new boss W. K. Weston, cost cutting at various levels resulted in increase in profits. Better financial management yielded the results. Three years later, the financial position stabilised somewhat. Commercial paper worth Rs. 15 crore (from Rs. 25.5 crore in the previous year) and a decline in cost of fund, interest charge during the year dipped to Rs. 6.8 crore.

To maintain its prominent position in the organised footwear market, the company revamped its systems. In 1999, it incurred a capital expenditure of Rs. 21.8 crore to modernise existing stores, opening new stores, and improving the work process.

If one looks at it from the profitability point of view, the return on equity in 1999 was 8.94 per cent. This is an improvement over the 7.44 per cent achieved in the previous year. At the same time, earning per share (EPS) went up from Rs. 4.7 per share to Rs. 5.9 per share. Dividend paid for financial year 1999 increased to Rs. 1.5 per cent per share, from Rs. 0.9 the year before.

During the past two years, Bata has launched shoes in the mid-price segment. But the question is: will it be able to sustain increased profits over a long period? In the volume game, it has not been able to introduce the designs that sell (for the upper segment).

During 1999, Bata achieved a turnover Rs. 774.6 crore, four per cent higher than the previous year's sales. Net profit grew by nearly 25 per cent to Rs. 30.4 crore. Leather footwear accounted for 58 per cent of gross sales, 30 per cent came from rubber footwear and 9 per cent from plastic footwear.

The brand is bound to grow, especially since it has emotional value for Indians. The labour problem also seems to be sorting itself out. Finally, things seem to be falling in place.

(Source: Abhishek Agarwal, "The Good Old Days," A & M, July 31, 2000).

In business management, the word 'strategy' started becoming popular during 1960s, but it is still a term with differing definitions and interpretations. According to Walker, Jr. Boyd, Jr. Mullins, and Jarreche, *a strategy is a fundamental pattern of present and planned objectives, resource deployments, and interactions of an organisation with markets, competitors, and other environmental factors.* Strategy refers to a game plan that corporations employ to compete successfully in the marketplace by establishing the objectives to achieve, specifying industries and product-markets to focus, and specify resources to allocate and activities to perform for each product-market to take advantage of environmental opportunities, and meet the threats to gain competitive advantage.

Strategic market planning (also mentioned as Strategic Planning or Strategic Market-Oriented Planning, or Strategic Marketing Planning in some texts) essentially refers to planning that is conceptually and functionally long-term, typically covering a period of five years or more for the entire corporation. *Strategic market planning is a process yielding a marketing strategy that is the framework for a marketing plan.* The aim of strategic market planning is to adapt, adjust, or reshape on an ongoing basis the corporation's different businesses to accomplish the target growth and profit objectives. The whole process involves keeping in focus the changing market opportunities and developing a viable fit between the corporation's objectives, resources, and competencies. This way the corporation attempts to help itself in selecting and organising its business(s) in a manner that would keep the business healthy despite upsets that may occur in any of its businesses or products due to uncontrollable environmental factors.

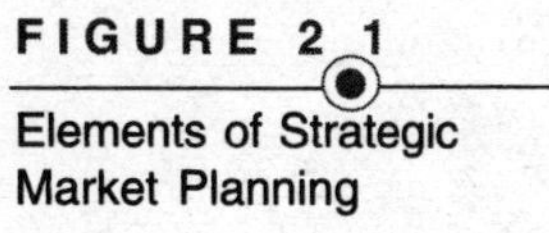

FIGURE 2.1

Elements of Strategic Market Planning

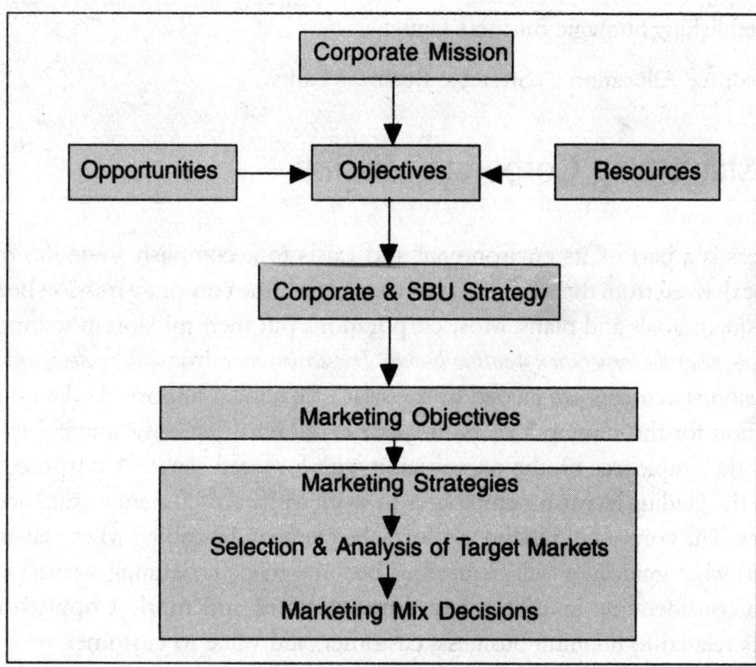

Strategic market planning is ***not*** the same as the annual marketing planning exercise. Strategic market planning refers to all aspects of an organisation's strategy in the marketplace, while marketing planning refers to developing a market plan that deals primarily with implementation aspects of the marketing strategy as it relates to the target market and the marketing mix variables.

Strategic market planning is undertaken at five levels:

1. Establishing Corporate Mission and Objectives
2. Determining Corporate and Strategic Business Unit Strategy
3. Setting Marketing Objectives
4. Developing Marketing Strategy
5. Developing Marketing Plan

Corporate Mission and Objectives

At corporate level, the top management has the responsibility to prepare statements with respect to corporate mission, policy, strategy, and goals. Within the boundaries of these statements, different strategic business units or divisions prepare their own respective plans. However, much depends on the corporate policy in this regard. In more decentralised corporations, business units enjoy considerable freedom to determine their own sales and profit objectives and develop appropriate strategies to accomplish these objectives. In some other corporations, the corporate management sets only the objectives for each business unit, while the strategies are developed at the business unit or division level. Another variation practised is that corporate management not only sets the objectives for the individual business units but also gets involved in developing each business unit level strategies.

Four planning activities are undertaken at corporate level:

1. Establishing Corporate Mission.
2. Establishing Corporate Objectives.
3. Establishing Strategic Business Units.
4. Resource Allocation to Strategic Business Units.

Establishing Corporate Mission

A business is a part of its environment and exists to accomplish some desired goals. What to accomplish should be derived from the mission statement. In fact, the corporate mission becomes the basis for developing all subsequent goals and plans. Most corporations put their mission in writing. *The mission statement is a long-term view of what the corporation wants to become. It describes the corporation's values, aspirations and reasons for being.* The best mission statements are guided by a vision – an almost impossible dream – that inspires and directs the organisation for the coming 5 years, 10 years or more. A really meaningful and inspiring mission statement provides the employees of the organisation with a shared sense of purpose, direction, and opportunity. It works as the guiding factor for employees to work with commitment toward accomplishing the organisation's objectives. The corporate mission is a formal statement describing what management wants the corporation to be and what guidelines will be used to become that. In defining a mission, the management must also take into consideration its **distinctive competencies** and **market opportunities,** besides answering the questions related to defining business, customer, and value to customer.

Mission statements need not be revised in a hurry every now and then in response to merely fluctuating economic conditions. It may become necessary or advantageous, though, to revise the mission if it has lost its relevance in defining an optimal course for a corporation, or to take advantage of new opportunities or respond to new market conditions. For example, formerly the mission of Amazon.com was being the largest online bookstore. Its mission has changed to becoming the largest online store, not just the largest online bookstore. When the top management is convinced about the irrelevance of mission, the famous management thinker Peter F. Drucker recommends answering some fundamental questions:

1. What is our business?
2. Who is the customer?
3. What is value to the customer?
4. What will our business be?
5. What should our business be?

Apparently these questions do not seem to be complicated at all. A casual approach to answering these questions is definitely going to be counterproductive. In fact, these are among the toughest yet most important questions that any corporation can answer. Creating or revising a mission statement is quite difficult because of the many complex variables that must be examined. However, having a mission statement can very significantly benefit the concerned organisation in at least five ways:

1. A mission statement sets a clear purpose and direction. This keeps the organisation on track and reduces any chances of drifting from its course.
2. It helps differentiate the organisation from competitors by describing its unique focus.
3. It keeps the organisation focused on customer needs rather than focused on its capabilities.
4. It sets specific direction and guidelines to top management for choosing from among alternative courses of actions such as which business opportunities to pursue.
5. It becomes the guiding *mantra* to all employees and managers, no matter where they are located in global operations.

EXHIBIT: 2.1: THE MISSION STATEMENT

The Mission Statement of Tata Group

- "At the Tata Group, our purpose is to improve the quality of life of the communities we serve. We do this through leadership, in sectors of national economic significance to which the group brings a unique set of capabilities. This requires us to grow aggressively in focused areas of business."
- "Our heritage of returning to society what we earn evokes trust among consumers, employees, shareholders, and the community. This heritage will be continuously enriched by formalising the high standards of behaviour expected from employees and companies."
- "The Tata name is a unique asset, representing leadership with a trust. Leveraging this asset to enhance group synergy and becoming globally competitive is the route to sustained growth and long-term success."

The Mission Statement of a Hypothetical Courier Company

- "The company is committed to People-Service-Leadership-Profit philosophy. We will provide extremely reliable, competitively superior, domestic air-ground transportation of goods and documents that require timely delivery, to earn above average profits. We will adopt latest techniques in our business and maintain leadership. We will maintain positive control of every package using electronic tracking and tracing systems. A complete record of each shipment and delivery will be presented with our request for payment. We will be courteous, and helpful to colleagues, clients, and the public. We will do our level best to have a satisfied customer at the end of each and every transaction."

The concept of corporate mission is dynamic and should neither be too general and vague or too narrow or specific in its scope. In case the mission is stated in a broad and general way, it may defeat the very purpose of its existence. The business may not be in a position to focus on any workable opportunity. For example, to state that the mission of ABC Company is "to benefit Indian consumers" is extremely vague. Or the company states that its mission is "to make light bulbs" is too narrow. In both these examples of mission statements, there is no mention of meaningful benefits to customers or any guidelines for the management.

Distinctive Competencies

Distinct competencies of an organisation refer to skills and talents in different functional areas such as production, finance, marketing, management, and utilisation of resources (financial, human, R&D, technological, and material). According to David Aaker, a sustainable advantage can be based on either the organisational assets or skills, such as financial resources, technical superiority, low-cost production, customer service and product support. Location, continuing product innovation, and overall marketing skills are all examples of sustainable competitive advantage. For example, Microsoft used its marketing and technical skills to create Windows operating system to make computers easier to use. Although Windows is now pre-installed on most personal computers, Microsoft continues to work to maintain its competitive advantage by improving Windows and introducing Windows compatible software. Maruti is known for providing quality autos at a reasonable price. Each succeeding generation of Maruti cars has shown significant quality improvements over previous models. Maruti has the largest service network in India. This has made Maruti cars the leaders in India with largest market share. According to David W. Cravens, companies can also gain competitive advantage through innovative breakthrough products, patents, low costs, strong sales force, or favourable brand equity. Sustaining competitive edge depends on a clear focus upon the assets and competencies and matching the distinctive competencies to the opportunities the company discovers in the market. This will lead to long-term performance gains.

Market Opportunities

An opportunity provides a favourable opening for the alert organisation to generate sales from identifiable market(s). Market opportunities emerge when a favourable combination of circumstances and timing allows an organisation to take action to reach a particular market with its offer. For example, factors such as technological innovations, changing consumer values, lifestyles, and preferences, etc., can throw up market opportunities. Being the first to take advantage of a market opportunity can be very rewarding and also expensive and sometimes risky as well. The lead-time that Leader Company has over later entrants can prove to be quite advantageous in terms of sourcing supplies, cost reduction, quality improvement, and gaining commitment from supply chain partners. Sabeer Bhatia of Hotmail fame spotted an opportunity in the Internet mail and became very successful. The introduction of the microwave oven threw up new opportunities for certain types of frozen foods. Entry of women in the workforce created an opportunity for opening day care centres and crèches in cities. Derek Abell has termed the often-limited periods of time as a **Strategic Window,** when market opportunities match the capabilities of a competing company operating in a particular market.

Opportunities are largely related to the environmental conditions and it is necessary to scan the environment to detect any changes that throw up promising opportunities. Just because some opportunity is spotted is not a good enough reason to go after it. The attractiveness of an opportunity needs to be assessed before taking any action. Several market factors determine the attractiveness of market opportunities. These factors may vary according to industry and product category and include factors such as market size, expected growth rate, as well as forces like competition, economic, political/legal, technological, and socio-cultural.

Establishing Corporate Objectives

The enterprise mission that provides a sense of direction with respect to where it wants to go and what it aspires to achieve in overall business, often also reflects much idealism. The next step is to establish a specific set of objectives (this text treats *objectives* and *goals* as synonymous).

- Objectives provide direction to stay focused on common purpose. Every activity is directed towards the objectives and every individual contributes to accomplish the objectives.

- Objectives coordinate the activities and keep them on the right track. They make behaviours in an organisation more rational and coordinated and thus more effective.
- Objectives serve as performance standards to compare actual results.
- Objectives provide a basis for motivation of employees to be result oriented because they know towards what ends they are working.

EXHIBIT 2.2: ORGANISATIONAL OBJECTIVES

Objective	Desired Results	Time Span
Increase market share from the present 13% by	2 per cent	One year
Increase sales from the present 10% by	5 per cent	Two years
Increase profits by	Rs. 3,000,000	One year
Decrease customer complaints from the present 5%	To 3 per cent	One year

With respect to long-range objectives, Peter F. Drucker argues convincingly for establishing objectives in eight key areas:

"A business must first be able to create a customer. There is, therefore, need for a marketing perspective. Business must be able to innovate or else their competitor will make them obsolescent. There is need for an innovation objective. All businesses depend on the three factors of production, that is, on the human resource, the capital resource, and physical resources. There must be objectives for their supply, their employment, and their development. The resources must be employed productively, and their productivity has to grow if the business is to survive. There is need, therefore, for productivity objectives. Business exists in society and community and, therefore, has to discharge social responsibilities, at least to the point where it takes responsibility for its impact upon the environment. Therefore, objectives in respect to the social dimensions of business are needed.

Finally, there is need for profit – otherwise none of the objectives can be attained. They all require effort, that is, cost. And they can be financed only out of the profits of a business. They all entail risks; they all, therefore, require a profit to cover the risk of potential losses. Profit is not an objective, but it is a requirement that has to be objectively determined in respect to the individual business, its strategy, its needs, and its risks."

(Peter F. Drucker, Management: Tasks, Responsibilities, Practices, 1974)

Corporate objectives are derived from its mission and specify what the enterprise wants to achieve. Wherever possible, objectives should be stated in quantitative terms and the time frame should be specified. Organisations can establish objectives in two basic areas: economic objectives and social objectives. Economic objectives may be related to market share, sales, profits, and reduction of customer complaints. The social objectives may relate to social commitments both to employees and society. Mission and objectives must be considered at each stage of strategic planning process.

Objectives should specify four important characteristics:

1. What is to be accomplished?
2. What is the starting point?
3. How much is to be accomplished?
4. In what duration it is to be accomplished?

Planning Corporate and Strategic Business Unit (SBU) Strategies

Corporate strategy determines how an organisation will accomplish its objectives. It specifies how the organisation will match its production, finance, R&D, human resources, marketing and other capabilities with identified opportunities to accomplish its objectives. By establishing Strategic Business Units (SBUs) and evaluating each in terms of current business and products, the organisation determines specific strategies for different business units and allocates appropriate resources. Most large corporations generally, and even medium and small ones have more than one independent business divisions or what is called the Strategic Business Units (SBUs). *A Strategic Unit may be a division, a profit centre, a product line or a number of related products, and in some cases a single product.* There are many examples of corporations having more than one division or business, for instance Tata Group, Reliance Group, Birla Group, Larsen and Toubro, ITC, Godrej, Philips, Samsung, Wipro and many others.

Hindustan Lever Limited Restructures

- Fast moving consumer goods (FMCG) giant Hindustan Lever Ltd. has announced a sweeping restructuring.
- The group's five strategic business units (SBUs) will be reorganised into two divisions – Home & Personal Care (HPC), and Foods, according to a corporate announcement posted on Bombay Stock Exchange website. The two divisions will operate with considerable autonomy.
- The HPC division will integrate the detergents and personal products businesses. It will have a management committee headed by Arun Adhikari, who will be designated managing director – Home & Personal Care. The Foods division will integrate the beverages, foods, ice creams, and confectionery businesses. It will have a management committee headed by S Ravindranath, managing director – Foods.

M. K. Sharma, D. Sundram, Arun Adhikari, and S. Ravindranath will constitute the national management for HLL, to be chaired by M. K. Sharma.

(Source: Times of India, April 16, 2004).

A superior way of defining business is to view it as a customer-satisfying process rather than a product/service producing entity. Prof. Theodore Levitt of Harvard argued that customer need-based definitions of a business are superior to product definitions. Products are transient, but customers' basic needs continue to last forever. As long as human beings exist on this earth, their needs will endure. As a result of coming up with strategic market definition of their business, some cola companies now see their competition as including non-cola soft drinks, tea and coffee, fruit juices, bottled water, and Indian brands of *sharbat* based on Ayurvedic or Unani formulations, as these are alternatives that can meet the consumers' basic need to quench thirst. These companies have now broadened their product portfolio and included branded bottled water and cold tea, etc., in their product mix.

According to Derek Abell, a business definition can be in terms of three dimensions: customer groups, customer needs, and technology used. The company can expand into additional businesses by keeping one or two of these dimensions constant and varying just one dimension. For example, customer group and customer need may remain the same, but by using new technology in the area of microchip and satellite communication, the company can better satisfy the existing and new customer groups and their present and emerging needs in a better way in several areas like communication, computing, design, research, etc. The cellular phone is satisfying various customer groups and their needs more conveniently, even when mobile by using this relatively new technology. Cellular phones provide services such as SMS, e-mail, instant checking of cricket scores, a camera, etc., to different customer groups.

Formation of Strategic Business Units (SBUs) helps in developing organisational strategy, more so in large diversified enterprises, by identifying those business units that have an opportunity to grow, those that need extra attention and resources, and those that should be harvested, divested, or eliminated. Managers use this analysis generally to examine the competitive position of SBUs or product, or product lines. Following are the four characteristics of an SBU:

1. It is a single business unit with its own mission of marketing distinct products/services to an identifiable group of customers.
2. It has its own competition with a well-defined group of competitors.
3. It can be planned separately from the rest of the organisation.
4. Each SBU has its own manager responsible for strategic planning, profits, and controls most of the factors affecting its performance.

Resource Allocation to Strategic Business Units

A number of tools have been proposed to help planning. The way financial portfolios are managed, based on similar ideas a number of ***business-portfolio*** evaluation models are available. Business-portfolio analysis helps managers in assessing the status of different business units. By analysing the profitability and growth rates of different Strategic Business Units, the management is helped in reaching a decision as how to allocate resources among them. These analytical models should not be taken as a complete substitute for managers' own judgement in this regard.

According to Roger A. Kerin, Vijay Mahajan, and P. Rajan Vardarajan, two of the best-known business-portfolio analysis models are the Boston Consulting Group model and the General Electric model.

Boston Consulting Group (BCG) Approach

Boston Consulting Group is a consulting company, which developed this growth-share matrix to evaluate the position of business units on the basis of market growth rate and relative market share. Annual rate of sales growth in an industry is the market growth rate and is shown on the vertical axis. The market growth rate of 10 per cent or more is considered as high. However, the growth rate in certain markets may far exceed 10 per cent. For instance, the rate of market growth in case of new and emerging industries may initially be much higher than 10 per cent. Relative market share, measured on the horizontal axis, represents the per centage of sales an SBU has in a particular market relative to the leader in that industry. This means the relative market share percentage of an SBU is measured against the total sales of the leader, and not the total industry sales. In the portfolio shown, for instance, the total industry sales are Rs. 100 million. The largest competitor's sales in this industry are Rs. 20 million. The sales of the SBU are Rs. 2 million. The market share of the SBU in question will be measured against the leader's sale, which is Rs. 20 million. In this example, therefore, the relative market share of the SBU being evaluated is 10 per cent. This way the relative market share can be shown as 0.1x (10 per cent), 0.2x, 0.5x and so on. When the relative market share is equal, it is shown as 1x. Beyond 1x, the relative market share 5x would mean that the SBU being evaluated has 5 times more sales than the nearest competitor. Similarly 10x would mean that the SBU has 10 times more sales than the nearest competitor.

FIGURE 2.2

Growth-Share Matrix developed by Boston Consulting Group

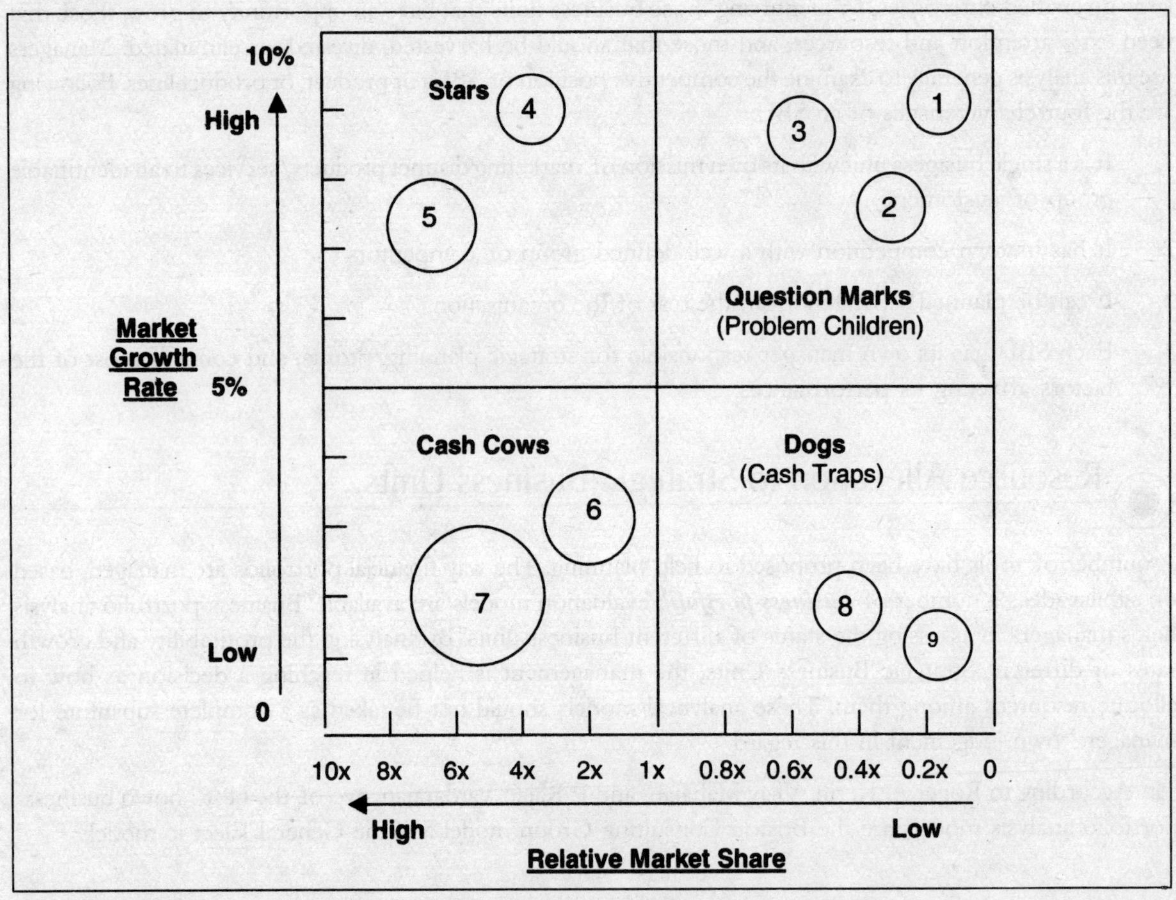

(*Source:* Adapted with changes from B. Hedley, "Strategy and the Business Portfolio.") *Long Range Planning,* February 1977.

FIGURE 2.3

BCG Matrix in a simpler form

		Relative Market Share	
		High	Low
Market Growth Rate	High	Stars (2)	Question Marks (3)
	Low	Cash Cows (2)	Dogs (2)

Based on BCG approach, the organisation can classify its Strategic Business Units into four categories of businesses: the Question Marks (also called Problem Children), Stars, Cash Cows, and Dogs. There are four main approaches to allocating resources to different types of Strategic Business Units: invest heavily, maintain or hold, build selectively, and harvest, divest, or eliminate.

The portfolio shown (Figure 2.2) has three Question Marks (SBU1, SBU2, SBU3). All these three Question Mark SBUs are operating in high market growth area but have very small relative market shares. SBU4, and SBU5 have qualified as Stars. These SBUs are operating in high growth area and are the market leaders. There are two Cash Cows (SBU6, SBU7). In a low market growth area, the Cash Cows have the largest relative market share. And, two Dogs are (SBU8 and SBU9) in an area with rapidly declining market growth and have very low relative share.

Question Marks (Problem Children)

These SBUs are operating in high market growth area and have a low relative market share. They are battling to make their presence felt by capturing a larger relative market share. Obviously, since the market growth rate is high, organisations like to enter in this segment. SBUs characterised as Question Marks are generally new and the categorization represents a period just after their launch. The Question Mark business is risky, since there is already a market leader in the business segment. Competition is likely to be intensifying as many other players in the industry see the market opportunity and enter the segment. Each question mark requires a lot of cash allocation (build strategy) to be spent on plant, machinery, human resources, product modification, market development, etc., to keep pace with the fast growing market and intensifying competition to capture the largest market share to become the leader. Since heavy cash outflows are involved to nurture these SBUs, decision-making requires consideration of corporate objectives, intensity of the competition, and the corporate financial muscle.

The strategic options for Question Marks are selective resource allocation for those that seem to hold future potential, as it probably would be unwise to dilute limited resources on too many risky SBUs. Also, harvesting can be used for non-promising Question Marks. Harvesting means cutting back all support costs to a minimum level and get the cash flow over the remaining period of the SBU's life cycle. The management may also consider selling (divest) the business to another firm or may decide to eliminate it. Many Indian banks and financial institutions seem to have decided to back up their credit card businesses with substantial investments. Sabeer Bhatia sold Hotmail.com to Microsoft, probably because he realised that it would be difficult to back it up with heavy resources in future in a high growth market with increasing competitive intensity.

Stars

Question Mark SBUs that successfully outmanoeuvre the competition and capture a substantial relative market share in a high market growth area become the leaders in this segment. There is two Star SBU in the portfolio shown and it is a very favourable situation as the Star SBUs generally turn out to be future cash-generators (Cash Cows). Stars have further growth potential and although Star SBUs generate, lot of cash, most of it is used to finance growth and meet competitive onslaughts. Competitors work hard to outperform and become the leaders in this high market growth area. To defend leadership position, Star SBUs spend substantial earnings to remain leaders in the high market growth rate area. The appropriate strategy the management generally opts for Stars is to invest heavily, as high relative market share in a high growth market means higher probability of future success. For instance Intel invests heavily in Pentium processors. Microsoft continues heavy investments in Windows, MS Office, and other software.

Cash Cows

Cash Cows are often former Stars. With declining market growth rate, yesterday's Star SBUs become today's Cash Cows. They are still leaders in the segment and enjoy economies of scale and also earn higher profit margins, generating substantial positive cash inflow for the organisation. As the market growth rate has slowed down, Cash Cow SBUs do not need financing for expansion. This cash is usefully employed in financing other businesses, such as promising Question Marks. Generally, Cash Cows have limited prospects for growth. However, it is necessary to keep Cash Cows healthy. In the portfolio shown, there are two Cash Cows. This is a favourable situation, as the organisation's vulnerability is low. For example, Hamdard's Roohafza, Classic Coke, Lux, Vicks, and many other strong Indian and multinational brands are Cash Cows. Cash Cow (SBU7) is in a stronger position than Cash Cow (SBU6). Had there been only one Cash Cow, say only SBU6 and it started losing relative market share, then it would hardly be able to generate surplus cash because it would itself need funds to maintain leadership position. The more the number of Cash Cows in an organisation's portfolio, the stronger the financial health of the organisation. 'Maintain' or 'hold' strategy is appropriate for strong Cash Cows as they generate lots of positive cash that can be invested in Question Marks and Stars. Before these Cows become dry, each should be milked to the maximum extent. For weak Cash Cows whose future is bleak, it is an appropriate strategy to harvest them by eliminating R&D expenditures and reducing promotional expenditures.

Dogs (Cash Traps)

These businesses occupy a position where the market growth is almost non-existent, negligible or even declining rapidly and their relative market share is also extremely low (SBUs 8 and 9). These Dogs were probably Cash Cows in the past but lost their glamour. Often a Dog SBU causes losses because in the firm has to allocate some funds keeping them operational. There are two Dogs (SBU8, and SBU9) in the portfolio above and this is having too many Dogs. Usually, a Dog business is viewed as unhealthy and is harvested, divested, or eliminated (if turnaround is not possible).

FIGURE 2.4
Characteristics and Strategies for SBUs in the Growth-Share Matrix

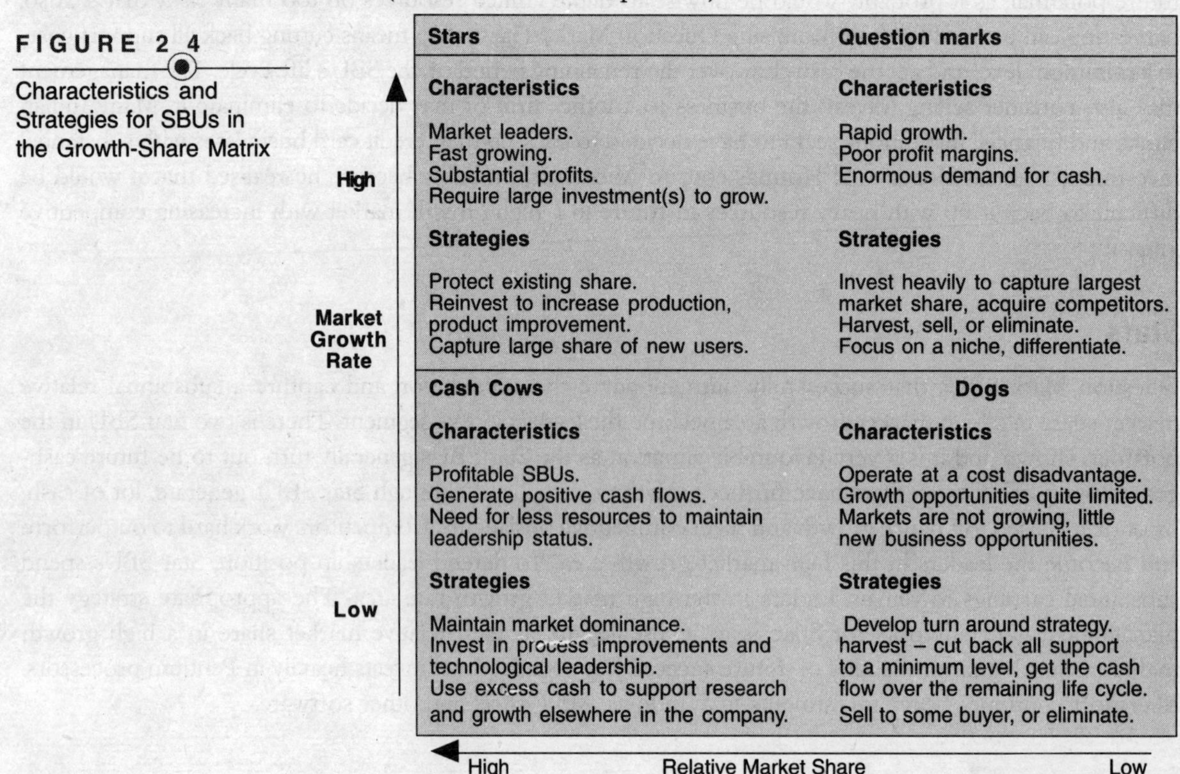

Stars
Characteristics
Market leaders.
Fast growing.
Substantial profits.
Require large investment(s) to grow.
Strategies
Protect existing share.
Reinvest to increase production, product improvement.
Capture large share of new users.
Question marks
Characteristics
Rapid growth.
Poor profit margins.
Enormous demand for cash.
Strategies
Invest heavily to capture largest market share, acquire competitors.
Harvest, sell, or eliminate.
Focus on a niche, differentiate.
Cash Cows
Characteristics
Profitable SBUs.
Generate positive cash flows.
Need for less resources to maintain leadership status.
Strategies
Maintain market dominance.
Invest in process improvements and technological leadership.
Use excess cash to support research and growth elsewhere in the company.
Dogs
Characteristics
Operate at a cost disadvantage.
Growth opportunities quite limited.
Markets are not growing, little new business opportunities.
Strategies
Develop turn around strategy.
harvest – cut back all support to a minimum level, get the cash flow over the remaining life cycle.
Sell to some buyer, or eliminate.
High
Market Growth Rate
Low
High
Relative Market Share
Low

(*Source:* Adapted with changes from William M. Pride and O. C. Ferrell, *Marketing,* 10th Ed).

It is necessary for companies to examine all aspects before reaching a decision that a harvest, divest, or eliminate strategy is appropriate for weak SBUs. (As you know, a SBU is an independent business and is likely to have several related products/brands, so the harvest, divest, or eliminate strategy may concern one or more of these). A decision to harvest a business reduces its future value and hence its sales price at which it can be sold in future. If the decision to divest a weak business is taken early, it is likely to fetch a better deal if it is perceived as having relatively more value for the buyer.

It seems the successful SBUs follow a typical life cycle pattern, similar to that of product life cycle. SBUs start as Question Marks and the successful ones become the Stars. As the market growth slows down, they become the Cash Cows, and finally, with loss of their glamour they become Dogs. The planners keep a sharp eye and critically examine not only the current position of SBUs but also their moving positions. What are your views about the likely moving positions in view of their present ones, particularly SBUs 3, 5, and 6 as shown in the portfolio? A healthy portfolio would be one that has one or two promising Question Marks. Too many Question Marks and just one Star and one Cash Cow is not very promising. More numbers of Stars and Cash Cows make the portfolio more attractive. Dogs are generally viewed as undesirable.

General Electric Approach

The General Electric approach appears to be somewhat similar to BCG matrix. General Electric developed this model with the assistance of McKinsey & Company. This approach is in fact an improvement over BCG growth-share matrix. The General Electric approach focuses on two important dimensions: industry attractiveness and business strength. This makes sense because businesses can succeed only when they enter attractive markets and possess the required business strengths to succeed in the selected markets.

There are nine cells in the model shown. The most favourable situation for an organisation is to be high on business strength in an attractive industry (SBU 1). Businesses in cells 2 and 4 are also favourable as both these are high and medium in one of the two factors. These SBUs (1, 2, 4) are said to be in **green zone** and the right strategy for these is to invest in developing strategies that would lead to growth. Of course, the degree of investment would vary according to overall value score of each SBU. SBUs 3, 5, and 7 represent high-low, medium-medium, and again high-low combination on two factors. SBUs in the diagonal position are said to be in **yellow zone** and the appropriate strategy is to protect their position. This is a strategy of defence to maintain their present market position as they generate positive cash flow (much like Cash Cows in BCG matrix) that can be used for other SBUs. SBUs 6, 8, and 9 are not in a sound position on both factors and are said to be in **red zone.** Harvesting is an appropriate strategy for SBUs 6 and 8 by curtailing resources substantially or selling them. SBU9 should not receive any resources, and probably the best strategy is to sell it.

FIGURE 2.5

Industry Attractiveness-Business Strength Model Developed by General Electric.

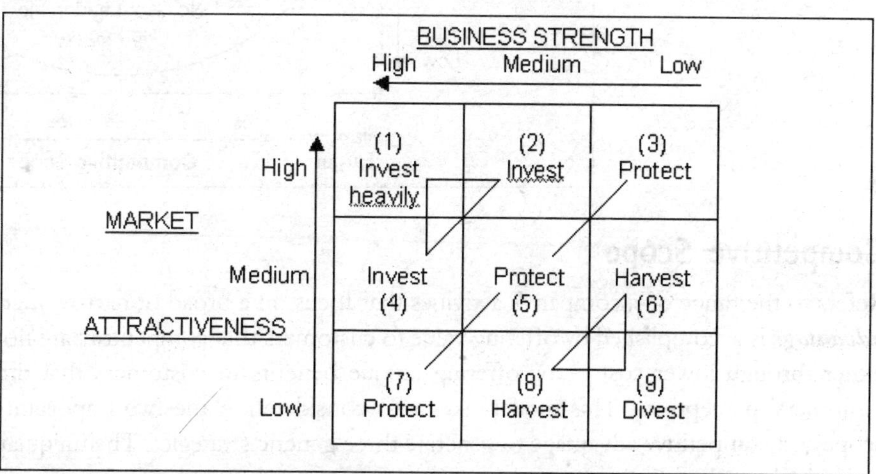

[*Source:* Derek F. Abbel and John S. Hammond, *Strategic Market Planning: Problems and Analytical Approaches,* (1979)].

The Significance of Portfolio Approaches

The portfolio approaches discussed here have been criticised on certain grounds. It is important to appreciate their usefulness as supplements to decision-maker's own judgement. They are used as diagnostic tools to assess a company's strong and weak areas. These approaches are not meant to serve as a substitute to a manager's own judgement or some kind of magic formula for success or quick-fix solutions for a company's problems. Donald L. McCabe and V. K. Narayanan report that despite criticisms of portfolio models about their usefulness, many organisations continue to use portfolio models that have been integral to their success.

The limitations being pointed out here are meant to serve as a signal for exercising caution while using portfolio models, because the results are sensitive to ratings and weights assigned to different evaluative criteria. These weights and ratings can be influenced by manipulation to produce a predetermined location in the matrix. Based on averaging process used in these models, two or more SBUs may occupy the same position in the cell while differing significantly in underlying ratings and weights. Also, some of the strategies recommended may be difficult to implement, such as harvesting and divesting. For example, harvesting and divesting an unprofitable SBU may not be possible if the economy is stagnating. Similarly, other strategies may adversely affect future growth opportunities; for example, a company might divest a Dog that it could have turned around and made a healthy SBU. Geoffrey Smith and Lisa Driscoll have reported the case of Remington Products. Victor Kiam bought Remington Products from Sperry Rand Corp. in 1980 for a price of US$ 25 million and within 10 years he turned this business into a US$ 250 million per annum company.

Porter's Generic Strategies

In his book, *Competitive Advantage,* Michael E. Porter recommends that businesses should (1) analyse and define the competitive scope of target market, and (2) define the competitive advantage. Then, choose a suitable strategy based on three considerations.

FIGURE 2.6
Porter's Generic Strategies Model

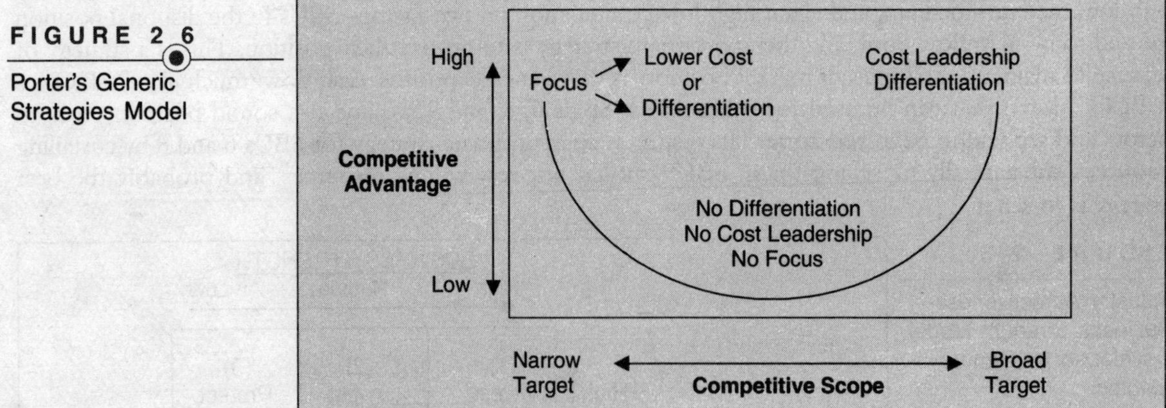

Competitive Scope

Refers to the range of a company's activities that focus on a broad or narrow market segment. ***Competitive advantage*** is accomplished by offering value to customers that competitors are not offering. This is possible either through lower cost or by offering unique benefits to customers that differentiate the product in customers' perceptions. This model takes into consideration the two important concepts of competitive scope and competitive advantage to generate three generic strategies. The unique point Prof. Porter stresses is that high market share may not be essential for financial success of a business. The three generic strategy considerations are appropriate for a wide variety of businesses across different industries:

1. Cost Leadership.
2. Differentiation.
3. Focus

Cost Leadership

Cost leadership strategy is generally adopted by large organisations or SBUs. The company targets a broad market and aims to become the lowest-cost producer of a standard product and produces large quantities, then prices it at a level that is less than the competitors' prices. This is achieved through production-efficiencies, purchasing, product design, technology, distribution, etc. This strategy could be somewhat risky in the long run because other competing companies will usually compete with still lower costs and prices and pose a problem for the company that adopted this strategy.

Differentiation

Strategy of differentiation involves developing a competitive advantage by offering a product that has broad appeal because, the product is perceived as persuasively valuable and distinct by customers, perhaps even unique in some way such as quality, innovative design, emotional dimensions, service, etc. And since customers value the appeal, the company can charge a higher price than competitors. Many ego-intensive or technically complex products enjoy this advantage such as Rolex watches, Caterpillar earthmoving equipments or Mercedes cars.

FIGURE 2.7
Porter's generic Strategy Model

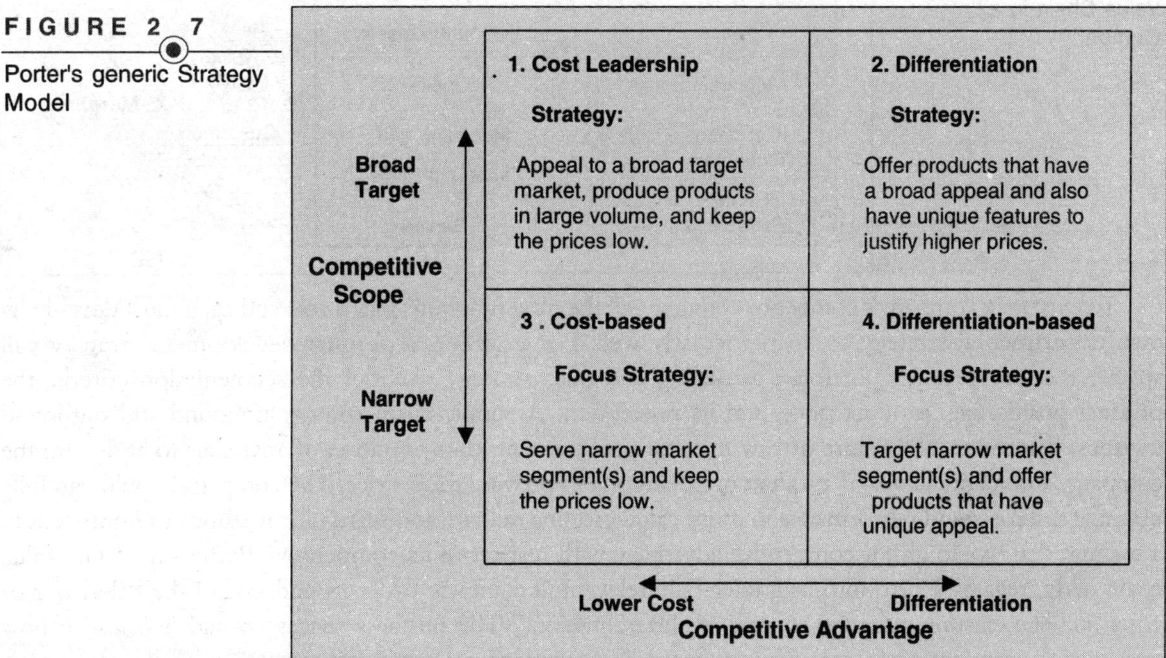

Focus

Focus strategy refers to accomplishing a competitive advantage in a part of market to satisfy customer needs either through cost leadership or differentiation by offering a low-priced product or a high-priced but highly distinctive product. The target segments are set apart by some factor such as geography or highly specialised needs and the company knows these segments rather intimately. Porsche autos and Apple computers are said to be following this strategy.

Usually, the companies in trouble are those that have nothing going for them either in terms of cost-leadership, differentiation, or focus.

Accordingly, Porter believes that businesses that don't have either cost leadership, differentiation, or focus going for them are the ones who find themselves in trouble.

Value Chain Analysis: Michael Porter views the total economic system in an industry as a value creating system and should be used to identify ways and means to deliver more value to its customers. Every business is involved in designing (product development), producing (operations), marketing, delivering, and supporting its product.

Nine strategically relevant activities go into creating customer value and also involve costs. Five of these activities are core functions and must be performed for a successful sale and include: (1) inbound logistics to produce the product (raw materials, etc.), (2) actual product production (operations), (3) shipping out finished product (outbound logistics), marketing and sales, and (4) servicing (service support). The remaining four activities are support activities to facilitate the functioning of the five core functions in the value chain and include: (5) finance, (6) accounts, (7) information technology, and (8) human resources.

The value chain begins with new product development that creates product specifications. Using these specifications, operations converts inbound supplies into finished products; marketing and sales generate demand by communicating with target customers and also brings in customer inputs; distribution makes the product available to customers, and service responds to customers during or after the sale.

FIGURE 2.8

Value Chain in a Company

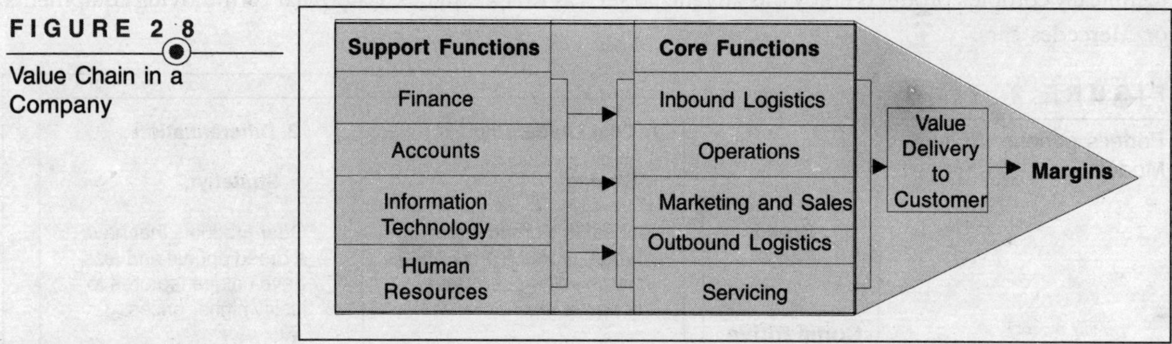

To execute a company's competitive strategy, all the nine functions play a role and each must develop its own departmental strategy to do particularly well. For example, a product development strategy will specify the new product portfolio; marketing and sales strategy specifies the segmentation criteria, the product positioning, product price, and its promotion. A supply chain strategy (inbound and outbound logistics) determines the nature of raw material procurement, transportation of materials to and from the company, and manufacture of product or operations to provide the service. The company should carefully examine the costs and performance in every value-creating activity and search for methods to improve it in a manner that would give it competitive advantage with respect to its competitors. Porter says, "The value chain disaggregates a firm into its strategically relevant activities in order to understand the behaviour of costs and the existing potential sources of differentiation." The business success would depend on how well each department performs and coordinates its activities with other departments.

Profit Impact of Market Strategy (PIMS)

Profit Impact of Market Strategy is perhaps a novel approach to strategic market planning and the development of competitive strategies. PIMS is a research programme developed by Strategic Planning Institute (SPI). The institute maintains a database of confidential operating and competitive data on about

3000 businesses for a minimum of four years. The data consists of about 100 items from each participating organisation and includes ***industry characteristics, competitive position, resource allocation, strategies***, and the ***operating results***. As a part of its inputs, each participating firm supplies its assumptions about the "most likely" changes in future rates of sales, prices, materials costs, wage rates, and equipment costs. The SPI analyses the data and prepares reports for member organisations to help them evaluate their present strategies and assess alternatives.

A Strategic Business Unit (SBU) serves as the unit of analysis in the PIMS studies:

> *"Each business is a division, product line, or profit centre within its parent company, selling a distinct set of products and/or services to an identifiable group of customers, in competition with a well-defined set of competitors, and for which meaningful separation can be made of revenues, operating costs, investments, and strategic plans."*
>
> [*The PIMS Programme* (Cambridge, Mass: Strategic Planning Institute, 1980)].

Unlike the other approaches to developing strategy, the PIMS furnishes both diagnostic and prescriptive information. According to Robert Buzzell and Bradley T. Gale, a large and diversified European firm was considering acquiring a US company. The managers of the European firm used PIMS database and models to simulate performance of the combined firms. This analysis was the most important piece of evidence in reaching the final decision to acquire the US firm.

EXHIBIT 2.3: EXAMPLES OF INFORMATION IN PIMS DATA BASE

Industry Characteristics	**Structure of production process**
Long-run market growth rate Short-run market growth rate Rate of inflation of selling price level Number and size of customers Purchase frequency and magnitude	Capital intensity (degree of automation etc.) Degree of vertical integration Capacity utilisation Productivity and capital equipment Productivity of people Inventory level
Competitive position	**Resource allocation**
Share of the served market Share relative to that of largest competitors Product quality relative to that of competitors Prices relative to those of competitors Pay scales relative to those of competitors Marketing efforts relative to those of competitors Pattern of market segmentation Rate of new product introductions	R & D budgets Advertising and promotion budgets Sales force expenditures **Strategic moves** Patterns of change in controllable elements **Operating results** Profitability results Cash flow results Growth results

The PIMS database indicates a strong link between market share and profitability: high market share companies earn higher ROI. The data also indicates that companies offering higher quality products tend to be more profitable than competitors. In this regard, Porter's model suggests that higher quality can justify higher prices. The PIMS model also suggests that lower costs have a positive impact on profitability.

Strategic Business Unit (SBU) Strategy

The strategic market planning focus at the corporate level concerns the growth and health of the total corporation with best possible allocation of corporate resources across all SBUs. At the business unit level planning, managers are concerned with successfully marketing their product(s) or services to ensure its short-term prosperity and healthy prospects in the long-term by evolving the right competitive strategies. Strategic business units need to be developed according to how well the corporation's strengths and skills match the SBU needs and success. Planning at this level concerns each individual Strategic Business Unit (SBU) separately within the boundaries of corporate mission, objectives, and strategies. At SBU level, managers can use any of the planning models to allocate available resources to products, product lines, or brands and adopt suitable objectives and strategies within the limits of corporate objectives and strategies.

Individual business units may have their own mission within the boundaries of corporate mission and objectives. Then, managers develop business unit level objectives based on corporate goals and strategies. For instance, if the corporate objective were to get a 15 per cent ROI and the strategy were to be cost-cutting to accomplish this objective during the next year, the business unit level objective would be cost-cutting. An important exercise undertaken by many businesses at this level is to conduct **Strengths, Weaknesses, Opportunities** and **Threats (SWOT)** analysis to spot the right opportunities to match the business unit's strengths and also identify weaknesses and serious threats and their likelihood of occurrence that may hamper the business unit's growth prospects. The assessment of strengths and weaknesses relates to internal factors that give the company certain advantages and weaknesses in meeting the needs of customers in the target markets. Business units generally monitor major macro forces such as demographic, economic, technological, socio-cultural, and political and legal. Monitoring of micro forces focuses on customers, competitors, and channel partners. These factors can often adversely affect the profitability of a company. Opportunities and threats are present in the *external* environment and strengths/weaknesses are *internal* to the company. Opportunities and threats are particularly considered by all competing companies, and sometimes even by non-competing companies as well because they represent issues that may be important. O. C Ferrell, George H. Lucas, and David J. Luck recommend that strengths and weaknesses should also be analysed relative to market needs and competition because this would allow the company to determine what it does well and what it needs to improve.

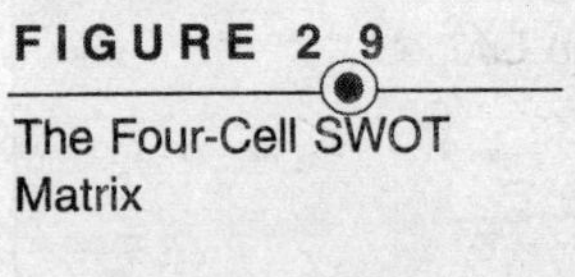

FIGURE 2.9
The Four-Cell SWOT Matrix

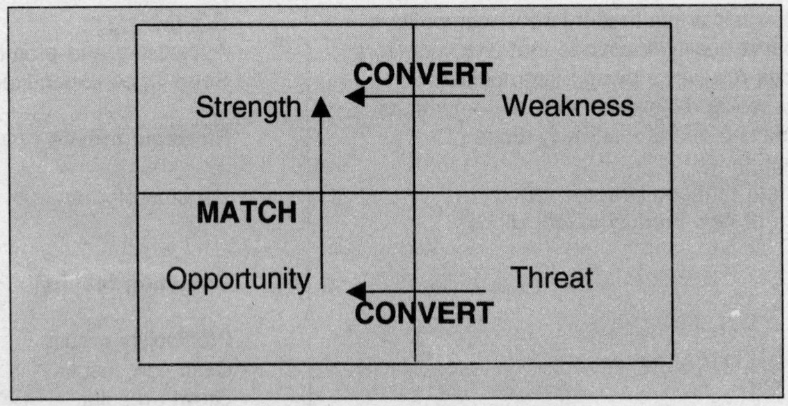

[*Source:* Nigel F. Piercy, *Market-Led Strategic Change,* (1992)].

Strengths relate to competitive advantage or distinctive competencies that give the company an edge in meeting the customer needs. For example, HLL in India has the widest distribution network in place, and Lux enjoys a very strong brand pull. Any strength is only meaningful to the extent that it gives an advantage to a company in meeting customer needs more effectively and completely. For instance, a company marketing a high quality product and having a highly trained and capable sales force (strength) may be of little use if customers are interested in low price and not in a high quality, expensive product. **Weaknesses** refer to any type of limitations that a business unit may experience in any area internal to a business unit, such as production, design, R&D, finance, human resource, marketing & sales, skills, etc. Besides the obvious, weaknesses should also be assessed from a customer perspective. There may be certain weaknesses that only customers can perceive but which the company cannot see. Relatively recent research suggests that logos used by some companies actually hurt the image of company's brands. An in-depth consumer research revealed that the two poorest performing logos were those of British Airways and American Express, and two of the three best rated were those of IBM and Mercedes-Benz ("Some Logos Hurt Brands," *Marketing News*, November 8, 1993).

As already mentioned while discussing market opportunities earlier, they represent favourable conditions in the environment that could hold some beneficial potential if addressed appropriately. **Threats** are those anticipated or prevailing conditions or barriers in the market-place that may adversely affect the chances of accomplishing company objectives.

SWOT Analysis of Apple

Strengths

■ Apple is a very successful company. Sales of its iPod music player had increased its second quarter profits to $320 million (June 2005). The favourable brand perception had also increased sales of Macintosh computers. So iPod gives the company access to a whole new series of segments that buy into other parts of the Apple brand. The sales of its notebook products are also very strong, and represent a huge contribution to income for Apple.

■ Brand is all-important. Apple is one of the most established and healthy IT brands in the World, and has a very loyal set of enthusiastic customers that advocate the brand. Such powerful loyalty means that Ample not only recruits new customers, it retains them, i.e., they come back for more products and services from Apple, and the company also has the opportunity to extend new products to them, for example the iPod.

Weaknesses

It is reported that the Apple iPod Nano may have a faulty screen. The company has commented that a batch of its product has screens that break under impact, and the company is replacing all faulty items. This is in addition to problems with early iPods that had faulty batteries, whereby the company offered customers free battery cases.

There is pressure on Apple to increase the price of its music download file, from the music industry itself. Many of these companies make more money from iTunes (i.e., downloadable music files) than from their original CD sales. Apple has sold about 22 million iPod digital music players and more than 500 million songs through its iTunes music store. It accounts for 82% of all legally downloaded music in the US. The company is resolute, but if it gives in to the music producers, it may be perceived as a commercial weakness.

Early in 2005, Apple announced that it was to end its long-standing relationship with IBM as a chip supplier, and that it was about to switch to Intel. Some industry specialists commented that the swap could confuse Apple's consumers.

Opportunities

Apple has the opportunity to develop its iTunes and music player technology into a mobile phone format. Motorola developed the Rokr mobile-phone device. It has a colour screen, stereo speakers and an advanced camera system. A version of Apple's iTunes music store has

Contd...

been developed for the phone so users can manage the tracks they store on it. Downloads are available via a USB cable, and software on the handset pauses music if a phone call comes in. New technologies and strategic alliances offer opportunities for Apple.

Podcasts are downloadable radio shows that can be downloaded from the Internet, and then played back on iPods and other MP3 devices at the convenience of the listener. The listener can subscribe to Podcasts for free, and ultimately revenue could be generated from paid for subscription or through revenue generated from sales of other downloads.

Threats

The biggest threat to IT companies, such as Apple, is the very high level of competition in the technology markets. Being successful attracts competition, and Apple works very hard on research and development and marketing in order to retain its competitive position. The popularity of iPod and Apple Mac are subject to demand, and will be affected if economies begin to falter and demand falls for their products.

There is also a high product substitution effect in the innovative and fast moving IT consumables market. So iPod and MP3 rule today, but only yesterday it was CD, DAT, and Vinyl. Tomorrow's technology might be completely different. Wireless technologies could replace the need for a physical music player.

In 2005 Apple won a legal case that forced Bloggers to name the sources of information that pre-empted the launch of new Apple products. It was suspected that Apple's own employees had leaked confidential information about their new Asteroid product. The three individuals prosecuted, all owned Apple tribute sites, and were big fans of the company's products. The blogs had appeared on their sites, and they were forced to reveal their source. The ruling saw commercial confidentiality as more important as the right to speech of individuals. Apple are vulnerable to leaks that could cost them profits.

(Source: www.Marketingteacher.com)

Andrew Campbell, Michael Goold, and Marcus Alexander ask a question: ("Corporate Strategy: is the SBU enhanced because the corporate strategy can contribute to the critical success factors of that unit?" A business can choose one or more growth strategies. H. Igor Ansoff has recommended four broad growth categories: market penetration, product development, market development, and diversification.

Growth Strategies

Intensive Growth: Intensive growth strategies are appropriate when **current products** and **current markets** show the potential for sales increase. There are three main strategic options that seem to be appropriate to accomplish intensive growth:

1. Market Penetration.
2. Market Development.
3. Product Development.

Market Penetration is a strategy of increasing sales of existing products in current markets. For example, Procter & Gamble reduced the price of its detergent Ariel in the Indian market to increase its sales among existing and new consumers in the current market. Depending on the product category, other approaches can be to increase advertising, sales promotion, personal selling and increase distribution network in the current markets.

FIGURE 2.10
Growth Strategies

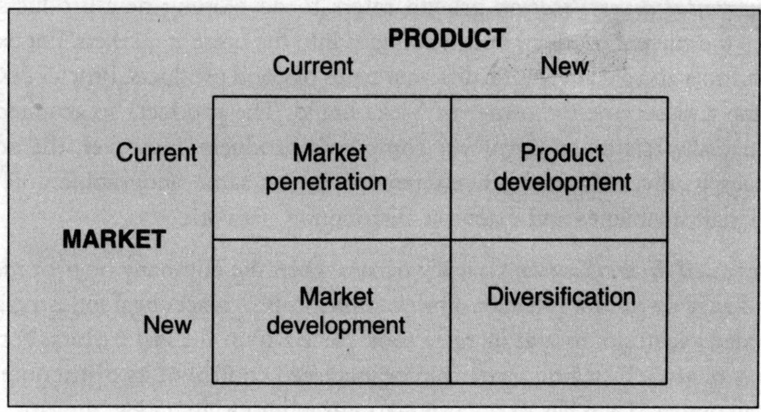

PRODUCT
Current
New
Current
Market penetration
Product development
MARKET
New
Market development
Diversification

Market Development

Strategy refers to increasing sales by introducing current products into new markets. This strategy often involves expanding business in new geographic areas. For example, with globalisation and opening up of Indian borders for businesses, many organisations have introduced their products in the Indian market. These companies were marketing these products in their domestic and other markets for quite sometime.

Product Development

Means increasing sales by improving current products in some way or developing entirely new products for current markets. For example, Gillette has modified its razor and named it Vector for Indian consumers. In auto industry, manufacturers regularly introduce redesigned or new products.

Diversification Growth

This strategy involves developing new products to be sold in new markets. Through this strategy, a firm with adequate resources can enter new, and expanding markets. Diversification strategy has some advantage over single-business companies because this way they can make better use of their managerial, financial, and technical resources and also spread their risk across a number of markets. The strategy can be implemented by internal development or by acquiring other firms.

FIGURE 2.11
Diversification Strategies

New Products	Markets: Present Markets	Markets: New Markets
Unrelated to Current Products	Horizontal diversification	Conglomerate diversification
Related to Current Products	Integrated diversification	Concentric diversification

Companies often diversify because their current sales are stagnating. Implementing diversification strategy generally requires considerable resources and often proves somewhat risky compared to other growth strategies. Michael E. Porter has reported one study of diversification strategies adopted by thirty-three large US organisations. This study found that the vast majority of the diversifications were mistakes. In nearly 20 % of the cases, these companies were taken over.

Horizontal diversification growth refers to developing new products that are technologically ***not*** related to the current products and introduced into the present markets. For example, HLL acquired Modern Foods in India and gained several different types of food products, Procter & Gamble purchased Richardson Hindustan and became the owner of Vicks brand. The products so acquired in the two examples are not technologically related to the buyer company's products. However, the acquisitions have helped these companies to diversify into other segments in the same geographic area and take advantage of their promotional capabilities and extensive distribution network.

Integrated diversification typically occurs when the company buys or merges with another firm in the same industry or product market. For example, in pharmaceutical industry, auto industry, IT industry and others, many acquisitions and mergers took place within the last 5 years. Forward integration occurs when the aim is to grow by taking ownership or increased control of its distribution channels such as Bata has its own retail outlets. Titan has its own showrooms in important cities. Similarly, Raymonds, Vimal Fabrics, and others have their own showrooms. Backward diversification refers to taking the ownership or control of its supply system such as when a newspaper buys a paper mill, or a petroleum products company has its own crude oil wells. Integrated diversification refers to buying or taking control of one or more competitors, such as the merger of two computer and computer peripheral companies, Compaq and HP.

Conglomerate diversification occurs when a company acquires a new business that has no relationship to its present technology, products, or markets. For example, a soft drink company might enter the computer hardware business.

Concentric diversification occurs when a company's technology and marketing of new products are related in some way to current products, but these new products are introduced in new markets only.

Dabur – 'Growth Natural' is the New Mantra

"For some time in the second half of 1990s, it appeared as if Murphy was running things at Dabur India Ltd.; everything that could go wrong, did. The Ayurvedic products major's forays into snack foods, chewing gum, cheese, cosmetics, and health insurance had failed. And, four of its joint ventures – with Spain-based Agrolimen for chewing gum; Israel-based Osem Foods, for snack foods; French Bongrain SA for cheese, and Boston-based Liberty Mutual for insurance – had run aground."

"It surprised no one, when, in 1999, the company announced it would implement a restructuring template prepared by McKinsey & Company. Dabur India Ltd. followed this up by exiting three of its joint ventures – General De Confiteria India, Excelsia Foods (snacks), and The Health Insurance Tie-up – discontinuing its Samara line of herbal cosmetics, and pulling out of veterinary products and bulk drugs."

"The company has returned to its original focus on family and healthcare, oncological drugs, Ayurvedic medicines, and health foods. Confesses G. C. Burman, 59, Vice Chairman and Managing Director, Dabur India Ltd.: "We diversified into unrelated areas and suffered. Now, we will focus only on core areas and grow through the natural route: Dabur India Ltd. is an Ayurvedic company, and it is as an Ayurvedic company that it will grow."

(Source: Paroma Roy Chowdhury, "Herbal Cure for Dabur," Business Today, Aug.–Sept. 2000)

Marketing Objectives and Strategy

Corporate mission, objectives, and strategy provide the foundation for planning activities in different business units and departments. ***Marketing objectives*** are determined on the basis of current business analysis and specify what is to be accomplished through marketing activities. As pointed out earlier, marketing objectives should be stated in clear, simple, and as far as possible quantitative terms so that all concerned understand without any ambiguity what they are focused upon achieving within a specified period of time and that against these standards, the results will be evaluated. Typically, marketing objectives in almost all businesses relate to either market share, sales volume, return on investment, customer complaints, or customer satisfaction levels.

Marketing strategy refers to actions for developing, pricing, distributing, and promoting products that meet the needs of specific customer groups. It determines the best use of the company resources to formulate an action plan to meet its objectives. Marketing strategy focuses on analysing and selecting target market, and developing suitable marketing mix for this target market.

TABLE 2.1

Three Options of Intensive Growth Strategy and Marketing Mix

		MARKETING–MIX			
SBU Strategy	**Marketing Strategy**	**Product**	**Price**	**Distribution**	**Promotion**
Market Penetration (1)	Increase sales of brand 'B' in the 18 - 24 - year old youth	Raise quality level. Add features desired by this segment.	Lower the prices below that of competitors.	Increase distribution outlets visited by this segment.	Offer coupons, advertise new prices. Target advertising to this group via media choice.
Market Development (2)	Find new uses for the product; enter new markets; enter into global markets.	Conduct research to discover new uses; new features desired by new markets.	Prices will depend on new uses and new markets.	Develop distribution in new markets; find global distribution partners.	Consumer education on new uses; use new advertising appeals for new markets.
Product Development (3)	Significantly improve existing products or develop new products.	Invest in consumer research and product development.	Increase prices on improved products.	For new products gain retailer cooperation to display.	Communicate improvements; advertise and use sales promotion.

Continuing with the example of Dabur in the box above, just for the sake of a simple example the statement of objectives and strategy might read:

- The objective of Dabur India, pharmaceutical division is to capture 25 per cent market share from the present 20 per cent by the end of December 2005.
- To capture this level of market share, the division will focus on its Ayurvedic specialities and will concentrate on building strong brands.
- Our target market would be the total domestic market. The segments would include general health conscious consumers, women, and children. Special purpose products would include skincare products, hair care, and oral care for men, women, and children.

Target market is a group of relatively homogenous customers who share similar types of specific needs and product preferences. Businesses that aim to satisfy the needs of all customers generally end up not satisfying the needs of any particular customer groups well. Careful target market selection may be the important decision for a company to achieve its marketing objectives. Defining the target market and developing the appropriate marketing mix are the keys to strategic marketing success. Just going by assumptions about the characteristics of target market and not knowing the set of product attribute preferences can prove to be a fatal mistake in case of many product categories. For example, Avanti moped was a sound product technically but mistakenly positioned and promoted as a family-two-wheeler. It failed miserably because the choice of target segment was inappropriate and ultimately resulted in huge losses and closure of the business. When analysing and assessing the potential target markets, managers also take into consideration company resources and skills to develop the right combination of marketing mix that would effectively satisfy the target market needs and that this would be consistent with the company's overall objectives.

Proper selection of the target market and knowing the preferences of customers serves as the foundation on which the appropriate ***marketing mix*** can be developed.

Developing Marketing Plan

A marketing plan is a formal written document, prepared detailing the activities essential to implement the chosen marketing strategies. It is a subordinate set of corporate strategy and specifies those specific marketing strategies necessary to achieve the objectives of the business unit and contribute to achieving overall corporate objectives. Some companies develop several marketing plans, one for each product/brand.

Many organisations develop short-term, mid-term, and long-term marketing plans. Sort-term plans cover a period of one year or sometimes even less. Mid-term plans generally focus on a period of two to five years, whereas long-term plans are relatively uncommon because they have limited value as the marketing conditions keep on changing rapidly. Various business decisions of strategic nature also grow in complexity and decisions concerning growth, profitability, and survival remain of paramount importance.

A marketing plan analyses the current marketing situation, assesses the market opportunities, threats, competitive strengths and weaknesses of the organisation. Based on the SWOT analysis, the management establishes marketing objectives, defines the marketing strategies and action programmes needed to accomplish the objectives. The plan also specifies the needed controls to monitor the implementation of the plan.

A marketing plan is never rigid in its scope. There is only one constant on which companies can count on that the marketplace will change. Despite the fact that some environments remain fairly stable from year to year–some other factors evolve slowly–but nevertheless, things can change suddenly and in fairly unexpected ways that would necessitate quick revision of plans. For example, if a new competitor enters the market, the company might need to revise some of its activities. We have seen when one soft drink company reduces the price of one or more of its different packs, the other companies immediately respond by matching the price reduction.

The best marketing plans are updated continuously in response to changing market conditions. To ensure proper implementation of planned programmes, companies evolve appropriate control mechanisms to help management take corrective actions as and when the need arises. In some companies, field salespersons submit daily reports and also there is a system of monthly and quarterly targets and reports from first-line and middle management personnel. Information flow on daily basis is facilitated because of laptop computers and Internet. Research data providing agencies such as Operations Research Group (ORG) in India furnish retail audit, brand share, and market share data in different markets on monthly basis. This data furnishes useful information for monitoring performance. Another control measure some companies use is to keep contingency plans ready for different types of reasonably serious but predictable emergencies. In the next chapter, some important aspects of proper implementation have been discussed.

TABLE 2.2

Contents of a Typical Annual Marketing Plan

1. ***Executive Summary:*** This section presents a brief summary of the marketing plan for senior managers who desire an overview.
2. ***Current Marketing Situation:*** This section presents an analysis of the trends and changes in the marketing environment, the market situation, customers, and competitors.
3. ***SWOT Analysis:*** This focuses on presenting an analysis of opportunities, threats, strengths, and weaknesses with respect to SBU (or different products/brands) for which the plan has been developed.

Contd...

4. ***Marketing Objectives:*** This section details the goals the marketing plan aims to achieve.
5. ***Marketing Strategies and Tactics:*** This portion describes the segmentation and target market, product, price, distribution, and promotion activities to be employed to accomplish the objectives.
6. ***Financial Schedules:*** This section usually mentions projected sales, expenses, and profits and the amounts allocated to different activities.
7. ***Time Schedules:*** This section mentions details when different activities will be undertaken during the plan period.
8. ***Controls:*** This section addresses the procedures for monitoring the plan over time for taking any corrective actions, if needed.

Summary

Strategic market planning refers to developing an outline of the methods and resources required to accomplish the corporate goals within a particular target market. In the process, it takes into consideration all functional areas of a strategic business unit that must be coordinated. A Strategic Business Unit (SBU) may be an independent business division, profit centre, a product line, or a single product within the parent corporation to identify areas for consideration in a specific strategic market plan. The outcome of strategic market planning process is a market plan that details the framework and entire set of activities to be performed and it is put into writing to direct and control an organisation's marketing activities.

An organisation's objectives should be derived from its mission that reflects what an organisation aims to become. The mission statement focuses on defining what business it is in, determining its customer, answering what is value to customer, and what business it should be in.

Environmental scanning is important as it brings to light the opportunities and threats faced by an organisation. The major considerations are evaluation of market opportunities and assessing the company's capabilities and resources. A favourable opportunity offers a chance to generate sales from the market if timely action is taken.

A number of analytical tools are available to help corporate managers in their planning efforts such as BCG approach and General Electric approach, Porter's Generic Strategies, and PIMS programme for assessing the health and resource allocation to different Strategic Business Units.

After corporate level planning, companies can adopt different business-unit level strategies to market products handled by each SBU within specific target markets. Growth strategies include market development, market penetration, and product development. In case a company decides to diversify, it has the options of horizontal diversification, conglomerate diversification, integrated diversification, and concentric diversification.

Marketing strategy refers to selection of target market, and developing the marketing mix that will meet the needs and wants of target customers and lead to creating satisfied customers.

The nature of strategic market planning is such that there seems to be an overlap to some extent among corporate strategy, business-unit strategy, and marketing strategy. However, marketing strategy is the most detailed and specific of the three levels.

A marketing plan is a written document that details the implementation and control aspects of marketing activities of an organisation. Most marketing plans include an executive summary, current marketing situation (environmental analysis), SWOT analysis, marketing objectives, marketing strategies and tactics, financial schedules, time schedules, and control mechanisms.

Questions for Discussion

1. What does strategic market planning mean? Explain the characteristics and importance of a good mission statement?
2. What are the steps of the strategic market planning? Explain their interrelationship.
3. How can the analysis of a company's opportunities and resources affect its marketing objectives and strategy?
4. How can companies develop sustainable competitive advantage? Explain with examples of Indian companies.
5. How can business-portfolio analysis models be used in developing company strategy?
6. Discuss the Boston Consulting Group approach to business-portfolio analysis for each type of SBU? What strategies would you consider?
7. Discuss Porter's Generic Strategies model. Identify an Indian company that you think has competitive advantage based on one of the four strategies.
8. Suggest how a company can increase its sales in the current target markets. How can the company increase sales in new markets?
9. Give reasons why a company should develop a marketing plan.

Projects

1. Select a diversified Indian company, collect information about its businesses, and suggest how many Strategic Business Units it should form. Give your reasons.
2. Identify the target market(s) of the following companies:
   (a) Bata, (b) Dabur, (c) Honda, and (d) LG Electronics.
3. Assume you have entered the manufacture and marketing of medium quality sports shoe manufacture. Draw up your marketing plan for the company.

Bibliography

1. Philip Kotler, "The Major Tasks of Marketing Management," *Journal of Marketing,* October 1973.
2. Philip Kotler and Sidney J. Levy, "Demarketing, Yes, Demarketing," *Harvard Business Review,* November-December 1971.
3. David Aaker, "Managing Assets and Skills: The Key to Sustainable Competitive Advantage," *California Management Review,* 1989.
4. Orville C Walker, Jr., Harper W Boyd, Jr., John Mullins, and Jean-Claude Jarreche, *'Marketing Strategy: A Decision-Focused Approach'* Tata McGraw-Hill, 4th ed. 2003.
5. Peter F. Drucker, *Management: Tasks, Responsibilities, Practices,* 1974.
6. David W. Cravens, "Gaining Strategic Marketing Advantage," *Business Horizons,* 1988.
7. Derek Abell, "Strategic Windows," *Journal of Marketing,* July 1978.
8. Derek Abell, *Defining the Business: The Starting Point of Strategic Planning,* Prentice-Hall, 1980.

9. Roger A. Kerin, Vijay Mahajan, and Rajan Vardarajan, *Contemporary Perspectives on Strategic Planning,* 1990.
10. Donald L. McCabe and V. K. Narayanan, "The Life Cycle of PIMS and BCG Models," *Industrial Marketing Management,* 1991.
11. Geoffrey Smith and Lisa Driscoll, "Victor Kiam, the Self-Sacking Quarterback," *Business Week,* February 1991.
12. Michael E. Porter, *Competitive Advantage: Creating and Sustaining Superior Performance,* 1985.
13. Robert Buzzell and Bradley T. Gale, *PIMS Principles: Linking Strategy to Performance,* 1987.
14. O. C. Ferrell, George H. Lucas, and David J. Luck, *Strategic Marketing Management: Text and Cases,* 1994.
15. Nigel F. Piercy, *Market-Led Strategic Change,* 1992.
16. Andrew Campbell, Michael Goold, and Marcus Alexander, "Corporate Strategy: The Quest for Parenting Advantage," *Harvard Business Review,* March/April 1995.
17. H. Igor Ansoff, *New Corporate Strategy,* 1988.
18. Michael E. Porter, "From Competitive Advantage to Corporate Strategy, *Harvard Business Review,* May/June, 1987.
19. J. Thomas Russell and W. Roland Lane, *Kleppner's Advertising Procedure,* 14th Ed.
20. Philip Kotler, *Marketing Management: Analysis, Planning, Implementation, and Control,* 9th Ed.
21. Steven J. Skinner, *Marketing,* 1994.
22. William J. Stanton, Michael J. Etzel, and Bruce J. Walker, *Fundamentals of Marketing,* 10th Ed.

Marketing Implementation & Control

CHAPTER 3

LEARNING OBJECTIVES

After going through this chapter, you will understand:

- What factors must be taken care of to implement a marketing plan
- The importance of internal and external marketing
- The concept of quality control
- Different approaches to organising marketing department
- Implementation of marketing programmes
- Different methods to control implementation; various marketing aspects

PepsiCo sold $3.6 billion worth of Pepsi, Diet Pepsi, Pepsi Max, and other beverage products outside the US market in 1995. This was 8 per cent more than the previous year, and its international operations earned $226 million, up 16 per cent from 1994. However, the Coca-Cola Co. continues to outsell PepsiCo nearly three cans to one outside the US, and it drives nearly 80 per cent of its earnings from overseas beverage sales, compared to PepsiCo's 6 per cent. Pepsi also trails Coke in the US. To gain market share and further differentiate itself from its archrival, PepsiCo plans to revamp its overseas marketing strategy with a complete redesign of the company's cans and bottles, a fresh advertising campaign, and a renovation of its overseas manufacturing and distribution systems. Projected cost of the overhaul would be $300 to 500 million.

Code-named "Project Blue," PepsiCo's plans call for updating cans and bottles designed for overseas markets from the familiar red, white, and blue labels used at home to a royal blue design with a futuristic, three-dimensional graphic of the company logo. According to PepsiCo officials, this is the first redesign of these products in five years, and the change is more radical than earlier changes. PepsiCo also plans to launch a new advertising campaign with celebrity endorsers to tout Pepsi around the word. The firm already features tennis star Andre Agassi and supermodel Cindy Crawford in some overseas ads.

The purpose of Project Blue is to refocus PepsiCo's overseas image and make it's marketing more consistent. These moves parallel a recent transformation in PepsiCo's overseas snacks division. For example, the firm's Doritos brand has been standardised globally in terms of shape, packaging, and positioning, although elements such as seasoning and thickness are still tailored for regional taste differences. These changes helped make Doritos the number one selling salty snack with $2 billion sales over twenty countries, including the US. Executives hope Project Blue will have a similar effect on PepsiCo's international beverage division, giving Pepsi a boost in the global cola wars.

Source: Lon Bongiorno, "The Pepsi Regeneration," Business Week, March 11, 1996; Robert Frank, "PepsiCo to Revamp Beverage Line Outside the US," Wall Street Journal, March 15, 1996.

As pointed out in the preceding chapter, marketing implementation and control activities are very important and focus on "how" of putting marketing strategies into action. It need not be emphasised that the surest way to making the best of marketing strategies unsuccessful is to combine it with bad implementation. However, we can't escape the truth that almost all marketing strategies turn out somewhat differently than intended. Based on views of Orville C Walker, Jr., and Robert W Ruekert it can be said that firms have two types of strategies, the intended strategy and realised strategy. The intended strategy is developed during the planning phase for implementation and the realised strategy is the one that actually takes place. During the process of implementing the intended strategy, the realised strategy happens and is often worse than the intended strategy.

The most common reason why this shift from the intended strategy sometimes happens is that managers fail to appreciate the importance of the fact that proper implementation is just as important as the marketing strategy. There is close relationship between the strategy and its implementation and can be viewed as two sides of the same coin. For example, several issues that involve both strategy and implementation include morale problems, employee compensation, performance appraisal, career development, etc. Robert Howard reports this relationship generally gives rise to three major problems:

- ***The responsibility for marketing strategy and its implementation are separated:*** This is often the key hurdle in the implementation stage of marketing strategy. Typically, it is the top management in the firm that develops the marketing strategies, and the responsibility to implement these strategies rests at the frontline of the firm. This distancing can hinder implementation because it is the frontline that daily interacts with customers, and not the top management. As a result of this, the top management may not appreciate the unique problems associated with implementing different marketing activities. Another reason that cannot be ignored is that it is always the human beings who implement the strategies, and in this situation the very personnel who are often responsible for implementation had no voice in formulating them. Consequently, these frontline personnel may lack motivation and commitment.

FIGURE 3 1

Separation of Strategy Planning and Implementation

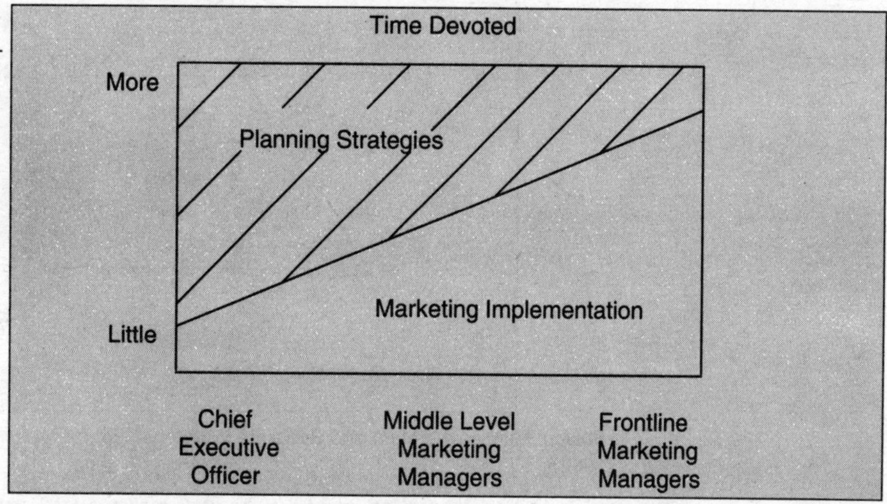

(Adapted with changes from O. C. Ferrel, George Lucas, and David J. Luck, *Strategic Marketing Management: Text and Cases,* 1994).

- ***Marketing strategy and its implementation are closely related:*** Firms that face this problem of difference between intended strategy and realised strategy almost always assume that planning marketing strategies comes first, followed by implementation. In reality, the formulation of marketing strategies and their implementation activities should be developed at the same time. It makes sense to appreciate that implementation activities may require modification or changes in strategies.
- ***Marketing strategy and implementation are constantly evolving:*** Keeping in view the dynamic nature of marketing environment, the shifts in customer wants, or competitive moves, etc., the strategy and implementation must remain flexible and be able to quickly respond to changes taking place in the market and its environment.

In a typical company, there are market information systems, strategic planning systems, finance, budgeting, and accounting systems, production and quality control systems, and performance appraisal systems.

McKinsey's 7-S Framework

The people-system in companies refers to the importance of human resources in the process of implementation and includes their quality, diversity, and skills. In this regard, their recruitment, selection, training, and motivation have great impact on the success of marketing strategies implementation. Closely linked to this is the art and skill of managing company personnel. The core element of marketing implementation is "shared values." Shared values and goals bind all the components of the firm together into a single, functional entity and are instrumental in successful implementation of marketing strategies. The main objective of a detailed mission statement is to clearly define the organisational philosophy and direction, that is, the shared values and goals of an organisation. McKinsey & Company's 7–S framework depicts this appropriately. According to this framework, strategy is just one of seven components that influence business success. In the absence of shared goals, different components of the company might pursue different objectives, thus limiting the chances of a company's success. In the presence of these seven elements, companies are usually more successful at strategy implementation.

FIGURE 3.2
McKinsey & Company's 7–S Framework

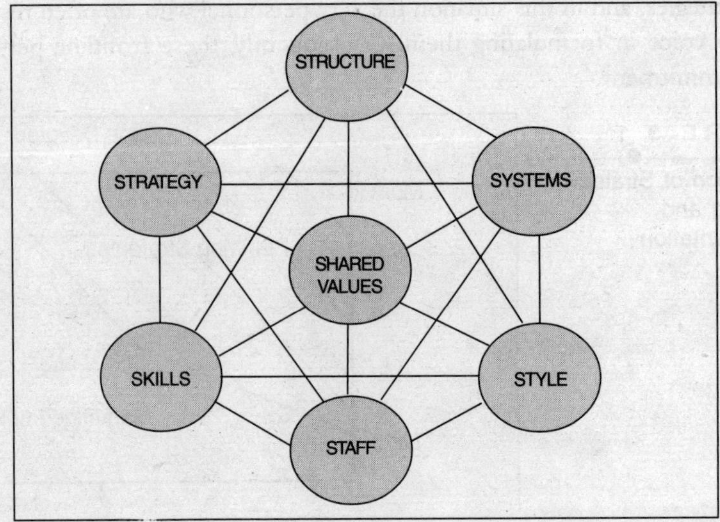

[*Source:* Thomas J. Peters and Robert H. Waterman, Jr., *In Search of Excellence*, Harper & Row (1982)].

1. Strategy is a coherent set of actions aimed at attaining a sustainable competitive advantage, improving the company's position with customers, or allocating resources.
2. Structure shows the company's organisation and depicts who reports to whom in the hierarchy.
3. Systems refer to the processes and flows showing how a company gets things done in its day-to-day functioning such as information systems, capital budgeting systems, manufacturing processes, quality control systems, and performance measurement systems.
4. Style refers to tangible evidence of what management considers as important, not by what it says, but the way management actually behaves.
5. Staff means all the people in a company. It is not about their individual personalities but about company demographics.
6. Skills refer to the capabilities that are possessed by a company as a whole, needed to carry out the company's strategy.
7. Shared values are the guiding values that almost all employees share, not merely the simple goal statements in determining corporate identity.

Components of Implementation

Marketing managers can adopt different approaches to implementing marketing strategies. In this regard, two general approaches to implementation are (1) internal marketing, and (2) quality control management. Both these approaches are not mutually exclusive and are often used when developing marketing activities.

Internal Marketing: Company employees are the internal customers, and external customers are all those individuals who patronise a company. Internal customers (company employees) are the ones who work to satisfy external customers. Thus, the needs of these two groups need to be met to ensure successful implementation. It is understandable, that if the internal customers are not satisfied, that external customers

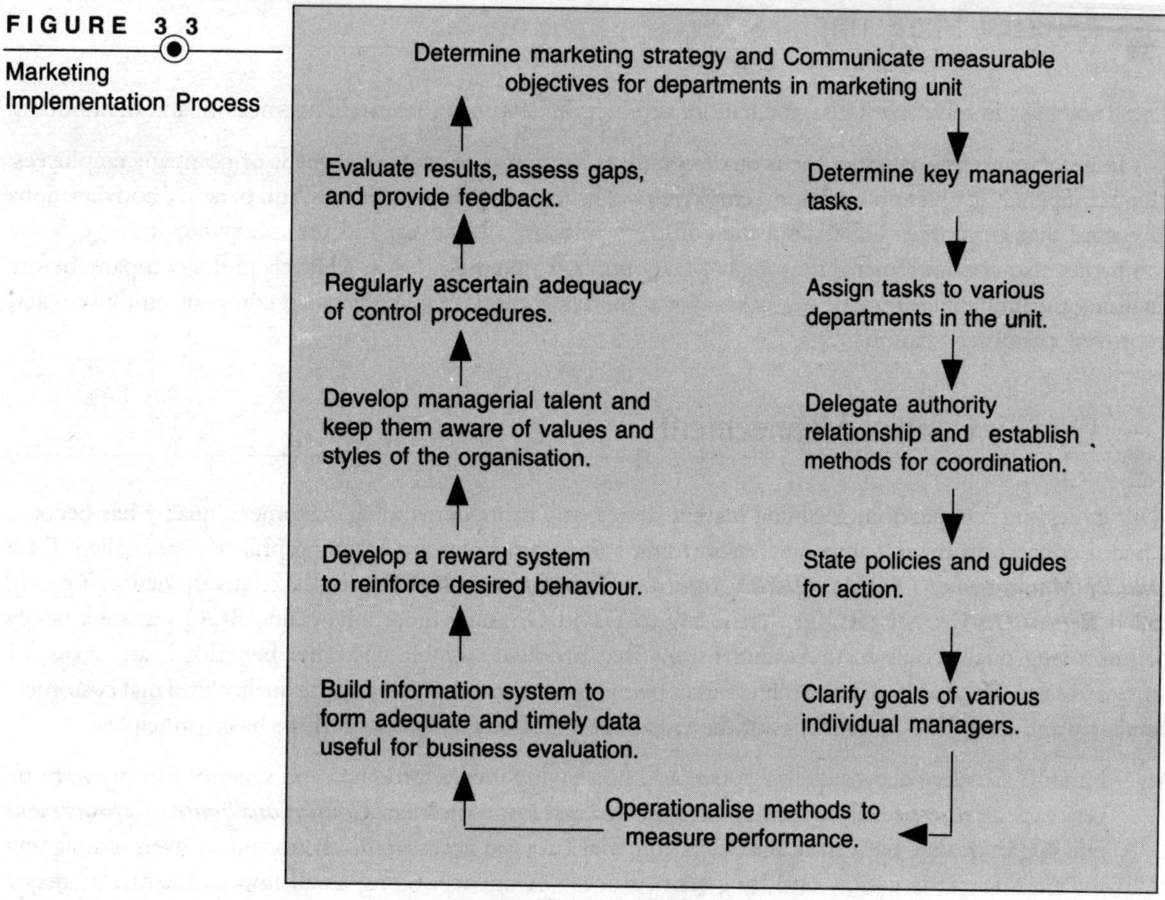

FIGURE 3.3
Marketing Implementation Process

may not be served in a manner that would result in their satisfaction. Companies, besides directing their communications to external customers, also use internal marketing to attract, train, motivate, and retain qualified and competent internal customers (employees). Internal marketing in itself is a management philosophy that coordinates the exchanges between the company and its employees to better accomplish successful company exchanges with external customers.

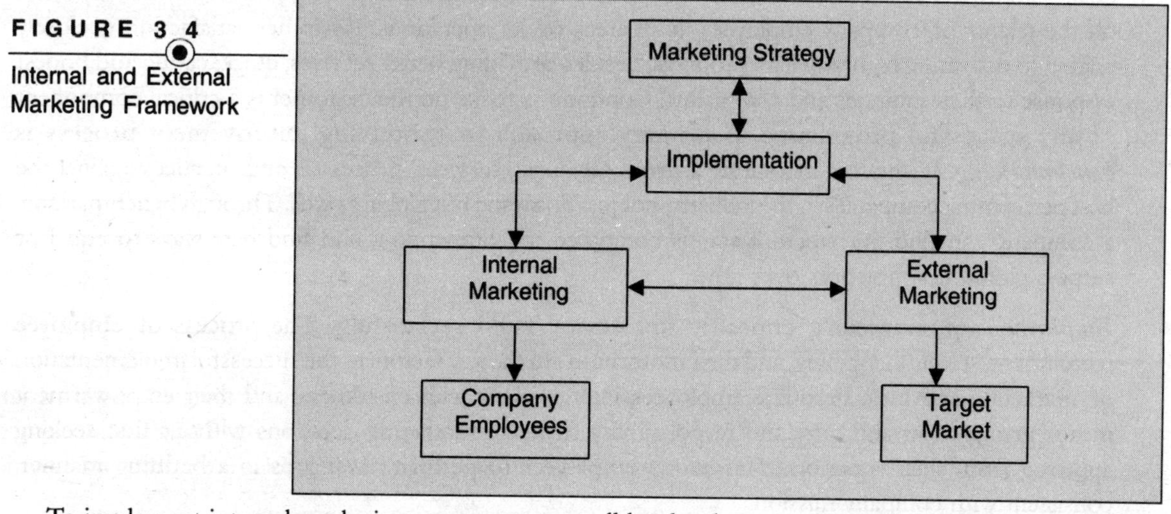

FIGURE 3.4
Internal and External Marketing Framework

To implement internal marketing, management at all levels takes necessary steps to making understand and accept their respective roles in the implementation of marketing strategy and the importance of delivering satisfaction to the company's customers.

External Marketing

These activities involve market segmentation, product development, research, promotion, and distribution.

Internal marketing activities focus on designing programmes to satisfy the needs of company employees. Many companies use planning sessions, employee workshops, appreciation letters, and personal conversations to ensure that employees understand the company mission, objectives, and the marketing strategy. Some companies also conduct formal meetings to take inputs from employees at all levels in the company before finalising the marketing strategy. All these efforts ultimately result in more satisfied company employees and improved customer relations.

Quality Control Management

With increasing competition, declining market shares, and more demanding customers, quality has become a major concern in many companies. As a result, some companies are adopting philosophies called ***Total Quality Management*** **(TQM)**, ***Quality Function Development*** **(QFD)**, and a relatively new approach, called ***Return On Quality*** **(ROQ)**. According to David Greising, those advocating ROQ pursue a policy of improving quality only in those dimensions that produce tangible customer benefits, lower costs, or increased sales. This focus on bottomline forces companies to ensure delivering the quality level that customers actually want. Joseph R. Janlonsky is of the view that TQM relies heavily on three basic principles:

- Philip B Crosby believes quality is free and not having quality products and services can prove to be very expensive, especially in terms of dissatisfied and lost customers. ***Continuous quality improvement*** building in quality, right from the beginning, may become necessary to the extent of even redesigning the product. It is a slow and long-term process of incorporating small improvements, as major advancements are often the result of an accumulation of these small improvements. All these approaches are directed at ensuring a company-wide uniform commitment to quality in all areas of the company to promote a culture that meets customers' perceptions of quality by coordinating efforts directed at delivering more customer satisfaction, encouraging and increasing employee participation and empowerment, forming strong supplier partnerships, and inculcating a company culture of ongoing quality improvement in all areas of its activities. Total Quality Management philosophy heavily relies on the talents of company employees in all areas of its operations. Customer satisfaction is closely related to delivering higher-quality products, besides providing better services, quick, caring and honest response to their inquiries and complaints. Continuous focus on the customer is a critical component of any successful programme. A primary approach to continuing improvement process is ***benchmarking.*** It involves measuring a firm's products, services, processes, and practices against the best performing companies in the industry, not just domestic but global as well. Through benchmarking, a company can find out where it stands compared to competition, and find best ways to equal or surpass global best practices over time.
- ***Employee empowerment*** is critical to implement TQM successfully. The process of employee recruitment, selection, training, and their motivation are the key factors to the successful implementation of marketing activities. Frontline employees interact daily with customers, and their empowerment means giving them authority and responsibility to make marketing decisions without first seeking approval from their superiors. This allows employees to perform their jobs in a befitting manner, consistent with company mission.

FIGURE 3.5
Principles of TQM

1. Quality must be perceived by customers.
2. Quality must be reflected in every company activity, not just in company products.
3. Quality requires total employee commitment.
4. Quality requires high-quality partners.
5. Quality can always be improved.
6. Quality improvement sometimes requires quantum leaps.
7. Quality does not always cost more.
8. Quality is necessary but may not be sufficient.
9. Quality drive cannot save a bad product.

- ***Quality improvement circles*** approach relies on teamwork by getting the best and the brightest employees from different functional areas as well as suppliers and customers and with a variety of perspectives. They are assigned to work on a quality improvement issue. It is well-known that suppliers can have a significant impact on a company's ability to deliver quality to customers. On the other hand, customers are in the best position to know what they and others in the same target market want and expect from the company.

The gains of TQM include financial benefits by reduction in operating costs, higher return on sales or investment, and the company may afford to charge a premium price rather than keeping the price competitive. TQM approach may not suit companies lacking the ability to invest substantial amounts of money, time, efforts, and patience in its implementation. TQM principles provide some useful structure for guidance to marketing managers committed to improving quality of products and services and deliver more satisfaction to customers. A word of caution here: some companies may run into serious problems if they overly focus or even fall in love with processes and how they are running business, and lose sight of customer needs and wants besides forgetting the reason why they are doing business. This would mean a serious deviation to inside-out view wherein the aim of TQM is to create an outside-in view of doing business.

Organising Marketing Department

To what extent a company's marketing chief has authority to plan and implement marketing strategies depends on how the marketing function is organised. The structure of the marketing department directly influences lines of authority, responsibility, and relationships. Steven J. Skinner is of the opinion that when customers are not satisfied, chances are that the fault lies in organisational structure. The structure of the company must be consistent with its marketing strategy. According to Trudy Heller, ***authority*** is the organisationally sanctioned right to make decisions without the approval of a higher-level executive. For example, when authority is delegated to the advertising manager to perform functions relating to advertising, the individual has the right to make whatever decisions are essential to perform those functions. These elements affect coordination among company personnel and ultimately affect how the individuals connect to perform the marketing activities.

Role of Marketing in Structuring

This aspect has been discussed in case of companies truly adopting marketing concept. With intensifying competition in domestic as well as global markets in almost all the industries, marketing activities gain importance and have become central to being competitive and successfully conducting business. According to Rohit Deshpande and Frederick Webster, Jr., the outcome of adopting a marketing concept is to develop and sustain a culture based on shared set of beliefs and values that focus on customer needs and wants for all company decisions about strategy and operations. As a philosophy of conducting business, marketing concept requires marketing to be closely coordinated with other functional areas such as design, production, finance, and human resources.

Ajay K. Kohli and Bernard J. Jaworski report that a marketing oriented company culture focuses on effectively and efficiently producing a sustainable competitive advantage by undertaking analyses of customers and competitors, and by integrating company resources to provide superior customer value, satisfaction and long-term profits.

As pointed out earlier, the organisational structure in a marketing oriented company has to take a totally different perspective. In the traditional company hierarchy, the CEO is the top authority and every level in the company is under the authority of levels above it. The frontline employees are answerable to frontline managers, frontline managers answer to middle level managers, and so on. In the marketing oriented company structure, too, each level must answer to the levels above it but answering to the next higher level means ensuring taking appropriate actions necessary so that each level performs its job effectively and efficiently. For instance, the CEO must ensure that middle level managers are provided with everything needed to perform their functions well, and the job of frontline managers is to ensure that frontline employees are competent, capable, and able to provide satisfying services to customers efficiently and effectively. The relevant marketing-oriented company structure has been shown in Figure 1. 3 to accomplish complete focus on customer needs.

Alternatives to Organising Marketing Department

Marketing department structure establishes the lines of authority and relationships among personnel and establishes who is responsible for taking which particular type of decisions, and for performing specific activities.

One of the most critical decisions about structuring authority is the issue of choosing whether to go for centralisation or decentralisation. In a ***centralised*** arrangement, the top-level managers make most of the major decisions and delegate very little decision-making authority to managers working at lower levels in the hierarchy. In sharp contrast, in a ***decentralised*** structure, authority to make decisions is delegated as far down the hierarchy as possible. Decision regarding choosing centralisation or decentralisation directly affects the concerned company's marketing operations. At one extreme, ***one marketing head*** makes all decisions and at another extreme ***all members*** of the marketing unit make all decisions. In actual practice, most marketing departments are structured somewhere in between these two extremes. Most traditional companies in India are centralised. Many of them are family dominated. In such companies, almost all marketing decisions are made at the top management levels. As companies start realising the importance and advantages of becoming marketing-oriented, centralised decision-making approach tends to prove increasingly ineffective and sometimes even counterproductive. To implement marketing concept, a decentralised structure approach is more suited to respond quickly and effectively to customer needs and wants. In a decentralised arrangement, managers divide the work into specific activities and delegate the responsibility and authority to managers in various positions in the marketing department such as sales manager, marketing research manager, distribution manager, advertising manager, etc.

There is no single approach to organising the marketing department that suits all types of businesses. Much depends on the number and diversity of products, target market, customer characteristics and their needs, the nature of competition, etc. Marketing activities can be organised on the basis of:

1. Functions
2. Products
3. Customer Groups
4. Regions

In real life marketing operations, companies often put in place some kind of carefully considered combination of functions, products, customer groups, taking into account regional considerations. This approach provides the marketing department with the flexibility required to prepare and implement appropriate marketing plans to match customer needs more effectively and efficiently.

Organising by Functions: This is a fairly popular approach to organising a marketing department. It also works well for some relatively less centralised businesses. Examples of organising the marketing department on the basis of functions include marketing research, product development, sales, advertising, distribution, and customer relations. All these functional managers report directly to the top marketing executive (Figure 3.6).

FIGURE 3.6
Organising by Functions

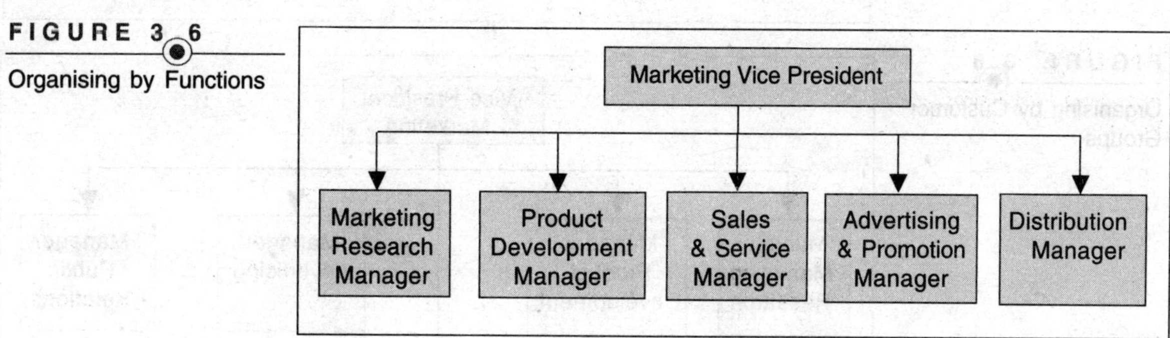

Organising by Products

Businesses operating with diverse product categories sometimes find it more appropriate to organise the marketing department by product groups. This arrangement provides the required flexibility to develop separate marketing programmes for different product groups. Procter & Gamble (*P&G*) operates with this arrangement. P&G has product category management arrangement to manage different product categories. Under each category manager, there are product managers. The product managers can also draw on the resources of the company's specialist staff in the area of advertising, research, distribution, etc. This approach, though providing flexibility, is somewhat more expensive as it creates more layers of management and increases the number of employees. However, in this arrangement each division is responsible for its own product planning, implementation of plans, monitoring performance, and corrective actions (Figure 3.7).

Organising by Customer Groups

This approach is appropriate for businesses that have several significantly different customer groups whose problems and needs are distinctly different. Some computer companies serve businesses, educational institutions, research laboratories, resellers, advertising agencies, home users, etc. Some other examples include companies such as Hyundai, Philips, Bajaj, and Larsen & Toubro, that serve many different customer groups. Such businesses require different marketing decisions and activities, as these highly diverse customer

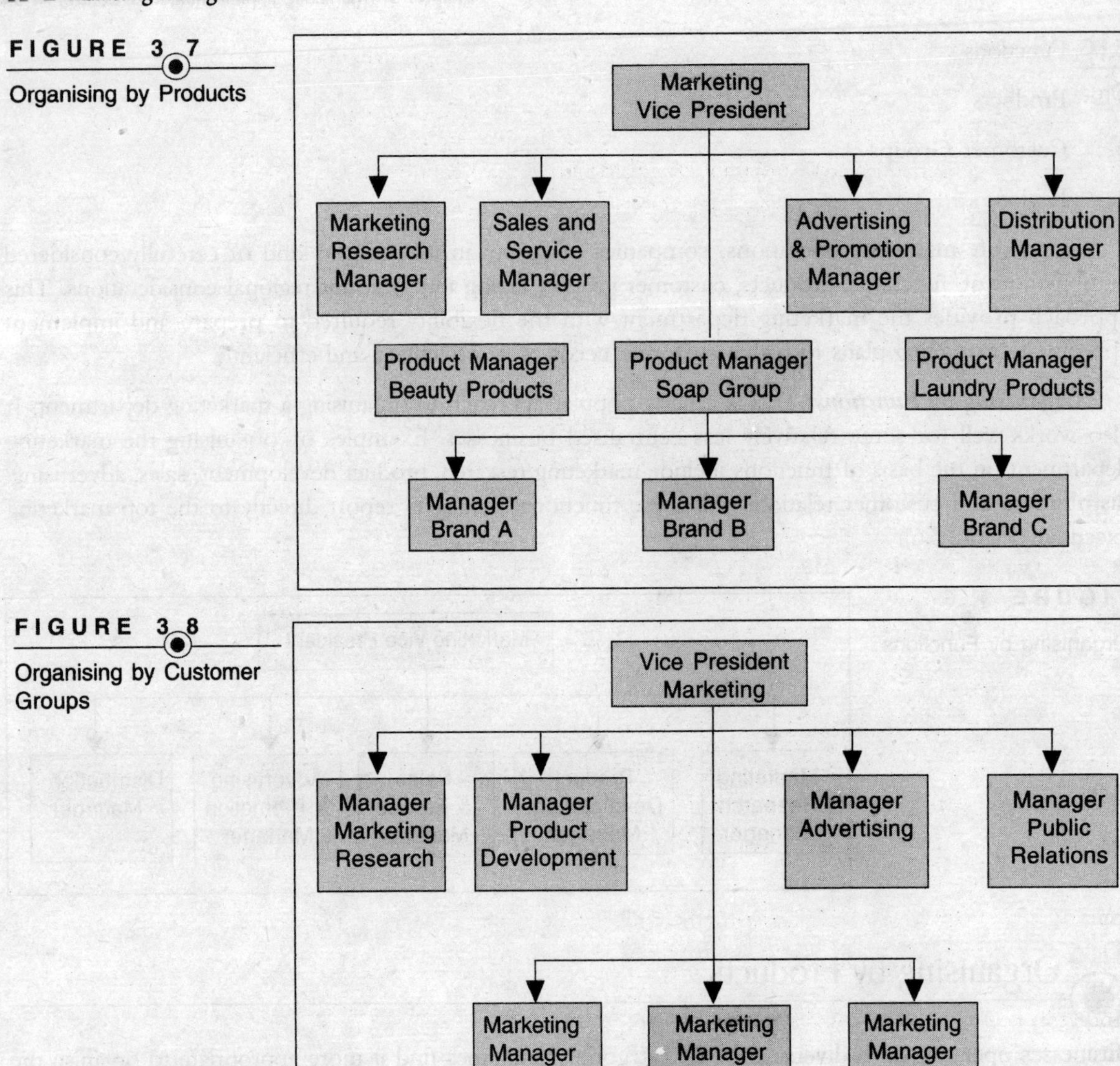

FIGURE 3.7 Organising by Products

FIGURE 3.8 Organising by Customer Groups

groups are considerably different in terms of their product and service needs. Marketing heads of these groups direct most marketing activities with respect to the specific customer group. These marketing heads report directly to top marketing executive in the company (Figure 3.8).

Organising by Regions

Large business houses that market products in domestic or in the global markets sometimes structure the marketing operations based on regional or geographic considerations. The markets may be divided on the basis of countries/regions, and the country or regional marketing directors report directly to the vice president marketing. This arrangement is appropriate for companies whose customer characteristics and needs differ in important ways in different regions. For example, fast food companies structure their marketing activities based on regional considerations. This facilitates closer contact with customers and responding quickly to market conditions (Figure 3.9).

FIGURE 3.9
Organising by Regions

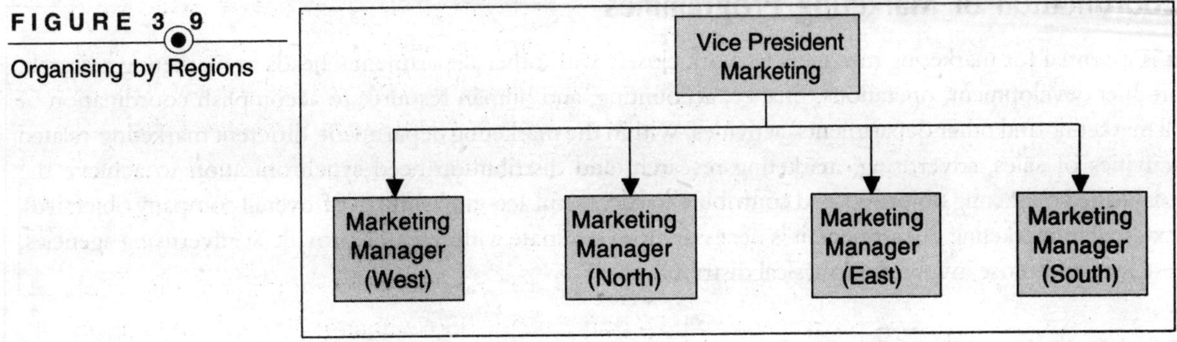

Implementation of Marketing Programmes

Effective implementation of marketing programmes essentially depends on:

- Marketing Personnel Motivation.
- Communication within Marketing Department.
- Coordination of Marketing Programmes.
- Establishing a Time Frame for Each Activity.

Marketing Personnel Motivating

This requires sincerity in finding out what are their physical, psychological, and social needs. It is necessary to learn what they think, feel, and want to accomplish. On the basis of these findings, suitable, fair, and ethical measures to motivate employees can be developed that are well understood by the department personnel. Developing the right combination of motivational tools is not easy and requires considerable deliberation. Any incentives to reward excellent or outstanding performance must be related to marketing goals. In the Indian context, many managers believe that money is the most important motivator and is considered as the first priority by most employees. However, other things such as recognition, prestige, autonomy, acquiring additional skills, and timely feedback about their performance are also important to most employees. An honest show of appreciation, and respect for the departmental personnel by the management goes a long way in motivating employees to be proud of their company and talk favourably about it as a good place to work. Satisfied and happy employees are an asset and are very likely to enjoy their work and be more productive.

Communication within Marketing Department

Timely and effective communication not only works to motivate personnel but also coordinates their efforts. Internal communication upward and downward concerns employees working in marketing research, sales, advertising, sales promotion, and distribution. Two-way external communication, includes package designers, resellers and, most importantly, customers. Equally important is internal upward communication with top management to ensure consistency with company mission and its overall objectives. This also is crucial to integrate activities with other company departments supporting marketing activities, such as finance, new product development, production, and human resource. All this requires establishing reliable and timely information system to support different types of activities such as planning, budgeting, sales analysis, performance evaluation, and preparation and delivery of timely reports.

Coordination of Marketing Programmes

It is essential for marketing managers to work closely with other departmental heads in marketing research, product development, operations, finance, accounting, and human resource to accomplish coordination of all marketing and other departments' activities. Within the marketing department, different marketing-related activities of sales, advertising, marketing research, and distribution need synchronisation to achieve the established marketing objectives and contribute to successful accomplishment of overall company objectives. External to marketing department, it is necessary to coordinate with research providers, advertising agencies, resellers, and those involved in physical distribution.

Establishing a Time Frame for Each Activity

It is imperative that all employees clearly understand what their specific responsibilities are. Unless all the employees understand this, they would not be sure about what is expected of them, or most of them may have only some vague ideas about what is expected of them. Not only must they understand their responsibilities thoroughly, they must be fully aware of the time frame for the completion of each activity. Activity completion time frame is quite visible at McDonald's. Each activity is related to preparing and delivering the burger to customers, right from taking the order of delivering the burger. All concerned employees know the specific time frame for the completion of their activities. Successful implementation of marketing activities requires establishing a time frame and involves several steps such as:

- Specifying different activities.
- Determining the time frame for the completion of each activity.
- Identifying activities requiring performance in a sequence and those that should be performed simultaneously.
- Establishing in what proper order the activities require performance.
- Assigning the completion responsibility for activities to managers, teams, or individuals.

Performance of all these activities requires well-thought out sequence and coordination among different departments involved in support as well as core functions to complete as scheduled. The activities scheduling work is fairly complex and time consuming and in modern day marketing the scheduling of different activities is generally accomplished with the help of quite sophisticated computer programmes. Scheduling helps in cutting down considerably on the time needed for implementing marketing strategies.

Mechanisms to Control Marketing Implementation

All the implementation control procedures relate to: (1) ***setting performance standards***, (2) ***measuring actual performance against these standards,*** and (3) ***taking corrective timely actions*** to reduce gaps between desired and actual performances. As long as most employees do not lose sight of company mission, objectives, marketing objectives, and overall value system, they generally exercise self-control and comply with group norms. Much really depends on employee motivation and commitment towards their responsibilities and overall company environment. This type of control is informal. The formal control, as already stated, involves setting performance standards, evaluation of performance against these standards, and remedial steps to control or reduce the gap between actual and desired performance. Bernard J. Jaworski reported that the kind of control that will dominate whether formal or informal largely depends on the prevailing environment in an organisation.

Setting Performance Standards

Developing marketing plans and controlling activities are closely linked. Statements made in the plan document with respect to accomplishing different goals clearly determine performance standards and provide control criteria. For example, if the marketing objectives included a sales increase by 10 per cent and this got translated into achieving a monthly sales of Rs. 5,00,000, then it becomes a performance standard. Performance standards can also be spelled out in terms of market share, reducing a certain percentage of expenditure in case of accomplishing an objective, improvement in product quality, reduction in customer complaints, or providing customer service, etc.

Measuring Actual Performance against Set Standards

Actual performance concerns not only different departments within the marketing unit but also some outside organisations contracted or hired for providing different goods and services such as advertising agencies, research providers, resellers, consultants etc. Measuring performance of individuals, teams, or departments within the marketing unit does not pose any problems. Performance of different departments within the marketing unit often significantly depends on the performance of outside assistance providers. The best that the marketing control process can do, in the case of external assistance providing firms, is to monitor their activities as closely as possible.

Taking Corrective and Timely Actions

For taking corrective actions to control or reduce the gap between set standards and the actual performance, there are a number of options available to marketing managers. In general, they can opt for steps to improve the actual performance, or totally modify or change the performance standards by making appropriate changes in the objectives, or develop a combination of these two general approaches. For example, to improve the sales performance, salespeople may be given additional training in some aspect of selling, or revise the sales targets.

Evaluation Problems

There is an overlap between marketing activities and other business activities and because of this, determining accurately the costs of marketing activities by marketing managers is nearly impossible. In the absence of accurate cost measurements of marketing activities, the question arises whether the exercise is worth the expenses involved. Besides, it is also true that it may be quite difficult to develop precise measurement standards. For example, to measure the sales results directly flowing from advertising is a very difficult proposition. Other problems include the cost of required information from outside firms; unavailability of information, the severity, and frequency of unpredictable environmental changes can adversely affect control of marketing activities.

Performance Evaluation Methods

Marketing objectives are often stated in terms of sales, costs, profits, product or brand awareness, etc. Performance evaluation always relates to measuring the accomplishment of objectives. Three general approaches to evaluation focus on sales, costs, and marketing audit.

Sales Analysis

Analysis of sales is extremely important for evaluation of marketing strategy and programmes. The sales data is conveniently available in almost all companies and is believed to be a reliable indicator of target market response to the company's marketing efforts. This sales data alone is insufficient and must be compared with the forecasted sales to provide a useful basis for analysis. Some companies also compare the sales data with industry sales and, more often, a particular competitor's sales and costs involved in achieving that sales level. For example, if the forecasted sales were Rs. 5,00,000 and the actual sales in the year for which the forecast was made were Rs. 5,25,000, then it tells the management the level of success of marketing strategy and programmes. It is also important to know the costs involved in achieving this sales level and for this, the budgeted expenditure is compared with actual expenditure. If the total expenditure were less by 5 per cent than budgeted, then it throws important light on the level of success of their programmes. Due weightage is given to price increases or decreases in evaluating the results.

The market share of any company's product or brand indicates the percentage of sales in that product industry. This provides the company a measure to compare its market share with those of its competitors reflecting the level of success of the company's marketing strategy. In India, research data providers such as ORG (Operations Research Group) offer this service at a fee to companies. If the level of sales volume declines but market share remains the same, it shows the overall impact of uncontrollable environmental factors on the product industry. In case a company loses some of its market share and the sales volume remains the same, and the sales volume and market share of one or more competitors increases, it means the industry's market is growing. It is a reflection on the marketing strategy or the implementation aspect of the strategy of the company.

Market share comparison is helpful but requires some caution. The reason is that objectives of all the firms in the industry are not necessarily the same and as a result of this, uncontrollable environmental factors do not affect all the companies equally hard. Sometimes, new entrants in the industry are not included in the research data provided by outside firms. These new entrants often affect the sales volume and market share of some companies in direct competition. Such a situation arose with a multinational pharmaceutical firm in India. The company was offering a drug for schizophrenic patients; normal doses of the drug often cause certain serious side effects in a sizeable percentage of patients, more so in the long-term treatment that almost all patients need. To control these side effects, a certain drug was offered by some other companies. A new entrant small company came out with a fixed dose combination of the two drugs and the original multinational started losing market share that was not reflected in the monthly research report provided by an outside agency. Market research conducted by the company was an eye opener for the management. The new entrant had taken away sizeable sales with that fixed dose combination. This forced the company to consider offering a fixed dose combination, but by the time it could introduce its new formulation, the new entrant had gained a strong foothold in the market.

Marketing Cost Analysis

It is no surprise that sometimes a company achieves its sales objectives but at a much higher cost than budgeted. Cost analysis is necessary to determine the costs incurred for performing different marketing activities. These costs can be compared with earlier costs with respect to performing the same activities to achieve a certain sales volume. Cost analysis makes it possible to evaluate the level of a strategy's effectiveness by comparing sales achieved and costs incurred even during the continuing implementation process or at its conclusion. By specifying where a company is incurring high costs, it becomes easier to determine profitable or unprofitable customers, products, or geographic areas.

Marketing cost analysis usually starts with a scrutiny of accounting records. These records are prepared by usually classifying different costs on the basis of how the money was spent, such as towards rent, wages and salaries, utilities, supplies, insurance, etc. These costs are listed on the basis of expenditure type and not by purpose and are called *natural accounts.* To illustrate the point, if the expenditure is incurred towards rent, it does not specify rent for what. The rent could be for a warehouse, production facility or some other purpose. To classify costs, marketing managers often reclassify some types of the costs by *purpose* of expenditure and these are called *functional accounts.* Such functional accounts include expenditure towards marketing research, personal selling, advertising, sales promotion, storage facility, order processing, and customer credit.

Cost analysis proceeds by generally reclassifying costs into natural accounts and functional accounts. Generally, four broad types of costs are considered:

- Fixed Costs
- Variable Costs
- Traceable Common Costs
- Non-traceable Common Costs

Fixed costs include rent, salaries, office supplies, utilities, etc., and refer to how the money was actually spent, but often do not mention which marketing functions were performed. For example, to mention that Rs. 5,00,000 was spent on rent annually does not explain rent for what? The analyst is unable to know if the rent was for storage facility or production facility.

Variable costs refer to costs that are directly allocated to perform some specific marketing activity such as advertising expenses incurred in different media to sell a particular product or service, or salaries of the sales force hired to sell a particular brand or product, selling in a specific geographic area, or to a certain customer group.

Traceable common cost can be attributed indirectly to some marketing function such as the cost of temporary support salesperson to man the toll-free telephone line and answer customer queries or handle customer complaints. This would be classified as a traceable common cost of selling a product or product line.

Non-traceable common cost cannot be attributed to a particular marketing function according to any logical criterion and is ascribed on an arbitrary basis such as taxes, interests, and the salaries of top management.

Much depends on the analyst's approach to cost analysis that determines to what extent these types of costs are considered in actual cost analysis. In case the analyst adopts the ***full cost approach,*** it will then include *variable costs, traceable common costs,* and *non-traceable common costs.* Full cost approach supporters believe that all costs must be considered in the analysis to get the correct profit picture. Those opposed to this point of view argue that since non-traceable common costs are ascribed on an arbitrary basis, full cost approach falls short of yielding actual costs as it uses different criteria for non-traceable costs. To avoid any inconsistency in using criteria, analysts may apply ***direct cost approach*** that considers *variable costs,* and *traceable common costs.* However, direct cost approach excludes non-traceable common costs because of arbitrary criteria used to determine these costs. Those against this approach are of the opinion that this approach is inaccurate because of the omission of one cost category.

Marking Audit

Marketing audit is the final method of marketing evaluation and refers to a thorough, systematic, objective examination of its objectives, strategies, organisation, and performance. The primary purpose of audit is to identify weak areas in executing marketing activities and recommends actions to improve performance in these areas. It also highlights activities where the company does well. Companies regularly conduct accounting or financial audit. Likewise, the marketing audit should also be conducted on a regular basis and not just when performance evaluation points to problems with the system, or when there is a crisis.

Marketing audit may focus on all of the firm's marketing, or it could include some specific marketing activity or activities. For example, the audit could be only for customer service, focusing solely on customer service objectives, standards, and comparing them achieved standards. Similarly, the audit might be conducted for sales, advertising, sales promotion, or any other activity. The extent of marketing audit depends on involved costs, number of target markets served, marketing mix composition, and environmental conditions. The audit findings can be useful to take corrective actions where required to be necessary such as target markets, opportunities, marketing strategies, marketing mix, etc. Marketing audit helps evaluation by undertaking the following:

- Describing the present activities and realised results in the areas of sales, costs, prices, profits and feedback with respect to other areas of performance.
- Analysing information about factors that may have an impact on marketing strategy such as environmental conditions, target customers, and competition.
- An analysis of opportunities, threats, and deciding suitable alternatives for marketing strategy.
- Develop a comprehensive database to be used in the evaluation of objective and achievements.

A company may use external consultants or company personnel. Hired auditors are more expensive though experienced in this specialised work, and not being from within the company, adopt an objective approach while devoting full time to this work.

The process of conducting marketing audit has no specific method or is bound by any set of rules or procedures. There are only some guidelines to develop a step-by-step plan to make marketing audit methodical and objective to accomplish the purpose. Professionals in this field often use a series of carefully designed relevant audit questionnaires to focus on the appropriate issues and interview diverse group of personnel from different departments of the company. These interviews start at the top management level and subsequently move down through other hierarchical levels. After the audit is complete, a comprehensive written report of findings is prepared and handed over to the top management. Many firms conduct marketing audits informally by attempting to verify operating results against set performance standards.

Marketing audits are expensive in terms of money and time involved. Small firms cannot afford comprehensive official auditing because of the expenses involved but such firms do evaluate performances in some way. Employees sometimes fear such comprehensive evaluations, more so by outside auditors.

William M. Pride and O. C. Ferrell have mentioned several possible dimensions of a marketing audit:

Part – I: Marketing Environment Audit

Economic – demographic

1. Company's expectations about inflation, material and supplies, unemployment, and credit availability in the short-run, intermediate-run, and long-run.
2. The forecast regarding trends, the size, age distribution, and regional population distribution and how it will affect the company's business.

Technological

1. Major changes taking place with respect to product technology and process technology.
2. Major alternatives that might replace this product.

Political - legal

1. Any laws being proposed that may influence marketing strategy and tactics.

2. Any need to watch central, state, or local government agencies. What is happening in the areas of environmental concerns, job reservations, advertising, price control, etc., that is relevant to marketing planning?

Cultural

1. Any shifts in public attitudes towards business and types of company's products.
2. Any major change in consumer values and lifestyles that have relevance for the company's target markets and marketing approaches.

Ecological

1. Any likely effect on the cost and availability of natural resources for the company.
2. Any public concern regarding the company's role in pollution and conservation, and what would be the company's tentative reaction.

Markets

1. Any noticeable shifts taking place in market size, growth, geographical distribution, and profits.
2. Any attractive market (but untapped) segments, and their expected growth potential.

Customers

1. Rating of the company by the present customers, prospects, and competitors about the reputation, product quality, service, price, and sales force.
2. How do different customer groups make their purchase decisions?
3. Any evolving needs of consumers in this market, and the satisfactions they seek.

Competitors

1. Major competitors, their objectives, strategies, major strengths and weaknesses, and their market shares.
2. Likely trends that can be expected in future competition and product substitutes.

Distribution and resellers

1. Main available distribution channels to make products available to customers.
2. The level of efficiency of these channels and the growth potential of different channels.

Suppliers

1. The forecast for the availability of important resources used in production.
2. Any emerging trends among suppliers in their selling practices.

Facilitators

1. The outlook for the availability of transportation, warehousing, and financial resources.
2. The effectiveness of advertising agency and the emerging trends in agency services.

Publics

1. Any opportunity and problem areas for the company.
2. The level of company success in dealing with its publics.

Part – 2: Marketing Strategy Audit

Business mission

1. Clarity of the business mission and its focus on satisfying customers.
2. Realism of the mission and its attainability.

Marketing objectives

1. Clarity of the corporate objectives statement (without any ambiguity, leading logically to the marketing objectives).
2. Clarity of marketing objectives, to guide marketing planning and performance measurement.
3. Appropriateness of marketing objectives with respect to the company's competitive position, opportunities, and resources.

Strategy

1. Soundness of marketing strategy for achieving stated marketing objectives.
2. Whether resource allocation is adequate, inadequate, or excessive for achieving set marketing objectives.
3. Allocation of resources to attractive market segments, territories, and products.
4. Allocation of marketing resources for the major marketing mix elements.

Part – 3: Marketing Organisation Audit

Formal structure

1. Appropriateness of formal structure of marketing department to empower employees to make decisions. Steps taken to ensure proper organisational culture.
2. Level of structuring of the marketing responsibilities along functional, product, end-user, and territorial lines.

Functional efficiency

1. State of communications and relations between marketing and sales in day-to-day working.
2. Effectiveness of product management system and managers' ability to plan profits (whether their focus is only on sales volume).
3. Whether there are any groups in marketing that need more training, motivation, supervision, or evaluation?

Interface efficiency

1. Any conflicts between marketing and manufacturing, R&D, purchase, finance, accounting, and legal that need attention.

Part – 4: Marketing System Audit

Marketing information system

1. Accuracy, sufficiency and timeliness of marketing intelligence system about developments in the market.
2. Adequacy of marketing research usage by company decision-makers.

Marketing planning system

1. Conception and effectiveness of the marketing planning system.
2. Soundness of marketing potential and sales forecasting measurements.
3. Soundness of setting sales targets.

Marketing control system

1. Adequacy and timeliness of control procedures, to ensure that the annual plan objectives are being accomplished.
2. Provision to analyse periodically the profitability of different products, markets, territories, and distribution channels.
3. Provision to periodically analyse and validate various marketing costs.

New product development

1. Appropriateness of company's arrangement to gather, generate and screen new product ideas.
2. Adequateness of company's concept research and business analysis before committing large sums of money in new ideas.
3. Whether the company carries out sufficient product and market testing before introducing a new product.

Part – 5: Marketing Productivity Audit

Profitability audit

1. Profitability level of the company's different products, served market segments, territories, and distribution channels.
2. Whether the company should enter, expand, contract, or completely withdraw from any business segments, and the short-term and long-term consequences on profitability.

Analysis of cost effectiveness

1. Level of different marketing activities costs, and their validity.

Part – 6: Marketing Function Audits

Products

1. The product line objectives, their correctness, and the level of achievement of objectives.
2. Need to phase out any particular products.
3. Any new products worth being added.
4. Any products that can benefit from quality, feature, or style improvements.

Price

1. The pricing objectives, policies, strategies, and procedures. Soundness of the prices set on cost, demand, and competitive analysis.
2. The customers' perceptions of the appropriateness of company's prices with respect to perceived product value.
3. Effectiveness of the company use price deals.

Distribution

1. Soundness of the company's distribution objectives and strategies.
2. Appropriateness of market coverage and service.
3. Degree of effectiveness of company's distributors, company sales reps, brokers, agents, etc.
4. Need to change the company's present distribution channels.

Advertising, sales promotion, and publicity

1. Appropriateness of the advertising objectives.
2. Appropriateness of the allocation of funds to advertising and the budget determination.
3. Effectiveness of the ad themes and copy. What do the customers and the public think about the advertising?
4. Appropriateness of the selection of advertising media and its effectiveness.
5. Adequacy of the internal advertising staff.
6. Adequacy of the funds allocated to sales promotion. Sufficiency and effectiveness of sales promotion tools such as samples, coupons, displays, and sales contests.
7. Adequacy of the budget for publicity, competence and creativity of the public relations staff.

Sales force

1. The company's sales force objectives.
2. Adequacy of sales force to achieve the set objectives.
3. The sales force organisation according to territory, market, and product. Enough or excess sales force for sales managers to supervise it.
4. Appropriateness of the sales compensation to provide adequate incentives and rewards.
5. The level of sales force morale, ability, and effort.
6. Appropriateness of the procedures for setting sales targets and measuring performance.
7. Competence level of the company's sales force compared with those of competitors.

Customer Service Audit

Identify customer service activities

1. Specific customer service activities, the company currently provides.

   Product-related: repairs, maintenance, and technical assistance.

   Pricing-related: credit, financing, and billing.

   Distribution-related: delivery, installation, and locations.

   Promotion-related: customer-service phone lines, and complaint handling.

2. Customer services are provided by the company or outside agency. If outside agencies provide these services, how is their performance?
3. Customer service needs or wants.

Review standard procedure for each activity

1. Existence of written procedures for each activity. Are these procedures up-to-date?
2. Existence of any verbal procedures for each activity. Consideration to include these in the written procedures or their elimination.
3. Regularity of customer-service personnel interaction with other functions to establish standard procedures for each activity.

Identify performance goals by customer-service activity

1. Existence of any specific quantitative goals for each activity.
2. Existence of any qualitative goals for each activity.
3. Contribution of each activity to customer satisfaction with respect to product, pricing, distribution, and promotion.
4. Each activity's contribution to the long-run company success.

Specify performance standards by customer-service activity

1. Internal, profit-based standards for each activity.
2. Internal, time-based standards for each activity.
3. Performance monitoring and evaluation internally by managers.
4. Performance monitoring and evaluation externally by customers.

Review and evaluate customer-service personnel

1. Consistency of the company's existing recruitment, selection, and retention efforts with the customer-service requirements established by customers.
2. The nature and content of company's employee training activities. Consistency of these activities with the customer-service requirements established by customers.
3. System of customer-service personnel supervision, evaluation, and reward. Consistency of these procedures with customer-service requirements.
4. Effect of employee evaluation and reward policies on employee attitudes, satisfaction, and motivation.

Identify and evaluate customer-service support system

1. Consistency of the quality and accuracy of company's customer-service materials with the image of company and its products such as instruction manuals, brochures, etc.
2. Consistency of the quality and physical appearance of company's physical facilities with the image of company and its products such as offices, furnishings, layout, etc.
3. Consistency of the quality and appearance of company's customer-service equipment with image of the company such as to repair tools, telephones, computers, delivery vehicles, etc.
4. Accuracy of the company's record-keeping systems. How readily is accurate information available when needed? What technology could be acquired to enhance record-keeping abilities such as bar code scanners, laptop computers, etc?

Summary

Marketing implementation is an important function of marketing management process. To achieve effectiveness in implementing marketing strategies and programmes, marketing managers must consider why the intended strategies do not turn out as planned. Actual marketing strategies often differ from the planned strategies. This happens because marketing strategy and implementation are inseparably related and constantly evolving and the responsibility for strategy development and implementation are separated. There is close relationship between the strategy and its implementation and they can be viewed as two sides of the same coin. Then, managers must also consider important implementation related issues like resources, systems, people, leadership, and shared goals to ensure the proper implementation of the strategies. The core element of marketing implementation is shared values and goals that bind all the components of the firm together into a single, functional entity and are instrumental in successful implementation of marketing strategies. The main objective of a detailed mission statement is to define clearly the organisational philosophy and direction, that is, the shared values and goals of an organisation.

Companies follow two major approaches to ensure proper strategy implementation. These are internal marketing and total quality management. Internal marketing refers to the coordination of internal exchanges between the firm and its employees to better accomplish satisfying external exchanges between the firm and its customers that include internal and external customers. The total quality management approach relies heavily on employee talents and participation to improve the quality of products and services. This involves perpetual quality improvement, empowered employees, and the use of quality improvement teams.

The organisational structure of a marketing department establishes the lines of authority and responsibility among marketing personnel. In a centralised organisation, usually only top-level executives make all the decisions; in a decentralised organisation, the authority to make decisions is delegated as far down in the hierarchy as possible. The marketing department may be organised on the basis of functions, products, markets, or other alternatives like a combination of different functions.

Empowerment is at the heart of TQM programmes, and employees are empowered to make decisions without the approval of higher authority. TOM's primary tools include measuring and evaluating the quality of a firm's products, services, or processes in relation to best performing companies in the industry.

Proper implementation of marketing plan depends on employee motivation, performing marketing activities, effective and efficient communications within the marketing department and other functional areas within the company, and other personnel involved in marketing outside the firm, the coordination of marketing activities, and establishment of a time frame for implementation. Motivation of employees depends on discovering employee needs and wants, and then developing appropriate motivational methods that help employees satisfy their needs.

Marketing control involves establishment of performance standards, evaluation of performance against laid down standards, and taking corrective and timely action to reduce discrepancies between desired and actual performance. Performance standards refer to expected levels of performance against which performance can be compared.

Control involves evaluation and effectiveness of marketing strategies, sales analysis, marketing cost analysis, and marketing audits. Sales analysis relies on sales results in terms of monetary value or market share to evaluate the firm's current performance.

Marketing cost analysis breaks down and classifies different costs to examine which costs are associated with specific marketing activities. It usually requires reclassification of natural accounts into functional accounts based on three broad categories, i.e., direct costs, traceable common costs, and non-traceable common costs. The direct-cost method includes only direct costs and traceable common costs.

The marketing audit is a thorough, systematic, and objective examination of a firm's marketing, mission, objectives, strategies, organisation, and performance. This attempts to unearth what functions a marketing department is doing well, pinpointing problems in the execution of functions, and recommending methods and means to improve these marketing functions.

Questions

1. Why does intended marketing strategy often differ from implemented strategy?
2. What are the major problems associated with the implementation of marketing programmes? Can these problems be minimised? Discuss.
3. What is the difference between centralised and decentralised marketing departments? Which one is more appropriate in your view to practice marketing concept?
4. Is there some way to empower employees in a company? Why is this believed to be important?
5. A market-oriented department is suitable for what type of companies?
6. Discuss internal marketing. Why do managers often believe that internal marketing is essential to implement marketing strategies more effectively?
7. What is the significance of employee-motivation in a marketing department?
8. Why is internal and external communication important for a firm in implementing marketing programmes?
9. Discuss the major steps involved in marketing control process.
10. What is sales analysis? What is its significance in the marketing control process?

Projects

1. You are a consultant for a small service company. How would you convince the owner of the need to conduct a customer service audit? What steps should be taken to conduct the audit?
2. A company has decentralised its product development and marketing operations to achieve better responsiveness to customers. How would you decentralise the following businesses? Would empowerment of employees be appropriate for:
   (a) Fast-food outlet.
   (b) Beauty parlour.
   (c) Speciality store.

Bibliography

1. Orville C. Walker Jr., and Robert W. Ruekert, "Marketing' Role in the Implementation of Business Strategies A Critical Review and Conceptual Framework," *Journal of Marketing,* July 1987.
2. Robert Howard, "Values Make the Company: An Interview with Robert Haas," *Harvard Business Review,* September – October 1990.
3. Robert R. Jablonsky, *Implementing Total Quality Management,* 1990.
4. Philip B. Crosby, *Quality is Free – The Art of Making Quality Certain,* 1979.

5. David Greising, "Quality: How to Make It Pay," *Business Week,* 8 August 1994.

6. Steven J. Skinner, *Marketing,* 2nd Ed. 1994.

7. Trudy Heller, "Changing Authority Patterns: A Cultural Perspective," *Academy of Management Review,* July 1985.

8. Rohit Deshpande and Frederick Webster, Jr., "Organisational Culture and Marketing: Defining the Research Agenda," *Journal of Marketing,* January 1989.

9. Ajay K. Kohli and Bernard J. Jaworski, "Marketing Orientation: The Construct, Research Propositions, and Managerial Implications," *Journal of Marketing,* April 1990.

10. Bernard J. Jaworski, "Toward a Theory of Marketing Control: Environment Context, Control Types, and Consequences," *Journal of Marketing,* July 1988.

Ethical and Social Issues in Marketing

LEARNING OBJECTIVES

After going through this chapter, you will understand:

- What is meant by ethical behaviour
- Which ethical issues are viewed as important in marketing practices
- How can companies encourage ethical marketing practices
- What constitutes social responsibility of businesses and what society actually expects from businesses

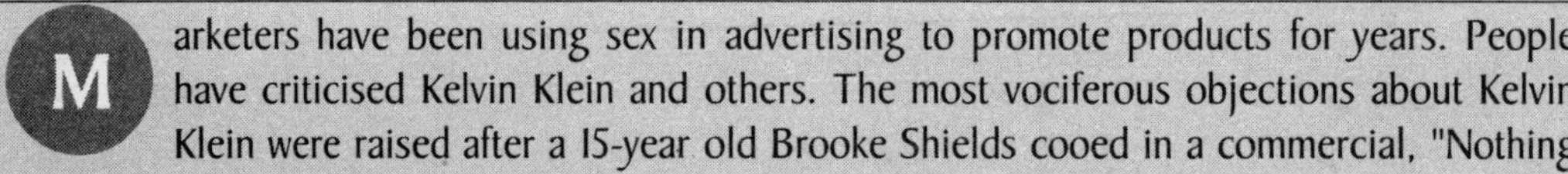

Marketers have been using sex in advertising to promote products for years. People have criticised Kelvin Klein and others. The most vociferous objections about Kelvin Klein were raised after a 15-year old Brooke Shields cooed in a commercial, "Nothing comes between me and my Kelvin Kleins." Many consumers think the designer's advertising in this campaign to sell Kelvin Klein jeans went too far.

Klein's 1995 spots featured young, scantily clad models in provocative poses. The print ads shot by the same Steven Meisel, who photographed Madonna's controversial book, Sex show some models revealing their underwear. In the television commercials, an off-camera adult male asks the model to take off articles of clothing and makes suggestive comments and queries.

Shocked consumers claimed the ads crossed the line into pornography, particularly because many of the models appeared to be under age eighteen. Several religious and children's advocate groups protested and threatened boycotts against Klein and retailers who carried the jeans. A coalition of church groups that promotes family values, even asked the US Justice Department to investigate, saying the ads "sexually exploit what appear to be children exhibiting them in a lascivious manner although the models are not completely nude." Many retailers responded to the protests by asking Klein to pull the ads.

The company refused to reveal the ages of the models appearing in the ads, but agents for some of the models insisted their clients were over eighteen years. Nonetheless, the Justice Department and the FBI examined whether the campaign may have violated laws against child pornography.

The public furore and retailer protests apparently worked. Klein announced in a full-page ad in The New York Times that the company was 'halting the misunderstood' campaign early.

Marketers will almost certainly continue to use sex to sell products as they have for years. A look at TV commercials and fashion magazines will show barely-dressed models (both female and male) in sensual poses hawking everything from mundane products to holiday sites.

Indian TV, magazines, and newspapers are no exception and frequently show ads for undergarments, condoms, bathing soaps, and many other products and services, which many believe to be sexually explicit.

Ethical Behaviour

Ethics is often misunderstood and generates controversies. There is need to examine the concept and support its application to marketing decisions that are acceptable and beneficial to society. The difficulty is that what is ethical for one individual may be unethical for another. Ethical conduct may also differ in different societies. In business context, employees are expected to live up to a set of laid down ethical standards. The real test of ethics people face is when things are not going well and pressures build. According to Andrew Stark, ethical challenges are mainly in two situations: (1) decisions in situations commonly called 'grey-areas' where the right decision is debatable, and (2) decisions for issues where the right course of action is clear but individual and company pressures, and circumstances force good-intentioned marketing managers in the wrong direction.

Ethics refer to values and choices and focuses on standards, rules and codes of moral conduct that control individual behaviour. Erik N. Berkowitz et al. maintain that: *ethics are moral principles and values that govern the actions and decisions of an individual or group.* In the marketing context, ethics is the moral evaluation of marketing activities and decisions as right or wrong. Whether a marketing behaviour is ethical or unethical is determined on the basis of commonly accepted principles of behaviour established by the society's expectations of conduct, various interest groups, competitors, company's own management, and personal and moral values of the individual. Each individual decides how to behave on the basis of these principles, and the public at large and various interest groups evaluate if the actions are ethical or unethical.

Many laws and regulations are put into force that determine what is ethical and permissible in marketing. However, not every issue is controlled by rules. Marketers are often faced with decisions regarding appropriateness of their actions, which are based on ethical considerations rather than what is within the law or industry guidelines. There is considerable overlap between what many consider to be ethical issues in marketing and the issues of manipulation, taste, and the effects of marketing conduct on values and lifestyles. In many cases, determining what is right and what is wrong can be extremely difficult. Many Indian companies frame codes of ethics, and these guidelines reduce the chance that an employee will knowingly or unknowingly violate the laid down standards. Such standards help dealing with customers and prospects that encourage violation of ethical behaviour. These codes are valuable guide to inexperienced executives in resisting pressures to ignore ethics in order to accomplish career goals.

Marketers often act in their own self-interest and certain actions may be within the law but still unethical. Marketing ethics go beyond just the legal issues and involve decisions fostering trust in marketing relationships at all levels; employees, customers, and competitors. Responsible marketers believe that if they do not act in the public interest, the public and customers will strike back at them with a vengeance. Violation of ethics adversely affects continued trust in marketing exchanges. Unethical behaviour can lead to loss of goodwill, showing up individuals and company in bad light, overshadowing good contributions to society and finally to loss of sales. However, despite the importance of ethics, there is a general feeling that ethical behaviour in marketing is declining. Robert A. Peterson, Richard F. Beltramini, and George Kozmetsky reported in their study that 80 per cent of surveyed college students thought that business ethics has deteriorated over the years, and 82 per cent think the situation would get worse.

Understanding Ethical Conduct

Among other reasons, one reason for many instances of unethical behaviour is that businesses generally do not understand how people make decisions when they face ethical dilemmas leading to ethical conflict and it is not clear whether to use one's personal values or the company's in a particular decision situation. An understanding of how people shape their ethical standards and what induces them to get involved in unethical conduct may be helpful in decreasing instances of unethical conduct. Three important factors presented in Figure 4.1 are understood to influence an individual's ethical behaviour:

- Individual Factors
- Organisational Factors
- Perceived Opportunity

Individual Factors

When marketing managers face ethically challenging situations and are unable to resolve them all alone, they experience ethical conflict, though they make decisions in their everyday lives based on their personal concepts of right or wrong. It is true that individuals can freely make – and do make – ethical choices in business situations. However, much depends on an individual's moral philosophies. According to O. C. Ferrell and John Fraderick, moral philosophies refer to rules or principles that individuals use to decide what is right or wrong. People learn these moral philosophies in the course of socialisation by family, religion, formal education, and social groups. The two major concepts relevant to marketing situations are ***utilitarianism*** and ***ethical formalism***.

FIGURE 4.1

Understanding Ethical Behaviour in Marketing Decisions

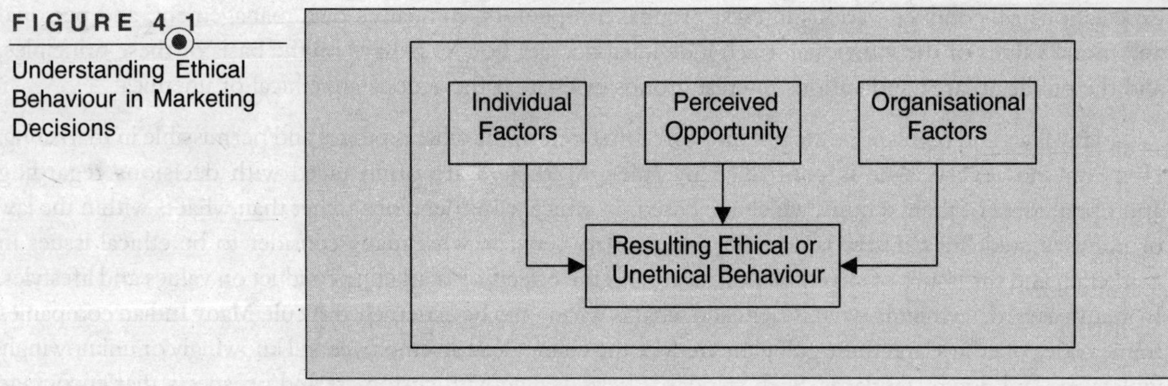

Utilitarianism is focused on maximising the greatest good for the maximum possible number of people. Marketing managers believing in utilitarianism are inclined to compare all possible options and choose the one that ensures the best outcomes for the maximum possible people. Here the outcome of a decision is judged by the consequences for all those affected by it.

Ethical formalism is concerned with intentions of an individual associated with a specific conduct and on the rights of the concerned individual. F. Neil Brady says that ethical formalism develops particular standards of conduct by examining whether an action can be viewed as consistent and adopted as a general rule without evaluating alternative outcomes. Here, the right or wrong is judged on the basis of whether the decision infringes on individual rights or universal rules.

Not everybody agrees on the correct moral philosophy that should be adopted in deciding ethical issues. Keeping in view the realities of the marketplace, it appears that marketing managers may use different moral philosophies across different situations. In situations of ethical dilemma, decisions based on different philosophies could result in different outcomes. Marketers sometimes change their moral philosophy. With an intense desire to succeed in the present day high-tension, competitive environment, it is not surprising that some marketing managers at times resolve to lie or deceive.

Organisational Factors

One must appreciate that people do not function in a vacuum. In most situations, choices are made in work groups or committees, or during everyday discussions with other employees. Interaction with associates serves as a learning process and influences how individuals resolve ethical issues. The extent of influence of this learning process depends on the strength of an individual's own values, perception of available opportunity, and the assessment of others' ethical or unethical conduct such as seniors, peers, and subordinates who influence the ethical aspect of decision-making process. Marketing managers face several ethical issues almost every day as a result of pressures arising from the marketing environment. A majority of managers involved in decision-making experience constant pressures to compromise ethics to accomplish company and personal objectives. Besides family and friends, the prevailing organisational culture is also a significant force that influences ethical decisions. Corporate culture refers to a set of values, beliefs, goals, norms, etc., shared by its members and expressed in every day working through work habits, and other activities. To a large extent, the attitude and behaviour of top management toward an organisation's commitment to ethics in its functioning heavily influences the ethical practices in an organisation.

The role of other company employees also influences decisions concerning ethical choices. If others expose an individual to rampant unethical behaviour in an organisation, it is very likely that the individual will behave unethically, particularly in ethically grey areas. It is no wonder that marketers learn the norms of organizationally acceptable behaviour from colleagues.

Perceived Opportunity

Opportunity refers to a set of conditions perceived as favourable that limit barriers or provide rewards. Most managers in marketing do not deliberately take advantage of every opportunity for unethical conduct in their companies. Of course, individual and organisational values do play an important role. In case an individual takes advantage of an opportunity to behave unethically and is not penalised or actually gets rewarded, the behaviour gets reinforced, and likelihood of repetition of unethical behaviour increases as other opportunities arise. For example, when a salesperson submits a false report of his day's number of calls and is not reprimanded, chances are such behaviour would be repeated in future. It may appear a hypothetical situation, but is often true in India that good firms allow their marketing executives to travel comfortably on company work and allow AC rail fares, but often others see them travelling in buses or in lower class rail compartments. The reason, they offer is that everybody else in the company does the same thing. Sales people are known to make false promises with customers to conclude a sale. Some products do not measure up to the claims made in the ads. O. C. Ferrell, Larry G. Gresham, and John Fraedrich report that opportunity to behave unethically is often a better predictor of unethical conduct than personal values. These are real life experiences but ultimately it is the organisation that suffers and also the credibility of the concerned individual takes a nose-dive. Presence of ethics related company policy and professional code of conduct also affect behaviour with respect to opportunity by prescribing acceptable behaviours. It is also true that if the rewards are significant and punishment mild, the chances of unethical behaviour increase.

Marketing Related Ethical Issues

Ethics in marketing practices is an important issue and needs developing understanding and awareness to bring improvement in its application. Ethical issue refers to some situation, problem, or opportunity that can be recognised and requires a person or organisation to select from among different actions that must be evaluated as right or wrong, or ethical or unethical. For instance when marketing managers or consumers feel manipulated or cheated, it becomes an ethical issue, irrespective of the fact that the action happens to be legally right.

Whatever the reasons for unethical instances, what is necessary after the issue is identified is that marketing managers must decide how to resolve it. This requires knowing most of the ethical issues related to marketing that often arise. In general, most issues relating to unethical behaviour occur in case of products and promotions.

Product-related ethical issues may include little or no information about safety, function, value, or use instructions. One example can be used of inferior materials, or components to cut costs without any information to customers. It is ethically wrong not to inform customers about the changes in product quality, as this failure is apparently a form of dishonesty. Issuing false medical certificates is unethical for medical practitioners as it raises questions about their honesty in general.

Promotion of products and services, etc., often furnishes a number of instances of a variety of situations that involve ethical issues, such as false and misleading advertising, and manipulative or deceptive sales promotions. There have been instances of misleading ads about obesity control and weight reduction programmes that mislead customers – and some went to the courts. Many ads are criticised for using excessive nudity to attract an audience. Use of bribery or false promises in personal selling situations is an ethical issue. Occasionally, media reports highlight cases of unethical practices by organisations involved in offering bribes to procure large orders. Such practices damage trust and fairness and ultimately harm the concerned organisation and tarnish its image.

Ethical Dilemma or Lapse?

- Unethical judgements lead to misleading and false advertising. Let us understand what is unethical and what is a lapse in the application of ethics.

- Ethical dilemma is the outcome of an unresolved interpretation of an ethical issue. We must appreciate the difference between "having a right" and the "right thing to do." For example, should advertisers strive to persuade not so well-to-do youth in urban and semi-urban areas to buy expensive sports shoes or branded jeans? There is no law against such advertising, but the socially and morally responsible behaviour may be to refrain, and so we have an ethical dilemma.

- It seems advertising professionals find ethics largely a matter of what is legal, which is why many consider advertising expensive jeans or sports shoes to all markets, including those who should not buy them, as "acceptable" ethical behaviour. We must appreciate that one can be ethical only when there is the option of being ethical. One cannot choose to be ethical when one cannot choose at all. Thus, ethics begins only where the law ends.

Ethical dilemmas can occur because advertisers typically sell brands, not just products. Even though functionally the products from different manufacturers may be the same, advertisers present their brands as being different from other brands. In this process, advertisers are tempted to create false differences. Another situation that creates ethical dilemma is when advertisers highlight only the good things about their brand but omit any mention of the shortcomings. Whatever is said is not false, yet the ad does not tell the whole truth, hence may be said to be misleading.

In contrast, ethical lapse is typically a clear case of illegal behaviour, not permitted by the law of the land. Plenty of laws govern what is legal in advertising, but laws ultimately reflect ethical judgements. As for the self-regulation, advertising and media associations, councils, and societies focus on legalities rather than philosophies. The eternal question of when, how, and by whom are these laws to be enforced in resolving ethical dilemmas and lapses still remains.

(Source: William F. Artens, Contemporary Advertising, 1999)

Encouraging Ethical Behaviour

American Marketing Association has its codes of ethics, and member organisations agree to abide by them. Individual organisations in India develop their own code of ethics. Some universities and management institutions in India offer courses in ethics or make it compulsory part of management courses. In the absence of formal written down codes of marketing ethics, there have been suggestions that Indian businesses should adopt AMA codes of ethics. Occasionally, there are seminars on topics such as "corporate governance" to promote ethical conduct in business. Codes of ethics refer to organisational rules and policies that serve an organisation's members in the shape of formal guidelines for professional conduct. This way, the employers help company members to better understand what is expected of them. Rewards and punishments associated with ethical or unethical conduct enforce code of ethics and limit the opportunities or tendency to engage in unethical behaviour. Fairness in the enforcement should help greater acceptance of ethical standards. A very short self-assessment test can assist an individual in determining whether a certain decision would be ethically right:

- **Is this decision right legally?** In case the answer is 'No', then one must stop there, as it can cause serious trouble.

- **Is this decision fair to all concerned?** If it is not fair to anyone concerned, then very likely it is not ethically right.
- **How will this decision make me feel about myself?** Unethical decisions generally give rise to feelings of uneasiness and guilt and when they become known to the public, they cause shame, and humiliation.

If top management of a business develops programmes to encourage ethical conduct, then such programmes become a force. Marketing people understand the policies that govern ethical conduct and can easily resolve any conflicting ethical issues. Tom Rusk and D. Patrick Miller suggest that an aggressive ethical approach to marketing should consider at least four fundamental values of interpersonal communication: (1) respect, (2) understanding, (3) caring, and (4) fairness. The application of these fundamental values entails five steps:

- Keep listening, don't argue, criticise, or defend yourself until you understand the problem confronting you.
- Identify the ethical issues involved in a decision that may affect colleagues, and customers. Understand the viewpoint of those who are involved.
- Ignore your anger and desire of power or prestige and develop as many alternatives as possible before analysing.
- Identify the best alternative from your point of view considering respect, understanding, caring, fairness, honesty, etc.
- Explain your decision to a neutral and trusted colleague, take time to reconsider, and consult before the final decision.

Irrespective of what businesses finally decide about framing a formal guideline to cover ethics in marketing practices, one aspect is of critical importance: the individuals character. Most cases of employees engaging knowingly in unethical conduct are traceable to the individual's character. People are expected to know at least what is clearly right or wrong and should have the courage to act accordingly. One often learns that it is not the compulsive need for some kind of gratification but greed that often motivates gainfully employed individuals to engage in unethical practices. One can understand some possibility of wrong judgements being made about grey areas, but there can't be excuses about knowingly engaging in unethical practices, and "everybody does it" cannot be the justification. Ultimately, each individual is responsible for her/his controllable behaviour.

Social Responsibility

According to Keith Davis and William C. Frederick, the society in which businesses exist, expects businesses to act as socially responsible members of the social community, besides producing products and services efficiently. Social responsibility of business refers to the obligation of a business to make deliberate efforts to maximise its positive contributions and minimise the negative impact on society as a whole and on various groups of individuals within the society. Social responsibility is a broader concept than ethics in marketing. The focus of ethics is on doing the right things in making business decisions by individuals and groups, and the social responsibility requires fulfilling the obligation to achieving a balance for all stakeholders within or outside the business. Archie B Carroll maintains that society expects business to earn profits, comply with the laid down laws, conduct their business ethically, and behave as responsible citizens. Many companies consider the costs involved in being socially responsible as right investments that need careful planning.

When one considers the major aspects of corporate social responsibility, the issues generally relate to economic, legal, ethical, and philanthropic concerns. The business responsibility of contributing to the economic growth and doing business within the given legal boundaries has long been acknowledged. In more recent times, philanthropic and ethical dimensions have acquired considerable recognition. Margaret A. Stroup and Ralph L. Newbert report that socially responsible companies try to learn and foresee society's expectations and determine actions that will be perceived as socially responsible, and accordingly allocate resources to accomplish objectives in this area and measure up to expectations.

FIGURE 4.2

Pyramid of Corporate Social Responsibility

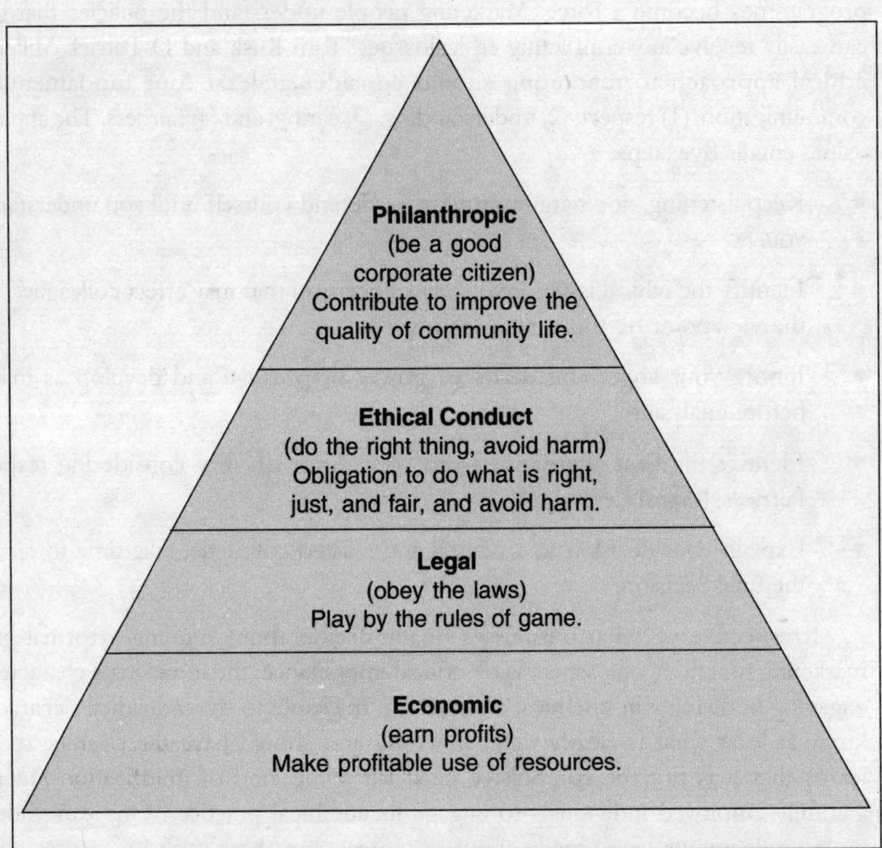

(*Source:* Adapted with changes from Archie B. Carroll, "The Pyramid of Corporate Social Responsibility: Toward the Moral Management of Organisational Stakeholders", *Business Horizons,* July-August, 1991.)

It is necessary for a company's success to determine and regularly monitor any changes that customers, employees, government regulations, competitors – what the society in general expects – in terms of social responsibility. According to Margaret Stroup, and Ralph L. Newbert, there is increasing recognition that for a company's survival and gaining competitive advantage, the long-term value of conducting business in a socially responsible manner outweighs short-term costs. The awareness of corporate social responsibility issues is far more in developed countries than developing countries. A survey of 1000 households reported that nearly 90 per cent respondents said that when quality, service, and price are similar among competitors, they are more inclined to buy from a company that enjoys a sterling reputation for social responsibility.

Society's Expectations

Customers purchase products or services with certain expectations. If they perceive the price as fair, the product or service satisfies their needs, causes no adverse effects, customers develop confidence and are more inclined to buy it repeatedly in future. If the purchase outcomes are contrary to expectations, customers are more likely to switch to other brands. In some extreme cases of dissatisfaction, customers form pressure groups that may lead to boycotts and adversely affect the company's business and reputation. Businesses sometimes market products without really knowing the long-run harmful effects of a product. For example, years after tobacco-based smoking products became popular, it has been discovered that tobacco smoking is associated with cancer and other medical problems, and society's attitude towards smoking is changing and marketers face new social responsibilities.

Under society's pressures central, state, and local governments promulgate laws and appoint various regulatory groups to prohibit undesirable and unacceptable business practices. Many such laws are framed in almost all developed and developing economies that regulate product safety, packaging, labelling, pricing, personal selling, advertising, fair competitive practices, environmental issues, etc. Companies that are truly conscious about their social responsibility, often engage voluntarily to improve or at least maintain society's well being. Their actions in this regard help building long-term relationship of trust and respect with employees, customers, and the society in which they conduct their business.

Businesses throughout the world meet the needs of society in various ways. Many Indian companies are conscious of their social responsibility and are providing facilities in the fields of healthcare, education, family planning, environmental concerns, sports, art and culture, etc., to contribute to the well being of society.

Social Responsibility Issues

Consumer Movement (Consumerism): It refers to several efforts by independent individuals, groups and organisations to protect the rights of consumers. There was rapid industrial growth in United States during the late 19th century leading to many undesirable conditions such as low pay, long working hours, false advertising, and sale of risky food and drugs. This led to consumers forming the 'Consumers League' in New York City. After this initiative, the consumer movement grew rapidly throughout the United States during 1920 – 1930. Subsequently, President John F. Kennedy declared that consumers have some basic rights and drafted a "Bill of Rights." It said, consumers have the right to safety, the right to be informed, the right to choose, and the right to be heard.

- ***The Right to Safety*** says that products must be safe for its intended use and marketers have an obligation not to market a product knowingly that could harm or cause injury to consumers. Marketers should have tested the product to ensure quality and reliability, and customers must have thorough and clear directions for its use.
- ***The Right to Be Informed*** means that consumers should have freedom to access and review all information about a product or service before buying it. Companies are required to print detailed information about ingredients and instructions for use (such as product labels, warnings, etc., on product packages).
- ***The Right to Choose*** refers to consumers' right to have the opportunity to choose and purchase a product or service at competitive prices, and should also be assured of satisfactory quality and service at a fair price. Competition should be free to flourish without permitting any one company to become so powerful that consumers have no opportunity to seek new and improved products or services.
- ***The Right to Be Heard*** ensures that while framing laws and policies, the government gives full and sympathetic consideration. It also promises that in case a consumer complains against a product or the marketer, she/he will get a fair treatment.

This major step by one country has created a lot more awareness among developed and almost all the developing economies. There is increasing awareness among consumers in most developing economies of the fact that they, too, can have or have certain rights to protect them against deception and damage for which some marketer is responsible.

Ecological Concerns

Ecology refers to the inter-relationship between the living things on earth and their environment. The issues concern our natural surroundings. Business managers must take deliberate steps to minimise any damaging impact of business operations on our environment. A very important issue today is the increasing pollution of air, water, and land with poisonous substances such as chemicals, sewage, and garbage. Manufacturing plants and ever increasing autos on the roads arc polluting the air with carbon monoxide and other harmful substances released in the air from burnt fuel. As a result, everybody is forced to breathe polluted air, though in the recent past, more stringent emission standards for autos have been laid down to control pollution caused by motor vehicles. Scientists have reported that ozone layer that protects us from dangerous ultraviolet rays of the sun is getting destroyed. The land is getting polluted because of industrial waste. In India, water pollution is a major concern, and even food grains and edible products have been reported to contain harmful levels of certain chemicals and pesticides. Governments, special interest groups, and responsible business firms are making attempts to control or solve these problems.

Green Marketing

Green marketing means developing environment friendly products and their packages to contain the negative effects on environment. This requires conservation of natural resources and controlling pollution. Some global and domestic companies are proactive and have taken steps in this direction. They develop product containers that are less harmful to environment, and use recycled materials. Todd L. Hooper and Bart T. Rocca believe that companies that perform excellently in green marketing will benefit in developing better relations with customers, regulating agencies, suppliers, and other firms in their industry.

To be effective, green marketing programme requires top management commitment, company environment to encourage green marketing, rewarding employees for reducing waste, developing new environment of friendly products, and making them available to consumers at reasonable prices.

Social Responsibility Issues – Indian Scene

Consumerism in India emerged as a result of different reasons than mentioned earlier in connection with the United States. It emerged as a reaction to adulteration, excessive prices of essential commodities, and serious shortages of products sometimes intentionally created by producers or traders. In the past, producers and marketers showed no concern for consumers; deceiving them by supplying unsafe or even fake products. Consumer Protection Act in India provides for:

- Right to Protection of Health and Safety
- Right to Be Informed
- Right to Be Heard
- Right to Improve the Quality of Life (Ecological concern)

Consumer Protection Act, 1986

A consumer is defined in this Act as anyone buying a product for personal consumption, and also in case the buyer is different but permits the use of the product or service by someone else. If anyone buys a product or service for resale purpose, then she/he is not a consumer. The objectives of the Act include: (1) Promoting and protecting consumer, consumer movements, and their organisations, (2) Facilitating consumer education, and providing protection against commercial malpractice, particularly that of traders, (3) The Act is to provide speedy and inexpensive redressal of consumer grievance and award compensation, wherever necessary.

Consumer Forums

The Act provides for establishing Consumer Protection Councils by the Central and State Governments. Dispute settlement takes place at three levels: District Forum, State Commission, and Consumer Dispute Redressal Commission (National level, established by the Central Government). Consumer Forums are required to mention reasons for their conclusions to avoid any arbitrariness and help higher Forum to examine the correctness of the given reasons. In case the consumer complaint is found to be correct, then the opposition party can be issued an order to remove the defect, or replace the defective product with a new one. The commission can order to withdraw an unsafe product and provide suitable compensation to the aggrieved party. The National Commission has the powers, over all the State Commissions, to periodically check the institution, disposal, the quantum of pending cases, and issue instructions regarding (1) adoption of uniform procedure in the hearing of cases, (2) copies of documents produced by opposing parties, (3) quick grant of copies of documents, and (4) generally monitoring the functioning of State Commissions and District Forums.

Competition Policy

A proposal to repeal the Monopolies and Restrictive Trade Practices Act, and winding up of MRTP Commission has been submitted to Government of India, along with a proposal to establish a new Competition Commission of India (CCI). The Competition Law should cover all consumers who buy products or services, irrespective of the purpose for which the purchase is made. The Competition Commission will receive all the complaints against the infringement of Competition Law from individuals, businesses, entities, and Central or State Governments.

Corporate Responsibility Issues

Some of the more relevant corporate social responsibility issues in India concern anti-pollution measures, adopting villages to achieve progress and development, starting and funding family planning programmes, making efforts to provide clean drinking water facilities in backward areas, providing vocational training to unemployed educated persons, providing educational healthcare sports facilities, and conducting tournaments to promote sports talent. The most important priority areas are population control, education, rural development, and poverty elimination.

FIGURE 4.3

Evaluation Concerns of Special Interest Groups

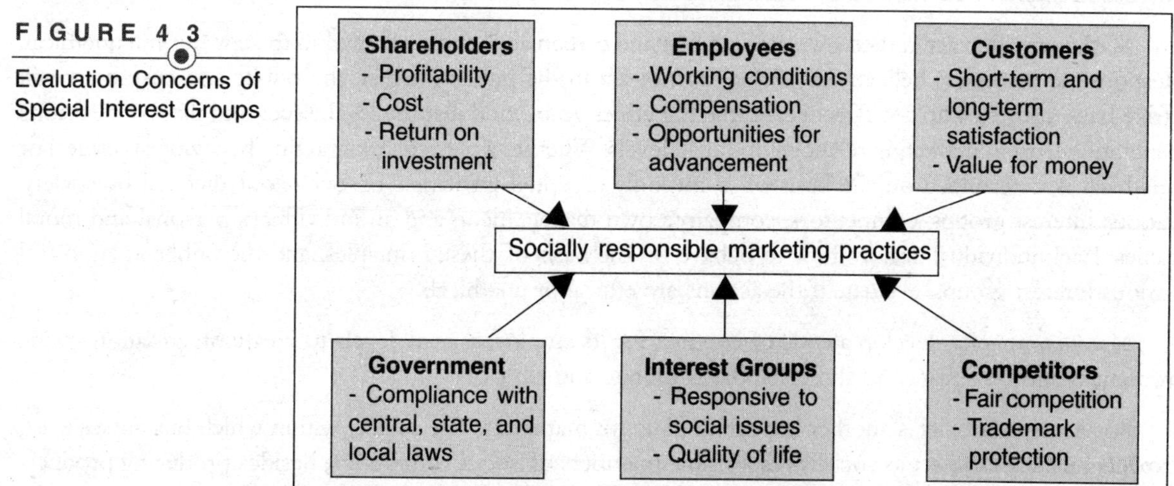

Titan Industries provides scholarships to underprivileged deserving students from Tamil Nadu for their education and vocational training. They also provide employment to physically challenged persons in factories located in Dehradun (UP) and Hosur (Karnataka).

Otis India helps mentally retarded, promotes spots for them. In 1995 World Special Olympics, the company sponsored 350 special athletes from Maharashtra. The company also voluntarily raises funds for the mentally retarded.

In this regard, some other names worth mentioning are Larsen & Toubro, Bajaj Auto, Sriram Investments, Associated Cement Companies (ACC), Mafatlal Group, Escorts Ltd., Godrej, Kirloskar, Hindustan Steel, and Sahara India. Such socially responsible companies have made important contributions to a variety of social action programmes.

Marketing activities are usually evaluated in terms of their effectives in achieving the desired objectives including acceptable social consequences. Various interest groups judge the results, depending on their own set of criteria. Organisations that believe in social responsibility pay close attention to feedback received from these diverse public and private interest groups. Such companies realise that these groups can and do speak against or in favour and their actions, which opinions can seriously affect the future of concerned firm. It was due to the complaints of competitors that Federal Trade Commission took notice of Microsoft's monopolistic practices. In late the 1970s and early 1980s, some pharmaceutical companies in India have suffered because of boycott by trade. The six major groups that keep a sharp watch on social responsibility issues, depending on their interests, are shown in Figure 4.3.

Summary

Ethics in marketing practices is an important issue, and many organisations need to develop an understanding and awareness of the grave repercussions adverse public opinion, and to bring about improvement in its application. Ethics refers to values and choices, and focuses on standards, rules, and choices in favour of strict moral conduct that affect individual or group behaviour. There is need to examine the application of the concept and support its application to marketing decisions that are acceptable and beneficial to society. The difficulty is that what is ethical for one individual may be unethical for another. Ethical conduct may also differ in different societies. In business context, employees are expected to live up to certain established ethical standards. The real test of ethics comes when people face hostile situations, when things are not going well, and pressures build. According to Andrew Stark, ethical challenges are mainly in two situations: (1) decisions in situations commonly called 'grey-areas' where the right decision is debatable, and (2) decisions for issues where the right course of action is clear but individual and company pressures, and circumstances force well-intentioned marketing managers in the wrong direction.

Marketers often act in their own self-interest and certain actions may be within the law but still unethical. Responsible marketers believe that if they do not act in the public interest, the public and customers will strike back at them with a vengeance. Marketing ethics go beyond just the legal issues and involve decisions generating trust in marketing relationships at all levels. Whether a particular marketing behaviour is ethical or unethical is determined on the basis of commonly accepted principles of behaviour dictated by society, various interest groups, competitors, company's own management, and an individual's personal and moral values. Each individual decides how to behave on the basis of these principles, and the public at large and various interest groups, evaluate if the actions are ethical or unethical.

Many companies develop a code of conduct for its employees at all levels to create organisation - wide awareness and compliance to these standards by one and all.

Social responsibility is another important issue for marketers. The society within which businesses exist, expects businesses to act as socially responsible members of social community, besides producing products and services efficiently. Social responsibility of business refers to the obligation of a business to make deliberate efforts to maximise its positive contributions and minimise the negative impact on society as a whole and on various groups of individuals within the society. The society expects business to earn profits, comply with the laid down laws, conduct their business ethically, and behave as responsible citizens. Many companies consider the costs involved in being socially responsible as right investments that need careful planning.

Under social pressures, central, state, and local governments promulgate laws and appoint various regulatory groups to prohibit undesirable and unacceptable business practices. Many such laws are framed in almost all developed and developing economies that regulate product safety, packaging, labelling, pricing, personal selling, advertising, fair competitive practices, environmental issues, etc. Companies that are truly conscious about their social responsibility often voluntarily undertake to improve or at least maintain society's well being. Their actions in this regard help in building long-term relationships of trust and respect with employees, customers, and the society within which they conduct their business.

Businesses throughout the world meet the needs of society in various ways. Many Indian companies are conscious of their social responsibility and are providing facilities in the fields of healthcare, education, family planning, environmental concerns, sports, art and culture, etc., to contribute to the well being of society.

The Consumer Protection Act in 1986 provides for Right to Protection of Health and Safety, Right to Be Informed, Right to Be Heard, and Right to Improve the Quality of Life (Ecological concern). The Act provides for establishing consumer protection councils at the State and Central Government level and District Forums at the district level.

Bibliography

1. Andrew Stark, "What's the Matter with Business Ethics," *Harvard Business Review*, May-June 1993.

2. Eric N. Berkowitz, Roger A. Kerin, Steven W. Hartley, William Rudelius, et al., 5th ed. "*Marketing,*" Irwin/MacDraw-Hill, 1997.

3. Robert A. Peterson, Richard F. Beltramini, and George Kozmetsky, "Concerns of College Students Regarding Business Ethics: A Replication." *Journal of Business Ethics,* Vol. 10, 1991.

4. O. C. Ferrell and John Fraedrich, *Business Ethics,* 1994.

5. F Neil Brady, *Ethical Managing: Rules and Results,* 1990.

6. O. C. Ferrell, Larry G. Gresham, and John Fraedrich, "A Synthesis of Ethical Decision Models for Marketing," *Journal of Macromarketing,* 1989.

7. Tom Rusk and D. Patrick Miller, *The Power of Ethical Persuasion: From Conflict to Partnership at Work and in Private Life,* 1993.

8. Keith Davis and William C. Frederick, *Business and Society: Management, Public Policy, and Ethics,* 1984.

9. Archie B. Carroll, " The Pyramid of Corporate Responsibility: Toward the Moral Management of Organisational Stakeholders," *Business Horizons,* July-August 1991.

10. Margaret A. Stroup and Ralph L. Newbert, "The Evolution of Societal Responsibility," *Business Horizons,* March-April 1987.

11. Margaret A. Stroup, Ralph L. Newbert, and Jerry W. Anderson, "Doing Good, Doing Better: Two Views of Social Responsibility," *Business Horizons,* March-April 1987.

12. "Good Guys Finish First," *Business Horizons,* March-April 1995.

13. Todd L. Hooper and Bart T. Rocca, "Environmental Affairs: Now on the Strategic Agenda," *Journal of Business Strategy,* May-June 1991.

Cases

Case I.I: Total Industries

Abhinav Kumar was totally unprepared for the news. And what surprised the 34-year-old scion of the Kumar family – which had interests in a range of industries including batteries, consumer durables, soaps and oils, and switchgears – was that it was his 36-year-old Wharton School classmate, Rakesh Bhatia, who gave him the scoop over their dinner meeting. Bhatia headed a small engineering company in Phoenix, Arizona (US), but was remarkably networked in the industry.

"I hear your competition just got bigger," he ribbed Kumar.

"What do you mean?" Kumar asked, surprised.

"Haven't you heard that PLT and Control Equipment are talking about a merger?" The two switchgear companies were competitors of the Rs. 1,750-crore switchgear division of Total Industries, Kumar's diversified family-managed company.

Kumar almost choked on his soup when he heard that. Such a merger would mean that Total would, overnight, lose its No.1 position in the industry, its 23 per cent market share in switchgears would be eclipsed by the combined 33 per cent share of PLT and Control.

"Who told you this?" Kumar asked.

"You are not going to believe this. It was a merchant banker sitting next to me on my flight from New York. In fact, this guy was flying down to Mumbai to meet the CEOs of the companies."

"Switchgears is our most profitable business, Rakesh. I can't afford to let any competitors to muscle us out of the market."

"That will happen if the merger happens. The new entity will have better bargaining power with their suppliers and customers; they may take a lead in product development, too."

"That has been our strength so far. We not only launch better products but also deliver better service at cost-effective prices."

Kumar excused himself to make a phone call. He called Manoj Kohli, the 42-year-old President of the switchgear division, on his mobile. "Manoj, can you postpone your Pune trip tomorrow. I need to meet you first thing in the morning." Manoj knew something big was afoot. With the meeting fixed for 9 am, Kumar returned to the table.

"I am just curious, Abhi, but tell me, how is the strategy process managed at your company?'

"Well, there is dad, me, and the four division heads. Typically, it's this group that does the strategising."

"So, I would be right in assuming that the process is more implicit than explicit."

"We do make our periodic business forecasts and reviews, and each division is clued into what is happening in the industry."

"How come they missed the news of the merger?" Rakesh asked Kumar. "But that's not what I am trying to say," continued Bhatia. "What you are describing is functional strategy. Every company has it. But what really works in the long run is a comprehensive competitive strategy that looks at the industry structure, maps the changing contours, predicts how competition will change, and puts together a response for your company."

Contd...

"I get your point. Although we are a Rs. 6,000-crore company, our focus seems to be on marketing battles and not competitive strategy. Had we done our homework, Total may have been merging with PLT or Control," conceded Kumar.

After the dinner was over, Kumar and Bhatia parted ways, promising to meet again before the latter left for Phoenix.

Kohli walked into Kumar's office at 9 am sharp. "What's up, boss?, he asked.

"PLT and Control are planning a merger," Kumar said matter-of-factly.

Wow! Who told you?"

"Rakesh. We met over dinner last night. It will take another three months for the deal to come through, but it is happening."

"Should we make a counter bid?" Kohli ventured.

"With our kind of stock price? It will cost us more than half the family's stake in the business to bid for either PLT or Control. The best bet is to get a defensive strategy in place."

"Let me get details about the merger. That will be essential before we plan our response," said Kohli.

"In any case, we are meeting again. And I have asked Srikant, Ratika, and Gunneen to be there too," said Kumar, referring to Total's Presidents of consumer durables, batteries, and soaps divisions, respectively.

"Is this about the merger?" questioned Kohli.

"No, but something to do with it. I think it is high time we got an explicit strategy together. Things are changing much too fast for us to be merely reactive. We need to plan ahead for the next 5 years at least."

Kumar's father and Total Industries Chairman, Deepak, was not scheduled to attend the evening meeting. But on an impulse, on the way to his squash club, he decided to join the brainstorming session. That explains why he landed up in shorts and sneakers. The meeting had not started when Deepak walked in.

"Thank you for joining us, Sir," Kumar said. He always addressed his father as 'Sir' in front of other executives. He then repeated the news of merger although, by then, almost everybody knew about it.

"In a way," Kumar said, "I am glad that the merger is happening. It has forced us to stop and examine the way we strategise. That is not to say that our strategies are ineffective or slow. We wouldn't be this big had it been so. But the point is, having become a conglomerate we cannot afford discrete strategies. The sum of our divisional approaches will – tomorrow – stop being equal to our corporate strategy. We need to formalise the process of strategy making, once and for all."

"We need a framework in which to examine where our business is going, and how to grow it," interjected Deepak.

"The basic dilemma in strategy," Kumar continued, "is similar to what we encountered during our vision creation process. What we have to ask ourselves, is whether our long-run strategy can be based on the present position of our divisions, or whether we should factor in the

Contd...

emergence of new forces like e-Commerce, economies of scale, disruptive technologies, and changes in the tradition configuration of the supply-chain."

"I guess it has to fit in with our vision of being No. I in each of the industries we choose to operate in," said Gunneen Roy.

"I agree," quipped Deepak.

"Me too," said Kumar. "But there doesn't seem to be any consensus on approach I spoke to several consulting firms this afternoon, before I asked two of them – Strategic Consultants Ltd. (SCL) and Transformation Consulting Group (TCG) to fax me details of what they could do for us."

"And what do they have to say?" asked Ratika.

"Diametrically opposing things. SCL says that our strategy must be based on data of what is, not projection of what will be. It also offers to identify all variables that impact the company's profits. But, I think a strategy should factor in the future. Besides, SCL won't help implement strategy."

"What about TCG?" Manoj wanted to know.

"TCG wants to look beyond today. Its aim is not to maximise the company's profits in today's markets, but to fundamentally re-configure our business portfolio."

"But do they agree on the formulation part?" asked Ratika.

"No, the SCL approach is top driven. It does not believe in involving employees at different levels in formulating strategy. It forms a team of two of senior executives, and two of its consultants. The team lays down the strategy. The TCG approach, in contrast, is bottom up. It seeks the active involvement of employees who are asked to define the kind of organisation they want their company to be."

A restless Deepak piped up. "Surprising, how divergent their approaches are!"

"TCG's methodology is also different, it comprises four phases: envisioning, external analysis, internal analysis, and developing an action plan. Phase I involves asking our employees where they see Total in another 10 years. Phase 2 entails asking managers from each of our four divisions their perceptions of our customers, competitors, and the macro-environment in 2010. They will be asked to define the customers, and the nature of competition."

"Sounds like a good idea," observed Roy.

"In Phase 3, internal analysis is aimed at enabling managers of individual businesses to look inwards and analyse our performance, and strategic options. The performance of the group would be measured both on financial parameters and non-financial parameters like customer satisfaction and product quality. The employees would, then, try and determine the options available to reach business looking at the past strategy, strategic problems, organisational capabilities, and constraints."

"How will these diverse views get synthesised?" queried Kohli.

"TCG has a framework for that Based on these findings, a summary of the strengths and weaknesses of Total will be arrived at. The final part of the phase involves defining the existing competencies and updating our vision. In the final phase, TCG would address issues like

Contd...

which core competencies to build, which product segments to tap, and what type of coalitions to form within the industry."

"Somehow, I am not convinced, said Deepak. "I fear that Total will end up being a guinea pig for testing strategy formulation. Yet, we do need an explicit strategy for tomorrow. I wonder what we should do."

TABLE 1: TOTALS' FOUR DIVISIONS

	CTVs			Refrigerators		
	Total	Nearest Competitor	Industry Average	Total	Nearest Competitor	Industry Average
Sales Growth	10%	8.5%	9%	7%	6%	6.5%
Profits Growth	8%	7. 5%	8%	5%	5.5%	6%
Product Launches	4%	5%	6%	2%	2%	4%

TABLE 2: CASH COWS

	Switchgears			Batteries		
	Total	Nearest Competitor	Industry Average	Total	Nearest Competitor	Industry Average
Sales Growth	23%	16%	20%	15%	16%	14%
Profits Growth	11%	9%	7.5%	13%	14%	12%
Product Launches	3%	2%	2%	2%	3%	3%

(Source: The case was referred by N. Balasubramanian, Visiting Professor & Chairman, CDOCTA, IIM-Bangalore, Business Today, May 7–21, 2000).

QUESTIONS

1. Identify the problems in this case.
2. Assume any data regarding strengths and weaknesses etc. What strategic options would you recommend for Total?

Case 1.2: The Body Shop and Marketing

The Body Shop recorded rapid growth during the 1970s and 1980s. However, its founder, Anita Roddick had publicly dismissed the role of marketing. It is well-known that she publicly ridiculed marketing for putting the interests of shareholders before the needs of society. She also held in similar low esteem the financial community that she referred to as "merchant wankers." While things were going very favourably, nobody seemed to mind her sceptical approach. After all, it was possible that she had actually found a new way of doing business, and the results so far stood to prove it. But how even such a famous and admired person as Anita Roddick could manage indefinitely without consulting the fundamental principles of marketing, wondered marketing experts and others. By the end of the 1990s, The Body Shop was experiencing bad times and the sceptics among the marketing and financial field were quick to point out the folly of its founder's apparently idiosyncratic ways.

From a high in 1992, The Body Shop shares dropped to a low witnessed at the start of 2003, despite the market index rising over that period. Profit remained similarly depressed, with performance in almost all European, North American, and Far Eastern markets stagnant.

Yes, everybody recognised that Anita Roddick has been the dynamo behind The Body Shop's success. From a small single outlet, she inspired and managed the growth of the chain to some 1500 familiar green-fronted establishments in 46 countries around the world. Yet, until the late 1990s, she continued to boast that The Body Shop had never used, or needed, marketing. Much of the company's success has been tied to its promotional approach by campaigning for the pursuit of social and environmental issues. But while Roddick campaigned for everything from physical torture of wives and Siberian tigers to the poverty-stricken mining communities of Southern Appalachia, the company was facing major problems in all its key markets.

Part of the problem of The Body Shop was its failure to fully comprehend the dynamics of its market place. Positioning on the basis of good causes may have been enough to launch the company into the public mind in the 1970s, but what it now needed was a sustainable long-term positioning. Other companies soon launched similar initiatives. For example, the Boots Pure Drug Company matched one of The Body Shop's earliest claims that it did not test its products on animals. Competitors had copied even the very feel of The Body Shop store that included its décor, staff, and product displays. How could the company stay ahead in terms of maintaining its distinctive positioning when many others had similar differentiation? Its causes seemed to become increasingly remote from the real concerns of shoppers. While most shoppers in UK may have been swayed by a company's unique claim to protect animals, it is not clear how many would be moved by its support for Appalachian miners? If there was a Boots or Superdrug store next door, why should a buyer shell out a premium price to buy from The Body Shop? The Body Shop may have pioneered a very clever business launching formula over twenty-five years ago, but the concept had been successfully copied by others. And these other companies had made enormous strides in terms of their social and environmental concerns and awareness.

Part of the company's problem has been blamed on the inability of Roddick to delegate. She is reported to have spent almost half of her time globetrotting in propagating support of her good causes, but did have a problem in delegating marketing strategy and implementation. Numerous capable managers who were brought in to try to implement professional management practices apparently gave up in bewilderment at the lack of discretion that they were given, and then left dismayed.

Contd...

The Body Shop's experience in America typified Roddick's pioneering style, which frequently ignored sound marketing analysis. She sought a new way of doing business in America, but in doing so she dismissed the experience of older and more sophisticated retailers – such as Marks & Spenser and Sock Shop, which came unscratched in what is a very difficult market. The Body Shop decided to enter the US markets in 1988 not through a safe option such as a joint venture or a franchising agreement, but instead by setting up its own operation from scratch, according to Roddick's principles of changing the business rulebook and cutting out the greedy American business community. But this was an exceedingly risky move. Her store format was based on the British town centre model. She did not bother to appreciate the fact that Americans spend most of their money in out-of-town malls. In 1996, the US operation lost 3.4 million pounds.

Roddick's critics claim that she has a naïve view of herself, her company, and business in general. She has consistently argued her philosophy that profits and principles don't mix, despite the fact that many of her financially successful competitors have been involved in major social initiatives.

The rift between Roddick's and others' view of the world was revealed in the results of an innovative independent social audit that The Body Shop commissioned in 1966. The company was prompted to commission the study after the report following media criticism that its social and environmental credentials might not actually be as good as the company claimed. The results highlighted eye-opening shortcomings in virtually every one of the company's stakeholder relationships. The company scored well in certain areas such as promoting human and civil rights, pollution control, product information, wages, and benefits, women's opportunities, and energy conservation; but it scored really badly on issues of corporate governance, relationships with shareholders, responsiveness to complaints of customer and franchises, accuracy of promotional claims, communication, and reaction to criticism.

Critics claim that had Roddick not dismissed and ridiculed the need for marketing for so long, The Body Shop could have certainly avoided future problems that it faced. But by 2000, it was paying the price for not having devoted sufficient resources to new product development, to innovation, to refreshing its product ranges, and to moving the business forward. It seems that heroes can change the rulebook when the tide is flowing with them, but adopting the disciplines of marketing allows companies to anticipate and react when the tide begins to turn against them.

N.B: The Body Shop was sold to L'Orcal, the world's largest cosmetics manufacturer, in March 2006, for £ 656 million. Dame Anita Roddick gained personally to the tune of £130 million. Since British and French companies have very divergent views on strategy and day-to-day management, it remains to be seen how successful the union will ultimately turn out to be. For The Body Shop, it's yet another chapter in its struggle to remain relevant in a changing world.

QUESTIONS

1. Analyse the significant issues in the case. Was Anita right in ridiculing the marketing?
2. How has Anita Roddick positioned The Body Shop and maintained its identity with social and environmental causes as a unique positioning approach?
3. Determine if Anita made any mistakes in running the Company? Was her approach to not modifying the company positioning right?
4. If you were in Anita Roddick's place, what would have you done for company's US operations?

Case 1.3: Kill Soft Glow?

Sunil Deo absent-mindedly ran his finger over the cake of soap before him. He traced the name 'Soft Glow' embossed on the soap as he inhaled its unmistakable sesame fragrance. It was a small soap, almost like a bar of gold. There were no frills, no coloured packaging, and no fancy shape. Just a golden glow and the fragrance of sesame and Lucida font that quietly stated 'Soft Glow'.

Deo smiled wanly and clasped the soap in his hands, as if protecting it from an unseen predator. He was wondering with quiet concern if the 30-year-old brand would last long. Romin India, where Deo was marketing manager, was taking a long, hard look at the soap, as it was proving to be a strain on resources.

There were conflicting stories about how Soft Glow was launched. Some said the brand was a 'gift' from the departing English parent company. Others claimed that it was created for the then chairman's British wife, as the Indian climate did not agree with her skin. They also claimed that the lady also coined the copy "The honest soap that loves your skin." The line had stuck, and has endured through three turbulent decades. Only the visuals had changed, with newer models replacing the older ones.

Romin India was basically a speciality products company producing household hygiene, fabricare, and dental care products. Soft Glow was the only soap in its product mix, and it was produced and marketed by Romin itself. Its reliable quality and value delivery had earned it a lot of respect in the market. Its equity was such that Romin was known as the Soft Glow Company. Indeed, the brand name Soft Glow denoted purity, reliability, and gentle skincare.

In 1994, Morten UK increased its stake in the Indian subsidiary to 51%. Within months, all of Moren's products were given a facelift, thanks to the inflow of foreign capital. New packaging, new fragrances, new formulations and more variants were introduced.

Only Soft Glow was left untouched. For, although it had a growing skincare business following some strategic acquisitions in Europe in the early eighties, Morten UK was not a soap company. The UK marketing team ran an audit of every brand and product in the company's portfolio. But when it came to Soft Flow, it faltered. "We don't know this one," officials at the parent company said.

"We don't want this one to be touched," Deo had said protectively, a sentiment that was endorsed by the managing director, Rajan Sharma. "Soft Glow is too sacred, we will leave it as it is," he said.

But the UK marketing team was confounded. What was a lone soap doing in the midst of toilet cleaners and fabric protectors, they wondered. However, they went ahead and agreed that their proposed revamp strategy would only look at up-gradation, not tinkering with what wasn't broken.

Indeed, for 30 long years no one had tampered with the Soft Glow brand, and Deo felt there was no reason to start now. Soft Glow, in his view, was a self-sustaining brand. That was a bit of an understatement because advertising for the brand was moderate and Morten India had never used any promotional gimmick for it.

Now, after four years of nurturing the other categories, Morten UK had decided to launch its Vio range of skincare products in India. But Soft Glow's presence and profile was a major

Contd...

roadblock to Vio's success. "It will create dissonance, confuse our skincare equity and deter the articulation of Vio's credo. It will stand out as a genetic flaw," argued the UK marketing head. "You need to do a rethink on Soft Glow. Ideally, we should just close it down."

Deo protested. "Why? It has such a strong equity and loyal following. So much has been invested in it all these years. Why give up all that?"

Rajan, however, had another idea. "Let us then extend the Soft Glow brand." He said. It was the simplest solution. Companies were now investing heavily in creating new equities for their brands. But in Soft Glow's case, Morten was already sitting on a brand with a terrific equity. He felt that extending this equity to other categories, such as skincare products would be successful.

But Soft Glow needed a new positioning before it could be extended. Till a few years ago, it had been in premium category, priced at Rs. 15. Then new brands with specific positioning and higher price tags entered the market. This created a level above Rs. 15 soaps and pushed Soft Glow down to the mid-priced range. Soft Glow's price was thus no longer commensurate with its premium position and image.

Over the years, Soft Glow had become so sacred a cow that Morten India had been too scared to do anything to it. As a result, the soap was left with a niche category of loyal users. This category neither shrank or increased, just kept getting older and older, and with it the brand also kept growing older. For example, when Deo's wife had her first baby at 25, her mother had recommended Soft Glow for her dry skin and also for baby's tender skin because it contained sesame oil. That was in 1979. Today, Deo's daughter had turned 21 and was being wooed by Dove, Camay, even Santoor and Lifebuoy Gold, with their aggressive advertising. Soft Glow had begun to lose its image of being contemporary as newer brands came in with newer values.

Today, at 46, Deo's wife still used Soft Glow, but when she recommended Soft Glow to her daughter, she said, "But Soft Glow is a soap for mothers, for older people."

That was a major problem. The Soft Glow brand had aged, and Morten India hadn't even been aware of it. While its equity had grown with its users, its personality had aged considerably in the last 30 years. "I don't think you can keep the personality young, unless you keep renewing the brand. The objective now is to widen your equity so that your image becomes young," continued Rajan. "For instance, if today you were to personify a Soft Glow user, it would be a woman of 45 years using the same brand for many years, who is averse to experimenting, very skincare conscious, very trusting, and very one-dimensional. As you can see, this is not a very competitive personality. These are the strengths of Soft Glow, but they are also its weaknesses," he analysed.

The context had changed. Today, youth demanded brands that stood for freedom and fearlessness. They demanded bold brands that dared to cure, not just preserve. "Preservation is for old people. Those are the attributes being presented in evolved markets," said Rajan. To make Soft Glow contemporary, the attributes had to be re-framed, he felt. "You can't make a young brand trusting, caring, loving, without adding other attributes to it. Today, youth stands for freedom, for laughter, for frankness, for forthrightness. That's what Close Up, Lifebuoy Gold, Vatika, and other brands propagate. So, either come clean and say it is for older skin which needs trust and kindness, or reposition the brand," said Rajan.

Repositioning was also necessary to address another anomaly in Soft Glow's image: its perceived premium. Morten India had been unable to do anything about Soft Glow slipping into the mid-price range following the entry of more expensive brands. Now, as Rajan mulled over the brand

Contd...

extension plan, Deo felt that Soft Glow's premium positioning was its core equity and that had to be maintained.

"If you are premium priced in the consumer's mind, your extensions are automatically perceived as premium. So, if you don't present the other products as premium, the consumer will not see them as extensions of the brand," he said. "For example, if you are to launch a shampoo which is priced lower than Sunsilk, but higher than Nyle and Ayur, then whatever the rationale, the consumer will not accept your product. "It is not the Soft Glow I know, "will be the feeling," he said. Deo felt that since premium positioning was one of Soft Glow's equity values, it would be very difficult to convince consumers that the brand was being extended without hanging on to this particular value. "Will they buy your rationale that the very same values and equity would now be available at a low price? To be in the premium segment now, you have to price it at Rs. 35 or 40, almost at par with Dove," he said. "With Dove retailing at Rs. 45, Soft Glow will be perceived as a cheaper option."

"We can't simply raise the price," said Rajan. "What are we offering for that increase? You can't add value because you don't want to tamper with the brand. The consumers will then ask, "Soft Glow used to be so cheap, what has happened now? The user will forget that 15 years ago, Rs. 10 was expensive, because all her comparisons would be in today's context," said Rajan.

"So what's the option?" asked Deo. "You don't have to be expensive to be premium," said Rajan. Soft Glow already has the image of a premium brand, thanks to its time-tested core values of purity, credibility, and reliability. What we can do is reinforce the premium through communication and positioning. In fact, we should have tinkered with Soft Glow long ago. That is what HLL did with Lux. It also launched a bridge brand, Lux International, in the premium category," said Rajan.

"How could we have done anything to the brand?" asked Deo. "The product had such a strong following. It stood for gold, for sesame oil, for its subtle earthy perfume. We changed the packaging periodically, but that's all we could do. Remember the time we brought out a transparent green Soft Glow with the fragrance of lime? It bombed in the market."

Rajan was not in favour of the premium positioning. It appeared very short-sighted to him, given the bigger plan to extend the brand. "Where are the volumes in the premium segment? He asked. "For some reason, every manufacturer feels that skincare can be an indulgence of only the moneyed class. As a result, there is a crowd in the premium end of the market. Do we want to be yet another player in the segment?"

Fifteen years ago, Soft Glow was perceived as a premium product. But today, global brands like Revlon, Coty, and Oriflame were delivering specific premium platforms. Soft Glow did not have a global equity. "Let us revisit the brand and examine what it stood for 15 years ago and examine the relevance of those attributes in today's context," suggested Rajan. "Soft Glow stood for care, consciousness, love, quality and all that. But today, are these enough to justify a premium position?" he asked Deo. "These attributes are viable in the mid-priced segment." He said.

"The mid-priced brand is the proverbial washer-man's dog," said Deo. "You don't know whether you are at the bottom end of the premium range or at the top-end of the low-priced range. You end up creating an image of being on the opportunity fence. It is a mere pricing ploy, with no strategic value."

Contd...

Rajan could understand Deo's fears. Some brands in a similar dilemma had managed to redefine their equity. For instance, HLL created a low-priced variant of Rin without incurring much dilution to the washing bar's equity. Rin was always perceived as a premium, high quality product that gave superior washing results. It was always several notches above Nirma. Rin was intended to be a stepping-stone for users to convert to Surf, a premium brand of HLL. Nirma users were people who upgraded from laundry soaps and were looking for a basic clean wash. Nirma stood for a different kind of personality – cheap, harsh, but effective. Rin, on the other hand, was sophisticated, gentle, effective, and expensive.

Deo and Rajan were faced with many critical decisions. It was risky to have a lone soap that did not fit in the overall image of the new business thrust. The UK team had recommended that Soft Glow should be discontinued. Deo had voiced a strong opinion that with appropriate changes in the formulations, an entry level Soft Glow Care, a medium-priced Soft Glow Plus, and a high-end Soft Glow Pearl would be an ideal solution.

QUESTIONS

1. Analyse the case and determine the significant issues.
2. Suggest an appropriate strategy keeping in view the company's core business and brand strength of Soft Glow.

Case 1.4: Real Juice Company

The company is in the business of producing and marketing fruit juices. Ritu Joshi and Rohit Jain were looking at the ad copy and turning it over and over again in their mind. The copy read, "The best fitness plan for you – real fruit, honest juice and no sugar." This was the main copy line. The more Ritu Joshi repeated this line in her mind, the more uneasy she became. "Something is wrong in this copy," she said to Rohit Jain, the marketing head. "We cannot say 'best for health' when we know for sure that the juice contains preservatives and food colour."

Rohit Jain said, "I don't see anything wrong with this. "But, don't you see? With food colour and preservatives added, we couldn't say it is best. This's what is wrong with it," replied Ritu.

Rohit said, "But this is hyperbole and permitted by law. There is nothing wrong in saying this. Haven't you noticed almost all detergent brands say 'for best wash', or 'whitest wash'? This is simply a way of claiming your brand's superiority."

"We are not talking about detergents, washes and fabrics. It is a health and fitness fruit juice. We could say something like 'a great way to plan your fitness programme' or something like that. We are saying, 'real fruit, honest juice, and no sugar' ... not a word about food colour and preservatives. Any consumer can contest our claim."

Rohit Jain thought for a moment then said, "Let us get the legal opinion from our lawyer, Amit Soni, to be on safe ground."

Amit listened to what Ritu had to say then said, "Companies use advertising to provide information to consumers and offer alternatives in a competitive market situation. Advertising is false when it says A = B and that isn't true. But if the ad is misleading, it falls under the category of unfair trade practice." Loudly reading the ad copy, Amit said, "Hyperbole such as best, newest, most effective way, are permissible and consumers are unlikely to take such claims with any seriousness. When a brand says its airconditioner is best or most efficient, consumers know that this is just a manner of speech and do not truly believe and put their money on such claims. In case a company tries to accord credibility to its claims, it goes beyond mere hyperbole. For instance, when the toothpaste says I am the best because I score 96 per cent whereas others score 80 per cent, then it is a claim that goes beyond hyperbole. The marketer is then trying to give it a scientific basis on a particular attribute. This enters the realm of false advertising and is misrepresentation under MRTP Act."

"Yes, Real Juice may pass the legal test, fine, but ethically it won't be correct," said Ritu Joshi. "Please understand. Here you are not making a claim," said Amit Soni.

"You think so? Then look at this," said Ritu Joshi, showing another campaign ad for Real Juice that showed a fitness instructor of some repute, holding a Real Juice orange can and his words were, 'I trust Real Juice for my fitness and good health...' "Now isn't that a solid claim on behalf of Real Juice," asked Ritu.

"It depends on whether the endorser is an expert," said Amit Soni. "If he were a doctor, a nutritionist, or a dietician then those words could connote a claim made by an expert and could be contested. For instance, if a doctor says that Real Juice is best for health then the question arises if the doctor has really conducted a test? Has he conducted the test in an independent manner? Did he conduct the test to deliver a certain result? Did somebody finance the test? That would amount to an unfair trade practice. If a complaint is lodged by a consumer that the

Contd...

ad is misleading, the MRTP Commission could grant an injunction that the ad be withdrawn."

Rohit Jain was thinking loudly about another campaign praising canned drinks, claiming that drinks in bottles faced a higher risk of contamination. The campaign was part of Real Juice's fitness and health positioning. Now he wondered if the manufacturers of bottled drinks could contest that claim.

Amit Soni said, "Comparative advertising is healthy but the advertiser must be clear about the claims to be made. In this case, you are saying that Real Juice is good because it comes in cans and bottled drinks are not as good. This is a direct attack on bottled drinks. Advertisers do not disclose all the parameters they have considered in their conclusion of 'best'. They may select some major ones, or they may choose to highlight the trivial ones and ignore the major ones. These things happen every day and are not strictly provided under the law. There must be prima facie evidence of damage or misrepresentation to establish a case of unfair trade practice."

"So, we are legally safe," said Rohit Jain. "We will reword this campaign, but our other campaigns have passed muster."

Ritu Joshi felt differently. She said, "Legally we may be safe, but we have to also take an ethical view." The Real Juice commercial showed an ailing old man. The wife proceeds to extract juice from some oranges, but the daughter-in-law sweeps everything aside and pours out Real Juice from a can.

Ritu Joshi said, "You know, this ad says to me 'Real Juice is convenient, Real juice is as good as fresh oranges, Real juice is good for the ailing.' That misleads."

"Don't be absurd," said Rohit Jain, "The proposition here is convenience."

"I am not being absurd," said Ritu Joshi, "We must not forget that our primary platform is health and fitness. This convenience angle is also creating an impression of 'also good for health'. I believe that as responsible advertisers, we have to be more concerned about the ethical aspects than merely the legal angle. This is where we come to the line between what is legal and what is ethical. We may be legally right but our act could be unethical if the words or pictures in the ad could lead the consumer to believe something that is not true. The aura of the fitness instructor used as the endorser creates an impression that the information is coming to consumers from an environment where there are people whose opinion consumers view as being correct. Otherwise, why use the instructor as the endorser."

QUESTIONS

1. Analyse the issues in the case.
2. What are your views about the ethical dilemma?
3. Why should marketers bother about ethics if the communications measure up to legal parameters?
4. How would you reword the copy of Real Juice so that it is ethical in your view, without weakening the core message theme?

Case 1.5: First Citizen Club

hen customers in an outlet of Shoppers' Stop pick up a pair of Florsheim shoes, they leave behind a distinct trail. The purchases made by a First Citizen Club (FCC) member are under the store's microscope. Shoppers' Stop wants to know what brand of shoes you like to wear. This process aims at building bridges to both its customers and suppliers, or perhaps even other manufacturers.

Shoppers' Stop uses customer preferences to gather valuable market reach data. Ajay Kelkar, senior manager marketing services says, "We are looking at the various ways in which we can work with our brands and customers."

In India, Shoppers' Stop is one of the first major chains that is working on ways to manage its customer related information to gain competitive advantage. Arvind Singhal, managing director of retail consultant KSA Technopak says, "Customer information capture, and an intelligent and rigorous warehousing and mining of transaction behaviour, is increasingly becoming one of the major success factors for successful retailers." Singhal cites the example of Wal-Mart, whose success has hinged on the way in which it uses its famously advanced customer shopping information.

Shoppers' Stop opened its first store in Mumbai in 1991. It launched its First Citizen Club Programme only in April 1994, drawing from the base of people that had been encouraged to drop their visiting cards in the previous years.

Any customer can become a FCC member by either paying an enrolment fee of Rs. 150 or making purchases worth Rs. 2,500 in a single day. The benefits to customers include reward points and updates on store events and merchandising, and information on the latest fashion trends through a monthly newsletter named First Update.

In the first year of this programme, the store enrolled some 4,000 FCC members. By 2000, FCC had 100,000 members and created member categories who could have a gold, silver, and a classic card. These cards bear different eligibility levels for different categories.

Pradeep Katya, senior manager, direct marketing say, "Beginners used to be targeted in a different manner, while high-frequency FCC members were already familiar with the experience. So the objective there is to grow in share of wallet."

About 2 per cent of the FCC members are gold cardholders, 25 per cent silver, and the rest have basic card. Around 15 per cent of the walk-ins on any day in any store are FCC members, and they account for nearly 40 per cent of the store's sales. According to Katyal, globally, large retailers sell as much as 60 per cent of their products in each category to loyalty customers. In India, the retail market is still fragmented, but Katyal expects the global trend will soon reach here as large and organised retailing grows in the country. Shoppers' Stop is clearly recognising that its FCC members are a precious database. For the chain is sitting on a cache of data on consumer buying habits. In fact, the quality of database isn't really derived from the information customers give upfront at the time of enrolment. That just covers the usual details like name, address, date of birth, spouse's name and date of birth, and their marriage anniversary. Katyal says, "Few people give out family details. But as long as we can communicate with them, it is sufficient." The real business starts when the FCC member starts making purchases.

Since the FCC programme is integrated in Shoppers' Stop enterprise resource package, every customer transaction at any checkout counter gets recorded. Over a period of time, then, the

Contd...

chain could ascertain whether a customer prefers Louis Philippe, Allen Solly, or whether he goes in for that Calvin Klein, or Armani after-shave.

"We can track consumers' psychographics by seeing when they buy and what kind of products or brands they buy. Now we are talking to other companies about this and they see value in it," says Kelkar. Singhal believes the store can, with a very significant investment in technology and management, use the loyalty programme-based transaction data to offer a more focused product mix in its stores, customise brand and product choices from one location to another, and delete slow-moving SKUs and substitute them with fast-moving ones.

Singhal says, "It can also use this information to generate a more direct Customer Relationship Management (CRM) effort, and give loyal shoppers enhanced service, and tangible and non-tangible benefits so as to generate higher sales per customer." The store is certainly open to the possibilities. Kelkar says that if they can understand their customers' psychographics and demographics, they can target products exclusively to them or even do limited launches for them, something they are currently discussing.

Some of the direct marketing thrust will be through the other link that the store has with its FCC base — the newsletter. Katyal claims that experience has shown the best advertisers in First Update tend to grab the best market share in that category.

So, now the chain is using the medium to promote its in-store label Shop, which accounts for 20 per cent of sales currently, but which Katyal and Kelkar would like to take to 50 per cent.

Consider the promo that Shoppers' Stop did for Espirit watches last year. FCC members were informed through a mailer that they could get a free Espirit watch if they bought goods worth rupees 15,000 within three months. Katyal says that against an estimated 1,500 watches, the store ended up giving 3,700 watches.

While each watch was worth Rs. 2,700, the promo brought in sales in excess of Rs. 5 crores for Shoppers' Stop. Katyal adds, "Generally, direct marketing has a 1-2 per cent success rate. We consider anything less than 12 per cent as a failure."

The store is also looking at going beyond such efforts. The back and front office teams are currently working on identifying the top-selling SKUs in every category. Shoppers' Stop will then use its database to profile buyers of that SKU, not on age or address, but by seeing what other products they are buying, and then targeting other buyers who have similar buying habits.

For example, in a simplistic scenario, if a large number of customers who buy Florsheim shoes also tend to buy Arrow shirts, the store could target other buyers of Arrow shirts and do a promo for Florsheim shoes with them.

The store has recently done market research for an FMCG company that is launching a fabric care product shortly. The brand wanted to understand the needs of people who buy a certain kind of apparel – say, a high-value shirt.

The FCC database was used for this research. In another case, channels like Hallmark and National Geographic are considering using the store's database for promotions. When Lakme sponsored a beauty week at the store earlier this year, it could interact with customers and gauge their responses to its products. Once the data warehousing tools are in place, Katyal and Kelkar plan to analyse the FCC data to give feedback to brands that are already selling at Shoppers' Stop. This could be done at a category level or with a specific brand.

Contd...

Brands could even use the information to clear inventory. For instance, if a producer has stagnant stocks of, say, 42-size shirts, the firm could use the database to target only those customers who wear that size.

On the other hand, the store could come up with a base of, say, bargain hunters and target events for them. Besides, if the suppliers have such information, they could quicken their response time for developing new products apart from improving their production planning for a more efficient replenishment cycle.

The store's customer base is essentially within the socio-economic classes A and B, and aged between 25 – 45 years. There's also the fact that the audience may be limited to a certain geographical area within the city – after all, Shoppers' Stop expansions are based on this catchment area premise. But Katyal says, "Most brands at the end of the day are targeting people who are in this age group and with a good disposable income.

Today, it is a buyer's market and marketers have to continuously add value for customers and convert first-time buyers into second-and-third timers.

QUESTIONS

1. How is Shoppers' Stop benefiting from FCC programme? Do you think the store is practicing CRM? Explain.
2. Why has it become necessary to develop cordial relations with customers? How can this help in enhancing customer satisfaction?

Case I.6: Life's Good for LG

G Electronics India's market share dropped in January 2005 — for the first time since the company was set up in 1997. But Managing Director Kwang-Ro Kim isn't worried.

"The dealers must have met their targets in December itself, so they took it easy in January," he explains.

Were it any other company, the managing director's insouciance would appear to border on foolhardiness. But this is LG, a company that can afford to take it easy.

Even after the blip in sales in January — LG's market share in refrigerators fell fractionally from 28.6 per cent the previous month to 28.1 per cent — the Korean consumer electronics brand is still the preferred white goods brand in India — across categories and sub-categories.

Whether it is refrigerators, air-conditioners, washing machines or colour televisions — LG's dominance over the white goods market is complete.

in volume term	LG		No. 2 player
Refrigerators	27.22	-	1.2 (Whirlpool)
Colour TVs	25.5	-	15.1 (Samsung)
Microwave ovens	41.4	-	19.7 (Samsung)
Washing machines	34.0	-	13.8 (Whirlpool)

That's pretty decent going for a company whose first experience in the Indian market was nothing short of disastrous. In its earlier avatar, the Korean company came to India as Lucky Goldstar.

This was in the early 1990s, and the rules at the time didn't permit foreign companies to start independent ventures. So Lucky Goldstar took on not one, but two joint venture partners. The first partnership ended acrimoniously while the second one never got off the ground.

In 1997, the Foreign Investment Promotion Board finally gave the Korean company permission to set up its own factory to make washing machines and refrigerators.

Re-christened LG Electronics, the new company — a 100 per cent subsidiary of the Korean 'chaebol — swung into action and set up a state-of-the-art manufacturing facility at Greater Noida, Uttar Pradesh.

There's been no looking back since then. In October 2004, LG set up a second manufacturing facility at Ranjangaon, near Pune, which makes white goods as well as cellular phones — the first GSM handset manufacturing facility in India.

Another facility, exclusively for GSM handsets, is being set up and will start operations in August. Turnover is also on the upswing: starting from Rs 150 crore in 1997, LG registered a turnover of Rs 6,500 crore last year and is targeting Rs 9,000 crore in 2005.

So, what went right?

Perhaps the most important step was to leave behind the baggage of the past.

As Lucky Goldstar, the company's biggest fault was that it did precisely what other white goods brands of the 1990s were doing: some half-hearted advertising and pushing the products only when the consumer entered the store.

Contd...

Activities that "pulled" potential buyers into showrooms were conspicuous by their absence. Once it got the permission to operate as a wholly owned subsidiary, though, all that changed. Within just five months, LG products were available across the country compared to the average two years competitors took for a nationwide launch.

An advertising blitzkreig followed. And the momentum hasn't let up since. LG is one of the most aggressive advertisers in the white goods industry, spending close to 5 per cent of its revenue on marketing activities — that's Rs. 130 crore last year.

A close tie up with cricket ensured the brand building exercise would score well on consumer recall — apart from signing on leading Indian cricketers, LG also launched a cricket game on one of its television models. Points of sales promotions were also extensively advertised to ensure customers were tempted to visit the stores.

Importantly, for LG, a nationwide launch meant just that. A penetrative distribution strategy ensured that products were available even in smaller towns and cities, breaking the chain of urban dependency that plagues most white goods manufacturers.

More than 65 per cent of last year's Rs 6,500 crore revenue came from non-urban sources; up from under 60 per cent the previous year. And what was the industry average? It was between twenty-five to 30 per cent. Add the fact that the rural markets accounted for a remarkable 30 per cent of total sales and it's clear that LG's strategy is working. "We push rural marketing," agrees Kim.

How does it do that? LG reaches into the hinterland through a pyramidal sales structure. Branch offices in larger cities set up Central Area Offices (CAOs) in smaller towns; these in turn reach out to even smaller towns and villages through Remote Area Offices (RAOs) — at last count, the company had 51 branch offices, 87 CAOs and 78 RAOs.

Each RAO has servicing, marketing and sales teams at its disposal and an individual budget for marketing activities in its territory. The executive in charge has independent decision-making powers — he can decide the tenor and scale of brand promotions in his area, without having to cross check every little detail from the head office.

Technology, too, is being used to the hilt to ease their jobs. The RAOs and CAOs are all electronically connected through a V-SAT and Intranet network.

And where earlier decisions about putting up large hoardings could be approved only after a visit from the head office, LG has provided all its branch managers digital cameras — now they just click images of suitable locations and get them approved electronically.

For customers, though, the direct approach is preferred. The advantage of an extended distribution network is that marketing executives can keep a finger on the pulse of the market. Promotions and finance schemes are designed to suit the needs of local customers.

In a small town in Uttar Pradesh, for instance, last year LG offered select households a free 15-day trial of a 50-inch flat screen television during the cricket season. The TV set costs close to Rs 1 lakh, but several families took the bait and considered buying the TV — at which point the showroom staff offered them carefully planned finance schemes.

Of course, it's not just the finance schemes that are tailor-made. LG has been careful right from the start to offer customers a "value-plus" proposition.

Contd...

Explains KSA Technopak Principal Harminder Sahni, "LG has always taken the stand that 'We're selling the AC, not the remote. The remote comes as part of the package." "Which is why, he adds, the company does not qualify as a "budget" models company." "LG does not sell no-frills products; it gives you all the bells and whistles," Sahni says.

LG recognised the need to do that early on. Kim — who's been with LG India since 1997 — points to a basic characteristic of Indian consumers: "They are very price sensitive. They want the best quality at reasonable prices." Accordingly, LG introduced its economy range in the country, which Kim predicted would be "easily accepted".

The company was ready to do battle on two flanks: it offered modern, features-packed products, at the same time keeping its margins wafer-thin. Even competitors accept the merit of the tactic.

"LG has been a price warrior while retaining its brand equity," points out Ajay Kapila, vice president, sales and marketing, Electrolux India. "Our success is the result of hard work and commitment. There's no miracle involved," says Kim.

The hard work was on the features, which were carefully chosen — and adapted — to appeal to Indian audiences. For instance, Kim points out that consumers in southwest India prefer big sound and big bass outputs.

Accordingly, LG India created Ballad, a flat screen television model that sells only in the subcontinent and comes equipped with 2,000 watt speakers.

Similarly, refrigerators in India have smaller freezers and big vegetable compartments — Indians prefer fresh food and a significant proportion are vegetarian. Colours, too, are chosen keeping market preferences in mind. White refrigerators, for instance, don't sell well in Kolkata and Punjab — while the sea air in Bengal corrodes the paint, the masalas used in Punjabi cooking discolour the fridge.

So LG offers a range of bright colours in these markets. The cricket game in TV sets wasn't the only "go local" innovation: LG also offered on-screen displays in five languages and large capacity semi-automatic washing machines that would suit Indian families.

The research for these adaptations and innovations is done in-house. LG invests significantly in local R&D — last year the company spent over Rs 100 crore on research.

"We want to be independent of Korea," states Kim. It's working towards that: already 70 per cent of its product line is produced locally, with the rest imported from China, Korea and Taiwan. In refrigerators, 95 per cent of the components are localised. All of which also help keep prices down.

But that was in the past. "Economy" and "value-for-money" are no longer going to be the cornerstones of LG's India strategy. In the next five years, says Kim, the company will concentrate on building itself as a premium brand, targeting 10 per cent of its earnings from super-premium products.

That includes products like the Whisen range of wall-mounted air-conditioners (Rs 50,000 and above), Dios refrigerators (Rs 65,000 and above) and X-canvas plasma TVs (Rs 1 lakh and above).

Contd...

LG has already set up 75 exclusive showrooms for these products, which were launched earlier this year, with more in the pipeline. This year it will spend upward of Rs 20 crore promoting the super-premium sub-brands. "High-end products need high-end outlays," smiles Kim.

Perhaps, but industry analysts have their doubts whether exclusive showrooms for such big-ticket items will bring in the bucks. "When it comes to consumer durables, people prefer comparison shopping. I will be surprised if the stores make money," comments KSA's Sahni.

Meanwhile, there's the imminent departure of the man who built up LG India to its present height. Kim, who was last year promoted as head of LG South West Asia, is likely to move up within the parent organisation some time soon. "I am preparing to leave," he admits. Will that make a difference to LG's growth curve? Kim doesn't think so.

"The system is working, so things will continue as they are," he says. That thought finds an echo in Sahni, who points out "Kim may be leading from the front, but LG couldn't have achieved what it has without a strong team."

The challenge now will be to integrate the new incumbent's working style with the existing culture of the organisation — and work on the new marketing strategy. If LG meets that head on, then, like its tagline says, Life's Good.

(Source: www.bsstrategist.com April 5, 2005).

QUESTIONS

1. Study the case and identify significant issues.
2. Conduct a SWOT analysis of LG.
3. What marketing strategies did LG adopt to be so successful in India?

PART 2

Marketing Environment Analysis

LEARNING OBJECTIVES

After going through this chapter, you will understand:

- Demographic Environment
- Economic Environment
- Competitive Environment
- Socio-cultural Environment
- Political-legal Environment
- Technological Environment

sage of helmets was very limited in India in the mid-1970s; they were not exactly popular. The early sales of available brands were low. There were just three brands: Blaze, Steelbird and Concorde. Blaze also manufactured helmets for other user groups, such as those used in different sports, e.g., polo or cycling. All helmets in sports line were manufactured to meet US standard specifications.

The domestic helmet market had grown to an annual size of nearly one million helmets by 2000. The domestic market for helmets is a derived demand stemming from increased sales of two-wheelers.

In India, all states have the authority to create their own helmet laws. As a result, helmet use was mandatory in some regions and optional in others. Helmet laws were enacted and retracted frequently, as local governments changed. In the year 2002, Delhi, Kolkata and Bangalore were the only three cities where helmet wearing was made compulsory because these three urban areas accounted for a large share of the two-wheeler market.

Subsequently, in some other states helmet wearing was made compulsory in selected cities. In some states helmets with only ISI mark were permitted. In Delhi, helmet wearing was also compulsory for the pillion rider.

The era of globalisation has begun and companies need to think globally while deciding to act locally. Within the last decade, the global economic and marketing environment has changed faster than ever before due to quantum leaps in science and technology. These developments have resulted in a quiet revolution – almost a transformation in managerial – and business practices.

High-tech products, technology, global sourcing, synergistic diversification, network building, shorter product life cycles, a culture of product and service quality including speed of response are the order of the day.

Domestic businesses in India no longer enjoy the comfort of protected economy, and competition from all sides is here to stay, liberalisation is gaining speed and privatisation of public sector companies is no longer a dream. Customer preferences are shifting; they are becoming increasingly discerning and value conscious.

Successful companies look beyond customer needs and wants and are sensitive to marketing environmental forces because a company operates within a generally uncontrollable external environment. It would be extremely dangerous for a company to be rejoicing and neglecting environmental forces when the company business is prospering and growing, customers are satisfied, and not much threat appears to exist from competitors. Environmental forces can pose serious threats to any business neglecting these forces.

Marketing environment includes all the forces that directly or indirectly influence marketing operations, by affecting an organisation's acquisition of inputs/creation of outputs such as human, financial, and natural resources and raw material, information, goods, services, or ideas. Sometimes, a distinction is made between macro and micro factors of environment. Macro influences consist of demographic, economic, socio-cultural, political-legal, technological, and natural factors. The micro influences include suppliers and distributors, competitors, customers, etc. Macro environmental factors are dynamic and a change in any one of them can induce changes in one or more of the others. The marketing environment includes six major forces:

- Demographic
- Economic
- Competitive

- Sociocultural
- Political-legal
- Technological

Scanning and Analysing Environment

Companies undertake environmental scanning and analysis to effectively monitor changes that may throw up opportunities and threats. ***Environmental scanning*** refers to systematically collecting information about environmental forces that affect the performance of not only the company but also all the players involved in the process of conducting businesses in the macro environment. Some players are less affected than others by the changes that take place in the environment. Companies ignoring or resisting such changes find themselves in very difficult situations. For example, Hindustan Motors and Premier Autos lost their dominant position to Maruti when it introduced a small car with a modern engine and low fuel consumption, and sold at a reasonable price. Ram Subramanium, Kamlesh Kumar, and Charles Yauger suggest that environmental scanning gives companies some advantage over competitors in taking advantage of changing trends. However, companies must know how to take advantage of such information in their strategic planning process. Scanning requires observation, collecting information from business, trade, government, general interest publications, etc. ***Environmental analysis*** means assessing and interpreting the gathered information through various sources, evaluation of information accuracy, resolve inconsistencies, assign importance to the findings, and forecast the impact of trends. This helps bring to light the opportunities and threats arising due to changes in the environment and successful companies take serious note of environmental changes and develop appropriate strategies.

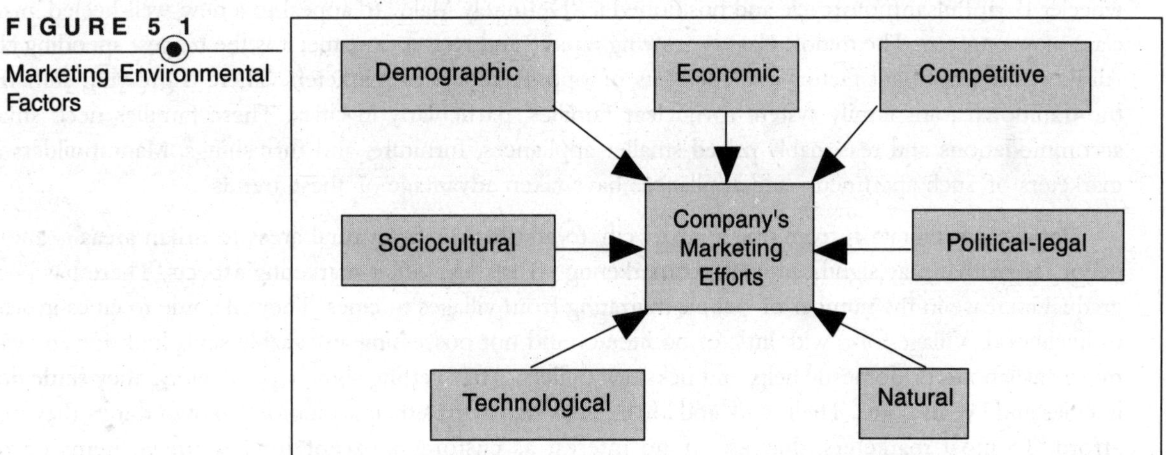

FIGURE 5.1
Marketing Environmental Factors

A well-managed company takes a reactive approach and attempts to prepare itself to respond quickly and appropriately to major changes in the environment. Carl P. Zeithaml and Valarie A. Zeithaml propose a second approach of being proactive toward environmental forces. Some marketing professionals argue that marketing environment forces can be controlled to some extent and believe marketing itself is an important force and can be put to use to induce change and extend its impact on environment. Philip Kotler recommends lobbying, legal action, advertising of key issues, and public relations that can help alter some environmental forces. One or the other of these approaches may suit different companies, while some other companies may prefer to use both approaches to suit their objective.

Demographic Environment

The size of population and its growth rate in urban, rural, state level, and nation is an important factor because people have needs and wants and constitute a market. However, just a large population with high growth rate does not necessarily mean growing markets unless supported by buying power and a willingness to spend. Other factors with respect to population in which marketers have interest include age distribution, gender figures, literacy levels, any changes in household patterns, and significant regional characteristics of their interest. The global population is growing and may exceed 7.9 billion by the year 2025.

India has the distinction of having the second largest population in the world. According to the census figures of 1991, the population of India was in excess of 846 million and the figures of last census in 2001 show the population to be more than 1027 million and growing at a little over 2 per cent per annum. In real figures, the population has grown by 180,713,000 between 1991 – 2001. The total population located in rural and urban areas is 736 million and 285 million respectively. A significant feature is that the middle class is growing fast; it is estimated that its size would be almost equal to the present population size by 2007. This is obviously a cause for jubilation for marketers. Another important factor is that there are more than 5,57,000 villages, spread all over the country over 70 per cent of India's population lives in rural areas.

More than 500 million Indians are young, that is, not over 30 years of age. The population aged 15 – 59 comprises 63.5 per cent, and only 8.2 per cent population is above 60 years of age. The trends show that the population of youth and older people is growing at a faster rate. The young population is an encouraging feature for marketers to develop products and promotions that address this market by attempting to get their feelings and emotions involved with their brands. For example, we see a clear shift of two-wheeler automakers towards introducing faster motorcycles for this segment. Bajaj introduced its two-wheeler Bajaj Pulsar motorcycle and positioned it "Definitely Male" to appeal to a new, well-heeled, macho class of youngsters. The middle class is growing rapidly and so is its income; it is the biggest spending class. All these are important factors and spell lots of opportunities for marketers. There is growing shift from the traditional joint family system to nuclear families, particularly in cities. These families need smaller accommodations and reasonably priced smaller appliances, furniture, and furnishings. Many builders and marketers of such apartments and appliances have taken advantage of these trends.

Population migration from one zone or city to another, or from rural areas to urban areas is another major factor that may significantly affect marketing efforts and other marketing aspects. There has been a gradual increase in the number of people migrating from villages to cities. They all come to cities in search of livelihood. Village folks with little or no literacy and not possessing any usable skills look for any work, mostly as labourers, domestic help, and rickshaw pullers. After getting some type of work, they settle down in cities and live in slums. Their work and life in cities transforms their aspirations to own things they can ill afford. To most marketers, they are of no interest as customers except for low-priced items of bare necessities.

Marketers are also interested in the literacy levels and the sex ratio of the population and woman's role. According to the 2001 census, the average literacy in India is 65.38 per cent. Literacy among males and females is above 75 per cent and 54 per cent respectively. By the end of 2002, the total number of universities, deemed universities, and institutes of national importance was 351. Besides these higher educational institutions the number of junior schools, higher secondary schools, colleges, and professional education institutions is 10,28,204. Positive changes in the literacy profiles of the population of a country are likely to mean better reading habits, higher readership and availability of magazines and newspapers, and more demanding and value conscious customers. According to 1998 – 1999 figures of the Ministry of Information and Broadcasting, Government of India, the total number of newspapers and periodicals published in different languages were 41,705.

The female population is nearly 50 per cent in India. More and more women are entering the work force and are also taking up professional careers. This has led to increased dual income homes, particularly in cities and the lady of the house is also more involved in most decisions that concern family, home appliances, and other major purchases. This rapidly increasing change has created the demand for time saving appliances and childcare service such as microwave ovens, washing machines, refrigerators, vacuum cleaners, crèches, and ready-to-eat foods. Accordingly, there is a shift in marketing communications targeting educated women for many products and services.

Economic Environment

The size of market only in terms of population is not enough. It is the people with buying power that really constitute a meaningful market. The economic environment is an important factor that influences the marketing efforts of just about every business and the overall economic conditions fluctuate in every country. Changes in general economic conditions affect supply and demand, income levels, current prices, and credit facilities. The general economic pattern is often described in four types of business cycles.

In case there is ***prosperity***, unemployment is low and people have disposable money or buying power because the income is relatively high. This offers the marketers an opportunity to increase the number of products pushed in the market, and take advantage of better economic conditions.

During ***recession***, unemployment increases and the total buying power of the population declines, consumers become tight fisted, pay more attention to saving, and business spending is adversely affected. Recession increases price sensitivity of customers, paying more attention to value, and try to confine purchases to basic and functional products. This forces many companies to reduce prices, offer more for the same amount of money, focus more on consumer research to learn what product functions they want and accordingly develop and offer such products.

A state of economic ***depression*** is said to prevail when unemployment is rampant, wages are very low, the total disposable income is at its lowest, and there is general pessimism about economy. Consumers are highly discouraged, scared, and angry. All this outlook and feelings seriously affect consumer spending, saving, and any investment by companies that may lead to economic losses. Many firms are compelled to curtail their businesses and some go out of business. There is a belief among some experts that the government's effective monetary and fiscal policies can help eliminate the possibility of depression from the business cycle.

Economic ***recovery*** refers to the business cycle stage when the economy moves from recession or depression to prosperity. Once again the unemployment decreases, disposable income of people increases, and consumers gradually shed their fears and pessimism towards economic conditions, and willingness to buy increases. To start with, approach of businesses is cautious and they try to maintain much flexibility in their marketing strategies.

The state of the economy determines consumers' buying power, which is affected by the availability of money to buy what customers need or want. For example, during inflationary periods, the buying power declines because the prices increase at a faster rate than personal income and more money is required to buy something. As a result of decline in buying power, most consumers spend less. The major sources of buying power include wealth, disposable income, and credit availability. The disposable income means income left after tax deductions. This means when taxes are low, the disposable income rises and when taxes are high, disposable income declines.

Discretionary income represents the money available after buying basic necessities such as food, clothing, and shelter. This category of income is important from marketers' point of view because people spend this money to buy expensive appliances, furniture, autos, costly durables, lifestyle products, etc. Availability of credit encourages people to buy now and pay later with expected future income. Though such purchases affect future buying power of individuals, the use of credit facility depends on the rate of interest charged. In case the rates are perceived as high, consumers postpone purchases.

India is a growing economy and the demand for different product and service categories is growing. The current average per capita income in India reported by A. C. Neilson is Rs. 21,000 (the exact figure is Rs. 20,860, according to 2003-2004 Economic Survey released by Government of India). However, the real spenders for medium to high-priced, or lifestyle products are in the middle and high-income bracket.

National Council of Applied and Economic Research (NCAER) reported a survey that detailed different income groups in India (Table 5.1). The level of income shown against each group refers to 1994-1995 figures at prices during the same period. Over the years, the level of income of different households has gone up, but so have prices.

TABLE 5.1
Number of Households in Different Income Brackets

Million Households	1994-1995			(Projections) 2006-2007		
Consumer groups & income	Rural	Urban	Total	Rural	Urban	Total
Very rich (Rs 2,15,000 and above)	0.30	0.70	1.00	1.60	4.50	6.10
Consuming class (Rs 45,000 – 2,15,000)	14.30	14.30	28.60	47.30	43.60	90.90
Climbers (Rs 25,000 – 45,000)	32.70	15.30	48.00	63.30	10.70	74.00
Aspirants (Rs 25,000 – 16,000)	39.70	8.30	40.00	14.70	0.70	15.40
Destitutes (Rs 16,000 and less)	28.90	6.10	35.00	12.20	0.50	12.70

(Annual growth in income at 6.70% in 1995-96 and at 7.80% from 2002-03 to 2006-07).

Another research report by NCAER in 1999 found that there are 15,05,528 households with an income of 5 lakh and above. In the top income bracket are 6515 households with income of one crore or more per annum, 20,863 households have income between 50 lakh to 1 crore, 98,289 households have incomes between 20 lakh to 50 lakh, 3,20,900 households enjoy incomes between 10 to 20 lakh, and 10,58,961 households are placed in the income bracket of 5 to 10 lakh. Majority of these higher income households are located in five states: Maharashtra, Delhi, Gujarat, Punjab, and Tamil Nadu. These figures are of significant interest to many marketers of medium to high-priced products and services. For example, some very expensive cars have been introduced in India and it is believed that the margins are so handsome that they would offset the disadvantage of low numbers sold.

Competitive Environment

In an open economy there is hardly a chance of not having competition and the nature and intensity of the prevailing competition influences the demand of a particular company's products and services. Competition in business terminology generally refers to the availability of other products and services by different marketers that are similar to or can be substituted for a particular company's products or services in the same market. Increasing popularity of Internet in urban areas and online services particularly in large cities is increasing the intensity of competition in the market place, by adding an entirely new dimension.

Four general types of competitive structures include monopoly, oligopoly, monopolistic competition, and pure competition. On one extreme is ***monopoly***, where a company markets a product that has no close substitutes and a particular marketer is the only source of supply. For example, before the economic liberalisation in India, the government was the only supplier of Petrol, LPG, and telephone service. The other extreme is ***pure competition*** that refers to a large number of marketers offering a homogenous product, a situation where no member can influence the price or supply, such as food grains. These are extreme situations and most businesses operate in a competitive environment in between these two extremes. In case of ***oligopoly***, there are few competitors such as Broadband Internet service providers. ***Monopolistic competition*** refers to a situation when many firms are marketing the same or similar products and each company attempts to differentiate its product to appeal customers that its product is a better choice. For example, Apple computers are highly differentiated with many substitutes.

The most common controllable competitive tool that many marketers use to gain competitive advantage is price. At a time when Surf was the only brand of detergent powder worth naming, Nirma used the price tool to get a strong foothold in a market dominated by HLL. It is reported in media (*India Today*, August 1, 2004) that Air Deccan is likely to offer from Bangalore to Delhi air travel an incredibly low airfare of Rs. 500. (Rs. 500 + Taxes Rs. 200 = Rs. 700). However, low-price in most cases fails to be long lasting as an advantage as sooner than expected, some competitors match or come out with still lower prices. Companies in a variety of industries take advantage of non-price tools as a competitive weapon such as distinctive product features, packaging, better product-quality, promotion, distribution, and service to differentiate their products from competing brands. For example, some marketers of a simple product like a toothbrush have created differentiation based on features. Sony sells its music systems by emphasising quality and is successful in charging higher prices. IBM focuses on research, quality, and service.

Sociocultural Environment

Sociocultural factors in every country have a significant effect on society and its culture(s). These forces have their impact on learned behaviours in everyday life including buying behaviour by influencing attitudes, beliefs, norms, customs, and lifestyles. Culture influences consumers through the norms and values established by the society in which they live. It is the broadest environmental factor that influences consumer behaviour. Cultural values are enduring and any attempts to change them generally fail.

The study of culture is concerned with a comprehensive examination of factors such as language, religion, knowledge, laws, art, music, work patterns, social customs, festivals, food, etc., of a society. In fact, culture includes everything that reflects its personality. However, culture does not determine the nature or frequency of instinctive drives but can influence how and when a particular drive will be gratified.

Individual and household lifestyles evolve within the given framework of culture. The boundaries set by culture on behaviours are referred to as norms, derived from cultural values and are the rules permitting or prohibiting certain types of behaviours in specific situations. Members of a society obey cultural norms without deliberation because behaving otherwise is viewed as not only unacceptable but unnatural. Culture is viewed as a mirror of both the values and possessions of its members. D. K. Tse and R. W. Belk believe that cultures are not static but evolve and change slowly over time. Availability of products and services popular in other cultures influence the desire of consumers. According to R. W. Pollay, D. K. Tse and Z. Y. Wang, the massive export and multinational advertising of consumer goods, especially heavily symbolic goods such as cigarettes, soft drinks, clothing, athletic gear, as well as experiential goods such as music, movies and television programming, impacts the culture and desired lifestyles of importing countries.

In the context of Indian culture, strong family bonds have been one of the core values and a major driving force in the Indian market. Members of a particular society hold some core beliefs and values that tend to persist over time. These values are often visible in marketing communications of different products in India showing a caring mother or housewife such as in ads for Maggi, Chayavanprash, Vicks Vaporub and many other products.

With the passage of time, particularly with the opening up of the economy, and increasing educational levels including the use of computers, and improved economic outlook, there is a change in how Indian consumers view themselves. They are increasingly acquiring new values and tastes because of their access to international media, cable and satellite TV channels, Internet, etc. A quite visible change is that the Indian consumer now is no more willing to postpone gratification of needs and wants. This has made credit schemes and credit cards offered by financial institutions popular particularly among urban consumers. The impact on market is that there is a spurt in the availability of products and services in almost all categories.

Within a given national culture, each society has several subcultures based on region, religion, language, age, gender, etc. All segments of a society do not possess the same cultural patterns and one can distinguish relatively more homogeneous groups and sizeable groups within the larger society. They have distinct beliefs, values, customs, that set them apart from the larger cultural mainstream. However, they follow most of the dominant cultural values and behaviours of the larger society. The diversity of subcultures in India is mind boggling, but only some are important from a marketers' point of view. Much depends on the relevance of a particular product category and marketers sometimes reap huge rewards in targeting subcultures. For example, the subculture of teens loves fashion, music, entertainment, and fast food. If a marketer successfully attracts teens now, there is likelihood that many of them will remain customers in the years to come. For example, teenagers constitute the major segment for soft drinks and snacks like Maggi and chips. When McDonald's opened its fast food outlets in India, within a short period of time there was much opposition to using beef in the burgers. The largest religious subculture, and some other smaller sub-cultural groups do not eat beef and are against cow slaughter. McDonald's had to reassure the concerned groups and stop using beef extract to flavour some of their burgers and introduce vegetarian burgers to adjust with this environmental.

Political – Legal Environment

Marketing decisions are influenced in important ways by the political and legal environment in any given country. Political, legal, and regulatory forces in a nation and its markets have close interrelationship. Legislations are passed; courts at different levels interpret legal decisions and different regulatory agencies are created and operated, in most cases by elected or appointed officials. The current laws, government agencies, and pressure groups put limits on marketing decisions and strategies of companies. Industries and organisations almost always maintain good relations with political officials to minimise the possibility of enacting unfavourable laws and regulations. Another major reason to stay on the right side of political power is that governments are the big buyer. In India public sector companies, armed forces, and other agencies participate in economic activities as buyers and sellers of different goods and services.

Some companies believe that such forces are uncontrollable and remain only reactive and adjust to conditions, while some industry associations openly protest against the actions of legislative bodies. It is important for industries and individual organisations to understand the political – legal forces and different political ideologies of groups at the state and central government levels.

The degree of political – legal intervention in business and industry varies across countries. For example, in India the extent of intervention is significant and the government decides the rules in respect of foreign private investment, imports, exports, advertising certain product categories such as tobacco products,

Monopolies and Restrictive Practices Commission (MTPC), etc. There is comparatively very low intervention in USA and the emphasis is on free economy.

Sometimes, major changes in the economic policy of a country can spell opportunities and threats. For example, after a major change in the economic policy in early 1990s, markets have opened up for foreign companies and private investors. Long ago, because of policy changes in India, Coca-Cola and IBM wound up their business in India rather than agreeing to adjust. Similarly, stricter laws concerning environmental pollution often restrict the activities of many businesses. In some developed economies, mandatory recycling laws opened up opportunities for recycling industry. In recent times, government agencies and pressure groups are turning against the use of non-biodegradable plastics.

Technological Environment

Technology refers to the application of knowledge and tools to solve problems and achieve more efficiency. It represents powerful forces that influence human lives in important ways. Technology has accomplished both desirable and undesirable wonders such as use of nuclear power for peaceful purposes, more advanced methods of surgery, safer and more effective medicines, fax machines, personal computers, Internet, antilock brakes and fuel injection, robots, lasers, space shuttles, digital watches and cellular phones that take digital photographs and download MP3 files from the Internet, and many more developments. On the negative side, there are weapons of mass destruction such as the hydrogen bomb, and nerve gas. Developments beneficial to human beings help businesses function and perform their tasks ever more effectively and efficiently and make it possible to offer exciting new products and services to customers. Within the last few decades, technology has been a major force in the development of economies to raise the standards of living in different countries.

Whenever a newer, better technology is introduced, many existing technologies become obsolete and are discarded. There are numerous examples of this. The vacuum-tube technology became obsolete with the coming of transistors. Use of computers and printers replaced manual typewriters and adversely affected the carbon paper industry. Television has hurt the film industry; digital and analog quartz watches have almost killed the traditional spring-powered watches. Notebook computers, Internet, voice mail, cellular phones, fax machines, hurt earlier communication technologies. The new telecommunications technology is making it possible for people to work from home or other non-traditional areas without going to office. This has introduced a new term – *telecommuting*. Businesses can now reach vast numbers of customers and potential customers more efficiently through a variety of newer communication tools. Increasing numbers of online services are offering low-bulk items and ticketing services in India. Many financial institutions are providing the facility of ATMS and credit cards, online banking and other financial services. Technological progress has influenced consumer tastes and lifestyles.

Companies often lose their market leadership as a result of failure to keep up with promising technological changes. Sometimes political forces influence policies and also the industry's response to the quantum of investment in R & D influences the technological developments. Joseph L. Bower and M. Clayton say that it is important for companies to determine when a technology is changing the industry and to define the strategic impact of the new technology.

Research is a chancy business and often requires huge expenditure. A drug company developed the first H_2 receptor antagonist to treat gastric ulcers and within a short time of two years, another drug company introduced an improvement and the first company had to withdraw its brand. To what extent companies can protect inventions from research also influences the use of technology. The security from imitation depends on how easily others can copy it without any violation of its patent. Unless companies are sure of being able to protect their major research products or processes, they are less inclined to market them and let the competitors take advantage by introducing them at low prices in markets.

A new technology may not always prove to be advantageous, unless the new technology creates successful products. A company that decides not to transform a new technology to its products may lose sales to a competitor that does use that technology. Sony kept on promoting its Betamax video system and kept its VHS technology proprietary while JVC licensed its VHS technology to many companies and quickly made Betamax obsolete. In this process, Sony lost millions of dollars. There was some debate in India whether CDMA or GSM mobile technology is superior. Nokia, the world leader in cellular phones has lost its market leadership in India in CDMA handsets to LG. About Nokia, Radhika Dhawan writes:

"Nokia has been tardy about starting off in the CDMA market, which is surprising since it has been one of the pioneers of this technology. It is now trying its best to claw back, opening a CDMA R&D centre in India. It is also pushing the envelope by setting new cooperation trends with operators."

– **Radhika Dhawan**, *Businessworld,* July 19, 2004.

Through technology assessment, managers attempt to evaluate and anticipate the impact of new products and processes on a company's operations, on other companies, and the society in general. Managers assess whether the benefits of using a particular technology are more than the costs to the company and to society at large.

Natural environment, is concerned with natural resources such as minerals, wood, coal, oil, etc. A large number of industries need natural resources as inputs. Governments in developed and most of the developing countries are concerned about the natural environment because industrial growth usually damages the quality of natural environment. The levels of air and water pollution in many cities around the world are touching the danger mark, and the ozone layer is gradually getting depleted. The "greenhouse effect" is leading to dangerous warming of the earth. Water shortage is reported in different countries, including India. Developed and rapidly developing economies depend heavily on oil and the reality is that oil seems to be dominating the world political and economic concerns, including the recent Iraq war. In India, much emphasis is on promoting the use of solar energy and other non-conventional sources of energy. Efforts are being made to produce bio-diesel, through harvesting of such plants as jojoba and jatropha, which are hardly, drought-resistant perennials whose seeds have a high oil content.

Summary

The marketing environment includes six major external forces: demographic, economic, competitive, sociocultural, political-legal, and technological that directly or indirectly affect a company's marketing activities. Changes in any one of them may trigger changes in one or more other factors and the combined total effect may influence acquisition of inputs such as personnel, financial resources, raw materials, and information. These changes may also influence a company's outputs of goods, services, or ideas.

The marketing environment is constantly changing and it is vital for marketing managers to undertake environmental scanning to monitor changes in these forces. Through environmental scanning, managers collect information about forces in the marketing environment. Assessing and interpreting this information helps marketing managers forecast opportunities and threats as a result of environmental fluctuations. There are two approaches of responding to anticipated changes: one is to be reactive and the other is to be proactive. Some companies prefer reactive approach and prepare themselves to adjust to changes, while some others may prefer to be aggressive and try to influence some forces, at least to some extent.

Demographic characteristics such as population and its growth rate, age-mix, gender, education, income, changes in family structure, and geographic shifts in population, etc., are important factors. The size of population is an indicator of market size to some extent.

Economic conditions determine the demand and influence marketing activities. Buying power and willingness to spend significantly influences consumer demand. The buying power depends on income, prices, tax structure, availability of credit, wealth, family size, and the economic outlook. The overall state of the economy depends on four general business cycles, namely, prosperity, recession, depression, and recovery.

Competition may include domestic and global players, in particular, the geographic market offering similar or substitute products. Several factors influence the intensity of competition depending on the type of competitive structure. The most common controllable marketing mix tool companies use to gain competitive advantage is price. However, price is often not a durable solution. Well-managed companies try to effectively differentiate their offer in meaningful ways. Increasing popularity of Internet in urban areas and online services particularly in large cities are increasingly introducing a different kind of competition in the market-place.

Sociocultural factors in every country have a significant affect on society and its culture(s). These forces have their impact on learned behaviours in everyday life including buying behaviour by influencing attitudes, beliefs, norms, customs, and lifestyles. Culture influences consumers through the norms and values established by the society in which they live. However, culture does not determine the nature or frequency of instinctive drives but can influence how and when a particular drive will be gratified. In the context of Indian culture, strong family bonds, and love for one's family have been core values and a major driving force in the Indian market. Members of a particular society hold some core beliefs and values that tend to persist over time.

Marketing decisions are influenced in important ways by the political and legal environment in any given country. Political, legal, and regulatory forces in a nation and its markets have close interrelationship. Legislations are passed; courts at different levels interpret legal decisions and different regulatory agencies are created and operated, in most cases by elected or appointed officials. The current laws, government agencies, and pressure groups put limits on marketing decisions and strategies of companies.

Technology refers to the application of knowledge and tools to solve problems and achieve more efficiency. It represents powerful forces that influence human lives in important ways. Whenever a new technology shows its impact, many existing technologies become obsolete. However, a new technology may not always prove to be advantageous, unless the new technology creates successful products.

Questions for Discussion

1. Why do you think environmental scanning and analysis of information so gained are important?
2. What are the major environmental forces? Briefly discuss each.
3. In your view, what business cycle are we in India experiencing currently? Give your reasons.
4. What factors influence the buying power of consumers? Discuss.
5. Discuss the impact of technology on marketing activities.
6. Discuss the impact on consumption patterns in the Indian society due to cultural changes as a result of latter day marketing activities.
7. In what ways are Indian cultural values changing? How are marketers responding to these changes?
8. Discuss how technology influences society. How does it affect marketing activities?
9. Discuss the changing role of women in Indian society? What impact do you see in marketing activities due to these changes?
10. Did the environment influence marketing activities of some foreign companies in India? How did they respond?

Projects

1. Interview some consumers or business people and identify two products or companies who are committed to maintaining environment.
2. Select an auto company of your choice. What steps would you take to compete successfully with another company offering the same product category?
3. You are in the business of running a fast food chain. MacDonald's and Pizza Hut are threatening your business. Discuss one major step you would take.

Bibliography

1. Ram Subramanium, Kamlesh Kumar, and Charles Yauger, "The Scanning of Task Environment in Hospitals: An Empirical Study," *Journal of Applied Business Research,* 1994.
2. Carl P. Zeithaml and Valarie A. Zeithaml, "Environmental Management: Revising the Marketing Perspective," *Journal of Marketing,* 1984.
3. Philip Kotler, "Megamarketing," *Harvard Business Review,* March-April 1986.
4. D. K. Tse and R. W. Belk, "Becoming a Consumer Society," *Journal of Consumer Research* (March 1989).
5. R. W. Pollay, D. K. Tse, and Z. Y. Wang, "Advertising Propaganda and Value Change in Economic Development," *Journal of Business Research,* 20 (1990).
6. Joseph L. Bower and M. Clayton, "Disruptive Technologies: Catching the Wave," *Harvard Business Review,* January/February 1995.

Information System & Marketing Research

LEARNING OBJECTIVES

After going through this chapter, you will understand:

- How marketing information system is organised and maintained
- Important data sources and their utility
- Need for marketing research and important steps involved in research process
- Types of research and major research tools and techniques
- Types of data and data collection approaches
- Use of marketing research

What do kids think? What do they feel? How do they take decisions? It is important for marketers to know, for kids do decide. And this is what the millennial round of New GenerAsians, Cartoon Network's survey on opinions, behaviour and preferences of kids in the Asia-Pacific region, has tried to unearth. There are rather some surprising findings. Or perhaps not surprising, for respondents were kids.

Says Anthony Dobson, Vice President, international research and strategic planning, Turner International Asia Pacific Ltd., "This survey is more comprehensive than the 1998 one. We have added two new countries, New Zealand and Vietnam. We also included ten cities in India and interviewed 2,045 kids in India. It is also user-friendlier and more brand-focused. I am sure business will find it extremely useful."

Conducted by A. C. Nielsen, kids were asked open-ended questions face-to-face. The fieldwork was conducted from October to December 1999. About 7,752 kids were interviewed, across four age groups: 7 - 9 years, 10 - 12 years, 13 - 15 years and 16 - 18 years. A region that has not been included, however, is West Asia.

One area was optimism. When asked whether there will be no pollution by the time the kid 'grows up', 17 per cent of the respondents in India thought it would 'definitely/probably' happen. In the entire region, 36 per cent thought it would 'definitely/probably' happen.

Internet access trends are interesting. In Singapore, 56 per cent of the kids had access to the Net. The figure was 38 per cent in Malaysia, 16 per cent in Thailand and 2 per cent in India (it has, however, shown commendable growth since 1998). The survey found kids in the entire region accessed the Net from school, most of the time.

Here is a look at aspirations. When asked at what age they will be able to afford mobile phones, Indian kids put the age at 21 years. In the entire region, the average was about 22 years. Also, in India, the latest trend (one which is everlasting) was watching TV for boys and trendy clothes for girls. And an overwhelming majority of kids in the Asia-Pacific said the best things about their lives were schoolwork and exams. Most agreed that achieving good grades was very important. Do kids hate school?

For Indian kids, Pepsi's was the favourite commercial, followed by Colgate, Close-Up, Coca-Cola and Pepsodent, soft drinks and toothpaste ads. Perhaps distribution has something to do with it, or these ads' themes.

As far as Weekly Pocket Money (WPM) goes, the average kid gets $1.5 in India, while it was $2.9 in Vietnam and $19.4 in Hong Kong. Out of this, Indian kids spent about 53 per cent of their WPM. The most spendthrift are kids in the Philippines. Chinese kids spent the least.

And the favourite jeans brand in India is 'Ruf N Tuf'. 'Action' is the favourite sports shoe brand. Watches show the same trend. Titan is the favourite brand. In the region, the average favourite is Casio. Now, the most talked about category - colas. Pepsi is the favourite, followed by Coke and Thums Up.

The survey is in-depth, no doubt. But is it accurate? Have kids given answers that parents want? Is it generic? Says Duncan Morris, director, A. C. Nielsen Media International, "Yes, there are dangers in face-to-face interviewing. But the size of the sample more or less evens out the discrepancies. Moreover, the data is really indicative."

The entire survey costs $1,200. Realising most companies won't want the entire study, Turner International also offers country topline findings for $300. And, really what do kids think?

(Source: Vivek Pareek, "Kids Will Be Kids," A & M, April 15, 2000).

Marketing success depends on making correct and timely decisions. Marketing managers need reliable and timely information about a large number of external and internal factors relevant to decision areas. Practically every decision area relevant to marketing requires the input of information. In a highly competitive business environment today, availability or otherwise of reliable and timely information might mean the difference between success and failure of a business enterprise. The society today is information based and businesses with access to superior and timely information can make better choices of markets, their offerings, do a better marketing planning job and ultimately enjoy a competitive advantage. Marketing is becoming a game where reliable and timely information, rather than raw marketing muscle wins the race.

In the absence of adequate knowledge about various factors that affect marketing, strategic decisions are likely to be misguided. For instance, products that have little chance of success may be introduced, that eventually fail, attractive product-markets may be overlooked and new markets may be entered despite conditions that make success unlikely, products may be targeted at wrong market segments overlooking the attractive opportunities for the same product in another market segment, pricing may be too high or low affecting sales adversely, promotional money may be poorly spent on inappropriate promotion mix elements, and choice of distribution channels may not be the most suitable. Most often, the errors in such decision areas are a result of ill-informed or under-informed marketing decisions.

FIGURE 6.1
Information, and MIS Planning

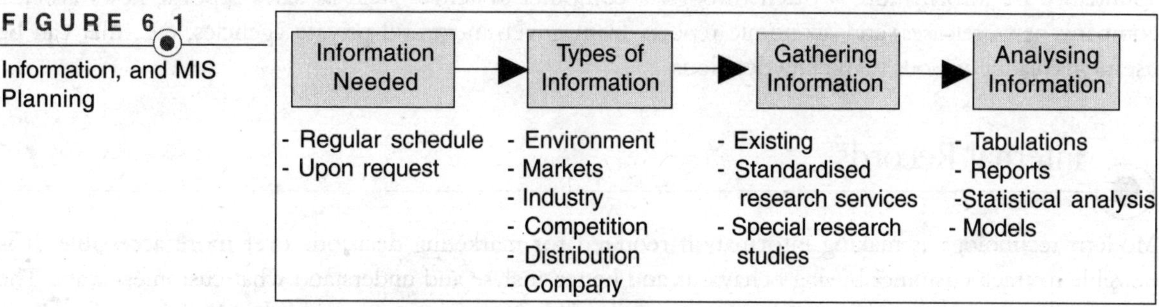

Rapidly changing marketing environments, expanding business boundaries of global and domestic companies, shifts in incomes, changing lifestyles and preferences of consumers, etc., have made marketers realise the need to have quick access to a large amount of reliable information to facilitate sound decision-making. Floyed Kemske believes that information will be the catalyst in the present global economy. The need for information and information technology has never been greater than now. Computers and other IT related products are being increasingly used by almost all the businesses, large or small. Despite this, many business establishments lack proper information systems.

Marketing Information Systems (MIS)

The term 'Marketing Information Systems' refers to a programme for managing and organising information gathered by an organisation from various internal and external sources. MIS assesses the information needs of different managers and develops the required information from supplied data in time regarding competition, prices, advertising expenditures, sales, distribution and market intelligence, etc. Information sources for MIS include a company's ***internal records*** regarding marketing performance in terms of sales, and effectiveness and efficiency of marketing actions, ***marketing databases***, ***marketing intelligence systems***, ***marketing research***, and information supplied by independent information suppliers.

FIGURE 6.2
Elements of MIS

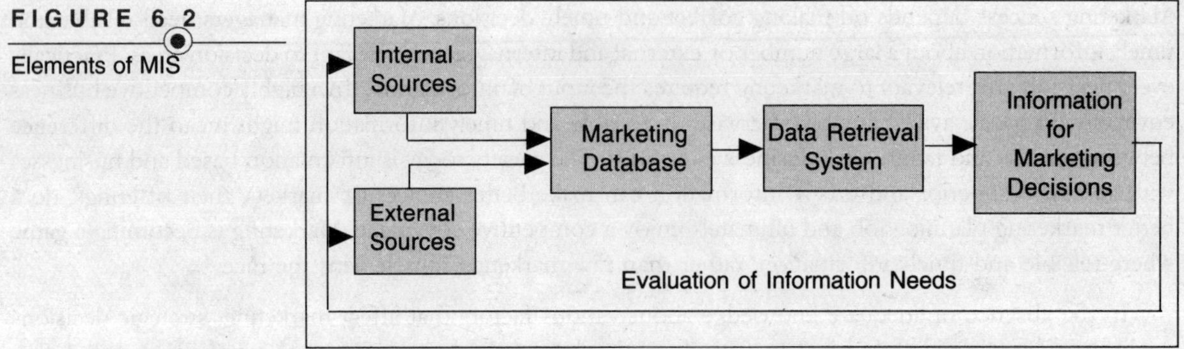

Databases

A database refers to the collection of comprehensive information about customers and prospects such as demographic and psychographic profiles, products and services they buy, and purchase volumes, etc., arranged in a manner that is available for easy access and retrieval. Databases allow marketers access to an abundance of information, – often through a computer system – such as sales reports, news articles, company news releases, and economic reports from government and private agencies, etc., that can be useful in making various marketing decisions.

Internal Records

Modern technology is making information required for marketing decisions ever more accessible. It is possible to track customer buying behaviour and better analyse and understand what customers want. The integration of various modern technologies is allowing companies to access valuable information. Ever increasing numbers of market researchers and managers are having access to e-mail, voice mail, teleconferencing, videoconferences, and faxes.

Internal database is the most basic starting point in developing a strong MIS. Marketers, not just the growing numbers of large retailers in our country, need information about what is demanded more by customers and what is not. Internal record systems help in tracking what is selling, how fast, in which locations, to which customers, etc. Availability of all such information relies on reports available on orders received from sales people, resellers, and customers, copies of sales invoices, prices, costs, inventories, receivables, payables, etc. Getting inputs and designing systems to provide right data to the right people at the right time is critical for marketing decisions.

- Tanniru R. Rao is a happy man. The president and CEO of Market Probe have enough reason. His market research firm is listed among the top 50 market research agencies in the world. Rao, however, believes that market research, in India, is still at a nascent stage.

- "You need more qualified people to do the field work and that is still not happening here," he says. Established in 1976, the company specialises in marketing research and customer loyalty studies with offices in Canada, Europe and the US. Recently, it started operations in India with centres in Mumbai, Bangalore and Delhi. With billings of $15 million for calendar year 1999, Market Probe is looking to spread the importance of specialised research in India. "In our business, long-term relations are essential and we make it a point to continue the relationship with our clients since, typically, our customer loyalty studies are continuous," says Rao. The

Contd...

timing is just perfect. Many Indian service-oriented companies are looking at customer retention and loyalty programmes to strengthen their brand and services. And what is Rao targeting?

"Automotive companies, banks and hotels, initially. Then, it would extend to other businesses as well," says Rao. But reliability is one issue that has always raised eyebrows when one mentions research reports in India. How is he planning to get over it? "We work with clients and offer tactical and strategic recommendations to satisfy their needs, as well as the needs of the customer with commitment from our end," explains Rao. The company already has clients such as Arvind Mills, BPL, Hindustan Lever and Reckitt & Coleman among other big names.

"Our first attempt will be to replicate our global customer base to India and also add new clients," adds Rao. With vast experience in customer satisfaction research, employee satisfaction research, new product development, brand health management and custom research tools to meet demands of clients, Market Probe is geared to face the challenge with its diverse and unique research. "Matured markets pose a problem as many people are not willing to speak. I guess India being still new to such research techniques, the response will be far better," explains Rao.

Rao, an alumnus from Indian Statistical Institute (ISI) and his team have developed new quantitative applications of Kruskal's Analysis for derived attribute importance and LISREL models for loyalty modelling and survival analysis for customer retention forecast. There are proprietary products too under the Market Probe stable that include Satisfaction Navigator (SATNAV) and Customer Retention Forecasting System (CRFS) based on company's experience and extensive client list. Not to be just left with quantitative research techniques, the company is also into qualitative research, wherein it has copyright tools and projective techniques such as Life maps, Auto Drive and Interactive Workshop Method to facilitate focused outputs for strategic management of brands. "We also plan to have research and training in India to facilitate spreading our research techniques in Asia and Pacific regions," adds Rao. With an international client list like AT&T, Xerox Corp, Kodak, American Express and General Motors, among other Fortune 500 companies, Market Probe is all set to make a definite impact in the Indian research scenario. "We are confident about our services and I feel that Market Probe will have a very favourable response from India," adds Rao.

(Source: Narain Krishnamurthy, "Stats and Facts," A&M, July 2000).

Accumulated data about customers in various internal records is an important source to build database such as customer inquiries, existing customers and past purchasing histories of these customers. The key information in this regard consists of RFM (Recency, Frequency, and Money) variables. Recency refers to the time of purchase, frequency reflects the number of times the customer made a product purchase from the firm, and money denotes the quantity and monetary value of the purchase. RFM helps analyse and develop a customer index that reflects which customers are more profitable for the business. *USP Age,* in its September 2004 issue has reported that BPCL has been compiling its database for the past four years and has a formidable collection of more than 1.4 million customers. Shopper's Stop has been compiling data of its regular customers through its loyalty programme, *First Citizen.* Further, a company in India can obtain a database for as little as 50 paise to Rs. 5 per contact. Companies involved in Direct Marketing such as Catalogue Selling and Mail Order Marketing are heavy users of databases.

External Sources

Census Bureau is one key source of information regarding various demographic variables. Besides Census Bureau of India, other sources include Newspapers, Trade Publications, Technical Journals, Magazines,

Directories, Balance Sheets of companies, Syndicated and published research reports. Various third party information suppliers offer a variety of information about customers as per marketer's requirements, for a price. For example, *Reader's Digest* markets a database covering 100 million households. It is one of the best databases to assess potential markets for consumer products. It lets *Reader's Digest* management know the likes and dislikes of many of its readers. Behaviour Scan is a single source information service that monitors consumer household televisions and records the programmes and commercials watched. This source is an example that screens about 60,000 households in 26 US markets. Many companies develop their own databases. According to Laurence N. Goal, a single source providing information about household demographics, purchases, television viewership behaviour, and responses to promotions is called a **single-source data**. When consumers from these households go shopping in stores equipped with scanner-installed computers, they present their credit cards to billing clerks for payment. This permits each customer's identification to be electronically coded so that the marketer can track his or her purchases.

Some Important Data Sources

1. **The Thomas Register:** It is the world's most important industrial buying guide for industrial products. Thomas Register of Indian Manufacturers is available in print, CD, and through Internet. It has 120,000 listings of 40,000 industrial manufacturers and service providers covering 10,000 different product and service categories.
2. **The Source Directory:** Source Publishers, Mumbai publish this directory. Currently Mumbai and Delhi editions are available. It provides contact information on ad agencies and related services, marketing and sales promotion consultants, market research firms, music companies, telemarketing, and different media.
3. **Yellow Pages:** Tata Press and GETIT yellow pages are leaders. Currently, yellow pages publications are available for all cities and major towns of India. New Horizons is a joint venture between Living Media and Singapore Telecom and have been publishing directories for specific businesses.
4. **Internet:** It is a source of extensive data on almost any subject. Different types of published data, research findings, statistics, and figures are available either free or on payment.

Computer Networks and Internet

Present day computer networks enable marketers to access data sources and customers with immediate information about products and performance. Through such networks, marketers can exchange e-mails with employees, customers, and suppliers. Online information services such as CompuServe and America Online typically offer their subscribers access to e-mail, discussion groups, files for downloading, chat rooms, and databases and other related research materials. Marketers can subscribe to "mailing lists" that periodically deliver electronic newsletters to their computer screens. This helps increased communication with a marketer's customers, suppliers, and employees and boosts the capabilities of a company's marketing information system. Online information services are available only to subscribers. However, the Internet allows global exchange of e-mails, discussion through newsgroups on almost any subject, downloading of files, chat rooms, etc. A well-maintained database enables a company to analyse customer needs, preferences, and behaviour. It also helps in identifying right target customers for its direct marketing efforts.

Data Mining and Data Warehousing

The term 'data mining' refers to automated data analysis of large amount of data stored in a data warehouse. This is similar to extracting valuable metals from mountains of mined ore. The purpose is to unearth – with the help of modern computing power – meaningful patterns of information that might be missed or remain undiscovered. Data mining creates customer database, which is extremely important for all narrowly defined target-marketing efforts. Data mining also leads to build database on resellers, distribution channels, media, etc. Data warehousing refers to storing subject-based, integrated, non-volatile, time variant data in support of managerial decisions. It can be viewed as a central collection of clean, consistent, and summarised information gathered from several operational systems. With increasing computing capabilities, organisations are collecting large amounts of a variety of information or data possibly faster than they can use, and for this reason all the collected data or information needs to be sorted, classified and warehoused, so that it can be retrieved when needed in a meaningful manner.

Marketing Intelligence Systems

In the current fast-paced business climate, keeping up with macro-environmental changes, and competition is becoming increasingly difficult. Marketing intelligence system refers to systematic and ethical approach, procedures, and sources that marketing managers use to gather and analyse everyday information about various developments with regard to competitors and other business trends in the marketing environment. This intelligence is collected from various sources such as newspapers, trade publications, business magazines, talking with suppliers, channel members, customers, other managers, and sales force people.

About competitive intelligence, the general idea is that more than 80 per cent information is public knowledge. The most important sources from which to obtain competitive intelligence include competitors' annual and financial reports, speeches by company executives, government documents, trade organisations, online databases, and other popular and business press. The company can take certain steps to obtain quality marketing intelligence. The company should take steps to train and motivate field sales personnel about the types of information to report regularly on any relevant developments in the market place. Besides sales force, the company can take steps to motivate channel members to pass along important intelligence. The company can also purchase competitors' products, and attend trade fairs.

Some important questions that managers should ask about competitive intelligence are:

- How fast does the competitive climate in our industry change? How important is it to keep our knowledge about these changes currently?
- What are the objectives of our company about competitive intelligence?
- Who are the important clients for competitive intelligence? To whom should the intelligence effort be reported?

With rapid developments in the area of software applications that run on PCs, it is becoming increasingly possible to keep track of client lists and the various kinds of contacts that are made with each client. Many such programmes keep track of clients' names, addresses, phone and fax numbers, e-mail addresses, personal details such as birthdays, likes and dislikes, product/brand usage, hobbies, club memberships, etc.

Most of today's information systems are computer applications in a sophisticated data-driven age. These enable marketers to be better informed about their customers, potential customers, and competitors. This helps marketers to be more productive and establish and sustain competitive advantage. New applications are being developed at a faster pace. The ultimate focus of most such systems is to enable marketers to know enough about any given customer and the competitive context, to fine-tune their marketing efforts to better serve the target market so that customer's needs are met perfectly. This is the ultimate dream for every marketer.

Marketing Research Process

While the Marketing Information System has its focus on managing the flow of relevant information to decision-makers in the marketing department, marketing research is concerned with the function of generating information for marketing decision-makers.

There are occasions when there are no easy answers for a variety of marketing situations that marketing managers face. Such situations may call for conducting formal marketing studies of specific problems and opportunities. Marketing research is intended to address carefully defined marketing problems or opportunities. It helps in identifying consumer needs and market segments, furnishes information necessary for developing new products and formulating marketing strategies, enables managers to measure the effectiveness of marketing programmes and promotional activities, develops economic forecasting, helps in financial planning, and quality control. Research undertaken without precisely defining the problem and objectives usually results in wasting time and money.

For conducting ***marketing research,*** companies develop systematic procedures for collecting, recording, and analysing data from secondary and primary sources to help managers in making decisions. Marketing research is different from ***market research***, which is information collected about a particular market or market segment.

In the process of marketing research, companies collect a lot of different types of information. David G. Bakken is of the opinion that it is easy to think of all these in terms of ***three Rs*** of marketing:

- Recruiting New Customers.
- Retaining Current Customers.
- Regaining Lost Customers.

To recruit new customers, the researchers study different market segments to develop the right products and services consumers need and want. To retain customers, the marketer may conduct customer satisfaction studies. Marketers realise that good relationship with customers is important for long-term positive sales results. Regaining lost customers can be a formidable problem. It needs innovative marketing and outstanding communications. The information collected with respect to the first and the second ***Rs*** helps regaining the lost customers.

Defining Marketing Research

"Marketing Research is the function which links the consumer, customer, and public to the marketer through information – information used to identify and define marketing opportunities and problems; generate, refine, and evaluate marketing actions; monitor marketing performance, and improve understanding of marketing as a process."

(Definition by American Marketing Association, according to Tull and Hawkins, 6th Ed.)

According to Tull and Hawkins, *"Marketing research is a formalised means of obtaining information to be used in marketing decisions."*

(Donald S. Tull and Del I. Hawkins, *Marketing Research,* 1993).

The six steps presented (Figure 6.3) should be viewed as an overall approach to conduct marketing research and should not be viewed as a fixed set of rules for each and every project. The decision-makers must consider each of the steps carefully and examine how they can best be adjusted to address a given problem or opportunity at hand. Various opportunities for error are present in the marketing research process and for this reason, it is important that all those who use research results be well-informed and critical users of information that results from such research results.

The difference between good and bad research is the quality of inputs. Ideally, the informed and critical users of research should ask some important questions *before* implementing the research and, if necessary, *after* the research is completed to be certain that the research is unbiased and results are reliable to help decision-making:

- Keeping in view the problem or opportunity, are the research objectives right? Will the data collected be sufficient to fulfil those objectives?
- Is the choice of data sources appropriate? Are readily available, cheaper data sources used where appropriate? Is qualitative research planned to support and ensure that quantitative research is on target?
- Is the planned approach to research design (qualitative and quantitative) appropriate to address the research objectives?
- Are the questionnaire scales appropriate and permit measurement necessary to accomplish the research objectives? Are the framed questions unbiased to conduct survey, interview, or focus group? Is the sample size suitable for research objectives? Do the sampling plan and respondent contact methods entail any known bias? Are the analyses appropriate as specified before conducting the research?

The research process involves defining a marketing problem or opportunity and establishing research objectives; decide research design; establish data collection approach; finalise sampling procedure; collect data; analyse data and present report.

FIGURE 6.3
Steps in Marketing Research Process

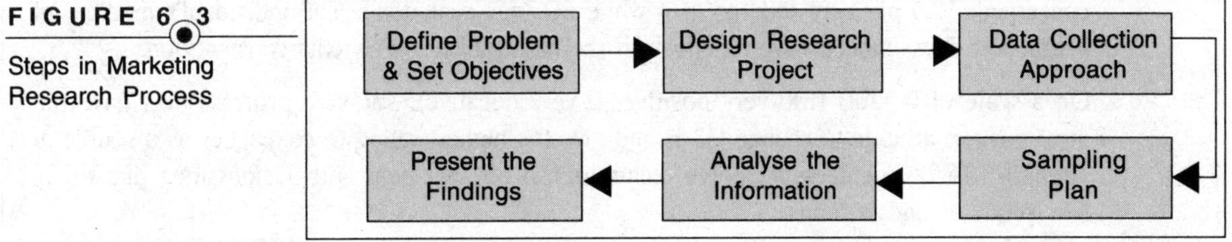

- Horizon 2000, a survey conducted by ORG-MARG on behalf of BBC World and Starcom, aims to reveal the ways and tastes of 'upmarket' India. The surveyed group forms 0.6 per cent of urban India and 5 per cent of SEC A, but with higher spend power – roughly three times that of SEC A. The target audience comprised professionals between 25 – 54 years in SEC A homes with monthly household income of more than Rs.8,000 and cable and satellite connection. The study covered the six largest metros – Mumbai, Delhi, Kolkata, Chennai, Bangalore and Hyderabad with a total sample of 4,791 respondents.
- The research incorporates detailing of occupation into doctor, lawyer, CA, engineer, software professional, architect, professor and scientists. It explores the target group on media interaction in terms of time spent on watching TV, programme genera and channels preferred and Internet

Contd...

usage; lifestyle in terms of daily schedule, breakfast habits, club membership, air travel, vacationing, type of house, work experience, banking, investment and alcohol consumption; attitude in terms of work, family, extroversion, and openness to change.

Jeremy Nye, head of research, BBC World, explains the need, "We spend a lot of money buying research studies – TAM, INTAM, IRS, and the Decision-makers Survey (DMS). We also have a six-monthly internal tracking. But we still felt there should be less duplication of data and more targeting of important sub-groups. Horizon tries to bridge the gap between the omnibus national surveys and the extremely specialised DMS."

Starcom revealed some topline results last year and most of the data is available for BBC World and Starcom clients. "This is not a "vow" survey," smiles Nye, "But what we have discovered is that there is a certain homogeneity among upmarket adults as markets and research cross geographical borders in the global economy."

Some of the results were intriguing. On a typical weekday, software professionals have the least free wake-up time in the morning, but surprisingly, sleep the most. They also compensate the most for lost sleep during the week, over the weekend. Lawyers have the most free wake-up time in the morning and also spend the least time away from home, along with the professors/ scientists. Doctors seem to be unlucky souls, with the most time spent away from home and the least sleep time.

The average value of durables owned by the target group is Rs. 3.3 lakh. The durable acquisition rate is highest among software professionals at Rs. 49,000 per year, while the durable purchase plan is highest among layers at Rs. 54,000 per year. Sixteen per cent are club members. The average spend for a vacation within India is Rs. 15,000, and Rs. 78,000 for a vacation abroad. Around 6 per cent of the target group vacationed abroad during the last year.

Ninety-five per cent of the target group watches news on TV, with infotainment and Hindi/ regional entertainment coming a close second (86%). As far TV viewership during Travel is concerned, 39.3 per cent indulge in it while 60.7per cent don't. The individual's medium of instruction does indeed have an effect on the nature of his/her media consumption.

On a scale of 0 –100 (100-very positive, 0-very negative), software professionals have the most positive attitude to change (33.5) and give the highest rating to colleagues as a source of strength (64.9), engineers welcome technological advancement and businessmen like to try new products and fashions.

(Source: A & M, January 15, 2001).

Define the Marketing Problem and Set Objectives

The starting step focuses on uncovering the nature and boundaries of a negative, or positive situation or question and calls for the marketing manager and the researcher to analyse the situation and carefully define the problem to be addressed. There is a popular saying, "A problem well-defined is half solved." However, the definition of marketing problem may not always be easy because the real issue may not be apparent to decision-makers and has to be identified and precisely defined.

Marketing departments, particularly in large organisations, Maintain Marketing Information Systems (MIS), which provide a continuous, and systematic flow of information for use in making marketing related decisions. Firms with inadequate information often find it difficult and time consuming to define the problem accurately and good research on the wrong problem is a waste of money and effort.

Problem Definition

The company's sales are declining and not producing the expected profits. Last year our market share slipped 10 per cent in men's jeans, and 12 per cent in men's footwear. Studies conducted show we are losing sales to other competitors in the same business and that customers are confused about our position in the market. We need to decide how we position ourselves in the future market place.

The statement clearly defines the specific and measurable problem that the research project has to address. All the five questions help specify relevant objectives for which the research should provide the information needed by the decision-makers to decide on a new positioning strategy for the marketer. This would facilitate the company in developing appropriate marketing plans, along with advertising and promotion strategies to communicate the new positioning to audiences in the target market(s) and hopefully regain the lost market position and increase profitability.

The research objective defines what information is needed to solve the problem. To design a promising research project, the first prerequisite is to refine a broad, indefinite problem into a precise researchable statement. A clear definition of problem and subsequent setting of relevant and precise objective(s) facilitates deciding what kind of basic research approach would be appropriate.

Going by the above mentioned problem definition, we can have a definite statement of research objective(s):

Research Objectives

We must find out: (1) Who are our customers? (2) Who are the customers of the competing brands? (3) What do these customers like and dislike about us and the competitors? (4) How are we currently perceived among customers? And (5) What must we do to clarify and improve the customers' existing perceptions?

Design Research Project

Marketing research design refers to the specification of methods for gathering and analysing the data necessary to facilitate identifying or reacting to a problem or opportunity. The users of research and those that conduct the research both should be aware why the research is being conducted.

To achieve accuracy and gain useful information through marketing research, the research design should be developed carefully and strict standards should be applied for collecting and tabulating the data. The advertiser must ensure that the collected data is valid and reliable to be useful. *Validity* means the research must actually measure what is being investigated. For example, if a market consists of 5 million people and the researcher shows a prototype of a mixer-grinder to just 10 individuals and 8 of them say they like it, it would mean 80 per cent favourable attitude. But a sample size so small is not enough for a minimum sample, and the prototype shown to them would probably bias their response. The test cannot be considered reliable because if repeated with another 10 individuals, it might get an entirely different response. *Reliability* of a test means that approximately similar results can be obtained if the research is repeated. For example, an entrance test for MBA is reliable in case a student scores similar marks after taking it a second time. Validity and reliability depend on a number of key factors, such as the sampling methods, the design of survey questionnaire, data tabulation approach, and the method of analysis.

According to Tull and Hawkins, many researchers have found it useful to consider three categories of research based on the type of information required. These are briefly discussed below:

Exploratory Research

This category of research aims at discovering the general nature of the problem and to correctly understand the involved variables. In case managers face serious doubts about the marketing problem and need more information about a problem, *exploratory research* ends to rely more on secondary data such as company's database, publicly available data, questioning experienced and knowledgeable persons inside or outside the company such as salespeople and resellers etc. It can be conducted with a very limited sample size such as convenience or judgement samples. Exploratory research studies are particularly useful in addressing broad problems and developing a more specific educated or informed guess, called a ***hypothesis***, which is a statement that specifies how two or more measurable variables such as age, attitude, and purchase behaviour are related.

Descriptive Studies

Such studies are more extensive in scope. In such studies, information is collected from a representative of respondents and the information collected is analysed by using statistical methods. Such studies generally demand much prior knowledge and assume that the problem is clearly defined. A lot of marketing research involves descriptive studies and may range from general surveys of consumers' age, education, occupation, market-potential studies, product usage studies, attitude surveys, and media research, for example, specifics such as how many consumers bought a Maruti Zen last month, or how many adults between the age of 18 to 25 visit McDonald's 4 times a week and how much they spend. Such studies could help developing new products or services. Accuracy is quite critical in such studies as the errors can lead to results that could prove to be misleading to marketing decision-makers. To minimise the chances of such errors, much care should be taken in sampling procedure, design of questionnaire, and information reporting.

Causal Research (Experimental Research)

As the name suggests, such research studies are conducted to establish cause and effect relationship between different variables. Suppose it is assumed that variable X causes variable Y. To prove or disprove this, the researcher must try to hold constant all other variables in the experiment except X and Y. If a marketer wants to learn the influence of rising income and change in lifestyle on purchases of a more expensive car model, the results may show that increasing income levels and lifestyle changes favourably affect the sales. Daniel C. Smith and C. Whan Park reported a study conducted to test the hypothesis that brand extensions increase new product market share. The researchers found that brand extensions do in fact contribute positively to market share.

Such research may be conducted in a laboratory setting such as central location to respond to experimental variables and might include interview rooms, one-way mirrors, video equipment, tape recorders etc. Such studies are called ***laboratory experiment***. For example, to determine the effect of various levels of sweetness in a soft drink on consumer taste preference, consumers may be invited to a taste room. The researchers would ask respondents to taste different versions of the soft drink and afterwards would be asked to rank the preference of each level of sweetness. In a laboratory setting, variables can be controlled. However, a laboratory setting is different from the real world, where many factors affect the choice in a market place.

A ***field experiment*** is undertaken in a natural setting such as a shopping centre. The field setting allows researcher to have a more direct test of marketing decisions but the respondents may be affected by factors not under the control of the researcher, such as weather conditions or other events. Suppose respondents are asked to evaluate planned future advertisements, their evaluation may be influenced and prejudiced by their earlier evaluation of competing advertisements. In a field experiment, it is not possible for researchers to control all variables except a few.

Data Collection Approach

There are four basic methods for collecting data in marketing research. These include *secondary data, observation data, survey data,* and *experimental data.* The nature of collected data can be put under either **secondary** or **primary** category.

FIGURE 6.4

Data Collection Alternatives

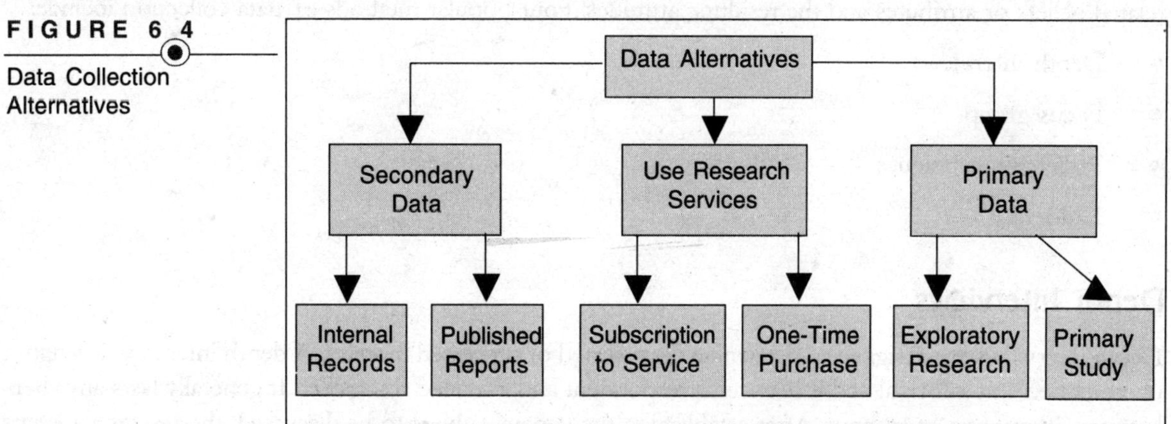

Secondary Data

Secondary data is any information originally generated for some other purposes rather than the current problem under consideration and can be either internal or external to the organisation. It includes findings based on data generated in-house for earlier studies, customer information collected by company's sales or credit departments and research conducted by outside organisations. The act of locating secondary data is called *secondary research.* Original research done by individuals or organisations to meet specific objectives is called *primary research.*

Sometimes, secondary data uncovers enough useful information related to the present problem that it eliminates the need to conduct primary research and collect primary data. In most cases, secondary data offers clues and direction for the design of primary research. Secondary data is relatively easily available, without much effort, time, and money. Company's information database, government agencies, industry sources, trade associations, marketing research firms, advertising agencies, and Internet are important sources of secondary data.

With the opening up of the Indian economy and the ever-increasing requirements of a variety of specific information by business organisations, a fairly significant number of large, medium, and small research suppliers are available. Some important research agencies include A. C. Nielsen, Taylor Nelsen Sofres MODE, IMRB, NCAER, NRS, IRS, and ORG-MARG.

Primary Data

In case the needed data are not available from secondary sources, it is dated, accuracy is doubtful, or unreliable, it becomes necessary for the researcher to obtain primary data through full-scale research. To collect primary data, the researcher undertakes either **qualitative research** or **quantitative research**.

Qualitative Research

Data collection techniques for qualitative studies include focus group, depth interviews and projective techniques. All these techniques relate to psychoanalytic and clinical aspects of psychology. The emphasis is on open-ended and free-response types of questions so that the respondents reveal their unconscious thoughts and beliefs. These techniques are frequently used in early stages of attitude research to learn product-related beliefs or attributes and the resulting attitudes. Four popular methods of data collection include:

- Depth interviews
- Focus group
- Projective techniques
- Laddering

Depth Interviews

Depth interviews are designed to determine deep seated or repressed motives. A depth interview is lengthy, unstructured and informal and is between a respondent and a trained researcher. It generally lasts anywhere between 30 minutes to an hour. After establishing the general subject to be discussed, the researcher keeps her/his own participation to the minimum possible level. The questions are general and respondents are encouraged to talk freely about their needs, desires, motives, interests, activities, emotions and attitudes, in addition to the product or brand under study. Questioning is sometimes indirect such as, "Why do you think some your friends use a Bajaj Pulsar motorcycle?" This method attempts to bypass the respondent's inhibitions about revealing inner feelings. Such studies furnish valuable ideas about product design, insights for product positioning or repositioning and marketing communications.

A new technique for probing respondents' inner feelings, called *autodriving,* involves exposing respondents to photographs, videos and audio-recordings of their own behaviour. This approach provides them with the opportunity of having a deeper look at self and commenting on their consumption related behaviour. This technique is believed to help in making the qualitative data more meaningful.

Interview results are interpreted by trained professionals and are subjective in nature rather than quantitative and for this reason there is increased possibility of bias. Another source of error is the small size of samples, which may not be representative of the entire population.

Focus Groups

Focus group is a popular technique for exploratory research and brings together about eight to ten people with similar backgrounds to meet with a moderator/analyst for a group discussion. The discussion is "focused" on a product, service or any other subject for which the research is conducted. The moderator/analyst guides the discussion encouraging the participants to freely discuss their interests, attitudes, reactions motives, lifestyles, and feelings about the product and usage experience, etc. These sessions generally last for two hours and are videotaped.

The sessions are usually held in specially designed conference rooms with one-way mirrors permitting the researchers to observe the session without inhibiting the responses.

Collage focus research is a variation of the focus group. The respondents are provided with scissors, paper, paste and magazines and are asked to make a collage representing themselves and their relationship with the product or service under study.

Focus groups can be helpful in:

- Generating hypotheses about consumers and market conditions.
- Suggesting refreshing new ideas.
- Checking an advertisement, product package, or product concept to determine any flaws.
- Understanding consumers' motivations, lifestyles and personalities.
- Doing a post-mortem on failed products.

Projective Techniques

Projective tests require the respondent to decide what the other person would do in a certain situation. These techniques explore the underlying motives of individuals who consciously or unconsciously get involved in rationalisations and concealment because they may be reluctant to admit certain weaknesses or desires. Projective techniques involve a variety of disguised tests containing ambiguous stimuli such as untitled pictures, incomplete sentences, inkblots, word-associations and other-person characterisations. The respondent taking the test is required to describe, complete or explain the meaning of different ambiguous stimuli. It is believed that respondents' inner feelings influence their perceptions of ambiguous stimuli. By taking the tests, they project their inner thoughts revealing their underlying needs, wants, aspirations, fears and motives, whether or not the respondents are fully aware of them. Some examples of projective techniques are:

- ***Thematic Apperception Techniques (TAT):*** Respondents are shown pictures or cartoons concerning the product or the topic under study and asked to describe what is happening in the picture. It is believed that respondents will actually reveal their own motivations, attitudes, personalities and feelings about the situation.
- ***Word Association Test:*** This is a relatively old and simple technique. Respondents are read a series of words or phrases, one at a time and asked to answer quickly with the first word that comes to mind after hearing each one. By responding in rapid succession, it is assumed that they indicate what they associate most closely with the word or phrase spoken and reveal their true feelings.
- ***Sentence Completion Test:*** The interviewer reads the beginning of a sentence and the respondent is required to finish it. This technique is believed to be useful in uncovering the images consumers have about products and stores. The information collected can be used to develop promotional campaigns.
- ***The Third-Person Technique:*** The interviewer asks the respondent to describe a third person. For this, respondents are presented with some information about the person. It is believed that when they describe a neighbour or a third person, they usually respond without hesitation and in doing so, they express their own attitudes or motives as they infer the attitudes or motives of someone else.
- ***Laddering (Means-End Chain Model):*** This is a relatively new research method for data collection. The assumption here is that very specific product attributes are linked at levels of increasing abstraction to terminal values. The consumer concerned has highly valued end states and chooses among alternative means to attain these goals, and therefore products are valued as the means to an end. Laddering uses in-depth probing directed toward uncovering higher-level meanings at attribute (benefit) level and the value level. According to Thomas J. Reynolds and Jonathan Gutman ("Advertising is Image

Management," *Journal of Advertising Research,* February/March 1984) it facilitates uncovering linkages between product attributes, personal outcomes, and values that assist to structure components of the cognitive network in a consumer's mind.

To illustrate how laddering works, we may consider a consumer who intends to purchase a diamond ring for his would be wife. Tangible attributes of diamond such as size and brilliance are projected into abstract and emotional values of love, and self-esteem. Diamond sellers keep the prices of diamonds artificially high through associating the size of the diamond and price to the size of your love and self-worth. The belief that consumption of products is instrumental in attaining more abstract values i.e., central to the application of this method.

Quantitative Research

There are three basic approaches to collecting data in quantitative study:

- Observation
- Experimentation and
- Survey

Observation

One important approach to gain an in-depth understanding of consumers is to observe their behaviour in the process of buying and using products. By watching consumers, researchers gain a better understanding of what a product symbolises to a consumer because in most cases consumers do not realise that they are being observed and their behaviour remains natural. Observational research provides valuable information, which is used in product advertising. It is also widely used by *experientialists* to understand the buying and consumption process.

Experimentation

In experimental studies, the researcher can test the relative sales appeals for package designs, prices, promotional offers and copy themes, etc., by designing suitable experiments to identify cause and effect. In such studies, called ***causal research***, only one *independent variable* is manipulated at a time and others remain constant. This ensures that any difference in *dependent variable* (results) is because of changes of independent variables such as consumers' attitudes or purchase behaviour and not due to the influence of any extraneous factors. For example, to determine whether the size of a magazine ad affects readers' attention, the size of the ad might be changed, keeping other variables such as message or appeal and the colour of the ads constant so that they would not influence the results.

Survey

In a survey for data collection, consumers are aware of the fact that they are being studied and participate actively. A survey can be conducted by personal interview, by mail, or by telephone.

Personal interview survey is a direct face-to-face interaction between interviewer and the respondent in home or in a retail shopping area (called *mall intercept).* A large amount of relatively accurate information can be obtained by this approach. A major advantage of this approach is the flexibility. The interviewer can modify the questions as per the situation and can also provide any clarifications to the respondent if necessary. The drawback is its high cost.

Mail surveys are conducted by sending questionnaires directly to individuals who complete it at their leisure and return it, usually in a postage paid envelope. Mail surveys can largely reduce respondents' reluctance to reveal sensitive information because they are seldom asked to identify themselves. The cost per respondent of mail survey is low and widely dispersed consumers can be covered, generating large amount of data. On the negative side, mail surveys can result in small number of responses because many consumers do not return the completed questionnaires.

Telephone surveys also provide interviewer-respondent interaction, though not face-to-face and can be a useful alternative to personal interview. The method is quicker and far less expensive than personal interviews. Telephone surveys work well when the objective is to learn about certain behaviour at the time of the interview, such as before or after viewing a TV programme. Telephone surveys generally generate higher response rate than mail or personal interview. The information collected during each interview is limited because of the difficulty of keeping respondents interested and on phone for extended period. Also, it is not possible to determine the intensity of respondents' feelings on telephone. ***SMS surveys*** are an emerging trend as an alternative to get two or three word answers, such as yes/no about something. In our country so far, more of SMS in this respect is used to get opinions about controversial issues, or as a tool to participate in some sales promotional contests that require short answers.

E-mail surveys are likely to emerge as an alternative to telephone surveys in more developed countries. Researchers can send questionnaires to individuals who provide their e-mail addresses and agree to participate as respondents. E-mail would also be relatively interactive and permit respondents to seek any clarification of specific questions, or raise their own specific questions. Email interviewing can offer the potential advantage of quick response and relatively lower cost than traditional mail or telephone survey where broadband Internet services are widely available. It is believed that since the number of PC owning households connected to Internet or online information services is increasing, marketing research in the future is likely to rely heavily on e-mail surveys.

TABLE 6.1

Advantages and Limitations of Data Collection Methods

	Personal interview survey	Telephone survey	Mail survey
Costs of data collection	High	Medium	Low
Time required to collect data	Medium	Low	High
Sample size for a given budget	Small	Medium	Large
Data quantity per contact	High	Medium	Low
Can reach widely dispersed sample	No	Maybe	Yes
Reach to special locations	Yes	Maybe	No
Level of interaction with respondents	High	Medium	None
Degree of interview bias	High	Medium	None
Presentation of visual stimuli	Yes	No	Maybe
Response rate	High	Medium	Low

Data Collection Instruments: The method of data collection depends on the type of research. The primary method of data collection for quantitative study is the ***questionnaire***. Researchers can use a questionnaire to conduct any of the three types of surveys (personal interview, mail and telephone).

A ***questionnaire*** consists of a set of questions presented to respondents for their responses. Constructing a good questionnaire requires considerable expertise. Typical problems include asking the wrong questions, asking too many questions and using the wrong words. Effective survey questions have three attributes:

focus, brevity and clarity. They focus on the topic of survey, are as brief as possible and they are expressed simply and clearly. The questions must be interesting, objective, unambiguous and easy to answer truthfully and completely.

FIGURE 6.5
Personal interview questionnaire to determine consumers' feelings toward a superstore

1. Do you intend to shop at (store name) between now and Sunday?

   Yes 1 No 2 (if No, proceed to Q. 5).

2. Do you intend to buy something specific or just look around?

   Yes 1 Look around 2

3. Have you seen any of the items you intend to buy advertised by (store name)?

   Yes 1 (continue) No 2 (proceed to Q. 5)

4. Where did you see these items advertised? Was it in (store name), you received in the mail, the pages of local newspaper, on TV, or somewhere else? (Specify one or more).

   a. In-store advertisement b. Local newspaper c. On TV
   d. Received in mail e. Somewhere else (specify) f. Don't recall

5. Please rate the (store name) advertising on the attributes listed below. Please tick the number that best reflects your opinion of how the ad insert rates on each attribute. Ticking No.4 will mean that you are neutral. Higher or lower number ticked will indicate, you believe it describes the (store name) ad insert.

Looks cheap	1	2	3	4	5	6	7	Looks expensive
Unskillful	1	2	3	4	5	6	7	Cleverly done
Unappealing	1	2	3	4	5	6	7	Appealing
Merchandise displayed unattractively	1	2	3	4	5	6	7	Merchandise displayed attractively

6. Please indicate all of the different types of people listed below you feel this (store name) advertising is appealing to:

Young people	Quality-conscious people	Bargain hunters
Low-income people	Conservative dressers	Budget watchers
Fashion-conscious people	Older people	Rich people
Middle-income people	High-income people	Women
Men	Office workers	Smart dressers
Career-oriented women	College going students	Others (specify)

Questionnaires include both questions that are relevant to the topic of study and are pertinent demographic questions. This facilitates analysis and classification of responses into suitable categories. Questionnaires are first pre-tested and any errors are removed before their widespread use.

The true purpose of a questionnaire itself can be *disguised* or *undisguised.* Sometimes the answers to a disguised questionnaire are more truthful than to an undisguised questionnaire because the former avoids responses that respondents may think are expected. There are two types of questions, *open-ended* and *closed-ended.* Open-ended questions require information in the respondent's own words and closed-ended questions require the respondent only to check the appropriate answer from the given list. Open-ended questions reveal more because they do not restrain respondents' answers but are difficult to tabulate and analyse. Closed-ended questions, which are checked by respondents, are relatively simple to code and interpret but reveal limited information based on alternative responses provided.

The most common types of questions are:

- ***Open-ended:*** (The respondent is free to express her/his opinion about the issue).
- ***Dichotomous:*** (The respondent can choose only one of the two alternatives, such as yes or no).
- ***Multiple-choice:*** (The respondent can make two or more choices).
- ***Semantic differential (scale):*** (The respondent can rate on the scale divided between 1 and 5, where 5 may represent excellent and 1 poor).

To develop an effective questionnaire, the following points should be considered:

- ***List specific research objectives:*** There is no point in collecting irrelevant data.
- ***The questionnaire should be short:*** Long questionnaires may tax the respondent's patience. The researcher may get careless or ignore some questions.
- ***Questions should be clear:*** There should be no chance of misunderstanding. Avoid generalities or ambiguities.
- ***First, prepare a rough draft:*** Sharpen and polish it.
- ***Opening statement should be short:*** Include interviewer's name, company name, and the objective of the questionnaire.
- ***Put the respondent at ease:*** Begin with one or two easily answered and inoffensive questions.
- ***Structure questions logically:*** Ask general questions first before moving to more detailed ones.
- ***Avoid questions that may be suggestive of an answer:*** Such questions bias the results.
- ***Include a few questions that crosscheck respondent's earlier answers:*** This helps ensure validity.
- ***Put personal questions concerning:*** age, income, education, etc., at the end of the questionnaire.
- ***Pretest the questionnaire:*** To be reasonably sure, it is necessary to pretest the questionnaire with 20 to 30 people.

Instead of using a questionnaire, sometimes researchers use a list of statements and ask respondents to indicate their degree of agreement or disagreement (called ***inventories).*** Sometimes, researchers use a list of product attributes or products and ask respondents to indicate their relative evaluations or feelings. Researchers also use ***attitude scales*** to collect this type of evaluative data. Attitude scales include Likert scales, Semantic differential scales, and Rank-order scales.

Likert scale is the most popular form of attitude scale, being easy to prepare and interpret and simple for respondents to answer. Use of this approach involves compiling a list of statements relevant to the attitude under study. The respondents are asked to check or write the number corresponding to their level of agreement or disagreement with the statement.

Semantic differential scale is relatively easy to construct and administer. It consists of a pair of bipolar pair adjectives (such as good/bad, like/dislike, expensive/inexpensive, sharp/blunt, aggressive/docile) or antonym phrases at both ends of the scale with response options spaced in between in five or seven points. Respondents are asked to mark the position on the continuum that most closely represents their attitude toward a product, concept, or company on the basis of each attribute. Semantic differential scale is useful for preparing graphic consumer profiles of the concept under study. It is also employed in comparing consumer perceptions of competitive products and measuring perceptions of existing product against perceptions of "ideal" product.

FIGURE 6.6

Example of a Likert Scale

	Strongly agree	Agree	Undecided	Disagree	Strongly disagree
Big Shopper is generally a progressive store.	____	X	____	____	____
Big Shopper is generally well stocked.	X	____	____	____	____
Big Shopper's merchandise is generally reasonably priced.	X	____	____	____	____

FIGURE 6.7

Semantic Differential Scale

Healthy	—	—	—	—	—	—	—	Unhealthy
Fresh	—	—	—	—	—	—	—	Stale
Soft	—	—	—	—	—	—	—	Hard
Expensive	—	—	—	—	—	—	—	Inexpensive
Young	—	—	—	—	—	—	—	Old
Old fashioned	—	—	—	—	—	—	—	Modern

Rank-order scales involve asking the respondents to rank items in order of preference against some criterion such as quality, value for money, or image. Rank-order scaling reveals important competitive information and helps identify areas of product design improvement.

FIGURE 6.8

Rank-Order Scale

The following are six brands of toothpaste. We are interested in learning your preference for each of these brands. Place a **1** alongside the brand that you would be most likely to buy, a **2** alongside the brand you would next be most likely to buy. Continue doing this until you have ranked all six brands.

______ Colgate Total
______ Pepsodent
______ Close-Up
______ Neem
______ Anchor
______ Vicco Vajradanti

Sampling Plan

A sample design addresses three questions: who is to be surveyed (sampling *unit*), how many to survey (sample *size*), and how should the respondents be chosen (the sampling *procedure*). Deciding whom to survey (*sampling unit*) requires that the researcher must define the target population (*universe*) that would be sampled. For example, if Sahara Airlines conducts a survey, should the sampling unit be business travellers, vacation travellers, or both? Should travellers under age 30 years be interviewed? Interviewing the correct target market or the potential target market is basic to the validity of research.

Investigating all members of a population is virtually impossible as the time and resources available for research are limited. However, the research must reflect the **universe** (the entire target population). Researchers obtain the needed amount of data through **sampling**. They select a limited number of units (**sample**) that they expect to represent the characteristics of a population. As a rule, the size of a sample must be large enough to achieve accuracy and stability. Larger sample size ensures more reliable results. Reliability though, can be achieved even with very small samples, such as 1% of the population. There are two broad types of sampling techniques: **random probability samples** and **non-probability samples**.

TABLE 6.2
Probability and Non-probability Samples

Probability sample	
Simple random sample	Every member of the population has an equal chance of being selected.
Stratified random sample	The population is divided into mutually exclusive groups (such as gender, age group),and random samples are drawn from each group.
Cluster or area sample	The population is divided into mutually exclusive groups (such as city, village) and the researcher draws a sample of the groups to be interviewed.
Non-probability sample	
Convenience sample	The researcher selects the most accessible population members to interview and obtain information (such as shoppers in a departmental store).
Judgement sample	The researcher uses her/his judgement to choose population members who are good prospects for accurate information (such as doctors).
Quota sample	The researcher finds and interviews a predetermined number of respondents in each of several categories (such as 50 males and 50 females).

Random Probability Sampling

The greatest accuracy is obtained from random probability samples because all units in a population have a known and equal chance of being selected. For example, in a lottery, when all the ticket numbers are mixed up, each number should have an equal probability of being selected. The difficulty with this method is that every unit (individual, or family, etc.) must be known, listed, and numbered to have equal chance of being selected. The task is often prohibitively expensive with customers of widely distributed products. Researchers use **stratified sampling** by dividing the population of interest into groups, or strata, based on some common characteristic and then conduct a random sample within each group. **Area sampling** is a variation of stratified sampling wherein researchers divide the population into geographic areas and select the units within the selected areas for a random sample.

Non-probability sampling: This sampling method is easier, less expensive and time consuming than probability sampling and for this reason, researchers use it extensively. This method involves the researcher's personal judgement and elements of the population do not have a known chance of being selected, so there is no guarantee the sample is representative and the researchers cannot be as confident in the validity of the responses. Most research situations in marketing or advertising require general measures of the data and non-probability method of interviewing suffices to find out the shopping preferences, customers' attitudes, image perceptions, etc. Non-probability sampling techniques include quota sampling, judgement sampling, and convenience sampling.

TABLE 6.3

Differences Between Qualitative and Quantitative Research

	Qualitative Research	Quantitative Research
Main techniques used for data collection	Focus groups and in-depth interviews	Surveys and scientific sampling.
Kinds of questions asked	Why? Through what thought process? In what way? What other behaviour or thoughts?	How much? How many?
Interviewer's role	Interviewer must think carefully and quickly frame questions and probes in response to whatever respondents say. Highly trained professionals required	Critical role is important, but interviewers need only be able to read scripts. They should not improvise or deviate. Little training needed, responsible personnel are most suitable
Questions asked	Position of questions may vary in sequence and phrasing from group to group and in different interviews. New questions are included and old ones dropped	No variation. Must be the question for each interview. Sequence and phrasing of questions must be carefully controlled.
Number of interviews	Fewer interviews but the duration of each interview is more	Many interviews to ascertain scientific sample that is worth projecting
Nature of findings	Develop a hypothesis, gain insight, explore language options, refine concepts, add numerical data, provide diagnostic for advertising copy	Test hypothesis, arrange factors according to priority, furnish data for mathematical modelling and projections

Deciding how many people should be surveyed (*sample size*) depends on the budget and the required confidence in research findings. As a rule, large samples give more reliable results than small samples. If the sampling procedure is credible, sample sizes of less than 1% of a population can give reliable results.

How should the respondents be chosen (*sampling procedure*)? If the researcher wants to project the findings to the total population, then a *probability sample* should be selected. If the findings are just to be "representative" of the population, then a *non-probability sample* can be chosen.

Analyse the Information

It is important to appreciate that raw data by itself does not serve the purpose of marketing research. After the research data has been collected, it is time to gain valuable insight from the findings. The researcher tabulates the data for analysis. At this stage, simple frequency counts or percentages are often used. Statistical analysis might consider using mean, median, mode, percentages, standard deviation, and coefficient of correlation. Computers make it possible to use more advanced analytical tools such as test of significance, factor analysis, multiple determinant analysis, and regression analysis.

Cross tabulation of data can show how males and females differ in some type of behaviour. Statistical interpretation reveals how widely responses vary and what is the pattern of distribution in relation to the variable being measured. When interpreting statistics, marketers rely on estimates of expected error from the true values of population. The analysis and interpretation aspect of marketing research calls for human judgement and intuition to accept or reject the research findings.

Present the Findings

Report writing requires taking an objective look at the findings to see how well the collected facts suit the research objectives to solve a stated marketing problem. It is very difficult and – in most cases quite unlikely – that research will furnish everything needed to solve the defined marketing problem. It is perhaps necessary to point out the lack of completeness and the reasons for it.

The research report presenting the results and recommendations is usually a formal, written document. To start with, the research report has an executive summary, as senior managers may not be in a position to go through the entire detailed report. The summary presents the main research findings and recommendations. The decision-makers can refer to the relevant details concerning issues of interest. When marketing decision-makers have a firm grasp of research methodology and procedures, they are in a much better position to integrate research findings and their personal experience. Besides executive summary, ideally the report should also include marketing problem and objectives, sampling procedure and sample size, tools for data collection, sources of data, analytical tools used, research findings and their interpretation, recommendations. It is not uncommon for marketing decision-makers to want the researcher to make a presentation using computer or transparencies. It is important for the researcher to be aware of the background and research abilities of decision-makers. There should be clear explanations in plain language without using complex research or statistical terminology so as to make it easier for research users. It can be helpful to talk with research users before writing the report.

Summary

Marketing success depends on making correct and timely decisions. Marketing managers need reliable and timely information about a large number of external and internal factors relevant to decision areas. Practically every decision area relevant to marketing requires the input of information. The term 'Marketing Information Systems' refers to a programme for managing and organising information gathered by an organisation from various internal and external sources. Its focus is on data storage, classification, and retrieval.

In the current fast-paced business climate, keeping up with macro-environmental changes, and competition is becoming increasingly difficult. Marketing intelligence system refers to systematic and ethical approach, procedures, and sources that marketing managers use to gather and analyse everyday information about various developments with regard to competitors and other business trends in the marketing environment.

Marketing research is the collection, analysis, and interpretation of data for guiding marketing decisions. It is characterised by detailed analysis of specific problems or opportunities related to marketing. The research process involves defining marketing problem or opportunity and establishing research objectives; decide research design; establish data collection approach; finalise sampling procedure; collect data; analyse data and present report.

Research design is an overall plan for gathering and analysing the data necessary to facilitate identifying or reacting to a problem or opportunity. In exploratory research, the existing information relevant to the problem is reviewed or informally investigated. Descriptive studies focus on understanding the characteristics of some phenomena underlying a specific problem. Causal or experimental studies are conducted either in a laboratory or in the field, and focus on investigating the relationships and involve manipulating only an independent variable to measure its effect on dependent variable, while controlling all other variables.

There are four basic methods for collecting data in marketing research. These include *secondary data, observation data, survey data*, and *experimental data.* The nature of collected data can be put under either secondary or primary category. Secondary data is any information originally generated for some other purposes rather than the current problem under consideration and can be either internal or external to the organisation. Primary data can be collected through surveys, or observation. Surveys refer to interviews on telephone, mail, or in person. Observation involves recording the exhibited behaviour of respondents.

Sampling addresses three questions: Who is to be surveyed, how many to survey, and how should the respondents be chosen. Deciding whom to survey requires that the researcher must define the target population that would be sampled. Sampling procedures are used to study human behaviour and also to estimate the likelihood of events not directly related with an activity. The greatest accuracy is obtained from probability samples because all units in a population have a known and equal chance of being selected. Non-probability sampling procedure involves personal judgement of the researcher.

Collected data is tabulated, and analysed to interpret its findings. Various statistical tools are used for interpretation and subsequently, a formal, written research report is usually prepared.

Questions for Discussion

1. Why should companies go for marketing research? Write a statement of research problem.
2. What has made marketing research important in the present day marketing?
3. What is a marketing information system? How can MIS serve marketing managers?
4. How are data for MIS collected? What are important external data sources in India?
5. What are the important steps involved in marketing research process? What are the main categories of research?
6. Briefly discuss qualitative research.
7. What are the methods used to conduct quantitative research?
8. What are different data collection instruments? Discuss different methods of conducting surveys.
9. Discuss situations in which it would be appropriate to use random sampling, quota sampling, and area sampling.
10. What is a questionnaire? Mention five points that should be kept in mind while preparing a questionnaire.

Projects

1. Develop a questionnaire to find out what four important services a beauty parlour should offer to females aged 18 - 25 among middle-income groups?
2. Develop a research plan to learn how a new management institution should position itself.
3. Conduct a survey to find out which TV channels are popular for Hindi movies among ladies in your locality.

Bibliography

1. Floyd Kemske, "Brains Will Replace BTUs," *Information Age,* June 1990.

2. Laurence N. Goal, "High Technology Data Collection for Measurement and Testing," *Marketing Research*, March 1992.

3. "Measure for Measure," *Marketing Tools,* 1994.

4. Daniel C. Smith and C. Whan Park, "The Effects of Brand Extensions on Market Share and Advertising Efficiency," *Journal of Marketing Research,* August 1992.

Measuring Market Demand

CHAPTER 7

LEARNING OBJECTIVES

After going through this chapter, you will understand:

- Market potential, company potential, and company sales forecast
- Demand measurement and methods of forecasting demand forecast

vents of the past few years suggest pizza deliveries as an indicator of political upheaval. On the day of the Soviet Coup, for example 260 pizzas were delivered to Boris Yeltsin and Crew, and on the day that Operation Desert Storm began, the Pentagon ordered 25 pizzas. While pizza deliveries as an indicator of political upheaval may seem far-fetched, one may think it equally strange that, in Japan, many believe that catfish can predict earthquakes.

Demand forecasters, while not relying on catfish and pizzas for data, have been accused of being just about the equivalent of witch doctors in the methods they use. In a survey conducted by the National Science Foundation, a majority of the research users questioned said that industrial marketing is more of an art than a science. Also, research has shown that most forecasters hate to predict bad news, because the opportunity costs of such a prediction can be high if sales are higher than expected.

Despite its limitations, demand forecasting is an integral part of the business world. An example of the company that used forecasting to steer a long period of sustained growth under differing market conditions is Alltel Corporation, whose basic business is cellular phone service. In the mid-1980s, signing up new subscribers were becoming more difficult for the cellular industry. Revenue growth for the industry slowed down from 71 per cent in 1989 to 36 per cent in 1990. Also, people who did subscribe were using their cellular phones less, and they were disconnecting at a higher rate than in past years.

These trends told Alltel to keep diversifying, and the company is now into manufacturing long distance, cable, and computer software. Alltel is particular about the cities to which it takes its cellular service and has chosen growing cities such as Atlanta, Georgia, and North Carolina for expansion.

Things have picked up in the cellular phone business, and the subscriber base has doubled since 1989. The industry has increased its profitability, provided better customer service, and produced new technologies.

(Source: Adapted with minor changes from Johnson, Kurtz, and Sheuing, Sales Management, 2nd ed. 1994)

At best, the future remains uncertain. It would be different from what it is now and different from what one expects it to be. Only seers know for sure what the future holds. Nevertheless, managers develop plans based on what they anticipate the future is likely to be. The future is inherently uncertain in the rapidly changing present day markets. Consumer needs, wants, and preferences shift; macro trends seem to be in a state of perpetual change; competitors come and go; and new technologies displace the old ones. Despite this, demand forecasting plays a key role in all kinds of planning and budgeting in each and every area of business and other organisations. Development of forecasts is usually spread over three stages. First of all, the forecast is developed for macroeconomic conditions. Developing forecast for the industry follows this, and finally the forecast for the company is prepared. Companies develop forecasts either internally or buy from outside sources such as independent research providers. If the forecast is developed internally, it is the marketing department that is responsible for preparing the sale forecasts.

A sales forecast refers to an estimate of sales in monetary terms or physical units, in a future period of time, under an assumed set of macro-environmental factors influencing the business unit for which the forecast is made, under a given marketing programme. The forecasts could be for the entire company, a division, a product line, or a single product/brand. Short-term forecasts are also called operating forecasts. Long-term forecasts, generally for three or more years, are used for planning production capacity and long-run financial planning.

Market Potential

Market potential (industry potential) refers to the highest possible expected industry sales of a product or service. Market potential often serves as a starting point for preparing a sales forecast. For instance, Samsung or Godrej would be interested in knowing the market potential for refrigerators. Assuming that 30 per cent of the households have enough income to buy refrigerators, this would be the size of the total market. To put it differently, the market potential represents the uppermost limit of market demand for a given set of anticipated conditions.

Company Potential

Company potential is a quantitative estimate of maximum possible sales opportunities for a company within a given market area for which the forecast is made under assumed ideal conditions and marketing efforts. This refers to the company's sales potential and represents its share of market potential. The absolute limit of company potential is the market or industry potential. Market share is the percentage of market controlled by a particular company or product.

Company Potential = Per cent Market Share ´ Market Potential

Company Sales Forecast

Company sales forecast represents the sales estimate that the company actually expects to achieve, based on market conditions, the company's resources, and its marketing programme. The sales forecast of a company is less than the total company potential because companies have limitations of resources.

Established and well-managed companies generally employ more than one method to prepare a forecast. There are two broad approaches: top-down and build-up (bottom-up). Under the top-down approach, a top manager or a group of managers prepares an overall forecast. Build-up approach is often used by decentralised organisations. Each region, district, and division prepares its forecast and all these are aggregated to create the forecast of the company as a whole. Let us consider a company that has four sales divisions; each division has five districts, and each district has five regions. Using a build-up approach, each region prepares its forecast; each region submits its forecast to the district; each district aggregates this forecast and forwards it to the division. At the division level the forecast from districts is aggregated, and finally at the marketing manager level the forecast from each division is combined, often with some necessary modifications, to culminate in the final forecast of the company.

FORECASTING METHODS

Two types of forecasting methods are used to prepare the sales forecast:

- **Qualitative or Judgemental Methods.**
- **Quantitative Methods.**

Qualitative Methods

Qualitative or judgemental methods consider factors related to expertise and human judgement. These methods are generally used in conjunction with some others to build more confidence in the forecast. Qualitative approaches have the advantage of adjusting to sudden shifts in environmental circumstances.

Jury of Executive Opinion

This is perhaps the oldest method to prepare a sales forecast. Robin T. Peterson found that it is still used by many companies. A committee of senior executives from various disciplines such as marketing, sales, marketing research, production, accounting, and advertising is formed and given the responsibility to develop the forecast. Each member provides an estimate of future sales, often along with written justification of their estimate. The opinions so collected are then analysed at a group meeting and synthesised through collective judgement of individual estimates.

This forecasting method is quite simple and uses the experience and expertise of senior managers from many functional areas. The limitations are that the forecast is reliable only to the extent of correctness of the judgements of committee members and also the extent of having sufficient uptodate market knowledge or current information on which to base their forecast. Besides, breaking down this forecast into more detailed estimates, such as product-wise or territory-wise estimates are quite difficult. This approach is quick and inexpensive, but hardly scientific.

Delphi Method

This approach is a slight variation from the executive opinion method. A group of experts expresses their views on different relevant issues such as the expected direction of future business conditions, technology, business activities, new product development, and expected market changes. These experts are often from academic and technical institutions, industry, and independent or government agencies, etc. The experts are kept apart and they give their individual anonymous forecasts. These forecasts are reviewed and compiled by the in charge of the group and returned for a second round of estimates. The experts are also informed of the groups' average estimates. This procedure is repeated till a consensus forecast finally develops. This method has the advantage of eliminating group pressures of a committee discussion. Used in conjunction with some statistical methods, it generally produces a reliable sales forecast, with fewer errors.

Sales Force Composite Method

This is a build-up method of preparing a sales forecast. The assumptions in using this method are that sales people are the company's ambassadors in close contact with customers and prevailing market conditions and best qualified to estimate future sales in their individual territories. The sales people are asked to estimate the sales in their territories for a specified future period. These forecasts from each salesperson are combined to prepare a composite sales forecast. At the regional level, some minor adjustments are often made in these figures.

The disadvantages of this method include: Poor judgement of sales persons about future sales, because of their emotional involvement. They may also become too optimistic or pessimistic due to their recent experiences. Some may report a lower figure as the forecast would affect their next year's sales quota and their judgement may be influenced either way by the recent sales success or otherwise. It is quite possible that many of them may not be aware and in a position to understand the impact of future macroeconomic conditions.

To manage these problems, providing all the relevant information to sales people and allowing them enough time to prepare their sales forecast could be helpful. The company may also train them in this function, and may also introduce some system of incentive to improve forecasts.

Survey of Buyers' Intentions

This method could be more appropriate for industrial markets, where the potential purchasers are well-defined and limited in number, are willing to cooperate, and their past record proves a consistent relationship between their buying intentions and actual purchases. The marketer can conduct a survey to collect potential customer responses. The sample of current or potential customers is asked how much of a particular product they would buy at a certain price during a specified future period. The sophistication of such surveys can vary from simple recording of buying intentions of customers to using advanced sampling and probability concepts.

The advantage of this method is that the forecast is based on direct contact with the market-place. However, the limitations are that the forecast reflects customers' intentions and actual buying behaviour may turn out to be different. The respondents may also deliberately overestimate their future needs to be certain of continued supplies. Their plans to buy may change in order to adjust quickly to change in the operating environment.

Quantitative Methods

The advantage of using quantitative methods of forecasting eliminates any subjectivity that is not possible with qualitative methods. The limitations include the nature and validity of assumptions used, and also, the mathematical approaches tend to generalise on the basis of past experience. There is hardly any scope to adjust to sudden shifts as may happen in case of high technology industries.

Simple Projection Method

In its simplest form, adding some fixed percentage of sales growth over the last year's sales arrives at the sales forecast. This approach may be appropriate for companies that have been experiencing a certain stable growth for the last several years, with little fluctuation. Companies using this method often stick to the average industry growth rate. Some companies use the following formula to arrive at the forecast:

$$\text{Next year's sales} = \text{This year's sales} \times \frac{\text{This year's sales}}{\text{Last year's sales}}$$

Time Series Analysis

Using this method, the forecaster studies the past sales data of the company and attempts to discover a pattern or patterns in the company's sales over time. In case a pattern is identified, it can be used to prepare a forecast. It is based on business cycle theory and assumes the past sales trends will continue in the future. It can best be used for long-term company forecasts and industry sales projections.

Time series approach generally involves ***trend analysis, cycle analysis, seasonal analysis,*** and ***random factor analysis.***

In case of **trend analysis**, the forecaster examines aggregate sales data, such as annual sales for a period of several years to find out whether the sales were mostly stable, rising, or falling. **Cyclic analysis** concerns studying sales figures for three to five years to find out if the sales fluctuate in a consistent, periodic manner. The forecaster undertakes **seasonal analysis** to examine daily, weekly, or monthly sales figures to determine the degree of impact of natural factors such as seasons or festivals. **Random factor analysis** examines sales variations due to non-recurrent or random factors such as impact of drought, floods, spread of seasonal diseases, and other natural disasters. For example, we have seen the impact of regional or widespread droughts on demand of a variety of products in India. The analysis is based on the assumption that these elements are combined in the following relationship:

$$\text{Sales} = T \times C \times S \times R \text{ (Trend} \times \text{Cycle} \times \text{Season} \times \text{Random factors)}$$

Time series analysis is viewed as an effective method of forecasting for products that have a reasonably stable demand, but not for products that experience highly fluctuating demand.

Regression Analysis (Correlation Method)

This method resembles time series analysis. The forecaster attempts to detect any relationship in historical sales data, that is, between past sales and one or more variables such as population, per capita income, or GDP. This requires the use of regression analysis to examine the statistical relationships among changes in sales over the past years and changes in one or more variables. Based on this analysis, the forecaster attempts to develop a mathematical formula that accurately establishes a relationship between company sales and one or more variables. The mathematical formula describes only the associational relationship and not the causal relationship. After the forecaster develops an accurate formula, the necessary information is inserted to develop the sales forecast.

The drawback of this method is that a forecaster can seldom establish a kind of perfect correlation between variables considered and sales. Some other factors such as sales force compensations or their motivation are often correlated with sales performance. This method is hardly of any use to forecast sales of new products because there is no past data available.

Econometric Models

These models represent economic theories in mathematical terms. These models can be verified with the help of statistical methods and are used to measure the impact of one economic variable upon another to predict future events. Application of econometric models to forecast is viewed as portraying the real world situations vividly reflecting the impact of multiple variables having their impact on sales of products or services.

In developing econometric models, sales are considered as the dependent variable influenced by many factors that perpetually interact and cause sales. Factors causing sales are independent variables and can be non-economic and economic in nature, such as natural factors, employment, income etc.

These mathematical models are believed to be more accurate but quite expensive to develop, complex in nature, and require the use of computers. These models are good for forecasting the demand for industrial products and consumer durable goods at industry level where replacement demand is an important factor. Generally, individual companies do not use econometric models to forecast their own sales.

Market Tests

This method involves making the product available to potential customers in one or more test markets to measure their response to price, promotion, and distribution. This method permits the evaluation of resulting sales volume in response to variations in price, packaging, intensity of various promotions, and distribution. Test results of consumer response are used to forecast sales for larger geographic areas.

This is a good method for forecasting sales of new products or existing products in new markets. Test market also furnishes information about actual customer responses rather than approximation of behaviours. The disadvantage of test market is that it is expensive and time consuming and may not reflect the response of total market.

Combination Methods: Based on their past experiences, many companies use only one method of sales forecasting that they have found to be reliable. Many companies believe that no single method is completely reliable and to have more confidence in the forecast, they use a combination of two or more methods. If the forecasts developed by using different methods do not show wide variations, the company develops more confidence in the forecast. Sometimes, just to verify the outcomes of one method, a company might use another method. But in the ultimate analysis, a forecast is only as good as its accuracy. If a particular method works for a company, it should probably stick to it.

Summary

Market potential refers to the highest possible expected industry sales of a product or service. Company potential is a quantitative estimate of maximum possible sales opportunities for a company within a given market area for which the forecast is made under assumed ideal conditions and marketing efforts. Company sales forecast represents the sales estimate that the company actually expects to achieve, based on market conditions, company's resources, and its marketing programme.

Qualitative or judgemental methods consider factors related to expertise and human judgement. These methods are generally used in conjunction with some others to build more confidence in the forecast. Qualitative approaches have the advantage of adjusting to sudden shifts in environmental circumstances. These methods include (1) jury of executive opinion, (2) Delphi method, and (3) sales force composite method.

The advantage of using quantitative methods of forecasting eliminates any subjectivity that is not possible with qualitative methods. The limitations include the nature and validity of assumptions used and also the mathematical approaches tend to generalise on the basis of past experience. There is hardly any scope to adjust to sudden shifts as may happen in case of high technology industries. These methods include (1) simple projection, (2) time series analysis, (3) regression analysis, (4) econometric methods, and (5) market tests. Econometric models are complex and require the use of computers.

All methods of forecasting have certain advantages and drawbacks. To eliminate risks and develop more confidence in forecasts, companies often use a combination of more than one forecasting method.

Questions for Discussion

1. What is the distinction among market sales potential, company sales potential and company sales forecast?
2. Why do companies believe in developing a sales forecast?
3. Suggest two methods of sales forecasting for an industrial products company. Give your reasons for their suitability.
4. Suggest two methods for developing sales forecast for a company dealing in mass consumption, non-durable products.

Project

1. You are planning to start a restaurant serving only vegetarian dishes. Obviously, you have no previous data. Develop a forecast for your first year sales.

Bibliography

1. Philip Kotler, *Marketing Management,* Pearson Education, 11th Ed., 2003.
2. "World's New Steel King," *Hindustan Times,* 26 October 2004.
3. Robin T. Peterson, "The Role of Experts' Judgement in Sales Forecasting," *Journal of Business Forecasting* (Summer 1990).

Consumer Behaviour - Personal and Organisational

LEARNING OBJECTIVES

After going through this chapter, you will understand:

- Impact of culture, subculture, family, social class, and reference groups on consumer preferences and behaviour
- Influence of motivation, perception, learning, attitudes, personality, demographic factors, lifestyle, situations, and involvement on consumers' buying behaviour
- The consumers' decision process steps
- In what ways do organisational consumers differ from personal consumers in their purchase decisions
- Different decision situations for business consumers and the decision process

The power of culture is a great influence in all decisions. And cultural creativity works the ultimate magic with consumers. Semiotic analysis is a form of focused desk research, which is done before touching base with consumers. One examines the communications of both the client and competitors: advertising, products, packaging, retail environments, promotions, historical and current. By evaluating the data, one can find out the cultural 'body language' unconsciously coded into brand messages. This allows one to see how consumers (consciously and unconsciously) use contexts, codes, myths and metaphors to make those all-important cultural connections with the brand and its spectrum of marketing messages.

Titoo Ahluwalia, Chairman ORG-MARG, while making a presentation in the Confederation of Indian Industry (CII) marketing summit held in Delhi said, "The rational and psychological levels in communication can be probed using conventional research techniques but the cultural level is more difficult to assess. That is because the culture is 'encoded' in everyday living and the average consumer cannot decode his own culture." With hypotheses developed by the semiotic analysis, one has an infinitely sharper and focused set of questions when one does get to talk to people. It helps market researchers in analysing and understanding the data much better. Says Sonia Pal, group product manager, MBL RCG, "Semiotics is used frequently in interpretations of the research we do. Even if there is no formal semiotic research phase in the study, we use semiotics to help us understand data better."

Semiotics looks at things through the other end of the marketing telescope: the cultural end. It bases the interpretation of what it sees firmly on the theory of consumers and culture. In semiotics, consumers are not independent spirits, articulating their original opinions and making their own individual buying decisions. By and large, consumers are products of the popular culture in which they live. They are constructed by the communications of that culture.

Neeta Gopal, Research Director, Probe Qualitative Research, gives an account of an actual instance where semiotics were used. She says, "In the late 1990s, we were involved in a re-launch of a leading malted food drinks brand. This brand was the market leader for ages. There was a new entrant, which was threatening its supremacy. So it was decided to go in for a re-launch of the brand. The shape of the bottle and the packaging was to change while the product was to remain the same. The new packaging was tested out with both mothers and children. The colours being tested out with consumers were bright yellow and dark purple, which were liked by the children but were rejected by the mothers. We tried semiotics to understand the cultural context behind the consumer's choice. It came out that MFD stood for food and nutrition that helped their child's growth. Bright colours like yellow and purple were creating a dissonance in the minds of the mothers." Strategically used, semiotic research can provide a ground plan, from which to structure and orchestrate all these other activities. Tactically, semiotic research can be focused on precisely how brand communications work. So specially designed programmes can have huge value for all forms of tactical creative development.

(Source: Sandeep Bhalla, "Culture Shock," A & M, October 15, 2000).

One of the very few aspects common to all of us is that we are all consumers and the reason for a business firm to come into being is the presence of consumers who have unfulfilled, or partially fulfilled needs and wants. Buyer behaviour is an extremely important and complex subject for any marketer. At the same time, it is important to appreciate that there is no unified, tested, and universally established theory on this subject. Buyer remains an enigma and her/his mind is viewed as a black box. Before businesses can develop marketing strategies, they must understand what factors influence buyer behaviour and how they make purchase decisions to satisfy their needs and wants. Understanding buyer behaviour and "knowing buyers" are not that simple. It is almost impossible to predict with one hundred per cent accuracy how buyers will behave in a certain situation. Buyers are moved by a complex set of deep and subtle emotions. Their behaviour results from deeply held values and attitudes; their perceptions of the world and their place in it, from common sense, impulse, or just plain whimsy.

"Consumer behaviour refers to the mental and emotional processes and the observable behaviour of consumers during searching, purchasing, and post consumption of a product or service."

Satish K. Batra and S. H. H. Kazmi, 'Consumer Behaviour', Excel Books, 2004.

Buyer behaviour has two aspects: the final purchase activity visible to any observer and the detailed or short decision process that may involve the interplay of a number of complex variables not visible to anyone. Actual purchase is just one activity, but the process is initiated several steps prior to a purchase and often progresses beyond consumption. In fact, purchase behaviour is the end result of a long process of consumer decision-making, influenced by many variables.

FIGURE 8.1
Various Factors Influencing Consumer Behaviour

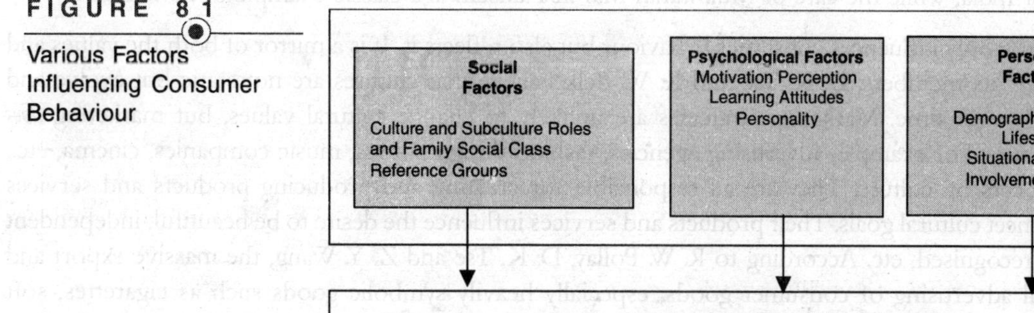

The terms 'buyer' or 'consumer' are used both for personal consumers and organisational consumers and refer to two different kinds of consuming entities. The **personal consumer** buys products or services for personal or household consumption for final use, such as salt, toothpaste, computer, gifts, etc.

The term **'organisational consumer'** includes for profit and not-for-profit organisations. They buy products, equipments, and services required for running these organisations, such as stationery, raw materials, computers, telephone services, advertising services, etc.

SOCIAL FACTORS

Social factors refer to forces that other people exert and which affect consumers' purchase behaviour. These include culture and subculture, roles and family, social class, and reference groups.

Culture and Subculture

Culture influences consumers through the norms and values established by the society in which they live. It is the broadest environmental factor that influences consumer behaviour. The impact of culture is automatic and almost invisible and its influence on behaviour is usually taken for granted. Culture operates primarily by setting somewhat loose boundaries for an individual within a society and by influencing the functions of different institutions such as family and mass media.

McCort and Malhotra define culture as "*the complex whole that includes knowledge, belief, art, law, morals, customs, and any other capabilities and habits acquired by humans as members of society.*"

Culture operates primarily by setting somewhat loose boundaries for individual behaviour within a society and by influencing the functioning of different institutions such as family and mass media. Within the given framework of culture, individual and household lifestyles evolve. The boundaries set by culture on behaviours are referred to as *norms,* derived from cultural values and are the rules permitting or prohibiting certain types of behaviours in specific situations. Members of a society obey cultural norms without deliberation because behaving otherwise is viewed as unnatural. For example, we are rarely aware of how close we stand to other individuals in a formal meeting. This norm is adhered to, though this well-defined distance varies from culture to culture. In India, kissing women in public is not an accepted norm, while in Western cultures it is quite normal. Persons flouting cultural norms face *sanctions* or penalties, which can be in the form of mild or severe social disapproval. There are any number of organised group reprisals in the rural areas of India, while the care of Mukhtaran Mai in Pakistan is a classic example of its fallout.

Culture not only influences consumer behaviour but also reflects it. It is a mirror of both the values and possessions of its members. D. K. Tse and R. W. Belk believe that cultures are not static but evolve and change slowly over time. Marketing strategies are unlikely to change cultural values, but marketing *does* influence culture. For example, advertising agencies, fashion design houses, music companies, cinema, etc., are all producers of culture. They are all responsible for creating and producing products and services designed to meet cultural goals. Their products and services influence the desire to be beautiful, independent and socially recognised, etc. According to R. W. Pollay, D. K. Tse and Z. Y. Wang, the massive export and multinational advertising of consumer goods, especially heavily symbolic goods such as cigarettes, soft drinks, clothing, athletic gear, as well as experiential goods such as music, movies and television programming, impacts the culture and desired lifestyles of importing countries.

Culture influences what people wear, what and how they eat, where they live, etc. It has a broad influence on their buying and usage behaviour of products and services, and the extent of their satisfaction with them. For example, Indians eat their food with their fingers and shun the fork-knife-spoon combination, while in many far eastern countries, chopsticks are used for this purpose. In some cultures such as that of India, where washing clothes is done by hands, manufacturers of laundry products offer washing soaps and detergent cakes to satisfy the needs of a majority of Indians. Culture also influences to some extent how consumers purchase products and use them, and this determines the development, pricing, promotion, and distribution of products. In western countries, with their full service supermarkets, some significant differences in shopping can be observed. For example, Americans are inclined to buy groceries from supermarkets, and in larger quantities. Europeans, however, tend to shop for groceries in small, specialised outlets such as dairy, bakery, and butcher's shops, and tend to buy smaller quantities. In India, even in cities having supermarkets and large departmental stores, most people tend to shop at smaller locality-based grocery shops. Because of cultural differences, McDonald's initially faced problems in Indian markets and had to make adjustments regarding what products they offered.

Since cultures are not static and change rapidly or slowly in different societies, this becomes quite an important consideration from the marketers' point of view. For example, traditionally the role of women in India was confined within the household. As a rule, they were married at an early age, looked after household duties and bore children. In urban India, at least, the role of women is gradually getting redefined. More and more women are acquiring higher and technical education and entering several professions, which, earlier, were the sole domain of men. As a result of this, dual income households are emerging, with smaller families and increased buying power. This has thrown up several important opportunities to marketers.

Such cultural changes in India can be directly attributed to the influence of Western cultures and media influence, which emphasise freedom and equality to women. Women's liberation has become a passionately debated issue and several women activist organisations have emerged and become quite active. Young men and women postpone marriage as long as they are employed or settled in some profession. Men are learning to share household responsibilities and be more cooperative in managing everyday family affairs.

Marketers are always concerned about cultural shifts and keen to discover new products or services that consumers may want. Women are trying to become more independent financially and are joining the work force in India. The number of dual income homes is increasing in urban areas. The need to provide care to children during work hours has resulted in the emergence of childcare services such as crèches, and day-care 'play' schools. The shift to nuclear families and smaller houses/flats has led to demand not only for time saving devices but also smaller gadgets for the kitchen. Cultural shift toward greater concern for health and fitness is leading to introduction of health and fitness services, exercise equipment, clothing, and a variety of health-and-fitness related foods and drinks.

Subcultures exist within a given dominant culture. Culture is viewed as consisting of basic patterns of behaviour that exist within a society at national level. Within this broad culture, one can easily distinguish relatively more homogeneous and fairly large groups that follow the dominant cultural values but also have other quite distinct beliefs, values, customs, and traditions that set them apart from the larger cultural mainstream. These represent the subcultures that may be based on religion, region, ethnic groups, language, age, gender, and many other differences. In India, we often differentiate subcultures when someone is described as a South Indian, Punjabi, Kashmiri, Gujrati, Bengali, etc. However, the diversity of subcultures in India is simply mind-boggling. These subcultures show significant preference for a particular type of diet, clothing, ceremonies, etc.

Out of several sub-cultures in India, only some are important from the marketers' point of view for formulating separate marketing programmes. Much depends on the relevance of a product category to a particular subculture. For example, cosmetics are popular among ladies, no matter to which subculture they belong. Similarly, jeans and T-shirts are very popular among urban and semi-urban teenagers irrespective of whether they are Hindus, Muslims, Sikhs, or Christians.

Religious groups can be regarded as sub-cultures because of traditions and customs that are tied to their beliefs and passed on from one generation to the next. The members of religious sub-cultures make purchases that are influenced by their religious identity, particularly products that are symbolically and ritualistically associated with the celebration of religious holidays, festivals, weddings, birth or death in the family, etc. For example, the bride in a Hindu family is dressed in a traditional crimson sari; the bridegroom wears a *sherwani, chooridar* and dons a *pagri*. Consumption of meat, beef, pork and alcohol is also determined by one's religion. Sikh religion does not permit use of tobacco products and shaving of hair.

McDonald's had a policy of adopting uniformity across global markets. After facing problems, it has now adopted products appropriate for particular cultures. When McDonald's entered India, it had to make the most dramatic changes. Eighty per cent of the Indian population is Hindu and they don't eat beef, so there is no *Big Mac* (which contains beef). In its place, there is *Big Maharaja,* which contains mutton. Many Hindus and almost all Jains are strictly vegetarian and for this segment McDonald's offers *Vegetable Burgers.* McDonald's also claims that only vegetable oils are used. The menu also does not contain any product containing pork because a sizeable population in India is Muslim and considers it unclean. It is the consideration of religious subcultures in India that compelled McDonald's not to use beef in their burgers. Some brands of toothpaste claim to be free from animal products to meet the needs of vegetarian subcultures.

Distinct ***regional subcultures*** arise due to climatic conditions, the natural environment and available resources, language and significant social and cultural events. Such groups can be identified as having distinct and homogeneous needs, tastes, lifestyles and values. Anyone who has travelled across India would have probably noted many regional differences in consumers' consumption behaviour, particularly with regard to dress, food and drink. For example, South Indians prefer to drink coffee, while most North Indians use tea. Dog meat is considered a delicacy in certain North-Eastern parts of India, which may shock consumers in other parts of the country. Given such clear differences in consumption patterns, marketers have realised that India is in no way a single market for at least some product categories.

Geography can significantly influence the type of food people consume and the dresses they wear. Conservative Brahmin families in India are generally vegetarian. However, Kashmiri Brahmins are basically non-vegetarian. Woolens and other warm clothes are worn by North Indians during winters but because of geographic conditions, South Indians have no need for warm clothes. Most areas in South Indian states are hot and humid and probably due to this reason there is maximum consumption of toilet soaps in this geographic region. While North Indians consume more wheat, South Indians prefer a variety of rice dishes. Traditionally, Tamilians prefer to wear a white shirt and *dhoti* or *lungi* and women are very fond of wearing bright coloured silk saris.

It is more relevant for marketers to study and understand sub-cultures on a regional basis, particularly language, food habits, festivals, gift giving, customs, etc. Some major Indian sub-cultural groups include Punjabi, Gujarati, Marwari, Marathi, Tamil, Oriya and Bengali.

Marketers have attempted to identify ***age subcultures*** because they produce unique sets of shared values and behaviours in a given society. As a subcultural group, they have experienced a common social, political, historical and economic environment, which is still evolving as foreign media channels impact them heavily via TV, magazine ads, movies, etc.

Those who are over 55 years of age account for a substantial portion of India's population. People who were born between the end of World War II and India's Independence are retired and are beginning to notice the physical effects of ageing. Various healthcare and nutrition products are promoted to them (*Chayavanprash, Kesri Jeevan* etc.). Members of this generation are often grandparents, some with sufficient current incomes to indulge their grandchildren. Retirement planning is important to this group and some builders have specifically targeted this group for small independent accommodations where all sorts of facilities that they look for are available. Promotions should be directed to them in ways commensurate with their values. Many older consumers do not want to be reminded that they are old and, therefore, they tend to react against advertising that separates them from the rest of the population. Ads featuring both youngsters and oldsters using and enjoying the product often work effectively. The key is to present older people in a matter-of-fact and realistic way (e.g., Pepsi commercial featuring kids, Sachin Tendulkar and Amitabh Bachchan).

Teenagers are known to be self-conscious and in search of self-identity. Most teenagers view themselves as kind, trustworthy, likable, funny, affectionate, intelligent, creative and active. Occasionally, their behaviour is rebellious against authority, tradition and what they consider as old-fashioned values. This influences their behaviour as consumers, particularly in urban and semi-urban areas in India. They need to be accepted for support and nurturing. Most teenagers prefer to wear modern casual dresses, sports shoes of known brands, want to own autos that project a macho image, listen to pop music and watch MTV. They spend family money and often influence family purchases.

This generation group (sometimes referred to in the media as GenY) seems to have its own language (highly influenced by American slang), way of speaking and expressions. They spend (both sexes) more money on clothes, stereo equipment, music tapes and CDs, entertainment and fast food. Young women spend most of their pocket money on cosmetics, clothes, beauty aids and jewelry. Young men spend more on jeans, sports shoes, stereo equipment, music CDs and tapes and motorcycles. Teenagers are emerging as a highly consumption-oriented subcultural group, particularly in urban areas.

For many products, friends are the most significant influence. This is known as 'peer pressure'. Nevertheless, parents are still an important factor affecting many buying decisions. The brand and store preferences of this cultural subgroup tend to be enduring. This market is particularly attractive to marketers because preferences and tastes formed during these years can significantly influence purchases throughout their life. To influence them as consumers, marketers need to use appropriate language, music, images and media especially in places where these young people 'hang out' (frequent) such as shopping malls, discotheques, pubs, fast food parlours, etc.

Rituals drive Market Opportunities around the World

- There are few rituals as curious as a beauty pageant. Recent globalisation of this phenomenon provides a vivid illustration of the connections among rituals, values, and consumption behaviour. Just ask the young women of India, most of whom look up to role models like Aishwarya Rai who win beauty contests, and move through modelling into a career in films.
- If rituals are about a culture affirming and expressing its values, then the rituals embedded in a beauty pageant are probably pretty obvious, and some would argue pretty superficial as well. Be that as it may, when Lara Datta was crowned Miss Universe in May 2000, many young women in India took notice and apparently approved of the outcome. The beauty pageant ritual and Miss Datta's subsequent emergence as a role model for women in India changed the way these women thought about themselves. With this change came a new set of values concerning personal appearance that no longer was restricted to traditional ways, but instead reflected a more international concept of beauty.
- Is there hard evidence from the marketplace that values have shifted in India? Without a doubt! Analysts estimate that India's "beauty market" is worth in excess of $1.5 billion and is growing 20% each year – which is twice as fast as this market's growth in United States and Europe. The cosmetics business in India is booming with familiar players like L'Oreal, Revlon, and Clarins in hot pursuit of the opportunity. Additionally, Indian women are participating in health and fitness activities as never before. Gyms are opening from Bombay to Calcutta – and to do the gym thing the right way, one also needs all the appropriate workout gear. Even cosmetic surgeons in India have seen their business benefit from the new passion for beauty. When values shift in a culture, consumption shifts are sure to follow. Look to rituals as a way to better comprehend when and where these powerful forces are likely to manifest in the marketplace.

Adapted from: "From the Runaway to Runaway Sales." Business Week, June 19, 2000).

Many products are typically associated with ***males or females***. For example, one hardly comes across any ads showing men using products traditionally associated with women or performing tasks such as changing diapers of kids. In India, shaving products, cigarettes, trousers, ties, motorcycles, etc., are products for males; bangles, bracelets, lipstick, sari, *bindi* and *menhdi,* etc., are ladies products. However, many products now are losing their traditional gender typing, such as financial services, cars, mobile phones, computer games, equipment, etc., that are now designed keeping women's preference in mind.

In developed and most developing countries, marketers are increasingly interested in targeting working women because they constitute a sufficiently large and growing market. They have a different set of needs compared to women who do not work outside their homes. Working women shop less frequently, spend less time shopping and are more brand and store-loyal. They are more likely to go shopping after office hours in the evening. After examining advertising response to financial services, Lynn J. Jaffe has reported that the use of a "modern" positioning strategy, that is, a focus on career and family, proved more effective with women than a more traditional positioning strategy of focusing on "nurturing and family."

In recent times, a number of advertisers have realised the importance of communicating appropriately with working women and mothers.

Roles and Family

All of us occupy some positions within family, groups, organisations etc. A role refers to a set of functions and activities that an individual in a particular position is supposed to perform, based on one's own and others' expectations. An individual may have several roles and sets of expectations placed on her/his behaviour. He can be a son, husband, father, employee, friend, teacher, and club member. These different roles influence a person's general as well as buying behaviour. For example, the father is a teacher and wants to buy a laptop computer, but the son who has just entered college wants a motorcycle and insists that father should postpone his computer purchase. Such a situation may have a bearing on an individual's buying behaviour.

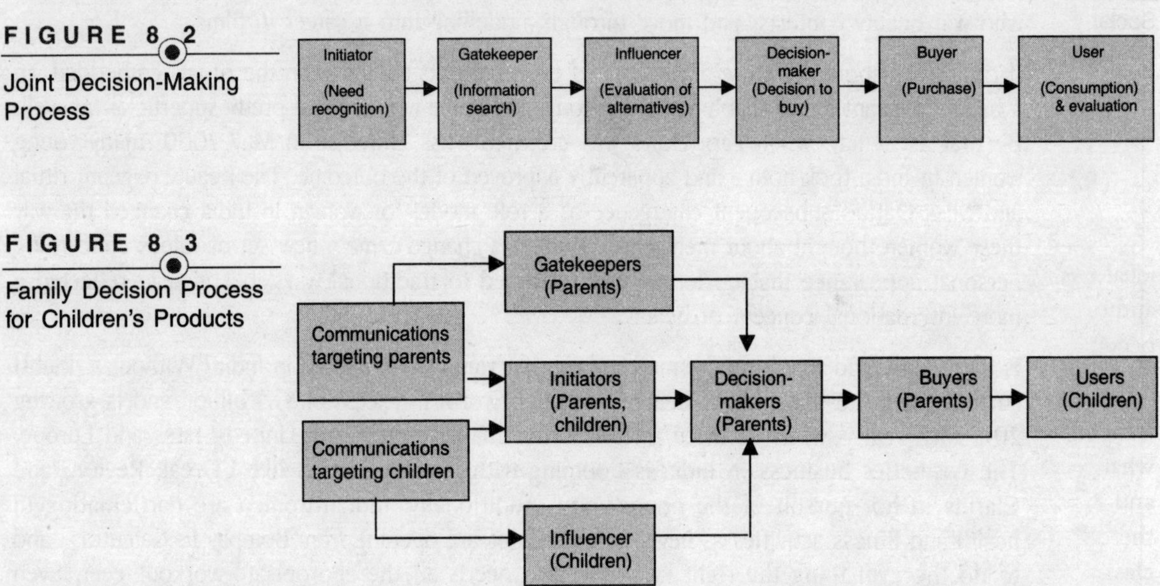

FIGURE 8.2 Joint Decision-Making Process

FIGURE 8.3 Family Decision Process for Children's Products

A person's changing roles in family lifecycle very significantly influence types of purchases and buying behaviour. Gradually, at least in urban areas women's roles are changing as many women are taking up different types of jobs. Increasing numbers are joining central and state governments in administrative positions; others are opting for professional positions such as engineers, doctors, and executives in business and industry.

In case of many products and services, husband and wife jointly make purchase decisions, particularly for durable goods. Children also now play a bigger role in some family purchases. When two or more family members are involved in making a certain purchase related decision, each may take up different role(s) such as initiator of the idea; gatherer of information regarding different brands; the decider selects specific brand and also perhaps the outlet; and finally, there is the actual buyer. Marketers need to know the influence of all these roles and develop a marketing mix that takes care of needs and wants of a target market.

Social Class

Many people like to think (and say) that all people are created equal. However, in all societies there are some people who are ranked higher than others. Social class can be viewed as a range of social positions in a society. 'Social class defines the ranking of people in a society into a hierarchy of distinct status classes; upper, middle and lower, so that the members of each class have relatively the same status based on their power and prestige.'

Social class means societal rank, which is one's position relative to others on one or more dimensions valued by society. Social class is based on demographic variables that others in society aspire for and hold in high esteem. These characteristics precipitate unique behaviours. Social classes range from the lower to the upper. Those with few or none of the socio-economic factors desired by society represent lower class, while persons who possess many of the socio-economic characteristics desired by the society constitute upper class. Individuals in different social classes tend to have different consumption patterns.

FIGURE 8 4

Social Class Results from Socio-economic Factors

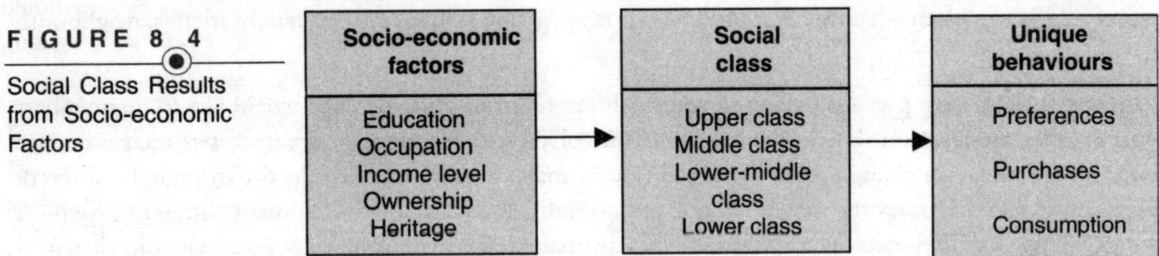

Social class is often measured in terms of social status. Subjective values set by a society determine the ideal types of people in that society. Important factors that determine the status in most societies include: authority over others; political, economic, military, or religious power; ownership of property, income, occupation, lifestyle and consumption patterns, education; public service, ancestry and connections.

Social class influences people and they may develop and exhibit common behavioural patterns. They may have similar desires, attitudes, preferences, and possessions. Consumers buy products not only for what they can do but also for what they mean, because products or services are seen to possess personal and social meanings in addition to their functional attributes. Our possessions such as the houses we live in, the cars we own, the clothing we wear, or the watches that appear on our wrists, are indicators of social class. Possessions of products or other signs of wealth have always been signs of achievement or status symbols. The things consumers buy become "symbols" that tell others who they are and what their social class is. In societies where financial wealth signifies status, possessions become an indicator of income and wealth, since others are unlikely to know how much one earns. Thus, there may be members at each social-class rung who aspire to achieve a higher status by acquiring those symbolic possessions that are marks of distinction enjoyed by a higher rung in the social status ladder.

Reference Groups

A reference group refers to a group of people with whom an individual identifies herself/himself and the extent to which that person assumes many values, attitudes, or behaviours of group members.

Almost all of us have several reference groups such as family, school or college related groups, work groups, club memberships, etc. Nearly the entire spectrum of consumer behaviour takes place within a group setting. In addition, groups serve as one of the primary agents of consumer socialisation and learning and can be influential enough to induce not only socially acceptable consumer behaviours but also socially unacceptable and even personally destructive behaviours. For example, group influences sometimes affect excessive consumption of alcohol, use of harmful and addictive drugs, shoplifting etc.

An individual can be a member of a reference group such as the family and would be said to be part of a *membership group.* This same individual may aspire to belong to a cricket club and would be said to be apart of an *aspiration group*. A *disclaimant group* is one to which an individual may belong to or join and then reject the group's values. An individual may also regard the membership in a specific group as something undesirable and to be avoided. Such a group is a *dissociative group*.

Membership groups and aspiration groups are viewed positively; disclaimant and dissociative groups are viewed negatively. Marketers advertise to appeal to the desire to be part of a group and very rarely appeal to the desire to avoid or disclaim a group. When they do, they do it for shock effect, to drive home the point in a dramatic manner. Even ad appeals used to encourage non-conformity are made on a positive note to being different from everyone else. Marketers tend to focus on membership and aspiration groups.

Group memberships and identity are very important to most of us. Apparently most of us do not like to think that we are conformists, but the truth is that we generally conform to group expectations most of the time. Marketers often advertise their products showing group settings such as family, friends, neighbours, etc.

In any society, most persons belong to several different groups and perhaps would like to be members of many other groups. Consumers who are actively involved with a certain group, treat it as their reference group. As the situation changes over time, individuals may base their behaviour on an entirely different group, which then becomes the new reference group. Individuals may belong to many different groups at the same time, but they use only one group as a primary reference group in a given situation such as immediate family, friends, co-workers, etc.

Consumers may change their behaviour to conform to beliefs and actions of reference group members. For example, new entrants to colleges in nearby cities from Indian villages are seen within a month or so to change their Kurta-Pajama to casual shirts, jeans, and sports shoes so as to appear more like other college students. In girls' colleges, other students often tease students wearing long shirt-shalwar combinations by describing them as "bahenjis" and such group pressure often compels them to leave behind conservative clothing and adopt more of those dresses that denote conformity to group norms. Some members of groups are accorded more respect because of their expertise, skill, knowledge, or status and assume the role of *opinion leaders* and may serve as role models. Marketers often identify such opinion leaders and develop advertisements featuring them as endorsers. According to Rebecca Piirto, opinion leaders have advanced education, are highly active members of their communities, are likely to have high income, and are heavy users of print media.

The degree of group influence depends on an individual's sense of identity, value systems, strength of involvement with the group and tendency of accepting influence of reference group. Reference groups may influence both purchase decision as well as the brand choice.

PSYCHOLOGICAL FACTORS

Psychological factors are internal to an individual and generate forces within that influence her/his purchase behaviour. The major forces include motives, perception, learning, attitude, and personality.

Motivation

This refers to driving forces within an individual produced by a state of tension caused by unfulfilled needs, wants, and desires. Individuals strive to reduce this tension through some appropriate behaviour that they expect will satisfy their needs. Much depends on individual thinking and learning in selecting the goals and the patterns of behaviour that they believe will satisfy their needs. Whether an individual's need is fulfilled leading to reduction of tension, depends on the course of action the individual takes.

FIGURE 8.5
Motivation Process

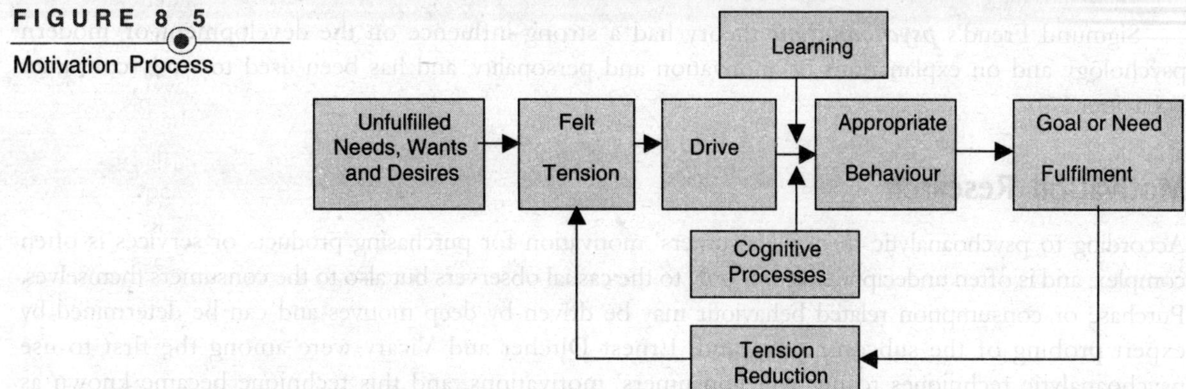

Consumers, at any given time, are generally influenced by a set of motives rather than just one motive. The strength of an individual's motives may vary at different times and occasions. For example, a person's motive for water and food would be much stronger after observing a twelve-hour fast than after having had water and food two hours earlier. Many different motives influence purchase behaviour at the same time. A middle-income group person buying a car might be motivated by several characteristics, such as transportation convenience, comfort, social distinction, and economy. This will have implications for auto manufacturing companies offering cars to consumers.

Every person has needs. Some of these needs are basic to sustaining life and are in-born with needs such as air, water, food, and shelter, etc. Acquired needs are learnt needs that we acquire as a result of being brought up in a particular culture and society. For example, needs for self-esteem, prestige, affection, power and achievement are all considered as learned needs. Motives may also be classified as utilitarian or hedonic. A consumer's utilitarian needs focus on some practical benefits and are identified with product attributes that define product performance such as economy or durability.

Hedonic motives relate to achieving pleasure from the consumption of a product or service and are often associated with emotions or fantasies. Hedonic needs are more experiential as they are closely identified with the consumption process. For example, a hedonic need might be the desire to be attractive to the opposite sex. The evaluative criteria for brands are usually emotional rather than rational (utilitarian).

Abraham Maslow's *hierarchy of needs* theory of human motivation is one of the most popular approaches to understand consumer motivations. According to this theory, there are five basic levels of human needs, arranged in a pyramidical hierarchy and based on relative importance of need level. These are:

Physiological: This is the most basic level of primary needs for things necessary to sustain life, such as food and water, shelter, clothing, and sex.

- ***Safety:*** This need level relates to safety and security from physical harm.
- ***Love and belonging:*** This concerns acceptance, belonging, satisfying relationships, love, and affection.
- ***Esteem:*** This relates for feeling a sense of accomplishment; and a need to gain recognition, status, and respect.
- ***Self-actualisation:*** This concerns the desire to realize one's potential and achieve whatever one is capable of—self-fulfillment.

According to Maslow, the lower order physiological and safety needs must be satisfied first before higher order needs become meaningful. After satisfying lower order needs, the individual attempts to satisfy higher order needs, such as esteem needs. In reality, the *lower order needs are a perpetual source of motivation for consumer purchase behaviour*.

Sigmund Freud's ***psychoanalytic*** theory had a strong influence on the development of modern psychology and on explanations of motivation and personality, and has been used to study consumer behaviour.

Motivation Research

According to psychoanalytic theory, consumers' motivation for purchasing products or services is often complex, and is often undecipherable not only to the casual observers but also to the consumers themselves. Purchase or consumption related behaviour may be driven by deep motives and can be determined by expert probing of the subconscious mind. Ernest Ditcher and Vicary were among the first to use psychoanalytic techniques to uncover consumers' motivations, and this technique became known as **motivation research**. Some of the methods used to probe the subconscious mind include:

In-depth interviews – the researcher asks a consumer to talk freely, using specific questions designed to gain insights into a consumer's motives, opinions, or ideas.

Projective techniques – pictures or designs are used to have an insight into consumer's motives, values, attitudes, or needs, which are hard to express. Respondents project these internal states on these pictures, designs or some other external object.

Association tests – the respondent is presented with a stimulus such as word, picture, or some other thing and asked to respond with the first thing that comes to mind.

Focus group – a small group of individuals from the target market are brought together to discuss a particular product, service, issue, or idea.

Human behaviour is said to be goal-oriented. Marketers are particularly interested in consumers' goal-oriented behaviour that concerns product, service or brand choice. They want consumers to view their products or brands as those that would best satisfy their needs and wants.

To satisfy any specific need, there are a number of solutions or goals. For example, to satisfy hunger any type of food is good enough but the individual consumer's goal may be a chicken roast. The goal selection depends on an individual's personal experiences, physical capacity and prevailing cultural norms and values and whether the goal object is accessible. Another important factor is the self-image the individual holds about herself/himself. A person acquires or would like to acquire products perceived as closely reflecting the self-image the individual holds. Specific goal objects are often chosen not only because they satisfy specific needs but also because they are perceived as symbolically reflecting the individual's self-image.

TABLE 8.1
Some Typical Motives

Hunger	Pleasure	Revenge
Safety	Taste	Manipulation
Rest/Sleep	Competition	Efficiency
Possession	Curiosity	Social distinction
Achievement	Power	Ambition
Parental protection	Sympathy	Physical activity
Approval of others	Respect	Economy
Play	Cleanliness	Leisure

Many of the needs of an individual remain dormant for long periods. The arousal of any particular set of needs at any given point in time gets triggered by an individual's physiological condition, emotional or thinking processes or due to situational factors.

- ***Physiological Arousal:*** Most of the physiological cues are involuntary and often arouse some related needs. For example, a person may heat up water on a store to take a bath, and may make a mental note to buy a geyser.
- ***Emotional Arousal:*** Sometimes latent needs are stimulated because a person gets involved in thinking or daydreaming about them. This occurs when consumers deliberate about unfulfilled needs. For example, a young man who wants to become a cricket player may identify with Sachin Tendulkar and use products endorsed by him commercially.
- ***Cognitive Arousal:*** Sometimes just random thoughts may stimulate arousal of needs. An ad "home away from home" may remind a person of home and he may suddenly become aware of his need to call his wife or children.
- ***Situational Arousal:*** A certain situation confronting a consumer may also trigger arousal. This can occur when the situation attracts attention to an existing bodily condition. For example, seeing an ad of Coca-Cola or a display suddenly makes one aware of being thirsty. The need would have been presented but was not strong enough to trigger arousal. Similarly, seeing a kitchen gadget in use may activate the need to buy that gadget.

Perception

Perception is the process by which an individual selects, organises, and interprets stimuli into a meaningful and coherent picture of the world. Stimuli may include products, packages, brand names, advertisements and commercials, etc. Perception is an individual process and depends on internal factors such as an individual's beliefs, experiences, needs, moods, and expectations. Perception is also influenced by the characteristics of stimuli such as the size, colour, and intensity, and the context in which it is seen or heard.

Perception includes three distinct processes:

- Sensation
- Information selection
- Interpreting the information

Sensation is the immediate, direct response of the sense organs (eyes, ears, nose, mouth, and skin) to a stimulus such as brand name, package, advertisement and so on. A ***stimulus*** is any unit of input to any of the senses. Marketers are interested in knowing the physiological responses of the consumers to various marketing stimuli such as visual and audio elements of a commercial or the design of the product package so that it would attract consumer attention.

Information selection refers to paying attention to particular stimuli. Sensory inputs are only part of the perceptual process. There are internal psychological factors that include a consumer's personality, needs, motives, expectations, and experiences. The individual psychological factors explain as to why people pay attention to some of the things and ignore others. For this reason it is not unusual that people select, attend, understand, and perceive the same stimuli in different ways. Consumers pay attention only to those stimuli that are relevant to their needs or interests and filter out the irrelevant ones. In a typical day we are exposed to a large number of stimuli but can remember only those that seem to be relevant to us and ignore all others.

Interpreting the information requires people to organise, categorise, and interpret the information registered by the senses. This process is uniquely individual as it is based on what individuals expect to see in the light of their experiences, the number of possible explanations they can think of, their personality, needs, motives, etc. The meaning attributed to a stimulus depends in part on the nature of stimulus. Some ads attempt to communicate objective, factual information in a straightforward manner, others are ambiguous and apparently seem to have no relationship with an advertised product and the individual will usually interpret the meaning in such a way that they serve to fulfil personal needs, wishes, interests, etc. An individual's interpretation of reality depends on clarity of the stimulus, past experiences, her/his motives, and interests at the time of perception. In a way, perception is a filtering process wherein internal and external factors influence what is received, and how it is processed and finally interpreted.

- ***Selective perception*** can possibly occur at the exposure, attention, comprehension, or retention stage of the perceptual process. Selective exposure can occur when a person chooses not to attend or ignore a stimulus, as happens during zapping and zipping. *Selective attention* is the outcome when an individual chooses to pay attention to certain stimuli and ignore others.

- ***Selective comprehension*** results when consumers interpret information on the basis of their attitudes, beliefs, motives, and experiences. For example, an ad that speaks against the preferred brand of a consumer may be interpreted as biased, untruthful, and the claims totally ignored. The information is often interpreted in a manner that supports the consumer's position.

- ***Selective retention*** is also a common phenomenon. Consumers do not retain all the information in their memory that the advertisement attempts to communicate even after attending and comprehending it. Advertisers use symbols, slogans, images, and associations to ensure that the information is available when it is time for purchase action.

Subliminal perception: As postulated by psychoanalytic theory, people are motivated below their level of conscious awareness. Stimulated below their level of conscious awareness, they perceive stimuli without actually being aware that they are doing so. Subliminal perception is the ability to perceive stimuli that are below the level of conscious awareness because the stimuli are either too weak or extremely brief to be consciously noticed. The stimuli are below the threshold of awareness but obviously not below the absolute threshold of the receptors involved. Constant repetition, not the strength or duration, is what makes them effective.

Learning

Learning is viewed as a relatively permanent change in behaviour occurring as a result information or experience, both direct and indirect. Schiffman and Kanuk have defined consumer learning as:

"The process by which individuals acquire the purchase and consumption knowledge and experience they apply to future related behaviour."

There are two basic approaches to learning: (1) behavioural approach, and (2) cognitive learning approach. The emphasis of behavioural learning is on external environmental stimuli, which are responsible for eliciting the behaviour and minimise the importance of internal psychological processes. Behavioural learning considers stimulus – response relationship as leading to learning, and cognitive learning is based on the premise that learning also occurs as a result of mental activity.

Classical conditioning (also called respondent conditioning) assumes that learning process is associative and there is relationship between a stimulus and a response. For example, the salivation resulting in dogs at the sight of food is not taught but is an innate reaction, as was demonstrated in Pavlov's experiments with dogs. Since this connection between food and salivation exists before the conditioning process, the food is termed as *unconditioned stimulus* and salivation as the *unconditioned response.* Pavlov showed that by pairing a neutral stimulus such as ringing a bell, with the unconditioned stimulus (in this case, food) for a number of repetitions, the dogs learned to salivate at the sound of ringing bell. And thus, the bell became a *conditioned stimulus* that resulted in *conditioned response,* that was similar to the original unconditioned response.

Two conditions are important for learning to occur through classical conditioning. The first condition is that unconditioned stimulus and conditioned stimulus must be close in time and space, and the second important condition is the *repetition.* There will be stronger association between the two, if the unconditioned and conditioned stimuli occur together more frequently.

Classical conditioning plays an important role in marketing as the consumers can be conditioned to develop favourable brand impressions. Marketers attempt to develop favourable associations of consumers' perceptions, emotions, and impressions for their products and services so that the reactions elicited are favourable. For example, the commercial of Liril soap shows quite pleasant settings. Classical conditioning can develop favourable emotional associations with the product or service. This is the reason that many ads use humour, popular music, or feature attractive personalities or exciting sports events.

Operant conditioning (instrumental conditioning) views the individual as an active participant in the learning process by acting on some aspects of the environment. The individual's response leads to getting a positive reinforcement (a reward) or negative reinforcement (punishment). According to operant conditioning, *behaviour is a function of its consequences.* A favourable consequence or reward with a particular behaviour is an important element of operant conditioning. Reinforced behaviour strongly cements the bond between a stimulus and response. For example, if a consumer experiences positive outcome after buying a product, the chances that this consumer will use the product again increase. Conversely, if the outcome is unfavourable, the chances of repurchase of the product decrease.

Cognitive learning theorists are of the opinion that a significant amount of learning takes place as a result of consumer thinking and problem solving. It is not unusual that we sometimes see the solution immediately when faced with a problem. More often, consumers are likely to search for information on which to base their decision-making and carefully evaluate what they learn in order to reach the best decision alternative. According to this theory, the kind of learning most typical of human beings is problem solving, which enables them to exercise some control over their environment. Consumer behaviour typically involves making choices and decisions. Mental processes such as perception, developing beliefs about different brands, and formation of attitudes are important to understand consumer decision-making process for many types of purchase situations.

Brand beliefs

- How likely is it that I will get a highly carbonated soft drink if I buy brand "B"?

  Very likely ___ ___ ___ ___ ___ ___ ___ Very unlikely

  Rate brand "B" by the following attributes:

- Highly carbonated ___ ___ ___ ___ ___ ___ ___ Not carbonated

  Indicate how well brand "B" is described by the following attributes:

- **Highly carbonated**

  Describes accurately ___ ___ ___ ___ ___ ___ ___ Does not describe

Attribute evaluation

How important is buying a highly carbonated soft drink?

Contd...

Very important ___ ___ ___ ___ ___ ___ ___ Not important

Indicate the degree of satisfaction that you would get from the following:

Highly carbonated

Very satisfying ___ ___ ___ ___ ___ ___ ___ Not satisfying

Think of your ideal brand of soft drink and rate it on the attributes listed below:

Highly carbonated ___ ___ ___ ___ ___ ___ ___ Not carbonated

Overall brand evaluations

Rate brand "B" as follows:

I like it very much ___ ___ ___ ___ ___ ___ ___ I don't like it

Which of the following brands do you prefer most? Which brands do you prefer as second, third, fourth alternatives, and so on?

Key brands of soft drink 1, 2, 3, 4 ———— .

Rate brand "B' as follows:

Very favourable ___ ___ ___ ___ ___ ___ ___ Very unfavourable

Intention to buy

What is the likelihood that you would buy brand "B" the next time you purchase a soft drink?

Definitely will buy _____

Probably will buy _____

Might buy _____ (Names of key soft drink brands to be listed)

Probably will not buy _____

Definitely will not buy _____

Attitudes

According to Krech and Crutchfield, "*An attitude is an enduring organisation of motivational, emotional, perceptual, and cognitive processes with respect to some aspect of our environment.*" In the context of consumer behaviour, Schiffman and Kanuk have defined attitude as *"a learned predisposition to behave in a consistently favourable or unfavourable way with respect to a given object."*

Consumers have attitudes toward many things that are relevant to products, brands, companies, celebrities, advertisements, etc. Attitudes are viewed as quite important in the object evaluation process, products, or companies and can be favourable or unfavourable feelings and behavioural inclinations. Research supports the assumption that attitudes strongly affect consumer behaviour.

Multi-attribute attitude models view an object as possessing many attributes that form a basis on which consumers develop their attitudes. According to this, consumers form attitudes toward a brand on the basis of their *beliefs* about the brand. These beliefs are developed by processing information based on personal experiences with the brand and from information collected from other sources. Information processing leads to thoughts or beliefs about products or brands which in turn lead to the formation of attitude that are used in the evaluation of products or brands.

A product has many attributes and an individual will process information and develop beliefs about many of these attributes. Favourable or unfavourable feelings are also developed on the basis of the beliefs held about these attributes. This attitude model can be put in an equation form as:

$$A_o = \sum_{i=1}^{n} b_i \, e_i$$

Where A_o = the person's attitude toward the brand

b_i = the strength of her/his belief that the brand

is related to attitude i

e_i = her/his evaluation or intensity of feelings

toward attribute i

n = the number of relevant beliefs for that person

To illustrate, a consumer may have beliefs (b_i) about various brands of fairness cream on certain attributes. One brand may be perceived as having 'X' ingredient and thus preventing pimples, without greasiness, and is flesh tinted. Another brand may be perceived as not having these attributes, but consumers may believe that it performs well on other attributes such as having sunscreen – protecting the skin from harsh sunrays – and also prevents wrinkles. To predict attitude, the marketer must know how much importance consumers attach to these attributes (e_i). Beliefs about specific attributes are called ***salient beliefs*** that marketers should try to identify.

Marketing managers can apply several methods to measure consumer attitudes. A simple method is to ask consumers directly. For example, a researcher might ask respondents what they think about the taste of a newly introduced soft drink. Researchers also have the option of using projective techniques employed in qualitative or motivation research to measure consumer's attitudes. Sometimes researchers prefer to employ available attitude scales to evaluate consumer's attitudes. Attitude scales comprise of a series of adjectives, sentences, or phrases about an attitude object to which respondents are required to respond.

Personality

Personality refers to a dynamic concept that describes the growth and development of an individual's whole psychological system, which looks at some aggregate whole that is greater than the sum of the parts. A frequently quoted definition of personality is the one given by Gordon W. Allport. According to him, "*Personality is the dynamic organisation within the individual of those psychological systems that determine his unique adjustment to environment.*"

There seems to be much controversy regarding the exact nature of personality. However, the concept of personality is viewed as very real and meaningful as personality characteristics help us describe and differentiate between individuals. Most authorities seem to be in general agreement that personality of an individual is made up of her/his inherited characteristics and the interactions with environment and moderated by situational conditions. It is the composite total outcome of an individual's psychological make up, motives, beliefs, attitudes, habits, and overall outlook.

TABLE 8.2
Measurement Scale of Self-concepts

	Ext.	Ver.	Som.	Nei-nor	Som.	Ver.	Ext.	
Rugged	___	___	___	___	___	___	___	Delicate
Excitable	___	___	___	___	___	___	___	Calm
Uncomfortable	___	___	___	___	___	___	___	Comfortable
Dominating	___	___	___	___	___	___	___	Submissive
Thrifty	___	___	___	___	___	___	___	Indulgent
Pleasant	___	___	___	___	___	___	___	Unpleasant
Contemporary	___	___	___	___	___	___	___	Non-contemporary
Organised	___	___	___	___	___	___	___	Unorganised
Rational	___	___	___	___	___	___	___	Emotional
Youthful	___	___	___	___	___	___	___	Mature
Formal	___	___	___	___	___	___	___	Informal
Orthodox	___	___	___	___	___	___	___	Liberal
Complex	___	___	___	___	___	___	___	Simple
Colourless	___	___	___	___	___	___	___	Colourful
Modest	___	___	___	___	___	___	___	Vain

Ext = Extremely, Ver = Very , Som = Somewhat, Nei-nor = Neither-Nor.
[*Source:* Naresh K. Malhotra, "A Scale to Measure Self-Concepts, Person Concepts and Product Concepts," *Journal of Marketing Research* (November 1981)].

Marketers consider four main theories of personality as more relevant to their purpose and include (1) Self-concept theory, (2) Psychoanalytic theory, (3) Social-cultural theory, and (4) Trait theory.

Most marketers consider ***self-concept theory*** as most relevant as it focuses on how the self-image or self-concept of individuals influences their purchase behaviour. Self-concept describes the totality of an individual's thoughts and feelings having reference to herself/himself as an attitude object. Each one of us has a self-concept. We see ourselves as individuals possessing certain attributes and qualities and value them. Individuals develop and alter their self-concept based on interaction of psychological and social dimensions. Research studies confirm that consumer purchases in many product categories are significantly influenced by their self-concept. According to Freud's ***psychoanalytic theory***, personality is the result of childhood conflicts between three fundamental components of personality: Id, Ego, and Superego. The id is entirely unconscious and is viewed as the source of strong basic desires and operates on 'pleasure principle'. It seeks immediate pleasure and to avoid pain. The ego represents an individual's conscious control to deal with the real world by developing capabilities of realistic thinking and tackle the environment in an appropriate manner. It operates on 'reality principle' and is capable of postponing the gratification to a time when it would be in a manner that is socially acceptable. The ego is believed to manage the conflicting demands of the id and the superego; usually striking realistic compromises. The superego constitutes the moral part of personality and represents the ideal rather than real. It defines what is right and good and affects an individual to strive for perfection. It often represses certain behaviour based on id that could disrupt the social system.

Marketers use many themes in advertising based on psychoanalytic understanding of personality such as fantasy, wish fulfillment, aggression, and escape from life's pressures. Examples of some of the product categories using some of these themes include perfumes, hair dye, skincare products, ready-to-wear garments, farmhouses, autos, and even some brands of laptop computers and cellular phones, etc.

TABLE 8.3
Consumer Innovativeness Scale

1. In general, I am among the last in my circle of friends to buy a new (Game CD*) when it appears.					
Agreement scale	5	4	3	2	1
2. If I heard that a new (Game CD) was available in the store, I would be interested enough to buy it.					
Agreement scale	5	4	3	2	1
3. Compared to my friends, I own very few (Game CDs).					
Agreement scale	5	4	3	2	1
4. In general, I am the last in my circle of friends to know the (titles of latest Game CDs).					
Agreement scale	5	4	3	2	1
5. I will buy a new (Game CD) even if I have not seen it yet.					
Agreement scale	5	4	3	2	1
6. I know the names of (new Game CDs) before other people do.					
Agreement scale	5	4	3	2	1

(*The product category and related wording can be changed to fit the researcher's objective).

Subscribers to ***social-cultural theory*** believe that social and cultural variables are more important than biological drives in the development of individual personality. They believe that childhood experiences in relating to others produce feelings of inferiority, insecurity, and lack of love. Their view is that individuals strive to win over the feelings of inferiority and search for ways to gain love, security, and relationships. Carl Jung, Freud's famous disciple believed that an individual's culture creates an accumulation of shared memories from the past such as caring and nurturing females, heroes, and wise old men.

It is fairly common for marketers to show some typical characters in advertisements that attempt to take advantage of positive shared meanings in a particular culture such as caring mother, devoted housewife, heroes with a macho image, *rishi* 's' and *sadhu* 's'.

Trait theory says that personality is composed of a set of traits that are relatively stable and describe a general pattern of behaviour. A trait is any distinct and relatively enduring characteristic in which one person differs from another.

Trait theorists construct personality tests and ask respondents to record their responses to many items. Respondents are required to mark 'agree' or 'disagree' with certain statements such as 'like' or 'dislike' certain situations or kinds of people. The responses are statistically analysed and reduced to a few personality dimensions. There are a number of standardised personality tests and evaluative techniques available. This makes using trait theory easier to study the relationship between personality and behaviour.

Personality tests that measure just one trait (such as self-confidence, or innovativeness) are called single-trait personality tests. Such tailor-made tests are increasingly being developed for use in the study of consumer behaviour.

PERSONAL FACTORS

Personal factors include those aspects that are unique to a person and influence purchase behaviour. These include demographic factors, lifestyle, and situational factors.

Demographic Factors

Demographic factors include individual customers' age, gender, education, occupation, income, marital status, family size, etc. These characteristics affect the purchase and consumption behaviour of persons. Demographic considerations have given rise to broad ways of looking at markets, such as child market, teenage market, youth market, and senior citizen market. Similarly, marketers also look at markets from the income angle: low-income group, middle-income group, high-income group, and dual income households. In general, income affects purchases because it determines how much people can afford to spend.

Buyer behaviour also varies among urban and rural consumers in conjunction with other characteristics such as education and income. It is believed that consumers with common demographic characteristics behave in relatively similar manner and tend to have similarity in many aspects, such as product and service preferences.

Demographic characteristics may affect purchase behaviour during specific stages of purchase decision process. In the present scenario, a person's age and income may affect the number and types of information sources used. For example, a university professor's and a taxi driver's income may be the same but their purchases of dresses and other discretionary products would be different. Composition of household and stage in family life cycle also influence purchase behaviour.

Younger generation in cities, with resources, use the Internet to search a variety of information and often make purchases online for some types of products. They are the ones who mainly patronise fast food outlets. The effect of occupation and education is also seen on consumer buying behaviour. Educated consumers seek more information and better quality products.

Lifestyle

Lifestyle is an indicator of how people live and express themselves on the basis of their activities, interests, and opinions. Lifestyle dimensions provide a broader view of people about how they spend their time, the importance of things in their surroundings, and their beliefs on broad issues associated with life and living and themselves. To some extent, people determine their own life styles, but the pattern is also influenced by demographic factors and personality.

Marketers use lifestyle research to segment markets, as lifestyles have strong effect on many aspects of consumer purchase decisions, including product needs, brand preference, media habits, and how and what types of shopping outlets they choose. Consumers in different countries and cultures may have characteristic lifestyles. For example, Indian women are home focused, less likely to visit restaurants, more price-sensitive, spend time preparing meals at home and are fond of movies. (Lifestyle is discussed in detail in later this chapter).

Situational Factors

Situational influences are temporary conditions or settings that occur in the environment at a specific time and place. Based on Russell W. Belk's study, situational influence refers to *all those factors particular to a time and place that do not follow from a knowledge of personal (intra-individual) and stimulus (choice alternative) attributes and that have a demonstrable and systematic effect on current behaviour.* This means that a situation is a set of factors outside of – and removed from – the relatively stable or permanent attributes of the individual consumer and also removed from the attributes of the primary stimulus object (an advertisement, or a product) to which the consumer is reacting, such as looking at an ad, or buying a product.

The consumption situation can become the basis for developing and positioning new products for specific consumer segments. For example, Timex introduced a line of watches for fitness segment. One of its models, Ironman Triathlon, is designed for joggers and swimmers and has features such as stopwatch to count time and laps and is water resistant up to 100m.

Subsequently, as computer usage spread in business, industry and government offices in India, Timex introduced a new line of watches, Timex Data Link watches, targeted at busy executives. These watches have the features of uploading phone numbers and appointments from an electronic day-planner or a personal computer to the watch's memory. This uploading can be accomplished by simply pointing the watch at the computer screen. Some other manufacturers have introduced watches that keep track of heart rate, pulse and blood pressure. Introduction of these watches is based on consumption situations.

Purchase occasions can also be related to certain situations such as birth, marriage, buying a new house, marriage anniversary, Diwali, Christmas, Mother's Day, Valentine's Day and others.

Purchase Situation may affect consumer decision about product selection. Three main factors particularly influence marketing strategy with regard to purchase situation:

In-store environment refers to stimuli present in the in-store environment and includes décor, sounds, aroma, lighting, dress and behaviour of sales personnel; product availability, shelf position, price deals, displays and physical space are important factors. According to R. W. Swinyard, store atmosphere has been shown to influence customers' mood and their willingness to visit and move around. In addition, store atmosphere also influences the consumers' judgements of the quality of the store and its image. B. Babin and W. R. Darden report that positive mood induced in the store enhances satisfaction with store, encouraging repeat visits and store loyalty. Such factors are particularly important in influencing unplanned purchases. C. Whan Park, Easwar S. Iyer and Daniel C. Smith have reported that in-store environment such as price changes, displays and sales personnel exert influence on consumer behaviour. A substantial part of sales promotion expenditures is devoted to in-store displays and promotions.

M. K. M. Hui and J. E. G. Bateson have reported that in-store crowding generally produces a negative effect for both the retail outlet and the consumer. When shoppers experience a feeling of being crowded, confined and claustrophobic, they tend to spend less time in the store by buying less, making quicker decisions and using less of the available information. This often leads to unsatisfactory purchases, unpleasant shopping experience and a decline in the probability of revisiting the store.

Service atmosphere is an important factor in influencing consumers' consumption behaviour. J. D. Herrington and L. M. Capella found that music, particularly the type consumers liked, increased their perception of how long they waited for a service. Music increased their emotional response to the service environment, to wait itself and also enhanced their willingness to continue using and recommending the service provider to others. Many services such as hairdressing, beauty parlour, bank, restaurant, dry cleaning and hospital, etc., require from a few minutes to a few days or weeks. It appears that the physical characteristics and the feelings as well as the images they create become increasingly important as hedonic motives and the time involved. Thus, physical characteristics of any of the above mentioned services might be more important than the intangible services provided.

Gift-giving Situation also influences consumer behaviour. Whether the product is purchased for personal consumption or for giving a gift also influences purchases. Marketers offer a wide range of products for gift-giving occasions.

Consumers are likely to be more involved while purchasing a gift than purchasing the same item for personal consumption. E. Fisher and S. J. Arnold have reported that consumers use different strategies and shopping criteria for gifts as against shopping for the same products for self-use. Gift-giving is more than just giving a physical product. Gifts are given as an expression of love and caring; gifts are also given to gain return favours and some social compulsions and ritualised situations, such as birthdays, are often independent of the givers' actual desires. Research shows that wedding gifts tend to be utilitarian such as durable, useful, based on newly-weds' need and often high performance; while birthday gifts are often enjoyable, unique, durable and tend to be fun. Thus, both gift giving and gift-giving occasions influence consumers' purchase behaviour. Also, the relationship between the giver and the recipient also influences purchase behaviour.

Consumers are particular about communicating the right message to the gift receiver and this may cause some anxiety because gifts carry symbolic meaning. The monetary value of the gift is either known or is knowable and can be interpreted as indicative of how much esteem the giver has for the receiver. On the one hand, the gift reflects the giver's image and thoughtfulness and on the other hand, it implies the giver's impression of the receiver's personality and image as reflected by the gift's image and functionality. S. Y. Park has noted that the meaning and nature of gift-giving is culture specific. It has also been described as a cultural ritual, often involving a sequence of symbolic behaviour. For example, the gift-giver buys a gift, removes its price tag, wraps the product, delivers it and tends to await a reaction. The outcome of gift-giving and receiving is a bond of trust and dependence between the parties.

Finding and selecting an appropriate gift often takes more time and consumer's involvement tends to be more even when the product type is less involving. To avoid any risk in product choice, consumers are likely to restrict their choice to a few well-known brands in a particular product category and also shop in stores with high-quality image.

Unanticipated Purchase Situations sometimes occur which are not anticipated. A common situation is when unexpected guests arrive and consumers have to rush for special shopping. A product failure or going out-of-stock are important situations and precipitate the need for making purchase decision. For example, the cooler fan suddenly stops working on a hot summer day, or the consumer finds a food item out of stock and may have to make a purchase trip immediately, if the item is really important. It frequently happens in India that consumers learn about sudden hike in the prices of fuel and rush to petrol pumps to get their auto tanks filled before the new prices become applicable.

Usage or consumption situation refers to the occasion of consumers' product use. When guests arrive, the type and number of items served during meals change than what is generally consumed in the family. People use different dresses to wear at home and at work. A consumer may use a particular brand of deodorant for a special occasion and another one for everyday use.

William O. Bearden and Arch G. Woodside identified seven consumption situations for beer:

- Entertaining close friends at home
- Going to a hotel or bar on Saturday night
- Watching a favourite sports event or TV programme
- Engaging in a sports activity or hobby
- Taking a weekend pleasure trip
- Working at home on the yard, house, or auto
- Relaxing at home.

Most of these situations are not unanticipated. Consumers know in advance that they would entertain friends or visit a hotel or bar. However, if friends drop in unexpectedly or the consumers take an unplanned trip, these situations may compel them to make some unplanned purchases quickly and even pay more than they ordinarily do, because of time pressures that inhibit shopping around for lower prices.

The amount of *time* available for purchase has a significant effect on consumer decision process. Generally, the less the time available, the shorter will be the information search. The less available information will most likely form the basis for decision and less than optimal purchase will be made. Being time pressured encourages brand loyalty and is a mechanism of avoiding risk. Shopping on the Internet has the potential of reducing the amount of time required to make a specific purchase and provides the consumer with almost total control over when the purchase is made. Though it is not a widely accepted practice among consumer circles in India; however, with the increase in Internet usage and dual-career households it is likely to grow more in urban areas.

Involvement Level

Consumer involvement is considered as an important variable that can help explain how consumers process the information and how this information might influence their purchase or consumption related behaviour. Judith L. Zaichkowsky has noted that there is no agreement about how to define involvement and measure the degree of involvement. However, there is wide agreement that the degree of involvement has a very significant effect on consumer behaviour. Zaichkowsky has done extensive review of involved problems in conceptualising and measuring involvement. She has observed that although there is no single precise definition of involvement, there is an underlying theme focusing on *personal relevance.*

Involvement Variables are believed to precede involvement and influence its nature and extent. These variables are believed to be the sources that interact with each other to precipitate the level of consumers' involvement at any particular time and situation.

The variables related to a person refer to that individual's personal needs, values, interests, experiences, etc. For instance, a person who is deeply interested in computers is very likely to have personal interest in computer related magazines, such as *Digit, PC Quest and Computers @ Home*, to learn about new developments in processors, hard drives and other related products.

Stimulus/object variable refers to products or stimuli that consumer perceives to be closely related to her/his values, experiences and interests and will stimulate higher degree of involvement. For example, in case of computers, one should not expect the same level of involvement for all consumers. Pradeep K. Korgaonkar and George P. Mochis found that the degree to which a consumer perceives differences in various product alternatives can also influence the level of involvement. The extent to which brands can be substituted, the number of brands available in a product category and performance features… all influence a consumer's perceived differentiation and affect the resulting degree of involvement experienced.

The extent of risk perception the consumer has with purchase decision can also influence the level of involvement. The perceived risk is the outcome of consumer's perception of the chances of potential degree of resulting unfavourable consequences from making a purchase decision, such as financial loss, or physical or psychological harm. As already discussed, researchers have suggested that the level of involvement may also be influenced by promotional messages and the media used.

Different **situations** that consumers face can also affect the degree of involvement, they will experience in making purchase decisions. For example, consumers buy candles for emergency use without much involvement at all but if the candles are needed for being placed on wife's birthday cake, the consumer may become more involved in the purchase. Consumers buy pens for everyday use without much involvement but if the pen is to be presented as a gift, then the level of involvement might increase significantly.

Involvement intensity refers to the severity of involvement as experienced by the consumer and is generally categorised as high or low. The direction refers to the focus of involvement and involvement variables will strongly affect this focus. The focus could be a product, service, advertisement, or purchase decision itself because of risk perception. *Persistence* describes the length of time, the consumer remains involved with the purchase decision. For example, car race enthusiasts seem to have an ongoing or enduring involvement in Formula-1 car races and their drivers. Photography enthusiasts seem to have a high degree of enduring involvement in cameras. On the other hand, a consumer's situational involvement is temporary. For example, a consumer may be highly involved in buying a gift for someone.

Response factors concern how a consumer behaves under involvement conditions of different intensity. These factors include different patterns of information search, information processing, evaluation of alternatives and post-decision actions. One may expect that consumers high in enduring involvement for a product will undertake regular, ongoing search for information and low involvement will result in little if any active information acquisition.

Purchase involvement is the level of concern for, or interest in, the purchase process stimulated by the need to consider a certain purchase. It is important to realise that consumer involvement can take many forms and a broad distinction is that it can be cognitive, such as a consumer may be motivated to learn about the latest specifications of the new iMac; or emotional, when a consumer is considering the purchase of a gift for his wife on their first marriage anniversary. A consumer may be very involved with a product category (coffee) or brand (Maruti Zen) and yet have very low involvement with a particular purchase because of brand loyalty, time pressure, or other reasons. Or, a consumer may have low involvement with a product such as car tyre but is highly involved because of her/his desire to save money. There are several broad types of involvement related to the product, the message, or the perceiver.

- ***Product involvement*** refers to a consumer's level of interest in a certain product. Marketers communicate many sales promotions to increase consumer involvement in a product. Tata Indica V2 sponsored a contest in which participants were to submit five words that describe the car starting with the letter "V."

- ***Advertising involvement*** refers to the consumer's interest in processing the ad messages. Television is said to be low-involvement medium and consumers process information in a passive manner. In contrast, print is a high-involvement medium as the readers actively process information.

- ***Purchase situation involvement*** may occur while buying the same item in different contexts. For example, when a consumer wants to impress someone, she/he may buy a different brand that reflects elegance and taste in a better way than the usual one that she/he buys.

Traditionally, consumer researchers have approached decision-makers from a rational perspective. The term ***consumer decision process*** brings to mind the image of an individual who is facing a clearly recognised problem and is carefully involved in evaluating the attributes of a set of products, brands, or services and very deliberately and rationally choosing the one that would deliver the maximum satisfaction at the lowest cost. Such a purchase decision begins to resemble a full-time job. For example, a consumer may literally spend days or weeks thinking about an important purchase such as a new house, even to the point of obsession. Richard W. Olshavsky and Donald H. Granbois note that such a process is not an accurate portrayal of many purchase decisions. If consumers followed this elaborate process for each decision, their entire lives would be spent making such decisions, allowing them little or no time to enjoy the things they actually buy. No doubt, some decisions are made in this manner, but many others involve little conscious effort and consumers seem to make snap decisions based on very little information. Because some purchase decisions are more important than others, the amount of effort consumers put into each one differs. J. C. Mowen found that the focus of many consumer decisions is on the feelings and emotions associated with acquiring or using the brand or with the environment in which it is purchased or used rather than its attributes. Whether consumer decisions are attribute-based or driven by emotional or environmental needs, the decision process discussed helps us gain insights into all types of purchases.

Researchers are increasingly realising that consumers actually possess a repertoire of decision strategies. A consumer evaluates the level of effort required to make a certain choice, then selects a strategy best suited for the occasion. This sequence is referred to as ***constructive processing*** and means that consumers adjust their degree of cognitive "effort" to the task at hand.

A large number of consumer-purchase decisions are related to apparently a single problem such as running low on laundry detergent or table salt. At other times, the problem may be associated with discarding the old car causing a feeling of inadequacy and buying a new but economical one to boost self-esteem, it being more in line with the present job status. The decision process may become further complicated when the consumer begins to consider the initial cost and the running cost and evaluates whether to buy a petrol or diesel driven vehicle. Finally, the consumer may wind up buying a higher-priced diesel model. In another situation, a consumer noticing a simple need for laundry detergent may want to economise and avoid one or more relatively expensive national brands and decide to buy a medium priced brand which is on promotion since she gets a small pack of toothpaste free along with the purchase.

There are various types of consumer-decision processes. It is useful to view purchase decision involvement as a continuum and as the consumer moves from a low level of involvement with the purchase situation to a high level of involvement, purchase decision-making becomes increasingly complex. Based on the amount of effort that goes into decision-making, consumer researchers have found it convenient to think that on one end is the habitual purchase decision-making or ***nominal decision-making*** and at the other extreme is ***extended decision-making.*** Many decisions fall somewhere in the middle and are characterised by ***limited decision-making.*** It should be kept in mind that the types of decision processes are not distinct but rather blend into each other.

FIGURE 8.6
Involvement Level and Types of Decision-Making

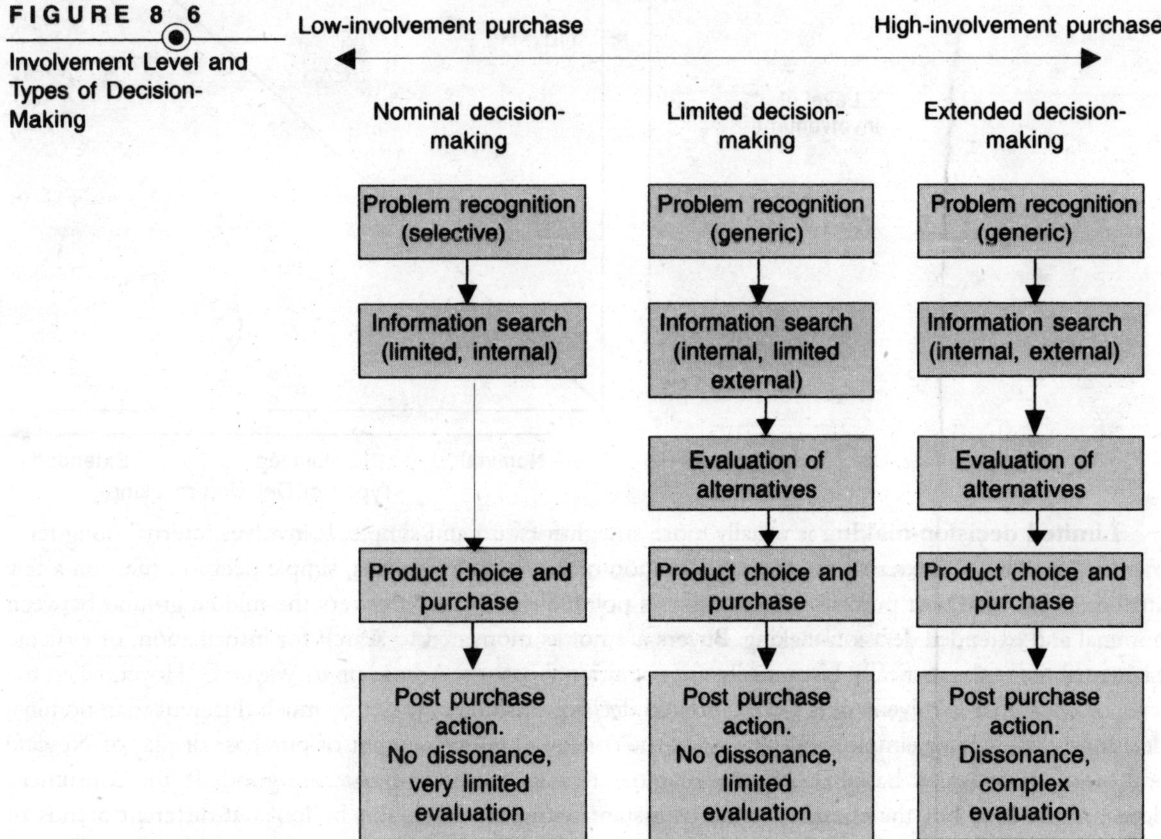

Nominal decision-making is also referred to as nominal problem solving, habitual decision-making, or routine problem solving. Recognition of need is likely to lead directly to an intention to buy. Information processing is very limited or non-existent. There is generally low-involvement with most low-priced and frequently purchased products, which are consumed on an ongoing basis and involve nominal decision-making. A problem is recognised, consumer's internal search from long-term memory comes up with a single preferred solution, the preferred brand is purchased and no brand evaluation occurs unless the brand fails to perform as expected. Some of these decisions are so nominal that the consumer does not even think of purchasing an alternative brand. Nominal decision-making is generally the outcome of continued satisfaction with a brand which was initially chosen after an extended decision-making process, or the consumer does not attach much importance to the product category or purchase. The consumer buys Aquafresh toothpaste without further consideration because it meets her/his overall needs, even though using the best available toothpaste is important to her/him. In the second situation, consumers may not attach much importance to salt or sugar they buy for household consumption. Having tried Tata Salt and found it satisfactory, they now purchase it repeatedly without any thought, when it is needed. In this category, sales promotions can lead to considerable brand switching.

Joseph W. Alba and J. Wesley Hutchinson note that such choices characterised by automatic behaviour are made with minimal effort and without conscious control. To some, such thoughtless behaviour may seem stupid, but it is actually quite efficient in most cases of routine purchases. The development of such routinised, habitual, or repetitive behaviours help consumers to minimise the time and effort devoted to mundane purchase decisions.

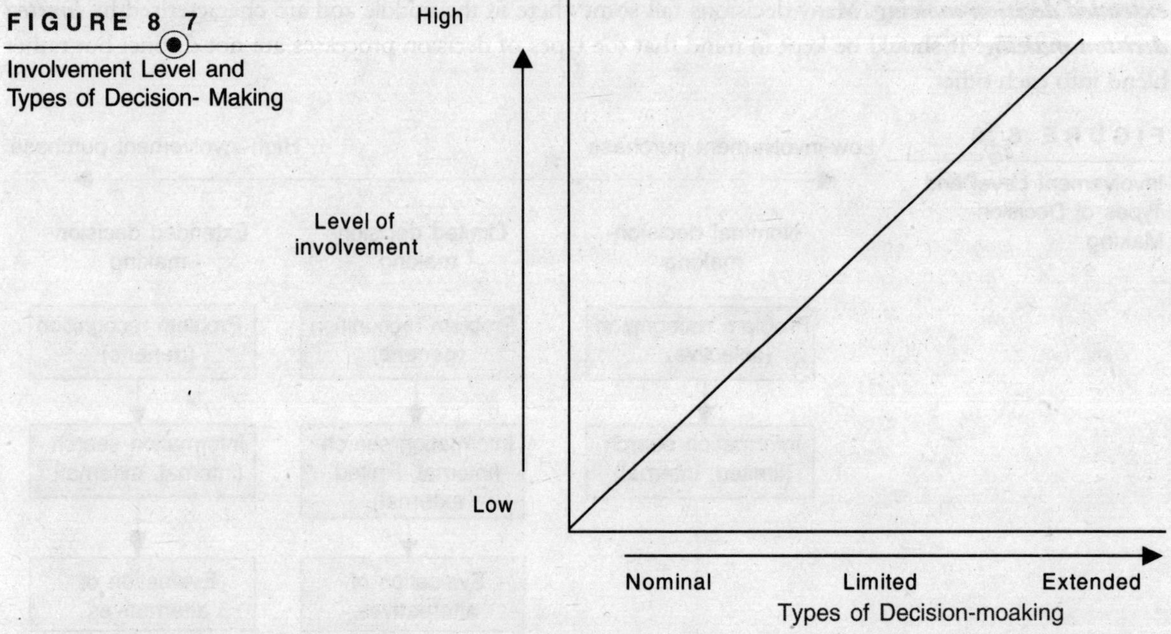

FIGURE 8.7 Involvement Level and Types of Decision- Making

Limited decision-making is usually more straightforward and simple. It involves internal (long-term memory) and limited external search, consideration of just few alternatives, simple decision rules on a few attributes and little post purchase evaluation. As pointed out earlier, it covers the middle ground between nominal and extended decision-making. Buyers are not as motivated to search for information, or evaluate each attribute enthusiastically, but actually use cognitive shortcuts. According to Wayne D. Hoyer, when the level of consumer involvement is lowest, limited decision-making may not be much different than nominal decision-making. For example, while in a store, the consumer notices a point-of-purchase display of Nescafé and picks up one pack based on her/his memory that its aroma and taste are good. If the consumer's decision rule is to buy the cheapest brand of instant coffee available, she/he looks at different brands of coffee for prices and buys the least priced brand. Sometimes, emotional factors may influence limited decision-making. For instance, a consumer may buy Colgate Total toothpaste instead of her/his regular brand just because she/he desires a change and not because of dissatisfaction with earlier brand. Such a decision may involve just reading of what is written on the carton and noticing that it has a slightly different flavour from the brand she/he had been using.

Extended decision-making corresponds most closely to the traditional decision-making perspective. Such decisions involve extensive internal (long-term memory) and external (outside sources) information search followed by a rigorous evaluation of several alternatives because consumers do not possess any meaningful information about the product or service and need lots of it. The evaluation often involves careful consideration of attributes of one brand at a time, and taking stock of how the attributes of each brand measure up to a set of desired characteristics. All this happens in response to a high level of consumer's involvement in making a purchase decision. Such complex decisions are relatively few and may relate to buying a computer, stereo system, washing machine, laser printer, or a new house. Post purchase evaluation is more likely to be complex and dissonance causing.

FIGURE 8.8

Continuum of Consumer-Decision-making

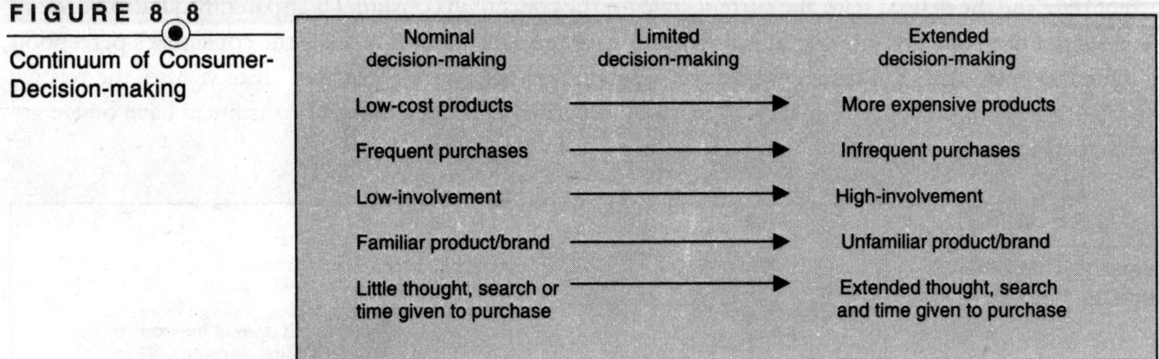

Extended decision-making may also be involved in certain emotional decisions such as choosing a birthday gift for the girl friend, decision to buy jewelry for the wife, choosing a designer dress, or buying a holiday abroad with family, etc. Some of these decisions may appear to be related to cognitive effort; however, the needs being met and the criteria being evaluated are largely emotions or feelings rather than product or service attributes. Because of the involvement of emotions or feelings, there is less external information to search for.

Consumer Decision-making Process

Consumer decision-making generally involves five stages: Problem or need recognition, information search, alternatives evaluation, purchase, and post-purchase evaluation.

Problem Recognition

Purchase decision-making process begins when a buyer becomes aware of an unsatisfied need or a problem. Problem recognition is a critical stage in consumer decision-making process because without it, there is no deliberate search for information. Rarely is there a day when we do not face multiple problems which individuals resolve by consuming products or services. We commonly face problems such as the need to replenish items of everyday consumption. For example, the consumer who runs out of milk, or cooking oil has a clear definition of the problem. Such problems are quickly recognised, defined and resolved. As another example of a routine problem, we can think of an individual who notices that the fuel meter of her/his auto is indicating very low level of fuel and goes to the first petrol pump on her/his way and gets the tank filled with petrol. Unplanned problem occurs when, for example, the refrigerator or some other major appliance breaks down. Recognition of a problem such as the need for a notebook computer may take much longer as it may evolve slowly over time.

The process of problem recognition combines some highly relevant consumer behaviour concepts such as information processing and the motivation process. First of all, consumers must become aware of the problem through information processing arising as a result of internal or external stimuli. This leads to motivating consumers; they are aroused and activated to engage in some goal directed activity (purchase decision-making). This kind of action in response to recognising problems and finding solutions to problems depends on the magnitude of the discrepancy between the current state and the desired or ideal state and secondly, the importance of the problem for the concerned consumer. The discrepancy and/or importance should be of sufficient magnitude to start the purchase process. Without perception of a problem by the consumer, there is no recognition of an existing problem and hence there is actually no need to engage in the process of decision-making. Since the consumer does not perceive any discrepancy between her/his current state and the desired state, the current state for the concerned consumer is apparently quite satisfactory and does not need decision-making. It is important to appreciate that it is actually the consumer's perception of the actual state that stimulates problem recognition and not some "objective" reality. Also, the relative importance is a critical concept in several purchase decisions because almost all consumers have budgetary or time constraints.

FIGURE 8.9

Stages in Consumer Decision Process

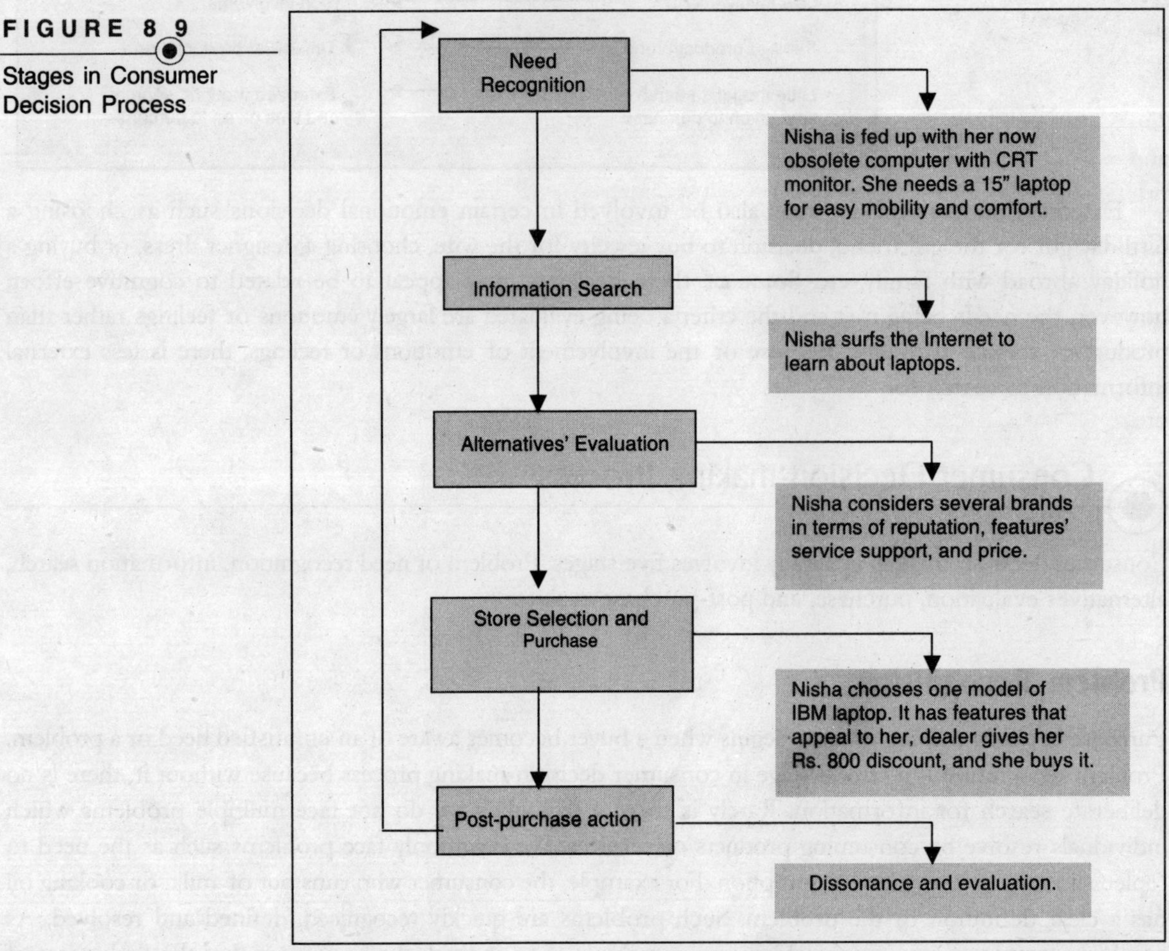

Routine problems are those where the difference between actual and desired states is expected to be felt and would call for immediate solution. For instance, convenience goods of everyday use are associated with this category of problem recognition. Both routine and emergency problems stimulate purchases of goods and services with a minimum time lag between purchase and actual consumption.

Emergency problems are possible but are unexpected and necessarily need immediate solutions. For example, say a consumer meets an accident while on his/her way to office, gets injured and the vehicle is badly damaged. In such an emergency, she/he needs a quick solution to reach a hospital's emergency room. Subsequently, she/he may plan to get the vehicle repaired or buy a new one.

Situations that can cause problem recognition include non-marketing factors and marketer initiated activities that can trigger the process of a consumer's problem recognition. The five of the most common situations are:

- ***Depletion of Stocks:*** Consumers use or consume certain types of goods every day on an ongoing basis such as groceries, toiletries and other convenience goods. No sooner has an item reached a stage, than it's about to run out, the consumer almost reflexively recognises the problem and must repurchase in order to continue fulfilling her/his need for the item. As long as the basic need for the item remains, problem recognition will keep on recurring as a result of its consumption.

- ***Dissatisfaction with Goods in Stock:*** Consumers frequently feel dissatisfied with products they own. For example, a consumer may be having chiffon saris, which are no longer in fashion and may be discontented and may desire to buy the ones currently in style. A family living in a small flat may feel that they need a larger accommodation. A student might recognise the problem that her/his computer is too slow, compared to more recent introductions.

- ***Environmental Changes:*** A family's changing characteristics are among the most significant situations and cause recognition of problems (different life cycle stages stimulate needs for different types of products). Similarly, reference group influences can also cause problem recognition.

- ***Change in Financial Situation:*** Any change in financial status almost always has an important relationship to problem recognition. Salary increase, promotion, bonuses, inheritances, etc., generally trigger spending on non-routine purchases. For example, after a promotion, the consumer may recognise that her/his auto is not reflective of her/his present status and may buy a more expensive vehicle. On the downside, if a consumer loses her/his job, then a new set of problems will be recognised and probably all future household expenditures would be affected.

- ***Marketer Initiated Activities:*** All marketers attempt to make consumers aware about their known and latent problems and convince them that they have the right solution to meet their needs. Advertising and other promotions focus on helping consumers in perceiving a difference of sufficient intensity between their desired state (ownership of the product) and their actual state (not owning the product). Marketers also attempt to influence consumers' perceptions about their existing state, for instance, the need to buy many personal care products. Women desire to use a soap to have fresh and smooth skin and the ad of Dove soap is designed to generate concern about the existing state of their skin. Dove claims to provide the desired benefits that presumably other soaps do not. Such ads aim to instigate consumers to question if the current state coincides with the desired state. Not all marketer-controlled messages succeed in this objective because of the consumers' tendency of selective exposure and selective perception.

Information Search

After problem or need recognition, consumers generally take steps to gather adequate information to select the appropriate solution. Information search refers to what consumer surveys in her/his environment for suitable information to make a satisfying purchase decision. Problem recognition is an ongoing process for consumers and they use internal and external searches to solve these problems. Consumers may also be involved in ongoing search activities to acquire information for possible future use. No sooner does a consumer recognises a problem, than she/he in a reflexive manner first thinks or tries to remember how she/he usually solves this kind of problem. The recall may be immediate or occur slowly as a result of conscious effort. This recall from long-term memory might produce a satisfactory solution in case of many problems, and no further information search is likely to occur. For example, to get relief from headache, the consumer recalls a brand of headache-remedy based on earlier experience and buys the brand. This is termed as *nominal decision-making*. Another possibility is that consumer recalls Dispirin and Novalgin but is not sure and picks up a book on home remedies and reads about different solutions. Or, the consumer perhaps asks a friend, or goes to the nearest medicine shop and seeks advice from the pharmacist as to which remedy would be effective and safe and buys the brand. The decision here would be based on internal and external information. This type of decision approach is called *limited decision-making*.

In case of high involvement purchases, the relative importance of external information search tends to increase. In general, it seems the type of information sought by a consumer depends on what she/he already knows. If the consumer possesses little knowledge about available alternatives, the tendency is to learn about the existence of alternatives and after acquiring sufficient information, to redirect efforts towards learning more about the attributes of available alternatives to develop suitable evaluative criteria and evaluate them. Purchase decisions of this type involving perceived risk, extensive information search, and serious evaluation efforts are called *extended decision-making.*

Sources of external information include:

- Relatives, friends, neighbours, and Chat groups.
- Professional information from handouts, pamphlets, articles, magazines, journals, books, professional contacts, and the Internet.
- Direct experience through trial, inspection, and observation.
- Marketer initiated efforts included in advertisements, displays, and salespeople.

Besides recalling and learning about the availability of different solutions, an important objective of information collection is to determine appropriate evaluative criteria. These criteria are the standards and specifications that the consumer uses in evaluating products and brands. The consumer establishes what features or attributes are required, to meet her/his needs. For several types of products such as computer, car, cell phone and others, these criteria may vary from consumer to consumer. In most cases, consumers usually undertake brand processing or attribute processing. Brand processing involves evaluating one brand at a time on several attributes, then a second, and so on in the evoked set. Attribute processing involves examining a specific attribute and comparing other brands on that attribute. In this manner, one by one, a second, a third, or fourth attribute may be selected for comparison.

The information collection yields an ***awareness set*** of brands/products. Awareness or consideration set is composed of recalled and learned about solutions. Awareness set contains *evoked set, inept set,* and *inert set.*

Evoked set is composed of those brands the consumer will evaluate to choose the solution of a particular problem or need. ***Inept set*** includes those brands that the consumer finds unworthy of consideration. ***Inert set*** is composed of alternatives that the consumer is aware of but would not consider buying and would treat with indifference.

Alternatives' Evaluation

Consumers' evaluative criteria refer to various dimensions; features, characteristics and benefits that a consumer desires to solve a certain problem. For example, a consumer's evaluative criteria for a laptop computer may include processor speed, operating system, memory, graphics, sound, display, software included, cost and warranty, etc. However, for another consumer the set of evaluative criteria may be entirely different from the same product.

Any product feature or characteristic has meaning for a consumer only to the extent that it can provide a desired benefit. Consumers who want to avoid dental cavities would use the toothpaste that contains fluoride in its formulation. For this particular consumer, fluoride content would probably be the most important evaluative criterion. Fluoride feature is important because it provides a desired benefit, otherwise it has no value. What is more important for marketers is to stress upon – and convince consumers about – the benefit that a particular feature provides rather than mentioning the feature only.

To evaluate different alternatives in the evoked set, the consumer examines products or brands against the desired set of criteria, and also those that are not desired. Consumers use either attitude-based choice that involves the use of general attitudes, impressions, beliefs, intuition, or heuristics and form overall preferences about brands, or attribute-based choice that requires the knowledge of specific attributes at the time of choosing a brand by comparing each brand alternative on specific attributes. This attribute-based choice process is cumbersome and time consuming. Generally, the importance of an optimal decision is related to the value of the product under consideration and the consequence associated with a non-optimal decision.

Some consumers are inclined to simplify the evaluation process and weigh only price heavily or only make the evaluation on the basis of a recognised brand name. It is important to appreciate that for many important personal consumption products, consumers make attitude-based choices. For example, for a notebook computer such as Acer's Ferrari 3000 series, many consumers are prepared to pay a premium price because of its looks and association with the Ferrari logo.

The purchase decision of certain products is primarily based on affective choice or what we call feeling-based purchases. For example, a young girl goes to a ready-to-wear clothing store to buy a dress, she would wear for the annual college dinner. She examines several dresses, tries a few and finally decides that in one particular dress she looks pretty attractive. She looks forward to making a great impression in the party and buys that dress. Such choices do not fit well with either attitude-based or attribute-based criteria and tend to be more holistic in nature. The brands are not divided into distinct components and each of them is evaluated separately from the whole. The evaluation is simply based on how the product makes the consumer feel while he/she is using the product or service. Probably most of us can recall certain purchases we made based on our overall feelings associated with product usage. Consumers imagine or picture themselves using the product or service and evaluate the associated feelings that this use will produce. For example, the ads of some products and personal care services such as mattresses, undergarments, massage, sauna bath and others aim at stimulating consumers to anticipate feelings that the consumption experience will produce and base their choice on these anticipated feelings.

Marketers' messages must attempt to furnish information and experiences by using suitable spokespersons to help develop a strong attitude-based position. Marketers' must also provide performance levels and supporting information to help those consumers who tend to develop preference based on attribute-based choice.

Store Selection and Purchase Decision

Making a purchase is often a simple, routine matter of going to a retail outlet where the consumer looks around and quickly picks out something needed. All consumers like to view themselves as intelligent shoppers and make decisions regarding the retail outlet choice in which they will shop. Generally, consumers decide about the make of the computer first then choose the dealer to buy it from. Frequently, it happens that consumers choose the retail outlet first and this influences their choice of the brand. For example, when consumers shop for clothes, they generally decide about a retail outlet first, or go to a market area where several such stores exist. Similarly, they often make a brand decision in the retail store when they shop for appliances.

Increasingly, consumers are exposed to product introductions and their descriptions in direct-mail pieces and catalogues, in various print media vehicles, on television and on the Internet and buy them through mail, telephone, or computer orders. In case of some product categories, Internet offers greater selection, convenience and lower prices than other distribution outlets for at least some consumers. So far, this in-home shopping is not so common in India but is on the increase. A large number of companies with websites are encouraging consumers to buy products through computer orders.

Retail outlet image and location has an obvious impact on store patronage and consumers' outlet choice often depends on its location. Consumers generally will choose the store that is closest. Similarly, the size of the store is also an important factor that influences consumers' outlet choice. For minor shopping goods or convenience items, consumers are unwilling to travel very far. However, for high-involvement purchases, consumers do not mind travelling to distant shopping areas. Retail outlets are also perceived as having varying degrees of risk. Consumers perceive less risk with traditional retail outlets compared to more innovative outlets such as the Internet.

Once the consumer has chosen a brand and selected a retail outlet, she/he takes the final step of completing the transaction. Traditionally, this would involve offering the cash to acquire the rights to the product. In developed and many developing countries, credit often plays an important role in completing the purchase transaction. Credit cards are popular in developed economies and are increasingly becoming popular in India and many other developing countries, as a convenient way of financing many purchases.

Many retail outlets overlook the fact that the purchase action is generally the termination of last contact that the customer will have with the store on that shopping trip. This presents the business an opportunity to create a lasting impression on the customer.

Post-Purchase Action

Consumers' favourable post-purchase evaluation leads to satisfaction. Consumers choose a particular brand, or retail outlet because they perceive it as a better overall choice than other alternatives that were evaluated while making the purchase decision. They expect a level of performance from their selected item that can range from quite low to quite high. Expectations and perceived performance are not independent and consumers tend to perceive performance in line with their expectations. After using the product, service, or retail outlet, the consumer will perceive some level of performance that could be noticeably more than the expected level, noticeably below expectations, or match the expected level of performance. Thus, satisfaction with a purchase is basically a function of the initial performance level expectations, and perceived performance relative to those expectations.

Consumers engage in a constant process of evaluating the things that they buy as these products are integrated into their daily consumption activities. In case of certain purchases, consumers experience post-purchase dissonance. This occurs as a result of the consumer doubting her/his wisdom of a purchase. After purchase, most products are put to use by consumers, even when they experience dissonance. Consumers experience post-purchase dissonance because making a relatively longer commitment to a selected alternative requires one to forgo the alternative not purchased. Thus, in case of nominal-decisions and most cases of limited-decisions, consumers are unlikely to experience post-purchase dissonance because in such decisions consumers do not consider attractive attributes in a brand not selected. For example, if a consumer purchases the least priced brand of toilet soap out of three alternatives that she/he views as equivalent on all relevant attributes except price, she/he would not experience dissonance. Generally, high-involvement purchases include one or more of the factors that cause post-purchase dissonance.

As one may expect, a positive post-purchase evaluation results in satisfaction and the negative evaluation causes dissatisfaction. In case the consumer's perceived performance level is below expectations and fails to meet the expectations, this will definitely cause dissatisfaction and the product or the outlet will be most likely pushed in the inept set and dropped from being considered on future occasions. Thus, the consumer is also likely to initiate complaint behaviour and spread negative word-of-mouth.

The consumer generally experiences satisfaction when the performance level meets or exceeds the minimum performance expectations. Similarly, when the performance level far exceeds the desired performance level, the consumer will not only be satisfied but also will most likely be delighted. Such an outcome tends to reduce the consumer's decision-making efforts on future purchase occasions of the same product or service to accomplish need satisfaction. Thus, rewarding purchase experience encourages consumers to repeat the same behaviour in future. A delighted consumer is likely to be committed and enthusiastic about a particular brand and usually unlikely to be influenced by competitors' actions. A delighted consumer is also inclined to spread favourable word-of-mouth.

Organisational Consumer

The goals of organisational buyers and personal consumers are different. Organisational goals are concerned with producing a good or providing a service, or reselling an item and all the purchases are made to effectively perform the organisational activities.

Webster, Jr., and Wind have defined organisational buying as 'the decision-making process by which organisations establish the need for purchased products and services and identify, evaluate and choose among alternative brands and suppliers."

(Frederick E. Webster, Jr.., and Yoram J. Wind, *Organisational Buying Behaviour*, Prentice-Hall, 1972.)

Organisational purchases are described as "rational" or "economic." Whether for-profit or not-for-profit, organisations make decisions ranging from routine replacement purchases, to frequently purchased commodity products such as pencils or paper. On the other extreme, the decisions might involve new, complex purchase decisions requiring careful problem definition, extensive internal and external search for information, a detailed and often highly technical evaluation process, a negotiated purchase and a long period of use and post-purchase evaluation.

Organisational buyer characteristics differ from final consumers in several important aspects.

- ***Group-based Decision-making:*** Many organisational purchases are often costly and complex and may involve a group of personnel from engineering, production, finance, purchasing and even top management in making a purchase decision.
- ***Technical Knowledge:*** Professional buyers, called purchasing agents in industrial, governmental and institutional organisations, make purchases and are highly knowledgeable about products or services. In case of resellers such as supermarkets, these individual experts are referred to as buyers and make purchases on their behalf.
- ***Rational Motives Dominate:*** Organisational buyers are generally strongly directed by rational motivations because of the technical nature of purchases involved. Such factors are usually economically based and can be translated into monetary terms to carefully weigh the costs and benefits. For example, factors such as quality specifications and consistency, assurance of prompt delivery, price, terms of credit, warranty and post-sale service, etc., are all rather objective criteria that influence buyers in their selection of vendor.

Decision Approach and Purchase Patterns

Organisational purchases and buying patterns differ from final consumers in many ways.

- ***Formality:*** Since many organisational purchases are likely to be complex and technical and financial risks are considerably high, buying behaviour is much more complicated as compared to final consumers. Due to these reasons, there is greater formality in decision-making and often proposals, quotation requests and purchase contracts are involved.
- ***Negotiations:*** In most cases of organisational buying, there are extensive negotiations between buyers and suppliers over a longer period of time. Some of the important reasons for lengthy negotiations

include (1) the product complexity requires that specifications must be carefully spelled out and agreed upon (2) the order size tends to be large and purchase price is important and (3) usually many people are involved in reaching a final purchase decision. According to Paul A. Dion and Peter M. Banting, negotiations tend to be a cooperative process between buyers and suppliers.

- ***Less Frequent Purchases:*** Organisations generally make purchases less frequently than do final consumers. Firms might buy capital equipment that will be used directly in the production process for a number of years. Similarly, computers, photocopying machines, printers etc., are infrequently purchased. Even office supplies consumed every day are purchased at intervals of a month or more. Raw materials and component parts are used continuously in production and replaced frequently but contracts for the sale and supply of these items are likely to be long-term agreements that are negotiated every few years.
- ***Reciprocity:*** Sometimes organisational buying transactions involve an arrangement in which two organisations agree to buy from each other. For instance, a computer software manufacturer might agree to buy computer hardware from a company that is buying its software and computer supplies.
- ***Service:*** In many instances, organisational products must be customised for a specific organisational buyer. Product support activities, such as service, installation, technical assistance and spare parts are critical.

Types of Decision Situations

The purchase decision process in organisations is significantly influenced by the complexity and difficulty of a given purchase situation. At one extreme, individuals or small groups make routine decisions without much effort because they are perceived as less complex and involve very little or no risk. At the other extreme end are organisational purchase decisions that are viewed as quite complex, entail much risk and have important implications for the organisation. The situation is slightly different in case of organisations as their purchases involve a larger range of complexity as compared with most individual or household decisions and involves three categories.

- ***Straight Re-buy:*** It is like making habitual purchase and involves an automatic choice, as happens when the inventory level reaches a predetermined reorder point. Most organisations maintain an approved vendor list. These are rather routine purchases to meet continuing and recurring requirements and are usually under similar terms and conditions of purchase. The purchases are of minor importance, involving little uncertainty because satisfaction exists with past products, terms and service. The buyer is likely to have limited purchase power such as purchase of paper for printers and photocopiers. The typical purchase process involves no search for information, no evaluation of alternatives, no consideration is given to long-term issues and procedural control is substantial.
- ***Modified Re-buy:*** These are somewhat important and involve limited decision-making. There is moderate level of uncertainty as the organisation wants to repurchase a product or service but with some minor modifications. There might be limited or many choices. For example, an ice cream producer might seek lower prices, faster delivery and higher quality of cream from suppliers to meet the changing market conditions. In case of a modified re-buy situation, competing suppliers may see an opportunity to obtain the company's business and regular suppliers might become more aggressive and competitive to retain a customer's business. P. Doyle, A. G. Woodside and P. Michell are of the opinion that new tasks and modified re-buy are rather similar but straight re-buys are quite different. The decision may involve limited information search, usually by speaking to a few vendors and moderate evaluation of alternatives that might probably involve one or few people.

- ***New Task:*** Such purchase involves extended decision-making, as the decision is new because the item is being purchased for the first time to perform a new job or solve a new problem. There is often a serious risk that the product may not perform as it should or that it will be too costly. New task purchase may involve development of product specifications, vendor specifications and procedures for future purchase of the product. In all such purchases, the organisational buyer needs a great deal of information and careful establishment of criteria on which to evaluate the product for purchase. This kind of purchase is quite significant for the supplier because, if the organisational buyer is satisfied with the new product and supplier's services, it may develop into a continuing profitable relationship between supplier and the buyer organisation.

Organisational buyers consider several factors when they make buying decisions, particularly the quality level, service and price. To ensure a certain quality level, industrial buyers establish a set of product-attribute specifications that they expect the products they buy to meet. In turn, suppliers try to conform to such standards and maintain an acceptable level of quality in the products that they supply. In case the raw material or component part supplied by the vendor does not meet given specifications, the organisational buyer may decide to switch to a different supplier.

For organisational buyers, service is another major concern and may include market information, inventory maintenance, on-time delivery, availability of repair services and replacement parts and credit. Many organisations view customer service as a strategic weapon in industrial markets. M. P. Singh notes that when the goods are same or similar, such as raw materials, different vendors may sell them at the same price and with same specifications. In such situations, the services offered by a supplier can be the best means of differentiating the supplier and gain competitive advantage.

TABLE 8.4

Categories of Organisational Buying Decisions

Buying situation	Level of effort	Risk	Buyers involved
Straight re-buy	Nominal decision-making	Low	Automatic reorder
Modified re-buy	Limited decision-making	Low to moderate	One or a few
New Task	Extended decision-making	High	Many

Product price is also an important consideration for organisational buyers because it affects the cost of the finished products and ultimately impacts selling prices and profit margins. However, buyer organisation is unlikely to compare alternatives only on the basis of price, since product quality and after sales services are equally important aspects in the purchase decision.

Organisational Buyer Decision Process

The size of a Decision-Making Unit (DMU) may vary according to how new, complex and important the purchase decision is; and how centralised, structured and specialised the organisation is. Large and relatively more formal organisations usually involve more individuals in a purchase decision than smaller and less formal organisations. For non-routine decisions, such buying centres are often formed on an *ad hoc* basis but for routine decisions, these centres are relatively permanent. In case of more important buying decisions, individuals from various functional areas and organisational levels take part in decision making than in case of less important purchase decisions.

The decision-making unit can be divided on the basis of functional responsibility and type of influence. Functional responsibility can include specific functions such as production, engineering, research and development, purchasing and general management. Each function evaluates the organisational needs differently and uses different evaluative criteria.

Problem Recognition

The first stage of organisational buying decision involves recognising a need or problem. Just like the consumer decision-making process, one or more people in the organisation perceive a difference of sufficient magnitude between the desired state and the actual state of affairs. Problem recognition may occur under a variety of internal or external circumstances such as breakdown of an old packaging machine, modifications to a currently manufactured product or the development of a new product that needs different packaging equipment. The organisation may also learn about the new packaging equipment from external sources through a visit to a trade fair, an advertisement seen in an industrial magazine, or a salesperson's call from a supplier.

Product Specification

In this stage, participants involved in the decision-making process assess the problem or need and determine what is required to resolve or satisfy it. The using department must prepare the detailed specifications of the product and communicate precisely what is needed. Product specifications may pertain to technical attributes, quality, durability, availability, warranty, support services, etc. For complex products, besides users, technical experts and financial executives will also be involved. For example, when a paint-spraying machine breaks down, in a two-wheeler auto manufacturing plant, engineers, technicians and machine operators assess the situation and determine the replacement needs. They finalise a set of attributes for a replacement machine, specify that it must paint 25 autos per hour, change colours of paint quickly and require only one operator. Finance executives then specify a price range for the machine.

Product and Vendor Search

At this stage, the organisation tries searching for possible products to solve the problem, and also to locate firms who may qualify to be suitable suppliers for those products. To collect information, the members of buying centre may look into company files and trade directories, contact suppliers for information, solicit proposals from known suppliers and examine catalogues and trade publications. Sometimes, in order to write specifications on complex products, the organisation must start with what products and vendors currently exist or, at times, the company may even decide to make the product in-house rather than buy it. Search efforts should generally result in a list of several alternative products and vendors. For example, the buying centre members of two-wheeler auto producer look for paint-spraying products that meet the set specifications and develop a list of paint-spraying machines available from various vendors.

Product and Vendor Evaluation

In this step, the buying centre makes an evaluation to determine which products meet the laid down specifications. Various vendors are also evaluated on criteria such as price, delivery, service, warranty, credit terms, etc. In our example of two-wheeler auto manufacturer, members of the buying centre evaluate the paint-spraying machines in the evoked set according to the evaluative criteria set by the engineers and technicians. The members also evaluate the vendors of these products to determine their ability to supply and provide after sales service. Some typical attributes listed below may be used by the buying centre for each vendor in order to choose the most suitable candidate.

- Overall reputation of the vendor
- Financing terms
- Vendor's flexibility in adjusting to buyer organisation's needs
- Experience with the vendor in comparable situations

- Technical service offered
- Confidence in the sales personnel
- Convenience of placing the order
- Data on reliability of the product
- Price
- Technical specifications
- Ease of product operation or use
- Preferences of principal user of the product
- Training support offered by the vendor
- Training time required
- Reliability of delivery date assured
- Ease of maintenance
- Expected post-purchase service from the vendor.

Product and Vendor Selection

Information gathered during evaluation stage is used to select finally the product to be purchased, as well as the vendor from which the purchase will be made. At this stage, the deciders and the buyers from two-wheeler auto manufacturer's buying centre finally decide to purchase a particular brand of paint spraying machine from XYZ vendor because the product and the supplier measure up to the established evaluative criteria. Terms and conditions, such as payments, delivery dates, warranties, etc., are both complex and critical in industrial markets.

Performance Evaluation

The last stage in purchase decision process involves an evaluation of the product as well as vendor performance. In case of organisational purchases, such evaluations are more formal than are household purchase evaluations. This stage is important in that it provides feedback so that the buying organisation and the vendor will be better able to work as a team. Management personnel from different departments may periodically rate the vendor's performance on criteria such as product quality, delivery and post-supply service. A major component of post-purchase evaluation is the service the seller provides during and after sale. Just like household buyers, dissatisfied organisational buyers may change vendors and/or engage in negative word-of-mouth. Suppliers seek to minimise dissatisfaction and to encourage those who become dissatisfied to complain to them and to no one else.

Summary

Consumer behaviour refers to action and decision processes of buyers involved in buying goods and services to satisfy personal or organisational needs. Social, psychological, and personal factors influence consumer purchase decisions. Social factors are forces exerted by other people and include culture and subculture, roles and family, social class, and reference groups. Psychological forces are internal to individuals that affect purchase behaviour and include motivation perception, learning, attitudes, and personality. Personal factors are forces unique to an individual consumer and include demographic factors, lifestyle, situational factors, and an individual's involvement in purchase.

Consumer decision-making process involves five stages that include need/problem recognition, information search, evaluation of alternatives, store selection and purchase, and post-purchase actions.

Need/problem recognition occurs when a consumer perceives a discrepancy between her/his desired state and the present state of sufficient intensity and stimulates consumers to achieve the desired state. This is strongly influenced by the individual's lifestyle. Besides marketer-controlled actions, other influences exerted by culture or subculture, social class, reference groups, financial condition, individual's development, motives, and emotions influence the desired state. As a result of need/problem recognition, consumers undertake information search to learn about available alternatives and make a reasonable purchase decision. Consumers, in a reflexive manner first search their stored information in long-term memory. In case no satisfactory answers are available, consumers engage in external search. Sources of external information include family, friends, reports, advertisements, Internet, etc. The outcome of information search also helps in developing the evaluative criteria for the solution. While evaluating alternatives, consumers make either attitude-based choice or attribute-based choice. Depending on the level of involvement in purchase, consumers either undertake the route of nominal decision-making, limited decision-making, or extended decision-making. Attribute-based choice is fairly complex and quite time consuming. The consumer buys the product after considering from where to buy. In the post-purchase stage, consumers evaluate products or services based on the pre-purchase expectations about the level of performance.

Organisation buying behaviour refers to decision-making processes by which organisations establish the need for products and services, and identify, evaluate, and choose among alternative products and suppliers. Buying behaviour of organisations differs in important respects from personal consumers. Their purchases are made to accomplish certain organisational goals and effectively perform the activities such as producing goods or services, or reselling an item. Organisational purchases are described as 'rational' or 'economic', and generally relate to considerably larger purchases and often more than one person is involved in decision-making.

Organisations make decisions ranging from routine replacement purchases to involve new, complex purchase decisions requiring careful problem definition, extensive internal and external search for information, a detailed and often highly technical evaluation process, a negotiated purchase, and a long period of use and post-purchase evaluation.

The organisational buying process involves problem recognition, information search, evaluation of alternatives and selection, final purchase, and the post-purchase evaluation is formal and extensive. Purchase is more important, and the terms and conditions agreed upon between buyers and suppliers are more important than in case of personal consumers. Buyer organisation satisfaction is dependent on a variety of criteria and is influenced by the opinions of many different persons. The supplier organisation has to satisfy these individuals according to criteria important to each individual.

Questions for Discussion

1. Discuss two situations, with examples, that show the influence of culture/subculture on consumer purchase behaviour.
2. Describe how reference groups can influence consumers' buying behaviour. Give two examples.
3. In what aspects roles and family can influence buying behaviour?
4. Discuss the impact of attitudes on consumer behaviour, with examples.
5. What are the important types of decision-making approaches that consumers use?
6. How can different situational factors influence the purchase behaviour?

7. What different decision steps are involved in buying behaviour? Do you think consumers may skip one or more of these stages?

8. What is post-purchase dissonance? Do consumers experience this anxiety after every type of purchase?

9. In what ways does organisational buying behaviour differ from that of personal consumers? Discuss the factors that influence organisational buying behaviour.

10. Discuss different types of organisational purchase situations. What type of purchase behaviour is likely to occur?

Projects

1. Visit a departmental store in your town and contact the purchase manager. Prepare a report on how purchases for the store are made.

2. You or one of your friends would have bought a desktop/laptop computer. Prepare a report for presentation discussing in detail the different buying decision steps undertaken.

Bibliography

1. D. J. McCort and Naresh K. Malhotra,"Culture and Consumer Behaviour," *Journal of International Consumer Marketing,* no. 2, 1993.

2. Rebecca Piirto, "The Influentials," *American Demographics,* October 1992.

3. Leon G. Schiffman and Leslie Lazar Kanuk, '*Consumer Behaviour*', 4th ed. 1991.

4. D. Krech and R. Crutchfield, *Theory and Problems in Social Psychology,* McGraw-Hill.

5. Gordon W. Allport, "Attitudes," in C. A. Murchison (ed), *A Handbook of Social Psychology.*

6. Russell W. Belk, "Situational Variables and Consumer Behaviour," *Journal of Consumer Behaviour,* December 1975.

7. D. K. Tse and R. W. Belk, "Becoming a Consumer Society," *Journal of Consumer Research,* March 1989.

8. R. W. Pollay, D. K. Tse, and Z. Y. Wang, "Advertising Propaganda and Value Change in Economic Development," *Journal of Business Research,* 20 (1990).

9. R. W. Swinyard, "The Effects of Mood Involvement, and Quality of Store Experience on Shopping Intentions," *Journal of Consumer Research* (September 1993); J. Baker, D. Grewal, and A. Prasuraman, "The Influence of Store Environment on Quality Inferences and Store Image," *Journal of the Academy of Marketing Science,* Fall 1994.

10. B. Babin and W. R. Darden, "Good and Bad Shopping Vibes," *Journal of Business Research,* March 1996.

11. C. Whan Park, Easwar S. Iyer, and Daniel C. Smith, "The Effects of Situational Factors on In-Store Grocery Shopping Behaviour: The Role of Store Environment and Time Available for Shopping," *Journal of Consumer Research* 15, (March 1989).

12. M. K. M. Hui and J. E. G. Bateson, "Testing a Theory of Crowding in the Service Environment," in *Advances in Consumer Research XVII* ed. M. E. Goldberg, G. Gorn, and R. W. Pollay, 1990, and S. A. Eroglu and K. A. Machleit, "An Empirical Study of Retail Crowding," *Journal of Retailing* (Summer 1990).

13. J. D. Herrington and L. M. Capella, "Effect of Music in Service Environments," *Journal of Services Marketing,* 10 (1996).

14. E. Fisher and S. J. Arnold, "More than a Labour of Love, "*Journal of Consumer Research* (December 1990).

15. S. Y. Park, "A Comparison of American and Korean Gift Giving Behaviours, "*Psychology and Marketing* (September 1998).

16. William O. Bearden, and Arch G. Woodside, "Consumption Occasion Influence on Consumer Brand Choice," *Decision Science*, 9 (April 1978).

17. Judith L. Zaichkowsky, "Conceptualising Involvement," *Journal of Advertising*, 15, 1986.

18. Pradeep K. Kargaonkar and George P Mochis, "An Experimental Study: Cognitive Dissonance, Product Involvement, Expectations, Performance, and Consumer Judgement of Product Performance," *Journal of Advertising*, 1982.

19. Richard W. Olshavsky and Donald H. Granbois, "Consumer Decision-Making," *Journal of Consumer Research*, September 1989.

20. J. C. Mowen, "Beyond Consumer Decision-Making," *Journal of Consumer Research* (Winter 1988).

21. Joseph W. Alba and J. Wesley Hutchinson, "Dimensions of Consumer Expertise," *Journal of Consumer Research* (March 1998).

22. Wayne D. Hoyer, "An Examination of Consumer Decision-Making for a Common Repeat Purchase Product," *Journal of Consumer Research* (December 1984).

Market Segmentation, Targeting & Positioning

CHAPTER 9

LEARNING OBJECTIVES

After going through this chapter, you will understand:

- The advantages of segmenting a market
- Requirements for effective segmentation
- Commonly used segmentation variables
- Frequently used market segment targeting approaches

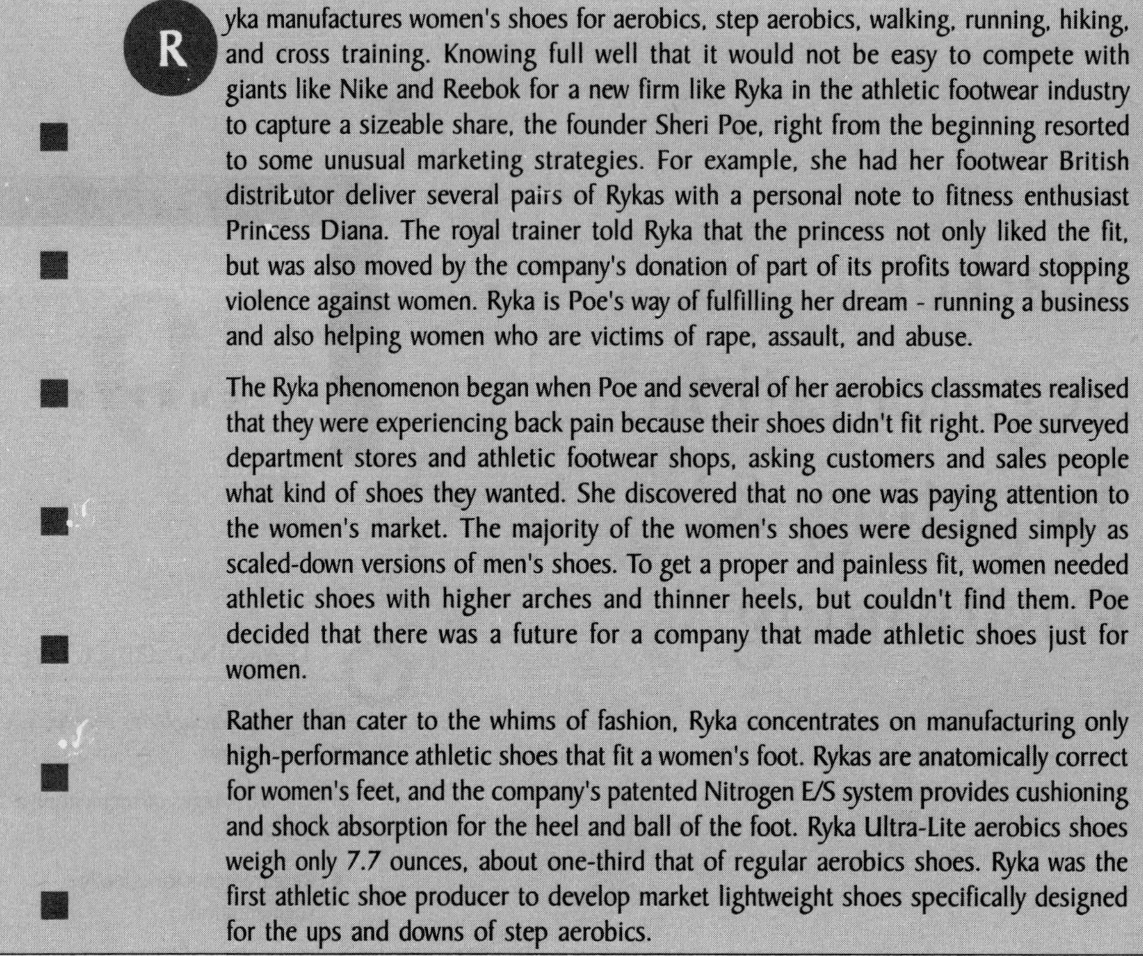

Ryka manufactures women's shoes for aerobics, step aerobics, walking, running, hiking, and cross training. Knowing full well that it would not be easy to compete with giants like Nike and Reebok for a new firm like Ryka in the athletic footwear industry to capture a sizeable share, the founder Sheri Poe, right from the beginning resorted to some unusual marketing strategies. For example, she had her footwear British distributor deliver several pairs of Rykas with a personal note to fitness enthusiast Princess Diana. The royal trainer told Ryka that the princess not only liked the fit, but was also moved by the company's donation of part of its profits toward stopping violence against women. Ryka is Poe's way of fulfilling her dream - running a business and also helping women who are victims of rape, assault, and abuse.

The Ryka phenomenon began when Poe and several of her aerobics classmates realised that they were experiencing back pain because their shoes didn't fit right. Poe surveyed department stores and athletic footwear shops, asking customers and sales people what kind of shoes they wanted. She discovered that no one was paying attention to the women's market. The majority of the women's shoes were designed simply as scaled-down versions of men's shoes. To get a proper and painless fit, women needed athletic shoes with higher arches and thinner heels, but couldn't find them. Poe decided that there was a future for a company that made athletic shoes just for women.

Rather than cater to the whims of fashion, Ryka concentrates on manufacturing only high-performance athletic shoes that fit a women's foot. Rykas are anatomically correct for women's feet, and the company's patented Nitrogen E/S system provides cushioning and shock absorption for the heel and ball of the foot. Ryka Ultra-Lite aerobics shoes weigh only 7.7 ounces, about one-third that of regular aerobics shoes. Ryka was the first athletic shoe producer to develop market lightweight shoes specifically designed for the ups and downs of step aerobics.

The concept of market segmentation emerged as an extension of the marketing concept in the latter part of 1950s. It is based on the simple observation that all the existing and potential consumers are not alike: there are significant differences in their needs, wants, tastes, background, income, education and experience, etc., and these characteristics change over time with lifestyle changes. Had they been alike, it would have eliminated the need to have different variations of the same basic product and one promotional campaign is all that would have been needed. For example, there would have been only one type of soap, one detergent, one car, one computer, one washing machine and so on.

A market is composed of individuals and they are rarely homogeneous in benefits wanted, purchase rates, and price and promotion elasticity. Their response rates of products and services and promotion programmes differ. Since consumers have dissimilar needs and wants in a market, it is called a heterogeneous market and most markets are heterogeneous. Differences in product preferences, size and growth in demand, media habits, and competitive structure of the market also affect the differences and response rates.

Market segmentation *is the process of dividing the total market into relatively distinct homogeneous sub-groups of consumers with similar needs or characteristics that lead them to respond in similar ways to a particular marketing programme.*

A ***market segment*** *is a portion of a larger market in which the individuals, groups, or organisations share one or more characteristics that cause them to have relatively similar product needs.*

Three-decision processes comprising market segmentation, target marketing, and positioning are closely related and have strong interdependence and essentially need to be examined carefully and implemented to be successful in managing a given product-market relationship. Peter Doyle cites an international example:

"In England, Japanese companies have outperformed their British rivals across a range of industries. A major reason for this was that the Japanese were better at managing the segmentation, targeting, and positioning relationships. Thus, only 13 per cent of the Japanese firms versus 47 per cent of the British were unclear about their target segment of customers and their special needs."

"All too often, the marketing directors of British companies remarked that they see their target market as being the whole market and since their products had wide appeal, there was no need to segment the market. As a consequence, Japanese concentrated their resources in specific high-potential segments, while the British tended to spread theirs thinly across the entire market. When British companies did segment, they did so at the lower, cheaper end of the market. This resulted in customers increasingly perceiving the Japanese, in contrast to the British, as offering quality and status."

When marketers provide a range of product or service options to serve diverse consumer preferences, they are more satisfied and happy. Market segmentation is a positive force for both marketers and consumers alike. In his book, *'Competitive Advantage'*, Michael E. Porter says:

"The competitive advantage of a firm lies in being everything to a select few. To be everything to everyone is a sure recipe for a strategic failure."

Requirements for Effective Segmentation

Five conditions must exist for segmentation to be meaningful:

1. A marketer must determine whether the market is heterogeneous. If the consumers' product needs are homogeneous, then it is senseless to segment the market.
2. There must be some logical basis to identify and divide the population into relatively distinct homogeneous groups, having common needs or characteristics and which will respond to a marketing programme. Differences in one market segment should be small compared to differences across various segments.
3. The total market should be divided in such a manner that comparison of estimated sales potential, costs, and profits of each segment can be done.
4. One or more segments must have enough profit potential that would justify developing and maintaining a marketing programme.
5. It must be possible to reach the target segment effectively. For instance, in some rural areas in India, there are no media that can be used to reach the targeted groups. It is also possible that paucity of funds prohibits the development required for a promotional campaign.

As more and more identifying characteristics are included in segmenting the market, the more precisely defined are the segments. However, the more divided a market becomes, the fewer the consumers are in each segment. So, at least in theory, each consumer can be considered as a separate segment. An important decision for the marketer is how far to go in the segmenting process. A market **niche** is composed of a more narrowly defined group of consumers who have a distinct and somewhat complex set of needs. A niche market is smaller in size but may prove to be quite profitable if served properly. Consumers in a niche are ready to pay a premium to the marketer who best satisfies their needs. For example, Apple computers serve the needs of a niche market, while PCs serve rather large market segments.

How Segmentation Helps

Segmentation studies are used to uncover needs and wants of specific groups of consumers for whom the marketer develops especially suitable products and services to satisfy their needs.

Marketers also use these studies to guide them in redesigning, repositioning, or targeting new segments for the existing product. For example, the heavy user adult market has been targeted for Johnson baby shampoo. For sensitive skins, Dove has come out with a variant, Dove Gentle Exfoliating Bar (it has a pH range of 6.5 - 7.5, almost neutral, neither acidic nor alkaline).

Segmentation studies help in identifying the most appropriate media for promotional messages. Almost all media vehicles use segmentation studies to determine the characteristics of their audience and publish their findings to attract marketers seeking a similar audience.

Bases for Segmentation

Markets are complex entities that can be segmented in a variety of ways. It is an important issue to find an appropriate segmentation scheme that will facilitate target-marketing, product positioning, and developing successful marketing strategies and action programmes.

A **segmentation variable** is a characteristic of individuals, groups or organisations that marketers use to divide and create segments of the total market. One approach to segmentation is on "*a priority*" basis. In this case, the marketer may assume that differences must exist among heavy users and light or medium users of a product category. Segmentation descriptors fall under four major categories and include ***geographic variables, demographic variables, psychographic variables,*** **and *behaviouristic variables.***

- Geographic variables focus on where the customers are located.
- Demographic variables identify who the target customers are.
- Psychographic variables refer to lifestyle and values.
- Behaviouristic variables identify benefits customers seek, and product usage rates.

Before collecting any data on the market, the basis for segmentation is analysed. The marketer can also assume that dual-income households are growing in urban areas and then develop a programme for this segment.

Selecting the right segmentation variable is critical. For example, small car producers might segment the market on the basis of income but they probably would not segment it on the basis of political beliefs or religion because political leanings or religious beliefs do not normally influence consumers' automobile needs. Segmentation variable must also be measurable to segment the market accurately. For example, segmenting the market on the basis of intelligence would be difficult because this characteristic cannot be measured accurately. Marketers can use one or more variables to segment the market.

Different variables are used to segment consumer markets. Broadly speaking, segmentation variables fall under two categories: *consumer characteristics* or *consumer responses.* The most popular bases for market segmentation include geographic factors, demographic factors, psychological characteristics, social/cultural variables; use related factors, use situation variables, benefits sought and combination of several segmentation bases called **hybrid** formats, such as demographic/psychographic profiles, geo-demographic variables, values and lifestyles.

FIGURE 9.1

Segmentation Variables

Geographic variables		Demographic variables	
Region	Nation	Gender	Family size
Urban, Rural	State	Age	Occupation
City size Climate		Race	Family life cycle
Terrain	Market density	Religion	Income
		Social class	Education
Psychographic variables		**Behaviouristic variables**	
Personality attributes		Usage volume, Occasion	
Motives		End use	
Lifestyle		Benefits sought	
		Brand loyalty	
		Price sensitivity	

Geographic Segmentation

Geographic segmentation focuses on dividing markets into different geographic units, such as regions, nations, states, urban, rural, etc. Customers located in different geographic areas vary in terms of climates, terrain, natural resources, population density, culture, service needs, sales potential, growth rates, competitive structure of the market, frequency of purchases for a variety of goods and services. For example, Jeeps are more popular in rural areas in India than in urban areas. Shopping malls are located only in larger cities in India, and raincoats are sold more in rainy areas. Geographic segmentation is used both in consumer and organisational markets, particularly where customers are not willing to travel far to acquire goods and services.

Geo-Demographic Segmentation

Many segmentation approaches involve both geographic and demographic descriptors. This approach is based on the premise that people who live close to one another are likely to have similar economic status, tastes, preferences, lifestyles and consumption behaviour. Geo-demographic segmentation is particularly useful when a marketer is capable of isolating its prospects with similar personalities, goals, interests, and in terms of where they live. For products, and services used by a wide cross-section of society, this approach may not be suitable. For example, some retailers who propose to open new stores are interested in knowing something about the people who live within a defined area whom they aim to attract.

Demographic Segmentation

Demographic characteristics are commonly used to segment the market. Factors such as age, sex, education, income, marital status, household life cycle, family size, social class, etc., are used singly, or in a combination, to segment a market. Shaving products for women are based on the demographic variable of gender. Toy manufacturers such as Funskool and Mattel Toys segment the market on the basis of age of children. Auto manufacturers segment the market by considering income as an important variable. Producers of refrigerators, washing machines, microwave ovens etc., take income and family size as important variables in segmenting the market. Ready-to-wear garment producers often segment the market on the basis of social class. Examples are Chiragh Din, Arrow, Van Heusen, Louis Phillipe, Levis and others. In general, the social class can represent lower, middle and upper class depending on education, income, status, etc. For example, an engineer and a clerk are considered as members of different social classes.

FIGURE 9.2

Socio-economic Pyramid of Indian Population

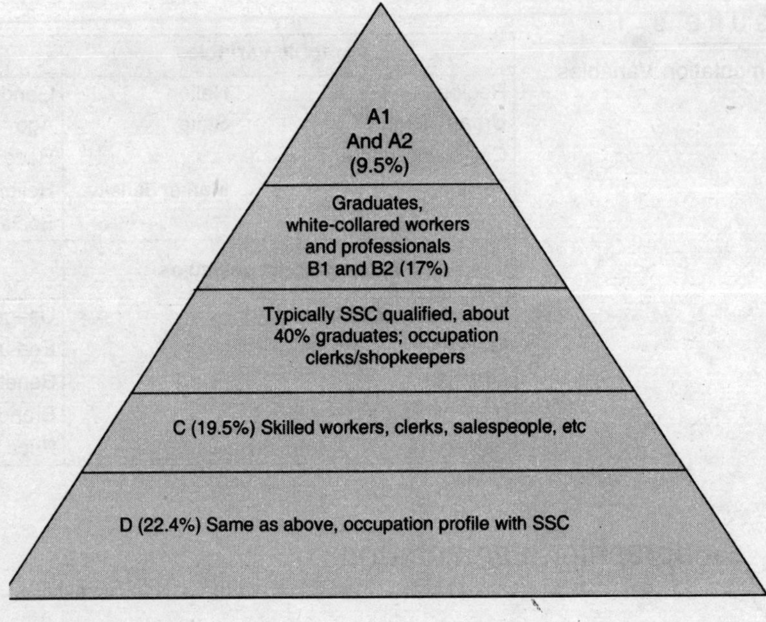

[*Source: A & M*, October (1991)].

Psychographics Segmentation

When segmentation is based on personality or lifestyle characteristics, it is called psychographic segmentation. Consumers have a certain self-image and this describes their personality. There are people who are ambitious, confident, aggressive, impulsive, conservative, modern, gregarious, loners, extrovert, introvert, etc. Some motorcycle manufacturers segment the market on the basis of personality variables such as macho image, independent and impulsive. Some producers of liquor, cigarettes, apparel, etc., segment the market on the basis of personality and self-image. Marketers, are often not concerned about measuring how many people have the characteristic as they assume that a substantial number of consumers in the market either have the characteristic or want to have it.

Lifestyle: It is an indicator of how people live and spend their time and money. What people do in their spare time is often a good indicator of their lifestyle. For example, John L. Lastovicka, John P. Murray, Erich A. Joachimsthaler, Gaurav Bhalla and Jim Sheurich in their study, were identified two lifestyle segments that were most likely to drink and drive: Good timers and problem kids. Good timers are partygoers, macho and high on sensation seeking. Problem Kids frequently display troublesome behaviours. According to Morris B. Holbrook, people who have an affinity for nostalgia, or the desire for old things, also represent a lifestyle segment and can be a key market for old movies, antiques and books. Surfing on the Internet has also created a new type of lifestyle. Another study by Rebecca Piirto of fashion consumers found six major groups: yesteryears (older consumers), power purchasers (married households with college degree), fashion foregoers, social strivers, dutifuls (highly practical) and progressive patrons (high-income/quality buyers). Consumers in different countries and cultures may have characteristic lifestyles. For example, Indian women are home focused, less likely to visit restaurants, more price-sensitive, spend time preparing meals at home and fond of movies.

AIO inventories are useful additions to demographic data but marketers have found the original AIO inventories as being too narrow. Now, psychographics or lifestyle studies generally include the following:

- Attitudes include evaluative statements about people, products, ideas, places, etc.

- Values refer to widely held beliefs about what is right/acceptable/desirable, etc.
- Activities and interests cover behaviours with respect to activities other than occupation to which consumers devote time and effort, such as hobbies, interests, social service, etc.
- Demographics cover gender, age, education, occupation, income, family size, geographic location, etc.
- Media preferences describe which specific media the consumers prefer to use.
- Usage rate focuses on measurements of consumption level within a particular product category and is generally recorded as heavy, medium, light, or non-user.

TABLE 9 1

Lifestyle Dimensions

Activities	Interests	Opinions	Demographics
Work	Family	Themselves	Age
Hobbies	Home	Social issues	Education
Social events	Job	Politics	Income
Vacation	Community	Business	Occupation
Entertainment	Recreation	Economics	Family size
Club membership	Fashion	Education	Dwelling
Community	Food	Products	Geography
Shopping	Media	Future	City size
Sports	Achievements	Culture	Stage in life cycle

[*Source:* Joseph T. Plummer, "The Concept and Application of Lifestyle Segmentation," *Journal of Marketing* 38 (January 1974)].

The sample size is often 500 or more individuals who provide this information and are placed in groups whose members have similar response patterns. According to F. W. Gilbert and W. E. Warren, most studies use the first two or three dimensions mentioned above to group individuals. The use of other dimensions provides more complete profiling of each group.

Generally, the AIO measurements are product or activity specific. For example, W. A. Kamakura and M. Wedel have reported a study related to fashion clothing which included 40 statements and respondents reported their degree of agreement or disagreement. Five of the statements are mentioned here:

- I like parties with music and chatting.
- I like clothes with a touch of sensuality.
- I choose clothes that match my age.
- No matter where I go, I dress the way I want to.
- I think I spend more time than I should on fashion.

In this study, statements relevant to activities and demographics were also included. General lifestyle studies can be used to spot new product opportunities, while product specific lifestyle analysis may help repositioning decisions regarding existing brands.

The VALS (Values and Lifestyles)

Stanford Research Institute (SRI) developed a popular approach to psychographics segmentation called VALS (Values and Lifestyles). This segmented consumers according to their values and lifestyles in USA.

Researchers faced some problems with this method and SRI developed the **vals2** programme in 1978 and significantly revised it in 1989. VALS2 puts less emphasis on activities and interests and more on a psychological base to tap relatively enduring attitudes and values. To measure it, respondents are given 42 statements with which they are required to state a degree of agreement or disagreement. Some examples of the statements are:

- I am often interested in theories.
- I often crave excitement.
- I liked most of the subjects I studied in school.
- I like working with carpentry and mechanical tools.
- I must admit that I like to show off.
- I have little desire to see the world.
- I like being in charge of a group.
- I hate getting grease and oil on my hands.

VALS2 has two dimensions. The first dimension, self-orientation, determines the type of goals and behaviours that individuals will pursue, and refers to pattern of attitudes and activities which help individuals reinforce, sustain, or modify their social self-image. This is a fundamental human need. The second dimension – resources – reflects the ability of individuals to pursue their dominant self-orientation that includes the full range of physical, psychological, demographic and material means such as self-confidence, interpersonal skills, inventiveness, intelligence, eagerness to buy, money, position, education, etc. The questions above are designed to classify respondents based on their self-orientation. Stanford Research Institute (SRI) has identified three basic self-orientations:

1. Principle-oriented individuals are guided in their choices by their beliefs and principles and not by feelings, desires and events.
2. Status-oriented individuals are heavily influenced by actions, approval and opinions of others.
3. Action-oriented individuals desire physical and social activity, variety and risk taking.

Based on the concepts of self-orientation and resources, Values and Lifestyle typology breaks consumers into eight groups. VALS2 suggests that a consumer purchases certain products and services because the individual is a specific type of person. The purchase is believed to reflect a consumer's lifestyle, which is a function of self-orientation and resources. People with most resources are at the top and the ones with least resources are at the bottom of this typology. Each of the eight groups exhibits a distinctive behaviour, decision-making approach and product or media usage attributes. VALS2 represents an interconnected network of segments, which means that adjoining segments have many similar characteristics and can be combined to suit particular marketing objectives.

FIGURE 9.3
Values and Lifestyle 2 (VALS 2)

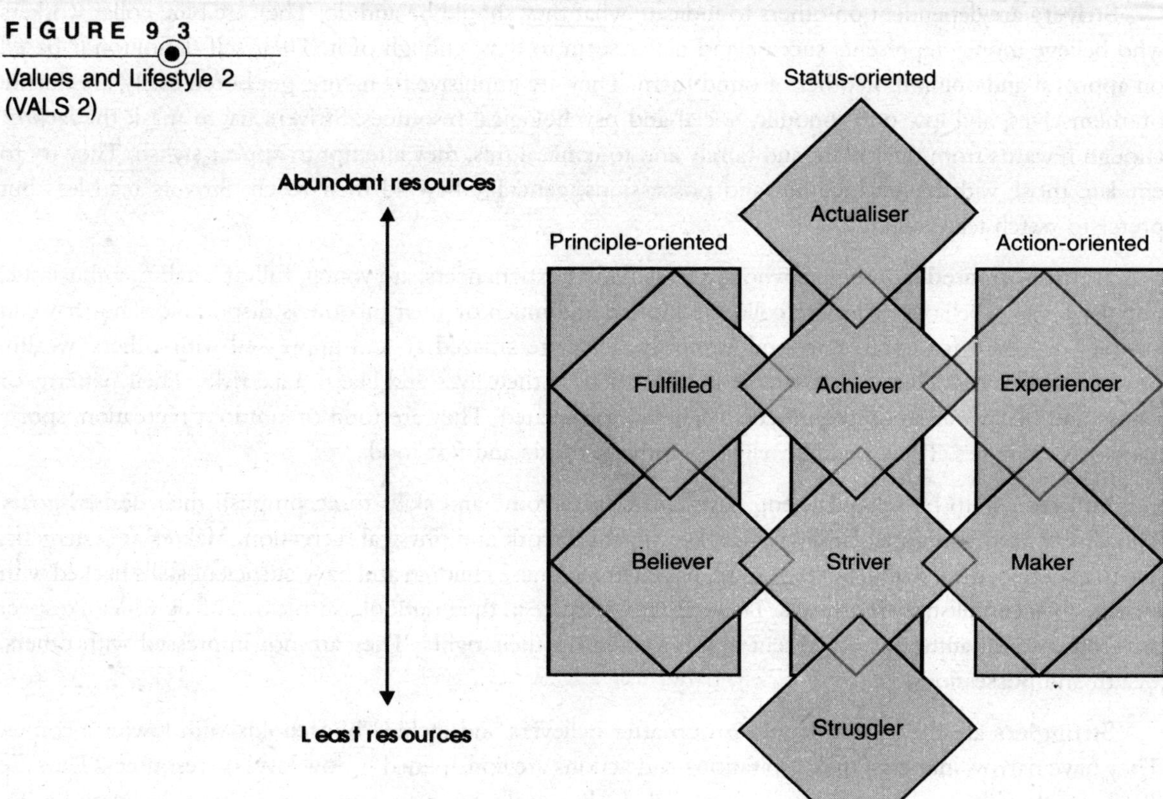

Actualisers have abundant resources. They are among the established or getting established leaders in business or government and are sophisticated and active with high self-esteem. Image is important to them as an expression of their taste, independence and character. They are interested in growth and seek to develop, explore and express themselves in many different ways. They have social and intellectual interests and are open to social change. They are guided sometimes by principles and at other times by desire and are fond of reading, but not fond of television and are sceptical of advertising.

Fulfilleds are mature in their outlook, are well-educated, reflective people who value order, knowledge and responsibility. They like their home and family; are satisfied with their careers and enjoy their leisure activities at home. Nearly 50 per cent of fulfilleds are in their fifties or older. They are open-minded about new ideas and accept social change. As consumers, they are conservative and practical. They purchase products for their durability, functionality and value.

Believers constitute the largest segment. They are not well-educated and the moral code of conduct is deeply rooted in their psyche and is inflexible. Their routines are established and largely influenced by home, family, religion and social organisation. Their behaviour as consumers is predictable and conservative. Their income is modest but enough to meet their needs. They are fond of watching much television and do little reading.

Status-oriented consumers value a secure place in society. Achievers make choices based on a desire to enhance their position or to facilitate their move to another group's membership for which they aspire. They are more resourceful and active. Achievers are inclined to seek recognition and self-identity through achievement at work and in their personal lives. They have high economic and social status.

Strivers are dependent on others to indicate what they should be and do. They are blue-collar workers who believe money represents success and never seem to have enough of it. Their self-definition is based on approval and opinion of others around them. They are impulsive by nature, get bored easily, are unsure of themselves, and low on economic, social and psychological resources. Strivers try to mask the lack of enough rewards from their work and family and to conceal this, they attempt to appear stylish. They try to emulate those with higher incomes and possessions, generally beyond their reach. Strivers read less but prefer to watch television.

'Action-oriented' consumers who are classified as experiencers, are young, full of vitality, enthusiastic, impulsive and rebellious. They are college educated and much of their income is disposable. They have an abstract disregard for conformity and authority. They are amazed at–and impressed with–others' wealth, prestige and power. They seek excitement and variety in their lives and like to take risks. Their patterns of values and behaviour are in the process of being formulated. They are fond of outdoor recreation, sports and social activities. They spend heavily on clothing, music and fast food.

Makers like to be self-sufficient, have sufficient income and skills to accomplish their desired goals. They live within traditional family values, like practical work and physical recreation. Makers are energetic, like to experience the world, build a house, have families, raise children and have sufficient skills backed with income to accomplish their projects. They are conservative in their outlook, suspicious of new ideas, respect government and authority, but resent any intrusion on their rights. They are not impressed with others' wealth and possessions.

Strugglers are the second largest group after believers and include households with lowest incomes. They have narrow interests; their aspirations and actions are constrained by low level of resources. They are ill-educated, with strong social bonds, low-skilled, chronically poor and concerned about declining health. They feel powerless and unable to have any impact or influence on events. As consumers, they show the strongest brand loyalties but are cautious and represent only a modest market. They watch a lot of television, read women's magazines and tabloids.

For several reasons, psychographic segmentation variables are used on a limited scale. To accurately measure psychographic variables is rather difficult compared to other types of segmentation bases. The relationships between psychographic variables and consumer needs are often difficult to document. Also, certain psychographic segments may not be reachable. For example, it may be difficult to reach introverted people at reasonable cost.

Behaviouristic Segmentation

Dividing the market on the basis of such variables as use occasion, benefits sought, user status, usage rate, loyalty status, buyer readiness stage and attitude is termed as behaviouristic segmentation.

Buyers can be identified according to the use occasion when they develop a need and purchase or use a product. For example, Archies greeting cards are used on many different occasions. User status, such as non-users, potential users, or first time users can be used to segment the market. Markets can also be segmented into light, medium, or heavy users of a product. Brand loyalty of varying degree can be presented among different groups of consumers and may become the basis to segment the market. There are consumers, who are very loyal to cigarette brands, beer and even toothpaste. Markets may also be divided on an imaginary Likert-type scale by considering level of product awareness such as unaware of the product, aware, interested, desirous, or contemplating to purchase the product. Based on attitude, consumers may be enthusiastic, indifferent, or hostile towards the product, and these differences can be used to segment the market.

Benefit Segmentation: By purchasing and using products, consumers are trying to satisfy specific needs and wants. In essence, they look for products that provide specific benefits to them. Identifying consumer groups looking for specific benefits from the use of a product or service is known as benefit segmentation and is widely used by marketers. For example, there are distinct groups of auto buyers. One group might be more interested in economy, the other in safety and still other in status.

Segmentation bases, such as demographics are descriptive. These variables are useful but do not consider why consumers buy a product. Benefit segmentation has the potential to divide markets according to why consumers buy a product. Benefits sought by consumers are more likely to determine purchase behaviour than are descriptive characteristics.

TABLE 9.2

Benefit Segmentation of Toothpaste Market

Principal Benefit Sought	Psychographic Characteristics	Behavioural Characteristics	Demographic Characteristics	Brands Much Favoured
Brightness of teeth (cosmetic)	Outgoing, active fun-loving, high sociability	Smokers	Teenagers, youngsters	Close-Up, Promise, Aquafresh
Decay prevention (medicinal)	Health conscious	Heavy users	Large families	Pepsodent, Colgate Total, Forhans
Taste (good taste, flavour)	Self-indulgent, hedonistic	Mint lovers	Children	Aquafresh, Colgate
Low price (economy)	Price-conscious, independent	Heavy users, deal prone	Men, traditional	Neem, Babool, Vicco Vajradanti

(Adapted with changes from Russel J. Haley, "Benefit Segmentation: A Decision Oriented Research Tool. *Journal of Marketing*, July 1963, pp. 30–35. Also, Haley, "Benefit Segmentation – 20 Years Later," *Journal of Consumer Marketing*, v'ol. 1, 1984, pp. 5-14)

Marketers should also appreciate that many benefits sought by consumers are subject to change with changing technologies, changing social values and competitive offers. This requires that marketers must constantly reassess benefit segments. The present scenario in the computer market is an example. With the introduction of faster and better products, the benefits consumers seek, are constantly changing. Benefit segmentation can be seen in the toothpaste market; fresh breath, decay prevention and whiter teeth are some examples and the leading brands involved are Colgate Total, Close-Up and Promise.

Demographic-Psychographics Segmentation (Hybrid Approach)

Demographic and psychographic profiles work best when combined together because combined characteristics reveal very important information about target markets. Demographic-psychographics information is particularly useful in creating consumer profiles and audience profiles. Combined demographic-psychographic profiles reveal important information for segmenting mass markets, provide meaningful direction as to which type of promotional appeals are best suited and selecting the right kind of advertising media that is most likely to reach the target market.

Segmentation Variables for Organisational Markets

Main approaches to segment organisational markets can be grouped under four heads:

- ***Geographic Location:*** This refers to customers' location in certain states, cities, or specified industrial locations. For example, the areas or regions where there are cotton textile manufacturers, or auto producers. Companies that process natural resources are often located close to the source to minimise transportation costs. Generally, international companies segment markets geographically.

- ***Customer Size:*** Business customer size can be based on factors such as number of production facilities, sales volume, number of sales offices, and number of employees. The customer size could be grouped as large, medium, or small on the basis of purchase value or other variables.
- ***Product Use:*** Segmenting market based on the type of use. For example, steel producers may segment their market, as do auto manufacturers, steel furniture producers, and construction companies. A paint manufacturing company might sell to customers in various industries.
- ***Type of Organisation:*** A company selling to several business organisations in a variety of industries may want to segment its market based on industry: For example, companies that are highly dependent on after sales service, are highly price sensitive, or which demand credit facility.
- ***Buying Behaviour and Situation:*** Business markets can be segmented on the basis of degree to which buying activity is centralised. A centralised buyer is likely to consider all purchases with a given supplier on a national or global basis, to be concerned about cost savings, and minimise risk. In a more decentralised company, the buyer is likely to be more concerned about the user's need, to emphasise quality, fast delivery, and to be less cost conscious.

In actual practice, companies generally use a combination of different segmentation variables to more accurately target an attractive segment.

Targeting Market Segments

Instead of aiming a single product and marketing programme at the mass market, most companies identify relatively homogeneous segments and accordingly develop suitable products and marketing programmes matching the wants and preferences of each segment. It should, however, be realised that all segments do not represent equally attractive opportunities for a company. Companies need to categorise segments according to their present and future attractiveness and their company's strengths and capabilities relative to different segments' needs and competitive situation. The following sequential steps present a useful framework, managers can use for this purpose:

- Establish criteria to measure market attractiveness and business strength position.
- Evaluate market attractiveness and business strength factors to ascertain their relative importance.
- Assess the current position of each potential segment on each factor.
- Project the future position of each market segment based on expected environmental, customer, and competitive trends.
- Evaluate Segment Profitability.
- Evaluate implications of possible future changes with respect to strategies and requirement of resources.

Segment Attractiveness and Business Strength Factors

The General Electric model has been briefly discussed (Chapter 2). The attractiveness of a market segment can be evaluated based on the company's current business strength and market potential assessment.

Determining the segment attractiveness requires, first of all, the degree of unmet, or partially met customer needs. More often it is difficult to get going with "Me-too" type of products in today's fiercely competitive markets. It also involves that the marketer estimate the segment size, growth rate, and the influence of various macro environmental factors that influence the demand in the market segment.

EXHIBIT 9.1: MARKET ATTRACTIVENESS FACTORS

Consumer Needs

- Determine if there are unmet or partially met needs.
- Market potential in monetary terms or units, and number of prospective customers.
- Might the segment serve as a platform for later expansion into related segments.
- Favourability of macro environmental trends.

It is also important to understand the company's business strength, to compete successfully as an industry. It would not be wise to enter an industry for which the company does not possess requisite strengths to be competitive and enjoy competitive advantage. The company should enter a segment where it can sufficiently differentiate its product from competitors and have resources to compete. Most new products or services need to be better or cheaper from consumers' point of view than the already available products or services.

EXHIBIT 9.2: BUSINESS STRENGTH FACTORS

Business Strength

- Can we meaningfully differentiate the product or service?
- Can we perform against critical success factors?
- Is the timing right considering the PLC stage of competing products?
- Strength and depth of management.
- Financial and functional resources (manufacturing, R&D, marketing, distribution, etc.)
- Brand image.
- Relative market share.
- Threat of new entrants and substitutes.
- Bargaining power of suppliers and buyers.
- Competitive rivalry.
- Industry size.

Assess Each Factor to Identify Segment Attractiveness

Each of the factors should be assigned a numerical weight to denote the factor's relative importance in overall assessment. Let us assume that a company wants to assess the fairness cream segment in India. Some users would rate each factor in the boxes, assigning a weight to each one.

EXHIBIT 9.3: ASSESSING THE FAIRNESS CREAM SEGMENT

	Weight	Rating (0 – 10)	Total
■ **Market Attractiveness Factors**			
Customers unmet needs	.5	10	5.0
■ Segment size and growth rate	.3	7	2.1
Macro factors trends	.2	7	1.4
■ **Total:**	**1.1**		**8.5**
Business Strength Factors			
Competitive advantage	.6	7	4.2
Capabilities and resources	.4	6	2.4
Industry attractiveness	.2	7	1.4
Total:	**1.1**		**8.0**

Rate Market Segments on Each Factor

This step requires quantitative and qualitative data to make an objective assessment on each criteria identified (Exhibits 1 and 2). It is extremely important to make a detailed analysis of major competitors with respect to their objective, strategy, resources, and marketing programmes. Another aspect to be carefully assessed is the evidence that, by entering the segment, the company can more completely satisfy unmet consumer needs in the target segment and gain competitive advantage. The scores entered below from Exhibit 3 show that the market segment for the company is promising for its fairness cream.

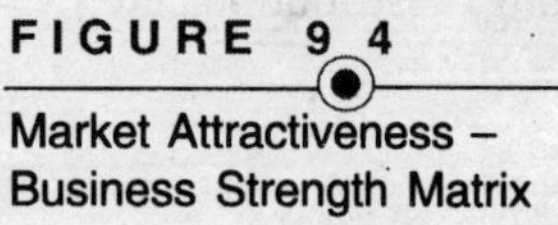

FIGURE 9.4

Market Attractiveness – Business Strength Matrix

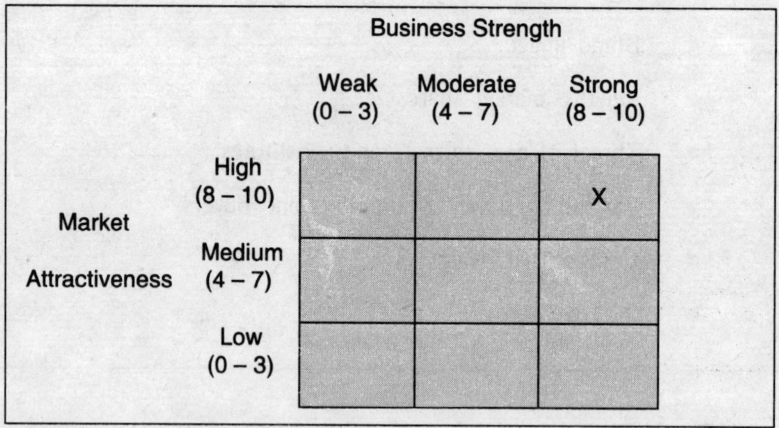

Assess Segment Profitability

The fact that a segment has positive attraction factors and the company has desired strengths does not necessarily mean that the segment can be served profitably. Many segments are large and the market is growing, but the customers seek low prices and the competing companies have a chance of making profits only by airtight control on their costs. It would be advantageous to enter a smaller segment if the customers are prepared to pay a price premium for a product or service for which cost of differentiation is less than the premium charged.

Plot Future Position for Each Segment

A company's management should assess the likely changes in the segment's attractiveness over the coming three to five years. This would require projecting the possible shifts in consumer needs, lifestyle, behavioural patterns, entry and exit of competitors, and changes in their strategies. The company management should also assess the possible changes in product or technology, shifts in macro trends, and bargaining power of customers. The company management should anticipate the possible shifts in its competitive position in the market assuming that the company would respond appropriately to projected environmental changes without making any changes in its basic strategy.

Choose Target Segments and Allocate Resources

Before making the final decision of choosing the market segment, it is necessary to examine that the segment is at least strongly positive on one of the two dimensions of market attractiveness and business strength and is at least moderately positive on the other.

A company may decide to enter a segment that otherwise does not currently appear to be a positive under certain conditions, such as when there is belief among the managers that the segment's attractiveness or the company's business strength is likely to improve in the coming few years, or they believe such segments would offer opportunity to enter more attractive markets in the coming years.

There are three basic targeting strategies:

- Undifferentiated Mass Marketing.
- Differentiated Multiple Segment Marketing.
- Single Segment Specialisation or Niche Marketing.

Undifferentiated Mass Marketing: This strategy involves ignoring any differences among consumers and offer one product or service to the entire market. This strategy of mass marketing focuses on what is common in the needs of consumers rather than what is different. For more than 90 years, Coca-Cola offered only one product version to the whole market and hoped that it would appeal to everyone. Hamdard offers its Rooh Afza based on this strategy. Undifferentiated marketing provides cost economies.

Differentiated Multiple Segment Marketing: The marketer decides to enter several market segments and develops separate offers for each. For instance, Maruti is producing different models of cars for various segments, Nike offers athletic shoes for different sports and Coca-Cola and Pepsi are offering different versions of their soft drinks. Companies producing toiletries are offering different versions of toilet soaps for dry skin, oily skin and normal skin. These companies expect higher sales volumes by offering product versions and a stronger position within each segment. Differentiated marketing strategy increases costs considerably.

Single Segment Specialisation or Niche Marketing: Many companies succeed by producing a specialised product aimed at a very focused market or a niche. This strategy also appeals to firms with limited resources. The company targets a segment and goes for a larger market share instead of a small share in a larger market segment. Recycled paper producers often focus on the market for greeting cards or wedding cards. Oshkosh Truck is the largest producer of airport rescue trucks. Concentrated strategy may involve more than normal risks. If a large competitor decides to enter the same segment, the going may become quite tough for the smaller company.

FIGURE 9.5

Three Basic Targeting Strategies

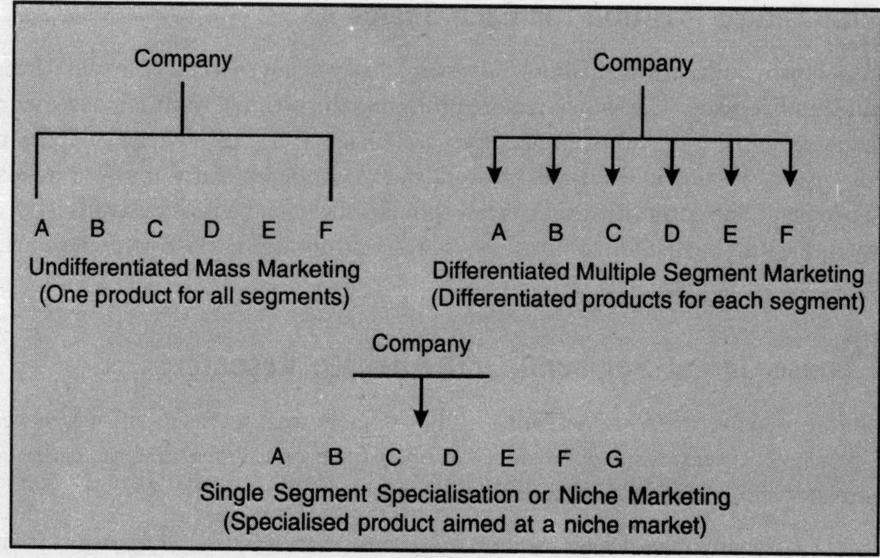

Some firms often target currently small *fast-growth segments*. Smaller competitors often favour this approach to avoid head on confrontation with larger companies while building volume and share. Venture capital firms often favour this strategy because it helps them to earn 30 – 60 per cent annual rates of return on investment. This approach usually requires strong R&D and marketing muscle to identify and develop products that would appeal to newly emerging user segments, and resources to finance rapid growth. Rapid and sustained growth is bound to attract powerful competitors. The aim of such firms should be to develop an enduring competitive position through its products, service, distribution, and costs by the time competitors start entering.

Undifferentiated mass marketing is more appropriate for uniform products, or when most buyers have similar tastes and react to marketing efforts in the same way. Products such as salt, sugar, steel, etc., are examples where companies often use undifferentiated mass marketing.

Differentiated multiple segment strategy makes more sense when the products can vary in design such as autos, cameras and computers. When producers of the same product category use segmentation, mass-marketing or undifferentiated marketing could be dangerous for a company. However, when others use undifferentiated or mass-marketing strategy, differentiated marketing can be adopted.

Single segment specialisation or niche strategy makes more sense when the company has the competence and resources to meet specialised, unique and somewhat complex sets of needs and also wants to avoid direct competition with larger firms pursuing larger segments.

Product Positioning

Why do consumers prefer one product to another? In today's over-communicated society and highly competitive markets, consumers have numerous options in almost all product categories. For example, consumers can buy a PC from IBM, Acer, Sony, Apple, HPCompaq, Zenith and others including low-cost assemblers. Every day, an average consumer is exposed to numerous marketing related messages and the marketer must successfully create a distinct and persuasive product or service image in the mind of the consumer.

Brand positioning is a major decision in marketing. It is believed to be the source from which all other decisions of the marketing mix should flow. The entire combination of marketing mix elements attempts to communicate the brand's "**position**" to consumers.

Product position and brand position are different in scope. According to Smith and Lusch, product position refers to the objective attributes in relation to other products, and brand position refers to subjective attributes in relation to competing brands and this perceived image of the brand does not belong to the product but is the property of consumers' perceptions of a brand. However, the terms 'product positioning' and 'brand positioning' usually mean the same thing.

Product positioning is a decision reached by a marketer to try to achieve a defined brand image relative to competition within a market segment. Product positioning decisions are strategic decisions and have an impact on long-term success of the brand. A product cannot exist unless it finds a place in the consumer's perception of the world of products around her/him. Any product or brand is noticed only when it occupies a particular point or space in the individual consumer's mind relative to other brands in the same product category. This perception of product is subjective and is governed by the individual's needs, values, beliefs, experience and environment. *The 'position' is the way the product or the brand is defined by consumers on important attributes.* Positioning is the perception of a brand or product it brings about in the mind of a target consumer and reflects the essence of that brand or product in terms of its functional and non-functional benefits as judged by the consumer. Maggi brand of noodles has been successfully positioned as the "two minute" noodle in the minds of target consumers and has created a distinctive brand image. HLL's soap, Lux, is hypothetically positioned as the "beauty soap" of female film stars and Dettol is the antiseptic for minor nicks and cuts, while possessing a plethora of uses, from preventing nappy rash to doubling as effective after-share lotion. BMW car is positioned as the "ultimate driving machine," and Volvo is positioned on safety and durability. As markets become more crowded and competitive with similar types of products, consumers rely more on the product's image than on its actual characteristics in making their buying decisions.

The right positioning is probably more important to the ultimate success of a brand than are its actual attributes. Marketers sometimes assign different images to the same product or service in different market segments or at times reposition the same product without actually making it any difference physically. They attempt to create a distinct position for their brand so that consumers perceive it as being different and occupying a niche, no other product does and thereby try to create a product image congruent with the relevant self-image of the target consumers. Marketers strive to differentiate their products or services by emphasising attributes that they claim to be better able to satisfy consumer needs and wants than competing brands.

Positioning theory is significantly different from target marketing. It puts emphasis on the target consumers' perceptions of brands in relation to other brands in the same product category. A major contribution of positioning theory is that it has introduced the concept of '**distance**' and '**dissimilarity**' between brands in the 'perceptual space' of the consumers. This concept can present many opportunities for perceived differentiation of products and brands. Prof. Levitt says that there is no such thing as a commodity; all goods and services are differentiable. To be meaningful, a differential advantage has to be persuasive and sustainable. Michael Porter points out: "A company can outperform its rivals only if it can establish a difference that it can preserve. It must deliver greater value to customers or create comparable value at a lower cost, or both." With rapid developments in science and technology, more and more brands in a given product category tend to become physically similar and more or less equal in performance. The product or brand manager has little choice but to fall back more and more on non-functional factors to distinguish her/his brand, and meaningful persuasive differentiation becomes an increasingly challenging task.

FIGURE 9.6

A Hypothetical Perceptual Map for Eight Cars

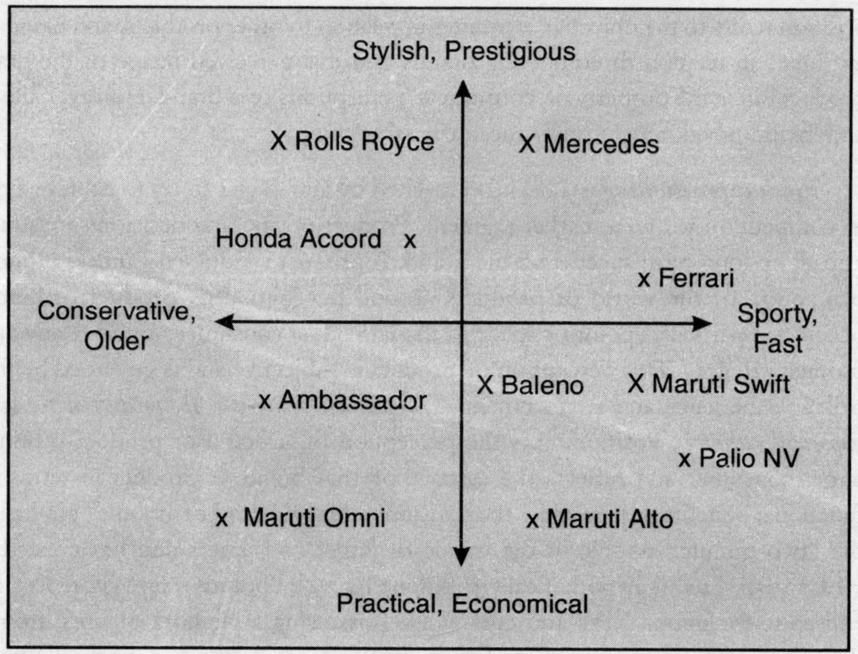

Brands can be expected to create loyal following only when they are perceived as different in some way, which is convincingly meaningful and persuasive for the members of the target segment, and this is what positioning exercise is meant to accomplish. It is not really what the product is or does but actually *what the marketer does to the mind of the consumer.*

To some extent, differentiation can be accomplished in all products based on tangible and intangible attributes. According to C. Merle Crawford, common bases used for positioning include:

- ***Features*** refer to objective physical or performance characteristics and are often used to differentiate products. For example, Amazon.com has a unique "I-click" ordering facility. Some autos claim "Zero to 100 Kph in 6 seconds." This sort of positioning is more common with industrial products.
- ***Benefits*** are directly related to products, such as Volvo's emphasis on safety and durability. "Sticks in a snap," Fevi Kwick. Fairglow soap is a "fairness soap."
- ***Usage*** includes end use, demographic, psychographic, or behavioural segments for whom the product is meant. It also includes product popularity. For example, Chayavanprash to build body resistance of children or elders, Farex for small kids, Bajaj Pulsar "definitely male" for customers of a certain psychographic profile.
- ***Parentage*** means the lineage denoting who makes the product. "Buying a car is like getting married. It's a good idea to know the family first," advises The Mercedes S Class model. Companies proudly trumpet their names, such as "SONY Vaio", "Tata Indica", "Fiat Palio," etc.
- ***Manufacturing process*** is often used to position the product. Some expensive watches claim to be "hand crafted," an appealing proposition in an age of mass produced artifacts.
- ***Ingredients*** are sometimes highlighted to create a position. For example, some garment manufacturers claim "One hundred per cent cotton," or "Hundred per cent Merino wool."
- ***Endorsements*** are made either by experts or a common person with whom the target customers are likely to identify. For example, Michael Jordan using Nike shoes, and the unforgettable Lalitaji (a savvy

middle class housewife concerned about family budget) and her enduring advice that "Surf Ki Kharidari Mein Hi Samajhdari Hai." (It's wise to buy Surf).

- ***Comparison*** with a competitor's product is a fairly common positioning approach. Avis compared itself with Hertz, stressing that it tries harder because it the *second*-biggest can rental *company*. Samsung Laser Printer compared itself with HP Laserjet ... and thereby jumped cleverly onto the came platform.
- ***Pro-environment*** approach to positioning aims to show that the company is a good citizen. Canon mentions on its packages, "Made from recycled material."
- ***Product class***, such as freeze-dried coffee shown as a product that is a different one from instant or regular coffee. Dove soap positioned as a moisturiser and not the toilet soap, and Pears as a glycerine soap.
- ***Price/quality*** is a powerful positioning technique. Zenith computers say "Multinational quality, Indian price."
- ***Country or geographic area,*** such as German Engineering, Russian Vodka, Benarsi silk sari, or Dehradun rice.

At least theoretically, consumers may consider several attributes in their evaluation of product or service alternatives. However, the number actually influencing consumer choice is typically small because they usually consider attributes of which they are aware and all differences among brands are not persuasive. The strength of a difference relates directly to the level of satisfaction it delivers. According to Kotler, a difference will be stronger if it measures up to the following criteria:

- ***Important:*** The difference from consumers' point of view is important because it delivers a highly desired benefit to sufficient number of consumers.
- ***Distinctive:*** The difference is quite clearly delivered in a well-defined way.
- ***Superior:*** Consumers perceive the difference to be superior to other alternatives offering the benefit.
- ***Pre-emptive:*** The difference is sustainable and cannot be copied easily.
- ***Affordable:*** The consumers can afford to pay for the difference.
- ***Profitable:*** The introduction of difference will turn out to be profitable to the company.

Jack Trout and Al Ries suggest that managers should ask themselves six basic questions to create a position for a product or service:

1. What position, if any, do we already have in the prospect's mind? (This information must come from the market-place, not the managers' perceptions).
2. What position do we want to own?
3. What companies must be outgunned if we are to establish that position?
4. Do we have enough marketing money to occupy and hold the position?
5. Do we have the guts to stick with one consistent positioning strategy?
6. Does our creative approach match our positioning strategy?

Marico

■ Consumer products major Marico is looking at extending the franchise of Saffola from cooking oils to salt.

Introduced about five years ago, Saffola salt was a low-key product. That changed when the company brought in actor Boman Irani to endorse the brand.

■ R. Chandrashekhar, category head, Marico said, "After healthcare, we started focusing on the preventive aspects of healthcare a while ago, which are blood pressure, and stress, among others. Salt, then, was a very natural extension of the brand."

■ Although the product has a limited reach at present of about 1.5 lakh households, Saffola and Parachute oil reaches 10 lakh households.

Chandrashekhar is hoping that at least a portion of these would move to the salt. Another reason he says for the increased focus on salt was that about 100 million Indians suffer from hypertension.

He admits that though salt was a largely commoditised category, the product was being positioned as a more premium product with a value add.

"There is increasing awareness in urban areas about iodised and low sodium salt, and this was a niche product aimed at niche audience," he says.

After being rather quiet on the communication front for the last five years, the company is, in addition to television commercials, also doing radio spots and has beefed up its retail strategy.

"In addition to the regular display and point-of-purchase material, we have also introduced dispensers at modern trade outlets, which are our key markets," said Chandrashekhar. Given the premium nature of the product, it would be marketed in urban areas only.

Apart from this, the company is also running a cross promotional offer with the oil.

The Process of Determining the Positioning Strategy

The exercise to determine the positioning strategy is not easy and could prove to be difficult and quite complex. It is important to fix a competitive point of reference by defining customer target market and nature of competition because arriving at the proper positioning requires establishing correct **points-of-parity** and **points-of-difference** associations.

Points-of-parity mean those associations that are not necessarily unique to the brand in some way but may in fact be shared with other brands. These associations can be of two types: *category points-of-parity* refer to those associations that consumers consider as being necessary within a certain product or category to make it a legitimate and credible offering. They may be necessary but not sufficient in themselves for brand choice. These attributes are minimally at generic product level and most likely at expected product level. For example, consumers might not consider a bank truly a "bank" unless it offers saving account facility, cheque books, fixed deposit, and a range of other services, convenient banking hours, ATM, etc. Over the years, facilities may change depending on technological developments and consumer trends, but the attributes and benefits that function as category can be seen to play the marketing game. *Competitive points-of-parity* associations attempt to discard or weaken competitors' points-of-difference associations, or other such type of benefit. If a brand offers the same benefit plus more in some other areas, the brand is likely to emerge stronger and have a better competitive position.

Points-of-difference refer to strong, favourable and unique associations for a brand in consumers' perceptions. These may be related to virtually any type of attribute or benefit association, functional, performance-related or imagery-related psychological considerations, to become a point-of-difference in the minds of consumers. They strongly associate these attributes and benefits with a brand, positively evaluate, and have a firm belief that they could not find these to the same extent in other competing brands. This is actually similar to USP concept pioneered by Rosser Reeves.

- Nivea created strong points of difference on the benefits of "gentle," "protective," and "caring' and became a leader in skin cream category. As the company leveraged brand equity into categories such as deodorants, shampoos, and cosmetics, Nivea found it necessary to establish category points of parity before the company could promote its extension brands' points of
- difference. Nivea's points of difference of gentle, protective, and caring were of little value unless consumers believed that its deodorant was strong enough, its shampoo would produce beautiful enough hair, and its cosmetics would be colourful enough. Once points of parity were established, Nivea's heritage and other associations could be introduced as compelling points of difference.

Seven Steps Need to be Taken to Reach a Decision about Positioning.

Identify Competitors: It may appear simple but it is not. This requires broad thinking. The competing products may not be restricted only to those which come from the same product category with which the brand competes directly. For example, Maggi competes not only with Top Ramen and other noodles, but also with all other products which are used as snacks. The marketer must consider all likely competitors, various use situations and usage effects on the consumer.

Assessment of Consumers' Perceptions of Competition: After defining the competition, it is important to determine how consumers perceive the competing products. To do this, a set of product attributes, such as product characteristics, consumer benefits, product uses or product users are chosen for comparison. The task is to identify relevant attributes to avoid any which would be superfluous. The most useful and relevant attributes are chosen which describe the brand images.

Kelly repertory grid is one approach to generate an attribute list. The respondent is given a deck of cards containing various competing brand names. The consumer is asked to separate all unfamiliar brand names. After this, three cards are then selected randomly from the remaining ones. The respondent is asked to pick up the two brands that are most alike and to describe the reasons for their similarity and why they are different from the third. The respondent is then asked to rate the remaining brands on the basis of attributes thus identified by her/him. This procedure is repeated a number of times for each respondent. This technique often generates a number of attributes. Once again, the redundant ones are separated from the long list of attributes so developed.

After obtaining a list of relevant attributes, most important, meaningful, and distinguishing attributes that influence the consumer's purchase decision, are selected. These attributes are the ones that represent the consumer's image of the competitive brands. Research by Russel J. Haley has shown the relevant attribute list of toothpaste as decay prevention, whitening capability, taste, colour, product and package attractiveness, and price.

Determining Competitor's Position: This exercise is undertaken to determine how all the competing brands, including the company's own are positioned and what is their relative position in the consumer's perceptual map — which are the competing brands that consumers consider as similar, and which are the ones considered dissimilar.

Marketing research can be used to plot a perceptual map that would show the position of different competing brands. Two-dimensional and multidimensional scaling techniques are available to help the researcher. (For a comprehensive discussion of these research techniques, the reader should refer to some good text on Marketing Research)

Analysing the Consumers' Preferences: The analysis so far discussed would determine where in the perceptual map the product should be positioned. The next step requires the identification of segments or clusters of customers who prefer this product location in the perceptual maps. Customers who value a certain set of attributes or benefits would form a segment. An ideal product would be the one that is preferred to over all others.

Making the Positioning Decision: Up to this point, it may become reasonably clear to make some subjective decision as to which position can be appropriate. In many situations, however, it may become necessary to rethink.

Positioning usually involves segmenting the market and choosing one or more segments. This would require ignoring the remaining parts of the market and focusing on selected part only. It is to be considered whether the selected segment or segments would support the brand entry. A specific chosen position may lead consumers to believe that this is what the product is for and those not looking for that specific benefit may not consider the brand. If the decision is for undifferentiated strategy, it may be possible to be general in positioning approach, encouraging consumers that they will get what they are looking for. For instance, the Toyota slogan, "I love what you do for me –Toyota," communicates to consumers that they will get whatever they are looking for in this brand.

Some companies wait to see the market development work done by the competitors and when the market is educated, they enter the market with suitable product modifications. This is what happened in case of cellular phones in India. Some currently strong brands entered the market later, only after companies like Ericsson had created product awareness and market development. Ericsson lost much money in the process and today Nokia, Samsung and LG have good market share, while SONY Ericsson, Panasonic and Motorola are trailing.

A major question, as already pointed out by Trout and Ries, is "Do we have enough marketing money to occupy and hold the position?" Often it happens in this game of creating a brand position that even a series of ads is not likely to be enough. For example, it took long and sustained advertising efforts to create a position for Kinetic Honda. It was only after the ads of Himalayan Rally, with comparative figures of performance, that the product could establish itself on reliability, ruggedness, and durability.

There is an old saying, "If it isn't broke, don't fix it." Many companies have learnt this the hard way. If an ad is working, changing it is usually unwise. Just because the managers are bored with some theme, it is not reason enough to change. Unless there are strong reasons to change the existing positioning of a brand, sticking with the current one is wise.

Writing a Positioning Statement or a Value Proposition

It is a statement expressed clearly and in few words that identifies the target market for which the product is intended. It also specifies the product category in which it competes and highlights the unique benefit it offers.

FIGURE 9.7

Example of a Positioning and Value Proposition Statement

Positioning Statement	Value Proposition
For upper-middle and upper class Indian families, Volvo is the car that provides the utmost in safety and durability.	1. Target market: Upper-middle and upper class Indian families. 2. Benefits: Provides safety and durability. 3. Price: 20 per cent above similar cars.

Monitoring the Position: How strongly and advantageously a position is maintained in the market should be monitored periodically by using tracking studies to measure the image of the brand or the company.

How Many Differences to Promote?

Successful positioning depends on effectively communicating the brand's differential advantage. The critical question is of how many differences to promote? Famous advertising Savant. Rosser Reeves said that a company should develop a Unique Selling Proposition (*USP*) for each brand and stick to it. The brand manager should pick a brand attribute, not being used by competitors, and tout it as "number one" on that attribute. Consumers have a tendency to remember "number one" better, especially in a cluttered advertising scene. For instance, 'Lux' is the beauty soap of female film stars. "Promise" toothpaste touts clove-protection for teeth, though almost all toothpastes contain clove oil. Some positions worth promoting are "Best quality", "Most advanced", "Best service", "Lowest price", etc. A firm that consistently promotes one of these positions and delivers the product or service as promised probably will become best known and remembered for its 'position'.

A *USP* is an outstanding advantage and the best strategy to create a product's position, provided it is not only persuasive for the consumers but also *sustainable.* For instance, Union Carbide developed the zinc chloride technology in India to produce batteries for torches and other products of everyday use. It could have been a *USP* but the company realized that soon it would be copied and wisely decided not to use it for positioning.

A number of advertising professionals believe that when the rule of *USP* was written, products did have genuine, tangible differences and it made really good sense to use *USP* in advertising. However, the times have changed. Products are reaching a uniformly excellent level of quality but the differences among brands in a product category are getting fewer and fewer. They say that *ESP* (Emotional Selling Proposition) or the *UEP* (Unique Emotional Proposition) has replaced *USP.*

There are others who say *USP* is not dead at all, but has become more important than ever before, given the need to be unique because of the ever increasing number of ad messages competing for attention.

As companies increase the number of claims for their brands, they begin to realise that this approach runs the risk of evoking disbelief and a loss of clear positioning. If a brand tries to be everything for everybody, it is likely to end up being nothing to anybody. The market situation has changed to a level where one size does *not* fit all and requires differentiated product and service offering.

Positioning Errors

A brand is a perceptual entity and exists in the perceptual world of customers. In their attempts to create a brand's position, strategists must guard against some *positioning errors* as suggested by Philip Kotler (*'Marketing Management'*, The Millennium Edition, Prentice-Hall of India).

- ***Underpositioning:*** This refers to a state of buyers having only a vague idea of the brand and considering it just another "me too" brand in a crowded product category. The brand is not seen to have any distinctive association.

- ***Overpositioning:*** In this situation, buyers have too narrow an image of the brand. Thus, buyers might think that Apple makes only very expensive computers when, in fact, Apple offers several models at affordable prices.

- ***Confused positioning:*** Sometimes, attempts to create too many associations or to frequently reposition the brand only serves to confuse buyers.
- ***Doubtful positioning:*** This situation may arise when customers find brand claims unbelievable keeping in view the product features, price, or the manufacturer.

According to Subroto Sengupta, positioning strategies revolve around answering the following four questions convincingly by the brand itself: The brand or product manager must determine which strategy is best suited in a given situation to position the brand or the firm, as the case may be:

1. **Who am I?** (The identity, lineage, family).
2. **What am I?** (The functional capabilities).
3. **For whom am I?** (Whom do I serve best).
4. **Why me?** (Why at all a consumer should choose me and not the other alternative).

Consumers are bombarded with information about products or services from all imaginable media. Re-evaluating products or services every time they make a buying decision is impossible. To simplify their buying process, consumers organise products or services into categories, that is, they "position" the products, services and organisations in their minds. A brand's "position" is the complex set of perceptions, impressions and feelings that the consumer associates with the brand compared with competing brands. These aspects may cover physical attributes of the brand, or lifestyle association, or use occasion, or the user's image, etc. Supposedly, if every consumer were to have a mental map of the product category, the location of a particular brand in that map, relative to that of competitor, is the position of the brand under consideration.

Consumers position the product anyway, with or without the help of marketers. It is advantageous for the marketer to plan the positions that will give their products the greatest advantage in the target markets rather than risk leaving the positioning to chance. The entire marketing mix is tailored to communicate the product's planned position. Some *popular positioning approaches* are:

Positioning by Corporate Identity

Companies that become tried and trusted household names, use their names to imply the competitive superiority of their new brands such as, Tata, Sony, Godrej and Seiko. Corporate credentials are added as a by-line. This offers a strong positioning and is used in line extensions or brand extensions.

Positioning by Brand Endorsement

Marketers use the names of company's powerful brands for line extensions, or while entering another product category. Lux, Surf, Titan and Dettol are some examples. These names have been successfully used to introduce new products. Whether it is corporate identity or brand name endorsement, both these answer the important question "Who am I?" or the potential consumer's questions, "Who are you? Do I know you?" Merle Crawford refers to this positioning as "parentage".

> *"Parentage...because of where it comes from, who makes it, who sells it, who performs it, etc. The three ways of parentage positioning are brand (Cadillac or Citizen printer), company (the Data general/ One or Kodak diskette), and person."*
>
> (Merle C. Crawford, *New Products Management,* 1987)

Positioning by Product Attributes and/or Benefits

This approach to positioning is probably the most common and involves setting the brand apart from competitors based on specific brand attributes or the benefits offered. Many products, such as autos, cameras and other durable product brands offer excellent examples. Some cars emphasize technical features such as MPFI, power windows, etc. Some others emphasize economy, safety, or reliability. The tag line for Tata Indica is "More car per car."

A product that is well made usually offers more than one benefit. In case of toothpaste, brands are positioned on cosmetic, medicinal, taste, or economy dimensions. Some brands are using one, two, or even three of the above-mentioned dimensions to create dual or triple positioning. Those consumers who are similar in important ways are more likely to cluster around the same product benefit. Colgate is positioned on fresh breath, decay prevention and taste. Close-Up is positioned on fresh breath and cosmetic benefit. Promise is positioned on gum care. These are examples of single, dual and triple positioning, all related to benefits.

Consumers buy products because they offer some kind of sought after benefit and not just because they are feature rich. Features become important to the consumer only when one or more of those features provide that special benefit(s) the consumer is seeking. Yoram J. Wind writes:

"Strongly linked to product feature positioning is benefit positioning, which is generally more effective than positioning, which describes product features without their benefit to the consumer."

(Yoram J. Wind, *Product Policy: Concepts, Methods and Strategy,* 1982)

The promised benefits answer the question "Why me?" or "Why choose me?" A brand's physical features or attributes become important when positioning lies more in offering a convincing reason why the brand will actually deliver the benefit it promises. In case of some brands, the functional differences compared to competing brands may be significant and the marketer would enjoy the inestimable competitive edge of a Unique Selling Proposition (*USP*), which promises some benefits that the competitors cannot. For example, Epson Inkjet printers use the *USP* of patented Micro Piezo technology. This is claimed to be superior and promises better printouts.

A brand is a composite entity and is perceived in terms of its functional and non-functional (emotional) benefits. Advertising professionals use Unique Emotional Value (*UEV*) in case of ego-intensive or feel-category products.

Positioning by Use Occasion and Time

The idea behind this approach for positioning is to find an occasion or time of use and sit on it. For example, Vicks VapoRub is to be used for a child's cold at night. Iodex is for sprains and muscle pains, Burnol ointment is for burns and Dettol antiseptic is for nicks and cuts. These brands have used this positioning for decades now without any serious challenge from competitors.

Positioning by Price-Quality

Price-quality positioning is quite a powerful approach, particularly in a developing economy such as India. In a large heterogeneous market like our own, consumers' quality expectation levels are different, depending on their socio-economic status. This offers many opportunities for price-quality levels and positioning.

FIGURE 9.8

Price Quality Positioning for TSF Footwear (Comfortable shoes, comfortable price)

For the top gun.
And the wannabe.
TSF
Comfortable Shoes.
Comfortable Price.

An excellent example is that of Nirma detergent powder. It has successfully used the price-quality positioning strategy. In the early 1970s, every ad of good quality detergents such as Surf had a strong demonstration effect on middle class housewives. They wanted to use it but were unable to afford it because of the price factor. Nirma positioned itself as a quality product that lathered well, cleaned well… and the price was nearly one-third that of Surf. The product promise was quality at the right price—a price-quality positioning. Timex used price-quality positioning for its quartz watches in USA and became a huge success, the largest selling brand there. Zenith uses price-quality positioning for its home PCs. These are examples of "value for money" that insist that an economically priced product does not necessarily mean bad quality.

When a consumer is satisfied with a particular value-for-money brand, consumer feels reinforced in her/his decision. This is a typical sequence of use—feel—learn, or it can be expressed as use—learn—feel. In such a situation, the advertising for the brand helps create an image that places the brand above its perceived rung on the price-quality ladder and makes the consumer feel really good about the wise decision.

Another dimension of price-quality positioning is that the product is positioned on high quality—where the price is kept high to communicate this high quality. In many product categories it is not possible to assess quality. For instance, the high price of a perfume becomes an indicator of its high quality. Premium brands positioned at the high end of the market use this positioning. For example Rolex, Omega, Mercedes, Rolls-Royce, Chanel No. 5 and many other brands use the strong price-quality positioning. This positioning can convincingly answer the questions "Who am I?" or "Why me?"

Positioning by Product Category

This positioning is used so that the brand is perceived as belonging to another product category. This is often a strong positioning strategy when the existing product category is crowded. The consumers then perceive the brand in a different context. Dan Sarel has described this sort of positioning as 'inter-set positioning' or 'macro-positioning'.

When Maruti introduced its van, it was initially positioned as a Van and advertised accordingly. Subsequently this vehicle was positioned as Maruti Omni, the spacious family car; no longer, was the erstwhile 'van' competing with other vans but with Ambassador and Fiat.

A classic positioning case is of soft drink 7-Up. For a long time, it was positioned as a beverage that had a "fresh clean taste" that was "thirst quenching." Research revealed that most consumers regarded it as a mixer beverage and not a soft drink. This positioning by consumers tended to attract only those who favoured 'light' soft drinks. 7-Up was later positioned as a real soft drink, not a common and familiar 'cola' but as an alternative to "colas", the "Uncola." This stands as an example of one of the most successful repositioning exercises ever, about equal to Rajdoot motorcycles, which was reborn as rugged rural vehicle ideal for tough terrain and perfect for 'doodhwalas'. Celebrity endorsement by film actor Dharmendra was the *grand finale* that considerably extended the Rajdoot's life cycle. The toilet soap, Dove, of HLL is positioned away from the toilet soap category. It's positioning in India is as a cleansing cream product for young ladies with dry skin.

A milk powder, with suitable additions and appropriate packaging, can be positioned as an 'energy drink' for sports people, or a 'health-drink' for convalescing people, or a drink for 'growing school going children', etc.

Positioning by Product User

The brand manager can determine a target segment for which the product will be positioned. Various segment bases can be considered. For example, Farex was initially positioned for two age groups: infants and old people. Later on the product was repositioned for infants from the age three months to one year and appropriate pack design changes were made.

FIGURE 9.9

Positioning by Product User

Dabur's Chyavanprash, the Ayurvedic tonic, is positioned for all ages, grandfather to grandchild. Another brand, Zandu Special Chyavanprash, is clearly positioned for families with small children to build up their resistance against coughs and colds. The product is basically the same, but both the brands are positioned for different demographic segments. These are examples of product brands positioned according to demographic fit.

Products can be successfully positioned according to psychographics, or behavioural aspects. Beauty and fashion products, footwear, autos, soft drinks, beer and many different products furnish good examples for psychographic fit. Similarly, heavy-users or light users, or consumers looking for certain benefits from product usage offer good opportunities to position the product. For example, Johnson & Johnson successfully positioned its baby shampoo for adults who were heavy users of shampoos. Cars are positioned on benefits such as, economy or safety. These positioning strategies persuasively answer the question "For whom am I?"

Positioning by Competitor

Probably the best and most widely quoted example of this type of positioning is by Avis, the car rental company. Avis gave a powerful reason to its potential customers "We try harder because we are No. 2." This positioning succeeded because Hertz held No.1 position in USA and Avis related to Hertz. People show a natural sympathy and inclination to support the underdog.

FIGURE 9.10
Positioning by Competitor

This is an offensive positioning strategy and is often seen in cases of comparative advertising. AMD (Advanced Micro Devices) have released ads showing comparison of their Athlon processor against Intel's Pentium, proving the superiority of Athlon. Apple computers compared their G. Power processors against Pentium, showing that G. Power processors are faster than Pentium. In an ad, the iMac's tag line was "Comparing this to a PC is nothing short of slander." These examples are loud and clear answers to the question "Why me?" based on functional attributes.

David Aaker and Gary Shansby have quoted the example of Avis in the following words:

"In most positioning strategies, an explicit or implicit frame of reference is the competition… perhaps the most famous positioning strategy of this type was Avis…The strategy was to position Avis with reference to Hertz as a major car rental agency and away from National, which at the time was a close third to Avis."

(David A. Aaker and Gary J. Shansby, *"Positioning Your Product", Business Horizons,* May-June 1982.)

Positioning by competitor may be used because the competitor enjoys a well-established image in the market. The marketer wants the consumers to believe that the brand is superior, or at least as good as offered by the competitor. It is like telling the people that you live next to some famous movie personality in Mumbai rather than getting involved in explaining the locality and streets.

Repositioning

No matter how well a product appears to be positioned, the marketer may be forced to decide on its repositioning in response to new opportunities or threats. The product may be provided with some new features or it may be associated with some new uses and offered to the existing or new markets.

FIGURE 9.11
Repositioning Milkmaid to prepare Desserts and Sweets

For example, earlier Nestle's Milkmaid was "Milkmaid Condensed Milk", a convenient form of milk for use as tea or coffee creamer or whitener. The sales of Milkmaid reached a plateau in 1980s and the company repositioned the product as ideal for preparing sweets and desserts. The pack design was smartened up and changed to suit this repositioning, which led to remarkably substantial gains in sales volume.

Johnson & Johnson repositioned their baby shampoos and lotions for the adult market by changing the promotional and packaging strategy. This was in response to grow opportunities due to lifestyle changes. It is often difficult to reposition a product or brand because of consumers' entrenched perceptions and attitudes. Some important positioning strategies have been discussed, but these are not all. Numerous other bases can be used to create a powerful brand position. A firm can differentiate its offer along the many possibilities related to product, image, service, or personnel.

Summary

The concept of market segmentation is based on the fact that all consumers are not alike. They differ in their needs, wants, desires, income, education, lifestyles and so on. Market segmentation is the process of dividing the heterogeneous market into relatively homogenous sub-groups of consumers with somewhat similar characteristics. When a marketer selects one of more segments and develops a distinct marketing programme to accomplish marketing objectives, it is called target marketing. There are certain conditions that must exist for segmentation to be meaningful. Many approaches are used for segmenting the market. Some of the popular bases for segmentation are geographic, demographic, psychographic and behavioural. Other specific approaches have been used and found to be quite effective, such as segmentation based on lifestyles. Lifestyle approach is based on studying how consumers spend their spare time, what they consider important in their surroundings, what are their beliefs on broad issues and their self image. Such data is generally combined with demographic variables to furnish a clearer picture about consumers. The marketer generally has options either to adopt undifferentiated marketing, differentiated marketing, or concentrated marketing.

Questions for Discussion

1. Why would a company want to segment a market?
2. What factors should be considered for effective market segmentation?
3. Discuss various bases of market segmentation.
4. What segmentations bases would you suggest to a manufacturer of ready-to-wear garments?
5. How should a company choose target markets?

Projects

1. You are a marketing consultant. A new company is planning to introduce a line of pre-cooked food items. It will be quite convenient and far less time consuming to prepare the meals within minutes. How should the company segment the market?
2. Interview the manager of a local departmental store and find out what socio-economic segments the store caters to.
3. Collect three advertisements for (a) consumer non-durable products, (b) consumer durable products, and (c) a service product. Determine to what segments the ads are directed at.
4. Collect two print advertisements of products which are directed at lifestyle segments. Describe the lifestyles these ads focus upon.

Bibliography

1. Peter Doyle, "Managing the Marketing Mix," in *The Marketing Book,* ed. Michael J. Baker, 1992.
2. John L. Lastovicka, John P. Murray, Erich A. Joachimsthaler, Gaurav Bhalla, and Jim Scheurich, "A Lifestyle Typology to Model Young Male Drinking and Driving, "*Journal of Consumer Research,* September 1987.
3. Morris B. Holbrook, "Nostalgia and Consumption Preferences: Some Emerging Patterns of Consumer Tastes," *Journal of Consumer Research,* September 1993.
4. Rebecca Piirto, Global Psychographics," *American Demographics,* December 1990.
5. Wendy Bounds, "New Cameras and Films for the Inept and Impatient," *Wall Street Journal,* January 29, 1996.
6. F. W. Gilbert and W. E. Warren, "Psychographic Constructs and Demographic Segments," *Psychology & Marketing,* May 1995.
7. W. A Kamakura and M Wedel, "Life-Style Segmentation with Tailored Interviewing," *Journal of Marketing Research,* August 1995.

Cases

Case 2.1: Psychographic Profiles – Key to Buyers' Mind

onsumer buying research has turned over a new leaf in India. The era of demographics seems to be on the backbench. Now, Marketing Research people are less likely to first ask you about your age, income, education, etc. Instead, there is a distinct shift towards inquiries about attitudes, interests, lifestyles, and behaviour – in short, a shift towards a study of consumers' minds called psychographics.

Pathfinders, the marketing research wing of Lintas, occasionally came out with its highly respected "Study on the Nation's Attitudes and Psychographics (P:SNAP)." The first in this series was released in 1987 with an objective to develop a database of lifestyles and psychographics information on the modern Indian woman. The second was in 1993, and the third in 1998. Pathfinders chose the Indian woman as the subject for the study because of the belief that more often than not, in urban areas, it is the woman who makes buying decisions.

The Pathfinders' study involves interviewing over 10,000 women over the entire country and segmenting them in clusters according to their beliefs, attitudes, lifestyles, and lastly their demographics profile. The idea is to identify groups of consumers with similar lifestyles who are likely to behave identically or very similarly towards products or services.

For advertisers and advertising agencies, this profile helps enormously. For example, an advertiser may want to give a westernised touch to a commercial. The profile of the target customer, as revealed by this study, tells the advertising people the perimeter within which she/he must stay, otherwise the ad may become an exaggerated version of westernised India.

For the purpose of this study, Pathfinders divided the Indian woman into 8 distinct clusters of varying values and lifestyles. Figures from two studies are available publicly and are given below:

Cluster	1987 (%)	1993 (%)
Troubled homebody	15.9	18.3
Tight-fisted traditionalist	14.8	10.0
Contented conservative	7.0	9.3
Archetypal provider	13.0	8.8
Anxious rebel	14.1	15.8
Contemporary housewife	19.2	22.1
Gregarious hedonist	8.7	6.6
Affluent sophisticate	7.3	9.1

The studies seek to track the macro level changes and movements within these 8 clusters in a period of time.

We note from the table that in 1987, 8.7% of the women in the sample group could be classified as "gregarious hedonist" – those who consider their own pleasure to be supreme in life. In 1993, this figure fell to 6.6%. The "troubled homebody" segment – those with large families and low-income, increased from 15.9% in 1987 to 18.3% in 1993.

Information such as this is obviously useful when it comes to assess the collective mood. That's why Pathfinders have an impressive list of clients for their P: SNAP, which includes Hindustan Lever, Cadbury, Johnson & Johnson, and Gillette.

Contd...

Profile Representative

The lady lives a 'good' life – she is a devoted wife, a doting mother of two school-going sons, and a god-fearing housewife. She has been living her life by the traditional values she cherishes – getting up at the crack of dawn, getting the house cleaned up, having the breakfast of 'Aloo Parathas' ready in time before the children's school-bus honks its horn, laying down the dress her 'government servant' husband will put on after his bath, and doing her daily one-hour Puja. She fasts every Monday for the welfare of her family, looks at the 'freely mixing' and 'sexually liberal' youngsters with deep disdain and cannot understand the modern young woman's 'greed' for money, jewelry, and jobs.

Her one abiding interest outside the household is the Ganesh Mandir that she has visited every Wednesday, ever since she got married. She lacks higher education and hence has little appreciation for the arts, the literature, and the sciences. Her ample spare time is spent watching TV, which is her prime source of entertainment and information.

Profile Representative

Shobha married young to the first person, she fell in love with, Prakash. Four children came quickly before she was quite ready to raise a family. Now, she is unhappy. She is having trouble in making ends meet on her husband's salary (Prakash is employed as a clerk in a private business and is often required to work late hours). She is frustrated, as her desire for an idyllic life has turned sour. She could not get education beyond high school and hence there are hardly any job opportunities for her. Her husband also keeps on complaining of the long hours of backbreaking work he has to put in. He consumes country-made liquor routinely.

Shobha finds escape in (Black and White) TV soap operas and films that transport her to the world of her dreams. She watches TV almost all through the day while her children roam around in the locality streets and cannot expect any help from their 'ever-grumbling' mother. Purchases are mostly limited to 'essentials' and any discretionary purchases are postponed till they simply must be bought.

Profile Representative

Neeru epitomises simplicity. Her life is untangled. It runs on a set timetable with almost clockwork precision. She works as a primary school teacher in a rural government school about 50 kilometers from her district town residence. She is married to a social worker in an NGO whose income is erratic. Her three children, two teenaged sons and a 10-year old daughter are getting school education.

The day begins with the lady getting up before anybody else and finishing the household chores as fast as she can. There is no room for delay, as the State government 'Express' bus, on which she travels to her school will be at the bus stop across the road precisely at 8.00 A.M. If she misses that, the next ordinary bus comes at 11.15 A.M, quite useless as it will reach her school only at 1.00 P.M. The school closes at 2.00 P.M. There are private Jeeps running sporadically, but the fare is high and Neeru does not believe in wasting hard earned money. Besides, she travels on her husband's 'free pass'. Neeru prides herself on her monthly savings of Rs.1000 for the last many years. The money will go toward the wedding of her daughter.

Profile Representative

For Vandana, saving money is 'inborn' discipline. When she was young and unmarried, she remembers her mother who was extremely tight-fisted and ran the household on under Rs. 800

Contd...

per month. It was the necessity of those times as her father retired at a princely salary of Rs. 1800 per month. All through her childhood, she saw deprivation and hardship. She would not join the annual class picnic in her school days as it meant 'avoidable expenditure'.

Now she is married and a mother of two school going children. The husband works in a bank as a clerk. He has taken all the loans that he could from the bank and invested the money in real estate. As a result of monthly deductions toward repayment of loans, his take home salary is now very little. But Vandana can manage. The school dresses are sewn by her at home, the stationery required comes from a wholesale market, and the books are second-hand from 'friends', cultivated for the purpose. On birthdays, Vandana prepares a sweet dish at home and they splurge on a film. There is a cow and calf at home, being kept as a source of revenue and milk. She sells half the milk to a neighbour and the family consumes the rest. Life in general is hard and frugal. There is a colour TV at home, but they disconnected the cable connection ever since the rates went up. Now they watch Doordarshan only.

Profile Representative

Daughter of a Freedom Fighter, Aditi has always fought her values and principles. People still remember when she walked out of the exam half in a huff as a mark of protest against mass cheating 'sanctioned' by the centre superintendent in a tough paper. While everybody else passed with high marks, Aditi failed.

Even though she repeated the paper, Aditi never learned to swim along the flow. She always swam against the current. She joined the Communist Party in her college and gave rousing speeches against the teachers and authorities. This resulted in her getting very poor marks and left her jobless.

Later, Aditi joined an NGO and now works on social issues. She says she is a creature of the mind, not materialism. Her favourite dress is a long flowing Kurta, and slacks. She wears loosened hair and chappals. She reads voraciously. Financially, she is independent and lives with her parents. Her disdain for the institution of marriage and contempt for the modern Indian male keep her single and unattached. She will continue to be so as she prefers to this status, but may adopt a baby later in life.

Profile Representative

Just 19, and Reema is already divorced. Her father is a wealthy businessman. During Reema's childhood, her father was mostly away in Dubai and Africa, trying to amass a fortune. That he did, but he lost out on his chance to be a good father. Both his children started feeling like 'orphans' after their mother got involved with another man.

Reema was ever longing for her family when along came Harsh, her private high school tuition teacher. Harsh was all of 32 and very caring. He was tall, handsome, and very popular in school and many girls had a crush on him. Reema was sixteen then and a great fan of Harsh. For her, Harsh was a prize catch as he combined the loving qualities of a father with a mix of being a good teacher. She was soon dazzled and surrendered in a physical relationship.

Marriage followed. She never understood how Harsh changed overnight from a caring father figure to a demanding husband. And she could never cope with the six hours she had to spend in the kitchen every day. Why should she do the cooking, she asked Harsh, as it was something that the 'Ayas' did? The reality of a humdrum middle-class existence hit her hard and she soon walked out of 'the hell'.

Contd...

Her father understood her need to recover and made her allowance rather generous. He bought her a red sports car and got her an admission in a private college. College is entertainment for her. She attends college only on days when there is some function like a cultural evening or the sports meet. Now, Reema spends on alcohol, dresses, parties, and holidays. She consumes a mood elevating drug every evening and keeps sending SMS messages on her mobile to her friends all through the night. For her, life means 'buying pleasure endlessly'.

Profile Representative

Shruti is an urbane woman. She is well educated and genteel. She is an officer in a nationalised bank, and is active in club affairs and community activities. Socialising is an important part of her life. She is a doer, interested in watching cricket, politics, and current affairs. Her life is hectic as she has a lot to do for home and office every day. Still, she often enjoys viewing movies on TV every week.

Shruti shops for sarees, jewelry, and cosmetics for herself on a regular basis. However, family needs come before her own needs. Her home is a double income household and she has one child. She has all the modern gadgets as a housewife could possibly want and her standard of living is upper middle-class.

Profile Representative

Momeeta was born Mamta, but elevated herself to Momeeta after marriage to a business tycoon. Momeeta is an elegant woman with style. She lives in Mumbai because that is where, she wants to be. She likes the economic and social aspects of big city living and takes advantage of her 'contacts'. She has built up many friendships and cultivated the city bigwigs by inviting them to the numerous parties she throws in her luxurious penthouse.

Momeeta is a self-confident, on-the-go woman, and not a homebody. She is fashion conscious and clothes herself in the latest designer dresses. Even at 40, she can carry off a mini with aplomb. She is financially very secure and hence does not shop with care. She shops for quality, exclusivity, and goes by the brand name, not the price. She frequently travels abroad, buys expensive gifts for friends, and has an international understanding on what is "chic" at the moment.

QUESTIONS

1. A manufacturer of personal care products in the premium category wants to develop various products. Which of the above types should the manufacturer target? Explain.
2. How is the above-mentioned information likely to benefit a marketer in selecting marketing communications?
3. Which of the above-mentioned segments are likely to respond to sales promotion? Explain.

Case 2.2: Shoppers' Stop

sk the company top brass what 'almost there' means. The answer: a premier Indian retail company that has come to be known as a speciality chain of apparel and accessories. With 52 product categories under one roof, Shoppers' Stop has a line-up of 350 brands. Set up and headed by former Corona employee, B. S. Nagesh, Shoppers' Stop is India's answer to Selfridges and Printemps. As it proudly announces, 'We don't sell, we help you buy.'

Back in 1991, there was the question of what to retail. Should it be a supermarket or a departmental store? Even an electronics store was considered. Finally, common sense and understanding won out. The safest bet, for the all-male team was to retail men's wear. They knew the male psyche and felt that they had discerning taste in men's clothing. The concept would be that of a lifestyle store in a luxurious space, which would make for a great shopping experience. The first Shoppers' Stop store took shape in Andheri, Mumbai, in October 1991, with an investment of nearly Rs. 20 lakh. The original concept that formed the basis of a successful marketing campaign for seven years is here to stay. And the result is an annual turnover of Rs. 160 crores and five stores, nine years later.

Everything went right from the beginning, except for one strange happening. More than 60 per cent of the customers who walked into Shoppers' Stop in Mumbai were women. This gave rise to ideas. Soon, the store set up its women's section. Later, it expanded to include children's wear and then, household accessories.

The second store in Bangalore came in 1995. The store at Hyderabad followed in 1998 with the largest area of 60,000 sq. ft. The New Delhi and Jaipur stores were inaugurated in 1999. All this while, the product range kept increasing to suit customer needs. The most recent experiment was home furnishings. Secure in the knowledge that organised retailing in global brands was still in its infancy in India, Shoppers' Stop laid the ground rules which the competition followed.

The biggest advantage for Shoppers' Stop is that it knows how the Indian consumer thinks and feels while shopping. Yes, feeling – for in India, shopping remains an outing. And how does it compare itself to foreign stores? While it is not modelled on any one foreign retailer, the 'basic construct' is taken from the experience of a number of successfully managed retail companies. It has leveraged expertise for a critical component like technology from all over the world, going as far as hiring expatriates from Littlewoods and using state-of-the-art ERP models. Shoppers' Stop went a step further by even integrating its financial system with the ERP model. Expertise was imported wherever it felt that expertise available in-house was inadequate.

But the store felt there was one acute problem. A shortage of the most important resource of them all, was trained humans. Since Indian business institutes did not have professional courses in retail management, people were hired from different walks of life and the training programme was internalised. By 1994, the senior executives at Shoppers' Stop were taking lectures at management institutes in Mumbai. The Narsee Monjee Institute of Management Studies (NMIMS) even restructured its course to include retail management as a subject.

Getting the company access to the latest global retail trends and exchange of information with business greats was an exclusive membership to the Intercontinental Group of Department Stores (IGDS). It allows membership by invitation to one company from a country and Shoppers' Stop rubs shoulders with 29 of the hottest names in retailing – Selfridges from the UK, C.K.

Contd...

Tang from Singapore, Lamcy Plaza from Dubai and the like.

With logistics I in place, the accent moved to the customer. Shoppers' Stop conducted surveys with ORG-MARG and Indian Market Research Bureau (IMRB) and undertook in-house wardrobe audits. The studies confirmed what it already knew. The Indian customer is still evolving and is very different from, say, a European customer, who knows exactly what he wants to purchase, walks up to a shelf, picks up the merchandise, pays and walks out. In India, customers like to touch and feel the merchandise, and scout for options. Also, the majority of Indian shoppers still prefer to pay in cash. So, transactions must be in cash as against plastic money used the world over.

Additionally, the Indian customer likes being served – whether it is food, or otherwise. The company's customer profile includes people who want the same salesperson each time they came to the store to walk them through the shop floors and assist in the purchase. Others came with families, kids and maids in tow and expected to be suitably attended to. Still others wanted someone to carry the bags. So, the shops have self-help counters, with an assistant at hand for queries or help.

The in-house wardrobe audit also helped with another facet of the business. It enabled Shoppers' Stop to work out which brands to stock, based on customer preferences. In fact, the USP of Shoppers' Stop lies in judiciously selected global brands, displayed alongside an in-house range of affordable designer wear. The line-up includes Levi's, Louis Philippe, Allen Solly, Walt Disney, Ray Ban and Reebok, besides in-house labels STOP and I.

Brand selection is the same across the five locations, though the product mix may be somewhat city-based to accommodate cuts and styles in women's wear, as well as allowing for seasonal variations (winter in Delhi, for instance, is a case in point). Stocking of brands is based on popular demand – recently, Provogue, MTV Style, and Benetton have been added. In-house labels are available at competitive prices and target the value-for-money customer and make up around 12 per cent of Shoppers' Stop's business.

Sometimes in-house brands plug the price gap in certain product categories. To cash in on this, the company has big plans for its in-house brands: From re-branding to repositioning, to homing in on product categories where existing brands are not strong. Competition between brands is not an issue, because being a trading house, all brands get equal emphasis.

The in-house brand shopper is one who places immense trust in the company and the quality of its goods and returns for repeat buys. And the company reposed its faith in regular customers by including them in a concept called the First Citizen's Club (FCC). With 60,000 odd members, FCC customers account for 10 per cent of entries and for 34 per cent of the turnover. It was the sheer appeal of the experience that kept pulling these people back.

Not one to let such an opportunity pass, the company ran a successful ad campaign (that talks about just this factor) in print for more than eight years. The theme is still the same. In 1999, a TV spot, which liked the shopping experience to the slowing down of one's internal clock and the beauty of the whole experience, was aired. More recently, ads that spell out the store's benefits (in a highly oblique manner) are being aired.

The campaign is based on entries entered in the Visitors' Book. None of the ads has a visual or text – nor any heavy-handedly direct reference to the store or the merchandise. The ads only show shoppers having the time of their lives in calm and serene locales, or elements that make shopping at the store a pleasure – quite the perfect getaway for a cosmopolitan shopper aged

Contd...

between 25 and 45. The brief to the agency, Contract, ensured that brand recall came in terms of the shopping experience, not the product. And it has worked wonders.

Value-addition at each store also comes in the form of special care with car parks, power backup, customer paging, alteration service and gift-wrapping. To top it all, cafes and coffee bars make sure that the customer does not step out of the store. In Hyderabad, it has even created a Food Court. Although the food counter was not planned, it came about as there was extra space of 67,000 sq. ft.

Carrying the perfect experience to the shop floor is an attempt to stack goods in vast open spaces neatly. Every store has a generic structure, though regional customer variances are accounted for. Each store is on lease, and this is clearly Shoppers' Stop's most expensive resource proposition – renting huge spaces in prime properties across metros, so far totalling 210,000 sq. ft of retail space. Getting that space was easy enough for Shoppers' Stop, since its promoter is the Mumbai-based Raheja Group, which also owns 62 per cent of the share capital.

(Source: Radhika Singh, "Stocking Up On Emotions," A & M, August 15, 2000).

QUESTIONS

1. What are the significant factors that have led to the success of Shoppers' Stop?
2. Draw the typical profile(s) of Shoppers' Stop customer segments.
3. How are Indian customers visiting Shoppers' Stop any different from customers of developed western countries?
4. How should Shoppers' Stop develop its demand forecasts?

Case 2.3: Mineral Water

n 1993, when Prakash Chauhan's Parle Agro entered the mineral water market with its brand, Bailley, market analysts thought it fit to keep their fingers crossed about its prospects. For one, the concept of bottled mineral water was not well established, with usages restricted to foreign tourists and jet-setting Indians. On the other, for whatever the market was worth, it was firmly within the stranglehold of Bisleri, owned by brother Ramesh Chauhan's Parle Exports. Bisleri enjoyed a clear first-mover advantage and was on its way to assume the generic brand status in a 3.5 million-case market (estimated at Rs. 36 crores).

For Prakash Chauhan, however, the market presented a very clear opportunity. Parle Agro had two well-entrenched brands in its portfolio, Frooti and Appy, which occupied leadership positions in the tetra packed fruit drinks market with a combined share of over 90 per cent. That meant that the distribution system was already in place and the new brand of bottled water from the same stable would have a readymade network of outlets throughout the country. Second, with very little investment required in terms of technology or infrastructure, the entry barriers were not very difficult to overcome.

However, as a new entrant, Bailley's task was formidable. Through the 1970s and 1980s, the mineral water category was a virtual, with only a handful of players catering to the sporadic demands of an equally small audience comprising travellers and a few affluent consumers. According to some estimates, travellers then accounted for 80 per cent of the sales volume. Research findings corroborated the fact that people associated the consumption of mineral water with foreign tourists, who were wary of consuming contaminated water. But for the average traveller, the price tag of Rs. 8-9 for a 1-litre bottle appeared unreasonable for a product which could be had for free and for which he had no clear need. Instead, most travellers carried their own water bottles. In any case, even though the concept of water filters had made its way into people's homes, the idea of carrying hygienic drinking water outside of home was accorded very low priority. Instead, travellers were quite content to consume tap water at railway stations or restaurants located near bus stops.

The biggest barrier was the high recall that Bisleri enjoyed. So much so that consumers who went to buy mineral water would actually walk up to the retail counter and say: "Ek Bisleri Dena." (Give me a bottle of Bisleri). Or even when the consumer did ask for a particular mineral water brand, the retailer would fish out whichever brand he had in stock and hand it over to the consumer. In essence, the brand awareness was low, and apart from localised competition, the small size of the market did not grant enough space for another national player to join the fray.

To thrive in such a scenario, the company had to expand the market. Here, new entrants and relatively smaller players were at a disadvantage because freight costs claimed a large part of the operating expenses, at times as high as 30–40 per cent of the total cost. Maintaining an efficient delivery system required both high volumes and investment in infrastructure. But raking in the volumes in a category where the scope for brand differentiation was low presented another formidable barrier.

Despite these barriers, when Parle Agro began exploring the market in detail, it realised that with increasing health consciousness the market was poised for a take-off. Added to that was

Contd...

the prospect of increasing tourist traffic, both domestic and foreign. But the existing capacities were not quite enough to serve the steadily increasing demand.

Since Parle Export's Bisleri was so strongly identified with the category, Parle Agro took great care to brand its new product carefully. Without being radically different, the company chose a name that was slightly anglicised to project a more upmarket image. The company also figured that the consumer took a little more time to articulate the name, which in turn made sure that recalling the name would be so much easier. But more than just the brand name, the company realised that to penetrate the market effectively, an efficient distribution system and competitive freight costs were important.

Bailley had learnt important lessons from the Bisleri experiment. Parle Exports' distribution system started out with its bottling plant in Mumbai. Later, it went ahead and added II more franchisees who had their own bottling plants in the metros and a few mini-metros. While this restricted the spread, it also resulted in a lopsided cost structure because the freight and handling costs to survive in the interior markets proved sufficiently prohibitive.

Parle Agro had a very clear game plan from the beginning. One thing was clear: distribution was the key to success. Mineral water being a logistics business and a voluminous item, transportation was expensive. Therefore, it was essential to locate plants across the country. But that was an expensive proposition. Also, differing sales tax, excise, and octroi rates across states makes it difficult to have uniform national pricing. A network of franchisees that was widely spread out was the only way to things would work.

Parle Agro established franchisees near the markets that it identified to attack. This meant they had to limit their focus to only a few markets initially. But that was fine for the company, as long as the freight cost was kept to the barest minimum. This structure also ensured that Bailley had shorter replenishment cycles and lower inventories for the plants. While Bisleri reverted to the same route later, Parle Agro simply doubled the number of franchisees. This allowed Bailley to penetrate the market quickly. All these franchisees were expected to set up PET bottle manufacturing facilities at the bottling plant as well. This was because packaging costs – bottle, pilfer-proof cap and so on – made up some 40 per cent of the total costs. This also did away with the uncertainty of bottle supply.

Parle Agro also decided to differentiate Bailley in terms of bottle design, since there was very little scope for differentiation in the product itself. Mineral water bottles, irrespective of brand, are made through the process of blow moulding. Since the preform-supplier of all those bottles was the same, all the mineral water brands available in the market had an identical design. To stand out, Parle Agro decided to standardise preform and cap designs for Bailley. The company set up a preform plant at Silvassa, which produced these moulds from PET granules that it buys from Reliance. These moulds are small test-tube like structures, which are sent to bottling facilities where they are blown, filled, and despatched.

Initially, the company introduced two pack sizes. 500 ml bottle was priced at Rs. 5 and was meant to induce trials, and was also most convenient for the individual traveller. The l-litre bottle was initially meant to spell safety and security for 'integrated consumers' who were genuinely into health and fitness. Thereafter, it was placed on the prestige platform for the achiever segment – those who like to make a fashion statement by drinking mineral water. The prestige aspect was fully exploited when the Bailley team hit upon the idea of exploring the

Contd...

wedding market. While caterers had reservations about whether the host would pick up the tab for water, Bailley salesmen did a fair amount of direct servicing to set the ball rolling. This has now turned out to be one of the fastest growing segments.

Side by side, Parle Agro's sales team also established franchisee networks in relatively inaccessible places such as Guwahati, Palghat, Jaipur, and Belgaum, which gave the company access to remote markets.

Another advantage was that while attacking these markets, the threat of any immediate retaliatory action from Bisleri was minimised. That was mainly because Bisleri was quite well established in the metros and such low-volume fringe markets were of very little interest to the company. Moreover, at the time Parle Exports was determined on paring down its investments on the mineral water brand and was content to let it piggyback on its existing soft drinks network. After the task of cracking the market open was through, Parle Agro devoted all its energies to exploit the non-traditional routes of increasing distribution width. It tied up with various long-distance bus operators who kept stocks of Bailley on board. A small incentive was given to bus operators and conductors to push the brand. The company also sought out restaurants or dhabas on Mumbai–Pune and Nasik–Pune route which had been neglected by other players. The company encouraged stockists to service these outlets, especially restaurants at which buses made their day or night-time halts.

Typically, the interior markets had far more players than could be accommodated. To fight the regional players, Parle Agro used a two-pronged approach at the outlet level. It offered better service cycles and better product quality.

In some cases, the company also resorted to an ingenious retail monitoring system, the Agro Retail Barometer to identify those outlets where competitive brands were not moving fast, so that the company could seize the opportunity to persuade the retailer to stock Bailley instead and push it.

Despite its aggressive stance, the Delhi market eluded Bailley for a long time. That was because it faced major problems in getting its franchisee set-up in Delhi right. While Bailley was widely available in the markets of Jammu and Uttar Pradesh, till December last year Parle Agro was not able to fix a big enough franchisee which would be able to service Delhi and adjacent towns. Despite that, till about a year back, Parle Agro was able to command a 20 per cent share nationally (against Bisleri's 45 per cent) with its persistent attempts to crack the areas that the leader wouldn't dare.

The company's aggressive marketing strategy seems to have paid off. For one, it successfully broke the monopoly of Bisleri and is now the leader in a number of regions including Maharashtra (especially Mumbai), Gujarat, West Bengal, Karnataka, and Goa, and a close second in many others. With a total production capacity of 120 million bottles per year, Parle Agro has mainly targeted towns with populations of more than one lakh, although Bailley is also available in towns with populations less than 50,000. Being a low-margin business, the company hasn't spent any money and effort on mass media advertising but has concentrated on educating consumers on the use of pure, hygienic water through direct mailers and other media. Participation in corporate events also gives it a lot of mileage and the brand is patronised by corporates such as the Taj Group of Hotels and Jet Airways.

But the main reason for Bailey's success has been the strength of its franchisee network. Following the example of the West, the company realised that the best growth strategy is not

Contd...

one that entails extra space, capital investments and added manpower, but franchising. Franchised operations provided it a quick expansion route, while keeping costs low and profitability high, and at the same time ensured deeper penetration and easy accessibility. Parle Agro now has a network of 18 franchisees. With regular monitoring of its decentralised operations and strict checks on quality, Parle Agro provides the overall expertise, cashing in on the local franchise's understanding of his area.

Today, the mineral water business has grown to a healthy Rs. 500 crore and is growing at a phenomenal rate of more than 50 per cent. Of this, unorganised sector players constitute about 40 per cent. Till four years ago, the market had only two national players; today, more than 168 are jostling for shelf space.

According to industry sources, a new label is launched every three months and one existing player recedes into oblivion. For all practical purposes, Bisleri and Bailley today dominate the organised sector. Bisleri leads the pack with a 40 per cent share by value. Bailley is a 60-crore brand and is the No. 2 player with a share of 22 per cent. In percentage terms, the brand is growing faster than the category, claims the company.

But the fact remains that even to this day, about 76 per cent of the mineral water consumption in the country is by travellers, and bottled water hasn't made inroads into middle class homes yet. For Bailley too, the biggest segment of consumers is that of travellers, followed by institutions and tourists. According to the company, the mineral water consumer is attracted by the benefits of easy accessibility, purity, and hygiene and only a small segment of consumers have evolved to the level of being loyalists of good brands.

The mineral water consumer is typically in the 25–35-years age group and is an educated, evolved person from SEC A and B.

The consumption pattern is changing, though. Mineral water is now served on trains, airlines, and parties. Besides the standard 1 litre bottle, Parle Agro has introduced bigger pack sizes to cater to a variety of needs. Bailley is available in 1 litre, 1.5 litre and 500 ml bottles, 20 litre jars and 200 ml glasses. The one-litre bottle sells the most.

While new players are making a beeline for this industry every day, hygiene continues to be the main plank of most brands. Worldwide, mineral water stands fortified with genuine minerals. However, it is different in India, since the Bureau of Indian Standards hasn't laid down any specifications. So what is predominantly available is purified water. Even techniques such as ozonisation and reverse osmosis are used only by a handful.

QUESTIONS

1. Study the case and identify major issues related to studying competition, as Parle Agro did.
2. What weaknesses of the competitor helped Parle Agro establish Bailley?
3. What is the typical profile of a mineral water consumer?
4. How do consumers shop for mineral water? What implications does it have for its distribution?

Case 2.4: End of All Work and No Play Culture?

Every year, about 100 million Japanese spend about $75 to see Mickey Mouse and wait two hours in line to rocket through Space Mountain at Tokyo Disneyland. They flock to hear Aron Narikiyo, "Elvis-san," a wildly popular Elvis impersonator. They ski, attend cultural events, go bowling, take juggling lessons, and play pachinko, a vertical version of pinball. What they also do in great numbers is shop. One hundred and twenty million Japanese consumers with rising disposable incomes translates into lots of buying power. Long considered a society of all work and no play, Japan finds both its culture and its consumers changing.

In the conventional picture of modern Japan, men work most of the time, and women are relegated to background positions of stay-at-home wives and mothers. Indeed, many older Japanese accept without complaint endless, unquestioned hard work. But the old ways are changing. Japanese men are discovering that fun is sometimes more important than earnest dedication to the workplace. And Japanese women are assuming professional roles outside the home. Declaring that its citizens should start enjoying life, the government officially shortened the workweek from forty-eight hours to forty and funded the Leisure Research and Development Centre to teach its citizens the value of leisure time. With more money to spend and more time in which to spend it, the Japanese are becoming active and experienced consumers, dedicated to make their country a seikatsu taikoku – a "lifestyle superpower."

Two of the most powerful groups of Japanese consumers are the more than 8 million Dankai Juniors, children of Japan's post-war baby boom, and women, whose status and affluence continues to grow. Raised during a prosperous time in an affluent society, young Japanese spend a lot of money on sports, audiovisual equipment, entertainment, and fashion. Although looking for value more than they did in the 1980s, these young consumers still splurge on new products that improve the quality of their leisure time. One of their favourite places to go for fun is Namco's Wonder Eggs, an arcade specialising in virtual reality games. As for tastes in fashion, this group prefers American and European styles and colours. To attract these trendy customers, some small shops in areas frequented by young people carry only imported clothing.

In today's Japan, women comprise about 40 per cent of the country's 64.5 million-person work force, and more than 50 per cent of mothers work outside the home. Following the Equal Employment Law of 1986, women began to pursue more education, entered a variety of professions, began earning their own salaries, and became champion consumers. Besides attending concerts and plays, travelling, engaging in sports, and frequenting "relaxation parlours," where the sounds of birds singing or waves crashing on the shore relieve stress, Japanese women shop. Choosy about labels, many Japanese women favour distinctive brands, such as Armani suits, Yves St. Laurent towels, and $1,600 Gucci handbags.

Benefiting from Japan's growing appetite for consumption, retailing – both upscale and value-oriented – is booming. To attract consumers by providing more spacious and attractive surroundings, venerable department stores and such as Mitsukoshi and Takashima are remodelling and modernising their interiors. New speciality shops are springing up, as are large shopping centres with avenues of stores and abundant parking space. Although many Japanese equate a good product with a high price tag, many others are becoming increasingly value-conscious, looking for high quality at low prices. Retailers are responding by opening giant discount stores. One of them, I World, is recording annual sales of over $180 million on discounted

Contd...

top-of-the-line brands such as Nordica and Sony. What the Japanese call "roadside chains," freestanding retail buildings, are springing up in the suburbs. Two such competing chains, Aoyama and Aoki, sell name brand men's clothing at lower-than-department-store prices.

When Japanese leaders commanded the country to relax, the leisure industry rushed to provide places to do it. Just as retailing is profiting from larger numbers of Japanese shoppers, the leisure industry is profiting from the greater amount of time that Japanese are spending on recreation. In one year alone, two hundred companies applied for permits to develop new theme parks. To enable ski enthusiasts to make one-day trips from Tokyo, a bullet train station opened at a popular ski resort, Gala Yuzawa. For those who prefer to schuss in climate-controlled comfort, indoor ski slopes are available within city limits. Built on top of one of Tokyo's numerous skyscrapers, the International AQuarium gives city dwellers a chance to escape temporarily to an undersea world. Having discovered the pleasures of camping, Japanese are pursuing this pastime in record numbers. American commercial camp-ground developer KOA recently opened its first Japanese compound in Okayama. Vacationers can swim, play tennis, visit the mini zoo, or join in recreational group singing at the Karoake Kabin.

With all these choices and more, people don't have trouble deciding how to have fun on a day off or a week-long break, but the Japanese are still novices at "hanging out." A Leisure Development Centre survey revealed that 40 per cent of respondents wouldn't know what to do with a month off. To help them, the National Recreation Association offers a one-year course on how to enjoy life. Many Japanese, however, are convinced that the art of having fun is "Made in the U.S.A."

QUESTIONS

1. What are the significant issues in this case?
2. "The changing role of Japanese women has influenced their buying behaviour." Discuss this statement in the light of what you have learned in this case.
3. To market leisure facilities in Japan, what aspects of Japanese consumers' behaviour is of interest?

Case 2.5: Wahaha – Taking the Fizz out of the Giant Cola Brands

hen Zong Qinghou, a Chinese farm worker, started a company of beverages and ice creams with two retired teachers in 1987, hardly anyone could have imagined that this company could give sleepless nights to global giants such as Coca-Cola and Pepsi Co. But the new company, Wahaha, the pride of many contemporary Chinese consumers, has managed to do just that.

Wahaha, one of the leading homegrown Chinese beverage brands, had revenues of US$1.37 billion (11.4 billion yuan) and profits of US$162.7 million (1.34 billion yuan) in 2004.

Wahaha, which is meant to mimic the sound of a baby laughing, demonstrates clearly what great brand stories are made of. The company started small, and in 1991, it merged with the state-owned Hangzhou Canning Factory. The 1996 joint venture with the Danone Group gave the company foreign investment to the extent of US$45 million. After dabbling in many product categories, it launched its trademark brand the 'Future Cola' in 1998 to compete against the global cola giants. Today, Wahaha's product portfolio includes milk and yogurt drink, purified and mineral water, carbonated soft drink, fruit and vegetable juice, sports drink, and iced tea including cognee (rice porridge), canned food and health products.

Wahaha has been careful in its strategy to compete against the global cola and food giants. As the fashion conscious Chinese consumers seem to prefer the global colas in the larger coastal Chinese cites, Wahaha has till now focused on rural and semi-urban Chinese areas. Further, the Wahaha brand has generously used home grown celebrities for all its products. This is in line with its overall strategy to position Wahaha as a patriotic company and to tap into the patriotic fervor of the Chinese consumers.

By projecting Wahaha's products as China's own, the Wahaha brand has carved out a clear positioning in the market against the global brands. But whether this strategy will work in the long run is a million dollar question and will require constant efforts to balance the brand promise and its careful delivery in a hostile and increasingly competitive Chinese marketplace.

QUESTIONS

1. What aspects of consumer behaviour have been discussed in this case?
2. What is likely to be the adoption process of Wahaha products among consumers?
3. Discuss the positioning strategy of Wahaha.

Case 2.5 Wahaha – Taking the Fizz out of the Giant Cola Brands

[illegible]

[illegible]

[illegible]

[illegible]

QUESTIONS

[illegible]

PART 3

Product Concepts

CHAPTER 10

LEARNING OBJECTIVES

After going through this chapter, you will understand:

- How products are classified
- Different product related concepts like product line and product mix and related decisions
- The concept of product positioning and its importance
- The process of developing a positioning strategy, and errors to avoid
- Frequently used positioning approaches

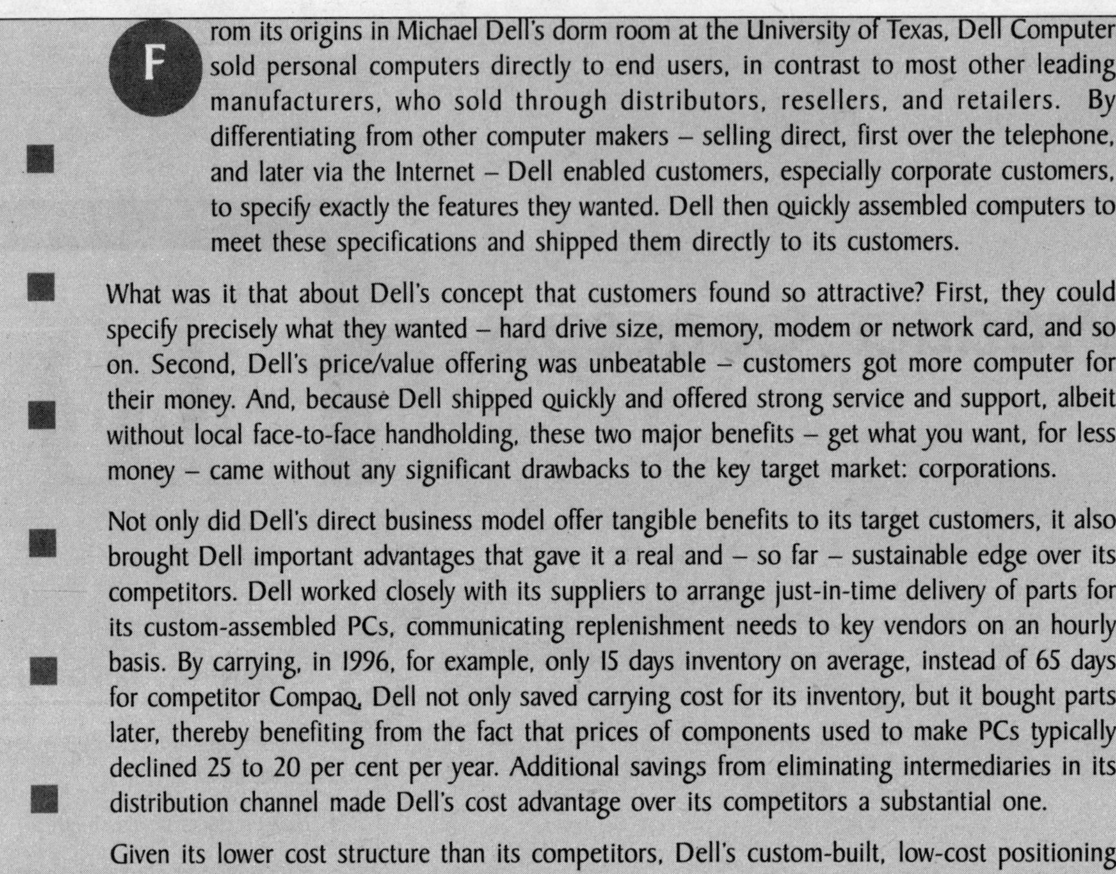

From its origins in Michael Dell's dorm room at the University of Texas, Dell Computer sold personal computers directly to end users, in contrast to most other leading manufacturers, who sold through distributors, resellers, and retailers. By differentiating from other computer makers – selling direct, first over the telephone, and later via the Internet – Dell enabled customers, especially corporate customers, to specify exactly the features they wanted. Dell then quickly assembled computers to meet these specifications and shipped them directly to its customers.

What was it that about Dell's concept that customers found so attractive? First, they could specify precisely what they wanted – hard drive size, memory, modem or network card, and so on. Second, Dell's price/value offering was unbeatable – customers got more computer for their money. And, because Dell shipped quickly and offered strong service and support, albeit without local face-to-face handholding, these two major benefits – get what you want, for less money – came without any significant drawbacks to the key target market: corporations.

Not only did Dell's direct business model offer tangible benefits to its target customers, it also brought Dell important advantages that gave it a real and – so far – sustainable edge over its competitors. Dell worked closely with its suppliers to arrange just-in-time delivery of parts for its custom-assembled PCs, communicating replenishment needs to key vendors on an hourly basis. By carrying, in 1996, for example, only 15 days inventory on average, instead of 65 days for competitor Compaq, Dell not only saved carrying cost for its inventory, but it bought parts later, thereby benefiting from the fact that prices of components used to make PCs typically declined 25 to 20 per cent per year. Additional savings from eliminating intermediaries in its distribution channel made Dell's cost advantage over its competitors a substantial one.

Given its lower cost structure than its competitors, Dell's custom-built, low-cost positioning in the market place allowed it to make an attractive strategic choice. Should it choose to reap higher margins than others in its industry, or should it keep prices low to gain market share? For much of its history, Dell made the latter choice, gaining share at the expense of its rivals.

Taking a narrow perspective, *a* product can be defined as a set of attributes assembled in a distinct and identifiable form. One can distinguish a product by a commonly understood generic name such as salt, steel, computer, entertainment, or crèche. Other attributes such as brand name and any added services are not a part of this description; for instance, both Dell and Zenith are the same product – a PC.

The need of marketing is to have a more comprehensive definition of product to understand clearly that consumers don't really buy attributes. What consumers really buy are specific benefits that they perceive as solutions to problems and satisfactions for their needs. Thus, consumers want the instant sticking benefit, and not just a thick liquid-filled tube named Fevi Kwik. It is important to appreciate that any product feature can be meaningful only to the extent it delivers an expected benefit and satisfaction. Therefore, a product that provides the desired benefits can be some other alternative than just a tangible good. For example, to relieve pain there can be several alternatives other than painkiller drugs.

This book adopts a sufficiently broad definition of product given by Philip Kotler. According to this definition, "*A product is anything, tangible or intangible, which can be offered to a market for attention, acquisition, use, or consumption that might satisfy a need or want.*" Thus, a product can be a physical entity (e.g., computer, shirt, or soap), some service (e.g., healthcare, tuition, or bank), a retail store (e.g., music store, locality grocer, or supermarket), a person (e.g., a singer, physician, or politician), an organisation (e.g., business organisation, trade organisation, or not-for-profit organisation), a place (e.g., village, city, or country), or idea (e.g., social issues, concepts, or population control). We use the word 'product' innumerably in everyday life.

While a product could represent many different things, a ***good,*** however, is a tangible object that can be seen and touched. A ***service***, unlike a good and in sharp contrast to it, represents an intangible product that may involve human or mechanical effort in its delivery. Services are being consumed increasingly by personal and organisational consumers and constitute a very important part of the economies of developed and developing countries. More people are employed in service jobs than in those that produce goods.

A product can be described at five levels:

- The first level is the ***core benefit*** that customers seek and is just a basic version of a product or service designed for the purpose of addressing and satisfying some fundamental need.
- The second level is a ***generic product,*** one that provides necessary attributes or properties to address the core need. At this level, depending on whether the product is durable, non-durable, or service, the product will have certain attributes such as a brand name, quality, styling, packaging, colour, and perhaps an instructions manual.
- The third level is the ***expected product*** that boasts of a set of attributes or characteristics that buyers normally expect in a product and which persuade consumers to buy it.
- The fourth level is the ***augmented product*** and refers to well thought out and deliberate additions of features, benefits, and services (such as in case of durable, complex products) delivery, installation, customer education and training, after sales service, guarantees or warranties, payment options, customer complaint redressal, etc. Marketers deliberately instigate the design and production of goods or services that meet or exceed customers' expectations.
- The fifth level is the ***potential product.*** This refers to all the possible augmentations and changes that the product can undergo.

Within markets of developed and developing countries, the competition is essentially hot at product augmentation level because most companies in an industry can successfully develop and produce satisfactory products at the expected level. Nearly 45 years earlier, Prof. Levitt wrote in 1960, "*The new competition is not between what companies can produce in their factories but between what they add to their factory output in the form of packaging, services, advertising, customer service, financing, delivery arrangements, warehousing, and things people value.*"

In their book, *Essentials of New Product Management,* Urban, Hauser, and Dholakia write that a company's products are often the most important links with consumers and critical means to accomplishing company objectives. The key variable in a marketing mix is the product. All decisions concerning other marketing mix elements must be coordinated with product decisions. There is general agreement that without a good product that meets consumer needs and wants according to their expectations, it is not possible to succeed in business. Totally new and breakthrough product inventions succeed only when consumers are convinced that they provide a better solution to their needs.

FIGURE 10.1

Five Product Levels

Level	Air-Conditioner
1. Core benefit	Cooling and comfort.
2. Generic Product	Sufficient cooling capacity and acceptable energy efficiency rating, reasonable air intakes, exhausts and so on.
3. Expected product	At least two cooling speeds, expandable plastic slide panels, adjustable louvers, removable air filter, vent for exhausting air, power cord at least 60-inches long, relatively safe refrigerant, one-year parts warranty and on-site service warranty, and five-years' warranty on the refrigeration system.

Contd...

4. Augmented Product	Optional features might include electric touch-pad controls, a display to show indoor and outdoor temps. and the thermostat setting, an automatic mode to adjust fan speed based on the thermostat setting and room temperature, and a toll-free number for customer service, one or two free-services, etc.
5. Potential Product	Silent operation, temperature completely balanced across the room, and energy self-sufficient.

Product Classification

Products can be grouped under one of the two general categories. ***Consumer products*** are those that we buy for our personal or family use or consumption. ***Organisational products*** represent those products that firms and institutions buy to produce other products, to resell, or to run day-to-day operations. Consumer products are purchased to satisfy personal needs and wants, and organisations buy products to accomplish organisational objectives. People buy some types of consumer products in which their feelings seem to play a dominant role in decision-making. Organisational products are said to be rational in purchase orientation and have nothing to do with feelings.

From the description above, it is apparent that same products can be consumer products and organisational products. For instance, when we buy a computer for personal use, it is a consumer product. But when a business entity or educational institution buys a computer for every day office use, it is considered an organisational product. Therefore, in the final analysis it is the buyer's use intention that determines whether a product is classified as a consumer product or an organisational product.

This classification is important to determine the segments of customers who the marketer decides to target in a certain market. This will influence the pricing, promotion, and distribution decisions. It needs to be emphasised that marketing efforts needed for personal consumers and organisational customers would be different in several important ways. The fact is that such a classification will have its impact on the entire marketing mix. A number of approaches have been used to classify consumer products. Traditionally, products have been classified on the basis of attributes such as durability and intangibility; or as consumer products and industrial products.

Consumer Products

Based on durability and tangibility, there are three categories:

Durable goods are tangible products and usually survive extensive use over prolonged periods of time, such as washing machines, footwear, autos, and clothes. Durable goods require a varied mix of promotional efforts, depending on whether they are bought by personal consumers for personal or family use, or organisational customers for its operations. Sales of durable goods are generally not as fast as in case of non-durable goods, though margins in durable goods are usually high. Some durable goods require more personal selling, warranties, credit facilities, and after sales service.

Non-durable goods are also tangible goods but usually get consumed in one or a few uses such as soap, wheat flour, candy, or soft drink. Non-durable goods are purchased and consumed on an ongoing basis and purchased without much effort. The marketer makes them available in as many locations as possible; margins are low, and advertising and sales promotion is heavy to develop top-of-the-mind recall, trial, and brand preference.

Services are intangible, inseparable, variable, and perishable products. A consumer cannot touch, smell, or taste them. Consumers can only experience them during or after delivery. Service quality assurance and service provider credibility are important aspects for consumers. Examples of some services are auto repair, beauty care, overnight courier, tour operators, etc.

The most widely used approach to classifying consumer goods puts them under four categories: convenience products, shopping products, speciality products, and unsought products. This approach is focused on considering characteristics of how consumers generally go about purchasing them.

Convenience Products: Products of this category are relatively inexpensive, consumed regularly on an ongoing basis, and purchased frequently. Consumer involvement in such product purchases is low and they buy them with little effort without making comparisons of available brands, such as eggs, bread, salt, matches, bakery products, flour, petrol, soft drinks, etc. Even when a preferred brand in this category is not available conveniently, consumer will readily buy a substitute brand. Sales promotions in this category can cause significant brand switching.

Marketing strategy for convenience products has several implications. It is important for marketers to make them available in a large number of retail outlets. Sales turnover is high and margins per unit are relatively low. Marketers have to spend large amounts of money for advertising and sales promotion because they expect hardly any promotional support from retailers. In fact, the reverse is usually true. Packaging of such products is also important because it should cause the product to stand out among many similar brands, particularly in large stores and supermarkets, and also in rural markets where the literacy rate is very low.

Shopping Products: These are items for which consumers willingly devote considerable time and effort because of their involvement in making the purchase, such as appliances, furniture, second-hand autos, music systems, TV, ready-to-wear garments, cameras, mobile phones etc. Consumers are concerned about product features, price, quality, service, and sometimes also about warranties/guarantees or even the retail outlet. These are products that generally last for a fairly long time and are less frequently purchased. Compared to convenience products, shopping products are relatively more expensive but most consumers are not particularly brand loyal.

Marketers adopt a selective distribution strategy and make shopping products available in fewer outlets, unlike convenience products. Since these products are purchased less frequently, their sales turnover is comparatively lower, and resellers expect large gross margins per unit. Such products are backed up with large outlay on advertising, sales promotion, and personal selling to advise customers. Usually, producer and reseller extend mutual cooperation for providing spare parts, service, and promotional activities.

Speciality Products: Products of this category have one or more unique and differentiated characteristics, and consumers seem to have strong brand loyalty. For such products, sufficient numbers of consumers are willing to make considerable effort in buying because of their high involvement, such as original paintings, designer dresses, luxury cars, professional cameras and expensive watches, etc. Brands such as Rolex watch, Porsche car, professional class Nikon camera, and Apple computer have achieved speciality product status among many consumers. Consumers plan such purchases with deliberation and they know exactly what they want and will not accept any substitutes. Buyers do not compare different alternatives and search out resellers(s) who carry the product they are looking for.

Marketers distribute speciality items mostly through a limited number of outlets and manufacturers often deal directly with appointed dealers. Speciality products are purchased infrequently, sales turnover is lower, and resellers require relatively higher gross margins. Promotional efforts are limited to advertising in high-end glossy magazines. There is often cooperative advertising and names of all the dealers frequently appear in ads.

Unsought Products: This category includes those products or services that consumers do not generally think of buying, or about which they are not aware, such as emergency repairs, emergency drugs, and insurance are some examples. Marketers undertake advertising to make people aware of the products they sell and also use personal selling. Sometimes personal selling takes the form of pressure selling to persuade customers to buy unsought products. Formerly, encyclopaedias available in print were viewed as unsought products and people generally did not think of buying them. Now, these are available on pre-recorded CDs at low cost, or as bundled software with some brands of computers.

Organisational Products

Organisational or industrial customers purchase products and services to achieve organisational objectives. The focus of buyers is mainly on functional attributes and benefits related to intended use. According to Webster Jr., organisational or industrial goods can be classified into seven categories based on their characteristics and intended use: ***raw materials, capital equipment, accessory equipment, component parts, process materials, consumable supplies*** and ***industrial services.***

Raw Materials: Raw materials include basic goods that become a part of a tangible product. These include natural products such as minerals, fruits, vegetables, cotton, wheat, crude petroleum, lumber, etc. Raw materials also include manufactured products, such as chemicals, steel, plastic, cement, fabric, etc. Organisations generally buy raw materials according to grades and specifications, and in large quantities, expect where JIT (Just In Time) supplies are received.

Capital Equipment: Products, called capital equipment refer to large machines and tools used for production work such as lathes, cranes, bulldozers, and stamping machines. Capital equipment is expensive and used in production work for considerably long periods of time. Purchase of any capital equipment constitutes a long-term investment. Such purchase decisions often involve top management and experts. Some capital equipment may be custom-made to be used for specific functions in a certain organisation, while other items are standardised and used to perform identical functions in different types of companies. Suppliers of capital equipment generally provide variety of necessary services that may include installation, training, repair, and to assist in maintenance.

Accessory Parts: Accessory parts are tangible products, usually less expensive, purchased more routinely, and are not as long lasting as capital equipment. These products do not become part of the final tangible product but are used in production and performing an organisation's daily office activities such as computers, fax machines, hand tools, motors, etc. They are usually sold through a limited number of outlets, and service requirements are not as many as with capital equipment. Producers of such products use a mix of promotional tools, such as mailing catalogues, advertising in industrial journals and, in some cases, personal selling as well.

Component Parts: Component parts are distinguishable and can be either completely finished items or those that need little processing before they become a part of larger finished tangible product, such as spark plugs and shock absorbers become parts of autos, computer hard drives, microchips, RAM modules, and monitors are component parts of computers. Organisations buy component parts according to industry standards, or in many cases according to their own planned specifications. Buyers expect supplies of specified quality and quantity to be delivered on schedule, so that planned production is not disrupted. Strong producers of component parts often use end-product advertising for consumers and also place their ads in industry and trade magazines and journals. For large branded product marketers, producers sell large quantities directly. To small non-branded assemblers, and independent service providers, component parts are sold through several resellers.

Process Materials: Process materials are also used in producing another final product and are mostly indistinguishable in the finished product, as in the case of cosmetics manufacturers who might purchase alcohol as an ingredient for some products. Organisations often place orders for large quantities of such materials based on their own specifications or some industry standards and supplies are made according to buyer's production schedules.

Industrial Services: As already mentioned earlier, services are intangible products and are required by organisations in different industries to run their operations, such as financial, legal, marketing research, advertising, training, consultancy, computer programming, maintenance and repair services, etc. Companies make decisions to provide required services internally or to purchase from independent service providers. In this regard, the decisions are generally based on frequency of needed services, extent of expertise and objectivity desired, and associated costs. Often companies buy some types of services on contract basis from outside service providers.

Product Line and Product Mix

Most companies generally market several products rather than just one or two. It is necessary for them to understand the relationship among all their products to coordinate their marketing of total group of products. ***Product item, product line,*** and ***product mix*** concepts help us understand the relationships among a company's different products.

A product ***item*** refers to a particular version of a product that is distinct, such as Surf Excel is a (premium) product item offered by Hindustan Lever Limited. A ***product line*** is a closely related group of products for essentially similar use, and technical and marketing considerations. Colgate product line includes Colgate Dental Cream, Colgate Gel, Colgate Total, Colgate Herbal, etc. ***Product mix*** is the total number of products that a company markets. ***Product mix consistency*** means how closely related different product lines are in end-use, production requirements, distribution, etc. A company may have many product lines in its product mix. The term ***product mix width*** refers to the number of product lines a company has. ***Product line length*** means the number of product variants available in a company's product line.

Product Line Decisions: Many companies start as a single product item or product line business. After getting a taste of success and with availability of more resources, companies decide to expand their product line and/or introduce newer product lines in consonance with market opportunities or in response to competitors' moves. For example, for quite some time, Nirma had only a single detergent brand and subsequently added a new product line by introducing a bathing soap. HLL realised the serious threat from Nirma washing powder and introduced cheaper versions of detergents.

Companies make decisions that concern either adding new items in existing product lines, deleting products from existing product lines, or adding new product lines. Another aspect relates to upgrading the existing technology either to reduce the product costs or to improve quality, for ***stretching*** (downwards, upwards, or both ways), or ***line filling.***

FIGURE 10.2

Selected Product Mix Elements in Just Three Product Lines of HLL

Product Mix Width (No. of Product Lines)

	Product Line – 1	*Product Line – 2*	*Product Line – 3*	*Product Line – 4*
	Bathing Soaps	Laundry Products	Beverages	Cosmetics
Product Line Length (Number of product item within a product line)	Dove Lux Pears Liril Rexona Lifebuoy Breeze Moti Hamam Jai	Surf Rin Sunlight Wheel 501	Lipton Green Label Brook Bond Red Label Taj Mahal Bru Taaza (Lipton) Super Dust	X Y Z

Product managers need to examine closely, the sales and profits of each item in a product line. The findings will help them decide whether to build, maintain, harvest, or divest different items in a particular product line.

Line Stretching: Product lines tend to lengthen over the years for different reasons such as excess manufacturing capacity, new market opportunities, demand from sales force and resellers for a richer product line to satisfy customers with varied preferences, and competitive compulsions. Lengthening of lines raises costs in many areas and decisions are based on careful appraisal. However, at some point in time somebody, often the top management intervenes and stops this.

- ***Downward Line Stretch:*** Companies sometimes introduce new products with an objective of communicating an image of technical excellence and high quality, and locate at the upper end of the market. Subsequently, the company might stretch downwards due to competitor's attack by introducing a low-end product in response to competitive attack, or a company may introduce a low-end product to fill up a vacant slot that may seem attractive to a new competitor. Another possibility is that market may become more attractive at low-end due to faster growth rate. For example, P&G introduced its Ariel Microsystem detergent at high-end assuring high quality. Customer response was not encouraging and the company saw more opportunities at lower end and introduced cheaper green alternative Ariel Super Soaker. Mercedes has offered its E Class model to compete at much lower price point than its high-end S Class models.
- Downward stretch sometimes poses risks. For example, low-end competitors may attack by moving into high-end, or for a prestige-image company introduction of a low-end model may adversely affect its product-image. Parker pen stretched downward and introduced ballpoint pen at low-price. This hurt Parker as a high-class product. Another risk is that introducing a lower-end item might cannibalise (eat away sales) the company's high-end item.

FIGURE 10.3

Line Stretching Decisions

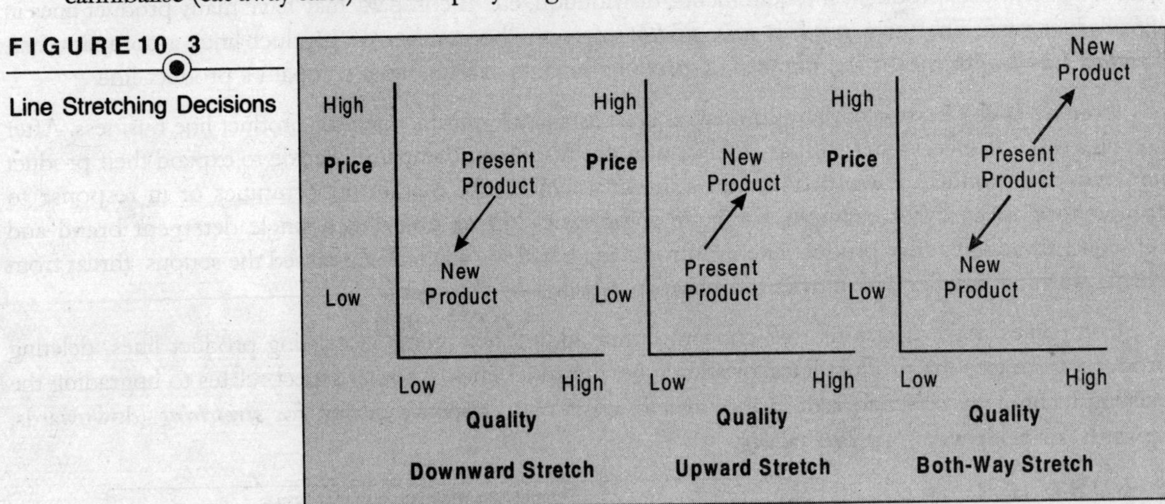

- ***Upward Stretch:*** In this situation, companies operating at low-end may opt to enter high-end because of better opportunities as a result of faster market growth, or the need to create an image of full line company. For example, Videocon entered the market with a twin-tub low-end washing machine. Subsequently, after the introduction of IFB automatic washing machine and entry of other players the market expanded. The average household income of middle class also showed positive trends. To take advantage of a market growing at the higher-end, Videocon also introduced an automatic washing machine. Maruti Udyog introduced its medium-priced models such as Maruti Zen, Maruti Esteem, Wagon R, Alto, and Swift after it had entered the market with its low-end Maruti 800 and Maruti Omni. Toyota introduced its Lexus luxury car as a standalone product (with no outward link to

Toyota) for just this very reason. It did not want it to be in any way affected by Toyota's no-doubt superb, but mass market image.

There may be certain risks associated with upward line stretching. These may include prospective customers' perceptions that the newcomer in the high-end category may not produce high-quality products, or competitors already well established in the high-end market may retaliate by introducing items in the low-end of the market. For example, long established footwear company Bata failed in its attempt when it tried upward stretch and finally introduced its Power line of economical sports shoes.

- ***Both-Way Stretch:*** Companies operating in the medium range of the market, may decide to stretch product line(s) both ways for reasons of opportunities arising in different market segments. The main risk is that it may prompt some customers to trade down. However, companies often prefer to retain their customers by providing low-end alternatives rather than losing them to competitors.
- ***Line Filling:*** A company may decide to lengthen the existing product line(s) by adding more items. The possible objectives leading to line filling may include realising incremental profits, meeting dealers' demands in response to their complaints that they lose sales because of missing items in the lines, excess capacity pressures, and trying to fill up vacant item slots to keep out competitors. For example, Videocon and some other TV and AC manufacturers have introduced models at various price-points right through high-end to low-end. Similarly, *IBM*, *HPCompaq*, Acer, and Sony etc., have introduced laptop PCs at various feature-price points ranging from high-end to low-end.
- Line filling may sometimes leads to cannibalisation, apart from confusing customers about the products' positioning unless the company succeeds in clearly differentiating each item meaningfully in customers' minds.

Line Pruning: Line pruning is just the opposite to line stretching and involves a deliberate decision to cut down the number of items in product line(s). Over a period of time, market conditions and customer preferences change, and companies find that some of their product lines contain some unnecessary variants and pack sizes. Another reason for line pruning can be the shortage of current production capacity. It is necessary for product managers to periodically review their product lines by examining sales and costs to spot items that are negatively impacting the profits. Procter and Gamble (P&G) was known to have very lengthy product lines but decided to rationalise and pruned its product lines. For example, the Head & Shoulders shampoo line had 31 items; P & G subsequently pruned this product line to only 15 variants. The company now believes that it is better to maintain simpler product lines and do away with unnecessary complexity. If the company can use any existing product formula or package to enter a new market, it can save precious resources and move faster.

Product Mix Decisions: Most business entities have many products in their portfolio. By dealing in many products, companies aim to serve a much larger and varied group of customers who look for solutions to different types of needs. This also helps to minimise the risks for a company across different products. For example, *ITC* diversified from tobacco-based products to hospitality products, financial services, and consumer non-durables such as edible oil and atta. Keeping in view the growing opposition from consumer advocates and restrictions being imposed by governments on certain types of promotional activities concerning cigarettes, *ITC* with only a single product line of different brands of cigarettes would have experienced high business risk.

Companies make decisions concerning product mix based on competitive situations, existing or emerging market opportunities, and changes in consumer lifestyles and preferences. As pointed out earlier, HLL faced competitive pressures from low-priced washing powders and introduced low-end brands at various price-points. In response to opportunities in medium-price segment of passenger cars, Maruti introduced suitable models. *ITC* introduced sports wear keeping in view the lifestyles of younger generation, seeing it as a logical extension of its positioning itself as a lifestyle products company. Bajaj Auto introduced its Pulsar motorcycle, and Apple computers introduced its iPods offering a high-quality portable digital music gadget. For quite some time, iPod was available as a high-end product. The market opportunities emerged and the company introduced medium-priced variants. These companies are operating in highly competitive markets and have two or more product lines. Moreover, there is a degree of convergence of various needs that are being met by products that combine the features of a mobile phone, camera, PDA, online communicator and music system.

Summary

A product is anything that can be offered to a market for attention, acquisition, use, or consumption that might satisfy a need or want. A good is a tangible product that can be seen and touched. In contrast, a service represents an intangible product that may involve human or mechanical effort in its delivery. Services are being consumed increasingly both by individual as well as organisational consumers.

Products can be classified as consumer products and organisational products. Consumer products are those that we buy for our personal or family use or consumption. Organisational products are those that are purchased by firms and institutions to produce other goods and services, or to resell and to run their day-to-day operations.

Consumer products can be grouped as non-durable, durable, or services. These can further be grouped as convenience products, shopping products, speciality products, and unsought products. Organisational products include raw materials, capital equipment, accessory parts, component parts, process materials, and industrial services. Purchase decisions are said to be more rational than emotional for such products.

Most companies market more than one product. A product item refers to a particular version of a product that is distinct. A product line is a closely related group of products for essentially similar use, and technical or marketing considerations. Product mix is the total number of products that a company markets. Product mix consistency means how closely related different product lines are in their end use, production requirements, and distribution. A company may have many product lines in its product mix. The term product mix width refers to the number of product lines a company has. Product line length means the number of product variants available in a company's product line.

Product positioning is a very important concept in Modern marketing. It is the decision by a marketer to try to achieve a well-defined and differentiated brand image relative to competition in a targeted market segment.

A brand exists only when it finds a place in consumers' perception of the world of products available in the market. This perception is subjective and is governed by a consumer's needs, values, beliefs, and experience. The position is based on a brand's functional and non-functional benefits as perceived by the consumer.

To reach a decision about positioning a product, managers should take steps to identify what are consumers' perceptions of competition and obtain a list of attributes that influence the consumer's purchase decisions. The analysis would determine where in the perceptual map the product should be positioned. The next step requires the identification of segments or clusters of customers who would prefer this product location in their perceptual maps. An ideal product would be the one that is preferred over all others.

Important positioning strategies revolve around answering certain questions convincingly by the brand itself and in more effective ways than competitors.

Questions for Discussion

1. What is the difference between tangible products and services? Give two examples of each category.
2. What important attributes would you look for in a medium-priced car?
3. How would you differentiate between a convenience good, shopping good, and speciality good?
4. How would you classify organisational products? Can an organisational product also be a consumer product?
5. On what basis can products be differentiated to decide a brand's position?
6. What is brand positioning? How does it differ from target marketing?
7. How can the use of positioning concept benefit the marketer? Mention some examples.
8. Discuss what you understand by positioning strategy.
9. Discuss some important positioning strategies with examples.
10. What make marketers reposition their brands? Discuss two examples of successful repositioning.

Projects

1. Collect some ads for different brands of cars in the Indian market. Determine how each car is positioned and whether the positioning is distinct.
2. Collect advertisements of two brands you believe have failed to create distinct positions. In your opinion, how should these have been positioned?
3. You are a consultant. A company wants you to position its brand of feature-loaded notebook computer. What steps would you take to decide the position?

Bibliography

1. Robert E. Smith and Robert F. Lusch, "How Advertising Can Position a Brand?" *Journal of Advertising Research,* February 1976.
2. Theodore Levitt, "Marketing Myopia," *Harvard Business Review,* July-August 1960.
3. Michael E. Porter, "What is Strategy?" *Harvard Business Review,* November-December 1996.
4. C. Merle Crawford, Richard D. Irwin, *New Product Management,* 1996.
5. Philip Kotler, *Marketing Management: Analysis, Planning Implementation, and Control,* 8th ed. (1997).
6. Fredrick W. Webster, Jr., *Industrial Marketing Strategy, 1984.*
7. Glen L. Urban, John R. Hauser, and Nikhilesh Dholakia, *Essentials of New Product Management,* 1987.
8. Theodore Levitt, "Marketing Success Through Differentiation – of Anything," *Harvard.*
9. *Business Review,* 1980.
10. Subroto Sengupta, *Brand Positioning: Strategies for Competitive Advantage,* 1990.
11. Dan Sarel, "Product Positioning – A Reassessment," *Theoretical Developments in Marketing,* (AMA, 1980).

New Product Development & Adoption Process

CHAPTER 11

LEARNING OBJECTIVES

After going through this chapter, you will understand:

- How do companies deliberately organise to develop new products?
- Different steps involved in developing a new product and launching it in the market
- How do consumers with different types of psychological make up adopt a new product and at what rate?
- Important factors that influence consumers in the adoption process
- The characteristics of innovators, early adopters, early majority, late majority, and those who are the last to adopt a new product.

Back in 2001, Nike introduced a range of slip-on sneakers - Presto, in India billed as T-shirt for the feet and referring to the comforts it offered. Close on the heels of Presto's launch, rival Reebok came up with what it called shoes with gears.

As it turned out, the "gear" system merely helped the users to adjust the fit of the shoes around the feet (in other words, loosen or tighten them) with the help of elastic shoestrings.

Now, it's the turn of German sportswear giant Adidas to take the technology driven marketing spin to a different level altogether. Its latest product, Adidas I, is the world's first "intelligent" shoe. It has a microprocessor chip, which Adidas claims can meet the individual comfort levels of an athlete by automatically adjusting the cushioning while he runs.

This feature, according to Adidas is the Holy Grail for the global sports footwear industry. Among several other things, Adidas can also lay claim to the fact that this is the world's first shoe which comes with an instruction manual, and a laptop-like case to carry the product around.

Priced at Rs. 12,499, Adidas-I is sold through just four outlets - South Extension Adidas store in New Delhi, in Gurgaon's MGF Mall, the Linking Road showroom in Mumbai and the Adidas store in Forum Mall in Bangalore.

Adidas claims that the shoe has a sensor capable of registering 20,000 readings in the blink of an eye, a processor capable of making 250,000 calculations in the beat of a bird's wing and a motor that spins faster than the rotors of a Blackhawk helicopter.

"Since no two runners are exactly alike, no two running shoes should be alike, either. Adidas-I solves this problem - it is a different shoe for every runner who wears it. It senses, understands and adapts to the needs, activity and environment of each runner who wears it, creating a running experience tailored uniquely for them," says Andreas Gellner, Managing Director, Adidas India.

The nerve centre of the shoe, a magnetic sensing system made up of a sensor below the runner's heel and a magnet at the bottom of the mid-sole, monitors heel impact forces 1,000 times per second as the runner runs.

The nerve centre then conveys the readings to the shoe's brain - a tiny microprocessor capable of making five million calculations per second to understand the runner's needs. The brain, using software written specifically for Adidas-I, then determines whether the shoe is too soft or too firm for the runner's movement and sends a command to the shoe's muscle.

A motor-driven cable system, the shoe's muscle then makes a physical change to the cushioning properties of the shoe as you run, adapting to ensure you have the correct level of cushioning for your needs at any given moment.

(Source: Business Standard, June 2, 2005).

The New Product

The human race has always wanted and looked for better, comfortable, and more satisfying things. Consumers' thirst for better and more efficient products and services seems insatiable. With the passage of time, the list of innovations keeps going on and on. Truly new breakthrough products are comparatively rare. During the last nearly three decades, some product innovations have created huge markets such as fax machines, computers, quartz watches, Internet, cellular phones, wonder drugs, etc. Innovations bring about a change in consumers' consumption patterns.

Companies spend huge sums of money and devote considerable time and energy to develop new products. It is reported that Boeing will spend $5 billion in developing a new 777 jet. If the new aircraft turns out to be a success, it will be extremely profitable for the company for many years afterwards. A new type of jet is under development by NASA that will be able to fly at speeds of Mach 10. In times to come, if this development can be adopted in passenger aircrafts, sixteen-hour distance will shrink to just one-hour. According to Cyndee Miller, after introduction in the market more than 80 per cent new products fail. Pam Weisz reported that nearly 22,000 were introduced in 1994. Of these, 90 per cent failed costing US companies about $30 billion. Many reasons are said to be responsible for such a high rate of failure. It is said that a major cause of new-product failure is lack of research. Besides lack of research, other common reasons for failure include design problems, and bad timing of product introduction. Developing new products could be both advantageous and risky for firms. Despite risks, failure to introduce new products is risky, too. Why have computers and cellular phones become so successful? Highly successful new products are always superior to competing products, are fine-tuned to consumer needs and wants, and enable consumers to do unique tasks. According to Robert G. Cooper and Elko J. Kleinschmdt, a unique and superior product becomes successful 98 per cent of the time. Products with moderate advantage have 58 per cent success rate, and products with minimal advantage only 18 per cent.

Connotations of the Term 'New Product'

The term '*new product*' has many connotations. So, what should we call a "new" product? Most definitions of new-product have a common feature that new products offer innovative benefits. Everett M. Rogers observes that some researchers have favoured a consumer-oriented approach in defining new products. Consulting firm of Booz, Allen, and Hamilton in their survey found that products introduced by 700 US companies over a period of five years were not equally "new." The study identified six new product categories based on their degree of newness as perceived by both the company and the customers in the target markets.

- ***'New to the World' Products:*** 10 per cent were true innovations, not just new to the company. Such products create an entirely new market.
- ***New Product Lines:*** 20 per cent constituted new product category for the company introducing it, but the products were not new to customers in the target market, as one or more competitive brands already existed.
- ***Additions to Existing Product Lines:*** 26 per cent were actually new items added in the existing product lines. These items may be moderately new to both the company and the customers in its established product-markets. They may help extend the market segments to which the product line appeals.
- ***Improvements in or Revisions of Existing Products:*** 26 per cent items provide improved performance or enhanced perceived value brought out to replace existing products. These items may present moderately new marketing and production challenges to the company. Unless these items represent technologically new generation of products, customers are likely to perceive them as similar to the products they replace.
- ***Repositioning:*** 7 per cent products are targeted at new applications and new market segments.

- ***Cost Reductions:*** 11 per cent products are modifications providing similar performance at low costs.

The degree of product newness to the company, its target customers, or both all help determine the extent of complexity and uncertainty involved in the engineering, operations, and marketing tasks necessary to make it successful as a new product. A truly new innovation both to the company and customers requires great expenditure of resources and efforts and also involves high degree of risk. Products new to consumers but not new to the company are often not so innovative in design or manufacturing. However, they may require high levels of marketing efforts to deal with uncertainty to build primary demand. Finally, products new to the company but not new to target customers generally do not pose much challenge or risk.

FIGURE 11.1

The degree of product Newness

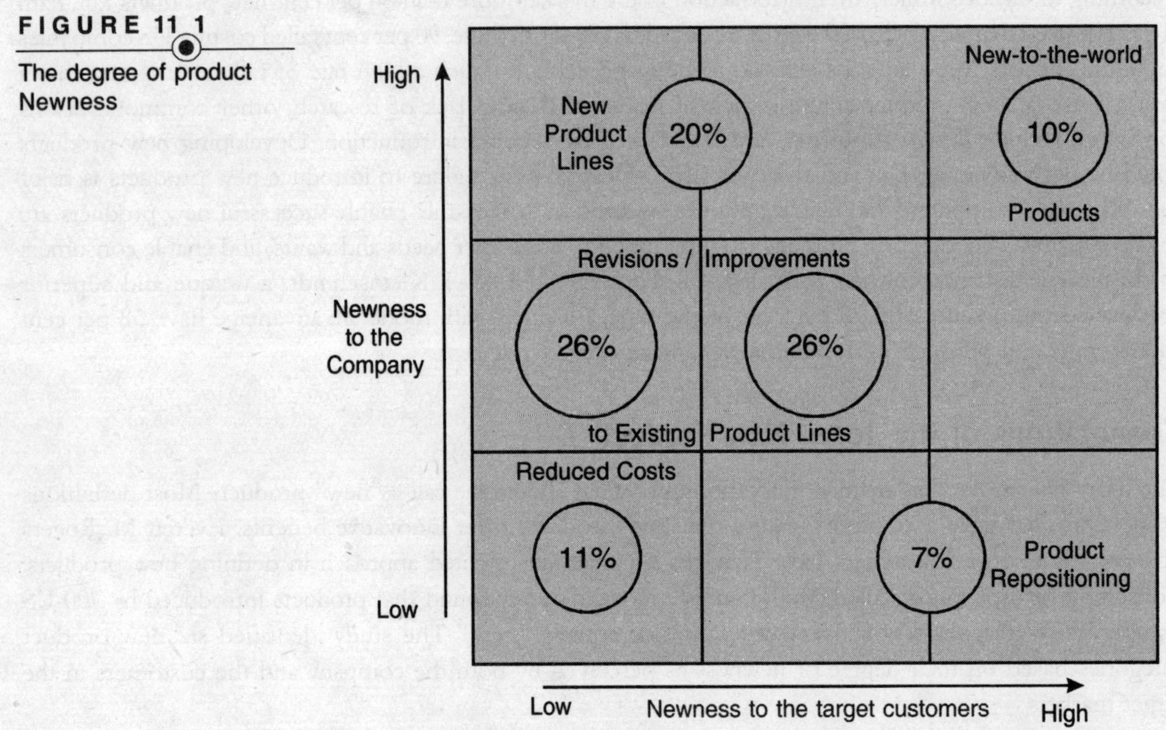

Source: New products management for the 1980s, (Booz, Allen, and Hamilton, 1982).

Several factors contribute to new product development and the primary objective of companies for developing most new products is to accomplish future profits and growth. Most of these factors relate to changes in the external environment such as new technology and intensifying competition from domestic and foreign firms, and changes in customer lifestyles and tastes, and also social and economic changes may bring new products to market. For example, growing anti-American sentiments of Muslims in some countries have given rise to new products such as Mecca Cola (*Times of India,* April 21, 2004).

New Technologies: New technologies have a substantial effect on a company's performance, or the product industry itself. Genetic engineering is having an impact on the pharmaceutical industry and newer and better medicines are being created. Rapid strides, in microchip technology are making highly advanced products available in the area of computing and telecommunications. Manual or electric typewriters have disappeared from developed and most developing countries, VCRs are practically obsolete, major camera manufacturers like Nikon and Canon have discontinued producing cameras (for sale in developing countries) that use film, preferring to focus only on digital technology. Broadband Internet is wiping out dial-up services, and Direct-To-Home (DTH) will adversely affect cable TV service providers.

Changing Customer Preferences: Consumer lifestyles and tastes are changing as a result of increase in literacy levels, exposure to other cultures, changing role of women, increasing shift from joint family system to nuclear families, availability of newer media, and impact of fast technological changes. We see a host of ongoing changes taking place in ready-to-wear garments, footwear, appliances, health foods, plastic money, and availability and consumption of many new services, etc. All these changes are a result of lifestyle changes.

Organising for New Product Development

Major innovations such as computer, cell phones, and the Internet occur now and again and transform the market place. It seems unlikely that any standard marketing approaches would have been instrumental in developing such innovations. For example, if potential customers had been approached to learn their likely interest in buying such unheard of products, probably they would not have understood the concept and its importance in their lives. Many innovative products are the result of presence of 'product champion' in a company. A champion perseveres and presses the case for a new product to be developed. Without such people, many innovations, we have today would probably not have been seen through to the development and finally the launch in market.

For organisations, it is proper to have a formal new product development process in place and more likely to be effective than adopting a haphazard approach to this critical activity.

New product development requires support from top management and budget allocation, definition of business activity, product categories of interest, and specific criteria of *ROI*.

It is interesting to note that 3M successfully develops and launches many new products each year. Its goal is to have each of its divisions produce at least 30 per cent of sales from products less than four years old. 3M has 3 important rules:

- The 15 per cent rule permits all employees to spend 15 per cent of their working time to be devoted to working on projects of personal interest. Three highly successful products – Post-it notes, Masking tape, and Micro-replication technology grew from this rule.
- The company expects some failures. The saying is, "You have to kiss a lot of frogs to find a prince."
- The company hands out Golden Step Awards every year to venture teams whose new product generates more than $2 million U.S. sales or $4 million in worldwide sales within three years of market launch.

Different companies manage new product development in several ways. In some companies, the responsibility is given to ***product management*** handling a product, product line, or several products that make up an interrelated group. Product managers generally have their hands full in managing existing products and beyond line extensions, have little time. Some companies have ***new-product management*** set up, reporting to category managers. This approach is relatively more professional. Some companies constitute a ***high-level management committee*** responsible for reviewing and approving new product proposals. Large organisations establish ***new-product department*** and the head is responsible for generating and screening new ideas, working with R&D, conducting market testing and commercialisation. The manager in charge has substantial authority and access to top management.

How to be Innovative When you are a Hundred Years Old

3M is a 100-year-old company that has discovered its own "fountain of youth." Yet it is no secret what it does to constantly renew itself. 3M is fast and successful in spinning out new products that offer innovative and practical solutions to customers' problems. This doesn't happen by chance. It is an ongoing priority of top managers. For example, 3M's chief set an objective that 30 per cent of sales should come from products that didn't exist four years' earlier. You can see the emphasis on innovation in even the quickest visit to 3M's website (3m.com). Current 3M innovations include respirators (for Dept. of Homeland Security "first respondents") radiant light film (for uses ranging from brighter cell phone displays to glittery signage), elastomers (which seal in aggressive chemicals in high temperature settings), and Filterate electrostatic fibres (which filter dust out of heating vents). Everywhere you look, there are past 3M innovations that are still being improved, including brands like Post-it-Notes, Thinsulate outdoor wear, and Scotch-Pop-Up Tape Strips.

3M motivates innovation by staying close to customers, rewarding new-product champions, and sharing ideas among divisions. Teams from marketing, operations, and R&D screen new-product concepts for the ones with the highest profit potential. Then everyone works to bring the best ones to market fast. 3M's Scotch-Brite Never Rust Wool Soap Pads show how this approach can succeed. Consumers told 3M marketing researchers that they wanted an improved soap pad. Ordinary steel wool pads leave rust stains on sinks and tiny metal splinters in dishpan hands. 3M screens new products for their environmental impact, so the R&D people developed a pad using plastic fibres from recycled plastic bottles. Experts from 3M's abrasives division figured out how to coat the fibres with fine abrasives biodegradable soap. Further marketing research refined the shape of the pads, and test markets evaluated details of the marketing plan. For example, tests confirmed that consumers liked the colourful package made from recycled paper and would pay more for Never Rust pads than they did for Brillo.

The managers varied the marketing plan for different countries. In mature markets, such as U.S. and Brazil, where steel wool pads already had a large consumer base, the objective was to capture share. In Japan, where steel wool is not commonly used, the objective was to pioneer the market and attract new customers. In a firm renowned for innovation, the launch of Never Rust pads was one of 3M's most profitable ever.

3M is also serious about how its innovations affect consumer welfare. When managers learnt that traces of chemicals in 3M's Scotchgard fabric protector might persist in the environment, they didn't wait for scientists to do more tests. They voluntarily pulled the popular product off the market – before they even knew if R&D could find a substitute chemical.

(Source: www.mhhe.com/fourps).

Some companies assign new product development to *venture teams*. It is a unit within the company responsible for creating entirely new products aimed at new markets. They are removed from their normal duties, given a budget, a time frame, and provided informal workplaces that may even be garages to work as a team and develop new products. The team handles all aspects of new product development, including R&D, engineering, production, finance and accounting, and marketing. Team members are generally drawn from different functional areas of the company. After their new product is successful, the members may return to their functional area or join a new or existing division to manage the product. Many companies, such as *IBM*, Xerox, and Boeing have used venture teams successfully. Christopher K. Bart reported that a major benefit of using venture teams is that, the number of products can be expanded rapidly and also the status and importance of new products are increased because the teams operate in a separate structure within the company.

TABLE 11 1

New product Development Phases

Phases	Marketing Activities
Idea Generation	Searching for new product ideas from internal and external sources.
Idea Screening	Select the most promising ideas and drop those with only limited potential. Study the needs and wants of potential buyers, the environment, and competition.
Concept Testing	Describe or show product concepts and their benefits to potential customers and determine their responses. Identify and drop poor product concepts. Gather useful information from product development and its marketing personnel.
Business Analysis	Assess the product's potential profitability and suitability for the market-place. Examine the company's research, development, and production capabilities. Ascertain the requirements and availability of funds for development and commercialisation. Project ROI.
Product Development	Determine technical and economic feasibility to produce the product. Convert the product idea into a prototype. Develop and test various marketing mix elements.
Test Marketing	Conduct market testing. Determine target customers' Reactions. Measure its sales performance. Identify weaknesses in product or marketing mix.
Commercialisation	Make necessary cash outlay for production facilities. Produce and market the product in the target market and effectively communicate its benefits.

Robert G. Cooper reported that some companies including Hewlett-Packard, 3M, and Lego use a method called *stage-gate system* for managing innovation process. In this system, at the end of each stage there is a checkpoint (gate) and the project team leader must bring a set of promising products that a company can have ready for customers. It is only after this that the product can pass on to the next stage. Senior manager critically reviews the criteria at each checkpoint to judge if the project merits to be moved to the next stage.

Before its launch in a market, a new product passes through several distinct phases and the process may vary across different companies. The steps involved in the development of a new product are presented in the Table 11.1.

Idea Generation

The focus in this first stage is on searching for new product ideas. Few ideas generated at this stage are good enough to be commercially successful. New product ideas come from a variety of sources. An important source of new product ideas is customers. Fundamentally, customer needs and wants seem to be the most fertile and logical place to start looking for new product ideas. This is equally important for both personal consumers and industrial customers. Other sources of new product ideas include scientists, resellers, marketing personnel, researchers, sales people, engineers, and other company personnel.

Producers of technical products sometimes study customers, making the most advanced use of supplied products and recognise the need for improvements. Toyota employees are said to contribute more than 2 million new ideas annually, and about 85 per cent of these are implemented. By studying competitors' products and services companies can find ideas.

Some other creative methods companies use to gain new product ideas include *brainstorming, synectics, attribute listing, forced relationship,* and *reverse assumption analysis.*

Sometimes, new product ideas just 'happen.' Akio Morita's story about the development of *Walkman* is well-known. He used to observe an employee carrying a heavy stereo record player with headphones. This prompted Morita to conceive the idea of a lightweight personal stereo.

No one was very hopeful about the idea. The doubts expressed, included the market potential, and the inability of such a stereo to record, but Morita was very optimistic about the market potential of such a stereo. When the experimental unit was ready, marketing people were not at all enthusiastic and said that it would not sell.

Everybody knows that SONY'S *Walkman* was a huge success. Morita writes:

"I do not believe that any amount of market research could have told us that the Sony Walkman would be successful; yet, this small item literally changed the music listening habits of millions of people all around the world. Often such a new product idea strikes us as a natural happening."

Source: Akio Morita, *Made in Japan,* Penguin, 1986.

Though there is need to be a market-driven company, product ideas sometimes arise quite by accident in laboratory tests. For example, researchers were seriously involved in developing a drug for angina (a heart ailment). However, undesirable side effects of the drug led to the development of a drug with huge market opportunity. Thus, the anti-impotency drug Viagra (sildenafil citrate) was born and became a major marketing success because it provided a solution for a major problem of a large number of consumers.

Idea Screening

The aim of screening is to reject the poor ideas as early as possible because the costs of new product development keep rising sharply with each successive development phase. Many companies use a standard format for describing new-product ideas by the review committee and includes descriptions of new-product idea, its target market, anticipated competition, assessment of market potential, price, estimate of development time, costs, and ROI.

Each promising idea is researched to assess its potential. Committee members sort out the ideas into three groups: promising ones, marginal, and rejects. The committee evaluates the ideas against a set of criteria. The criteria seek the answers to questions such as:

- Does the product meet a genuine need?
- Would it offer customers a superior value?
- Can it be distinctively communicated?
- Does the company have enough resources in terms of know-how and finance?
- Will the new product bring in expected sales volume, sales growth, and ROI?

These criteria differ across different companies.

The extent to which a company responds to new product ideas depends much on its financial resources, availability of production capacity to meet with likely demand, availability of suitably trained personnel, and availability of raw materials and components required for producing the new product.

Time is another major consideration because the development process can take a long time from idea generation to production and market launch. Some developments can take as little as a few months while others can take years of effort to finally launch the product in market. This is particularly true for cases where safety testing is prolonged, such as new drugs. Screening should ensure that the new product would not cannibalise existing company products. The new product should fit within the company's overall marketing strategies.

The screening or filtering stage discussed here depicts it as a purely rational process. D. Forlani, J. W. Mullins, and O. C. Walker found some evidence that the final selection of ideas for further development is typically affected by intuitive and feeling factors, and non-analytical judgement processes were found to have a significant affect. While screening the idea, the company must guard against *drop error* and *go error.* A drop error occurs when the company rejects, an otherwise promising idea from further consideration because it is easy to see some fault in the ideas of other people. A go error occurs when an otherwise poor idea is allowed to pass through by the company and moves into development and commercialisation phases.

Concept Testing

Concept testing of a new product idea refers to a more detailed version of the idea. It involves describing the product concept through oral or written description and the benefits to a small number of potential customers, and make an assessment of their responses regarding the product. For a single product idea, a company can test one or more concepts of the same product. It is a low-cost procedure and helps the company to decide whether to commit considerable resources in research and development. Positive consumer response to product concept, also helps decide which particular product attributes and benefits are most important from a potential customer's point of view.

Concept testing proves useful in most cases, but in certain cases it may not be appropriate. In case the major benefit of a product is something intangible and subjective, concept testing often fails. It is difficult to communicate the concept of such a product in a way that respondents would be able to visualise in such a product. Similarly, it is difficult to test a new service unless it can actually be demonstrated being performed. For instance, it would have been very difficult to test the concept of a fax machine just because potential users would not have been able to visualise and understand its technology. Because of this difficulty, some concepts with huge potential of success are killed before further consideration. Concept testing is difficult in case of major innovation simply because customers have no experience of such an idea.

The more clearly, the concept is presented and resembles the final product, or helps consumers visualise the experience with it, the more reliable its testing. Some firms use *rapid prototyping* (a computer-aided design programme) to design small appliances and produce plastic models. This helps potential customers seeing the model and comprehending the concept easily. Some companies use virtual reality to test new product concepts. The questions those respondents answer after the new product concept is presented to them, focus on a product's ability and degree of meeting a consumer need, clarity of benefits and their extent of believability, as to whether the product sounds superior to existing solutions, its perceived value relative to proposed price, and the respondent's purchase intention. The questions asked vary considerably, depending on the type of product concept being tested.

Customer preferences for alternative concepts can be measured through *conjoint analysis* wherein respondents are asked to rank varying levels of product's attributes to determine the most attractive product offer.

FIGURE 11.2

Concept Testing of a New Mosquito Repellent

Product Description

A consumer product company is considering the development and launch of a new mosquito repellent. This product would consist of a liquid dispenser, much like deodorant containers, you are familiar with. The mosquito repellent easily comes out from the nozzle and rapidly spreads in vapour when its push-button release is pressed lightly. Only a small amount of repellent is dispensed with each press and is mildly perfumed. The chemical used is completely non-toxic for humans and pets. Only 5 ml. of repellent is enough for a room measuring 14x12 sq. feet and its effect persists for two days after the room is sprayed just once.

Please answer the following questions:

1. How do you feel about using this type of product in your home?
2. What major advantages do you see over existing products that you currently use to get rid of mosquitoes?
3. What attributes of this product do you particularly like?
4. What suggestions do you have for improving this product?
5. If it is available in pressurised 300 ml. containers at an appropriate price, how likely are you to buy his product?

   Very likely Moderately likely
   Unlikely
6. Assuming that a container will last for 15 days in a 3-bedroom house, approximately how much would you pay for this product?

Business Analysis

It is an assessment to determine the new product's potential contribution to the company's sales, costs, and profits and for this reason a financial analysis is necessary. An income and expenditure statement needs to be prepared and requires secondary and primary data from the market concerning consumer surveys. The aim of this financial analysis is that the new product should at least break even over a period of time. Obviously, at this stage any forecasts can be based on crude approximate assumptions about likely sales volume, the selling price, distribution costs, and production costs. This is not only difficult but also speculative part of the process, and this stage is particularly difficult for innovative and new-to-the world products.

The evaluation process focuses on answering a number of questions such as: Does the product fit in with the company's existing product mix? Is the demand likely to be strong and enduring enough to justify its introduction in the market? What kind of change with regard to environment and competition can be anticipated and what is likely to be the impact on product's future sales, costs, and profits? Are the R&D, engineering, and manufacturing capabilities of the company adequate? In case there is need to construct new facilities, how quickly can they be built and what would be the costs involved? Is the finance available or can it be obtained consistent with a favourable ROI?

Accurate sales forecasting at this stage is difficult. Companies use break-even analysis to assess how many units must be sold to customers before any profits start. They also sometimes use payback analysis to determine the time to recover investments. Companies often use sensitivity analysis to assess the impact on overall profitability of changes in underlying assumptions.

Product Development

This stage refers to when the new product concept moves to test stage. The company determines the technical feasibility to produce it at costs low enough to sell it at reasonable price. If the answer is negative, the costs incurred so far are lost and the company may gain perhaps some useful information. This phase involves substantial increase in the investment of resources. The product concept is converted into a prototype/working model to evaluate its acceptability. The prototype development may take anything between a few days to even years in some rare cases. Advanced modern virtual-reality technology greatly helps to speed up the development process.

A critical decision at this stage is, how much quality to build into the product. Higher quality often requires better quality materials and expensive processing. This adds to product costs and consequently its selling price. It is necessary to ascertain target customers' views on acceptable price range of the product. In this regard, the quality of existing competing brands should also be considered. Product development is expensive and only few products concepts reach development stage.

The prototype should reveal its tangible and intangible attributes that consumers might associate with it to meet their needs and wants. Marketing research and concept testing reveal product attributes that are important from a consumer's point of view. The product design should be such that it must communicate these characteristics.

Laboratory and field tests are conducted for the product's performance, convenience, safety, and other functional characteristics. Testing consumer responses to intangible elements of a new product is difficult. This is particularly an issue when developing new services. The product should be subjected to rigorous and lengthy enough testing for verifying its functional attributes. The term *alpha testing* refers to conducting laboratory tests, and *beta testing* means that a sample of customers use the product prototype and give their feedback. Many computer companies offer customers to download a new or modified software for testing, that remains functional for a limited period of time. Apple computer subjects its PowerBook to many rigorous tests and one such test involves heating the computer notebook in ovens to 140 degrees. 200 Gillette employees test company products such as razors, blades, shaving creams, or aftershave under instructions of technicians every day and afterwards fill out a questionnaire.

If the product qualifies as sufficiently successful and considered eligible for test marketing, then marketers make decisions about branding, packaging, labelling, pricing, and promotion during test marketing.

Test Marketing

Test marketing is essentially a limited introduction in some carefully selected geographic area that is viewed as representing the intended market. Test marketing is a sample launching of the entire marketing mix. The aim is to assess how large is the market and determine the reactions of consumers and resellers in an authentic setting. Most companies use test marketing basically to lessen the risk of product failure. Test marketing can furnish valuable information about buyers, dealers, and effectiveness of promotional efforts.

Test marketing is a fairly time-consuming process and has to be conducted for a sufficiently long period to collect reliable information. The period of testing may be anywhere between a few months to one year. Much depends on the company's investment level and risk perceptions as well as time pressures. Designing the programme for test marketing involves making a number of decisions:

- **Where and in how many markets should the test marketing be carried out?** Markets should be a representative of target markets. Marketers generally consider two to six markets in which to conduct test marketing.

- **What should be the duration of test marketing?** Much would depend on the nature of the product. For example, in case of consumer non-durables, average repurchase period should be considered.
- **What to test?** Marketers are interested in information that concerns consumer response to promotion, trial rate, usage, satisfaction level, repurchase, and reseller reactions.
- **What criteria should be used to determine success or otherwise?** The decisions would concern trial rate, repurchase rate, adoption, and frequency of purchase.

Companies use various testing methods. Some of the more popular ones are:

Sales-Wave: Consumers are offered free samples for trial and they may also be exposed to one or more ads. Subsequently, they are offered the product at a reduced price. The product may be re-offered three to five times. The number of consumers who select the product again, and their satisfaction level, is recorded.

Controlled Test Marketing: An independent research providing company is hired and it is asked to test the product by placing the product in a geographic area and in the specified number of stores. The research firm decides the product's price, promotion and store displays, etc. Finally, electronic scanner data is collected at the check out point. The research firm also interviews a sample of customers to learn their responses.

Simulated Test Marketing: A sample of thirty or more customers is interviewed to determine their familiarity and brand preference in a particular product category. This sample is then shown a mixed bundle of commercials or print ads of company's test-product as well as competing brands. Consumers are then given a small amount of money and invited in a store to buy any item. The researcher notes how many of these consumers buy the test-brand and competing brands. This points out the advertisement's relative effectiveness against competing ads of other brands. Subsequently, consumers are interviewed to learn their reasons for buying or not buying the company's product. A free sample of company's product is given to consumers who did not buy the test-product and some weeks later are interviewed on telephone to learn their responses concerning satisfaction and purchase intentions. This is a good method to evaluate the effectiveness of ads and trial rate of the company's product.

Test Market: The company test-marketing, the new product selects a few cities representing target markets, employs all final national launch promotional tools, including advertising and sales promotion, etc., and also employs sales force to motivate resellers to keep the product. It is like a mini national launch, and is quite expensive.

Other methods companies use to conduct test marketing include laboratory tests, demonstrations, and putting the product in exhibitions and trade fairs.

Some methods of test marketing expose a product to natural marketing environment to make an assessment of its acceptability to target consumers and its sales performance. By testing a product in a limited area, the company can learn about any weaknesses in the product or other marketing mix elements. This is of great advantage to the marketer as it provides an opportunity to correct the shortcomings. A product shortcoming after a nationwide launch can be very expensive for a company. Through test marketing, a company can try varying pricing, advertising and promotional mixes, as well as different types of packaging.

Test marketing involves risks, too. Besides being expensive, competitors may attempt to interfere by increasing advertising and other promotions, and lowering prices. This may affect the accuracy of test results. In case the product seems to be a success, competitors may copy it without spending heavy resources and introduce their product, while the original product is still in testing stage. Simulated test marketing ensures relative safety because of its quicker speed, lower costs, and tighter security. According to Leslie Brennan, Gillette's Personal Care Division spends less than $200,000 for a simulated test.

Commercialisation

The decision to commercialise involves the largest costs to a company. Quite often, a new product replaces an old one that may still have a customer base and mistakes can occur. This is what happened when Coca-Cola replaced its existing Coke with a new formulation. There was error in interpreting the results of marketing research and ultimately the company had to reintroduce the earlier version as 'Classic' Coke.

After reviewing the results of test marketing, it is determined if any changes in the marketing mix are needed before its full-scale introduction. Cyndee Miller reports that only 8 per cent of new-product projects reach the commercialisation stage. During this stage, the plans for full-fledged production and marketing must be refined and set, and budgets for the new product must be prepared. The size of manufacturing facility would be a critical decision. Marketing is another area of major consideration. To launch packaged consumer products nationwide, the company needs huge resources to undertake advertising and promotion for at least one year. Timing of market entry of a new product is also important. Microsoft spent more than $200 million on its media advertising campaign when it introduced Windows 95.

Companies generally do not launch new products overnight, but adopt the *rollout* method. They introduce the product in stages. It is first introduced in a region (it could be a country for global players) and subsequently in adjoining areas, states, or countries. Cities where test marketing has been conducted are sometimes chosen as the initial marketing area as a natural extension of test marketing. The major factor that may favour this approach is if the product fails, the company will suffer smaller losses. Also, if the company does not already have a wide network in place, it would take considerable time to set up a distribution network.

NEW PRODUCT ADOPTION PROCESS

New product introductions and their adoption, particularly in case of new-to-the-world products often takes a very long time. Customers are sometimes suspicious, even sceptical about adopting new products.

New-to-the-world products bring about changes in consumers' use or consumption patterns. For example, a comparatively recent innovation is Internet shopping, which has altered the way we buy certain types of products. Other innovations may radically change the way we use products or services. For example, microwave ovens have changed the way, food is cooked and e-mail, voice mail, and cellular phones have changed the way we communicate.

Blade Runner

- In a country of more than a billion people, only 3.8 billion shaving blades are sold every year. And of these, an overwhelming 97 per cent is double-edged blades. That doesn't leave much scope for twin-blades, does it? Gillette India doesn't seem to agree.
- In October 2003, it introduced the Gillette Vector Plus in another effort to slice open the market for twin-blade shaving systems. The USP: The product claims to take care of the perennial issue of hair clogging between the blades.
- Take a look at how the Indian market for twin-blades has shaped up. Since Gillette introduced the first twin-head shaving system, the 7 O'Clock PII, in the mid-1980s, the market has grown three-fold: From an estimated Rs 200 crores in 1986 to Rs 600 crores in 2002.

  Twin-blades, which were just 3 per cent of the value (Rs 6 crores) in 1986, have increased to nearly 28 per cent of the value (Rs 168 crores). And Gillette commands nearly 80 per cent of the twin-blade market. But that's still only 80 per cent of a minuscule 114 million units market.

Contd...

- The biggest and the most obvious reason for the preference for the archaic double-edged blades is cost. For the price of one low-end disposable twin blade, you can buy a pack of 10 double-edged blades.

  Gillette did try to get around that problem earlier: In 1993, it introduced the Gillette Presto, a disposable twin-blade, at price points as low as Rs 7.

- However, as products like the Presto encouraged a large number of trials, they had limited usage. For instance, analysts point out that buyers in smaller towns used twin-blades as rarely as Indian consumers use contact lenses — only for special occasions.

- There's another important - but less considered - reason for the lack of enthusiasm for twin-edged razors. That is the low frequency of shaving by Indian men. According to a survey conducted by the company, the average shaving frequency of Indians is 1.7 times a week.

  In comparison, the average in countries like Germany is as high as 5.2 times a week. The preference for stubble affects sales of twin-edged razors for a surprising reason. First, Indians have a strong beard growth and shaving once every three to four days will mean that the beard lengths are longer.

  That results in hair-clogging between the two blades of twin-blade systems. Gillette executives point out that clogging of hair leads to a poor quality of shaving. It also results in faster use-up rates of the blades as customers used various means to clean the blades. Consequently, two out of three users who had tried twin blades went back to the low-end double-edged blades.

  Flat blades have no such problem: The shaving system ensures that the double-edged blade can be taken out and washed. "Double-edged consumers are not happy with their shaves. But hair clogging is the biggest barrier for consumers to upgrade to twins," points out Sachin Gopal, general sales director, Gillette India. Gillette could have still taken care of the hair-clogging issue if running water were available throughout the country. However, research shows that only 25 per cent of shavers use running water, the rest shave using a mug as an accessory.

  Will Vector be a plus point for Gillette India?

  (Adapted from: www.bsstrategist.com)

The diffusion process identifies *innovators* in the introductory phase of a product's life cycle; there are *early adopters* during growth period, the *early majority* and *late majority* adopt the product in its maturity period and *laggards* (late adopters) are the last to adopt the product. These life cycle phases are important, because they are linked to different marketing strategies during the product life cycle.

During the introductory phase, the marketer's objectives are related to establish distribution, building brand awareness among members of the target market and encouraging trial to begin the adoption process. As the product gains some acceptance, the marketer can define its early adopters. The company now tries to strengthen its foothold in the market by shifting from the objective of creating brand awareness to one of broadening product appeals and increasing product availability by increasing its distribution.

As the product matures, competition intensity gradually increases and sales begin to level off. The marketer starts emphasising price appeals, starts sales promotions and may consider modifying the product to gain competitive advantage. Majority of the adopters enter the market at this stage largely because of the influence of early adopters. The majority that has already gone through the process of product adoption does not rely much on mass media any more for information. When the product is viewed to have entered its decline phase, lower prices become more relevant and the marketer considers revitalising the product, or adopts the strategy of harvesting or divesting. It is during the decaying maturity and the decline phase of the product life cycle that laggards enter the market.

FIGURE 11.3

Product Lifecycle Phases of Adopter Groups

PLC stages	Introduction	Growth	Maturity		Decline
Adopter groups	Innovators	Early adopters	Early majority	Late majority	Laggards
Percentages	(2.5%)	(13.5%)	(34.0%)	(34.0%)	(16.0%)

Adoption Decision

The adoption of an innovation requires that an individual or a group of consumers decide buying a new product. The diffusion of adoption starts when early adopters influence their reference group members and other acquaintances. Therefore, it is reasonable to view adoption as the first step in the process of a product's widespread acceptance in the target market.

The adoption of an innovation is likely to be a reasonably involving decision for most of those who are among the first to buy the product and can be represented by a hierarchy-of-effects model. Thus, the adoption process is basically a term used to describe extended decision-making by consumers when a new product, service, or idea is involved. For example, the decision to buy a *DVD* writer or have laser eye surgery will most likely be a high-involvement decision. Most modified or upgraded new products probably trigger limited decision-making. In case of low-cost, low-risk new products, consumers' involvement level is likely to be low.

The process shows that the consumer becomes aware and recognises the need for the product. In the next step, to acquire knowledge about the product, the consumer gets involved in information search. The third step is brand evaluation. Next is trial of the product before making a purchase decision and finally, the consumer decides whether to adopt the product or not. As a consequence of using the product, the consumer makes post purchase evaluation. In this process of adoption, product trial is more important than in most other decisions because the perceived risks are likely to be much higher with the use of a new product. Certain types of products or services are difficult, or even impossible to try on a sufficient basis such an electric cars or laser eye surgery.

Post purchase evaluation is likely to have important implications because of the expenses involved or the complexity of many products and the rapid changes in technology. For example, if many adopters had discontinued the use of personal computers after their first purchase as a result of unfavourable post purchase evaluation, the market for PCs would be shrinking instead of expanding rapidly. As a result of favourable evaluation, many of the PC adopters have either upgraded their old machines or discarded their original machines and bought third or fourth generation computers.

FIGURE 11.4

Adoption Process and Extended Decision-making

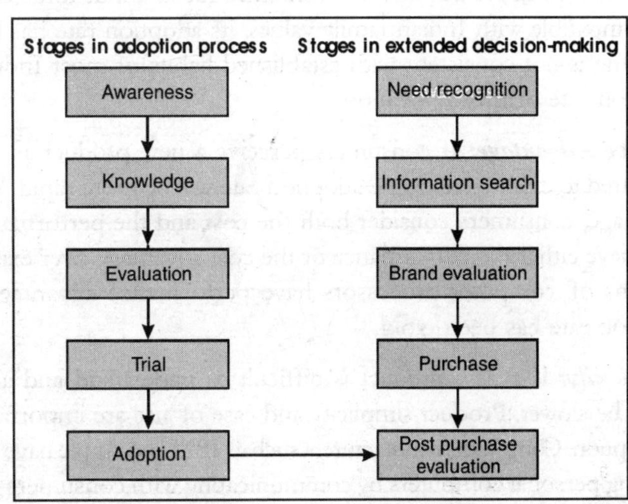

The outcome of consumers' decision process can be adoption or rejection of the product. Many consumers' evaluation of cellular phones has led them to rejecting this wonderful product, because they consider the convenience of keeping a cellular phone not worth the expense involved. Apple Computers introduced their Cube, which was believed to be something unique in computer design. However, the company discontinued the model because of consumers' rejection of the product. When Apple introduced their range of iMacs, another breakthrough in computer design, consumer response was overwhelming.

Factors Affecting New Product Adoption Rate

The chances of a product's adoption and subsequent diffusion are largely dependent on its nature. The rate at which the diffusion of an innovation takes place is a function of the following 10 factors:

1. ***Type of Target Group:*** The target market for the new product is an important factor in influencing the rate of adoption. Some groups are more inclined to accept change than others. In general, affluent, young and highly educated groups tend to try and accept new products readily.

2. ***Number of People Involved in Decision-making:*** This refers to whether the decision is made by an individual or a group. If fewer individuals are involved in making the purchase decision, the adoption is likely to spread more rapidly. When two or more family members are involved in making the purchase decision, the adoption rate will be slower than purchases that primarily affect one individual.

3. ***Extent of Marketing Efforts Involved:*** The rate of adoption is very significantly influenced by the extent of marketing efforts undertaken. No matter how wonderful a new product, unless sufficient numbers are informed and convinced of what it can do for them, the adoption process would be adversely affected. Thus, the rate of new product adoption is not completely beyond the control of the marketer.

4. ***Need Fulfillment:*** The more involving and obvious the need that the new product satisfies, the faster the rate of adoption. The rate of adoption of antidandruff shampoos has been fast as they gained rapid trial among those who were uncomfortable with dandruff. Sildenafil Citrate (Viagra), the male impotency drug gained rapid trial and its adoption rate has been very fast. Rogaine, believed to be a cure for certain types of hair loss or baldness, gained rapid trial among those who felt uncomfortable with their hair loss problem.

5. ***Compatibility:*** This refers to the degree to which the new product is consistent with the individual's and group's needs, attitudes, beliefs and past experiences. The more its consistency, the faster its adoption rate. Microwave ovens were introduced about three decades back in India but since it was not compatible with Indian family values, its adoption rate has been rather slow. Internet banking or shopping is not consistent with established habits of most Indian consumers, resulting in very slow adoption rate of this innovation.

6. ***Relative Advantage:*** If consumers perceive a new product as better in meeting their relevant need compared to existing ones, the adoption rate will be more rapid. While considering the relative product advantage, consumers consider both the cost and the performance. To be successful, a new product must have either the performance or the cost advantage over existing alternatives. For example, newer versions of computer processors have performance advantage over earlier ones and hence their adoption rate has been rapid.

7. ***Complexity:*** If a new product is difficult to understand and also difficult to use, its adoption rate would be slower. Product simplicity and ease of use are important factors in speeding up the process of adoption. Computer manufacturers such as IBM and Apple have tried to overcome the initial complexity of using personal computers by communicating with consumers that their computers are user-friendly.

8. ***Observability:*** This refers to the ease with which consumers can observe the positive effects of adopting a new product. The rate of adoption will be more rapid if the positive effects are easily observable. Products such as cellular phones, fashion items, and autos are highly visible.
9. ***Triability:*** It is the degree to which a product can be tried before adoption. This is much less a problem with low-cost or low-risk items such as cold remedies, but cellular phones, fax machines, computers, etc., can be demonstrated in actual use and tried on a limited scale. If consumers can purchase a product in small quantity, then trial is relatively easy and the rate of adoption is rapid.
10. ***Perceived Risk*:** The more risk associated with trying a new product, slower the rate of adoption. The risk in adopting a new product can be financial, physical, performance, or social. For example, when microwave ovens were introduced, consumers expressed worries about physical risk from radiation. Technological improvements and consumer education overcame this perceived risk. Initially, adopters of personal computers perceived economic and performance risks which have been largely overcome by decreasing prices and improved software. In case of fashion items, consumers feel social risk until opinion leaders in consumers' peer group adopt them. The most effective way to reduce perceived risks in adopting a new product is through trial. Free samples are an effective tool in case of consumer non-durables — low cost items such as detergents, toothpaste, etc. Sony offered trial of its high-priced innovation ProMavica electronic photography system. It distributed 150 prototypes to large newspaper and magazine publishers. This allowed publishers to try and experience the product and encouraged its rate of adoption.

Time Factor and Diffusion Process

Time is an important component of new product diffusion and concerns the *time of adoption* of a new product by consumers considering, whether consumers are earlier or later adopters and the *rate of diffusion*, that is, the speed and extent with which individuals and groups adopt the new product.

Time of Adoption: Everett M. Rogers examined more than 500 studies on the rate of new product adoption and concluded that there are five categories of adopters classified by time of adoption:

1. Innovators.
2. Early Adopters.
3. The Early Majority.
4. The Late Majority.
5. Laggards.

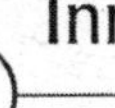

Innovators

Innovators constitute, on an average the first 2.5 per cent of all those consumers who adopt the new product and are technology enthusiasts. They seem to have an eagerness bordering almost an obsession to try new products and ideas. They are venturesome risk takers, willing to live with bugs and deficiencies. According to Thomas E. Weber, innovators represented the primary market for the WebTV developed and marketed in 1996. By the end of that year's holiday season, only about 30,000 to 100,000 of the 97 million households with TVs had purchased WebTV. Innovators tend to be younger, better educated, have higher incomes, are cosmopolitan and active outside of their community as compared to non-innovators. They also tend to be less reliant on group norms, use other innovators rather than local peers as a reference group, are more self-confident and make more extensive use of commercial media, sales personnel and professional sources in learning of new products.

Early Adopters

Early adopters tend to be opinion leaders in local reference groups and represent, on an average the next 13. 5 per cent who adopt the new product. They admire a technologically new product not so much for its features as for its ability to create a revolutionary breakthrough in the way, things are normally accomplished. Though they are not among the earliest individuals to adopt the product, yet they adopt the product in the early stage of its life cycle. They are successful, well educated and somewhat younger than their peers. They tend to be more reliant on group norms and values than innovators and are also more oriented to the local community rather than having a cosmopolitan look. They are willing to take a calculated risk on an innovation but are concerned with failure. Early adopters also use commercial, professional and interpersonal information sources. Since they tend to be opinion leaders, they are likely to transmit word-of-mouth influence and, due to this reason, they are probably the most important group in determining the success or otherwise of the new product.

The Early Majority

The early majority tend to be deliberated and cautious with respect to innovations and represents 34.0 per cent. They look for new products that offer incremental, predictable improvements of an existing technology. They adopt innovations earlier than most of their social group but only after the innovation is viewed as being successful with others. They tend to collect more information and evaluate more brands than is the case with early adopters and, therefore, the process of adoption takes longer. They tend to be price sensitive and like to see competitors enter the market. They are socially active, somewhat older, less well educated and less socially mobile than early adopters and are seldom leaders. They rely heavily on interpersonal sources of information and are an important link in the process of diffusing new ideas because of their position between earlier and later adopters.

The Late Majority

The late majority (34.0 per cent) are somewhat sceptical about innovative products. They are conservative, wary of progress, rely on tradition and generally adopt innovations in response to group norms and social pressure, or due to decreased availability of the previous product rather than positive evaluation of the innovation. They tend to be older, with below average income and education and have less social status and mobility than those who adopt earlier. In many developing countries, consumers who are just now learning to use the Internet are late majority consumers. They tend to place high value on bundled products that include everything they need to connect to the Internet.

FIGURE 11.5

Adoption Rate and Product Life Cycle

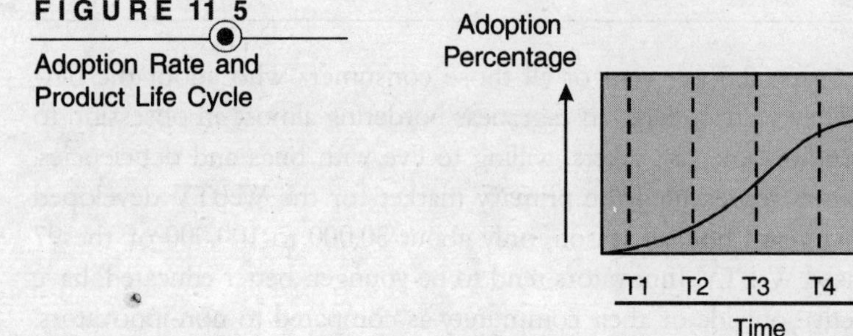

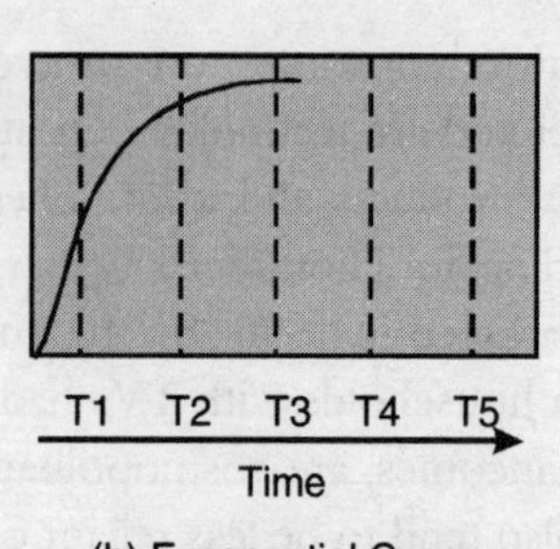

Contd...

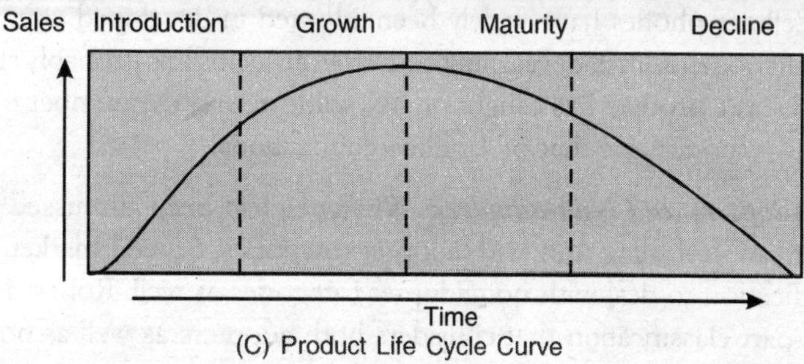

(C) Product Life Cycle Curve

Laggards represent the last 16.0 per cent of adopters. Like innovators, they are the least inclined to rely on the group's norms. Laggards are tradition bound, tend to be dogmatic and make decisions in terms of the past. By the time they adopt an innovation, it is old and has been superseded by something else. They tend to be suspicious of new products and alienated from a technologically progressing society and adopt innovations with reluctance. In the personal computer market, consumers who can afford and have yet to buy a PC are likely to be regarded as laggards.

Adoption rate curves for different products vary significantly and depend on the type of product. In case of major innovations, fewer individuals will adopt early but more will be in the late majority and laggard categories. Several diffusion patterns have been identified. Two of the more important ones are shown in Figures 11.4 (a) and (b).

The third figure (c), is a typical life cycle curve and depicts sales of a product rather than cumulative adoption rate of an innovation. In case of fads, they come quickly in the public eye, are adopted with great enthusiasm and, subsequently, their decline is fast. Their acceptance cycle is very short and they tend to attract only a limited following. Generally, fads do not last long because either they do not satisfy a strong need or fail to satisfy it well. Mainly, it is the amount of media attention, along with some other factors, that influence their adoption.

Product life cycle and product diffusion rate are related but different concepts. Product life cycle deals with sales of the product over time. The PLC curve may decline as consumers decide not to purchase the product on future occasions. Thus, although an innovation such as the rotary dial telephone may have been adopted in an entire market, it has been replaced by another innovation, the touch-tone phone. Diffusion, on the other hand, focuses on the *percentage of the market that has adopted the product.* Complete diffusion is achieved when 100 per cent of the market has purchased the product. Adoption curve generally continues to increase or at least level off over time.

In case there is frequent revitalisation of the product, the product experiences periods of decline and subsequent growth. Such products require adoption of new technology at each phase of technological improvements. For example, computers and their peripherals are passing through continuous upgradations at short intervals.

FIGURE 11.6

Adoption of cellular phones

Cellular phones have widely been adopted in developed countries. However, their adoption is rapidly gaining momentum in developing countries. It seems it is probably still among early adopter groups. However, in India, the product has caught on like wildfire, and the number of subscribers has crossed the 100 million mark — about twice that of landline connections.

Adopters and Non-adopters: Whatever has been discussed so far is based on Everett M. Rogers' classification dealing only with adopter categories. Several marketing studies have used a simple three-part classification to deal with non-adopter categories as well. Robert L. Anderson and David J. Ortinau used a three-part classification that considers both adopters as well as non-adopters:

1. Early adopters
2. Later adopters
3. Non-adopters

According to this three-part classification, the early adopters include innovators of five-part classification of Everett M. Rogers; the later adopters include both early and late majority as well as laggards. The non-adopter group provides for the possibility that a significant number of consumers in the market may simply decide not to purchase the new product.

Rate of Diffusion: Rate of diffusion of a new product refers to the cumulative level of adoption of an innovation over time among groups. For example, about four decades have passed since TV was introduced in India and not even 70% households own a TV set. Adoption of some even cheaper new products are much slower in Indian rural markets. Most of the households in rural India do not own a telephone connection. Even in cities, so far, the use of automatic teller machines has not witnessed rapid growth. In developed and emerging economies, the speed of adoption of innovations seems to be increasing. In a study, Richard W. Olshavsky found that such consumers are adopting new products comparatively much more readily than they used to. There are four major reasons that explain why innovations are adopted more quickly:

1. With the increase in household disposable income, new products are likely to be more affordable.
2. Rapid technological advances require quicker adoption cycles.
3. As technology is becoming more standardised, it reduces consumers' risk perception associated with the adoption of a new product. The rate of adoption of Pentium processor based PC was fairly quick because of the acceptance of *DOS* (operating system) as the industry-wide standard.
4. Information regarding innovation is communicated rapidly and is accessible to the consumers conveniently. Obviously, the more quickly consumers become aware and gain knowledge about a new product through mass media and Internet, the faster is the reach of communication to various other consumer groups, aided by visibility of use and word-of-mouth publicity.

Culture may have an important influence on the diffusion of innovation. Two concepts are worth considering in this regard: *cultural context* and *cultural homogeneity.*

Low-context cultures are those that rely primarily on verbal and written communication in transmitting meaning. They place more value on individual initiative and rely more on mass media for communication. The concept of heterophilous groups can be applied to low-context cultures, which are more disparate, with wider differences among groups. United States and Western Europe would be described as low-context/heterophilous cultures.

High-context cultures rely primarily on non-verbal communication, with little difference in norms, values and socio-economic status among groups. The emphasis on non-verbal communication means that such cultures will place more value on interpersonal contacts and associations. In high-context cultures, more value is placed on group than on the individual, the emphasis being on subscribing to the norms and long-standing rituals of society. Most of the Far Eastern countries would qualify as high-context/homophilous cultures.

One would expect the rate of adoption to be rapid in high-context/homophilous cultures because of their uniformity, leading to relative ease of transmitting information from one dissimilar group to another. Another important aspect is that the credibility of information on new products, services, or ideas is higher because the source is more likely to be friends or relatives rather than commercial mass media.

Hirokazu Takada and Deepak Jain conducted a study to compare the rate of adoption of calculators, washing machines and air-conditioners in Japan, South Korea and Taiwan (considered as high-context cultures) and United States (considered low-context culture). They reported that in most cases, the rate of adoption was faster in all the three high-context cultures than it was in the United States.

Summary

It is essential for companies to develop new products for the sake of their survival. Researchers have identified six categories of new products depending on their newness to the world, to the consumer, or to the company. New products also include repositioned or upgraded products.

Successful new product development requires a company to establish an effective set up for new product development. Companies organise for new product development on the lines of product managers, new product managers, new product committees, new product departments, or new product development venture teams.

New product development involves seven stages: Idea generation involves searching for new product ideas; idea screening refers to selecting the potential ideas, concept testing is presenting product concepts and product benefits to target customers to assess their responses to identify and eliminate poor product concepts, business analysis step assesses the new product's profit potential and compatibility with markets, test marketing involves testing the product in some types of settings to evaluate consumer responses towards the product and the marketing programme, and commercialisation is full-fledged product launch in the market. Use of modern virtual reality technology may be of help to shorten the duration involved in new product development.

The adoption process refers to the decision process through which consumers adopt a new product. Diffusion is the manner in which innovations spread over time to other consumers through communications across a market. Innovators adopt the product in its introductory phase of life cycle; early adopters during growth phase, early and late majority during its maturity period, and laggards are the last to adopt the product. These life cycle phases are important because they are linked to different marketing strategies during the product life cycle.

Adoption of an innovation requires that individual or a group of consumers decide buying a new product. The process of adoption starts when early adopters influence group members and other acquaintances. Adoption of an innovation is a reasonably involving decision for new adopters and is best described by the hierarchy of effects model. Post purchase evaluation is likely to have important implications.

Communication is a key-element that influences diffusion across markets, as early adopters rely on mass media for information about new products. Subsequent adopters show greater reliance on friends and family to help them to evaluate new products, and word-of-mouth publicity increases in importance.

Members of low-context cultures rely primarily on verbal and written communications in transmitting the meaning, place more value on individual initiative, and rely more on mass communication. High-context cultures rely primarily on non-verbal communication, with little difference in norms, values, and socio-economic status among groups. Members of such cultures place more value on interpersonal contacts. One would expect rapid rate of diffusion in high-context cultures, as the credibility of information providers is high.

Questions for Discussion

1. What is the significance of innovations for the society?
2. If developing new products is risky, why do companies bother to spend huge sums of money in this effort?
3. Define a new product. Give example of three products you consider as new.
4. What steps would you recommend for generating new product ideas for a car manufacturer?
5. Evaluate different methods companies use to conduct test marketing.
6. Why do companies conduct test marketing when the product concept has already shown promising potential?
7. Discuss the adoption process of an innovation.
8. What is the role of communications in the product adoption process?
9. What are the personality characteristics of early adopters?
10. Discuss the characteristics of different types of innovators.

Projects

1. What type of innovations are the products mentioned below? Identify the characteristics of people who adopted these products?
   (a) Cellular phone
   (b) Notebook PCs
   (c) Wristwatch with camera.
2. Check up advertisements and prepare a list of three products as you consider as innovations, that were introduced within the last ten years. Assess the reasons for their success or otherwise.
3. Select an innovation, which has just entered or is soon likely to be introduced in the Indian market. Why, in your view, would it be adopted quickly/very slowly/or fail?

Bibliography

1. Miller Cyndee, "Survey: New Product Failure is Management's Fault," *Marketing News*, February 1993.
2. Weisz Pam, "1994's New products Winners and Sinners, a la Consumer Panels," *Brandweek*, December 1994.
3. Rogers Everett M, *Diffusion of Innovation*, 4th Ed. 1995.
4. Cooper Robert G and Klein Schmidt, *New Product: The Key Factors in Success*, (AMA, 1990).
5. Christopher K. Bart, "Organising for New Product Development," *Journal of Business Strategy*, July-August 1988.
6. E. Dahan and J. R. Hauser, "The Virtual Customer," *Journal Product Innovation Management* 19, (2002).
7. Forlani D, J. W. Mullins, and O. C. Walker, "New Product Decision Making: How Chance and Size of Loss Influence What Marketing Managers See and Do," *Psychology and Marketing*, 2002.

8. Miller Cyndee, "Little Relief Seen for New Product Failure Rate," *Marketing News,* June 21, 1993.

9. Stern Gabriella, "To Outpace Rivals, More Firms Step up Spending on New Product Development," *Wall Street Journal,* October 28, 1992.

10. Weber Thomas E, "Why Web TV Isn't Quite Ready for Prime Time," *Wall Street Journal,* January 2, 1997.

11. Anderson Robert L and David J. Ortinau, "Exploring Consumers' Post-Adoption Attitudes and Use Behaviour in Monitoring the Diffusion of a Technology-Based Discontinuous Innovation," *Journal of Business Research,* 17 (1998).

12. Olshavsky Richard W., "Time and Rate of Adoption of Innovations," *Journal of Consumer Research* 6, (March 1980).

13. Takada Hirokazu and Deepak Jain, "Cross-National Analysis of Diffusion of Consumer Durable Goods in Pacific Rim Countries", *Journal of Marketing* 55 (April 1991).

Branding, Packaging & Labelling

CHAPTER 12

LEARNING OBJECTIVES

After going through this chapter, you will understand:

- A brand is much more than suggested by its classical definition.
- The concepts of brand equity, brand personality, brand image, and identity.
- There are different types of brands.
- Importance of brand name selection.
- Different branding strategies.
- Significance of packaging and labelling.

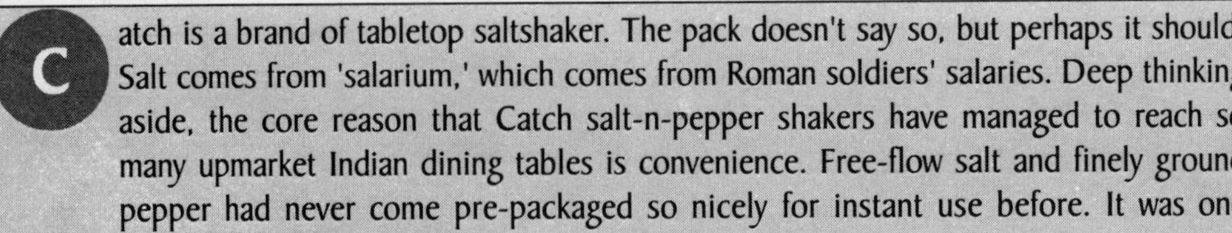

Catch is a brand of tabletop saltshaker. The pack doesn't say so, but perhaps it should. Salt comes from 'salarium,' which comes from Roman soldiers' salaries. Deep thinking aside, the core reason that Catch salt-n-pepper shakers have managed to reach so many upmarket Indian dining tables is convenience. Free-flow salt and finely ground pepper had never come pre-packaged so nicely for instant use before. It was one terrific idea, and everyone knew it was bound to succeed.

The salt came first, in the year 1987. The Delhi-based Dharam Pal Satya Pal (DS) group is better known for its Baba, Tulsi, and Rajnigandha Paan Masala. Catch was launched by a subsidiary of DS, Hi Tech Foods Ltd. Satya Pal had this vague hunch that branded free-flowing table-salt was exactly what many Indian homes wished they had access to, but didn't. The more he thought about it, the better the idea began to crystallise. Getting cooking salt out of a 1- kg bag, putting a portion into a shaker - and then having it turn soggy in the monsoons - was simply too much of an inconvenience. Pepper - it had to be crushed manually or turned into a fine powder in a grinder, and then part of that powder filled in a shaker. The question was simply how cheaply the idea could be launched, and how many consumers would be willing to pay for it.

In hindsight, it looks obvious. It was to take a product as basic as salt and deliver it in a more user-friendly form to customers. That is the thing about great ideas - they are so simple and elegant. But the point is, it was the late 1980s, several years into the 'consumer boom', and no one had done it before. The 60-year old DS Group, with a 75-crore turnover, had an enterprising brain in Satya Pal, who went ahead and did it. Today, his two sons, Ravinder Kumar, chairman, and Rajiv Kumar, managing director, DS Group are busy building on the success.

Catch, as a brand has already achieved the distinction of having made it to the upmarket Indian table, which is often the biggest hurdle for most enterprises.

Success was not a simple matter of executing a terrific idea. It took hard work, as all business ventures do, and plenty of bold thinking. The idea may have been the result of gut feel, but everything else followed a statistically valid process. Hi Tech carried out a random survey of the urban Indian market, and decided to aim Catch at two well-defined segments. One segment chosen was premium Indian households in SEC A and B cities, and the segment included hotels and restaurants, which would use the product in large volumes. Hi Tech built itself a national distribution network that covered some 1,600 premium outlets in India's A and B class cities. Even 30-odd regulars per outlet would be a decent start.

Catch was launched at a price of Rs. 6 for a 200-gm pack. For a product that had stirred price passions in the past, this was an audacious premium over regular salt. The market leader, Tata iodised salt, was selling at Re 1 per pack for one whole kg and local merchants were selling loose salt at less than that. So Rs. 6 was quite a price, spelling big risk. A bigger one than the price ratio will suggest at first glance, because low-priced salt is seen by most in India as something of a fundamental right, and anything extra, be it taxes, in-built costs or margins, being viewed askance by the 'aam janta' (common public), as extortion.

As Ashok Agarwal, vice-president, DS Group, says, "We did not have any competitors, as the brand was a high-priced commodity packaged for convenience." And luckily for it, the urban Indian household made a rational choice, and found that the free-flowing benefit and added

Contd...

convenience value outweighed the price. The rest of the family was also impressed, which was a key factor, and so were guests. The product was so well packaged that it became a status symbol and an instant success. Price analysts would have been shocked. Never before had the Indian market accepted a product at thirty times the per-gram price, for packaging.

Within months of launch, it was clear that Catch was on its way into the marketing history books. It wasn't all packaging, insists the company. The salt used in Catch was seawater salt (sub-soil salt is another source). Sourced from the Gujarat coast, DS was getting it processed at its NOIDA refinery plant, near Delhi, into a pure white, crystalline form of sodium chloride (no magnesium chloride or other hygroscopic salts) that could resist moisture and thus continue to flow freely. This is also the tack adopted by Captain Cook salt, which came later in 1991, and made free-flowing proposition for 1-kg packs.

"Our process," says Agarwal, "includes filtering the impurities out, precipitating and crystallising the salt, then purifying it by removing the water absorbing organic materials to make it free-flowing. The high sodium chloride content (99.5% plus) differentiates free-flowing salt from common salt. Catch's packaging keeps it free-flowing throughout." This is why look-alikes didn't click. DS had invested Rs. 60 lakh in its original plant. Another Rs. 2 crore was put in subsequently (for state-of-the-art iodisation and crystallisation machinery).

The finished salt crystals coming out of the plant were of various sizes. While the larger crystals went into the consumer pack, the finer leftovers were bought by potato chip manufacturers and used in such brands such as Uncle Chipps, Binnie's, and PepsiCo's Hostess. This made the business all the more exciting. Britannia started buying fine salt from DS in 1997.

Within four years Catch's launch, Hi Tech touched a turnover of Rs.1 crore. The company also introduced a 100-gm pack of Catch salt.

(Source: A & M)

Branding is a major decision issue in managing products. Well-known brands have the power to command price premium. Today, the brands Mercedes, IBM, Sony, Canon and others enjoy a huge brand-loyal market. According to *Business Week,* the Intel brand is one of the top 10 global brands, with a brand equity value of more than US 30 billion dollars.

The history of branding goes back centuries in time, when craftsmen wanted to be identified for their skills and placed their distinct and identifiable marks on goods they crafted. This was the earliest form of branding to build reputation of particular artisans by word-of-mouth. Buyers learnt to look for distinctive marks just as we look today for brand names and trademarks on products. According to George S. Low and Ronald A. Fullerton, such marks have been found on early Chinese porcelain, on pottery jars from ancient Greece and Rome, and on goods from India dating back to 1300 B. C. The origin of "brand" is the Norse word *brandr,* that means, "to burn," and owners of livestock mark their animals to identify them.

Branding has always been an important aspect of marketing. Distillers in the16th century burned or put their brand name on the wooden containers. This identified the whisky of one distiller from that of others. The branding evolution continued and the real boost for branding came in the middle of the 20th century. American Marketing Association defined brand as *"a name, term, sign, symbol, or design, or a combination of them, intended to identify the goods and services of one seller or group of sellers and to differentiate them from those of competition."* Thus, according to AMA definition, the key to be able to create a brand is to choose a name, term, sign, symbol, logo, design, package, or other attributes to identify a product from those of others.

As noted earlier, most competition in developed and developing economies is essentially hot at product augmentation level, because most companies in an industry can successfully develop and produce satisfactory products at the expected level. Nearly 45 years earlier, Prof. Theodore Levitt wrote, "*The new competition is not between what companies can produce in their factories but between what they add to their factory output in the form of packaging, services, advertising, customer service, financing, delivery arrangements, warehousing, and things people value.*" Thus, a brand is much more than what AMA definition describes. It is a product, but one that adds other dimensions differentiating it in some way from other products designed to satisfy the same need (Kevin Lane Keller, *Strategic Brand Management,* 2nd ed. 2003). These other differences include not only tangible and rational aspects related to brand performance, but also intangible, emotional, and symbolic meanings consumers perceive the brand represents.

Brands live in the minds of consumers and are much more than just a tag for their recognition and identification. They are the basis of consumer relationship and bring consumers and marketers closer by developing a bond of faith and trust between them. The promise of brand is consistent with reliable quality, service, and overall psychological satisfaction. The marketer has to establish a mission for the brand and a vision of what the brand is and can do. It is crucial for the marketer to consider that it's an offering of a contract to the consumer about how the brand will perform, and it must be an honest contract. All these factors add value not only for the consumer but also for the marketer. Brands identify the source or maker of a product. This allows consumers to assign responsibility to a manufacturer or distributor. Based on their past experience of use, brands are a means of eliminating search costs, risks, and simplify product purchase decision process.

Brands are believed to be the real generators of wealth of 21st century and determine the market value of business entities. Gillette, Lakmé, Hit, and Goodnight are different names, but there is one thing common among them. They are all brands which other companies have bought. Procter & Gamble has bought Gillette for $57 billion, Hindustan Lever Ltd. bought Lakmé for Rs. 78 crores, Godrej bought Goodnight and Hit for Rs. 131 crores. The prices paid for these brands are many times more than their tangible assets.

A ***brand mark*** refers to that part of brand which is not made up of words, but can be a symbol or design such as swoosh mark of Nike, or Golden Arches of McDonald's. A ***trademark*** is a legal registration indicating the owner's exclusive right to use a brand or some part of brand. A ***trade name*** is the full and legal name of a firm, such as Maruti Udyog Ltd., and not the specific name of a product.

Brand Identity

Different brands vary in the power and value they command in the market place. Many brands are largely unknown to consumers and for some others, there is very high level of awareness in terms of name recall and recognition. David A. Aaker defines brand identity as, "*a unique set of brand associations that the brand strategist aspires to create or maintain. These associations represent what the brand stands for and imply a promise to customers from the organisation members.*" *Brand identity* and *brand image* are sometimes used interchangeably in different texts. Brand identity refers to an insider's concept reflecting brand manager's decisions of what the brand is all about. Brand image reflects the perceptions of outsiders, that is customers, about the brand. From customers' point of view, it is the image they have of a brand that matters. Brand image is the sum total of impressions created by the brand in the consumer's mind. This includes a consumer's impressions about the brand's physical characteristics, its performance, the functional benefits, the kind of people who use the product, the emotions and associations it develops, and the imagery or the symbolic meanings it generates. To put it differently, how a consumer perceives a brand in its 'totality' is the brand image and encompasses both physical and perceptual components. It is a concept that drives customer behaviour with respect to brand.

According to Jean-Noel Kepferer, a brand is complex symbol and capable of conveying up to six dimensions or meanings:

Physique: Physique dimension refers to the tangible, physical aspects. The physical dimensions are usually included in the product such as name, features, colours, logos, and packaging. The physique of IBM brand would be data system, servers, desktop PCs, notebooks PCs, and service, etc.

Personality: Marketers deliberately may try to assign the brand a personality; or people on their own may attribute a personality to a brand. It is not surprising that people often describe some brands by using adjectives such as "young," "masculine," "feminine," exciting," "rugged," "rebel," "energetic," etc., as if they are living persons. Brands usually acquire personalities because of deliberate communications from marketers and use of endorsers. Bajaj Pulsar ads communicate "Definitely male." The personality of Boost is seen as young, dynamic, energetic and an achiever.

Culture: Culture includes knowledge, belief, rites and rituals, capabilities, habits, and values. A brand reflects its various aspects and values that drive it. Culture manifests various aspects of a brand. For instance, Apple computers reflect its culture. It is a symbol of simplicity, and friendliness. Its symbol (munched Apple) connotes being different from others and not following the beaten path. Mercedes symbolises disciplined, efficient, high quality German engineering.

Relationship: Brands are often at the heart of transactions and exchanges between marketers and customers. The brand name Nike is Greek and relates to Olympics, and suggests glorification of human body. "Just Do It" is all about winning, the unimportance of age, and encourages us to let loose. Apple conveys emotional relationship based on friendliness. Relationship is essentially important in service products.

Reflection: This refers to defining the kind of people who use it. It is reflected in the image of its consumers: young, old, rich, modern and so on. For example, Pepsi reflects young, fun loving, carefree people. The reflection of Allen Solly's brand is a typical young executive. However, it does not by any chance mean that they are the only users. The concept of target market is broader than reflection.

Self-Image: This means how a customer relates herself/himself to the brand. Self-image is how a customer sees herself/himself. The self-image of users of Bajaj Pulsar motorcycle is believed to that of being tough, young males. Users of Nike see their inner reflection in the brand's personality.

Brand Equity

Brand equity is one of the popular and potentially important concepts in marketing that emerged in the 1980s. It has raised the importance of the brand in marketing strategy. Many scholars have expressed their views in defining brand equity. David A. Aaker defines brand equity in the following words:

"Brands have equity because they have high awareness, many loyal consumers, a high reputation for perceived quality, proprietary assets such as access to distribution channels or to patents, or the kind of brand associations (such as personality associations)."

David A. Aaker, *Managing Brand Equity,* (Free Press1991).

Kevin Lane Keller defines brand equity:

"Brand equity is defined in terms of marketing effects uniquely attributed to the brands – for example, when certain outcomes result from the marketing of a product or service because of its brand name that would not occur if the same product or service did not have the name."

[Kevin Lane Keller, "Conceptualising, Measuring, and Measuring Customer Based Brand Equity," *Journal of Marketing,* (January 1993)].

Iconic Brands

All companies aspire to build brands that eventually get etched in the culture of the society and become cultural icons. But very few companies are able to achieve this iconic status. Contrary to popular perception, iconicity does not happen by chance, but rather has to be carefully planned and executed. A look at some of the most iconic brands in history such as Coca-Cola, Harley-Davidson, Giorgio Armani, Apple, Aman-Resorts and Singapore Airlines reveals some very common characteristics. All these brands fulfilled three important requirements of being an iconic brand:

Create an identity myth: For any brand to attain iconic status, it has to create an identity myth. Every society invariably goes through phases of prosperity and crisis. Brands that resonate and show direction to the masses through the brand stories and brand activities get etched into the culture. These brands, by creating an identity for themselves, provide identity to the whole society.

Involve multiple storytellers: Dissemination of brand information through the many participants of the society is critical for an iconic brand. The four major authors of these brand stories are: companies, the culture industries, intermediaries and customers. Each of these authors facilitates the brand to blend into the fabric of the society. By associating the brand and its identity with the prevalent events in the society, these authors create an iconic stature for the brands.

Weave powerful brand stories: Great brands always have resonating stories that touch the lives of consumers. These stories could be of the brand's unique history (Shanghai), myth (Jim Thompson), culture (Harley-Davidson), fashion icon (Giorgio Armani), struggle (Li Ning), and underlying philosophy (Singapore Airlines). These brand stories offer consumers a good reason to elevate the brand beyond their mere utilitarian role in the market.

One of the important results of developing an iconic brand is the growth of brand communities. Brand communities are largely imagined communities that represent a form of human association situated within a consumption context. Brand communities are collections of active loyalists, users of a brand who are committed, conscientious and almost passionate. There is an intrinsic connection between members and the collective sense of difference from others not in the community. Members of the brand community practice rituals and traditions that perpetuate the community's shared history.

Brand communities are liberated from geography, commercial in nature, possess communal self awareness and are committed; that facilitates the brand to attain long term acceptability in the society and ensures that the brand attains iconic state.

By being an important resource for consumers, brand communities provide wider social benefits to consumers through interaction and provide social structure to the relationship between marketer and consumer.

(Source: Martin Roll, Official Weblog for Asian Brand Strategy, February 22, 2006).

The power and value of different brands varies in the market place. There are clearly two extremes in this regard. On one extreme are brands that customers largely do not know. They are unknown faces to a large number of customers. Next in hierarchy are brands for which customers have fairly high levels of awareness. Enjoying a better status in the hierarchy are brands with high degree of acceptability among customers. Further on, there are brands for which customers have high degree of preference. At the other extreme, there are those brands that command a high degree of brand loyalty. A *brand loyal* customer would not accept a substitute and would go elsewhere to acquire that brand.

Jagdish N. Sheth, Banwari Mittal, and Bruce I. Newman define brand loyalty in the following words:

"Brand loyalty is the biased behavioural response, expressed over time by some decision-making unit, with respect to one or more alternative brand out of a set of such brands, and is a function of psychological processes."

(Jagdish N. Sheth, Banwari Mittal, and Bruce I. Newman, *Consumer Behaviour,* 1999).

Loyalty is at the heart of equity and a very important brand equity asset. Few customers are fiercely brand loyal to this degree. Based on customer's degree of commitment toward brands, David A. Aaker categorised customers in five groups based on their attitudes toward a brand, from the indifferent or switcher at one extreme and most committed on the other extreme. The other three categories fall in between the extremes:

1. No brand loyalty. Such customers will change brands, particularly for price reasons.
2. Satisfied but change the brand. They are satisfied with the brand but apparently have no reason to remain attached with it.
3. The customer is satisfied and stays with it because changing brand would incur costs.
4. Customer values the brand and considers it as a friend.
5. Customer is devoted to the brand with intense feelings.

Brand equity is highly related to categories of customers that fall into categories 3, 4, and 5. Brand loyalty is an area of key interest for marketers because it has the ability to have a dramatic impact on marketing performance. Brand equity and associations can add or subtract value for customer and the company. The assets of brand equity, such as perceived quality and associations can boost customer confidence in buying decision and provide use satisfaction, or even delight.

- Brand loyalty of consumers provides insulation against attacks by competitors.
- The company can afford to charge higher prices than competing brands.
- Leverage brand into extensions.
- Gets channel support and cooperation.
- Attract new customers due to strong positive word-of-mouth.

> ■ The Giorgio Armani brand owned and run by the founder designer Giorgio Armani has earned the much hallowed space in the fashion industry through its superior design, relevant themes and trends. It maintains the aura of a real luxury brand. Not only has Giorgio Armani become one of the most respected and known brand names in the fashion and luxury brand industry, it ■ is also one of the most highly valued fashion companies in the world with a value of nearly 3 billion Euros.

Each level of loyalty implies a different equity asset and different kinds of marketing challenges. The indifferent customer does not attach any importance to the brand and buying is done on the basis of price, switching with indifference. The second category of buyers are satisfied habitual buyers but are vulnerable because of extra benefits from competitors. The third is a some what safer category of customers. They are satisfied but switch only when competitors are able to overcome the switching costs for them. Customers of the third category seem to have a negligible element of attitudinal commitment to the brand. Fourth level of loyalty denotes that customers have some level of emotional attachment to the brand as a result of prolonged usage, use experience or perceived high quality. They consider the brand as a friend. The fifth, and last category are customers committed to the brand, what Sheth and Mittal posit as "an enduring desire to continue the relationship and to work to ensure it continues." The brand has a personal significance and customers perceive it as a part of themselves. They identify with a brand so much that it becomes a source of self-expression. Such fanatical loyalty is a huge asset for the company, as it ensures future revenue stream.

There would be lesser marketing costs. When customers are not loyal to the brand, the equity is not likely to exist. Brand is clearly an asset capable of generating revenue streams. Equity is all about financial value of a brand.

FIGURE 12.1

Components of Brand Equity

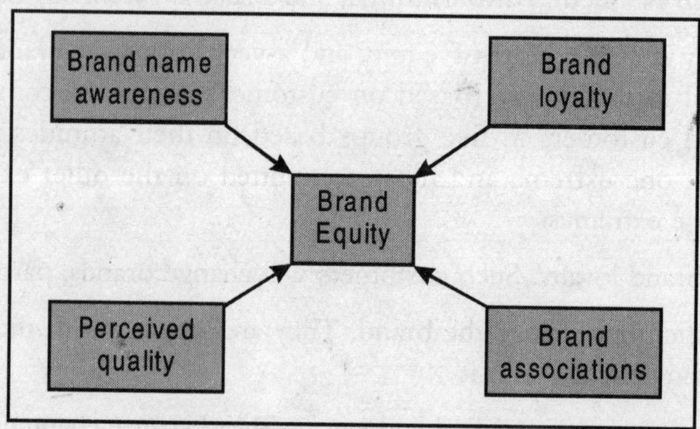

(*Source:* David A. Aaker, *Managing Brand Equity: Conceptualising on the Value of Brand Name,* (1991).

According to Kevin Lane Keller, the challenge marketers face in building strong brands is to make sure that customers get the right type of experiences with brands of products and services, and to ensure the brand's related marketing programmes evoke the desired thoughts, feelings, images, beliefs, perceptions, opinions, values, etc. To build positive brand equity, a brand needs to be managed carefully. David A. Aaker says, besides actual proprietary assets such as patents and trademarks, the four major elements underlying brand equity are brand awareness, a brand's perceived value, positive associations with a brand, and brand loyalty among consumers (Figure 12.1). These tasks require continued investment and focus on R&D, effective advertising, and excellent consumer and trade service. Very old but excellently managed brands seem to be eternal and defying the concept of brand life cycle, e.g., Lifebuoy, Dettol, Lux, Bournvita, Colgate, Coca-Cola, and Gillette, P & G believe that well-managed brands are not subject to brand life cycle.

Walfried Lasser. Banwari Mittal, and Arun Sharma identified five dimensions of customer-based brand equity:

- ***Performance:*** The aspect of brand equity focuses on the physical and functional attributes of a brand. Customers are concerned about how fault free and durable the brand is, based on their judgement.
- ***Social image:*** This focuses on what social image the brand holds in terms of its esteem for customer's social and reference groups.
- ***Value:*** This refers to the customer's value perception of the brand. This is the ratio between what are the involved costs and the perceived delivered value.
- ***Trustworthiness:*** This means the customer's extent of faith in the brand's performance, quality, and service. This reflects reliability of the brand, that it would always take care of customer's interest and the people behind the brand can be trusted.
- ***Identification:*** To what extent customers feel emotionally attached to the brand. Their association with the brand is important because it matches their self-concept and aspirations. This means psychological association with what the brand stands for in the customer's perceptions.

Brand Image

Brand image is the key concept intervening between the brand and its equity. It is the driver of brand equity. The image of a brand can adjust brand value upwards or downwards. When the coconut oil is "Parachute', its value moves upwards. This shift is the result of brand name. The name adds visual and verbal dimensions in consumer's mind and acts as intervening variable moving the value upwards. The name Rolex, or Omega add radical value to the product. A customer who is not familiar with brands like Rolex or Omega will most probably assess the value of these brands as just another watch (a product) because these brands mean nothing to her/him. In such a case, these brands are unlikely to alter value because there is no intervening variable between the brands and their valuation.

A brand exists as a complex network of associations in a consumer's mind. Alexander L. Biel proposed that types of brand associations can be *hard* and *soft* and brand sub-images consist of three elements: *image of provider, image of product,* and *image of user.*

Hard Associations: Hard associations include consumer's perceptions of tangible or functional attributes of a brand. These involve brand's physical construction and performance abilities such as economy, quality, reliability, sturdiness, etc. For example, the hard associations of an automobile can include its power, speed, fuel economy, etc.

Soft Associations: Associations of this type are emotional in nature. Such associations can be positive or negative. A motorcycle can be visualised as male, tough, exciting, youthful, etc. For instance, Bajaj Auto has managed to associate its Pulsar motorcycle with maleness, toughness, youthfulness and excitement. As a consequence of negative associations, consumers associate Indian Airlines with dullness, old age, indifference and inefficiency.

- ***Image of provider:*** This refers to the image of manufacturer. Consumers also carry in their memories a network of associations about companies. For example, Apple computers create associations such as unconventional, exciting, user friendly, creative, innovative, and cool. When consumers visualise Delhi Cloth Mills (DCM), the kind of associations that may emerge are likely to be old, dull, cloth; Rath Vanaspati (vegetable oil): Unchanging, and unexciting. An inappropriate corporate image may tarnish the image of an otherwise good product.
- ***Image of product:*** Products also carry an image of what they carry and have aspects such as functional characteristics, technology intensiveness, emotionality, old, or modern that go with them. Products such as laundry detergents, cold remedies, mosquito repellents etc., tend to be driven by functional attributes and rationality. On the other hand, fashion clothing, perfumes, cold drinks, expensive watches, and many alcoholic beverages tend to be associated with emotions and substantial symbolism. Therefore, brand image has to be shaped within structural limits imposed by the product image.
- ***Image of the user:*** The brand image brings to consumers' minds the image of its users. The image of brand may indicate the age, sex, occupation, lifestyle, interests, and personality attributes. For example, the image of Raymond suitings is that of a "complete man." The user image dimension reflects the brand's personality. According to Leon G. Schiffman and Leslie Lazer Kanuk, a study found that beer, coffee, cigarettes, cars, credit cards, haircuts, legal services, scotch, sneakers, and toothpaste were found to be masculine. Products perceived as feminine included bath soaps, shampoo, facial tissue, clothes dryers, washer, and dishwashing liquid.

Brand image management requires determining brand concept. This concept embodies the central meaning of the brand that the company chooses and is derived from basic consumer needs. The more strongly the brand satisfies these needs, the more differentiated and strong the brand image customers carry. These needs can be put under three broad groups.

Functional needs refer to performance related aspects of customer's living. These needs may relate to solving existing problems or avoid future problems. For example, the need to get rid of dandruff, have relief from cold, insuring for health, or protection against burglars. Some examples of functional brands include Bisleri (pure and safe water), Pepsodent (fights germs causing dental problems), Fevi Kwick (bonds in a snap), and Dispirin (relief from headache).

Symbolic needs are learned, needs as a result of living in a society and include wants for esteem, self-enhancement, identification with desirable groups, etc. Some examples of symbolic brands include Raymond (the complete man), Omega (the sign of excellence), Louis Philippe (upper crest), and Ruggers (be casual).

Experiential needs refer to sensual gratification that comes from brand usage experience. People seek pleasure through their senses, including cognitive stimulation and variety. Some examples of experiential brands include Mother Dairy (pleasure of taste), Armani (the power of smell), Ford Ikon 'Josh' (driving experience), Dove (doesn't dry your skin), Gillette (the best a man can get), and Fisher Price Toys (cognitive stimulation).

Types of Brand

There are several brand options that include manufacturer brand (also called national brand), private brand (also called distributor, reseller, store, or house brand), or a licensed brand.

Manufacturer brands are initiated by manufacturers and identify the producer. This type of brand generally requires the initiator involvement in its distribution, promotion, and pricing decisions. The brand quality is assured and guaranteed, and the aim of promotion mix is to build company and brand image and encourage brand loyalty.

The major feature of ***private brands*** is that they are resellers initiated brands. Manufacturers are not identified on the products. Wholesalers and retailers use private brands to develop more efficient promotions to build store image and generate higher gross margins. Shoppers' Stop is a private brand. Wholesalers or retailers have the freedom and advantage of buying specified quality at an agreed upon cost from the manufacturer without disclosing manufacturer identity. In most markets around the world, manufacturer brands dominate. In developed countries such as U.S., supermarkets average more than 19 per cent private brand sales. The trend of private brands is slowly catching on in India. This is likely to speed up with increasing numbers of large retail stores appearing in major cities of the country. Mukesh Ambani's Reliance Retail is planning to invest Rs. 25,000 crores into its forthcoming retail operations.

Paul S. Richardson, Alan S. Dick, and Arun K. Jain found that formerly, consumers viewed brands in a category in a ladder-like manner. The top rung was occupied by the most preferred brand and the remaining brands were arranged in descending order of preference. There are now indications that consumer perceptions of brand parity are replacing the brand ladder.

Licensed brand is a relatively new trend and involves licensing of trademarks. Entering into a licensing agreement, a company allows approved manufacturers to use its trademark for a mutually agreed fee. The royalties may range anywhere between 2 per cent to 10 per cent or more of wholesale revenues. The company obtaining the license would be responsible for all production and promotional activities, and would bear the costs in case the licensed product fails. The benefits of this arrangement can bring extra revenues, free publicity, new images, and protection of trademark. For example, P&G licensed its Camay brand of soap in India to Godrej for a few years. The disadvantage is that the licensing company loses its control on manufacturing and at times this may hurt the company's name and lead to overstretching the brand.

Some manufacturers prefer to have branded products as well as their *generic brands.* Generic brands indicate only the product category, such as aluminium foil. Another form of generic brands is that the generic name of the product is mentioned and the manufacturing company's name is written just to conform to legal requirements, such as paracetamol, or tetracycline. They do not include any other identifying marks. Generic brands are usually sold at lower prices than their branded versions. Generic brands are fairly common in the drug industry.

Brand Name Selection

The choice of brand name is fundamentally important because it often captures the key concept or association of a product in a compact and economical manner. Brand names can be an effective way of communication because they become attached to the products in consumers' minds. It is critically important to be very careful in selecting the brand name, as changing this brand element in future is extremely difficult. Brand name selection for a new product is certainly a combination of art and science. Companies have four strategic options in choosing a brand name:

Company Name: Companies that have built a reputation for product quality and commitment to customer satisfaction and have become household names sometimes use this strategy. All products are sold under the company name. This approach is less expensive, as it avoids research to select an appropriate name. It does not require heavy advertising expenditures to create brand name awareness. The name takes advantage of good corporate image. Many Indian and global companies use this approach. For example, Nirma, Escorts, HMT, Philips, GE, Mercedes, LG, Samsung, Sony, Canon, Nikon and others use this approach.

Individual Names: Some firms adopt this policy and each brand has its own individual name. The advantage is that the company does not tie its reputation to the product. In case the product fails, or its quality is low, the company's name or image is believed to be safe. The company can introduce lower quality products under an individual name without diluting the image of its higher quality product. For example, HLL introduced a low-priced detergent (Wheel) without hurting Surf.

The company also uses separate brand names for its range of bathing soaps (Lux, Liril, Pears, Dove, Moti, etc.). Procter & Gamble also uses this approach for its products (Ariel, Tide, Head & Shoulders, Pantene, and Vicks). The company searches for new names for its individual brands and this could mean name research expenses.

Separate Brand Family Names: Some companies producing many different products adopt this approach to select brand names. Such companies use different brand names for a category of products. For example, Denim brand of HLL has several products: Denim Deo, Denim Shaving Cream, After Shave, Denim Soap, and Denim Talc. The company's Orchid brand includes several women's beauty products. HLL's Lakmé brand has several personal care products.

Combination of Company Name and Product Name (also called umbrella or endorsement brand names): Some companies follow this policy, such as Maruti Esteem, Maruti Zen, Fiat Palio, Ford Ikon, IBM ThinkPad, Acer TravelMate, Apple Powerbook, Hamdard Roohafza, etc.

Desirable Qualities of Brand Names: Kim R. Robertson is of the view that brand names selected are simple and easy to pronounce; familiar and meaningful; and are different, distinctive, and unusual. Kevin Lane Keller, Susan Heckler, and Michael J. Houston caution that brand name elements that are highly descriptive of the product category or its attributes and benefits may be potentially quite restrictive. For example, attempts at extending the Burnol brand so far have failed because of consumers very strongly associate Burnol with burns.

Sometimes a unique name becomes intimately connected to a product category and may threaten a company's exclusive rights to that name. For example, consumers now use names Aspirin, Xerox, Luna, Scotch Tape, Surf, and Dalda to describe product category. Xerox means photocopy, Aspirin means acetylsalicylic acid, Luna means any moped, Scotch Tape means adhesive tape, Surf is synonymous with detergent category, and Dalda is any vegetable oil. In other words, the brand names have metamorphosed into generic names that cover entire categories of products.

Apple PowerBook is quite an effective name for a laptop PC. The word combines "book," denoting a small product that holds a lot of information and "power." Right from 1984, Apple has used the power plank to promote its computers. This power theme is also associated with the processors it has developed over time: Power processors G3, G4, and G5.

The following qualities of a brand name are considered desirable:

- The name should be suggestive of some product benefit, such as Fair & Lovely, No Marks, Hajmola, Fair Glow, and Roohafza.
- The name should be suggestive of product or service category, such as Himalaya Ayurvedic Concepts, Kleenex, Tatafone, Businessworld, and First Flight.
- The name should be suggestive of imagery that projects qualities, such as Gillette Mach 3, Nike, Moods, etc.
- The name should be simple and easy to spell, pronounce, recognise, and remember, e.g., short names like Lux, Surf, Tide, and Vim.
- The name should be distinctive, such as Apple, Kodak, Sony, Palio, etc.
- The name should not resemble or suggest negative associations in other languages and countries.

To choose a brand name, companies generate a comprehensive list of possible names. Each name is evaluated for its merits, and ultimately a few most suitable ones are left. These names are tested with target consumer groups to arrive at a final choice.

Companies sometimes hire outside marketing research firms specialising in this field. These specialist firms use techniques such as brainstorming sessions and extensive computer databases, sounds, etc. Name-research process employs a variety of tools and techniques, such as *association tests* (images that emerge in the mind's eye), *learning tests* (ease of pronouncing the word), *memory tests* (is the name remembered well?), and *preference tests* (the most preferred names). Research also ensures that the chosen brand name has not already been registered.

Building brands are not easy. It usually requires huge expenditures and effective communications. Keeping in view the product category, its target markets, and competitive situations, companies use an array of communication tools that include advertising, public relations/publicity, trade shows, event marketing, sponsorships, celebrity endorsements, factory visits, social cause marketing, etc.

Branding Strategies

With the passage of time, successful companies grow and the number of products handled by most companies also grows. These companies face the question as to what kind of branding relationships these products will have. The branding strategies that companies adopt reflect this relationship. There is no best branding strategy and the choice is not easy. Different companies adopt different strategies, and since there is no best strategy for all types of products, a company may adopt different branding strategies across its product mix.

Companies differ in their approaches to branding. A casual look at Western World and Eastern World shows that companies of the Western World generally adopt product-branding strategies (one product one brand or many products many brands). At the top of this approach are three giant and familiar companies, P&G, HLL, and Xerox. Eastern companies, such as those from South Korea and Japan adopt a mega branding approach. The company tagline covers all products "Chips to Ships." Examples are Hyundai, Samsung, LG, Hitachi, Mitsubishi, Toyota, etc. These two general approaches reflect customer or market-oriented logic, or cost-oriented logic.

Companies enlarge their product mix by either stretching existing product lines or adding new product lines, or both. In these situations they either use existing brand names or use new brand names, or some combination of company name and product brand name. The six branding strategies discussed here can be termed as generic branding strategies, each having its own set of pros and cons.

Product Branding Strategy

This approach is driven by customer-orientation. The thinking focuses on customer perception and information processing and the company believes the most effective method to differentiate its offer in a customer's mind is to give the product an exclusive position and identity. What the brand represents is clearly comprehended and internalised by its target market. Placing several products under one brand name may cause confusion among consumers. Al Ries and Laura Ries say:

> *"A successful branding programme is based on the concept of singularity. It creates in the mind of the prospect the perception that there is no product on the market quite like your product."*
>
> (Al Ries and Laura Ries, *The 22 Immutable Laws of Branding,* 1998).

This strategy focuses on promoting the brand exclusively so that it reflects its own personality, identity, associations, and image. The brand does not take on company associations and any benefits from its name.

Procter & Gamble is an ardent follower of product branding strategy in its purest form as shown in (Figure 12.2). Hindustan Lever Ltd. also largely follows product brand strategy, but shows some shifts by leveraging established brand names into areas outside its product category. Actually, very few companies follow only product branding strategy. HLL has brands such as Dove, Lux, Rexona, Lifebuoy, Liril, Pears, etc. Dove moisturises skin, Lux is the toilet soap of film stars, Rexona is a gentle soap with natural oils, Lifebuoy fights germs, Liril is 'the' freshness soap, and Pears is the 'original' translucent glycerine soap. It is worth noting that both P&G and HLL use separate brand names for products that are in the same product category (Ariel and Tide are detergents; Lux and Liril are soaps).

Product branding approach is also followed by ITC for its tobacco-based products. At the product level, most cigarettes generally tend to be the same and what counts really is the perceived differentiation among consumer groups who show strong brand preference. This is more distinct in the upmarket segments. The basic product by itself does not offer much opportunity for differentiation. This differentiation has to be created in consumers' perceptions of a brand. This is the major reason why ITC adopts the product differentiation approach for cigarettes. ITC's brand portfolio of cigarettes includes India Kings, Classic, State Express, Benson & Hedges, Gold Flake Kings, Wills, Navy Cut, etc. Each brand is highly differentiated and occupies a distinct position. However, ITC seems to have diluted its product branding approach in case of its powerful Wills brand and has extended the brand into ready-to-wear clothes.

Product branding delivers certain advantages. It helps to create an identifiable brand enjoying a unique position and directed at a well defined target segment, and the company can cover an entire market composed of several segments by creating multiple brands each addressing a different segment. This leaves very little chance of creating confusion among consumers. Product branding is especially advantageous when products are similar, such as detergents, or soaps.

By extending established brands in other categories, a company tries to minimise its risks and excessive promotional expenditures. When a new product is given a familiar and established brand name, consumers are likely to feel more confident about the new product such as HLL extended the Lux name to introduce its shampoo. HLL's brands Signal (toothpaste), and Blue Seal (peanut butter) failed and most people did not even know these were from Hindustan Lever Ltd. All brands of P&G are stand-alones in all of its SBU's, leaving the company to venture into many unrelated fields.

FIGURE 12.2

Product Branding Strategy of P&G (incomplete list)

Brands	Category	Position
Ariel	Detergent	High-tech detergent.
Tide	Detergent	Whiteness no other can deliver.
Head & Shoulders	Shampoo	Antidandruff shampoo with micro ZPTO
Pantene	Shampoo	Healthy & Shiny hair.
Whisper	Sanitary Napkin	Hygienic protection.
Vicks	Balm	Clear blocked nose by touch therapy.
Old Spice	After shave	Sign of manliness.

The major disadvantage of product branding is excessive costs that may be as high as Rs. 5 to Rs. 50 crores in building a successful brand in India. In developed markets, these costs may run into hundreds of million dollars. Another disadvantage is that new brands miss the opportunity of exploiting the strengths of a powerful company name or its brands

Line Branding Strategy

The term 'line branding' is altogether different than what product line refers to in the context of product mix. Companies often have several product lines in the product mix. For example, Gillette India has three product lines: personal care, oral care, and alkaline batteries. In line branding, products share a common concept. Line brands start with a single product conveying a concept and later the brand name extends to other complementary products. The core concept remains unchanged. For example, the core concept of Denim brand is, "The man who doesn't have to try too hard." All products sporting the Denim brand name share the same concept. Lakmé concept is "the source of radiant beauty." The brand concept appeals to a distinct target group of consumers and Lakmé offers a number of additional products that go together, complement each other, and form a whole such as winter care lotion, cleansing lotion, body lotion, lipsticks, eye make up, and nail enamels. All products in line branding draw their identity from the main brand. Park Avenue is also an example of line branding with several products that complement each other addressing the upward mobile man.

Line branding strategy aims to satisfy customer's complementary needs that surround the core need. The core customer need that Lakmé aims to fulfil is 'need to be beautiful' and all products surrounding this need complement each other. The brand takes care of total needs rather than just offering one or two fragmented items. The company focuses on promoting only the main brand concept that builds and reinforces all related items without incurring much additional expenditures. The company can also extend brand without much investment in promotion. The negative side is that success and ease sometimes tempts a company to over extend and weaken the brand.

Range Branding Strategy

This strategy seems to resemble line branding but is significantly different. It is also called brand extension. Product categories are different but brand name is the same, such as carrying the brand name Maggi is a range of different products: noodles, sauce, soup, Dosa mixes, etc. The range represents the area of expertise, which is fast food. In line branding, every product originates from the "product concept."

Lakmé concept is "the source of radiant beauty," and all products surround this core product concept. Line branding is restrictive to brand expansion into products that do not surround this core product concept and complement each other in this regard. In case of range branding, it is not the product concept but "the area of expertise." This strategy permits expanding into products that do not complement each other. For example, a company's area of competence might be microprocessors, and it can develop expertise in some other area over time such as software and expand its brand. Himalaya Drug Company has range of Ayurvedic home remedies like Health Care, Body Care, Skincare, Hair Care, etc., under Ayurvedic Concepts. Certainly, deep cleansing lotion does not complement digestive capsules, and antiseptic cream does not complement face wash. The focus is on expertise. Himalaya Drug Company's area of expertise is 'Ayurvedic medicines' and it can use its expertise to expand the brand to products that do not complement each other. This means range branding covers many different products under one brand banner. Promotional expenditures are low because promoting one brand helps all products in the range. However, the same brand name for too many products may lead to overstretching, may confuse consumers and weaken the brand.

Umbrella Branding Strategy

In general, umbrella branding is favoured among Eastern World companies but is not exclusively confined only to this part of the world. Giants like GE and Philips are examples of non-Eastern companies that use umbrella branding. The approach is driven by economic considerations. The company name itself is the brand name for all products across diverse categories. Investment in building one brand proves far more economical than investing in building several brands. The brand transfers the advantages of brand awareness, its associations, and goodwill. Ever increasing number of brands, and information overload makes it a very difficult to get noticed. Consumers are more likely to take notice of something familiar.

Apparently, umbrella branding appears to be flawless, but it has several disadvantages. A major shortcoming with this approach is that it is not customer or market focussed. Cost advantage does not get translated into better margins. It is a low-cost strategy but earnings are also low. Research indicates that average profit of top Eastern companies adopting umbrella branding is much lower as compared to top Western firms.

Umbrella branding may be suitable when markets are viewed as homogeneous, operating at a higher level of aggregation. But when markets are composed of distinct segments in terms of buyer needs and preferences, companies start offering specialised need solutions to different segments. This precipitates a difficult situation for companies using umbrella branding. From the consumer's point of view, a specialist brand is appealing and makes more sense. This is the reason that auto companies offer small and mid-sized cars such as Alto, Esteem, Santro, Getz, Palio, etc.

Sharing a common brand name can be risky in case there is a problem with one category. This may negatively influence consumer perceptions in other products sharing the same identity. Also, it is difficult to stretch brands upwards (as happened in case of Maruti Baleno). Downwards stretch in case of Parker failed because of Parker's high-end image. Horizontal stretching is relatively less likely to pose too much of a threat.

Double Branding Strategy

This approach combines umbrella branding and product branding. Along with the product brand name, the company name is associated to create double branding, such as Tata Indica and, Bajaj Pulsar. Tata is the company behind Indica car brand. Maruti also follows this strategy. Both names are equally important and are given equal status in the brand's communication. Double branding serves two objectives. The product gains from the company name awareness, expertise, and reputation. And Pulsar adds some unique value of its own: "Definitely male." This is customer focus and the brand can communicate something in addition to what Bajaj name stands for in customers' perceptions and appeal to a new segment. The product's brand name helps differentiate the offer.

It is only the company's area of expertise and image that may restrict how far it can go in using this branding approach. Double branding works as long as brands are consistent with expertise domain of the company. Beyond this domain, the brand may become a burden. Two or three-wheeler autos are categories that have greater consistency in the area of company's expertise domain. But if the field of expertise is not consistent, such as trucks, or computers, double branding may not always be a suitable branding strategy.

Endorsement Branding Strategy

This is a minor variation of double branding strategy. The product brand name gains a dominant position, while the company name merits a lower profile. The company name appears in smaller letters and takes a back seat. The brand largely seeks to exist on its own. The company name is mentioned to identify who owns it just by way of endorsement to the product brand, such as Godrej Cinthol, or Nestlé Kit-Kat identify the owners of these brands.

In case of double branding, the company name is an integral part with equal status. Endorsement signifies assurance of quality by transferring certain associations that increase consumers' trust. The aim is not to pass on the company's expertise domain. Customers ask for Fair Glow, or Chocos and not Godrej's Fair Glow, or Kellogg's Chocos. Company name acts as a familiar signage to reassure consumers by communicating the company's associations and image.

Endorsement branding is nearest to product branding, allowing more freedom to the brand to get its own distinction. When endorsement branding is tried in inconsistent areas, it is quite likely to fail. For example, some time back Nestlé launched Mithai Magic and it did not work.

Factors Influencing Branding Strategies

A company must carefully examine its situation before making a decision about adopting a certain branding approach. Six factors seem to be more relevant and include the assessment of market size, competitive situation, company resources, product newness, and innovativeness and technology.

- ***Market Size:*** In a large and expanding market, some minimum investments are necessary to build up brand to a level that its sales generate sufficient revenues to support its growth. If the market size is smaller and the growth is very low, achieving sizable sales would not be easy. This would extend the payback period. Large investment in promotion is not called for and would also further extend payback period. In this situation, taking assistance from an established name may be desirable. This would reduce expenditure on promotion in brand building and may favourably reduce payback period.
- ***Competitive Situation:*** When the competition is intense, customer-focus gains importance to win their confidence. It becomes necessary to strongly differentiate the brand and be a specialist in some meaningful and persuasive way. This requires communicating specific customer benefits and brand's matching personality dimensions. Individual brand identify creation gains importance. It may be desirable for companies to choose between product branding, endorsement branding, or double branding, depending on available resources.

  In case the level of competition is low, companies may not be motivated to create distinct brand identity for each brand and simply a company's identification may seem desirable. Thirty or forty years ago, brand building was not a priority concern in India. More concern about branding became apparent only after economic liberalisation in our country.

- ***Company Resources:*** Branding in most cases is a highly expensive proposition. It is certainly not meant for resource-starved companies. Commitment to branding suits firms having deep pockets to create and support brands in the long-run. The companies opting for umbrella branding aim to create a common equity pool and their products exploit this equity. Most companies in this group tend to ensure consistent product quality and high degree of customer service.
- ***Product Newness:*** As companies grow, they tend to add new products to expand product mix. The marketplace is getting more and more crowded because of brand multiplication and customers tend to group them into categories to simplify their purchase decision. This crowding makes it increasingly difficult for marketers to make brands distinct.

  Creating a unique, differentiated identity and image for some product boasting really unique attributes and benefits require focusing on brand building. This requires adopting a branding strategy that suits this objective, such as product, endorsement, or double branding and certainly not umbrella branding as it may dilute and cloud image and confuse customers.
- ***Innovativeness and Technology:*** Really innovative products sometimes emerge from new technology. A breakthrough innovation embodies risks both for customers and the concerned company. Companies perceive risks of uncertainty about a product's success. High on a company's agenda are effective communications of product's uniqueness and to protect the company's equity. Such potential risks favour strategies towards product branding continuum such as product, or endorsement branding. Highly innovative companies such as 3M, Apple, and DuPont adopt either product branding or endorsement branding.

  Failures of innovations are less likely to damage company equity. Product branding is risk minimising but expense-intensive branding approach. However, customers seek more assurance because of their risk perceptions. A company's reputation can help reassure customers and speed up adoption process and for these reasons, endorsement branding or double branding may be desirable, such as Apple G5 processor, or *AMD* Athelon XP+ (these processors boast of futuristic 64-bit chip technology). Choosing a branding approach for innovative products depends much on what the company's approach has been in the past and how confident the company feels after conducting market testing.

Packaging & Labelling

Some texts consider packaging so important that they place it in the marketing mix as a fifth 'P.' Most texts consider packaging as a part of product policy. Packaging includes all activities that focus on the development of a container and a graphic design for a product. A package may have three levels; the *primary package* is the container of the product such as a bottle, jar, or tube, the *secondary package* is the box of cardboard or some other material containing the primary package; and the last is *shipping package* that contains more units of secondary package.

Packaging of a product is important and can make a product more visible, desirable, versatile, safe, or convenient to use. Good packaging has the power to influence customers' attitudes and purchase decisions. Often, customers have one of the strongest associations with a brand based on the looks of its packaging. Package attractiveness can become an important means of brand recognition. Also, the information conveyed or inferred from the package can help build or reinforce valuable brand associations.

Packaging is much more than just putting the product in a container and covering it with a wrapper. Packaging materials serve the purpose of not only protecting the product but also keeps it in functional form, such as milk, juices, and sprays. Packaging helps preventing damage and loss. Packaging also helps to check tampering. A reusable package often makes a product more desirable. In a country like India, reusable packages are often used in sales promotion, such as Bournvita container was a glass jar that could be used for other purposes, or 4kgs Surf was packaged in a plastic bucket. Housewives used the container (bucket) to wash clothes and for other purposes.

Packaging Considerations: A variety of packaging materials, processes, and designs are available. Marketer's primary concern is to consider the costs involved. With increasing incomes, customers show different degrees of willingness to pay more for improved packaging. The question is of how much target, consumers are willing to pay, and research can determine this.

Companies also need to consider how much consistency they desire among packages of the firm's products. If the aim were to promote an overall corporate image, the company would prefer to have similar packages or include one major design characteristic. Some companies prefer to use family packaging for different product lines. The package's promotional aspect includes symbol, contents, features, uses, advantages, and precautions. The package design, colour, texture, shape, etc., also communicate a product's desirable images and associations. An expensive perfume cannot communicate the image of luxury and exclusiveness if its package is ordinary or cheap looking.

Brian Wansink found that a larger package size could increase product consumption by 7 to 43 per cent. Colours carry diverse meanings in different cultures. Marketer should carefully study this aspect, while choosing packaging colours. Pastel colours are viewed as feminine and dark colours as masculine. The need to create a tamper proof packaging would depend on the nature of product and extent of its necessity. Companies should conduct a variety of tests to ascertain that the package stands intact under normal use conditions, colours are harmonious and written words are legible, and consumer and dealer responses are favourable. The package should be convenient for transportation, storage, and handling. A cumbersome package may sometimes discourage resellers from stocking and displaying a product.

Present day environmental concerns are also a consideration. Many consumer pressure groups in developed and developing countries show increased environmental concerns. Discarded plastic packaging is a major source of garbage. Many packages are thrown away indiscriminately, such as crumpled cans and broken bottles, which can be seen almost anywhere in Indian cities. The problem of waste is rampant across almost all countries of the world. Experts point out that plastic is non-biodegradable and paper requires valuable inputs from forests. Some companies are shifting to environment friendly packaging and some others are using recycled (and recyclable) material for packaging.

Labelling

Labelling is closely related to packaging and is used in many different informational, legal, and promotional ways. A label may be a part of package or it may be a tag attached to the product. Depending on the product category and specific laws of the country, the label might include only the product's brand name or more detailed information desired by the marketer, or conforming to the legal requirements. The label can facilitate product identification by presenting the brand and a distinct graphic design. The labels perform a descriptive function relating to a product's source, its contents, important features and benefits, use instructions, cautions or warnings, storage instructions, batch number, date of manufacture, and date of expiry.

Many product labels contain a *Universal Product Code* (UPC). It consists of a series of thin and thick lines that identifies a product, and provides pricing and inventory information. An electronic scanner reads this *UPC* information at retail check counter that is used by retailers and marketers for inventory and price control purposes.

Summary

A brand is a name, term, sign, symbol, or design, or a combination of them, intended to identify the goods and services of one seller or group of sellers and to differentiate them from those of the competition. The key to be able to create a brand is to choose a name, term, sign, symbol, logo, design, package, or other attributes to identify and differentiate a product from others.

At a higher pedestal, brands live in the minds of consumers and are much more than just a tag for their recognition and identification. They are the basis of consumer relationship and bring both consumers and marketers closer by developing a bond of faith and trust between them. The promise of brand is consistent with reliable quality, service, and overall psychological satisfaction. Brands are believed to be the real generators of corporate and stakeholder wealth in the 21st century, and determine the market value of business entities.

Brand identity refers to a unique set of brand associations that the brand strategist aspires to create or maintain. These associations represent what the brand stands for and imply a promise to customers from the organisation members.

Brand image reflects the perceptions of outsiders, that is customers, about the brand. From customers' point of view, it is the image they have of a brand that matters. Brand image is the sum total of impressions created by the brand in the consumer's mind. This includes consumer's impressions about the brand's physical characteristics, its performance, the functional benefits, the kind of people who use the product, the emotions and associations it develops, and the imagery or the symbolic meanings, it generates. In other words, how a consumer perceives a brand in its 'totality' is the brand image and encompasses both physical and perceptual components. It is a concept that drives customer behaviour with respect to brand.

Brands have equity because they have high awareness, many loyal consumers, a high reputation for perceived quality, proprietary assets such as access to distribution channels or to patents, of the kind of brand associations. Brand equity is the marketing and financial value associated with a brand's strength.

Brand loyalty refers to a customer's favourable attitude towards a specific brand. Loyalty is at the heart of equity and a very important brand equity asset. Depending on the level of customer's loyalty strength, there is increased likelihood that a consumer will purchase a specific brand consistently on future purchase occasions. Fiercely brand loyal customers are generally the few, who would not accept a substitute and would go elsewhere to acquire that brand.

A manufacturer brand is initiated by producer and facilitates firm's association easily. A private brand is reseller-initiated brand. Manufacturer is not identified on the product. Wholesellers and retailers use private brands to develop more efficient promotions to build store image and generate higher gross margins. Some manufacturers prefer to have branded products as well as their generic brands. Generic brands indicate only the product category, such as aluminium foil, or paracetamol.

Selected brand names should be simple and easy to pronounce; familiar and meaningful; and should be different, distinctive, and unusual.

Companies differ in their approaches to branding. As companies grow, they enlarge their product mix by either stretching existing product lines or adding new product lines, or both. In these situations they either use company name, existing product brand names, new brand names, or some combination of company name and product brand name. The six generic branding strategies include product branding, line branding, range branding, umbrella branding, double branding, and endorsement branding. Each branding strategy has its merits and demerits.

Packaging includes all activities that focus on the development of a container and a graphic design for a product. A package may have three levels; the *primary package* is the container of the product such as a bottle, jar, or tube, the *secondary package* is the box of cardboard or some other material containing the primary package; and the last is *shipping package* that contains more units of secondary package.

Packaging of a product is important and can make a product more versatile, safer, or convenient to use. Packaging can influence customers' attitudes and purchase decisions. Environmental concerns are also an important consideration. Many consumer pressure groups in developed and developing countries show increased environmental concerns. Labelling is closely related with packaging and is used in many different informational, legal, and promotional ways. The label can facilitate product identification by presenting the brand and a distinct graphic design. The labels perform a descriptive function relating to product's source, its contents, important features and benefits, use instructions, cautions or warnings, storage instructions, batch number, date of manufacture, and date of expiry.

Questions for Discussion

1. Elaborate on what constitutes a brand. What is the significance of brand for marketers?
2. Do you think the standard definition of brand completely covers all dimensions of what a brand stands for?
3. How does branding benefit consumers?
4. Explain what you understand by the term 'brand equity'.
5. What do you understand by brand loyalty? Do you think in the modern marketplace where most products are perceived as being more or less similar, brand loyalty exists?
6. Distinguish between brand identity, brand personality, and brand image.
7. What important factors should be considered while choosing a brand name?
8. What are the advantages and disadvantages of product branding compared to umbrella branding?
9. What is the significance of packaging and labelling in modern day marketing?

Projects

1. Study the different brands of Godrej. What branding strategy/strategies are used? Do you think Godrej's strategy/strategies are advantageous for the company?
2. Contact a brand manager of some consumer product company and study the branding strategies adopted by that company.
3. You are a consultant and a company has hired you to suggest branding strategies for its range of cosmetics, software it develops, and its high-end computer notebooks. How would you proceed to discharge your brief?

Bibliography

1. "The Top 100 Brands," *Business Week,* August 2002.
2. Low George S. and Ronald A. Fullerton, Brands, Brand Management, and the Brand Manager System: A Critical Historical Evaluation," *Journal of Marketing Research,* (May 1994).
3. Levitt Theodore, "Marketing Myopia," *Harvard Business Review,* July-August 1960.
4. David A., Aaker *Building Strong Brands,* 1996.
5. Kepferer Jean-Noel, *Strategic Brand Management: Creating and Sustaining Brand Equity Long Term,* 1st South Asian Ed., 2000.

6. Keller Kevin Lane, *Strategic Brand Management: Building, Measuring, and Managing Brand Equity,* 2nd ed., 2003.

7. Biel Alexander L., "How Brand Image Drives Brand Equity," *Journal of Advertising Research,* 1992.

8. Schiffman Leon G. and Leslie Lazer Kanuk, *Consumer Behaviour,* 1997.

9. Walfried Lasser, Banwari Mittal, and Arun Sharma, "Measuring Customer Based Brand Equity," *Journal of Consumer Marketing,* 12, (1995).

10. Richardson Paul S., Alan S. Dick, and Arun K. Jain, "Extrinsic and Intrinsic Cue Effects on Perceptions of Store Brand Quality," *Journal of Marketing,* (October 1994).

11. Robertson Kim R., "Strategically Desirable Brand Name Characteristics," *Journal of Consumer Marketing,* 6, (1989).

Cases

Case 3.1 Look Ma, Fair Hands

Case 3.2 Harley-Davidson

Case 3.3 Saree State of Affairs

Case 3.4 Haier Brand

Case 3.5 New Product Introductions - 2002 - Why have many failed?

Case 3.1: Look Ma, Fair Hands

he glow on Rakesh Kumar Sinha's face is hard to miss — and it's all due to FairGlow, the fairness soap from the Godrej stable. No, Sinha isn't a user, but as vice president for sales and marketing at Godrej Consumer Products, he has reason to be bright — again.

For the past three months, FairGlow has been growing at close to 40 per cent; Sinha claims that the advertising support for the brand has also doubled since last year. Agency Mudra, which handles the brand, says there will be "interesting activities" around the brand in the next few weeks.

The activity is urgently needed. FairGlow may be erupting like Etna at the moment, but until the last quarter of 2004, the brand bore a closer resemblance to Haleakala, the world's largest dormant volcano. Within two years of its launch in 1999, FairGlow had become a Rs 100-crore brand.

But now the entire fairness soaps category — Godrej FairGlow, Hindustan Lever's Fair & Lovely soap and Emami Naturally Fair herbal fairness soap— has shrunk to Rs 80 crore.

In comparison, fairness creams, which were around Rs 550 crore, crossed Rs 800 crore by end-2004. Even in the Rs 4,000 crore soaps market, the fairness segment has a minuscule 2 per cent value share (just 1 per cent in volume terms).

Although FairGlow still has the lion's share of the fairness segment, its 60 per cent share works out to just Rs 48 crore, which is less than half its earnings in year two.

In other words, even if FairGlow keeps up its scorching 40 per cent growth, it will take another two years or so for it to regain its 2001 position. So, is Sinha happy because FairGlow is getting a second opportunity to score?

When FairGlow soap was launched in December 1999, the dice were heavily loaded in its favour. The foremost reason is that most Indians associate beauty with fair skin.

Even the competition's research bears that out: According to a 1998 Hindustan Lever study, 78 per cent of women in India aspired to be two shades fairer because they believed it made them more attractive and confident.

"It is a colonial hangover," comments Ashish Mishra, head strategic planning, Mudra.

The decision to promote the fairness proposition as a soap also made strategic sense; in India, creams had a penetration of only 25 to 30 per cent.

On the other hand, soaps enter over 95 per cent of Indian households. And FairGlow was priced at Rs 11 for a 75-gram bar, compared to Rs 26 for a 25 gram tube of Fair & Lovely cream. "We offered fairness through a soap, which was more convenient to use at no extra cost," says Sinha.

With high expectations from the product, Godrej planned a high visibility launch. On the launch day, FairGlow created a "surrogate roadblock" on television channels (the 40-second television commercial ran simultaneously on all channels within a five- to 10-minute time frame to ensure that even viewers who surf channels during commercial breaks caught a glimpse of the brand).

Contd...

Then, the product was advertised on all top rated programmes such as Kaun Banega Crorepati and Kyunki Saas Bhi Kabhi Bahu Thi. "The opportunity was big because it was a true innovation," says Mishra.

But there were huge credibility issues to be tackled: The stay-on proposition of creams — once applied, creams stay on all day — while soaps are washed off within seconds of application.

Sinha argues, "The same is true with hair conditioners or a face wash, which are also washed away. But consumers still believe that they work." True, but fairness soaps had to contend with an established category (launched in 1975) like fairness creams. For hair conditioners and face washes there was no close alternative product.

Godrej's solution was simple: It tailored its commercials to focus on customer testimonials. The result, within a year of launch, FairGlow was selling between 400 and 500 tonnes a month (a volume share of 1 per cent in the toilet soaps segment).

How did HLL, whose Fair & Lovely had more or less created the market for fairness products, react? Within a couple of month of FairGlow's launch, HLL retorted with a prolonged teaser campaign for Lux Sunscreen soap. The new variant was launched in March 2000 — and withdrawn barely a few months later.

In the second half of 2000, battle-lines had been drawn between the soap and the cream. FairGlow and Fair & Lovely aired similar television commercials on the marriage theme; only, Fair & Lovely launched two ads in response to FairGlow's single ad spot.

"We could not match their advertising muscle," admits Sinha. Instead, Godrej resorted to offers like buy-three-get-one-free in end-2000.

Even as Fair & Lovely and FairGlow fought it out on TV screens, the sun was eclipsing over the toilet soaps industry.

Consumers were downgrading to the sub-popular category: In 2000, while the popular category grew by just 1 per cent, the sub-popular category was clipping along at a brisk 15 per cent. FairGlow being an offering in the popular segment of soaps, was naturally going to be hit.

Then, in December 2000, a year after the launch of FairGlow soap, it committed a vital strategic mistake. It extended FairGlow into creams with the proposition, Bedaag gorapan (spotless beauty).

But instead of being considered a natural brand extension, the move further fuelled a suspicion that consumers had harboured — fairness soaps may not be as effective as creams.

Importantly for Godrej, it lost the high ground of innovation that it had made its USP. Sinha admits that if he could change one thing about FairGlow's past, "We would never venture into creams".

Even as FairGlow's brand extension backfired, HLL engaged in battle on another flank — it launched Fair & Lovely soap. Naturally, the already thin dividing line between cream and soap further blurred.

Fair & Lovely's soap was a high profile launch with its theme, Ek tukda chand ka (A piece of the moon). While a barge backlit by the moon floated on the sea off Mumbai's Marine Drive, practically every hoarding in prominent places hollered the benefits of Fair and Lovely soap. But at Rs 15 per cake, (nearly 50 per cent more expensive than FairGlow), HLL's new battering ram did not find too many takers.

Contd...

Analysts say that HLL used the soap as merely a flanking strategy to guard its cream user-base. "The idea was that even if consumers bought a fairness soap, it would be from the same brand basket," says one analyst. HLL executives did not meet The Strategist for this article.

Still, HLL did not rest after its soap launch. Over the next two years, the company launched several new Fair & Lovely cream variants.

FairGlow, on the other hand, was still fighting consumer perception that soaps may not work. It launched a "money-back challenge" to build up credibility in 2002. Fair & Lovely reacted by offering two soaps for the price of Rs 20 (coming down to the FairGlow price).

The sales graphs, though, remained dim. By mid-2004, FairGlow put the cap on its cream misadventure. It followed with an ad campaign in late-2004 that illustrates the efficacy of the soap. That's paid off dividends, and sales are currently up. Whether they'll be able to reach their previous highs, though, is anyone's guess.

(Source: www.bsstrategist.com, February 22, 2005)

QUESTIONS

1. What is the positioning of FairGlow soap? Why is this positioning likely to appeal to Indian consumers?
2. Why was the extension of FairGlow to face cream a bad decision?

Case 3.2: Harley-Davidson

nyone interested in motorcycles is definitely familiar with the name Harley-Davidson. It was one of the few companies that had been pushing the innovation process even before the idea of 'innovation' became popular. William Harley and Arthur Davidson opened a small motor-shed in Milwaukee in 1903. The idea behind the venture was to find a way that would ease the physical efforts needed to ride a motorcycle, this needed innovation to be meaningful. The first motorcycle they built, made it easier to go uphill, and this feature led to instant success of their product.

By 1905, Harley-Davidson was regularly producing these bikes, nicknamed the 'Silent Grey Fellow'. An uncle extended a loan and the partners built their first shop. In 1907, Harley-Davidson was incorporated as a company and produced 150 bikes in the first year. Inspired by the success of their initial efforts, other family members assisted the partners, and an upgraded version of the bike was developed by 1909. This model had a new engine, known as the 'V-twin' (because the engine had two cylinders arranged in a 'V' angle).

The new product was different in two innovative ways. First, the 'V-twin' engine produced a deep-throated, distinct rumbling sound that no other motorcycle at the time made. Second, the engine could manage a speed of over 60 mph. This was a technical breakthrough at that time. This was a major success and the sales increased to 1, 149 units in 1909 and to 9,500 units by 1912. Japan was the first country where the motorcycle was exported at this time.

The success attracted many new manufacturers to the market and in 1913, there were as many as 150 competitors in the US market. Harley-Davidson had the first-mover advantage. During World War I, Harley-Davidson sold 20,000 motorcycles to the US forces. It was during this period, that the company began to make its mark in racing competitions.

In 1916, Harley-Davidson took another important step and launched 'The Enthusiast' magazine for its customers. The idea was to provide its customers with the latest information on the company's products and the motorcycle industry. The magazine was also a platform for Harley-Davidson customers to voice their views and opinions (The Enthusiast is still continuing in the 21st century).

The company kept its focus on innovation and up-gradation technologies, introduced front-brake system and the unique teardrop-shaped gas tank. These innovations and sales strategy helped beat competition successfully. Harley-Davidson emerged as the world's largest manufacturer of motorcycles, with dealers in 67 countries. The Great Depression of 1930s put many motorcycle companies out of business and this helped Harley-Davidson stay in business, coupled with exports and supplies to US postal service and police departments.

During the early 1940s, only Harley-Davidson and Indian (producer of the Ghost range of motorcycles) were two companies that remained in business. Harley-Davidson prospered from military purchase during World War II. It produced more than 90,000 motorcycles for the US military. This was a record level. The company earned the coveted Army-Navy "E" award for excellence in wartime production. From the year 1947 onwards, Harley-Davidson began producing biker gear like leather motorcycle jackets and accessories such as boots, shoes, and clothing.

In 1952, the company launched the K-model in the market. In 1953, Indian closed its operations and Harley-Davidson became the sole manufacturer of motorcycles in the country. Harley-Davidson's popularity and sales grew rapidly in the late 1950s and 1960s as it brought out a

Contd...

new range of 'super-bikes' – the Sportster (1957), Duo-Glide (1958), Electra-Glide (1965), and Super-Glide (1971). These 'loud and heavy-weight' bikes soon became the symbol of counterculture in the US. Added to this, the freedom-loving and carefree attitude of people in the 1960s gave rise to 'bike culture,' of which Harley-Davidson was an integral part. Tattooed motorcycle enthusiasts travelling across the US in groups on their Harley-Davidson 'chopper' Peter Fonda's blockbuster movie 'Easy Rider' epitomised. The biker culture and raised Fonda to iconic status rivalling that of his legendary father, Henry Fonda motorcycles in black leather gear became an image increasingly associated with the culture.

Reportedly, part of Harley-Davidson's success was due to Davidson's innovative idea of setting up a network of dealers that would sell only H-D (Harley-Davidsons) motorcycles. The company was able to attract a large number of dealers to this network as it promised them a handsome share in profits and also offered product guarantees. It was during late 1950s and 1960s that H-D bikes became a fashion and lifestyle statement. By late 1960s, the company was popular as a rebel and brand and its 'bad boy' image appealed to the rebel inside the largely male clientele.

In 1965, Harley-Davidson went public from family ownership. It was at this time the Electra-Glide – the first motorcycle with an electric starter – was introduced to replace the Duo-Glide. In 1969, American Machine and Foundry (AMF) Company acquired Harley-Davidson. By the mid 1970s, the quality of H-D motorcycles began declining as AMF kept pushing Harley-Davidson for sales increase. Thus, against 14,000 units in 1969, H-D had to produce 75,403 vehicles in 1975. As a result, quality had to be sacrificed. Problems intensified when high-quality, low-priced Japanese motorcycles from Honda, Suzuki, and Kawasaki hit the US market.

By 1980, H-D was on the brink of bankruptcy and AMF decided to sell it. In 1981, thirteen members from the management purchased the company from AMF in a leveraged buy out funded by the US-based financial services major Citicorp. However, within the first year of buy out, the overall demand for motorcycles declined, hurting H-D badly.

The reputation of H-D motorcycles had taken a severe beating in the market. Its prices were reportedly 30 per cent higher than the Japanese models. As a result, the company's market share declined from 80 percent in 1969 to below 20 per cent in 1979. The financial position of the company was also very bleak. In order to cut costs, the company had fired almost a third of its manpower. The company, reportedly incurred losses to the tune of $50 million in two years after the buy out. According to industry observers, apart from the external problems, the failure to invest in innovation was one of the main causes that were pushing the company towards oblivion.

At this stage of Harley-Davidson, the US government announced policy changes that restricted the imports of Japanese motorcycles, and Harley-Davidson got a respite for five years. The company had to make considerable improvements in its business processes to sustain itself in the market in the long-run. The H-D management accepted the challenge and embarked on what analysts referred to as the 'path of adopting innovation' as a tool to improve the company's performance at all levels, including marketing and customer relations, organisational changes, product, process, and manufacturing.

Harley-Davidson was quite aware of the fact that its brand was its biggest strength and decided to leverage the same for boosting growth. It also knew how successfully The Enthusiast magazine had contributed to 'enhancing the customer experience'. H-D management decided to reinvent that practice and established the Harley-Davidson Group (HOG) in 1983. The main aim of

Contd...

HOG was to involve customers in a way that would forge stronger relations and bonds between the customers and the company.

Every H-D owner was given a one-year free membership to HOG. This proved to be an extremely insightful business decision as over 33,000 members joined the group in a short span of time. Through HOG, the company organised several motorcycle rallies and tours. These rallies involved giving customers trial rides, letting them interact with company officials, and selling new bikes and merchandise. H-D thus encouraged customers to have trial rides of their motorcycles and share 'their excitement of riding a H-D'. Over the years, HOG not only served as a primary customer-relations tool but also allowed H-D to demonstrate and promote new products to its customers. Aware of the critical role dealers played with respect to customer service, H-D took various initiatives. In 1983, H-D organised a three-day dealer-training programme, which came to be known as 'Harley-Davidson University'. Through this training programme, trained its dealers to develop their business and leadership skills to be able to sell more effectively. Subsequent training programmes focused on other areas such as retail management, inventory control, merchandising, and customer service.

In 1983, the company launched a trademark-licensing programme for its dealers, which helped the company eliminate the problem of bootlegged merchandise. In the following years, H-D published several fashions and collectibles catalogues featuring its merchandise. During the 1980s and early 1990s, the company also began to sell its merchandise, especially clothes, through popular retail stores in the US, such a J. C. Penney and Bloomingdales. All this helped in capitalising on tough image of the brand. Another move the company made was to set up 'Harley-Davidson Cafes' at places where its dealer stores were located, to attract a larger number of people. In yet another innovative move, the company set up Eaglemark Financial Services Inc and Harley-Davidson Financial Services Inc (HDFS) in 1991 and 1993 respectively. Through these, the company offered wholesale insurance and financing programme. The services included motorcycle inventory planning, parts and accessories trade acceptance, and commercial insurance brokerage to its dealers in the US. These subsidiaries also offered dealers and customers a credit card called the 'Harley-Davidson Chrome Visa' card. Dealers were also given special discounts and 120-day delayed billing terms to help them cope with sales fluctuations.

In 1995, encouraged by the resounding success of HOG initiative, H-D launched the 'Buell Riders Adventure Group' (BRAG), an exclusive club for Buell motorcycles. Like HOG, BRAG also aimed at enhancing the customers' overall experience by bringing motorcycle enthusiasts together to share their on-the-road experiences. Based on customer feedback, H-D had also expanded into niches that were looking for other than heavyweight vehicles from the company such as customised touring, sports touring, and sport-street motorcycle categories. H-D also produced a number of models in other than 'grey' colours. This helped company to attract repeat purchase. In 1990s, when H-D realised that a lot of women were buying its motorcycles and merchandise, the company began offering products to suit the tastes of its new customer profile.

H-D ensured that production did not exceed the demand for its motorcycles. This led to an increase in demand to such an extent that in the late 1990s, customers had to wait for six to eight months for buying H-D motorcycle. The craze and 'halo' of Harley-Davidson motorcycles was such that old H-D models were fetching prices 25% - 30% higher than the list price for the new models.

Contd...

According to industry observes, the positive impact of H-D's innovation philosophy was to use technology and engineering to support the processes that aimed at enhancing the overall customer's experience. The company worked on the premise that the customer's experience transcended the product. Product is no doubt the core, but Harley-Davidson sold its customers the total 'H-D riding experience'. Harley-Davidson sums this up the 'two riders sharing the same Harley-Davidson experience on different generations of motorcycles, and both of them longing for the next great product to further enhance their experience'.

QUESTIONS

1. Study the case and determine the significant issues that shed light on the importance of innovation.
2. What factors have been responsible for Harley-Davidson becoming a cult?
3. What is Harley-Davidson's positioning? What is the secret of the fanatical customer loyalty to Harley-Davidson?

Case 3.3: Saree State of Affairs

t's a brand that put faces like Aishwarya Rai and Madhu Sapre on the beauty map. Way before that, back in the 1970s, textile brand Garden Vareli, owned by the Rs. 650-crore Mumbai-based Garden Silk Mills, set new standards for the fashion industry by launching chic sarees and dress material.

Two decades down the line, few women would want to be spotted buying — leave alone wearing — a Garden saree. In the past five years, sales of Garden sarees have dropped by 50 per cent. Until about five years ago, 25 shops in Mumbai alone — not counting the company's own showrooms — stocked the brand.

Today, the product is retailed only at company-owned showrooms. Garden operates through franchisee operations with outlets in about 104 locations across the country and six company-owned showrooms (four in Mumbai and one each in Bangalore and Surat).

Why did Garden stop blooming? Ask company officials and their reply is stock: The brand is still flourishing and there's no downward trend.

But says Kamlesh Pandey, former creative head, Rediffusion DY&R (Garden's erstwhile agency), who was involved in the launch of the brand, "Garden started as an individualistic brand. It was known as an artist's brand. But somewhere along the way, it lost its way. It could not embrace the changes in the market-place as the company's passion got dissipated." In short, the brand failed to age gracefully.

The problem was one of complacency and lack of innovation. Says an industry observer, "Garden was an aspirational brand until about 15 years ago. Then, its image went for a toss because it was neither innovating in terms of new designs and prints nor re-inventing itself."

While lack of innovation was the root cause for the decline of the brand, there were many more creases that Garden should have ironed out. To begin with, the company could not take the brand beyond sarees and dress materials.

In 1997, Garden launched ready-made men's shirts and trousers under the Vareli brand name, while its sarees and dress materials were already selling under the Garden Vareli label. With such strongly feminine associations, the men's wear brand came apart at the seams.

Agrees Garden Silk Mills General Manager, marketing, Paresh V. Chothani, "People always confused the word 'Vareli' for an Italian company and thus it was always perceived as a dress material brand. We needed to separate the identities of the two brands."

To do just that, Vareli was removed from the brand name in 1998. The company has since been selling its sarees and dress materials under the "Garden" label alone and focusing on strengthening it.

Meanwhile, although Vareli still sells men's-wear, it remains a completely neglected brand, accounting for barely 5 per cent of the company's sale of fabric.

Textile industry analysts aren't too convinced that the brand name was the only reason for the failure of Garden's foray into men's-wear.

They cite the example of Vimal, the competing brand from Reliance Industries, which in spite of its feminine association, was able to reach across all fabric categories, such as sarees and materials for dresses, suits and shirts.

Contd...

The true culprit, therefore, was the image of the brand. In fact, one reason for the erosion of Garden's brand equity has been its increasing reliance on bargain or spot sales; the company holds 20-day discount sales twice a year at all its outlets.

Besides, Garden is no longer seen as a brand that is fashionable or stylish. "All loyal customers of Garden are grandmothers now," dismisses a Mumbai-based retailer.

Pandey points out that Garden's earlier target customers were working women who were urban, educated and fashion conscious, in the 18 to 25 age bracket.

As these customers grew older, unfortunately, the brand also aged, instead of reaching out to the newer generations of customers. In the meantime, the demands of the target audience changed.

Consider this. Today, Garden retail outlets are visited only by women in the B and C socio-economic categories or those looking for low-priced outfits for daily wear: Garden sarees sell for between Rs 200 and Rs 2,000, while dress materials retail in the range of Rs 250 to Rs 850.

Says Chothani, "Till 2002, our saree business was growing at 18 to 20 per cent a year. But since the demand for sarees has been gradually fading, in the past two years, we have shifted focus to dress materials."

Until December 2001, 65 per cent of the company's sales came from sarees, with the balance made up by dress materials. By this year-end, the balance will even out more: The share of dress materials in total sales is likely to increase to 45 per cent.

Garden may consider that a step in the right direction, but it may be a case of too little, too late. For the problem extends beyond just Garden. Over the years, the demand for sarees per se has dropped.

Up to the late 1980s, sarees were the preferred wear for office-going women; today, the dress of choice is more likely to be salwar-kameez or western outfits.

With sarees being increasingly reserved as special occasion-wear, there's little room for the ordinary or garden variety of saree — customers demand more dressy and ornate varieties.

But Garden never invested in upgrading its sarees to that level; it's stuck to its hopelessly-outdated designs and image.

Also, while Garden has always manufactured polyester and silk fabric, consumers have moved on to more contemporary materials like linen, cotton and denim. And increasingly, the trend is for ready-made garments rather than tailored outfits.

As Pandey puts it, "Garden should have grown beyond the realm of sarees and dress materials. It had the potential to become a complete fashion house. But it never made any effort to stay on top while it could have easily encashed on the brand."

One way of ensuring that would have been increased brand visibility — but Garden's performance in that area has been dismal. Its last television advertising campaign was in 1995. With a minuscule advertising and marketing budget of about Rs 3 crore, the brand now depends on print ads and hoardings for its recall.

Contd...

Ironically, at the same time, smaller saree brands like Parag, Kunwar Ajay and Prafful sarees — which used to be in the unorganised sector — have grown exponentially in the past five years, riding on the cable and satellite wave.

Clearly, in today's time of cut-throat competition, visibility means electronic media. To quote Pandey, "If it's not on air, it's not there."

Chothani disagrees. He says, "We don't really need to be present on television as our brand is a heritage one. So, we don't need to make its presence felt; people remember Garden from its early days. Besides, promoting a brand is an expensive exercise these days."

Garden's current advertising agency, Publicis Ambience, on the other hand, is busy attempting to modernise the brand and make it a desirable fashion garment.

Says Elsie Nanji, vice chairman and chief creative officer, Publicis Ambience, "To keep the brand in sync with the times, through our latest print and outdoor ads, we are showcasing latest cuts, accessories and new ways of draping a saree."

Industry observers, however, think it will take more than that to revive the brand. "It will need an excellent communication strategy and a complete breakthrough, other than a huge investment," says a Mumbai-based analyst who tracks the textile sector.

Garden does seem to realise that — and perhaps does not feel equal to the task just yet. Tellingly, it has taken a step back from branding to manufacturing yarn.

Garden ventured into manufacturing polyester filament yarn in 1997 and at present, 60 per cent of the company's revenues come from its yarn business and the rest from fabrics.

While the company currently produces 50,000 tonnes of yarn a year, there are plans to expand to 80,000 tonnes over the next year.

Of course, it's not quite ready to let go of the textile business. Plans are afoot to revive the Vareli men's-wear brand.

According to Chothani, the Vareli brand range will be retailed through exclusive "Vareli" showrooms instead of the existing Garden showrooms.

The company plans to set up about six franchised stores for selling just the Vareli range. But with Vareli accounting for just 5 per cent of the company's revenues, Garden is not aiming very high.

Points out Chothani, "It's a slow-growth area. Also, our current infrastructure is more suitable for production of women's wear."

QUESTIONS

1. What are the significant issues in this case? What went wrong with Garden Silk Sarees?
2. How can Garden make its brand contemporary? Suggest a plan to revive Garden's business.

Case 3.4: Haier Brand

Haier is the world's 4th largest white goods manufacturer and one of China's Top 100 electronics and IT companies. Haier has 240 subsidiary companies and 30 design centers, plants and trade companies and more than 50,000 employees throughout the world. Haier specializes in technology research, manufacture, trading and financial services. Haier's 2005 global revenue was RMB103.9 billion (USD12.8 billion).

Guided by business philosophy of CEO Zhang Ruimin, Haier has experienced success in the three historic periods — Brand Building, Diversification and Globalization. At the 21st anniversary of founding of the Haier Group December 26, 2005, Haier announced its 4th strategic development stage of Global Brand Building. In 1993, Haier brand was officially recognized as a famous brand and in 2005 valued at RMB70.2 billion. Since 2002, Haier has consecutively been ranked first in the row of China's most valuable brands for manufacture of 15 products, including refrigerators, air-conditioners, washing machines, televisions, water heaters, personal computers, mobile phones and kitchen integrations. Haier was ranked first of China's Top 10 Global Brands by China State Bureau of Quality and Technical Supervision (CSBTS) for refrigerators and washing machines. On August 30, 2005, Haier was ranked 1st of China's Top 10 Global Brands by the Financial Times.

Haier has been widely recognized as a leader of 9 products in terms of domestic market shares and the 3rd player of 3 products in the world market and world-class company in the fields of home integration, network appliances, digital and large-scale integrated circuits and new materials. Haier has long attached significance to innovation in satisfying the demands of worldwide consumers and realizing win-win performance between Haier and clients. Haier has currently obtained 6,189 patented technology certificates (819 for inventions) and 589 software intellectual property rights. Haier has hosted and taken part in modification of about 100 China's technological standards. Haier invented technology, incorporated in the Safe Care water heaters and dual-drive washing machines, has been proposed to the IEC Criteria.

Haier's "OEC", "Market-chain" and "Individual-goal combination" management performances have been recognized worldwide. Haier's experiences have also been introduced into case studies of business mergers, and to financial management and corporate cultures of many foreign educational institutes, including Harvard University, University of Southern California, Lausanne Management College, the European Business College and Kobe University. Haier's "Market-chain" management practice has also been recommended to the EU for Case Studies, and its "Individual-goal combination" management concept has been recognized by worldwide management researchers as a feasible solution of commercial over stocks and accounts overdue.

Facing fierce global market competition, Haier has launched the global brand building strategy and updated the spirit, "Create resources, worldwide prestige" and work style "Individual-goal combination, swift action and success", with an aim to gain global recognition and sustainable development.

Haier is an example of how an Asian company can build a brand and take it beyond its national market. Haier brand which is built on quality and a commitment to offer innovative products at a competitive price, exports to over 150 countries around the world, has 13 factories spreading from Philippines to Iran to the US and recently became the no. 1 refrigerator maker in the world, overtaking Whirlpool.

Contd...

Haier traces its history back to the Qingdao General Refrigerator factory, which was founded in 1958 as a cooperative to repair and assemble electric appliances. Till Chinese entrepreneur Ruimin Zhang took charge of the factory in 1984, the company struggled with its quality and incurred huge losses. Haier attracted tremendous publicity when Zhang smashed faulty refrigerators with a sledgehammer, to send out a message about his commitment to quality. Today, Haier commands approximately over 30% share of the Chinese market in white goods and had revenues of US $9.7 billion as of 2003.

True to that event, Haier has built its brand on quality. Haier's strategy has been to establish a leadership position in the domestic market before venturing into global markets. Unlike most players who concentrate on the low end of the market by offering cheap products, Haier has focused on offering innovative products at a competitive price and the brand is starting to see results. A case in point is that Haier is the leading brand in the US in mini-refrigerator category.

Haier's commitment to quality and innovation is evident by the 18 international product design centers that it has established in Los Angeles and Tokyo which are in turn supported by production facilities in US, Japan and Italy.

Though it is common to see charismatic CEOs such as Sir Richard Branson, Steve Jobs and Bill Gates leading the brands in the western world, it is hardly the case in Asia. Many Asian executives shy away from publicity. Ruimin Zhang has set an example to many Asian companies about how the CEO can take charge of the brand and be the chief brand ambassador. Zhang's aggressiveness to build his brand, his commitment to quality and his business acumen has attracted much deserved global accolades.

Ruimin Zhang was placed nineteenth among the twenty-five most powerful people in business outside the US by Fortune magazine in 2003 and Haier was ranked the most admired Chinese brand in 2004 by a Financial Times/Pricewaterhouse Coopers survey.

QUESTIONS

1. Analyse the Haier case and identify significant issues.
2. Discuss Haier's branding strategy.

Case 3.5: New Product Introductions – 2002 – Why have many failed?

New products are the backbone of any organization's progress. New products are the lifelines for profitability. New products are the accelerating factor for a company's supremacy in the market. New products help the company to fight the competition better. Therefore, many progressive companies are giving more emphasis to launching of new products. But how many products are successful and what are their roles in 2002? What was the impact they registered in 2002? This article reviews the same.

Many progressive companies have introduced many new products in 2002. As usual, Cipla took the lead in launching of the new products and registered over 29 crores sales from them. The company-wise number of new products introduced, and sales generated, is given below:

Company	No. of New Products introduced	Volume generated by new products incl. line extn.(In crore)	Sales/Average New Product/Year (In crore)
Cipla	123	28.7	0.23
Ranbaxy	78	25.0	0.32
Glaxo	5	4.3	0.86
Nicholas	31	10	0.32
Sun Pharma	25	9.6	0.38
Alkem	57	13.5	0.24
Dr. Reddy's Lab	17	9.8	0.58
Zydus Cadilla	39	8.1	0.20
Boots	2	1.3	0.65
Novartis	14	2.9	0.21
Industry	1621	362.2	0.22

From the above it is quite surprising to note that many products introduced during 2002 could not get listed in ORG as top 300 products or even cross 1 crore in sales. Year-wise performance of new products are given below:

Year	No. of New Products listed among Top 300 during the first year of launch
1999	7
2000	3
2001	NIL
2002	3

From the above it is quite disturbing to note that the number of products listed in Top 300 are going down day by day. Why are the new products introduced by pharmaceutical companies not doing well? What could be the reasons?

Compatibility with Company's Product Mixes

Many times, new products are selected irrespective of their compatibility with product mix, e.g., a company that is strong in selling Antibiotics and B-complex, suddenly decides to introduce cardiac range products with their existing field force. The success rate becomes less because of the different mindsets of medical representatives. The compatibility is very important. During 2002, many new products could not register more sales because of this compatibility problem and mindset of representatives.

Contd...

Half-hearted Efforts

Many companies introduce products because they have to do so. They have no proper planning as well as no follow-up. With more new products being introduced, field force also gets confused and is unable to increase sales.

Company	No. of new products incl. line extn.	New products (Per Month)
Cipla	123	10
Ranbaxy	78	7
Sun	25	2
Alkem	57	5
Nicholas	31	3

Thus, from the above table it is clearly visible that we should re-look at our strategy, at our working norms, working patterns. New product requires money. New product requires time to take root. Haphazard introduction of new products lead to wastage of these two prime resources. Therefore, to improve the above, a strategy formulation should be planned with proper market research.

Faulty Strategy Formulation

Many times, it its seen that companies are launching new products but not launching the brand. Company's strategy should be to develop the brand, not the product. Companies often develop a product, thereby creating a market for others to get their share. Therefore, efforts should be to launch a brand, not a product. How many of us are doing these? By selling a product we are getting some share of the prescriptions but by creating a brand, we are getting a share of the mind as well as prescriptions.

No clear cut UCP

Unique Customer Perception is very important in getting quick response. Azithromycin, despite having good molecular benefits cannot be perceived as a better molecule compared to Roxithromycin. The same holds true for Esoprazole, which did not get much success compared to Pentaprazole, even though Esoprazole is a better product. The proper survey should be conducted before the launch of the product. How many companies are doing proper surveys?

Lack of Market Research

It is saddening to know that market research department is losing its impact and place in pharmaceutical industry. Many pharmaceutical companies are not doing research on the impact of the promotional thrust, concept taste, product taste, etc. This lack of research which may be due to time constraint have led to faulty introduction of many new products and colossal loss to the company.

New products are the backbone of any progressive company. If it is so, then why are many companies still failing to take a step to look at their failure rate? Why has our standard of evaluating new product success rate come down? Marketing professionals should re-look at their activities and learn from experiences so that during 2003, a number of new products introduced soon have a better success rate. (Source: Dr. R.K. Srivastava, Marketing Consultant, on Internet).

QUESTION

Analyse the causes of new product failures in Indian drug companies. How can companies overcome this problem?

PART 4

Marketing Communications

CHAPTER 13

LEARNING OBJECTIVES

After going through this chapter, you will understand:

- Communications process
- Important communications models relevant to promotion planning
- Message related concepts
- Media and communication systems
- Determining marketing communications budget
- Marketing communications mix elements
- Selection of promotion mix and feedback

hen Microsoft Corporation launched Windows 95, its new operating system for personal computers; the company turned its debut into a worldwide marketing event. On the day the product was introduced, a four-storey-high Windows 95 balloon sailed over Sydney Harbour in Australia as musicians and dancers performed. Across the globe, The Times of London printed its first fully sponsored edition in its 307-year history. All 1.5 million copies of the paper were bought by Microsoft and were distributed free along with an advertising supplement. In New York City, a Windows 95 light show was created for the Empire State Building. Consumers lined up at retail stores around the world to be the first to buy the new software the moment the clock struck midnight on August 23, the first day it was available.

Microsoft's worldwide launch of Windows 95 is another example of how companies are looking beyond their borders and developing marketing and promotional programmes for global markets. Nearly 80 per cent of the world's population lives in developing areas, and consumers in these countries represent an enormous market for all kinds of products and services.

The world's largest markets are developing in Asia and marketers are using a variety of integrated marketing communication techniques to pursue the opportunities in countries like China, India, and Thailand. Intel is placing television and billboard ads throughout China to establish brand awareness for its microprocessors, which serve as the brains of personal computers. The company also distributed a million bike reflectors - which glow in the dark with words "Intel Inside Pentium Processor' - in China's biggest cities. Citicorp's Citibank unit has captured 40 per cent of Thailand's credit-card market, relying primarily on a sales force of 600 part-timers who are paid a fee for each applicant approved.

Global marketers are also recognising the tremendous opportunities for selling sports in Asia. From Bombay to Beijing to Bangkok, foreign sports promoters, broadcasters, and consumer product companies are pouring millions of dollars into sports. Companies are lining up to take advantage of integrated marketing opportunities associated with corporate sponsorship of sporting events. Yonex Corp pays $2 million annually to be the exclusive sponsor for Indonesia's national badminton team. Hiram Walker, R. J. Reynolds, and Rado Uhren sponsor golf, tennis, and auto racing events. Master Card, Pepsi, Gillette, and Canon have all signed four-year $2.6 million deal to sponsor Asian soccer. Nike sponsors, four teams in China's new professional soccer league - including one owned by the People's Liberation Army. Broadcasters such as Fox Sports network (which is a part of Rupert Murdoch's Star TV Asian satellite) and ESPN are purchasing the broadcast rights for popular Asian sports such as badminton, cricket, and soccer, as well as golf and volleyball.

Companies are recognising that emerging markets in Asia as well as other parts of the world offer tremendous opportunities for growth. They also know that advertising and other promotional tools will play an important role in reaching the new global consumers.

Source: Various sources such as Wall Street Journal, August 7, 1996; Business Week, August 7, 1996 etc.

The marketplace is becoming an increasingly complex arena of competitors' activities within a rapidly changing international environment. Companies try to be heard in these sophisticated and cluttered market conditions. They make every effort to speak with clear voices about their activities, products, and services. It is critically important to ensure that whatever is communicated, reaches their intended audiences in a clear and consistent manner. Communication is a unique tool used by marketers in an attempt to persuade consumers to act in a desired manner. The purpose of communications is to directly or indirectly influence individuals, groups, and organisations to facilitate exchanges by informing and persuading one or more audiences to accept a company's products and/or services. Organisations' indirectly influence exchanges by communicating suitable information about their activities and products/services to interest groups such as current and potential investors, regulatory agencies, financial institutions, and society in general. Marketing communications help a company to justify its existence and maintain a positive and healthy relationship with different groups.

Everyone knows what communication is, yet definitions of communication vary in different textbooks. There always has been a search to formulate more precise definitions of communication. After examining 126 definitions of communication, Dance and Larson concluded:

"Although there are several points of difference in many definitions of communication, upon at least one aspect the vast majority of scholars seem to be in relative agreement. Most students view communication as a process."

Frank X. Dance and Carl E. Larson, *The Functions of Human Communications: A Theoretical Approach* (Rinehart and Winston, 1976)

Terence A Shimp and Wayne Delozier say, *"Communication can be defined as the sharing of a common meaning."*

Terence A. Shimp and Wayne Delozier, Promotion Management and Marketing Communication (Dryden Press, 1986).

Donald Baak says, "*Communication occurs when the message that was sent reaches its destination in a form that is understood by the intended audience.*"

Donald Baak, "Communication Process," *Consumer Behaviour,* 1998.

The current view about marketing communications is an interactive dialogue between the organisation and its audiences, and that every type of brand contact with customers is important because it communicates something that can strengthen or weaken customers' view of the company. Communication can be written or spoken, a picture, an illustration, a product demonstration, some kind of body language, or a combination of verbal and visual. Communication could also be symbolic, such as brand name, high price, a memorable company logo, striking packaging and its colour, promotion, distribution outlet decor, and the dress and behaviour of sales personnel, etc., communicate some special meaning. Suitable communications can trigger favourable feelings and emotions that put consumers in a more receptive frame of mind that may encourage and lead to purchase action. In fact, communications can work as a bridge between marketers and consumers and also between consumers and their socio-cultural environments. It is important for companies to appreciate that just reaching the audiences with a message is not enough, but also ensuring how quickly and effectively the customers can reach the company. This is the only way to ensure a continuing and interactive dialogue with customers.

Communication as a process would mean that it has a beginning, middle and ending. That is, communication is the transmission of a message from a sender to a receiver by means of a signal of some sort, sent through a channel of some sort communicating the intended idea and meaning. No matter how great an idea, it is useless until it is transmitted and understood by others. Communication must include both the *transference* and the *understanding of meaning.*

The marketing communications support the marketing plan and help the target audience understand and believe in the advantage of marketer's offer over competition. This is possible only through designing and implementing persuasive communications. Marketing communications has an *external flow* and an *internal flow.*

- ***External flow:*** The external flow of marketing communications is directed at the past, current and potential customers; at the channel members; at competing and non-competing firms and at various other audiences who may influence the firm's operations such as government agencies, private agencies and experts in the field. The communications mix may include advertising, personal selling, direct mail, point-of-purchase display, warranties, product updates and publicity, etc. Such communications help in developing and maintaining mutually healthy relationships with different audiences outside the company.
- ***Internal flow:*** This aspect of marketing communications flow involves various departments in the company, all the company employees and stockholders. When the company is introducing new products or dropping some existing products, product prices are revised, or company enters new markets or enters new distribution outlets, company employees often need to know what the marketing is doing. Convincing and persuasive marketing communications can help in influencing employee perceptions and shape their morale and performance. If the employees feel that their company is producing highly regarded advertisements, they are motivated to work harder, their turnover decreases and they become a source of effective public relations. Different departments, such as research, engineering, production and marketing need to share product information among them. Stockholders also need to be informed about various marketing actions, as they must be comfortable with the information that marketing decisions are in their best interests and buying company stocks would be a positive investment.

Irrespective of the fact whether the flow is external or internal, effective communications require reaching the right people with the appropriate information through the right sources at the right time. The integrated strategy should be:

- To make an assessment of the relative importance that members of audience place on certain categories of information, such as, is it the objective information with facts and figures that they want? Or, are emotional appeals desirable to induce action?
- To select most appropriate communication vehicles to deliver the information to audience. This would require finding out which media vehicles are used by the audience regularly, which ones are trusted most and whether the audience turn to different vehicles for high involvement product categories.
- To assess what the marketer's position is in relation to competing sources. For example, the members of the audience may heavily rely on information from friends or the published reports, or may also be open to some new sources of information.
- To determine guidelines about the mix of communication techniques and allocate resources. This would depend on the communication objectives and the resources available.

Strategy implementation requires a clear understanding of the needs and wants of target audiences and a great deal of data concerning competitors, news media, available communication techniques, and government policies before implementing communication strategy.

Communication is the soul of promotion activity and understanding communication is essential to better managing a marketing communication programme.

Communications Process

In any communication there are four basic components, a source, a destination, a medium and a message (Figure 13.1). The source, as the initiator or sender of the message, may wish to communicate a feeling, an attitude, a belief, or some fact to another person or persons. To accomplish this, the initiator must first find some way to *encode* the desired message so that it will accurately convey the message to the desired destination. The source may use words, pictures, symbols, some kind of familiar body language, or some other recognizable code or signal. Whatever the method, the important goal of the source or sender is to encode the message in a way that will maximise the likelihood that the receiver will interpret it in a way that would enable the receiver to understand the intended meaning.

The source or sender must then find a suitable channel or medium through which to transmit the message (sent message). In marketing, the potential channel alternatives are many and varied; therefore, considerable deliberation must be taken to select the channel with characteristics most appropriate to the type of message involved. To make the message delivery efficient, the channel must have direct access to the receiver and be relatively free from noise and distortion.

FIGURE 13.1

Communications and Feedback Mechanism

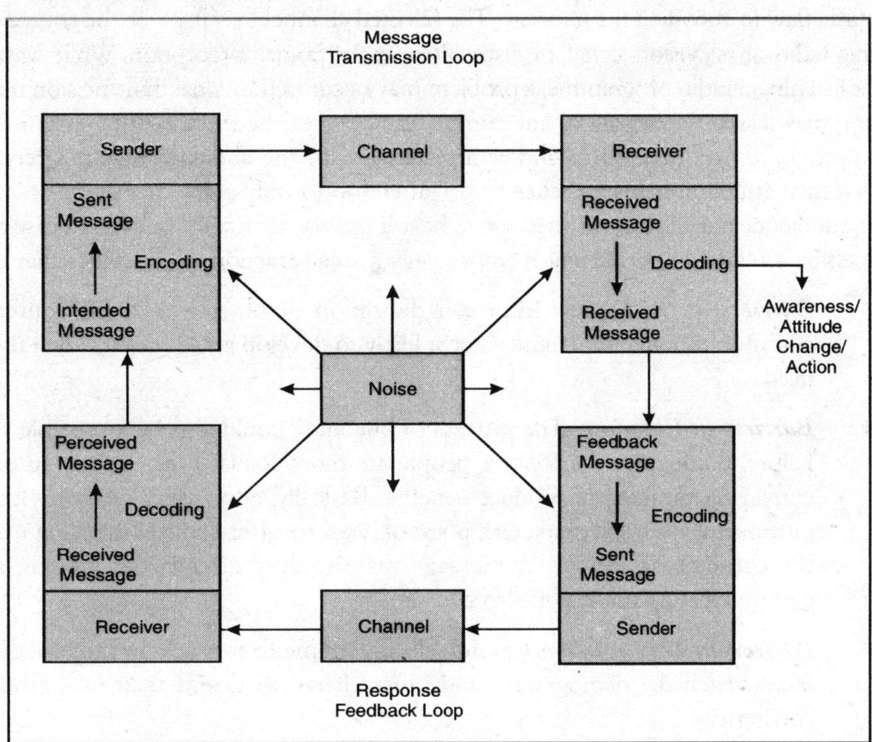

The sent message may reach one or more receivers. Rarely, if ever, are received messages identical to sent messages. Channel characteristics and noise present in the system are important factors that account for this difference. For example, it is quite difficult to accurately reproduce colours and textures on audio-visual medium and in newspapers, and for this reason the received message may differ from the original sent message.

The sender's message after being received by the target audience is transformed into a perceived message. The perceived message (decoded message) is the outcome of receiver's information processing activities leading to interpretation of thoughts or meanings by the receiver. Several factors affect *decoding*. The nature of the relationship between the sender and receiver, the sender's and receiver's experiences, attitudes, values, biases and the context in which the message is perceived, will influence the decoded message and also influence any meaning derived by the individual from it. Any actions or changes in the receiver's attitude will be the result of this perceived message.

The feedback loop (Figure 13.1) recognises that the communications process is a two-way information flow. This shows that the feedback can be viewed as the beginning of another communication in which the receiver of the communication can be thought as the message sender. The sender's and receiver's roles are reversed as they interact with each other. The feedback mechanism helps the original sender to monitor how accurately the intended meaning of the message was conveyed and received. In case of many marketing communications, mass media is used to reach widely scattered audience and in such situations, accurate feedback information is rare and very difficult to obtain.

Barriers to Communication

The element of *noise* in the communications process refers to any type of unplanned disruption or interference that may hinder the communications. The source of noise may be other competing messages vying for audience attention. The sender may have difficulty in formulating the intended message, or there may be some flaw in encoding the message. The selected channel may itself be the source of noise, such as distortion in a radio or television signal, or distractions at the point of reception. While watching a programme on TV or listening a radio programme, a problem may occur in the signal transmission that interferes with reception and may lessen the impact of any commercial. Any of the three factors, *selective attention, selective distortion,* or *selective recall* may play a role and as a result of this, the audience may not receive the intended message. Selective attention helps audience to pay attention to only some messages. Because of selective distortion, the audience may distort the message to hear it the way they want to hear. In case of selective recall, audience members retain, in permanent memory, only a small fraction of messages that reach them.

- ***Barriers at the Source:*** Improper definition of objectives at the source is a barrier of effective communication. This failure is most likely to develop an ad message that does not focus on consumer needs.
- ***Barriers in Encoding:*** The process of encoding could also be a possible factor for communications failure. Sometimes the creative people are more focused on creating an original ad message than in conveying meaningful product benefits. Basically, advertising creativity needs to be disciplined and purposeful from the marketer's point of view to offer some compelling reasons to consumers to buy the product or service. A message may be very effective in gaining attention but may fail in communicating the benefits to consumers.
- ***Barriers in Transmission:*** Careful selection of media to reach the target audience is essential. Marketers must match the demographic and other characteristics of their user group to the profile of media consumers.
- ***Barriers in Decoding:*** A failure to develop a distinct product positioning or ad message related to consumer needs is likely to create barriers in the decoding process. Consumers selectively ignore messages that fail to stimulate their interest. Besides competitive advertising clutter, continued use of the same ad for a long period is often boring to the audience and may prove to be a barrier and decrease ad effectiveness.

Clutter due to competing messages in almost all media is a major barrier for marketing related communications. Ever increasing number of ads and commercials inhibits consumers in the decoding process. Attention and recall of ads drops off with the increase in the number of ads. Raymond R. Burke and Thomas K. Srull have reported that more exposure to competing ads inhibits consumers' ability to remember the advertised brand and concluded that greater similarity between brands and between advertising themes, confuses consumers and makes retrieval of specific brand information from memory more difficult.

One easy solution for marketers to combat consumer confusion is to increase the frequency of a message and create a lasting impression. This solution is particularly effective if the product message is closely tied to consumer needs. This is the reason that marketers of soft drinks, toothpaste, soaps, dry battery cells and many other products maintain increased advertising frequency. It is also true that if two brands are equally rated, the one that advertises more is purchased more frequently.

According to Wilbur Schramm, the likelihood that the receiver will attend to any message is explained by the equation:

$$\text{Likelihood of Attention} = \frac{\text{Perceived reward strength} - \text{Perceived punishment strength}}{\text{Perceived expenditure of effort}}$$

In the evaluation of communications process, marketers must seek answers to four questions:

- Have communications objectives been set to reflect consumer needs?
- Has there been proper encoding of product benefits?
- Has the message been transmitted to the target audience by utilising the right media?
- Did consumers decode the message in the manner the marketer intended?

Communications Objectives (Marketing Communication Models)

Marketers seek any one or more of the following responses to their communications:

- ***Cognitive Responses:*** The audience should pay attention to message and comprehend it. This refers to thinking, belief, and other rational aspects.
- ***Affective Responses:*** The message should lead to formation of new attitude or bring about a change in attitude. This represents feelings such as liking and preference.
- ***Conative or Behavioural Responses:*** The message should achieve some degree of desired change in behaviour, such as product trial or purchase action.

Researchers and scholars have developed several marketing communication models to suggest how message recipients move through a series of sequential steps to finally purchase decision. 'Noise' due to competing messages, psychological, or social factors hinders the smooth progress through the stages and the probabilities of communication success decline in each stage, reducing the chances of actual purchase.

Hierarchy Models

Marketing communications model implying that consumers pass through a series of sequential steps leading to purchase of a product or service are called hierarchy models (Figure 13.2). The **AIDA** model was developed in 1920s (E. K. Strong), suggesting that an effective sales presentation should attract attention, gain interest, stimulate desire, and precipitate action (purchase). Ideally, an ad would prove to be really effective if it takes this route, however, in the real world of advertising, ads rarely take the consumer all the way from awareness through purchase. This model, however, suggests the desirable qualities of an effective ad.

FIGURE 13.2
Four Best-Known Hierarchy Models

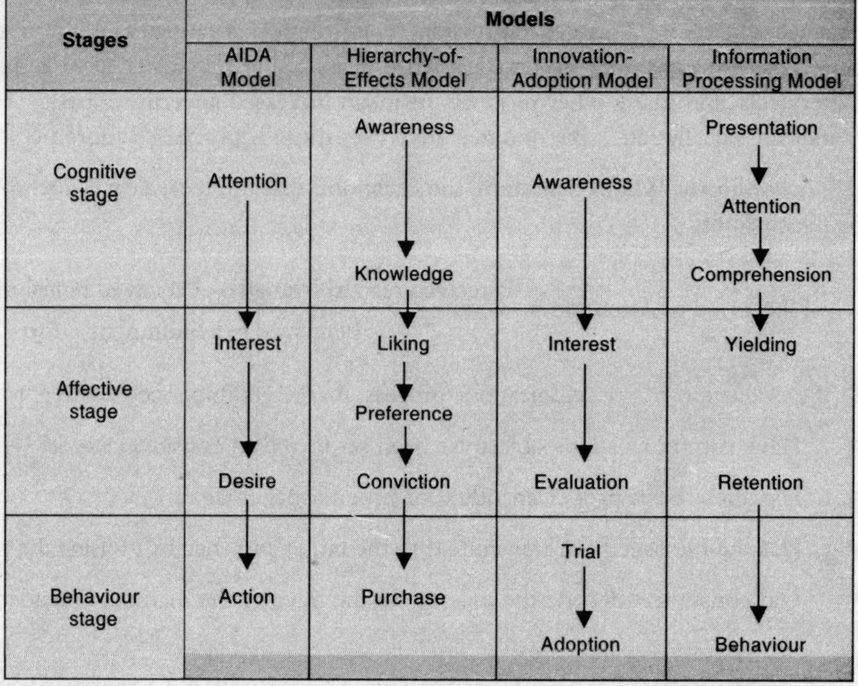

Stages
Models
AIDA Model
Hierarchy-of-Effects Model
Innovation-Adoption Model
Information Processing Model
Cognitive stage
Attention
Awareness
Knowledge
Awareness
Presentation
Attention
Comprehension
Affective stage
Interest
Desire
Liking
Preference
Conviction
Interest
Evaluation
Yielding
Retention
Behaviour stage
Action
Purchase
Trial
Adoption
Behaviour

Hierarchy-of-effects model: Research findings, in the area of consumer behaviour and communications has led many scholars to view communications effects in terms of hierarchy-of-effects model and many such models have been developed over the years. Hierarchy-of-effects model developed by Lavidge and Steiner has stood the test of time well and is the best known. This model helps in setting promotional objectives and provides a basis for measuring results. This model also suggests that communication produces its effects by moving the consumer through a series of steps in a sequence from initial awareness to ultimate purchase of product or service. This sequential order indicates the basic premise that communication effects are elicited over a period of time and that advertising may not precipitate the desired effects immediately because a series of effects must occur before the consumer possibly moves to the next stage in the hierarchy.

Innovation-adoption model: According to Everett M. Rogers, this model evolved from work on diffusion of innovations. The model depicts various sequential steps and stages that a consumer moves through in adopting a new product or service. Marketers face the challenge of creating awareness and interest in the product or service among target audience and evaluate it favourably. The best way to persuade consumers to evaluate a brand is by inducing product trial or sometimes product-in-use demonstration. This can lead to product adoption as a result of consumer satisfaction or rejection if the consumer is not satisfied.

Information processing model: William McGuire developed this model, which assumes that target audiences are information processors and problem solvers. The first three stages in the model; presentation, attention, and comprehension are similar to awareness and knowledge, and yielding means the same as liking. Up to this point, there is similarity with Lavidge and Steiner's model. The next stage, retention is unique to this model and is not present in any other model. Retention refers to the ability of the consumer to accept and store in memory the relevant information about the product or service. Retention of information is important, because most communications, except some types of sales promotions, are designed to motivate and precipitate action not just immediately and the retained information is used at a later time to make purchase decision.

Implications for managers: Any stage in the response hierarchy may serve to establish communications objectives and the effects can be measured. The targeted audience may be at any stage in the hierarchy and the communicator's tasks may be different in each stage. For example, popular and mature brands of the company may require only reminders to reinforce consumers' favourable perceptions. Every day there are ads about products such as, Coke, Pepsi, brands of toilet soaps, detergents, and many other products, which are in mature category and enjoy popularity among consumers.

If the research reveals that a significant number of target audience have low level of awareness about the brand and its benefits, then the task is to increase awareness of the brand, attributes, and the resulting benefits.

All the four models presented in Figure 13.2, show that in each case the starting stage is **cognitive**, leading to **affective** stage and finally to **conative** or **behavioural** stage. This progression shows the following sequence:

Learn (Cognitive) → Feel (Affective) → Do (Conative)

These hierarchy-of-effects models are sometimes referred to as **standard learning models**. The consumer is considered as an active participant and gathers information through active learning. This type of learning is usually more relevant when consumer is highly involved in the purchase situation and perceives much differentiation among competing brands. Communications for these types of products or services usually are detailed and attempt to furnish a great deal of meaningful information to target audience.

The research in the last more than two decades has shown that this high-involvement sequence may not hold true in case of different product categories. Some convenience products that are consumed daily and purchased routinely do not require high-involvement of consumers.

Brand managers should know how the decisions about each independent variable could influence the stages of response hierarchy. There are examples of ads that used sex appeal, humour, or celebrities as endorsers to attract consumers' attention. Such ads are generally quite successful in attracting the audience attention but often are ineffective in brand name or brand message recall.

FIGURE 13.3

The Persuasion Matrix

Steps in Persuasion Matrix (Dependent variables)	The communication components (Independent variables)				
	Source	Message	Medium	Receiver	Destinatio
Message presentation			(2)		
Attention	(4)				
Comprehension				(1)	
Feeling/Conviction		(3)			
Retention					
Behaviour					

(Adapted with changes from William J. McGuire, in "An Information Processing Model of Advertising Effectiveness," in *Behavioural and Management Science in Marketing*, ed. Harry J. Davis and Alvin J. Silk, Ronald Press, 1978).

Persuasion matrix (Figure 13.3) can help to evaluate the following communications-related decisions:

1. ***Receiver/Comprehension:*** Comprehension of a message by the consumer is an important prerequisite in precipitating the desired behaviour. The marketer must know the important characteristics of the target market to develop a message that would be clear and understandable. Less educated audience may experience difficulty in interpreting a complicated message. For example, in rural India it would be futile to use complicated language to communicate the ad message. The use of familiar symbols and words of commonly spoken language can make the message more comprehensible.

2. ***Medium/Message Presentation:*** Various media are available to communicate a message. *Femina* magazine reaches a large number of educated urban, upper class and fashion conscious women. *India Today* is a very respected popular general interest magazine, while a different segment patronizes *Economic Times*. Then, there are special interest magazines. There are quite a good number of satellite TV channels, besides radio and other media. The marketer must know which is the appropriate medium to reach the target market to ensure that the message is presented to the right audience. A wrong choice may mean considerable loss of money and no message impact.

3. ***Message/Feeling, Conviction:*** The communicator would like to choose the type of message that will create favourable attitudes and feelings most likely to precipitate the desired action. The message content can focus on the rational or emotional approach. Humorous messages attract consumer attention and put them in a pleasant mood. Music can add emotion and make the consumers more inclined towards the message. The marketer may favour a brand comparison approach, or use sex or fear appeals. There is a wide choice in developing an appropriate message for the target audience.

4. ***Source/Attention:*** Which source will be most effective in getting consumer attention? In the present promotional scenario, it is a formidable challenge for marketers to break through the clutter and capture attention. Marketers use well-known personalities in sports, film and other fields to attract the target audience's attention. If a product or service is to be presented effectively to consumers, then there must be a message that catches the consumers' attention. Without a message, there is no communication and without consumers' attention, no amount of communications can succeed.

Persuasive Communication

Communication among people takes place almost constantly and in innumerable number of ways. Persuasive communication, however, is a specific type of communication in promotion. If a particular ad is intended to achieve an intermediate objective, such as to build awareness, deliver information, or remind the target audience, the ultimate objective of promotional strategy is to persuade the audience towards some desired goal of the marketer. Persuasion through advertising or PR/publicity requires longer period of time and may involve several intermediate steps, while personal selling or sales promotions take much less time and a shorter route.

Marketing objectives are based on company objectives, and persuasive communication objectives are based on marketing objectives. It is essential to coordinate the activities of all communications elements towards achieving these objectives and to ensure this; each component of promotion mix is guided by a set of communication objectives. The communications mix objectives are often sequential. The first step might be to create product, brand, or company name awareness among the target audience, next providing important and meaningful information, then to change impressions, perceptions and attitudes and finally creating conviction and precipitating favourable behavioural change. Desired change in behaviour is the primary indicator of successful persuasive communication. Effective persuasion requires considerable sensitivity towards others to understand their information processing and decision-making.

Message Design

Marketing is all about satisfying consumer needs and wants at a profit and at the same time protecting the larger and long-run interests of society. The message is often considered as the most vital component in the communications process. The message is the thought, idea, attitude, image, or other information that the marketer wishes to convey to the targeted audience. How a message is presented is critically important in determining its effectiveness. Brand or promotion managers must focus on what will be the message content, how this information will be structured for communication and what kind of message appeal will be appropriate.

Message Appeals

Through the use of a variety of appeals, a marketer attempts to communicate and influence the purchase and consumption behaviour of the existing and potential consumers. One of the most critical decisions about message-design involves the choice of an appropriate appeal. Some communications are designed with the intent of appealing to the rational, logical aspect of the consumers' decision-making process, and others attempt to stimulate consumers' feelings with the intent of evoking some desired emotional response. Many professionals believe that effective promotional message is created by combining practical reasons for purchasing a product or service with emotional values of the audience.

Often the promotional appeals are classified as *rational appeals, emotional appeals,* and *moral appeals.* Rational appeals are those that focus on the audience's self-interest and are directed at the thinking aspect of decision-making process. Such appeals attempt to show that the product or service will produce the desired benefits. Examples are ad messages that promise economy, assurance of resale value, quality, durability, reliability, and ease of use, etc. Rational appeals are particularly relevant for industrial buyers who choose products according to some of the mentioned criteria. In case of general consumers, they confidently rationalise most of their purchases even when the purchase decisions are based on emotional grounds. Most of us probably have a keen desire to be regarded as rational human beings and for this reason, we usually extend socially acceptable reasons for our purchases.

Emotional appeals are put under two categories: positive emotional appeals, and negative emotional appeals, depending on what kind of emotions are to be triggered. Love, affection, joy, pride, humour, prestige, status, etc., are some examples of positive emotional appeals. Examples of negative emotional appeals are fear, shame, guilt, embarrassment, rejection, etc. Such appeals motivate audience to do things they should do, such as cleaning teeth (Colgate commercial), or to stop doing things they should not, such as smoking and using other tobacco products.

Moral appeals attempt to draw audience attention to what is "right." Moral appeals are generally used to urge people to support social causes such as, environmental concerns, population explosion, donating money to help victims of some natural calamity, or equal status for women, etc. The aim of all marketing communications is to capture audience attention, hold interest, precipitate their desire, and elicit desired action. This requires focusing on four important message issues: what should be said, how should it be said and what would be the message execution style, and who should say it (spokesperson).

Fear Appeals: Fear is an emotional response to some actual or perceived threat or danger. Advertisers use fear appeals in some situations to evoke the desired emotional response and motivate audience to take steps to remove the threat. Some people humorously call these as "slice-of-death" ads. Toothpaste, mouthwash, deodorants, helmets, anti-dandruff shampoos, water filters, fire extinguishers, life insurance and a large number of other products and services use explicit or implicit fear appeals.

In some situations, it appears to be quite reasonable for advertisers to consider using fear with the explicit purpose of persuading the audience to elicit a favourable response. Fear is a powerful motivator, but only up to a point. Ad messages using fear appeals have promoted social causes as well, such as wearing helmets while driving two-wheeler autos, safe driving, paying taxes, the dread of drugs, dangers of smoking and AIDS, etc.

It is advantageous for the marketer to understand how fear operates, what level of fear to use in communications and how different types of target audiences may respond to fear appeals. The nature of fear is such that as a stimulus it tends to create negative emotions, but may stimulate positive drives among target audience. Fear appeals are particularly useful for products or services that do not interest consumers, or are considered bothersome. For example, mostly young two-wheeler riders particularly dislike wearing helmets, or not many consumers are enthusiastic about buying insurance policy, or respond to different kinds of vaccination programmes. According to a theory proposed by Michael L. Ray and William L. Wilkie, the relationship between the intensity of fear in an advertising message and its persuasive impact on target audience is such that as the amount of fear rises, the message acceptance increases. But this increase in message acceptance occurs only up to a point of fear intensity. Once this point is reached, any further increase in the amount of fear will fail to enhance message acceptance. On the contrary, the effect of increased fear beyond this point would increasingly decrease message acceptance.

Earliest research on response to fear extended the explanation that strong fear invoking messages led consumers to set up perceptual defence mechanisms to filter out the frightening aspects of the communicated message and while doing so, the consumers reject the entire message.

Later experiments suggested that mild fear appeals are not effective because they lack sufficient intensity to motivate consumers to bring about a change in attitude. Higher levels of fear in messages also tend to yield very little desired effect among consumers because of perceptual defence mechanism by consumers as already mentioned. This analysis sought to explain why fear appeals of only moderate intensity work; it was opined that they provide sufficient motivation and do not activate perceptual defence mechanism, leading to message acceptance and attitude change among consumers. This became known as the "inverted U" argument.

Brian Strenthal, C. Samuel Craig and others have argued that perhaps it is inappropriate to draw general conclusions about any given level of fear appeal because numerous factors may influence how consumers will respond to a given fear appeal. According to them, for example, the following factors may influence the audience response to fear-evoking messages in advertising:

- 'Highly credible sources' are more likely to be effective in using mild to moderate fear to influence audience attitudes because the consumers would refrain from counter-arguing that they often use to protect themselves from fear generating advertising messages.
- 'Audience characteristics' may determine the degree to which they will be persuaded by fear appeals. Consumers having high self-esteem can cope with tension and do not feel particularly vulnerable to the frightening consequences. They appear to be persuaded by fear appeals of high intensity. For example, many people working in coalmines consider their occupation very risky and may not be susceptible to fear appeals, low or high. In a country like ours, a large number of consumers are somewhat fatalistic in their outlook about life and believe that no matter what anyone says, life will take its own course.
- There is some evidence suggesting that fear of social disapproval may be more effective in influencing actual behaviour than the fear of physical harm. Presence of some degree of humour in the ad environment can help to focus audience attention on it and can effectively to distract their attention from strong fear appeal and the actual message may become more persuasive.

- Fear appeals are likely to be more persuasive when the audience attention is focused on the specific threat and what practical steps should be taken to avoid the fearful consequences. Messages not suggesting a solution to the audience are less likely to be persuasive.

The fourth point as above has led to the development of 'protection motivation theory' by Ronald Rogers. According to this theory, four processes influence and determine how an individual will actually respond to a message that uses fear appeal. The individual will:

- Determine how severe is the threat to her/him
- Determine the likelihood of the threat to occur
- Determine what kind of action will be able to nullify the threat (the coping response)
- Determine her/his own capabilities to carry out the coping response behaviour.

The outcome of this threat-evaluation in relation to the above mentioned factors would lead to the individual's 'protection motivation'. In essence, this means adopting certain behaviours to protect oneself against dangers. The actually intended behaviour to cope with a threat is different from fear itself, which is an emotion felt by the individual.

Protection motivation is an attractive concept for the advertisers as it suggests guidelines for developing ads to motivate audiences to respond to fear appeals. Based on this theory, the communication using fear appeal should:

- Provide information about the seriousness of the threat,
- Suggest the probability of its occurrence,
- Indicate effective behaviour to cope with the threat, and
- Show the audience how easily the coping response can be used.

For example, Khaitan Kitchen fans used a fear appeal. The ad headline warns, "Are you cooking or being cooked?" The body copy goes on to say, "Every housewife knows how miserable she feels when she cooks. It makes her irritable and saps her energy. Khaitan presents a simple, efficient and inexpensive offer. Khaitan Fresh-Air-Fan. It drives out smoke, smells and heat and brings in fresh air. The chances of dampness are eliminated. And this prevents cockroaches and other insects from breeding in your kitchen."

The fear appeals facilitate attention and interest in the message and may motivate the audience to resolve the threat. Increasing the intensity of fear from mild to moderate can generate increased persuasion. On the other hand, high intensity of fear produces inhibiting effects and the audience may emotionally block the message by rejecting it, using selective perception or selective distortion.

Fear appeals are more effective when the target audience is more self-confident and prefers to cope with threats instead of avoiding them. Non-users of products are more likely to take notice of fear appeals than product users and for this reason, fear appeals may prove more effective at keeping non-smokers away from cigarettes, etc., than persuading smokers to stop smoking.

Humour Appeals: Humour generates feelings of amusement and pleasure and, for this reason it has a potential for the feelings to become associated with the brand, and affect consumer attitudes towards the brand and probably its image. Humour can also affect information processing by attracting attention, improving brand name recall, creating a pleasant mood and reducing the chances of counter-arguing. The positive side of humorous ads can be summed up in the following points:

- Humour attracts attention

- Humour can help increase ad message retention.
- Source credibility can be enhanced with humour.
- Audience attitude towards the ad can be enhanced with the use of humour.
- Humour may diminish the chances of counter-arguments because it distracts the audience from making cognitive responses.

Critics argue that humorous ads draw attention to the funny aspects in the ad, but distract the audience from the brand and its attributes, thereby hurting ad effectiveness. Amitava Chattopadhyay and Kunal Basu have reported that if the consumers have a negative prior evaluation about the advertised brand, a humorous ad could actually prove to be less effective than a non-humorous ad. Marc G. Weinberger and Charles S. Gulas conducted a comprehensive review of studies on ads using humour and concluded that humour in ads usually increases audience attention and liking of the ads but appears not to increase message comprehension and persuasion. Humour appears to work best for low-involvement and "feel" category of products but not for "think" type of products.

A difficulty in using humour is that what appears to be humorous for one person, may sound outright silly or even irritating to another. Frequent repetition of humorous ads is often irritating to the audience. Humour is related to feeling and to build feeling associations, advertising requires frequent repetitions and the tendency for some in the audience to get irritated is enhanced. It is particularly important with humour to have a good understanding of the target audience.

Some types of ads are humorous and others are not. Humorous ads can be created by the inclusion of jokes, anecdotes, satire, understatements, puns, irony, etc. The use of humour is culture-bound and tastes for different kinds of humour vary considerably. What could be a humorous ad message in Western culture may not necessarily mean the same thing in more conservative eastern cultures. Some evidence suggests that better-educated and professional persons are likely to be best suited for humorous messages. Based on Gestalt principle of contrast, humorous commercials seem to work best when presented in an action-adventure setting. There are contrasting views and many qualifying conditions on the effectiveness of humour and for these reasons, perhaps it would be wise for the advertisers to use humour very selectively for products and audiences that seem to be most suitable for this approach.

Sex Appeals: Marketers have always had a traditional worry that consumers are being flooded with too many advertising claims. This, coupled with ever-increasing competition from new products, has convinced many advertising people that sex is a necessary ingredient in advertising. Sex appeals in advertising range from blatant nudity to subtle devices that only a trained observer can recognise.

The use of sex in advertising seems to have become somewhat discouraged because of public fear of AIDS and this has caused advertisers to turn to more romantic themes. It is believed that sexual imagery is unlikely to disappear from print ads and TV commercials, but is likely to be managed more subtly than previously.

It is very difficult to predict the audience response to ads with sexual appeals, but advertisers still use it. The reasons are obvious. There are few appeals in advertising that probably can equal the attention-arresting magic of sex appeals. Many psychologists are of the opinion that proper manipulation of sex appeals can trigger subconscious human desires that result in the purchase of products or services. Readership studies reveal that sex stimulates immediate interest of both genders.

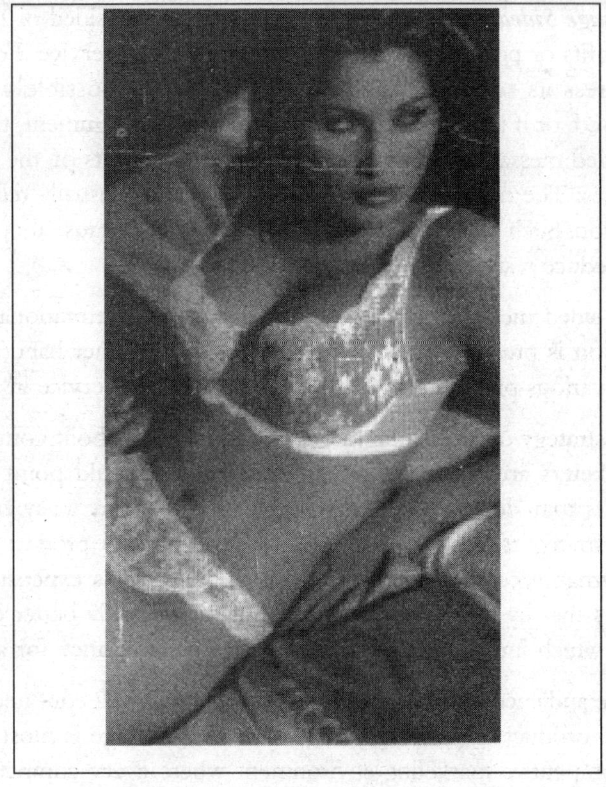

FIGURE 13.4
Sex Appeal Can be Effective in Capturing Attention

Message themes related to sex may attract audience attention but they rarely generate curiosity about the product being advertised (Figure 13.4). There are indications that audiences' interest stops with sex only and the ad message is hardly, if ever, processed deeply. If sex appeal has no relevance to the advertised product, it completely fails in creating any persuasive impression on the target audience. In fact, the advertiser may be sacrificing message persuasiveness for stopping power of the ad.

The responses of men and women are totally different toward sex appeals in advertising. The perceptions of men, for example, about sexiness of an ad depend on the degree of nudity shown. However, the romantic content in the ad is the primary determinant of sexiness for women. There are differences between men and women concerning brand recall when sex appeals are used. Studies show that women could tolerate ads with high levels of sexual arousal and still recall the brand names, while men, in a similar situation, could not remember anything about the product. Better ad recall scores are generally obtained for ads that use sex appeal in a functional fashion, such as ads for undergarments of ladies.

For using sex appeals, the advertiser must be sure that the product, the ad, the target consumers and the sexual message themes and other elements all match up. If sex is relevant to the product, it can be an extremely strong copy theme. The ads of Candico's Mint-o After Smoke, Kohinoor and Kama Sutra premium condoms are good examples of ads using sex appeal in relation to products and their functionality.

Message Structure

Message structure refers to how the elements of a message are organised. Extensive research has been conducted to understand how the message structure influences its effectiveness and includes message sidedness, order-of-presentation, conclusion drawing and verbal versus visual message characteristics.

Message Sidedness: A message can be either one-sided or two-sided. A one-sided message mentions only benefits or positive attributes of the product or service. For example, advertisements of Maruti 800 only address its advantages and don't mention any possible weaknesses. If the audience is favourably predisposed, or if it is not likely to hear an opposing argument, then a one-sided message is most effective. A two-sided message presents not only the strong points of the product or service, but also admits to any weaknesses. The negative part of the information is usually relatively unimportant compared to positive information. Such messages become more effective because they help to increase the source credibility and thereby reduce resistance to message acceptance.

Two-sided messages can be refutational or non-refutational. In a refutational message, the negative information is presented first then refuted. On the other hand, a non-refutational message would simply mention various pros and cons about the product or service in a straightforward manner.

The strategy of presenting negative information about company's own product is not very common. The marketers are fearful that such an approach could point out the deficiencies of the product and consumers may develop a negative evaluation and shy away from buying it. However, this could be a powerful strategy if refuting a negative factor enhances the product value. In case of Khaitan fan advertisement, the Chairman accepts at the very outset that the fan is expensive and subsequently goes on to prove to customers that by paying a little more, they are actually better off because of the superior quality of the product, which implies trouble-free, superior performance for a long time.

If the audience is critical, unfriendly or hostile, well educated, or if it is likely to hear opposing claims about the product or service, then a two-sided message is most likely to be more effective especially in a highly competitive marketing environment where every competing brand claims superiority over others. Robert E. Settle and Linda L. Golden propose that claim credibility can sometimes be made more authentic by actually 'disclaiming' superiority of some product features in relation to a competing brand. For example, the Khaitan Marathon fan ad claims superiority about its features but admits that it is more expensive than other fans. Research findings suggest that two-sided messages containing both pro and con arguments about the brand serve to inoculate or immunise consumers against arguments that may be raised by competitors. This strategy actually helps provide consumers with counter-arguments to dilute any attacks by competing brands.

Two-sided messages are often seen in the case of comparative advertising, where the name of one or more competitors are openly mentioned for the purpose of claiming overall superiority or superiority on a selective attribute basis. To enhance credibility, the advertiser usually mentions an independent research organisation as the supplier of comparison data.

One-sided messages tend to confirm what the audiences already believe about the brand and therefore consumers generate cognitive responses in the form of support arguments, which reinforce their initial position. When the audiences are not favourably predisposed, a two-sided message is more effective because it acknowledges their initial position and the consumers tend to view the advertiser as more honest or credible. This minimises the audience's use of counter arguments as the advertiser is perceived trustworthy, which should then result in more acceptability of the advertiser's message.

Order of Presentation: Order of presentation of message arguments is an important consideration in the design of promotional message (Figure 13. 5). Important message arguments can be presented in the beginning of the message, in the middle, or at the end. Research shows that items presented in the beginning or the end of the message are remembered better and stand a much better chance of recall than those presented in the middle.

Climax versus Anticlimax Order: When the strongest message arguments are presented at the end of the message, it is called climax order. But when the most important message points are presented at the beginning of the message, it is referred to as anticlimax order.

The main message points when presented in the middle are called pyramidal order. Based on research findings, the following guidelines can help in deciding the message order.

- When the audience is likely to have low-involvement in a product category, an anticlimax order tends to be most effective.
- In case of audiences having high level of interest in the product category, a climax order tends to be most effective.
- The least effective order of presentation is believed to be pyramidal order.

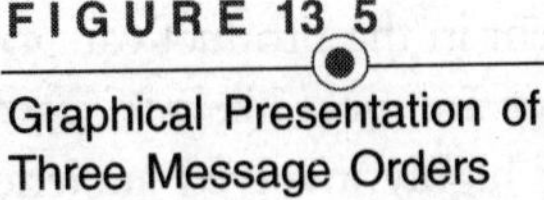

FIGURE 13.5

Graphical Presentation of Three Message Orders

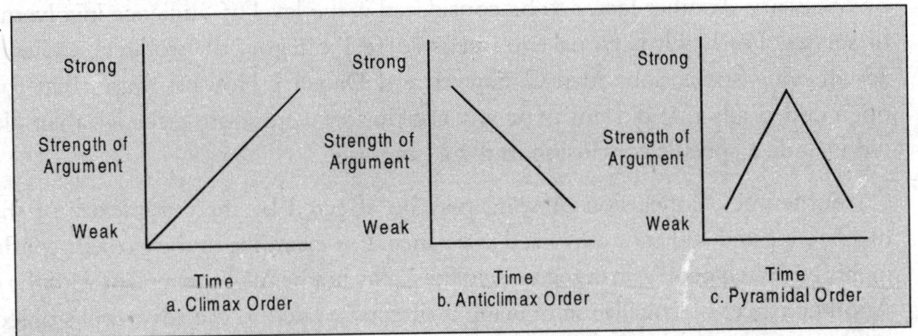

In the first situation, where the consumers' involvement is likely to be low, the stronger, more interesting points in a message have the greatest chance of attracting audiences' attention. For this reason, the strong and more interesting points should be presented in the beginning of the message (anticlimax order) and the advertiser would be in a much better position to get the ad message across and expect to create better effect on the audience. The advertiser, however, must take care that the remaining part of the message should not "put off" the audience totally.

When the audiences are likely to be highly interested in an ad message, there is no need to include the strongest and most interesting message points in the beginning as the audiences would attend to the message anyway and therefore, the climax order is more appropriate in such situations. The strong points taken up at the end of the ad message would most likely exceed the audiences' expectations created by the points at the beginning. This may prove to be very helpful in increasing the persuasiveness of the message.

In general, it is appropriate for message designers to use the anticlimax order for low-involvement product categories and climax order for messages of high-involvement products or services. If the target audience is opposed to the advertiser's position, presenting strong arguments first can reduce the chances of counter-arguments. In such a situation, presenting weak points first might lead to such strong counter-arguing that strong points that follow would not be acceptable to the audience. In some cases, perhaps it may be appropriate for the advertiser in both types of message ordering to present brand name and important selling points at the beginning as well as at the end of the message.

Apparently, there seems to be very little or no justification for a pyramidal order in delivering advertising messages.

Recency and Primacy Effects: When many competing messages are involved, as is the case in print or TV ads, different advertisers often consider primacy effect and recency effect. The primacy effect occurs when the message presented first creates greater opinion or attitude change. But if the message arguments presented last produce greater opinion or attitude change, it is recency effect. It appears that both primacy and recency effects work at different times. So far, research findings are not conclusive on this issue. There are advertisers who believe either in primacy or the recency effect and accordingly decide about the message order or the ad placement.

Conclusion Drawing: It is an important issue for marketers to decide whether the message should allow the audience to draw their own conclusions about the product or service or the message should draw a firm conclusion for the audience. Research shows that drawing a firm conclusion or leaving the conclusion drawing to audience largely depends on the nature of target audience, the type of product or service and the nature of communication situation.

Highly educated audiences prefer to draw their own conclusions and are quite likely to be irritated when the ad message attempts to explain the obvious or draws simple inferences for them. When the audience is less educated or lacks the ability to draw a conclusion, there is a possibility of making incorrect inferences or failing to draw any conclusion from the ad message, in which case stating the conclusion may be necessary. Another factor to be considered is the level of audience involvement in the product category or service. For highly personal ego-intensive 'feel' category of products, audiences are most likely to resent ads drawing conclusion. Alan G. Sawyer and Daniel J. Howard found that for highly involved audience open-ended ads that did not draw any conclusion were more effective than closed-ended arguments that did include a specific conclusion in the ad message.

Sometimes, conclusion drawing may be affected by the complexity of the product where even the highly educated audience may need assistance. For example, in the present conditions in our country, many highly educated people, in certain disciplines, may not be fully conversant with the complexities of computers. Another aspect of conclusion drawing is directly related to the advertiser's objectives. If the ad is expected to trigger immediate action from consumers, then the message should draw a firm conclusion. For instance, a number of ads prompt consumers to take immediate action and include some sales promotional incentive. As opposed to this, if the objective is to create long-term effects, repeated ad exposures using open-ended messages allow the audience to draw their own conclusions. A good number of ads for leading computer brands, autos, highly visible personal products, etc., use open-ended ad messages. The Quantum Institute ad message headline says, "A starting salary of Rs 27 lakhs? What exactly do they teach you at Quantum?" The sub-headline of Aptech Computer Education ad message reads, "Where else can you get the real global advantage?" The audience is left to draw the conclusion by answering the posed question, leading to either acceptance or rejection of the offer.

Verbal versus Visual Messages Characteristics

No one can deny the importance of visual and non-verbal elements in advertising. A good number of ads use very little written information and mainly focus on visual elements to covey the message. Pictures used in ads convey meaningful information and also reinforce the ad claims. According to Andrew A. Mitchell, the verbal and visual portions in an ad have their influence on ad processing by audiences, who often develop images based on illustrations and pictures. Research by H. Rao Unnava and Robert E. Burnkrant has shown that verbal information was low in imagery value while the pictures, providing examples increased immediate as well as delayed recall of the product attributes. Advertisers often create ads where the visual image supports the verbal appeal to develop strong and persuasive impressions in the audience's mind.

Message Source

The company seeking to promote a product or service is the ultimate message source. Sometimes the message source identity may be quite clear, but at other times the company may use some distinctive individuals as the apparent message source. A message source is quite distinct from the message itself and the distinct individual may have considerable impact on the communication effectiveness. If the target audience identify with endorser and perceive closer link between the source personality and a product, the stronger the message effect. Quite a few companies marketing consumer durable and non-durable products are using popular sports persons and film stars in their advertising to endorse their products. It has been a common sight to see Sachin Tendulkar, Rahul Dravid, Saurav Ganguly, Amitabh Bachchan, Shahrukh Khan and many others – the list goes on and on – endorsing some well-known brands. Companies expect to derive three types of benefits from endorsers:

- Endorsers increase viewing of TV ads and readership of newspapers and magazines, etc.
- Endorsers can influence positive attitude change towards a company and its brands because of their credibility.
- Endorser's perceived personality characteristics, can get associated with a brand's imagery.

Consumers associate varying degree of credibility with different information sources. It is believed that more credible the source, the more persuasive the endorser is likely to be in influencing the acceptance of ad message by the audience. Endorsers in ads are viewed as "source" of information and influence audience's acceptance of message content because of their credibility and attractiveness. Besides this, it is also believed that endorsers possess some symbolic attributes which consumers associate with the brand. By purchasing, owning and consuming those brands, consumers see themselves as possessing those desired attributes. There was a news article that a youngster died while trying to emulate a risky jump taken by Salman Khan in an ad of ThumsUp. Coca-Cola ads use endorsers who portray an image of being "young" and "modern." While companies are investing huge sums of money in the concept that sports people of today and yesterday are good endorsers, they are also recognising that choosing a celebrity endorser is no longer a matter of personal taste. Several companies have learned the hard way that high priced endorsers have been suspected of involvement in messy scandals and controversies. The cricket match fixing suspicions have seemingly brought into the wrong kind of limelight, some famous sports persons who were the endorsers for some multinational brands.

For a number of companies using sports people as endorsers, risk management has become a major consideration. Some companies are moving away from controversial sports personalities and are putting their money on those who would attract attention to enhance the product or company image. It has become imperative that a company must select the right spokesperson to deliver a persuasive message through appropriate media to make the promotional campaign effective. The marketer has control over some communication elements such as, source, message and media etc. William J. McGuire's persuasion matrix helps advertisers to assess how the independent variables interact with consumer's response process.

Source here means the person involved in communicating the marketing related message, directly or indirectly. Companies take due care in selecting the source. They are quite aware of the fact that source characteristics have considerable effect on the marketing communications and select individuals whose traits will maximise the message influence on the audience.

The source in a marketing communication can be a salesperson, in an ad the key source can be a celebrity, announcer, spokesperson or a common consumer, etc., who endorses or demonstrates the product in an advertisement, and in publicity the source is the writer of a news insert.

Source Credibility: Source credibility means the extent to which the audience perceives the source as having relevant knowledge, expertise, or experience and believe that the source will provide unbiased and objective information about the product or service.

The element of credibility has two important dimensions — expertise and trustworthiness. A person with more expertise in any field is considered more credible than the one with less expertise. In this sense credibility is directly related to knowledge. But this source, with more expertise also has to be honest, unbiased, ethical, and one who could be believed. This is trustworthiness. For any reason, if the audience thought that a particular source, in spite of being knowledgeable, lacks honesty, or may be biased, then the source would be less effective. For example, as the source is being paid and the audience may perceive that the source has underlying motives for favouring a position, the source's trustworthiness is likely to be compromised and the influence will be reduced. The source's knowledge, reputation and prestige are considered as the cognitive dimension of credibility and attractiveness and popularity as the affective aspect of trustworthiness. This means that the consumers' approach to source credibility can be rational as well as emotional.

A source that is portrayed as being similar to the audience in terms of background, social status, lifestyle, opinions, activities and attitudes could be liked and identified with. People have a tendency to like those whom they consider as similar to themselves. For example, Lalitaji of Surf ad is portrayed as a typical housewife who is concerned with managing the family budget.

A source may be considered as high on one dimension of credibility, such as competence but low on another. In today's political scenario, many of the politicians are considered as experts of the game, but biased in their viewpoints. A motorcycle ad showed Sachin Tendulkar as the endorser. He is very famous and probably the best cricket player in the world, but as far as expertise about motorcycles goes, the consumers are not sure. They may also wonder if Sachin Tendulkar would really be using a motorcycle instead of some really expensive cars. Many may consider that the advertiser paid money to get the endorsement.

Besides the familiarity and likability (called a 'Q' rating), other types, such as celebrity, expertise, a typical satisfied consumer and announcer must also be considered in selecting an endorser.

Source Expertise: Research findings show that expert and trustworthy endorsers are more persuasive than others considered less knowledgeable or trustworthy. A credible source's message influences beliefs, opinions, attitudes and behaviour because the audience believe that information from such a source is accurate and becomes integrated in the belief system of individuals and may be maintained even after the message source is forgotten. An expert is likely to be the best choice when the product nature is technical and consumers need to be assured about safety and reliability. This is a typically high-involvement decision situation and consumers need solid reassurance.

Marketers use a number of approaches to communicate source expertise. Endorsers are often chosen for their expertise and experience in a particular product or service area. The sources can be scientists, doctors, professors, engineers, athletes, famous musicians, artists, a typical housewife and many others. Research shows that celebrity endorsers are most persuasive when they are knowledgeable, qualified and experienced to talk about what they are endorsing.

Source Trustworthiness: Expertise is fine, but consumers must also be convinced about the expert's trustworthiness. Finding endorsers with an image of being trustworthy is at times difficult. Such figures hesitate to endorse a brand because of the potential effect on their reputation and image. It often helps if trustworthy individuals say things that are not only favourable to the brand but also talk about some insignificant limitation of the product, as no product can be thought to be one hundred per cent perfect. This is making a two-sided argument, which is generally more effective with a literate audience. Michael A. Kamins is of the opinion that a two-sided argument by the endorser works better than one-sided argument in an ad. To impart an aura of trustworthiness, advertisers sometimes use disguised brands, which the endorser compares. Most consumers are sceptical of such techniques, so they have very limited value in enhancing perceptions of trustworthiness.

Another approach to enhancing credibility is to use the company chairman or chief executive officer as the spokesperson in the firm's advertising. Many advertisers believe that the ultimate commitment to quality and customer service is to use *CEO* or the company president as the spokesperson. Eric Reidenback and Robert Pitts have suggested that the use of company president or *CEO* can improve consumer attitudes and increase the likelihood that they will enquire about the company's product or service. For example, the ad of Khaitan Marathon fan used the Khaitan chairman as the spokesperson.

Marketers use a typical satisfied consumer (Lalitaji in Surf ad), which often is the best choice when consumers strongly identify with the role involved. A typical satisfied consumer is considered as sincere and trustworthy. In case of some personal care products, the ad depicts two friends involved in a conversation about how a particular product or brand brought about the most desirable but unbelievable change. To add an element of maximum naturalness in the situation, it is useful to use a hidden camera and capture the natural reactions of the endorsers with which the audience can identify. Research shows that an endorser's effectiveness is related to the type of product being endorsed. To select a professor type to endorse a detergent is quite meaningless. Choosing an attractive female film star to endorse a skincare product makes much sense but care should be taken to assess in a pre-test that the endorser does not detract the audience attention from the product message.

Limitations of Credible Source

A number of research studies have shown that a high credibility source is not always an asset and a low credibility source is not necessarily a liability. Both types of sources can be equally effective when they argue for a position opposed to their own best interest. A highly credible source is particularly influential when the audience is not in favour of the ad message. But when the audience's initial attitude is favourable or neutral, a highly credible source is less important.

According to Darlene B. Hannah and Brian Strenthl, a low credibility source may be as effective as a highly credible source because of *sleeper effect.* It has been suggested that because of *sleeper effect,* the persuasive impact of a message increases with the passage of time. The explanation is that though the initial ad exposure effect of low credibility source is negative, with the passage of time this negative association breaks down resulting in an increase in the overall message impact over time. Noel Capon and James Hulbert, however, have reported that many studies have failed to demonstrate the sleeper effect. Advertisers usually feel more comfortable with using credible sources and consider it a safer and more reliable strategy.

Source Attractiveness: Attractiveness of a source surrounds similarity, familiarity and likability. Similarity is an assumed resemblance between the source and the members of audience and familiarity means the knowledge of the source through exposure. Likability is the affection developed for the message source as a result of physical appearance and behavioural aspects. Consumers often admire the source's looks and other personality traits and thus the source's attractiveness becomes persuasive through a process of *identification.* This means that the audience develops a need to search for some type of resemblance or relationship with the source.

The identification with source helps in developing similar beliefs, attitudes, preferences, or behaviour. Messages coming from someone, with whom consumers identify are often more persuasive. Advertisers use slice-of-life commercials and hope that the consumer tells herself/himself, "I can see myself in that situation." A health-insurance commercial, for example, showed an emergency situation requiring the patient's immediate hospitalisation. The expenses involved were expected to be high but the patient's wife is not worried because she had already bought that insurance policy for her family. Many consumers are likely to realise that this is a familiar situation for middle class families and they may identify with the patient's wife. This can help to establish a bond of similarity between the source and the target audience, increasing the source's persuasiveness in communicating the message.

Advertisers use celebrities as endorsers to break through the advertising clutter. They believe that celebrities have stopping power and draw attention to advertising messages. For instance, commercials that use Sachin Tendulkar or Shahrukh Khan as the endorsers are more likely to be effective in capturing the attention of the target audience. Marketers think that a popular celebrity cannot only influence the audience feelings, attitudes and purchase behaviour positively, but can also enhance the product image or performance in consumers' perception.

Overexposure: According to Valerie Folkes, consumers are often sceptical of endorsers because they know that the endorsers are paid to appear in an ad. This problem is relatively more serious when the same endorser appears in ads by different companies, leading to overexposure. Marketers often include some clause in the contract banning the endorser from appearing in any other ad for a period of time to check overexposure, but such clauses are generally expensive. When a celebrity appears in many different ads, the credibility of the endorser goes down. It is not unusual, to view in TV commercials in our country the same rather senior looking lady in the role of a mother, or mother-in-law endorsing a detergent, a cooking medium, a hair-oil or an Ayurvedic cough-remedy. The same familiar faces are seen in too many ads for different products. The point being emphasised is that consumers are unlikely to be impressed with such ads.

Likability: Advertisers often use physically attractive persons in their ads as a passive or decorative model to compel audience attention. Attractiveness generates positive influence and can lead to favourable evaluations of products as well as ads. The relevance and suitability of the model depends on the nature of the product. For example, Cindy Crawford appears in Revlon ads. Since physical appearance is quite relevant for cosmetics and fashion clothing, attractive female models are more appropriate for such products.

Message Execution Style

The message needs to be powerfully presented with regard to headline, copy, visuals, colour, sounds, and non-verbal cues. William Bernbach strongly believed that the element of message execution is just as important as the message. There are various ways in which a message can be presented in different promotion mix elements, such as factual message, scientific or technical evidence, testimonial, demonstration, comparison, slice-of-life, lifestyle, fantasy, humour, etc.

Communications Media

In an advertising context, the medium means the channel used to communicate the messages, for example, the broadcast media and the print media. Both these media are non-personal in nature. The various media used by advertisers to communicate with audiences are different in a number of aspects, such as the type of audience, the number of audience they can reach, costs and qualitative factors, etc. There are basic differences among media concerning the rate and the manner in which the information is communicated and can be processed by audiences. When the readers are in a position to read as long as they desire and process the ad message at their own convenience, such as ads appearing in newspapers, magazines, or direct mail, the information processing is 'self-paced'. On the other hand and in sharp contrast, the information from broadcast media of television and radio cannot be processed at the audiences' convenience because it is 'externally paced' and the rate of transmission of the messages is controlled by the medium itself. These differences in the processing rate for print and broadcast media are important and have significant implications for advertisers in media choice. In case of personal selling, the salesperson is the message carrier and can make adjustments according to the situation and customer requirements. This allows face-to-face dialogue between the salesperson and the customer.

Print media offers the advantage of being self-paced and makes it easier for the message recipients to read and process a detailed and complex ad message. It is often advantageous for advertisers to use print media in case of high-involvement products that require a rather lengthy copy in an attempt to communicate detailed information. Broadcast media, in most cases, are more appropriate for shorter messages. For example, TV is more suitable when pictorial information along with words and movement is important. Often shorter and attention arresting messages on broadcast media are followed by print ads to furnish more detailed and complex information. For immediate recognition of the ad message in print, advertisers use the same version of the ad as in broadcast media.

Marshall McLuhan says, "The medium is the message." This means that an ad message is interpreted and influenced by the environment in which it is received and communicates an image that is independent of the message content. This effect is known as *qualitative media effect.* For example, the ad for a designer dress for women is likely to have more of an impact in a magazine like *Femina* or *Vogue* than *India Today* or *Reader's Digest.* The image of media vehicle is independent of the type of message it carries and can have significant effect on reactions to message.

The nature of a broadcast media programme in which the commercial appears can also affect the consumers' reactions. Marvin E. Goldberg and Gerald J. Gorn have reported that consumers react more positively to TV commercials seen during happy programmes than those evoking sadness. For example, Coca-Cola never advertises during TV news-breaks because bad news is inconsistent with its image. It also does not advertise during programmes of excessive violence because it thinks that the image of Coca-Cola is of a fun and joy product. In general, advertisers tend to avoid programmes that are more likely to create a bad mood among the audience. Huge amounts of money are spent to advertise on popular sports programmes, such as Olympic Games, World Cups and Grand Prix, etc., where positive mood is generated.

Advertisers are also concerned with clutter in media environment. Besides the actual programmes in broadcast media, there are large numbers of commercials competing for the consumers' attention. This clutter is quite annoying to consumers and poses difficulties to advertisers in effectively communicating ad messages. The problem is more intense during prime time or popular TV shows due to the increasingly popular trend of shorter commercials of 10 or 15 seconds duration.

Types of Communications Systems

Different communications systems vary in complexity, level of communicator and receiver contact, feedback time and adjusting to feedback. The types of communication can be basically classified under two heads, interpersonal communication and impersonal communication. The impact and influence of each differs significantly.

Interpersonal Communication: Communication occurring at a personal level between two or more people is termed as interpersonal communication. This communication may be face to face between two people, on the telephone, or through mail.

Informal communication concerning products or services is more likely between two friends. Such word-of-mouth communication is likely to be highly persuasive because one friend apparently has nothing to gain from the other friend's future reactions. For this reason, marketers realise that positive word of mouth about their product or service can be very beneficial. On the other hand, negative word of mouth can be disastrous, more so because it is difficult for marketers to control this situation. In many situations of high-involvement purchases or before buying services, consumers often rely more on informal communication.

FIGURE 13.6

Characteristics of Different Types of Communications Systems

Communication	Characteristics			
Types of Communications	Complexity	Contact	Feedback time	Adjustments
Mass Communication	High	Low	Long	Low
Interpersonal	Low	High	Short	High
Organisational	Moderate	Moderate	Moderate	Moderate
Public Communication	High	Low	Long	Moderate

Formal interpersonal communication takes place between a salesperson and a potential customer. The salesperson is the sender of the message and the customer is the receiver. This communication, when face-to-face, tends to be more effective because the salesperson can immediately notice the customer's reaction, verbal or non-verbal, indicating whether the intended message is received. In case of telephonic communication, only the words or voice tones, etc., do provide quick feedback. Mail also permits feedback but it is slower and much depends on the receiver's willingness and ability to answer.

Marketers are increasingly realising that non-verbal messages are sometimes more important than verbal messages particularly in personal selling and advertising.

Feedback, both verbal and non-verbal, in interpersonal communications, enables the message initiator to have some indication concerning acceptance of message and if required, the sender can explain, repeat, or modify the message in more detail. Marketing communicators are generally quite attentive to feedback and modify messages based on what they see or hear from the audience. It is only through feedback that the message initiator can know the impact of intended message, and for this reason feedback has been shown as an integral part of communications model.

Impersonal Communication: Communications directed to large and scattered audience is called impersonal communications. An example of impersonal communications is mass communication, such as advertising or publicity. There is no direct contact between the sender and the receiver. The organisations, both for profit and non-profit, are usually the source of mass communications. They develop and transmit suitable messages through specific departments or spokespersons. These messages are usually meant to reach targeted audience or audiences to inform, influence, or persuade them. For example, a toilet soap or detergent marketer may wish to persuade individuals and households to use its brand of toilet soap or detergent. Generally, the objective of marketing communications is to induce purchase of a product, to create a positive attitude toward its product, to impart the product a symbolic meaning, or to convince that it can satisfy consumers' needs or wants in a better way than the competitive products.

The typical mass media used are newspapers, magazines, billboards, radio, television and transit media, etc. Mass communication is used both by profit and non-profit organisations. Marketing organisations use mass communication usually for commercial purposes, while non-profit organizations' objectives are social or cultural in nature.

In case of mass communication, feedback is just as important as in interpersonal communications. Since large sums of money are involved in mass communications, most managers consider feedback quite essential in this case than in interpersonal communication.

Communications initiating organisations must develop some reasonably reliable method to determine whether the messages are reaching the intended audience, understood in a proper manner and successful in achieving the set objectives. Generally, the inferences are drawn based on indirect methods. How the audiences respond toward an advertised product or service is inferred from the results. If the response shows positive results, it is concluded that the message has been persuasive.

Marketing companies often try to measure the effectiveness of their messages by conducting audience research. The objectives may be to know which newspapers are read, which television programmes are watched, or which ads does the target audience remember.

In developed and many developing countries, new means of *interactive communication* permit the audiences of mass media to provide direct feedback. Some television news programmes conduct opinion polls by requesting viewers to use a toll free number to register reactions such as agreement or disagreement about an important issue of the day. Similarly, direct marketers often ask viewers to ring for information or place the order on the telephone. With increasing use of Internet, many companies with websites provide product information and accept orders from customers. Many companies provide toll free numbers for the convenience of customers to discover and correct any problems as swiftly as possible to maintain brand image and reliability.

Budget Allocation to Marketing Communications

Rarely, if ever, are theoretical approaches to budgeting used. In practice, firms use one or more methods developed through practice and experience that have been somewhat resistant to change for more than a decade. Some firms use more than one method, and approaches to budgeting vary among companies depending on size and sophistication of the company.

FIGURE 13.7

Top-down and build-up budgeting approaches

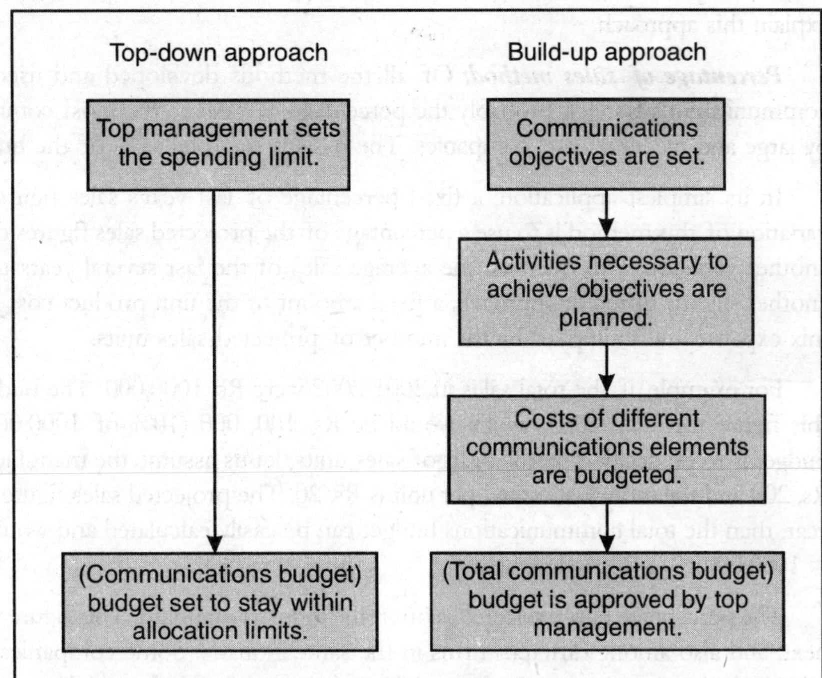

In practice, companies use two totally different approaches to budget setting, **top-down approach** and **build-up approach** (also called bottom-up approach). In case of top-down approach, the budgetary amount is established by higher management and passed down to various departments. There is no real theoretical base for this approach. Top-down methods of budgeting include the affordable method, arbitrary allocation, percentage of sales, and competitive parity method.

Top-down methods are judgmental in approach and the budget is apparently not linked to the objectives and the strategies decided to attain them. The build-up approach takes into account the company's communications objectives and budget is allocated on the basis of what is considered essential to accomplish the goals. This approach includes objective and task method, and quantitative models.

The affordable method (also called **all-you-can-afford method**): This is quite a simple method. After all other allocations have been made to cover other relevant company expenditures whatever is left is allocated to communications considering that, this is what the firm can afford to spend. No consideration is given to what is expected of communications. One may reasonably think that the chances of under or overspending are high with this method.

This approach is fairly common among small firms; high-tech firms in particular focus on new product development and engineering and believe that if the product were good it would sell on its own. Surprisingly, this method often produces good results. If a company is doing proper allocation to other elements of business, then probably the amount left over for communications is adequate to meet the company's advertising needs.

The thinking seems to be "we can't be hurt with this method as we are allocating what we can afford and not get into any financial problems." This method is not based on sound decision-making principles.

Arbitrary allocation: This method of budget allocation seems to have no theoretical basis. The management determines the budget on the basis of what is felt to be necessary, however, there are no criteria to defining what is really meant by "necessary" in the context of advertising budget allocation. This method does not offer any advantages but is used by many firms. It lacks any systematic thinking that may reflect some relationship with advertising objectives. Probably the managers believe that some amount should be spent on advertising and pick up a figure as advertising budget. Apparently there is no basis to explain this approach.

Percentage of sales method: Of all the methods developed and used to determine the marketing communications budget, probably the percentage of sales is the most commonly used method, especially by large and medium sized companies. The basis is the total sales of the brand or product.

In its simplest application, a fixed percentage of last year's sales figure is allocated as the budget. A variation of this method is to use a percentage of the projected sales figures of the next year as the base. Yet another variation is to calculate the average sales of the last several years to decide budget allocation. In another slightly different approach, a fixed amount of the unit product cost is taken as the communication mix expense and multiplied by the number of projected sales units.

For example, if the total sales in 2001-2002 were Rs. 1000,000. The budget may be decided as 10% of this figure for 2002-2003, which would be Rs. 100, 000 (10% of 1000,000 = 100,000). In case the ad budget is to be decided on the basis of sales units, let us assume the manufacturing cost per pair of jeans is Rs. 200 and the money allocated per unit is Rs. 20. The projected sales figure is 50,000 jeans for the coming year, then the total communications budget can be easily calculated and would be Rs.1000,000 (50,000 ´ 20 = 1000,000).

The percentage figure selected is often the industry standard. This figure varies from one industry to the next, and also among different firms in the same industry. Some companies allocate a small percentage of sales as the communications budget, while some others decide for a higher percentage. Actual rupee amounts spent vary considerably depending on the individual company's total sales figure. If the company's sales are substantially high, even a small percentage figure would mean significantly more spending on communications compared to another company with lower sales figures in the same industry.

Those who favour percentage of sales method point out that it is simple, straightforward, easy to implement and the expenditures are directly related to the funds available. If a company's sales were more in the last year, presumably more funds are available to be spent on communications this year. It is safe and ad spending remains within reasonable limits, sales increases will lead to budget increase and sales decreases will result in reduced budget. Regardless whether past sales or the projected sales are taken as the basis for calculation, it is easy to arrive at the budget figure. Unless there are unprecedented changes in sales, managers will have a fair idea of the budget parameters.

There are some serious disadvantages as well with percentage of sales method. The basic premise of this method is that sales are the cause of advertising, or just another element of promotion mix that help generate sales. It ignores the possibility that sales may decline because of too little communications, or that promotion mix may take advantage of rising sales potential. What if an aggressive firm wishes to allocate more funds to marketing communications? Percentage of sales method ignores this possibility, which often may be the need in marketing warfare. This is possible only if the manager is willing to deviate from the industry standards in allocating more funds to marketing communications.

Since the communications budget is dependent on sales only, decrease in sales decreases the budget at a time when increase in budget may be most needed. Reduced budget may further push the sales trend downward. Robert Settle and Pamela Alreck have reported that some of the successful companies spent additional funds during recession and achieved higher growth in sales and market share compared to those who decreased the advertising budget.

Marlboro cigarettes were introduced in 1920s. The brand share was only one per cent in early 1950s. The company invested heavily in building brand image in 1954 (cowboy country) and now the brand share among young smokers is in excess of 60% in the USA.

Perhaps the most effective way to use percentage of sales method is to examine not only the past sales figures but also the forecasted sales.

Competitive parity method: Many advertisers base their promotion mix budget allocation on competitor's expenditures. Such information is easily available in trade journals and business magazines. Adopting this approach, managers decide budget amounts by matching competitor's percentage-of-sales allocations. The logic behind this approach is that the collective wisdom of the firms probably generates communications budgets that are quite close to optimal. Not everyone would be too far from what is adequate in a given industry. This method also takes into view the competition leading to stability in the market-place and minimising the chances of promotional wars.

There are disadvantages in using competitive parity method. First, it ignores the fact that each firm allocates budget to accomplish specific communications objectives to solve certain problems, or to take advantage of the present or emerging opportunities. The inherent assumption seems to be that all the firms have similar communications objectives, and their allocations are correct, which may be far from reality. Second, the method assumes that all firms will have equally effective communications programmes because the expenditures are similar and ignores the contributions of media and creative executions.

There is simply no guarantee that what the firms in the industry spend on promotion mix is the optimal level and that they will continue to pursue their existing strategies. The market realities indicate that conditions do change over time and the chances are that the firms may not be spending at the optimal level. The situations of individual firms are quite likely to be sufficiently unique and the practices of the competitors should not be followed.

The information on competitive promotional expenditure is available only after the money has been spent and there is no reason to believe that a competitor will not increase or decrease its own expenditures, regardless of what other firms do. Coca-Cola and Pepsi have already shown that promotional wars are likely to continue when strong competitors respond to each other's increased outlays.

Competitive parity method is quite popular among firms but it is used in conjunction with percentage-of-sales or some other methods. It is always wise not to ignore what the competition is up to, but to emulate them blindly could be disastrous.

Some of these top-down methods are popular and commonly used and some others are used less frequently. The purpose is to acquaint the reader with the advantages and limitations of these methods. The major shortcoming of top-down methods is that their approach is judgmental and leads to predetermined budget allocations, which may have no relationship with communications objectives and formulated strategies to accomplish them.

It seems more logical to approach budgeting by first considering what the company's promotional objectives are and then allocate whatever money is deemed necessary to accomplish these objectives.

Objective and task method: Setting objectives and budget decision are linked together and should be considered simultaneously. For example, it does not make sense to have an objective of creating awareness among 200 million audiences in the target market unless the firm is prepared to allocate minimal budget amount required to achieve this goal. The objective and task method is based on *build-up approach*. Three steps need to be taken:

- Defining the communications objectives to be accomplished,
- Deciding specific strategies and tasks necessary to achieve them, and
- Estimating the costs involved in putting these strategies and tasks in operation.

The total of all the associated costs is the base to determine the advertising budget.

Implementation of objective and task method in determining the communications budget requires a higher degree of managerial involvement. The whole process must be monitored throughout keeping in view, how well the objectives are attained and suitable changes in strategies made, if deemed is necessary. This approach represents an attempt to introduce intervening variables such as awareness, knowledge, or attitude formation, etc., which are presumed to be indicators of immediate and future sales.

The major difficulty is to determine which are those specific tasks required and the costs associated with each. For instance, if the objective is to accomplish an awareness level of 60% among target audience, what specifically are those tasks that need to be performed to achieve this level of awareness? How much will it cost to perform these tasks? It is difficult to know precisely what is required. Past experience, though, serves as a good guide in case of existing products.

The method does not rely on past sales figures, forecasted sales, what the competition spends, and considers only those factors, which are under the marketer's control. This budget is also viewed as appropriate for setting method is particularly well suited to new product introduction when communications must be developed more or less from scratch. It is difficult to implement this method, however, it is fairly popular among large companies.

The experimental approach: The promotion or brand manager uses tests and experiments in one or more selected market areas. The purpose is to determine the impact of input variations that might be used. The feedback data from these experiments and tests is used in determining the non-personal methods of communications budget. A brand may be simultaneously tested in several market areas with similar population, level of brand usage and brand share. Different expenditure levels are kept for each market. Brand awareness and sales levels, etc., are measured before, during, and after the test in each market. Results are compared and estimates can be developed on how the budget variations might influence the communications results nationwide. The managers may decide any level of budget depending on the firm's advertising objectives. Apparently, the experimental approach removes the difficulties faced by other budgeting methods.

The major drawbacks of this approach are the expenses and time involved. The advertiser also cannot control the environmental variables that may influence the outcome of such tests. The development and use of quantitative techniques, which are often used in deciding advertising and other budget allocations but have met with limited success.

Mathematical models are far from perfect and have not been able to get wide acceptance in the industry. Many firms lack such capabilities and also the process is expensive and time consuming. Normally, quantitative models are limited to larger companies with strong computer and statistical departments.

There is no universally accepted method; companies differ in their approaches to determining the promotional budgets. All methods suffer from one or the other drawback, however the use of objective-and-task method seems to be on the increase. Another method that is relatively popular is the percentage-of-sales method. Most companies in practice generally use some combination of approaches to arrive at a more useful and relatively accurate budget figure.

Marketing Communications Mix

The major elements of marketing communications mix (also called promotion mix) include advertising, sales promotion, personal selling, public relations and publicity, and direct marketing. Each element of communications mix has its own unique attributes and associated costs.

Advertising: Advertising is any paid form of non-personal mass communication through various media to present and promote products, services, and ideas, etc. by an identified sponsor.

Advertising can be extremely cost effective because it can reach a large population at a low cost per person and the message can be repeated several times. TV commercials combine movement, visuals, sound, and colour. A company can attempt to enhance its own image and that of its brand by including celebrity endorsers in its ads appearing in various media.

TV advertising is expensive in terms of actual target audience reached. TV commercials are usually very brief to furnish meaningful information to audience. Advertising can rarely provide rapid feedback, measuring its effect on sales is difficult. Advertising clutter in almost all media is making advertising less capable of attracting consumer attention.

Sales Promotion: More recently, the Council of Sales Promotion Agencies has offered a more comprehensive definition, "*Sales promotion is a marketing discipline that utilises a variety of incentive techniques to structure sales-related programmes targeted to customers, trade, and/ or sales levels that generate a specific, measurable action or response for a product or service.*"

Examples of sales promotions include free samples, discounts, rebates, coupons, contests and sweepstakes, premiums, scratch cards, exchange offers, early bird prizes, various trade deals, etc. All such offers generally include specified limits, such as offer expiry date or a limited quantity of merchandise. Sales promotions are aimed at either increasing immediate sales, to increase support among marketer's sales force, or gain the support of resellers of company product.

Personal Selling: Personal selling is a face-to-face paid personal communication and aims to inform and persuade prospects and customers to purchase products, services, or accept ideas of issues. It involves more specific communication aimed at one or several persons.

Personal selling is most effective but also more expensive than other promotion mix elements. It provides immediate feedback, allowing sellers to adjust their sales messages to improve the impact on customers. Personal selling helps sales people to determine and respond to customers' information needs and also interpret body language.

Public Relations and Publicity: Public relations is a broad set of communication activities employed to create and maintain favourable relationships with employees, shareholders, suppliers, media, educators, potential investors, financial institutions, government agencies and officials, and society in general, such as annual reports, brochures, events sponsorship, sponsorship of various programmes beneficial for society.

Publicity is a tool of public relations. It is non-personal mass communication, but not paid for by the benefiting organisation for the media space or time. It appears in the form of news story about an organisation, its products, or activities. Some common tools of publicity include news releases, press conferences, and feature articles.

Unpleasant situations arising as a result of negative events may precipitate unfavourable public reactions for an organisation. To minimise the negative effects of such situations leading to unfavourable coverage, companies have policies and procedures in place to manage help any such public relations problems.

Direct Marketing: Direct marketing is vending products to customers without the use of channel members. It is a system by which firms communicate directly with target customers to generate the response or transaction. The response may be to generate an inquiry, a purchase, or even a vote. Direct marketing uses a set of direct-response media, such as direct mail, telephone, interactive TV, print, Internet, etc. Through these media, direct marketers implement the communication process.

Most companies use primarily conventional promotion mix elements to move products through intermediaries, many companies are adopting direct marketing as well to reach customers directly to generate immediate behavioural response.

Selection of Promotional Mix

Different organisations vary in their composition of promotion mix. No matter which element of promotion mix or a combination they choose, they aim to inform, persuade, or move customer closer for making a buying decision. Depending on the type of customers and the kind of product, consumers sometimes rely to some extent on word-of-mouth communication from personal sources.

Product Characteristics: Promotion mix for non-durable consumer products includes advertising, sales promotion, personal selling, and public relations. Many other products used both by personal consumers and also by industrial buyers such as computers, get advertising, sales promotion, and personal selling. Advertising and personal selling are used for many consumer durable products such as home appliances, autos, tractors, housing, etc. Industrial products, such as aircraft and heavy earth-moving and construction equipment are mainly sold through personal selling.

Product life cycle stage is another consideration. During the introductory stage, advertising and publicity are most cost-effective. Advertising and publicity are powerful tools for creating awareness. Personal selling is very helpful in creating comprehension among consumers and gaining distribution coverage. Sales promotion can induce trial during introductory stage of life cycle. During growth and maturity stages of consumer products, heavy emphasis on advertising becomes necessary and in some cases sales promotion is also used. Industrial products during these stages often require personal selling coupled with sales promotion. During decline stage, firms generally decrease promotional support, particularly advertising.

Market Characteristic: This aspect is particularly important for industrial products. Allocation of promotional funds in order of priority goes to personal selling, advertising, sales promotion, and public relations. If business buyers are located only in certain geographic areas, and are large buyers then personal selling is more cost effective. Companies operating in consumer markets, allocate more funds to sales promotion, advertising, personal selling, and public relations in order of priority. Generally, personal selling is more appropriate for high involvement expensive, complex, and risky products.

Pull and Push Strategies: Promotion mix decisions also depend on the choice of promotion strategy. In case of **pull strategy**, a marketer directs its communications to consumers to develop strong consumer demand for the product or service. This is primarily accomplished through advertising and sales promotion. This induces consumers to ask resellers of the product. Retailers in turn go to wholesalers or the producer to buy the products. This strategy intends to pull the goods down through the channel by creating demand at the consumer level. This strategy suits strong high-involvement brands, when consumers perceive high differentiation between brands, and the brand choice is made before going to the store. With **push strategy**, the manufacturer promotes the product only to the next institution down the marketing channel. Each channel member promotes to the next channel members down the line. This strategy usually involves using personal selling and trade sales promotions to motivate resellers to stock the product and sell the product to consumers. In certain cases, retailers pass on part of the benefit to consumers to clear the stocks early. Push strategy is suitable when the brand loyalty is low, consumers are aware of brand benefits, and purchase decisions are made in the store.

Integrated Marketing Communications

Different marketing and communication functions are generally managed as totally separate entities and such companies do not realise that marketing communication tools should be coordinated for communication effectiveness and present a consistent image to target markets.

Many companies recognise the need for increased strategic coordination of different promotional elements. *Integrated Marketing Communication* (IMC) is an attempt to coordinate various marketing and promotional activities to make marketing communication to target customers more effective and efficient. The first definition of IMC by American Association of Advertising Agencies says:

"... a concept of marketing communications planning that recognises the added value of a comprehensive plan that evaluates the strategic roles of a variety of communication disciplines - for example, general advertising, direct response, sales promotion, and public relations - and combines these disciplines to provide clarity, consistency, and maximum communications impact."

Don E. Schultz, "Integrated Marketing Communications: Maybe Definition Is in the Point of View," *Marketing News* January 18, 1993.

However, Don E. Schultz advocates for an even broader perspective that considers *"all sources of brand and company contact that a customer or prospect has with a product or service.* It requires firms to develop a total marketing communications strategy that recognises how all of a firm's marketing activities, not just promotion, communicate with its customers.

To fully appreciate IMC perspective, one has to look through the consumer's eyes. Many consumers' views of advertising include not only the advertising in TV, print, and other media but they also consider door-to-door selling, shopping bags, and even community sponsored events as advertising. The perceptions of consumers about a company's image, its products, or services depend on a number of other elements than promotion alone. Besides advertising, personal selling, sales promotion, PR/publicity, direct marketing, and messages on the Internet etc., other elements such as, package design, price of the product or service, selected distribution outlets, displays, news reports, word-of-mouth, gossip, experts' opinions, and financial reports also communicate powerfully.

All such communications, whether sponsored or not, create an integrated product in consumer's mind. This means that consumers, on their own, integrate all brand-related messages originating from the company or any other source and this determines their perception of the company.

What marketers must understand is that everything they do or do not do sends a message. Every corporate activity has a message component. According to Duncan and Moriarty, consumers and other stakeholders receive four company/brand related messages (Figure 13.8).

FIGURE 13.8

Say, Do, Confirm Model

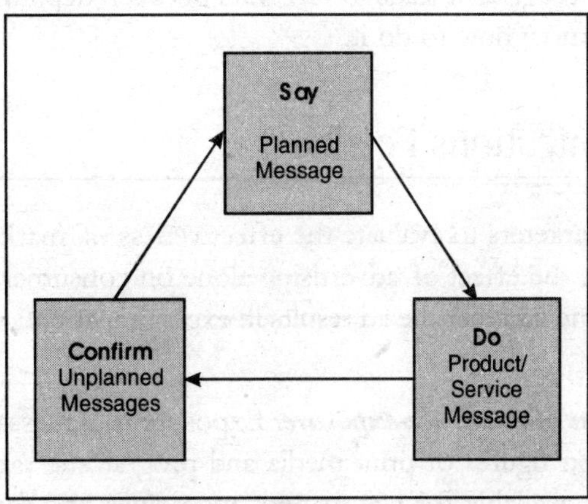

1. ***Planned messages:*** Planned messages are *say* messages, representing what companies say about self. These messages represent typical marketing communications such as advertising, personal selling, sales promotion, direct marketing, publicity, etc. Such messages often have the least impact because they are viewed as marketer controlled and self-serving. Planned messages should aim to accomplish the predetermined set of communications objectives. This is the most basic aspect of Integrated Marketing Communications (IMC).

2. ***Product messages:*** Product or service messages are *do* messages, as they communicate what the company does. Messages from product, its price, and distribution elements are referred to as the product messages. Customers and others receive totally different messages from Rs 75 lakh BMW and Rs 2.36 lakh Maruti 800. Product messages cause great impact because when a product performs as promised, the consumer gets a positive and reinforcing message. On the other and, if there is a gap between the product's performance and the communicated promises, the customer is more likely to get a negative message.

3. ***Service messages:*** Company's employee interactions with consumers also become a source of messages. In many service-providing companies, customer service personnel are supervised by operations, and not marketing. The service rendered sends messages, which have greater impact than the planned messages.

4. ***Unplanned messages:*** Such messages are *confirm* messages as they represent what others say and confirm/not confirm about what the company says and does. Companies have little or no control over the unplanned messages that result from employee gossip, news stories not under the control of the company, comments that traders or competitors pass on, word-of-mouth communications, or major disasters. These unplanned messages, favourable or unfavourable, may influence consumer attitudes quite significantly.

The objectives of integrated marketing communications are to coordinate all of a company's marketing and promotional efforts to project and reinforce a consistent, unified image of the company or its brands to the market-place. The IMC approach is an attempt to improve over the traditional method of treating promotion elements as totally separate activities. IMC is an increasingly helping company to develop most suitable and effective methods to contact customers and other interested groups.

Thomas R. Duncan and Sandra E. Moriarty have called IMC as one of the "new generation" marketing approaches being used by companies to better focus their marketing efforts in acquiring, retaining, and developing relationships with customers and other stakeholders. A very important and fundamental reason, besides others, is the value of strategically integrating different elements of communications functions and take advantage of the resulting synergy among different tools in developing more effective and efficient marketing communication programmes. Experts say that IMC is one of the easiest ways to maximise return on investment in marketing and promotion. Tom Duncan and Steve Everett report that applying IMC in practice is tough as it leads to turf wars between departments and though companies want to adopt this, they do not know how to do it.

Communications Feedback

Feedback helps marketers to evaluate the effectiveness of marketing communication. It is difficult in most cases to determine the effect of advertising alone on consumer purchase behaviour and due to this reason marketers determine whether the ad results in exposure, attention, comprehension, message acceptance and retention.

- ***Measurement of Audience-exposure:*** Exposure to a message can be measured by taking into account the circulation figures of print media and programme rating for broadcast media. These figures are conveniently available for newspapers, magazines and for different broadcast media programmes.

- ***Measurement of Audience-attention:*** These figures are measured by recognition of a message by the audience. Consumers are asked whether they have seen a particular message and can they associate it with a brand or manufacturer. Research agencies conduct recall and recognition tests in case of broadcast media to ascertain whether consumers recalled relevant message regarding the brand or company.
- ***Measurement of Audience-comprehension:*** This is measured with the help of aided or unaided recall tests for specific message points in the communication. Researchers probe consumers to determine the level of comprehension of a message.
- ***Measurement of Audience's Message Acceptance:*** Consumers' attitudes towards the brand are good indicators of message impact. This can be done by measuring their attitudes towards the brand before and after the exposure to ad message. Researchers compare matched groups of consumers exposed to the message and those not exposed to the message to determine the impact of advertisement on audience attitudes.
- ***Measurement of Audience's Message-retention:*** Average consumers are likely to retain a message in their memory if it was successful in making an impact. They do not pay attention to messages that are not relevant to them. They are also likely to forget messages over time unless they are repeated.

William J. McGuire has presented an advertising processing model that depicts the types of feedback that each step can possibly provide. These steps typically assume that as consumers move from exposure to other intervening steps, the probability that they will buy the promoted product increases with each succeeding step (Figure 13.9).

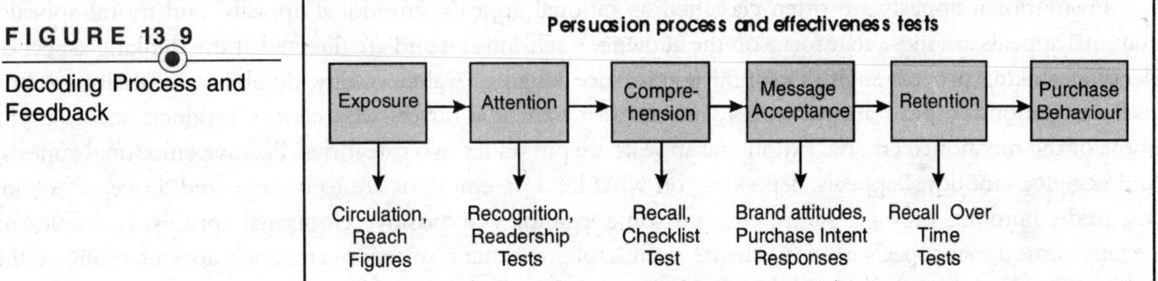

FIGURE 13.9
Decoding Process and Feedback

Technological developments have created opportunities to help in establishing a link between consumers' exposure to company or brand related messages and their subsequent attitudes and purchase behaviour. In case of company products, electronic scanners record sales at checkout counters and furnish useful data.

Despite several developments, it is still difficult to precisely record the impact of advertising and other promotions on consumer purchase behaviour. A major reason is that besides marketing communications, there are several other variables that influence consumers' purchase behaviour.

Summary

The purpose of communications is to directly or indirectly influence individuals, groups, and organisations to facilitate exchanges by informing and persuading one or more audiences to accept a company's products and/or services.

The current view about marketing communications is that it is an interactive dialogue between the organisation and its audiences and that every type of brand contact with customers is important because it communicates something that can strengthen or weaken customers' view of the company.

In any communication there are four basic components: A source, a destination, a medium and a message. The source encodes the desired message so that it will accurately convey the message to the desired destination. The source may use words, pictures, symbols, some kind of familiar body language, or some other recognisable code or signal.

The source must then find a suitable channel or medium through which to transmit the message. To make the message delivery efficient, the channel must have direct access to the receiver and be relatively free from noise and distortion. The decoded message is the outcome of receiver's information processing activities leading to interpretation of thoughts or meanings by the receiver and depends on the relationship between the sender and receiver, the sender's and receiver's experiences, attitudes, values, biases and the context in which the message is perceived.

The element of noise in the communications process refers to any type of unplanned disruption or interference that may hinder the communications. The source of noise may be other competing messages vying for audience attention, sender's difficulty in formulating the intended message. Any of the three factors, selective attention, selective distortion, or selective recall may play a role and as a result of this the audience may not receive the intended message.

The AIDA model suggests that an effective sales presentation should attract attention, gain interest, stimulate desire, and precipitate action (purchase). Hierarchy-of-effects model helps in setting communication objectives and provides a basis for measuring results. This model also suggests that communication produces its effects by moving the consumer through a series of steps in a sequence from initial awareness to ultimate purchase of product or service. This sequential order indicates the basic premise, that communication effects are elicited over a period of time and that a message may not precipitate the desired effects immediately because a series of effects must occur before the consumer possibly moves to the next stage in the hierarchy.

Promotional appeals are often classified as rational appeals, emotional appeals, and moral appeals. Rational appeals are those that focus on the audience's self-interest and are directed at the thinking aspect of decision-making process such as economy, assurance of resale value, quality, durability, reliability, ease of use, etc. Rational appeals are particularly relevant for industrial buyers who choose products according to some of the mentioned criteria. Emotional appeals are put under two categories: Positive emotional appeals, and negative emotional appeals, depending on what kind of emotions are to be triggered. Love, affection, joy, pride, humour, prestige, status, etc., are some examples of positive emotional appeals. Examples of negative emotional appeals are fear, shame, guilt, embarrassment, rejection, etc. Such appeals motivate the audience to do things they should do. Moral appeals attempt to draw audience attention to what is "right." Moral appeals are generally used to urge people to support social causes.

The aim of all marketing communications is to capture audience attention, hold interest, precipitate their desire, and elicit desired action. This requires focusing on four important message issues: What should be said, how should it be said and what would be the message execution style, and who should say it.

Message structure refers to how the elements of a message are organised. A one-sided message mentions only benefits or positive attributes of the product or service. A two-sided message presents not only the strong points of the product or service, but also admits to any weaknesses. The negative part of the information is usually relatively unimportant compared to positive information. When the strongest message arguments are presented at the end of the message, it is called climax order. Drawing a firm conclusion or leaving the conclusion drawing to audience largely depends on the nature of target audience, the type of product or service and the nature of communication situation, for less educated customers drawing a conclusion may be necessary. For a highly involved audience, open-ended messages are more effective than closed-ended specific conclusion in the message.

Companies use different methods to determine promotional budget that include all-you-can-afford, percentage-of-sales, competitive parity, objective-and-task, and experimental methods. The most scientific approach is objective-and-task method.

Major promotion mix elements include advertising, sales promotion, personal selling, public relations publicity, and direct marketing. Each has its advantages and limitations. Advertising is any paid form of non-personal mass communication through various media to present and promote products, services, ideas, etc. by an identified sponsor.

Sales promotion is a marketing discipline that utilises a variety of incentive techniques to structure sales-related programmes targeted to customers, trade, and/or sales levels that generate a specific, measurable action or response for a product or service.

Personal selling is a face-to-face paid personal communication and aims to inform and persuade prospects and customers to purchase products, services, or accept ideas of issues.

Public relations is a broad set of communication activities employed to create and maintain favourable relationships with employees, shareholders, suppliers, media, educators, potential investors, financial institutions, government agencies and officials, and society in general, such as annual reports, brochures, events sponsorship, sponsorship of various programmes beneficial for society. Publicity is a tool of public relations. It is non-personal mass communication, but not paid for by the benefiting organisation for the media space or time. It appears in the form of news story about an organisation, its products, activities, etc.

Direct marketing is vending products to customers without the use of channel members. It is a system by which firms communicate directly with target customers to generate the response or transaction. Selection of promotion mix elements depends on the nature of product and target market characteristics.

Questions for Discussion

1. How would you define marketing communications? What are the main elements of communications process?
2. Explain hierarchy model. For what kind of purchases do these models fail, when it comes to explaining the steps consumers take in making buying decisions?
3. What is message appeal? Illustrate your answer with three examples each of rational and emotional appeals.
4. Emotional appeals are appropriate for what kind of products? Give your reasons.
5. What is the significance of message source?
6. How do market and product characteristics affect promotion mix?
7. What are the different methods for promotion budget determination? Which is the best method, in your view?
8. How do advertising and publicity differ? Which one of these is more effective and why?
9. What is the major strength of sales promotion? Under what situations is sales promotion more appropriate?
10. What is integrated marketing communications? How can a company apply this concept?

Projects

1. A start up, low-budget company wants to market its detergent powder in a phased manner. Suggest what promotional method(s) should it adopt, and why?
2. Collect three print ads, one each for a durable, non-durable, and service product. Identify the appeals used in these ads. Do you think they are appropriate?

3. Advertising aims either at informing, persuading, or reminding consumers about a product or service. For accomplishing each of these objectives, collect three ads that address at least one of these objectives. Do you think the ads are effective?

Bibliography

1. Schramm Wilbur, "How Communication Works, in *The Process and Effects of Mass Communication,* ed. Wilbur Schramm and Donald F. Roberts, 1971.
2. Burke Raymond R. and Thomas K. Srull, "Competitive Interference and Consumer memory for Advertising," *Journal of Consumer Research,* June 15, 1988.
3. Strong E. K., *The Psychology of Selling,* McGraw-Hill, 1925.
4. Lavidge Robert J. and Gary A. Steiner, "A Model for Predictive Measurements of Advertising Effectiveness," *Journal of Marketing,* (October 1961).
5. Rogers Everett M., *Diffusion of Innovation,* (Free Press, 1962).
6. McGuire William J., "The Nature of Attitude and Attitude Change," in *Handbook of Social Psychology,* 2nd. Ed. G. Lintzey and E. Aronson, (Addison Wesley, 1969).
7. Kamins Michael K., "Celebrity and Non-Celebrity Advertising in a Two-Sided Context," *Journal of Advertising Research* (June-July 1989).
8. Reidenback Eric and Roberts Pitts, "Not All CEOs are Created as Advertising Spokespersons: Evaluating the Effective CEO Spokesperson," *Journal of Advertising,* (1986).
9. Hannah Darlene B. and Brian Strenthal, "Detecting and Explaining Sleeper Effect," *Journal of Consumer Research,* (September 1984).
10. Capon Noel and James Hullbert, "The Sleeper Effect: An Awakening," *Public Opinion Quarterly*, (1973).
11. Valerie Folkes, "Recent Attribution Research in Consumer Behaviour: A Review and New Direction," *Journal of Consumer Research,* (March 1988).
12. Settle Robert E. and Linda L. Golden, "Attribution Theory and Advertiser Credibility," *Journal of Marketing Research* (March 1974).
13. Kamins Michael A. and Henry Assael, "Two-Sided versus One-Sided Appeals: A Cognitive Perspective on Argumentation, Source Derogation, and the Effect of Disconfirming Trial and Belief Change," *Journal of Marketing Research,* (June-July 1987).
14. Sawyer Alan G. and Daniel G. Howard, "Effects of Omitting Conclusions in Advertisements to Involved and Uninvolved Audiences," *Journal of Marketing Research,* (November 1991).
15. Mitchell Andrew A., The Effect of Verbal and Visual Components of Advertisements on Brand Attitudes and Attitudes Towards the Advertisement," *Journal of Consumer Research,* (June 1986).
16. Unnava H. Rao and Robert E. Burnkrant, "Am Imagery Processing View of the Role of Pictures in Print Advertisements," *Journal of Marketing Research,* (May 1991).
17. Ray Michael L and William L Wilkie, "Fear: The Potential of an Appeal Neglected by Marketing," *Journal of Marketing,* (January 1970).
18. Strenthal Brian and C. Samuel Craig, "Fear Appeals Revisited and Revised," *Journal of Consumer Research,* (December 1974).
19. Chattopadhyay Amitava and Kunal Basu, "Humour in Advertising: The Moderating Role of Prior Brand Evaluation," *Journal of Marketing Research,* 27 (November 1990).
20. Weinberger Mark G. and Charles S. Gulas, "The Impact of Humour in *Advertising*: A Review," *Journal of Advertising,* (December 1992).

21. Council of Sales Promotion Agencies, "Shaping the Future of Sales Promotion," 1990.
22. McLuhan Marshal, "Understanding Media: The Extensions of Man," (McGraw-Hill, 1966).
23. Madden Thomas J. and Mark C. Weinberger, "Glamour in Advertising: A Practitioner's View," *Journal of Advertising Research,* (August-September 1984).
24. Goldberg Marvin E and Gerald J. Gorn, "Happy and Sad TV Programme: How They Affect Reactions to Commercials," *Journal of Consumer Research,* (December 1987).
25. Settle Robert and Pamela Alreck, "Position Moves Negative Times," *Marketing Communications,* 1988.
26. McGuire William J., "An Information Processing Model of Advertising Effectiveness," in *Behavioural and Management Sciences in Marketing,* ed. Harry J. Davis and Alvin J. Silk, 1978.
27. Council of Sales Promotion Agencies, "Shaping the Future of Sales Promotion," 1990.
28. Thomas R. Duncan and Sandra E. Moriarty, "A Communication-Based Model for Managing Relationships," *Journal of Marketing* 62, (April 1998).
29. Duncan Thomas R. and Sandra E. Moriarty "*Driving Brand Value: Using Integrated Marketing to Manage Stakeholder Relationships,*" McGraw-Hill 1997.

Advertising & Sales Promotion

CHAPTER 14

LEARNING OBJECTIVES

After going through this chapter, you will understand:

- Relationship of product life cycle stage and the type of advertising
- Classification of advertising
- Planning and managing advertising
- Selection of advertising appeals
- Developing a media plan and types of available media
- Evaluation of advertising effectiveness
- What is sales promotion and its types
- Sales promotion planning and evaluation

On the occasion of Superbowl 1984 (American Football event), Apple computer's 60-second commercial introducing Macintosh computer was telecast. Many fans watching the sports event may have missed the historic moment because the commercial was aired during a commercial break, when many viewers went to their refrigerators. It was a tremendous gamble as the commercial was not only bold but also quite unusual, and Apple paid half a million dollars for the airtime. Yet Apple sold nearly 50% more Macintosh computers in the first 100 days than it had projected. It was such a successful commercial that its portions were replayed on news and entertainment shows. Advertising Age magazine in its issue of January 1, 1990 declared the commercial to be the "TV commercial of the decade."

Audiences who viewed the commercial were interested and excited about this new and affordable technology. Just a day after the event, besides thousands of telephone calls to Apple's switchboard from prospects, many consumers went directly to retail outlets looking for the home computer and a substantial percentage of them made spot purchases.

At this time Apple's cofounder, Steven Jobs was the chairman. The process began when Steven Jobs gave the marketing director a newspaper clipping about the marketing of the movie Star Wars. George Lucas, the film's producer, had done such good advance work with marketing and promotion companies to create a big stir when the film was released that it appeared to be an instant hit. Steven Jobs wanted the same kind of marketing for the Macintosh.

The commercial grew out of a brainstorming session for 30-minutes among three top members of Apple's advertising agency, TBWA/Chiat/Day. The key idea was to create a world straight out of George Orwell's novel '1984', in which a Big Brother government watches and regulates every move a citizen makes. Apple wanted audiences to connect the industry giant IBM with Big Brother and to greet the introduction of Apple Macintosh with the same enthusiasm they felt when the rebellious woman in the commercial raced through the audience of clones and smashed the TV screen projecting Big Brother's face.

Everyone in the agency and Apple liked the " big idea," and Apple invested the money to give the commercial feature-film quality production. Apple had planned to introduce the Macintosh at its shareholders' meeting on January 24th, the Superbowl event on January 22nd seemed to be the perfect setting during which to air the commercial. However, Apple's board of directors were concerned about the huge cost of airtime and the company's image and told the marketing department to shelve the idea. Luckily, Apple could not find anyone to buy its airtime, so the commercial was aired. And Macintosh quickly became the only real alternative to IBM personal computers and their clones.

An enthusiastic response of this degree to a single ad is rare. The ad planning and execution was acclaimed as nothing but excellent. However, most cases of advertising take time and generally many ads before the consumers respond in a manner satisfactory to the advertiser. Apple has produced ads that consistently use the underlying theme of "power" that Apple products provide to the consumer.

The history of advertising goes back to nearly 3000 BC. Communication has been a part of the selling process ever since the exchange of goods started between people. The basic reason for using advertising was the same as it is now. Modern advertising is largely a product of the twentieth century. The contribution of modern technology and research has led to high degree of sophistication in advertising.

Advertising is the structured and composed non-personal communication of information, usually paid for and usually persuasive in nature, about organisations, products, services, ideas by identified sponsors through various media.

First, advertising is a highly structured form of communication and employs both verbal and non-verbal elements. These elements are composed to fill predetermined space and time formats that are controlled by the sponsor.

Second, the focus of advertising is directed to groups of people rather than to individuals and for this reason it is non-personal or mass communication. The groups might be personal consumers, organisations, resellers, etc.

Third, most advertising is paid for by sponsors for the media time or space it uses to communicate its messages. However, sometimes public service messages are carried in media for which no payment is made.

Fourth, although most advertising messages are intended to be persuasive to accomplish the desired selling function, some ads appear only to inform people, examples being legal announcements, change of address, obituaries, etc., without any persuasive intent. They are ads all the way because they satisfy other aspects of definition.

Fifth, an ad identifies its sponsor. The identification of the advertiser does not remain unknown. The very purpose of advertising is to create awareness and distinction about a company or brand. The real-world sponsor is legally responsible for the created advertisement. Publicity may not be openly sponsored.

One cannot think that advertising is neutral. All advertisements are controlled by the marketers and are intended to serve the advertiser's interest in some way.

Advertising is an important element of promotion mix in most companies' marketing programmes. Almost all companies, whether large or small, domestic or multinational in the consumer goods, and services marketing and many industrial goods manufacturers use advertising. Most consumer goods companies depend heavily on advertising to sell their products.

Product Life Cycle and Advertising

The developmental stage of a product determines the role of advertising. As products pass through various stages of their life cycle, the manner in which the advertising presents the product to target audiences depends largely upon the degree of a product's acceptance by consumers. Based on the concept of product life cycle, one may differentiate three stages:

Introductory Stage: In this stage, the marketer develops a new product and there is no assurance that consumers will perceive a need for it. Unless consumers perceive a need for the product, it will not sell. The job of advertising is to introduce the idea that the product is better able to meet the consumer needs than the existing solutions. It must effectively communicate that the new product has overcome the limitations of earlier alternatives that consumers tolerated for long. The role of ad message in this stage is to furnish product knowledge, change existing habits, develop new usage, cultivate new standards of living, and implant a new way to look at existing approaches of problem solution.

Competitive Stage: The consumers have accepted the product and the competition has moved into the market-place sooner rather than later. The consumer faces the question, "Which brand should I buy?" Generally, in the early stages of competition, the combined total effect of competitors creates significant growth for the product category. The key objective of advertising is to clearly and convincingly differentiate the company's brand and effectively communicate its position.

Reminder Stage: When products reach maturity in their life cycle and are widely accepted, they are in their reminder stage. Marketers may not feel much need for competitive advertising, as consumers already know all about the product. Some consumers like it and some others don't like it, or may be neutral. However, if marketers do not advertise, consumers are likely to forget about it and switch to other alternatives being advertised regularly. This is sufficient reason to switch to reminder advertising and keep the brand in front of consumers for top-of-mind recall.

Advertising alone almost never "sells" products, services, or ideas. It "**helps**" to sell through persuasion. For any reason, if a product is not available in the distribution outlets, the "greatest advertisement" cannot sell this product. If the consumers perceive that the product is overpriced, or does not meet their requirements, then advertising won't be able to sell such a product. No amount of advertising will persuade consumers to buy a bad product a second time. Advertising cannot sell anything that is not perceived by the audience as needed, wanted, or desired.

Types of Advertising

Scholars have proposed various approaches to classifying the vast variety of advertising. An understanding of these would help managers in choosing the most appropriate type of advertising to achieve their objectives.

Consumer Advertising

Most non-classified advertising is **display advertising** and is found throughout the newspaper and on many magazine pages, and generally uses headlines, illustrations, white space, coupons, and other visual devices besides the copy text. Display ads appear in all sections of the newspaper except the editorial page, obituary page, and classified section. Most newspapers get approximately 70 per cent of the advertising revenues from display advertising. Two types of display advertising in newspapers are **national** and **local**.

National Advertising: The marketer of branded product or service, sold through different outlets in the distribution channel mostly uses this type of advertising. Apparently the term 'national advertising' conveys mass marketing effort. In reality, this does not necessarily mean that the product is sold nationwide. The objective is to communicate brand features, benefits, advantages or uses and to create or reinforce brand image so that consumers will be predisposed to buy it.

National advertisers realise that under certain conditions, it is better to advertise in regional or local media rather than mass media. As more and more national advertisers are able to identify and reach narrowly defined market segments; there would be more regional or local advertising. For example, they may select regional/local newspapers, television stations, radio, or outdoor media because of differences in the regional language. The advertiser would still be classified as a national advertiser as the purpose of the ad is to encourage purchase of the advertised product at any outlet carrying the item. The national advertiser's prime interest is in establishing long-run favourable attitudes and building brand equity.

Retail (Local) Advertising: The manufacturer has little concern where his product is purchased. The goal of the retail advertiser differs from that of national advertiser. The retailer advertises to encourage patronage by consumers and build store loyalty among them. Generally, a retailer is not really concerned with any specific brand. The general approach in retail advertising is "buy at our store." The sale of any specific brand is not the concern of the retailer unlike the national advertiser.

The retailer's advertising must convey the image of the type of store, particularly to attract certain type of consumers. To achieve these objectives, retailers often communicate price information, service and return policies, and the range of merchandise available. Some retailer ads are aimed specifically at building the store traffic. The retailer advertises to precipitate relatively, a quick response to most of this local advertising.

Co-operative Advertising: Manufacturers of consumer durable goods, or speciality products often show special interest in their dealers' advertising. Help to identify the dealers in different geographic markets, ads are put in local media under their names. The manufacturer often provides the dealer with the material and guidelines to develop ads for print, television, or radio commercials. This ensures that the message is in line with, what the manufacturer wants to communicate. The manufacturer and the dealer usually share the media costs and hence, the name 'co-operative advertising'.

End-Product Advertising: There are many products that are rarely purchased direct by consumers. They are usually bought as a part or ingredient in other products. For example, branded products such as Teflon (DuPont), Pentium (Intel), Samsung Monitors, and many others are used in the manufacture of other end products. Advertising of such products is called 'end-product advertising' (also called *branded-ingredient advertising*). Manufacturers whose branded parts or ingredients are used in producing usually other branded or unbranded consumer products, often undertake this type of advertising. Successful end-product advertising helps to create demand for the ingredient that helps in the sale of another product, such as Intel promotes its Pentium processors. The sustained existence of consumer demand for such ingredients encourages companies to use them in their consumer products. End-product advertising may take national or international dimensions and can be very advantageous to companies who can successfully do it.

Direct-Response Advertising: This type of advertising encourages the consumer to respond either by providing feedback to the advertiser or placing the order with the advertiser either by telephone, mail, or the Internet. Such advertising uses direct mail, catalogues, direct-response print advertising, direct-response broadcast advertising, telephone, and Internet. Some of these methods to reach the consumer are viewed as part of sales promotional techniques.

Classified Ads: Classified ads are arranged under subheads that describe the class of goods or the needs, ads seek to satisfy. Such ads provide a community market place for goods, services, and opportunities of every type, from real estate, autos to matrimonial, domestic help, coaching, employment, and business opportunities etc. Classified display ads run in the classified section of the newspaper but use illustrations, larger type sizes, white space, borders, colour, and photos. For example, *Ascent* section of *Times of India* is devoted to employment ads and in some ads, it uses colour and photos, too.

Advertising to Business and Profession

This type of advertising is aimed at re-sellers, and professionals such as, architects, lawyers and doctors, etc. The media used is direct mail or professional journals.

Trade Advertising: Trade advertising is used to promote products to re-sellers, encouraging them to stock the product. Manufacturers emphasise the profitability to retailers and the consumer demand that will ensure the high turnover of the product. In case of mass distributed products, the manufacturer is interested in increasing the number of retail stores that stock the brand. The objective is to achieve maximum distribution. In this situation, the advertising is aimed to create brand awareness among re-sellers, which is followed by sales people or by offering some trade incentive.

Industrial Advertising: Manufacturers are buyers of machinery, equipment, raw materials and consumer products etc., needed in producing the finished products they sell. The advertisements of this category use media such as, industry publications, direct mail, telephone, Internet, and trade fairs.

Industrial advertising is directed at a specialised and relatively small-sized target audience. Though the buyers are few, the purchases by each one are relatively huge. The audience of such ads is composed of experts in their fields and hence advertisements contain details and specifications of products meant for a specific manufacturing segment. This helps to reduce personal selling costs, efforts, and speeds up sales of industrial products.

Professional Advertising: Professional advertising is directed towards people who are not the final consumers. Many professionals such as architects, engineers, and medical consultants, etc. often take the final purchase-decision on behalf of their clients. The advertising media comprises professional journals, direct mail, and in rare instances mass media.

Corporate or Institutional Advertising: Corporate advertising is an extension of public relations and does not promote any specific product or service. Corporate advertising aims to build and maintain the image of a company or an institution. Organisations and brands are meant to strengthen mutual credibility. Brands by themselves often lose their significance unless their association with the marketer produces authenticity.

The corporate image is something that customers perceive when the name of the company is seen or heard. Corporate communications reach several audiences, such as company employees, current customers, potential customers, non-users of company products or services, channel members, shareholders, suppliers, financial institutions, and government agencies.

Major changes in the economic and political scenario, affecting business and industry may often warrant *advocacy* or issue based advertising. Advocacy advertising refers to company's views on issues that affect its business and to protect its position in the market place. In other cases the company presents its viewpoint about a national cause such as the literacy movement or the company may list its social contributions, or emphasise its socially oriented policies. Such advertising usually does not attempt to sell anything directly but gives a face to the company and attempts to develop a positive relationship by influencing public's reaction towards the company and its products, services, sales force, and job offers. Much of the contemporary, corporate advertising serves as the support function to promote a company's products or services.

Some of the important objectives of corporate advertising include:

- To create and maintain corporate identity in public.
- To counter negative attitudes towards the company.
- To enhance company image.
- To associate the company with some worthwhile national or social cause.
- To overcome negative company image.

Non-product Advertising

Idea Advertising: Advertising being a powerful communication tool is often used to influence special interest groups and sway public opinion. Environmental issues, population explosion, declining natural resources, road safety measures, child labour, human rights, dowry, equal status to women, and many other issues are examples for which mass media advertising has increased in the recent years.

Service Advertising: Marketing of services is on the increase as more and more specialists in different fields are available. There is a need for medical and healthcare services, financial and educational services, childcare services, hospitality services, transportation services, repair and maintenance services, psychiatric and counselling services, domestic help, and many other services. The need for a variety of services seems to be ever increasing.

Service advertising is more difficult than product advertising. What the service provider is trying to sell is basically the expertise in some fields. Services are intangible, inseparable, and there is no transfer of ownership. Service industries are so alike that it is difficult to meaningfully differentiate among competitors.

Surrogate Advertising

The dictionary meaning of 'surrogate' is a delegate; a substitute, a person appointed to act for another. In advertising context when the laws of a country do not permit advertising of a certain product category, the advertisers take the shelter of brand extension. For example, advertising of alcoholic drinks in India is not permitted. To bypass this, some manufacturers of whisky or similar products launched brands of soda under the same brand name as that of their popular whisky, such as Bagpiper soda, or McDowell soda.

Important Players in Advertising

There are five major players in Advertising: Advertisers, advertising agencies, media organisations, collateral service providers, and target audiences.

Advertiser: It is an organisation or individual that usually initiates the process of advertising. The advertiser is the final authority, who makes final decisions regarding the target market, the media that will carry the ad message, the size of the advertising budget, and the duration of the ad campaign. Without an advertiser, there would be no advertising.

Advertising Agency: Most advertisers hire an outside independent agency to plan, develop, and implement part or all their advertising efforts. Advertisers use an outside agency because they believe the agencies have strategic and creative expertise, media knowledge, talent, and ability to negotiate good deals for the advertiser.

A typical *full-service agency* has five functional departments: Accounts management, creative services, media services, marketing services, and administration department.

Creative boutiques are small agencies and specialise only in preparing creative execution of client marketing communications.

Media-buying services specialise in buying media for clients. They often deliver media related services espouser and knowledge at a low cost because they buy large chunks of media and get discounts from media organisations.

Industry-focussed agencies concentrate on certain fields such as agriculture, healthcare, drugs and pharmaceuticals, and computers etc.

Some of the large organisations have their own *advertising department,* or an *in-house agency*. Advertising department has an advertising manager as its head and may have brand managers handling one or more brands. The advertising manager organises the staffs the department, selects the advertising agency and coordinates with other departments as well as deals with outside businesses. The advertising manager is responsible for all activities concerning advertising; creation, production, placement in media, and results. An *in-house agency* is an independent business, owned by the company and performs all or most functions that an outside agency does and earns media commissions. This arrangement offers closer control over advertising and is believed to offer more economy.

Media Organisations: Media organisations perform a vital function by providing information and entertainment to their audiences and thereby serve as the right platform for ad message that reach specific target audiences. They sell space and time to advertisers or ad agencies, assist in media selection and analysis, and help with production.

Collateral Service Providers: These independent freelance service providers assist advertisers, advertising agencies, and the media. They include copywriters, graphic artists, photographers, marketing researchers, songwriters, printers, telemarketers, direct-mail production houses, and public relations consultants etc.

Target Audiences: The target audience has a direct bearing on the overall advertising strategy; product and its positioning, communications media, and advertising message. The advertiser spends huge amount of money to collect reliable data concerning these aspects, to make the right choices. Ultimately, the success or otherwise, of advertising depends on the target audience's response.

Planning and Managing Advertising

Advertising must fit nicely into the marketing plans and can occur at three levels. The company can have an annual advertising plan, or the company may have an annual plan and advertising campaign plan that is closely focused on solving a specific communications problem. The third choice is to develop a copy strategy for an individual ad that runs independent of any campaign. The advertising plan and ad campaign are similar in outline and structure.

A campaign is an interrelated and coordinated set of promotional activities that focus on some single theme or idea and is built to accomplish some predetermined objective(s). An ad campaign includes a series of ads placed in different media based on an analysis of marketing and communication situations. An advertising plan aims at matching the right target audience to the right message and presents it in the right medium to reach that audience.

Usually, a campaign theme is developed to last for a long time, but depending on an advertiser's short-term objectives it could be short as well. Many campaign themes last only for a very short time because either they prove ineffective, or lack respond to changes in competitive or other marketing conditions. Some advertisers change their campaign themes often while some successful campaigns may last for years. For example, Nike has been using "Just do it" for quite sometime, and DeBeers theme "Diamonds are forever," has been continuing for a very long time, and "Marlboro country" campaign has continued for more than 40 years.

Advertising planning and managing steps include *situation analysis, identifying target audience, determining objectives, setting budget, advertising strategy implementation,* and *evaluation.* In most cases the ad agency's accounts executive develops the advertising plan or campaign.

Situation Analysis

Marketing plan provides the details pertaining to brand share, anticipated market conditions, competitors' share and past moves, and any legal constraints concerning the product category. The first step is to research and review the current business situation that is relevant to advertising. The aim is to analyse important current trends affecting the market, competitors' share and past moves, consumer behaviour, the company itself and earlier advertising and its impact, and the important attributes of product or brand and making sense of all this information and analysis to determine what should be done for the future success of the product or brand. It is difficult to achieve perfection in analysis and there will always be some aspect that is overlooked or improperly analysed, but it is best to analyse the situation to identify communication problems that hinder successful marketing of the product or brand and what advertising can do to create or take advantage of the opportunities. Clearly identifying the communication problem that advertising can successfully address is at the heart of advertising planning.

In case of new product situation, more in-depth analysis of various aspects of the market would be needed and involve research of some kind. Good advertising starts with a clear understanding of marketing goals based on thorough market analysis and the aim is to explore the answers to the two basic questions: Where are we today? And, how did we get here?

Target Audience

A critical decision is to define the specific target audience for the product or service and involves finding and precisely defining those variables that indicate who and where are the best prospects in respect to demographic characteristics, geographic location, psycho-graphic variables, and behavioural patterns. Typically, this is larger than the target market. For example, the advertiser may target the heavy users but many light and non-users are also exposed to the message. Ned Anschuetz found that brand popularity cuts across all levels of purchasing frequency. It will also be necessary to find out the accessibility of the target audiences. Obviously, how the target audience is defined would influence the message and media strategies. Consumer research may be needed to find out:

- Who buys the product?
- What do they really buy?
- When do they buy?
- Who is the end-user?

Knowing the target audiences' lifestyle, motivations, and behavioural patterns, etc. helps in deciding whom the advertiser wants to reach, and also helps creative people to write messages for real audiences and communicate more effectively.

Advertising Objectives

Objectives help communications between the ad agency accounts executive and the creative team members, and help coordinate the efforts of copywriters, media specialists, media buyers, and professionals involved in advertising research. Objectives also provide a standard against which the results can be measured.

Sales are a convenient and really attractive advertising objective for many managers but they are usually unsuitable for most advertising managers because advertising is just one factor among many others that influence sales. Other factors that may have a significant effect on sales are product features, price, distribution, personal selling, publicity, packaging, competitors' moves, and changing buyer needs, etc.

Many experts recognise the fact that advertising creates delayed or *carryover effect* and no matter how much money is spent on advertising, it may not necessarily have an immediate impact on sales. The carryover effect creates additional difficulty in determining the precise relationship of advertising and sales. Darral G. Clarke found that for low-priced, mature, and frequently purchased products the carryover effect of advertising on sales lasts, up to nine months.

Understanding specific consumer problems is often the key to developing appropriate advertising campaign. Advertising creates its most powerful impact when it is used to solve narrowly defined

Short-term advertising objectives are realistic and long-term objectives are ambitious. Advertising communications objectives can be put in a pyramid form. First the lower-level objectives, such as awareness, knowledge or comprehension are accomplished. Subsequent objectives may focus on moving prospects to higher levels in the pyramid to elicit the desired behavioural responses such as, associating feelings with the brand, trial, or regular use etc. It is easier to accomplish ad objectives located at the base of the pyramid than the ones towards the top. The percentage of prospective customers will decline as they move up the pyramid towards more action-oriented objectives, such as regular brand use. Irrespective of the fact whether the brand is new or established, the pyramid can be used to determine appropriate advertising objectives. What is required is to determine, where the target audience lies with respect to the various levels in the pyramid. Some possible objectives can be:

- Increasing the percentage of target consumers who associate specific features or benefits with company's brand.
- Increasing number of target consumers who prefer company's brand rather than competing brands.
- Increasing company's brand usage rate among existing consumers.
- Encouraging company's brand trial among non-users.

Objectives for a Detergent Brand

- Objective I: Create awareness among 90% of target audience. Use simple message and repetitive advertising in print and broadcast media.
- Objective 2: Create brand interest among 70% of target audience. Use informative message about brand's features and benefits.
- Objective 3: Generate positive feelings about the brand among 40%, and preference among 25 per cent of the target audience. Build favourable attitudes by conveying useful brand information, and sampling, etc.
- Objective 4: Obtain trial among 20% of the target audience. Use brand sampling, and coupons along with advertising.
- Objective 5: Maintain regular use among 5% of the target audience. Use reinforcing ads.

Russell H. Colley proposed DAGMAR (*Defining Advertising Goals for Measured Advertising Results)* approach. He also proposed 52 advertising objectives. Colley believed communications effects are the logical basis for setting advertising objectives.

"Advertising's job, purely and simply, is to communicate to a defined audience, information and a frame of mind that stimulates action. Advertising succeeds or fails depending on how well it communicates the desired information and attitudes to the right people at the right time and at the right cost."

DAGMAR approach proposes that communications objectives be based on a hierarchical model with four stages:

- ***Awareness:*** Involves making target audience aware of the existence of the brand or company.
- ***Comprehension:*** The purpose is to develop an understanding among audience of what the product is and what it would do for them.
- ***Conviction:*** The objective is to create a mental disposition among target audience members to buy the product.
- ***Action:*** To motivate target audience to purchase the product or service.

FIGURE 14.1

Effect of Advertising on Consumers

Behavioural Dimensions	Steps Toward Purchase	Advertising for Various Stages
Conative The realm of motives. Ads stimulate or direct desires.	**Purchase** ↑ **Conviction**	POP advertising. Testimonials Price/quality appeals
Affective The realm of emotions, attitudes, and feelings	**Preference** ↑	Comparative ads. Argumentative copy.
	Liking ↑	"Image" copy. Status, glamour appeals.
Cognitive The realm of thoughts. Beliefs.	**Knowledge** ↑	Descriptive copy. Slogans, jingles, etc.
	Awareness	Ad repetition, teaser ads.

(Figure based on Lavidge and Steiner Model)

It is interesting to note that advertising communication objectives *awareness, knowledge or comprehension, liking, preference,* and *conviction* are all mental responses, not visible to an observer. One can easily appreciate that, advertising objectives in terms of audiences' purchase behaviour are fundamentally just two: Product trial and repeat purchase. Both of these are observable and measurable.

Budget Allocation

Advertising objective setting may be significantly influenced by the limitations of the budget. Budget decisions are critical as the money spent on advertising may mean, the difference between success and failure. The greatest power of advertising lies in its cumulative, long-term reinforcement effect. It builds consumer preferences and goodwill, which helps to enhance the reputation and value of the company's name and its brand. As an element of marketing communications mix, advertising is an investment in future sales. (For detailed discussion of budget allocation methods, see Chapter-17, Marketing Communications).

Unfortunately, budget allocated to advertising is considered as current business expense, cutting into profits, rather than an investment. For this reason when a firm faces tough times, the axe falls on advertising expenditures like other expense items. This is understandable but short-sighted, as this may affect the brand's image and erode its equity.

According to Robert D. Buzzell and Frederick D. Wiersema, market share is a prime indicator of profitability.

- Additional advertising normally increases sales, but at some point, however, the rate of return declines.
- Sales response for advertising may build over time, but it is not durable, and a consistent investment is important.
- There are minimum levels of ad expenditure below which, advertising expenditures have no effect on sales.
- There will be some sales even if the marketer does not advertise.

- Culture and competition impose saturation limits and beyond this no amount of advertising can increase sales.

Setting advertising budget is not an easy task. There is no way to be absolutely certain that a company is spending the right amount. Some critics say that large consumer packaged goods marketers tend to spend too much on image advertising without really knowing its effects. They overspend as a form of "insurance" against not spending enough. Industrial companies generally underspend on advertising, underestimating the power of company and product image in pre-selling and tend to rely too heavily on their sales forces to bring in sales.

Marketers should consider some specific factors when setting the advertising budget:

- ***Product life cycle stage:*** New products typically need large advertising budget to create awareness, develop preference, and induce product trial/purchase. Mature brands usually require lower budget as a ratio to sales.
- ***Market share:*** Brands enjoying high market share usually need more advertising push as a percentage of sales compared to low-share brands. Taking share from competitors requires larger advertising expenditure than just maintaining the current status.
- ***Intensity of competition and clutter:*** In a market with many competitors and high spending on advertising, there is bound to be advertising clutter. A brand must advertise more heavily to be seen and heard above the noise in the market.
- ***Advertising frequency:*** When many advertising repetitions are needed to communicate the brand's message to the target consumers, the advertising budget must be large.
- ***Product differentiation:*** When a brand cannot be differentiated significantly and resembles other brands in a product category, it requires heavy advertising to set it apart from its competitors. Ama Carmine found that high amount of advertising perceived by consumers is often interpreted as an indicator of product quality. Consumers reason being that because of high quality the advertiser is backing the product with high intensity of advertising.

Advertising Strategy Implementation

Advertising strategy has four important elements of creative mix: Identifying the target market and defining the audience, deciding the product's positioning, developing advertising message, and selecting the communication media. Advertising objectives determine what is desired in terms of consumer response, and advertising strategy describes how to accomplish the objectives. Product positioning (Chapter 10) has been discussed in detail and target market and audience have been briefly discussed earlier in this chapter.

Advertising Message

We have looked at various message aspects (Chapter 17). Some creative authorities have suggested different methods to develop effective advertising messages. Some of the best-known creative approaches used are attributed to David Ogilvy, William Bernbach, Rosser Reeves, Leo Burnett, and Jack Trout and Al Ries.

Great ads give advertisers more advertising effectiveness per unit of money spent. Great advertising results by creating a combination of *"ad liking"* and its "*strategic relevance.*" While the text and the visuals carry the ad message, behind the creative team's choice of tone, words, and ideas, lies an advertising strategy. When the ad is completed it must have relevance to the sponsor's strategy otherwise it will fail. Great advertising always has a strategic mission to accomplish and is the key element that serves as a guide to great creative work.

Account executive from the advertising agency prepares a *creative brief* to communicate the strategy to the creative team. It is a simple written statement of the most significant issues to consider and guide the team in the development of an advertisement or campaign. The statement addresses the following issues:

- ***Who?*** Who is the potential customer in terms of geographic, demographic, behaviouristic, and psychographic qualities? What is the personality profile of a typical prospect?
- ***Why?*** Does the consumer have specific needs and, wants the ad message should focus upon and appeal to? There are two broad categories of appeals. *Rational appeals* are directed at the consumer's practical, functional need for the product or service, whereas the *emotional appeal* aims at the consumer's psychological, social, and symbolic needs.
- ***What?*** Are there any special features of the product or service to satisfy the consumer's needs? What factors support the product claim? How is the product positioned? What image or personality of the brand can be created or has been created? What perceived strengths or weaknesses of the brand need to be addressed?
- ***Where, when, and how?*** In which market area, what time of the year, and through what medium will these messages be delivered?
- ***What style, approach,* or *tone?*** Will the campaign use? Generally what will the copy say?

Creative brief only identifies the benefits to be presented to the consumers but how these benefits will be presented is the domain of creative specialists.

The real challenge to the creative specialists is to come up with the *big idea* to use in the ad. More and more products and services in their category are perceived as similar and unable to offer anything unique. In most situations it is difficult to find something really interesting to say. In this respect David Ogilvy, considered to be one of the most creative copywriters ever to work in the advertising business, has said:

"I doubt if more than one campaign in a hundred contains a big idea. I am supposed to be one of the more fertile inventors of big ideas, but in my long career as a copywriter I have not had more than 20, if that." David Ogilvy, *Ogilvy on Advertising*, New York: Crown 1983.

David Ogilvy: Increasing numbers of competing brands in many product and service category do not seem to offer anything unique in terms of features or benefits. All of them, seem to be almost similar and difficult to differentiate on a functional or performance basis. To find or create a unique benefit or feature as a major selling idea is very difficult. The creative strategy in such situations is based on the development of a strong brand identity by emphasising psychological meaning or symbolic association with certain values, and lifestyles etc. This type of advertising is referred as *image advertising.*

In his famous book, *Confessions of an Advertising Man,* David Ogilvy popularised the idea of *brand image.* He argued that the brand's image or personality is particularly important when competing brands are similar. He said:

"Every advertisement should be thought of as a contribution to the complex symbol which is the brand image. If you take that long view, a great many day-to-day problems solve themselves."

David Ogilvy, *Confessions of an Advertising Man,* 1963.

David Ogilvy has further argued that in the long-run it pays to protect a favourable image even if some appealing short-run programmes (sales promotions) are sacrificed in the process. He goes on to say:

"The greater the similarity between brands, the less part reason plays in brand selection. There isn't any significant difference between the various brands of whiskey, or cigarettes, or beer. They are all about the same. And so are the cake-mixes and the detergents, and the margarines. The manufacturer who dedicates his advertising for building the most sharply defined

personality for his brand will get the largest share of the market at the highest profit. By the same token, the manufacturers who will find themselves up the creek are those short-sighted opportunists who siphon off their advertising funds for promotions."

David Ogilvy, *Confessions of an Advertising Man.*

Ogilvy used prestigious individuals to convey the desired image for the product in some of his most well-known campaigns and when possible, he would use testimonials from celebrities. He even used Queen Elizabeth, Winston Churchill, and Mrs. Roosevelt as the endorsers.

He prescribed the following eleven commandments for creating advertising campaigns:

1. What you say is more important than how you say it.
2. Unless your campaign is built around a great idea, it will flop.
3. Give the facts. The consumer isn't a moron; she is your wife. You insult her intelligence if you assume that a mere slogan and a few vapid adjectives will persuade her to buy anything. She wants all the information you can give her.
4. You cannot bore people into buying. We make advertisements that people want to read. You can't save souls in an empty church.
5. Be well mannered, but don't clown.
6. Make your advertising contemporary.
7. Committees can criticize advertisements, but they cannot write them.
8. If you are lucky enough to write a good advertisement, repeat it until it stops pulling.
9. Never write an advertisement, which you wouldn't want your family to read. Good products can be sold by honest advertising. If you don't think the product is good, you have no business to be advertising it. If you tell lies, or weasel, you do your client a disservice, you increase your load of guilt, and you fan the flames of public resentment against the whole business of advertising.
10. The image and the brand: It is the total personality of a brand rather than any trivial product difference, which decides its ultimate position in the market.
11. Don't be a copycat. Nobody has ever built a brand by imitating somebody else in advertising.

David Ogilvy, *Confessions of an Advertising Man* (Portions of some points excluded).

In many product categories and services, image advertising has become increasingly popular and is used as the main selling idea. For example, image advertising is used for soft drinks, perfumes, watches, cigarettes, two and four-wheeler autos, ready-to-wear clothing, beauty care services products, and airlines etc.

William Bernbach: The primary function of an advertisement is to communicate a persuasive message and David Ogilvy's prescription for copywriters is *"what you say is more important than how you say it."* William Bernbach had a radically different approach and said *"execution can become content, it can be just as important as what you say."* He emphasised the ad execution elements. His ads communicated a feeling that the consumer is bright enough to understand what the advertising is saying. The copy was honest and any heavy repetitions were avoided. The message approach was clean and direct. He believed that one should be as simple, as swift, and as penetrating as possible, and the advertisement should stand out from others and have its own character. In his own words:

'Why should anyone look at your ad? The reader doesn't buy his magazine or tune in his radio and TV to see and hear what you have to say... What is the use of saying all the right things in the world if nobody is going to read them?" And,

believe me, nobody is going to read them if they are not said with freshness, originality and imagination…If they are not, if you will, different."

Source: Martin Mayer, *Madison Avenue,* Pocket Books, 1958.

FIGURE 14.2
Bernbach positioned Volkswagon car as "small" and very high quality

Bernbach frequently used humour in advertising. He believed in rewarding the reader positively through humour. A copywriter Robert Fine of DDB Needham, now part of Omnicom group said:

"We recognise that an advertisement is an intrusion. People don't necessarily like advertisements, and avoid them if possible. Therefore, to do a good advertisement you're obligated, really to reward the reader for his time and patience in allowing you to interrupt the editorial content, which is what he bought the magazine for in the first place. This is not defensive. It just takes into account the fact that an advertisement pushes its way uninvited into somebody's mind. So entertainment is sort of repayment."

Frank Rowsome, Jr., *Think Small,* Ballantine Books, 1970.

His ideas, among other things, made the ugly-looking Volkswagon one of America's most talked about automobile success. The ad itself had nothing extraordinary. A black-and-white picture of that simple car, no woman draped over the fender, no mansion in the background. A one-word headline: 'Lemon.' And the simple self-effacing copy that began, "This Volkswagon missed the boat. The chrome strip on the glove compartment is blemished and must be replaced. Chances are you couldn't have noticed it; Inspector Kurt Kroner did."

Volkswagon was a totally new voice. In a very self-deprecating manner it managed to say to the people, how stringent its quality norms were. Copywriting is the truth about a product said in a refreshing manner. The idea should contain an insight into human behaviour, with which a reader can relate. Copywriting is more to do with ideas than pompous looking words.

Some ads of Volkswagon, viewed as classic, had headlines "Ugly is only skin deep," "Think small," and "Lemon." The ads were well accepted and read by large numbers. Common people talked about these ads. The ads were also picked for many creative awards.

The true essence of writing advertising copy is reflected in the classic William Bernbach paradigm. It says:

"The truth isn't the truth until people believe you, and they cannot believe you if they do not know what you are saying, and they cannot hear what you are saying if they do not listen to you, and they will not listen to you if you are not interesting, and you will not be interesting unless you say the truth."

Rosser Reeves: Rosser Reeves of Ted Bates agency (now part of Saatchi group) developed the concept of Unique Selling Proposition *(USP)*. His book, *Reality in Advertising* is considered an important contribution and has significantly influenced advertising. His approach was to write to create sales, rather than for aesthetic appeal. Reeves mentioned three characteristics of *USP:*

1. Each advertisement must make a proposition to the consumer. Not just words, not just product puffery, not just show window advertising. Each advertisement must say to reach reader: "Buy this product and you will get this benefit."
2. The proposition must be one that the competition either cannot or does not offer. It must be unique either in the brand or in the claim.
3. The proposition must be strong enough to move the mass millions, that is, pull over new customers to your brand.

Rosser Reeves, *Reality in Advertising,* (1961).

Reeves proposed that each product develop its own *USP,* which should dominate the ad and be emphasised through whatever repetition is necessary to communicate the *USP* to the target audience. Reeves relied heavily on product research to develop and support *USP.* He believed that once an effective *USP* is found, it must be retained for as long as possible.

Reeves approach of *USP* was undoubtedly successful, but this requires finding out a truly unique product or service attribute, benefit, or inherent advantage that can be used in developing the claim. Another aspect that advertisers must consider is whether the *USP* offers them a *sustainable competitive advantage* that cannot be copied easily. In many product categories, companies can quickly match a brand feature for feature, and this makes the *USP* approach somewhat obsolete. *USP* is a good theory as long as one can really find a unique and persuasive, but sustainable claim.

Leo Burnett: His approach to determining the major selling idea is termed as *"Inherent drama."* This approach focuses on finding out the product attribute that made the manufacturer to produce it, and the product benefit that motivates the consumer to purchase it. Burnett believed that the inherent drama is hard to find but it is always there, and constitutes the most interesting and believable of all advertising appeals.

He believed that the foundation of advertising should be based on consumer benefits with an emphasis on thé dramatic element in communicating these benefits. He reflected *"common touch"* in advertising, using plain ordinary people. His approach vividly contrasted that of David Ogilvy, who used prestigious personalities to convey the desired brand image. Leo Burnett said in a speech given before the Chicago Copywriters Club:

"Not only is great copy "deceptively simple" – but so are great ideas. And if it takes a rationale to explain an ad or a commercial – then it's too complicate for that "dumb" public to understand. I am afraid too many advertising people blame the public's inability to sort out commercial messages or advertisements in magazines on stupidity. What a lousy stupid attitude to have! I believe the public is unable to sort out messages, not just because of the sheer flood of messages assaulting it every day but because of sheer boredom! If the public is bored today – then let's blame it on the fact that it is being handed boring messages created by bored advertising people. In a world where nobody seems to know what's going to happen next, the only thing to do to keep from going completely nuts from frustration is plain old-fashioned work! Having worked many, many years for peanuts and in obscurity, I think I know how a lot of writers feel today and I sympathise with them, but I also wonder if a lot of writers aren't downright spoiled."

Leo Burnett "Keep Listening To That Wee, Small Voice", *Communications of an Advertising Man,* 1961.

Some of the famous ads created by Burnett's agency using *'inherent drama'* approach are for McDonald, Hallmark cards, and Kellogg's cereals etc.

FIGURE 14.3
Some successful long-running ad campaigns

Company/Brand	Ad campaign theme
Amul	"Taste of India."
De Beers	"A diamond is forever."
BMW	"The ultimate driving machine."
Nike	"Just do it."
Wills cigarettes	"Made for each other."
Videocon	"Bring home the leader."
Philips	"Let's make things better."
BPL	"Believe in the best."
Woodland shoes	"Leather that weathers."
Maggi	"2-Minute noodles."

Al Ries and Jack Trout: In early 1970s, Al Ries and Jack Trout introduced the concept of *"positioning."* Positioning theory acknowledges the importance of product features and images, but insists that what is really important is how the brand is perceived and ranked against the competition in the consumer's mind. Positioning approach became a popular basis of creative strategy development. Using cola as a frame of reference, Al Ries and Jack Trout say:

"To find a unique position, you must ignore conventional logic. Conventional logic says you find your concept inside yourself or inside the product. Not true. What you must do is look inside the prospect's mind. You won't find an'uncola' idea inside a 7-Up can. You find it inside the Cola drinker's head."

Al Ries and Jack Trout, *Positioning: The Battle for Your Mind,* McGraw-Hill, 1986.

Products or services can be positioned on the basis of attributes, price/quality, usage or application, users, or product class. Any of these can kindle a novel selling idea that becomes the basis of the creative strategy. The creative outcome may help the brand occupy a particular position in the minds of the target audience.

Some of the more recent advertising personalities who have had significant influence on contemporary advertising include Hal Riney, Lee Clow, Jay Chiat, Dan Weiden, Jeff Goodby, Rich Silverstein.

Anthony Vagnoni writes:

"The modern creative kings don't write books, rarely give interviews or lay out their theories on advertising. They have endorsed no set of rules, professed no simple maxims like Mr. David Ogilvy's famous "When you don't have anything to say, sing it." If pronouncements and books are out of the window, what has replaced them is a conscious desire to lift the intelligence level of advertising. Today's leaders see advertising as an uplifting social force, as a way to inspire and entertain."

Anthony Vagnoni, "The Might Be Giants, *Advertising Age,* (April 1998).

Goodby and Silverstein describe their creative formula as doing intelligent work that the public likes to see and that has a sales pitch:

"Advertising works best when it sneaks into people's lives, when it doesn't look or feel like advertising. It's about treating people at their best, as opposed to dealing with them at their lowest common denominator."

Anthony Vagnoni, "Goodby, Silverstein Do 'Intelligent Work' with a Sales Pitch," *Advertising Age,* April 1998.

Lee Clow says:

"No rulebook will tell you how to target the masses anymore. The best of us understand the sociocultural realities of people and how they interact with the media. If we didn't, we couldn't make the kinds of messages that people would be able to connect with."

Anthony Vagnoni, "Having Ad Bosses Focus on the Work Key to Cult of Clow," *Advertising Age,* April 1998.

Creative professionals often use these approaches as the basis of developing creative strategy for ad campaigns. However, these approaches are not the only ones. Many other approaches are available and individual agencies are not limited to any particular creative approach. The real challenge to the creative specialists is to find the "big idea" and use it in developing an effective creative strategy.

Advertising Appeals: The advertising appeal is the central message to be used in the ad. David Martin, founder of The Martin Agency, is of the opinion that desires are part of our basic nature. Humans will always have a need for food and drink; for rest, comfort, and security; and for social sense of worth, independence, power, and success. He says human nature is constant and has in-born instincts such as fear (self-preservation), hunger (food and drink), sex (love), and rage (anger). And nature has given them five senses: Sight, sound, smell, taste, and touch. These instincts and senses are often the basis for developing advertising appeals.

The selection of primary appeal is the key to any ad campaign. Many research techniques, such as concept testing, focus group, and motivational research, can be used to determine which appeal to use. The selected appeal should have the power to attract the attention of consumers, arouse their latent desires or influence feelings, and thus speak to human needs or wants that can be met by the advertised product, service, or cause. How this particular appeal is turned into an effective advertising message depends on the *creative execution style.*

William Weilbacher says:

"The appeal can be said to form the underlying content of the advertisement, and the execution, the way in which that content is presented. Advertising appeals and executions are usually independent of each other, that is, a particular appeal can be executed in a variety of ways and a particular means of execution can be applied to a variety of advertising appeals. Advertising appeals tend to adapt themselves to all media, whereas some kind of executional devices are more adaptable to some media than others."

William M. Weilbacher, *Advertising,* 2nd Ed. (1984).

A large number of different appeals can be used as the basis for advertising messages. At any point in time only two types of elements make up a brand. The *rational elements* stem primarily from the question *"what"* the product or service does and speak more to the left or rational side of the brain. The *emotional elements* originate from *"how"* the product or service is expressing itself, and address more to the right or intuitive-nonverbal side of the brain. Thus, most of the appeals can be grouped as:

Rational Appeals: These appeals address the consumer's self interest and focus on negatively originated motives (problem removal or problem avoidance) as happens when we run out of something and experience a negative mental state. To relieve those feelings we actively seek a new or replacement product. These are also referred as informational motives because the consumer actively seeks information to reduce the mental tension. These could also be called *"relief"* motives because they relieve the negative state. The appeals emphasise product or service features and benefits, such as quality, performance, economy, durability, value, convenience, comfort, and health etc. The message content emphasises facts, learning, and the logic of persuasion.

William Weilbacher has identified several types of rational appeals. Some of them are:

- *Feature appeal.*
- *Competitive advantage appeal.*
- *Favourable price appeal.*
- *News appeal.*
- *Product/service popularity appeal.*

Emotional Appeals: Emotional appeals relate to customers' social and psychological needs and stir up positive or negative emotions that can motivate purchase of a product or service. The appeal promises a reward rather than the removal or avoidance of some negative situation. This reward could relate to *sensory gratification*, *intellectual stimulation*, and *social approval.* They could also be referred as *"reward"* motives.

Emotional appeals can be used in many ways in the creative strategy. Advertisers attempt to depict the characters in ads or commercials as experiencing some kind of emotional benefit or outcome from using the product or service. Emotional appeals are used to evoke positive feelings that may get transferred to the brand. Research supports the belief that ads and commercials that generate positive mood among the audience are better remembered and stand a relatively better chance that the advertised product or service will be evaluated favourably.

Many advertising professionals believe that there may be few occasions when purely rational or emotional purchases are made and creative specialists attempt to combine the two types of approaches. According to Ogilvy and Raphaelson:

"Few purchases of any kind are made for entirely rational reasons. Even a purely functional product such as laundry detergent may offer what is now called an emotional benefit – say, the satisfaction of seeing one's children in bright clean clothes. In some product categories the rational element is small. These include soft drinks, beer, cosmetics, certain personal care products, and most old-fashioned products. And who hasn't experienced the surge of joy that accompanies the purchase of a new car."

David Ogilvy and Joel Raphaelson, "Research on Advertising Techniques That Work and Don't Work," *Harvard Business Review,* (1982).

In most purchase situations, consumer decisions are based on a combination of both rational and emotional motives, only the degree of each varies depending on the product or service category and the buying situation. Attention must be accorded to this fact in creating effective advertising.

The concept of *emotional bonding,* developed by McCann-Erickson Worldwide and Professor Michael L. Ray, uses the premise that consumers develop three levels of relationships with brand(s):

1. Consumers *think* about brands in respect to product benefits.
2. Consumers assign a *personality* to a brand.
3. Consumers develop *emotional bonds* with brands.

Thinking relationship occurs through a rational learning process and can be determined how successful an ad has been in communicating the product information. At the thinking relationship level, consumers are not particularly brand loyal and brand switching is quite common. The product or services are typically those that are purchased for rational motives to solve or avoid a problem.

At the second level consumers assign a personality to a brand. A brand may be thought of as a male, young, fun loving or adventurous person. The brands may be perceived as masculine or feminine, modern or old-fashioned, timid, aggressive, or self-assured etc. Based on an assessment of overt and covert stimuli in the advertising, audiences determine the personality of a brand. For example, Bajaj Pulsar personality is that of a rough and tough, aggressive young male. The ads of Bajaj Pulsar motorcycle say "definitely male."

The third level of consumers' relationship with brands develops on the basis of emotional attachments. They develop powerful *emotional bonds* with certain brands. For example, Harley Davidson motorcycles. Advertisers aim to develop the most powerful emotional bonding between their brands and the target consumers.

Advertising Execution: is the way an advertising appeal, is used in an ad message. What is to be communicated through an ad message and how it is executed is very important. David Ogilvy emphasised the importance of what is said in advertising, and Bernbach strongly believed that the element of message execution is just as important as the message. There are many ways in which an advertising message can be presented.

Factual message or straight sell: This type of message is based on factual information about the product or service and the approach is often used with rational. The main focus is on product or service and the ad attempts to communicate its specific attributes and/or benefits to the target audience. The products or services involved may be of high or low involvement category, however, the consumer needs are rational and concerned with problem solving or problem avoidance. The print ad of Gillette Gel puts a straightforward message "One drop for smoothest shave."

Scientific or technical evidence: This approach is often used to introduce new products and describe technical products. Advertisements include technical information, scientific evidence, or endorsements by well-known agencies to support the product or service claims. For instance, certain brands of toothpaste used medical reports on how fluoride content helps check dental cavities.

Testimonial: Some advertisers prefer to use a satisfied customer who praises the product or service based on personal experience with its usage. Such an ad execution can use well-known personalities or ordinary satisfied customers. This style of execution can be particularly effective if the target audience identify with the person delivering the testimonial. The familiar ad of Surf with Lalitaji is an excellent example.

Demonstration: The product may be demonstrated in actual use, or it may be shown in some sort of staged demonstration with the explicit purpose of highlighting the key advantages of product or service. To demonstrate the product in action, TV is the most suitable medium as the benefits can be shown right on the TV screen with movement.

Comparison: Comparing features, performance, reputation, and other characteristics of two or more brands is a popular basis for advertising execution. This approach offers a direct way of communicating a brand's particular advantages. Advertisers also use this execution approach to position a new, or less-known brand by comparing it with the industry leaders. This is an effective way to communicate the competitive advantage.

Slice of life (problem solution): Slice-of-life commercials dramatise real-life situations. Often the situation encountered is of personal nature, such as pimples, bad breath, body odour, dandruff, or less than satisfactory laundry detergent etc. A friend, relative, or colleague drops the hint; the product is tried and the next scene shows a happy satisfied consumer.

Lifestyle: Advertisers use lifestyle approach to present the user rather than the product or service. The focus is on who uses the brand rather than any product attributes or benefits. Many ready-to-wear garment ads address the message to young, contemporary, and outdoor type characters. Likewise, ads of soft drink usually show active, young, fun-loving, and ambitious people. The commercial attempts to create excitement and motivation to identify with people of this lifestyle.

Fantasy: This approach is based on the need of consumers to find emotional escape to offset daily routines. This is fairly popular for emotional types of appeals. Certain cosmetic ads often use fantasy appeals to create pleasant images and symbols that consumers associate with the product or service.

Animation: Cartoons, puppet characters, and demonstrations with computer-generated graphics are some of the techniques used to communicate difficult ad messages and reach certain specific target groups, such as children. The way some common pain, or cold and cough remedies affect the human system is difficult to explain verbally. Animated pictures of pain, cold and cough, with the help of computer graphics simplify the subject and it becomes relatively easy to understand the demonstration.

Humour: Many advertisers tend to use humour as the basic approach when their major concern is to attract attention to the product or service. Humour evokes feelings of amusement and pleasure and may favourably affect the information processing by audience. A good example of humour is in the execution of Centre Shock chewing gum commercial.

Combination: In actual practice, most commercials use a combination of various execution techniques to present the advertising message. Humour is quite adaptable to most execution-techniques. Slice-of-life ads are often used with the intent of demonstrating a product. It rests with the creative personnel to determine whether more than one execution style would be better suited in creating the advertisement.

Creative writing of headlines is also very important to draw readersattention. The headline must put forth the main appeal, theme, or proposition, giving powerful reason to read the ad further. Other important elements of ads such as ad size, colours, visuals, and body copy should be paid due attention. Several factors influence the type of headline used such as creative strategy, advertising situation, and its relationship to body copy, and the visuals, etc.

There is no formula that can be recommended for writing an effective headline. Copywriters use several different approaches. Typically, copywriters use a headline that presents the "big idea" most successfully. Frequently used headlines include: Benefit headline (Jeevan Samridhi), information/news headline (Alto makes its debut outside of Japan for the first time – India), provocative headline (Don't buy DVD unless…), question headline (Do you just hope for the best?), and command headline (Buy Your Matiz Today) etc.

Research findings suggest that less than 50 per cent of the exposed readers take notice of an excellent ad, 25 per cent might recall the advertiser, and less than 10 per cent will go through the body copy.

Media Plan

Advertising media selection is an important element in the success of an advertising programme. Media planning involves a series of decisions in delivering the ad message to the largest number of the target audience in the most effective manner at the lowest cost. Three important steps involved are media objectives, media strategy, and media selection.

After closely analysing the media habits of target audience, geographic area, and media timing, the planners formulate a particular combination that would serve the reach, frequency, and impact objectives successfully and effectively.

Media class is the general category of message delivery system for carrying the ad message to a selected audience, such as print media, broadcast media, or outdoor media etc.

Media vehicle is the specific message carrier within a medium, such as *Times of India, Outlook, Star Sports.*

Media reach is a measure of the number of different audience members or households exposed at least once to a media schedule within given period of time. Reach is also called Opportunity to See (OTS).

Media frequency is the average number of times that an individual or household is exposed to a message carrying media vehicle within the specified time period.

Media impact refers to the qualitative value of an exposure through a given media vehicle. It is the intrusiveness of the ad message, such as the ad for a ladies' perfume is likely to have more impact in *Femina* than in Computer magazine.

Media scheduling is concerned with timing the insertion of ads in the selected media vehicles. There are three major media scheduling approaches. *Continuity* refers to a continuous pattern of advertising that can mean every day, every week etc. during an advertising cycle. This is suitable where continuous reminder is important. *Flighting* is less regular advertising messages. There are intermittent periods of advertising and no advertising and often suits seasonal, expensive, or durable products. *Pulsing* combines continuity and flighting. The advertising follows a continuous schedule, but during certain periods it is stepped up. For example, during major sports events we see there is a spurt in the ads of cold drinks.

Media planners have to determine the most cost-effective combination of reach, frequency, and impact. To create awareness, or for infrequently purchased products, reach is an important consideration. Frequency is important when the product nature is complex, competition is more intense, or top-of-mind recall is necessary for every day use products. Since the media budget is fixed in most cases, media planners strike a balance between reach, frequency, and advertising cycles.

So far, there is no known way of determining how much reach is required and what frequency can provide the desired level of awareness, attitude change, or purchase intention. Decisions in this area are not always based on any hard data. Joseph W. Ostrow believes that establishing frequency goals for an advertising campaign is a mix of art and science but with a definite bias towards art.

Most advertisers have settled at three ad exposures as the last number and ten exposures as the maximum number. Less than three exposures are assumed to give insufficient reach and more than ten are viewed as overexposures. Despite these assumptions, there is no guarantee that a level of three to ten exposures will ensure effective communication.

Selection among Major Media Types

Media planners consider certain factors in making their choices among major media to achieve the desired reach, frequency, and impact. Media planners consider the following factors:

Target Audience Media Habits: For instance to reach younger urban audiences, TV, magazines, and FM radio are more effective.

Product Characteristics: Products that require demonstration, or want to be presented in slice-of-life format need TV as the medium. Women dresses are best presented in glossy magazines that reproduce good colour quality.

Message Characteristics: A product message involving a great deal of technical data might require some specialised magazines.

Media Costs: Television is considered as most expensive. With the rising number of advertisers seeking to reach their customers through TV, cost of TV time is rising rapidly. Newspaper is relatively less expensive, and considering the coverage, radio is least expensive. In terms of ad durability and repetition, billboards are quite inexpensive.

A major present day communication problem is time famine. Consumers not only have less time to pay attention to advertising messages but also less inclination. For selecting specific media vehicles in a most cost-effective manner, planners compare costs within a specific media class.

For broadcast media: Costs are compared in terms of Gross Rating Points (*GRP*). This is a numerical figure indicating how many potential audience members are likely to be exposed to a series of commercials. This combines programme rating (Programme Rating indicates the percentage of households owning a TV who view a programme) and the average number of times (Frequency) these households are reached during a given period.

TABLE 14.1

General Characteristics of Major Media Types

Media	Advantages	Disadvantages
Television	Offers mass coverage. High level of reach. Combined impact of sight, sound, and motion. Prestige value. Low cost per exposure. Attracts attention.	Offers low selectivity. Short span of message life. High cost. High production costs. Creates advertising clutter. Waste coverage.
Radio	Local coverage. Lower cost. High frequency. Focused segment selection. Low production costs.	Only audio. Noise. Low on attention getting. Message short lived.
Newspapers	Mass coverage. Low cost, large space. Short lead time for ad placing. Ad position choice possible. Good for current ads. Reader controls exposure. Coupons can be inserted.	Short life of advertisement. Clutter. Low attention getting. Poor production quality. Selective exposure.
Magazines	Potential for focused segmentation. Very good production quality. Longevity of message. High information content. More readers per copy.	Long lead time for ad placing. Only visual. Low frequency. Lack of flexibility.
Outdoor	Good for specific location. High repetition. High visibility.	Short exposure time. Short message. Poor image.
Direct mail	High level of selectivity. Reader controls exposure. High information content. Opportunity for repeat exposures	High cost per contact Clutter. Often thrown as junk mail.
Internet	User controlled. Increased attention and involvement.	Limited creative capabilities.

Magazine space is sold primarily on the basis of pages or some increment of a page and calculated on the basis of cost per-page per-thousand circulation. The Cost Per Thousand (*CPM*) is calculated as under:

$$CPM = \frac{\text{Cost of Space}}{\text{Circulation}} \times 1000$$

Media buyers use MR to compare the cost of *newspaper* space. A milline rate is the cost in rupees per line of standard dimensions to reach a circulation of one million. Alternatively, the cost of space is calculated in terms of rupees per square inch or centimeter per-column. Newspaper with higher circulation figures charge more per-unit of space.

$$GRP = \frac{1000{,}000 \times \text{Rate per Agate Line}}{\text{Circulation}}$$

$$GRP = \text{Reach} \times \text{Frequency}$$

Evaluation of Advertising Effectiveness

Advertising agencies usually pretest ads or commercials and also conduct post-testing. Some major pretesting and post-testing methods are mentioned briefly.

Pre-Testing Methods

Print Advertising

- ***Direct Questioning***: The researcher using this method asks respondents specific questions about the ads.
- ***Focus Group:*** A group of 8 to 10 people participate in a moderated but freewheeling discussion and interview.
- ***Portfolio Test:*** One group of respondents is exposed to a portfolio of test ads interspersed among other ads and editorial matter. Another group sees the portfolio without the test ads.
- ***Order-of-Merit Test:*** Respondents see two or more alternative ads and arrange them in rank order.

Television and Radio Advertising

- ***Central Location Test:*** Respondents see test commercial film in a central location, such as a shopping centre.
- ***Clutter Test:*** Test commercials along with non-competing control commercials are shown to respondents to determine their effectiveness, measure comprehension and attitude shifts, and detect any weak points.
- ***Trailer Test:*** Respondents see or listen to commercials in trailers at shopping centres and receive coupons for the advertised products.

Post-testing Methods

Recall refers to a measure of the proportion of a sample audience that can recall an ad as having seen. In *aided recall,* respondents are shown certain ads with the name of the sponsor or brand concealed and then asked whether their previous exposure was through reading, viewing, or listening. In *unaided recall,* respondents are asked, without prompt, whether they read, saw, or heard advertising messages. ***Day-after-recall (DAR)*** is the most popular method of post-testing used in broadcast industry. Since these are field tests, the natural setting is believed to elicit more realistic responses.

Recognition refers to whether a respondent can recognise an advertisement as having seen before. Such tests are conducted by mail survey in which questionnaires are mailed to 1000 households picked from a mailing list or telephone book.

FIGURE 14.4

Gallup & Robinson Impact Test

Objective: Tracking recall of advertising appearing in magazines to assess performance and effectiveness.

Method: Test magazines are placed in participants' homes and respondents are asked to read the magazine that day. A telephone interview is conducted the second day to assess recall of ads, recall of copy points, and consumers' impressions of the ads. Sample size is 150 people.

Output: Three measurement scores are provided:

- Proven name registration – the percentage of respondents who can accurately recall the ad.
- Idea communication – the number of sales points the respondents can recall.
- Favourable buying attitude – the extent of favourable purchase reaction to the brand or corporation.

FIGURE 14.5

The Starch Readership Report

Objective: Determining recognition of print ads and comparing them to other ads of the same variety or in the same magazine.

Method: Samples are drawn from 20 to 30 urban areas reflecting the geographic circulation of the magazine. Personal interviewers screen readers for qualifications and determine exposure and readership. Samples include minimum of 200 males and females, as well as specific audiences where required. Participants are asked to go through the magazines, looking at the ads, and provide specific responses.

Output: *Starch Readership Reports* generate three recognition scores:

- Noted score – the percentage of readers who remember seeing the ad.
- Seen-associated score – the percentage of readers who recall seeing or reading any part of the ad identifying the product or brand.
- Read-most score – the per centage of readers who report reading at least half of the copy portion of the ad.

FIGURE 14.6

Day-After-Recall-Test (ASI Market Research)

Objective: Determining the ability of the commercial to gain viewer attention, communicate an intended message, associate the brand name with the message, and affect purchase behaviour.

Method: Interviews are conducted the day after the commercial airs in numerous cities throughout (country name). The sample is 200 people who confirm that they watched the programme in which the ad was placed. All individuals are asked if they remember a commercial, then what they can remember about it.

Output: Scores reflecting unaided and aided recall, indicating that viewers remember the commercial and can relate details about it.

Inquiry refers for checking the effectiveness of ads appearing in various print media on the basis of which consumers respond by requesting for more information. The researchers can test an advertisement's attention-getting value, readability, and comprehension. The results also indicate that the person not only saw or read the ad but also took some action, which is relatively stronger indicator than recall or awareness.

Sales Promotion

Sales promotion utilises a variety of incentive tools for a predetermined, limited period of time in order to stimulate trial, increase consumer or trade demand, and motivate and reward sales force, such as samples, coupons, discounts, premiums, refunds and rebates, contest and sweepstakes, trade deals, and sales contests for sales people etc. In most cases, the objectives are generally short-term sales related rather than long-term brand building.

There are some distinct differences between sales promotion and advertising. Sales promotions are generally short-term and offer an incentive. This incentive is over and above the normal product and changes the price-value equation in favour of consumers. These incentives are either 'same for less' or 'more for the same.' Sales promotion is essentially a selling process acceleration tool to maximise sales volume.

Advertising is an indirect approach to induce product trial without offering any incentive. Its main aim is to create brand awareness, develop favourable brand attitudes, build brand image and develop brand preference among consumers. The objectives of most advertising are long-term brand image.

Reasons for Sales Promotion Growth

The role of sales promotion has increased dramatically within the last 15 years. Consumer goods firms and many services are high users of sales promotions. No definite figures are available, however, it is estimated that 60 – 70 per cent of the total advertising and sales promotion budget goes to sales promotion. Increased sophistication and more strategic role and focus have elevated its importance in promotion mix of many companies.

Intense Competition: Intensifying competition in almost all consumer product categories has led to greater use of sales promotions because consumer respond favourably to the promotional incentives. An obvious reason for favourable consumer response is that they save money. Buying a brand on sale or display simplifies decision-making process.

Brand Proliferation: Products are becoming more and more standardised. Every year, numerous new brands are introduced and most do not seem to have any significant point of meaningful or persuasive differentiation to become the basis of sustained advertising. Thus, companies find no option but to depend heavily on sales promotion to induce product trial of these brands with the fond hope that initial trial may lead to repeat purchases at full price.

Declining Brand Loyalty: Consumers today are getting better educated, are more selective, and have become less loyal to brands than in the past. They purchase products based on price, value, and convenience. Even otherwise, loyal consumers switch back and forth among a set of brands they perceive as almost equal.

Growing Power of Resellers: The shelf space available with resellers is limited. They demand extra incentive to let the product enter their store and occupy some space. Companies who desire prominent shelf space have to offer some incentive to retailers. Obviously, when consumers enter a store, products prominently displayed attract their attention and consumers often make many unplanned purchases.

Advertising has Become Less Effective: Consumer markets are becoming more fragmented and traditional mass media advertising is less effective. The costs of mass media have escalated considerably. A 10-second spot on prime time TV might cost more than Rs.100,000. Audience are bored with advertising clutter and avoid looking at ads. Some people even consider advertising as an intrusion in their privacy. Sales promotion increases the attention-getting power of ads.

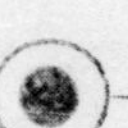

Sales Promotion Tools

Sales promotions are announced both, by manufacturers and retailers. Manufacturer announced promotions might be directed at consumers, resellers, or both. Manufacturers may also announce sales promotion for its sales force. Sales promotions may also originate from retailers aimed at consumers. The retailer-originated promotions' main objective is to increase store traffic rather than sell any specific brand. Manufacturer announced consumer promotions constitute "pull" strategy and retailer promotions are based on "push" strategy. Sales promotions are more effective when combined with advertising and "pull-push" strategies are used at the same time.

Consumer Promotions

Sales promotions directed at end-users are called consumer sales promotions. Usually, consumer promotions are either "same for less" or "more for the same" type and may get translated into a straight price-cut or added value. 'Interest promotions' may or may not require the purchase of anything such as free samples, free premiums, contests, and sweepstakes. The objective of such promotions is to stimulate consumer interest in products, services, activities, and special events.

"Consumer franchise-building" promotions are those which reinforce consumer brand preference and include a product-related selling message, such as in case of free premiums, free samples, coupons and patronage awards. "Non-franchise building" promotions include price discounts, price-packs, premiums not related to the purchased product, contests and sweepstakes, and ad refund offers. Some commonly used consumer promotions are briefly discussed:

Price Discount (also called cents-off): The customers pay a certain amount less than the regular price of the product or service if purchased within a specified period. This can yield short-term sales increase, can serve as an incentive to try a new product, and can also help product sales during off-season.

Bonus-Pack: An additional quantity of the purchased product is offered free with standard pack. The producer may develop special larger-sized pack containing more product quantity but the price is proportionately low. A variation of this offer is "buy two, take one free." These offers are generally limited to low-bulk items or ready-to-wear dresses, and sometimes footwear. There are stray cases when a buyer would get a 14-inch TV free with the purchase of a 21-inch TV.

Samples: It is an offer of some amount of product or service free or at a very nominal price. One major concern of the marketer is to put the product in the consumer's hand, which often is the key to success in many product categories and some services. The main objective of sampling is to induce initial product trial and let the consumer have the first hand experience with the product or service. Sampling is probably the most successful approach when the product is new, is not a market leader to induce trial.

Premiums: A premium (gift) is a reward given to the consumer for performing a particular act, generally purchasing a product or service. The premium may be free or available to the consumer by paying a price well below the regular market price. Getting a printer free with the purchase of a computer, or getting a Swiss knife well below the market price when the consumer purchases a microwave oven, are typical examples of premium.

Refund or Rebate (the terms are used interchangeably): Rebate offer, refers to some amount of money repaid to customers sometime after the purchase when a customer submits the specified proof-of-purchase to manufacturer. The manufacturer "refunds" part of the price paid by the customer via mail.

Frequent-User Reward: These are incentives to reward those, who frequently purchase the product or service, such as frequent-flier incentives to air passengers. The purpose is to encourage repeat purchases or repeated visits to a particular retail store. Locality grocery or general stores use this approach on an ongoing basis for their regular customers to encourage store loyalty. Usually such programmes cover a fairly long period to offer customers ample opportunity to respond favourably.

Coupons: Coupons can be viewed as certificates offered by manufacturers or retailers that entitle the owner to some stated savings or claim on the specified thing. Coupons bear a date of expiry and cannot be redeemed after that date. Coupon is a versatile tool and can be used to accomplish many different sales promotion objectives.

Consumer Contests, Sweepstakes, and Games: These promotions often generate considerable interest, excitement, and enthusiasm among consumers. Individuals compete based on their analytical or creative abilities. The participants can win cash, jewelry, trips, or some merchandise. A panel of judges examines the contest entries and the best one or more entries are declared as winners. In a sweepstakes, participating consumers' names are put in a draw. A game offers something to consumers such as missing numbers or letters to complete a certain numbered digit or product or brand name. A consumer who does it within the promotion period, wins the prize.

Exchange or Buy-Back Offers: Some consumer durables once bought are not replaced for a very long time in India. To encourage such consumers to replace their old products with a new one, companies or their authorised dealers offer buy-back or exchange offers. The manufacturer or the dealer pays some reasonable amount for the old product and sells a new one. Often this new product is offered on convenient interest-free installments.

Point-of-Purchase Displays: In-store presentations and exhibitions of products along with relevant information fall under this category. The message is clearly "come and get it, we have it." There is a saying in Hindi "Jo Dikhta Hai Woh Bikta Hai," (whatever is displayed, gets sold). Producers often supply such displays to retailers. Retailers like to use *POP* materials if they are attractive, informative, and capable of having impact. Effective displays stimulate customer interest, increase store-traffic, and often encourage unplanned purchases.

Trade Promotions

Trade promotions are directed at resellers (distributors, dealers, wholesalers, and retailers). Trade sales promotions are part of "push" strategy of producers. The objectives of trade sales promotions are different from consumer promotions. Producers realise the importance of retailer support. They are in the final contact in distribution chain and can influence customers in more ways. Consumers sometime seek retailer's suggestions before making a purchase and retailers in many cases can influence the product choice. The main objectives of trade promotions include:

- Build strong relations with channel members.
- To stimulate in-store merchandising support, such as arranging displays, shelf space, feature advertising etc.
- Gain distribution of new products.
- Gain support for existing brands.
- Manipulate levels of inventory held by wholesalers and retailers.
- ***Trade Allowances:*** The purpose of trade allowances is to offer financial incentives to resellers in order to motivate them to make a purchase. A trade allowance can be offered in a variety of ways:
- ***Buying Allowances:*** A producer pays a reseller some fixed amount or money or discount for purchasing a certain minimum quantity of product within the specified period of time. The payment may be given in the form of a cheque from the producer or a discounted invoice.
- ***Free Goods:*** Reseller is required to buy a certain number of product cases and for each case purchased, a certain amount of free quantity of the same product is offered. For example, the offer might be, "One pack containing one dozen of product free on purchase of 12 packs".
- ***Slotting Allowances (also called stocking, or introductory allowance):*** This is the money paid to retailers to stock new products. William L. Wilkie, Debra M. Desrochers, and Gregory T. Gundlach found that retailers justify this by pointing out the costs they incur by stocking so many new products every year and to cover risks associated with new products. Many firms are uncomfortable with this type of allowance.
- ***Buy-Back Allowance:*** Producers sometime offer retailers the opportunity to re-stock. This promotion immediately follows another type of deal and offers incentives for new purchases. After the first promotion if the inventory levels with retailers are very low or almost depleted, producers may offer this second incentive to build inventory level to normal with retailers.

- *Advertising Allowances:* The manufacturer pays the dealer or retailer a certain amount of agreed upon money to advertise the producer's product. This amount can be a fixed rupee amount or a percentage of gross purchase during a specified time period.
- *Display Allowance:* This is a direct payment of money or free goods to the retailer for each item purchased if the party agrees to set up a *POP* display, or running in-store promotional programme as specified by the marketer. The marketer requires the retailer to sign an agreement specifying the activity to be performed before the allowance is given.
- *Contests and Incentives:* Manufacturers sometimes use trade contests and special incentives to stimulate greater support and selling effort from dealers and salespeople and achieve sales targets, and other objectives. The prizes might include items such as TV, stereo, and trip to exotic places etc. Sometimes these contests and incentives are offered to sales people of the distributors, dealers, wholesalers, or retailers. These rewards involve cash payment to sales people to specially sell the producer's product. This type of cash payment is called **push money** or **SPIFF**.
- *Cooperative Advertising:* The manufacturer agrees to share a certain amount of media costs with the dealer for advertising his products. This deal is usually based on product quantity purchased. The dealer must show proof that the ads were released then only the payment is made. Most of these ads appear in newspapers.
- *Dealer Loader:* A dealer loader is a premium that a marketer gives to retailers for buying a specified quantity of a product. A dealer loader may be a premium to retailers for just buying the specified product quantity or the condition may be to display it for the duration of promotion and afterwards the item is given to retailers as premium.
- *Training Programme:* Manufacturers impart training about their own brands to the sales staff of wholesaler or retailer at their (wholesaler's or retailer's) location. Michele Marchetti and Andy Cohen reported that Microsoft launched a training programme "Helping Clients Succeed" aimed at value-added resellers. The three-day workshop was designed to help resellers, better understand Microsoft Software.

Internet Promotions

The number of companies using Internet promotions is increasing. Contests and sweepstakes are among the most commonly used to motivate people to visit marketers' Internet sites. America Online frequently conducts prize promotions to attract users to its advertisers' areas. The prizes may range between substantial sums of money to daily prizes including merchandise decorated with the online service's logo. In India, some popular Internet promotion sites are Hungama.com and Contest2win where companies such as Pepsi, Cadbury, Sony, and Levis frequently run online contests and offer exciting prizes. This trend is gradually catching up in our country with increased availability of Broadband Internet and more and more households acquiring computers.

Promotions that Blur the Line

Some promotions such as *speciality advertising, event marketing and sponsorship* are activities that blur the line between advertising, sales promotion, and public relations.

Speciality Advertising: Promotional Products Association International has now given a new definition to this term:

"A medium of advertising, sales promotion, and motivational communication employing imprinted, useful, or decorative products called advertising specialities, a subject of promotional products.

Unlike premiums, with which they are sometimes confused (called advertising specialities), these articles are always distributed free – recipients don't have to earn the speciality by making a purchase or contribution."

Speciality advertising is often viewed both a means of advertising and sales promotion. According to *Promotional Products Association International,* the increased use of speciality advertising makes it the fastest growing of promotional methods. These items normally have a promotional message printed on them.

It is used to reinforce the name of an existing company, product, service, or brand. Speciality advertising is used in creating awareness, as reminders, to thank customers for patronage, introduce new products, and often support other forms of product promotions. Advertising speciality items include ballpoint pens, pen stands, calendars, key rings, matchboxes, T-shirts, caps, coffee mugs, glasses, bags, and numerous other items with advertiser's name or brand name printed on them.

Event Marketing and Sponsorship: It has become quite a popular promotional approach and is often considered as a part of sales promotions, especially if a product is sold through the event. However, the objectives and decisions concerning such events are often the responsibility of public relations manager. Event marketing refers to promotion where a marketeer or brand is linked to an event or an activity based on a theme, and aimed at creating some experiences by associating a brand personality with a certain lifestyle. Companies often associate their product with a sporting event, festival, music concert, or fair. Marketers sometimes create their own events to celebrate milestones, such as 50th anniversary, or new product-introduction event where they organise some contest and winners get a pack of new product. An *event sponsor* develops sponsorship relations with an event and extends financial support to obtain in return the rights to display brand name, company logo, or advertising message and to be identified as a financial supporter of the event.

Sales Promotion Planning Guidelines

Planning process starts with situation analysis. To start with, the promotion planners must first consider the corporate policy with regard to sales promotion. Joseph S. Mair has recorded one such policy statement in *Handbook of Sales Promotion*, ed. Stanley M. Ulanoff. The policy says:

1. "Sales promotion is an integral part of the marketing mix."
2. "Sales promotion should be used as an offensive weapon in the brand's marketing arsenal, not merely as a defensive reaction when a problem arises."
3. "Sales promotion should extend and reinforce the brand's advertising and positioning, whenever possible."
4. "Sales promotion should be developed as campaigns, not as single, unrelated events."
5. "Good sales promotions are built upon sound strategic planning."

The first step in promotion planning is situation analysis. This would include product or brand performance analysis, competitive situation including the promotion activities of major competitors, distribution situation, and consumer behaviour with respect to sales promotions. Political/legal aspects concerning sales promotion are also considered. Based on marketing objectives and strategies, the promotion objectives would be developed. It is critically important to set unambiguous and measurable objectives and these should be developed in coordination with advertising and other promotion mix elements. The next step would be the allocation of budget to sales promotion out of the combined total budget for advertising and sales promotion.

Considering the objectives and the budget allocation, each promotion event must be carefully created. There is vast choice of promotion tools, and the combination of these tools seems to be endless. Each sales promotion tool has its own advantages and disadvantages and these may change when different tools are combined.

Sales Promotion Objectives

Some of the important objectives of sales promotion include:

- Increase sales volume
- Attract new customers
- Launch new product and increase trial
- Encourage repeat purchase
- Clearance of excessive inventories
- Motivate dealers to stock and sell more
- To gain advantageous shelf-space
- To increase store traffic
- To block competitors' moves
- Motivate sales force

Important Considerations in Sales Promotion Decisions

Once the objectives are set, there are some important decision areas that must be considered critically:

Type of Promotion to Use

There are three types of promotions that can be used, singly, or in combination:

(a) Consumer promotion

(b) Trade promotion, and

(c) Sales force promotion

There are two major approaches for consumer and trade promotions:

(1) Same for less, and

(2) More for the same

Immediate Value Offer vs Delayed Value Offer: Sales promotions can offer immediate value to consumers or the re-sellers, such as a discount, extra goods, or a premium. The delayed value promotions reward the consumer or re-seller sometime after the purchase of the product or service, such as rebates, contests and sweepstakes, frequent flier offer, or after making multiplc purchases. Immediate value offers produce a stronger impact, stimulate customers for unplanned purchases, and encourage brand switching at the point-of-purchase. For example, there is significant brand switching in toiletries, laundry products, soft drinks, and cooking oils, etc.

Delayed value offers produce a weaker response because the reward for behaviour is possible after some time lag. However, the effect of delayed value offers is longer lasting. When a customer is required to collect proof of multiple purchases, there is a reminder of the product and the customer is also exposed to longer duration of product usage.

Price-Cut vs Extra Value Offer: The manufacturer or the retailer may offer "same for less" in the form of a price discount on the promoted product. Or, there could be an offer of extra value, which would be "more for the same". For example, a special bonus-pack that contains more quantity of the same product without any increase in the price, or a premium offered free with the purchased product. This extra value offered is independent of the promoted product and has more value to the customer than the cost to the marketer. Such premiums can be quite helpful in building the long-term brand strength of certain brands. Consumer promotions, which frequently offer price cut, or extra quantity of the same product, generally degrade the perceived value of the brand and may weaken its brand strength.

Manufacturers of high-involvement products prefer not to offer straight price discounts because this approach may disrupt the price-quality perception of customers, who may develop some negative evaluation of the product. Straight price reductions may be used only in case this type of promotion is common to the category. In general, price cuts are limited to low-end products in a product-line and prove to be more effective. A variety of "more for the same" or extra-value promotions can be used for expensive high-involvement products. For example, some computer manufacturers are adding accessories in their offer.

In case of low-involvement products, major portion of sales promotion budget is allocated for rewarding the consumers at the time of purchase by cutting the price or offering extra quantity of the product (immediate value offer). This is especially true if the product category is susceptible to unplanned or impulse buying and variety seeking; offers that encourage consumers to buy multiple units; continuity promotions, such as in-pack or on-pack coupons; and interest promotions that excite consumers, such as contests and sweepstakes.

Should the promotions be run on higher priced or lower-priced products, the products that contribute more to the sales or those that contribute less? In case of consumer non-durable products, would it be advantageous to come out with special promotion packs, or the promotion should be run on regular packs? Answers to these questions are likely to be significantly influenced by considering the consumer and trade behaviour, competitive situation, and co-ordination with advertising and personal selling.

Which Product to Promote

Resellers perceive **inventory risk** associated with stocking or not stocking the product on promotion. The following conditions may be the cause of risk perception:

- When the consumer demand for the product is unpredictable.
- When the inventory holding costs are high.
- When the product is seasonal.
- When the product is likely to go out of fashion quickly.

Choice of Market Areas

Strong brands are good traffic builders and when such brands are inexpensive and low bulk to transport and store, there is considerable forward buying and diversion in non-deal areas by the trade. Sales promotions of similar value should be announced at the same time everywhere. Higher inventory risk would require that promotions be developed for separate markets. Excess product stocks from one market can be shifted to another market with more sales potential.

Promotion Timing, Duration, and Frequency

When the product or brand inventories are less than normal in trade channels, the objective of the promotion would be to build inventories. When the inventories with the traders are high, then the objective would be to clear the inventories. It is inadvisable for the producer to announce a promotion, when the retailer shelves are full with the competitive brand, because the promotion is quite likely to prove unprofitable. If the product use were linked to weather conditions, then this factor would affect the consumer demand and the timing of promotion.

The duration of consumer promotion should be such that a larger per centage of customers get exposed to the promotion offer. In case of some product categories, interval between two successive purchases may give an idea about the duration. Low-involvement products are usually purchased more frequently and hence the duration of the deal for this category can be shorter.

In case of high-involvement category products, to induce a sense of urgency, the duration of the offer can be short. To attract the second wave of customers, it may prove to be advantageous to announce the extension of the deal period.

Frequency of promotion depends on competitive situation, deal sensitivity of customers, the interest of the trade, and the complexity of the promotion offer. Very frequent promotions of high-involvement category products may create negative impressions about the quality and price relationship of the product. Trade deals often become necessary to motivate dealers to arrange displays and participate in contests.

Rate of Discount, Terms and Conditions

What should be the minimum level of benefit in terms of price-cut or value addition that would attract the attention of the target customers to induce the desired change in purchase behaviour? Planners have to ascertain the j.n.d (Weber's Law) and answer this question.

A smaller discount figure on high priced products would translate in high monetary figure and would appear significant enough to attract customer attention and is likely to influence purchase behaviour. In case of low priced products, a higher percentage figure can be associated with the purchase of multiple units of the product. Generally, the price elasticity of low priced products is high because consumers do not perceive much difference between brands, and do not mind switching to another brand. Customers can also stock more units of low priced and low bulk products in response to promotion offer. Higher discounts should be considered to achieve large short-term sales of low priced products. Strong brands in general do not involve any inventory risk, serve as traffic builders, and would not require higher discounts.

In case of trade promotion, the producer may specify the minimum purchase value or the quantity of product to avail the benefit of promotion. Payment terms may be specified, or the terms may be related to display arrangement and its timing. Consumer promotion may require coupon expiry date, or rebate claim date. Contests and sweepstakes would require spelling out the conditions of participation, etc. Depending on the specific type and technique of promotion, market conditions, and consumer response pattern, there would be different terms and conditions associated with sales promotion.

Protection from Competition

Sales promotions in general are easily imitated by competitors and legally there is nothing that any manufacturer can do about such moves. The very purpose of gaining short-term competitive advantage is lost to the manufacturer. For example, if a marketeer announces "one cake of soap free with three cakes purchased" and other competitors announce the same or some similar deals on their brands then the advantage is likely to be lost. One way to gain some protection is to develop a promotion, which would be complex to copy and allow reasonably lengthy start to the innovator. Another way is to join hands with other well-known non-competing firms and develop an exclusive joint promotion (tie-in promotion) that cannot be imitated in a hurry. For example, Ariel and Vimal Suiting developed a joint promotion.

Promotion Evaluation

Sales effect before, during, and after the sales promotion can be measured by studying the sales figures. In case of objectives related to trial purchase, or change in consumer awareness and attitude as a result of increase in perceived value of the product, measurement may be difficult.

Pretesting can be conducted by using focus groups and consumer panels. Portfolio test is relatively expensive but a more effective method. A portfolio of sales promotions is prepared and shown to consumers in person and their responses are noted. It is often quite helpful to evaluate the response of resellers before implementing the promotion programme. The simplest way is to seek resellers' opinion and suggestions.

Concurrent testing is done when the sales promotion is in progress. Concurrent testing may permit the promotion manager to modify the sales promotion if needed. In case of consumer contest the response to promotion can be adjudged by the number of entries received at some interval and if need be the contest period can be extended.

Post-testing assesses the change in consumer awareness and attitude. To assess this, telephone calls, questionnaire mailed to consumers, and personal interviews can be used. To measure the sales effect, sales figures before the promotion period can be compared with figures at the end of promotion, and one month after the promotion ends. It is very likely that the sales in the month following promotion will come down. If the sales return to pre-promotion levels then perhaps, the sales jump was because of brand switchers and deal prone consumers. However, if the regular sales settle at higher than normal period levels then definitely the promotion proved successful in increasing the long-run sales by attracting new customers and perhaps also attracted customers away from other competing brands.

Summary

Advertising is the structured and composed non-personal communication of information, usually paid for and usually persuasive in nature, about organisations, products, services, ideas by identified sponsors through various media. Companies may handle advertising programme by themselves or hire independent outside advertising agencies for the purpose.

The developmental stage of a product determines the role of advertising. As products pass through various stages of their life cycle, the manner in which the advertising presents the product to target audiences depends largely upon the degree of a product's acceptance by consumers.

A campaign is an interrelated and coordinated set of promotional activities that focus on some single theme or idea around which the campaign will be built to accomplish some predetermined objective(s). An ad campaign includes a series of ads placed in different media based on an analysis of marketing and communication situations. An advertising plan aims at matching the right target audience to the right message and presents it in the right medium to reach that audience.

Advertising planning and managing steps include *situation analysis, identifying target audience, determining objectives, setting budget, advertising strategy implementation,* and *evaluation.* In most cases the ad agency's accounts executive develops the advertising plan or campaign.

Accounts executive prepares a creative brief to communicate the strategy to the creative team. It is a simple written statement of the most significant issues to consider and guide the team in the development of an advertisement or campaign.

A critical decision is to define the specific target audience for the product or service and involves finding and precisely defining those variables that indicate who and where the best prospects are in respect to demographic characteristics, geographic location, psychographic variables, and behavioural patterns.

Advertising aims at achieving one or more objectives such as making target audience aware of the existence of brand or company, to develop an understanding amongst the audience about the product, what is it and what it would do for them, to create a mental disposition among target audience members to buy the product, or to motivate target audience to purchase the product or service.

The advertising appeal is the central message to be used in the ad. The selected appeal should have the power to attract the attention of consumers, arouse their latent desires or influence feelings, and thus speak to human needs or wants that can be met by the advertised product, service, or cause. Rational appeals address the consumer's self interest and focuses on problem removal or problem avoidance. Emotional appeals relate to customers' social and psychological needs and stir up positive or negative emotions that can motivate purchase of a product or service. Emotional appeal promises a reward rather than the removal or avoidance of some negative situation. How this particular appeal is turned into an effective advertising message depends on the creative execution style?

Media planners have to determine the most cost-effective combination of reach, frequency, and impact. To create awareness, or for infrequently purchased products, reach is an important consideration. Frequency is important when the product nature is complex, competition is more intense, or top-of-mind recall is necessary for every day use products. Planners strike a balance between reach, frequency, and advertising cycles within the budget constraints.

Sales promotion utilises, a variety of incentive tools such as samples, coupons, discounts, premiums, refunds and rebates, contest and sweepstakes, trade deals, and sales contests for sales people etc. for a predetermined, limited period of time in order to stimulate trial, increase consumer or trade demand, and motivate and reward sales force, In most cases, the objectives are generally short-term sales related rather than long-term brand building.

Sales promotions directed at end-users are called consumer sales promotions. Such promotions include discounts, free samples, premiums, rebates, contests and sweepstakes etc. The objective of such promotions is to stimulate consumer interest in products, services, activities, and special events.

Trade promotions are directed at resellers. The objectives of trade sales promotions are to build relations with channel members, to stimulate in-store merchandising support, gain distribution of new products, gain support for existing brands, and manipulate levels of inventory held by wholesalers and retailers. These promotions include various trade allowances, trade contests and incentives, cooperative advertising, dealer loader, and training programmes etc.

Questions for Discussion

1. What is advertising and what is its role during different product life cycle stages?
2. Briefly discuss different types of advertising.
3. What are the different methods of setting advertising budget determination? Which one would you recommend to a consumer product company?
4. Why is it important to identify and define target market for an advertising programme?
5. What factors media planners should consider in developing a media plan?
6. What is an advertising appeal? Discuss two methods of advertising execution styles.
7. How would you pretest a print ad?

8. How would you conduct post-testing of a TV commercial?
9. What major factors should be considered in developing a sales promotion programme?
10. Discuss three important consumer promotion tools.
11. Discuss various methods of trade sales promotions. In your view, which method is more suitable?

Projects

1. Collect three print ads and identify the kind of appeals they use. Do you think the appeals are appropriate?
2. Create an advertising plan for a brand of consumer durable of your choice.
3. View a humorous commercial and write down a report on its different aspects. Do you think it is effective in communicating the desired message?
4. Develop a complete sales promotion programme for a new brand cellular phone.

Bibliography

1. Ned Anschuetz, "Point of View: Building Brand Popularity: The Myth of Segmenting to Brand Success," *Journal of Advertising Research,* January-February 1997
2. Darral G. Clarke, "Econometric Measurement of the Duration of Advertising Effect on Sales," *Journal of Marketing Research,* (November 1976).
3. Russell H. Colley, "Defining Advertising Goals for Measured Advertising Results," *Association of American Advertisers,* 1961.
4. Robert D. Buzzell and Frederick D. Wiersema, "Successful Share Building Strategies," *Harvard Business Review,* (January/ February 1981).
5. Ama Carmine, "The Effect of Perceived Advertising Costs on Brand Perceptions," *Journal of Consumer Research,* September 1990.
6. Joseph W. Ostrow, "Setting Frequency Levels: An Art or a Science?" *Journal of Advertising Research,* (August-September 1984).
7. Joseph W. Ostrow, "What Level Frequency?" *Advertising Age,* Nov 1981.
8. William L. Wilkie, Debra M. Desrochers, and Gregory T. Gundlach, "Marketing Research and Public Policy: The Case of Slotting Fees," *Journal of marketing & Public Policy,* 21, (2002).
9. Michele Marchetti and Andy Cohen, "In Search of Microsoft's Softer Side," *Sales and Marketing Management,* 151, (1999).
10. Joseph S. Mair, "The Big Event and Sales Campaign," in *Handbook of Sales Promotion,* ed. Stanley M. Ulanoff, (McGraw-Hill 1985).
11. *Promotional Products Association International,* (Irving, 1996).
12. *Promotional Products Association International,* 2000.

Personal Selling

CHAPTER 15

LEARNING OBJECTIVES

After going through this chapter, you will understand:

- The nature of personal selling and its significance
- Steps involved in personal selling process
- Activities involved in managing sales force
- Performance evaluation of sales people

lthough the early 1990s have been difficult for IBM, during the 1970s and most of the 1980s, IBM was considered to be one of the finest sales and marketing organisations in the world. Much of the credit for this went to F. G. Rogers, who became IBM's senior marketing executive in 1974 when he was selected IBM's Vice President of Marketing. This capped a career begun as an IBM sales person in 1950 after his graduation from college.

Rogers's sales and marketing approach reflected IBM's dedication to the customer. In his book 'The IBM Way', Rogers wrote: "At IBM everybody sells ... Every employee has been trained to think that the customer comes first - everybody from the CEO, to the people in finance, to receptionists, to those who work in manufacturing."

Under Rogers's direction, IBM developed comprehensive sales training and management programmes that emphasised product and customer knowledge, and most importantly, a high level of service support after the sale. IBM's sales people were taught to provide solutions to their customers in addition to selling equipment. Rogers emphasised that "customers, rather than technology, establish the direction at IBM.

Rogers's personal commitment to quality carried through to the IBM sales force. He believed in spending time and money to find quality sales people. After finding these people, IBM provided them with a demanding sales training programme. Role-playing and other sophisticated training approaches were used to prepare sales trainees for market place conditions. Sales people were taught to concentrate on what a product would do, not what it was. This enabled them to understand customers' problems and to offer sensible solutions. IBM rewarded its sales people by providing them with meaningful and challenging assignments, paying salaries and incentives based on a "pay for performance" philosophy, and rewarding superior performance through honours and recognition.

Under Rogers's sales leadership, IBM became known as a company that maintained a close working relationship with customers. Rogers and IBM's commitment to customer service and quality became the benchmark by which other sales organisations were judged.

Source: Sales management, by Johnson, Kurtz, and Scheuing, McGraw-Hill International, 1994.

Personal selling is a critical aspect of a company's promotional strategy. According to Ginger Conlon, personal selling is often said to be the "last 3 feet" of marketing function. In most selling situations this is approximately the distance between the sales person and the customer whether across the retail counter or the table. This brings in the human element in marketing transactions and a bond or partnership between the sales person and her/his customers can be one of the most valuable assets that a company holds in the marketplace. The sales person can create the confidence in the company, makes it possible for the customer to act quickly, and simplifies the handling of individual customer problems.

Sales people and the customers interact face-to-face and the likelihood of any distractions is minimised and the buyer generally pays close attention to the sales message. This direct and interpersonal communication lets the sales person immediately receive and assess the feedback from the customer. This allows for more specific adjustment of the message. The message being communicated can be adjusted to tackle the customer's specific needs or wants. It offers the opportunity to develop long-term familiarity and relationship. The sales person becomes the company face for the customer who they personally see, know and interact with. The emphasis accorded to personal selling varies across companies depending on a variety of factors such as the nature of product or service and the type of industry. Marketers of Industrial products generally place more emphasis on personal selling and it plays a nominal role in companies selling low-priced consumer non-durables.

Role of Personal Selling

It is important to determine the role of personal selling and this is possible by examining the following factors:

- ***Information to be Exchanged:*** Personal selling may be used to create product or service awareness, knowledge, product demonstration, inducing trial, and closing the sale. During this process it may be necessary to answer questions, remove doubts, and meeting potentially unmet needs or wants.
- ***Product Nature and Selling Situation:*** Personal selling is appropriate when the product nature is complex and requires application assistance such as complex machinery, aircraft, or pollution control systems. Personal selling is suitable while, selling to large retail stores or supermarkets. Other situations include where price is negotiated for expensive products such as property or appliances, distribution channel is direct to end users, product training and assistance is needed by channel members, and product needs to be "pushed" through personal selling, and information needs of buyers cannot be met completely through mass communications, such as life insurance.
- ***Cost Effectiveness:*** Personal selling is the most expensive of all promotion mix elements. However, it is appropriate for industrial products where a single purchase may run into several lakhs of rupees. Even certain expensive consumer durables such as cars, or home appliances require personal selling at dealer showroom level.

Personal Selling Tasks

Personal selling involves a variety of responsibilities. Thomas R. Wotruba believes that personal selling function is constantly evolving in response to changes in marketing environment. These evolutionary stages are:

- ***Provider Stage:*** Personal selling function is limited for accepting orders from customers for the seller's available range of offerings and delivering it to the buyer.
- ***Persuader Stage:*** Selling activity involves an attempt to persuade customers in a face-to-face communication to buy the seller's product or service.
- ***Prospector Stage:*** Personal selling activities involve identifying selected potential customers who are perceived as having a need for the seller's product or service, and also have the resources and authority to buy it.
- ***Problem Solving Stage:*** Personal selling involves participation of customers in identifying their problems and suitable solutions and then offering the sellers' solution, that matches the needs of the customers and is an effective solution for buyers' problems.
- ***Procreator Stage:*** This type of personal selling also involves problem-solving approach and needs customer's active participation. The discussion leads to develop a tailor made offer unique to a particular buyer. For instance, installing electrical fixtures in a production facility requires company sales person to discuss the whole situation and then with mutual consent designs the installation plan.

Sales Force Organisation

Sales force structuring has important implications. Most companies structure their sales force based on geography, customers or products, or some combination of these factors. For a company marketing just a single product category and selling to different scattered customers in one industry, a territory-based structure would be suitable. If a company manufactures several different product categories and sells to different types of customers, it might find a customer type based sales force.

Territory Based: It is a fairly common approach for structuring the sales force. Field sales people are assigned the responsibility for direct or missionary selling in a given geographical area. This sales structure is fairly common among FMCG companies. The sales person would sell the company's full range of products and each territory is treated as a separate profit centre for the purpose of analysis and evaluation of sales personnel. The selling expenses are generally low because the sales person operates in a limited area.

Product Based: The sales people concentrate all their efforts on particular product lines, brands, or individual items. This is often the case with companies who have adopted product management, or brand management system. Product based structure suits companies with highly unrelated and technically complex products and in large numbers. For example, marketers selling mainframe computers have product based sales force structure, or companies dealing in complex laboratory equipment, often have product specialists.

Customer Based: Those favouring customer based sales force structure believe that it is better to focus on customer needs and build close relationship with clients. The customers may require specialised knowledge of their industry. Companies selling to diverse industries might structure their sales force based on customer types. Xerox, IBM, and Compaq*HP* are customer-based organisations. Some large publishers of textbooks have separate sales people who are specialist in different disciplines, and some large office equipment manufacturers use sales people serving only educational institutions. Auto parts manufacturers have separate sales people for *OEM* and replacement market.

Personal Selling Responsibilities

Prospecting: It is the process of locating new potential customers and involves following the leads and separating prospects from suspects. The sales person collects possible information, about the prospect and determines the best way of approaching her/him. The sales person determines the prospect's needs and wants, the company products or services can satisfy. Another important aspect of prospecting is to ascertain whether the individual has the resources and authority to take the purchase decision.

Recommending the Solution: The sales person recommends the company product or service to solve potential customer's problem. This requires presenting information, the prospect had not thought of or had no access to the information regarding the alternative solution. The sales person demonstrates the company's capabilities and why the company and its product or service is the right choice for the prospect. Obviously, at this stage the corporate image building advertising and other promotional activities help the sales person.

Closing Sales: In the final analysis, closing sales is the most important ultimate step. Despite all efforts if the sales person fails to close the sales, the call is wasted for that occasion.

Follow Up: The responsibility to serve the customer does not end at sales closing. It is economical and relatively easier to keep current customers than attracting new ones. Post sales follow up helps sales persons in developing customer relationship, generating repeat sales, and sell firm's additional products or services to the same customer. Post purchase follow up is an important step in satisfying customers.

FIGURE 15.1

Major Types of Sales Jobs

Creative Selling (Order getters): Sales jobs of creative nature require high levels of selling skills and preparation. Creative selling requires prospecting, assessing the situation, identifying the prospect's needs, making a presentation of the need satisfying product or service, and closing the sale. The salesperson establishes the first contact on behalf of the company and is responsible for completing the sale. The sales person seeks new customers, focuses on existing customers and encourages them to buy more company products.

Order Taking: After the creative sales person has completed the initial exchange, the order takers complete most sales transactions and maintain relationship with their customers. Order takers sell on a routine basis to regular or established customers. This requires ongoing follow-up to ascertain that the customer is completely satisfied. Sometimes the order taker may be involved in modified rebuy that may require some creative selling. If a major purchase is involved, the creative salesperson again takes over. Order takers are sometimes categorised as *inside order takers*, and *field order takers*. Inside order takers work in the office and take orders by phone, mail or the Internet, and field order takers go to customers and take the orders.

Missionary Selling: This involves essentially a more supportive role played by the salesperson. The salesperson performs all the functions involved in creative selling but may not be required to take the orders. They call on customers and middlemen and attempt to develop goodwill and stimulate demand, help middlemen to train their salespeople, and some firms may require them to book orders as well from resellers and customers. Missionary salespeople are also called the *detailers* and are most often employed in pharmaceutical industry.

Technical Specialists: Technical salespeople are often specialists and technically qualified persons. They are usually more skilled in showing the technical details of their product. The technical specialists provide the product details and not primarily trying to persuade the customer to buy it.

Characteristics of Top Sales Performers

A survey conducted by *Sales & Marketing Management* of 209 sales persons from 189 companies in 37 different industries found the following ten traits of top sale performers:

- ***Ego Strength:*** Possesses a healthy self-esteem that helps salesperson to bounce back from rejection.
- ***A Sense of Urgency:*** Has a sense of urgency and wants to get it done now.
- ***Ego Drive:*** Possesses a combination of self-esteem and enduring competitiveness.
- ***Empathy:*** Has the ability to place herself/himself in another person's shoes?
- ***Assertiveness:*** Has the ability to be firm, lead the sales process, and communicate her/his point of view?
- ***Willing to Take Risks:*** Is willing to innovate and take chances?
- ***Sociable:*** Has a friendly disposition, and interested in others?
- ***Abstract Reasoning:*** Possesses the ability to comprehend concepts and ideas.
- ***Creativity:*** Possesses the ability to think differently.
- ***Scepticism:*** Has a slight lack of trust and suspicion of others?

MANAGING SALES FORCE

Determination of Sales Force Size

Companies have to determine the size of the sales force they need. Walter J. Semlov's is the oldest and best-known method to determine the size of sales force. According to this formula, a company may add more salespeople until the last additional member equals the profit of the sales volume, the sales person is expected to produce. He expressed this approach to calculating the size of the sales force in a simple formula:

$$S(p) - C = 0$$

Where:

S = Expected sales volume each additional salesperson will produce.

p = Expected profit margin on sales.

C = Total cost of maintaining the additional salesperson in the field.

The main weakness in this formula is ascertaining the accuracy of sales volume the additional salesperson will produce. There are also certain complex quantitative models available to determine the sales force size.

Sometimes companies determine the sales force size by making calculations as under:

- Total number of customers in classes (A+B) based on their estimated sales volume.
- Multiply each customer class with its call frequency to determine the workload.
- Average number of customer calls per salesperson per day.
- Total number of working days in a year.
- Divide the total number of calls in a year by the average number of calls per salesperson per year.

Example:

A Class = 1000 × 48 (Annual Call Frequency) = 48,000

B Class = 4000 × 24 = 96,000 = 144,000 Calls per year.

Average number of calls per salesperson per day = 5

Total number of working days in a year = 300

Annual average calls per salesperson = 5 × 300 = 1500

$$\text{Sales Force Size} = \frac{\text{Total Calls in One Year}}{\text{Annual Average Calls Per Salesperson}} = \frac{1{,}44{,}000}{1500} = 96$$

Recruitment & Selection of Salespersons

It is important for companies to employ and maintain an effective sales force. The management first develops a set of qualifications that each applicant must satisfy to be considered. Recruitment and selection process involves developing a list of sales positions and selecting candidates to fill the vacancies. Companies can recruit from several sources, such as personal recommendations, educational institutions, employment agencies, advertising the vacancies, and other sources.

The process of selection varies widely from one company to another. It could be just one personal interview, or a more detailed process involving a preliminary interview, group discussion, written test and detailed personal interview, and physical check up. Whatever be the recruitment and selection process, it should satisfy the company needs to ascertain specific information about potential candidates. Through experience companies develop more confidence in a recruitment and selection procedure that has been found to be more appropriate for a particular company. Recruitment and selection of salespeople is an ongoing activity and not just one-time decisions. As things keep on changing in marketing environment, companies develop different marketing strategies accordingly, and salespersons should be available with required new skills.

Training Sales Persons

It is not uncommon in some companies to send the selected candidates into the field without any formal training. This often leads to sales people having bad experiences and some decide to leave the job. This also causes companies to waste money.

To design a training programme, the management focuses on determining the following training-related issues:

- The aim of the training programme.
- The course content.
- Methods to be used.
- Who should conduct the training?
- The place where training will be conducted.
- Duration and time of training.
- Training evaluation.

Well-managed companies arrange training programme for newly selected salespersons. The training period may range between a few weeks to few months. The training programme for fresh salespeople is generally comprehensive. The course contents might cover company policies and procedures, job responsibilities, company products, their benefits, and applications, problems, services, warranties, terms and conditions, distribution, selling skills and methods. For experienced salespersons, there might be refresher courses for existing products/services, for new -products, and certain selling skills.

Companies use a wide range of training methods depending on the training objectives and may include lectures, role-plays, demonstrations, case method, videotapes and films, and on-the-job training etc. The training programme may be conducted by the managers in sales, senior salespeople, technical experts within the company, or outside experts.

Sales Force Compensation

Sales force compensation programmes vary considerably across industries and also within the same industry. Before determining the compensation programme, the company must examine the importance and value of salespersons to the company's selling efforts based on objectives, tasks, responsibilities, and required qualifications and experience. The company should develop a compensation plan that would attract, motivate, and retain top-quality sales persons. It should give adequate income security, incentive for achieving more, freedom, and allow management of the necessary level of control. The compensation should be fair, flexible, economical to the company, easy to administer and understand by salespersons. The company should also consider what is generally the going rate in the industry.

Companies take care to reimburse sales persons for selling expenses, offer certain employee benefits, and provide an adequate income. Generally, compensation programmes use one or more of the three basic approaches.

Under *straight salary* system, salespersons receive a specified monetary payment per month or per week. The salary may be raised at specified intervals (every year or every two years etc.).

In case of *straight commission* plan a set per centage of sales or different levels of percentage on different levels of sales are used.

Under *combination* approach, salespersons are paid both a fixed salary and commission on sales volume. Most companies use a combination compensation plan. The reason for this plan's popularity is that it provides all that is required for a good system of compensating salespeople, both, financial security and incentive for higher than average performance. In additions to, salary and incentive, some companies provide additional perks such as company car, telephone, and laptop computers to their salespeople.

Motivating Sales Persons

Motivating sales force refers to making deliberate efforts so that salespeople do their jobs well. The first-line manager plays an important role in accomplishing this objective. The majority of salespersons require encouragement and special incentives because of the very nature of field working. Their working hours are irregular and they usually work alone, face tough competition from sales personnel of other companies, and moreover hardly succeed on every call.

The manager must understand the behaviour of salespeople to lead and motivate them to obtain high levels of productivity. According to Kenneth Blanchard, to motivate salespersons, managers need to acknowledge and reward achievements and progress more often than just once a year. The sales management must appreciate the fact that salespeople are human beings and they have needs and wants, and accordingly create a climate that allows them to satisfy these needs and wants in an agreeable manner. Company should provide congenial working conditions, reasonable job security, opportunity to achieve more and excel. Salespersons are more likely to be motivated to do well if they really believe that their efforts will result in appropriate rewards. Research findings indicate that money, recognition, respect, promotion, personal growth, and a sense of accomplishment are important motivators for salespersons. The importance of these factors varies across countries and cultures.

The rewards should be both financial as well as non-financial (psychological) for outstanding performance and achievements. Occasional sales contests, appreciation letters, and sales meetings are also helpful in motivating salespersons.

Sales Quotas

Companies develop annual sales forecasts (Chapter – 7). Sales management assigns quotas to different sales regions based on potential. Typically, the total of these sales quotas is a little more than the forecasted figures. The whole idea is, if some sales personnel fail to achieve their sales quota, the company might still be achieving its sales targets. This is believed to be an approach to stimulate better performance from sales personnel.

Regional managers further divide the quota among area managers according to the potential of different areas. Finally, area managers allocate quotas to salespersons operating in their sales territories. Area managers remain in closer contact with their salespersons and have deeper understanding about their capabilities and their territories. Based on these factors and company policy they may set higher but attainable quotas, modest quotas that majority of the salespersons can achieve, or variable quotas based on individual salespersons' capabilities.

In some companies there is a general approach to quota setting and area managers determine the percentage increase in area quota as compared to last year's achievement. The area managers add one or two per cent from their side in the assigned quota, to be on the safer side and divides this among salespersons based on their last year achievement. Salespersons generally consider this approach as fair because everyone gets the same percentage increase in last year's achievement.

There is always a possibility that the quota set, might be less than what an individual is capable of achieving and also the quota might be high to achieve. Accuracy of sales forecasts under the assumed set of controllable and uncontrollable market conditions may also influence the sales performance of salespeople.

Eilene Zimmerman reports that some companies are doing away with quota system. This is because salespersons are focused on achieving more sales to earn incentives. As a result they often ignore customer service and long-term satisfaction.

Performance Evaluation of Salespersons

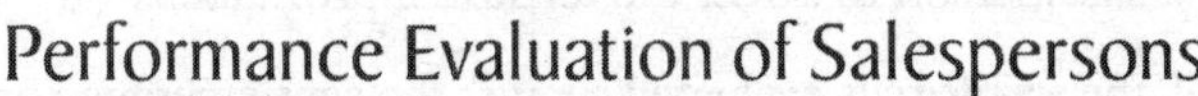

Evaluation of any business activity is ideally related to set objectives and standards. The areas of performance evaluation with respect to salespersons, generally focus on some combination of knowledge, skills, performance, and personal characteristics. The evaluation criteria vary across industries and from one company to another. Well-managed companies establish standards for evaluating sales performance and also the intervals at which this would be formally done.

Johnson, Kurtz, and Scheuing mention some generally accepted principles of evaluation salespeople:

- Must be realistic and reflect territories, competition, experience, and sales potential etc. as they are.
- Salesperson must know when and how performance is evaluated.
- The evaluation must show a salesperson, what needs improvement and how to do it.
- It must be motivating and stimulate the salesperson to improve.
- It must furnish useful information about a salesperson and the work territory.
- The salesperson must be involved in her/his evaluation.
- It must be based on objective evaluation standards and not opinions.
- It must take into consideration the changing market conditions.
- It must be specific to fit the company and the salespeople.
- It must be economical.

Most companies use only quantitative criteria to evaluate the performance, and some other believe in making quantitative as well as qualitative evaluation of salespeople. Quantitative criteria focus on measuring the nature and desired levels of performance, and qualitative aspects appraise those performance characteristics that affect sales results. Various factors on which salespeople have very little or no control also affect sales performance, such as level of promotional support given to salespeople from the company, competition, and changing economic conditions.

Many companies require their salespeople to submit weekly or monthly work plan, or the frontline managers in consultation with individual sales representatives develop these work plans. Each individual representative is given a copy. Based on this, each sales person submits her/his coming week's work plan showing the planned calls on different customer categories, and the route plan.

Sales representatives submit *daily* or *weekly work reports and expense reports.* These are a rich source of data and managers can determine the call average, types of customer contacted, average revenue per call, average cost per call, number of orders procured per month, new prospects contacted per month, cost and sales ratio for each salesperson.

Generally frontline managers work 2-3 days with each sales representative in a month or two. They also submit their work reports after discussing various aspects with the salesperson. These reports often reflect comments about certain work habits and specific characteristics that affect sales performance and require improvement.

Quantitative Standards: Some of the main quantitative standards considered include:

- ***Quotas:*** This can be in monetary value terms or product units that the salesperson is required to achieve within the specified period. Quotas measure sales volume, gross margin, net profit, expenses, selling and non-selling activities, or some combination of these.
- ***Ratio of Selling Expenses:*** Depending on individual territorial conditions and territory potential, an analysis of selling expense ratio can help a salesperson to affect the territorial profitability.
- ***Territorial Market Share:*** Market share of the territory is evaluated against the set percentage of total market. All companies in the industry may not have similar individual territorial demarcation. At the time of quarterly, half-yearly, or final evaluation, industry sales are matched with the company territory/ or state sales.
- ***Call Average Per Customer Class and Total Average:*** Compared against set targets.
- ***Average Cost Per Call:*** This reveals per call profitability.
- ***Average Order Size Per Call:*** This shows whether more profitable customers calls were made.
- ***Non-Selling Activities:*** Some companies set standards for activities such as number of prospects, arranging sales displays, or conducting film shows etc.

Non-Quantitative Standards: These job aspects affect performance but in their evaluation a subjective element cannot be ruled out. These may include:

- Product and Customer Knowledge.
- Customer and Trade Relations.
- Quality of Sales Presentation.
- Communication Skills.
- Punctuality.
- Marketing Intelligence.
- Job Attitude.
- Cooperation.

Personal Selling Techniques

Personal selling has been around since ancient times. The objectives and the manner, it requires to be implemented have evolved over the years. In today's highly dynamic and competitive market conditions, the role of a salesperson is not just limited to persuading customers to buy products but also adopting ways to build long-term customer relationship.

Prospecting

The first requirement in personal selling is narrowing down the selling effort to the targeted customers. Prospecting involves developing and following all the leads to identify potential target customers and this requires hard work and proper time management.

Some companies provide prospect lists or customer relationship database to make it easier for salespeople. Customer enquiries from different territories through various sources, including company website can be passed along to salespersons. Companies can also acquire lists from commercial sources providing this service. Other sources to generate leads can be current customers, suppliers, resellers, trade association members, various directories, or cold calling (calling unannounced on offices and individual households) etc.

Pre-Approach

Once the salesperson identifies a set of prospects and customers, the salesperson should try to learn as much as possible about the individual or company needs. In case of a company, the salesperson should collect as much information as possible about the company's products, competition, market, potential sales volume, the purchase procedure, who is involved in influencing purchase decision, who is the final authority for making purchase decision, and their personal traits. Salespersons scan company web sites, consult industrial reports, and explore acquaintances. Kirk Smith, Eli Jones, and Edward Blair report that properly organised salespersons usually develop some system because they have too many demands on their time.

The salesperson should consider the available facts and set specific call objectives that have measurable outcomes. The call objectives may not always be to make a sale. The aim might not always be to get an order but it could be to qualify the prospect, information collection, or to get a sales order. In selling situations where multiple calls are needed, specific objectives should be set for every stage. The salesperson should also determine the suitable approach method and time. In certain cases this may require a phone call or a letter first. In some companies, telemarketing personnel get an appointment for the salesperson's call.

Approach

It is extremely important for the salesperson to determine how the customer should be greeted. The first impression is not just important but crucial to the success of a sales call. The salesperson must look and act like a professional.

A salesperson should select an approach that suits her/his personality and judgement about the specific sales situation. Homer B. Smith has recommended different approaches. Some proven techniques include:

- ***Ask Questions:*** Questions should preferably be relevant to sales presentation.

- ***Use a Referral:*** Preferably someone favourably known to the potential customer.
- ***Offer a Benefit or Service:*** This can be quite effective if relevant to customer's need.
- ***Complement the Prospect:*** It is a good way to establish rapport if there is anything the prospect has achieved.

FIGURE 15.2
Missionary Selling, (A Medical Detailer)

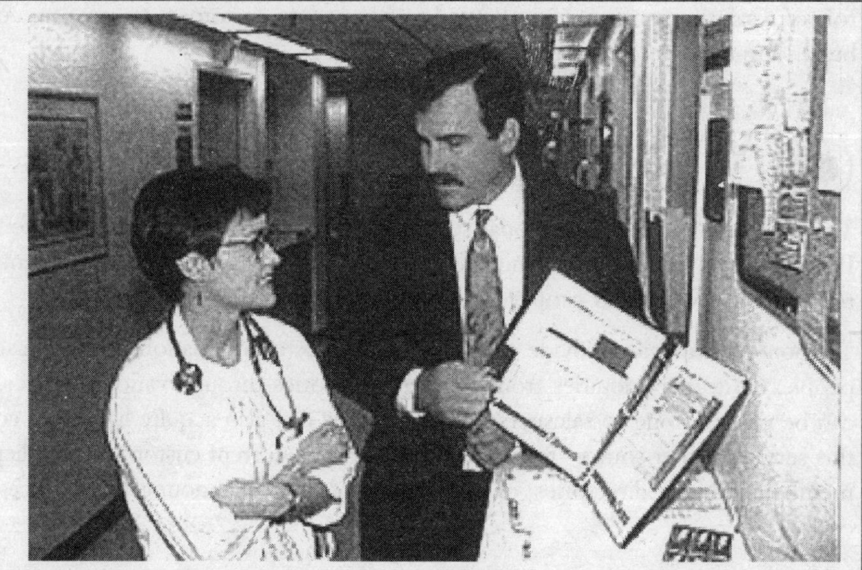

Sales Presentation

Relevant to prospect needs, the salesperson presents the product/service story according to the AIDA model (capture *attention*, hold *interest,* stimulate *desire,* and get *action*). The salesperson describes product/ service features, their advantages, benefits (economic, technical, service, and social or psychological), and the total value prospect gains from making the purchase. James E. Lukaszewski and Paul Ridgeway report that, to be effective with the prospect, the salesperson should ensure that the sales presentation is clear, concise, and well prepared.

Salespersons can use different approaches to making sales presentation. The oldest method is the *stimulus-response* theory of learning (sometimes called *canned presentation*). This approach reflects the belief that a customer will buy a product or service if exposed to the right stimuli, such as words, terms, pictures, and actions etc. The salesperson memorises the sales presentation, including when to do what, and with customer after customer repeats it.

A variation of stimulus-response based approach is *formulated presentation.* The salesperson identifies the prospect's needs and then makes a formulated presentation. Not much attention is given to encouraging the prospect involvement in the sales presentation proper.

The *need-satisfaction* approach starts with first determining the prospect's specific product or service related needs and tailors the presentation addressing those needs, although encouraging the prospect to participate in the presentation and do most of the talking.

Sales presentations can be made more meaningful with use of visuals, samples, video cassettes, computer-based simulations, testimonials, examples, guarantees, and demonstrations. It is useful to leave brochures and booklets. For group presentation, now with technological advancements it is useful to make Powerpoint presentations prepared by professionals and offer the advantage of downloading them on the laptops of audience. Such professionally prepared presentations can use animation to clarify what cannot be explained by words.

Handling Objections

All salespersons, encounter sales resistance and this resistance often takes the form of objections. Some of these objections may be rational, or may be purely psychological. These may include product price and quality, company reputation, preference for competing brand, postponing purchase, and irritation towards salesperson etc. A salesperson should be prepared to face such objections. However, no matter how well-prepared a salesperson is, there is always a chance that a customer may raise some objection for which the salesperson has to come up with a solution immediately on his own. The salesperson must possess a good degree of presence of mind. In most situations a good product and competition knowledge, and an understanding of human behaviour is of considerable help to salespersons.

The salesperson should maintain a calm approach, be positive and make sure the true nature of prospect's concern is understood. This requires first listening carefully, asking questions to clarify the issue, and them understanding the true nature of objection. However, if the prospect doesn't really need the product, or has no resources to buy it, the salesperson must thank her/him for the time taken and leave business card with the assurance of great service any time in future.

Closing the Sale

Closing refers to asking for the order. After making an effective sales presentation, the salesperson is ready to ask for the order. Closing is the sum total of all the sales presentation steps. It is the very reason for which the prospect was contacted. Many salespeople, perhaps because they lack confidence, feel uneasy, fail to perceive the positive cues indicating the prospect's readiness, and fail to take the step of asking for order.

Salespersons should learn to interpret meanings of queries, comments, statements, or prospect's body language signals. As soon as possible, the salesperson must try to close the sales. During the presentation, at some point the salesperson may use a *trial close.* This involves assuming that the prospect is ready to buy and might ask which model, size, colour, financial terms, quantity, and delivery etc., the prospect prefers. The prospect's response to such questions indicates how close the prospect really is for making the purchase. The salesperson might also indicate the advantage of buying now, or offer some incentive to act just then. The salesperson may also repeat strong points of agreement and take a decisive and confident approach and ask for an order.

In most business-to-business (B2B) buying situations, salespersons need to be skilled negotiators during the sales presentation. The negotiations may involve factors concerning price, quality, service, delivery, payment terms etc. The salesperson should be able to negotiate and work out a final settlement to which both buyer and seller are willing to agree to its terms and conditions. It is a win-win situation for both the parties when negotiations are concluded successfully.

Follow Up

Post-purchase follow up is very important in building customer confidence and long-term relationship with the company. The salesperson contacts customer to learn if there are any problems and answers any questions that the customer does. He also contacts customers regularly to ascertain that they are happy with their purchase and offered services. Relationship selling not just focuses on selling the product but to understand changing customer needs, and solving their problems. All the company departments must understand the value of customer and provide appropriate backup to sales people to strengthen this relationship. As long as both the customer and the seller are successful in achieving their goals, the relationship continues to prosper.

Summary

Personal selling involves a face-to-face communication with prospects and customers. The message being communicated can be adjusted to tackle the customer's specific needs or wants. This brings in the human element in marketing transactions and a bond or partnership between the salesperson and her/his customers can be one of the most valuable assets a company holds in the marketplace.

Most companies structure their sales-force based on geography, customers, products, or a combination of these factors. For a company marketing just a single product category and selling to different scattered customers in one industry, a territory-based structure would be suitable. If a company manufactures several different product categories and sells to different types of customers, it might find a customer type based sales force.

Creative selling requires prospecting, assessing the situation, identify the prospect's needs, make presentation of need satisfying product or service, and close the sale. The order takers complete most sales transactions and maintain relationships with their customers. Missionary selling involves essentially a supportive role from the salesperson and may not be required to take the orders. They call on customers and middlemen and attempt to develop goodwill and stimulate demand.

Technical salespeople are often specialists and technically qualified persons.

Prospecting involves locating new potential customers and identifying their needs, and also ensures if they have the resources and authority to make the purchase decision.

The salesperson recommends the company product or service to solve potential customer's problem. This requires presenting information the prospect had not thought of or had no access to the information regarding the alternative solution. The salesperson demonstrates the company capabilities and why the company and its product or service is the right choice for the prospect.

Closing sales is the most important ultimate step. Despite all sorts of efforts if the salesperson fails to close the sales, the call is wasted for that occasion.

Post sales follow up helps salespersons in developing customer relationship, generating repeat sales, and sell firm's additional products or services to the same customer. Post purchase follow up is an important step in satisfying customers.

Recruitment and selection process involves developing a list of sales positions and selecting candidates to fill the vacancies. Companies can recruit from several sources, such as personal recommendations, educational institutions, employment agencies, advertising the vacancies, and other sources.

Fresh salespeople may require comprehensive training and experienced salespersons might have refresher courses. Motivating sales force refers to making deliberate efforts so that salespeople do their jobs well. Salespersons are more likely to be motivated to do well if they really believe that their efforts will result in appropriate rewards.

The rewards should be both financial as well as non-financial for outstanding performance and achievements. Occasional sales contests, appreciation letters, and sales meetings are also helpful in motivating salespersons. Sales force compensation is based either on straight salary, straight commission, or combination of salary and commission. Most companies use a combination compensation plan.

Salespeople have attainable quotas and performance evaluation is often based on knowledge, skills, performance, and personal characteristics. Companies use quantitative and qualitative criteria to evaluate the performance. Work and expense reports furnish rich source of data for evaluation.

Personal selling techniques include prospecting, pre-approach, approach, sales presentation, objections handling, closing sales, and follow up.

Questions for Discussion

1. How personal selling differs from advertising? Discuss the changing role of personal selling.
2. What is the importance of prospecting? Discuss some approaches to prospecting.
3. Differentiate between the role of a missionary sales representative and a technical salesperson.
4. Why is it important for sales management to pay special attention for motivating salespersons?
5. If you were a front line manager what steps would you take to motivate your team members?
6. What are the implications of different compensation plans? Which compensation method would you recommend to a bank for marketing its credit cards?
7. Discuss the advantages of different systems of compensation methods. Which one would you adopt for your company salespersons?
8. Briefly describe the personal selling techniques.
9. Discuss in detail the importance and two methods of handling objections?
10. Should getting the order be the single most important concern for the sales person? Or his responsibilities extend further?

Projects

1. Contact a pharmaceutical sales representative and study how the individual works in the field. Prepare a report about missionary selling activities.
2. Visit the sales office of an Indian FMCG company. Meet the sales executive and learn how the performance of salespersons is evaluated. Prepare a report.
3. Contact an Eureka Forbes salesperson. Go with her/him in the field and study the sales presentation steps. Write a critical report.

Bibliography

1. Ginger Conlon, "cornering the Market," *Sales & Marketing Management,* March 1997.
2. Thomas R. Wotruba, "The Evolution of Personal Selling," *Journal of Personal Selling & Sales Management,* 11 September 1991.
3. Walter J. Semlov, "How Many Salesmen Do You Need?" *Harvard Business Review,* May-June 1959.
4. Kenneth Blanchard, "Reward Sales People Creatively," *Personal Selling Power,* March 1992.
5. Eugene M. Johnson, David L. Kurtz, and Eberhard E. Scheuing, *Sales Management,* McGraw-Hill, 1994.
6. Eilene Zimmerman, "Quota Busters," *Sales & Marketing Management,* January 2001.
7. Homer B. Smith, "The First Three Minutes of a Successful Sales Approach, *Personal Selling Power,* 10, 1990.
8. James E. Lukaszewski and Paul Ridgeway, "To Put Your Best Foot Forward, Start by Taking These 21 Simple Steps," *Sales & Marketing Management,* June 1990.

Public Relations and Publicity

CHAPTER 16

LEARNING OBJECTIVES

After going through this chapter, you will understand:

- The significance of public relations in promotion mix
- In what way public relations affects promotion programmes
- Setting objectives and managing public relations programmes
- Role of publicity
- Measuring results

Many a time, the PR approach is to view media as news vending machines instead of the larger role that the media can play. This rules out possibility of media playing a larger the part in shaping the perceptions about a company. So in effect, what does the PR approach do? It makes sure that there is a high visibility in the media and that there is the frequent splash in the pages every once in a while. But there is an inherent tightrope that organisations will have to walk by adopting this route. Visibility in the media means that one is directly in the public glare, where if any volatility in statements is sensed, the degree of difficulty in the self-extrication becomes all the more difficult. This is also the common hurdle that several companies falter at, so regularly. A case that readily comes to mind is that of HLL, when it advertised about Wheel detergent powder, the product with lemon. And the campaign really did wonders for HLL in terms of generating huge sales for the brand. But the high visibility proved to be HLL's undoing, when Nirma proved comprehensively - through laboratory tests and a messy court trial - that wheel contained no trace of lemon! The amount of negative publicity that was generated for HLL through this single episode, will continue to haunt it for a while. After all reputation scars cannot be hidden once tainted, the company or brand will continue to be referred to, albeit unfairly, by the same murky credentials that had pulled it down.

(Source: Part of an article by Avis in A & M, titled "For that Good Name" October 15, 2000).

Sometimes jokingly, actors who generally perform the roles of a villain in movies say, "There is no such thing as bad publicity." It may or may not be true for such characters trying to get their names in the public, but certainly bad publicity for any marketing organisation is worse than no publicity. Companies spend large sums of money and devote much time to protect or defend themselves from negative news and try to develop noticeable positive messages. Public relations efforts tell the organisation's "story" to its public.

'Public relations' is defined in a variety of ways by different authors. Institute of Public Relations, UK defines it in the following words:

"Public relations practice is the deliberate, planned, and sustained effort to establish and maintain mutual understanding between an organisation and its public."

According to Raymond Simon, perhaps the most comprehensive definition has been offered by *Public Relations,* which is the weekly newsletter of the industry:

'The management function which evaluates public attitudes, identifies the policies and procedures of an organisation with the public interest, and executes a programme of action (and communication) to earn public understanding and acceptance."

In modern open market economies, the role of public relations is more marketing oriented to promote business organisation and its products or services. These companies view public relations as primarily a marketing communications function, a part of Integrated Marketing Communications (*IMC*) process. Public relations activities create awareness, inform and educate, develop customer understanding, foster trust and favourable attitudes towards the company and its products, and promote acceptance. *Marketing Public Relations* (*MPR*) programmes create impact in many ways:

- ***Generate Excitement in Market Before Advertising Campaign:*** Companies announce new and exciting product introductions. This offers an opportunity to get publicity and generate anticipation among customers. This helps in increasing advertising effectiveness.
- ***Introducing a New Product:*** Jack Neff, Clara Dipasquale, and Jean Halliday report that Gillette primarily uses public relations when introducing its new products. Initially there may be no advertising.

John Scully left Apple Computers in a bad shape and Steve Jobs rejoined Apple Computers. He unveiled the new computer model named iMac on May 6, 1998 to awestruck reporters. This generated a continuing buzz and in August the machine went on sale and was an instant success.

- ***Advertising Itself Becomes the News:*** When Apple released its commercial on the occasion of Super Bowl, 1984, the commercial itself became the topic of publicity and besides print media coverage, parts of commercial were shown by some TV channels.
- ***Influence the Opinion Leaders:*** These opinion leaders may be experts in science and technology, professors, doctors, or beauticians etc.
- ***Defend Adverse Product Consequences and Convince Consumers:*** Sometimes companies face the problem of adverse publicity about their products or the company. For example, Coca-Cola and Pepsi containing pesticides. These companies used public relations programmes to counter such reports. The case of Johnson & Johnson Tylenol is well-known, where different public relations approaches benefited the company.
- ***Build the Company Image and Create Favourable Brand Opinion:*** Speeches by Bill Gates and Steve Jobs attract global media attention.

A major reason for increasing use of marketing public relations is the decreasing power of advertising. In developed countries such as US, a fairly large number of companies use *MPR*. Gillette goes to the extent of requiring its brand managers to allocate a separate budget for *MPR* and reasons for not using *MPR*.

Well-planned public relations offer some major advantages that include:

- Can be very effective in new product launch.
- It is a highly targeted way of reaching the desired audience.
- It is far more cost effective than advertising.
- It gets endorsements from independent, objective third party having no association with the product or company.
- It is viewed as highly credible.
- It breaks through advertising clutter.
- It supports advertising campaigns.
- It bypasses consumer resistance to company sales efforts.
- It helps image building.
- It can generate immediate inquiries about new products.

The disadvantages include:

- It has no control over media.
- There is no guarantee of media time or space.
- Lacks standard effectiveness measures.

Managing Public Relations

Corporations exist in communities. They are very concerned about public attitudes towards them. Negative attitudes tarnish the company image, adversely affect sales and employee morale and no company wants to be viewed as socially unacceptable. Many organisations and independent research firms conduct surveys to assess public attitudes. Findings can furnish important inputs to determine *MPR* objectives and develop targeted programmes. According to Raymond Simon, the better a company understands a problem, the better it can develop communications to deal with it.

Earlier, public relations tools were not formally designed and generally included press releases, press kits for trade shows, and new product announcements. The fact is that public relations should be viewed as an ongoing process with definite policies and procedures as is the case with other promotional programmes to take advantage of opportunities and deal with problems.

Scott M. Cutlip, Allen H. Center, and Glenn M. Broom recommend four steps for planning a public relations programme: (1) Identify and define public relations problem, (2) Develop a plan and programme, (3) Implement the programme, and (4) Evaluate the programme effectiveness.

Many firms have internal public relations officer or department. Other companies hire independent outside professional PR agencies to handle specific projects or all public relations functions.

The first step is to determine the target audience because the objectives could be totally different for each different public segment. The target audiences may be internal or external.

Internal audiences are employees of the company, company shareholders, and unions. All these groups have their stakes in the company and are also referred as internal stakeholders. Employees in different locations, unions, and shareholders should receive relevant information regularly about company activities.

FIGURE 16.1

Internal and External Audiences

Internal Audiences	External Audiences
Employees.	Channel members.
Unions.	Customers.
Shareholders.	Media.
	Financial Institutions.
	Special-interest groups.
	Government.
	Local community.

External audiences include channel members, customers and other important groups. Customers may be strongly influenced positively or negatively by promotional campaigns or publicity. Channel members can directly affect a company's operations and mass media promotions, and company sales people maintain relevant information flow. Media may or may not report publicity, and great care should be taken to release interesting information to print and audiovisual media. Financial institutions lend money and are interested in financial well being of the company and also the goodwill company can generate. Lastly, government, special interest groups, and communities keep a watch that concerns environmental pollution, harassment of women employees, or any other unfair treatment of employees.

Setting Objectives

Marketing Public Relations (*MPR*) can serve to accomplish a variety of promotional objectives. Some of them are:

- Build Excitement Prior to Product Introduction.
- Build Strong Consumer Awareness and Launch Product.
- Influence Opinion Leaders.

- Build Company and Brand Image.
- Counter Negative Publicity.

Programme Implementation

After conducting research, identifying target audience, and setting objectives, programmes are developed and delivered to audiences to accomplish the objectives.

Press release and press conferences can be a very effective way of communicating with large numbers of target audiences. However, the appropriate topic should be carefully chosen to be of major interest to the target group to gain coverage. Business organisations call press conference when they have newsworthy new product introductions or some have planned some exciting event. Some sports wear or auto companies issue press release when they sign up some famous sports or movie personality. Individual educational institutions, or a group of them arrange conferences where both media and target audiences are invited. Besides furnishing all the relevant information, authorities also conduct interviews and grant on the spot admissions. The aim is to provide a number of stories addressing various audiences.

Personal interviews are also arranged to clarify company position. Steve Ballmer, President Microsoft, appeared in several personal interviews to present the company position when facing a legal case brought against the company by the U. S. government. Sometimes in large business houses, there are controversies regarding controlling rights among various family members, some of them appear for personal interview to explain their side.

Event sponsorship is both, part of sales promotion and also a tool of public relations. (Chapter-16). Event sponsorship blurs the difference. Corporate sponsorships of charities and worthwhile causes is popular form of public relations to build corporate image. As part of *MPR*, many sports events such as Olympics, World Cups, Cricket matches between countries and other important events have corporate sponsors. Sahara India is the sponsor of Indian cricket team. Many companies marketing smoking products, liquors, autos, soft drinks, airlines, and high-tech products etc., sponsor events. Some of these, such as soft drink companies often create their own events. Such events get considerable visibility among target audiences and put company or brand's name in front of the consumers. Increasingly companies are finding event sponsorship as an effective public relations tool. A good example of sales promotion (consumer contest) combined with event is the Gold Jewelry Contest by well-known Mumbai jewellers, Tribhovondas Bhimji Zaveri (See box "Gold Jewelry Contest").

Community involvement may be in the form of participation in community events, such as participation in religious festivals. After Tsunami tragedy, many corporations and trade associations came forward to help victims with time, money, and other type of assistance. Media devoted free airtime to aid victims by coordinating activities, announcing programmes, and food drop activities to help victims.

Gold Jewelry Contest

Tribhovondas Bhimji Zaveri, Mumbai organised a contest to boost sales during the lean season. A jar, full of gold coins, was placed in a large attractive fish tank with exotic species of fishes. Anyone who bought jewelry worth just Rs. 5,000 could participate and was required to guess the correct number of gold coins. The contest was to run for a month. The first prize was diamond jewelry worth Rs 2 lakh. The prize to runner up was gold jewelry worth Rs. 1 lakh. There were 100 consolation prizes too.

Contd...

> To popularise the contest, MPR was adopted. Model Aditi Govitrikar, who had just been crowned Mrs. World was a befitting choice to launch the contest at the showroom. Key journalists from print and TV were invited to the launch. Govitrikar launched the contest by unveiling the fish tank, providing a very interesting photo opportunity. Immediately after the launch, a media release with her photograph was disseminated to media in Mumbai. Within a week there was an extensive coverage with Govitrikar's photograph in English, and other language media. Even a business daily, The economic Times carried the photograph prominently on its back page. The contest received an overwhelming response.
>
> To award the winners, an event was organised at Cricket Club of India at which Tribhovondas Bhimji Zaveri, contest winners, participants, key customers and media were invited. Photographs of winners along with media release was sent to various publications and some of them gave good coverage.
>
> (Source: Based on a report by Meera Gidwani in USP Age, June-July 2004).

Corporate advertising (discussed in Chapter – 18) focuses on building company image in the public mind. Companies also undertake *advocacy advertising,* and *cause-related advertising* in an attempt to create some favourable distinction among the public.

PUBLICITY

Publicity is an important tool of public relations effort and both terms are used as synonymous. Publicity is concerned with generation of news about a company, product, service, or person in print or broadcast media. 'Public relations' is a deliberately organised long-term programme to communicate positive information about the company and its activities. Publicity is generally a short-term affair, and not always under the company's control because it is not paid for by the company and hence may not be favourable. Publicity of both types, favourable or unfavourable, often comes from outside sources, other than the company.

> **Public Relations Reliance Group**
>
> - The late Dhirubhai Ambani understood the power of media and value of rewarding shareholders with higher dividends and bonus shares. Shareholders were his best ambassadors. In those license raj days, their success or failure depended on good relations with government, and used public relations effectively.
> - When Central Bureau of Investigation (CBI) raided the Ambani residences years ago, the mainline dailies carried their denials, not the story. Ambani used public relations to build bridges with shareholders and, journalists, and bureaucrats.

Publicity, as everyone believes, originates from independent sources that do not have any stake in the company and is considered highly credible. Consumers consider information through publicity as more objective. All other promotional elements are company controlled and viewed as less reliable. Publicity is a very powerful weapon and can make or break a product or even company. After news reports of harmful levels of pesticides in Coke and Pepsi, there was a substantial drop in the sales. Very large segments of consumers across all ages were highly concerned and upset. TV news channels invited audiences from various sections of society, particularly younger groups and parents, and arranged discussions and this negative publicity was not under the control of these soft drink producers.

Consumers perceive the medium in which publicity appears, endorses the information. Often we read news articles in auto magazines that a certain car has won the award of "Car of the Year" and readers believe, it reflects the perceptions of the quality of the selected car by that magazine.

Publicity can work for business organisations (see box). A high level of favourable publicity has made iPod from Apple Computers a top seller. Marketers like to have as much control as they can over publicity time, place, and content. Some companies do this through *video news release*. This is a publicity story produced by publicity consultants so that news channels can air it as a news item.

Advantages of publicity include high credibility, news value, significant word-of-mouth messages from interpersonal sources, and perception of having media endorsement of media.

Disadvantages include lack of control by the concerned company most of the time, the timing of news release is almost entirely up to media, not always reported the way provider wants it, and there might be errors due to omissions, and inaccuracy.

Measuring Results

Walter K. Lindenmann says that measurement can be at three levels. The measurement at the basic level evaluates actual PR activities undertaken, next level concerns measuring audience perception and comprehension of message, and the final stage relates for measuring the resulting changes in terms of perceptual and behavioural aspects.

So the main areas of measurement focus on determining target group's awareness levels, perceptions and attitudes, and changes in behaviours. One way to determine the effectiveness of a programme is personal observation and evaluation by one's superiors at all levels of the company. The measurement can also be done by outside consultants who conduct surveys to assess public opinion, and conduct focus group research to assess the programme success. It is also required to examine total number and ratio of positive and negative articles over time by publication, and reports on news channels etc.

Summary

'Public relations' refers to the management function, which evaluates public attitudes, identifies the policies and procedures of an organisation with the public interest, and executes a programme of action (and communication) to earn public understanding and acceptance.

Public relations activities create awareness, inform and educate, develop customer understanding, foster trust and favourable attitudes towards the company and its products, and promote acceptance.

Business organisations are very concerned about public attitudes towards them. Negative attitudes tarnish their image, adversely affect sales, employee morale and no company wants to be viewed as a bad citizen.

Internal audiences for public relations are employees of the company, company shareholders, and unions. External audiences include channel members, customers and other important groups. All of these groups either have direct stakes or are influenced by the activities of the concerned organisation.

Managing public relations involves setting objectives, developing and implementing suitable PR programmes such as press release and press conferences, personal interviews, sponsoring events and involvement in local community programmes, and corporate advertising etc.

Publicity is an important tool of public relations. Publicity is concerned with generation of news about a company, product, service, or person in print or broadcast media. 'Public relations' is a deliberately organised long-term programme and publicity is generally a short-term affair, and not always under the company's control, and not paid for by the company. It may or may not be favourable.

Areas of measurement focus on determining target group's awareness levels, perceptions and attitudes, and changes in behaviours.

Questions for Discussion

1. What is PR? What is its role in modern day businesses?
2. Distinguish between *MPR* and publicity.
3. What is internal and external public? How are these groups affected by PR?
4. Discuss why PR and publicity may have more impact than other promotional mix elements.
5. Discuss the advantages and disadvantages of *MPR* and publicity.
6. What steps should be taken in managing PR activities?

Projects

1. Go to a company office and learn what PR activities they undertake.
2. What steps Coca Cola and Pepsi Co. undertook to counter negative publicity? Write a report.
3. You are area PR manager in an airlines and there is passenger plane crash. What steps would you take to handle the crisis?

Bibliography

1. Raymond Simon, *Public Relations, Concept and Practices,* Second Ed. 1980.
2. Jack Neff, Clara Dipasquale, and Jean Halliday, "Ries Thesis: Ads don't build brands, PR does," *Advertising Age,* July 15, 2002.
3. Scott M. Cutlip, Allen H. Center, and Glenn M. Broom, *Effective Public Relations,* 8th Ed. Prentice-Hall, 2000.
4. Walter K. Lindenmann, "An Effectiveness Yardstick to Measure Public Relations Success," *Public Relations Quarterly,* 38 (1993).

Direct Marketing

CHAPTER

17

LEARNING OBJECTIVES

After going through this chapter, you will understand:

- Role of direct marketing in modern businesses
- Direct marketing objectives and media selection
- Different approaches to direct marketing
- Direct selling

Sangam Direct comes from HLL stable and offers a revolutionary way to shop. It offers everything, a kirana store, over the phone, by e-mail or on Internet. The consumer has 3,500 stock keeping units available to her/him and by dialling 5555 0000, the customer can order monthly grocery and supermarket supplies and have them delivered at the doorstep next day at a convenient time. A range of interesting deals, promotions and extensive customer relationship management and loyalty programmes bring the customer month after month. The delivery is free if the billed amount is Rs. 400 or more, or else there is a delivery charge of Rs. 20. Outside of the deals at the moment, there is a one per cent discount on MRP and a five per cent discount on unbranded goods.

A consumer has to call the number or register online. After a brief registration process, a customer-care representative designated as Personal Shopper leads the caller through the process. This Personal Shopper is trained, friendly voice that speaks the consumer's language.

After the first order is placed, an order history called My List is generated. This helps the company to understand consumer's buying habits. It sets the benchmark for the next purchase and helps to design company's loyalty programme. On future calls the consumer is taken through My List again and requested modifications are made. The customer can quickly place the order or take time to consider best deals. The discount service and innovations linked loyalty programme is base on spending and more importantly, regularity of purchases.

At the back end the clout of large-scale retailer comes into play. The discounts and deals come, courtesy, company promotions and the benefits of non-involvement of intermediaries and scale. Branded products are bought from distributors and stocked. Grains and commodities are procured, cleaned, weighed electronically and packed. The products are put in distribution centre, which is linked to call centre. The orders are downloaded and the pick-list comes out. The orders are picked and assembled and sealed in a plastic tote with an invoice inside. The seal is opened in front of the consumer at the delivery time convenient to consumer, 24 hours after placing the order. The consumer can pay by cash, check, or credit card (approved on a wireless device).

Marketing has been hectic in pilot Thane region since 2001, when the service was launched. The service now covers part of Navi Mumbai and has been extended to Dadar and Matunga within the city. It indeed is a revolutionary shopping model and HLL plans to pan it out to other Indian cities after its launch in Mumbai. Is India ready for it yet? While kirana stores frown on the concept they leave it to the consumer who knows best and will decide, they believe.

(Source: USP Age, June-July 2004).

Marketeers always search for new and effective tools to reach customers with their messages. The interactive media such as the cellular phone and Internet are important additions. Most companies around the world rely more on traditional promotion mix elements such as advertising, personal selling, and sales promotion to reach customers and sell their products and services through some system of resellers. They believe these traditional promotion mix elements are effective in creating awareness and knowledge, and building brand image. Some marketeers tried reaching customers directly with these tools on a one-to-one basis to assess whether this can stimulate immediate behavioural response and now direct marketing is a rapidly growing discipline in marketing. Direct marketing may or may not involve middlemen to distribute products. Direct marketing is primarily concerned with the promotion area.

The *Dictionary of Marketing Terms* defines direct marketing as:

"The total of all activities by which the seller, in effecting the exchange of goods and services with the buyer, directs efforts to a target audience using one or more media (direct selling, direct mail, telemarketing, direct-action advertising, catalogue selling, cable TV selling, etc.) for the purpose of soliciting a response by phone, mail, or personal visit from a prospect or customer."

Peter D. Bennett, ed., *Dictionary of Marketing Terms* (AMA, 1988).

According to Direct Marketing Association:

"Direct marketing is an interactive system of marketing which uses one or more advertising media to affect a measurable response and/or transaction at any location."

Direct Marketing, October 1990.

Direct marketing uses a set of all major direct-response media including print, TV, Internet and cellular phones as the tools to implement communications and accomplish its objectives. *Direct Marketing Association Economic Impact,* 2002 reported that purchases of products and services through direct-response advertising exceeded $2 trillion and projected to reach 2.8 trillion by 2006. All sorts of products and services marketers, including major retailers, business-to-business (B2B) and industrial marketers use direct marketing methods.

The adoption of direct marketing in India is gradually picking up. According to *USP Age* July 2004 issue, no definite figures are available about the size of the direct marketing industry, but there are very clear indications that it is growing across various industries, including financial and other services. O&M has a direct marketing arm, OgilvyOne is a separate direct marketing division of O&M and about 10 per cent Ogilvy and Mather business comes from handling accounts, which want them to create direct marketing programmes. Some other names of direct marketing outfits in India include *HTA* Direct, Saatchi & Saatchi Direct, Grey's Direct, AP Lintas Global Market Links, Contract Direct, Mudra Diversified, K&D Corvo Direct, Direct Response, *FCB-ULKA*, McCann Erikson, Datamatics, and Rediffusion *DYR*'s Wunderman Cato Johnson etc.

A number of factors are promoting the attractiveness of direct marketing. The main factors are:

- Availability of consumer credit cards.
- Availability of professional agencies.
- Competitive Pressures, Rising Media Costs, and Market Fragmentation.
- Increasing family incomes, including dual-income families.
- Technological advances.

Some marketers such as Amway, or online marketers like Dell computers, Amazon, and eBay, etc. rely solely on direct marketing to generate consumer response. In many other cases marketers use direct marketing and integrate it with other promotion mix elements such as advertising, personal selling, sales promotion, and public relations. Some authors, such as Schultz, Tannenbaum, Lauterborn, and Roman, refer to this shift toward combining all promotional elements by other names as well such as *Integrated Marketing Communications (IMC), maximarketing,* and *Integrated Direct Marketing (IDM).* According to Ernan Roman, combining promotional mix elements within a closely defined time frame enhances message to reach and impact.

Direct Marketing Decisions

For successful implementation of direct-marketing, marketers must establish objectives, specify target market, choice of strategies, and set evaluation criteria.

Direct-Marketing Objectives

Objectives of direct marketing usually focus on seeking direct response in terms of behaviour. Order response rate varies across product categories and prices but in most cases, usually a 2 per cent order placement is viewed as good. Some organisations use direct marketing to inform and educate customers about product/service in anticipation that it may precipitate future actions, reminding about offers, image building, maintain customer satisfaction, strengthen relationship, and reassure customers about purchases.

Market Segmentation

Market segmentation and targeting the right customers are critical to the success of promotional programme. Customers can be grouped on the basis of age, sex, income, education, lifestyle, and stage in family life cycle etc.

Other more focused criteria relate to purchase history of customers. Most direct marketers finalise their mailing list based on *RFM (Recency, Frequency, Monetary value)*. This means elapsed time after last purchase *(R)*, purchase frequency *(F)*, and monetary purchase value *(M)*. This would specifically require data to be entered each time there is a transaction between the customer and the company so that the company can track, how recently purchases have been made, how often they are made, and how much money is spent. The goal is to focus efforts and reach most promising customers.

Direct marketers use a *database*. It is much more than just names and addresses and is used to identify and profile the company's best customers and effectively target the customer segments.

Ongoing database updating helps companies identify trends and buying patterns. This information, can be used by the companies to strengthen relationship with its customers by satisfying their needs and wants more effectively.

The database should provide the answers to the following questions:

- Where do they live?
- How did they make contact first time?
- What have they purchased?
- How often have they purchased?
- What is the monetary value of their purchases?
- How do they order or purchase, through the Internet, mail, phone, or in person?
- What is known about them and their families, occupation, education, children, interests, attitudes, and payment histories etc.?
- In case of B2B, who are the influencers, users, deciders, and purchasers?
- Location of corporate office and branch offices.

Well-managed companies usually develop and maintain their own database. Many independent research suppliers sell this kind of information. Database helps in developing a mailing list that minimises waste coverage as much as possible. A good database is crucial to the effectiveness of direct marketing. If a direct marketing company buys database from outside sources, it is worthwhile to pay a little more for a good database that has been well researched and segregated than to pay for a list of names and addresses.

FIGURE 17.1

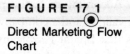

Direct Marketing Flow Chart

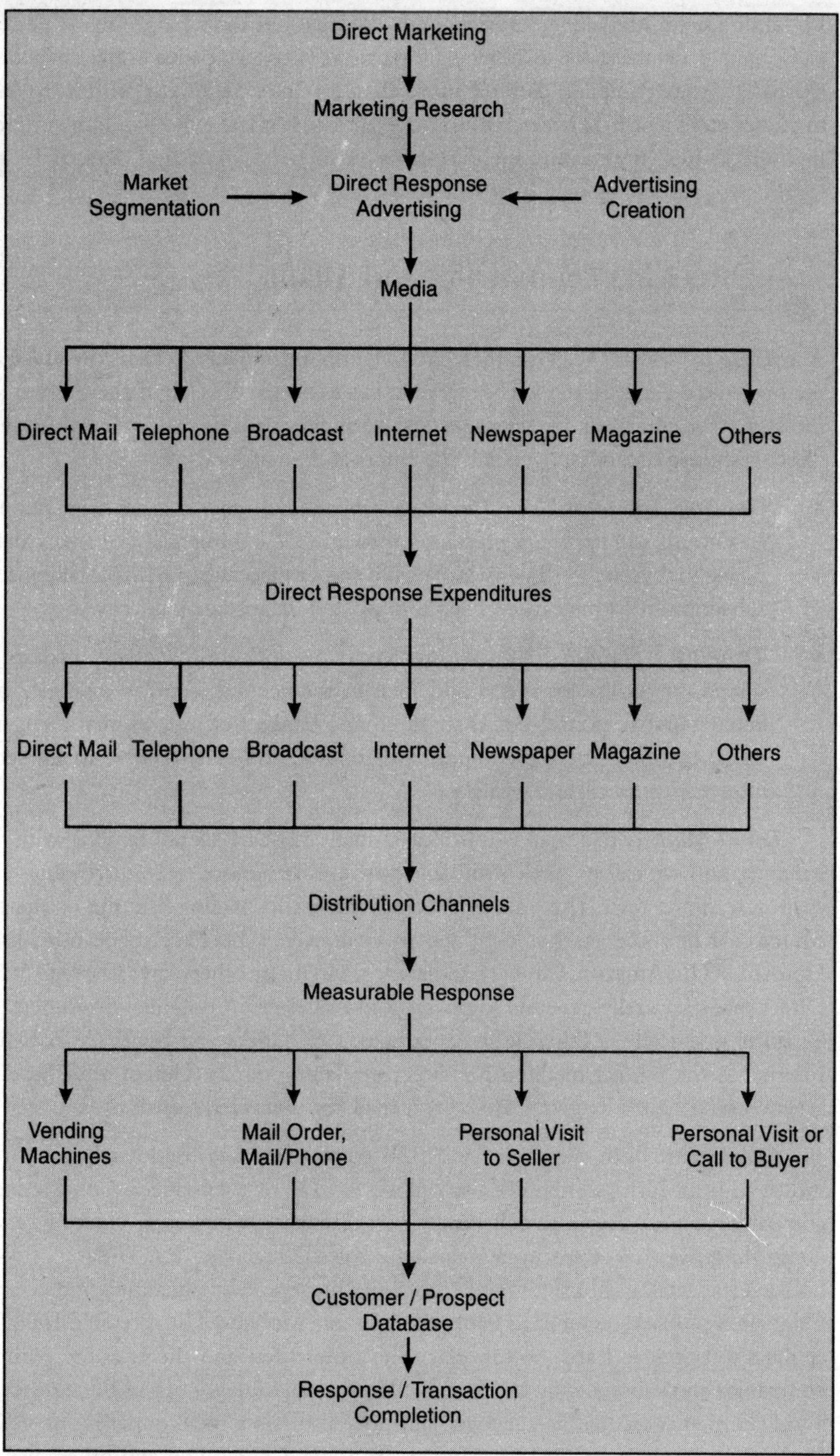

(*Source:* G. Belch and M. Belch, *Advertising and Promotion*. Based on figure by Martin Bair, Henry R. Hoke, Jr., and Robert Stone).

Many direct marketing outfits lack database of their customers or prospects. According to Sandeep Mittal of Direm Marketing Services, some databases in India have only 30 per cent validity and a company can obtain a database for as little as 50 paise to Rs 5 per contact. He further says that Bharat Petroleum Corp. Ltd., has compiled data on more than 14 lakh customers within the last four years, and a direct marketer can identify between two to three lakh customers, who would be interested in the company's new high-grade fuel, Speed. Shoppers Stop has also been compiling data of its regular customers through loyalty programme, namely First Citizen.

Direct Marketing Offer and Media

According to Edward L. Nash, there are five important decision areas: Product, offer, medium, distribution method, and creative strategy. The marketer has to decide on each of these issues and develop the appropriate message to be conveyed. Direct marketers use all the available major media such as direct mail, telemarketing, direct-response broadcasting, print, the Internet, E-mail, and others.

- ***One-Step Approach:*** The marketer uses the medium to obtain an order. For example, exercise equipment and household items are presented through TV commercials, or many magazines insert subscription forms in their issues. The viewer or the reader places the order by calling a toll-free number. Magazine subscription forms can be filled and posted in postage-paid envelops.
- ***Two-Step Approach:*** This may involve the use of more than one medium. This may be done to first screen, or qualify prospects and then in the second step the marketer makes the effort to elicit a behavioural response. For example, many banks first use telemarketing to determine the potential based on interest, employment, and income and then follow-up by sending an agent with more information to close the sale.

Direct Mail: Direct mail is unsolicited mail, most of us are familiar with. For some of us it is fairly irritating and we call it "Junk mail" and throw it or ignore without reading. Companies of all sizes and shape use direct mail. This mail is generally based on mailing lists the companies buy from independent sources, or in some cases is confined to customers who have made purchases earlier. Google, Yahoo, Hotmail, *AOL*, Amazon, Fabmart, Indiatimes, and many others have vast lists of home and e-mail addresses. Direct mails generally generate lower response rates from potential customers. The cost of direct mail as e-mail is practically nothing. John Goodman, *CEO* India and South Asia, Ogilvy & Mather believes the Internet is the perfect medium for direct marketing. *HLL* (Denim aftershave, Lux), Hyatt Regency, and several banks have effectively used direct mail for their credit cards.

Catalogues: Both, consumer and B2B companies may send catalogues of their entire product lines, mostly in print form, sometimes also online, as CDs, or even videos. Considering the global scenario, many companies use catalogue to sell variety of merchandise including clothing, and cosmetics. According to *Direct Marketing Association* forecast, catalogue sales has reached $16.3 billion in 2006. Internet has particularly boosted the catalogue business and companies present their catalogues and accept orders over the Internet. Catalogues of marketers such as Fabmart, Amazon, McGraw-Hill, Prentice-Hall, Dell and others are available at their websites and anyone can place the order then and there. Some companies started as catalogue companies and subsequently also branched into retail outlets, such as Firstandsecond bookseller initially had a website that presented its catalogue but now also has a retail outlet in New Delhi. Anjali Textiles, Otto-Burlingtons Mail Order (P) Ltd., Mothercare India, Charag Din and others use catalogues.

Some authors make a distinction between manufacturer-originated and trading house-originated direct mail marketing by using either direct mail or catalogue. If the marketer is a manufacturer, it is called Direct Mail Marketing, and when the source is a trading house, it is called Mail Order Marketing or Mail Order Business.

Broadcast Media: Direct marketer can use television and radio. Almost entire advertising with respect to direct marketing occurs on television. This type of advertising is either in the form of direct-response advertising, or support advertising. *Direct-response advertising* encourages customers to place orders by using a toll-free telephone number. Support advertising informs customers generally to take part in sweepstakes or expect something in mail. An interesting example of support advertising is on NDTV news channel. Airtel encourages customers to use its cellular service and make two calls then answer a simple question of the day. The winner gets Rs 100,000 for correct answer. The message is broadcast by NDTV and also the winner of the day is announced by NDTV in its news.

Some companies use a new form of direct-response advertising on cable and satellite called *infomercials*. These are lengthy commercials ranging between 30 to 60 minutes and resemble documentaries. Indian TV viewers are quite familiar with lengthy commercials about losing weight, and portable exercise equipments and satisfied users testifying the great benefits they derived and ease of use. Of course a toll-free number is included to place the order immediately. Infomercials have been reported to be quite effective, audience watch them and place orders.

Widespread use of credit cards and availability of toll-free telephone numbers in more developed countries has promoted *teleshopping*. Some TV channels exclusively sell products and services 24 hours a day, such as Home Shopping Network. The programme host offers low prices on a variety of items including jewelry, kitchenware, fitness products, insurance, and CDs, etc. Customers sitting in their homes make their purchases by calling a toll-free number and the ordered item is delivered within 48 hours. *QVC* is a major shopping channel so far covering U. S., Germany, and Japan reaching 84 million households.

So far it seems there are no daylong teleshopping programmes in India. Some programmes being aired in India are actually infomercials. Important names connected with such programmes include Dees' Home Shopping (DD, and C&S channels) offers home appliances, car accessories, fashion wear, footwear, beauty care products, air tickets, and groceries etc. Teleshopping Network (*ATN*, DD, Sun, local C&S), and United Teleshopping (DD National) are the other two names. So far the maximum time allotted in India to such programmes is limited to about 5-hours/day.

Print Media: Newspapers and magazines are not considered to be 'sound choice' for direct marketing. There are too many ads competing for attention. Specific interest newspapers focused on financial matters, or sports and hobby magazines are sometimes used.

Telemarketing: Direct marketing through telephone is called telemarketing. It gives the marketer a better chance of influencing the prospect and win a customer. As mentioned earlier, it is most often used in the screening process. Companies hire several telephone-callers, mostly girls, or operate through hired agents. Call centres have become a real arena of telemarketing activity. Several teams of 5 to 6 members are formed and for each team there is a supervisor. Individual team members sit in front of a computer terminal wearing a headset. They call different telephone numbers from a list and present the sales talk based on pre-tested script and update information on the computer screen.

Unless handled carefully, telemarketing can irritate call recipients and actually harm the brand. According to Dr. C. R Sridhar, CEO, SRS-ICON Brand Navigation, instead of generating sales, telemarketing could damage your company's brand equity if not handled properly. We receive calls from well-known multinational banks, asking if Mr … is home. The caller does not know that it's not a Mister but a lady. Then, they would call you at odd hours when you are engaged in some serious work requiring concentration. There is tragedy at home, and you receive a call greeting you with a good morning or good afternoon and would ask you to buy something. You keep on receiving bill after bill when you have not even used the credit card and the period expired and they renewed it without your consent. No one pays attention to your complaints and you still keep on receiving calls from different locations offering some additional benefit.

Electronic Shopping: Infomercials and home shopping use TV channels. Electronic shopping is an online information retrieval and shopping service through computers. Internet is the newest medium for direct marketing. It can be used to access information, communication, entertainment, and a means of transaction. Direct marketing through Internet involves business in "market space" as opposed to physical "market place."

Direct Selling: Some authors consider direct selling as the additional element of direct marketing, often called *Multilevel Marketing* (*MLM*). Some well-known players in this field include Amway, Oriflame, Avon, and Modicare. The selling steps are the same as discussed earlier. In this situation the salesperson directly sells to customers only in their homes. Any additional distribution channels are not involved. In India, Eureka Forbes has been very successful and is the leader in this field. Their salespeople call on homes and make presentation and demonstrate water filters and vacuum cleaners, book orders and ensure installation etc.

The Case of IBM Locked Box Mailer

- IBM was loosing market share to competition in 2003. There was need to reinforce its leadership in the industry and reinforce IBM's commitment to its customers. IBM needed to establish strong differentiators, such as superior technology with its critical customers. One aspect of superior IBM technology is security – which is crucial to business today. The communication objective was to focus on establishing the fact that no other PC offered as much online and data security as IBM PC and drive sales.

- Another objection was to collect more information through this communication from the prospect to update and validate its database. This offered an ideal opportunity talking to key customers, such as chief executives, chief information officers, and chief financial officers within the top 300 customer organisations in India. They are the ones who are fastidious about the kind of technology they implement at a macro level that concerns networks, servers, storage and so on. But when it comes to PC, the level of involvement is not as high as it ought to be.

- To demonstrate the impregnable security of IBM PC, OgilvyOne mailed out a locked briefcase that had a six-digit combination lock. Recipients were challenged to crack the combination. In case they were unable, they had to visit a specially designed website and fill in the personal and organisational details to access the code. Inside the briefcase were a letter, a brochure, and a CD that contained detailed information on security trends and issues, and IBM's military-level, foolproof security solutions.

  About 59.2 per cent of the recipients logged on to the IBM Website to access the secret code and open the briefcase. Follow-up calls to the target audience gauged feedback as highly positive. Customers wrote back to IBM lauding the pack and for bringing such an important issue to the fore. A total of 574 packs were mailed out to 297 unique organisations and 340 recipients logged on to the IBM website. That exercise drove sales and did not use a shred of media.

  (Source: USP Age, September 2004).

Multilevel marketing employs a multi-tried, independent sales people, who double as distributors to sell the products. The company practicing this approach recruits a core group of sales people who also function as distributors. They are introduced to the company by a member of the core group. Each of these salespeople are required to buy an assortment of products of a minimum fixed value, generally within Rs. 2000 at a time. They sell them directly to consumers, who can also enroll as independent operators linked within the chain. After selling the first consignment, the sales people can buy another lot from the company. Each salesperson-cum-distributor is supposed to recruit next rung of operators or consultants as they are called, working as salespersons-cum-distributors, under the salesperson who introduced them to the company.

The first salesperson-cum-distributors earns the commission at two levels, the first commission is on products that she/he sells directly, and is made up of the difference between selling price and the price the consultant pays as distributor. The second part is the certain percentage of share of the commission that the distributors working under her/his earn.

Advantages of Direct Marketing

- Direct marketing offers the advantage of reaching large number of well-defined target customers and almost eliminates waste coverage.
- Good quality databases are available from independent suppliers and the marketer can segment customer groups with considerable precision.
- Direct marketer can personalise the message.
- Direct marketing can deliver almost perfect offers to customers.
- Marketer can build desired frequency level based on media.
- Direct marketing offers creative flexibility in different media.
- Direct marketer can quickly develop a list of specific profiles for direct mail.
- Direct marketing is more effective in building customer relationship.
- It is very cost effective considering the sale generated per contact.
- The results can be measured most accurately.

Measurement of Direct Marketing Effort

The objectives of direct marketing in many cases are related to purchase behaviour and the marketer knows in no uncertain terms, the number of orders received. For non-behavioural response objectives, traditional measurement methods are used.

Summary

Direct marketing is an interactive system of marketing and uses a set of all major direct-response media including print, TV, Internet and cellular phones as the tools to implement communications and accomplish its objectives. Some companies use direct marketing to inform and educate customers about product/service in anticipation that it may precipitate future actions, reminding about offers, image building, maintain customer satisfaction, strengthen relationship, and reassure customers about purchases.

The adoption of direct marketing in India is gradually picking up and there are very clear indications that it is growing across various industries, including financial and other services.

Most direct marketers finalise their mailing list based on recency, frequency, monetary value. This means elapsed time after last purchase, purchase frequency, and monetary purchase value. This would specifically require data to be entered at the time, there is a transaction between the customer and the company. The goal is to focus efforts and reach most promising customers.

Direct marketers use a database to identify and profile the company's best customers and effectively segment and target the customers. A good database is crucial to the effectiveness of direct marketing. This information, companies can use to strengthen relationship with its customers by satisfying their needs and wants more effectively.

Direct mail is unsolicited mail and is generally based on mailing lists, companies buy from outside sources, or in some cases is confined to customers who have made purchases earlier.

Both, consumer and B2B companies may send catalogues of their entire product lines, mostly in print form, sometimes also online, as CDs, or even videos to sell variety of merchandise including clothing, and cosmetics.

Direct-response advertising encourages customers to place orders by using a toll-free telephone number. Support advertising informs customers generally to take part in sweepstakes or expect something in mail.

Infomercials are lengthy commercials ranging and resemble documentaries. Infomercials have been reported to be quite effective, audience watch them and place orders. Another direct marketing approach on TV is to use teleshopping. Customers sitting in their homes make their purchases by calling a toll-free number and the ordered item is delivered within 48 hours.

Direct marketing through telephone is called telemarketing. Companies hire several telephone-callers, mostly girls, or operate through hired agents. Unless handled carefully, telemarketing can irritate call recipients and actually harm the brand.

Questions for Discussion

1. What is direct marketing? How it differs from traditional marketing approach?
2. Describe database and its development. What is the significance of database in direct marketing?
3. Briefly discuss various methods that can be used for direct marketing.
4. What is direct-response advertising? Discuss two examples of direct-response advertising.
5. Critically evaluate the value of direct mail as a means of reaching customers.
6. Discuss telemarketing critically and point out its advantages and disadvantages.
7. What are the advantages and disadvantages of direct marketing?

Projects

1. Identify one infomercial. Analyse different aspects of message presentation and evaluate its effectiveness.
2. You are the marketing manager of a computer manufacturer. Device a direct marketing plan to sell the computer notebooks to high-end customers.
3. Prepare a Powerpoint presentation for telemarketing a coaching service for any subject(s) for students aspiring to go to IIT for their engineering education.

Bibliography

1. Don E. Schultz, Stanley I. Tannenbaum, and Robert F. Lauterborn, *Integrated Marketing Communications,* (Business Books, 1993); Ernan Roman, *Beyond Maximarketing: The New Power of Caring and Daring,* McGraw-Hill, 1994); *Integrated Direct Marketing: The Cutting Edge Strategy for Synchronising Advertising, Direct Mail, Telemarketing, and Field Sales,* (Business Books, 1995).
2. Sandeep Mittal of Direm Marketing Services, *USP Age, September* 2004.

3. Edward L. Nash, *Direct Marketing: Strategy, Planning, Execution,* Third Edition, McGraw-Hill, 1995.

4. *Direct Marketing Association,* 2002.

5. John Goodman, CEO, Ogilvy & Mather, India and South Asia, *USP Age,* September 2004.

6. Dr. C. R. Sridhar, "Telemarketing: A Brand Killer," *USP Age,* March 2005.

Cases

Case 4.1: Taj Hotel

Right from early 1900s, the Taj stood for class and comfort. It was a place where viceroys of the Empire arrived and departed amidst scenes of splendour, typical of Raj. From the very beginning it was one of the wonders of the Orient! Singapore's Raffles, Hong Kong's Peninsula, and Frank Lloyd Wright's Imperial did not come up to the level of the Taj in spite of their rich ancestry. The reason the hotel towered over the rest was because of the amazing attention to detail that was paid by its founder, Jamsetji Nusserwanji Tata himself. It was a time when Indians were not allowed to enter most of the prestigious hotels and clubs. Legend has it, that this was one of the reason why Tata went ahead with the project though he was, at that time, busy with plans to industrialise India. He made sure that the Taj would have its own laundry, an aerated water bottling plant, electroplating for its silverware, a Mora silver burnishing machine, a crockery washing plant and elevators. The hotel was completed at a cost of 500,000 pounds in 1904.

The Taj Intercontinental (the new wing) was built in 1971 and rapidly after that came the Lake Palace, and Rambagh Palace at Udaipur and Jaipur respectively. The company pioneered the concept of conversion of century-old palaces into hotels! Today this has become an USP of the Taj group, and a new logo is being designed to incorporate the palaces aspect of the product. In mid 1970s, the chain expanded to Chennai (Taj Coromandel and Fisherman's Cove) and For Aguada at Goa. Here too, Taj scored over the others with its timing. At that time, Goa was not a tourists' paradise.

Around the same time it set up Ganges Varanasi and started international flight kitchens too. The end of the decade saw the coming up of the Taj at Delhi. This last marked the start of an ethnic style in hotels with international standards. By this time it appeared that nothing could halt the phenomenal growth of the Taj. In the 1980s, two more hotels were built in Delhi, two in Bangalore, and one each in Chennai, Ooty and Agra. Next came Jaimahal Palace Hotel in Jaipur as well as the New Delhi Flight Kitchen. The new hotels were built taking the original Taj as the model hotel. The Indian Hotels Co. Ltd. is the parent company. The chain is managed by the The Indian Hotels Co. Ltd., the Indian Resort Hotels, Ltd., the Oriental Hotels Co. Ltd., Piem Hotels Co. Ltd., and the Benares Hotels Co. Ltd.

There was hardly any direct advertising to attract consumers. In fact, this element of marketing mix was absent till about 1999. The brand being an established one, advertising was not considered to be necessary. Secondly, the company was conservative and media shy for many, many years.

But nothing can go forever without a blemish. And so it was with Taj too. Cracks became evident when recession loomed large over the Indian economy. Excess capacity made some of the ventures unprofitable, especially overseas ones.

Managing Director Krishnakumar has it pat. "The vision for the Taj Group is for it to be a select chain, present globally, Asia, perhaps, in character, but absolutely international in terms of systems and processes and with a strong West European focus. The way forward was to make sure that the entire Taj team is imbued with the missionary zeal to sell the brand." International travellers form the bulk of the market for the Taj, particularly in the metros. Even the profile of Indian consumers is changing. In smaller cities, such as Hyderabad, though, the foreign element is a little lower but overall, the Taj has a higher dollar rate of revenue – approximately 70 per cent comes from international guests.

Contd...

As far back as 1990s, it was realised that formal market research was must to help understand the consumer better. Though it always had access to research done by independent research agencies, such as the airline and travel industry, it was about seven to eight years since, the group had carried out extensive research to understand current lifestyles. The research attempted to discover whether the future customer would be more egalitarian, more democratic or would she/he wish to be pampered? The findings revealed that the customer would like exclusivity, more than anything else. On the other hand, research also indicated that the company's existing consumer base of traditionalists – those who liked the Taj because it was understated, yet classy – was shrinking.

By the mid 1990s, the renovation was in full swing. Units across the country were refurbished. It meant overhauling entire floors. Rooms were revamped, business centres rebuilt. More than a handful million dollars were reportedly spent on renovation – just in the lifestyle (luxury segment)! It was anticipated that the business was likely to become big (and those using it were likely to be non-traditionalists) and the Taj went ostentatious with its new business floors. It meant putting in optic fibre cabling, remote control systems and giving the business guy a lounge where he could relax and even have breakfast. It included a mini-business centre too.

Initially, fax machines were installed in the rooms and later Internet and laptops. Not only mobiles were provided on hire, the Taj dropped communication charges by 33 per cent.

It was only when the product was ready, was a major advertising campaign developed. Earlier, the advertising had been restricted to the major feeder markets; the US, UK, Germany, Singapore, and Hong Kong and the advertising emphasised hardware aspects of the hotel. The new campaign developed a specific brand identity for the hotel. It also marked out three separate entities that the Taj Group comprises – Business, Leisure, and Luxury.

Though the concept of these sub-brands had come into existence five years ago, today, they are operationally different. Which means that though the heads of these three divisions sit at head office, their 'territory' is scattered geographically.

There are other changes. Unprofitable ventures were hived off. The sales and marketing functions were separated. The HRD department modernised, with emphasis on performance and career succession planning. The organisation was made flatter and more compact. Moreover, a continual benchmarking against international standards was made part and parcel of the culture of the Taj.

More emphasis was placed on business segment, as the profits are higher here (it being less price-sensitive comparing to luxury segment). In the business segment, 17 new cities, and towns will soon have the Taj Presidency hotels, also, new properties will come up in Goa, and Jodhpur and one is stated to come up near Sahara airport in Mumbai. The group has also acquired Hotel Blue Diamond in Pune.

Though, the Taj has a high un-aided recall, it has launched a corporate campaign to reinforce its new identity. The ad (made by Rediffusion) shows the Taj symbolised by an enigmatic woman who stands for both hospitality and efficiency. This identity was developed after extensive research on the consumer's attitude towards the Taj. Over 60 in-depth interviews were conducted in the metros by client agency. The parameters were based not on quantity but quality. The focus of research was on things that go into creating images of wonderful hospitality, such as the quality of check-in, the smile, the greeting, or the welcome drink etc.

The insights gathered were analysed extensively and a cleat slot, which the Taj could occupy when global competition arrived, emerged. The slot was an emotional one. This was translated

Contd...

into creating a distinct personality of the Taj as caring, efficient, and enigmatic. The line went, "She is the Taj." The base line was, "Nobody cares as much." Today, after a century since it was established, the Taj is all set to conquer.

Economic Times of December 15, 2004 reported in its 'Brand Equity' that among hotels, Taj is ranked as 'number one brand followed by Oberoi Hotels, ITC Hotels and Hyatt, respectively.

QUESTIONS

1. Analyse the case and determine the positioning of Taj. Do you think the advertising theme that is appropriate to reflect what it aims to communicate?
2. Why did Taj spent large sums of money to renovate its hotels?
3. Suggest an appropriate theme for an alternative campaign than the present one.

(Source: "The Crown's Subjects," A & M, February 15, 2000).

Case 4.2: Starbucks

tarbucks started in Seattle in 1970 as a gourmet coffee retailer, selling fresh ground coffee beans to local coffee lovers. Starbucks CEO, Howard Schultz spotted an unfulfilled market need for cafes serving gourmet coffee directly to consumers. This proved to be a sound market penetration strategy and led to a large loyal consumer base.

Entrepreneurs in India discovered the romance of coffee at Starbucks and a few coffee chains, such as Barista, Café Coffee Day, and Qwiky's have sprung up in metro cities. People of all age groups are extending enthusiastic welcome to this new entrant and drinking coffee like never before. Coffee lovers have always been lyrical about the virtues of this beverage – coffee inspires poetry and inflames prose; it is capable of firing passion, and stir people to romance, and drown a lover in dreams. The word coffee originates from Turkish kahvelt, which is wine prepared from fermented juice of ripe coffee cherries. Traditionally, coffee cafes in countries like Italy, France, Vienna, or London were the points where philosophers, writers, painters, and musicians spend hours savouring their coffee and let their creative juices flow.

In India – cafes or addas in Calcutta (now Kolkata) acquired the status of their legendry counterparts of 19th century Europe, where artists of various descriptions and anarchists, with dry hair and a kind of seriousness peculiar to them jostled together with their khadis and jhollas. Being seen sitting in a café with a cup of coffee for hours together discussing their favourite and hot topics was a kind of distinction for being progressive.

Times changed, and today's cafes reflect the befitting ambience of contemporary times, yet each café reflects a distinct character. Barista is brightly lit with orange coloured tabletops, Italian furniture, and music resounding in the air. Qwiky's has transparent glass walls through which consumers contemplate the buzz of the world, so that they are part of it and yet away from it. There is a message board on which a consumer can scribble a line to loved one. In addition, there is a Buddhist bell to sound one's satisfaction by ringing it. Prices suit every pocket, ranging between Rs. 10 and Rs. 150, and the brew is lip smacking variety of imported toppings.

For some, coffee sitting is incidental to hawking a lifestyle. The emphasis is on merchandising, such as T-shirts, greeting cards, and wristwatches. Each of the cafes plans a portal and a guest loyalty programme. With this high demand boom in coffee retailing, the image of coffee is changing from old-fashioned to young and modern. Harish Kapoor, vice president marketing at Tata Coffee says, "These are part of a coffee movement. There will be a third place for families to be in besides home and office." Shivaram, a college student says, as he zooms in on his motorcycle into Café Coffee Day, "My parents actually love this. Rather than being in pubs, this is more acceptable as an alternative. So I get a coffee allowance and hang around with friends."

For Amalgamated Bean Coffee Trading Co. (ABC) owned by Siddharth Hegde of Karnataka, Café Coffee Day represents forward integration. Three generations of the family have been in plantation business. The family owns 2,500 acres plantations and 50 depots that buy beans from 10,000 traders. ABC is one of the largest coffee export houses. This provided the company an opportunity to build its own brand of coffee. The firm decided on a genetic name to enhance recall value – Coffee Day. Retail section head, Narendra says, "We decided to enter the filter coffee segment, where freshness and choice of blend are critical. It is here you get real feel of coffee."

Regional marketeers, such as Narasu, Padma, and Vivekanand of Mysore dominate the market. At their points of sale where coffee beans are roasted, exude an aroma of fresh coffee, but the firms give little or no thought to customer convenience.

Contd...

So, Coffee Points stepped in and set up shop in residential localities in small 120 sq. ft spaces where customers find a place to leave their shopping bags, and actually step in the shop and choose the blend. 50gm samples and leaflets were distributed in the neighbourhood. In the past four years, over 400,000 households have been targeted. Coffee Points' pricing during introduction period was slightly below regional players' prices, and the customer response was phenomenal. The head of café division, P. Murali says, "Today we dictate the price."

Riding the crest of 1996 Internet wave, the first café was opened as cybercafe on Brigade Road in Bangalore with a leased line and terminals. Narendra says, "We exploited the compatibility between coffee and the cyberworld. Now, however, the two terminals are incidental. It is coffee that dominates." Today, there are 14 cafes in the south; 300 are being planned in three years' time all over the country, and also international airports.

Prices of coffee and light snacks are reasonable. Murali says, If we increase the price of a cup of coffee by one rupee, with a sale of 100,000 cups per day, I will improve my margins by Rs. 3.5 crore a day." Promotions vary from jazz festivals to distributing coffee recipes. Recently the cafe's have started to organise art exhibitions at the cafe's to promote local talent.

Unlike Hegde of Coffee Day, who were coffee people, for the owners of Qwiky's and Barista, coffee retailing was niche in the market waiting to be exploited. Shashi Chimala, CEO of the Chimaiyo Chain, master franchise for US-based Qwiky's says, "When I returned from the US, I missed cafe's. It is a place where you can connect with the community. In India, cafe's did exist in five-star hotels, where accessibility was limited to a few."

Chimala, an IT person, had no experience selling coffee. Inspired by Howard Schultz's book on the romance of selling coffee and realising that the domestic market holds potential, Chimala moved into coffee retailing. He says he does not want to push a particular type of coffee bean. He says, "We are enhancing an experience."

Starbucks has 5,000 outlets in the US and is a multi-billion dollar company. It opened in Chennai in 1999, aiming to sell 100,000 cups in the year but actually sold 3.65 lakh cups. Chimala says that Starbucks targeted 13 – 30 years-old but soon realised age was no bar for a cup of coffee. The outlets regular clientele included UC consul general Bernard Alter, Ford's managing director Phil Spender, housewives, and children. Besides coffee pubs, Qwiky's Islands are a store-within-a-store concept, which can be placed in shopping malls, book shops, or multiplexes.

Qwiky's chain has a tie-up with Dubai-based Landmark to open coffee kiosks in all its Life Style stores. H. Ramanathan, Life Style's MD says, "It is a win-win situation. Both of us share the core value giving our customer the best retail experience." To strengthen the brand, Qwiky's has a brand partnership with MTV where VJs are regular visitors. Chimala has also acquired Confidence Trading, a company belonging to Marugappa group, to distribute equipment and food necessary for the gourmet coffee business.

As coffee retailers roll out expansion plans, the market is getting segmented, Ravi S. Deol, president and CEO of Barista says, "We are enhancing as a fine café, not just a coffee pub like Qwiky's or Café Coffee Day. Out target customers include professionals, working couples, and families who detest the loud ambience of coffee pubs." Its softer ambience and higher price distinguish it from others. Barista takes its name from the Italian term for a coffee brew master. According to Deol, his brew master are trained under genuine baristas; the Cimpelli machine differs from the automatic dispensers in other cafes and the coffee bean is treated in a way that gives coffee a richer, sweeter taste. Deol believes that three crucial elements – the bean, the dispensing of the brew, and the actual brewing – makes Barista tick.

Contd...

He says people spend 45 minutes on an average in his café and 70 per cent are repeat customers. Many have been weaned away from the cold glitter of the five-star hotels. Reiterating the bond between books and music lovers, Barista has small bars in music retail chains, Plant M and Crossword. To fuel the boom, Barista plans to sell out a training school for Indian brew masters, coffee-tasting clubs, and coffee appreciation sessions.

Bijoor of Tata Coffee is glad that evangelists have boosted the coffee market that has been so far unexplored. He says this shot in the arm and other branding efforts are the need of the hour if Indian coffee is to survive. Bijoor attended the seventh Asian International Coffee Conference in Thailand and has just returned. He says, "Coffee has never seen such bleak days." Coffee prices have shot down to an all time low. He points out that supply is 114 million bags, of 60kg each, this year, where demand is 97 million bags. He says that if stocks carried forward it will be tragic for coffee prices.

Traditionally, once in ten years there used to be a correction of stock by bad weather in Brazil or Columbia. But this correction is not expected. Besides the demand-supply problem, another reason for the volatile is speculative funds, which have moved into commodities such as coffee when meals and stocks fare badly. In fact, Bijoor says coffee is the second largest traded commodity after petrol. The cumulative effect of these external conditions like trading sentiment, weather, and health of economy presents a bleak picture for coffee growers. "We need to build an Indian brand with a coffee ambassador to improve the image of Indian coffee," says Bijoor

Consumers in developed countries stress the need for quality, consistency, and new offering. Bijoor says that instead of crying hoarse about low prices and low realisations, coffee producers need to work on their image and lobby with the International Coffee Organisation to fund a generic promotion in the country, for after all India is nascent market with the world's second largest population.

He says that Tata Coffee applies innovative ways to build its brands. For example, it built the world's largest coffee mug to toast 50 years of Independence. The mug was 20 feet high, with a five-foot handle made of food-grade fiberglass. It not only entered the Guinness Book of World Records, but also featured on national and international television. Tata Coffee is now installing coffee machines in shopping malls, petrol stations, and railway stations to enhance visibility. Bijoor does not rule out setting up its own cafes in the future.

The speculation of Starbucks' impending launch in Indian market has warmed up the café market. Coffee Day is expected to invest Rs. 100 crore over the next three years. Qwiky's has plans to set up 55 coffee pubs and 90 islands. For this it might tap the capital market. Barista is contemplating opening 100 cafe's at a cost of Rs. 65 crore. Lakshmi Venkatachala, chairperson of Coffee Board, says, "In India, there is tremendous potential to improve domestic coffee consumption considering rising per capita income in the urban middle-class." For log, Vindhya divide was thought to mark the boundaries between kapiland and chailand. Not anymore. The coffee bean is converting people all over India with cafes whisking up many different aromatic coffee combinations.

QUESTIONS

1. Study the promotional approaches in this case to promote coffee brands by different cafe's in India. If you were to develop a promotional approach for the anticipated new player Starbuck, what would it be?
2. In your view what kind of promotional approaches should be adopted to increase category consumption in India?
3. What theme would you suggest to promote coffee as a category?

Case 4.3: Pizza Hut

Pizza Hut has a sense of occasion, of being there at the right time. Be it a heart-shaped pizza on Valentine's Day or a special promotion during the Cricket World Cup, Pizza Hut is on the ball – with eye catching promotions. In the summer of 2000 in New Delhi, Pizza Hut launched its innovative Pizza Pooch menu as well as a Birthday Party package exclusively for kids in the 6 – 10 years age group. Senior marketing manager, Tricon Restaurants International said, "There is a specific reason to cater to this segment. Though, at this age children are under their parents' guidance, they perceive themselves to be teenagers and have the ability to choose or demand a particular brand of their own choice."

The $ 20 billion Tricon Restaurants that owns Pizza Hut, Taco Bell and Kentucky Fried Chicken (KFC) has nearly 29,000 outlets globally. The largest number of Pizza Hut outlets is in Paris, followed by Moscow and Hong Kong. Pizza Hut started operations in India nearly seven years ago with just a single outlet. It has realised the cultural differences in India and importance of religion in the consumption pattern of certain sub-cultures. Today it has spread in several cities and it also has a 100 per cent vegetarian restaurant in Ahmedabad.

Innovative promotional activities and a popular logo have helped Pizza Hut expanding. The senior marketing manager said, "Our focus is not just on offering a great pizza but also on providing excitement and good customer service." The manager further emphasised on the customer focused operations and intensive research done to find customer needs and satisfaction. Besides, Pizza Hut conducted in-house research on psychographics of Indian consumer that led to the use of cartoon characters in campaigns. The Indian Market Research Bureau (IMRB) also carries out regular surprise checks at different outlets to monitor the quality of service. Moreover, a regular test, CHAMPS (Cleanliness, Hospitality, Accuracy of order, Maintenance, Product quality and Speed of service) is conducted in-house.

The company says that its Pizza Pooch birthday package is full of fun and excitement. What is unique in the package is the nominal price of Rs. 125 per child that offers much more than only goodies in the main menu. The birthday party includes a well-decorated area within the Pizza Hut outlet with several gifts for the children. Moreover, the party is conducted by a trained host with lots of games, prizes and a special gift for the birthday child. Pizza Hut, better known as a family restaurant, takes the onus of relieving parents of the cumbersome job of clearing up the mess after the kiddies have enjoyed themselves thoroughly.

The Pizza Pooch menu, on the other hand, includes a wholesome delicious meal and a gift for the child. The menu has been intricately designed with pictorial games. A free set of crayons is provided to keep the children occupied while their parents dine. The campaigns created by HTA are eye-catching with cartoon characters on the mailers, hoardings and print advertisements where the cartoon characters are aimed at matching varying moods of kids. The birthday part concept is not entirely original – local fast food major Nirula's has been doing it for years as does KFC.

(Source: A&M, August 15, 2000)

QUESTIONS

1. Do you think Pizza Hut promotion is successful? Give your reasons.
2. Suggest one alternative promotion to attract girls to Pizza Hut. Why do you think this would be successful?

Case 4.4: Body Shop International

Anita Roddick lived in England and was bored with managing her restaurant and an eight-room hotel in her hometown. She was planning to do something new and more exciting and came up with an idea of producing and selling shampoos, skincare creams, and other body lotions made from fruit and vegetable oils rather than animal fats. She believed that it would be good idea to capitalise on selling "natural" cosmetic to the ageing generation like herself who distrust advertising and sales type, and demand product information, and are loyal to socially responsible companies.

The more she considered this idea, the more convinced she was about its soundness. She borrowed a loan of $7000, hired a local chemist to develop animal-fat-free creams and body lotions. She opened her first shop in Brighton, and Body Shop came into existence. By 1993, more than seven hundred Body Shop stores were operating around the world. In the US, out of the total of seventy-eight Body Shops, sixty-four were franchised.

Body Shop does no advertising, but relies on in-store selling and promotion to communicate with consumers. Faith Popcorn, a consultant with Brain-Reserve says, "Ninety-nine per cent of Fortune 500 chief executives have never walked into a Body Shop, yet this is what business will be like. And it is so contradictory to the way we are used for marketing."

Body Shop has adopted the strategy of providing product information to customers without a sales pitch. Sales people are expected to develop a forthright relationship with customers, tell them about the history of lotions, and provide accurate product information. Leaflets offer tips for skincare, and a manual containing product information is available in each store. Pamphlets scattered throughout stores also tell customers about Body Shop's recycling programme, whereby customers can bring in used Body Shop bottles and get them refilled. Roddick also uses the stores to push Body Shop's social agenda, a variety of causes including "Save the Whales" and Amnesty International. With her long-running social campaign, Roddick intends for her company to demonstrate what she calls the new business consciousness.

Body Shop International prides itself on its knowledgeable staff. Courses in product ingredients, teach sales people about properties, structures, and sources of cosmetics. Employees are taught to serve the needs of customers who are culturally foreign. Training is also available to help franchises and partnership shop owners get involved in community projects. Work force training efforts are measured by employee attitude. Roddick also displays slogans and messages around the stores to motivate employees. One of her favourite is "If you think you are too small to have an impact, try going to bed with a mosquito." Even Body Shop trucks are used as rolling billboards for pithy slogans.

Not everyone is impressed with Body Shop's approach to selling products. The British press has become especially critical of Roddick and her husband. A London daily, the Independent, wrote: "They represent causes attractive to the liberal conscious. Yet this goodness is used to, remorselessly, to sell vanity products. You wash your hair in global concern. And it is debatable whether the wizened peasants on the walls are dignified or patronised." Although there may be some debate about Body Shop's approach, most agree that selling in general will incorporate some aspects of it in the decade ahead.

Contd...

QUESTIONS

1. How do environmental concerns fit into the strategy of Body Shop? Is it a sound approach in selling personal care products? Explain.
2. What approaches Body Shop adopts to train its sales people and motivate them?
3. Would you say Body Shop uses relationship selling? Explain.
4. Is it wise for Body Shop not to advertise its products in mass media? Explain.

Case 4.5: From Direct Selling to Direct Marketing

For years Avon lady was a fixture in American neighbourhoods. Selling door-to-door built Avon into the world's largest manufacturer of beauty products. Avon operates in 135 countries and besides the cosmetics it also sells jewelry, home furnishings, and baby-care products. Avon pioneered the idea of hiring housewives for direct selling cosmetics in the neighbourhood. But in 1980s, as millions of women began to work outside the home, the cosmetics maker's pool of customers and sales representatives dwindled, and its sales faltered. By 1985, its profits were half what they had been in 1979.

Consumer research showed that many women thought Avon's make-up was "stodgy," its gifts products overpriced, and its jewelry old-fashioned. So the company created a more contemporary line of jewelry, lowered the prices of its giftware to offer more items under $15, and expanded its lipstick and nail polish colours.

On the selling side, recruiting sales people had become problematic, much as it had for other direct sellers like Mary Kay Cosmetics and Premark International's Tupperware division. To attract sales representatives and boost productivity, Avon improved incentive-compensation plans and offered free training programmes for recruits. As a result, Avon's direct-sales business – which accounts for 70 per cent of sales and 85 per cent of operating profits – experienced a dramatic turnaround. Within a year sales rose 17 per cent, to $2.9 billion, and profits jumped as much as 25 per cent.

Today more than 450,000 sales representatives work for Avon and fill out some 50,000 orders daily. Sales exceed $3.5 billion a year. Nonetheless, Avon estimates that at least ten million women in the US who are interested in buying from Avon are unable because no sales representative is calling. To win back some of the customers and attract new ones, the company has begun mailing catalogues directly to potential customers nationwide. The move represents growing concern at Avon that its core market has matured. The growing number of women joining work force means that fewer of them have time to meet with Avon representatives. Although Avon remains the nation's largest direct seller of beauty products, supermarkets and discount stores are stealing market share. Avon hopes that mail-order catalogues will help to reach "stranded" customers.

The plan is to send catalogues to people who have moved or who no longer are active buyers. They can then order directly through the company or through a salesperson. Initial expectations are modest. Avon hopes catalogue sales will reach $25 million the first year. In the long run, Avon hopes to penetrate major cities and suburbs, the places where much of the female work force is absent at prime selling times. Avon is also increasing the use of toll free numbers in conjunction with this strategy.

Source: Pat Sloan, "Avon Looks Beyond Direct Sales," Advertising Age, February 22, 1993.

QUESTIONS

1. What are the significant issues in the case?
2. Do you think Avon's approach in response for changing conditions is right for products that need personal contact by saleswomen?
3. Suggest any other solution than what Avon is planning to do.

Case 4.6: Bahenji Turns Bold

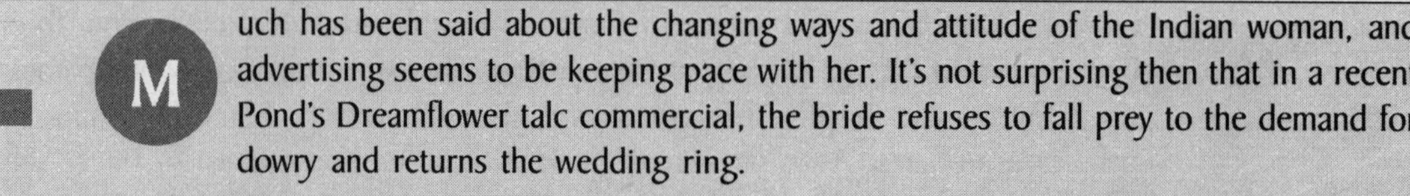

Much has been said about the changing ways and attitude of the Indian woman, and advertising seems to be keeping pace with her. It's not surprising then that in a recent Pond's Dreamflower talc commercial, the bride refuses to fall prey to the demand for dowry and returns the wedding ring.

She's applauded and also finds a suitor among her admirers. In fact, a quick ad scan reveals that Indian advertising is increasingly showing women rubbing shoulders with men and taking up more challenging jobs.

Clearly, the advertising agencies are handling the gender issues with sensitivity. Recently, Ogilvy & Mather altered its commercial for a private sector bank based on a single complaint that was posted on the agency's website.

The earlier tag line stated something to this effect: "agar mere pass paison ka pedh hota to mein apni beti ki shaadi ek Raj Kumar se karta aur bete ko padhne videsh bhejta" (If I had a tree of money I would have married my daughter to a prince and sent my son abroad to study).

The complaint, that the ad is discriminating, was also made to the Advertising Standard's Council of India (ASCI).

O&M was quick to react and altered the ad to say: "Agar mere pass paison ka pedh hota to mein apni beti ko videsh bhejta aur bete ka business shuroo karwata" (if I had a tree of money I would have sent my daughter abroad to study and helped my son to set up a business).

Though Abhijit Awasthi, senior creative director, O&M, says that neither he nor any member of his team (including women) felt that marrying one's daughter to a prince connotes encouraging dowry, but the agency readily changed it.

"The bank is among our esteemed clients and we could not let its image erode even if one out of 200 million viewers has been offended," says Awasthi.

Ad makers agree that the advertising must reflect social changes. Santosh Desai, president, McCann-Erickson, says that ads are changing for two reasons: one, women are becoming more assertive and confident.

Secondly, trade and voluntary bodies like women's organizations are watching the advertising fraternity closely. "Consumers are not ready to pardon even the occasional lapses," he says.

Desai points out that even the fairness cream; Fair & Lovely commercials have been upgraded to suit the new environment. The cream's older ads showed a woman fetching a good groom after using the cream.

Later, the ad showed a girl becoming an airhostess. In another fairness cream ad she is not content being an airhostess: "into conchae kaki nahein" and she goes on to become a pilot. In the Fair & Lovely ad the product user is offered the role of the lead actor by filmmaker Rakesh Roshan.

"Not that being a housewife is inferior but advertising has to reflect the change in aspirational levels. Sometimes ad-makers dictate and lead the society, for instance the Fair & Lovely ad shows a woman cricket commentator. So far, there is none in India," says R. Balakrishnan, national creative director, Lowe.

Contd...

Coyness in advertising the sanitary towel category is also passé. The new lot of commercials feature busy working women with little time to waste.

In a Whisper's ad, Perizaad Zorabian is confidently rushing for a full-day film shoot on the second day of her periods, while in another one a reporter is getting ready to enter a packed cricket stadium to cover the match.

"Old anxieties and insecurities are dying out and the new ads are bringing the woman out of her inner world," observes Desai.

Ad makers claim the idea behind all advertising is to reflect aspirational and heroic values and most feel that today's women match men in financial prowess and intellect.

"They are an intelligent universe. And yes, it certainly helps to show them as they are in real life today," says Meenakshi Bhalla, vice president, O&M.

(Source: Sangeeta Singh, "Bahenji Turns Bold," Business Standard, June 25, 2005).

QUESTIONS

1. What is the new profile of Indian women according to the above case?
2. What do you think, how this will affect business communications?

PART 5

Marketing Channels and Physical Distribution

CHAPTER 18

LEARNING OBJECTIVES

After going through this chapter, you will understand:

- Important channel functions and common types of channels for consumer and industrial products
- Intensity of desired market coverage affects channel arrangement
- Channel-Related Terms and Conditions
- What is meant by vertical and horizontal marketing system
- Causes of channel conflict and its management
- Physical distribution, inventory, management, warehousing, and transportation arrangements

Compaq Computer Corporation designs, manufactures, and makes its own line of computers for home and professional use. Compaq is the largest manufacturer of IBM compatibles and thus is a major competitor of IBM, one of the market leaders. Compaq's sales doubled between 1986 to 1987, and net income tripled in 1988. This growth allowed the company to exceed $1 billion in annual sales in only five years, making it among the fastest growing companies in the history.

Part of Compaq's success can be traced to a very effective distribution network. One of its largest distributors, Business land accounted for 7 per cent of Compaq's revenue; Compaq's products made up 15 percent of Business and's sales. Thus, it came as a surprise to the industry when Compaq announced in April 1989 that it would no longer distribute through Business land. In response to the decision, Business land stock dropped almost by 10 percent. Shortly after the announcement, industry analysts harshly criticised Compaq for the decision, saying that the break was the worst thing to happen to Compaq in a long time.

May be it was. In October 1999, CEO and co-founder Rod Canion announced the company's first-ever quarterly loss and the layoff of 1,700 employees, or 14 percent of the work force. Compaq had never before laid-off an employee. Most industry observers attributed Compaq's problems to price, not distribution. Because of intense price wars, the firm's market share, revenues, and earnings had fallen faster than the competitors'. Although Canion blamed Compaq's problems on the recession and hoped to ride it out, the chairman of the board, Benjamin Rosen believed the company to be in "a crisis, almost a life-and-death situation." Canion was removed from his position.

Eckhard Pfeiffer was named CEO, and he restored the company to its lofty position nearly as quickly as it had fallen. In June 1992, Compaq announced an extended line of PCs including forty-five newer models, bringing to seventy-six the total number of models. The firm's across the board cut of upto 32 per cent rocked the industry. The price of Compaq's high-quality machines was much closer to that of inferior clones. Third quarter sales jumped 50 per cent, to $1.1 billion, and earnings quadrupled to $72 million.

With new products and increased sales, Compaq is exploring new distribution alternatives. The firm more than doubled its worldwide outlets to more than 9,000, adding office supply discounters like Office Depot and Circuit City as well as computer stores. Plans are also underway to begin selling certain products through mail-order companies.

(Source: Based on a case in Marketing, by Steven J. Skinner, 2nd ed. 1994.)

Producing and offering a good product or service to customers at a reasonable price is not the whole story. The third 'P' of traditional marketing mix represents *place*. Place decisions concern marketing channel or distribution channel arrangements. It is crucial to ensure availability of goods and services to customers when they want, at places they want, and in the right quantities. This is an integral part of satisfaction delivery to customers and marketing channel arrangements can have dramatic implications for competition in a product market. Most marketing channels are composed of intermediaries who perform a number of very useful functions. These intermediaries or channel members include firms and individuals, such as wholesalers, retailers etc. that facilitate the distribution of goods or services to ultimate customer. Wholesalers buy larger quantities of products and resell to retailers, and industrial customers. In turn, retailers buy from wholesalers and sell to consumers for personal or home use. Each channel member performs a set of different functions within the overall channel structure. Channel members cooperate with each other and earn profits and success. Bowersox and Cooper define marketing channel in the following words:

"A marketing channel is a system of relationships existing among businesses that participate in the process of buying and selling products and services."

Marketing channel decisions are critical and influence all other marketing mix decisions. These decisions are usually long-term and determine product's market presence and ensure customer's accessibility to the product. The same product may require different approaches to set up channel arrangements if different customer segments view it differently. For example, a computer is a consumer product as well as an organisational product and may require separate approaches to establish channels for different segments. Marketing channel decisions are often harder to change than price, promotion, and product decisions. Legal contracts may limit changes and developing effective relationships with channel members, often takes longer and costs more. It may also be hard to move retail outlets and wholesale facilities once they are set up. E. Raymond Corey writes in his book:

"Normally it takes years to build (distribution channel), *and it is not easily changed... It represents a significant corporate commitment to large numbers of independent companies whose business is distribution – and to the particular markets they serve."*

Channel Functions

Most manufacturers do not sell their products directly to end-users. Between the end-user and the producer, there are channel members performing a variety of functions. Some of these resellers such as wholesalers and retailers purchase from producers, take ownership title, and in turn resell the products to parties or consumers at the next level. They are called merchants. In contrast brokers, agents, and producer's sales-persons search and negotiate with buyers on behalf of the producer and do not acquire ownership title to merchandise. Other channel members work as facilitators in the process of distribution and include transporters, privately owned warehouses, banks, and others who neither negotiate with buyers or sellers on behalf of producer nor take ownership tile of merchandise.

A single channel member may perform all these functions in certain situations. However, in most of the situations, channel members at different levels are involved in performing the following functions jointly:

- ***Channel Members Create Utility:*** Marketing channels create *time, place,* and *possession utility.* Time utility refers to making products available to customers when they want them. They create place utility by making products available in locations, where customers desire them to be available for buying. Possession utility means customers having access to obtain and have the right to use or store for future use. This may occur through ownership or some arrangements such as rental or lease agreements that entitle the customer the right to use the product.
- ***Channel Members Facilitate Exchange Efficiencies:*** Channel members offer exchange efficiencies and help reduce the exchange costs by providing certain functions or services. Let us assume that three customers seek to buy products from four producers. If there are no middlemen involved, the total transactions with three customers will be twelve. If these four producers sell to one reseller, the total transactions for producers will come down to four (one for each producer), and in turn the reseller will handle three transactions with customers. The costs of three transactions for each producer are likely to be more than just one transaction with reseller for each producer. In this situation just one reseller serves both producers and the customers. Cost is a major factor coupled with better service to customer needs for using channel intermediaries.

- ***Channel Members May Reduce Discrepancies and Separations:*** For most customers, producers are located far from them and customers may want different product assortment and quantity of the manufacturer's produce. Customers too may not be very clear about their product choices and channel members help adjust these discrepancies.

  Assortment discrepancy refers to the difference between the product lines a company produces and the assortment customers want. A company may be specialist in producing cricket balls only, but a typical cricket enthusiast would also be interested in cricket bat or gloves, and other complimentary products and may not prefer to shop for these items elsewhere. The resellers adjust these discrepancies.

  Quantity discrepancy means the difference between what quantity is economical for the company to produce, which in most cases is quite large. The cricket ball manufacturers might be producing 10 or 15 thousand balls in a given period. The average buyer would buy far less number of balls at a time. Channel members may also help in handling this discrepancy. Middlemen collect and accumulate products from various producers. Wholesalers buy in bulk, break it into different grades or qualities desired by different customer groups, and sell smaller quantities to retailers, who sell to the customer one or few units at a time.

- ***Other Functions:*** Distribution channels share financial risk by financing the goods moving through pipeline and also sometimes extend the credit facility to next level operators and consumers as well as handle personal selling by informing and recommending the product to consumers, and partly look after physical distribution such as warehousing and transportation, provide merchandising support, and furnish market intelligence.

The main criticism about using intermediaries is that this increases prices. Customers prefer lower prices and would like the channels as short as possible. The assumption is that lower the number of intermediaries, the lower the prices. This thinking ignores the fact that channel members perform certain functions and producers cannot escape these functions by not involving intermediaries. The functions and associated costs are simply transferred to producer.

Types of Channels

Many different distribution path alternatives have been developed because a certain channel type may be appropriate for one product but may not be suitable for others. Various channel types may be classified generally as channels used for consumer products or industrial products.

Consumer Product Channels

Companies producing consumer products may use several different types of channels. Producers can choose *zero-level channel* (also called direct-marketing channel). This approach involves moving product direct from producer to customer. Zero-channel system does not involve resellers. Examples include company owned stores, telemarketing, mail order, and door-to-door selling etc. Sara Lee, Amway, Avon cosmetics, Eureka Forbes, Amazon and others use zero-channel. This is a quite simple arrangement but may not be the most efficient or economical means of distributing products to consumers (Figure 18.1, A). Sumit K. Majumdar and Venkatram Ramaswamy suggest that faced with making strategic choice of going direct to the consumer or using channel partners, a company must weigh the benefits to consumers against the transaction costs involved in using intermediaries before going direct to consumers.

FIGURE 18.1

Marketing Channels for Consumer Products

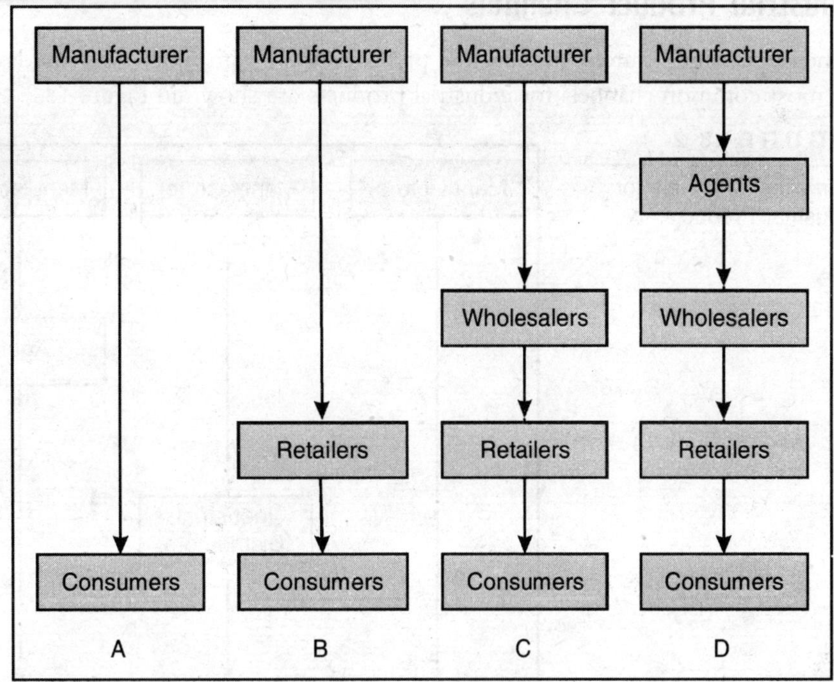

One-level channel (B) moves products from the manufacturer to retailer. Retailer makes these products available to consumers. Large retailers such as supermarkets and chain stores prefer to buy large quantities of goods from manufacturers. ***Two-level channel*** (C) has been quite popular among consumer product companies since long. Between a manufacturer and consumers there are two types of channel intermediaries – wholesalers and retailers. The goods pass from producer to wholesalers, then to retailers, and finally to consumers. This channel arrangement is a practical option to producers who sell to millions of consumers in several geographic areas through few thousand to lakhs of retail shops including the locality *kirana* stores. In India, there are an estimated 12 million grocery outlets. Wholesalers of all shapes and sizes cater to large number of retail stores, including rural markets. Tobacco products, tea, and laundry products etc. are typical examples where wholesalers and retailers operate between manufacturers and consumers. ***Three-level*** channel arrangement involves intermediaries at three levels. The manufacturer does not handle any distribution functions and appoints sole agents with substantial resources or C&F agents. They have their own network of wholesalers, and retailers all over the country. This kind of arrangement may also be on territorial basis. C&F agents handle only distribution functions. Sole selling agents may also handle personal selling on behalf of producer besides taking care of distribution. This is a fairly common practice in India among pharmaceutical manufacturers lacking resources to handle personal selling and distribution functions.

Another channel option is ***strategic channel alliance***. This refers to an arrangement when another company through its own marketing channels sells the products of one producer. For example, a soft drink company may distribute the bottled water of another manufacturer, or a domestic company might distribute the product of a foreign company.

Traditional channels discussed above refer to forward movement of products from producer to consumer. Some producers must also plan for channel intermediaries performing the role of *reverse-flow channels* to retrieve products that customers no longer want. For example auto firms, drug companies, toy manufacturers, and others sometimes have to recall products due to defects, breakage, safety reasons, and repairs during warranty period. They, including producers, help in reversing the flow of certain types of containers for reuse, computer circuit boards for refurbishing and resale, paper, cardboards, and metals etc. for recycling.

Industrial Product Channels

Sometimes manufacturers of industrial products work with more than one level of wholesalers. Four of the most common channels for industrial products are shown in Figure 18.2.

FIGURE 18.2

Marketing Channels for Industrial Products

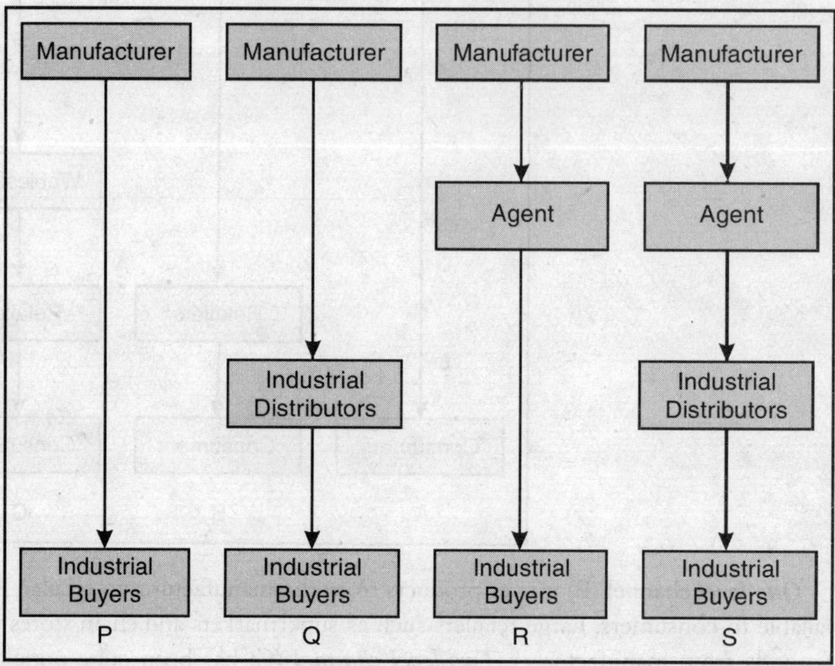

A large number of industrial products, particularly producers of expensive and technically complex equipment sell directly to industrial buyers (Figure 18.2, P). IBM sells its mainframe computers direct to business buyers. Companies producing standard industrial items, such as hand tools, and small operating equipment usually operate through industrial distributors (Q). Industrial distributors may carry a wide variety of product lines and items from different manufacturers, or some may specialise and carry only limited number of lines. James D. Hlavecek and Tommy J. McCuistion reported that this distribution channel suits producers making products with broad market appeal, easily stocked, sold in small quantities, and needed on demand to avoid high losses.

The advantages industrial distributors offer include selling services at low cost, extend credit to customers and develop close relationship, and provide market intelligence to manufacturers. They also minimise financial burden of manufacturer by holding adequate inventories in the market. The disadvantages include lack of control because industrial distributors are independent firms, they also carry competing brands and manufacturer cannot depend on them to push a specific brand. They generally avoid stocking expensive and slow moving items and may seek special incentives. In case of industrial channel three (R), an independent firm works as producers' representative or agent on a commission, usually sells complimentary products of several companies in specific territories. The agent does not acquire ownership title to the products.

Agents offer the advantage of their considerable technical and market information and have an established number of customers. They can be very useful for seasonal industrial products, more so because agents are paid only commission on sales. When the company cannot afford a full-time sales team, agent can be an asset.

The problems include little control on agents, because of commission system they often focus on large buyers, and may not adequately follow up customers when it reduces productive selling time.

Using two intermediaries, selling agent and industrial distributor(s) is useful when manufacturers wish to operate in large geographic areas and do not want to employ sales people, demand for products is seasonal, or when starting coverage of new geographic area without expanding sales force.

FACTORS AFFECTING SELECTION OF MARKETING CHANNEL SYSTEM

In developing distribution strategy, any producer should be able enough and flexible in responding to the changing market conditions. A company has to take into account a number of factors that influence channel design decisions. This includes product, company, customer, competition factors, PLC stages, objectives, and desired market coverage intensity and control etc.

Channel Objectives

A company's channel objectives aim at what the company seeks to accomplish through marketing channels. Most companies have some general objectives and in addition to these may also have some specific ones because of their peculiar circumstances. Some general objectives can be:

- Convenience to customers.
- Effective target market coverage.
- Cost-effective distribution.

Specific objectives may relate to the nature of the product such as custom-made machinery, perishable nature of product, products requiring installation and maintenance like cooling or heating systems, or expensive and bulky items such as mainframe computers, turbines and generators etc. Some major factors that affect objectives are discussed below:

End Customer: This may mean considering the geographic locations of customers and their preferences to buy locally, or their inclination to feel more at ease going to a particular type of store such as a retail store capable of providing the much needed after sales service, or a music store like Planet M for buying music CDs and DVD. Customers may favour buying from large retail stores or discount stores. Decisions with regard to suitable marketing channel would depend on marketing research on buyer behaviour patterns. Rural customers in India generally prefer buying tractors and other agricultural equipment, and two-wheeler autos etc., from dealers nearer to their locations and who are capable of providing satisfactory after sales repair services. This is equally true for B2B markets. For example, producers of computer servers and notebooks need to determine whether business buyers prefer to deal directly with company's direct sales force or would prefer specialist distributor nearer their location. In international markets it may be necessary to use a local agent with intimate understanding of the market and cultural aspects.

Product Characteristics: Perishable products, such as milk, fruit juices, and fresh food products etc. require short marketing channels. This has implications for storage and transportation of products. Highly complex products may need personal contact between the producer and the buyer, such an installation of high technology machinery and all related repairs and services are to be performed by the producer without using an intermediary. Heavy equipment such as cranes and earth moving machinery are generally distributed direct to buyer, or through exclusive industrial distributor.

Company Factors: Available company resources are an important consideration to make the product available where customers normally shop for the product category. If the available finances are insufficient, the company cannot afford maintaining its own sales force and will use wholesalers instead. Companies producing a very limited range of products, or seasonal products will use a wholesaler route. If the product is very expensive such as mainframe computer system, it will have little option but to use its direct sales force. The producer has also to consider its core competence. If the competence area does not include marketing and distribution, then it would be suitable to use specialist channel intermediary. A company may want to protect its image among target customers and have exclusive company showrooms to have full channel control. The desired level of control on marketing channel can also affect channel decision.

FIGURE 18.3

Producer Reliance on Intermediaries

Factors	Less Reliance	More Reliance
End Customer		
Lot size	Large	Small
Location	Concentrated	Wide-spread
Number	Few	Many
Special needs	Frequent	Infrequent
Producer Resources	Extensive	Limited
Product Characteristics		
Perishability	High	Low
Cost	High	Low
Bulk	Large	Small
Technology	Complex	Simple
Competition	Weak	Strong
Alternative Channels	None	Many

Competition: If competing producers already have exclusive deals with certain intermediaries, then the company has to look for alternative marketing channels with desired market presence and penetration. Timex watches initially had exclusive tie up with Titan showrooms for sales and after sales service. After parting company with Titan, Timex selected supermarkets to put its products on shelf rather than going through watch retailers, or opening its own retail outlets. Deccan Avionics tied up with Hindustan Petroleum to sell air tickets to passengers at its retail petrol outlets.

Product Life Cycle Stages: Distribution decisions need to be modified keeping in view the PLC stage of a product. As a product passes through different PLC stages, it attracts different adopter groups. Accordingly, distribution decisions should take into consideration the market growth rate and the value addition by intermediaries. During introductory phase, specialist stores may add value, speciality or dedicated stores may be appropriate during growth stage, during maturity and decline stages, low cost channels and discount stores may be appropriate.

Intensity of Market Coverage

A company must determine the distribution coverage intensity a product should get, what number and kinds of channel in which the product will be sold. This will depend on the nature of product, target market, and availability of other competing products. Three major coverage strategies include *intensive, selective*, and *exclusive* distribution.

Intensive Distribution: A company uses all available distribution outlets for making its product available to consumers. This system does not offer any control on distribution outlets. These products are generally low-cost convenience products such as bread, soft drinks, chewing gum, tea, laundry soaps and detergents, toothpaste, toilet soaps, and petrol and diesel etc. These products are used routinely and on an ongoing basis and require no post sale service. To meet consumer demand efficiently, intensive distribution is necessary and companies use all available distribution channels that offer deep market penetration in every geographic area. This is necessary because availability is important and may generally have direct relationship to sales because there is no brand loyalty, consumers want to buy immediately in the nearest location where they live and do not devote any time to search, they buy whichever brand is easily and conveniently available, substitution and brand switching is common. Consumer product companies such as HLL, P&G, ITC, and Nirma etc. use intensive distribution. HLL objective for its Lifebuoy bathing soap is to make it available in 80 per cent of the Indian rural markets. Companies producing fertilisers and insecticides have to ensure intensive distribution to make products available within few kilometers to farmers living in rural India. Such companies use C&F agents, distributors, wholesalers, sub-wholesalers, retailers and village shops. Speedy availability is critically important.

Selective Distribution: Companies use selective distribution, which means using more than a few and less than all available outlets in a market area to distribute products. This offers some degree of control at a relatively less cost than intensive distribution. High-involvement products such as consumer durable items that include TV, washing machine, refrigerators, stereo systems, PCs for home and personal use, branded clothing, and sports wear etc., use selective distribution. These products are infrequently purchased, are more expensive than convenience products, and consumers are willing to devote time in searching various retail outlets to compare product price, features, design, and style etc. Selective distribution is suitable when product requires post-sale service from the outlet, such as PCs, Printers, Cell phones, and air conditioners etc. Selective distribution is also suitable when product differentiation at the outlet level is important. Some companies use company owned showrooms such as Raymonds, Titan watches, Vimal fabrics, and Bata shoes etc. Many firms producing industrial products, such as hand-tools use selective distribution.

Exclusive Distribution: This type of distribution means using one or very limited few outlets. Allen J. Magrath writes that exclusive distribution offers producer tighter image control. The producer can also maintain control over dealer's sales and service activities. It is called exclusive because it involves *exclusive dealing* arrangement and often includes exclusive territorial agreements and the intermediary does not handle any other competitors' products. The manufacturer hopes, the resellers would be more committed for selling the product and providing excellent customer service, carry complete inventory, send their personnel for training, and participate in promotional activities. This type of arrangement is quite suitable for products, which are infrequently purchased and consumed over long period of time. Products suitable for exclusive distribution include expensive cars, branded jewelry, high-priced wristwatches, designer dresses, exclusive perfumes and expensive fashion products. Porsche, Christian Dior products, Rolex watches, Professional Nikon cameras, and French perfumes etc., are sold through exclusive dealers. Both parties benefit from exclusive distribution and this system is often used as an incentive to dealers when only a limited target market is available. It requires closer ties between the producer and the dealer.

Channel Terms and Conditions

The producer stipulates terms and condition and responsibilities of channel partners to develop better mutual understanding and usually include price policy and trade margins, payment terms, and territorial demarcation, guarantee and returns policy, and mutual responsibilities etc.

Price policy and trade margins should be fair and require manufactures to establish a price list, trade margins and allowances. Intermediaries' margins should be sufficient enough so they can earn a reasonable margin for their efforts and high return on investment. Simplicity and clarity help in avoiding strained relations between the produce and intermediaries.

Payment terms include any discounts on quantity and early payments. This may also include guarantees producer offers against defective goods or breakages during transit, or price declines, and producer policy on taking back date expired products.

Territorial demarcation establishes territorial boundaries and rights of company appointed distributors or dealers. This avoids conflicts and strained relations between dealers operating in different territories, and also between the producer and the dealers. Mutual responsibilities and services should be clearly laid down in case of exclusive dealerships or where the producer has franchise arrangement. The producer should also clearly state what kind of promotional support, standards, services, records the dealers or franchisees must maintain, and what the dealers and franchisees should expect from the producer in terms of training and other mutually beneficial activities.

Evaluation of Channel Alternatives

In making a decision about channel alternatives, producers' evaluation criteria is generally based on some combination of the following factors:

- Product characteristics.
- Buyer behaviour and location.
- Severity of competition.
- Cost effectiveness and channel efficiency.
- Degree of desired control on intermediaries.
- Adaptability to dynamic market conditions.

Channel Selection and Training

After determining the most appropriate channel alternative, the producer selects the most qualified parties and arranges for their training. In case of exclusive dealerships and franchisees where personal contact with customers and service delivery are important, company appointed dealers play an important role. They practically become the company for the customers and any negative impressions may severely damage company image and reputation. Companies vary in their ability to attract top rung dealers. For a respected name like Tata, it was not difficult to attract qualified intermediaries to handle Titan showrooms. Others try but may not attract the better ones. No matter what, the company should at least be able to identify some criteria that distinguishes better agents/dealers, such as duration in business, financial strength, lines handled, number and quality of sales or technical personnel, growth and profit record, and service reputation etc.

Producer must carefully outline **training programmes** for dealers. They have to be competent to provide excellent service to customers. The purpose of imparting training is to sharpen dealers' product knowledge and selling skills to better serve and satisfy customers. Apple arranges training programmes for its dealers and authorised service providers. Some companies, such as Hyundai conducted training programme for its dealers at parent company's headquarters in Korea before launching its Accent in India. Microsoft arranges structured training for third-party service engineers and they complete a set of courses and then appear in a test. Those who clear the exam are awarded a certification recognising them as Microsoft Certified Professionals. To provide excellent service to customers, all manufacturers of complex technical machinery and consumer durable appliances train their dealers' personnel.

Motivating Intermediaries

Motivating channel intermediaries is a challenging task for producers, but essential to obtain best possible performance from them. Getting cooperation from intermediaries is the main challenge for producers. As in other situations, developing motivational programmes for intermediaries begins with first, understanding their needs and wants. Bert Rosenbloom writes in his book that intermediaries base good relationship on cooperation and partnership.

Motivation programmes for channel intermediaries focus mainly on financial and non-financial rewards. Financial rewards usually include higher margins, extended credit facilities, bonuses and allowances, special deals, and sharing intermediaries' promotional expenses. Intermediaries sometimes pass on part of their better margins to customers as inducements.

Non-financial rewards include training programmes at company expenses in India and abroad for intermediaries in areas such as technical skills and service. Company also arranges training in India in areas of selling and territory management, human resource, and to acquaint them about company's future outlook, plans and policies. Other non-financial rewards include sales and display contests, recognition for outstanding performance, company paid holidays in India and abroad, spending money on arranging lavish distributors/ dealers' meet at exotic places. To name a few manufacturers who conduct training programmes are Reliance, *ITC*, Bajaj Electricals, Parle Exports, Videocon, Godrej-GE, Phillips, and others.

Performance Evaluation of Intermediaries

Producers must periodically evaluate performance of dealers against laid down and agreed upon parameters. The evaluation criteria differ across industries and from one company to another in the same industry. Companies may use a set of criteria that may include some combination of factors with differing weight given to each element in order of its importance, such as achievement of sales targets, average inventory maintained, performing promotional activities, customer service, and attending training programmes etc.

In certain cases, it may not be easy to terminate the contract with dealers due to legal implications. In certain industries, trader groups form trade associations and without the approval of their apex body that looks into such matters, a company cannot terminate dealership.

The purpose of evaluating intermediaries' performance is to plan ways to improve performance of individual parties. In certain cases, a company might decide to terminate a dealer. Periodically the producer should also evaluate the effectiveness and suitability of the selected channel system with major changes in the marketing environment.

Channel Modification

Evaluation of channel system in place may sometimes make it necessary for the firm to modify it as a result of changes in buyer behaviour, market conditions, availability of new and more effective and suitable alternatives, and later *PLC* stages. For example, when Wipro introduced its PCs for home users the first time in 1997, its authorised dealers used sales people to call on prospects and sell its computers. When Apple launched its computers in India, the company appointed authorised dealers with service facilities. Subsequently, with negligible or no demand in many areas, dealers were not interested to carry on and the company did away with dealers in these areas. Authorised dealerships were maintained in metros and few other large cities. To focus on its targeted tech-savvy customers with in-store product demonstration, full range of products, software, accessories, and staffed by Apple trained specialist, Apple opened its own Apple Store in Bangalore. Later, with increasing acceptance and popularity of its iPod and launch of low-priced Macs, the company opened its own Apple stores in some other important locations. Tobi Elkin reported that roughly 25 per cent Apple's sales comes through *www.apple.com*, its own retail shops are a natural choice.

A particular marketing channel is unlikely to remain appropriate throughout the entire life cycle of a product. As mentioned earlier, different adopter groups acquire products during different product life cycle stages. For instance, innovators and early adopters of cell phones were from the business and moneyed class and cell phones were available at few places. Now three-wheeler auto driver and even locality vegetable shops use cell phones and retail stores dealing in electronic goods to sell these phones and prepaid service cards.

FIGURE 18.4

Meland M. Lele Matrix

Market Growth Rate	Value Addition by Channel: High	Value Addition by Channel: Low
Low	**Introduction** Personal Computer Lobbyist store *Designer Apparel* Boutiques	**Decline** Personal Computer Mail order *Designer Apparel* Discount stores
High	**Growth** *Personal Computer* Speciality stores *Designer Apparel* Better departmental stores	**Maturity** *Personal Computer* Mass merchandisers *Designer Apparel* Mass merchandisers

Miland M. Lele proposed a matrix (Figure 18.4) by studying changes in the case of PCs and designer apparel channels at different stages in the product life cycle and suggested how a company should consider market growth and value addition by the channel. During introductory period of innovative products and designer apparel, specialist channels attract innovators and early adopters. Early and rapid growth period shows growing interest and higher-volume speciality stores and up-market departmental stores providing services are appropriate. Growth slows down during maturity stage and companies place their product into lower-cost mass merchandisers. Finally, in the decline stage least-cost channels such as mail order resellers and discount stores sell the product.

Over a period of time, existing channel loses its relevance and the gap between existing and ideal system widens. In case of low-entry barrier industries with high intensity of competition, channel arrangement changes over a period of time. These changes could be addition or dropping of some individual resellers, particular market channels, or developing an entirely new channel structure.

Vertical, Horizontal, and Multichannel Marketing Systems

With the passage of time and changes in business environment and strategies, marketing channel systems evolve and new wholesaling and retailing institutions appear. The traditional marketing channels we discussed include members who are independent entities and no party has complete control over others in the channel system. Each seeks to maximise its own profit goals without much concern for others in the same system. Some recent changes in channel systems that have emerged include *Vertical Marketing Systems (VMS), Horizontal Marketing Systems,* and *Multichannel Marketing Systems* (also called hybrid channels).

Vertical Marketing System (VMS)

Vertical marketing system refers to an arrangement in which the whole channel focuses on the same target market at the end of the channel. This includes producer, distributors, wholesalers, and retailers acting in an integrated manner. Any channel member, a manufacturer, distributor, wholesaler, or retailer can become a *channel captain* who helps direct the activities of the entire channel and tries to eliminate or resolve conflict. The channel captain assumes the leadership role because the captain is either the owner, a franchisee, or wields so much power that all others cooperate. This single channel captain concept seems quite logical since *VMS* offers economies of scale due to its size, bargaining power, and eliminates duplication of services. Such a system also makes sense because if in the end, the customer does not buy the product, the entire channel suffers. Channel captain arranges for the necessary functions to be performed in the most effective manner. There are three types of *VMS* – *corporate, administered,* and *contractual.*

- ***Corporate VMS*** refers to the producer's ownership of the entire channel, right from manufacturing to wholesaling, and retailing. One may say the company is going direct. In India Vimal Fabrics, Titan watches, and Bata etc., are some examples. Manufacturer can accomplish this through vertical integration (acquiring firms at different levels of channel activity). This offers greater buying power, stable sources of supplies, better control of distribution and quality, and lower executive overheads. Many experts feel that it is difficult to be good at performing such diverse functions and it is better to stick to what they know and do best. It is better to concentrate on ways to gain increased cooperation from channel members for effective and efficient distribution rather than entering into so many functions.
- ***Administered VMS*** is achieved when some members because of their position, size and power in the industry are in a commanding position to secure cooperation and support from resellers at different levels. Members informally agree to cooperate with each other on matters like routine ordering, sharing inventory and sales information over networks, standardise accounting, and integrate their promotional activities. The agreement is informal and the members retain some of the flexibility of traditional distribution system. Companies with strong brands command substantial market power and are able to get cooperation from resellers at different levels of distribution. Several examples can be cited such as Hindustan Lever Ltd., Procter & Gamble, Maruti Udyog, ITC, IBM, Sony, Apple, and TELCO etc.
- ***Contractual VMS*** consists of independent businesses at different levels in the channel including production and distribution, and is most popular. Members agree to cooperate with each other by entering into contract that spells each member's' rights and obligations and gain economies of size and sales impact. Contractual *VMS* can be franchiser, wholesaler, or retailer sponsored, such as Coke and Pepsi have bottlers with distribution set up, some educational institutions appoint franchisees, Body Shop, Shahnaz Herbal, some retail chains, and others.

Horizontal Marketing Systems

Horizontal marketing system occurs when two or more related or unrelated companies working at the same level come together to exploit marketing opportunities. By coming together they have the option to combine their capital, production capabilities, marketing strengths to gain substantial advantage than by each company working alone. This kind of joining forces is viewed as symbiotic relationship and can be between non-competitors as well as competitors. This arrangement can be on a temporary or permanent basis. Some competing credit card businesses, competing banks, retail petrol businesses, and consumer goods companies have joined hands. Auto manufacturers have joined hands with finance institutions to finance customers. Coca Cola and Nestle joined hands to pool Coke's marketing and distribution strengths in global markets and Nestle's strong brands, Nescafe and Nestea to market ready-to-drink coffee and tea worldwide, TVS-Whirlpool and Onida joined hands to market washing machines, Whirlpool manufactured the machines and Onida promoted and distributed them. Horizontal marketing system particularly offers efficiencies and economies of scale in promotion, marketing research, and bringing together specialists.

Multichannel Marketing System

Some companies use several marketing channels simultaneously to reach diverse target markets. This system is also called ***hybrid channels*** or ***multichannel***. Each channel involves different group of intermediaries. Hybrid or multichannel marketing arrangement is also called by another name, ***dual distribution***, when a company uses two or more channels to distribute same products to the same target market. Hybrid channels may involve selling direct to large sized customers, use telemarketing to reach medium sized customers, direct mail selling to small customers, retailers sell to personal consumers, and company also uses online selling. The online bookstore operating from Delhi, ***www.firstandsecond.com*** sells online to the same target market and also has retail shop in Delhi. LG sells its goods through retailers, company shop, and online. Coca Cola supplies direct to McDonald's, and the fast food chain sells no other soft drinks but Coca Cola. Think of other places where you can buy Coca Cola or Pepsi? Kelly Shermach is of the opinion that hybrid or multichannel distribution can maximise market exposure. Multichannel distribution can sometimes cause dissatisfaction among wholesalers and small retailers in the face of competition from large stores who buy directly from producers.

Channel Conflicts and Cooperation

Traditional channel intermediaries are still typical and very important in most industries in our country. The goal of all channel members is to distribute products profitably and efficiently. However, at times they disagree about the methods to accomplish this goal. It is fairly common among channel members to make little or no effort to cooperate with each other. In general, their relationship is limited for buying and selling products from each other. Each member is interested in only doing, what is considered to be in its own best interest without worrying about others.

According to Louis W. Stern and J. L. Heskett, *"Channel conflict is a situation in which one channel member perceives another channel member(s) to be engaged in behaviour that prevents or impedes it from achieving its goals. The amount of conflict is, to a large extent, a function of goal incompatibility, domain descensus, and differing perceptions of reality."*

To manage conflict, it is first of all necessary to understand the *type, cause,* and *intensity* of the conflict.

Types of Conflict

In any distribution channel arrangement there can possibly develop three kinds of conflicts:

- *Vertical channel conflict refers* to a situation when conflict occurs between members at different levels within the same distribution channel, such as conflict between the producer and distributors, or between wholesalers and the retailers. This is between parties one-level up or one-level below each other.
- *Horizontal channel conflict* describes a conflicting situation developing between channel members at the same level, such as when one stockist starts price-cutting and others at the same level start complaining, or when stockists start sending goods to other stockists' designated territories in adjoining or other territories.
- *Multichannel conflict* results when the producer has established two or more different channels to sell the product to the same target market. For example, a computer company may have its own retail showroom, authorised dealers, and also sells online. The conflict may arise if the company store or online prices are lower than what dealers charge for the same products.

Causes of Conflict

It may not always be easy to resolve conflicts. The best that can be done in certain cases is to minimise the seriousness of the conflict. Major causes of conflict include *goal incompatibility, roles and rights ambiguity,* and *differing perceptions.*

- ***Goal incompatibility*** is a major cause of conflict between producer and the channel members. Channel members almost always want to earn hefty margins on products they sell. The producer's goal might be to keep the price low and go for rapid market penetration to capture a larger market share and earn profits in the long-term. The dealers may want to have more margin and profitability in the short-term. Such situations often create strained relations and both sides start accusing each other. In some extreme cases, demands for more margins have led to entire channel boycotting a company's products.

- ***Roles and rights ambiguity*** refers to situations when the company sells its products to same customers directly, and the channel members also sell products to the same group of customers. This may occur when a producer uses multichannel arrangement. For example, if both the company sales force and dealer 's sales people sell products to institutions, an unnecessary conflict may arise because there is no clarity regarding such situations.

- ***Differing perceptions*** about the economic outlook may sometimes become a cause of conflict between the producer and the dealers. The company may be optimistic about the economy and income growth in Indian middle class and want dealers to carry higher than usual inventories. Companies may also appoint more dealers and may come out with line extensions. The dealers, on the other hand may be pessimistic and refuse to comply what company wants and may oppose appointing more dealers. All this may give rise to a conflict.

Intensity of Conflict

This refers to how serious is the conflict. In some cases, the intensity of conflict might be just minor and at other times, the severity might demand immediate attention from the producer otherwise the consequences might be serious if it is not resolved. For example, managing incidences of price-cutting or territory jumping can be handled relatively easily. In other instances if channel members threaten to boycott company products, the consequences of sales loss might be serious. In such situations postponing or delaying negotiations with channel members to resolve conflict can lead to considerable loss of sales, market share, and goodwill. The company must take the initiative to resolve the conflicting issue.

Managing the Channel Conflict

Most companies, particularly *FMCG* companies have large dealer networks right up to far-flung rural areas. In certain other industries, many companies use multiple channels and conflicts develop occasionally. Managing conflict in certain cases may be quite a demanding task. Conflict magnitude can range from minor to serious leading to termination, lawsuits, or company boycotts. The frequency of conflicts can range from infrequent disputes to long drawn bitter relations. The frequency and seriousness of conflict determines how speedily the situation must be managed. Authorities have suggested several approaches for effective conflict management.

- ***Regular Communication:*** Regular communication between producer and channel members can minimise the chances of conflict. Top and middle-level management executives of forward-looking companies maintain regular personal contacts and also arrange formal meetings once or twice a year to listen to them and understand channel dynamics, resolve channel problems, and acquaint them with future plans. Some companies also develop in-house newsletters containing updates on market conditions and company's perspective. These newsletters are regularly mailed to their appointed dealers.

- ***Forming Dealer Councils:*** There are some misgivings about forming dealer councils that this may turnout to be a platform for dealers to unite and pressurise manufacturer with some unreasonable demands. It is difficult to completely rule out the possibilities. However, if these councils are formed on regional or state basis and company remains focused on the laid down agenda, listens and accepts constructive suggestions, these councils can be an effective means of managing conflicts.

- ***Co-option:*** This approach refers to include channel association leaders in the company's advisory council or board of directors etc. to win the channel support. This can be quite an effective method to minimise conflicts if the channel concerns and opinions are listened to.
- ***Arbitration and Mediation:*** When conflict becomes serious or other efforts have not been successful, then each party can send their representative or a team of representatives to meet and resolve the conflict, or conflicting sides can approach a neutral third party to listen to both sides and resolve the conflict. Sometimes conflicting sides approach government agency to resolve dispute, or finally conflicting sides may approach the court of law for deciding the matter.

PHYSICAL DISTRIBUTION

The term physical distribution is more appropriate to outgoing (outbound logistics) or forward movement of products, services, and information from a firm's manufacturing facility to customers, and involves defined network of transportation links, warehousing and storage, and finally delivery at the destination in a cost effective manner within the desired time. Some texts use terms *supply chain management*, and *logistics management* which are much broader concepts than physical distribution. As discussed earlier, supply chain management starts from the supplier of raw materials, then conversion at factory into finished products, storage at warehouses, and finally, supply to distribution channels to meet the demand of end-user for a finished product at an acceptable cost and service level. Physical distribution starts in a forward movement of goods from the company's production facility to end-user, and supply chain management starts before physical distribution. According to Stern, El-Ansari, and Coughlan, *"The term logistics management and supply chain management are widely used to describe the flow of goods and services and related information from the point of origin to the point of consumption,"* Some authors view *logistics* as the transporting, sorting, and handling of goods to match target customers' needs with a company's marketing mix – within individual companies and along a channel of distribution. Thus, logistics represents the value chain of a company, the starting point is the procurement and at the end of the chain is the customer. Logistics management includes both materials management and physical distribution. More and more companies are realising the importance of managing the entire supply chain rather than just transportation and warehousing decisions alone. The focus of managing supply chain is on removing inefficiencies and hurdles in meeting customer demand at the time when it occurs.

The concept of physical distribution is based on the highly acclaimed study of Howard T. Lewis, James W. Culliton, and Jack D. Steele of Harvard University in 1956. It says that entire transportation, storage, and product handling activities of a business and the total channel set up should be coordinated as one system that aims to minimise distribution costs for a particular customer service level because lower costs and better service contribute for increasing customer value. Often, one channel member manages physical distribution on behalf of all involved channel members. Tom Richman reported a trend toward centralisation, where one channel member in the supply chain assumes responsibility and authority for physical distribution for the entire channel.

Meeting Customer Service Requirements: Marketing strategy aims at satisfying customers' needs and wants. Physical distribution is invisible to most consumers. They pay attention to it only when something goes wrong and it may be too late for the company to cheer them. It is not unusual in India, particularly for service providers failing to meet customer service delivery expectations.

Physical distribution systems must meet the factory needs towards supply chain and the customers. First of all it is necessary to find out what are customers requirements and what competitors are providing. Customers want timely delivery, efficient order processing, willing suppliers to meet emergency needs, progress report, proper handling of products, post purchase services, prompt replacement of defective goods, and warranties. Customers' inventory requirements affect the expected level of physical distribution service. The company must determine the relative importance of these aspects. Paying attention to customer needs and preferences is necessary for increasing sales and getting repeat orders. For example, an auto manufacturer with a low inventory of replacement parts requires fast, dependable supply from suppliers of component parts. Repair service facility and time for car buyers is very important. Anne G. Perkins found that even when the demand for products is unpredictable, suppliers must be prepared to respond fast to inventory needs. Under these situations, distribution costs may be a minor consideration compared to the importance of service, dependability, and timeliness.

Most customers are concerned with speedy and dependable delivery of what they want and don't care how a product moves from a manufacturer to the point of delivery from where they acquire it.

Minimising Total Distribution Costs: Companies strive to minimise their distribution costs associated with order processing, inventory management, materials handling, warehousing, and transportation. However, decreasing costs in one area often increases them in another. The company has to develop an economical system without compromising the minimum guaranteed service delivery level and to achieve this trade-offs between service level and costs becomes unavoidable. Taking a systems approach to distribution, the focus from lowering costs of individual activities shifts to minimising overall distribution costs. Adoption of total cost approach requires analysing costs associated with distribution alternatives, such as comparing inventory levels against warehousing costs, materials cost against expenses involved with various modes of transportation, and all distribution costs against customer service requirements. Lowest overall distribution system cost should be compatible with company's stated minimum expected level of customer service objectives. This requires trade-offs costs because higher costs in one area of distribution system may be necessary to obtain lower costs in another. In many cases accounting procedures, asking customers to rank their preference and employing statistical procedures, and computer simulations are used to determine total costs.

Curtailing Time-Cycle: Time-cycle refers to the time it takes to complete a process. It is an important objective of physical distribution to reduce time-cycle to reduce costs and increase customer service. Many businesses such as overnight delivery companies, and major news media strive to slash time-cycle to gain competitive advantage. For example, FedEx overnight delivery service conducts research and employs new techniques and procedures to be the fastest overnight delivery service. FedEx offers its customers package-tracking software so that they can track the progress of their package. In such situations, speed is important than costs.

Order Processing

The receipt of order and transmission of sales order information is an important function of physical distribution. In developed and developing countries, computerised order processing furnishes a database for all channel members to increase their productive efficiency. Efficient order processing contributes to customer satisfaction, reduces costs and time-cycle, and increase profits.

Order entry starts when customers or sales people place purchase order by telephone, computer, or mail. Electronic ordering system reduces procurement costs. After receiving order, it is passed on electronically or by whatever system is in place to warehouse to verify product availability, to credit department for checking prices, terms, and customer's credit rating. After credit department's approval, warehouse personnel assembles the order. If the product is out of stock, production order is sent for manufacturing or the customer is offered a substitute.

After assembling the order and packing for shipment, the warehouse arranges delivery though an appropriate carrier. The customer is sent an invoice, inventory records are updated, and order is delivered.

Order processing can be manual or electronic depending on which approach offers more speed and accuracy within cost limits. In India, so far electronic order processing is not very common with many smaller businesses. Manual processing is suitable for smaller volumes. Electronic Data Interchange (*EDI*) is very suitable for integrating order processing with production, inventory, accounting, and shipping. It links marketing channel members, facilitators, and provides convenience to member to cut down paper work and sharing information on invoices, orders, payments, inquiries, and scheduling among all members.

Managing Inventory

Inventory managing involves building and maintaining enough product assortments to meet the customer demand. Investment in inventory forms a significant part of company assets and affects physical distribution costs in a major way. Very little inventory can create shortages of products or out-of-stock situation. This is detrimental to company and can lead to brand switching, lower sales, and the most serious consequence of losing customers. When too much inventory of products is carried, particularly of slow moving products, costs and risks of product obsolescence, damage, or pilferage increase. To strike a balance, companies focus on determining when and how much to order.

To find out when to order, the marketer must know the order lead time, the usage rate, and the safety stocks required. Order lead-time refers to average time lapse between placing the order and receiving supplies. The usage rate represents the rate at which the inventory of product gets sold during a specified time period. Buffer stock is the extra inventory that is maintained to guard against out-of-stock situation from increased demand or to cover longer lead-time than expected. Following formula can be used to calculate when to reorder:

Reorder Point = (Order Lead Time × Usage Rate) + Buffer Stock

To illustrate, let us assume that order lead-time is 15 days, usage rate is 2 units per day, and buffer stock is 10 units. The point to place the order is when there are 40 units in stock.

In certain cases, marketers employ a fixed order-interval approach and stocks are ordered at predetermined intervals when rate of usage is fairly constant and cost per unit is small.

To determine how much to order, it's necessary to examine inventory carrying costs and order processing costs. Considering both sets of costs determines Economic Order Quantity (*EOQ*), which is the order size that has the lowest total of both inventory carrying and order processing costs. However, the aim of minimising total inventory costs must be weighed against meeting or exceeding customer service level objectives.

Some organisations use ***Just-in-Time* (*JIT*)** approach in countries where this is possible. This system means that products arrive as and when they are needed for use in production process or for resale. This allows companies to maintain very low inventory levels and purchases at that time are also in smaller quantities. JIT system reduces physical distribution costs, especially inventory and handling related costs.

Handling Materials

Physical handling of products is necessary for efficient warehouse functions, transportation from the point of manufacture to final points of consumption. The nature of product often influences how a product should be moved and stored. For example, perishable goods, liquids, and gases have unique characteristics that determine their movement and handling.

Techniques and procedures used for material handling can increase warehouse capacity, reduce the number of times a product is handled, improve customer service, and their satisfaction. Various activities such as packaging, loading, movement, labelling systems must be coordinated to reduce costs and increase customer value and satisfaction. Correct internal packaging of materials is important to prevent any damage during handling and transportation. Companies use different methods of loading such as unit loading or containerisation. Unit loading is grouping one or more boxes on a pallet and use forklifts, trucks, or conveyer system. Container helps consolidate many items within the large inside space of one huge box, which is sealed at its originating point and opened after arriving at its destination.

Warehousing

Warehousing is an important physical distribution function and refers to the design and operation of facilities for storing and moving goods. Producers have to make arrangements to store products until they are sold because production and consumption cycles differ. Warehousing functions offer time utility and help companies to adjust for dissimilar production and consumption rates. Of necessity, mass produced products create a much greater stock of products than can be sold in the market immediately and companies store excess stocks till the time, customers are ready to buy. Warehousing is also necessary for seasonal products such as woolens and others.

Warehousing function is not just limited to storing of items. Wagonloads and truckloads of products are received at warehouses where, they are broken down into smaller quantities for customers, or smaller lots received are sometimes consolidated into bulk loads for shipping economically. Some basic physical distribution functions of warehouses are given below:

- Receiving goods and assuming responsibility.
- Recording quantity of each item and marking with codes, tags, or physical property etc.
- Sorting goods to store in an appropriate area.
- Dispatching goods for storage.
- Holding products in properly protected condition until needed.
- Recalling and picking products ordered by customers from storage.
- Collecting for a single shipment, checking for completeness or explaining omissions.
- Dispatching suitably packaged shipment to the right transport vehicle along with necessary documents.

The ***choice of warehouses*** can range between company's own dedicated warehouses or share space with others in third party owned warehouses. A company can also decide to have some kind of combination of both. By making the right choices, a company may minimise physical distribution costs. The firm decides the number, location, and which type of warehouse is most suitable.

Company Owned Warehouses: Companies operate these for sorting and shipping its products. These are usually leased or sometimes purchased when a company has justification to have its own warehouse in a geographic market area based on substantial and stable demand to make long-term commitment to fixed facilities. When products require special handling and storage features and control of warehouse design and operation, a company may have its own warehouse.

Cindy Muroff reported that to reduce inventory costs, companies are striving to move products as quickly and directly as possible from producer to customers.

Third Party Warehouses: Some companies construct warehouses and offer on rent, or offer rented space to producers, such as cold storage for vegetables and fruits etc., to farmers and wholesalers in such businesses. Sometimes third party warehouses also provide distribution services such as receiving and unloading products or reshipping.

Third party warehouses such as Tech Pacific and RS Components and Controls (India) Ltd. are particularly useful for firms with seasonal production, low-volume storage needs, for producers with inventories that must be maintained in many and widely spread locations, companies entering new markets, or despite own warehouses need additional storage space. In contrast to company-owned warehouses involving fixed costs, third party warehouses have variable and sometimes lower costs because storage space is purchased only when needed. Flexibility in storage location and space utilisation makes third party warehouses an attractive alternative. Businesses offering warehouse facility realise that most companies prefer not to tie up their capital in such fixed costs. Besides, over the years the value of their property may appreciate many times over.

Sometimes these third party warehouses are also referred as *distribution centres*. Going strictly by the definition of distribution centre operated in developed and in some developing countries, a distribution centre is large, centralised warehouse that receives goods from manufacturers and suppliers, regroups them into orders, and ships them to customers quickly. The main focus is on faster movement of goods rather than storage. Many distribution centres are highly automated with computer-directed robots, forklifts, and hoists collecting and moving products for loading docks.

Transportation

Companies are concerned with transportation decisions because choices affect product pricing, delivery time, and condition of goods when they arrive at destination. Transportation is the most expansive of physical distribution function and offers the time and place utility value to the product. Product availability and on-time deliveries depend on transportation choice and have direct impact on customer service and ultimately satisfaction.

There are five main *transportation modes* for moving goods that include *railways, roadways, waterways, airways,* and *pipelines.* Each of these offers certain advantages. Some companies prefer to use a combination of these modes, depending on product nature, delivery schedule, and geographic locations.

Railways

Railways carry heavy, bulky goods, that need shipping to long distances over land, such as mineral ores, lumber, sand, farm products, heavy and bulky machinery, chemicals, petroleum, and autos etc. Railways are particularly efficient for transporting full wagonloads at lower rates and require less handling.

FIGURE 18.5

Typical Means of Transporting Various Products

Railways	Roadways	Waterways	Airways	Pipelines
Coal Lumber Chemicals Autos Steel Grain	Paper goods Clothing Computers Livestock Cement Scooters	Petroleum Iron ore Chemicals Grain Bauxite	Overnight mail Flowers Emergency parts Instruments Perishable food	Oil Natural gas Chemicals Processed coal Water

Roadways

Trucks are providing a tough competition to railways. Roadways offer most flexible schedules of all major modes of transportation. Trucks can go almost anywhere, including rural market areas where just *kachcha* roads are available. To reach Indian rural markets in some areas where trucks cannot be used, tractors with trolleys and bullock carts are used to haul goods for short distances. Trucks are generally used to transport small shipments of high-value goods. Trucks are unique in a way that they can move goods directly from factory or warehouse to customer. Trucks transport goods much faster than railways, they are relatively more expensive and somewhat vulnerable to bad weather conditions and accidents. Common goods carriers are often criticised for loss and damage to freight and for delays.

Waterways

For heavy, low value, non-perishable goods such as ore, and petroleum etc., waterways is the cheapest mode of transportation. Water carriers offer large capacity. Ocean going vessels can move thousands of containers, powered barges travel along inter-coastal routes and inland rivers to haul more than a railway wagonload. Waterways are slow, less dependable than other transportation means, and limited in the number of locations served. In colder regions, it may come to a standstill during freezing weather. Droughts and floods can create problems for inland waterway transportation of goods. Waterways are often used in conjunction with railways and roadways.

Airways

This is the fastest of all modes of transportation, most expensive, and relatively quite dependable. Perishable, low-bulk, high value products, such as overnight packages, emergency parts and supplies are frequently shipped by air. New jet cargo planes can carry goods weighing few thousand kg. FedEx, *DHL*, United Parcel Service, *TNT*, Overnight Express, Elbee Airlines etc., are some well-known names of air cargo service providers. Some airlines carry a combination of passengers, mail, and freight. Some kind or road carrier is used to pickup goods at the airport. The high cost is a major limitation of airways as goods carrier.

Pipelines

Pipelines are the most automated means of transportation and usually carry petroleum, natural gas, and chemicals. A company or group of companies generally own the pipeline for transporting the product. Pipelines offer uninterrupted movement at a relatively low-cost. They are dependable, fuel-efficient, and involve less losses and damages. The use of pipelines is limited. They are extremely slow means of transportation and serve very limited number of locations.

Selection of transportation mode is based on considerations of cost, speed, dependability, load flexibility, accessibility, and frequency.

Cost comparisons of various alternatives determine whether higher cost alternative such as airfreight carrier is worth the benefits.

Marketeer determine ***speed*** by taking into account, the total time a carrier has possession of goods and this includes the time required for pickup and delivery, handling, and movement between point of origin and final point of delivery.

Dependability is important for marketers and depends on consistency of service provided by a mode of transportation. Dependability, along with speed directly affects inventory costs, and loss of sales because of non-availability of the company's product.

Load flexibility means the extent to which a carrier can offer suitable equipment and conditions for transporting specific goods and can adapt to moving other products that require controlled conditions, such as temperature and humidity control, or transporting liquids, or gases etc., that require special equipment or facilities for shipment.

Accessibility is a carrier's ability to transport goods over a certain routes or network such as truck routes, or rail lines etc. There may be some carrier that can access areas that competitors do not, such as a carrier may differentiate its service by guaranteeing access to certain rural areas in India and might be very attractive to some marketer.

Frequency determines how often a marketer can use a specific mode of transportation to send its goods. A company using rail or ship must adjust to limited schedules, but roadways may provide desired frequency.

Outsourcing Physical Distribution

Recent non-conventional approach to physical distribution is outsourcing total physical distribution. Marketers make arrangements with outside physical distribution service providers and allow them to operate independently, more like an extension of the company's physical distribution arm. They may handle only physical distribution or may also function as a distribution channel. Outsourcing may help to achieve more efficiency, better service standards, and cost effectiveness compared to company's own handling of all physical distribution functions. Air express companies provide such services and should not be confused with couriers or freight forwards. Just one agency handles all responsibility to move freight faster and provide convenience of door-to-door transportation. Some of them even offer additional warehousing facility and function as a complete system. In India, AFL, Elbee, and Blue Dart are some examples of companies providing air express services.

Summary

Distribution channels are composed of wholesalers, retailers etc., and facilitate distribution of goods or services to ultimate customers. Channel decisions are usually long-term and determine product's market presence and ensure customer's accessibility to the product. Merchants take ownership title. Brokers, agents, and salespersons do not acquire title to merchandise. Producers can go direct or may involve two or more channel levels to serve end-users.

In developing distribution strategy, companies consider factors related to customer, competition, *PLC* stages, objectives, and desired market coverage intensity and control etc. Intensive distribution uses all available distribution outlets. Selective distribution is using more than a few and less than all available outlets in a market area. Exclusive distribution involves exclusive dealing arrangement with intermediaries.

Producers' select channels generally based on considerations of product characteristics, buyer behaviour, competition, cost effectiveness, desired control, and adaptability to dynamic market conditions. Motivation of channel members focuses mainly on financial and non-financial rewards. Dealers' performance criteria include sales target, inventory maintained, promotional activities, customer service, and attending training etc.

Vertical marketing systems focuses on the same target market and includes producer, wholesalers, and retailers acting in an integrated manner. A channel captain directs the activities of the entire channel. Corporate *VMS* refers to the producer's ownership of the entire channel. Administered *VMS* members informally agree to cooperate with each other on routine ordering, sharing inventory and sales information, accounting methods, and integrate their promotional activities. Contractual *VMS* involves independent firms at different levels entering into contract that spells each member's rights and obligations and cooperate with each other. Horizontal marketing system involves two or more companies working at the same level come together to exploit marketing opportunities. Using several marketing channels simultaneously to reach diverse target markets is called hybrid or multi-channel system. Methods to resolve conflict involve forming dealer councils, communication, arbitration and mediation, or go to court of law for deciding the matter.

Physical distribution manages the flow of products from producers to consumers in a cost-effective manner. To satisfy customers' needs, a company must set customer service standards. Order processing involves order entry, handling, and delivery. Inventory management and control helps to develop and maintain adequate assortment of stocks to meet customers' requirements. The *EOQ* (Economic Order Quantity) is thc optimum order size that minimises the total cost of ordering and maintaining inventory. Materials handling refers to packaging, loading, and movement systems using nit loading or containerisation. Warehouses provide storage facilities for products until customers need them. Warehouses also perform functions, such as sorting, marking, and assembling goods for shipment. A company may operate its own warehouses or hire from other outside parties. A distribution centre is a large, private warehouse designed to provide movement of goods, in and out of storage as fast as possible. Five major modes of transportation include railways, roadways, waterways, airways, and pipelines. A new trend is outsourcing physical distribution.

Questions for Discussion

1. What are marketing channels? What is the difference between merchant middlemen and agent middlemen?
2. Describe different channel systems for consumer products with examples of products that are distributed by these channels.
3. Describe the major functions of marketing channels. Why are distribution channels more suitable for performing these functions?
4. Why some marketeers use more than one channel?
5. Explain the difference between intensive, selective, and exclusive distribution.
6. Under what conditions would you suggest using channels with different intensities?
7. Under what conditions would using franchise system be appropriate?
8. What are the most common types of channels industrial marketeers use? Describe the products and situations that prompt manufacturers to use these channels.
9. Describe the characteristics of different types of *VMS*.
10. Why do conflicts develop between channel members? Suggest a method to resolve conflict between a producer and a wholesaler.

Projects

1. Go to a supermarket and study what kind of channel system is being used. Write a report with suggestions.
2. Open the web page *www.apple.com* and study how the company distributes its computers and other products. Write your findings.
3. Study the *IBM* site and also visit an authorised *IBM* dealer. Why does *IBM* use multichannel marketing? What are the views of dealer about this arrangement?

Bibliography

1. D. J. Bowersox and M. B. Cooper, *Strategic Marketing Channel Management,* McGraw-Hill 1992.
2. E. Raymond Corey, *Industrial Marketing: Cases and Concepts,* Prentice-Hall, 4th ed. 1991.
3. Sumit K. Majumdar and Venkatram Ramaswamy, "Going Direct to Market: The Influence of Exchange Conditions," *Strategic Management Journal,* June 1995.
4. James D. Hlavecek and Tommy J. McCuistion, "Industrial Distributors: When, Who, and How?" *Harvard Business Review,* March-April 1983.
5. Kelly Shermach, "Retail Catalogues Designed to Boost In-store Sales," *Marketing News,* July 3, 1995.
6. Allan J. Magrath, "Differentiating Yourself via Distribution, "*Sales & Marketing Management,* March 1991.
7. Bert Rosenbloom, *Marketing Channels: A Management View,* 5th ed. 1995.
8. Tobi Elkin, "Apple Gambles with Retail Plan," *Advertising Age,* June 2001.
9. Melend M. Lele, "Change Channels in Your Product Life Cycle," *Business Marketing,* December 1986.
10. Louis W. Stern and J. L. Heskett, "Conflict management in Inter-organisation Relations: A Conceptual Framework," in Louis W. Stern (ed.), *Distribution Channels: Behavioural Dimensions,* (Houghton Mifflin, 1969).
11. Louis W. Sterns, Adel I. El-Ansari, and Annet T. Coughlan, *Marketing Channels,* Prentice-Hall, 5th ed. 1996. (The reference is, " Philip Scary and James Coakley, "Logistics Organisation and the Information System," *The Journal of International Logistics Management,* Vol. 2 (1991).
12. Tom Richman, "How 20 Best-Practice Companies Do It," *Harvard Business Review,* September-October 1995.
13. Anne G. Perkins, "Manufacturing: Maximising Service, Minimising Inventory," *Harvard Business Review,* March-April 1994.
14. Cindy Muroff, "Private Warehouses Take A Tumble," *Distribution,* July 1993.

Wholesaling and Retailing

CHAPTER 19

LEARNING OBJECTIVES

After going through this chapter, you will understand:

- What is wholesaling and major types of wholesalers
- Retailing function and major types of retailers
- Speciality stores, shopping malls, retail chains, and non-store retailing
- Factors to consider store location
- Building right kind of store image and importance of atmospherics, service, and price

Modern Silk House started as a bit of a lie in Lucknow in 1937. It was not a mere silk house, but rather a department store that catered to the needs of British families living in India at that time. It stocked products such as watches, cutlery and crockery. It also stocked some silk offerings. But most of the clothes were western and the material on offer, meant to be sewn in into western outfits - they were of either silk or cotton because there were no blends at the time. "The name Modern Silk House was a suggestion by a astrologer," recalls Chander Jashnani. "My father stuck with it because the jyotshi said my father will prosper in the silk business."

The Jashnani's prospered all right. When the British left India, Modern Silk House turned closer to the business that its name suggests. It began to stock an exquisite array of saris, most of which were made of rich silks. Soon its fame grew far and wide and it had celebrities as customers visiting the shop. "By the early 1950s, our fabrics had become very popular and we had royalties visiting us regularly," recalls Chander Jashnani. 'Pandit Nehru's sister and the princesses of Rajasthan were our clients. Besides there were others - the nawab of Rampur and his family, the women of the royal houses of Pilibit, Awadh, Kotwara, and Balrampur came to check out Jashnani's goods.

Since then Modern Silk House has attracted the cream of the society. Women belonging to elite industrialists' families such as Mafatlals, the Piramals as well as those from top bureaucracy are regular visitors to Modern Silk House. Besides, the company has now set up a network of outlets in major cities such as Mumbai, Pune, Delhi, Gurgaon, Hyderabad, Jaipur, Chennai, and Kolkata.

Back in Lucknow, there are seven designers who work in a design studio and sketch out exclusive designs for the company. No design is replicated - therefore each sari is one of a kind. That exclusivity coupled with quality fabric and fine craftsmanship have contributed to an exclusive club for the company.

(Source: "Revealing Wraps," USP Age, June-July 2004).

Wholesaling is concerned with the activities of individuals and establishments that sell to retailers and other merchants, or to industrial, institutional, and commercial users, but do not sell in large amounts to ultimate consumers. Wholesaling excludes those engaged in production, farmers growing agricultural products, and retailers. Unlike retailers, wholesalers are not much concerned with promotional activities, store atmospherics, and location because usually they deal with business buyers rather than ultimate consumers. Wholesalers usually handle large transactions, and operate in a larger market area. The wholesaling activities are just variations of marketing activities, such as gathering and providing information, buying and selling, grading, storing, transporting, financing, and risk sharing etc. Wholesalers add value for customers and suppliers.

All through wholesalers have dominated marketing channels in underdeveloped, developing, and developed countries. The factors that favour their importance in distribution channels include distant locations of producers from final customers; most products are manufactured before specific orders from customers, and intermediaries and final consumers demand varying quantities in terms of packages, and forms. According to Harry G. Miller, effective functioning of wholesalers as a part of marketing channel, especially in developing countries contributes directly to the economic potential and growth by providing links to an extended market base. It is common perception that goods move from producer to a wholesaler, then to retailers where consumers buy them. The process is more complicated in reality. Products can move through the hands of several manufacturers and wholesalers and may never end up at a retail store because the end user may be in a business and not a consumer.

FIGURE 19.1
Wholesaler Functions for Producers and Customers

Functions for Producers	Functions for Customers
Market Coverage.	Product Availability.
Sales Contacts.	Assortment Convenience.
Inventory Holding.	Bulk-breaking.
Order Processing.	Credit Facility and Finance.
Market Information.	Customer Service.
Customer Support.	Technical Support.

As producers are becoming larger, many of them bypass the wholesalers. Producers' sales force is believed to be more effective at selling, but the costs of maintaining a sales force and performing functions normally handled by wholesalers are sometimes higher than benefits derived from firm's own sales staff. Wholesalers often handle many product lines from different producers and are able to spread sales costs over more products than most producers. Wholesalers also help retail dealers to select the inventory. They often understand market conditions better and experts are at negotiating. They generally offer a wider range of products from different producers to retailers while most producers' salesperson offer only a few products. As mentioned in previous chapter, wholesalers buy large quantities and deliver to customers in smaller lots, and undertake physical distribution activities such as transportation, materials handling, inventory planning, warehousing, and communication.

Large retail chains very often take up functions handled by wholesalers. The growing trend of e-commerce is making things easier for consumers and producers as increasingly many businesses in developed and fast developing countries are moving toward this new-age marketing mantra.

Major Types of Wholesalers

A variety of wholesalers are operating and new types emerge in response to changes in marketing environment to meet different types of needs of manufacturers and retailers. They are classified in three major classes: (1) merchant wholesaler, (2) agents and brokers, and (3) manufacturer's sales branches and offices.

Merchant Wholesalers

These are independent businesses that take title to goods and assume risks associated with ownership and generally buy and resell products to industrial or retail customers. They sometimes specialise by certain type of products or customers. Producers often prefer to rely on merchant wholesalers when selling directly to customers is not economically feasible. They provide market coverage, sales contacts, gather market information, carry inventory, process orders, and provide customer support. They are called by different names, such as distributor, dealer, jobber, assembler, exporter and importer. They are divided into two subtypes: full-service and limited-service wholesalers.

Full-Service Merchant Wholesalers: They are resellers performing a wide range of wholesaling functions. According to Donald J. Bowersox and M. Bixby Cooper, their customers rely on them for ensuring product availability, desired assortments, bulk breaking, financial assistance, and provide technical advice and service. Some trading areas in large cities are known as wholesale bazaars, where many wholesalers have their set up.

- ***General merchandise wholesalers*** carry a wide product mix, such as cosmetics, laundry products, tobacco products, drugs, and non-perishable foods etc. They have very good contacts with retailers, such as grocery stores, appliance stores, hardware shops and paint stores, etc.
- ***Industrial distributors*** offer supplies and accessories mostly to industrial or institutional buyers rather than retailers.
- ***Limited line-wholesalers*** carry a narrow product mix limited to few product lines with extensive assortment, such as smoking products, tea and coffee, chewing tobacco products *(gutkha),* lighting fixtures, pharmaceutical products, and health and beauty aids.
- ***Speciality-line wholesalers*** carry usually a single product line, or just a few items in a product line, such as fruit, spices, eggs, fragrances, or carpets etc. Speciality wholesalers have deep understanding of particular customer requirements, have extensive product knowledge, and offer depth of choice.
- ***Rack jobbers*** are full-service, speciality-line wholesalers and retain the title to products. They specialise in hard-to-handle assortments. They display their products in display-racks in large departmental stores and supermarkets, mark products, replenish products in shelves, and record inventory and sales. They raise a bill to store only for the sold products and generally operate on consignment basis and take back unsold products. For example, a large retail store or supermarket might rely on a rack-jobber to arrange magazines and paperbacks, it sells.

Limited-Service Merchant Wholesalers: These wholesalers take ownership title to merchandise, specialise in only a few wholesaler functions and offer very few services to customers. They often make no delivery to customers, do not offer credit facility, or gather market information. They are compensated at lower rates and earn lower margins compared to full-service wholesalers.

- ***Cash-and-carry*** wholesalers usually deal with small retailers, and accept only cash payments. They generally deal in few fast moving items, such as groceries, electrical supplies, building materials, or office supplies. They exist because full-service wholesalers refuse to extend credit to small businesses that may have trouble paying their bills.
- ***Truck wholesalers*** transport a limited line of products direct to customers for on the spot inspection and purchase. They usually have regular schedules and routes. This is usually seen in India where company appointed pharmaceutical dealers conduct so called “taxi tours” in rural areas and sell to medicine retailers and village medical practitioners on the spot. In developed countries, truck wholesalers promptly deliver perishable merchandise such as fruits, fresh vegetables, and potato chips etc., that other regular wholesalers prefer not to carry. They serve small grocery retailers, supermarkets, restaurants, canteens etc., and do not extend credit but help retailers to keep a tight control on inventory.
- ***Drop-shippers*** take title to products they sell but do not take possession, or deliver the merchandise. They first book the order and then select a producer and pass on the order to producer for shipping the merchandise on agreed upon terms and delivery schedule directly to the customer. Drop shippers commonly sell bulky products, such as lumber, marble, and coal etc., for which handling would be expensive and possibly damaging. In developed countries, company websites and Internet is posing serious threats to drop-shippers and progressive ones are setting up heir own websites and charge fees for referrals.
- ***Mail-order wholesalers*** widely distribute their catalogues to sell their products generally to smaller industrial, institutional, and retail buyers that might not be called on by other middlemen. Customers place orders by mail, telephone, fax, or e-mail. These wholesalers sell non-bulky products such as jewelry, cosmetics, computers, books, CDs and DVD etc. They require payment by credit card or cash-on-delivery.

Agents and Brokers

Agents and brokers form the second major category of wholesalers. They negotiate purchase and speed up sales but do not take title to merchandise. They perform fewer services for producers and work on commission, generally based on product price. **Agents** represent buyers or sellers on an almost permanent basis. **Brokers** are employed to represent buyers or sellers temporarily. Both agents and brokers usually specialise for certain categories of products or customers, know their customers or markets well and provide valuable service to producers.

Manufacturer's Agents: They sell products of several non-competing manufacturers that are complementary and offer complete product lines. Such agents can be individuals or small businesses with few sales people and work almost as members of producers' sales force round the year, except that they are independent. They work on the basis or a formal written agreement with each manufacturer that explicitly outlines specifies sales territories, selling prices, order handling, delivery, services, warranties, and commission rates etc. They cannot exercise any control on producers' pricing or marketing policies. They do not extend credit facility or may not be able to provide technical advice to buyers or sellers.

- ***A selling agent*** is an independent middleman who enters into a contract with manufacturer to sell a manufacturer's entire product lines or specified line. They do not take title to merchandise and usually perform important marketing functions, such as marketing research, pricing, promotion, and distribution etc. A selling agent generally provides more services than any other type of agent. They often assume functions for more than one non-competing manufacturers at a time and generally are not bound by territorial limits. They handle products like chemicals, metals, pharmaceuticals, and industrial equipment and machinery etc.
- ***Commission merchants*** take goods on consignment in truckload quantities from local producers and negotiate sales in large markets. After concluding the sales, they deduct their commission and selling expenses and forward the balance to the marketer.
- ***Export*** or ***import*** agents are basically manufacturers' agents who specialise in international trade. These agents operate in every country and help international companies adjust to unfamiliar foreign conditions and markets.

Brokers, as mentioned earlier usually have a temporary relationship with buyers or sellers only for the duration while, a certain deal is negotiated. What brokers sell is; their information about what buyers need and what supplies are available. They have no role in financing, taking physical possession of goods, setting prices, and assume almost no risks. They just offer buyers or sellers specialised knowledge about specific goods and established network of contacts and help negotiate sale. They earn a commission from the hiring party only if the transaction is completed. Some brokers also work as export and import brokers.

Manufacturers' Sales Branches and Offices

Manufacturers set up Sales branches and offices to improve selling, promotion, and inventory control. ***Sales branches*** carry inventory and provide support services to manufacturer's sales force, particularly in areas with concentration of large customers and considerable demand. They provide promotional support, extend credit facility, and arrange delivery etc. ***Sales offices*** do not carry inventory and operate much like agents and in addition to manufacturer's products may sell other complimentary products produced by other firms.

RETAILING

The word 'retail' has its origin in French word *retaillier* and means 'to cut a piece' or 'to break bulk'. Retailing covers all the activities involved in the sales of products to final consumers for personal, family, household use and not for business. These activities include anticipating what consumers' want, developing assortments of products, acquiring market information, and financing. A retailer is a business and can be an individual, chain store, departmental store, supermarket, speciality store, small locality shop, *paan-bidi* kiosk, or a service retailer etc., who links the producers and the final consumer. Retailing is responsible for matching final consumer demand with supplies of different marketers. Manufacturers who sell directly to ultimate consumers are performing retailing activity. In case of service retailing, the retailer is also the producer of service, such as dry cleaner, beauty parlour, or a fast food joint.

Retailers primarily get their sales volume from retailing. The value added by retailers is important both for final consumers and marketers. Retailers add value, provide service and help consumers in making product selections. The image of a retailer can enhance product value though, contributing to consumers' experience, availability, or convenience. Retailers provide technical advice, demonstrate, deliver, extend credit, and provide after-sales repair services etc. Retailing is not confined to stores only but it also takes place door-to-door, through mail, Internet etc.

Retailing is a high-intensity competition industry and second largest globally. The reason for its popularity lies in its ability to provide easier access to a variety of products, freedom of choice, and many services to consumers. The size of an average retail store varies across countries depending largely on the level of a particular country's economic development. The largest retail store in the world is Wall-Mart of *USA* and the second largest is Carrefour of France. The Indian market is dotted by traditional market places called *bazaars* or *haats* comprising of numerous small and large shops, selling different or similar merchandise. A *bazaar* in India is a long street in a city or town and a central place of commercial activities. In Indian rural areas, these *bazaars* also occur on fixed weekdays where buyers and sellers converge from other nearby villages and often seem like festive events. Traditionally, the small retailers in India have played a major role in all sectors and unorganised retailers outnumber organised ones.

Within the last 10–12 years there have been major changes in the general retailing scenario. For example, now ready-to-wear garments market has seriously affected what used to be strictly a made-to-order market for clothing. Almost all other retail businesses are undergoing changes with the passage of time.

According to a better-known theory of retailing – *wheel of retailing* proposed by Malcomb McNair (Figure 19.2), new retailers often enter the marketplace with low prices, margins, and status. The low prices are usually the result of some innovative cost-cutting procedures and soon attract competitors. With the passage of time, these businesses strive to broaden their customer base and increase sales. Their operations and facilities increase and become more expensive. They may move to better up-market locations, start carrying higher-quality products, or add services and ultimately emerge as a high cost-price-service retailer. By this time newer competitors as low-price, low-margin, low-status emerge and these competitors too follow the same evolutionary process. The wheel keeps on turning and department stores, supermarkets, and mass merchandisers went through this cycle.

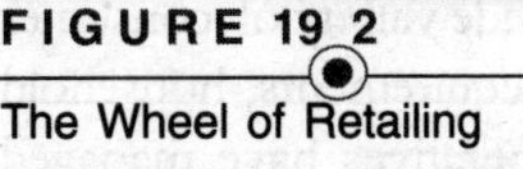

FIGURE 19.2

The Wheel of Retailing

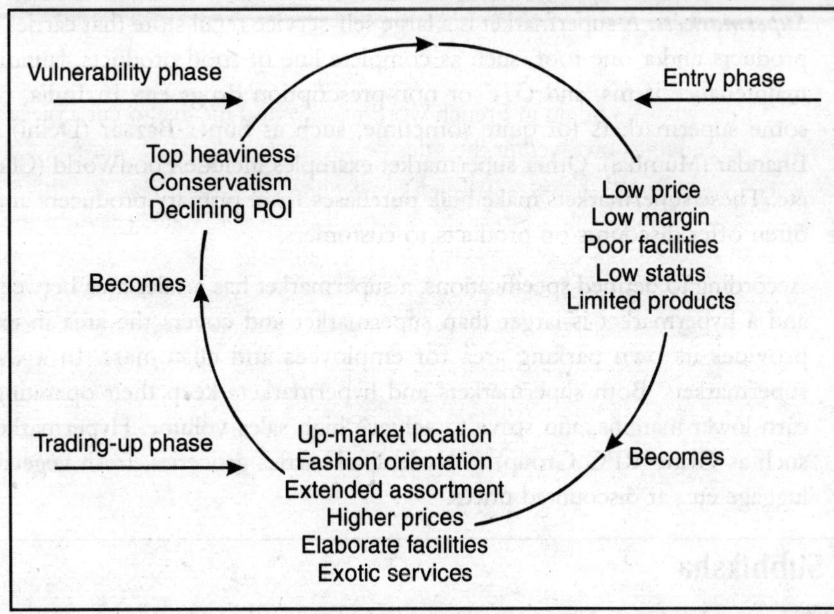

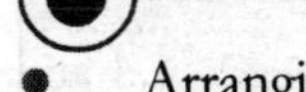

Functions of Retailers

- Arranging Assortment
- Breaking Bulk
- Holding Stock
- Channel of Communication
- Promotional Support
- Extending Services

Major Types of Retail Stores

There is no universally accepted method of classifying retailers. Various schemes have been proposed to categorise retailers based on (a) number of outlets, (b) margin *vs* turnover, (c) location, and (d) size. Because of the overlap of classification criteria, some stores may qualify as under two different categories at the same time. An independent store is a single retail unit owned by an individual, partnership, or corporation. Usually independent stores tend to be small and are owned by individuals. Traditional independent stores are known as *kirana* shops in India. A retail chain store is a part of a multiple retail outlet business. When any type of other stores start spreading in more locations, they can be called as retail chains of that specific type. Franchise store is contracted with the parent company under specified conditions.

I. General Merchandise Retailers

General merchandise retailers carry a variety of product lines, with considerable depth. Some major types of these stores include supermarkets and hypermarkets, discount stores, and department stores.

- ***Supermarkets:*** A supermarket is a large self-service retail store that carries a wide variety of consumer products under one roof, such as complete line of food products, laundry requirements, household maintenance items, and *OTC* or non-prescription drugs etc. In India, cooperatives have managed some supermarkets for quite sometime, such as Super Bazaar (Delhi), Apna Bazaar and Sahkari Bhandar (Mumbai). Other supermarket examples include FoodWorld (Chennai), Foodland (Mumbai) etc. These supermarkets make bulk purchases from primary producers and keep the prices low. They often offer discounts on products to customers.

  According to defined specifications, a supermarket has a sales area between 25,000 and 50,000 sq. ft., and a hypermarket is larger than supermarket and covers the area in excess of 50,000 sq. ft. and provides its own parking area for employees and customers. In a way hypermarkets are large supermarkets. Both supermarkets and hypermarkets keep their operating expenses and prices low, earn lower margins, and strive to achieve high sales volume. Hypermarkets in India are coming up, such as Giant (RPG Group) in Hyderabad carries groceries, fresh vegetables, home appliances, and luggage etc., at discounted prices.

Subhiksha

■ Subhiksha, a discount store, started with just a single store at Chennai in 1997 and now it has stores located in Tamil Nadu, Pondicherry and Karnataka. Future expansion will include other cities, such as Delhi, Mumbai, and Ahmedabad. This retail chain is mainly organised on discount store concept but also provide home delivery service to some extent. The aim of the stores is to
■ meet all monthly household consumption needs with monthly income of about Rs 5000.

- ***Discount Store:*** These stores are self-service, standard general merchandise retailers regularly offering brand name and private brand items at low prices, earn lower margins, and push for high sales turnover. The characteristics of true discount stores include: (1) selling products at discounted price, (2) carry standard international, national or store brands to build image, (3) operate as no frills attached, self-service stores to minimise operational costs, and (4) preferred store locations are low-rent areas and attract customers from other near and distant stores, too. Discount stores carry a wide, but carefully selected product assortment including household items, appliances, clothing, appliances, food items, toys, and sports goods. The world's largest and best-known discount store is Wal-Mart. In India, the idea of discount is not new. Almost all sorts of retail stores offer discounts once in a while, particularly on the occasions of major festivals. Perpetual discount stores are Subhiksha of Chennai and Margin Free Markets of Kerala.

- ***Department Stores:*** A department store is large retail store organised into several departments, offering a broad variety and depth of product lines. The product mix may include food products, appliances, clothing, furnishing, and other household goods. To facilitate marketing efforts and internal management, related product lines are organised under different departments, such as apparel, cosmetics, home furnishings, and appliances etc. Buyers of each department may be fairly autonomous and work as self-contained businesses. Department stores are service-oriented and their total offerings include personal assistance, delivery, credit, merchandise return, and pleasant atmosphere. Macy's, Sears, J. C. Penny, and Nordstorm are well-known departmental stores in *USA*. Department stores are believed to have reached a stage in their life cycle where they have entered the decline phase due to competition from other retailers, such as discount stores. Some of them have started weekly discount sales, introduced their own store brands to cut down costs, mail-order services, and no-questions asked merchandise return policy.

Pantaloon Stores

Pantaloon Retail India Ltd. belongs to Pantaloon Group. PRIL opened its first department store in Kolkata in 1997. The company now owns 14-retail outlets based on department store format in Kanpur, Chennai, Hyderabad, Secundrabad, Nagpur, Thane, and Ahmedabad and has become a chain store. Pantaloon stores carry broad product mix, deep assortment, and extends high level of customer service. These stores have separate departments carrying clothing and accessories for women, children, and men. Household section carries gift items, textiles, and furnishings. The leading brands include John Miller, Pantaloons, T–2000, Scotsville, Annabelle, Ajile, and Bare, etc.

Now your neighbourhood chai wala and samosa wala will soon have competition. Pantaloon Retail India has entered the food court business with a chai and samosa outlet. Christened Chamosa, this new format is currently being tried out at some of the existing malls in Mumbai.

Confirming the development, Pantaloon Retail India MD Kishore Biyani says, "We are experimenting this new business model. Initially we have just tried it in our stores in Mumbai. Following the success of this initiative we will then expand it to high traffic areas." The company has opened a kiosk at Phoenix Mills, Lower Parel, and claims that it has so far received an encouraging response.

In India, food-retailing business is still going through teething troubles. Some Industry observers said that given the size of the brands that Pantaloon has built like Big Bazaar, it is unviable to have both share the same retail space. This has forced, industry sources said Biyani, to explore the smaller format store like Chamosa and smaller brands like Indus League's Indigo Nation and Scullers to garner business. Pantaloon Retail has over 39 stores that include Big Bazaar, Food Bazaar, Central, and Pantaloon. It has set itself a target of over Rs. 1000 crore by 2005-2006. Biyani has been on an acquisition spree to expand its business model. Pantaloon Retail India has picked up a 15.7% stake in Mumbai-based Galaxy Entertainment for making a foray into leisure and entertainment business.

(Source: Chamosa store details from Times of India, June 10, 2005).

In India and other developing countries the trend of department store is picking up. Many leading independent retailers such as Appeal (Delhi), and Baniya Store (Jammu), and other new entrants are showing inclination to open department stores. Department stores are usually part of a retail chain and located within planned shopping centres or traditional up-market shopping centres. Most department stores in India carry women's, men's, and children's clothing and fashion accessories, and household appliances. Sahkari Bhandars are "Indianised" version of department stores. Akbarally's is department store with three branches in Mumbai, and Shoppers' Stop has 14 stores located in different cities in the country. Kids Kemp is speciality department store for infants, children, and teenagers in Bangalore and specialises in ready-to-wear garments with several attractions for children and claims to be the largest store of its kind in the world. Most department stores in India are located in large cities. The leading examples of fashion related department stores in India are Ebony (7 stores), Globus (4 stores), Pantaloon (14 stores) and Lifestyle (3 stores).

Large numbers of independent unorganised retailers with small retail outlets are unlikely to get hurt by organised retail players enjoying buying power among members. Manufacturers and suppliers would not like to compromise on the retail penetration because of the operations of very limited number of organised large-volume retailers. Small independent retailers provide important services to their customers even in remote rural markets in India. In cities, locality retailers take orders on telephone, deliver merchandise at home, extend credit facility, and offer low prices. A significant advantage is that they are just around the corner and have developed strong relationships with their customers and enjoy the huge benefit of customer loyalty.

Shop-in-Shop

Timex Watches Ltd. experimented with shop-in-shop concept in department stores. The company has named it Club Timex Stores and has over 62 shops in department stores. The aim is to cash in on the opportunity offered by increasing department stores in India.

2. Speciality Stores

Speciality stores carry a narrow product mix and deep product lines. It seems the number of chain speciality stores is increasing.

- ***Speciality Retail Stores:*** As the name suggests, speciality stores carry a narrow product mix with depth of assortment within the line. The emphasis is on a limited number of complimentary products and a high level of customer service. Speciality stores often sell shopping goods such as jewelry, apparel, computers, music systems, and sporting good etc. Traditionally, independent speciality retailers in India operate in specialised market centres that attract large number of customers. These stores are viewed as experts in the kind of products they sell and carry a definite image.

  Examples of speciality stores include Gautier (furniture), Titan (watches), and Tribhuwandas Bhimji Zaveri (jewelry) etc. Chirag Din, Van Heusen, Shopper's Stop and Raymonds, Louis Vuitton, Body Shop, and Tanishq etc., are all speciality stores. Sometimes speciality stores are called as *single-line, limited-line,* or *super-speciality stores* depending on the degree of narrowness of product lines they carry. For example, Shopper's Stop is a *single-line* store and carries only ready-to-wear garments for the family. Raymonds showrooms carry clothing and accessories for men and is referred as *limited-line store.* Keeping in view the degree of narrowness of product lines Chirag Din, Benetton, Zodiac and Van Heusen etc., sell designer clothes for men, and are viewed as *super-stores.*

Khadi Speciality Store

- Tropical Clothing Company (P) Ltd. of Kolkata owns retail stores under the brand name Khaddar, carrying Khadi garments. The company has retail outlets in Kolkata, Patna, Chandigarh, and Bangalore, and has plans to expand to other cities. Khaddar is one of the pioneers and its garment range covers 70 per cent in women's wear category. The prices range between about Rs 300 and 600. Little promotion is used and there is more reliance on word-of-mouth communication.

- ***Off-Price Retailers:*** These stores buy manufacturers' seconds, factory overruns, off-season production, returns, or left over goods at less than wholesale prices and sell to consumers at very low retail prices. Off-price retailers generally offer clothes, and shoes, or second-hand used items. Their aim is to turn their inventory nine or more times in a year and sometimes attract department stores customers and price-sensitive customers familiar with brand names. A variation of this format is manufacturer's own outlet that sells overstock and unsold merchandise. Some ready-to-wear clothes manufacturers adopt this approach in India.

- ***Category Killers:*** These are huge speciality retailers that dominate single product line or category and compete on the basis of very low prices and enormous product availability. These are called category killers because they expand rapidly and capture sizeable market shares, and business of other smaller, high-cost retailers. Examples include Home Depot, Tower Records, Office Depot, Sports Authority, and Vishal chain. They are able to buy file cabinets, electronic goods, bathroom tiles, and pet food etc., in large volumes and sell at prices even lower than large competitors.

3. Shopping Malls

The largest mall in *USA* is Minnesota Mall, having four hundred stores, fourteen movie theatres, seven restaurants, five nightclubs, and 97-acre theme park. Shopping malls are a relatively recent happening in India. There were 25 operational malls in 2003 and the projections are that by the end of 2006, the country might have 220 malls and is unlikely to remain restricted only in metros or large cities. There is a possibility that malls will spread in non-metro cities, such as Ludhiana, Chandigarh, Jaipur, Ahmedabad, Lucknow, and Indore etc.

Malls are believed to inspire fashion-based shopping by upwardly mobile and rich families in stark contrast to need-based shopping in case of lower, and lower middle-class families shopping at supermarkets and discount stores. Shopping malls typically deal with several bases and product categories and provide a large variety of merchandise and services. Some well-known malls include Spenser Plaza (Chennai), Crosslands (Mumbai), Ansal Plaza (Delhi), Sahara Plaza in Gurgaon, etc. More have come up in Kolkata, Gurgaon etc.

4. Retail Chains

As mentioned earlier, a retail chain operates multiple retail outlets under common ownership in different cities and towns. Most retail chains carry general merchandise and are also seen in services retailing under contractual franchise agreements. To some extent the purchasing function and decision-making are coordinated or centralised. Chain stores generally have considerable bargaining power because of large purchase volume. These chains generally receive new items no sooner they are introduced, get appropriate selling and service support, they often buy directly from producers and bypass wholesalers and get best prices. Dominant chains sometimes manage exclusive selling rights for certain products and manufacturers may produce goods under the store brand name. Examples of retail chains in India include Shoppers' Stop, Spenser, Westside, Globus, Escorts-Nanz, McDonald's, FoodWorld, Nilgiris, various brands of retail petrol outlets etc.

5. Non-Store Retailing

As the name suggests, non-store retailing is not conducted from a store but takes place outside traditional store environment. Store retailers operate from a fixed-point-of-sale location, use mass media advertising, maintain store décor, and arrange product displays to attract and sell products to walk-in and other customers. In case of certain products they provide alteration or installation services. Non-store retailers don't have to select any location for visibility or accessibility. They access to prospects and customers by using certain direct approach methods.

Non-store retailing involves accessing prospects and customers directly through direct response advertising, mail, telephone, catalogues, Internet, vending machines, and door-to-door selling, etc. The method of payment and delivery vary across different types of non-store retailers. (Also see Chapter 17).

Spenser Plaza

- Spenser Plaza owned by RPG group, is the largest shopping mall located in Chennai. It is an amusement complex with facilities like virtual reality theatres, pool tables, bowling alleys, swimming pool, beauty parlours, and restaurant.
- RPG also owns other chains – FoodWorld, Health & Glow, and Music World. The Rs. 7,500 crore RPG Enterprise is heavily investing in retail business. It is getting onto the hypermarket segment in a big way. The company intends to invest Rs. 300 crore to open 20 Spenser's Hypermarkets by 2006. The business will be managed by Great Wholesale Club Ltd., a wholly owned subsidiary of Spenser. RPG Enterprise currently has a total shopping space of 6.40 lakh sq. ft. This will double to 15 lakh. Currently, the retail business contributes Rs. 550 crore. In the long-run, the retail business is expected to contribute 25 per cent to the groups projected turnover of Rs. 10,000 crore by 2006-2007.

STRATEGIC ISSUES IN RETAILING

To enter retailing is easy and still easier to fail. To survive and be successful in retailing needs catering to customers. Their costs and profits depend on their type of operation, product lines, and level of service. Personal consumers make purchases for a variety of reasons. Sometimes the reasons seem to be obvious, and at times seem to be non-rational, vague and may be just social or psychological in nature, such as to escape boredom, to socialise, to kill time, or to learn if there is anything interesting or new. Retailers particularly consider target market and retail store location; merchandise variety and assortment; store image and atmospherics; services, price level and promotion.

Target Market and Store Location

Identifying target market is essential to determine all other aspects of retailing decisions, such as location, merchandise mix, pricing, store atmospherics, promotional efforts, and level of service. Location decision is quite significant because it dictates the area of customer coverage and it is the least flexible strategic issue. Retailers must consider the characteristics of their target customers, their income levels, lifestyles, needs, service requirements, and the image of the store.

A retailer may decide to locate in a shopping centre, or have a *freestanding store* away from a shopping complex in a separate stand-alone building, near shopping complex, on a highway, or residential locality. It would need to pull customers on its own strength, such as a small grocery store or *paan-bidi* kiosk near a highway petrol pump or *dhaba*. Most retailers prefer to select locations adjacent to roads with high level of pedestrian traffic. Convenience goods retailers prefer locations where there is high level of pedestrian and vehicular traffic, and available transportation facility. Locality and corner shops like to be located inside thickly populated colonies. Other considerations relate to availability of parking in the surrounding area, cost or rent of the location, and condition of the building. The retailer must also examine the characteristics of existing stores, whether the location is in a planned shopping area, or unplanned area. For example, locality shopping area or corner shop is more suitable for carrying convenience goods, medicine, shopping goods, and personal care items. Speciality stores draw customers from even distant localities.

Changes in socio-economic conditions and technological advancements have led to the newer retail formats and competition has intensified in retailing. It is important for decision-makers to consider retail outlet positioning. This involves reviewing critically the target market characteristics, to what extent they are getting the desired products and services, and what can distinguish the retail outlet as compared to others. Different retailers vary in positioning themselves. A retailer could position itself as high-quality, premium-price product store with many services. On the basis of one or more differentiation attributes such as quality, price, assortment, specialisation, special services, convenience, atmospherics, entertainment etc., can position itself.

Merchandise Variety and Assortment

The kind of product assortment a retailer intends to carry must match the expectations of the target market customers. Merchandise variety generally means breadth of product lines and assortment refers to different models in the same or different brands in a category. This decision will also affect decisions about sources of supply. Some retail outlets like to keep limited assortment only of fast moving, low-priced items, and an entertainment electronics speciality store is likely to carry a large and complete range of different branded systems, offering very deep assortment of models, styles, sizes, and prices. Convenience goods are frequently and habitually purchased, require little or no selling effort, generally carry low unit prices, and sold in numerous retail outlets, including supermarkets. Such goods are generally purchased in easily accessible locality stores.

Shopping goods are purchased relatively less frequently, are relatively more expensive, customers are inclined to compare price, quality, and features etc., and require more selling efforts on the part of the retailer. For such stores, the quality of store traffic is more important and often depends more on the character of the outlet than the products it sells.

The consumer of shopping goods is prepared to travel some distance to see what is available and compare and evaluate the different attributes of the products. However, easy accessibility in a shopping centre and also from residential areas often proves advantageous.

Speciality items are usually expensive, used for extended periods of time, and bought infrequently. Customers know what they want and travel to store location to by the brand. A retailer has to carefully decide what merchandise variety and assortment it would carry, because a jumbled image does not help in creating persuasive distinction.

Store Image and Atmospherics

It is necessary for a retail outlet to project the right image by stimulating interest and confidence among its target customers. Physical design elements of a retail store that appeal to customers' emotions create a certain favourable position and store image, distinct from other stores. This would require proper location, consideration of traffic congestion, exterior storefront appearance, display windows, and entrance etc. These aspects are particularly important for first impressions because customers often judge a store by its outside appearance. If it appears attractive, friendly, and inviting, customers are more likely to come inside the store. Interior considerations include lighting, floor carpets, colour, fixtures, product assortment, store layout, sounds, dress and manner of store personnel, the kind of customers store that attracts, and movement space etc.

Obviously, a high-end store and discount store are likely to project different type of image. Other factors that affect store image include prices, luxury and novelty, reputation for credibility, number of services offered, and promotional activities etc.

How consumers perceive a store can be an important determinant of what kind of customers are likely to patronise it. Consumers from lower economic groups like to shop at small, low-price, and friendly stores. Affluent customers like to visit and are seen shopping at exclusive stores offering high-quality products and carrying prestigious labels. It is important for a retailer to consider multiple factors to create a desired store image. Management of a retail store must ensure that the store atmosphere is consistent with the tastes of its target market.

Services, Price, and Promotion

Service mix includes pre-purchase, and post-purchase services, such as accepting customers' orders on telephone or by mail, advertising and promotions, helpful sales personnel, gift-wrapping, delivery, returns, installations, extending credit, and repairs etc. To differentiate themselves from competitors meaningfully, retail stores often use services. Many high-quality consumer durable products fail to capture sizeable market share because stores carrying them fail to deliver desired level of repair services. For example, though Fiat Palio is said to be a good and sturdy car but lack of widespread and convenient service points has discouraged potential customers. Customers prefer to patronise retail outlets with reputation for delivering high levels of desired services.

Price is also a critical differentiating factor and needs to be carefully determined in relation to target customers, the nature of product mix, desired level of service, and what kind of competition exists and anticipated. High-end stores generally keep higher margins and sell low volumes, and offer many services; discount stores depend on low-margins, high volume, and little or no services. Locality stores operate on low-margins, some service, and friendly relations. Some retail outlets announce low prices on some items and attract store traffic. Most retail stores use advertising in local media, run sales promotions, reward regular customers, and arrange displays etc.

Summary

Retailing is a fast growing business and its structure varies across countries. It covers all the activities involved in the sale of products to final consumers for personal, family, household use and not for business. These activities include anticipating what consumers' want, developing assortments of products, acquiring market information, and financing. A retailer is a business and can be an individual, chain store, departmental store, supermarket, speciality store, small locality shop, *paan-bidi* kiosk, or a service retailer.

The wheel of retailing theory says that new retailers often enter the marketplace with low prices, margins, and status. The low prices are usually the result of some innovative cost-cutting procedures and so attract competitors. With the passage of time, these businesses strive to broaden their customer base and increase sales. Their operations and facilities increase and become more expensive. They may move to better up-market locations, start carrying higher-quality products, add services and emerge as a high cost-price-service retailer. Newer low-price, low-margin, low-status stores emerge and follow the same evolutionary process.

Major types of retail stores include supermarkets, discount stores, department stores, speciality stores, off-price retailers, category killers, shopping malls, and retail chains. The distinction of retailers is based on the variety and assortment they carry, number of stores they operate, contractual agreement with principles to sell the product or service or use brand names, and the level of services offered.

Non-store retailing activities take place outside traditional store environments unlike fixed-point-sales-operations. These non-store selling activities fall under the category of direct marketing. To enter retailing is easy and still easier to fail. To survive and be successful in retailing needs catering to customers. Their costs and profits depend on their type of operation, product lines, and level of service. Retailers must consider several aspects when developing strategies. Location of store is a critical issue as it determines the business area from which customers will be attracted. Consumers are psychologically affected by the store's image, atmospheric aspect and its environment.

The kind of product assortment a retailer intends to carry must match the expectations of the target market customers. This decision will also affect decisions about sources of supply. Some retail outlets like to keep limited assortment, only of fast moving, low-priced items, and an entertainment electronics speciality store is likely to carry a large and complete of different branded systems, offering very deep assortment of models, styles, sizes, and prices. Convenience goods are frequently and habitually purchased in easily accessible locality stores. Price is also a critical differentiating factor and needs to be carefully determined in relation to target customers, the nature of product mix, desired level of service, and what kind of competition exists and anticipated.

The nature of retailing is changing due to technological and socio-economic changes. Successful retailers will have the insight and matching resources in adopting new systems that speed up transactions, reduce costs and prices, and deliver more service to customers.

Questions for Discussion

1. What is the significance of retailers in marketing channel?
2. How retailers and wholesalers differ in terms of different functions they perform?
3. Differentiate between mass merchandisers and speciality store. Mention two examples of each from India.
4. What are the major distinctions between department stores and discount stores?
5. How does a supermarket differ from a speciality store? Name two supermarkets and two speciality stores.
6. Do you think the organised retailers will gradually eliminate locality retail and *kirana* shops in India? Give your reasons.
7. Discuss three major types of non-store retailing in India. Have you ever purchased products from a non-store retailer? Why?
8. If you were to open a speciality retail store, what factors would you consider?
9. What is the importance of store exterior and atmospherics?
10. Discuss some new retailing trends in India with examples.

Projects

1. Visit some locality retail stores and prepare a report about the kind of product assortment, pricing they use? Suggest methods to improve their performance.
2. A lady wants to open a small retail store, specialising in high quality, high-price children clothing. What suggestions do you have regarding her choice of location and competition factors she should consider?
3. Study and classify the retail store formats existing in the central business area of your city. What are the major differences between them in terms of strategies adopted?

Bibliography

1. Harry G. Miller, "Micro-Enterprise Development: The Role of Wholesaling in Developing Countries," *International Journal of Technology Management*, 9 (1994).

2. Donald J. Bowersox and M. Bixby Cooper, *Strategic Marketing Channel Management,* McGraw-Hill, 1992.

3. Stephen Brown, "The Wheel of Retailing: Past and Future," *Journal of Retailing,* Summer (1990).

Cases

Case 5.1: Bypassing Practice

rvind Sood, like most entrepreneurs, dreamt a lot. He dreamt customers would eagerly phone Woodstock Acoustic Systems in India. To order the latest, custom made stereo speakers. He saw demand rising and rising, cash flowing, and his technicians producing superior quality products that were delightful and appreciated by the Woodstock customers, and favourable word-of-mouth spreading.

Arvind had a degree in mechanical engineering from Delhi School of Engineering, but his hobby was always acoustics. Like most entrepreneurs he had taken a long time in developing his dream. It was during the course of completing his studies in engineering that he became interested in audio science and devoted time to his hobby. Just after completion of his studies, Arvind started working on creating stereo speakers in his garage. He named his enterprise Woodstock Acoustic Systems. He would design a pair of speakers and invite a couple of his friends to listen and give their opinions. Occasionally, on the recommendations of his friends, one or two customers would come and after demonstration would buy a pair. After a year, his parents told him that he had spent enough time working on creating his ideal stereo speakers, and now he should look for a job to start his career.

It was a Friday, and Arvind had spent nearly Rs. 50,000 taken from his parents and was down to his last Rs. 10. He was seriously contemplating to take up some job because so far nothing fruitful had come out of his dreams. He looked fondly at the two pairs of speakers he had finished designing only a week back, when his landline phone rang. The voice said, he was Ajay Suri and had heard about his speakers from some friends. He asked for an appointment on Monday, the 15th June 2001 to discus few things regarding his stereo speakers. The meeting was fixed for 4 pm on Monday at Arvind's place.

All through, Arvind had focused on creating something delightful for "audio addicts," – the people who love to listen to music and appreciate high-quality stereo equipment at a reasonable price. These people were fastidious about sound quality but were unable to afford very expensive brands of well-known companies such as Bose or others. They were young, well educated, upwardly mobile in their careers, and would be affluent in about 6 – 10 years, and would prefer to buy a set of speakers now rather than wait.

As scheduled, Ajay Suri arrived at the appointed time. He said he had heard about Woodstock Acoustic Systems from a friend of a friend. He wanted to have a first-hand experience of his stereo speakers. Arvind took him to his garage office and played couple of Indian classical music tapes. Ajay Suri afterwards asked Arvind if he was interested in selling these two pairs of speakers, and how much is the price for each pair. Arvind said, "These are the latest that I have designed and are of very high-quality. I have not decided about the price yet but might sell, but it depends on how much you are prepared to pay for a pair." Arvind put his hand in his trouser pocket and touched a 10-Rupee note. He was thinking if Suri says he would buy a pair for Rs. 1500, he would sell. He thought, "I need some money." Suri was silent and thinking. Arvind was feeling nervous and stared at something that was not there on the floor.

Suri spoke, "I will buy both the sets for Rs. 8000 each, cash. But there is a condition." "And what is that condition?" asked Arvind reflexively, not really believing his ears. His heart seemed to be racing at 100 km per hour.

"Well, every month you will sell me five such pairs at this price for six months. You will not sing contract with anyone else during this period in Delhi market. I might ask for more number of

Contd...

pairs, but that we will see later." "Further, I will give an advance for the next two pairs that I will pick up in about two weeks, or may be earlier. So, keep them ready by the end of the next week." He paused for a moment then said, "If it suits you." "In fact, I will call you after about ten days to learn when should I really come to collect the pieces." That was the evening, three years ago.

For the first year, he sold his speakers only to Suri, who had a music equipment showroom in South Extension. After the first two months, Arvind employed two qualified workers and his supply of speakers to Suri's showroom had climbed to 120 pairs per month in six months time. He learnt that Suri was also attracting customers to his showroom from adjoining areas of Delhi.

In two years Arvind had established his manufacturing unit in Okhla Industrial Area and had 30 full time workers. He personally tested each pair of speakers produced and was stickler to quality. Now Woodstock Acoustic Systems was supplying to six music showrooms in Delhi and sold to trade customers approaching directly from other states. So far he had not established system of distribution in any market, except for six regular showrooms of Delhi.

Arvind had been for some time, thinking about establishing some streamlined distribution system. He knew that most manufacturers distribute their equipment primarily through stereo dealers. Whatever little experience he had gained, Arvind did not think much of this, he felt that the dealers too often played hardball with producers, and forced them to accept thin margins. In general, the dealers concentrated on a handful of well-known manufacturers who provided mass produced models. This kept those firms that offered high quality customised products from gaining access to the market. Perhaps most disturbing, Arvind felt that the established dealers often sold not what was best for customers, but whatever they had in inventory in a given period.

Arvind's dream was to provide high-end stereo speakers directly to audio-obsessed, and device a method of bypassing the established dealer network. It was clear that he wanted to go directly to end customers, thereby avoiding dealer mark-ups and offer top quality products and service at reasonable price.

Arvind was now 28 years of age and set out to turn his dream into reality. Some customers who know about Arvind's work and Woodstock Acoustic Systems had become enthusiastic supporters and invested Rs. 4.5 million in Woodstock.

Approximately 370 stereo-speaker makers compete for Rs. 5000 crore market in the country for audio equipment. Nearly 230 of these manufacturers sell to the low-and-mid-range segments of the market. This accounts for 90 per cent of the market's unit volume and about 50 per cent of its value. In addition to competing with each other, Indian manufacturers also compete with Japanese and American firms that offer products at affordable prices. The remaining 140 or so producers compete for the remaining 10 per cent of the market's volume and 50 per cent of the value – the high end – where Arvind hopes to find his customers.

To serve the audio-addicts segment, Arvind offers only the highest-quality speakers. Woodstock has two models: the Elite and Percy. The Elite stands 18 inches high, weighs 8 kg and designed for stand mounting. The floor standing Percy is 46 inches high and weighs 38 kg. Both models feature custom-made cabinets that come in natural or black oak, and walnut. Arvind can build and ship two pairs of Elite speakers or one pair of Percy speakers all by himself in a single day. In order to have adequate parts inventory, Arvind has to spend Rs.1.5 million of his capital on the expensive components.

Arvind set the price of Elite and Percy at Rs. 35,000 and 73,000 per pair respectively. He selected these prices to provide a 50 per cent gross margin. Arvind believes that traditional

Contd...

dealers would sell equivalent speakers at retail at nearly twice those prices. Customers can call Woodstock on a toll-free number to order speakers or get advice directly from Arvind. Woodstock pays for shipping or any return freight via First Flight. Round trip freight for a pair of Percy costs Rs. 9,500.

Arvind offers to pay for the return freight because a key of his promotional strategy is a 30-day, in-home, no obligation trial. This trial period allows customers to listen to the speakers in their actual listening environment. In a dealer's showroom, the customer must listen in the environment that is at best artificial and often feels pressure to make a quick decision.

Arvind believes that typical high-end customers may buy speakers more for "non-rational" reasons. They want a quality product and good reproduction of sound, and also to convey an image. For these reasons, Arvind has tried to create a unique image through the appearance of Woodstock speakers and to reflect the image in all of company's marketing. He has spent money on distinctive stationery, business cards, a brochure, and a single display ad. He also designed a laminated label he places just above the gold-plated input jack on each speaker. The label reads, "This speaker was handcrafted by (the technician's name who assembled the speaker goes here in her/his own handwriting). Made in India by Woodstock Acoustic Systems, Delhi."

To spread the word, Arvind concentrates on producer reviews in trade magazines and on-trade shows organised for high-end Hi-Fi systems (including foreign brands). Those who attend the show cast ballots to select the, "Best Sound at the Show." In the balloting, among 160 brands, Percy finished twelfth. Among the top ten brands, the least expensive was priced at Rs. 94,900, and four of the systems were priced from Rs. 340,000 to Rs. 735,000. A reviewer of Hi-Fi systems in an issue of industry magazine Stereoline evaluated Woodstock's speakers and noted, "The overall sound was robust and dynamic, with a particularly potent low end. Parts and construction quality of speakers appeared to be first rate. Definitely a company to watch."

Arvind made plans to invest in a slick, four-colour display ad in Stereo Review magazine with highest circulation. He also expected another favourable review in Stereoline magazine.

Reflecting on his first year of operations and the difficulties Arvind faced, he realised that he has learned a lot. He faced typical challenges an entrepreneur encounters. There were quality problems with the first cabinet supplier. Then, he ran short of a key component after a mix up with a second supplier. He tried hard to avoid debt, but had to borrow Rs. 2.5 million from a bank. Prices for his cabinets and some components had risen, and product returns had been higher than expected. The price and cost increases put pressure on his margins, forcing Arvind to raise his prices (to those mentioned above). Despite the price increases, his margins were less than the targeted 50%.

All things considered, Arvind felt good about his progress. The price increase does not seem to have affected demand. The few ads and particularly word-of-mouth seem to be working. Arvind receives an average of five calls per day, with one in six calls leading to a sale. Arvind also feels the stress of log hours and the low pay. He is not able to pay himself a high salary. His total salary for the year was Rs. 480,000.

Arvind reaches over his table and picks up his most recent projections. It seems this year will earn a profit of about Rs. 9 lakhs. Perhaps he is going to make it. As he puts back the projections on the table, Arvind's mind drifts to his plans of introducing two new models Minnow (Rs. 168,000 per pair) and the Rostuk (Rs. 340,000 per pair). He knows that there is a

Contd...

considerable potential in the foreign market for his speakers. Should he use the same direct marketing strategy for foreign markets, or should he consider distributors. The dreamer is visualising.

QUESTIONS

1. Why did Arvind establish a direct marketing channel?
2. What objectives and constraints have shaped his channel decision? If you were a consultant, what distribution channel strategy would you recommend Arvind for domestic and foreign markets?

Case 5.2: Distribution for FMCG Companies

Today, money talks in bottom lines. In case of FMCG companies, this is precisely what is driving a serious search on the right marketing and distribution strategies, questioning established beliefs in target consumers, and figuring out what really Indian market means for their brands.

One can think of it as a search for an approach that would be specific to each company. Clearly, a move away from the established marketing and distribution paradigm that FMCG companies in India earlier believed was the mantra for success – the HLL model. With nearly a million retail outlets, 7,500 distributors and a bag full of products focused on every possible price point, HLL addresses virtually every income and geographical segment in India.

The challenge for the others was to come up with a similar system in as short a time as possible. But replicating HLL is no easy task. The basic problem that confronts marketers of every description trying to get on HLL curve is the heterogeneity of the Indian market , in terms of geographical and income diversity.

Given this situation, HLL's task of building diverse markets comes with associated costs. Arranging rural and small town distribution system, establishing new product at different price points takes both time and money. This, in turn, means that at the initial stage of setting up a product or a distribution network, companies have to take a hit at their bottomline.

Industry analysts point out that the main reasons for multinationals organisation other than HLL, going in for a revamp of their strategies is a renewed emphasis by their parent on sharing the bottomline rather than focusing on topline growth. This revamp shows the deep pockets of parent ready to support sales growth at the cost of low margins. For Indian companies too, profits are becoming important, forcing them to take a second look at their existing approaches.

For instance, P&G, in a marked shift from its earlier focus of going after sales targets by aggressively exploiting distribution cover, is streamlining its distribution network and the company has named it as Operation Golden Eye. Proctor & Gamble's director public affairs, Ashok Chhabra says, "The traditional distribution system in India operates on the lines of a command economy. Companies decide on a supply target and then somehow push this to the consumers. This leads to tremendous waste in resources, which ultimately hurts the consumers. We are moving to a demand-based model, which enables us to reduce the quantum of waste."

While company officials are unwilling to comment on the specifics of the revamp, industry insiders point to the fact that P&G is cutting the size of its distributor cover to roughly one-tenth and is getting out of rural markets. "The company is focusing on class A and B towns and getting out of smaller population clusters," says a competitor. Only for a limited set of products, like Vicks Action 500 and some detergent sachets, P&G will not have much of its distribution presence in rural areas, he points out. "The company is reducing the number of price points at which it offers its products. For example, it has reduced the number of pack sizes in which it markets its detergent, Ariel."

An analyst, who tracks FMCG companies for a foreign brokerage, points out that between 1993 and 1996, Nestle added roughly 350,000 retail outlets to its distribution network; the majority of them in smaller towns and rural areas. Nestle also added quite a good number of products and variants in its portfolio – 31 in 1997 as compared to just three in 1993. The operating margins dipped sharply in 1992, when they were at around 13.5 per cent. By 1996 they had dropped to 11.5 per cent.

Contd...

Nestle is now revamping its product and marketing strategies. The emphasis is on products in which it was traditionally strong – milk products and beverages. This would be accompanied by a strategy of weeding out low margin products from the portfolio. The soya-based health drink, Bonus was discontinued from 1998, the axe is likely to fall on other products too.

Instead of trying to make its products available to as many consumers in as many markets as possible, like HLL, Nestle has identified a sharply defined target segment that it would focus on in its marketing and distribution efforts. According to company sources, Nestle has identified about 1,443 million households as its target group – or roughly 55 per cent of the urban population. These would, in turn, be split into two groups – 63 million individuals in the primary target group making 11.5 million households; and 81 million individuals in the secondary target group comprising about 15 million households. These target groups currently have a per capita annual consumption of Nestle's products of a value of Rs. 77 (The urban average consumption is Rs. 42).

If one places HLL and P&G at two ends of the spectrum, Dabur is thinking of a strategy that falls in between these two. Dabur's plan is to follow the HLL's basic track "because we have entry level FMCG products, we are trying to catch the consumer at the point where he is transiting from unbranded to branded products," says Sunil Duggal, vice president healthcare business. Yet, Dabur has taken a leaf out of P&G book by reducing the number of distributors. For towns with population of less than 20,000, the company has cut down on the number of distributors because it was uneconomical. Instead, it has appointed what Duggal terms as "super stockists." A super stockist differs from a distributor in that the party services 10 to 15 stockists, who are in turn to supply to retailers. If there is central theme in the way companies are reworking their distribution and marketing strategies, it is a focus on the products they are trying to market. Each product has an associated profile of customer groups that in turn determines its demand. "Instead of expanding distribution to increase demand for product, it is the demand that should drive the distribution," says Shunu Sen, chairman of Quadra Advisory.

Hasit Joshipura, General Manager Sales at HLL elaborates, "HLL has been a pioneer in creating and evolving a market of products like soaps and detergents. Our product portfolio has been geared towards the mass market. It is not necessary for a company with a different kind of product portfolio to follow our marketing and distribution model."

And where does it leave HLL? With less competition in the rural-urban markets, is its first mover advantage so strong that it can sit back and rake on the money without much effort? Joshipura emphatically says, "No competitive advantage is permanent. We have to constantly change and innovate to stay afloat."

What are the alternatives? If the HLL marketing and distribution model is not everybody's cup of tea, one option is to stop looking beyond the city lights as P&G seems to have decided for most of its products and keep the product space limited to the higher-ends of the urban income spectrum. The other option is to focus on specific demographic segments and tailor all the marketing and distribution efforts for them, as Nestle has decided. A third alternative seems to be in the choice of distribution channel. "Companies which do not want to build large distribution and retail networks beyond the urban areas can fall back on wholesale distribution," suggests Joshipura.

In a wholesales distribution system, companies off-load their products on a large wholesaler, usually offering a larger discount than they would offer to regular distributors. Smaller retailers

Contd...

buy the products directly from the wholesaler. This eliminates the need for a distributor with a large sales force, ultimately resulting in lower cost for the producing company. Nirma soap is an example that is distributed largely through wholesale segment, and contrasts with price peer, Lifebuoy, which goes into the same markets but through a large distributor and retailer network.

While each all of these models have their inherent advantages, there are disadvantages too. Most industry insiders point out that while wholesale distribution does cut down costs, brand building and customer recognition suffer in the long-run.

The experience of consumer companies in developed markets have proposed models that provide for streamlining distribution and sales networks in tune with consumer needs. P&G executives tout the Efficient Consumer Response (ECR) model, which they claim, forms the basis for P&G India strategic revamp.

P&G India CEO, Helmut Meixner described the ECR model in a recent speech: "The ultimate objective of ECT is to maximise consumer satisfaction by optimising the entire supply chain, rather than potentially sub-optimising the total by focusing on one element at a time." This may sound like a jargon but the model actually does throw up some specific recommendations like reducing the number of product variants.

Ultimately, it has all got to do with the product and the consumer it can successfully proposition. Surely, more models will emerge or evolve out of the existing ones.

(Slightly modified from Brand equity, Economic Times, 7-13 April 1999).

QUESTIONS

1. Study the different distribution approaches discussed in the case. Highlight the advantages and disadvantages of different systems.
2. All the four companies in this case are FMCG marketers. Why have they favoured different approaches for the distribution of their products?

Case 5.3: Oceanic Needs to Cut Distribution Costs

ceanic Home Appliances Ltd. is a Rs. 125 crore manufacturer of refrigerators and air conditioners. The company has been in the market for the last 11 years and at present, commands a market share of 28 per cent for refrigerators and 21 per cent for air conditioners.

The national distribution manager for this company, Rajeev Sehgal is a worried man today as he looks through the various cost analysis sheets sent to him by the strategic planning head, Sanjeev Chopra. The papers contain information on the inventory, the costs related to transportation from warehouse to depots and analysis of distribution costs of Oceanic vs Competitors. The data was collected from various sales depots spread across the country; the internal reports from the finance division and the invoices and delivery records. The details of the competitors' distribution strategies and costs were also being presented, though in brief. The cost comparisons were made in a way so that even a layman can understand.

After carefully studying all the breakdowns and details, Rajeev started making his own notes for an urgent review meeting called by the Managing Director, Uday Singh, next day at 10 am. All the national and regional heads for distribution, finance, and business development were to attend the meeting.

The meeting was called to review the existing distribution strategy; its consequences, and decide the future course of action.

When Sehgal had joined the company, it had a distribution strategy of supply based on demand from dealers. The distribution was a centralised process under the direct control of the national distribution head. The company had six regional offices across the country and each had three sales depots under it. The simple strategy put in practice was like this: based on demand estimates by the regional offices, goods were dispatched to these 18 sales depots. These goods were stocked, until the dealers demanded supply, having confirmed orders from the customers. A typical regional office serviced about 35 – 40 dealers and the total dealers under Oceanic in the country numbered 230. The system worked under tremendous pressure as last minute demands from dealers, unexpected increase or decrease in sales, political and economic fluctuations and competition often disturbed this not-so-appropriate strategy. Within six months of joining Oceanic, Sehgal was on a major revamping exercise for the entire distribution and inventory management system. He was quick to spot the negative fallout effects of this existing system: First, the dealers were not receiving stocks in time and the dealers, eager to do business, began to prefer and push brands of competitors. Second, the company offered a 20-day credit for its air conditioners while the arch rival company offered a 40-day credit. This was incentive enough for dealers to prefer competing brand to that of Oceanic. The impact of these factors was visible as sales volume gradually dropped to 13 per cent in that year.

Sehgal resolved the issues one by one. First, he increased the dealer margin by one per cent. Second, he started the practice of diverting stocks from one sales depot to another, which faced shortage in supply. Sehgal also increased the stock holding of all sales depots by 5 per cent. In six months time these changes began showing results. In the next one-and-a-half years the company's share for refrigerators rose to 20 per cent and 12 per cent for air conditioners from previous year's 14 and 8 per cent respectively. This strategy worked well for Oceanic for the next 3 years without any major problems. Of course, occasionally there was last minute rescheduling and

Contd...

redirecting of stocks or transfer of stocks was delayed for some problems like transporters' strikes etc. Overall, Sehgal excised complete control over quantity and stock movement. The market share for both the products showed a healthy growth and sales volumes were good enough to pose profits year after year. The dealers were happy with increased margin and the waiting period for the product was six days compared to an industry average of 10 days, and goods were available at sales depots all the time.

The strategy, however, drew a different set of problems. The recent cost review meeting revealed that transportation costs of the company had increased to 9 per cent over the normal 4 per cent of the total sales volume in the last three years. Also, the sales and distribution costs of Oceanic were 7.5 per cent of sales as compared to industry average of 6.5 per cent. The strategy of supplying products at market and dealers' demand had made them very happy but this had strained the stock movement. As this strategy involved transportation of goods from plant to depots as well as from one depot to another, it increased the transportation and insurance costs.

In the meeting, managing director Uday Singh started off by saying, "the profits have been good in the last few years, however we have to rely on short-term loans to fund our working capital. The high distribution costs have upset the higher sales and to revamp our working capital management, we must look at these costs carefully. The three major issues raised by our auditors are:

1. The time between the date of sending the product to depot and date of invoicing from dealers is high. On an average it is 20 days.
2. The stock movement is higher and the costs for transportation are 9 per cent as against industry average of 5 per cent.
3. The sales and distribution costs are 7.5 per cent of sales as compared to industry average of 6.5 per cent.

We need to look for an alternative to our existing strategy as we can't afford more costs.

Sehgal presented his strategy, "Today, the consumers can get a product within 6 days time as against 10-day waiting period of other companies. The dealers prefer our brands and it must be seen as a great achievement. Today, we are at number three position in the market because of easy access of our products." Finally, the distribution head south and east region started to speak. "I suggest creation of regional warehouses to meet the demand. The depots should narrow down its other work activities and concentrate on paper work only. The warehouse will move goods directly to dealers against confirmed orders. This should reduce inventory and transportation costs to a large extent." Sehgal argued the advisability of this alternative, "Our ultimate aim should be to develop market responsive systems, which will eventually meet the demand of consumers in the next few years. A system like this would reduce costs but increase the waiting period at end-user and dealer level. Speed of delivery is critical in a competitive market."

QUESTIONS

1. Analyse the major issues in the case. Is Sehgal right in stressing customer responsive systems at the risk of higher costs and inventory problems?
2. Prepare a suitable distribution strategy for Oceanic that will both retain efficiency and reduce costs.

Case 5.4: FoodWorld

Household groceries at walking distance, at economical prices is FoodWorld's USP. Where from do you get your vegetables and groceries? Pop this question to any housewife, and the most likely response is from the neighbourhood vendor selling on a pushcart, or a nearby market, which houses groceries. But both these options make no allowance for hygiene and comfort. This germ of a thought is what set the process for the conception of FoodWorld in Chennai in 1996. From there on, FoodWorld, a joint venture between Dairy Farm International and RPG Gardinier, has gone to add four cities – Bangalore, Pune, Coimbatore, and Hyderabad – at 41 locations.

Raghu Pillai, managing director, FoodWorld says, "We started in Chennai because of the developed retail market, good real estate prospects and cosmopolitan atmosphere. We have the most comprehensive range of products at the most competitive prices." Lower pricing is a function of the volume that the store generates. It gets close to a million customers a year. The throughput in a store ranges from Rs. 20,000 lakh to Rs. 17 crore a month. It has plans to touch the Rs. 1000 crore figure by the year 2003-2004. Says Pillai, "From humble beginnings, today FoodWorld has 12 outlets in Chennai, 14 in Bangalore, 9 in Hyderabad, 4 in Pune, and 2 in Coimbatore. It occupies a total retail space of 100,000 sq. ft and has additional 100,000 sq. ft of warehousing facility. Not content to sit on its laurels, FoodWorld has chalked up plans of setting up 100 stores by December 2000. But instead of venturing into new cities, FoodWorld will consolidate itself in the already existing locations.

Normally groceries, food, and vegetables is a low interest area. So building a brand is much more difficult. To generate and retain interest, FoodWorld runs a host of contests and promos. It has a 52-week promotional calendar with a variety of schemes to attract consumers. Pillai says, "At any given time, there are 150 – 200 products at a certain level of discount."

The layout of the store is designed keeping convenience in mind. For example, pulses are kept at the front, rice at the back, while vegetables to be kept on top. The execution enables vegetables on the top of a basket during a purchase. FoodWorld sources most of its branded groceries from traditional C&F agents, rice from the rice mills, fruit and vegetables from the neighbouring villages or the mandi.

Some of the problems encountered are assessing the best location, attaining economic viability and leveraging synergies. As all volumes are aggregated in the state, generating large enough volumes to leverage it as an advantage is a difficult task. The infrastructure of cold chains and basic infrastructure is missing. Getting trained people to man, the stores has proved another challenge. FoodWorld has the largest number of employees from government and municipal corporation schools.

In India, on an average, there is one retail outlet per thousand people. The industry is poised to grow at 5 – 10 per cent per year over the next 25 years. But to grow at this rate, retail has to grow across all categories of the spectrum.

(Source: A & M, September 30, 2000).

QUESTIONS

1. What external factors FoodWorld exploits to ensure successful existence and expansion of its retailing activities?
2. What is likely to be the impact of so many sales promotions on FoodWorld in the long-run?

Case 5.5: The Hidden Flavour

'It's probably on your mind but not on your body'. In April this year, Tamariind (yes, it's two 'i's after all) had the Indian yuppie raring to emulate Hrithik Roshan's perfectly turned out 'V'. But not a clue existed on retail availability of the product. A perplexing situation that S. Kumars Nationwide planned to remedy by end-September this year with about 20 exclusive stores and an equal number of shopping-stops.

Tamariind will be retailed through three formats – exclusive stores called Tamariind Flavour Zones, large format stores such as Shoppers' Stop, Zarapkars, Eternia and so on, and regular multi-brand outlets throughout the country. The exclusive stores are considered important for the brand image, as also to house the entire range and reinforce the proposition of Total Wardrobe Solutions (TWS) from head to toe. Large format retailing is expected to deliver volumes while multi-brand outlets deliver reach and penetration. The visual merchandising plan, of course, would be executed on the basis of the layout of each individual outlet. S. Kumars promises the salient features of modern retailing in terms of consumer-friendly outlets with complete liberty to touch and feel the product and sales staff who assist the customer in his purchase process and don't just sell the merchandise.

Keeping in mind the brand name, the merchandise has been divided into five lines, each identified as distinctive flavour and of course accessories, oops, flavoursories. The 'power flavour' comprises office wear. The 'fusion flavour' is a range of bolder office-wear, which could double up as subdued casuals. The 'lounge favour' offers knitted coordinates while the 'cool flavour' comprises the usual casual wear. Which leaves 'flash flavour' in distinctive colours and prints. The warehousing is done at Bhiwandi, near Mumbai, while the distribution is done through a number of agents across the country who hold stocks in basic items for immediate replenishment as well as book orders and forward it to central warehouses for dispatch.

Thus, after manufacturing and distributing textiles for over 50 years, the Rs. 700 crore S. Kumars Nationwide has made its ready-to-wear foray. The configuration of the two businesses is entirely different. According to Nitin Kasliwal, managing director S. Kumars Nationwide, "The entire readymade business needs a far more proactive approach and a far deeper understanding of consumer preferences, which change very fast. Thus, the entire business is about imagery." But retailing success depends not just on getting the target audience to identify with a brand to aspire for but actually buying it. In the already crowded Rs. 6,000 crore men's wear market, with an expected rate of growth of 15 per cent per annum for the next five years, a lot depends upon the retail ambience and the customer experience at the point of sale. The Tamariind retail strategy, therefore, incorporates 75 per cent pull and only 25 per cent push. Add Kasliwal, "This business is about communication, association, and visibility, unlike the textile business, which generally reaches a crescendo only during the main season time. The difference also lies in the fabrics."

Keeping all this in mind, the still nascent retail strategy adopted by S. Kumars aims to combine mass penetration with the long-term vision of a phased launch of the five ranges (designed by John Paul Vivian) within the next two years and fulfil its promise of TWS, which S. Kumars claims has not been so far offered by any brand in India.

Meenal Sinha, of Percept, says, "The brand has been launched after conducting an in depth survey of the buying habits of the Indian male. Today's consumer is more enlightened and looks for brand values and not just the functional aspect of the product. We are positioning

Contd...

Tamariind as the latest dress code for the young achiever, focusing on the flavour he can identify with." S. Kumars is all set to have at least 200 exclusive showrooms across the nation over a four-year period. In the near future, the company plans to launch clothes for every segment and achieve a target of Rs. 400 crore in three-years time.

QUESTIONS

1. What are the significant issues in this case?
2. Evaluate S. Kumars retailing strategy and determine its soundness or otherwise.
3. Is the positioning decision taken, the correct one to create the desired brand image of Tamariind?

PART 6

CHAPTER 20
Pricing Concepts, Strategies and Price Setting Approaches.

Cases

Pricing Concepts, Strategies and Price Setting Approaches

CHAPTER 20

LEARNING OBJECTIVES

After going through this chapter, you will understand:

- The meaning of price in general terms
- Importance of pricing objectives and factors that affect pricing decisions
- Information businesses need before setting prices
- Different pricing strategies and price setting methods
- Selection of suitable pricing approaches

Yes, the pricing does create a new customer. Nabankur Gupta, corporate advisor and director, at the Raymond Group, believes the customer is now at the centre of any marketing plan. "The customer decides the product price, where to buy, and the kind of communication he wants," he says. "The customer determines the balance between a product and its price."

In items of everyday use, price is the determining factor, which is why people rush to hypermarkets, such as Big Bazaar, where items of everyday use are available at discounted prices. The FMCG industry seems to have understood the customer's psyche very well; which is why they keep reducing the prices of toothpaste, soaps, detergents, edible oil etc., or top it with an interesting offer like buy one get one free.

The runaway success of sachet products, kick-started by Velvet shampoo, is also a clear indicator that if a desired product is available in an affordable price, everybody will lap it up. The strategy of pricing of Coke and Kitkat at Rs. 5 seems to have worked well indicating that price matters.

In items of everyday use, even the upper classes are price conscious. On a given day, it is not uncommon to see more than 800 cars parked outside Big Bazaar, located at Mumbai's Lower Parel. This is a clear indication that the upper class is price conscious when it comes to certain categories. Take for example, Lever's Sangam Direct, the supermarket-on-the-phone. It is proving to be quite popular with this segment.

Often, there is a fine distinction even in mass-market products, between charging premium pricing with a narrow base or an inclusive price, which reveals a market size that leaves everyone dazed. Take the telecom industry, for example. The industry presumed carrying a mobile phone to be a luxury, charged over Rs. 14 per minute of talk-time. Some where along the line, telecom players sensed that this market was driven by social factors than by businessmen, and decided to get into the volume game by drastically slashing talk-time charges and the result is for all to see. Today, there are nearly 50 million mobile phones in the country and this segment is growing by 25 per cent per year.

But when it comes to status symbol or snob value then price is irrelevant. Here the reverse works. The more costly a product, better it is perceived to be. Flashing a platinum card, wearing a Cartier glass, talking on a Nokia Vertu, carrying a Louis Vuitton bag, driving around in a Porsche becomes a fashion statement. When quite a lot of people can afford to buy a Calvin Klein, how will you distinguish yourself? You buy a Patek Philippe, which is in a league of its own. In Italy, there have been stories of people tightening their belts so that one day, they could buy their dear Ferrari. That's brand, the very antithesis of price.

(Source: Selected excerpts from USP Age, April 2005).

Price setting is a very critical area in marketing mix decisions of a company. The meaning given to price sometimes creates pricing difficulties. It is the only element that generates revenues for the company, and all others involve only costs. The aim of marketing is to facilitate satisfying exchanges between the marketer and consumers at a profit.

Price represents the value that is exchanged in a marketing transaction. A marketer usually sells a specific combination of need-satisfying product or service, and additional services like warranty. Donald Lichtenstein, Nancy M. Ridgeway, and Richard G. Niemeyer say that in most marketing or guarantee etc., transactions price is very evident, and buyers and sellers are aware of the value that each must part with in order to complete the exchange. However, price may not always be in monetary terms. *Barter* is the oldest form of exchange and still used occasionally for a variety of goods between countries. From the earliest times, when people learnt to engage in barter to affect exchanges, settlements were based on bargaining. Bargaining is still used in markets in majority of the countries. Certain websites, such as Priceline.com and eBay.com basically use the idea of bargaining between buyer and seller for a variety of products and services.

Pricing exercise begins with an understanding of corporate mission, target markets, and marketing objectives. Based on these factors, pricing objectives are developed. Management must examine the costs to determine how much flexibility it has in establishing prices and the lowest price level essential to meet profit and other company objectives. Determining the role prices play relative to other marketing mix variables sets boundaries and guidelines for pricing decisions. Pricing decision should take into consideration the impact on other items in the product line, promotional decisions, and distribution channels. There are two types of pricing decision situations; new product pricing, and adjusting prices of existing products. Pricing strategies of particularly new products are high-level responsibility shared by marketing and other top-level executives.

Buyers have limited resources and their interest in price, reflects their expectations of a product's ability to deliver the desired satisfaction they may derive from it. Customers must evaluate whether the utility value gained is worth the buying power sacrificed in an exchange. After the dawn of money economy, with the passage of time, buyers in almost all present day societies have learnt to assess goods, services, and ideas etc., in terms of financial price to measure the value usually used in exchange.

Price is everywhere all around people. For a variety of marketing situations price is expressed in different terms. For example, insurance companies charge a *premium*, colleges charge a *tuition*, a lawyer or physician charges a *fee*, taxis charge a *fare*, banks charge *interest* for a loan, *taxes* are paid for government services, a *toll* is charged for some bridges etc.

Pricing should never be seen as an isolated component of a company's marketing decision-making. Companies spend large amounts of money on product development, promotion, and distribution and face risks. Price is often the only marketing mix element that can be changed quickly to respond to changes in demand or competitive moves. Developing new products or modification of existing products, any changes in promotional programme, or distribution system involves much time and efforts. As mentioned above, price is the only element directly related to total revenue generation. A miscalculation of selling prices in high turnover and low profit margin in businesses can have a large impact on a company's profits. The following equation is significantly important for the entire company:

Profits = (Prices × Quantities Sold) – Total Costs

Thus, prices have impact on a company's profits and are important for its long-term survival. Price also has a psychological impact on customers and can reflect product quality and user status. This is especially true for ego intensive products. A company can highlight the product quality and user status by keeping the price high.

For most companies, setting prices can be a complex task involving both scientific analysis and intuitive trial and error. This is particularly true when a company launches a new product and there are no historical data or precedent on which to base expectations of how much consumers are prepared to pay for the product.

Price Competition: There is tremendous price competition in free market economies all around the world. A company can use price to compete by changing its prices or by reacting to price changes by competitors. This influences decisions concerning other marketing mix variables. Typically, price-based competition occurs when consumers cannot readily differentiate between competitive offerings. In this situation companies use price as a tool to differentiate its products from competitors' products to beat or match prices set by competitors. To adopt this competitive approach, a company should be low-cost producer. In case all competitors charge the same price, then the company producing at the lowest-cost would be most profitable. Companies adopting price-based competition tend to market standardised products and are generally adept at frequently adjusting prices or quite willing to do so.

A company adopting price-based competition can exercise flexibility in making adjustments to changes in company's costs or product demand. Over the time period, most companies manage to lower costs at varying levels and are able to adjust prices. Too frequent price reductions sometimes lead to price wars and weaken companies. In India, Coke and Pepsi occasionally indulge in price-cutting, attempting to take advantage. The day, one of them announces price reduction, the response of the other company is immediate and apparently neither firm gains advantage.

Non-Price Competition: Non-price competition focuses on other than price factors of a product such as distinctive product features, quality, service, packaging, and promotion to make it meaningfully differentiated from competing brands. The company attempts to add more value to its brand to push sales rather than changing its price. It is important that consumers must be able to perceive these distinctions and view them as important. When we go to buy an otherwise ordinary product toothbrush, we find significant differences in prices ranging between Rs. 5 to Rs. 38. Major companies differentiate their brands on the basis of bristle-head flexibility and tiny shock absorbers to benefit teeth and gums. This approach is more appropriate when customers primarily do not buy a product only for price reasons such as those products, the customers consider a commodity. When the customers prefer a brand because of its features, quality, or service, they are less likely to shift for competing brands and sales are less dependent on price. Despite this, a company cannot completely ignore prices of competitive products. Price is an important marketing mix element even when market environment and product nature favours non-price competition.

Pricing Objectives

Pricing objectives focus on what a company wants to achieve through establishing prices. These objectives should be clear, concise, and understood by all involved in pricing decisions. Pricing objectives affect decisions in various other functional areas such as finance and production etc., and must be in accordance to company's overall mission and objectives. There is diversity of objectives and generally companies have multiple pricing objectives. Some of these objectives may be short-term and others long-term. Besides, to respond to changing market conditions, companies generally alter pricing objectives as and when desirable. Most companies do not lose sight of the fact that price is a strategic tool and do not simply let costs or the market determine the prices. Some major types of pricing objectives are shown in Figure 20.1.

Survival: This is the broadest and most fundamental pricing objective of any company because staying in business is important under difficult conditions such as overcapacity, intense cut-throat competition, and changing consumer's wants and preferences. Most firms will tolerate difficulties but only as long as prices cover variable costs and even a small part of fixed costs, they can stay in business and device methods of adding value.

Profit: Many companies set profit maximisation as their pricing objective. Profit maximisation is likely to be more beneficial over the long-run. The firm, however, may have to accept modest profits or sometimes even losses over the short-term. The major problem with maximisation objective is that it is difficult to measure, whether profit maximisation has been accomplished. It is almost impossible to establish what could be the maximum possible profit. Because of this difficulty, maximisation objective is rarely set and companies settle down to a profit figure or some percentage change over previous period that its decision-makers view as optimum profit.

Return on Investment (ROI): *ROI* is also a profit objective and aims at achieving some specified rate of return on company's investment. Large companies such as Tata or Reliance are in a better position to set pricing objectives in terms of *ROI*. They may decide to establish pricing objectives usually independent of competition than do smaller companies. Return on investment pricing objectives are set by trial and error because all relevant cost and revenue data are not available to project the ROI at the time of price setting. ROI pricing objectives do not take into account of competitive prices and consumers' perceptions of price.

FIGURE 20.1

Pricing Objectives and Typical Company Actions

Objectives	Typical Actions
Survival	Price adjustment to enable company to increase sales volume to meet company expenses.
Profit	Determine price and cost levels that permit company to realise maximum profits.
Return on Investment	Determine price levels that allow company to yield targeted Return on Investment.
Market Share	Adjust prices to maintain or increase sales volume relative to competitors.
Product Quality	Company sets prices to recover R&D expenditures and high product quality. Establish high-quality image.

Market Share: A large number of companies establish their pricing objectives in terms of market share that they want to capture of the total industry sales. The objectives can be to maintain existing market share or increase in percentage terms. Companies want to maximise market share believing that a higher sales volume will consequently bring down unit cost and lead to higher profits in the long-run. The prices are set at the lowest possible level to generate higher sales and larger market share. As the unit costs dip, prices are further reduced. Intel follows a different approach. When it develops a faster better processor, it keeps the prices high aiming to skim the market. Subsequently, with decreasing unit costs, it keeps lowering its prices at intervals to capture the largest market share. Both market share and product quality influence a firm's profitability. Because of this reason, companies often state their pricing objectives primarily in terms of market share. Maintaining or increasing market share may not necessarily be dependent on growth in industry sales.

Product Quality: A company might have the objective to be a product quality leader in the industry. Consumers directly relate price to quality, particularly in case of products that are ego intensive of technology based. Such companies consistently strive and maintain high quality and accordingly set higher prices to cover quality and high cost of research and development. Caterpillar, Nikon, and Canon products set prices high to reflect quality.

Factors Affecting Pricing Decisions

A number of different internal and external factors affect pricing decisions and this may pose some complexity. In general, there is uncertainty about how consumers, competitors, resellers etc., would react to prices. Price considerations are important in market planning, analysis, marketing mix variables, demand forecasting, competitive structure, costs, and government actions. To illustrate the point, let us just look at one factor, the competitive market structure and what kind of affect this single factor can have on pricing decisions. However, it is necessary to appreciate that all internal and external factors interact to influence pricing decisions.

Competitive Structure: The market conditions vary considerably and market structure affects not only the pricing decisions within a company but also the kind of likely response from other players in the same industry. Much depends on the number of buyers and sellers operating in a market and the extent of entry and exit barriers. These factors affect a company's level of flexibility in setting prices.

FIGURE 20.2

Number of Buyers/Sellers and Their Influence on Market

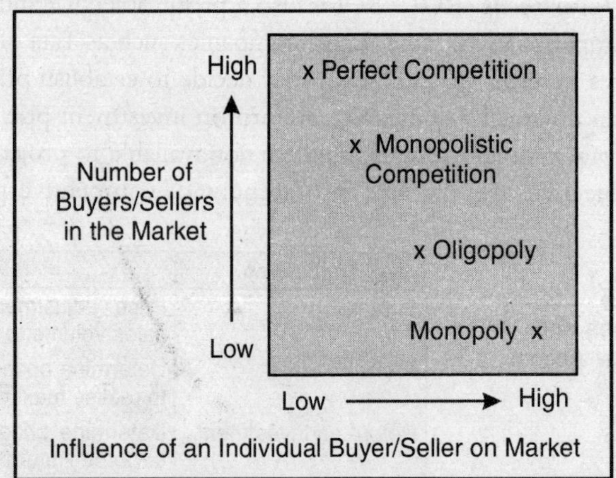

A non-regulated *monopoly* can set prices at any level it determines to be appropriate. However, in case of regulated monopoly there is less pricing flexibility and the company can set prices that generate a reasonable profit. In case of *oligopoly,* there are few sellers and market-entry barriers are high, such as auto industry, computer processor industry, mainframe-computer, and steel industry etc. If an industry member company raises its price, it hopes others will do the same. A similar response is likely to result when a company reduces its price in an attempt to increase its market share, other companies too follow suit and the initiator company gains no appreciable advantage. *Monopolistic* market structure means numerous sellers with differentiated offerings in terms of tangible and intangible attributes, and brand image. This allows a company to set different price than its competitors. In most successful cases, the nature of competition is likely to be based on non-price factors. Under *perfect competition* there are very large number of sellers and buyers perceiving all products in a category as the same. All sellers set their prices at going market price as buyers are unwilling to pay more than the going market price. Sellers have no flexibility in price setting.

PRICE SETTING PROCEDURE

The steps involved in price setting include:

(1) Development of Pricing Objectives

(2) Determination of Demand

(3) Estimation of Costs

(4) Examining Competitors' Costs, Prices, and Offers

(5) Selecting a Pricing Strategy

(6) Selection of Pricing Method

(7) Final Price Decision.

Development of Pricing Objectives

In the beginning of this chapter various pricing objectives have been looked at. Developing pricing objectives is necessary because all subsequent decisions are based on objectives. Objectives must be consistent with company's overall objectives and marketing objectives. As stated earlier, companies generally have multiple pricing objectives keeping in view their short-term and long-term interests. No company can remain satisfied with just one unchanging pricing objective. All companies typically alter their pricing objectives over time in response to changes occurring in the market-place. In terms of priority of objectives, most companies set their pricing objectives in terms of profit optimisation, market share, or return on investment.

Determination of Demand

Demand determination of a product is the responsibility of marketing manager, aided by marketing research personnel and forecasters. Demand and competition typically set the upper limits of price. Demand forecasts furnish estimates of sales potential of a product reflecting the quantity that can be sold in a specified period. These estimates help in examining the relationship between product's price and the quantity likely to be demanded.

The Demand Curve: For most products, there is inverse relationship between price and the quantity demanded. Higher the price, lower the demand and vice versa. As price goes down, the quantity demanded goes up. When the price is raised, the quantity demanded goes down. This fundamental relationship continues as long as the marketing environment, consumers' buying power, willingness to buy, and authority to buy remain stable.

FIGURE 20.3

Classic Demand Curve Showing Price-Quantity Relationship

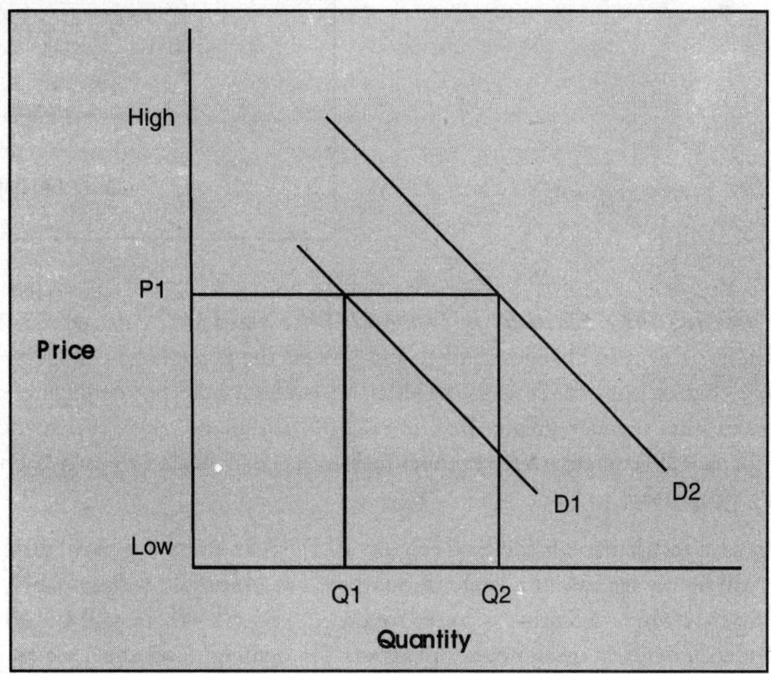

The classic demand curve (Figure 20.3) (*D1*) shows the expected quantity of a product that will be sold at different prices, provided other factors remain constant. Demand of a product depends on other factors in the marketing mix that include product quality, promotion, and distribution. Some kind of improvement in one or more of these factors may shift the demand to, say, demand curve (*D2*) and an increased product quantity (*Q2*) will be sold at the same price (*P1*).

There are certain exceptions to the classic demand curve that do not conform to this concept. In stock markets, when the share prices decrease, the demand for the specific shares also decreases and demand increase with rising prices of shares. Another illustrative example relates to ego intensive or prestigious products such as perfumes or lifestyle products that sell more at high prices than low prices. Such products are viewed as desirable mainly because their use reflects buyers' status. If the prices of Rolex watches or Channel No. 5 perfume fall drastically, these products will most probably lose their status appeal.

Figure 20.4 presents the relationship between price and quantity demanded in case of status reflecting or prestige products. When the price is raised from (*P1*) to (*P2*), the quantity demanded increases from (*Q1*) to (*Q2*). Even in case of prestige products, beyond a certain price level, if the price is raised steeply the quantity demanded goes down from (*Q2*) to (*Q1*). In case of such products, price has direct relationship to demand within a certain tolerable range.

FIGURE 20.4

Price/Quantity Relationship for Status Products

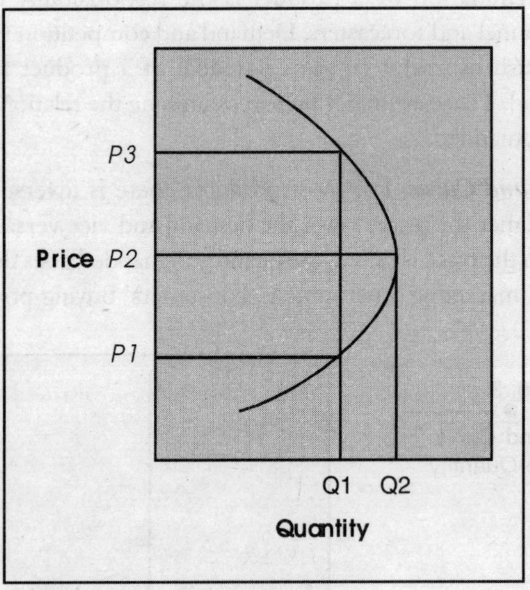

Assessing Price Elasticity of Demand: Price elasticity of demand helps in examining the extent of demand sensitivity to changes in price and reflects the percentage change in quantity demand relative to per centage change in price. In case the demand is elastic, the per centage change in demand due to a small change in price is much greater than in case of inelastic demand. If demand is elastic, lowering of price by a company will generate more revenues as long as costs related to manufacturing and marketing do not rise out of proportion.

In case the demand is inelastic (Figure 20.5), when there is a small raise in price, say, from (*P1*) to (*P2*), there will be no significant change in demand. For essential products, such as water supply, electricity, and cement etc., when the price is raised from (*P1*) to (*P2*) there will be no significant change in quantity demanded. For most discretionary products the demand is elastic such as low and medium segment cars, or furniture etc., the quantity demanded decreases considerably from (*Q1*) to (*Q2*) if the price rises sharply from (*P1*) to (*P2*).

Price setting can be a little easier after determining price elasticity of demand. An examination of the total revenues as prices change can give a fair idea whether a particular product demand is price elastic or inelastic. If the demand falls by 10 per cent by raising the price 2%, then the price elasticity of demand is – 5. The negative sign shows inverse relationship. If the demand falls by 3% when the price is raised by 6%, the price elasticity of demand is – 1/2. In case the demand is less elastic, the company can benefit by raising the price.

$$\text{Price Elasticity of Demand} = \frac{\%\ \text{Change in Quantity Demanded}}{\%\ \text{Change in Price}}$$

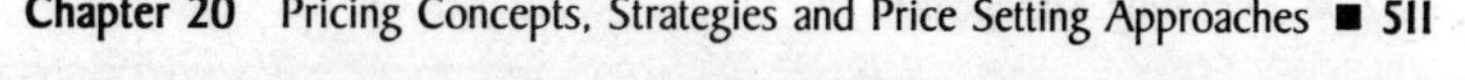

FIGURE 20.5
Demand Elasticity

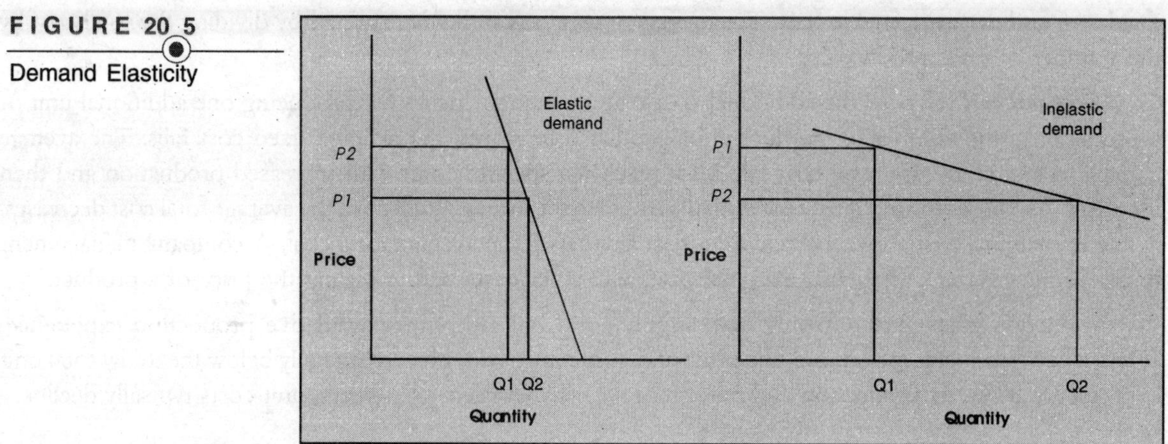

As a result of availability of many alternatives in a given product category and ever increasing competition, consumers are becoming more sensitive to prices. Customers' price sensitivity varies and demand curve reflects the probability of what product quantity the target market is likely to purchase at different prices. Price elasticity can change over time and over price ranges. It can also be different for a price decrease than a price increase because elasticity is the result of consumer behaviour. Generally, customers' show very high levels of price sensitivity in case of products that they buy frequently or products that cost more. They are less price-sensitive to low-cost items or those they buy infrequently. For some types of products, consumers consider initial purchase cost, operating cost, and maintenance cost for the total period of ownership. Thus, a car may be priced higher, but it may give high fuel efficiency, and involve low maintenance cost. Customers often consider the *total costs of ownership* and in such cases may show less price sensitivity to initial purchase cost. Generally, customers with higher incomes show less price sensitivity to products that are viewed as positively distinctive; have more quality, prestige, and exclusiveness.

Estimation of Costs

Over the long-run, prices must exceed average unit costs to earn a profit. Cost set the lower limits of price. The reality of free market economy is such that customers now pass up certain brand names in case they pay less without sacrificing quality. The purpose of price setting for a company is to set a price to cover costs involved in a product's production, selling, and distribution and some desired level of profit for its efforts and risks. A product's costs set the lowest point below which a company would not set price and demand sets a ceiling on the price.

Fixed costs do not vary with changes in the number of units produced or sales revenues. The cost of hiring a production facility does not change if a company switches from one shift to two shifts in 24 hours, or because the company sells its total increased produced quantity. *Average fixed cost* is calculated by dividing the fixed costs by the total number of units produced.

Variable costs, as the name suggests, vary directly with the level of product quantities produced or sold. Such as, the extra costs that occur because of wages for a second shift, the costs of more raw materials, and electricity etc., to produce more quantities represent variable costs. Variable costs are usually constant per unit. The *average variable cost* per unit produced is calculated by dividing the total variable costs by the number of units produced. The average variable cost is typically relatively high at the start but gradually declines as a company achieves efficiencies in production and purchasing. The average variable cost again rises at some point in time as company hires more workers and purchases more materials to produce more units.

Total cost is the sum of total fixed cost and total variable cost. *Average total cost* is the sum of average fixed cost and average variable cost. The average total cost can be determined by dividing the total cost by the number of units produced.

Marginal cost refers to the additional cost that a company incurs for producing one additional unit of a product. As the number of product units produced increases, the average fixed cost falls. The average variable cost and average total cost fall, till it reaches a specific point with increased production and then increases. As long as the marginal cost remains less than the average total cost, the average total cost decreases. A rise in marginal cost above average total cost also raises the average total cost. A company management must examine average total cost, marginal cost, and other costs before setting the price of a product.

Production costs vary not only with supply costs but also with cumulative production experience. When a new product is introduced, the price may sometimes be set just marginally below the initial total unit cost (Figure 20.6). As production and sales improve, say between 1 – 3 years, unit costs typically decline.

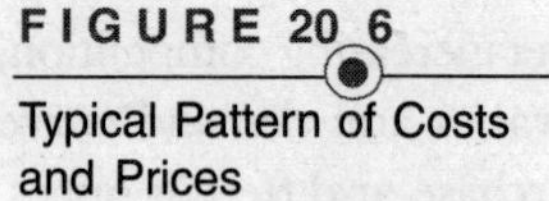

FIGURE 20.6

Typical Pattern of Costs and Prices

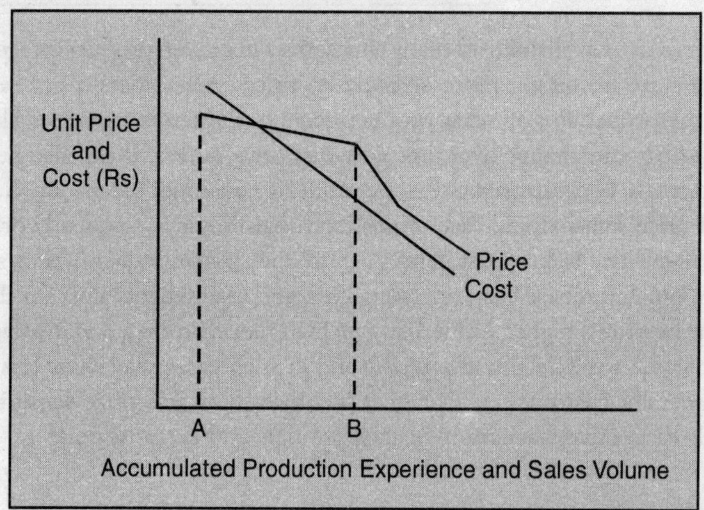

A company can earn high profits at least in the short-run if the price does not reflect these declining costs. As the prospects of high profits attract competition, the prices settle to a more reasonable level above costs. Between A and B (Figure 20.6) costs decline at a rate that is greater than decline in price. This results because of experience and economies.

Break Even Analysis is the point at which the cost of making a product is equal to the revenue generated from selling that product. If a watch manufacturing company has total annual costs of Rs. 1000,000 and in the same year the company sells Rs. 1000,000 worth of watches, it has broken even. An illustration of relationship of costs, revenues, profits, and losses involved in determining the breakeven point is shown in Figure 20.7. We can see in the illustration that at 40000 units sold, the company breaks even.

$$\text{Break Even Point} = \frac{\text{Total Fixed Cost}}{(\text{Unit Price} - \text{Average Variable Cost})}$$

Total Cost = Rs. 40,00,000.

Unit Price = Rs. 400

Average Variable Cost = Rs. 300

$$\text{Break Even Point} = \frac{40,00,000}{(400 - 300)} = 40,000$$

FIGURE 20.7

Break Even Analysis

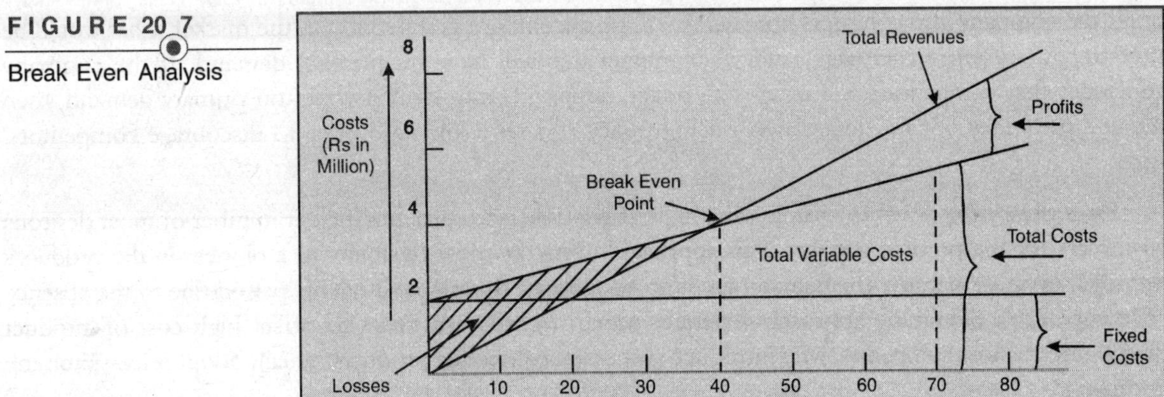

Examining Competitors Costs, Prices, and Offers

Examining the market demand and company costs, a range of possible prices can be considered. However, the company must also examine the cost, prices, and possible responses of competitors in the industry. Learning, competitors' costs, prices, and offers is an ongoing function of marketing research. When one company dominates an industry, it may set the tone for price decisions in the industry, such as De Beers Consolidated Mines Ltd., or Intel in case of computer processors. The company must appreciate that other companies in the industry can change their prices in reaction to prices set by the company. Obviously, the nearest competitor is the first choice to consider for setting a price. The first step is to ascertain what positive differentiation features the company's offer contains and not offered by the nearest competitor. The second step is to a ascertain the worth of additional positive features to consumers and this worth should be added to the competitor's price to set the company's product price. If the worth of positive differentiation features of competitor's product is more and the company's product does not have those features in its offer, then the value should be subtracted from competitor's price for setting the company's product price. This exercise can help whether to keep the price higher, or lower than the competitor, or the same.

Selecting a Pricing Strategy

A pricing strategy is a course of action framed to affect and guide price determination decisions. These strategies help realising pricing objectives and answer different aspects of how will price be used as a variable in the marketing mix, such as new product introductions, competitive situations, government pricing regulations, economic conditions, or implementation of pricing objectives. More than one pricing strategy may be selected to address the needs of different markets or to take advantage of opportunities in certain markets.

There are many different strategies companies adopt for accomplishing pricing objectives. Some of the important ones and often used are discussed here.

New Product Pricing

The base price of a new product is easily adjusted in the absence of price control by government. A pioneer can set the base price high to recover product development costs quickly. While setting the base price, the company also considers how quick will be the entry of competition in the market, what would be the strength of entry campaign, and what impact this will have on primary demand. If the company concludes that competitors will enter with heavy campaign, with limited effect on primary demand, then the company may opt for penetration pricing policy and set a low base price to discourage competitors' entry.

Price skimming refers to charging the highest possible price that a sufficient number of most desirous customers for the product will pay. This approach offers the most flexibility to a pioneer in the product's introduction stage because the demand tends to be inelastic during most of this period due to the absence of competitors. Skimming approach generates much needed cash flows to offset high cost of product development. Most companies, who introduce successful pioneering products, usually adopt price-skimming approach.

Price skimming can generate quick returns to cover up the product's research and development costs. This strategy restricts product's market penetration because only the most desirous customers buy the product. Possibility of earning large margins encourages competitors to enter the market.

Penetration pricing approach requires the price to be set less than the competing brands and aims at market penetration to capture large market share quickly. Companies adopt this strategy when the demand tends to be elastic. Sometimes companies use penetration pricing to rapidly capture a large market share. Increased demand makes it necessary to produce more and this decreases per unit production costs. Low unit production cost puts the marketer in an position of advantage to further decrease the price, and thereby make it difficult for aspiring new competitors to enter the market. Besides, a low unit price is likely to be less attractive to competitors because the lower per unit price results in lower per unit profits. With this approach it becomes difficult to raise price subsequently. Some marketers initially skim the market and later set a penetration price. A lower price makes the market less attractive to potential new entrants.

Psychological Pricing

Psychological pricing approach is suitable when consumer purchases are based more on feelings or emotional factors rather than rational, such as love, affection, prestige, and self-image etc. Price sometimes serves as a surrogate indicator of quality. Technological advancements are making product differentiation difficult and many companies attempt to differentiate their offers based on non-functional product attributes, such as image and lifestyle etc. Psychological pricing is not appropriate for industrial products.

Marketers set artificially high prices to communicate a status or high quality image. This pricing method is appropriate for perfumes, jewelry, autos, liquor, and ready-to-wear garments etc. John C. Groth and Stephen W, McDaniel found that marketers use prestige pricing and consumers associate a higher price with higher quality. Acer and Sony have adopted this type of pricing for their range of Ferrari and Vaio Lifestyle notebook PCs. Apple adopts this method of pricing for its high-end PowerBook laptop computers. This pricing method requires creation of strong brand image through promotion programmes that reinforce the brand's quality and image of total exclusiveness.

Price perceptions are significantly influenced by the brand's perceived quality and extent of advertising. Paul W. Farris and David J. Reibstein studied 227 consumer businesses to examine the relationships among relative price, relative quality, and relative advertising and found that:

- Brands with high relative advertising but with average product quality were able to charge premium prices successfully than brands that were relatively unknown.
- Brands with both high relative advertising and high relative product quality could charge the highest prices. Brands with low ad budgets and low quality realised the lowest prices.

- The positive relationship between high relative advertising and high relative product quality was very strong during later life cycle stages for market leaders.

Odd-Even Pricing: Marketers sometimes set their product prices that end with certain numbers. The assumption is that this type of pricing helps sell more of a product. It is supposed that if the price is Rs. 99.95, consumers view it not as Rs.100 and certain types of consumers are attracted more by odd prices rather than even. This assumption is not supported by substantial research findings, but still odd prices seem to be far more common than even prices. Also, supposedly even prices favour exclusive or upscale product image and consumers view the product as a premium quality brand.

Promotional Pricing

Companies can choose a variety of pricing techniques to motivate consumers to buy early. As the name suggests, these techniques are considered as an important part of sales promotions. Some of these techniques include loss leader pricing, special event pricing, low-interest financing, longer payment period, cash rebates, free auto insurance, warranties, increased number of free services, etc. Generally, these techniques do not lead to significant gains because most competitors can copy them in a hurry: To illustrate, just three techniques are briefly discussed.

Loss Leader Pricing: Sometimes large retail outlets use loss leader pricing on well-known brands to increase store traffic. By attracting increased number of consumers to store the retailers hope that sales of routinely purchased products will rise and increase sales volume and profits. This compensates for the lower margins on loss leader brands. Firms whose brands are chosen as loss leader oppose this approach as the image of their brands, gets diluted and consumers resist paying list price to retailers selling the same brands.

Superficial Discounting: It is superficial comparative pricing. It involves setting an artificially high price and offering the product at a highly reduced price. The communication might say, "Regular price was Rs. 495, now reduced to Rs. 299." This is a deceptive practice and often used by retailers. Occasionally we come across advertisements that show Rs. 495 crossed (X) and a fresh price written as Rs. 250.

Special Event Pricing: This involves coordinating price cuts with advertising for seasonal or special situations to attract consumers by offering special reduced prices. For example, before the beginning of a new session for young children at school, we see ads of shoes generally viewed as part of uniform.

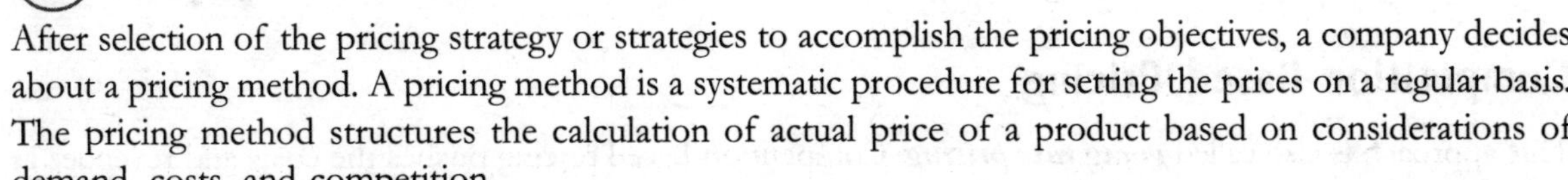

Selection of a Pricing Method

After selection of the pricing strategy or strategies to accomplish the pricing objectives, a company decides about a pricing method. A pricing method is a systematic procedure for setting the prices on a regular basis. The pricing method structures the calculation of actual price of a product based on considerations of demand, costs, and competition.

Cost-Based Pricing

Cost-based pricing methods are fairly common. Price is determined by adding either rupee amount or a percentage to the product's cost to achieve the desired profit margin. Cost-based pricing methods do not take into consideration factors such as supply and demand, or competitors' prices. They are not necessarily related to pricing policies or objectives.

Markup Pricing: In markup pricing a certain predetermined per centage of product's cost, called *markup,* is added to the cost of the product to determine the price.

Let us suppose a watch manufacturer has the following costs and sales forecast:

Fixed Costs = Rs. 40,00,000

Average Variable Cost Per Unit = Rs. 300

Forecasted sales = 40,000 units.

The watch manufacturer's unit cost is given by:

$$\text{Unit Cost} = \text{Average Variable Cost} + \frac{\text{Fixed Cost}}{\text{Unit Sales}} = 300 + \frac{40{,}00{,}000}{40{,}000} = \text{Rs. } 400$$

If the watch manufacturer aims to earn 20 per cent markup on sales, the markup price is given by:

$$\text{Markup Price} = \frac{\text{Unit Cost}}{(1 - \text{Desired Rate of Return})} = \frac{\text{Rs. } 400}{(1 - 0.2)} = \text{Rs. } 500$$

The watch manufacturer would sell its watches to resellers at Rs. 500 per unit and earn a profit of Rs. 100 on each unit sold. If the resellers want a markup of 20 per cent on their selling price, they would sell for Rs. 625 per unit. Prescription drugs are generally sold at very high markup prices. Manufacturers also use markup prices on speciality items, and seasonal products.

***Target Return Pricing* (Cost-Plus):** Some companies use target-return pricing method and find out the price that would ensure a certain fair rate of return on investment (*ROI*).

Supposing the watch manufacturer has invested Rs. 8 million in business and wants a 20 per cent return on investment.

Then the target-return price can be calculated by:

$$\text{Target Return Price} = \text{Unit Cost} + \frac{\text{ROI} \times \text{Capital Invested}}{\text{Forecasted Unit Sales}}$$

$$= \text{Rs. } 400 + \frac{0.2 \times \text{Rs. } 80{,}000{,}000}{20{,}000} = \text{Rs. } 1200 \text{ Price Per Unit}$$

The watch manufacturer will get 20 per cent ROI if the company sells forecasted units. With the help of breakeven analysis, the company can examine different prices and their likely affect on sales volumes and profits. This method ignores considering price elasticity as well as competitors' reactions to prices.

Competition-Based Pricing

This approach is also called ***going rate pricing***. Competition-based pricing pushes the costs and revenues as secondary considerations and the main focus is on what are the competitors' prices. This pricing acquires more importance when different competing brands are almost homogeneous and price is the major variable in marketing strategy, such as cement or steel.

Depending on the level of product differentiation a company can achieve, the company can keep the price higher, lower, or the same as the nearest competitors. This approach may make it necessary to adjust prices frequently. However, this approach can help to keep prices stable in the industry.

Demand Based Pricing

Companies using this method mainly consider the level of demand. The price is high when the product demand is strong and low price when the demand is weak. This approach is fairly common with hotels, telephone service companies, and museums etc. The marketer must be in a position to accurately estimate the product amount consumers will demand at different price levels. Demand based pricing can help a company to achieve more profits if consumers perceive product's value sufficiently above its cost. Demand based pricing can be favourable when the company is able to accurately estimate demand at different prices, and it is often quite difficult to forecast the demand accurately at different prices.

Perceived-Value Pricing

Many companies perceived-value pricing. In this approach the price is based on customer's perceived value of a product or service. The company must deliver the promised value proposition, it communicates to its target customers. And of course, it is important that customers must perceive this value. Marketers carefully use different elements of promotion mix to communicate effectively and enhance customers' perception of product or service's perceived value.

Customers' perceptions of value depend on elements such as company image, trustworthiness, reputation, product performance, quality assurance, channel members' image, warranty, post sale services etc. Also, much would depend upon, how much importance each customer places on these different elements. Depending on individual customer's value assessment some will be loyal buyers, some will be value buyers, and still others will be price-buyers. Companies adopt different strategies for these groups. Loyal buyers, companies work hard to build relationship. For value buyers, companies make efforts to keep innovating new value and effectively communicate this. For price-buyers, companies offer a stripped down product and few services. Some companies have a uniform policy of offering high-quality products at lower prices. Zenith Computers has this policy and offers good-quality desktop and laptop computers at lower prices.

Product Range Pricing

Many companies sell a range or line of products and price of each individual item should consider the prices of other products in the range.

Optional Additional Items: These additional items or features a customer may or may not choose to add to the main product purchased. The basic stripped-down product carries a low price, and the margin on additional components is more. For example, some computer and auto companies keep a lower price for the basic model and for additional components such as *LCD* monitor, larger *RAM*, power windows, or power steering etc., charge additionally.

Captive Product Pricing: Some companies produce products that need the use of ancillary products such as razors and manufacturers of Inkjet or Laser printers. Gillette manufactures different types of razors and for each type the company has different blades that fit a particular type of razor. The razor is priced low but the margins are high on blades. Inkjet or Laser printer manufacturers sell their printers at a low initial price and price their ink or toner cartridges at a price to earn higher margins.

Two-Part Pricing

This pricing method is fairly common with service providing companies. They charge a fixed price for providing the basic service plus a variable usage rate. For example telephone service providers charge a monthly fixed price plus variable per call charges for calls beyond a certain number. Internet broadband service providers charge a fixed amount for cable model installation and variable charges for number of usage hours. The pricing decision for such firms involves problems about deciding how much to charge for the basic service and what rates should they keep for variable usage. The fixed price should be at a level that would attract sufficient number of customers and profits can be earned through varying usage charges.

Bid Pricing

This type of pricing involves submitting either a sealed or open bid price from the marketer for buyer's consideration. The buyer notifies potential suppliers to submit their bids by a fixed date. The buyer evaluates these quotations in terms of quoted prices, product specifications, and the ability of suppliers to deliver specified products according to the buyer's schedule when and where needed. Usually the lowest bidder is awarded the contract. Generally, central, state, or local government departments, and construction companies use this method.

Discount Policies

Discounts refer to reductions from list price that a seller gives to buyers. These buyers either give up some marketing function or provide the function themselves. Discounts can be useful in developing marketing strategy. Marketers use various types of discounts. Some of them include the following:

Sellers offer *quantity discounts* to *encourage* customers to buy more quantities. The seller gets one or more of the advantages such as getting more of customer's business, shifting some of the storing function to buyers or reducing selling and shipping costs. Cumulative quantity discounts apply to total purchases over a given period of time – such as one year – and the discount increases with the increase in purchase quantity. Cumulative discount encourages customers to repeat purchase and reduces the customer's cost for additional purchases. This helps build customer relationship and loyalty. A *cumulative quantity discount* is generally attractive to business buyers who don't want to increase their inventory costs. Individual orders are smaller but the total quantity purchased during the given period goes up. *Non-cumulative discount* is applicable to individual orders. This type of discount encourages buyers to buy larger quantities in one go and the buyer is not obliged to repeat purchase from the same seller. Such a discount is usually a price cut, but sometimes it can be in the form of free goods. *Seasonal discount* encourages customers to purchase earlier than present demand requires. This can help fluctuating sales to stabilise. This type of discounts helps manufacturers to shift storing function further along the channel. *Cash discount* is a reduction in price and aims to encourage business buyers pay the bills quickly. A *trade* or *functional discount* refers to price reduction given to resellers for the job they are going to perform. Trade discount is offered by manufacturers to wholesalers and/or retailers, and by wholesalers to retailers and is deducted from the suggested retail price to cover their cost for retailing function and their profit margin.

Allowance Policies

Allowances are like discounts and offered to consumers or channel members either to do something or accept less of something.

Advertising allowance is given to resellers to encourage them to advertise producer's products in the local market. ***Stocking allowance (slotting allowance)*** is offered to resellers to get the shelf space. A producer sometimes offers ***push money*** (SPIFFS) to sales people of a wholesaler or retailer for aggressively selling the company's particular products. A ***trade-in (exchange) allowance*** is given when customers bring in used durable products and buy the company's similar new products. This is an easy way to reduce the effective list price.

Price Discrimination

Many companies sell the same product or service to different customer groups at different prices. Price discrimination enables some customers or segments to pay less. This brings in more overall contribution to company than if one price is charged to all. For example, Indian Railways offers reduced railways fares to senior citizens. Some airlines offer reduced fares to more frequent users of their service, or passengers in luxury and economy class pay different fares. Some companies charge reduced prices for larger quantities purchased, or many branded computer sellers offer students and teachers their products at reduced prices. Coca-Cola supplies its coke to McDonald's at reduced prices. To practice price discrimination for short-term, sales promotion techniques, such as coupons, or short-term discounts etc., are also used.

Changing Prices

No matter how carefully a product's price has been set, there would be occasions in a product's life cycle to change the existing price for a variety of reasons such as need for additional business, product improvement, sales slow down, loss of market share, competitive pressures, economic conditions, and change in government policies etc.

A company may require price increase because of over-demand, and cost inflation squeezing profit margins. Under favourable market conditions, a company raising its brand's price successfully can earn substantial profits. For example, if the existing profit margin is 3 per cent of sales, an increase of just 1 per cent in price will mean a rise of 33.3 per cent in profit margin if there is no change in sales volume (see Figure 20.8).

Before increasing or decreasing the price of a brand, the company must consider possible reactions of the customers, competitors and others.

Consumer's interpret price decreases, or increases, in different ways based on their perceptions that vary considerably. Their perception about price being high, fair, or low has significant influence on their buying intentions and post-purchase satisfaction. For example, seeing the explosive growth of cheap ballpoint pens, Parker Pen introduced low-priced pens. To say the least, the results were quite discouraging because Parker's image was inconsistent with low-priced pens. Price decrease may also be perceived as indicating that the product is not selling well, the company is facing some financial trouble, it is not of high quality, or a new model would replace the existing one and the company is trying to clear the existing stocks. An increase in brand's price could be interpreted that the quality has been improved, or customers really like the brand and consider it offering high value. Many consumers perceive that high-quality products tend to cost more and price increase may become an indicator of higher quality. A careful analysis of price elasticity, company and brand image, availability of substitutes etc., can help the company in determining the possible effects of price rise or decrease.

FIGURE 20.8

Positive Effect of Price Increase under Favourable Conditions

Existing		After 1 per cent Price Increase
Price	Rs. 20	Rs. 20.20 (1 per cent price increase).
Sales	1000 units	1000 units.
Revenue	Rs. 20,000	Rs. 20,200.
Costs	Rs. 19,400	Rs. 19,400.
Profits	Rs. 600	Rs. 800 (Revenue – Costs).
Increase in profits		33.3%.

Competitors in an industry with limited number of players are most likely to react if the product is homogeneous and consumers are knowledgeable about the category. A company must attempt to judge how other companies in the industry will interpret and react. If the company is a leader, others may simply follow the leader. When leaders face a price-cut attack from smaller companies in the industry, they consider several options such as to maintain existing price, maintain price and add value, decrease the price, increase price and improve quality, or launch a low-priced fighter line. The appropriate response would depend on careful analysis of market situation, product's importance for the company, its stage in life cycle, competitor's objectives and resources, and consumer sensitivity toward quality and price etc.

In general, the kind of responses from leaders or followers include no change, limited change, or a move to match or exceed the change made by the competition. Competitors may respond with a combination of price and non-price changes such as heavier promotion or addition of new product features, or service benefit.

Final Price Decision

Final price setting is guided by company's pricing policies. The final price is set according to company's pricing objectives and the needs and wants of target customers to accomplish the marketing and company objectives.

Summary

Price setting is a very critical area in marketing mix decisions of a company. It is the only element that generates revenues for the company, and all others involve only costs. The aim of marketing is to facilitate satisfying exchanges between the marketer and consumers at a profit.

Pricing should never be seen as an isolated component of a company's marketing decision-making. Companies spend large amounts of money on product development, promotion, and distribution and face risks. Price is often the only marketing mix element that can be changed quickly to respond to changes in demand or competitive moves. Developing new products or modification of existing products, any changes in promotional programme, or distribution system involves much time and efforts.

In any economy, price influences the allocation of resources. In case of individual firms, price is a major factor that determines the success of marketing efforts. In many purchase situations, price is an important factor to consumers that influences the value of a product or service. But defining price precisely is very difficult. In general we can think of price as the money and/or other items with utility needed to acquire a product or service.

For most companies, setting prices can be a complex task involving both scientific analysis and intuitive trial and error. Pricing objectives focus on what a company wants to achieve through establishing prices. Survival is the broadest and most fundamental pricing objective of any firm because staying in business is important under difficult conditions such as overcapacity, intense cut-throat competition, and changing consumer wants and preferences. Many companies set profit maximisation as their pricing objective but because of certain difficulties, maximisation objective is rarely set and companies settle down to a profit figure or some per centage change over previous period that its decision-makers view as optimum profit. Return On Investment (*ROI*) is also a profit objective and aims at achieving some specified rate of return on company's investment. This pricing objective is set by trial and error because all relevant cost and revenue data are not available to project the *ROI* at the time of price setting. A large number of companies establish their pricing objectives in terms of market share, they want to capture of the total industry sales. The objectives can be to maintain existing market share or increase in percentage terms. Companies want to maximise market share believing that a higher sales volume will consequently bring down unit cost and lead to higher profits in the long-run. A company may have the pricing objective to be a product quality leader in the industry and set the product price high to communicate high product quality.

Besides pricing objectives, other important factors that influence price setting relate to various aspects of market structure, such as demand, competitive reactions, marketing mix strategies for elements other than price, and costs.

A pricing strategy is a course of action framed to affect and guide price determination decisions. These strategies help to realise pricing objectives and answer different aspects regarding to how will price be used as a variable in the marketing mix, such as new product introductions, competitive situations, government pricing regulations, economic conditions, or implementation of pricing objectives. More than one pricing strategy may be selected to address the needs of different markets or to take advantage of opportunities in certain markets.

There are two approaches for setting price of a new breakthrough product: Price skimming and penetration pricing. Price skimming means the company charges a price that customers who are in dire need of the product, will pay. Penetration price is a lower price charged to penetrate the market and capture a large sales volume quickly. Psychological pricing aims to encourage purchases that are based on emotional rather than rational responses. Promotional pricing approach means that it is coordinated with promotional efforts.

A pricing method is a mechanical procedure for setting prices for specific products on a regular basis. The methods include cost-based pricing, demand-based pricing, and competition-oriented pricing. In case of cost-based pricing, accompany determines price by adding a monetary value or percentage to the cost of the product. This cost-based approach includes two common pricing methods – cost-plus and mark-up pricing. Demand-based pricing relates to the level of demand for the product. When the product demand is strong, the price is high, and the price is kept low when the demand is weak. In case of competitor-based pricing, costs and revenues become secondary to competitor's prices.

No matter how carefully a product's price has been set, there would be occasions in a product's life cycle to change the existing price for a variety of reasons such as need for additional business, product improvement, sales slow down, loss of market share, competitive pressures, economic conditions, and change in government policies etc. Before raising or decreasing the price of a brand, the company must consider possible reactions of customers, competitors and others.

Final price setting is guided by company's pricing policies. The final price is set according to company's pricing objectives and the needs and wants of target customers to accomplish the marketing and company objectives.

Questions for Discussion

1. There is usually inverse relationship between the price of a product and the quantities sold. Explain the reasons for this kind of relationship.
2. Does product quantity demanded always decrease when the price is raised? Illustrate your answer with examples.
3. Discuss price elasticity of demand for commodities, shopping products, and status products.
4. What important factors should a marketer consider before setting a product's price?
5. Using examples, discuss the advantages and disadvantages of cost-plus pricing.
6. What is breakeven analysis? Why is it important?

7. What is price skimming? Under what conditions price skimming and price penetration is advisable?
8. Discuss psychological pricing strategy. Illustrate with examples the application of psychological pricing strategy.
9. Compare cost based and demand based pricing methods with examples.
10. What is promotional pricing? What are its advantages and disadvantages?

Projects

1. Choose a company of your choice and show how it uses price discrimination.
2. Go to a manufacturing company and study the price setting procedure it adopts. Evaluate its strategic approaches and methods.
3. Visit retail stores and determine how they decide retail prices for cosmetics range and men's ready-to-wear range.

Bibliography

1. Donald Lichtenstein, Nancy M. Ridgway, and Richard G. Netemeyer, "Price Perceptions and Consumer Shopping Behaviour: A Field Study," *Journal of Marketing Research,* May 1993.
2. John C. Groth and Stephen W. McDaniel, "The Exclusive Value Principle: The Basis for Prestige Pricing," *Journal of Consumer Marketing,* 10 (1993).
3. Paul W. Farris and David J. Reibstein, "How Prices, Expenditures, and Profits are Linked," *Harvard Business Review,* (November-December 1979).

Cases

Case 6.1: The Big Advantage

Ten-year old Praveen is hooked on to Candico's big Bubble Gum after his cousin introduced him to it a few months ago. Now he asks retailers only for the big Bubble Gum. The reason: "It is the only bubble gum with which I can blow large bubbles. Ask my friends," he says. Loyalty from numerous such children has enabled Candico to become India's number one bubble gum company. Candico (I) Ltd., part of the Sancrop Group, ran full page advertisements in November, 1999, with claims of selling 60 lakh bubble gum pieces a month. Competitors such as Perfetti and Jayco have not responded to these claims. It is this silence, which Candico sees as a vindication of its stand. The vehicle behind its stupendous success has been big Bubble Gum, the 50 paise gum. Launched in June 1999, the market for big Bubble Gum exploded in a span of five months.

What is the winning formula behind this magic?

Shivkumar, chairman and managing director Candico, goes back into history to find the answer. "The company was conceived in 1976, the confectionery division being launched in 1986. The company split up into Candico (I) Ltd., (confectionery) and Bakeman's (bakery products) in 1996, as we realised that liberalisation had unleashed great potential in both these sectors and we needed to focus on each."

Candico was chosen as the company name as it was 'easy, pronounceable and promised top-of-the-mind recall.' Candico has a world-class plant in Nagpur spread over an area of 250,000 sq. ft. This plant can manufacture four of the five categories of confectioneries that Candico is into, namely sweets, candies, mouth fresheners and gums. The company is not into chocolates – though it is a growing market – because of logistical problems.

The plant with a capacity of 40,000 tonnes per year is, according to Kumar, "the largest in this part of the country, West Asia and South Asian countries." The plant is totally imported. Interestingly, Candico even has a manufacturing arrangement with Nestle and Nutrine, its competitors. This speaks volumes of Candico's trustworthiness as a quality manufacturer. Kumar adds in a lighter vein, "In the market, I ask my employees to kill their products but we give them complete quality during manufacturing."

To get its message across, Candico launched a Young Consultants Programme (YCP) in 1997. The company invited responses for recruiting 12 children as product consultants. These children were supposed to sample, taste and design new products, and were to receive of Rs. 24,000 per annum for their services. Full-page advertisements were run. The campaign reached a readership of eight lakh. Though the target audience was children it appealed to elders who, in turn, passed on the message to their children. The company derived a two-pronged benefit following this strategy. It got publicity, and collected a database of three lakh. Kumar admits candidly, "If we had said, we are going to make bubble gums, no one would have noticed." This database helps the company in market research. Every product, which goes on the floor, is tested against this target audience group. The company makes it a point to update this databank constantly and it receives 30 – 35 letters daily from children. Candico responds to every letter and birthday cards are sent out signed personally by Kumar. Candico had two options before it embarked on its strategy. First, take on Perfetti and Jayco head-on, which would have meant spending huge sums on promotional campaigns. The other option was correspondence with 18,000 children. 10,000 questionnaires were sent out enquiring about the price, look, colour and flavour they preferred.

Contd...

The answers showed that children were comfortable in the 50-paise slot. If the company could give a bubble gum, it was giving its customers value for money. Based on this feedback, Candico launched big Bubble Gum. The lower price enabled Candico to take on the unorganised sector and, more importantly, it captured a large part of the market as 'it was giving the quality and size of a rupee at 50 paise'. Candico, with its lower pricing strategy has targeted the 2,100 tonnes a month market for bubble gums in one rupee segment. Extra costs on marketing and sales were cut. Company's margins were cut, which were advanced to the consumer. "MNCs would not be able to afford this cost so we will be able to maintain market share," is Kumars's judgement on the matter.

Has the company compromised on quality due to low prices? Kumar counters the claim by saying, "We have a technical collaboration with Eurobase, a Belgium company, which provides us with the base of bubble gum." A wholesale pack of big Bubble Gum displays this prominently, as an assurance of quality. Candico's main competitors are Perfetti and Jayco. Perfetti has Centre Fresh and Big Babool. Jayco has Boomer. All these are priced at Re. 1 a piece.

Candico's logic is simple. If children can be satisfied at half the price, the rupee segment would be wiped out. According to Kumar, "Perfetti sells 910 tonnes per month, Candico 525 tonnes per month, while the rest of the 2,100 tonnes a month (organised market) is held by Jayco, Chicklets, and Wrigley's. The unorganised market is difficult to compute. Candico's share has increased multifold since big Bubble Gum's launch in June 1999. Inane sounding names such as Loco Poco (means 'mad' in Spanish), Jumbo Gumbo, Americano, Freedom, and big Bubble Gum for its products have been chosen with a purpose. Kumar says, "Bubble gum is not a serious buy, it is leisure buy, so simple names such as Freedom, which is an expression of an attitude have been used. We want to be in the mind before we are on the shelf."

Advertising and promotions are an important part of Candico's market strategy. Six per cent of the company's outlay is spent on advertising and promotions. Candico's advertising account is being handled by Ambience. The brief is to project Candico as 'a sweet company.' This would carry Candico beyond being a mere bubble gum company. The target market is composed of children in the age group of 4 to 17-years. Candico has gone for promotions in a big way. For instance, customers can exchange six wrappers for a postcard of their favourite star (cricketers and film stars). For retailers, the company offers over 250 kg of silver in the shape of 51,000 silver coins and other prizes to be won. A prize coupon inside every dispenser enables retailers to win prizes.

The company's marketing team keeps a track of the happening trends and preferences of children. As bubble gums are casual purchase, customers are not bound by brand loyalty. Grabbing their attention is a challenge. And grabbing the attention of kids is not child's play. Freebies such as tattoos, stickers, cricketers' and film start's posters fulfil their role as magnets quite admirably. The company's database from the YCP also helps it keep a tab on changing customer preferences. Kumar says, "The marketing team has to constantly think about innovation. We fail sometimes, but most of the time we succeed." Kumar is not boasting when he says that.

Candico has 1,000 distributors and a reach of around 2.2 lakh retail outlets. It is trying to increase this by 25 per cent in the next three to six months. The company has a marketing field force and distribution team of 250 each. Its marketing infrastructure covers all the major states for all its products. Moreover, the company is zeroing in on the SEC B and SEC C categories.

This enables Candico to reach out to a larger group. Kumar explains, "It is not as if we cannot reach out to higher income group, but we realise that volumes lie in the categories which we are

Contd...

targeting." What about the rural areas then? As of now, Candico's products are easily available in towns with a population of 25,000. In towns with a lesser population, Kumar says, "We are there but these areas are not very well covered. But we can double or triple our coverage in these places."

Candico is also looking at export markets earnestly. At present, the company is going for the countries in South and West Asia. Explaining the rationale, Kumar says, "The buying pattern in these countries is more or less the same as in India. Moreover, these are growing markets. We are getting requests to manufacture for the American markets, but presently we do not have the line and energy to go into these markets as a private label." Candico is presently exporting to Nepal, Srilanka, Bangladesh, and the Maldives. Achal Khaneja, deputy general manager Candico says, "We export 90 tonnes a month to Nepal (ten trucks). In the rest of the markets we are close to 90 tonnes."

Over the years, high levies on bubble gum have been a major grouse for manufacturers of this product. Though taxation on bubble gums is 16 per cent compared to eight per cent on other confectioneries, Candico is not perturbed. "It is still a virgin market and as we have not covered enough, I have no reason to complain. Only when the market reaches saturation can I ask for the Government help," is what Kumar feels.

Candico presently has a turnover of around Rs. 84 crore. Since it is also into private labelling, Candico's share would come to around Rs. 75-76 crore. In 1996-97 and 1997-98, Candico's turnover was Rs. 65 crore and Rs. 74 crore respectively. Though Candico is into gums, sweets, candies and mints, it is concentrating on bubble gums. Kumar admits candidly, "As it is not possible to devote equal attention to all the categories simultaneously, our primary focus is on gums. Once we have carved a niche in the gums arena, we will concentrate on other categories."

And what are the plans for future? Candico plans to include seven to ten products every year to ensure a growth rate of 40 per cent per annum. Its plan of achieving a target of over 200 crore by the turn of the century now seem far fetched. Pontificating on the future, Kumar says, "We have not touched even the tip of the iceberg. We have capacities for growth for the next three years. Our Nagpur plant manufactures 825 tonnes per month, and with minor equipment balancing this can go up to 1,000 tonnes."

According to the projections made in a recent report by consultancy firm McKinsey, the Indian confectionery market will grow to Rs. 6,400 crore (present estimates peg the market at Rs. 1,500 crore) by 2005. "As long as Americans teach us the American way of life, bubble gum sales are here to stay and boom," jokes Kumar. "More seriously," he adds, "chewing has always been a part of Indian tradition, we are only converting it into a pocket holding opportunity." Candico's big Bubble Gum, illustrates the point being made by market analysts for years. In a country like India, the road to success involves, targeting volumes with low-priced goods. In that case, Candico has the right ideas.

QUESTIONS

1. What are the significant issues in the case?
2. Evaluate Candico's strategy. What external factors have been kept in mind while developing the strategy?
3. Is the competitive advantage of Candico sustainable in the long-run? Explain.

Case 6.2: When Fortune Smiles

hat helped a new entrant become a market leader in the edible oils market?

In just three years, a new brand — launched by a new company — has become the leader in the Indian edible oils market. Adani Wilmar Limited (AWL) introduced the Fortune brand of soya oil at the end of 2000.

By December 2003, the brand had slid into the top slot — with 17.25 per cent of the 265,706 metric tonnes edible oils market — dislodging the erstwhile leader Agrotech Foods, which slipped to a 12.9 per cent volume share.

"AWL just swept the market," admits a rival. Another executive from a competing company describes the Fortune brand as an "overnight behemoth".

How did AWL (a 50:50 joint venture between an Indian export company, Adani, and Singapore-based oil traders, Wilmar Trading) earn such a formidable reputation and reach such a position?

It was a mix of all elements like product differentiation, backward integration and entering the market at the right time.

What really helped the new entrant gain a foothold in the slippery oil market was a carefully planned back-end system that was in place before the late 2000 launch. At that time, the competition had varied sourcing models.

For instance, Marico Industries, which markets brands like Saffola and Sweekar, followed flexible sourcing models: A large part of what Marico markets, is refined at its own refinery, while the rest is outsourced.

Others like Agrotech (sellers of Sundrop) outsourced their entire manufacturing process, while the GCMMF (Gujarat Cooperative Milk Marketing Federation), marketer of the Dhara brand, owns eight to 10 refineries across the country.

In contrast, AWL opted for an integrated manufacturing model that would allow it to control the entire manufacturing and packaging process.

"Our main learning from existing players was that there was enough scope to cut down on expenses like logistics and operating costs," says Pranav Adani, executive director, AWL.

That's where the choice of location proved critical. AWL's parent company, Adani Exports, already co-owned, with the Gujarat government, a port at Mundra, in Kachchh district of Gujarat.

So AWL invested Rs 150 crore and set up its oil refinery at Mundra. The port was connected to the refinery and packaging plant through a pipeline. (Competitors, in contrast, operated out of hinterland-based refineries and transported oil from the port to the plants through trucks.)

The pipeline delivered several benefits. First, there was minimum spillage of oil during transportation from one facility to another.

Then, logistics costs at the production-end were also done away with. That immediately brought down AWL's logistics costs to 10 or 15 per cent lower than the competition. Company sources say that this helped shave off a rupee from the selling price of a litre of oil.

Contd...

Crucially, the proximity to the port and the pipeline helped slash AWL's time-to-market — after the crude oil reaches the port, it takes the company 10 to 15 days to get the final product to the market.

Otherwise, claim company officials, the time-to-market would shoot up to 30 days. The result: AWL's operating costs were 8 to 10 per cent lower than competition. "The integrated manufacturing set up is AWL's biggest advantage," says one competitor.

AWL had the infrastructure in place, but a critical question was still unanswered: Which category should it enter? It was easier to see the paths it shouldn't take. The maximum competition was in sunflower oil, which accounted for 59.3 per cent of total volumes.

The largest-selling edible oil brands were also sunflower oils: Agrotech's Sundrop, which had a 15.8 per cent share, and Marico's Saffola and Sweekar, which together accounted for 11.8 per cent of the total market.

If Fortune were to make a quick impact, it would have to choose a market close to its production facility, which would help leverage the cost advantage. But the market for mustard oil was in north and east India and, while the west preferred groundnut oil, brands like Dhara were too well entrenched there.

So, AWL decided to enter soya oil. "Our pre-launch market surveys had shown that there was a clear need for a lighter, healthier and affordable oil. Soyabean oil fitted the bill," says Anghsu Mallick, general manager, sales and marketing, AWL.

Also, competition in the segment was limited — soya oil was just about 11 per cent of the edible oils market in 2000. The only organised players in the category were Ruchi Soya Industries (its brand Ruchi had an 18 per cent market share) and Agrotech (Crystal, 5 per cent).

"Most players shied away from the soya segment after the failure of Vital," points out a market observer. The reference is to a Godrej Foods' brand that was launched in the late 1980s and flopped dismally.

One reason for Vital's bombing was the odour of soya oil: The oil's fishy smell put off many potential consumers. AWL kept this in mind before launching Fortune.

"If we had to grow the market for soya oil, we had to make it smell and taste as good as sunflower oil," says Mallick. The company found that the reason for the smell was that soyabeans required more deodorisation than other oilseeds.

So AWL introduced a "double deodorisation process" at its refinery. The process involved deodorisation of refined oil at two different temperatures, while other refineries deodorised at a single temperature.

AWL began by test-marketing Fortune in Rajasthan. "It was a good test market: Rajasthan is a soya-consuming market, and it is close to the refinery," recalls Mallick.

But the next step was to set up a distribution network. By 2001, AWL had roped in 600 distributors with a reach of 90,000 outlets (now 2,200 distributors and 300,000 outlets). Then AWL focused on B- and C-class towns where big brands are considered expensive.

Even now, 70 per cent of the 2,200 AWL distributors are from small towns. "We tried to pick more distributors who had the resources but did not deal with big companies," explains Mallick. This ensured that distributors would pay more attention to promoting the new brand.

Contd...

Price was also critical in drawing in consumers. Thanks to rising international prices of sunflower oil in the late-1990s — close to half the sunflower oil consumed in India is refined from imported crude oil — prices of sunflower oil brands in India rose from an average of Rs 40 a litre to Rs 60 a litre between 1998 and 2000.

Sundrop hiked its prices by 40 per cent during that time and, as admitted by an Agrotech official, "market shares did suffer as a result of that."

Soybean prices, however, did not increase as much. The price differential between soya and sunflower was widest in early 2001, when soybean was roughly $325 and sunflower was roughly $500 per tonne (Crude prices). Leveraging the cost advantage, AWL priced Fortune soya oil at around Rs 40 a litre, which was almost Rs 15 lower than the competing sunflower oils.

"This price difference meant a lot to the discerning housewife, so the brand gained presence quickly," says a market observer.

AWL's pricing strategy — which it later carried over to its brand extensions — was simple enough. The product was launched at a price significantly lower than the competition, which was later brought on par with the market price.

"Lower prices induce customers to switch, but our market research also indicates that they equate dirt-cheap prices with bad quality. Once we grow to account for at least 25 per cent of the market, we increase the prices," says Mallick.

It also helped that AWL padded Fortune's entry with a heavy advertising campaign where it spent nearly Rs 35 crore in the first two years as it took the brand national.

The budget was big enough to ensure Fortune was noticed, but it was also to AWL's advantage that, at the time, no other soya oil brand had a noteworthy presence on television. And the sunflower oil brands like Saffola, Sweekar and Sundrop were being promoted on the health platform.

Initially, therefore, Fortune's communication emphasised the lightness of the oil, rather than direct health benefits. The storyboard of the first campaign, which was launched in May 2001, featured a newly married man dreading a heavy meal at his parents-in-law's home.

But, to his surprise, he wolfs down much more than he expected, since the food is cooked in — naturally — Fortune soya oil. The jingle sang "Fortune Hai Light. Thoda aur chalega." (Fortune is light, so a little more is welcome).

The cans started flying off the shelves almost immediately. Between January and March 2001, 1972 metric tonnes of Fortune soya oil were sold, equal to the then leading soya brand, Ruchi.

By June end of that year, Fortune sales had shot up to 2,802 metric tonnes, overtaking Ruchi, whose sales declined to 827 tonnes. In the first year of launch (January-December 2001), AWL garnered a 35 per cent volume share of the soya market; by 2003, that figure had gone up to 47 per cent.

Meanwhile, the soya oil segment has grown within the total edible oils market, from 30,640 metric tonnes in 2001 (11 per cent of the total market) to 80,422 metric tonnes in 2003 (30 per cent of the market). "The steadily growing market shares do suggest that Fortune was able to override the taste apprehensions related to soya," says the market analyst.

Contd...

A new advertising campaign in February 2002 also contributed to AWL's good fortunes. This time round, the communication showed a doubting housewife to play up the health benefits of soya, turning the spotlight on Omega 3 (a compound in soybean oil that is beneficial for the heart, eyes and skin); the term found instant recall with consumers.

"The campaign was aimed at driving away all apprehensions associated with soya oil," says Jayesh Ravindranath, executive director, Triton, the ad agency for Fortune.

Meanwhile, AWL had moved ahead to the next logical step. In September 2001, the company entered regional markets in other oil categories such as double-filtered groundnut and cottonseed, all under the Fortune umbrella. "In the Indian market, you can't be a national brand if you overlook regional markets," explains Mallick.

Initially, regional variants were pushed piggybacking on the equity created by the advertising for the soya brand.

"The overall advertising for the Fortune brand centered around the goodness of the soybean variant, although no variant was specifically mentioned in any of the advertisements," a rival points out. For instance, the doubting housewife campaign played up the Omega 3 aspect, while showing other variants at the end of the commercial.

Now, however, the communications approach is changing. "We realise that we cannot over-focus on one success," accepts Mallick. Soya may be the flag-bearer for the company but it may not necessarily do well in regional markets that are skewed towards other tastes like mustard or groundnut.

In this case, Fortune soya can piggyback on the strength of other variants in regional markets. For instance, the company launched its raw mustard oil variant — Kachi Ghani — in August 2003 and is propping it with exclusive television campaigns in east India.

But problems could soon creep in. As its brands have grown, AWL has abandoned the low price strategy — and with it, its biggest advantage. The health plugs, too, seem to have been forgotten — the recent forays into mustard oil and vanaspati (hydrogenated vegetable oil) have drawn criticism from industry observers.

Mallick defends the decision. "Largely, 'healthy' oils in the Indian context also mean nutritious, not just light. And we can't ignore regional tastes if we want to be a national brand," he says.

That's an ambition that is yet to be realised. AWL is yet to make a mark in the southern markets, which leans towards consumption of sunflower and coconut oil.

In fact, sunflower oil continues to dominate the edible oils market in India, accounting for 44 per cent of the total market (although that's lower than its 59 per cent share in 2001).

At present, AWL accounts for only 4.5 per cent of national sunflower oil volumes, while the south-based Kalisuri Mills (which owns the Goldwinner brand) leads the market with a 26 per cent market share, followed by Agrotech , which hogs 21 per cent of the volumes. And it is this category that could well decide whether Fortune will retain its sheen.

If Fortune kicked up action at the lower end of the market, competitors have brushed up their act at the other end. Curiously, none of the competitors has plunged into the soya segment, in spite of the lure of volumes.

Contd...

"Segments like soya mean low margins. Our focus is the top-end of the market, where our margins are much higher," says Harsh Mariwalla, chief executive officer, Marico.

Instead, most oil manufacturers are pinning their hopes on blended oils to change their fortunes.

Marico Industries has already tried its luck in the blended oils segment in 1998 with "Tasty Blend", a corn and kardi blended variant of its 40-year-old brand Saffola (which at Rs 99 a litre, is the costliest brand in the market).

Marico took another shot at the premium-blended market with the recent launch of Saffola Gold. Company sources don't rule out the possibility of more launches in the premium blend segment.

While Marico has successfully tied in its blends with its existing brand, Agrotech's brand name — Sundrop — isn't proving as amenable to variations: The association with sunflowers is too strong.

Instead, it launched various blends with sunflower oil: Sundrop Nutrilite (sunflower and soya) was launched in 2001, while Sundrop Super-Lite (sunflower-palm blend) was launched the following year.

Recently, a premium rice and sunflower variant was also launched. "The blended oil variants are helping us recover our market share," confirms a company source. Clearly, it helps to blend well.*

(All figures from the AC Nielsen Retail Audits).

(Source: www.bsstrategist.com June 18, 2005).

QUESTIONS

1. Identify the major issues in this case.
2. Analyse the pricing strategy for Fortune. Do you notice any weaknesses? Explain.

Case 6.3: Dell Uses Price as a Competitive Weapon

Michael Dell, just a student selling made-to-order personal computers over the phone from his dormitory room at the University of Texas, had a huge ambition of taking on IBM. In 1984, Dell quit his studies to pursue his quest full-time. He had only $1000 as seed money.

Dell Computer's share in the domestic PC market had crossed that of IBM by the end of 1996. Dell was the leader by 2001 with more than 25%, surpassing Compaq's 13%, HP's 10%, and 8% of Gateway's.

Dell's meteoric rise has revolutionised the industry. Dell created a new business model. Instead of focusing on the usual strategy for computer companies of product innovation, Dell's approach focused on keeping the prices low and delivery times short.

Dell buys components directly from manufacturers, assembles them to meet individual customer's specifications, and then delivers the product in record time. Rather than selling products through retail outlets, Dell relies on direct sales approach and catalogues. Additionally, Dell has embraced the Internet like no other company. Today, Dell sells computer equipment of worth over $50 million via web every day.

Dell's success has compelled its competitors to reconsider their business strategies. In order to compete with Dell, other PC makers are compelled to reduce their prices and employ methods to cut down their costs. Profit margins are shrinking across the industry, and many analysts wonder whether (a) Dell will be able to continue decreasing its prices to gain market share, and (b) whether any competitors will go out of business trying to keep pace.

Michael Dell adopted the direct sales model and was able to eliminate middlemen, keep prices low, and make product deliveries faster than its competitors. In 1988, Dell Computers sold its stocks in public. By 1993, Dell Computers became one of the five top manufacturers of PCs in the world. Its stock, which sold originally for $8.50 per share, was worth $100 in 1995.

Dell was one of the first companies to sell its products over the Internet, www.dell.com in 1996. Meanwhile Dell Computers continues to expand into foreign markets, such as Central America and China, and introduces new products like workstations and network servers. Dell Computers, which became the top sellers of PCs in 2001, has now revenues in excess of $50 billion.

The advent of the Internet facilitated the direct sales approach of Dell Computers also had given it a means of reaching customers and suppliers. Dell computer uses the Internet not only to promote and sell but also orders components and parts from numerous, sometimes even on an hourly basis. Using the Internet for procurement has facilitated Dell Computers to keep very low inventory and deliver made-to-order PCs with pre-loaded software in as little as three days. Customers are delighted because they get what they want and Dell is not left with any unwanted computer stocks.

Dell maintains stock for just four days of operations, while Compaq carries stocks for 24-days. This difference gets translated into enormous cost advantage for Dell. Besides, Dell has the advantage of delivering finished product fast, it collects payments from clients before long it pays suppliers. This would mean that the company would make money as a result of its positive cash cycle even if it did not turn a profit on its product sales.

Contd...

Dell Computers maintains close contact with its suppliers and is able to pass along cost savings to its customers in as little as one day. A Dell executive explained, "Michael focuses relentlessly on driving low-cost material from the supplier through the supply chain to our customers." Once Michael Dell noticed that one supplier had brought pastries to a meeting. Michael Dell complained, "Take those back and let us knock the price off the next shipment of materials you bring in. We don't need food. We want a better price." Dell's emphasis on cost control, has led to expense ratios that are much lower than competitors. Dell Computer's ratio of ten cents for every dollar compares favourably to 21 cents for HP.

In an attempt to capture more market share, Dell slashed prices by 20% in late 2000, forcing competitors either to follow suit or lose sales. Many competitors tried to match Dell's prices, but changed their tactics within a few months. Most companies were forced to lay off employees. By 2001, the market shares of Compaq, Hewlett-Packard, and Gateway had dropped and Dell's share increased by almost one-third.

Compaq was the market leader and had been aggressively slashing the prices as well as cutting down the inventory and increasing direct sales efforts. Dell had enormous cost advantage and Compaq was unable to keep up with Dell, and was acquired by Hewlett-Packard in September 2001.

Gateway has been persistent in its efforts to match Dell. Gateway returned to profitability in 2001 by focusing on higher-margin products, and decided to aggressively recapture the market share it had lost in the PC sector. In early 2002, Gateway announced another round of price cut on its brand of PCs. It did sell more units, but because of the lower prices, generated less revenue, and in turn, incurred big losses.

Both, IBM and HP declared the price war "irrational," elected to lose market share rather than reduce prices and harm profitability. Dell's assault was well timed. The economy and stock market were declining, making investors and analysts to accept lower earnings reports. Consumers too had become more price-sensitive and were eager to find the best deal. Despite price slashing, by late 2001 Dell was still profitable with earnings of $1.8 billion for the year. The rest of the players lost in excess of $2 billion. Michael commented, "When we sell these products, we make money. When our competitors sell them, they lose money."

Dell apparently gained on its competitors, but according to some observers the company may have paid a heavy price to do so. The profit margins for Dell slid down to less than 6% of saies and all those competitors who tried to match Dell's prices also experienced similar declines in margins. Dell too was forced to cut down 5,000 jobs.

Way back in 1992 when the PC was still in its growth stage of life cycle, Compaq slashed prices in its efforts to be the leading PC seller in the United States. The company achieved its objective and increased its revenues, but profitability suffered and never returned to its original levels. Today, the PC seems to be in its maturity stage of life cycle, making it difficult to increase sales. The PC segment is saturated to a great extent, and corporate users are keeping their larger computers for longer periods of time before upgrading. One industry analyst observed, "It used to be that you quote prices and people would buy more. There aren't customers for their stuff at any prices."

Significant product innovations are one way to boost sales, but declining profits are discouraging investments in technology. Compaq's R&D spending fell from 6% of revenues in 1991 to 3.5% in

Contd...

2000. Two years later Compaq suspended development of its Alpha chip as a result of budget limitations. Dell spends just 1.5% of revenues on R&D. It seems price competition is killing any significant innovation. Dell executives claim that the company is being innovated by developing new cost cutting methods. Others in the industry disagree. The CEO of Sun Microsystems puts it bluntly, "Dell is a grocery store. They are not in the PC business any more than Safeway is in the food manufacturing business."

It actually appears like grocery business because Dell is counting on selling other organisation's innovations. Intel and Microsoft, two of Dell's suppliers will continue putting substantial amounts of money into R&D. Dell plans to incorporate the advances they come up with in its products with higher profit margins. In a totally different move, Dell decided to offer an unbranded desktop PC to dealers that primarily serve small enterprises in the United States.

Dell Computer is always interested in expanding its share of PC market. When it had nearly 25% of the domestic market and 16% of the global market, Dell started looking for new ways to increase its revenues. Dell has been traditionally a strong player in the corporate sector, but after it slashed its price in 2001, many consumers discovered Dell for the first time. Taking advantage of this trend, Dell began running a new series of commercials featuring "Steven" and the tagline, "Dude, you are getting a Dell." Also knows as "The Dell Guy." Steven (played by Benjamin Curtis) became a popular spokesperson for the company. Michael Dell even started personally promoting company's products on OVC, the home-shopping channel. These efforts have facilitated Dell more than double its share of the global consumer PC market from 7% in 200 to 16% in 2002.

In their efforts to improve profitability several of Dell's competitors, including IBM, and HP are using new approaches for pricing products other than PCs. Dell has recently acquired selling space within the stores of major retailers such as Sears. As Dell establishes new distribution approaches, readies new products, and targets new markets, other companies in the computer industry may have to be more creative and come up with better pricing strategies to be competitive in the industry.

QUESTIONS

1. Study the case and identify Dell's pricing objectives. What is likely to be the impact of Dell's pricing approach on the computer industry?
2. In your view, how should the competitors respond to Dell's pricing policy?

Case 6.4: Procter & Gamble Tries New Pricing Strategy

Seven consumer goods firms, including Kraft, General Food, Quaker Oats Co., and Colgate-Palmolive are experimenting with pricing strategies that appear to achieve the same goals as everyday low pricing. But most of these firms deny they are initiating everyday low pricing strategies. Not to be confused with everyday low pricing by retailers like Wal-Mart Stores, the strategy used by manufacturers, eliminates the varying prices they offer retailers as a part of trade promotion deals. Proctor & Gamble, however, did use everyday low pricing, when it reduced the listed prices on many of its best-selling brands.

The goal of Proctor & Gamble's everyday low pricing strategy is to give better value to consumers who have suffered through a recession. But although the strategy is designed to give greater value to consumers, many retailers have openly protested. Vice President of corporate affairs by Big Y Foods said, "We are not happy with Pig's everyday low pricing programme. It takes away our flexibility as a retailer. Basically, P&G is saying we have one option – take it or leave it. We are therefore leaving it when we can."

Most warehouse clubs and mass merchandisers prefer to everyday low pricing. On the other hand, many supermarket chains, including Jewel Food Stores and Supermarket General's Path mark, have publicly or privately expressed dissatisfaction regarding Proctor & Gamble's policy. Those retailers who operate with a "high-low" prices with frequent specials are particularly upset.

Proctor & Gamble has felt the pressure but says it will not back out. The firm believes that, the programme will benefit everyone – Proctor & Gamble, retail stores, and consumers – because it results in lower operating costs and lower prices. In theory, the strategy frees trade promotion money for additional promotional spending directed toward consumers. Proctor & Gamble put the Tide and Cheer detergent brands under the everyday low pricing programme; the entire laundry detergent line is now under the plan.

Most other packaged goods marketers are watching Procter & Gamble and silently applauding its efforts. They also favour everyday low pricing as an alternative to expensive trade promotions, but do not have the resources to weather the potential backlash from retailers. Many companies are testing pricing programmes with different names but all designed for the same reason, to reduce trade promotion spending and increase promotion to the final consumer. Meanwhile, the entire industry is hoping that P&G is successful.

(Source: Based on a case study in Marketing, 2nd ed. by Steven J. Skinner).

QUESTIONS

1. Study the case and determine the significant issues in the case.
2. Examine the pricing practice of P&G. Do you think it can spoil P&G's relation with retailers and harm the company in the long-run?

PART 7

CHAPTER 21
Product Life Cycle

CHAPTER 22
Competition Analysis and Strategic Options Across PLC Stages

Cases

Product Life Cycle

CHAPTER 21

LEARNING OBJECTIVES

After going through this chapter, you will understand:

- Different stages through which most products pass during its existence.
- Each stage depicts particular market behaviour towards the product and accordingly sales volumes increase or fall.
- There are different strategic options for each stage of a product's life cycle.
- Implications of the product life cycle concept

Some called it the ultimate in design from Apple Computer. Forget the good-looking iMacs that were a hundred times better than the plain-vanilla desktop personal computers. This was even better. Priced in India at Rs. 122,130, this computer was probably the smallest desktop computer, packing in the most power. It was equipped with a 450 MHz processor, 1 MB to 1.5 MB RAM, 20 GB hard drive, DVD video, and operated at a processing speed of 4 gigaflops (where anything over 0.6 gigaflops is termed as supercomputer). "Just five years ago, supercomputers of about the same power cost around Rs. 10 crore, but all that has changed now," said Naren Ayyar, managing director - SAARC countries, Apple Computer International Ltd.

The G4 Cube in itself was a breakthrough in computer design. It was extremely quiet, with a noise level of only 19 decibels. This was due to the absence of an electric fan for cooling, that's usually present in all other computers, and accounts for the trademark hum.

The Apple G4 Cube instead used a simple principle of physics to cool the computer. The computer had about an inch of free space below it, covered on three sides, but open at the back through which air entered. On the top of the computer was a vent. The centre of the computer was hollow, and all the components were built around it. The simple principle of hot air rising from the vent above cooled the computer. Connections to the Cube were made without any clutter at the base of the machine, by means of simple connectors. Getting on to the Internet too, did not require too many connections, due to Apple's patented 'Airport' wireless Internet connectivity.

To go with the Cube, Apple also had a sleek, transparent keyboard, and a new transparent mouse. The mouse was also a breakthrough in design, as it did not incorporate the standard trackball that's present in other mice. Instead, it used an optical sensor to judge movement in any direction. So much so, that each time the mouse was moved it gave off a red light, that made it look very futuristic. Then again the entire surface of the mouse had been made click-able, thereby making it versatile to various users. The mouse moved by scanning the surface on which it was placed 1,000 times per second, and hence could judge movement in any direction. This made it much more accurate than the traditional mouse, as well as, virtually maintenance free.

The speakers that came with the system too, were revolutionary, and were manufactured using Harman-Kardon audio technology, that made for the good audio quality. Apple offered a choice of displays with the Cube, ranging from 17 inch studio display, a 15 inch studio display, and a 22 inch full flat cinema display, ranging between Rs. 32,600 up to Rs. 310,590. These display units have pure clean lines and are see - through in design.

(Author's note, "It seems apple had introduced a product that was highly advanced and unique in many respects in its time. However, for some reason the Apple's G4 Cube did not click and was discontinued in its introductory phase. It had a very brief life cycle. As the experts say, the rate of failure new products is extremely high and more than 80 per cent products fail.")

Source: Based on an article by Roshun Povaiah, A & M, October 15, 2000.

There is general agreement that products have life cycle much the same way as living organisms do. This concept of life cycle applies to product category, sub-category, and brands in the sub-category. For example, computer represents a product category; desktop, and laptop represent product sub-category, and Apple

PowerBook, and Sony Vaio are brands in the sub-category. A product is introduced among consumers, and if consumers perceive it as meeting their needs and want, it experiences a period of growth. Subsequently, it reaches the stage of maturity and when it loses its appeal, its decline starts and eventually is may be taken off the market (demise). The classical product life cycle curves are depicted as "S" shaped and generally divided in four stages: Introduction, growth, maturity, and decline. Some authors distinguish more than four stages. For instance, Chester W. Wasson views an additional stage of *competitive turbulence* or shake-out at the end of growth period and just before the start of maturity phase. During this competitive turbulence, the growth rate starts declining and leads to strong price competition. This may force some companies to exit the industry or sell out.

Many products do not follow the typical life cycle pattern because of discouraging results just after introduction phase. Other products never seem to die such as autos, TVs, telephones, steel, and cement etc. The shape of life cycle curve may differ considerably from the typical "S"-shape among industries and within industries. J. E. Swan and D. R. Rink have identified as many as twelve different types of life cycle curves. Within an industry generally one or very few life cycle curves are typical. Probably, the most common phases are growth-decline plateau (Figure 21.1) since a large majority of products are in their maturity stage, such as home appliances. The most common example of *cycle-recycle* pattern can be observed in products of pharmaceutical companies where products are promoted heavily at the outset. Heavy promotion is repeated when sales seem to drop. *Innovative-maturity* or scalloped pattern portrays situations when new innovative features are added or new uses are discovered as has happened in case of Scotch tape and Nylon over the years. The *classical "S" curve* describes those products that pass through all stages to their demise, such as many prescription drugs.

Other special product life cycle variations concern *style, fashion,* and *fads*. Kotler defines a style as representing a basic and distinctive means of expression that appears in a field of human endeavour, such as formal, or causal clothing. Chester Wasson defines fashion as a currently accepted style in a given field that a large number of customers adopt. The life cycle of products in fashion is unpredictable. Fads are a kind of fashion that people adopt very quickly, with great enthusiasm, the fads climb the peak of tide early, and their decline is equally fast.

The concept of product life cycle is concerned with the sales history of a product. It portrays the changes in sales and profits over time. Most products generally follow the classical "S" shaped curve when their sales are pitted against time. It is necessary to assess the life cycle of a product category and sub-category while examining the life cycle. Often the product sub-category has greater relevance than its category while studying the life cycle of a product. The fact is that the life cycle of a brand has to be studied along with its sub-category, and category to have a clearer picture. Examining the life cycle of Apple PowerBook or Sony Vaio would make sense only when it is studied along with the life cycle of laptop computers. Studying life cycle only at a particular brand level without taking into account the product sub-category's position would not consider the entry and exit of competitors, additional resources deployed by them, and their marketing strategies.

FIGURE 21.1 Common Product Life Curves

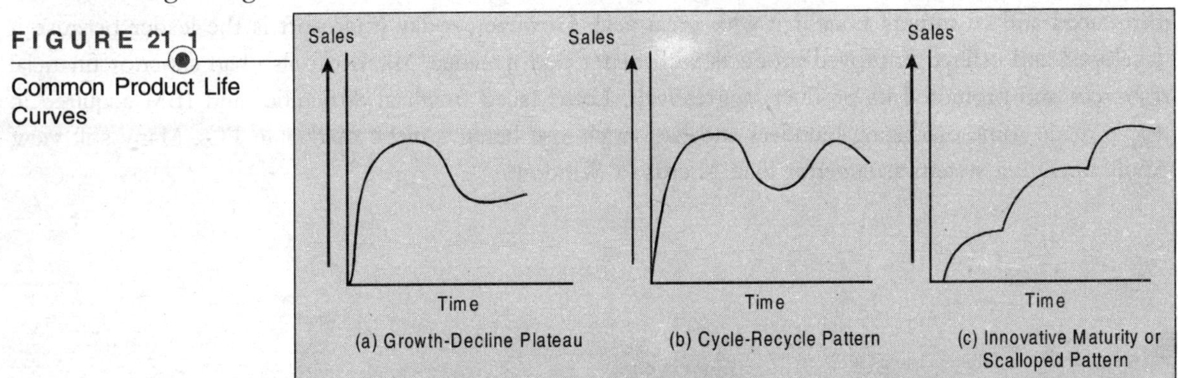

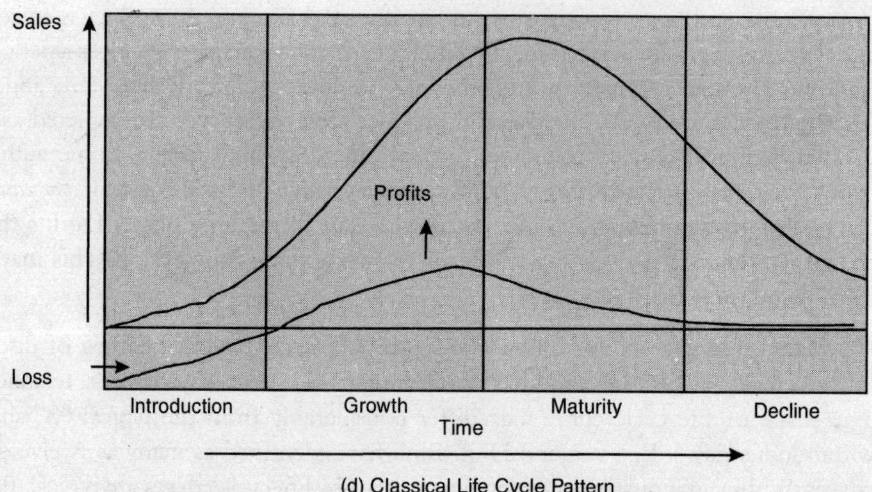

(d) Classical Life Cycle Pattern

It is interesting to note that profits from a product are highest before the sales peak. This means that sales maximisation does not necessarily get translated into profit maximisation. Profits maximise before the sales are highest because the intensity of competition increases at the end of growth period and before the start of maturity stage. This is what has been referred to as competitive turbulence. Most competition is generally from followers and tends to attract consumers from product pioneer with low prices, additional features, better service, larger distribution, and larger promotion outlay such as advertising and sales promotion. To maintain its market share, the pioneer fights back competition and has to spend more money on adding features, marketing communications, and distribution, or even price reduction to remain competitive. All these activities eat away the profits.

Whether to Be a Pioneer or Follower?

The question whether to be a pioneer or a follower often confronts companies. Being a pioneer can be highly rewarding, but entails high risks and expenditures. Entering the market as a follower can also turn out to be advantageous if a company can bring in superior technology, and higher quality.

Many research reports support the view that being a pioneer or "first-mover" offers several key advantages. A study conducted by Gregory S. Carpenter and Kent Nakamoto found that 19 out of 25 firms who were leaders in 1923 stayed as leaders even after 60 years.

There are also examples of successful followers, such as Microsoft who was not a pioneer with products like Word, Excel, and Powerpoint. Lotus 1, 2, 3 was the leading spreadsheet software, WordPerfect and other programmes led the word processing category, and Apple's Macintosh was the first affordable PC introduced and customers bought it with great zeal. However, today Microsoft is the leader because it developed and offered improved products with better performance. Microsoft also had superior financial resources and promoted its products aggressively. Lotus faced financial difficulties and IBM acquired it. Apple made some marketing blunders and had to choose being a niche marker in PCs. Many still view, Apple operating system as superior than Microsoft Windows.

FIGURE 21.2

Pioneer and Follower Advantages

Pioneer		Follower
1.	First choice of market segments.	• Can bring in superior technology.
2.	Influence on consumer attitudes and choice criteria.	• Can take advantage of pioneer's product mistakes.
3.	Pioneer defines the rules of the game.	• Ability to take advantage of pioneer's positioning mistakes.
4.	Switching costs higher for early adopters of pioneer's product.	• Ability to take advantage of pioneer's marketing mistakes.
5.	Gaining distribution advantage.	• Can take advantage of pioneer's resources limitations.
6.	Economies of scale and more experience.	
7.	Possibility of pre-empting scarce resources and suppliers.	

Introduction Stage

After successful test marketing of a new product, the company introduces the product in the market with full-scale marketing programme. The introductory stage is viewed as fairly risky and quite expensive because large amounts of money is spent on advertising and other tools of marketing communications to create consumer awareness in sufficiently large numbers, and encourage trial. For truly new products, any direct competition may be very little or non-existent and the company's primary objective is demand stimulation for the category rather than its brand. Profits are mostly negative in this stage, or in some exceptional cases they may be very little.

Marketing Mix Elements During Introductory Stage: There is a vast difference between pioneering a product category and a sub-category. Introducing a product category is relatively challenging, expensive, time consuming and quite risky. For example, introduction of computers would have been extremely difficult than introducing its sub-category, PCs. This is evident from the comments made by Thomas Watson, Chairman IBM, *"I think there is a world market for maybe five computers."* Similarly, introducing telephone would have proved a challenge compared to the introduction of cellular phones (sub-category). The introduction phase is likely to be long even for relatively simple product categories such as packaged goods. Generally, product sub-category and brands appear in the market during late growth and maturity period and are likely to have shorter introductory as well as growth periods. The aim of every company is to move quickly through the introduction stage and for this research, engineering, production, are critically important to ensure the availability of quality products. The company must be able to provide promptly post-purchase service and availability of spares, if required. To encourage trial and repeat purchase, consumer goods companies use a combination of demonstrations on TV, samples, special introductory prices, and coupons. The company also tries to gain distribution and shelf space with retailers.

FIGURE 21.3

Strategy Elements Adopted by Successful Pioneers, Fast and Late Followers

These Companies ...	Adopted One or More of these Strategy Elements
Successful Pioneer	- Large entry scale. - Broad product line. - High product quality. - Substantial promotion expenditure.
Successful Fast Follower	- Larger entry scale than pioneer. - Leapfrogging the pioneer with superior: 1. Product technology 2. Product quality 3. Customer service
Successful Late Follower	- Focus on peripheral target markets or niches.

(*Source:* Simmons Market Research Bureau. www.smrb.com.)

The product line at this stage is almost always limited to one or a few to minimise production and inventory costs. During this stage, the company attempts to differentiate and position its new product to gain competitive advantage over solutions that customers were buying previously to satisfy target need and want.

Various factors affect pricing decisions of a new product, such as new product's perceived value to consumer; how fast competitors can copy it; the availability of close substitutes; the effect of price on sales volume, and costs. Generally, for a pioneering product, or a significantly improved new product, companies adopt high-price high-promotion strategy. However, depending on objectives, a company can use any one of the two important pricing strategies during introduction of a new product: Skimming pricing strategy, or penetration pricing strategy.

Skimming Pricing: For this strategic decision to be effective the product awareness is viewed as low, those who are aware or become aware are willing to pay a high price to own the product. This strategy can also be appropriate when the market size is large and not much time is available before the competition appears. Similarly, this strategy can also work in niche markets where customers are relatively insensitive to price, and owning the product is important, such as Apple computers keeps its prices high when it introduces a new product. Typically, this has been the case with computers, printers, Internet, new software, and cell phone etc. Initially, these durables and Internet services were priced quite high. The company's objective is to gain as much margin per unit as possible. This helps company to recover its new product investment relatively fast.

Penetration Pricing: This strategy allows the company to strive for fast market development and the focus is on long-term objectives of market share and profit maximisation. Price is kept low and promotion is high. The market is seen as large and characterised by intense competition, and consumers who are aware or become aware are very willing to buy the product at an affordable price. In fact, the market is viewed as price sensitive. Nirma and some other companies used this strategy in India. Most Japanese and Korean companies use this strategy. This strategy can also work when the market is large and any serious threat from competition is not anticipated. In this age of rapid strides in science and technology, the competition is almost always around the corner and it is rare to have such an opportunity. This can work with me - too product launches, but for a company that has invested millions in the development of a new product, probably it would prefer to recover its investment and earn profits early.

During introduction, particularly for mass-market, small-value products, *promotion* expenses for advertising, sales promotion, and sales force are high in terms of percentage of total sales. The foremost communication task at this stage is to build awareness about the unique features and benefits and ensure product availability. This is expensive but necessary to convince customers to try the product.

The importance of *distribution* set up is particularly significant for consumer product companies. The availability of consumer products at convenient locations where consumers generally shop for such products is quite important, keeping in view the large amounts spent on promotion to make consumers in the target market aware and induce new-product trial among customers. Most firms use their established distribution network for a new product.

Growth Stage

The growth stage of life cycle is characterised by a sharp rise in sales. Only a small percentage of new products introduced survive to reach the growth stage. Important improvements in the product continue, but at reduced rate. Increased brand differentiation is attempted primarily by adding new features. Product line expands to attract new customer segments. The intensity of competition increases, and competitors offer increased choices to consumers in terms of features, packaging and price. During the later part of growth stage, market share leader particularly endeavours to lengthen the period of growth stage by improving product quality, adding new features, lowering costs, adding new segments, and trying to increase product usage rate. Due to the combined total efforts of all competing companies, market expands and more customers start buying the product. Seeing the trends of increasing demand, more resellers are willing to carry the product and generally prices are reduced.

Near the end of this stage, there is a drop in the overall growth rate and typically the prices are significantly reduced. Generally, weaker companies start exiting the market and strong competitors capture more market share. This results in major changes in the industry's competitive structure. Strong companies evaluate their product lines and eliminate their weaker items, start promotional pricing, and strengthen their reseller relationships. What happens to a company during this period depends much on how well the product has been positioned with respect to target customers, the state of distribution system, and relative costs per unit.

Marketing Mix Changes During Growth Stage: At the *product level,* the line expands by making available products with differing features, and at different prices. The main focus now is on creating meaningful and persuasive differentiation relative to other competing brands in the category. The *prices* tend to decline, more so during competitive turbulence period because of price competition. Generally price differences among different brands narrow down. The level of price decrease would depend on cost-volume relationship, level of concentration in the industry, and the fluctuations in raw material costs. *Promotion* expenditures cover advertising, sales promotion, personnel selling etc. aimed at increasing demand for the company's brand (selective demand) and not really much concerned with category demand (primary demand) building. Companies try hard to build positive consumer attitudes toward their brand, communicating unique features and benefits. Another objective of communications is to address newly targeted segments. As a percentage of sales, costs of promotion generally decrease. However, during the later part of the growth stage, promotion costs may increase particularly for low-share consumer goods companies to maintain their distribution system by offering consumer and trade incentives. Companies try to develop their *distribution* network. This is true both for consumer and industrial companies to provide increased product availability and service at the lowest cost. Many firms now try to build some kind of direct-sales system to expand their market share. If a company succeeds in accomplishing this, it definitely puts competitors at a disadvantage. It is necessary to gain some degree of success at the distribution level before the maturity stage. Channel members often tend to disinvest in less successful brands during maturity stage.

Maturity Stage

Most products after surviving competitive battles, winning customer confidence and successful through growth phase enter their maturity stage. The sales plateau, and this flattening of sales usually lasts for some time because most products in the category have reached their maturity stage, and there is stability in terms of demand, technology, and competition. Sales slow down, competition is intense; price and promotional wars erupt, and profits decline. The demand for the category is at its highest during maturity. Strong market leaders manage to gain high profits and large positive cash flows because they have the advantage of lower-cost and have no need to expand their facilities. In general, if the maturity stage is protracted, a company cannot ignore the possibility of changes in the marketplace, the product, the distribution, production processes, and the nature and structure of competition.

Marketing Mix Changes During Maturity Stage: Different brands in the *product* category tend to be more similar due to technical maturity. Companies use every trick available either to increase users or rate of usage or both, to gain volumes. Some companies try to carve out a niche in a market segment and become a niche specialist and earn high profits. Attempts to modify product gain more importance and only a major breakthrough in R&D or engineering can help in differentiating the product, or reducing product costs can have significant payout. One option is to add value that benefits the consumer to make it easier to use the product. For example, Radio-Internet connectivity for laptop PCs, or voice-activated dialling for cell phone is convenient for consumers. Firms are increasingly using additional *services* in an attempt to differentiate the offering. *Prices* and expenditures on promotion during the maturity stage generally remain stable. However, the *promotion* emphasis shifts from advertising to various tools of sales promotion such as discounts, coupons, premiums, and store promotions etc. The impact of experience on costs and prices narrows down. Severity of competition to gain market share leadership or defend leadership position forces prices down. For consumer goods companies, distribution and shelf space acquire more importance.

FIGURE 21.4

Product Life Cycle Stages, Characteristics and Standard Responses

	Introduction	Growth	Maturity	Decline
Characteristics				
Market Growth Rate (Rs)	Moderate	High	Insignificant	Negative
Technical Change In Product Design	High	Moderate	Limited	Limited
Market Segments	Few	Few to many	Few to many	Few
Competitors	Few	Many	Limited	Few
Profitability	Negative	High	High for Market-share leaders	Low
Company's Standard Responses	Stimulate primary demand	Gain market share	Gain market share	Harvest
Product	Improve quality	Continue quality improvements	Concentrate on features	No change
Product Line	Narrow	Broad	Hold line length	Reduce line length
Price	Skimming or Penetration	Reduce	Hold or reduce	Reduce
Promotion	High	High	High or reduce	Reduce
Distribution	Selective	Intensive	Intensive	Selective

Decline Stage

Decline stage sets in when customer preferences change due to the availability of technologically superior products and consumers' shift in values, beliefs, and tastes to products offering more value. The number of competitors dwindles and generally few product versions are available. Those who stay, may cut their promotional budgets and further reduce their prices. The onset of decline stage may be gradual or fast. There may still be a small residual segment that remain loyal to the product.

Sales take a nosedive, costs increase, and profits are almost non-existent. All these factors create overcapacity. If the industry has low-exit barriers, many companies leave the market. This may increase the sales volume of remaining companies to the extent that their exit may be delayed, and for a short time strong contenders may even prosper.

Marketing Mix Changes During Decline Stage: In this stage if the decline is slow and exit barriers are low, *prices* tend to remain stable because there are still some enduring profitable segments, customers are fragmented and weak in bargaining power, and there are only few single-product competitors. In case the exit barriers are high and decline is fast and erratic, price-cuts are stiff, there are no enduring segments, only a few large single-product competitors are present, and customers exercise high bargaining power. Consumer goods companies try to persuade distributors to continue keeping the product. Companies consider the options of harvesting or divesting the product.

Implications and Limitations of Product Life Cycle Concept

Product life cycle concept shows a framework to spot the occurrence of opportunities and threats in a product market and the industry. This can help firms to reassess their objectives, strategies, and different elements of marketing programme.

A new product launch requires investment of considerable resource, and most companies have to contend with substantial short-term losses. During the growth stage, sales rise rapidly and competition increases, and large investments are required. The company that captures largest share of the market should have lowest per unit cost because of economies of scale and experience. If the market-share leader reduces the price, it discourages aspiring new entrants and low-share firms. Such low-share firms as well as new entrants have not only to invest to take advantage of market growth but also to increase market share. The "first starter" company is likely to lose some market share during this stage but its sales keep on increasing.

During the maturity phase, companies with larger market share enjoy the rewards of their earlier investments. Product price is sufficient to keep even high-cost companies in business because they do not need investments, as was the case during growth stage. Most competitors are content with the present position and do not try to increase their market share. Market leader keeps investing to improve product and attain more efficiency in production, marketing, and physical distribution.

The major weakness of product life cycle concept is that it is prescriptive in nature and focuses on strategies based on assumptions about different life cycle stages. Besides, it is difficult to tell what stage the product is in. A product may seem to have reached the maturity stage but it might be a temporary phase before it takes another upsurge. It ignores the fact that market forces drive the PLC reflecting consumer preferences, technology, and competition. Mary Lumpkin and George Day have strong views that greater emphasis on competitive issues and understanding the dynamics of competitive behaviour can help better understand how product-market structures evolve.

Summary

There is general agreement that products have life cycle much the same way as living organisms do. This concept of life cycle applies to product category, sub-category, and brands in the sub-category. The classical product life cycle curves are depicted as "S" shaped and generally divided into four stages: Introduction, growth, maturity, and decline. Some authors distinguish more than four stages. There are many other life cycle patterns that include growth-decline plateau, cycle-recycle pattern, and innovative maturity or scalloped pattern

The concept of product life cycle is concerned with the sales history of a product. It portrays the changes in sales and profits over time. Most products generally follow the classical "S" shaped curve when their sales are plotted against time. It is necessary to assess the life cycle of a product category and sub-category while examining the life cycle. Profits maximise before the sales are highest because the intensity of competition increases at the end of growth period and before the start of maturity stage.

Being a pioneer can be highly rewarding, but entails high risks and expenditures. Entering the market as a follower can also turn out to be advantageous if a company can bring in superior technology, and higher quality. With appropriate application of strategy elements, followers can be successful and surpass pioneers.

Each PLC stage requires different strategic elements. During introduction the sales growth is slow and profits are almost always non-existent because company spends large sums of money on product improvement, promotion, arranging distribution, and enlarging production facilities. The successful product during growth stage shows rapid increase in sales and increasing profits. The competition intensifies, and companies try to capture the largest market share. During the maturity phase sales growth slows down and profits may stabilize or decrease. Weak companies may start leaving the market, and market leader still spends money to remain a leader. The last stage is decline, and the product sales and profits take a nosedive. Companies generally think of harvesting or divesting.

Questions for Discussion

1. Describe different stages of product life cycle. Do all product follow this pattern?
2. What is the importance of product life cycle for companies?
3. Suggest marketing strategies for a consumer durable product during its growth, and maturity stages.
4. Identify the stage of life cycle of computer notebooks in India. Give your reasons.
5. What are the advantages of being a pioneer company and a follower company in a product category?
6. How might a company's promotion mix differ during different stages of product life cycle?
7. For what types of products companies might stress life style and fashion in their marketing programme?
8. Identify three products which you think are in their decline stage of life cycle. Why do you think companies are not discontinuing them?
9. Identify one brand that has entered its decline stage. Do you think it is permanent? Can there be some remedy to spark life in it?
10. Name two products and two services that you think are in their introductory stage. What are their chances of success to reach growth stage? Give your reasons.

Projects

1. Go to a super market. Identify two new products and write a report about customer response.
2. Take the help of Internet and prepare a report on changes that have taken place in PC life cycle.
3. Look into the history of Lux toilet soap. Identify its stage in life cycle and write a note giving reasons for its present life cycle status.

Bibliography

1. Chester R. Wasson, *Dynamic Competitive Strategy and Product Life Cycles,* 1978; Chester Wasson, "How Predictable Are Fashions and Other Product Life Cycles?" *Journal of Marketing,* July 1968.
2. J. E. Swan and D. R. Rink, "Effective Use of Industrial Life Cycle Trends," in *Marketing in the 80's,* (AMA, 1980).
3. Philip Kotler, *Marketing Management,* 12th Ed. 2003.
4. Gregory S. Carpenter and Kent Nakamoto, "Consumer Preference Formation and Pioneering Advantage," *Journal of Marketing Research,* August 1989.
5. Frank R. Kardes, Grumurthy Kalyanaram, Murali Chadrashekran, and Ronal J. Dornoff, "Brand Retrieval, Consideration Set Composition, Consumer Choice, and the Pioneering Advantage," *Journal of Consumer Research,* June 1993.
6. Mary Lumpkin and Gorge S. Day, "Evolutionary Processes in Competitive Markets Beyond the Product Life Cycle," *Journal of Marketing,* (July 1989).

Competition Analysis and Strategic Options Across PLC Stages

CHAPTER 22

LEARNING OBJECTIVES

After going through this chapter, you will understand:

- The nature of competitive forces
- Impact of bargaining power of different groups and availability of substitutes
- Customer perception of value
- Meeting competition
- Offensive and defensive strategies
- Different strategic choices across product life cycle

Global trade in textiles and apparel is expected to increase from US$ 356 billion in 2003 to US$ 600 billion by 2010. The textile industry accounted for 22% of India's Rs. 2,551 billion exports in 2002-03 and 17 per cent of India's total exports of Rs. 1,070 billion during April-July 2004. It has been predicted that post-January 2005 (Refer Exhibit I for details about MFA) India's share in apparel exports would increase from 2.5 per cent in 2003-04 to 5 per cent by 2008. In 2003-04, 75 per cent of India's apparel exports were to USA, the European Union and Canada (Refer Figure I). India's share in the global textile trade was forecasted to grow the fastest of all countries, post-MFA, as its quota allocation in developed countries during the MFA was among the lowest.

India has a proven advantage in raw material availability as the world's third largest producer of cotton, second largest exporter of cotton textiles among low cost countries, and fourth largest exporter of synthetic yarn and fabric. India produces all varieties of cotton. In 2003-04, the industry accounted for 21 per cent of global spinning capacity and 33 per cent of global weaving capacity. The industry contributed about 25 per cent share of the world trade in cotton yarn. The industry has high levels of operational efficiencies in spinning and weaving: Around 96% for spinning and 85-90% for weaving. The skilled manpower available in India has been relatively low-cost in an industry where labour contributes the largest component of manufacturing cost in textiles (Refer Figure II for data on labour cost component of textile units of various countries). "India has a cost advantage of 40% over the US and 30% over 'garment conversion centers' such as Mexico due to lower labour cost," said Rajinder Gupta (Rajinder), Managing Director, Abhishek Industries Ltd.

The wide availability of skilled labour in India has been another differentiator. India has been adept at traditional apparel-making skills like embroidery, mirror work and beading, design and at making complex garments. Some Chinese buyers are planning to manufacture part of their value added products in India.

Export orders from major retail companies have risen only by 5-6%. Moreover, these orders have been contracted at prices 5% lower than the existing ones. While slackening retail sales in the US has been cited as a reason, there are several other reasons why overseas buyers like Wal-Mart, Target, GAP and J.C. Penney have not increased sourcing from India for the season beginning January 2005. There is a lack of clarity in the price ranges that Indian players can offer to the buyers, and they are also unsure of the volumes they can offer. While the big players have already scaled up capacities, it amounts to only a small part of the textile industry. A KSA Technopak study found that in fiscal 2002-03, organized textile makers produced only 3.6 per cent of all fabric production which accounted for about 5.5 per cent in terms of value, while the remaining came from the unorganized sector that mostly used outdated powerlooms or handlooms (Refer Table I for details on technology usage by the weaving ?sector in 1998). On the revenue side, excluding the output of producers like Reliance Industries, Indorama Synthetics India (Indorama) and Grasim, total revenues of the top 20 companies associated with textiles and apparels in India did not exceed US$ 2 billion. No more than 15 apparel exporters have revenues in excess of US$ 22 million; another 30 between US$ 1 million and US$ 22 million; while none of the rest touch the million-dollar mark. It has been noted that as there haven't been many exporters who can handle large orders, international retailers have been looking at China and Vietnam. "The $50-billion figure was first mooted by the government five years ago. But the investments have started flowing in only recently," said IndoRama Managing Director O.P. Lohia while speaking about the need to expand and upgrade. While the average turnover of China's top 10 textile firms was US$ 600 million in 2004 that of the top 10 firms in India was around US$ 300 million. "Firms have not achieved much economies of scale, and their overheads and cost of labour are still high," said Adil Raza (Raza), Country Manager, J.C. Penney, (India). ???

(Source: www.icfai.org)

Since late 1980s we have witnessed the increasing awareness and impact of competition in India in almost all product categories, including many types of services. Competitive forces promote new thinking and innovations in every area of business activity. In a highly competitive global economy, with changing consumer wants, lifestyles, and preferences, companies must carefully and on an ongoing basis assess their competition. Generally companies view and analyse competition both from an industry and a marketing perspective. An industry represents a group of companies that offer a product or class of products that are viewed as close substitutes to satisfy a need category, or a set of needs.

Industries are classified according to the number of firms selling similar products and the degree of product differentiation. When there are many businesses selling a certain product, product differences and price consideration are very likely to be important as compared to only one business selling that product. The industries have been divided into four types according to economists view of competition: Pure Monopoly, Oligopoly, Monopolistic competition, and Perfect competition. With the passage of time, however, the industry's competitive structure can change.

Pure monopoly refers to a situation when there exists only one business selling a particular product or service in a defined geographic area. Without regulation, a monopoly can charge unreasonable prices, provide no service, and may undertake little or no promotional efforts. A regulated monopoly is required to charge reasonably lower price and offer some service in public interest.

Oligopoly exists when few companies are marketing products, which could be highly differentiated or standardised but these companies control most of the supply such as oil or cement. It is difficult for such companies offering standardised product to charge higher than the going rate price. They can obtain competitive advantage by cutting their own costs and matching the going price. In case of differentiated oligopoly, companies attempt to differentiate products on the basis of features, quality, styling, image, and services as in case of computers, cell phones, autos, and washing machines etc.

Monopolistic competition refers to a situation when the marketers can differentiate their products or services partially or completely, such as beauty clinics, hotels, cars etc. These competitors specialise in meeting the special needs of customers in a superior way and charge very high prices.

Perfect competition exists when the number of competitors is very large and they are offering the same product or service such as food grains or basic banking services. There is no opportunity to differentiate their offer and prices for all competitors remain the same.

For the purpose of analysis one may define markets and industries at the industry, product class, and product type levels. The problem with industry level analysis is that, it will include large number of non-competing products. For example in automobile industry, Hero Honda two-wheelers and Leyland trucks are non-competing products. In case of product class, the products involved may serve diverse markets or segments, such as pain remedies. Product types represent the sub-sets of a product class (pain remedies) such as aspirin, and paracetamol.

Marketers generally select product type as the basis of analysis for marketing planning because these products are viewed as close substitutes for one another. It is advisable in analysing the market and competition to keep in focus the consumer need, but this practice seems uncommon among marketers. In their study Bruce H. Clark and David B. Montgomery reported that managers tend to view what companies sell in defining competitors rather than what customers need. Managers also tend to identify fewer companies as competitors and generally omit the new companies. In reality, the range of a firm's actual and potential competitors is much broader and the chances are that a company stands more of chance to get hurt by potential competitors or new technologies than the players already competing.

The trend in our country shows that more than 50 million customers, both individuals and business people, are hooked on cell phones and the market is growing rapidly. This seems like an attractive market. But are cell phone manufacturing, and cellular services attractive industries?

Michael Porter calls the trends that shape attractiveness of industries as the *driving forces*. According to him these forces include: (1) changes in the industry's long-term growth, which directly impact investment decisions and competitive intensity, (2) changes in key buyer segments, which affect the demand and strategic marketing programmes, (3) diffusion of proprietary knowledge, which controls both the rate at which products become more alike and the entry of new companies, (4) changes in cost and efficiency, derived from scale and learning effects, which have the potential of making entry more difficult, and (5) changes in government laws and regulations, which can affect entry, costs, bases of competition, and profitability. Studying the trend data with respect to these five forces can help to determine whether an industry is attractive to enter and stay there. This also helps making strategic marketing decisions that enable the company to compete effectively.

Competitive Forces

Michael Porter has identified five interactive competitive forces that determine an industry's long-term attractiveness:

- Present competitors.
- Potential competitors.
- The Bargaining power of suppliers.
- The bargaining power of buyers.
- The threat of substitute products.

Rivalry among Present Competitors

Rivalry takes place among companies that produce close substitute products and when competitors try to improve or maintain their position. Whatever action one company takes and affects others. The greater the competitive intensity in an industry, the less attractive it is to current or would-be entrants. As the intensity of rivalry increases, generally the profitability starts decreasing. This happens when the industry has many strong, or aggressive competitors, investment required in fixed and working capital is high to produce sales, or exit barriers are high. This is likely to precipitate price and promotional wars. Competitors operate at or near capacity as much as possible. Rivalry is also high when there are many small firms in the industry without a dominant player. Competition also intensifies if there is little or no product differentiation, as is the case with TV sets, or car and two-wheeler tyres.

FIGURE 22.1
The Determinants of Industry Attractiveness

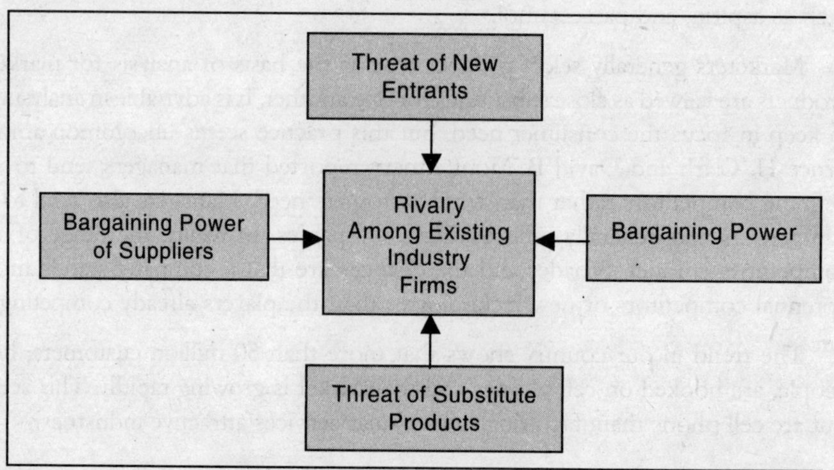

Threat of New Entrants

New entrants can become a source of competition, particularly when they are bigger. Michael Porter is of the opinion that the degree of attractiveness of an industry varies according to its entry and exit barriers. For new entrants it takes time to obtain the volume and learning required to accomplish a low relative cost per unit. The entry becomes even more expensive, posing the problem of cost disadvantage if the companies already present in the industry are vertically integrated, or the existing firms share their output with their other related businesses. The most attractive industry would be, where the entry barriers are high and it is easy to exit without incurring heavy costs. The situation is more complicated in industries where both entry and exit barriers are high, profit potential is high, but even low-performing companies are compelled to stay and try to fight it out. The situation does not entail any serious risk when both entry and exit barriers are low and returns are low but stable. The worst situation is when entry barrier in an industry is low but exit barriers are high (Figure 22.2). Barring aside favourable market conditions when firms enter the industry, during bad times there is severe overcapacity and every player has to contend with depressed returns.

Bargaining Power of Suppliers

Generally suppliers exercise bargaining power through higher prices, or reduced supply. The effect could be quite significant, particularly when the number of suppliers in the industry is limited, when the supplied product is an important input, switching costs and prices of substitutes are high, or when the suppliers are organised and can realistically threaten forward integration. The bargaining power is changing in many industries with the development of just-in-time relationship with suppliers. Such relationship with suppliers has turned into a cooperative partnership, leading to lower transaction and inventory costs, and improved quality.

In case the bargaining power of key suppliers in an industry is very high, the overall attractiveness of the industry is viewed as low.

FIGURE 22.2

Entry and Exit Barriers

		Entry Barriers: High	Entry Barriers: Low
Exit Barriers	High	Returns High but Risky	Returns Low and Risky
	Low	Returns High and Stable	Returns Low but Stable

Bargaining Power of Buyers

It is no surprise that buyers in any industry always want more for less. They look for improved product quality, and additional services at lower prices. Thus, they can affect competition within an industry. The success of buyers bargaining power grows when (1) the number of large buyers is quite limited, they are concentrated, or organised, (2) switching costs are favourably low, (3) threat of backward integration, (4) when the product represents just a small part of buyer's cost, and (5) buyers earn low profits and the product involved product cost is an important part of their costs, then buyers will bargain more determinedly. The greater power of large volume buyers in an industry makes it less attractive.

Threat of Substitute Products

Those alternative product types that perform essentially the same function are called the substitutes, such as different cooking oils, laundry products, headache remedies, or postal and courier services. Availability of substitutes puts a limit on prices companies can charge and the profit margins are restricted, more so when supply position is such that it exceeds the demand. More recently, we have seen this happening in the case of cellular phone services in our country. It is also likely to happen in case of Internet services. Industries of this type are unattractive when there are many existing or potential substitutes. Increasing competition and technology upgradation may adversely affect prices and profits.

Analysis of competition reveals a set of primary competitors and the potential ones. The analysis must ascertain their characteristics with particular focus on their strategies, objectives, and their strengths and weaknesses.

The strengths of a competitor may be in the area of its size, R & D, technology, costs, marketing systems, promotional aspects, dealer network and loyalty, customer service etc. For example, a major strength Maruti (*MUL*) enjoys its after sales service and customer satisfaction. A careful analysis may also reveal weakness in one or more of the same areas.

Porter recommends that competitor's analysis should also consider the level of satisfaction the competitor has about its existing position in the industry. In case the satisfaction level is low, it is quite likely that its stance would be aggressive to improve its position to reach the desired level. However, its satisfaction with its existing position is more likely to guard its exiting position. Much is likely to depend on the level of satisfaction it derives from its exiting position.

FIGURE 22.3

Indian Cell Phone Service Industry and Five Forces

Forces	Impact	Reasons
Rivalry among present competitors.	Rivalry is moderately high, moderately favourable.	Product differentiation through new features and services; customer switching costs are low.
Threat of new entrants.	High threat; moderately unfavourable.	Rapid pace of technological change may bring new players based on new technologies; satellites, packet switching.
Bargaining power of suppliers.	Supplier power is high, moderately unfavourable.	Government has control on price of additional bandwidth.
Bargaining power of buyers.	Buyer power is low; very favourable.	Even large customers have little power to set terms and conditions in this oligopolistic industry.
Threat of substitute products.	Threat of substitute is high; moderately unfavourable.	New multimedia devices could replace cell phones.
Note: In this hypothetical analysis, only two forces are favourable and three are unfavourable. The cell phone industry is not particularly favourable under these situations.		

The five competitive forces discussed in this chapter get affected over a period of time. Due to this reason the strength of each of the factors varies as the industry passes through its introductory stage to finally the decline. During the fast growth period, the competitive forces are likely to be weak. This presents many opportunities for competitors for increasing market share. During the early maturity period, the overall growth slows down and competitive forces are at the peak, compelling some weak companies to exit. During full maturity, if the leader holds a strong position, competition usually slackens. In case the leader holds a weak relative position, then there would be intense price competition. In a declining industry, there is likely to be considerable rivalry among the existing competitors. Intensity of rivalry would much depend on the exit barriers and the rate of decline.

Factors that make a difference between success and failure of companies within an industry, are called *critical success factors* and they differ in different industries. In many cases these factors are often related to marketing mix elements (product, price, distribution, and promotion). Examining the fit between an industry's critical success factors and the presence or absence of these within the company can determine whether an industry is attractive for the company or not.

COMPETITIVE STRATEGIES AND PLC STAGES

The three basic performance objectives, companies choose keeping in view the competition include *share position, sales growth,* and *profit performance.* Depending on the prevailing and anticipated market conditions, some companies will adopt offensive strategies and some will choose defensive strategies to suit objectives. Businesses evaluate market attractiveness and competitive advantage before making a choice of strategic moves.

Market Attractiveness: The factors that make a market attractive include market size, market growth; competitive intensity, profit potential, accessibility to market, and fit with company's core competencies. These aspects can be grouped under three heads: Market Forces, Competition, and Market Access (Figure 22.4).

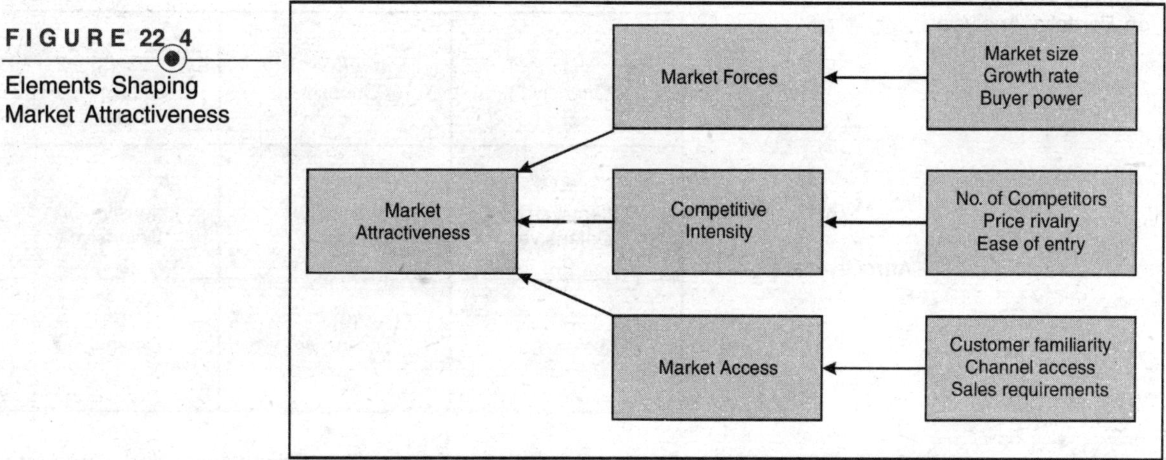

FIGURE 22.4
Elements Shaping Market Attractiveness

Competitive Advantage: There are various elements that determine competitive advantage of a business and include differentiation advantage, cost advantage, and marketing advantage. According to L. W. Philips, D. R. Chang, and R. D. Buzzell, other forces go into shaping these competitive advantage elements of a business. The three dimensions of competitive advantage shown (Figure 22.5) include three forces underlying each element of competitive advantage and include product related aspects, cost related factors, and competencies in various areas of marketing functions.

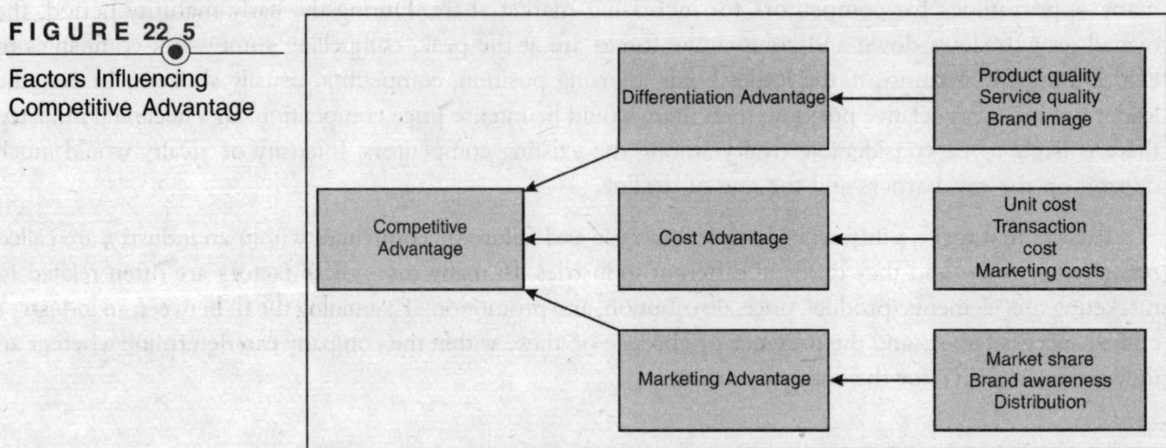

FIGURE 22.5
Factors Influencing Competitive Advantage

Offensive Strategies

Offensive strategies are most likely to be adopted by competing businesses during growth stage of product-market life cycle (early growth and rapid growth stages) and aim at sales growth and increase market share, and improve profit position in future. Defensive strategies are more likely to be adopted during later stages of product-market life cycle (late growth, early and late maturity) and usually focus at protecting market share and increase short-term sales returns and profits.

FIGURE 22.6
Strategy Choice Based on Portfolio Analysis

Market Attractiveness \ Competitive Advantage	Low	Medium	High
High	(1) Offensive	(2) Offensive	(3) Offensive OR Defensive
Medium	(4) Offensive OR Defensive	(5) Offensive OR Defensive	(6) Offensive OR Defensive
Low	(7) Defensive	(8) Defensive	(9) Defensive

Adoption of offensive strategy depends on a combination of market attractiveness and competitive advantage. Companies are more likely to adopt offensive strategies to gain competitive advantage and market share when the company's competitive advantage is either average or below average. The company may decide to gain competitive advantage and market share in the existing product-markets and/or enter new markets with no recognised market share. Another strategic objective favourable for offensive strategy might be when the marketer aims at cultivating an emerging or underdeveloped market where it has established a strong competitive advantage.

Using the market attractiveness and competitive advantage portfolio (Figure 22.6), a marketer can spot six positions where offensive strategy could be adopted. These are cells 1, 2, 3, 4, 5, and 6. Four of the cells (3, 4, 5, and 6) with average market attractiveness and one with highest attractiveness and highest competitive advantage could also use a defensive strategy. A marketer could decide whether to use offensive or defensive strategy based on more detailed information, such as an offensive strategy may be called for depending on the company's sources of relative competitive advantage. Alternatively, a defensive strategy to protect the current business position may be a better choice for accomplishing desired performance objective of the company. A defensive strategy is sometimes more suitable in some cases when the company aims to gain optimum market focus, minimise investment, and earn more profits.

It makes sense to adopt offensive strategies in a company's existing markets because the company has already gained some knowledge about the target customers and competitors, and is capable enough to serve these markets. The company should take advantage of the existing market position and adopt offensive strategies to further penetrate and develop these existing product-markets where it has a presence.

The basic offensive strategies include investing for sales growth in existing markets, improving competitive position or investing and entering new markets (Figure 22.7). Each of these strategies will have a different set of objectives and sub-strategies to achieve the desired results.

FIGURE 22.7
Offensive Strategies

Strategy	Basic Strategy (A) Invest to Grow Sales In Existing Markets	Basic Strategy (B) Invest to Improve Competitive Position	Basic Strategy (C) Invest to Enter New Markets
Objective	Grow in Existing Market	Improve Revenues	Diversify to Grow
Different Strategies to Implement Central Strategies	Grow market share Grow revenue per customer Enter new market segment Expand market demand	Improve customer loyalty and retention Improve differential advantage Improve marketing productivity Build marketing advantage	Enter related new markets Enter unrelated new markets Enter new emerging markets Develop new markets

Defensive Strategies

Generally businesses with high market share in growing or mature markets opt to adopt defensive strategies with the objective of maintaining cash flow and short-term profitability. Without defending their position and profitability, companies would face short-term difficulties in terms of profitability and lack resources to take advantage of opportunities by entering growing markets with offensive strategies.

The fundamental aim of defensive strategy is to protect profit position of the business and important share positions that justify investment. Defensive strategy is also appropriate for a secondary objective, which is to manage profitability of the business that is losing the potential for high growth profitability.

FIGURE 22.8
Defensive Strategies

Strategies	Basic Strategy (A) Protect Position	Basic Strategy (B) Optimise Position	Basic Strategy (C) Increase Cash Flow Harvest, or Divest
Objective	Maintain Profit	Maximise Profits	Cash Flow
Different Strategies to Implement Central Strategies	Protect market share Develop customer retention Enter new market segment	Maximise net profits Reduce market focus Improve marketing productivity	Manage for cash flow Harvest or Divest for cash flow Enter new emerging markets

Choosing Competitors

In an industry there are likely to be several competitors, all with different profiles based on their size, resources, objectives, strategies, and areas of strengths and weaknesses. The competitor chosen might be basically either strong, or weak. Some of the these competitors might be categorised as "good" or "bad." Good ones follow industry rules, develop realistic assumptions about its future growth, they price their offers reasonably based on lower costs and advocate others to keep costs low, favour product differentiation, focus on a portion of the industry and favour a healthy industry. Bad ones ignore these healthy practices and adopt practices that upset the healthy balance in the industry.

Customer Perceptions of Value: It is believed that customers choose a brand from a set of available alternatives based on their perceptions of its value. This value is the sum total of quality, benefits (functional and image), costs, and service. It is believed that the brand that exceeds all others on the chosen criteria is purchased. The steps involved in assessing customers' value perception include:

- Identify major attributes and their relative importance from customers' point of view. Assess consumers' perceptions of the company's and competitors' performance on these attributes. Evaluate the company's one or two major competitors in a market on these attributes.
- Deliver customer value, and periodically conduct customers' value perception studies.

The analysis will reveal four types of competitors in an industry, including the company itself. Some of the major characteristics of *market leader, market follower, market challenger,* and *niche marketer* are briefly discussed below:

Market Leader: The firm enjoys the largest market share and generally leads others in, new technology introduction or up-gradation, new product introduction, generally setting the changes in price, promotional practices, and level of distribution coverage. Such a firm is very likely to device offensive or defensive strategies to fight tooth-and-nail to maintain its position and stay the leader.

Market Follower: Many companies in product industries that are capital-intensive and deal in products viewed as homogeneous such as cement, steel, and chemicals etc., prefer to stay follower. They usually copy the leader and present similar offers to customers in terms of quality, price, and service. Opportunities to create any meaningful differentiation of their offer are very little, and price sensitivity is considerable. Any attempt to pose a challenge to the leader requires huge investments. Those who try for challenging the leader, often take the route of expansion through acquisitions. For example, according to a news item in *Hindustan Times*, Mittal Steel Co., became the largest steel producer in the world by acquiring some other steel businesses in the industry.

Market Challenger: Any other competing firms, whether second, third, or further down below in rank in the same product-market might decide to become the challenger. Much depends on the individual company's assessment of the leader's objectives, strategies, strengths and weaknesses, and also the firm's assessment of its own resources, strengths and weaknesses and objectives to challenge the leader. The strategies that a challenger may adopt is to go for head-on frontal attack, attacking in an area where the leader has a weakness, called a flank attack, or adopt guerrilla methods, that is, attacking in random corners in an attempt to weaken the competitor's market power.

Niche Marketer: A niche market is a very small sub-segment of a segment where customers seek a distinctive set of attributes resulting in certain most desired benefits. A niche marketer focuses on customer needs in this small sub-segment and customises its marketing effort to that group of target customers. These customers are prepared to pay a premium price to the niche marketer who best satisfies their needs. The niche usually does not attract competitors.

STRATEGIC OPTIONS FOR GROWTH MARKETS

Market Leader Strategies

Market leader is either a pioneer or at least one of the first few entrants who first developed the product-market. Generally, the leader's objective is to maintain its leading share position despite the entry of new players. Maintaining early market share-lead in growing markets is challenging because of increasing number of competitors, fragmentation of market segments, and threat of product innovation from competitors. A company can maintain its market share in the presence of competitors only when its sales grow at a rate that is equal to overall market growth.

To gain and maintain leading market share a business needs to retain its existing customers by building brand loyalty to ensure they make repeat or replenishment purchases. The business should stimulate selective demand among later product adopter groups and makes sure of capturing larger product-market share of the growing market.

With a view to speed up the expansion of product-market, the business may stimulate the primary demand, particularly when the product adoption process is slow because of complex product nature, or high product switching costs for customers. By expanding total market, it is the leader who gains maximum if it can maintain its high market-share position.

Market Share Expansion: One of the most attractive strategic options for a market leader is often to grow its market share. Coca Cola has managed to grow its volume at the rate of 7-8 per cent. In large industries, an increase of one share-point is often worth millions in monetary terms. For example, one share-point in soft drinks is in excess of US$ 120 million and for this reason the competition intensity among colas is of the highest order. David Zymanski, Sunder Bhardwaj, and Rajan Verdarajan report that many factors influence a company's ability to grow market-share and earn profits. For example, the cost of gaining share growth might far exceed the revenue gains. It is easy to get caught up in share wars without considering the unprofitable possibility of winning the battle of market share but losing the war for revenues. A business should consider four major factors:

1. ***Possibility of Competition Act 2002, or similar laws such as Anti-trust Action in U.S.A.:*** The merger of Jet Airways and Sahara Airlines drew investigation. Similarly, the protracted investigation of Microsoft is well-known. The risk reduces the attractiveness of increased share gain.

2. ***The cost involved in market share gain may rise and exceed the revenues:*** Robert D. Buzzell and Bradly T. Gale found that 31 per cent of the 877 market-share leaders in the PIMS database experienced loses in relative share, and leaders were particularly likely to experience losses when their market share was very large. This may happen, for example, because of additional expenses involved in public relations exercise, existence of unattractive market segments, customers refusal to accept what is offered leading for disliking the business and their loyalty to competitors, and customers unique product feature preferences etc. Sometimes market leaders find it more appropriate to decrease their market share by taking it easy in less profitable segments and cutting down on maintaining market share.

3. ***Selecting and using an inappropriate marketing mix strategy:*** Apple computers introduced its Cube but could not sell much despite advertising and other communications. Avanti Garralli Moped did not sell because its advertising was addressing the wrong segment. Robert D. Buzzell and Frederick D. Wiersema identify three areas to excel in order to gain successfully, increased market share: (1) New Product Development, (2) Product Quality, and (3) Marketing Expenditure.

4. ***Increased number of customers may put a strain on the company's resources and hurt service delivery and product value:*** Linda Hellofs and Robert Jacobson found that share growth might affect customer perceptions of product quality.

A business leader can adopt *defensive* or *offensive* strategies to *maintain share-position, increase market share*, or *expand product-market*. Depending on the situation a market leader faces, the strategic move options include:

- Position Defence Strategy
- Flanker Strategy
- Confrontation Strategy
- Pre-emptive Strategy
- Market Expansion Strategy
- Contraction or Withdrawal Strategy

Position Defence Strategy: Almost always, the market share leader adopts *position defence* strategy. This strategy focuses on perpetually strengthening an existing position like a fortress and repulsing attacks by existing or future competitors. The share leader must take care not to leave any area exposed to a flank attacker, and determine which areas are most important to defend. By investing to support and maintain existing leadership position, the business can improve the feeling of satisfaction among present customers, and make the offer more attractive to new customers.

Fair & Lovely Menz Active

- All the big players in the Rs. 700 crore fairness products market in India admitted that at least 25% of their users were male. Emami launched its Fair & Handsome skin lightening cream for men. HLL has now hit back with Fair & Lovely Menz Active.
- "We have always been aware that a significant male user base existed within Fair & Lovely itself, and hence there was always need to launch a variant that understands and takes care of unique requirements of men," says vice president, Skin Care, HLL.

(Source: The Brand Reporter, March 13 – 31, 2006)

Possibly the most important measure a market leader can adopt is to continue modifying its product and add innovative features. Hindustan Lever Limited introduced its top of the line Dove Gentle Exfoliating Bar that has pH range between 6.5 and 7.5, which is almost neutral unlike other toilet soaps that are alkaline with 9 pH or above. This can block moves by competitors to differentiate their offer by incorporating features or performance improvements not offered in leader's products. It would add to the competitive edge if the leader also reduces costs to discourage price-competition.

In addition to adding new features, the market leader should take steps to improve customers' perceptions about the product. The focus of marketing communications should shift for building selective demand of company's brand. The sales promotion efforts should be directed to induce trial among late adopters, and repeat purchase among the existing customers.

Another important aspect the leader must consider is to focus on increased pot-purchase service in case of durable products to strengthen its position.

The leader should expand its distribution reach to ensure increased product availability and make efforts to minimise any possibility of 'out of stock situation' at retail level, or shorten product delivery time.

It makes good sense to build strong customer relationships right from the start in industrial and consumer durable product categories to build loyalty and ensure repeat or replenishment purchases. This relationship becomes very important during maturity stage of product-market life cycle when the competition becomes quite intense to win over established customers.

Flanker Strategy: The market leader adopts this strategy to outsmart a *challenger* who simply decides to bypass the leader's fortress and attempts to capture a territory where the leader so far has not been able to develop a strong presence. This may happen when the product-market is fragmented with distinct segments and the leader's product-brand does not meet the needs and wants of some of those attractive segments. This may happen when a competitor with appropriate resources and strengths differentiates its offer that appeals to, one or more of these segments, where the leader so far is not established. In this situation, the challenger captures a big chunk of the share.

To defend exposed flank against the challenger's attack, a leader might develop a *fighting brand* (also called Flanker brand) to compete against the challenger's brand. For example, this is what Hindustan Lever did when Nirma detergent made inroads in HLL Surf market share. Depending where the challenger focuses, the leader can introduce a higher quality brand at higher price, or lower-quality brand at lower than the challenger's price to appeal to the segment thus, protect the leader's main brand.

A market leader first ensures position defence and simultaneously adopts flanker strategy. Obviously this requires investments and the company should have sufficient resources to fully commit to adopting both strategies at the same time.

Confrontation Strategy: IBM was the leader in commercial PC market but in mid 1980s the company lost market share to competitors like Compaq. Compaq computers cost almost the same as IBM but offered customers more features or better performance levels. Later, Dell computers adopted direct distribution and offered customised machines at lower prices. The customers could choose components and place order online.

When a market leader is attacked directly, it may have no recourse but to adopt confrontation strategy. A confrontation strategy is often reactive in nature. It is not very common to gain reliable intelligence sufficiently well in time to become proactive and develop suitable marketing programme before the challenge occurs. The leader often decides to meet or beat the competition by offering more desirable product features of a competitor. The leader incorporates product improvements, increases promotional efforts, and sometimes lowers the prices. In case of products with high purchase rates or where the product diffusion process is long drawn, the leader should perhaps adopt a penetration pricing strategy right in the first place. This would pre-empt lower-price competitors from entering the market, and would also ensure competitive advantage of the leader and obviate the need to adopt confrontation strategy.

This strategy requires investment to accomplish process improvements to reduce unit costs, improvements in product quality, customer service, or develop more advanced versions that offer greater value to customers. For example, Maruti was facing attacks from other manufacturers and share erosion in its hatchback car segment. The company has introduced a more advanced car in this segment, Maruti Swift that offers more value to customers.

Market Expansion Strategy: The main objective of this strategy is to capture a large share of new customer groups who have different needs and preferences than the segment where company has been operating with initial offer. This is a proactive and more aggressive version of flanker strategy to defend leader's market share position by expanding the total market. This protects the company from future competitive threats. In case the company has abundant resources and competencies, market expansion strategy is particularly suitable where the market is fragmented

This strategy calls for product line extensions, new brands, or alternative products at different price-quality points. For example, Intel has processors at different price-quality points in its four brands: Pentium D, Xeon, Pentium, and Celeron for different market segments in a fragmented market with different set of needs and preferences and leads with the largest share in the global processor market. Similarly, Nike has sustained leading share of the athletic shoe market. It has developed a series of several line extensions that offer technical, design, and style features to satisfy customer preferences covering almost all the sports.

Another approach, a market leader may adopt in certain product categories is to develop a specialised sales force to deal with different user groups. Yet another approach a leader can adopt is to retain several customer groups is to retain the basic product but vary other elements of marketing programme to make the offer attractive and appealing.

Pre-emptive Strategy: This is an offensive strategy to defend leadership position before a competitor even starts attacking the market-share leader. A company can use pre-emptive strategy in several ways. A company can introduce several new products and announce it much in advance before the actual launch in the market. According to R. J. Calantone and K. E. Schatzel, a market leader's action of pre-announcing is deliberate to discourage competitors from attacking. Bayes, Jain, and Rao have called such new-product pre-announcements by high-tech companies, much in advance of their actual introduction, as "Vapoware."

Contraction or Withdrawal Strategy: If the market happens to be highly fragmented and new entrants have more resources than the leader, it might be difficult for a market leader to defend properly in all market segments. The firm may not have enough resources and have no options but to decrease or take no action in some market segments. The company focuses its efforts on segments where it has maximum competitive advantages or highest segment attractiveness and potential for growth.

Market Follower Strategies

Following pioneers in a product-market, there are late entrants. Of course, not all followers in a growth market dream of becoming the market-share leader leaving behind the pioneer. Many competing businesses enter the market, especially those with limited resources and competencies and may decide to enter a distinct segment of the larger market, overlooked by other entrants, and build a successful business. It resembles a kind of niche strategy that avoids head-on competition with larger players and may have some degree of success.

Most market structures have share leaders, followers, and niche marketers. A firm that has second largest share in a market and is a close follower has an interesting strategic choice whether to challenge the leader with an offensive strategy. Another strategy option is to protect its share position and maximise profitability. Much will depend on the competitive advantage of the leader and its pledge to defend its position, follower's resources, and the short-term profit needs of the follower.

Many businesses prefer to stay followers rather than challenge the share leader. This is particularly true for more homogeneous industries such as food grains, fertilisers, chemicals, cement, and steel etc. Businesses in these industries have low opportunities to differentiate their offer; price sensitivity is high, and service quality is almost similar. Followers prefer to copy the leader and present similar offers to customers, and market shares remain stable.

Market-share followers try to retain their customer base, try to acquire new customers but avoid any moves that might attract retaliation from competitors. Some commonly adopted strategies are:

Counterfeit Strategy: This type of follower makes duplicates of leader products and sells at very low prices through grey market and dealers of doubtful integrity. For example, some operators in East Asian countries, duplicate/pirate software, music and movie CDs, Apple Computer, top selling novels, and some brands of expensive watches etc.

Adapter Strategy: This business takes or copies a leader's product, improves it and sells in different markets. The differentiation is in terms of features, packaging, pricing, and distribution. Some firms pick up product ideas from established leaders and implement them in a different country with some modification.

Research findings show that number one and two share-leaders earn the maximum *ROI*, and others may run into negative ROI. This is the reason that P&G aims to be either number one or two in a business otherwise the business is not worth being in.

Market Challenger Strategies

A challenger visualises capturing the market-share leadership in an industry. Many challengers have successfully overtaken the leader and some others have gained share points. There was a time when GM was the largest producers of cars but today Toyota leads the pack. Maruti Udyog was nowhere when Hindustan Motors and Premier Auto (Fiat) were the largest share companies. Today, Maruti produces and sells more cars than Hindustan Motors and Fiat in India.

A challenger has two basic strategic options to consider. In markets where the share leader and others have already cornered a very large portion of the potential market, there is no choice for a challenger but to capture some demand from other competitors' existing customers. A challenger could try head-on confrontation with chosen competitor by adopting various marketing activities aimed at giving it an advantage. Or a challenger can decide to leapfrog over the share leader by offering new generation products with more benefits to encourage existing customers to trade in their existing brand for a new one. This could also bring to fold a large share of late adopters in the mass market.

In the early growth stage of product-market where no one has so far captured a clear leading share position of potential customers, the option for the challenger is to attract a substantial share of potential first-time customers. This could be a better choice in case overall market is heterogeneous and much fragmented, and the share leader has been successful in capturing a strong position in only one or few segments. The key would be successful differentiation of the offer from those of current competitors, and make it more attractive and appealing in underdeveloped segments.

There are five major competitive strategies for a challenger that may be used singly or in combination and include *frontal attack strategy, leapfrog strategy, flanking attack strategy, encirclement strategy,* and *guerrilla attack strategy.* Most of these strategies seem similar to share maintenance strategies.

Whom to Attack?

It is necessary for a challenger to decide which competitor to attack. There are several options to choose from. Choosing whom to attack requires careful analysis and comparison of strengths and weaknesses of different competitors:

- Attack the market-share leader
- Attack another follower
- Attack one or more smaller competitors
- Avoid direct attacks on any established competitor

Frontal Attack Strategy: In case the market for a product category is relatively homogeneous, there is an established market leader, few untapped but unattractive segments, then the challenger has no choice but to go for frontal attack with matching product, price, promotion, and distribution. This may succeed when most current customers have weak or no brand preferences or loyalties. In this situation even superior resources are no insurance of success if simply the challenger imitates the targeted competitor's offer.

To succeed, attaining lower costs or differentiated position in the market can give a competitive advantage to a challenger. Sustainable cost advantage can help to cut down prices to attract target customers of the chosen competitor, or it can maintain prices and go for more extensive promotion.

To implement these strategies, certain factors must be favourable. Price challenge may work only if a challenger has one or more sustainable advantages such as superior technology, good and continuing relations with low-cost suppliers, or some source of synergy with other business divisions of the company. A challenger should also assess the target competitor's resources before launching a promotional blitz. If the chosen competitor has no resource constraints, then it can retaliate aggressively. A large and better trained sales force can accord a competitive advantage to a challenger in certain industries where sales force plays a key role in a company's marketing programme.

The best approach for a challenger is to meaningfully and persuasively differentiate its product or relevant services that do a superior job in meeting the needs and preferences of most customers. In such a situation, strong promotion and/or attractive price can do wonders. Adopting this strategy, Dell Computers has out performed big competitors in PC market. Dell differentiated itself by offering customers to choose PC configuration, deliver the computer at home, and at lower prices.

Low-price might favour a low-price challenger if the target competitor has built a reputation of high quality. In such a case the target competitor might not be willing to reduce price, as it is likely to send wrong signals to customers about brand image.

Leapfrog Strategy: This strategy is adopted in an attempt to gain an important advantage over the current competitors. A challenger launches new generation, persuasively differentiated products that are far more advanced and offer more desirable features and benefits to customers than the existing alternatives. Digital watches, portable music, and digital cameras are some examples. Citizen introduced watches that do not require a battery change. Leapfrog strategy works well in attracting repeat or replacement purchases from competitor's existing customer groups, and new purchases from other adopter groups of customers.

There is also a chance that this strategy may sufficiently delay any retaliation from established competitors. Target competitors have already committed large sums of money in their existing operations that have achieved a measure of success. Change to a new technology, takes time and large investments. This may make them reluctant to switch over to a new technology.

A challenger might succeed with leapfrog strategy when it has a reasonably sustainable advantage by having a technology that is superior to target competitor's; design and process capabilities to offer superior and appealing products, and resources to back promotion programmes effectively to convince existing customers that the benefits of new product outweigh the cost of switching. Apple, for example has tried this approach to attract PC users to Apple desktops and notebooks.

Flanking Attack Strategy: This strategy is suitable when a market can be meaningfully divided in more segments and a challenger cannot match the competitor's resources in a frontal attack. The target competitor(s) is well established in some primary segment, and the available brands fall short of delivering desired satisfaction to the customers in one or more segments. To start with, a challenger focuses its resources and capabilities on one large untapped segment and attempts to corner a sizable share of the total market. This approach may generally require attractive product features, and services highly desired by customers. In addition to this, suitable pricing, and effective promotional policies to attract customers are necessary to speed up brand demand.

In case a challenger can't offer unique product features, then it can differentiate its services to meet special customer needs, and offer convenient distribution. Dell offered convenient and speedy direct distribution to customers and PCs are delivered at the doorstep. Some cosmetic businesses have started home delivery of ordered products keeping in view the working women group.

Encirclement Strategy: A challenger applies flanker strategy to attack several small, and untapped or underdeveloped segments at the same time. The challenger attempts to surround the target competitor's brand from all sides, offering a variety of alternatives to several peripheral segments in a market. This strategy may be successful when a market is fragmented and there are varied application, or geographic areas and have distinct needs and preferences.

To apply this strategy, a challenger needs to develop a varied line of products with desired features to suit the preferences of different market segments. For example, Cadbury-Schweppes sells a wide variety of flavoured soft drinks that appeal to unique preferences of several segments. The company has stayed away from cola drinks to avoid drawing competition from Pepsi and Coke.

Guerrilla Attack Strategy: Guerrilla attack strategy may suit a challenger with relatively limited resources and where other strategies are not possible. The challenger makes a series of surprise attacks in limited geographic areas against its established target competitor. The whole objective is to demoralize the target competitor and establish safe and lasting foothold.

A challenger can apply a variety of tactics. These include sales promotion, heavy local advertising, and merchandising efforts. Price-cutting sales promotions in small geographic areas are a good means of encouraging brand switching among customers, particularly in consumer markets and often difficult to counter quickly by a large competitor. Similarly, appropriately targeted direct mail or Internet marketing can be effective in implementing this strategy. In some cases guerrilla raids discourage a larger competitor from further expanding its product-market share or undertake other aggressive actions.

STRATEGIC OPTION FOR MATURE AND DECLINING MARKETS

During the later part of product life cycle growth stage, the competitive intensity is very high and businesses that survive this transition or shakeout, stage face new challenges as market growth stage shows signs of stagnation. With the onset of maturity phase, total volume stabilises, there is excess installed capacity in the industry, businesses experience growing pressure on costs and profits, first-time customers decrease, and repeat or replacement sales account for larger share of sales volume. All competitors try to hold their current customer base. The success of a business during this stage depends largely on its ability to lower costs, or come up with some persuasive differentiation in product features or delivering superior customer service.

A business should always consider that all market segments and all the available brands do not mature at the same time. A product-share leader in a mature market might adopt strategies to gain sales volume by promoting new uses for its old product and/or encourage customer to use it more often, or use more of the product per use occasion. Most strategies attempt to follow the following equation:

Sales Volume = Number of Users × Usage Rate

A product-market or brand matures because of technological advances, changing demographic variable, changing taste and preferences, lifestyle changes, and development of substitutes. It is unwise for managers to support a dying product too long or to divest it in a hurry. Application of suitable strategy can produce sales volumes and profits in declining stage of PLC.

If the exit barriers are low, a leader might consider aggressive price-cutting and promotion to speed up the exit of weaker competitors, or the leader might buy out weaker brands and make better capacity utilisation. Lastly, a business might decide to harvest a mature product to increase cash flow over the remaining period of its life cycle.

Strategic Traps During Shakeout Period

According to Michael Porter, the ability of a firm to survive the shakeout period or transition from growth stage to maturity depends to a large extent on its ability to avoid strategic traps. Common traps are:

- Failure to anticipate transition or shakeout from growth to maturity.
- Business not having any clear competitive advantage as growth slows.
- Assuming that an early advantage will insulate the business from price or service differentiation.
- Sacrificing market share in favour of short-term profits.

The first, and the most obvious trap would be not to notice the happenings that indicate the onset of the shakeout period. A firm should develop an accurate forecast of the slow down in sales growth rate and accordingly hold production capacity to its sustainable scale. Fareena Sultan, John U. Farley, and Donald R. Lehman report that models can forecast when the replacement sales begin to be more than the first-time sales, both for consumer durable and industrial goods markets. It is almost impossible to forecast shakeout period in consumer non-durable market because slow growth might be the result of shifts in consumer preferences and availability of substitutes.

Number two trap is not having a clear competitive advantage when the market is passing through the transition period. During the product-market growth period, survival of a business may not be very difficult even without a clear competitive advantage in terms of differentiation or cost advantage. Firms not having competitive advantage find it difficult to retain market share and sales volume as growth slows down.

A third trap is not to recognise the increasing importance of price or service. It would be wrong to keep focused only on initial product differentiation and believe this will protect the business from price or service competition. Entry of more competitors initiates product improvements and feature difference decreases as the industry nears maturity. As technological differentials become smaller, differences in price and service acquire greater importance to customers. Ming Jer Chen and Ian C. McMillan found that firms achieving success due to technological edge or other differentiation often disregard aggressive pricing or other marketing practices even when the earlier differentiation becomes less meaningful. This delays meeting the aggressive stance of competitors and lose market share. For example, in the face of market slow down Dell adopted aggressive pricing policy and overtook more powerful competitors.

A fourth trap results from ignoring aggressive pricing. Many businesses attempt to maintain their earlier profitability to keep focused on short-run profits and lose market share, decreasing marketing efforts, R&D, and other investments to maintain economies of scale. Focusing and improving on these aspects is critical for ensuring future success during market maturity stage.

Two sets of strategic options are important for success in mature markets:

1. Developing and implementing strategies to strengthen competitive advantage, customer satisfaction, and loyalty.
2. Effectively implement flexible and creative marketing programmes aimed at achieving growth or profit as conditions change in product-markets.

Mature Markets

Current Market Share Maintenance Strategies: Maturity stage of markets can continue for prolonged periods of time. In early stage of maturity, a business should aim to maximise profit flow over the remaining period of product-market. The most important goal is to *maintain and protect market share.* It is essential to retain the firm's share of repeat or replacement purchases from current customers. This is important because in a mature product-market, the number of new customers is not sizeable as compared to the existing customers.

Some of the defensive or offensive strategies discussed earlier in this chapter continue to be relevant here to retain customers. The most suitable approach for a market-share leader is to continue sustaining its position applying *position defence strategy*. This requires for enhancing customer satisfaction and loyalty, as well as simplifying and encouraging repeat purchases. Such as actions that focus on improving product quality, service quality, and reduce costs. In case, markets are more fragmented, a business might expand product lines, and applying *flanker strategy* add one or more *flanker brands* to protect business from competitive attacks.

Other competitors with small shares should avoid prolonged direct confrontation with large share firms. A small business can adopt *niche strategy* and focus on a smaller customer segment, with specialised needs and preferences. A niche strategy could be very favourable when a small sub-segment is less attractive to larger firms, or when the niche marketer can create a solid differential advantage, or brand preference among customers.

Volume Growth Strategies

Growth rate in mature markets flattens. When this flattening of growth occurs due to the availability of substitute products, or a definite shift in customer tastes, or changes in lifestyles etc., it is very difficult to make a market bouncy. This slow down is because of unsuitable current marketing programmes, such as very narrow segmentation or limited offerings, then aggressive marketing strategies might be successful in extending the product-market life cycle into renewed growth and additional volume growth can be pursued as an objective.

A business has choice of several strategies that can be adopted singly or in combination to gain additional volume in a market that is viewed as mature. These volume growth strategies include *greater penetration strategy, prolonged use strategy,* and *market expansion strategy.*

Greater Penetration Strategy: Sales volume of a market segment depends on (a) the number of customers in the market segment, (b) the proportion of customers in that segment who actually use the product, and (c) average rate at which customers use the product and make repeat purchase. In case the product usage rate is very high among actual users but only a relatively small portion of potential customers in the segment buy the product, a business might focus on increasing the market penetration. This strategy better suits a market leader than smaller firms with less known brands.

The business should find out the reasons why potential customers are not interested in the product. The business might learn that potential customers are aware about the product but it does not offer them sufficient value worth their effort and expense. The obvious solution is to incorporate features to deliver desired benefits through line extension. For example, a quite large number of Indian customers do not have running tap water to clean razors. Gillette introduced a special twin-blade razor, Vector Plus for Indian customers. It is easy to clean this razor in water kept in a mug or cup.

A business may increase product value by offering services that enhance its performance or use convenience for potential customers. Driving schools in many Indian cities offer additional service to learners to help them to get the driving licence. Many businesses offer extended services to their customers. Acer service to customers includes picking up its notebooks for repair and delivering back to customers.

Modifications in existing product or line extensions should be supported with more aggressive and effective promotional efforts. For example, a consumer goods firm may use a combination of advertising to stimulate primary demand among target customers and combine it with sales promotion to induce trial. BSNL has offered non-users of its broadband Internet, a two-month free trial with free downloads. An industrial goods business may offer additional sales incentive to its sales force for creating customers out of non-user groups and open new accounts.

In case distribution can improve customer access to product or service, a firm can expand or create more convenient accessible channels. Indian Railways has made it convenient to book passenger tickets online or through cell-phone and delivered at the customer's address. Wait listed passengers would be accommodated in next higher class free of additional charge. Booking offices have been opened in different locations in larger cities. Maruti Udyog has the advantage of widespread dealer network and service stations across the country.

Prolonged Use Strategy: A prolonged use strategy makes sense when a market is well penetrated but the average use per consumer is less frequent and/or use per occasion is low. For example, a shampoo marketing firm discovers through market research that market penetration is good but an average consumer uses a shampoo just twice a week and the quantity used is just about 5ml per use occasion. In situations like this, a strategy of prolonged and/or more quantity use per occasion may increase sales volume.

A firm might convince customers that the usage of shampoo five times a week gives better protection against dandruff, or on each wash occasion it is better to apply shampoo once and wash then apply a second time to derive more benefits. Sometimes firms successfully promote new uses for its products, or for new segments. Milkmaid increased its volume by promoting its product use to prepare sweets and desserts. Johnson & Johnson promoted the use of its baby shampoo and toilet soap for persons with sensitive skins and increased volume.

In case of low-involvement product categories, a business can move inventories closer to the consumers. If there is no Coke at home then a customer is unlikely to spend time or effort and buy another cola brand. Another approach is to offer larger pack sizes and minimise out of stock situation at home. Also, with more stock at home, the consumption rate may also increase (such as soft drinks, ice cream, protein powders, and detergents etc.).

For some products, package design can help to increase their consumption. For instance, a large number of customers prefer to buy single serving sachet packs of shampoo, *gutkha* (a mixture of tobacco and other ingredients), instant adhesives (Fevi Kwik), coffee, and other products. Even cell-phone service firms are offering short-time service usage packs.

Various sales promotions can help loading customers with product inventories by encouraging large volume purchases, such as quantity discounts, buy-one-take-one free, large value prize contests and scratch cards, or frequency purchase incentive programmes. For example frequent flier programmes by various airlines help customers stay loyal. Maruti Udyog announced large discount to Maruti car owners if they buy a second Maruti car.

In case of some products it is difficult to change characteristics and this discourages more frequent use, such as high calorie foods. Increasingly food product firms have focused on reducing calories to encourage more frequent usage by health conscious customers.

In case of industrial products businesses it may be necessary to have new technology to overcome product limitations for identified applications. Sales engineers or technical advertisers might visit industrial firms to advise the application and advantages of using new technology.

Market Expansion Strategy: Market expansion strategy makes sense and can gain substantial additional volume growth when a mature industry is heterogeneous and fragmented, and some market segments are not so well developed. The strategy focuses on acquiring new customers in these underdeveloped or new segments. This strategy suits leaders and also smaller firms (provided they have resources and competencies to focus on niche segments) in domestic or foreign markets.

The application of this strategy requires strengthening a firm's current position in these market segments and gain experience-curve benefits and operating synergies. This kind of expansion in a mature industry may not be a viable approach for a leader to increase volume growth because the larger firms have already gained national market coverage. Small *regional firms* in domestic market might consider this alternative of expanding their operations in other regions of national market to improve share and volume growth. Such a move entails the risk of retaliation from established competitors, national or geographic. A suitable approach for regional firm is to acquire smaller businesses in other regions. This can work when, (a) a small, low-profit business sells its assets at less than cost of capacity involved for the acquiring firm, and (b) the acquiring firm gains synergies by combining regional operations and committing additional resources and improves profitability of the acquired business.

Another approach to expand in the domestic market is to develop totally new customers or application segments. For example, a hand-made paper business selling its paper in consumer market might expand in business market. It might expand its distribution to reach other regional segments in domestic market without making any modifications in the product and no additional expense on promotion. A watch producing business, distributing through retailers might approach to chain stores to sell its watches. In certain cases, product modification may be necessary.

Some regional players produce private label brands for large retailers, such as Shoppers' Stop, Bata, Amway, and Wal-Mart etc. This is an attractive but somewhat risky option to achieve volume growth for small firms with relatively weak brands and excess installed capacity. The risk relates to relying on one or a few private label customers who have high bargaining power and might switch to other low-cost suppliers. Private label brands typically compete with low-price and this situation may suit only a low-cost position of the supplier in an industry.

Large firms with leading market shares in mature domestic product-markets have opportunities for geographic expansion in less developed but accessible foreign markets. Businesses can enter foreign markets in various ways (discussed in Chapter 24) from as simple as relying on import agents to entering into joint ventures, or establishing wholly owned subsidiaries. The sequence might involve first entering a country with a very low level of development, then to a developing country, and lastly to developed economies. Gradual sequencing might help in reducing risks and costs and gain marketing experience. Japanese businesses are viewed as masters of this game plan (Seiko, Citizen, National, Canon, Suzuki, Toyota, Honda, and others) and have entered large number of developing and developed markets in the world and have gained substantial market shares.

Many global companies plan their expansion in developing countries as the disposable income rises. This is particularly important for discretionary products, such as soft drinks, fast foods, and cosmetics. Coca Cola believes that its future growth would come from countries in Asia, South America, and Africa.

Declining Markets

Most product-markets enter a decline phase in their life cycle, but not all markets decline at the same time. Excess capacity is a burden and competitors fight to hold volume. They differ in their levels of strengths and weaknesses. Here again the basic dimensions of product-market attractiveness and competitive strengths hold good and determine the suitable strategy choice.

According to Kathryn R. Harrington, attractiveness of declining markets depends on a set of three factors: (1) conditions of demand including the rate and reliability of forecasted future decrease in volume, (2) exit barriers (ease with which weaker competitors can leave the market), and (3) rivalry and intensity of future competition within the market.

Demand conditions have a significant affect on strategy choice. Demand decline occurs due to several reasons, such as technological advances create substitute products, demographic shifts can lead to shrinking markets, changes in customer needs, preferences, and lifestyles, and high rise in the cost of consumables or complementary products.

The reasons of demand decline influence both the speed and predictability of that decline. For example, demographic shifts are likely to cause gradual decline in demand, but a shift due to technologically superior alternative can be very fast. Obviously, it is easy to predict a switch to superior substitute, while it is difficult to predict a change in customer tastes.

A slow and gradual decline gives enough time to weaker businesses to withdraw from the market. For those who stay, overcapacity is not a problem and cut-throat competitive actions are less likely to obtain profits, but not so if the decline is quick and erratic. In case the decline is predictable and certain, it is easy to withdraw conveniently and overcapacity does not become a problem. But if the uncertainty is high about whether the demand might decline, or increase, overcapacity may lead to predatory competitive actions.

Exit barriers are the second important factor that influences strategy choice. If the exit barriers are high, it is less favourable for a competitor to exit the product-market. Weaker businesses find it difficult to leave a product-market as demand falls, excess capacity builds, and competitors engage in aggressive price cuts and even promotional efforts in attempting to increase their volume and keep their units costs low. This leads to volatile competitive behaviour of firms.

Firms have some highly specialised assets unique to a particular business and these are difficult to divest because of low liquidation value. Potential buyers for such assets are businesses who would use them for a similar purpose as the seller firm, and this is quite unlikely in a declining product-market. Businesses may have no option but to stay or sell the assets for their scrap value. The problem further gets complicated and unattractive when the assets are relatively new and not fully depreciated. Other exit barriers include assets that are used in shared production facilities in firm's other business units, and reluctance of managers to admit failure and divest a business that no longer delivers acceptable returns.

Rivalry and intensity of future competition is the third factor to consider in making a strategic choice. In a declining market, there may still be some pockets with significant demand but it may be unwise to pursue them in the face of future intense competitive rivalry. Other factors, such as bargaining power of customers and their ease of switching to substitutes, and diseconomies of scale may not be favourable to get involved in intense price competition.

Decision to Divest

During the product-market decline stage, a firm finds the situation unattractive and it has a relatively weak competitive position. The business sees an opportunity of recovering a major portion of its investment by selling its business in the early stages of product-market decline and not later. In the early stages of market decline there is some uncertainty about the future direction of demand in the market among potential buyers. The likelihood of finding a willing buyer may not be difficult. By opting for an early exit, the firm may obtain a higher liquidation value. Quick divestment may not be possible if the exit barriers are high. This decision also has some risks. The firm might be wrong about future forecast of product-market.

Marketing Strategies for Competitors Who Stay in Declining Market

Strategies for declining markets include *harvesting strategy, maintenance strategy, survival with profits strategy,* and *niche strategy.*

Harvesting Strategy: The aim of this strategy is to generate cash quickly by maximising cash flow in a relatively short period. The company avoids any additional investment in business, reducing marketing and other operational expenses, and in some case raising prices. The strategy is to divest the business and some loss of sales and market share is likely to occur during the implementation period. The efforts should be to keep the sales and market share decline as slow as possible and steady.

This strategy works best when the business is relatively strong at the beginning of the decline stage and still a share of current customers buy the product even with reduced marketing support. This strategy is also appropriate when the decline is slow and steady and competitive intensity is not likely to be very severe. The business should try improving efficiency of sales and distribution, and reduce advertising and promotion expenses to the minimum necessary level.

Maintenance Strategy: With high level of uncertainty about future sales volumes in a declining market, a firm having leading market share might adopt this strategy. The business continues with its earlier strategy that succeeded during maturity stage of product-market, till the time the future of declining market becomes more obvious. The business has to reduce either price or increase marketing expenditure to hold market share in a declining product-market. Often this results in reduced short-run margins and profits. This a kind of stop-gap arrangement. When its certain that market decline will continue, the business should switch to some other strategy to gain cash flows over the remaining period of product-market life cycle.

Survival with Profits Strategy: In a declining product-market, this strategy may suit a business with strong share position and a sustainable competitive advantage. The firm invests to gain more product-market share and become the market leader till the remaining part of market decline period.

The conditions suitable for this strategy include certainty of slow and gradual decline in demand, and sustained demand continues in several pockets of the market and is likely to continue in future for a period of time. This strategy also makes sense when a company in declining product-market has shared facilities, programmes, or common customer groups with other divisions in the firm.

Improving market share is often possible for a strong share leader in a declining market because other competitors may be preparing to harvest or divest. The firm should aggressively cuts prices, or increase advertising and promotion. It may also introduce line extensions aimed at existing pockets of demand and make it increasingly tough going for smaller competitors seeking niches. The firm may purchase smaller competitors and either improve their productivity or scuttle them to avoid unnecessary excess capacity.

Niche Marketer Strategies: Becoming a niche marketer is a refusal to becoming a follower. Even when most segments in a product-market are expected to decline, a niche strategy may be a viable alternative. The firm should have a strong competitive position in a target segment and have competencies to hold sustainable competitive advantage to pre-empt competitors. It is often a good strategy to avoid direct competition with larger businesses that pursue several larger market segments. For example, Apple is a niche marketer serving customers having specialised needs. TAG Heuer watches serve the specialised needs of auto race enthusiasts. A niche marketer gains limited sales volume and earns high margins per unit of sales, and a mass marketer gains high sales volumes and lesser margins.

A niche share firm is a market leader in many ways. It is simply the share leader in a more narrowly defined and potentially profitable sub-segment of a larger segment. Niche marketer can adopt defensive strategies to protect its share position.

Summary

Generally companies view and analyse competition both from an industry and a marketing perspective. An industry represents a group of companies that offer a product or class of products that are viewed as close substitutes to satisfy a need category, or a set of needs.

Marketers generally select product type as the basis of analysis for marketing planning because these products are viewed as close substitutes for one another. It is advisable in analysing the market and competition to keep in focus the consumer need, but this practice seems uncommon among marketers. Managers tend to identify fewer companies as competitors and generally omit the new companies. In reality, the range of a firm's actual and potential competitors is much broader and the chances are more that a company stands to get hurt by potential competitors or new technologies than the players already competing.

Rivalry takes place among companies that produce close substitute products and when competitors try to improve or maintain their position. Whatever action one company takes affects others. Greater the competitive intensity in an industry, less attractive it is to current or would-be entrants. Five important forces should be considered while analysing the attractiveness of industries and these include present competitors, potential competitors, bargaining power of suppliers, the bargaining power of buyers, and the threat of substitute products.

During different stages of product-market life cycle, market leaders, followers, challengers, and niche marketers have several strategic choices depending on the prevailing and forecasted market conditions.

During growth stage the competition starts increasing in intensity. Near the end of growth stage, there is a period of transition from growth to maturity and firms surviving this stage enter the maturity phase of the life cycle. It is advantageous for business to develop sustainable competitive advantage during the growth stage to be successful during the maturity phase.

Competitive intensity is at its highest during early maturity to hold share position and profitability. Normally the share leader stands a better chance of earning large profits by adopting suitable marketing strategies and programmes.

During decline phase of life cycle, the options are to divest, harvest, or stay longer for the remaining part of the decline.

Questions for Discussion

1. In what type of competitive market structure does Maruti Udyog operate?
2. Why is competition a concern for marketers?
3. What is the influence of competitive market forces in determining long-term market attractiveness?
4. Distinguish between monopoly, oligopoly, monopolistic competition, and perfect competition.
5. A leading beverage marketing company wants to start sandwich and coffee outlets in large cities all over India. What products and companies should it consider as competitors?
6. What competitive strategies are suitable for market share leaders?
7. Under what market conditions is it appropriate to stay in a declining product-market?
8. Discuss defensive strategies.
9. Discuss two strategies suitable for a challenger in detergent market.

Projects

1. You are a consultant and have been hired by Airtel to conduct a competitive analysis. Prepare a report.
2. Consider a business where in you have access to its market information and competitors. Suggest a strategy it should apply. Give your analysis and reasons.

Bibliography

1. Bruce H. Clark and David B. Montgomery, "Managerial Identification of Competitors," *Journal of Marketing,* July 1999.
2. Michael Porter, *Competitive Strategy,* 1980.
3. L. W. Phillips, D. R. Chang, and R. D. Buzzell, "Product Quality, Cost Position, and Business Performance: A Test of Some Key Hypotheses," *Journal of Marketing,* 47 (January 1983).
4. R. J. Calantone and K. E. Schatzel, "Strategic Foretelling: Communication-Based Antecedents of a Firm's Propensity to Pre-announce," *Journal of Marketing,* 64 (January 2000).
5. B. L. Bayus, S. Jain, and A. G. Rao, "Truth or Consequences: An Analysis of Vapoware and New Product Announcements," *Journal of Marketing Research,* 38 (February 2001).
6. Robert D. Buzzell and Frederick D. Wiersema, "Successful Share-Building Strategies," *Harvard Business Review,* (January-February 1891).
7. Robert D. Buzzell and Bradly T. Gale, *The PIMS Principles: Linking Strategy to Performance,* 1987.
8. Linda Hellofs and Robert Jacobson, "Market Share and Customer's Perceptions of Quality: When Can Firms Grow Their Way to Higher Versus Lower Quality," *Journal of Marketing,* 63 (January 1999).
9. Michael E. Porter, *Competitive Strategy,* 1980.
10. Freena Sultan, John U. Farley, and Donald R. Lehman, "A Meta-Analysis of Applications of Diffusion Models," *Journal of Marketing Research,* February 1990.
11. Ming Jer Chen and Ian C. McMillan, "Nonresponse and Delayed Response to Competitive Moves: The Roles of Competitor Dependence and Action Irreversibility," *Academy of Management Journal,* 35 (1992).
12. Kathryn R. Harrington, *Managing Maturing Businesses,* 1988.

Cases

Case 7.1: Off Colour

Despite periodic makeovers colour cosmetics brand Tips and Toes is losing its sheen.

Reinventing a brand is always a challenge in a market where product life cycles are as short as four or five months, driven by fickle trends and seasons.

A strong case in point is Tips and Toes, launched by Paramount Cosmetics in 1979, which started as a nail colour brand and then grew to include lipsticks and other cosmetic and toiletry products.

After a series of brand extensions and re-launches, the brand is looking for some "divine" inspiration to make its mark in an increasingly competitive business. The latest avatars of Tips and Toes are the Goddess and the Eve Divine ranges, which hit the market early this year.

However, neither of the products has acquired many converts. Brands like Lakmé, Revlon and Lissome (a new entrant in the economy segment) are still far more visible on a cosmetic retailer's shelves.

A visit to any marketplace in Mumbai shows that at least four out of 10 retailers think that the brand has been phased out. And the remaining don't want to stock the brand anymore.

This marks a stark colour contrast to the 1980s when the brand enjoyed tremendous equity as the only other organised player apart from the Tata-owned Lakmé in the cosmetics business. It rose to dominate about 30 per cent of the nail colour market.

But over the years, it has been chipped out of the reckoning. Lakmé continues to dominate the cosmetics market with a 50 per cent share, followed by Revlon at 12 per cent and Maybelline at 8 per cent.

Tips and Toes is a small player selling at only 2,000 outlets. A competitor asserts, "The brand has fallen out of our consideration over the past five or six years."

So why did the colour start fading from Tips and Toes' performance? This was partly a result of excise anomalies. Back in the 1980s, to encourage small-scale industry, manufacturing units with turnovers of more than Rs 15 lakh were subject to excise duty of 120 per cent.

As a solution, Paramount Cosmetics divided its own manufacturing outfit into 27-odd units to meet the small-scale criterion. But in 1997, excise duty was standardised to cover all manufacturing units irrespective of their turnover.

Obviously, it no longer made sense to stick to the model of manufacturing at so many small units of its own.

"Paramount was late to realise that it would be better to outsource its manufacturing and concentrate on marketing, given the increased levels of competition in the cosmetic market," says a market watcher.

On the other hand, Lakmé was quick to outsource its production in 1995. Previously, the company manufactured at its Deonar plant, a Mumbai suburb. Paramount followed suit only in the year, 2000 when it outsourced to three manufacturers.

The problems of manufacturing consolidation impinged on marketing strategies too. During the 90s, as competition started making its mark, Paramount was consistently late to market.

Contd...

This is a major issue in a business like colour cosmetics where fashions change every few months. Players like Lakmé, Revlon and Maybelline launch at least two new ranges in a year.

For example, the mid-1990s saw the launch of an imported matte format lipstick brand called Personi, which set off a fashion for matte lipsticks in India.

Distributors recall that Lakmé and Gala were the first to launch their matte ranges almost immediately. But Tips and Toes launched its matte collection only in 1998.

Again, while the colour trend shifted to lighter and glossy colours in 2001, Tips and Toes largely stuck to the dark shades like red and maroon — and this continues even in its Goddess collection.

"We also create colours in line with the market but our study shows that regular shades (reds and browns) are still the faster moving shades," explains Hitesh Topiwala, director, marketing, Paramount.

Also, when others were pushing their economy ranges, Tips and Toes lost the opportunity although it was in a position to do so after cutting costs by outsourcing its new nail colours.

It was only in 2002 that the company launched its range of "mini" nail colours priced at Rs. 18. This was much after the launch of Elle 18 — Lakmé's economy brand launched in 1995. And where Lakmé targeted the faster growing market for teenagers through Elle 18, Tips and Toes sharpened its focus on women aged between 20 and 35 years.

"Our understanding and experience of the changing needs of the Indian women made us move from teenagers to a young woman," says Topiwala.

Also, brand extensions have been slow in coming. For example, in the early 1980s, Tips and Toes was restricted to nail colours while Lakmé had forayed into lipsticks and basic skincare and make-up products like compact powder and winter-care lotion. When Paramount finally started expanding its range, it made too many mistakes.

For instance, the company launched its lipstick brand under the name Kiss'n Tell because research showed that Tips and Toes brand name suggested only nail colours. That turned out to be a bad decision because customers felt shy about asking for it by name at shops.

The company then tried to correct its mistake by calling its lipsticks "Whisper". But Proctor & Gamble had already got that brand name registered for its sanitary products. Thus, Paramount eventually had to bring in its lipsticks under the fold of Tips and Toes brand name.

In the event, this was actually a good thing because Paramount could not summon up enough resources to market its subsequent extensions under different brand names — a skincare brand Enriche and a men's toiletries brand called Instinct among them — adequately.

Compare this with Lakmé, which launched all its ranges under the umbrella brand. Former company officials recall that there were bottlenecks in the distribution network too. This was partly because of the over-abundance in shades that the company supplied in the market.

Till recently, the company focused on pushing quantity rather than learning from the competition and launching seasonal ranges.

For example, in the 1980s, Tips and Toes had an exhaustive shade card running into 80-odd shades compared to Lakmé's modest 48 shades.

Pushing a large number of shades in the market was difficult when only a few moved fast according

Contd...

to season and trend. Inevitably, this led to overstocking at retail stores.

"To add to it, neither did the company take back the returned stock nor did it increase visits to replenish stock," recalls a former Mumbai-based distributor, who distributed the brand till the late 1990s.

Even as Tips and Toes finally trimmed its colour portfolio down to 21 lip colour shades and 37 nail colours, its emphasis on darkish colours like maroons and browns has stayed in spite of the trend moving towards floral shades, say retailers.

The company says that it has corrected the problem of the backlog of slower moving shades piling at stores now.

Says Topiwala, "With the Goddess range, we have learnt which shades move faster. Accordingly, the shades are taken off the shelves in about three-four months' times and replenished with the faster moving stock."

Pricing was another big issue. Back in the early 1990s, the company had launched another range of premium colour cosmetics called Cloud Nine targeted at teenagers. But the premium pricing didn't help simply because teenagers couldn't afford it.

Later, Lakmé launched Elle 18 — its colour cosmetics targeted at teenagers, which was priced economically. For instance, while Lakmé lipsticks and nail colours cost Rs 58 and Rs 39 in the mid-1990s, an Elle 18 lipstick cost about Rs 35 and Rs 25. Paramount cut Cloud Nine prices to take on Elle 18 but eventually had to discontinue it.

Then, when Tips and Toes made a comeback with the Goddess range, it could have done better by focusing on the B and C class cities, say market watchers. This is because Tips and Toes is 20 per cent cheaper than brands like Lakmé.

Currently, Tips and Toes is present in only two or three key cities in Maharashtra, Karnataka, Andhra Pradesh, Tamil Nadu and Delhi.

"We target metros and A class cities only because Tips and Toes is essentially an urban brand. Also, women in smaller towns are influenced by urbane imagery, so it's essential to maintain this positioning," says Topiwala.

But for that, Paramount will have to fight for its share of consumer mind-space. Despite spurts of advertising in women's magazines, the brand has stayed in the shadows through most of the 1990s. Though Paramount claims it spends about 15 per cent of its turnover on ads and below-the-line activities, lack of consistent mass-media advertising has pushed the brand onto the sidelines. Tips and Toes distributors and retailers in Mumbai vouch for that.

"The more visible the brand is, the more customers ask for it. Demand is directly proportionate to advertising in the mass media," says one of them. Will Tips and Toes listen to its past to add colour to its dull present?

(Source: www.bsstrategist.com June 18, 2005).

QUESTION

1. Study the case and identify the stage of Tips and Toes life cycle. What mistakes Paramount Cosmetics committed for its brand Tips and Toes.

Case 7.2: Video Games

The rise of personal computers in the mid 1980s spurred interest in computer games. This caused a crash in home Video game market. Interest in Video games was rekindled when a number of different companies developed hardware consoles that provided graphics superior to the capabilities of computer games. By 1990, the Nintendo Entertainment System dominated the product category. Sega surpassed Nintendo when it introduced its Genesis System. By 1993, Sega commanded almost 60 per cent of Video game market and was one of the most recognised brand names among the children.

Sega's success was short lived. In 1995, Saturn (a division of General Motors) launched a new 32-bit system. The product was a miserable failure for a number of reasons. Sega was the primary software developer for Saturn and it did not support efforts by outside game developers to design compatible games. In addition, Sega's games were often delivered quite late to retailers. Finally, the price of the Saturn system was greater than other comparable game consoles.

This situation of Saturn's misstep benefited Nintendo and Sony greatly. Sony's PlayStation was unveiled in 1994 and was available in 70 million homes worldwide by the end of 1999. Its "Open design" encouraged the efforts of outside developers, resulting in almost 3,000 different games that were compatible with the PlayStation. It too featured 32-bit graphics that appealed to older audience. As a result, at one time, more than 30 per cent of PlayStation owners were over 30 years old.

Nintendo 64 was introduced in 1996 and had eye-popping 64-bit graphics and entered in more than 28 million homes by 1999. Its primary users were between the age of 6 and 13 as a result of Nintendo's efforts to limit the amount of violent and adult-oriented material featured on games that can be played on its systems. Because the company exercised considerable control over software development, Nintendo 64 had only one-tenth the number of compatible games as Sony's PlayStation did.

By 1999, Sony had captured 56 per cent of the video game market, followed by Nintendo with 42 per cent. Sega's share had fallen to a low of 1%. Hence, Sega had two options, either to concede defeat or introduce an innovative video machine that would bring in huge sales. And Sega had to do so before either Nintendo or Sony could bring their next-generation console to market. The Sega Dreamcast arrived in stores in September 1999 with an initial price tag of $199. Anxious gamers placed 300,000 advance orders, and initial sales were quite encouraging. A total of 1.5 million Dreamcast machines were bought within the first four months, and initial reviews were positive. The 128-bit system was capable of generating 3-D visuals, and 40 different games were available within three months of Dreamcast's introduction.

By the end of the year, Sega had captured a market share to 15 per cent. But the Dreamcast could not sustain its momentum. Although its game capabilities were impressive, the system did not deliver all the functionality Sega had promised. A 56K modem (which used a home phone line) and a Web browser were meant to allow access to the Internet so that gamers could play each other online, surf the Web, and visit the Dreamcast Network for product information and playing tips. Unfortunately, these features either were not immediately available or were disappointing in their execution.

Contd...

Sega was not the only one in having the strategy of adding functionality beyond games. Sony and Nintendo followed the same approach for their machines introduced in 1999. Both Nintendo's Neptune and Sony's PlayStation 2 (PS2) were built on a DVD platform and featured a 128-bit processor. Analysts applauded the move to DVD because it is less expensive to produce and allows more storage than CDs. It also gives buyers the ability to use the machine as CD music player and DVD movie player. As Sony marketing director commented, "The full entertainment offering from Play Station 2 definitely appeals to a much broader audience. I have friends in their 30s who bought it not only because it's a gaming system for their kids, but also a DVD for them." In addition, PlayStation 2 is able to play games developed for its earlier model that was CD-based. This gives the PS2 an enormous advantage in the number of compatible game titles that were immediately available to gamers.

Further enhancing the PS2's appeal is its high-speed modem and allows the users easy access to the Internet through digital cable as well as over telephone lines. This gives Sony the ability to distribute movies, music, and games directly to PS2 consoles. "We are positioning this as an all-round entertainment player," commented Ken Kutaragi, the head of Sony Computer Entertainment. However, some prospective customers were put off by the console's initial price of $360.

Shortly after the introduction of Neptune, Nintendo changed its strategies and announced the impending release of its newest game console, The GameCube. However, unlike the Neptune, the GameCube would not run on a DVD platform and also would not initially offer any online capabilities. It would be more attractively priced at $199. A marketing vice-president for Nintendo explained the company's change in direction, "We are the only competitor whose business is video games. We want to create the best gaming system." Nintendo also made the GameCube friendly for outside developers and started adding games that included sports titles to attract an older audience. Best known for its extra ordinary successes with games aimed at the younger set, such as Donkey Kong, Super Mario Bros, and Pokemon, Nintendo sought to attract older users, especially because the average video game player is 28. Youthful Nintendo users were particularly pleased to hear that they could use their handheld Game Boy Advance systems as controllers for the GameCube.

Nintendo scrambled to ensure there would be an adequate supply of GameCubes on the date in November 2001, when they were scheduled to be available to customers. It also budgeted $450 million to market its new product, as it anticipated stiff competition during the holiday shopping season. With more than 20 million PlayStation 2 sold worldwide, the GameCube as a new entry in the video game market would make the battle for market share even more intense.

For almost a decade, the video game industry had only Sega, Nintendo, and Sony; just three players. Because of strong brand loyalty and high product development costs, newcomers faced a daunting task in entering this race and being competitive.

In November 2001, Microsoft began selling its new Xbox, just three days before the GameCube made its debut. Some observers felt the Xbox was aimed to rival PlayStation 2, which has similar functions that rival Microsoft's Web TV system and even some lower level PCs.

Like the Sony's PlayStation 2, Xbox was also built using a DVD platform, but it used an Intel processor in its construction. This open design allowed Microsoft to develop the Xbox in just two years, and gave developers the option of using standard PC tool for creating compatible games. In addition, Microsoft also sought the advice of successful game developers and even incorporated some of their feedback into the design of the console and its controllers. As a result of developers'

Contd...

efforts, Microsoft had about 20 games ready when the Xbox became available. By contrast, The GameCube had only eight games available.

Microsoft online strategy was another feature that differentiated of the Xbox from the GameCube. Whereas Nintendo had no immediate plans for Web-based play, the Xbox came equipped with an Ethernet port for broadband access to Internet. Microsoft also announced its own Web-based network on which gamers can come together for online head-to-head play and for organised online matches and tournaments. Subscribers to this service were to pay a small monthly fee and must have high-speed access to the Internet. This is a potential drawback considering that a very low percentage of households world over currently have broadband connections.

By contrast Sony promoted an open network, which allows software developers to manage their own games, including associated fees charged to users. However, interested players must purchase a network adapter for an additional $39.99. Although game companies are not keen on the prospect of submitting to the control of a Microsoft-controlled network, it would require a significant investment for them to manage their own service on the Sony-based network.

Initially the price of Microsoft's Xbox was $299. Prior to the introduction of Xbox, in a competitive move Sony dropped the price of the PlayStation 2 to $299. Nintendo's GameCube already enjoyed a significant price advantage, as it was selling for $100 less than either Microsoft or Sony products.

Gamers eagerly snapped up the new consoles and made 2001 the best year ever for video game sales. For the first time, consumers spent $9.4 billion on video game equipment, which was more than they did at the box office. By the end of 2001 holiday season, 6.6 million PlayStation 2 consoles had been sold in North America alone, followed by 1.5 million Xbox units and 1.2 million GameCubes.

What ensued was an all out price war. This started when Sony decided to put even more pressure on the Microsoft's Xbox by cutting the PlayStation 2 price to $199. Microsoft quickly matched that price. Wanting to maintain its low-price status, Nintendo in turn responded by reducing the price of its the GameCube by $50, to $149.

By mid 2002, Microsoft Xbox had sold between 3.5 and 4 million units worldwide. However, Nintendo had surpassed Xbox sales by selling 4.5 million GameCubes. Sony had the benefit of healthy head start, and had shipped 32 million PlayStation 2s. However, seven years after the introduction of original PlayStation, it was being sold in retail outlets for a mere $49. It had a significant lead in terms of numbers of units in homes around the world with a 43 per cent share. Nintendo 64 was second with 30 per cent, followed by Sony PlayStation 2 with 14 per cent. The Xbox and GameCube each claimed about 3 per cent of the market, with Sega Dreamcast comprising the last and least market share of 4.7 per cent.

Sega, once an industry leader, announced in 2001 that it had decided to stop producing the Dreamcast and other video game hardware components. The company said it would develop games for its competitors' consoles. Thus Sega slashed the price of the Dreamcast to just $99 in an effort to liquidate its piled up inventory of more than 2 million units and immediately began developing 11 new games for the Xbox, four for PlayStation 2, and three for Nintendo's GameBoy Advance.

As the prices of video game consoles have dropped, consoles and games have become the equivalent of razors and blades. This means the consoles generate little if any profit, but the

Contd...

games are a highly profitable proposition. The profit margins on games are highly attractive, affected to some degree by whether the content is developed by the console maker (such as Sony) or by an independent game publisher (such as Electronic Arts). Thus, the competition to develop appealing, or perhaps even addictive, games may be even more intense than the battle among players to produce the best console. In particular, Nintendo, Sony, and Microsoft want games that are exclusive to their own systems. With that in mind, they not only rely on large in-house staffs that design games but they also pay added fees to independent publishers for exclusive rights to new games.

The sales of video games in 2001 rose to 43 per cent, compared to just 4 per cent increase for computer-based games. But computer game players are believed to be a loyal bunch, as they see many advantages in playing games on their computers rather than consoles. For one thing, they have a big advantage of having access to a mouse and a keyboard that allow them to play far more sophisticated games. In addition, they have been utilising the Internet for years to receive game updates and modifications and to play each other over the Web.

Sony and Microsoft are intent on capturing a portion of the online gaming opportunity. Even Nintendo has decided to make available a modem that will allow GameCube users to play online. As prices continue to fall and technology becomes increasingly more sophisticated, it remains to be seen whether these three companies can keep their names on the industry's list of "high scorers,"

QUESTIONS

1. Considering the concept of product life cycle, where would you put video games in their life cycle?
2. What are the implications of each product's life cycle stage?
3. Should video game companies continue to alter their products to include other functions, such as e-mail?

Case 7.3: Beyond the Bullet

How successful has Siddhartha Lal's game plan for Royal Enfield Motors been?

Almost two years ago, Siddhartha Lal, chief executive of Royal Enfield Motors, the two-wheeler division of Eicher Group, told The Strategist ("Biting the Bullet", November 6, 2001) about his elaborate comeback plans for the company's ailing business.

It had suffered a loss of Rs 1.6 crore over a sales turnover of Rs 142 crore. Lal's immediate concerns were to cut costs and streamline the company's finances.

But broadly, he told us that the attempt was to make Royal Enfield the leader in the higher-end bikes segment.

Towards this end, his priorities were to step up marketing efforts, widen the distribution network, provide consumers with new, improved models every six months and to stay focused on the needs of the niche segment of 250cc-plus bikes.

Two years on, how successful have Lal and his team been? Certainly, sales has improved. From 20,487 bikes in 2000-01 and 22,770 in 2001-02, domestic sales crossed the 25,000-mark in 2002-03 with 26,610 bikes.

No small achievement, considering that in the past two years the market has expanded to accommodate 10 more models, taking the total to 30.

But at the same time, the domestic motorcycle market has grown about 30 per cent between 2000-01 and 2002-03 and Royal Enfield's market share in these two years has shown a marginal increase from 0.72 per cent to 0.79 per cent.

The company says that this is primarily because Royal Enfield caters to the niche audience (bulk sales lie in the 100cc plus segment).

Fair enough, but then Bajaj Auto's Pulsar, the 175cc bike launched in March 2001 (though not in the same category of 250cc plus bikes) and considered a power bike, has average sales of about 29,000 bikes a month.

Yamaha Motors' 125cc cruiser Enticer (launched in July last year) sold around 54,000 bikes in a year. Royal Enfield, on the other hand, sold just over 28,000 bikes (including exports) in 2002-03. Sales have grown by 15 per cent, but volume remains dismal.

Lal says that the biggest achievement for the company is that it has been able to overcome the financial loss, it was facing two years ago.

The company's sales turnover has increased to Rs 169 crore from Rs 142 crore, a 19 per cent growth. And Royal Enfield has made a profit of Rs 7.92 crore against a loss of Rs 1.6 crore in 2000-2001.

Lal says that a lot of changes that the organisation underwent in the past two years were internal. The objective was to streamline costs and return to profitability.

Broadly, for this, the company closed its unit in Jaipur (the only one outside Chennai) last year; reduced manpower substantially and cut material costs. Even while it saved on costs in these areas, it shifted its investment focus to product development and marketing.

Contd...

Says Lal, "Now that the bottom line is secured, we are on the right track. With this, we now have a single-track focus — making our current operations very efficient and investing in future areas."

Two years ago, Lal had committed a new model every six months. The company has kept its promise, more or less.

It launched three new models (all 346 cc) in two years — the Bullet Electra in August 2001, the Thunderbird (a cruiser) in April 2002 and the (reworked) Machismo in April 2003.

"It is not important to have a launch every six months, but what we want is to create a pull in the market with each launch. We are actually trying to come out of the syndrome where people would say that Royal Enfield had just that one old, black bike — the Bullet — all the others are modifications."

But that's exactly what industry observers are saying: that Royal Enfield's models are reworked versions of the original Bullet in the 1950s. They say changes are mostly cosmetic.

"The technology that Royal Enfield is using is vintage — of the mid 1950s. Technically, the Bullet today has the same frame, same engine, same shock absorbers, same suspension — almost everything is the same. Even in the new bikes, frills may have been added, but technically, there is no big change," says Tutu Dhawan, an auto industry analyst.

Lal doesn't completely disagree with Dhawan, but says Thunderbird and Machismo use a new engine which is more contemporary with a modern 5-speed left-shift gearbox.

While the frame hasn't changed, he points to several style changes in the Thunderbird — in the mud guard, the side panel and the tank, for instance. That may not be enough, warns Dhawan.

"At a time when most auto companies are offering their products with technologies at par with international standards, minor upgrades cannot take Royal Enfield a long way. Either it revamps its technology completely — go the Ducati, or the Triumph way — or die a slow death."

Royal Enfield seems to be listening. The new bike to be launched in April 2004 will be completely new, says Lal, even though it will also be in the 350cc plus category.

"It will not have one visible part that will be common with the current range of bikes," he adds.

More importantly, the engine will be new — not a modification of earlier versions, but built from scratch.

Company sources say it has been developed keeping in mind the needs of the power bike segment (250cc plus); the engine is now at the execution stage. This engine may soon replace the engines on Royal Enfield's other bikes as well.

Stepping up marketing was the second key priority for Lal two years ago. Royal Enfield is primarily identified with the Bullet; it doesn't help that the company advertises very little, and has no television ads.

That will change next month when Royal Enfield will launch what Lal calls a "relatively large" TV ad campaign for Bullet Electra. In the past two years, it has also had two print ad campaigns for Thunderbird and Bullet Electra.

"You need to understand our target audience to understand our marketing efforts. We are not targeting the absolute mass market," explains Lal.

Contd...

"We see a huge trend towards upgrading bikers. People who've already owned a bike look for a bit more from their machines and are also willing to pay a bit more. With domestic sales of about 26,500 bikes a year, I think that we have only skinned the surface of this segment, we can definitely have two, three, even four times this volume."

"We want an additional 10,000 to 15,000 people. To get that number, do we need to reach 10 million people? Probably no. But we do need to reach 50,000 to 100,000 people much more effectively," says Lal.

So, instead of continuous, big-budget ad campaigns, Royal Enfield is concentrating on motorcycling activities focused on potential audiences in colleges, institutions and corporations. These activities include adventure rides, weekend drives, motorcycling clubs and so on.

The third area of priority that Lal talked about was to widen the company's distribution network. In the past two years, there has been no significant change in the number of dealerships across the country — in 2001 there were 220 dealers, there are now 224 dealers.

The company says that this is because some 20 dealerships were cancelled and almost the same number added.

Royal Enfield now claims to be making substantial investments in providing better infrastructure and training to dealers. "More than the numbers, the idea is to improve the quality of dealerships," says Lal.

The dealers don't seem to be satisfied with Royal Enfield's efforts. Many dealers in semi-urban areas that also caters to rural audiences (both segments form 65 per cent of the company's sales; semi-urban 35 per cent, rural 30 per cent) say that interest rates on finance schemes are high and the packages are not flexible enough.

Royal Enfield has a nationwide tie-up with ICICI Bank for finance of its vehicles. In Gurgaon, Haryana, it charges a flat interest rate of 14 per cent, which is much higher than the rate charged by banks associated with motorcycle manufacturers.

Associate Bank, for instance, has a tie-up with LML; it charges between 7.5 and 11 per cent. Similarly, Bajaj Auto Finance has packages with even zero per cent finance on many two-wheelers.

A substantial number of Royal Enfield customers are from rural areas, but dealers complain that banks are not too keen on financing such customers given the difficulties in paperwork and record keeping.

"This cuts down on our market," says a dealer in Gurgaon. Lal admits there is not much Royal Enfield can do in these cases, but adds that the company is working on better finance packages with ICICI Bank and some local banks.

So, where does Royal Enfield go from here? Lal says the company will be focusing on three areas. First, is to work on the existing brands and make them much stronger.

Second, he says, is a market-led strategy: "The up graders in the market are the most important for us, so our next family of bikes will squarely address that segment — in around three years time we'll be addressing this segment much better."

And third is a strategy to create new markets, where again Royal Enfield will be looking at the needs of up graders — providing more power, more fuel economy, more comfort or more individuality in bikes, more maneuverability or using it in multi-conditions.

Contd...

Royal Enfield is also keen on expanding its exports. About 7 per cent of the company's total sales come from exports.

"The market in the West is largely untapped. We have a brand that people are willing to accept in these countries. To cater to their demands we need to look at bigger and more powerful bikes," says Lal.

Exports also mean higher margins: The same Bullet 500 that sells in India for Rs 70,000, fetches over Rs 2 lakh in the UK and the US, and even then it's considered a relatively cheap bike. Lal is clear that Royal Enfield will not rest on the Bullet's laurels.

"We understand that it's not the same old Bullet that will take us through the ages. That's definitely not our position. We are moving on."

(Source: www.bsstrategist.com June 18, 2005).

QUESTIONS

1. Analyse the competitive profile of Bullet Motorcycle in the two-wheeler auto industry.
2. In the present scenario, evaluate Siddhartha Lal's game plan for Bullet's revival.
3. Do you think there are any favourable factors that may help Bullet's revival? Explain.

PART 8

Marketing of Services

CHAPTER 23

LEARNING OBJECTIVES

After going through this chapter, you will understand:

- What are services and what are their special characteristics
- The extended marketing mix of services
- How services have been classified
- Developing marketing strategies for services
- Significance of people, physical evidence, and process in services
- How to achieve service quality differentiation
- Service quality evaluation and monitoring service performance

n Air India passenger reports, "I was to fly Air-India from Delhi to New York. In my hotel room, I was getting ready in a leisurely manner, confident that I had plenty of time – until the phone rang. The hotel told me that I had the timing wrong. The flight was leaving an hour earlier than the time written on the ticket. I tried arguing, half-drenched under the shower, that my ticket had to be correct. The hotel staff said they had the airline at the other end and I could speak to them. I did. After a quick confirmation, I rushed out – I had barely an hour to reach the airport and check-in.

The check-in counter was deserted but for a couple of people before me. The lady at the counter took what seemed to be eternity before my turn came. I was convinced she would not let me board. Anxious, I asked her the time of the flight. In a very placid voice she said it would leave as per the time written on my ticket! I told her that I had spoken to Air-India earlier, and had been told that the flight time on my ticket was wrong. She had no answer. I boarded the plane, still smelling of soap. Just before take-off, while I was cursing the whole incident, the check-in lady appeared, apologised for the mix-up and upgraded me to first class. I promptly forgave Air-India.

On board I met a friend. We were chatting in the alley with a drink, when a purser got us a bowl of mixture. What customer service, I told myself. My friend and I took turns to hold the bowl because we were also holding our drinks. After a while, the same purser joined us. He decided to get friendly, and started eating the mixture from the same bowl. We were taken aback by his friendliness, not to mention the un-professionalism.

"Last January, my wife and I boarded the national carrier from New York to Mumbai via Paris. It was the thick of winter with temperatures near zero. You won't believe this, but the plane did not have enough blankets! There were a few that were given to people with young children. When tempers flew, the pursers – burly men in their 50s, with hair awkwardly dyed – asked passengers to "complain to the authorities." The plane landed at Paris airport but was not taken to a gate. It was parked in the middle of the tarmac, where they opened the doors to get the plane cleaned and pantry filled up. It was snowing and for that full hour snow kept coming inside the plane. Only frayed tempers kept us warm.

It is people who make up an organisation. It baffles me to think of the low self-esteem of those who don the Air-India uniform and live this image. All airlines fly the same planes, get their lease, finance and insurance from the same agencies, use the same aviation fuel, take off and land at the same airports and get their food from the same catering service. Why then, does one set of people produce world-class service and another opt for mental poverty? Explanations apart, it is a pride thing."

(Source: Businessworld, October 18, 2004).

Services as products are widely used today by ultimate consumers, businesses, and non-profit organisations and are usually provided through the application of human and/or mechanical efforts directed at people or objects. As economies grow, the demand for services keep on increasing in numerous areas such as in education, health, finance, telecommunications, travel and transportation, entertainment, marketing research, advertising, fast food, maintenance and repair, childcare, domestic help and so on. The demand for services has become an indicator of the economic growth of a country and as economies shift from the developing to the developed stage, they will show higher demand-shift for existing and newer services. The reasons are obvious. The demand for services at the personal consumer level is related to increase in per capita income. If we look at the dual income households as a case in point, both husband and wife are employed, spare time available for domestic activities is limited, the earnings are more, and they hire domestic service providers to make life easier. Major factors contributing to the increased demand for services include economic affluence, leisure time, life expectancy, working women, product complexity, complexity of life, and new technologies etc.

Considering the domestic scene, during the past nearly 15 years, services have increasingly become more important in Indian economy and the competition in service industries is gaining momentum. Perhaps because of this reason the role of services marketing is becoming more relevant in our fast developing economy.

Defining Services

Several definitions of services have been proposed. According to Berry and Parasuraman *"A service is an intangible product involving a deed, a performance, or an effort that cannot be physically possessed."*

Christian Gronroos has proposed a more comprehensive definition of services:

"A service is an activity or series of activities of more or less intangible nature that normally, not necessarily, takes place in interactions between the customer and service employees and/ or physical resources or goods and/or system of the service provider, which are provided as solutions to customer problems."

[(Christian Gronroos, *Service Management and Marketing,* (Lexington Books, 1990)].

Characteristics of Services

The issues associated with marketing of services are somewhat different than goods marketing. This is because of typical characteristics of services. According to Christopher H. Lovelock, typical characteristics of services include (1) Intangibility (2) Inseparability of production and consumption (3) Heterogeneity (4) Perishability (5) Client-based relationship, (6) Customer contact.

Intangibility: Unlike most physical products, where a prospective buyer can examine the physical dimensions, aesthetic looks, and other aspects, a pure service cannot be assessed using any of the physical senses. Many promotional claims about tangible aspects of a product can be verified by examining the product before buying. Intangibility of services means there are no such aspects and a service cannot be seen, touched, tasted, or smelled. For example, it is not possible for an aspiring student to see, touch, taste, or smell education that students get in a management institution from attending classroom lectures and completing a variety of assignments. Similarly, a lady going to a beauty parlour for a facial cannot know how would she look afterwards unless the service is performed. It is not possible to examine a sample of surgery before buying and consuming it. The consumer experiences the reliability, expertise, attentiveness, and personal care of staff etc., only when a service has been bought and consumed. Physical products have certain benchmarks against which quality can be evaluated but any quality parameters can often be defined in the minds of consumers. Much depends on the expectations of customers.

Intangibility of services poses some problems for service marketers. A service marketer sells a promise to customers and customers are forced to place some degree of trust in the service provider to get the expected level of service performed.

Marketers also face problem in communicating with customers about pure services because there is nothing tangible to put in ads or display in a store. Where tangible products are an important part of service offer, the problems may not be so challenging. The visible part gives customers some basis to assess quality. For example, an auto service garage may have reassuring tangible cues to build customer confidence, but there is really nothing tangible to show in case of life insurance. Lack of tangible aspects increases the degree of uncertainty among consumers while considering competing offers. It is interesting to note that wherever possible, service marketers strive to add tangible physical evidence to their service offer and pure tangible product marketers often try to augment their products by including elements such as assured post-purchase service.

Pricing of services also poses problems. In case of tangible products there are raw material and labour cost to have some pricing base, in case of many services determining the cost of producing and delivering the service is very difficult. For example, to determine the price of producing and delivering a massage or haircut is very difficult. Besides, marketers may face difficulty for justifying the prices of services to customers because customers cannot evaluate services before their actual consumption.

FIGURE 23.1

Service Characteristics

Intangibility	Difficult to evaluate, Marketer sells a promise, Difficult to advertise, Difficult to justify prices, Goods augmented with intangible services.
Inseparability	Activities of service production and consumption are simultaneous, Consumers must participate in production. Consumer does not take physical possession of service, Role of service provider critical.
Heterogeneity	Considerable variation in man-based service quality, Quality control difficult, Difficult to standardise service delivery.
Perishability	Services cannot be stored. Very difficult to balance supply and demand, Unused capacity lost for ever, Considerable variation in demand.
Client-Based Relationship	Success depends on satisfied customers in the long-run, Customer relationship maintenance is critical. Retaining a group of satisfied customers essential.
Customer Contact	Service providers' commitment critical to delivery, High-level of employee training and motivation essential to success, Service marketers try to change high-contact services into low-contact services without affecting customer satisfaction.

Inseparability: In case of tangible products, their production and consumption are two separate activities and consumers are not a part of the process of production. Goods are generally produced in some central location at different times, stored, and transported to those locations where there is existing or potential demand. Inseparability of services refers to the fact that service production and consumption cannot be separated. Both, the production and consumption of services take place simultaneously. Tangible products can be bought, taken to home, stored, and consumed after sometime. This characteristic of services has implications for marketing.

Because of inseparability, the role of service provider becomes very important in the process of delivery and in some extreme cases of personal customer care must participate in the production of service. For instance, the patient must be present and participate in a surgery; a consumer must be present in a face uplift service. Mary Jo Bitner reported that for services such as education, healthcare, and hairstyling, the service provider is the service in the eyes of consumer. The service marketer must pay careful attention to proper training of service personnel.

Heterogeneity: With technological advances, most tangible products can now be produced with high degree of consistency. However, people-based services are usually susceptible to variability, or variation of quality. It is very difficult to ensure service consistency because of the very nature of human beings. Tangible products offer the opportunity of inspection and rejection before delivery but this is normally not possible in case of services.

Service marketers' greatest concern is about the variability in production standards of services, where consumers are highly involved in service production process and monitoring it is impractical such as personal healthcare. In case of machine-based services, such as telecommunication, it is possible to operate services at highly standardised level. The variation in service quality can occur in four ways: (1) variation from one marketer to another, (2) from one service to another in the same company, (3) from one outlet to another within the same company, or (4) the service delivery of the same employee can vary from customer to customer, day to day, or even hour to hour in the same day. Generally, equipment-based services are viewed as less variable than those requiring high levels of personal involvement in the production process.

In general, variability of service poses some problems to marketers in building brands. Service organisations try to minimise variability and focus on improving methods to select, train, motivate, and control service personnel. Companies also try to customise services to match the specific needs of consumers in an attempt to gain advantage. Wherever possible, marketers are shifting to equipment-based services to minimise heterogeneity. For example, increasingly different banks are installing ATMs to do away with human intervention and many banks are upgrading their systems to offer online-banking services etc. These are methods to change high-contact services into low-contact services.

Perishability: Very few services face a constant pattern of demand through time. Most services show considerable demand fluctuations. D. L. Kurtz and L. E. Boone observed that the utility of most services is short-lived. Unlike physical goods, services cannot be stored. Tangible product manufacturers can stock unsold products to be sold in future. By contrast the unsold service capacity of one occasion cannot be stored to be sold on future demand occasions. For example, if any passenger seats in an airlines flight remain unsold, these vacant seats cannot be sold after the flight departs and the capacity cannot be stored to meet extra demand on some other occasion and is wasted for that particular occasion. For these reasons, service marketers face problems in managing supply and demand. Airlines use sophisticated system of seat reservations to ensure full occupancy by manipulating the prices several times for each flight to maximise revenues. Service demand is also time or season sensitive and many services such as passenger trains, roadways, and movie theatres etc., face peak-demand and off-peak demand problems. Every vacant seat means loss of revenue on that occasion and non-availability of service involves opportunity cost.

Client-Based Relationships: According to Paul Peter and James H. Donnelly, the success of certain services depends on developing and maintaining interaction with customers that causes satisfaction and leads to repeat purchases over time. For example, lawyers, accountants, and financial consultants view their customers as clients. These professional service providers are successful only to the extent that they maintain a group of clients who retain them as advisors on an ongoing basis. Satisfied customers recommend them to others and through positive word of mouth, these professionals build a satisfactory list of satisfied clients. It is only through delivery of high-degree of service satisfaction that the customers become loyal to the service provider. Many customers repeatedly use the services of a particular insurance agent on an ongoing basis and through their word of mouth the insurance agent builds a long list of clients.

Customer Contact: This refers to those services where interaction between service provider and the consumer is necessary for service delivery. In these situations, service delivery employees become the source of creating satisfied customers. One of the major principles of customer contact is that satisfied employees lead to satisfied customers, and vice versa. Research studies indicate that employee satisfaction is the single most important factor in delivering high service quality. Thus, paying attention to training and motivating employees for customer-centered performances can help minimise customer contact problems. Service companies are trying to minimise customer contact problems by shifting high-contact services to low-contact ones by taking help of modern technological advances. This often creates the problem that service becomes more impersonal and the nature of human beings is such that they like personal contact.

Classification of Services

The distinction of pure goods seems to have disappeared or disappearing fast in today's business environment. Most of the products that we buy are combination of goods and services. Products can be good-dominant or service-dominant. For example, sugar is a good-dominant product and education is a service-dominant product. It is helpful to appreciate that tangibility and intangibility are two extremes of products on a continuum. Good-dominant products are viewed as tangible products and service-dominant products are called intangible products. At the middle point of the continuum will be products, which are equally good and service dominant, such as a restaurant. Knowing where the product lies on the service continuum is important in determining the marketing strategies for service products. Theodore Levitt observed:

"There is no such thing as service industries. There are only industries where service components are greater or less than those of other industries."

FIGURE 23.2

The Service Continuum

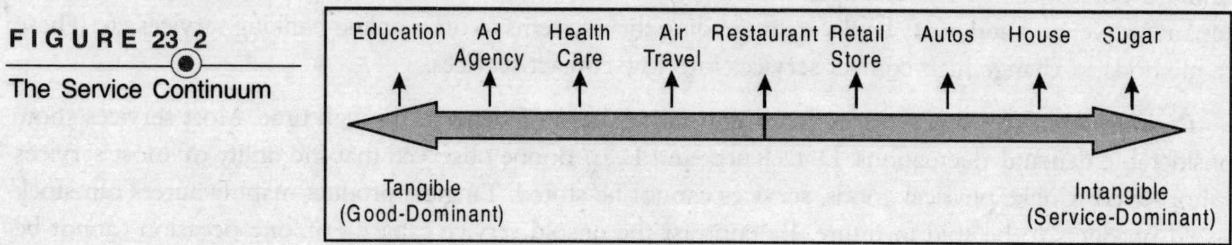

Service products are a very diverse group and include large number of industries such as health care, education, repairs, beauty parlours and barber shops, hospitality, surface and air travel, transportation, day care, legal services, financial services, business consulting, accounting, domestic services, and many others. Leonard L. Berry, David R. Bennet, and Carter W. Brown say that classifying services helps managers better understand customer needs and provide insights into marketing of services. Despite considerable diversity, services can also be classified on the basis of different categories:

- Type of market.
- Degree of labour intensiveness.
- Degree of customer contact.
- Skill of service provider.
- Goal of service provider.

Type of market or customer refers to whether the marketer serves ultimate consumers or the organisational market. It is important because the buying decision process of personal consumers and organisations differs and accordingly the marketing mix is generally adjusted for a service. For example, the tuition provider has to make adjustments while, privately coaching one or two students and when delivering classroom lectures in an educational institution.

FIGURE 23.3

Classification of Services

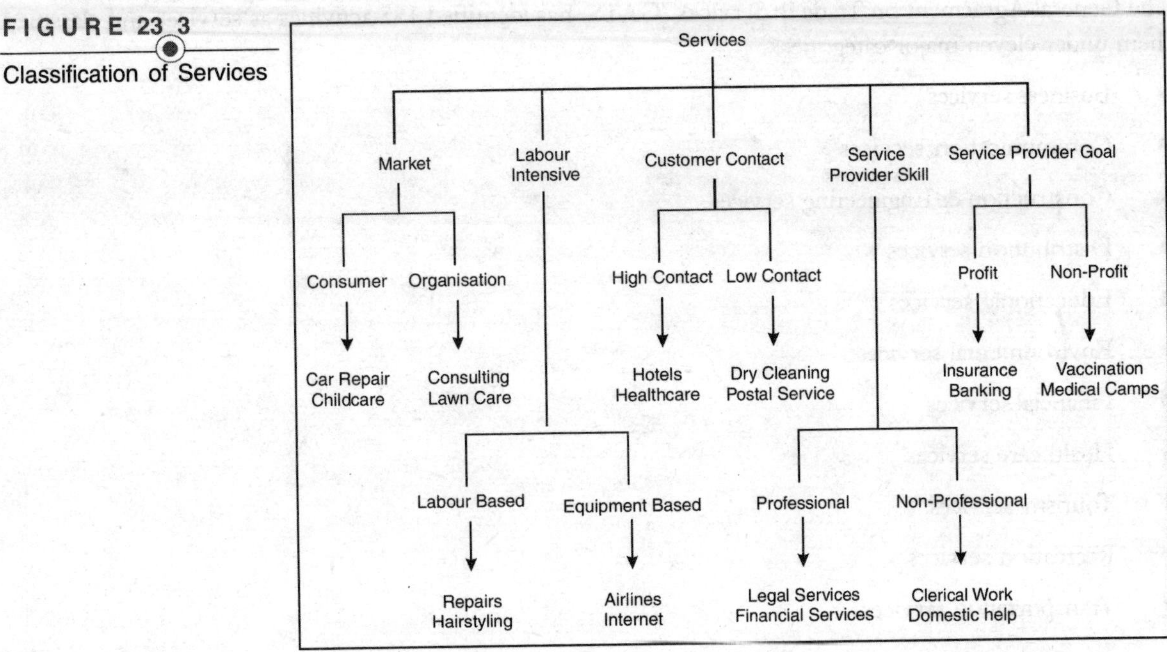

[*Source:* Adapted with slight modification from Christopher H. Lovelock, "Classifying Services to Gain Strategic Marketing Insights," *Journal of Marketing,* (Summer 1983)].

Degree of labour intensiveness is more in case of people-based services such as education, hairstyling, and repairs. Quality of service depends heavily on service delivery person's knowledge and skills. In case of telecommunications, transportation, and air travel etc., there is more reliance on equipment-based delivery. People-bases services, as mentioned earlier, are generally more heterogeneous than equipment-based services. Consumers often identify service provider as the service itself and service firms must pay special attention to selection, training, and motivation of service personnel. For example, the nursing attendants represent a hospital to many consumers.

Degree of customer contact is more in people-based services, such as hotels, restaurants, and beauty parlours etc. In case of high-contact services, actions are generally directed at individuals and consumer must be present, during service production. The physical appearance of service facility becomes a critical element in consumer's overall evaluation of service and attracting the customers. For example, an unclean consultancy chamber of a physician is likely to put off patients. Physical appearance in case of low-contact services, such as courier services, or dry cleaning is not that important because the customer does not have to be present during service delivery.

Skill of service provider is more important in case of complex professional services such as heath care or legal services. In these situations the customers often do not know what the actual service or its cost will be until the service is completed. Different laws or professional associations often regulate professional services. For example, the clerks in a hospital's record office do not need knowledge of medical subjects and skills to perform their jobs, but doctors do.

Goal of service provider relates to offering services for profit or not-for-profit. The objectives of non-profit organisations are not stated in financial terms and the users are generally donors or clients. For example, some NGOs offer legal services to needy persons of very low-income group who cannot afford hiring lawyers, or free medical service camps are organised for poor population in cities and villages. Governments organises vaccination drives free of charge.

The General Agreement on Trade in Services (GATS) has identified 155 activities as services and classified them under eleven major categories:

- Business services
- Communication services
- Construction & Engineering services
- Distribution services
- Educational services
- Environmental services
- Financial services
- Healthcare services
- Tourism services
- Recreation services
- Transportation services

Developing Marketing Strategies for Services

The aim of marketing is to satisfy customer needs and a marketer strives to deliver a complete offer that may involves a combination of some tangible and intangible products. We know services are intangible and cannot be defined in terms of their physical attributes. This poses difficulties for at least first time consumers to understand offerings and evaluate other service alternatives.

A service marketer must therefore develop strategies that satisfy needs and wants of customers. First of all the firm must determine the needs and wants of customers it aims to satisfy and select a target market. The next important step is to develop a suitable marketing mix for this target market. It is necessary to view the unique characteristics of services in developing marketing strategies for services.

The ***marketing mix for services*** is an extended one and includes *7Ps*. The first four marketing mix elements are the traditional *4Ps* that work well for tangible products. The additional three elements are important and require attention in services marketing. In addition to these *4Ps* (Product, Price, Place, and Promotion), B. H. Booms and M. J. Bitner suggested three more *P*s for service products marketing and include ***people, physical evidence***, and ***process***.

People of a service organisation involved in production and delivery of services are a vital element of the marketing mix. Service people are an important consideration because they are the ones who provide most services. Service employees sometimes become almost a distinction for some businesses and they become the business. Parasuraman and Berry observe that a service firm can be only as good as its people. If the people don't meet customers' expectations, then neither does the service. If these employees are taken away, the company may be left with few assets with which to gain competitive advantage. The actions of service employees have a much more direct affect on the output that customers receive. Sound selection, training, and motivation of service delivery personnel can mean the difference between a service business's success and failure. Satisfied customers are more likely to repeat purchase the service and spread favourable word-of-mouth. A committed service employee should ideally be competent, caring, responsive, has initiative, and problem-solving ability and attitude. In labour-intensive industries where workers must perform their tasks 'live' in front of customers, the performance of workers can have a major impact on service quality perception.

Physical evidence reduces the risk perception by customers by offering tangible evidence of the promised service delivery. Tangible evidence of service quality can take a number of forms. At its simplest level, the evidence could be a brochure that gives pictorial evidence of infrastructure and physical facilities of a management school, or a holiday brochure gives evidence of hotels and resorts. The appearance and smiles of airline staff and stewardesses provides some indication of the nature of service. For example, every McDonald's outlet right from the exterior to interior and employees evoke confidence in the kind of service a consumer can expect, and actually gets.

Process is of critical importance to consumers in high-contact services. Diners in a restaurant can be significantly affected by the manner in which staff serves them and the amount of waiting time involved in the service production process.

FIGURE 23.4

Services Involve Three Types of Marketing

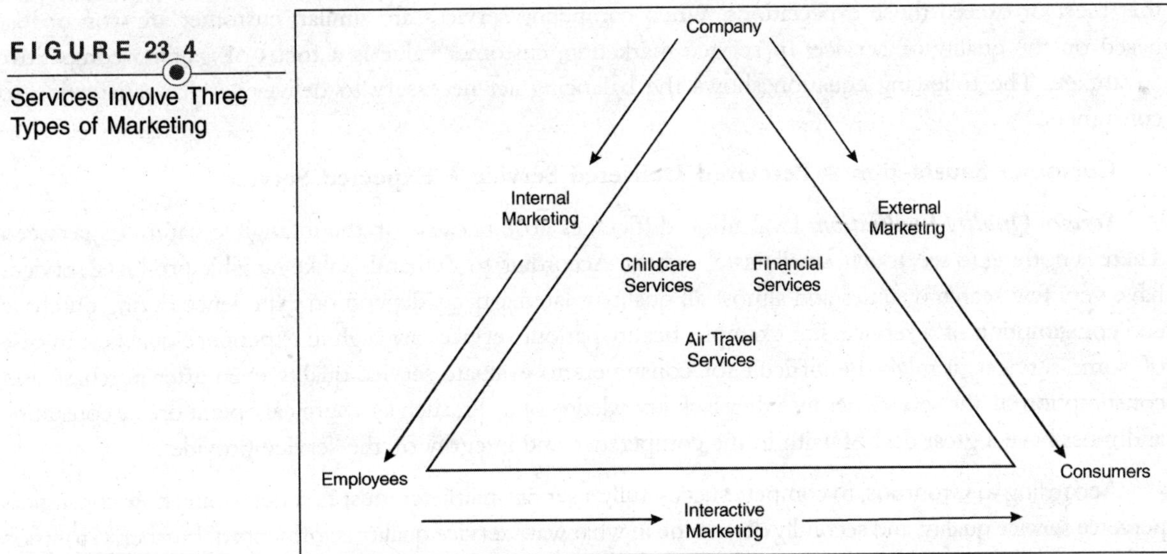

G. L. Shostack defined 'service encounters' as the period of time during which consumer directly interacts with a service. Of any number of possible service encounters, some are likely to be very critical to successful completion of service delivery process. Bitner, Booms, and Tetreault called these encounters as critical incidents, referring to specific interactions between consumers and service marketer's personnel that are specially satisfying or dissatisfying. Consumers' satisfaction or dissatisfaction can also be the result of interaction with service provider's equipment used in service production and delivery.

Service marketers can choose among different processes to deliver their services to consumers. Where service production and delivery process is complex and includes multiple encounters, it is necessary for a service marketer to consider the service in its totality and determine how different elements relate to each other.

Gronroos developed a service-quality model, which is an important contribution to services-marketing strategy. According to him, marketing of services involves three types of marketing: External, internal, and interactive marketing (Figure 23.4).

External marketing focuses on normal product development, pricing, distribution, and promotional activities. Internal marketing refers to the activities that focus on hiring, training, and motivational aspects of employees. Finally, interactive marketing describes the level of employee skill and commitment in serving the consumers. In this, the employee satisfaction becomes a critical factor. Disgruntled and dissatisfied employees are unlikely to be motivated to deliver at their peak performance level.

Service Quality and Differentiation

Delivering high-quality services is one of the most challenging tasks service organisations face. The quality of service is tested at each service encounter. The nature of service is such that it makes their evaluation difficult. Zeithaml, Parasuraman, and Berry define service quality as the *customers' perception of how well a service meets or exceeds their expectations.* It is the level of conformance of service to customer specifications and expectations. Consumers form service expectations based on past experiences, marketing communications, and word-of-mouth and it is the consumer who finally judges the service quality. This forces service marketers to take an outside-in approach and evaluate their service quality from consumer's point of view. Service marketers must determine what benefits consumers expect to receive, and then develop their service products that meet or exceed those expectations. When competing services are similar, customer are won or lost based on the quality of service. In service marketing, customer value is a focus of gaining competitive advantage. The following equation shows the balancing act necessary to deliver service satisfaction to consumers.

Customer Satisfaction = Perceived Delivered Service 3 Expected Service

Service Quality Evaluation: Evaluation difficulties arise because of the intangible nature of services. There is nothing to see, touch, smell, taste, or hear. According to Zethaml, unlike tangible products, services have very few search qualities and almost all quality-related aspects depend on experience during purchase and consumption of a service. For example, beauty parlour services are high in experience qualities. In case of some services, it might be difficult for consumers to evaluate service quality even after purchase and consumption of the service because they lack knowledge or skills, such as a surgical operation, or consulting and must have a great deal of faith in the competence and integrity of the service provider.

According to Gronroos, to compete successfully a service marketer must first determine how consumers perceive service quality, and secondly determine in what ways service quality is influenced. Further, Gronroos argued that functional quality dimension of service is more important than technical quality. This means the interactive aspect of service marketing (interaction between service employee and consumer) is the most important component of service quality.

Managing consumers' perceived service quality requires matching consumer expectations and the perceived service quality. To keep the gap between consumer expectation and perception minimal, service marketer's promises and communications must not be unrealistic compared to the service that customers will actually receive. Secondly, management must understand what factors affect the technical and functional dimensions of service and how consumers perceive these dimensions of service quality.

To develop greater understanding of the nature of service quality and deliver high-quality services, Parasuraman, Zeithaml, and Berry developed a model that shows major requirements for delivering high-quality service (Figure 23.5).

FIGURE 23.5
Model of Service-Quality

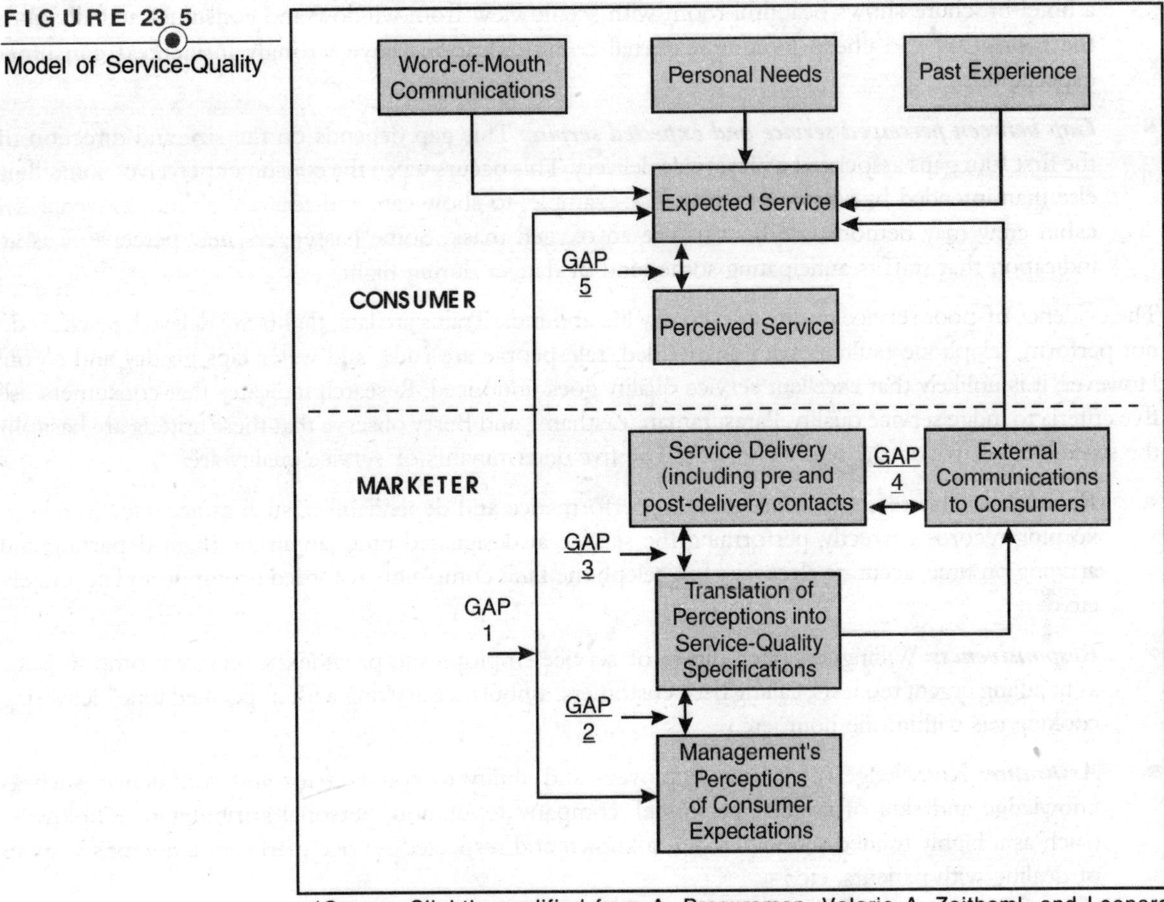

(*Source:* Slightly modified from A. Prasuraman, Valarie A. Zeithaml, and Leonard L. Berry, "A Conceptual Model of Service Quality and Its Implications for Future Research," *Journal of Marketing,* Fall 1985).

This model clearly shows that consumers' quality perceptions are influenced by a series of five gaps. Any of the five possible gap points can be the cause of unsuccessful service delivery and management must take steps to close these gaps.

- ***Gap between consumer expectation and management's perception:*** Service firm's management does not always correctly perceive consumer expectations. For example, a hotel management may perceive that consumers prefer low-priced accommodation, but consumers may be more concerned about comfortable and clean beds and good room service.
- ***Gap between management's perception and service-quality specification:*** The management might correctly perceive consumers' expectations but may not establish a performance quality standard. The hotel management may instruct employees to provide "fast" service without specifying it in terms of specific time limit standard.
- ***Gap between service-quality specifications and service delivery:*** Service personnel might be poorly trained, lack skill, or may not be motivated to meet the laid down standards. For example, the room service may take longer than specified time.
- ***Gap between service delivery and external communications:*** This refers to discrepancy between communications to consumers describing the service and the service actually delivered. Consumers form their expectations based on service marketer's advertising and statements of company reps. If

a hotel brochure shows beautiful room with scenic view from window and consumer actually finds the room dull and cheap looking, external communications have wrongly influenced consumer expectations.

- ***Gap between perceived service and expected service:*** This gap depends on the size and direction of the first four gaps associated with service delivery. This occurs when the consumer perceives something else than intended by service provider. For example, to show care and reassure airlines passengers a cabin crew may demonstrate how to use an oxygen mask. Some passengers may perceive it as an indication that staff is anticipating some kind of danger during flight.

The evidence of poor service quality in everyday life abounds. Trains are late, flights are delayed, teachers do not perform, telephone faults remain unattended, salespeople are rude, and water taps go dry and so on. However, it is unlikely that excellent service quality goes unnoticed. Research indicates that consumers use five criteria to judge service quality. Parasuraman, Zeithaml, and Berry observe that these criteria are basically the same irrespective of the type of service. The five determinants of service quality are:

- ***Reliability:*** This refers to consistency in performance and dependability, such as accuracy in billing, keeping records correctly, performing the service at designated time (an airline flight departing and arriving on time, accurate electricity bill, telephone fault complaints recorded promptly and accurately, etc.)
- ***Responsiveness:*** Willingness or readiness of service employees to provide the service promptly, (such as handling urgent requests, calling back customers, ambulance arriving within specified time, delivering cooking gas within one-hour, etc.)
- ***Assurance:*** Knowledge of service employees and ability to convey trust and confidence, such as knowledge and skill of contact personnel, company reputation, personal attributes of employees, (such as a highly trained school teacher, a known and respected service marketer, a doctor's manner of dealing with patients, etc.)
- ***Empathy:*** Caring and individualised attention provided by service employees to customers, (such as attentively listening to customer needs, caring about customer's concerns, a nurse counselling a post-surgery patient, etc.)
- ***Tangibles:*** Physical evidence of the service. Appearance of physical facilities, appearance of service employees, equipment or tools used to provide service, (a clean and professional looking doctor's consulting clinic, the cleanliness in a restaurant, alert waiters, good-looking and courteous air hostesses, etc.)

Service marketers seek ways to *differentiate* their service offers. This acquires more significance because of intangibility characteristics. In the absence of physical differences, competing services are likely to appear quite similar to consumers. One option to create differentiation is to augment the service with attractive features that can be promoted. For example, in highly competitive credit card services, some banks have started offering their cards free of any renewal charges. Some banks offer fixed deposit schemes that customers can operate as savings account. Some banks have extended hours of banking and still others keep their branches open on Sundays. Union Bank of India introduced 'Insured Recurring Deposit', adding Life Insurance to recurring deposit. Ideally, augmentations should be such that cannot be easily copied by competitors. In any case, the service provider who regularly adds innovative features important from consumers' point of view gains a succession of temporary competitive advantages and earns a reputation of being the leader in introducing innovations. For example, FedEx has been the first to install software to make it easier for customers to track packages in transit.

In case of certain services, a firm can differentiate itself on the basis of faster, reliable, and on-time delivery. BPL Mobile released a series of ads in magazines and differentiated itself on attributes of fairness, reliability, and speed of service, '1-Second Billing' (Figure 23.6).

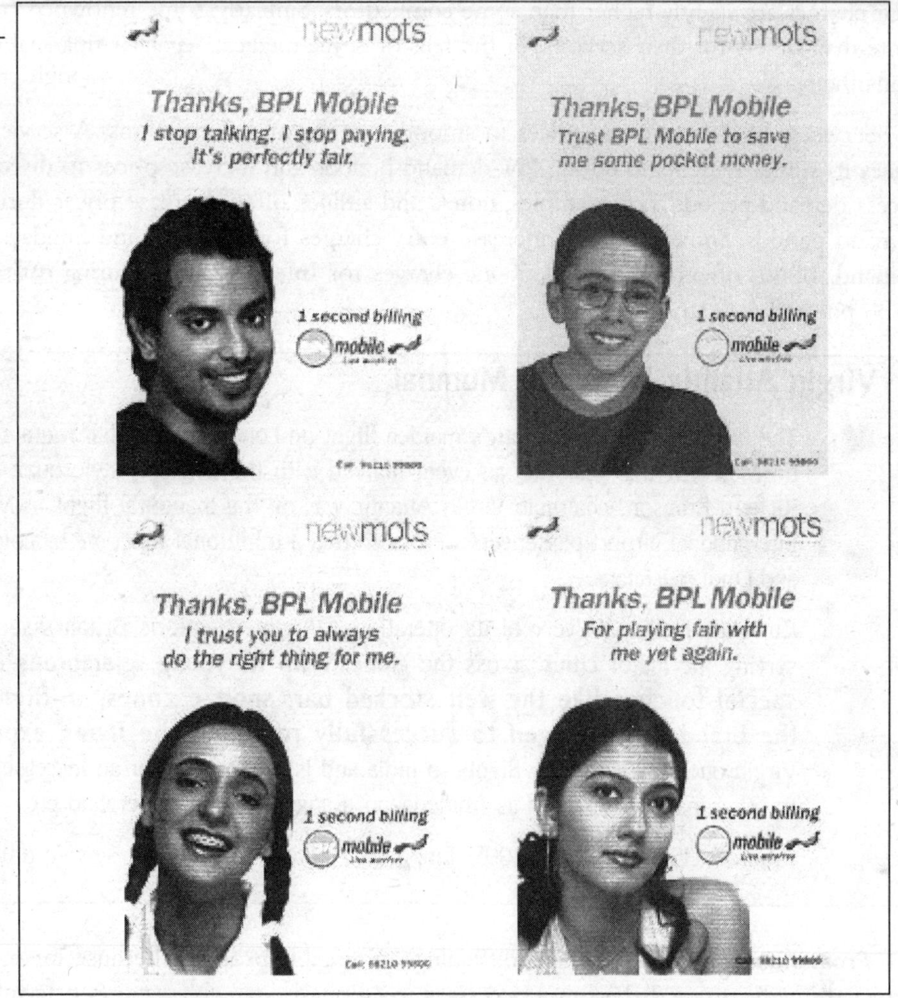

FIGURE 23.6

BPL Differentiates itself with 1-Second Billing Service

Windsor Manor Hotel, Bangalore is committed for providing room service within 30-minutes of placing the order and the guest will not be billed for the service if the order is not served within the specified time. Some other hotels specify their time limits for services such as check-in, baggage-delivery, checkout and other services.

Other successful approaches to differentiate service include service personnel expertise and commitment, adding confidence evoking physical dimensions to services such as latest gadgets, or emphasising service process itself such as laser surgery or online banking etc. Organisations can use branding, logos, and symbols to create differentiation. The golden arch of McDonald's, Lamp and folded hands of Life Insurance Corporation (*LIC*), Virgin Atlantic Airways, Singapore Airlines, FedEx, DHL, IIMs, IITs, Indian Institute of Sciences, Taj Hotels, Hyatt Hotels, and Apollo Hospitals etc., are some examples.

Price may function as an important factor influencing consumer choice of service, more so when consumers perceive certain services as basically the same. For example, consumers may perceive various airline services as similar, and the airline with lowest price may be selected. For example, Air Deccan or Southwest Airlines offer bargain prices, keep their costs as low as possible, use fuel-efficient planes, have more flights on busy short-distance routes, and cut down amenities. In case, consumers perceive services as dissimilar, they may be agreeable to pay more for high-quality, more reliable and dependable service. Services that have snob appeal always keep their prices high to retain customers from specific segments. For example, FedEx and DHL are perceived as more reliable where on time consignment delivery is critical and their charges are slightly higher than some competitors. Similarly, some renowned consulting firms charge more than others for their services, or the fees of some medical, legal, or financial consultants are higher than others.

Service providers also use prices to smooth out demand fluctuations. A service provider may lower prices to stimulate demand during low-demand periods and increase prices to discourage demand during excess demand-periods. For examples, hotels and airlines often decrease prices during off-season or low-demand periods. Some museums increase entry charges for Holidays and Sundays to discourage excess demand. BSNL offers reduced telephone charges for Internet surfers during off-peak demand between 10.30 pm and 6.30 am.

Virgin Atlantic Flies into Mumbai

The landing of Virgin Atlantic's maiden flight on London – Mumbai route after Delhi – London on March 31 this year was an event marked with the Branson style buzz and excitement. Sir Richard Branson, chairman Virgin Atlantic was on the inaugural flight to Mumbai. At the CST International airport passengers were accorded a traditional welcome by colourful Lavni dancers and Dhol musicians.

Currently in the 21st year of its operations, Virgin Atlantic is Britain's second largest airlines serving the major cities across the globe. **With its young, glamorous crew and its many special touches like the well stocked bar, snooze zones, in-flight beauty therapy, the brand has managed to successfully re-define the flying experience.** Currently Virgin operates 10 weekly flights to India and is negotiating for an increased presence by flying to other major cities such as Ahmedabad, Bangalore, and Hyderabad etc.

(Source: USP Age, April 2005. Emphasis Author's to highlight service differentiation).

Promotion of services is more difficult than tangible products because intangibles cannot be easily depicted in advertising. It becomes necessary to emphasise tangible aspects or symbols that can be easily perceived and understood. Service companies sometimes use well-known and credible spokespersons, or even common satisfied consumers authenticating the service. Where services are labour-intensive, using actual service personnel in ads as spokespersons has a positive effect on service contact personnel, their motivation, and commitment.

Personnel selling can be very effective because it provides interaction between salesperson and consumer and properly trained and motivated sales force can help to reduce consumer uncertainty, reassure consumers, reduce consumer anxiety, and build company image.

Contests, rebates, and coupons may have some role in promoting services. Consumers view publicity as more reliable source of information about services because publicity is believed to be objective and unbiased and coming from an independent source.

Distribution of services in most cases is direct because of inseparability of service production and consumption. Low-contact services, such as film processing and printing can be offered through different retail outlets. The outlet serves only as a collection centre and the film is sent to some other place for processing and printing. Certain laundry and courier services outsource the functions of collection and distribution to independent outlets. In these examples the presence of consumer is not required during service production and delivery.

Another approach for distribution of some other services is to appoint franchisees, such as some weight reduction services like Personal Point, VLCC, beauty parlours, and other services such as, coaching centres, computer and management educational services, travel agencies, hotel chains, car rentals, legal and financial services, packers and movers, fast-food outlets, and maintenance and repair services, etc.

Monitoring Service Performance

For top performing service companies, monitoring both their own and competitors' performance is a regular exercise. Service companies can use several methods to monitor their performance, such as ghost shopping, putting in place an efficient system of receiving consumer complaints and suggestions, and conducting surveys etc. Research indicates that speedy and satisfying resolving of consumer complaints wins more customers' loyalty as compared to normally satisfied customers. Some service firms install a toll-free system and encourage consumers to register their complaints or suggestion. This helps companies to correct mistakes and improve their service performance standards to better satisfy consumers. It is also necessary for service companies to monitor on an ongoing basis service personnel satisfaction and attitudes. The interactive phase of services marketing is seriously influenced by service delivery employees level of satisfaction in their jobs and commitment.

Summary

A service is an activity or series of activities of more or less intangible nature that normally, not necessarily, takes place in interactions between the customer and service employees and/or physical resources or goods and/or system of the service provider, which are provided as solutions to customer problems.

Unique characteristics of services include intangibility, inseparability of service production and consumption, heterogeneity, perishability, client-based relationship, and customer contact.

The marketing mix for services is an extended one and includes *7Ps*. In addition to the popular *4Ps*, product, price, place, and promotion, additional 3*Ps* for service products include people, physical evidence, and process.

Service production and delivery personnel are a vital element of the marketing mix. If the people don't meet customers' expectations, then neither does the service. Sound selection, training, and motivation of service delivery personnel can mean the difference between a service business's success and failure. Physical evidence reduces the risk perception of the customers by offering tangible evidence of the promised service delivery. Tangible evidence of service quality can be physical facilities or service employees. Process is critical and can significantly affect service production process. It is the period of time during which consumer directly interacts with a service. Consumers' satisfaction or dissatisfaction can also be the result of interaction with service provider's equipment used in service production and delivery. Marketing of services involves three types of marketing: External, internal, and interactive marketing.

External marketing focuses on normal product development, pricing, distribution, and promotional activities. Internal marketing refers to the activities that focus on hiring, training, and motivational aspects of employees. Finally, interactive marketing describes the level of employee skill and commitment in serving the consumers. In this, the employee satisfaction becomes a critical factor. Disgruntled and dissatisfied employees are unlikely to be motivated to deliver at their peak performance level.

Service quality is the difference between the customers' perception of how well a service meets or exceeds their expectations. It is the level of conformance of service to customer specifications and expectations. Consumers are the final judges of the service quality and the interactive aspect of service marketing is the most important component of service quality.

Managing consumers' perceived service quality requires matching consumer expectations and the perceived service quality, and depends on reliability, responsiveness, assurance, empathy, and physical evidence of the service.

Price may function as an important factor influencing consumer choice of service, more so when consumers perceive certain services as basically the same. In such instances, service providers keep prices low and use cost cutting methods. In case consumers perceive services as dissimilar, they may be agreeable to pay more for high-quality, more reliable and dependable service.

Promotion of services is more difficult because of intangibility characteristic. Emphasise on tangible aspects or symbols that can be easily perceived and understood. Service companies sometimes use spokespersons to authenticate service satisfaction. Personnel selling can be very effective because it provides interaction between salesperson and consumer and properly trained and motivated sales force can help to reduce consumer uncertainty, reassure consumers, reduce consumer anxiety, and build company image. Contests, rebates, and coupons may have some role in promoting services. Consumers view publicity as more reliable source of information about services because publicity is believed to be objective and unbiased and coming from an independent source.

Distribution of services in most cases is direct because of inseparability of service production and consumption. Low-contact services, such as film processing and printing can be offered through different retail outlets. The outlet serves only as a collection centre and the film is sent to some other place for processing and printing. Certain laundry and courier services outsource the functions of collection and distribution to independent outlets. In these examples the presence of consumer is not required during service production and delivery.

Good service companies monitor their performance by conducting surveys, and putting in place an efficient system of receiving consumer complaints and suggestions etc. Speedy and satisfying complaint resolving, wins more customers' loyalty as compared to normally satisfied customers.

Questions for Discussion

1. What is service? Name three labour-intensive services and two services where consumer presence is not necessary.
2. How do services differ from tangible products?
3. Define high-contact services. What are the marketing implications for high-contact services?
4. How do consumers judge service quality? What a service marketer should do to ensure service quality?
5. Discuss the major approaches to classifying services.
6. Discuss the marketing mix for a beauty parlour.
7. What are the major elements of service quality? Why is it difficult for consumers to evaluate service quality?
8. What is the importance of tangibles in service marketing?
9. How can services be differentiated?
10. What is the significance of external, internal, and interactive marketing in services?

Projects

1. Go to a hotel of your choice, observe and find out in what services hotel distinguishes itself. Discuss what steps hotel takes to ensure high-quality services.

2. Interview five consumers of a restaurant. Learn the strong and weak points of restaurant services. If you were the manager, what steps would you take to improve consumer perceptions about the weak areas of service?

3. Discuss with five of your friends who have the same cable connection for viewing television programmes. Learn how satisfied are they with the services of cable service provider? Prepare a report and suggest ways to improve this service?

Bibliography

1. Theodore Levitt, "Production Line Approach to Service," *Harvard Business Review*, September-October 1972.

2. Leonard L. Berry and A. Parasuraman, *Marketing Services: Competing Through Quality*, (Free Press, 1991).

3. Mary Jo Bitner, " Evaluating Service Encounters: The Effects of Physical Surroundings and Employee Responses," *Journal of Marketing*, April 1990.

4. Paul Peter and James H. Donnelly, *A Preface to Marketing Management*, 6th ed. 1994.

5. D. L. Kurtz and L. E. Boone, *Marketing*, Dryden Press, 1981.

6. Leonard L. Berry, David R. Bennet, and Carter W. Brown, *Service Quality: A Profit Strategy for Financial Institutions*, (Dow Jones-Irwin, 1989).

7. B. H. Booms and M. J. Bitner, "Marketing Strategies and Organisational Structures for service Firms," in *Marketing of Services*, ed. J. Donnelly and W. R. George, 1981.

8. G. L. Shostack, "Planning the Service Encounter," in J. A. Czepiel, M. R. Soloman, and C. F. Suprenant, (eds.), *The Service Encounter*, 1985.

9. M. J. Bitner, B. H. Booms, and M. S. Tetreault, "The Service Encounter: Diagnosing Favourable and Unfavourable Incidents," *Journal of Marketing*, January 1990.

10. Christian Gronroos, "A Service Quality Model and Its Implications," *European Journal of Marketing*, 18 (1984).

11. Valarie A. Zeithaml, A. Prasuraman, and Leonard L. Berry, *Delivering Quality Service: Balancing Customer Perceptions and Expectations*, (Free Press, 1990).

12. Valarie A. Zeithaml, "How consumer Evaluation Processes Differ Between Goods and Services," in *Marketing of Services*, ed. James H. Donnelly and William R. George, 1981.

13. A. Parasuraman, Valarie A. Zeithaml, and Leonard L. Berry, "A Conceptual Model of Service Quality and Its Implications for Future Research," *Journal of Marketing*, 1985.

International Marketing

CHAPTER 24

LEARNING OBJECTIVES

After going through this chapter, you will understand:

- Levels at which companies may decide to get involved in international marketing
- Different approaches to entering foreign markets
- Important factors that companies must consider before deciding to enter foreign market(s)
- Special considerations in choosing the marketing mix elements

n China, knowledge of the company behind a product or service is key to everything, whether it's in a consumer or business-to-business market, or whether you are trying to get the government to accept your products or services.

It is often that Chinese consumers are in a drift. But the rise of the middle class, particularly in the urban areas, is changing all of the buying habits. Fifty-six per cent of those surveyed in 2000 were optimistic about the economy, compared with 41% in the U.S and 43% in Australia. Only 13% were pessimistic compared to 25% in the United States, and 24% in Australia.

There is a growing recognition of brand names and a growing preference for them. It becomes important because the bureaucratic mind wants to know that it has made a safe decision in picking a particular company for a joint venture. So it is in our interests to make that as many people as possible to know about our companies and who we are.

In fact, most studies show that American products lag behind those from Japan in the Chinese market, even though Marlboro is the single biggest advertiser.

Never assume that the Chinese public will know the name of your company or brand. Even the name Coca-Cola had to be introduced to China while McDonald's had to explain what a hamburger is.

There are good reasons to emphasise that you are a multinational corporation, because of the quality perception. There is a hierarchy of quality in China. Imported is best, second best is a joint venture product, third is a product that is the result of technology transfer, and a poor fourth are the locally produced goods. They are almost always regarded as poorly made and liable to breakdown.

You should never assume anything when it comes to China. People have assumed it was OK to talk publicly about a deal, only to find the Chinese government angry at them for going public too early.

You may assume you have got a contract, and then you find that it was just the beginning of negotiations.

If your company is thinking of registering its brands and properties in China, then register now. One large company came to us because one of their franchises had registered its title. The Chinese didn't recognise the difference. As a result, the company had to have an internal battle and incur significant loss in recovering its title.

Media relations in China are just as important as they are anywhere else. Yes, there is controlled media but less so than in the past. Foreign investment and business coverage tend to be positive so take advantage of it.

Personal relationships are absolutely a key factor. There are old friends and new friends. The second time, even if there is a one year gap in between, you are old friends. The result that interviews produce is better than a news release because if a journalist looks at a piece of paper, they simply don't have a personal sense of that company.

A lot of the Chinese media firms require their journalists to go for four types of verifications before concluding that this particular piece of news is real.

Ceremonies are extremely important in China. Especially when you are entering the market, you need to take advantage of every opportunity you can to get your company known in China and make its commitment to China known. So a signing ceremony is an opening, and all of these are important.

Contd...

Banquets are also a strong tradition; they often form the final step in negotiations and can serve as a "thank you." Failure to host one can be misconstrued, for example leading to questioning of the importance of your company in the Chinese market.

Relationships with media are also facilitated over meals. Often the media is included in a banquet following an opening or signing ceremony. Alternatively, your company may opt for a private, smaller banquet with its new partner and appropriate officials, and have media entertained by your PR firm and/or the company's public relations staff. This is generally more appropriate for business-to-business or industrial marketers.

Finally, don't refuse a Chinese host's request to taste each and every banquet dish. And don't forget to give a small personal memento (noting lavish) to your Chinese hosts.

(Source: Dian Terry and Rachel DeWoskin, A & M, April 30, 2000).

Countries use trade to speed up their economic growth. The increasing importance of international marketing is the outcome of current changing structure of competition, and changing demand patterns in markets across the world. Whether businesses like it or not, protectionism of markets is disappearing from large number of countries. Domestic market, large or small, now has to be shared with a variety of offerings and their marketers. Companies are unavoidably involved with foreign customers, competitors, and suppliers within their own domestic markets. For almost all players, large or small, it has become necessary to seek foreign markets for their products and services to survive and grow.

With the opening up of economies, increasing levels of incomes, barrier-less communications and travel, and technological advances, people in a large number of countries throughout the world want the same things. They want modern appliances, fast-food restaurants, latest in fashions, ever increasing convenience in life, high-quality services and so on. As a result of these powerful shifts in trends, organisations must be prepared to be competitive in an increasingly interdependent global environment. Whether a firm chooses to compete directly or not it gets affected by other foreign competitors who do. For a company producing refrigerators or traditional *Rajasthani namkeen*, there seems to be no way out but to compete in the global market. Businesses are able to communicate throughout the world at the speed of sound using data, text, voice, or image.

Definition of International Marketing

A brief definition of international marketing by Vern Terpstra:

"International marketing is the performance of marketing activities across national borders."

Vern Terpstra, *International Marketing*, 4th ed. Dryden Press, 1987.

Phillip Cateora defines international marketing in the following words:

"International marketing is the performance of business activities that direct the flow of company's goods and services to consumers or users in more than one nation for a profit."

Philip R. Cateora, *International Marketing*, 9th ed. McGraw-Hill, 1997.

The definitions apparently point to minor difference between domestic and international marketing. No doubt, international marketing involves all those basic activities necessary for operating in domestic market. But the task of an international marketer involves more complexities than faced by a domestic marketer because when a business decides to cross the borders of domestic country, it faces a variety of complications due to uncontrollable factors associated with major differences in macro-environmental factors, such as cultural, social, political/legal, economic, competitive, logistics, infrastructure etc. Each foreign market will have its own peculiarities relating to these characteristics, which are often unique and influence strategies of international marketers. The uncertainties associated with various uncontrollable factors of different countries create the need to closely study and monitor operating environment in each new country.

Levels of International Marketing Involvement

Some companies decide to keep their degree of involvement in international marketing low-key and some other may become totally involved. According to Cateora, a business firm may choose one of the five distinct levels of commitment to international marketing. Companies generally move gradually through different phases of involvement in international marketing. The reasons are obvious. Risks can be minimised by gradually committing more financial resources to a particular foreign market based on accumulated experience. Temporary, low level of involvement means low financial risks. However, it is not necessary for every company to follow the sequence of phases and some companies may bypass one or more stages:

- ***No Involvement:*** The firm has no active commitment to seeking customers in international markets, but the products may reach foreign markets via other means. The firm may sell only to foreign traders or companies that come directly to the firm, or domestic wholesalers sell the firm's products in other countries on their own initiative. These types of unsolicited buyers approaching the firm often trigger the firm's interest in seeking more sales in foreign markets.
- ***Infrequent International Marketing:*** At this level, the firms may sell any temporary surplus production to foreign buyers, but international marketing activities are reduced as soon as domestic demand increases. There is negligible or no intention of continuing international market presence. Company makes no adjustments in organisational structure or in the products it sells.
- ***Regular International Marketing:*** Companies in this phase develop regular international marketing strategies to achieve set goals. The firm undertakes operations in foreign markets by either seeking foreign middlemen, may have its own sales force, or have sales subsidiaries in selected countries. At this stage, generally company makes investment in management, production capacity, and marketing goods continuously in foreign markets. The company begins to depend on profits from foreign operations.
- ***International Marketing:*** Companies at this level have full commitment and involvement in international marketing operations. They look for potential markets throughout the world and sell goods and services in various countries. They often set up production facilities in foreign countries and become international or multinational companies and depend on revenues from these markets.
- ***Global Marketing Operation:*** The firm is fully committed and involved in the international marketing activities. While a multinational company views the world as a series of different markets with unique characteristics, and develops separate strategies for each market, the global company views the entire world, including the domestic country, as one big market for products and services. The global company considers the common market needs and wants and attempts to maximise returns through global standardisation of its business operations. The production is planned to meet the demand of the total world market.

As a result of globalisation, firms involved in international marketing operations reflect the dynamic patterns of competitiveness, interdependence of economies of counties, and ever increasing number of competing businesses from developed and developing countries.

Markets in different countries of the world show varying levels of evolution for products. Regina Fazio Maruca found that consumers show preferences for different products based on cultural peculiarities. They differ in the ways that they satisfy their sets of needs and wants. Prof. Levitt said that global marketing involves developing marketing strategies as if the entire world were one large market. He believes there are substantial market segments with common needs for standardised products with high quality, and at reasonable prices. Richard A. Kustin believes that competition in the future will require global marketing rather than international or multinational marketing. A study by David K. Tse, Kam-hon Lee, Ilan Vertinsky and Donald A. Wehrung about the importance of cultural differences in marketing concluded that the process of globalisation on the supply side has begun. There is ample proof that demonstrates there are market segments in most countries of the world showing similar preference and demands for the same products. Companies, such as Coca Cola, McDonald's, Intel, Sony, IBM, Xerox, Microsoft, Hyundai, LG, Samsung, Levi Strauss, Toyota cars, Revlon, Rolex watches, Nike shoes, and many others that sell relatively standardised products to satisfy needs of customer in different countries across the world.

Despite what proponents of global marketing observe and report, it definitely does not mean that global marketing approach should be adopted uniformly for all types of products. Much depends on the nature of products and cultural imperatives. In case of some products, adaptation may not be a suitable strategy and in others adaptation may be necessary. According to A. Tansu Baker, segmenting international market involves for identifying market segments with similar wants and preferences that can be satisfied with the same product and using elements of marketing mix that can be standardised, and go for adaptation of required elements of marketing mix if there are important cultural differences requiring adaptation approach.

International Market Entry Strategies

The approaches to international marketing include exporting, contracting, joint ventures, and direct ownership.

Exporting

Exporting is selling products to one or more foreign countries and is an indispensable part of all international marketing. Exporting is fairly popular with small companies. This involves little risk or investment on the part of the exporting firm and represents the lowest level of involvement in international marketing. Most companies involved in international marketing first start as exporters and companies generally rely heavily upon home country production to supply goods to foreign markets. Exporting companies sell their goods either directly to importers in foreign markets or operate through export agents. Export merchants or agency performs most of the marketing functions involved in selling in foreign markets. According to Joseph V. McCabe, export agencies can assist firms with limited resources at low-cost and help avoid significant investments. Also, exporting involves minimal time and effort on the part of exporting producer. The drawback is that the exporter has little or no control on exporting agency. Some firms export through company's own sales branches located in foreign markets. This enables them to control sales effort more completely and streamline distribution.

Sometimes a distinction is drawn between direct and indirect export. *Direct export* means that the producer itself performs the tasks involved in exporting. *Indirect export* refers to selling company products in its own country to another party operating as an exporter. The difference is in the level of involvement in export operations and related costs, risks, and benefits.

Many companies station their buying representatives, or send their buying teams in India and other countries to procure goods. In this type of exporting, as in case of selling to export merchants, the company is not involved in completing any export procedures and avoids taking any risks. Sometimes these representatives or visiting teams suggest ways to adapt products, provide specifications, and designs or styling etc.

Contracting

Various approaches with regard to contracting involve legal relationship that international marketers enter into, to quickly establish market presence in a foreign country. Licensing, contract manufacturing, and franchising are fairly popular approaches. *Licensing* is an alternative to exporting, or involving any direct investment in foreign markets. The company granting the license permits the licensee to manufacture goods under the brand name of the company, and the use of patent rights, trademarks, raw materials, production processes, and provides necessary technical know-how. This arrangement involves making a down payment to licensor and may also include a royalty on sales. Licensing is an appropriate approach, when a company wants to avoid a direct involvement in international marketing. This approach can help overcome tariff barriers and import restrictions. This is a good approach to enter foreign market with little or no investment and risks. The drawback is that licensee may learn all about the product and processes and start independently after the expiry of license agreement.

FIGURE 24.1
Major Approaches to Operating in International Markets

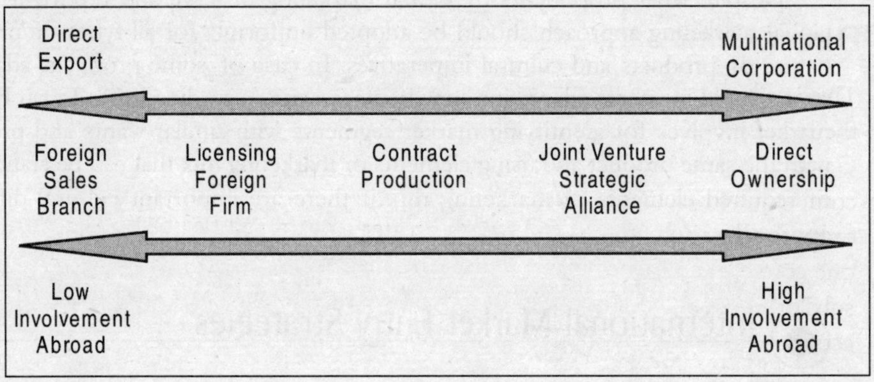

Licensing arrangement may take a variety of forms, such as granting licenses for using production processes, using trade name, or it could be for distributing the licensor's imported products. This arrangement poses problems of finding, controlling, and motivating licensees.

In case of *contract manufacturing*, the company enters into contract with a foreign firm to supply products to the international company, which are sold in the producers' country. For example, Reebok gets its sports shoes manufactured by firms from Indonesia, China, Taiwan, South Korea, Malaysia, Thailand, and Philippines. Indian firms include Phoenix Overseas, Liberty, Woodland, and some others. Reebok provides technology and designs and buys the entire output. The company aims to buy nearly thirty million pairs of shoes annually from contract manufacturers. Many other multinational marketers in industries, such as automobile, photographic equipment, electronics, computer parts, apparel, multinational retail chain business and others, use contract manufacturing.

Joint Venture

Forming a joint venture is a more important and popular approach for carrying on international marketing. A joint venture is a partnership between a domestic company and a foreign business house, or it can be between two countries. Joint venture partner minimises risks associated with political, economic, and cultural aspects.

A joint venture can be an attractive option to an international marketer when the company can take advantage of specialised skills of local partner, avail the facility of local partner's distribution set up, wholly owned subsidiary is not permitted, and the international marketer gains access to protected markets. For example, a huge multinational like General Motors formed a joint venture with Jinberi Automobiles of China to manufacture light commercial trucks. Many brands of companies from other countries are manufactured and marketed in China at prices that would not be possible if these brands were imported.

The newest form of joint ventures in partnership is called *strategic alliance* in which two or more firms join hands to create competitive advantage on worldwide basis. In industries such as autos, airlines, insurance, and computers etc., strategic alliances are fairly common to meet the every increasing competition. According to Harvey Arbelaez and Rafik Cuplan, Strategic International Alliance (SIA) is a way to provide support for weaknesses and increase competitive strengths. Strategic alliances at international level attract partners to take advantage of opportunities to enter and expand into new markets, gain access to new technology, cost efficiencies in manufacturing and marketing, access to marketing channels, and suppliers. For example, Jeffery Ball, Todd Zaun, and Norihiko Shirouzu report that Daimler Chrysler, Mitsubishi, and Hyundai have entered into a joint venture to develop a "small-car engine" to be used in one million cars of these auto companies. An engine is one of the most expensive car component and since margins on small cars are very thin, this type of strategic alliance provide savings for all the companies and allows them to compete on other features.

Direct Ownership

This level of involvement in international marketing entails owning a foreign subsidiary or division. This is the highest level of commitment to international marketing by multinational companies, such as Procter & Gamble, Nestle, Sony, Canon, Nikon, LG, Samsung, Toyota, Pfizer, GlaxoSmithKline, and IBM etc. The company is the sole owner and does not compromise on any aspect of the business, including manufacturing or marketing programmes and enjoys greater control and flexibility. The parent company is often based in one country and carries manufacturing, management, and marketing operations in different countries. The subsidiaries may be autonomous and allowed to operate independently of the parent company to adjust according to local environmental conditions, usually operating under local management.

Opportunity Analysis

Different foreign countries may present vastly different opportunities and risks in comparison to what a company has been exposed to in the domestic market. The company should consider in general terms factors such as political stability and cultural attributes to determine whether a market merits further analysis. PEST framework (political/legal, economic, social/cultural, technological) is useful to assess the potential opportunities of different foreign markets.

Political/Legal Considerations: At the national level, stability of political system and laws enacted by government determine the legal and economic boundaries within which businesses will operate and influence marketing opportunities for companies from other countries. Following factors need to be considered:

- Unstable political systems generally make markets very risky and unattractive for firms interested in foreign markets.
- The host country's legislation may protect domestic companies against foreign competition, government may restrict imports or make it difficult to get clearance, and in some countries trademark protection may be difficult.
- Host government may restrict currency movements and profit repatriation from foreign operations may be difficult.

The international marketer has also to consider regional trading blocks such as Association of South East Asian Nations (ASEAN), European Free Trade Association (EFTA), and North American Free Trade Agreement (NAFTA) etc. SAARC countries are trying to strengthen the trade association.

Economic Considerations: A company seeking foreign markets has to evaluate the economic conditions of the host country. These dimensions will include infrastructure, level of economic development, and competition etc.

Study of infrastructure would evaluate the foreign country's ability to provide transportation, power, and communications. Depending on the nature of product, the international marketer will need certain levels of infrastructure development. For example, a company may need efficient Internet availability, warehousing, and courier services to do business. Companies will need newspapers, TV, and other communication media to efficiently and effectively reach customers.

The company would consider GDP per capita, and income distribution at present and also what is likely to be the scenario in future. In general, as GDP and per capita income figures rise, the demand for most goods and services also increases. Income distribution may reveal some attractive rich niche markets. For example, India and Indonesia have relatively low per capita income, but there are small and wealthy niche markets with ability to pay for branded luxury goods.

For the last few years India has been gradually lowering the import duties and has freed selected goods completely from any duties, interest rates have been lowered, direct and indirect taxes are being rationalised, entry barriers are lowered, public sector undertaking are being privatised, and limits of Foreign Direct Investment in many sectors have been increased. These sweeping reforms are making India an attractive destination for large number of international marketers.

Social/Cultural Considerations: It is crucial for an international marketer to understand the society's cultural values in a host country. Study of culture will include various aspects of material, religion, social, beliefs and behaviour, aesthetic, education, and language dimensions. Individual consumers from different cultures patronise different products and may respond in different ways towards the same product. Kazuo Nukazawa reported that appreciation of differences in cultural dimensions is a fundamental requirement for being successful in international marketing. For example, when Mattel Toys introduced its famous Barbie Doll in Japan, customers did not buy it. Later the company introduced a modified Barbie Doll with slightly oriental eyes and girlish figure, the sales rapidly picked up.

In some countries, religion is a powerful influence on purchase behaviour of local consumers, such as acceptance of certain type of foods and clothing. For example, McDonald's entered India and opened its first outlet in Jaipur. After facing problems, it had to make many dramatic changes and adapted products appropriate for dominant cultural groups in India.

Eighty per cent of the Indian population is Hindu and they don't eat beef so there is no *Big Mac* containing beef. In its place there is *Big Maharaja,* which contains mutton and for strictly vegetarian consumers McDonald's offers *Vegetable Burgers.* McDonald's also claims that only vegetable oils are used. The menu also does not contain any product containing pork because a sizable population in India is Muslim and considers it unclean.

Inadvertent Offence

There are in excess of 1.2 billion Muslims in the world, yet multinational companies often offend them. An incident in 1994 involved the French fashion house of Channel which unwittingly desecrated the Koran by embroidering verses from the sacred book of Islam on several dresses shown in its summer collection. The designer said, he took the design, which was aesthetically pleasing to him, from a book on India's Taj Mahal palace and that he was unaware of its meaning. To placate a Muslim group that felt the use of the verses desecrated the Koran, Channel had to destroy the dresses with the offending designs along with negatives of the photos made of the garments. Channel certainly had no intention of offending Muslims since some of the most valued and important customers belong to that religion.

Source: Based on a report in Wall Street Journal, January 21, 1994.

Difference in language often discourages companies from entering foreign markets. Literal translation of a brand name or communications message in a foreign language may sometimes mean something quite ridiculous to consumers in a foreign market.

Technological Considerations: Considering technological aspects is necessary when getting involved in international marketing operations. Companies requiring the use of technically sound infrastructure need to evaluate host markets on this dimension. At any given time, all countries do not reflect the same level of technological development. For instance, in some countries there is considerable shortage of power and this consequently influences demand for electrically operated products. A major concern of businesses is communications facilities that differ across different countries of the world. Communications influences speed of response to customers, suppliers, and others. Many countries lack dependable communication services, such as modern broadcasting and postal services, landline and mobile phones, fax, Broadband Internet, courier, transportation and travel etc. Due to lack of technological advancements, much of technology used for marketing communications cannot be used in many countries. For companies using high technology, availability of skilled manpower is necessary to produce goods and services in the local market.

Key Decision Areas

International marketers may have to modify or replace domestic marketing practices. Lack of statistically reliable secondary data in a foreign market may pose difficulties in assessing the country's market attractiveness. Availability of reliable data generally depends on the level of country's economic development. In certain countries lack of reliable lists makes collecting primary data difficult, coupled with problems of unfamiliar language. Other important considerations mainly relate to selecting appropriate marketing mix. Based on the extent to which a company can adjust its marketing mix, different companies adopt different strategies.

Product: Some companies reflect the belief that the world is a single market and consumers everywhere have the same needs, wants, and product preferences etc. Product standardisation can yield important economies of scale. Customer visiting markets in other countries can immediately recognize a brand and understand what it stands for. For example, if Coca Cola or Pepsi tasted different in other countries, it would confuse customers. Gillette sells the same razor blades worldwide; IBM sells the same laptops, Intel sells the same processors everywhere, and Microsoft sells the same operating software everywhere in the world.

The best bet for standardisation is in the area of durable products, particularly durable business goods such as computers, earth moving machines, and aircrafts etc. Consumer durable goods, such as TV, cameras, mobile phones sets, and small appliances may pose very slight difficulties in extending totally unchanged into foreign markets.

The most challenging are personal products to standardise, such as beauty care products, wearing clothes, and food etc. International marketers adopt a strategy called *product adaptation* and modify a successfully selling product to suit the requirements of another country. For example, Procter & Gamble modified Max Factor cosmetics with brighter shades to suit Latin American preferences. The global fast food chain McDonald's modified its burgers to suit preferences of Indian consumers. Ford and Hyundai studied the weather and road conditions in India and designed suitable air conditioners and shock absorbers. Another approach is to *invent* a totally new product or modify a product for a particular foreign country. For example, Gillette has introduced a modified version of twin-bladed Gillette Sensor shaving system to suit the shaving habits of large number of Indian consumers and named it Vector Plus. Kellogg's developed Basmati rice flakes specifically for Indian consumers. Sometimes companies introduce an earlier product version more suited to the country's needs or stage of development. For example, Panasonic sold its basic version of washing machine to Videocon in India in 1988. Some companies are selling their less advanced models of laptop computers in India.

Companies have to take care about using the same brand names in different countries because translation of the brand name and its symbol in the host country might carry very funny or even harmful meanings.

Product packaging is also important while dealing with international markets. In developed and rapidly developing countries, supermarkets and self-service stores cater to a very large number of customers and packages work as silent persuaders. Package size should be determined based on buying habits of consumers in a country. Some countries prefer packages made of recyclable materials. In certain countries, consumers prefer reusable containers. For perishable items, the packaging has to be developed according to a country's climatic conditions.

Advertising and Promotion: The debate over standardisation *versus* localisation began many years ago. In case of standardised advertising a number of companies have been very successful. For example, Gillette introduced its Sensor shaving system and has used the same theme globally, "The Best a Man Can Get," and when the company introduced its Mach3 triple-bladed shaving system, it used the same theme in all countries.

On the subject of standardisation not everyone agrees with Prof. Levitt, particularly with respect to advertising. Many scholars and professionals argue that products and advertising messages must be designed or at least adapted to the needs and preferences of consumers in different countries. Differences in language, tradition, values, beliefs, lifestyle, music, usage pattern, media availability, and legal restrictions etc., make it extremely difficult to standardise advertising. Some scholars and experts say, cultures around the world are becoming more diverse and advertising can do its job within a given cultural context.

According to Rebecca Fannin, advertising standardisation may be suitable under the following conditions:

- Brands or ad messages can be adapted for visual appeal, such as Boeing aircraft or Apple's iMac desktop computers.
- Brands that are promoted with image campaigns using sex or wealth appeal, such as liquor, jewelry, cosmetics, or cigarettes.
- High-tech products and new-to-the-world products that have nothing to do with cultural heritage of the country, such as TVs, calculators, or computers.
- Products identified with nations, if the country has built a reputation in the field, such as Swiss watches, German autos, and French wines.
- Products that appeal to market segment having similar taste universally, such as elite rich around the world buy very expensive jewelry, clothing, and autos etc.

MNC Ads Go Back to Global Roots

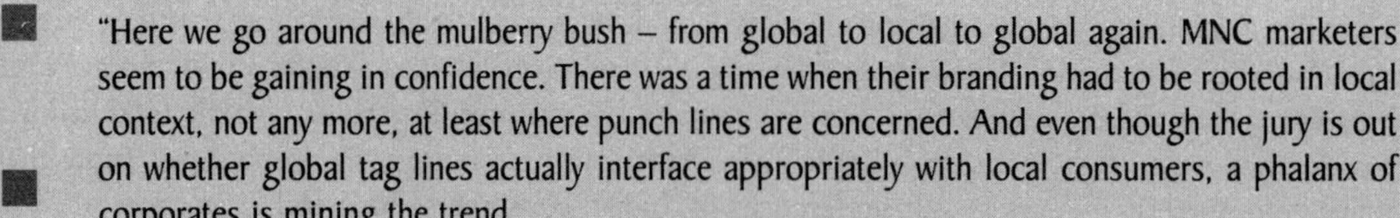

"Here we go around the mulberry bush – from global to local to global again. MNC marketers seem to be gaining in confidence. There was a time when their branding had to be rooted in local context, not any more, at least where punch lines are concerned. And even though the jury is out on whether global tag lines actually interface appropriately with local consumers, a phalanx of corporates is mining the trend.

In Reebok's new global campaign, 'I Am What I Am', Rahul Dravid, Irfan Pathan and company may have replaced Lucy Liu and Rapper J-Z in TV promos the American faces are still stamped on some print campaigns.

Contd...

Sony's new global slogan 'Like No Other', and Pepsi's 'Do the Dew' are other cases in point. Or take McDonald's, which had to junk its first-ever global TV commercial after it bombed in almost every market, but didn't withdraw the catch line 'I Am Loving It'. Now even Coca-Cola has, reportedly, set aside $400 million this year to shift local brand campaigns to global initiatives that can cover continents. So what really gives?

Advertisers feel the idea is to consolidate the diffused brand equity across markets. Says Prasoon Joshi, regional creative director South and South East Asia, McCann Erickson, which handles Coca-Cola: "Local flavour in communication is required when one is introducing an alien idea or product in a new market. Today most of the brands used in our daily life are global. And locals are at ease with their global image and stature. A unified brand communication, thus, makes sense."

Apparently, today's young consumers are on the same bandwidth when it comes to attitude, aspiration and lifestyle."

(Source: Archana Shukla, Times of India, May 23, 2005).

The second approach is to "Think Globally, Act Locally." Such companies use the same theme globally but adapt the advertising copy in different countries to respond to differences in language, market conditions, and other factors. Many international marketers use a strategy called *pattern advertising.* The advertisements follow a basic approach, but ad themes, copy, or even visuals are adapted to suit local market conditions. For example, the Dove soap uses the same product positioning in all countries but its advertisements include local female models in India, Australia, or European countries.

The third approach international marketers adopt is producing a variety of global pool of ads for all markets with a similar theme and format and invite managers from regions or countries to select those ads which in their judgement will work best in their country. Some companies allow more autonomy to managers in adapting global campaign themes to local conditions. William Echikson reported that when Douglas Daft joined Coca Cola Company as CEO in 1999, he announced a new strategy and allowed managers more freedom in different countries to adapt their marketing and advertising to local conditions.

Many global marketers are trying to build global brands; there is evidence to suggest that most are doing so by adopting a localised approach. Ali Kansu found that most consumer durable goods producers of USA used a localised approach to advertising with some standardised messages. Jan Jaben found that "think globally, act locally" is still dominant advertising strategy for international marketers, but with a slight revision: "Think Globally, Act Regionally." In general, managers are of the view that it is important to adapt ad contents, such as language, message content, models, scenic background, and symbols to suit local cultural dimensions.

Sales promotion programmes of international marketers are best handled locally. This is necessary because many countries have specific laws governing the use of different tools of sale promotion.

Price: Determining what price to charge for a product in a foreign country is complex and may involve trial and error. Multinational companies encounter several problems and must deal with price escalation, transfer prices, dumping penalties, and grey markets. Setting prices is particularly complicated for an exporter facing currency conversion, if any service is included in price, and often little control on prices set by resellers. Depending on the added cost of transportation, tariffs, importer margin, dealer and retailer margin to exporter's production costs, the price escalation may be two to five times more in another foreign market to earn profits. *Transfer price* refers to price set for goods shipped to company's subsidiary abroad. Charging high price will result in paying higher tariff, and charging less than product costs or less than the firm charges in its domestic market may attract *dumping* duty. Grey marketing occurs when an importer buys a product and rather than selling it in an agreed low-price country, sells it in other geographic markets to take advantage of price differences. For example, in some South Eastern countries widely used PC software is sold at a fraction of original software prices.

Differences in price charged in different countries for an identical brand is a growing concern. Price differences are the outcome of strength of demand, the complexity of distribution system, and the differences in taxes. Internet and other means have made it easy for consumers to learn about the price differentials, this makes the job of resellers quite complex. An exporter may quote prices in seller's country currency or that of buyer. Quoting prices in buyer's currency entails the risk of its decline and the exporter or importer may suffer a loss.

An alternative to currency pricing is engaging in *counter trade* or *barter*. Instead of making any payments in either county's currency, the buyer foreign country arranges to trade in domestically produced products in exchange for imported goods. This may happen for two reasons: (1) less developed countries may not have reasonably stable currency, often called "hard" currency to buy necessary capital goods, such as equipment and trade in less sophisticated domestically produced goods such as coffee, timber, food grains, or oil, or (2) a country lacks marketing infrastructure to encourage international trade. Counter trade is associated with less developed economies; it is typical of some high-value business-to-business international trade.

Distribution: As can be expected, the distribution system varies across countries. For example, the distribution of goods for exporters to Japan is fairly complicated as more levels of resellers are involved and product price to consumers shoots up. In broad terms, the purpose of distribution of goods and services to points where consumer buy them is quite similar in different markets. Right distribution strategy is as crucial for success in foreign markets as it is in the domestic market. The international marketer strives to choose the best distribution network and many exporters prefer to enter into partnerships with companies that are already established in foreign markets.

Summary

International marketing is the performance of marketing activities across national borders. The difference between domestic marketing and international marketing is the manner in which different activities are handled. It is crucial for companies to do business in other foreign markets. With the opening up of economies, increasing levels of incomes, barrier-less communications and travel, and technological advances, people in a large number of countries throughout the world want the same things.

In general, a business firm may choose one of the five distinct levels of commitment to international marketing: (1) no involvement, (2) infrequent international marketing, (3) regular international marketing, (4) international marketing, and (5) global marketing. The highest level of commitment to international marketing is global or multinational marketing. There are several approaches to enter foreign markets.

Exporting involves the lowest level of commitment to international marketing. Contracting involves licensing or contract manufacturing. Licensing is an arrangement in which the international marketer granting the license permits to the licensee to manufacture goods under the brand name of the company, patent rights, trademarks, raw materials, production processes and provides necessary technical know-how. This arrangement involves making a down payment to licensor and may also include a royalty on sales. In case of contract manufacturing, the company enters into contract with a foreign firm to supply products to the international marketer, which are subsequently sold in the producer's country. A joint venture is a partnership between a domestic company and a foreign business house, or it can be between two countries. Joint venture partner minimises risks associated with political, economic, and cultural aspects. Strategic alliance is a form of joint venture in which two or more firms join hands to create competitive advantage on worldwide basis. Direct ownership is the highest level of commitment to international marketing by multinational companies. The company is the sole owner and does not compromise on any aspect of business, including manufacturing or marketing programmes and enjoys greater control and flexibility. The parent company is often based in one country and carries production, management, and marketing operations in different countries. The subsidiaries may be autonomous and allowed to operate independently of the parent company to adjust according to local environmental conditions, usually operating under local management.

Because of the uncertainties of foreign markets, international marketers study these markets to assess political/legal, economic, social/cultural, and technological factors.

After initial analysis and assessment of various macro factors, the most critical decisions relate to marketing mix variables. The two most important variables in this regard are product development and promotional aspects.

There is much debate over standardisation of product and promotion to gain economies of scale. The other view is that consumers in different countries differ in many important aspects and product and promotion adaptation is the right approach. Various authorities and professionals suggest three approaches.

One is to adopt global approach for products. This means no product modification or adaptation is required for certain types of consumer and B2B products. Another approach is product adaptation keeping in view the consumer preferences and behaviour in specific countries. Yet another choice is to invent a totally new product for a foreign country suitable to its specific conditions.

With respect to advertising, some companies view a standardised approach as the best because consumers need the same things everywhere. Some experts say that this might be appropriate for some types of products.

The second approach is to think globally and act locally, and companies use the same theme but adapt the advertising copy in different countries to respond to differences in language, market conditions, and other factors. A variation of this approach is called pattern advertising in which the advertisements follow a basic approach, but ad themes, copy, or even visuals are adapted to suit local market conditions. The third approach international marketers adopt is producing a variety of global pool of ads for all markets with a similar theme and format and invite managers from regions or countries to select those ads which in their judgement will work best in their country. Some companies allow more autonomy to managers in adapting global campaign themes to local conditions.

Sales promotion programmes of international marketers are best handled locally. This is necessary because many countries have specific laws governing the use of different tools of sale promotion.

Questions for Discussion

1. In your view, what cultural differences in India can cause problems for a fast-food chain opening its outlets?
2. What is international marketing? How does it differ from domestic marketing?
3. What factors make the task of international marketer more difficult than domestic marketing?
4. Why should a company seek foreign markets, when it has established business in domestic market?
5. What are the major approaches to entering international markets? Which one would you recommend to a new company?
6. How do political/legal, cultural/social, and economic factors affect international marketing?
7. What is the difference between standardising the marketing mix and customising the marketing mix? What conditions do favour standardisation?

8. How can an international marketer determine the suitability of a particular product for a new foreign market?
9. Identify two Indian companies that in your view can purse global marketing. Give your reasons.
10. What kind of product and promotional strategy Nokia, Nestle, and Coca Cola adopt in Indian market?

Projects

1. A leather goods manufacturer has appointed you as the export manager. Identify two countries and entry strategies, product standardisation or adaptation for those countries.
2. Contact a jeweller operating in international markets. Study the company's operations and prepare a report with suggestions.
3. Visit a pharmaceutical company in India having international business. Learn what is their mode of operation and what standards they must adopt for countries where they export generic medicines.

Bibliography

1. Philip R. Cateora, *International Marketing,* 9th ed. McGraw-Hill, 1997.
2. Regina Fazio Maruca, "The Right Way to Go Global: An Interview with Whirlpool CEO David Whitwam," *Harvard Business Review,* March-April 1994.
3. Theodore Levitt, "The Globalisation of Markets," *Harvard Business Review,* May-June 1983.
4. Richard A. Kustin, "Marketing Globalisation: A Didactic Examination of Corporate Strategy," *International Executive,* January-February 1994.
5. David K. Tse, Kam-hon Lee, Ilan Vertinsky, and Donald A. Wehrung, "Does Culture Matter? A Cross-Cultural Study of Executives' Choice, Decisiveness, and Risk Adjustment in International Marketing," *Journal of Marketing,* 1988.
6. A. Tansu Baker, "A Marketing Oriented Perspective of Standardised Global Marketing," *Journal of Global Marketing,* 7 (1993).
7. Joseph V. McCabe, "Outside Managers Offer Packaged Export Expertise," *Journal of Business Strategy,* March-April 1990.
8. Harvey Arbelaez and Rafik Cuplan, "An Assessment of Colombian Managers' Perceptions of International Strategic Alliances," *The International Executive,* March-April 1995.
9. Kazuo Nukazawa, "Japan and the USA: Wrangling Towards Reciprocity," *Harvard Business Review,* May-June 1988.
10. Jeffery Ball, Todd Zaun, and Norihiko Shirouzu, "DaimlerChrysler Ponders 'World Engine' in Bid to Transform Scope into Savings," *The Wall Street Journal,* January 8, 2002.
11. Rebecca Fannin, "What Agencies Really Think of Global Theory," *Marketing & Media Decisions,* December 1984.
12. William Echikson, "For Coke, Local Is It," *Business Week,* July 2, 2000.
13. Ali Kansu, "International Advertising Strategies: Global Commitment to Local Vision," *Journal of Advertising Research,* January-February 1992.
14. Jan Jaben, "Ad Decision-Makers Favour Regional Angle," *Advertising Age International,* May 1995.

Rural Marketing

CHAPTER 25

LEARNING OBJECTIVES

After going through this chapter, you will understand:

- The peculiarities of rural conditions, including the size of rural population, socio-economic conditions, literacy levels, and their sources of income
- Implications concerning product, packaging, pricing, distribution and promotion
- Some examples of pioneering work by companies such as HLL and ITC to reach rural consumers

busalesh and Aditi Pany warn, "Don't Romanticise The Village"

"A recent NCAER-Business Standard survey, which shows that the rural markets are growing faster than urban the markets in certain product categories, has triggered much debate. To infer from its findings that the rural economy is surging ahead would be simplistic and inadequate.

Rural India presents a baffling dichotomy of images – on the one hand we see persisting poverty and on the other we see corporate giants betting big on the growing potential of rural markets. The fact is that rural India is anything but a homogeneous category.

The importance of the rural sector has been on the decline. Agriculture accounted for 59% of the gross domestic product shortly after Independence, as against 13% and 28% in the case of industry and services, respectively. Today, agriculture accounts for 24% of GDP, while the other two make up 25% and 51%, respectively. However, the proportion of workforce in the three sectors hardly changed over this period, moving from 74:11:15 to 57:18:25. This suggests a relative income advantage to the workforce in the organised manufacturing and services sectors.

The relative productivity ratios of 1: 3.4: 4.2 per unit of labour in agriculture, industry, and services respectively seem nonconductive to equitable social and economic development. Clearly, economic reforms have succeeded in transferring capital from inefficient to efficient sectors, but have yet to achieve a corresponding transfer of labour. Although poverty declined from 70% during the 80s to around 40% in 90s and further declined to about 26% in 1999-2000, we still have 260 million people (13 times the population of Australia) living below the poverty line.

So, what explains the recent corporate euphoria about the latent potential of rural markets? It is only partly correct to attribute increasing penetration of consumer durables and expendables into rural markets to income growth.

Owing to sustained increase in real agricultural wage rates and growing importance of non-farm income, rural incomes have indeed improved. According to NSS data, the real daily wages of regular wage and salary earners in rural areas increased by an average of 5.8% per annum between 1993-94 and 1999-2000. The wage of casual workers also increased, albeit at a smaller rate of around 3.3%.

Although rural India is still dependent on monsoons, non-farm incomes account for a significant proportion of household income. According to an NCAER survey, non-farm income in rural India was about 34% of total household income in 1993-94, evenly spread across consumption expenditure categories.

Another factor impacting the increased purchasing power of rural markets is the rural-urban Terms-of-Trade (TOT). Notwithstanding the debate over methodological issues, most evidence suggests that TOT remained in favour of agriculture in the 1990s. In addition, as a result of falling prices of urban goods (durable and expendables) due to more efficient technology and improved economies of scale, the purchasing power of the rural markets increased, irrespective of their income growth.

Greater media penetration has influenced the aspirations and expectations of the rural rich and middle class, reflected in their changing consumption habits. But to infer from all this that poverty alleviation is proceeding at an equally rapid pace would be incorrect.

Contd...

With saturated urban markets, corporate India is only now turning to the better offs of the rural society. Although not as striking as in the urban sector, rural inequality as measured by the Gini ratio for per capita consumption expenditure is a discernible feature. It is important to note that while the Gini ratio – measured on a scale of 0-1 where 0 denotes complete equality – for the rural sector has improved marginally from 0.28 in 1993-94 to 0.26 in 1999-2000, that for the urban sector has actually worsened. In some of the Northeastern states such as Assam and Sikkim, rural disparities have widened. The wealthier states of Haryana, Punjab, Maharashtra, show greater disparity than the poorer states of Bihar, Bengal and others.

The rural economy is not just heterogeneous, but is also subject to a variety of influences. Companies seem to turn a blind eye to the millions of people below poverty line who are leading a landless, in fact asset-less existence and barely have the minimum resources necessary for survival. Though, poverty is indeed declining, let us not be deceived into believing that poverty is fast disappearing and that the onset of a consuming class in rural areas is real and vast.

The availability of data that can accurately decompose market growth into cash-income growth vis-à-vis relative income growth would benefit both marketers and policy makers immensely."

(Source: Abusaleh Shariff and Aditi Pany, Times of India, May 26, 2005.The writers are with the NCAER).

The topic of rural marketing apparently seems to be India specific. In reality, the rural marketing conditions in certain respects are equally applicable to other neighbouring countries in various stages of economic development.

Marketing principles are the same for rural or urban markets. It is the approach to applying these principles that requires adjustments according to specific opportunities and constraints resulting from a host of rural conditions in India that a marketer faces.

Many otherwise successful companies, domestic or foreign, consider that Indian rural market has large and rapidly growing potential but the challenges involved in accessing these markets appear to be formidable. For example, the rural market is vast and highly scattered, communication facilities are poor, transportation and warehousing poses difficulties, buying power of most households is very low, and masses are largely illiterate etc.

Considering the size of *rural population*, almost 70 per cent Indians live in rural areas. Census of India reported the total Indian population in March 2001 was 1027 million and growing at about 1.9 per cent. That is, each year Indian population increase by more than the total population of many countries of the world. Incidentally, the population growth rate in urban areas is less and higher in rural India. Over the last two decades, the rural population has marginally decreased in terms of percentage to total population, but has increased in absolute numbers. In 2001, out of total Indian population the share of rural population was 736 million.

Population Distribution

There are more than 5,70,000 villages in India of varying sizes based on the number of persons living in different habitations. Some other sources put the figure of villages at 6,30,000. Details based on Census of India, 2001 about 5,57,137 villages are given in Table 25.1.

The number of rural households is in excess of 120 million and accounts for over 70 per cent of total households in India. The urban population of India lives in 3,200 cities and towns, and just 9040 villages have population of 5,000 or more (see Table 25.1). The remaining 5,48,097 villages have less than 5,000 people in each village. One can clearly see the pattern in the concentration of demand. In urban areas the demand is limited in just 3,200 cities and towns and the rural market demand is highly scattered in our vast country.

TABLE 25.1

Village Size by Rural Population

Population Range	No. of Villages	Proportion to Total (%)
Less than 200	1,20,073	21.95
200 – 499	1,50,722	27.05
500 – 599	1,35,924	24.40
1000 – 1999	94,486	16.96
2000 – 4999	46,892	8.42
5000 – 9999	7,202	1.29
10,000 and above	1,838	0.33
TOTAL	5,57,137	100.00

Socio-Economic Conditions

Rural population is culturally heterogeneous. They differ in their religious beliefs, cultural factors, customs, traditions, social patterns, linguistic factors, literacy level, and incomes. The major religious groups in rural India include Hindus, Muslims, Christians, Buddhists, and Sikhs. All these groups are further divided in hundreds of castes, and sub-castes. Each religion has its own structure based on hierarchy. Accordingly, there is a wide variation in customs and traditions of each group. What is right for one group is embarrassing or even offensive to the other religious groups, caste, or sub-caste people. It is said that the dialect, if not the language, changes after every 50 to 100 miles in India. In certain areas a hybrid of two or more languages may be noticed. Similarly, there is a wide diversity in the dressing and food habits across the country.

The literacy level in rural India is estimated to be about 30 per cent. A large percentage of the literate population belongs to the primary or high school level. In the year 2001, the literacy rate for males was 61 per cent and 32 per cent for females among the rural people. Over the years government has paid much attention to rural educational programmes. Year after year the literacy rate is rising and today, the educated young in villages are already large in number and around 40 per cent of the graduating from colleges, are from the rural background. They are the real decision-makers and not very different in terms of education, exposure, attitudes, and aspirations from others located in smaller cities and towns. A large number of students appearing in the competitive examinations for different administrative services have rural backgrounds.

Signs Speak Louder

- What do the sun, the moon and the stars symbolise to the city stickler? Ask a rural person the same question and she/he will say that sun symbolises life, the moon, love and the stars control the destiny. With such perceptions and interpretations, symbols become a very vital consideration for effective rural communication.
- It is easy to understand why certain successful brands in the rural markets have brand names depicting numbers or animals or symbols – 555 soap, monkey brand tooth powder, Gemini tea (with the elephant), Cheetah fight matches. Or sheru beedi, and tiger mark cigarettes. The easy

Contd...

association and recollection of such brands should be well understood, to realise the significance of semeiotics in the rural markets.

Another way to understand the effectiveness of 'semeiotics' in the rural context is to study the success achieved by local brands. These are successful, because of high semeiotic content, which have built a whole series of associations in the consumer's mind.

The dictionary meaning of 'semeiotics' is the study of signs, symbols and interpretations. "In the rural context, the interpretation of these signs and symbols becomes the deciding factor to build the brand value and image," says Maithali Ganjoo of ORCN (Ogilvy Rural Communication Network). Semeiotics primarily works best for products that have low-involvement at the time of purchase, and have very frequent usage.

Mnemonics also becomes crucial to nurture and retain place in the mind space. The shelf life of FMCG products is short enough for most to remember these products by their symbols, colours, and names or a combination of these elements. The low level of literacy in rural India acts positively for signs and symbols along with visual hooks, to succeed. The factors that most influence a consumer are the ones that make her/him feel, think, and associate with the products.

This is evident when Rose brand tea leaves, makes the rural consumer think and feel fresh, and thus associate with a common product such as tea. Tortoise mosquito coil is another player which was able to succeed with its brand name and logo, which was well-registered and received, rurally. Here are other factors to be considered, like size of the logo, shades of the colours and also the significance of the combined effect. Hence, it is not surprising to note that ITC sells its Goldflake brand with a yellow cover in the South, where it is associated with prosperity and purity, compared to a golden one in the North, because in the North, yellow is often associated with jaundice and ill-health.

(Source: Some portions deleted. A & M, November 30, 1999).

Rural consumers are believed to be somewhat more conservative and tradition-bound than their urban counterpart. However, the increasing levels of education, over exposure to the media and is the free modern city environment influencing their lifestyles, particularly that of the youth. The outlook of the younger generation seems to be changing with regard to customs and traditions. The contributory factors in this process of change include rising levels of income and its distribution, growing rate of education, exposure to television and cinema, relatively more frequent travel to cities and interaction with urban population, and the ever increasing presence of corporates in the rural markets. Most of the rural people expect some products, such as motorcycle, TV, VCR, wristwatch, pressure cooker, etc. to be given to them as dowry. As a result of this, during the marriage season the sales of these products increases substantially. Most of the rural consumers are relatively price sensitive and less inclined to buy unfamiliar brands, and bargaining in case of most products is common.

The attractiveness of rural markets is the result of the socio-economic changes taking place as a result of increase in farm productivity. Concerted programmes by government such as green revolution, rural electrification programme, rural development programmes, increase in irrigation facilities, application of technology, use of modern farming methods, and low-interest bank financing etc., have greatly helped in increasing the farm productivity and consequently the income of the farmers.

Some companies and banks have adopted some villages for an integrated rural development plan. Fertiliser producing companies saw an opportunity of increasing fertiliser consumption by adopting villages for development, others such as ITC, TELCO, and TISCO extended their hand voluntarily as a part of their social commitment to adopt villages and take care of their development. The Integrated Rural Development Programme focuses on education, health, modern farming techniques, development of land, development of the village industry and craftsmanship, and cooperative marketing of farm and rural produce.

Agriculture has considerable importance in India. It produces around 20% of GDP, feeds over a billion people, and employs 66% of the workforce. Over the years, due to focused efforts towards the improvement of agriculture by the government, agricultural productivity has improved to the point where, not only our country is self-sufficient but also an exporter of a variety of food grains. Yet most of the Indian farmers are still under the poverty line.

When compared to the earlier income levels, within the last decade and a-half, rural incomes have grown many folds. However, the income of an average rural consumer is much lower than an average urban consumer. The distribution of wealth in rural India is very uneven. Land holding of only 13 per cent farmers account for 37 per cent of cultivated land, and just 10 per cent of the rural population accounts for sales of nearly 37 per cent consumer goods. Rural people working in project towns serve as source of many new purchases and communication of ideas. Some of these people maintain regular link with towns and cities. During the crop sowing and harvesting time, they stay in their villages and take care of their agricultural interests, and during off-season they work in nearby towns and cities on daily wages or as temporary workers.

The estimation of the major *sources of income* includes agriculture (59%), agricultural wages, (16%), business and craft (9%), non-agricultural wages (8%), and salaries, and others (8%). Obviously, the prosperity of the rural people is tied with agricultural income and consequently their capacity to spend. However, unfortunately, the agricultural output is dependent on monsoon in our country.

A well regarded national daily, *The Hindu,* reported on October 11, 2001:

"Trends indicate that the rural markets are coming up in a big way and growing twice as fast as the urban, witnessing a rise in sales of hitherto typical urban kitchen gadgets such as refrigerators, mixer-grinders, and pressure cookers. According to National Council of Applied Economic Research (NCAER), there are as many 'middle income and above' households in rural India as are in the urban areas. There are almost twice as many 'lower middle income' households in rural areas as in the urban areas. At the highest income level, there are 2.3 million urban households as against 1.6 million households in rural areas. As reported by Mr. Shivakumar, Business Head, Personal Products Division of Hindustan Lever Limited, the money available to spend on FMCG products by urban India is Rs.49,500 crores as against Rs.63,000 crores in rural India."

"As per NCAER projections, the number of middle and high income households in rural India is expected to be 80 million to 111 million by 2007. In urban India, the same is expected to grow from 46 million to 59 million. Thus, the absolute size of rural India is expected to be double to that of urban India. The study of ownership on goods indicates the same trend. It segments durables under three groups – (1) necessary products – transistors, wristwatch, and bicycle, (2) emerging products – B&W TV and cassette recorder, (3) lifestyle products – CTV and refrigerators. Marketers have to depend on rural India for the first two categories for growth and size. Even in lifestyle products, rural India will hold a significant position over the next five years."

Besides the well established products in rural markets, such as textiles, bathing soaps and laundry consumables, medicines and personal care products, packaged tea, tobacco products, agricultural inputs and capital goods, ready-to-wear garments and footwear, sewing machines, pressure cookers, refrigerators, ornaments and jewelry, wristwatches, bicycles, petrol and diesel driven two, three, and four wheeler autos, fire arms, radio, B&W and CTV, fans, desert coolers, and air conditioners etc., the demand for a variety of products, both non-durable and durable consumer goods is steadily increasing over the years. The aspirations of rural consumers show a definite positive change and the latest products that have entered into the rural areas include telephones, computers, cellular phones, and the Internet.

The land owned farmer, trader/shopkeeper, and employed people such as government employees, teachers and self-employed service providers are the ones who buy more expensive durable items, such as CTV, refrigerators, motorcycles etc. in the rural areas. Comparatively, the employed people seem to have more potential for high-priced durable goods than traders and shopkeepers. Similarly, those who work in towns and cities but have their permanent homes in villages have more inclination to buy these consumer durable goods. This difference in consumption behaviour is probably the result of more exposure to city life and influence of colleagues.

The potential of rural market is immense and according to studies by NCAER and ORG-Marg, the market is growing five times faster than the urban market. According to BS Corporate Bureau, New Delhi, August 21, 2003:

"Today, real growth is taking place in the rural-urban markets, or in the 13,113 villages with population of more than 5,000. Of these 9,988 are in seven states – Uttar Pradesh, Bihar, West Bengal, Maharashtra, Andhra Pradesh, Kerala, and Tamil Nadu. For manufacturers, these are the markets to look out for. NCAER estimates that an average rural Indian household will have five major consumer appliances by 2006, almost double of that, it had five years ago."

TABLE 25.2
Consumption Comparison of Four Products in Rural and Urban Markets

	Urban Market	Rural Market
Shampoo	718 Tonnes	2257 Tonnes
Lipstick	131 million units	250 million units
Nail Polish	81 million units	270 million units
Mosquito Repellents	79 million units	173 million units

Further, NCAER puts rural market for consumer goods including vehicles at Rs. 11,000 crores. Inclusive of agricultural inputs, the total size of rural market is estimated to be more than Rs. 31,000 crores, and nearly 68 per cent of the market remains untapped due to various reasons ranging from inaccessibility to lack of awareness. A comparison of just four products in rural and urban areas shows the relative consumption size.

Key Decision Areas in Rural Marketing

Marketing in rural India requires hard work. According to Mr. Shivakumar of HLL, four factors determine the demand in rural India: (1) access, (2) attitude, (3) awareness, and (4) affluence. All these aspects, boil down to understanding the psyche of rural consumer in this highly heterogeneous market, overcoming a variety of difficulties related to infrastructure and developing suitable marketing mix. In general, the following factors need to be taken care of:

- Segmentation and targeting
- Product planning
- Pricing
- Distribution
- Promotion

Rural Market Segmentation: A marketer has certain important sources of data available and can consider several variables, to segment these markets. There are no hard and fast rules regarding what variables to choose. The following variables seem to be relevant to most of the rural areas in India and can be considered in determining the different market segments:

- Geographic location
- Population density
- Gender, age, occupation, income levels
- Socio-cultural considerations
- Language and literacy level
- Lifestyle, benefits sought
- Nearness to an urban area/industrial town

Some of the rich sources of data on rural consumers in India include reports from Centre for Monitoring Indian Economy, Thompson Rural Market Index developed by Hindustan Thompson Associates that covers 26 relevant variables including area of the district, demographic profiles, agricultural data, occupation, commercial banks, and electrification etc. The National Council of Applied and Economic Research (NCAER) data on rural households, consumers, and consumption levels is also a good source. Private market research agencies active in conducting rural research are available, such as ORG-Marg, Ogilvy Rural Communication Network, and Lintas etc.

As an example, The MICA Rural Market Rating collects some valuable data such as the number of shops in a district, availability of doctors, the number of LPG connections, and whether roads provide linkage to villages. MICA uses digital maps showing railway lines, roads suitable for motor vehicles, and the location of about 42,000 village *haats, mandis, melas,* or even the festivals celebrated at all the places including the *Tehsil* and the district.

Companies planning to adopt rural marketing, realise the need of generating superior data on rural marketing system, the *haats, melas, mandis,* and on village and small town income levels as well as consumption patterns. With appropriate data at their disposal, they can device methods about how to use these market places and occasions to communicate with consumers effectively, such as arranging live demonstrations of their products. Obviously, the key ingredients of successful penetration into the hearts and pockets of the rural consumers involves long-term commitment, backed with innovation and specialised strategies.

Product Planning: Companies have to consider whether the existing successful products available in the urban areas can be marketed in the rural markets without any modification. It is advisable for companies to first determine what consumers in the rural markets need and want, and then select products from the available ones. Of course, much depends on the nature of the product under consideration. For example, some soap makers use advance technology to coat one side of the soap bar with plastic to prevent it from wearing out quickly. Consumer durable products in general may not require any modification. But in case of some products such as tractors, pumps, and two-wheeler autos, the availability of service in convenient locations may be every important. In the case of certain non-durable consumer products, the marketer may learn that the existing pack sizes may not be suitable because of prices, and the marketer may introduce a smaller pack that would be readily acceptable. For example, in case of *Paan Masala,* tea, shampoo and even toothpaste, sachet packaging has been quite successful in the rural markets. According to an ORG-Marg data, 95 per cent of total shampoo sales in rural India are small sachets.

In case of certain products, a marketer may need to differentiate the brand according to important regional disparities, not necessarily in terms of product design or content. The differentiation may be in terms of packaging, communication and association with the brand. Package design, including symbols, logos, and colours are important for product recognition. The visual elements of the brand are very important in rural markets. For example, the palm tree is the symbol for Dalda. For rural consumers, particularly the uneducated, this palm tree stands for real Dalda brand. Similarly Nirma girl, Lifebuoy, and Lux communicate the powerful association with the brand. The brand has to be made relevant by understanding the local needs.

The Rajdoot motorcycle was designed, keeping in view the road conditions of rural India. Titan watches specifically developed its low-priced 'Sonata' watches keeping in view the rural market. Arvind Mills appropriately chose the name Ruff and Tuff for its brand of jeans. First, the company introduced its ready-to-stitch denim product successfully for just Rs. 195, keeping in mind the young rural consumers. The ready-to-stitch kit included denim trouser-length with specific stitching instructions for the tailors, the branded zipper, buttons, and rivets. Later, the company assessed the increasing opportunity for its finished product and introduced the Ruff and Tuff brand of jeans.

The rural consumers seem to be more brand-conscious than many of their urban counterparts. They stick to the brands, they have seen being used by their elders and the ones they have had experience with. Cheaper product substitutes and generics are often looked upon with suspicion and rejected, particularly by uneducated consumers. They evoke feelings of uncertainty and the fear of being taken for a ride. The educated and the young consumers are the ones who are inclined to experiment with new products and brands.

Pricing: The rural consumer in general, is price sensitive, or more appropriately, value conscious. Apparently, this has much to do with the income level of most of the consumers. The marketer will have to examine ways to make the product affordable to a large number of consumers in the rural markets. In case of a large number of non-durable consumer products, it is possible to design smaller pack sizes or unit sizes. A lot of FMCG and consumer electronic companies are aggressively targeting rural consumers. Most companies have started tinkering with pack sizes and creating new price points. Toiletries, washing products, packaged cooking medium, salt, spices, and OTC products etc. are sold in smaller packs in the rural markets. For example, the launch of the Rs. 5 mini Coca Cola reaped rich dividends in terms of sales and the bottles were expected to account for 50 per cent of the firm's sales in 2003. This pricing strategy increased price compliance from 30 per cent to 50 per cent in rural markets and reduced the overall costs by 40 per cent.

In case of consumer durable and farm machinery, such as motorcycles, TVs, refrigerators, tractors, and pumps etc., the marketer may make arrangements with some banks for financing customers at low rates of interest or make arrangements with his dealers to offer products on installments.

Distribution: Distribution is critical to penetrate rural markets for success. This is also the most challenging constraint for the marketers. This is an area that can determine a critical competitive advantage. For example, the rural market of Coca Cola grew at 37 per cent in 2003 over 2002, against 24 per cent growth in the urban areas. The per capita consumption in rural areas has doubled during 2001-2002.

Those of us who hail from rural areas and others who have had the opportunity of visiting rural areas in different parts of the country can very well appreciate the challenges marketers face. The first constraint relates to aspects of ***physical distribution.***

It is quite well-known that, transportation infrastructure in most parts of the rural India is in poor shape. We have the third largest system of railways in the world, but still many parts of our country are completely inaccessible. More than half the villages out of 5,70,000 or 6,30,000 have no proper roads. Continued rural development programmes are making some headway, many areas can only boast of *kuccha* roads, and deeper interiors have hardly any roads except for footpaths. These are challenging difficulties that perhaps discourage many aspiring marketers. Lack of roads poses problems in delivering goods in the rural areas. Same is the case with storage facilities in many parts of the country. To access rural markets, not well connected by rail or roads, makes the marketers think of other less conventional approaches and the costs escalate by as much as 50 per cent on an average compared to the urban areas. A company seriously interested in penetrating the rural market needs a network of C&F agents and distributors located at the right strategic places for facilitating the availability of products to the consumers at places where they shop. In the theory at least, a direct channel to villages will be most appropriate.

Enterprising companies make arrangements to use a combination of all available, conventional and unconventional modes of transportation to deliver supplies at their destinations, such as trains, trucks, delivery vans, tractors with trolleys, two-wheeler autos, bullock carts, water transport, or even hire labourers to carry the shipper packs and to distribute its goods.

Pioneers in rural marketing like HLL and ITC maintain a fleet of company owned delivery vans to facilitate distribution in the rural areas. This ensures frequent direct contact with their dealers and retailers and has its visibility and promotional value in the rural markets.

The second set of difficulties relates to the organising of an effective and efficient ***distribution channel***. Many companies give serious thought to uneconomic operational costs involved in transportation, servicing distribution points, and selling costs. Unlike urban areas, the distribution channel in most of the rural markets is composed of one or more levels. This is essentially the consequence of distance between the manufacturing locations and the rural market and the scattered nature of the customers. Usually at a minimum, there would be three tiers involved in addition to company sales branch office, and include a wholesaler or C&F agent in a town nearer to the rural market, a multi-level distributor, and finally the village level shopkeeper. This escalates the operational cost and any company that can manage to come up with an alternative with a shorter chain will have a competitive advantage.

In many areas, the number of available dealers is limited and finding an appropriate dealer may be difficult due to limited demand. Most dealers do not seem to have a reasonable turnover to make their operations attractive. Whatever extra a company spends in reaching these markets does not result in any kind of attractive incentive to the channel members down the link and moreover, there is really no assurance that all concerned will be benefited.

In order to efficiently and cost-effectively target the rural markets, the aspiring companies have no other option but to cover, whatever independent retailers are available, since in these areas, the retailer influences purchase decisions and generally stocks a single brand in a product category. In such circumstances, being the first on the shelf and developing a privileged relationship with the retailer shop owner is a source of competitive advantage to the consumer product companies.

The rural market areas need banking facilities and so far, the penetration of banks is limited to some of those smaller towns, which are connected and accessible by roads and where banks expect to have reasonable dealings. Of course, banks too have to take into account their operational costs and returns. Such banks in rural areas are something like one bank for about thirty or fifty villages. At the small village level, not connected by accessible roads, there are no banks. The main difficulty this poses is, non-availability of credit facility and trade transactions that the banks facilitate.

For a large number of consumer goods, a typical village shop is unique. There are more than 3.6 million shops in the rural areas of the country. For any given product, the stocks are very limited because the shopkeeper has to maintain an inventory of a large number of products. The demand for many of these products vary considerably and it becomes difficult to establish any kind of pattern. Consequently, the inventories for many items are carried for a longer period of time. The supplies from various sources are off and on, generally involving longer lead-time, and sometimes the shopkeeper makes trips to the feeder town in a hurry to replenish the much needed products. These factors block money and increase operational costs of the village retails. Any chance of earning more margins by increasing retail price at the shop level is self-defeating as consumers are otherwise quite sensitive to prices. Similarly, there is no way of increasing retail turnover. It is estimated that the average daily turnover of a rural shop may be within the range of Rs. 300 to Rs. 500 and that too when the shopkeeper extends credit to its customers. This whole description makes the picture of retailing in rural markets gloomy to an extent as if it a losing proposition. Not really so. These rural retailers generally have their best ups during festivals, on *haat* days, and *melas* etc., when people from the adjoining deep interior villages congregate. They do earn a profit but nothing substantial because the average turnover is limited. The picture is gradually improving with increase in the rural income.

The Hindustan Lever Ltd. Approach

- Data on rural consumer buying behaviour indicate that the rural retailer influences 35% of the purchase occasions. Therefore, sheer product availability can determine brand choice, volumes, and market share.
- Project streamline was conceptualised to significantly enhance our control on the rural supply chain through a network of rural sub-stockists, who are based in these villages. As part of the project, higher quality servicing, in terms of frequency, credit and full-line availability, would be provided to the rural trade. Thereby, giving us a substantial competitive edge over the next decade.

The principle of Project Streamline is to leverage our scale and organisational synergy to increase reach in markets. The pivot of Streamline is the Rural Distributor (RD) who has 15-20 rural sub-stockists attached to him. Each of these sub-stockists is located in a rural market. The sub-stockist then performs the role of driving distribution in the neighbouring villages using conventional means of transport such as a tractor, bullock cart et al.

From 1998, the project has been rolled out in select states of the country where the terrain or poor stage of market development typically makes any distribution system unviable. The Streamline system has extended direct HLL reach in these markets to about 37% of India's rural population from 25% in 1995. Most important, the number of HLL brands and SKUs stocked by village retailers has gone up significantly. Having done that, the project now aims to expand our coverage to 50% of the rural population by 2003.

Distribution will acquire a further edge with Project Shakti, the HLL's partnership with Self Help Groups of rural women. The project, that started in 2001, already covers over 5,000 villages in 52 districts of Andhra Pradesh, Karnataka, Madhya Pradesh, and Gujarat and is being progressively extended. The vision is to reach 100,000 villages, thereby, touching about 100 million consumers. The SHGs have chosen to adopt distribution of HLL's products as a business venture, armed with training from HLL and support from the government agencies concerned and the NGOs. A typical Shakti entrepreneur conducts business of around Rs. 15,000 per month, which gives her an income in excess of Rs. 1,000 per month on a sustainable basis. As most of these women are from below the poverty line, and live in extremely small villages (less than 2,000 population), this earning is very significant, and is almost double of their past household income. For HLL, the project is bringing new villages under direct distribution coverage. Plans are being drawn up to cover more states, and provide product/services in agricultural, health, insurance, and educational spheres. This will both catalyse holistic rural development and also help the SHGs generate even more income.

This model creates a symbiotic partnership between HLL and its consumers, some of whom will also draw on the company for their livelihood, and helps build a self-sustaining virtuous cycle of growth."

(Source: Adapted with changes from www.hll.com/HLL/knowus/bs_ruralmark.html).

Companies committed to rural marketing will have to device ways to improve the viability of targeted rural outlets. This long-term commitment would involve developmental marketing and then, perhaps firms will cooperate to ensure, that outlets manage to carry non-competing product lines.

Promotion: Rural marketing poses several problems with regard to various methods available to the marketers for communicating effectively in different areas of the country. As we have seen the rate of literacy among rural consumers is low and this limits the use of printed word. The masses in rural areas are highly traditional, with high regard and compliance for deep-rooted customs. Any language or its variations including dialect has its limitations and this is also true for a variety of symbols. Any communication can simply serve little or no purpose unless it uses local language and idioms. The availability of variety of familiar mainstream media also poses problems. According to HLL, mass media reaches only 57 % of the rural population.

Gradually the reach of TV is expanding in the rural areas and now has become a prime medium. Recent introduction of Direct to Home (DTH) facility has further increased the TV penetration in the rural areas. Other media useful in rural areas include cinema, radio, some print media, *kathputli* shows, *nautanki,* festive occasions such as Dussehra, Diwali, Navaratrey, local festive occasions such as *kajri* song competitions, *Aalah* singing, and rural sports events such as *Dangals*, Kabddi and Kho-Kho matches etc.

Using symbolic association of products or events with deities, movie heroes, and local folklore heroes etc. can have special significance in influencing consumer attitudes, awareness, and product recall.

Communicating with the rural consumers effectively requires, a comprehensive understanding of the rural consumers in different parts of the country, appropriate creative approaches, additional funds, and focused efforts. Some companies, such as HLL, ITC, Colgate-Palmolive, Godrej and others employ audio-visual vans. These vans provide marketers comprehensive means of promotion with the added advantage, that company-owned mobile units are totally under the control of the firm. These vans screen films and also show other audio-visual materials and carry ready stocks to deliver at the outlets.

Jain TVs and Video-on-Wheels, a private firm, offers mobile audio-visual communication vehicles for hire. The reach of these vehicles is great and covers villages having 20 or more households. This is a much sought after service by more than 300 mostly consumer product companies who do not want to commit funds to the company-owned promotional vehicles. The companies use them for a variety of purposes such as demonstration of product including sampling, on-the-spot-trial, selling products to retailers, and collecting market information.

Hindustan Lever Limited – Project Bharat

"Creating distributive reach is not sufficient to tap the rural market. Market development can be a difficult task because in rural India, both consumption and penetration is low. For instance, only three out of ten people in rural areas, use toothpaste or talcum powder, or shampoo and skin care products, and only six use washing powders. Even in categories with high penetration, such as soaps, consumption is once per five bathing occasions.

Mass media reaches only 57% of the rural population. Hence, generating awareness means, utilising targeted unconventional media including ambient media. We have been utilising events such as fairs and festivals, haats et al, as occasions for brand communication. Cinema vans, shop-fronts, walls and wells are other media vehicles that we have utilised to heighten brand and pack visibility.

We are tying up with various Non-Governmental Organisations, United Nations' Development Programme (UNDP), and voluntary organisations to propagate health and hygiene message. The goal is to reach 2,35,000 villages up from the current 85,000; 75% of the population up from 43% today; and a message reach of 65% up from the current TV reach of 33%. In the process we aim to increase access, influence attitudes, create a channel to raise awareness of its brands and catalyse affluence in rural India.

Contd...

Project Bharat, the first and largest rural home-to-home operation, to have ever been mounted by any company, sought to address many of these issues. The exercise was started by our Personal Products Division in 1998, and covered 13 million households by the end of 1999.

This path-breaking venture aims to facilitate the doubling of our share of the rural consumer's wallet in three years. The model is unique, in that it influences all the variables that influence growth. This model triples physical reach, doubles communication reach, creates a platform for influencing attitude changes and raising incomes.

In the course of operation, company vans visited villages across the country and distributed sample packs comprising a low-unit-price pack each of shampoo, talcum powder, toothpaste, and skin cream priced at Rs. 15. The distribution was supported by explanation of product usage and video show, which was interspersed with product communication. Thus we generated awareness of its product categories and the availability of affordable packs.

Consumers were also made aware of the superior benefits of using our products vis-à-vis their current habits, and the affordability of the pack sizes on offer. The project, thus, successfully addressed issues of awareness, attitudes and habits. Hopefully, as consumers in rural areas get exposed to such value-added, value-for-money alternatives, they will continue to buy into the categories. The project saw a 100% increase in penetration, usership, and top-of-mind awareness in the districts targeted.

However, sampling once is not adequate to convert non-users. So Personal Products Devision rolled out a follow-up programme, the Integrated Rural Promotion Van, to once more target villages with a population of over 2000."

(Source: Adapted with changes from www.rediffcom/money/2003/aug/21 rural.htm).

Personal selling has special significance in the rural markets. First of all, companies would do better to appoint sales people who hail from the concerned rural areas because they would be the ones who are completely familiar and conversant with local conditions including language and culture. Living or working for such sales people in these areas, and mingling and understanding rural customers would not pose any problems. They are more likely to feel at ease and evoke confidence amongst customers and develop beneficial relationships.

The sales persons need not resort to pressure selling techniques. They are more likely to be effective, if they adopt a position of a consultant with empathy. The salesperson should start by trying to understand in general terms the problems and needs that the company's products or services can solve, suggest more than one alternative, and explain the pros and cons of these alternatives.

A company from Maharashtra dealing in seeds for agricultural crops, vegetables, and fertilisers appointed a salesperson in a certain state. This salesperson would regularly visit the farming community in the designated area and discuss about general farming difficulties related to different crops, seeds from which source were used, if any fertilisers were used, and what was the yield etc. He did not try to sell anything in particular but just made certain attractive suggestions and learned about what the farmers thought. With the passage of time, rural people developed more confidence in this sales person who was not persuading them to buy anything but just making suggestions in general terms that benefited them. After this stage was reached, the sales person proposed trying what his company offered and asked farmers to see the results. Some of the farmers adopted his suggestions and reported better results. Over a period of time, this sales person was a sought after consultant and many farmers eagerly awaited his next visit, sent messages inviting him, asked solutions and suggestions, and this gentleman was regarded as their trusted man for a variety of crop related matters. In the following two years, the territory belonged to him and the farmers regarded him as a messiah.

A Novel Rural Marketing Initiative by ITC – e-Choupals

- "ITC is India's private company with annual revenue of US$2 billion. Its International Business Division was created in 1990 as an agricultural trading company; it now generates 150 million dollar in revenues annually.

- ITC launched e-Choupal in June 2000 that places computers with Internet access in rural farming villages; the e-Choupals serve as both a social gathering place for exchange of information and as an e-commerce hub. It has also created a highly profitable distribution and product design channel for the company – an e-commerce platform that is also a low-cost fulfillment system focused on the needs of rural India. The e-Choupal system has also catalysed rural transformation that is helping to alleviate rural isolation, create more transparency for the farmers, and improve their productivity and incomes.

It has become the largest initiative among all Internet-based interventions in rural India. e-Choupal services today, reach out to more than 3.1 million farmers growing a range of crops – soyabean, tobacco, coffee, wheat, rice, pulses, shrimp – in over 31,000 villages through 5050 kiosks across six states (Madhya Pradesh, Karnataka, Andhra Pradesh, Uttar Pradesh, Maharashtra, and Rajasthan).

ITC made significant investment to create and maintain its own IT network in rural India and to identify and train a local farmer to manage each e-Choupal. The computer, typically housed in the farmer's house, is linked to Internet via telephone lines, or increasingly by a VSAT connection, and serves an average of 600 farmers in 10 surrounding villages within a radius of five kilometers.

Each e-Choupal costs between Rs. 1,40,000 and Rs. 2,80,000 to set up and about Rs. 4,500 per year to maintain. Using the system costs the farmers nothing, but the host farmer, called a Sanchalak, incurs some operating costs and is obliged by a public oath to serve the entire community; the Sanchalak benefits from increased prestige and a commission paid to him for all e-Choupal transactions. The farmers can use the computer to access the daily closing rates on local mandis, as well as to track global price trends or find information about new farming techniques – either directly or, because many farmers are illiterate, via the Sanchalak. They also use the e-Choupal to order seed, fertiliser, and other products such as consumer goods from ITC or its partners, at prices, lower than those available from the village traders; the Sanchalak typically aggregates the village demand for these products and transmits the order to an ITC representative. At harvest time, ITC offers to buy the crop directly from the farmer at the previous day's closing price; the farmer then transports his crop to an ITC processing centre, where the crop is weighed electronically and assessed for quality. The farmer is then paid for the crop and for the transport. "Bonus points," which are exchangeable for products that ITC sells, are given for crops with quality above the norm. In this way, the e-Choupal system bypasses the government-managed trading mandis.

The farmers' benefit from more accurate weighing, faster processing time, and prompt payment, and from access to a wide range of information, including accurate market price knowledge, and market trends, which help them decide when, where, and at what price to sell. Farmers selling directly to ITC through an e-Choupal, typically receive a higher price for their crops than they

Contd...

would receive through the mandi system, on average about 2.5% higher. The total benefit to farmers includes lower prices for inputs and other goods, higher yields, and a sense of empowerment. The e-Choupal system has had a measurable impact on what farmers chose to do. In areas covered by e-Choupals, the percentage of farmers planting soyabean has increased dramatically, from 50 to 90% in some regions, while the volume of soyabean marketed through mandis has dropped as much as half. At the same time, ITC benefits from net procurement costs that are about 2.5% lower by saving the commission fee and part of the transport costs, it would otherwise pay to traders who serve as its buying agents at the mandi, and ITC has more direct control over the quality of what it buys. The company reports, that it recovers its equipment costs from an e-Choupal in the first year of operation and the venture is profitable.

In mid-2003, e-Choupal services reached more than one million farmers, in nearly 11,000 villages, and the system is expanding rapidly. ITC gains additional benefits from using this network as a distribution channel for its products and those of its partners and a source of innovation for new products. For example, farmers can buy seeds, fertiliser, and some consumer goods at the ITC processing centre when they bring in their grain. The Sanchalaks often aggregate the village demand for some products and place a single order, lowering ITC's logistics costs. The system is also a channel for soil testing services and for educational efforts to help farmers improve crop quality. ITC is also exploring partnership with banks to offer farmers access to credit, insurance, and other services that are not currently offered or are prohibitively expensive. Moreover, farmers are beginning to suggest – and in some cases demand – that ITC should supply new products or services or expand into additional crops, such as onions and potatoes. Thus farmers are becoming a source of product innovation for ITC."

(Source: Internet: Adapted with minor changes from ITC's e-Choupal and Profitable Rural Transformation).

The speech of Mr. Sushil Kumar Jiwarajka, chairman FICCI-Western Regional Council, sums up very appropriately, the status of rural marketing in India (some portions excluded):

"While we accept that the heart of India lives in its villages and the Indian rural market with its vast size and demand base, offers great opportunities to marketers, we tend to conclude that the purse does not stay with them. Nothing can be far from the truth. Rural marketing involves addressing, around 700 million potential consumers, over 40 per cent of the Indian middle-class, and about half the country's disposable income. According to a NCAER study the consuming class households in both, rural and urban is equal. The recent NCAER publication "The Great Indian Middle Class" further reveals that the Indian middle-class consisted of 10.7 million households or 57 million individuals of which 36 per cent lived in rural areas. No wonder, the rural markets have been a vital source of growth for most of the companies. For a number of FMCG companies in the country, more than half their annual sales come from the rural market.

Although with the substantial improvement in purchasing power, increasing brand consciousness, changing consumption pattern and rapid spread of communication network, rural India offers a plethora of opportunities all waiting to be harnessed, the marketers lack the in-depth knowledge of the village psyche, strong distribution channels and awareness that are indeed the prerequisites for making a dent into the rural market.

Moreover, vast cultural diversity and vastly varying rural demographics, poor infrastructure – be it inadequate roads and highways or the unavailability of telephones and electricity, low income levels, low levels of literacy, often tend to lower the presence of the corporates in the rural markets.

Thus, although the rural markets must be alluring, tapping the vast potential calls for a systematic psychographic analyses and an appropriate marketing mix to meet the consequent challenges of availability, affordability, acceptability, and awareness.

To achieve success in rural India, companies need to establish rural market development programmes. There is a need to innovate and adapt products that suit the rural operating conditions. The rural consumers need to be educated regarding new concepts relevant to the environment and usage habits that will improve their quality of life.

In addition to focusing on targeted promotions and advertising, there is an urgent need to work on economical packaging, dual pricing and special sizes of FMCG and household products. IT can be considered as an important marketing tool.

Moreover, corporates need to place emphasis on retailers directly, rather than depending on the wholesalers for distribution in the rural market, as this has not proved to be very effective and a proactive marketing medium.

There is a need to generate, superior data on rural marketing system, the *haats, melas, mandis,* and on village and small town income levels and consumption patterns. They need to learn how to use the existing market places for live demonstrations of their products. The ingredients for successful penetration into the hearts and wallets of village consumers include long-term commitment, cost re- engineering and sustained innovation and specialised strategies.

I would like to mention that despite the hurdles that the rural economy presents, corporate-rural partnership can overcome these and bring about positive results for both the entities. Partnership needs to extend beyond agri-business. It is not only the FMCG but also the financial and insurance sector that needs to come forward."

(*Source:* Internet: "Rural Marketing Summit 2004," October 5-6, 2004, Mumbai).

Villages that have population of under 1,000 really prefer weekly shandies, not shops. For the rural shopper, the best choice comes from weekly bazaars. The thousands of weekly haats, bazaars, and shandies (as they are known in the South) attract millions of rural buyers to make loads of purchases. And the demand increases with the festive season. Ideally, these outlets creep up every week, providing the consumers, immense choices. "The haats are the oldest outlets to purchase household goods and for trade," says Pradeep Lokhande of Rural relations.

With varying populations, one shop or a few shops cannot really cater to all the consumer's needs. Thus, it makes sense to have weekly outlets that cater to the needs of the consumers in these regions. These markets themselves vary, in name, from region to region, but are startlingly similar in the wares that are up for sale. Adds Lokhande, "Many marketers have still not understood the potential these outlets actually have."

Frugal though the rural consumer's life is, success from these weekly outlets is that much more pertinent. What attracts the consumer is, the freshness of the produce, buying in bulk for a week and the bargaining power. Household goods, clothes, durables, cattle, jewelry, and even machinery is available, making haats and shandies a tough market to compete with.

"Big players think that promotion at the haats is enough to build their value," feels Lokhande. Most assume that exposure at these outlets leads to penetration and, thereby, rise in market share.

Contd...

FIGURE 25.1

A Typical Haat, Bazaar, or Shandy

Does this really happen? Not exactly. The haat or shandy is just a vehicle for promotion and learning. It is nothing but a big marketplace that changes its location every week. "These markets are very organised, with shopkeepers having pre-assigned spaces for themselves, to sell their wares," adds Lokhande. A typical market is in an open field with ample space for displaying all sorts of goods. "The markets start early and are over by lunch, after which, the entertainment begins," he says. These markets are so successful, that many marketers use them as test pads to launch new products.

Pradeep Kashyap, director, Marketing and Research Team (MART), who has conducted many studies on these markets, says, "These markets have high potential that the corporates are now waking up to." The scope that these markets offer to distribution, is something that has to be seriously considered. For urban players, who have stockists and distributors that don't service remote areas, this form of selling can be a boon. A simple re-distributorship arrangement can be worked out.

The haats and bazaars also cater to farming equipment and raw material requirements. Another reason why these markets are so handy, is that the barter practice still 'lives' here. If you have a cow that you don't really need, you can exchange it for a stove – something you need. The entire market can be related to large departmental stores in the cities, where the advantage is a one-stop shopping exercise. The convenience of haats is that, they offer goods conveniently, and in a variety of choices. A basic advantage is the sale of second-hand durables as well.

But one thing holds true. Psychologically, it is the conservative approach to living that is inculcated in most of the Indian village dwellers that adds to the huge success of haats and shandies.

(Source: Narain Krishnamurthy, "Market is Frenzy," A & M, March 31, 2000).

Summary

More than 70 per cent of the Indian population lives in rural areas. Studies reveal that the consuming, class households in the rural equals the number in urban that is, 10.7 million strong households or 57 million individuals, out of which, 36 per cent live in rural areas and constitute a huge market. No wonder, the rural markets have become a vital source of growth for most companies. For many FMCG companies in the country, more than half their annual sales come from the rural market.

Urban markets are becoming intensely competitive for most companies and almost all product categories face stiff competition. Rural markets offer substantial growth opportunities and have gained importance in stature and many believe rural markets as the real market of the new millennium for businesses domestic or multinational.

The conditions that an aspiring rural marketer faces, appear to be highly challenging because of peculiarities of cultural, social, and economic dimensions, and the lack of facilities related to infrastructure. Understanding highly varied conditions in different parts of the country is an essential prerequisite for a marketer who wishes to make any inroads in rural markets.

Companies are appreciating the facts that approaches have to be tailored according to specific needs of rural people and this requires making adjustments in marketing mix elements. Products are to be modified in a number of ways, new products suited to rural consumers are to be developed, price adjustments are required, distribution difficulties are to be overcome, and novel means and approaches adopted for communicating effectively with the rural consumers.

The rural marketing is essentially developmental marketing and needs long-term commitment from the companies. Some companies have experimented with novel approaches and are reaping the benefits. They have devised ways to empower rural consumers and have made efforts to raise their standard of living.

Questions for Discussion

1. Why rural marketing in India has become such a hot topic for different businesses?
2. Is rural marketing any different from marketing in urban areas? Illustrate with examples.
3. What problems companies face in the rural markets?
4. How will you segment rural markets for a toothpaste, shampoo, and fairness cream?
5. In what ways are the rural consumers different from the urban consumers?
6. Why should a FMCG company consider product modification? Discuss two products that a company modified for the rural markets.
7. Would you prefer introducing a generic version of a detergent or prefer to use a brand name? Why?
8. In rural India, which particular media mix will you suggest to communicate effectively with consumers?
9. Suggest some unconventional media options to communicate with the rural consumers?
10. "Rural marketing is developmental marketing." Explain with examples.

Projects

1. You have joined a TV manufacturing company as "Manager Rural Marketing." Your product is superior and economically priced. The company's top brass feels advertising will not produce the desired results. What would be your promotional plan?
2. During your vacations, visit a rural area away from the urban market. Contact whatever retail outlets are available and study how companies make arrangement to deliver goods to them, or how they procure supplies.
3. Locate on the Internet a company involved in marketing fertilisers. Study the method of distribution, the company uses. Why do you think the method is appropriate?

Internet and Marketing

CHAPTER 26

LEARNING OBJECTIVES

After going through this chapter, you will understand:

- How the Internet is affecting markets and marketers
- How it affects the audience freedom, quantity and quality of information
- How the use of the Internet is influencing customisation, prices, and distribution channels
- Impact on communication and marketing research
- New approaches to promotions

eff Bezos quit his job on Wall Street in 1994 and started Amazon.com to sell books online. By 2001, the sales reached $3 billion. After building the book business, Bezos began adding other product categories. Music CDs and videos were the first additions. He wanted consumers to be able to buy 'anything and everything' at Amazon.

- Within days of its entry into the toy business in 1998, Amazon became the number one online toy retailer.
- Amazon faced scrutiny from business partners regarding its continual expansion into additional product categories in its quest for greater sales.
- Despite objections, no other online retailer has been as adapt, or innovative at finding ways to personalise the very impersonal process of buying products online. Amazon introduced the world of e-commerce to "collaborative filtering" technologies. In this high-tech form of marketing, the purchase of a consumer is recorded and scrutinised to allow Amazon to make recommendations based on that person's unique tastes.
- The fact that Amazon is still in business when so many dot.coms have failed, is almost certainly a tribute to Bezos persistence. Interestingly, Amazon's original products have been its most successful. In the first quarter of 2002, sales of books, music CDs, and videos amounted to $443 million, or more than half the Amazon's total revenues.

Technological developments, such as telephone, television, and personal computers etc. have influenced marketing in various ways. The latest and perhaps the most profound impact on business and marketing has been, the introduction of the Internet. We can think of Internet as a worldwide means of exchanging information and communicating through a series of interconnected computers. It is a medium and at the same time a space similar to physical space where, all sorts of activities take place, right from freely available information on almost any subject under the sun to and a variety of marketing activities. Besides, Internet is a business too.

Marketing activities on the Internet are actually a part of e-commerce or e-business. The Internet is changing the way, businesses undertake their marketing tasks. This wonderful technology provides marketers with faster, more efficient, and powerful ways to handle designing, promoting and distributing products, doing research, and collecting loads of market information almost instantly. It is difficult to forecast, what lies in future with respect to the full potential of this technology as the possibilities seem to be endless, and changes are being introduced at a much faster pace. The development in this field is so fast, that by the time this matter is printed and is in the reader's hands, chances are that an exciting something new would have been added to the Internet application, to interact with people and doing business with them. Many people believe that the Internet enables businesses, respondents, and customers close to real-life like interaction.

The *Internet* emerged from a U.S government project in 1970. The purpose was to develop some system of communication that would link researchers all over the world and allow them access and exchange of information. In 1989 *World Wide Web* (WWW) was developed. Web makes it possible for its users to share a complete range of communications including text, graphics, and audio messages. Any person or a company can create and register a *website* that includes a homepage and other information, containing files and anyone can access this website through a unique address and access the collection of available data contained in the web files. Today, web has become indispensable, for much of the communication that occurs between marketers and consumers in a large part of the world is through the Internet. Anyone with a computer and the Internet connection can access websites sitting anywhere in the world and buy or sell products and services.

Electronic networking refers to the linking of companies or individuals and can be accomplished by using some form of telecommunications. Companies or individuals can create an *electronic network* to share a variety of ideas, information, views, data, and perform various tasks. In business firms, when computers of company employees or departments are linked via Internet, this arrangement is known as *intranet* or *local electronic network*. A company, for example, can create an intranet by linking computers of designers, engineers, production executives, accountants, executives in marketing, sales, and advertising etc. to exchange information and inputs. The functionality of such local networks gets considerably enhanced when these computers are connected to a powerful central computer, called a server, that is capable of storing large databases that the participants can access through their computers.

Bharat Matrimony

- Bharat Matrimony group, the online matchmakers, has announced the launch of a classified portal called IndiaList.com, targeting the Rs. 1800 crore classifieds market in India.
- A company release said that, IndiaList.com is an online marketplace for buyers and sellers. From real estate, jobs, automobiles, electronics, computers to health, marriage, food, apparels and household products, the site is a place to advertise listings of every kind.
- "There are over 25 potential classifieds categories, which could not have been individually addressed due to their size. We have brought in all those segments under IndiaList.com, which will give the required presence and impetus to maximise our share of the Rs. 1800 crore classifieds market," Murugavel Janakiraman, CEO, Bharat Matrimony group, said in the release.

"There is a huge potential for internet to deliver classifieds services and it would become the undisputed leader in that space," he added.

Registration on IndiaList.com is free. However, the advertiser needs to be a registered member to post an ad on the site. Each member on the site is provided with a personal management area where they can monitor their responses and activities. Each ad that is posted on the portal needs to be validated, which may take about 24 hours. The advertisers will be notified about the acceptance or rejection of their ad through e-mails.

Besides online matrimony business, Bharat Matrimony group has also expanded into other online businesses like jobs (clickjobs.com) and property (IndiaProperty.com). The ISO certified Bharat Matrimony.com has over 7.5 million members worldwide.

Companies create their corporate website and post vast amount of information on it that includes product description, operating instructions, invitation to suppliers to submit bids on company's planned purchases, and contacting sales people. Some information on websites may be accessed by anyone and everyone while other may be restricted and accessible only to those with a password. This allows the companies to make some information accessible only to suppliers, customer, or distributors. Most companies producing consumer products consider ***electronic information*** (e-information) as a necessary form of communication – much like advertisements but with more information than any form of ad can carry.

Several important developments after the appearance of the Internet, made it possible for firms to take advantage of this new technology as a marketing tool. ***Web browser*** provides the Internet visitors a necessary application programme to view and interact with different websites. Two of the very well-known web browsers are the Netscape Navigator and the Internet Explorer. A very large number of websites came into existence and it became necessary to prepare an electronic directory. One of the most popular directory today is Yahoo (Yahoo stands for "Yet Another Hierarchical Officious Oracle") and contains hundreds of thousands of websites and millions of website pages. A ***portal*** such as Excite, Sify, or

Indiatimes is just a communication outfit or gateway to other websites and works as an entrance or guide to the World Wide Web. A typical portal offers a directory of large numbers of websites, a search engine such as Google to find out other websites and information, to connect to e-mail, look at stock rates, read weather report, access news and other information a user is looking for.

The Internet usage by business houses and consumers has grown by leaps and bounds over the years and today any firm worth its name in developed and developing countries is now maintaining some kind of Internet presence. Most business-to-business marketers consider having a website as a dire necessity for their business to flourish.

The level of Internet penetration in developed countries is quite high. The current estimates show that the number of Internet users in India is approximately 11 million. As the number of PC users in India is increasing rapidly and so are the Broadband Internet service providers, the rate of Internet user growth is expected to be healthy in the coming years. So far, easy availability of Broadband Internet and usage costs are a limiting factor for large number of consumers.

Effects of the Internet on Markets

Audience Freedom: Prior to the usage of the Internet by marketing companies, communications were traditionally under the control of the sellers. Of course companies kept in mind the target audiences, but the decision was always theirs, about when, what, and where with respect to messages they used in their communications with customers. Even the sales people were guided with regard to messages and their scheduled visits to the customers. The picture seems to be reversed with respect to marketing related interactions online. It is the Internet user who decides to use the computer, locate a website, and also decides what pages to consider or ignore. For example, a potential customer for a laptop computer, may visit any one or more number of computer seller websites and choose which pages to read or ignore, including accessories, independent software sellers, and service facilities etc. and on every page there would be direct and indirect promotional messages. Other traditional mass communication methods for the same product offer little more than, to just building brand.

Quantity and Quality of Information: The available information on the Internet about any item is extensive in terms of quantity and quality and a customer is in a much better position to compare various alternatives, to choose what is more suited to her/his specific needs and wants. Books from various publishers are available in bookstores, publishers sell them online, and independent stores also sell the same books online. A buyer can look at various sites and choose the one with right price, sitting at home. Internet has made it possible for customers to track shipments sent through FedEx at every stage of their journey. Customers are in a much better position to compare prices and make use of this information in negotiating with traditional sellers.

Speedy Customisation: Few years back, customisation in case of consumer items was rare and limited to made-to-order jewelry, watches, or cars etc. and these were expansive products. Now companies, such as Dell Computers and some others, offer buyers the choice of speedy customisation. Internet has made customisation possible and practical as it speeds up the whole process. Formerly, it would have required getting the required customisation details from customers, procurement, information sharing with production and all this took much time. Auto manufacturers and even some ready-to-wear garment producers are now using the Internet and right from selling stores to suppliers, all are interconnected and whatever parts are needed by the manufacturer or whatever designs or styles of apparel are demanded, are being produced and supplied quickly.

Customisation almost completely eliminates the inventory maintaining costs. Otis Port reported that increased production efficiency, decreased inventories, and lower transportation costs are shifting auto manufacturers from mass to customised production and marketing and this could reduce vehicle prices by almost 30 per cent.

Flexible Prices: In case of certain consumer products and services, the norm of fixed prices is becoming flexible. Internet makes it possible for customers to post their specifications with respect to the product or service and at what price it would be acceptable, and then sellers make offers to buyers. Internet auction sites are available where a prospective customer can record her/his bid. eBay is the largest online auctioneer with about 40 million registered sellers and buyers selling or bidding for more than 125 million diverse items, including retired ships or submarines. Air travellers post their travel details and specify ticket prices and sellers make offers. There are no fixed prices, buyers and sellers interact in real time and prices are determined.

Distribution Channels are Becoming Shorter: Unlike traditional marketing channels that involve more levels, Internet has made it possible to skip one or more levels or create direct-to-customer channel in case of many durable and non-durable product categories and services. In case of direct marketing, we have seen how Internet is changing the shopping scenario. In the preceding chapter we have discussed the role e-Choupals which are playing in eliminating middlemen. Many large retail chain stores are buying direct from the manufacturers thus, eliminating wholesalers' roles.

Customer Communication: Promotional messages from producers are viewed as biased as firms have self-interest with regard to selling a product or service. Independent information sources are viewed as objective and credible because the independent third party gains or loses nothing from a buying decision. The Internet has tremendously enlarged the scope of exchanging word-of-mouth information from third parties. The Internet makes available unlimited information through chat rooms, forums, and independent evaluations from other users of a product or service. Many firms make these individual evaluations and opinions available on their sites for customer convenience and as a tool in building customer confidence.

Marketing Strategy and the Internet

Marketing Research: The information the marketers gather using marketing research techniques has direct impact on market segmentation, targeting, and promotional approaches etc. Companies use the Internet to collect a wide variety of detailed information about visitors of websites. IntelliQuest and Millward Brown joined hands to develop a research tool that collects online information on demographics, psychographics; location of web access, media usage, and purchase habits. Also, an electronic device called a ***cookie*** typically collects the information on users. This is connected to users' file, about this electronic device, the user usually is not aware, and collects information on what is visited, how many times visited, and where the user clicks etc. Collection of all such information by using traditional research approaches would involve much manpower, time, and considerable expenditures. Traditional market research approaches, such as surveys or focus groups are conducted on web swiftly, at low cost, and large geographic reach. Internet can use graphics and visual images of product in use. These images can be shown from different angles that customers look at. Of course, similar to conventional mail surveys, it is not certain who completed the information. Another disadvantage is that, it is difficult to ensure that respondents really are from the target group in which the marketer is interested.

A technique called ***clustering*** is used to track the web pages visited, amount of time devoted to a page, and what items are purchased by individuals while moving through the website. This type of information is used in creating clusters of site visitors with similar behavioural patterns. When behaviour of new visitors resembles to a certain cluster, they can be easily moved to products they are more likely to be interested in and purchase. This facilitates segmenting and targeting. The largest online bookstore Amazon.com developed a similar technique to recommend books or any other items based on a visitor's selection, or previous purchases. For example, if on the previous occasion visitors bought books on marketing from Amazon.com and also examined some books on, say tarot, or adventure. The next time a visitor clicks on marketing books, the site would also suggests some books on tarot, or adventure.

Marketing Channels: Marketers using web to sell products are increasingly realising the benefits of developing closer links with end customers. They have also appreciated the advantage of eliminating all or some middlemen from the distribution channel for both, business and consumer, products and the impact on costs. Marketers of several types of products can even bypass their own sales force. Companies are in a better position to decide what product selection to present, how to present, and what level of service to offer in each case. Further, it is a big plus point, that consumers can directly and quickly communicate with marketers about their product usage experience and give suggestions.

Despite several advantages from marketers' point of view, bypassing sales people or some level of channel partners may become a source of tension in many cases. For a company employing sales force, sales made to customers via Internet, directly affects commission of the sales people. This becomes a cause of heartburn. Majority of sales people resent such moves, particularly when this affects large chunk of sales in their territory. Business-to-business marketers such as Cisco and Dell use the web to track and distribute sale leads to sales people in real time.

Established manufacturing companies have some kind of channel arrangement in place. When such a company bypasses one or more channel partners, it frequently becomes a cause of conflict. Besides, by changing the distribution arrangement to make a product available to customers, affects both individuals and firms and the level to what extent customers are treated fairly is not really clear. Such changes are bound to upset the existing business of channel parties. Some of the moves manufacturers have considered for avoiding conflict related to Internet use in channel functions include the following:

- Target a market segment with specialised needs. For example, a company might target customers, who need customised personal care products, cosmetics, computers, autos and others.
- Use Internet for generating customer leads. For instance, an auto manufacturer might collect leads for potential customers and pass them on to channel members, or direct customers to channel members in specific cities.
- Offer different products online. For instance, a computer manufacturer may sell its desktops through channel members and offer its laptops online. Or it may decide to sell servers to businesses directly through sales force and make direct supplies. It is necessary for the company to clarify its policy as to which products it would sell online and for this, a traditional channel arrangement is not suitable due to a number of reasons. For example, IBM sells some products directly and others through channel members.
- A company may involve channel partners in online sales. For example, Amway in some countries started selling online and protected the interests of its independent salespersons by asking them to direct all the customers to the Amway website. For all sales made this way, the salespersons receive a commission.
- Companies sell the product online at retail prices. Whether a customer buys online or goes to a retailer, same price is charged. This only helps in expanding the market and any kind of cost advantages for the concerned company are not there.

Resolving Channel Conflict at Mattel

In 1999, Mattel moved into e-commerce, when it began selling select products from its Fisher-Price infant and preschool toys online. This move raised eyebrows among the retailers, who were worried that the online sales would eat up their sales. Retailers grew more displeased when Mattel started selling Barbie toys and apparel on its Barbie.com site in September 2000. In addition to selling Barbie merchandise on Barbie.com, Mattel mailed its first Barbie catalogue to some 4 million households that month. One top toy seller executive said, "We are supposed to be partners and this is obviously competitive." Retailers were particularly upset because the simultaneous unveiling of the e-commerce-enhanced Barbie.com and the launch of catalogue came just before the holiday shopping season.

Mattel insisted that its site was designed as a "self-funding marketing and advertising tool" that built relationships with parents and children, than as a device for direct competition. At the time of Barbie.com launch, Christina DeRosa, vice president of the Website and media content for Mattel's Barbie division, said, "We have been at the forefront of marketing for 40 years, so we have to be at the forefront of this new medium. The Internet has become a compelling part of a girl's life. When that happens to your consumer base, you have to think about it." The site was an instant hit. During its first month of operation as an e-commerce portal, Barbie.com attracted 548,000 unique visitors.

Mattel could not afford to alienate retailers, since half the company's revenue came from only five retail chains. To appease the retailers, Mattel voluntarily limited the number of products available on Barbie.com and in the catalogue. Mattel pointed out that in addition to toys and apparel, the site offered less widely available items, such as Barbie brand bath and body creams, house furnishings, and books, that would not cannibalise retail sales. To drive traffic to stores, Mattel printed information about the nearest retailers according to zip code in each catalogue and included a store locator on Barbie.com. Additionally, Mattel did not advertise the e-commerce features of its site. Finally, the company assured its retailers that online and catalogue sales would account for less than 1 per cent of Barbie's overall sales in 2000.

(Source: Lisa Bannon, "Selling Barbie Online, May Pit Mattel vs Stores," Wall Street Journal, November 17, 2000).

At the retail level businesses, the retailer is the last link in the distribution chain and hence using the Internet by a retailer has nothing to do with other channel members. Many retail organisations in the world are using the Internet to sell their merchandise. Some enterprising new breed middlemen have invested in creating their own websites. These electronic middlemen facilitate transactions between the buyers and the sellers through the Internet. eBay is one such site that facilitates transactions and gets its revenues from ads on its site. The entire negotiation takes place between the buyer and the seller. eBay simply provides the cyberspace for negotiations and transactions.

So far, whenever any established firm makes use of the Internet for transactions, without exception, it has some level of impact on the existing channel relationship and adjustments may be moderate to severe, depending on the product category, existing channel arrangement, and consumer preference.

Promotions: Websites have become much more creative than being simply online catalogues. Now they promote products and try to create brand images, use sales promotions, and even sell products and services.

The number of websites keeps on increasing everyday. What if a company creates a website that nobody visits. It is like opening a show room that no prospective customer comes to. Another situation can be, those who enter the showroom are not the target customers. They are not the ones who would buy the available merchandise. The number of websites is numerous and unless a company's website is visited by the right customers, it amounts to having wasted the money in creating the website. Search engines cannot keep track of all the available websites.

Visits to websites are deliberate and initiated by the visitors who can be customers, suppliers, or competitors, looking for particular products or information of their interest. In case of mass media marketing communications, such as advertisements, there is no passive exposure. What happens in case of traditional mass media marketing communications such as TV, or radio commercials, or outdoor media, people get exposed to them without really looking for such ads. In case of the Internet, the visitor initiative is very important.

The Internet marketers have to make their websites attractive to the right target audience so that, they are motivated to visit their specific websites. Developing and maintaining a website requires considerable effort to attract visitors to the site and encourage them to return again and again requires creativity, effective marketing and regularly updating the site. Depending on the product category and the company's marketing objectives for the Internet, a website can be just a simple source of information about the company and its products or a powerful tool to build brand image, a means to offer samples, or generating sales leads.

In general, the communication objectives may relate to creating awareness, generating customer interest, provide information, help in building a strong brand, a powerful image or stimulate product trial by consumers.

To accomplish their objectives, Internet marketers use many approaches, some of which include:

- ***Banners:*** A banner ad is a boxed-in promotional message that often appears at the top of the web page. If a visitor clicks on the banner ad, she/he is transported to the advertiser's home page. This is the most used form of Internet promotion. Banners can be used to create brand recall or recognition. Other names given to banners include *side panels, skyscrapers,* or *verticals.* Experienced web visitors ignore banners and many experts believe that their usefulness is very limited and their use seems to be declining.
- ***Sponsorships:*** This is another common advertising approach on websites. The advertiser is given a permanent place on host's website and pays a sponsorship fee to the host. Some sites are targeted at specific segments, such as iVillage is targeted at women. This site has many sponsors who offer special deals and offer advice to target visitors. The use of sponsorship sites is increasing and is more popular than banners.
- ***Pop-Up and Pop-Under:*** When a visitor accesses a web page, sometimes a window appears either in front or underneath the web page, the visitor is viewing. Pop-ups become visible as sooner the web site is accessed and pop-under becomes visible only when the visitor closes the browser. Pop-ups are usually larger than a banner but smaller than full screen. Website visitors often get irritated with pop-ups and consider them as intrusion.
- ***Portal Use:*** Some portals give a prominent place to a company's offer for a fee. When a visitor follows directed search, the marketer's name appears prominently at or near the top of the list. For example, when anyone uses Yahoo's search engine to locate a toy marketer, the name of K-B Toys is displayed prominently.
- ***E-mail:*** Companies send e-mails to Internet users to visit the company web site. It can be effective only when the target customer is appropriate otherwise it becomes "junk mail."

Apple Computer's "Switch" Campaign

Apple developed 'Switch' campaign to attract Windows users to Mac computers. Apple has taken the integration of web and TV to a new level. TBWA/Chiat/Day developed eight 30-second TV spots. These spots feature regular people talking about their switch from Windows to Macintosh – and of course, about how happy they are for having done so. The $75 million ad campaign has been integrated with a new Apple site (apple.com/switch) by directing viewers to the site for more information. Once at the site, consumers can actually view the TV commercials. The commercials appear in the same quality as they would on TV, and they have become a hit – in one case, creating a new crush named Ellen Feiss, whose homework was eaten by a PC.

(Source: Mylene Mangalindan, "Now TV Ads in Returns on Web Sites," The Wall Street Journal, February II, 2002).

- ***Interstitials:*** These ads appear on the computer screen while a visitor is waiting for a site's contents to download. The opinion about the effectiveness of interstitials is divided. Some believe they are irritating and a nuisance than a benefit, but some others believe that the recall rate of interstitials is better than pop-ups.
- ***Push Technologies:*** Some companies provide screen savers to its website visitors, that allow the firms to directly "hook" the visitor to their websites. This is an approach to "push" a message to the consumers rather than wait for consumers to locate it. These new technologies are known as ***push technologies*** or ***web-casting technologies*** and open web pages or news updates and may also have video and audio content.
- ***Sales Promotions:*** Many companies effectively use sales promotions such as contests and sweepstakes to generate consumer interest. For example, Pepsi Co. used a contest for its Mountain Dew named "Play Street Dash" (www. pepsizone_yahoo.co.in).

Increasingly, more and more companies are using many of these promotional methods. However, attracting consumers is only one objective. Internet visitors are believed to be an impatient lot and holding them to the site is a challenge. Internet users in general, are comparatively more educated and from middle and upper income bracket and a larger percentage of young people using Internet live in urban areas. The use is gradually spreading to smaller towns and even some rural areas in India have been provided access. So far, the infrastructure facilities and costs of Internet are a major deterrent in its faster spread. Many companies are gradually spreading their network of broadband Internet services in different parts of our country and the future holds much promise.

Use of the Internet to promote products is new and evolving. The businesses still have much to learn about how to attract visitors, keep them glued to the site for sufficient time, and sell to them. With more research input and experience, companies will develop more effective approaches about online marketing efforts.

Many companies initially thought, that web marketing could replace retail stores for customers or sales people in case of business-to-business selling. Over the years, experience has proved that it is very difficult to eliminate the services extended by middlemen. The major areas of concern for online marketers include tackling the problems associated with returned products, payment, and performance complaints. For example, eBay simply brings the buyers and sellers together to facilitate transactions and if a buyer was dissatisfied, the buyer has no place to go. These firms are making efforts to avoid or solve such sticky problems.

Service back up is also a major problem for companies aspiring to move into Internet marketing. Ann Grimes reports that quite a few successful Internet retailers combine online access with physical store and consider it the best formula.

Security is also an issue. It seems that a very high percentage of people have never made an online purchase. Many experts believe that security and privacy are major issues and visitors fear that credit card numbers can be stolen because there have been many publicised instances. There also have been serious incidents when hackers have broken into marketers' databases to steal account numbers. The Internet is something impersonal unlike retail stores where consumers interact with store employees face-to-face. This 'impersonal' characteristic makes consumers hesitant and less agreeable to share personal or credit card information. So far, ensuring complete security and secrecy on the Internet is very difficult for online marketers.

Summary

Technological developments, such as telephone, television, and personal computers etc. have influenced marketing in a large number of ways. The latest and perhaps the most profound impact on business and marketing has been, the introduction of the Internet. We can think of Internet as a worldwide means of exchanging information and communicating through a series of interconnected computers. This wonderful technology provides marketers with faster, more efficient, and powerful ways to handle designing, promoting, and distributing products, doing research, and collecting loads of market information almost instantly.

Electronic networking refers to linking companies or individuals and can be accomplished by using some form of telecommunications. Companies or individuals can create an electronic network to share a variety of ideas, information, views, data, and perform various tasks. Internal electronic networks are called intranets.

The commercial application of the Internet became possible with the creating of World Wide Web and several tools to access websites. These include browsers, directories, and portals. Firms create their corporate website and post vast amount of information on it that includes product description, operating instructions, invitation to suppliers to submit bids on company's planned purchases, and contacting sales people. Some information on websites may be accessed by anyone and other may be restricted and accessible only to those with a password. Anyone with a computer and the Internet connection can access websites sitting anywhere in the world and buy or sell products and services. Customers enjoy greater control of interaction with marketers and have the easy access to comparing prices. More product customisation and flexible pricing is possible. Consumers have access to more quantity and quality of product related information, not directly under the control of markers.

Use of the Internet permits companies to collect marketing research information at reduced costs and manpower involvement. Wherever feasible, companies have shortened distribution channels to reach the customers and are using variety of methods to minimise any possibility of channel conflict or sales force complaints.

Internet marketers have to make their websites attractive to the right target audience so that they are motivated to visit their specific websites. Developing and maintaining a website requires considerable effort to attract visitors to the site and, to encourage them to return to it again and again requires creativity, effective marketing and regularly updating the site. Depending on the product category and the company's marketing objectives for the Internet, a website can be just a simple source of information about the company and its products or a powerful tool to build brand image, a means to offer samples, or generating sales leads. To achieve promotional objectives, companies use banners, sponsorships, pop-ups, pop-under, e-mails, interstitials, push technologies, contests and sweepstakes etc.

The major concerns companies have relate to service backup and security related to transactions on the Internet. It is particularly security from consumers' point of view that discourages them from recording credit card or personal information on website.

The Internet will continue to grow and evolve. So far, the costs of using the Internet and the widespread unavailability of broadband are a major deterrent in its faster spread in India. Many companies are gradually spreading their network of broadband Internet services in different parts of our country and the future holds much promise.

Questions for Discussion

1. How has the use of Internet benefited the marketers?
2. In your view, what are the attributes of an effective website?
3. Internet marketing may be appropriate for what kind of products? Why?
4. Discuss with example, how Internet has benefited marketing research.
5. What are the disadvantages of Internet use in marketing? Suggest some methods to tide over the problems.
6. Do you think Internet can replace traditional retailers? Explain with examples.
7. Discuss three promotional methods that companies use to communicate with the consumers through the Internet.
8. In your view, is Internet a better medium to advertise home appliances than television? Explain.
9. Discuss the advantages and disadvantages of the Internet as an advertising medium. Give suitable examples.
10. Has the use of Internet benefited rural marketing in India? What future for Internet marketing do you foresee in India?
11. Why should companies such as Sony and IBM be concerned about their existing channels? When they sell computers to customers online?

Projects

1. Visit Sony, Dell and IBM. Note down the differences in their websites promoting their laptop computers.
2. Go to portals, Indiatimes.com and sify.com. Study the banner ads on both links. In your view, what are the objectives of the banner ads and what factors can make those banners effective or ineffective?
3. Interview two or three of your friends or neighbours, who shopped on the web. Find out why they preferred web shopping? Did they buy or not? why?

Bibliography

1. Otis Port, "Customers Move into the Driver's Seat," *Business Week,* October 1999.
2. Ann Grimes, "What's in Store," *Wall Street Journal,* July 15, 2002.

Cases

Case 8.1: Service Differentiation at British Airways

Since, 1990s, international airlines saw increasing competition and providing services became a major factor to differentiate and a key to success. Carriers lost billions of dollars and needed to raise the airfares. Some airline executives believed that improved service package would make increased fares more acceptable to the customers. Adopting this approach, companies started focusing on services rather than competing on price dimension. No one did it better than British Airways and in an annual poll conducted by a magazine, business travellers rated British Airways as providing the best service.

British Airways has come a long way since 1982 when it lost $1 billion, an industry record. When Colin Marshall took over as CEO in 1983, everyone in the industry made fun and laughed at the carrier. Comedians referred to it by its initials BA, as "Bloody Awful." Employees' morale had hit rock bottom, thousands of employees were laid off, and those remaining were embarrassed to work for the world's worst airline. Marshall's first challenge was to restore pride. To send a clear message to the employees and potential customers, he ordered newly designed uniforms for all personnel. The planes were repainted with bright stripes with the motto "To fly to serve."

Marshall ensured that the airline lived up to its new motto. He launched a major campaign to change the employee's attitude towards the service. He guessed, that many passengers, especially business travellers, wanted better service. He therefore, required all employees to participate in a two-day seminar, "Putting People First," which put the airline employees in the role of the customers. In the seminar, employees discussed their own experiences with poor service.

Immediately, British Airways worked to overcome more obvious problems, such as uninteresting food, poor cabin service, and insufficient legroom. But Marshal also examined the less obvious. For example, the research revealed that passengers like to be called by names. BA employees spent several months observing passengers on flight from London to Glasgow and Manchester. The customers' satisfaction score went up about 60 per cent when ticket agents addressed customers by their name. This was the beginning and BA ticket agents were expected to call customers by name whenever the opportunity arose. Multilingual employees were placed at the London's Heathrow Airport to help passengers. British Airways set up booths at JFK Airport in New York City so that they could videotape the passengers' comments about British Airways service. Finally, at present, the airline changes flight schedules according to the customers' convenience.

British Airways also revamped its Concorde flights. Marshall decided to use British Airways' seven Concorde aircrafts, which were losing money. This was to symbolise, the revitalised image of the airline. The company redecorated the planes and hiked fares by 30 per cent more than the first class fares that conventional jets charge. Since Concorde could cross Atlantic Ocean in half the time it takes by other jets, British Airways concentrated its advertising on the importance of time to business travellers. As an outcome, BA's Concorde achieved over 60 per cent occupancy, which was the break-even point on transatlantic routes.

British Airways also invested $40 million to improve first-class service. The airline redesigned cabin interiors and put a video terminal at each seat. The new wine cellar offered an improved selection; menu allowed first-class passengers to eat when they wished.

In discussing service, the British Airways CEO recalled the famous Twentieth Century Limited, the train that ran from New York to Chicago. Conductors would pay to the passengers $1 for

Contd...

every minute the train was late, no matter who or what was to be blamed. Air traffic delays and weather problems would make it next to impossible for airlines to make the same offer. Marshall said, "We could promise to make the delays completely painless with concentrated service attention. Think how many customers you could acquire for life, if and when the guarantee is cheerfully, quickly, and easily paid." The improvements at British Airways drew the attention of managers from other airlines and other service industries. The changes also turned the company around. In 1991, profits for British Airways were at an industry high of $496 million. Its average revenue per passenger, $396, was among the best in the industry. In terms of passengers carried and miles flown, British Airways became the largest international airline in the world.

British Airways would like to provide its much lauded service to the passengers across the world. In July 1992, it finalised an agreement with US Air to form a transatlantic alliance. But it withdrew its $750 million bid for 44 per cent of US Air, as it became clear that the U.S. government would not approve the deal. The proposed deal resulted in protests from major U.S. airlines, which claimed that the British would have a substantial head start in becoming the first global airline. British Airways second bid of $300 million for 19.9 per cent of US Air was approved in March 1993. Together, the two carriers were to serve 339 cities in 71 countries.

QUESTIONS

1. Analyse the case and identify reasons that made the British Airways a laughingstock in the industry? Why was it necessary to change the employees' attitude toward service?
2. What effect the new alliance would have on the services offered by other airlines?
3. Why would a passenger pay 30 per cent more to fly the same destination?

Case : 8.2: Bharat Sanchar Nigam Limited (BSNL)

In 1985, Posts and Telegraph Department (P&T) was reorganised under two separate entities – The Department of Post Services, and The Department of Telecommunications (DoT).

The DoT services included, basic telephony to Indian consumers, such as local and national long-distance telephony, ISDN, data networking, satellite and public telephones. In 1986, as part of DoT, two corporations were created – Mahanagar Telephone Nigam Limited (MTNL) and Videsh Sanchar Nigam Limited (VSNL). MTNL jurisdiction covered telecom operation in two important metro cities – Delhi and Mumbai. Videsh Sanchar Nigam Limited was responsible for the Overseas Communications Services (OCS) and served as international telecom service provider in India. The telephone-density at this stage was less than one telephone per 100 people because of large population base, lack of infrastructure, low standard of living, and the lack of resources to cover our large country. Even by early 1990s, there were large number of villages without a single telephone connection. Even in the cities, there were considerably long waiting lists for telephone connection.

In May 1994, the government decided to open the Indian market to foreign telecom players and spelled out its National Telecom Policy. The main objectives were to provide, at least one telephone line each, in more than 600,000 villages in the country, make telephones available on demand, and improve the telephone-density to 2.5 lines for 100 people by 1997. It was because of this policy that cellular phones were introduced in the country. The first two companies in this business were Essar and Bharti. For the initial few years the market was not very enthusiastic due to lack of awareness among the people, lack of infrastructure-related facilities, non-supportive government regulations, and above all the high tariff call rates and handset prices.

By the close of the century, the industry had undergone many structural changes and the demand for cellular phone services was picking up. The government realised the need for a new telecom policy and regulatory framework, and the new telecom policy was announced in April 1999.

DoT nearly had monopoly status in the landline telecom business and its profits had increased from Rs. 1300.28 crores in 1990 to Rs. 7300.22 in 1999. The competition in the industry intensified as never before, and the government decided to give DoT a free hand to compete with private companies in the industry. In October 2000 a new corporation was created to handle DoT's service function under the name Bharat Sanchar Nigam Limited (BSNL). In 2001, BSNL had an increase of 18.87 per cent in its subscriber base, and the number of subscribers jumped from 28.12 million in 2000 to 33.41 million and profits soared to Rs. 63.12 billion on revenues of 235 billion.

Despite this impressive growth, in the beginning of the 21st century BSNL was facing problems. Large number of subscribers were leaving BSNL and it was a serious cause of concern. According to industry observers, besides the factors such as intensifying competition and regulatory framework, which were beyond BSNL control, there were other problems that could be controlled by BSNL but, BSNL did not do so. The most important among these, were faults in the network, and complaints of poor service quality.

The number of faults per 100 mainlines per year in BSNL's landline network were reported to be more than 150 as compared to the worlds average of 25. Even in low-income countries, average number of faults were 140. In addition, BSNL customer service left quite a lot to be desired. It was different till 1994 when customers had no other alternative but to use BSNL services and

Contd...

live with these service problems. The entry of private companies like Bharti, Essar, and Tata during early 2000s changed things drastically for BSNL. These companies offered much better services than BSNL had ever provided and subscribers began leaving BSNL for these companies.

Meanwhile the popularity of cellular services had increased due to the strategies adopted by cellular operators. This too hit BSNL badly during the early 2000s. In December 2001, Bharti introduced IndiaOne, a STD service that offered large discounts to customers. Bharti offered 60% of the amount received on every STD call to cellular operators who routed their calls through IndiaOne, while BSNL offered only 5%. This motivated major cellular operators to use IndiaOne to route their STD calls instead of BSNL This further, led to a substantial decline in BSNL revenues.

When cellular companies reduced their STD charges to benefit the customers, BSNL revenues were further affected negatively. BSNL responded by cutting down its STD charges to the extent of 62% in January 2002. BSNL expected that increased traffic would offset the decrease in rates. The traffic, however, rose only by 10 – 15% and the company stood to lose Rs. 30 billion in the first 6 months of 2002. The company's revenues from long-distance calls fell from Rs. 99.66 billion in 2000 to Rs. 71.91 billion by the end of 2001.

BSNL realised that to survive in the long-run it would have to reorient its strategies. The growth in cellular market was attractive. From 1.2 million in 1999, it had grown to 10 million by early 2002, and BSNL decided to expand and diversify by entering the cellular market. This appeared to be a timely decision.

BSNL developed plans to introduce its cellular services by April 2002. It finalised contracts with the vendors for hand set supply to be given along with post-paid connections. However, before the launch of BSNL cellular service, Promod Mahajan, the then Telecom Minister intervened and asked the vendors to drop hand set prices further. This delayed the launch by a few months, though the prices were actually just marginally reduced. This delay gave enough time to the competitors to establish themselves even more strongly and BSNL lost many potential customers.

BSNL launched CellOne and Excel (post-paid and prepaid connections respectively). In terms of reach, this was India's largest cellular service till then. The service was to be launched across the country in two phases. The first phase was to be completed by December 2002 and the company planned to cover all major cities and towns in all the states. The second phase aimed to cover other remaining areas by December 2003. BSNL could attract about 3,50,000 customers within the first two months of the launch and an additional 3,50,000 more subscribers by the close of 2002. This was nearly half the total cellular subscriber base. By January 2003, BSNL captured 7.5% of the total cellular market.

This rapid acceptance of BSNL was due to its extensive reach, low tariffs, and service offerings such as free incoming calls and free roaming within India, and waiver of airtime charges on STD calls for areas further than 500 km. Director, Commerce and Marketing, BSNL said, "First, our tariffs are the lowest anywhere in the world. Second, we are expanding in areas so far untouched by private companies. Third, we leverage our strength of vast nationwide network to offer high quality service.

BSNL offered its post-paid service at a low rate of Rs. 325 per month without any security deposit. This was in sharp contrast to other private sector companies who required customers

Contd...

to deposit between Rs. 1500 and Rs. 2000 as security deposit for post-paid connections. BSNL's Excel, the pre-paid service, was also made available at attractive rates in different price ranges. Additionally, BSNL also offered value added services, such as caller ID and roaming for free in contrast to private companies who were charging for these services.

A very favourable factor for BSNL, that contributed to rapid acceptance of its cell phone service has been its extensive infrastructure. Private companies are at a disadvantage in this regard. Setting up infrastructure involves high costs. This has been the main reason that they have not spread their network to small towns and villages. BSNL has more than 37,000 exchanges and covers nearly 95% of the entire country.

BSNL subscriber base grew rapidly in early 2003 and it had more than 2 million customers in its net. Soon, the company encountered capacity overload problems because its technology could not support such a large subscriber base, and the company was quick to upgrade its technology and infrastructure.

A variety of criticisms surfaced. BSNL was accused of taking undue advantage of huge financial resources and its extensive infrastructure discouraged competitors by offering services at very low prices. Some analysts pointed out that the BSNL prices were less than the costs incurred by some private firms. BSNL charged Rs. 1.20 per minute for its outgoing calls, while private firms charged Rs. 1.99 per minute on an average. BSNL also offered free incoming calls to CellOne customers if the call originated from either another CellOne or from a BSNL landline connection. Private firms, such as Essar or Bharti could offer free incoming calls only if the subscriber belonged to their own network. Further, BSNL waived airtime charges of Rs. 2 on long distance calls that had to be paid for by customers of other cell phone companies. Yet another BSNL advantage was, that it did not have to pay 8 – 12% of its revenues as interconnect charges of the government.

For the private companies, the license terms stipulated that all their calls had to be routed only through BSNL, and private firms had to pay BSNL for using its network. Private firms considered it as an unfair government policy and wanted the government to permit them to route their cell-to-cell calls directly without involving BSNL network. Private companies, such as Reliance and Shyam Telelink also criticised BSNL for delays in providing the required number of interconnect points. BSNL maintained that delays were due to certain technical problems, but private players saw it as a deliberate strategy of BSNL to attract customers of private companies.

The BSNL customers were not satisfied with its services. They said that though BSNL had an established infrastructure and wide reach, the quality of its cellular services was inferior to private companies. Reportedly, many customers complained that it was very difficult to connect to a BSNL cell phone through other cell phone services. The voice quality was poor because, compared to private cell phone operators, such as, Hutch and Airtel were using 32k chip and BSNL was using 16k Chip. BSNL also did not provide the facility of downloading different ring tone, pictures, or sending text messages to other cell phone users in India or abroad. Customer services and fault rectification was nothing but unsatisfactory. BSNL cell phone connections were not available easily and customers were required to go to BSNL office several times to acquire a connection.

To revamp its strategies, BSNL set up about 3,200 customer service centres across the country to facilitate customers' access to easy connections, to provide convenient fault repair service and third party transfers. It also set up 81 quality assurance centres in cities, such as Hyderabad,

Contd...

Bangalore, Kolkata, and Chandigarh etc. These centres examined the quality of all telecom supplies made to BSNL and periodically conducted marketing research to evaluate the services of BSNL and competitors, as perceived by customers. Call centres were set up across the county to answer the customer inquiries and furnish information. The company planned to offer customer added services by mid 2003, such as sports news, news, weather forecasts, stock market quotes, and jokes through text messaging.

To increase its coverage and reach all the user segments, BSNL entered WLL market in late 2002 with its Tarang service. This service was offered in four customer friendly tariff packages and acquired a customer base of 1.4 million by 2003. With the entry of Reliance in WLL market, BSNL decided to revise the tariff rates of Tarang to counter lower Reliance rates. BSNL became the market leader in the WLL segment by March 2003 with a subscriber base of 1.4 million customers as compared to Reliance and Tata's 0.96 and 0.15 million respectively.

By March 2003, BSNL became the second largest cellular company after Bharti with subscribers numbering 2.3 million and the company sources believed that it would not be long before BSNL will surpass Bharti and become the market leader in cellular phone services.

The view of its competitors and some analysts were however different and they expressed their doubts about BSNL's subscriber growth rate, as they believed that BSNL had overstated the number of its subscribers. The reason for these doubts – the initial pre-paid BSNL connections was priced at Rs. 200 and recharge card was priced at Rs. 300 – Rs. 2000 depending on the package a customer bought. This was at least Rs. 100 more than the initial pre-paid connection and reportedly, many customers were purchasing a new connection rather than paying for a recharge card. Hence, BSNL seemed to be simply recounting its customer base and the customer base became exaggerated than the actual numbers. Another reason for doubts was the fact that, according to a TRAI order all cellular service firms started providing free incoming calls to all subscribers from April 1, 2003 and this was expected to terminate competitive advantage that BSNL had enjoyed to attract customers.

By early 2003, the competition had intensified considerably. Bharti and Hutch waived away the charges for value added services like caller ID and also slashed STD tariffs to Rs. 2.99 per minute. These private companies also cut down their airtime charges for STD calls to 50 paise and air charges for ISD calls were completely waived off.

BSNL lost approximately 20 – 25% of its STD tariffs to private companies because of reduced cell-to-cell STD tariffs. Idea cellular entered the market with even more reduced tariffs. Private players also offered various value added services, such as news updates, weather forecast, stock market quotes, airline schedules, and facility of checking the status of railway reservation.

BSNL faced additional problems in its landline phone segment. In March 2003, the government announced that it would not reimburse a part of the costs that BSNL incurred in rural areas, beginning April 2003, which was expected to have adversely affected BSNL finances.

TRAI dealt a further blow to BSNL in April 2003 with a new tariff scheme according to which the BSNL landline rentals were increased and free calls reduced, pulse rate was reduced to 2 minutes from earlier 3 minutes, and the landline to cell phone call charges were increased. These moves were expected to hike customers' bills by 30 – 40 %. There was a general belief among the analysts that these moves will shift BSNL subscribers to private cell services.

Contd...

In May 2003, TRAI again revised tariff plans to benefit the customers. Fixed cell charges of BSNL were reduced to half as compared to the earlier scheme, and the rental charges and free calls were also altered marginally. TRAI also ordered BSNL to start paying license fee and spectrum charges like all other private companies. Many industry analysts argued that paying license and spectrum charges could wipe out the operating profits of BSNL, and the company might even incur losses for 2003, as the company was already burdened with huge salary bills, interest, and tax.

The telecom industry was adjusting to rapid changes on the regulatory and competitive fronts even in June. Companies in a landline, WLL, and cellular were modifying and introducing new tariff plans to attract more customers. The negative developments on the regulatory front for BSNL indicated that the future was unlikely to be a piece of cake.

QUESTIONS

1. What made BSNL enter cellular phone business? What strategies BSNL adopted to establish itself in the cellular market?
2. What decisions or factors helped BSNL to establish itself as market leader in the cell phone business?
3. What steps BSNL should have taken to retain its cellular service consumers?

Case 8.3: Kentucky Fried Chicken

By mid 1950s, fast food franchising was still in its infancy when Harland Sanders began his cross-country travels to market "Colonel Sanders' Recipe Kentucky Fried Chicken." He had developed a secret chicken recipe with eleven herbs and spices. By 1963, the number of KFC franchises had crossed 300. Colonel Sanders, at 74 years of age was tired of running the daily operations and sold the business in 1964 to two Louisville businessmen – Jack Massey and John Young Brown, Jr. – for $2 million. Brown, who later became the governor of Kentucky, was named president, and Massey was named chairman. Colonel Sanders stayed in a public relations capacity.

In 1966, Massey and Brown made KFC public, and the company was enlisted on New York Stock Exchange. During late 1960s, Massey and Brown turned their attention to international markets and signed a joint venture with Mitsuoishi Shoji Kaisha Ltd. in Japan. Subsidiaries were also established in Great Britain, Hong Kong, South Africa, Australia, New Zealand, and Mexico. In the late 1970s, Brown's desire to seek a political career led him to seek a buyer for KFC. Soon after, KFC merged with Heublein, Inc., a producer of alcoholic beverages with little restaurant experience and conflicts quickly arose between the Heublein management and Colonel Sanders, who was quite concerned about the quality control issues in restaurant cleanliness. In 1977, Heublein sent in a new management team to redirect KFC's strategy. New unit construction was discontinued until existing restaurants could be upgraded and operating problems eliminated. The overhaul emphasised cleanliness, service, profitability, and product consistency. By 1982, KFC was again aggressively building new restaurant units.

In October 1986, KFC was sold to PepsiCo. PepsiCo had acquired Frito-Lay in 1965, Pizza Hut in 1977 with its 300 units, and Taco Bell in 1978. PepsiCo created one of the largest consumer companies in the United States. Marketing fast food complemented PepsiCo's consumer product orientation and followed much the same pattern as marketing soft drinks and snack foods. Pepsi soft drinks and fast food products could be marketed together in the same restaurants and through coordinated national advertising.

The Kentucky Fried Chicken acquisition gave PepsiCo the leading market share in three of the four largest and fastest growing segments in the U.S., quick-service industry. By the end of 1995, Pizza Hut held 28 per cent share of $18.5 billion, U.S pizza segment. Taco Bell held 75 per cent of $5.7 billion Mexican food segment, and KFC held 49 per cent of the $7.7 billion, U.S chicken fast food segment.

Japan, Australia, and United Kingdom accounted for the greatest share of the KFC's international expansion during the 1970s and 1980s. During the 1990s, other markets became attractive. China with a population of over 1 billion, Europe and Latin America offered expansion opportunities. By 1996, KFC had established 158 company-owned restaurants and franchises in Mexico. In addition to Mexico, KFC was operating 220 restaurants in the Caribbean, and in the Central and South America.

Many cultures have strong culinary traditions and have not been easy to penetrate. KFC previously failed in German markets because Germans were not accustomed to take-out food or to ordering food over the counter. KFC has been more successful in the Asian markets, where chicken is a staple dish. Apart from the cultural factors, international business carries risks not present in the U.S. market. Long distances between headquarters and foreign franchises often make it difficult to control the quality of individual franchises.

Contd...

In some countries of the world such as, Malaysia, Indonesia and some others, it is illegal to import poultry, a situation that has led to product shortages. Another challenge facing KFC is to adapt to foreign cultures. The company has been most successful in foreign markets when local people operate restaurants. The purpose is to think like a local, not like an American company.

As KFC entered 1996, it grappled with a number of important issues. During 1980s, consumers began demanding healthier foods, and KFC's limited menu consisting mainly of fried foods was a difficult liability. In order to soften its fried chicken chain image, the company in 1991, changed its name and logo from Kentucky Fried Chicken to KFC. In addition, it responded to consumer demands for greater variety by introducing several new products, such as Oriental Wings, Popcorn Chicken, and Honey BBQ Chicken as alternatives to its Original Recipe fried chicken. It also introduced a dessert menu that included a variety of pies and cookies.

Soon after KFC entered India, it was greeted with protests of farmers, customers, doctors, and environmentalists. KFC had initially planned to set up 30 restaurants by 1998, but was not able to do so because its revenues did not pick. In early 1998, KFC began to investigate the whole issue more closely. The findings revealed that KFC was perceived as a restaurant serving only chicken. Indian families wanted more variety, and the impression that KFC served only one item failed to enhance its appeal. Moreover, KFC was also believed to be expensive. KFC's failure was also attributed to certain drawbacks in the message it sent out to consumers about its positioning. It wanted to position itself as a family restaurant and not as a teenage hangout. According to analysts, the 'family restaurant' positioning did not come out clearly in its communications. Almost all consumers saw it as a fast food joint specialising in a chicken recipe.

KFC tried to revamp its menu in India. Cole Slaw was replaced with green fresh salads. A fierier burger called Zinger Burger was also introduced. During the Navaratri festival, KFC offered a new range of nine vegetarian products, which included Paneer burgers. Earlier, KFC offered only individual meals, but now the offerings include six individual meals, two meal combos for two people, and one family meal in the non-vegetarian category. For vegetarians, there are three meal combos for individuals, and meals for couples, and for families.

KFC also changed its positioning. Now its messages seek to attract families who look not only, for food, but also some recreation. Kids Fun Corner is a recreational area within the restaurant to serve the purpose. Games like ball pool, and Chicky Express have been introduced for kids. The company also introduced meal for kids at Rs. 60, which was served with a free gift.

Over the years, KFC had learned that opening an American fast food in many foreign markets is not easy. Cultural differences between countries result in different eating habits. For instance, people eat their main meal of the day at different times throughout the world. Different menus must also be developed for specific cultures, while still maintaining the core product – fried chicken. You can always find original recipe chicken, cole slaw, and fries at KFC outlets, but restaurants in China feature all Chinese tea and French restaurants offer more desserts. Overall, KFC emphasises consistency and whether it is Shanghai, Paris, or India, the product basically tastes the same.

QUESTIONS

1. Analyse the case and determine the factors that have made KFC's a success global business.
2. Why are cultural factors so important to KFC's sales success in India and China?
3. Spot the cultural factors in India that go against KFC's original recipe; KFC Fried Chicken.
4. Why did Kentucky Fried Chicken change its name to KFC?

Case 8.4: Dilly & Best International

illy & Best (D&B) is a large 40-year old company operating in 35 countries of the world. Many of its items, such as Sparkle toothpaste, Up Flow shampoo, and Darlin diapers have high brand recognition throughout the world. In 2003, the company had international sales of $8 billion. This was a growth of 12 per cent over the previous year's sales. About 30 per cent of the company's profits came from U.S. market.

The company is a big spender on advertising in overseas markets and adopts aggressive marketing strategies. The main focus remains on striving to improve its market share in all the markets where it has its presence and believes that its brands should be among the top three in a given product category. Other than the U.S. market, amongst the very important markets, are Europe and Asia. In the last 10 to 12 years, the company has not been successful in making much progress in some specific but attractive markets, such as Japan. The company has faced several marketing problems in Japan regarding its otherwise successful brands elsewhere, such as Darlin diapers. The women prefer diapers from local manufacturers that they consider more comfortable and hygienic. Other items include kitchen and laundry products, where the company has been facing problems.

The research revealed that the company had not made a careful study of the Japanese culture and all the sales people were Americans who also lacked any understanding of Japanese culture and how to deal with women buyers. To rectify these mistakes, a major move was to employ local people in sales job and in managing the sales force. Most of the U.S. born and bred sales people were adjusted in U.S. or Europe. The company also made some changes in packaging and colours, which the research had revealed to be more appropriate in Japan. These adjustments worked well and the company introduced some other brands with features most sought, by the Japanese consumers.

The one lesson it learned was that it is better to hire local employees who understand the finer aspects of the local culture and went ahead to create a balance of both cultures in its offices all around the world. Now, its diapers brand has a market share of 27 per cent as against 30 per cent of the leading local brand. D&B is in the process of launching three new products in Japan and is running test marketing for three. The company's objective is to determine the need for adaptation if any and launch the product that will best suit the local conditions and generate favourable response.

In Europe, D&B is very successful with its Sparkle, Up Flow, and a brand of detergent, Arrow, which is the leader in most markets wherever it has been introduced. The company has built a strong brand image for Arrow and has two variants. Constant innovation, adaptation to local preferences, and aggressive media usage has helped the company to retain a market leadership position with 40 per cent market share. In three countries, including Japan, the diapers and toothpastes of D&B are number two brands and the company is planning to use its well-developed distribution channels to launch four more products in personal hygiene and cosmetic product categories.

As D&B seeks to further expand its presence in foreign markets, it faces various hurdles. Other than different needs and preferences of local customers, some legal and trade barriers are always there to tackle. There are different regulations regarding weight, colour, and food clearance faced by D&B in most of the countries.

Contd...

Recently, the company was compelled to shelve its major expansion plan in an European country, when the company was not allowed to build a production facility and warehouse unless D&B formed a joint venture with a local company. The company, however, chose not to enter into a joint venture and instead decided to continue with present marketing set up.

QUESTIONS

1. How can a company determine potential problems and restrictions in a foreign market?
2. Is product adaptation strategy necessary for all types of products? What factors makes it necessary to undertake product adaptation in a foreign market?
3. What factors a company must examine before entering a foreign market?

Case 8.5: Nestle

There was a time when the Swiss company, Nestle Corporation was just a chocolate maker. It is now the world's largest food company and the largest producer of coffee, powdered milk, and frozen dinners. With the purchase of Perrier for $20.7 billion, Nestle became the world's largest producer of mineral water, with 20 per cent of the world market. After passing Mars, the company also became the number one in candy. Nestle achieved its success through intensive global expansion. Only 2 per cent of Nestle sales comes from Switzerland, the other 98 per cent comes from various foreign countries.

One of the first multinational corporations, Nestle, now has production facilities in more than 60 countries. Its products can be found almost anywhere around the globe. In Europe, where, Nestle has experienced the greatest success, sales of instant coffee, mineral water, yoghurt, frozen foods, cold cuts, candy and cereal bars are roughly $10.2 billion. The company's sales in North America are approximately $6.7 billion, for products such as Nestle instant coffee, Carnation Coffee-mate, and non-dairy creamer.

QUESTIONS

1. Look for information about the company on the Internet and study its strategies that have made it successful.
2. Prepare a report for presentation.

Case 8.6: FMCG Company Implements Rural Marketing

The Lever Brothers entered India through the export route in 1888. The first product marketed was Sunlight laundry soap. Lever Bothers merged with Margarine Unie of Netherlands to form Unilever Ltd. in the United Kingdom. The same year, Unilever Ltd. established Hindustan Manufacturing Company in India to produce edible oils. Initially, the majority of the company's revenues came from soaps and Vanaspati (vegetable oils). In 1932, Vanaspati accounted for nearly 75% of India's production of almost 6,000 tonnes.

In 1933, Lever Brothers (India) Ltd. was incorporated as a wholly owned subsidiary of Unilever Ltd. of U.K. Two years later, United Traders was formed for importing and distribution of toilet products. Subsequently in 1956, the three subsidiaries – Hindustan Manufacturing Company, Unilever Ltd., and United Traders were merged to form Hindustan Lever Ltd. (HLL). In late 1950s the company started modernising its facilities and expanded its manufacturing capacity for vanaspati by buying factories in Trichy (Tamil Nadu), Shamnager and Ghaziabad near Delhi border but located in Uttar Pradesh. By 1960, HLL's annual vanaspati production went up to 3,36,000 tonnes.

HLL launched Lux soap in 1961. Between 1960 and 1970 HLL launched Anik (clarified butter), Sunsilk shampoo, Rin washing bar, Clinic shampoo, Liril bath soap. In 1975, the company entered oral care market and introduced Close-Up toothpaste. A major step HLL took was to establish 70 medium and small-scale production units in rural areas for manufacturing detergents and soaps.

The company diversifies in chemicals manufacturing with plants at Maharashtra, West Bengal, and J&K. Between 1983 and 1989, there was much expansion and HLL moved into agro-products, introduced a new variant of Lux soap, Lifebuoy Personal, and Breeze soaps, the company set up a new manufacturing facility in collaboration with National Starch Corporation, USA, and also set up a new synthetic detergent plant and a toilet soap plant.

In 1991, HLL launched Lifebuoy Plus and Le Sancy soaps. In 1992, HLL added Pepsodent and Mentadent G toothpastes. Between 1992 and 1996, HLL bought many businesses, such as Tomco, Kwality, Kissan, and Lakme. In late 1990s, HLL entered a 50:50 joint venture with U.S based Kimberly Clark Corporation and formed Kimberly Clark Lever Limited (KCLL) that produced diapers and sanitary napkins. HLL also formed joint venture named Lever Johnson with S.C Johnson & Co of USA. This company marketed pest repellents and disinfectants.

Between 1991 and 1994 "value for money" was the buzzword among most FMCG companies in response to global recession and India was no exception. Growth in urban markets was badly hit and even rural markets showed signs of slowing down in terms of both value and volumes. This became evident from the earlier growth of 52% in 1996, which slid down to 29% in 1997. Despite these conditions, HLL managed to launch 10 brand extensions and new products in 1996, followed by 6 brand extensions and new products in 1997.

HLL had a market share of 50 – 60% in FMCG sector in 1996, which increased to 62% by 1998. The company launched a few more new products and re-launched some existing ones with innovations. The company set up new distribution outlets to double its reach in the rural markets, and also set up 10 new factories – including two each, for packaged tea and personal products, and one each for soaps and detergents.

Contd...

The Indian FMCG sector faced a tough year in 2001, because of the economic slow down to 4% in India from previous year's 6.4%. However, HLL was able to post significant gains in both, the rural and the industrial markets. This resulted from company's focus on "Power Brands" aimed at sustaining profitable growth in slow-growth markets. The company maintained its leadership position in most of the product categories it marketed. The company had Rs. 17.57 billion sales in i992, which increased to Rs. 109.71 billion in 2001. Profit after tax improved from Rs. 958 million to Rs. 15.4 billion in 2001. HLL stood out as the company that had shaped India's FMCG market over the decades. The company had built some of the most successful brands in India and its advertising campaigns were talked about among the Indian advertising professionals. Out of more than 110 brands in its product mix, HLL called the 30 best selling brands as the "Power Brands" and included Lux, Breeze, Lifebuoy, Fair & Lovely, Lakmc, Axc, Ponds, Sunsilk, Clinic, Surf, Rin, Wheel, Vim, Lipton, Brooke Bond, Close-Up, Pepsodent, Kissan, Annapurna, Dalda, and Kwality. These brands enjoyed high awareness and usage rates among the Indian households. Many of these products, particularly those in categories like fabric wash, personal wash, and beverages had more than 50% of their sales volumes from rural markets.

HLL used both, wholesalers and retailers to penetrate the Indian rural markets. It employed a fleet of motor vans to cover small towns and villages to access retailers in rural areas and induced them to stock HLL products and display promotional material in their shops. In many small towns, HLL appointed about 7,000 redistribution stockists, who carried bulk stocks and serviced retailers in over 10 lakh scattered villages.

Despite these pioneering efforts of HLL to expand its consumer base in rural areas, a large part of the rural market still remained untapped. In a new move, HLL set up a target of contacting 16 million new village households by 1999. This was to be achieved by focusing on the sales, marketing, and production of Power Brands in the rural markets. The plan was to address key issues in a phased manner related to availability, awareness, and overcoming existing attitudes and habits of the rural consumers. The idea was also to approach consumers with penetrative pricing of the products.

In 1998, the initiative was named Project Streamline to focus on some selected states of the country. It focused on the rural distribution system, to enhance HLL's control over the rural supply chain and increase the number of rural retail outlets from 50,000 in 1998 to 100,000 in a time span of one year.

The Streamline Project targeted places that had poor development base and hardly any kind of distribution was available. The project was to be implemented with the help of a rural distributor, who had 15 – 20 rural sub-stockists working with him/her. The sub-stockists performed the role of driving distribution in the neighbouring villages using unconventional means of transportation, such as bullock carts and tractors. HLL, aimed at providing higher service quality to consumers in terms of supply frequency, full-line availability, and credit facility. This project helped HLL, increase the availability of brands and the Stock Keeping Units (SKU) stocked by village retailers. As a result, the reach increased to 37% in 1998 from 25% in 1995.

Encouraged with the results, in mid 1998, HLL's personal products division launched another campaign called Project Bharat. This was to be carried out till the end of 1999. It was a direct marketing effort aimed at addressing the issues of awareness, attitudes, and habits of rural consumers and also to achieve deeper penetration level of HLL products in the rural markets. It was the first of its kind and the largest rural home-to-home operation to have ever been taken

Contd...

by any business house in India. The company implemented direct marketing exercise in the high potential districts of India and attracted first-time users. Company vans visited villages and sold bundled packs containing just one unit each of small packs of detergent, toothpaste, face cream, and talcum powder. It was a low unit-price bundled pack for Rs. 15. During the campaign, company sales personnel also explained to the people how and when to use these products with the help of a video show. The communication also focused on superior benefits of using these HLL products, a compared to their current habits. This was particularly meaningful in creating awareness about HLL's product categories and availability of packs at affordable prices. HLL very well appreciated that just one sampling campaign would not be meaningful, so the company started a follow up campaign called Integrated Rural Promotion Van to further enhance the awareness among the rural consumers in villages having a population of 2000 and above. Simultaneously, another programme followed targeting villages with less than 2000 population. This was a real market development exercise and under this programme, HLL provide self-employment opportunities to villagers through Self-Help Groups. The Self-Help Groups consisted of 15 – 20 villagers from below the poverty line households (with less than Rs. 750 per month household income). They were provided with an opportunity to take micro-credit from banks. Using this money, they could buy HLL's products and sell them to village consumers, thereby generating income and employment for themselves. These Self-Help Groups operated like direct-to-home distributors and helped the company to increase the reach of products.

Besides this, HLL tied up with NGOs, UNDP, and other voluntary organisations in 1999 to create awareness about health and hygiene in villages. The company set a goal of accessing 2,35,000 villages from the existing 85,000 and covering 75% of the population from the existing 43%.

To further augment the campaign effectiveness, HLL aimed at reaching 65% reach through TV, from its current 33% and encouraged primary education in villages with the help of V-Sat connections.

By the close of 1999, the company had covered 13 million households through Project Bharat. The campaign turned out to be highly successful and increased rural penetration, awareness, and usership of HLL products in the targeted districts. This also helped HLL to record better growth rate than the industry average. The growth of shampoo was 15-16% in rural areas as compared to 4-5 per cent recorded in urban markets. Similarly, the growth in the skincare market was 14% in rural areas as compared to just 7-8% in urban markets.

In 1999, HLL launched a nationwide Community Dental health campaign in association with the India an Medical Association to promote toothpaste. As part of the project, several infomercials were launched to increase dental hygiene awareness and also to highlight common dental problems and their causes. These dental hygiene-related infomercials were aired on Doordarshan. Nearly 200 fairs were organised mostly in the rural areas. Various dental health programmes as well as dental health education and check up modules were organised at public health centres. Indian Medical Association representatives and local public health centres conducted various educative demonstrations on good brushing habits, and dental hygiene issues.

The dental health programme was conducted for three years and by the end of 2000, some 50 districts were covered in various states. The campaign aimed to increase the direct reach of toothpaste in rural India to 1,25,000 villages by the end of 2001 from the existing 40,000. The collaborative IMA – Pepsodent programme increased the dental care penetration in the country to 58 – 60% from earlier 48%.

Contd...

Project Millennium was yet another campaign launched in 2000 aiming at increasing HLL's share in tea market. The company planned ways to tap chai-ki-dookan (tea vendors). The company provided affordable tea packets that were having suitable blend of tea to appeal to the rural consumers' taste of kadak chai (strong tea). The company test marketed a specifically designed product 'chai-ki-goli' (small tea ball) which was to be dropped in boiling water-milk combination and was fully soluble. The price for four-ball pack was just Re. 1.

In a survey conducted by the Centre for Industrial and Economic Research in December 2000, named "Emerging Market Trends", it was found that HLL had overtaken both Colgate-Palmolive and Nirma in increasing brand awareness and penetration in rural households. HLL had achieved 88% market penetration as compared to 56% of Nirma and 33% of Colgate-Palmolive. In fact, in many product categories, HLL had achieved the highest rural penetration level.

In August 2001, HLL went on to participate in a rural communication programme 'Grameenon ke beech' (amidst villagers). The Rural Communications & Marketing handled this programme. This agency specialised in rural advertising and marketing. Other major companies, such as Colgate-Palmolive, Mahindra & Mahindra, and Parle also participated in this programme. During the first phase, 1000 villages and 2,000 satellite villages in 22 districts of western U.P. and 13 districts of central U.P were covered within a period of 6 months. The programme combined many activities, such as setting up company stalls, product briefings, demonstrations, lucky draws, interactive games, magic shows, and screening of popular Hindi films, and product commercials.

The Project Shakti of HLL started in late 2001, first focused only in Andhra Pradesh for a period of 6 months and then came to a conclusion by March 2002. The project's aim was to create a sustainable partnership between the company and the low -income rural consumers by providing them access to micro credit, and opportunity to provide work as HLL's distributors. This programme helped self-help groups and also achieved an increase of 20% in the consumption of company product in the areas covered. Encouraged with the results, the company planned to expand Project Shakti in the states of Gujarat Maharashtra and Madhya Pradesh in the coming period.

HLL's efforts continue, but there have been questions as to how long HLL and other FMCG companies would be able to sustain such activities in rural markets before their attraction for rural markets starts waning. This has to be seen, after all rural markets too, will become crowded and reach the saturation point.

QUESTIONS

1. What major challenges companies face in accessing rural markets in India? How did HLL accomplish acceptance and growth of its products in rural markets?
2. "Rural marketing in India is developmental marketing." Comment with examples from the case.

Case 8.7: ITC's e-Choupal and Profitable Rural Transformation

Rural India is a difficult business location. Transport, electric power, and information infrastructure are inadequate. Business practices are underdeveloped or outdated. Lack of access to modern resources has resulted in an under-trained workforce. Rural society is structured around subsistence and is unprepared for modern products and services. These constraints, along with many others, have dissuaded most companies from taking on the challenge of rural commerce. Yet, such an engagement can serve a dual agenda; bridging rural isolation and the resulting disparities of education and economic opportunity, while at the same time creating a potentially large profit opportunity for the organization, willing to tackle the inefficiencies. The key question is how modern resources and methods can be practically deployed to profitably overcome rural constraints. Also important are the social impacts of such an engagement.

ITC's e-Choupal initiative began by deploying technology to re-engineer procurement of soy and other crops from rural India. It has gone on to serve as a highly profitable distribution and product design channel. The effort holds valuable lessons in rural engagement and demonstrates the magnitude of the opportunity while illustrating the social and development impact of bringing global resources, practices, and remuneration to the Indian farmer.

THE PARADOX OF INDIAN AGRICULTURE

Agriculture is economically and socially vital to India. It contributes 20% of the GDP, feeds a billion people and employs 66% of the workforce. Agriculture's share of GDP has shrunk steadily but at 20% it remains a critical component of the economy.

Yet, despite this economically vital role, Indian agriculture has until recently been regulated in an archaic fashion that limits its productivity. Non-optimal farming practices and capricious weather patterns left post-Independence India with an under-performing agricultural sector, acute food shortages, and dependence on food imports. Legislation from this period brought heavy government intervention in agriculture, including control of land ownership, input pricing, and regulation of product marketing. Produce could only be sold in government-recognized locations to authorized agents. Processing capacities, private storage, future trading and transport were restricted. The result was corrupt and inefficient systems, in which starvation existed alongside granaries overflowing with food stocks of over 60 million metric tonnes. At the same time, the unprofessional business environment made the sector unattractive to modern companies and blocked their influence in rationalizing the market.

High Production yet Impoverished Producers

The goal of being self-sufficient in food supply brought Indian agriculture into the mainstream of political and social consciousness. The Green Revolution brought great strides in agricultural productivity to some parts of India and made the country a net exporter of most food grains by the mid-1970's, thus resolving previous famine paradoxes. However, the Indian farmer did not progress correspondingly. After independence, the government parcelled and redistributed larger land holdings to rectify historical inequities and entrust ownership to end cultivators, thus encouraging productivity. In subsequent years, ownership ceilings were legislated and inherited land was partitioned into smaller lots, such that by 2003, the typical Indian farm is a very small-scale operation with total landholdings often measured by fractions of an acre. Unable to realize economies of scale, most Indian farmers are very poor as a result of land redistribution policies. In 1993, agricultural labourers in most states made barely enough to keep a three-person family above the poverty level.

Contd...

In recent decades, the economy has been growing far more rapidly in non-agricultural areas, especially the service sector in urban areas. From 1993 to 2003, the (primarily urban) service sector has seen its share of national GDP rise by 11.6%, while rural agriculture has seen its share of GDP decline by 5.01% over the same period. There is a vast disparity in access to education and opportunities between the urban and the rural India. This means that farmers rarely know of non-agricultural opportunities and likely would not have the resources to pursue them even if adequate information were available. Remedying this asymmetry of opportunity will require providing rural India with both the knowledge of opportunities and the ability to pursue them. ITC's e-Choupal is an example of how a commercial venture can provide a channel for knowledge and opportunity, bringing global resources and practices to Indian villages as well as higher incomes for farmers, and helping to create the conditions for many other enterprises to cater to the rural market.

ORIGIN OF e-CHOUPAL

The ITC group is one of the India's foremost private sector companies with a market capitalization of around US$4 billion and annual revenues of US$2 billion. ITC has a diversified presence in tobacco, hotels, paperboards, specialty papers, packaging, agri-business, branded apparel, packaged foods and other fast moving consumer goods.

Spurred by India's need to generate foreign exchange, ITC's International Business Division (IBD) was created in 1990 as an agri-trading company aiming to "offer the world, the best of India's produce." Initially, the agricultural commodity trading business was small as compared to the international players. By 1996, the opening up of the Indian market had brought in international competition. Large international companies had better margin-to-risk ratios because of wider options for risk management and arbitrage. For an Indian company to replicate the operating model of such multinational corporations would have required a massive horizontal and vertical expansion. In 1998, after competition forced ITC to explore the options of sale, merger, and closure of IBD, ITC ultimately decided to retain the business. The Chairman of ITC challenged IBD to use information technology to change the rules of the game and create a competitive business that did not need a large asset base. Today, IBD is a US$150 million company that trades in commodities such as feed ingredients, food-grains, coffee, black pepper, edible nuts, marine products, and processed fruits.

Corporate and social responsibility is an integral part of ITC's philosophy, and ITC is widely recognized as dedicated to the cause of nation building. Chairman Y. C. Deveshwar calls this source of inspiration "a commitment beyond the market."

"ITC believes, that its aspiration to create enduring value for the nation, provides the motive force to sustain growing shareholder value. ITC practices this philosophy by not only driving each of its businesses towards international competitiveness but by also consciously contributing in enhancing the competitiveness of the larger value chain of which it is a part."

This view of social consciousness allowed ITC to recognize the unique opportunity of blending shareholder value creation with social development. The social impact of the e-Choupals as envisioned by ITC ranges from the short-term provision of Internet access to the long-term development of rural India as a competitive supplier and consumer of a range of goods and services in the global economy. The sustainability of the engagement comes from the idea that neither the corporate nor social agendas will be subordinated in favour of the other.

THE OILSEED COMPLEX

Edible oil from vegetable sources is a fundamental part of the Indian diet. The oilseed complex refers to the class of crops from which edible oils are extracted. The complex is further classified

Contd...

into traditional oils (groundnut, rapeseed/mustard seed, safflower) and non-traditional oils (sunflower, soy, cottonseed). The process of oil extraction varies by oilseed, but consists of two basic stages: mechanical crushing and solvent extraction to obtain residual oil. The residue, called de-oiled cake, is sold as animal feed. Because of its low oil content, The extraction of soy oil is done almost exclusively by the solvent extraction process.

In the 1970's, oilseed production stagnated. By 1980, imports accounted for 32% of the domestic supply. Following the Green Revolution in wheat and rice, the government of India turned regulatory attention in the early 1980's to oilseeds, sharply limiting imports. Protectionism brought substantial gains in domestic production, doubling oilseed output to 21 million metric tonnes by 1994 and increasing the reliability of supply. About 40% of the increased output came from the introduction of new crops, especially soy and sunflower. Soy, thus represented an important innovation in the Indian oilseed complex, resulting in better utilization of scarce resources and greater cropping intensity. Soy was exempted from the Small Scale Industries Act to allow for processing in large-scale, modern facilities. Nonetheless, the industry remains dominated by small farmers. Some three million soy farmers produce about five million tonnes of soybeans annually.

When ITC entered the soy industry in the 1990's produce was generally bought and crushed by small crushers who also functioned as traders. ITC began with buying and exporting de-oiled soy cake. Within a year, the company realized that it needed greater presence to better understand the product dynamics. ITC then began renting processing plant time and buying soy directly from the local mandis. ITC's procurement has grown rapidly and has seen the introduction of professional business practices, transparency, and formal contractual relationships between agents and buyers.

PRODUCTION CHANNELS PRIOR TO THE e-CHOUPAL

There are three commercial channels for soy, traders, government-mandated markets (mandis), and producer-run cooperative societies for crushing in cooperative mills. In addition, farmers traditionally keep a small amount of their crops for their personal consumption and get the produce processed in a small-scale crushing-plant called a ghani. The system varies among states and the districts, as does the per centage of produce going through each channel, but on an average, 90% of soy crops are processed through traders and mandis.

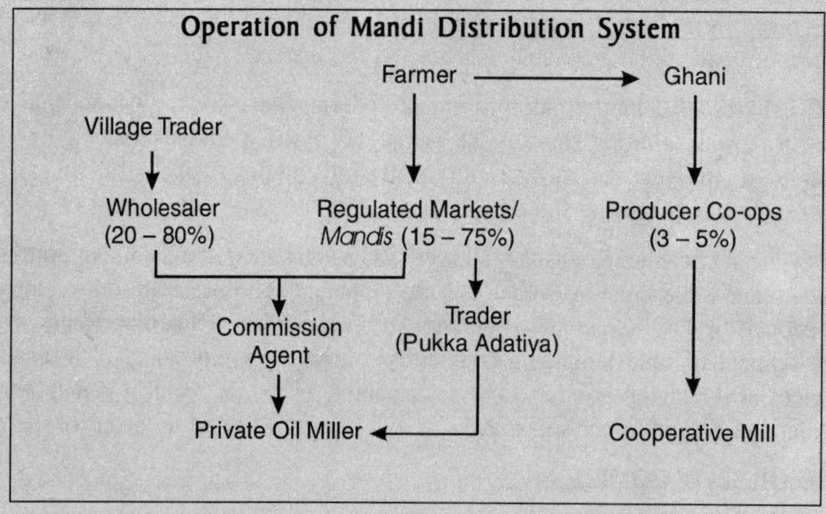

Contd...

The Agricultural Products Marketing Act legislated the creation of mandis to enable a more equitable distribution of the agricultural gains among producers, consumers, and traders. The mandi is central to the functioning of the marketing channel, and acts as a delivery point, where farmers bring produce for sale to traders. In the soy growing areas of Madhya Pradesh, a mandi typically serves around 700 square kilometers, although the area served by a mandi varies from state to state. With traditional grains, large portions are used by the farmer or bartered for different crops. But since soy is not native to the Indian palate, its major market is the crushing plant and nearly the entire crop must be exported. This makes the mandi a vital part of the soy chain.

Mandi trading is conducted by commission agents called adatiyas (brokers who buy and sell produce). They are of two types: kachha adatiyas are purchasing agents that buy only on behalf of others and pukka adatiyas who finance trade as representatives of distant buyers and sometimes procure crops on their own account. All the adatiyas belong to the Agarwal and Jain community, an economic class distinct from farmers. This community manages grain trade across the entire country including south India, a remarkable feat considering the vast cultural and social diversity across the nation. The lack of professional competition combined with the communal stranglehold on rural trading has made commission agents extremely wealthy. Commission agents from medium sized mandis can possess assets and incomes in millions of dollars. The adatiyas established and grew the soy industry on the basis of familial and community trust, with buying and selling based upon oral agreements. Their expansive personal networks within the industry and their financial influence make them a formidable presence.

Mandi Operation Process

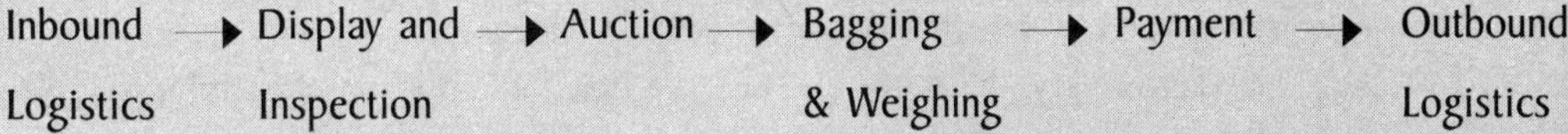

The operation of the Mandi consists of a number of different stages, from the logistics of transporting grain to the market to quality inspection, auction, bagging and weighing, and payment. Based upon local information within the village, farmers decide in which of the nearby mandis to sell. They transport their crops to the mandis in carts drawn by animals or tractors. Very often, to avoid peak-time crowds, farmers will arrive at the mandi, the night before they intend to sell. When the mandi opens in the morning, farmers bring their carts to display areas within the mandi.

The inspection by buyers is by sight. There is no formal method of grading the produce and the only instrument used is the moisture meter; the crop is not tested for oil content.

Once potential buyers have inspected the produce, a mandi employee conducts the auction, where commission agents place bids. The auctions are typically open, oral auctions with incremental bidding. The auction represents a stark contrast from the buyer's and seller's perspectives. For the farmer, the moment is pivotal: a scant 30 seconds assesses the results of six months of investment and hard work and establishes the value of one out of the two or three paydays he will have in the year. For the commission agent, on the other hand, the moment is routine; he has many more carts of produce to buy and his margin is assured irrespective of the price.

Once the price has been established by the auction, the farmer moves the cart to the weighing area run by the buying commission agent. In most cases, the weighing area is in the mandi

Contd...

complex. In some cases, especially if the mandi is small, the weighing area may be at the commission agent's home near the mandi. Here, the produce is transferred from the cart into individual sacks. The sacks are then weighed, one at a time, on a manual scale. After weighing, the full value of the grain is calculated. The farmer goes to the agent's office to collect a cash payment. The agent pays a mandi fee (1% of purchase value in Madhya Pradesh) to the mandi. The bagged produce is then loaded on to the buyer's trucks and transported to the processing plant.

Limitations of the Mandi System

The mandi system does not serve the farmer well, and is burdened by inefficiency. Just because the farmer does not have the resources to analyze or exploit price trends, the timing of the sale may not result in the optimal price for the crop. Moreover, since the actual sale price is determined at the auction, by the time the farmer gets the price, it is too late to go to another mandi to make his sale. Other expenses and inefficiencies exist; the overnight stay near the mandi costs the farmer money; most crops are displayed in open air courtyards, and are therefore subject to being negatively affected by the weather; the inspection process is unscientific and often arbitrary, tending to favour the buyer, and generally does not provide an incentive to farmers to invest in better seed or farming practices that lead to higher quality—even though quality, especially oil content, matters to soy processors.

In addition, farmers find the auction process demeaning. Agents belong to a close-knit community that is socially and economically distinct from the farmers' community. While they may not collude in pricing, they do collude in establishing the practices of the trade that uniformly favour agents and exploit the farmers' situation. The farmers also bear the cost of bagging and weighing the crop, which is done by mandi labourers—part of whose compensation is the sale of spilled produce. Needless to say, these labourers ensure that some portion of each lot is spilled.

Farmers feel that the weighers consistently under-weigh their produce by applying practiced and timely nudges to the scale. Historical intimidation and long queues waiting behind them, dissuade the farmers from protesting. To add to this exploitation, the farmer is never paid the full purchase price up front, but is paid a partial amount and asked to return to the mandi later for the remainder. Farmers are not paid interest on the remaining sum—although crushers pay agents usurious rates for the privilege of delayed payment—and repeating the trip to the mandi costs farmers time and money. Since the crop has already been delivered, however, the farmers are at the agents' mercy.

Apart from the exploitation of the farmer, there are other inefficiencies in the system. The multiple points of handling, in the supply-chain requires the produce to be bagged, which takes four to five times longer to be unloaded at the processing plant than un-bagged produce. Traders generally do not have the capacity to store and manage different qualities and grades of produce, inhibiting efforts to produce better crop grades. Pricing is set locally at the mandis, and is not reliably tracked or reported nationally, resulting in a lack of information that reduces the opportunity for arbitrage and leads to market inefficiency. In addition, regulatory restrictions tend to limit arbitrage to small geographic areas.

The mandi system also does not serve well, trading companies such as ITC; its inefficiencies make the mandi far from being an optimal procurement channel. From the company's point of view, the key problem is the agent's control of the market and the resulting distortions of price and

Contd...

quality. Agents purchase grain on a trading company's behalf. Some of the produce they buy is of good quality and therefore commands a premium price, while other crops are of poor quality and therefore sell at a discount. In any given day, an agent purchases produce with a range of crop quality at a range of prices. The agent often mixes the different quality crops together and charges the trading company a single price near the higher end of the price spectrum.

Not only does the agent inflate the price to trading companies, he also inflates the price at the mandi. As we have seen, high-quality produce is used to make an entire lot of lower quality produce acceptable. Because of its value to agents, agents pay an inflated premium for high-quality produce, which drives high, the crop price at the mandi for the day. Very few farmers actually get the price for top-quality produce, but this price acts as a benchmark for the next day's pricing, thereby inflating the mandi price over a period of time and increasing costs for trading companies.

Additionally, the trading company establishes a daily price range for its agent to buy within. If the agent's average buy price that day is lower than the low end of the established price, the agent sells the grain to the trading company at the established low price and pockets the difference. If, however, the average buy price is higher than the trading company's established high price, the agent will still buy the produce but will report to the company that since its price was not high enough, no grain could be bought. The agent will store the grain and sell it to the trading company the next day when the established price has been raised to make-up for the previous day's procurement shortfall. Commission agents therefore capture the entire benefit of intra-day price shifts. The agents therefore, operate without risk of loss or profit. Officially, the agents' commission is 1% of ITC's price. In reality, ITC estimates that the agents' operating margin is around 2.5-3%.

As a result of the commission agent structure in the traditional mandi system, ITC had no direct interaction with the farmer. This gap created a range of supply-chain issues, including limiting ITC's knowledge of its crops, suppliers, and supply risks, as well as limiting the company's ability to improve crop quality and quantity by bringing modern agricultural practices to the farmers.

The company developed its e-Choupal strategy as a way to communicate directly with the farmer and to bypass the inefficiencies arising out of the agents' intermediation, thereby achieving "virtual vertical integration."

VISION AND PLANNING BEHIND THE e-CHOUPALS

Implementing and managing e-Choupals is a significant departure from commodities trading. Through its tobacco business, ITC has worked in Indian agriculture for decades, from research to procurement to distribution. ITC's translation of the tactical and strategic challenges it faced and its social commitment into a business model demonstrates, a deep understanding of both, agrarian systems and modern management. Some of the guiding management principles are:

Re-engineer, Not Reconstruct

The conventional view of transforming, established business systems begins with the failures of the current system and develops means to change it. ITC took a different approach by looking at the successes of the current system and identifying, what they could build on. ITC

Contd...

not only retained the efficient providers within the mandi system but also created roles for some inefficient providers. This philosophy has two benefits. First, it avoids "reinventing the wheel" in areas where ITC would not be able to add value through its presence. Second, it recruits and engages members of the rural landscape thereby making their expertise available to ITC while preventing their expertise from being shared with ITC's competition. A good example of this, in action, is the role created for the commission agents as discussed earlier.

Address the Whole, Not Just One Part

The farmers' various activities range from procuring inputs to selling produce. Currently, the village trader services the spectrum of farmers' needs. He is a centralized provider of cash, seed, fertilizer, pesticides, and also the only marketing channel. As a result, the trader enjoys two competitive benefits. First, his intimate knowledge of the farmer and village dynamics allow him to accurately assess and manage risk. Second, he reduces overall transaction costs by aggregating services. The linked transactions reduce the farmers' overall cost in the short-term, but create a cycle of exploitative dependency in the long-term. Rural development efforts thus by far have focused only on individual pieces rather than, what the entire community needs. Cooperatives have tried to provide agricultural inputs, rural banks have tried to provide credit, and mandis have tried to create a better marketing channel. These efforts cannot compete against the trader's bundled offer. Functioning as a viable procurement alternative, therefore, must eventually address a range of needs, not just the marketing channel.

An IT-Driven Solution

From the conception of the model, an IT-based solution was recognized as fundamental to optimizing effectiveness, scalability, and cost. Information technology is 20% of all the effort of ITC's e-Choupal business model, but is considered as the most crucial 20%. The two goals envisioned for IT are:

- Delivery of real-time information independent of the transaction. In the mandi system, delivery, pricing, and sales happen simultaneously, thus binding the farmer to an agent. e-Choupal was seen as a medium of delivering critical market information independent of the mandi, thus allowing the farmer an empowered choice of where and when to sell his crop.
- Facilitate collaboration between the many parties required to fulfil the spectrum of farmer needs. As a communication mechanism, this goal is related to the commitment to address the whole system, not just a part of the system.

It should be noted, that ITC did not hesitate to install expensive IT infrastructure in places where most people would be wary of visiting overnight. It is a manifestation of the integrity of rural value systems that not a single case of theft, misappropriation, or misuse has been reported among the almost 2,000 e-Choupals.

Modularity of Investments, in Size and Scope

ITC managed its investments modularly along the scope and scale axes in what it terms "rollout-fix-it-scale up" and "pilot-critical mass-saturation." This incremental control of investment levels along with the clarity of revenue streams and the social import were critical in getting board approval for the initiative.

Contd...

Risk Assessment and Mitigation

ITC identified the following risks as it designed the business model:

- Radical shifts in computing access will break community-based business models.
- The **sanchalaks** are ITC's partners in the community, and as their power and numbers increase, there is a threat of unionization and rent extraction.
- The scope of the operation: The diversity of activities required of every operative and the speed of expansion create real threats to efficient management.

Managing Bureaucracy

When the e-Choupals were conceived, they faced a fundamental regulatory obstacle. The Agricultural Produce Marketing Act, under whose aegis mandis were established, prohibits procurements outside the mandi. ITC convinced the government that e-Choupals would operate according to the spirit of the Act and thus e-Choupal procurement was in line with its goals. Since ITC would not be using the mandi infrastructure for its procurement, and would have to incur its own costs with the e-Choupal infrastructure, the government offered to waive the mandi tax on the produce procured through the e-Choupal. However, ITC recognized that the tax was a major source of revenue for the government and local mandis and, as ITC's competition was also subject to the tax, the tax itself was not making ITC uncompetitive. ITC therefore, chose to continue paying the tax rather than risking the relationships with the government and the mandis.

THE BUSINESS MODEL

The model is centered on a network of e-Choupals i.e., information centres equipped with a computer connected to the Internet and located in rural farming villages. e-Choupals serve both, as a social gathering place for exchange of information (choupal means traditional village gathering place in Hindi) and an e-commerce hub. A local farmer acting as a sanchalak (coordinator) runs the village e-Choupal, and the computer usually is located in the **sanchalak's** home. ITC also incorporate a local commission agent, known as the sanyojak (collaborator), into the system as the provider of logistical support.

ITC has plans to saturate the sector in which it works with e-Choupals, such that a farmer has to travel no more than five kilometers to reach one. The company expects each e-Choupal to serve about 10 villages within a five kilometer radius. Today, its network reaches more than a million farmers in nearly 11,000 villages through 2,000 e-Choupals in four states (Madhya Pradesh, Karnataka, Andhra Pradesh, and Uttar Pradesh), and the network is expanding rapidly. Of the e-Choupals in Madhya Pradesh, the one in Khasrod services about 500-700 farmers in 10 villages; another e-Choupal in Dahod services 5,000 farmers in 10 villages. The average usage is about 600 farmers per e-Choupal in the soy cropping area, with fewer in wheat, coffee, and shrimp.

The critical element of the e-Choupal system, and the key to managing the geographical and cultural breadth of ITC's network, is the sanchalak. ITC channels virtually all its communication through the local sanchalak. Recruiting a local farmer from the community for this role serves several purposes:

- For generations, individuals and institutions have betrayed the Indian farmer. Trust is the most valuable commodity in rural India. No transaction will happen without trust,

Contd...

irrespective of the strength of the contract. The sanchalak is selected to provide this vital component in ITC's system.

- ITC need not invest in building and securing a physical infrastructure such as a kiosk for housing the e-Choupal computer.
- The sanchalak is trained in computer operation and can act as a familiar and approachable human interface for the often illiterate farmers, and other villagers.
- ITC expects to leverage the profit-making power of the small-scale entrepreneur.

Sanchalaks indicate three equally-weighted motivations for assuming their role: A means to help their community, a profitable business for themselves, and a means of getting access to a functional computer. The sanchalaks receive a commission for every transaction processed through the e-Choupal and also benefit from increased social status that accompanies the position—a significant advantage in rural Indian life. ITC insists, that sanchalaks should not give up farming, for this would compromise the trust that they command. To ensure that sanchalaks serve their communities and not just themselves, ITC projects the role as a public office: Hence the title "sanchalak," and a public oath-taking ceremony, where the sanchalak takes an oath to serve the farming community through the e-Choupal. Successful sanchalaks usually have a number of common characteristics, including risk-taking ability and the willingness to try something new, ambition, and the aspiration of earning additional income through the e-Choupal. Sanchalaks are usually from well to do families with status in their communities, able to read and write, and are part of an extended family, large enough so that they can find time to service the e-Choupal.

The sanchalaks undergo training at the nearest ITC plant. They receive education on basic computer usage, the functions of the e-Choupal Website, basic business skills, as well as quality inspection of crops. For the sale of products through e-Choupal, the sanchalaks receive product training directly from the manufacturer with ITC involving itself only in product design and facilitation. Nonetheless, their role requires considerable entrepreneurial initiative and entails some operational costs, between US$60 and US$160 per year, for electricity and phone-line charges; the latter of which are gradually declining as ITC replaces phone-based Internet connections with a VSAT system.

Selecting and training of the sanchalaks is just the first step. Most of them do not have retail experience and may lack motivation to actively promote ITC products. ITC employs a variety of motivational techniques to encourage sales. One technique is to hold a ceremony, where sanchalaks are presented with their annual commission checks and public announcements of earnings are made. Stories how sanchalaks spent past commissions and serve to demonstrate the income potential and spurs non-performers to work. The zeal to perform sometimes leads to territorial disputes, but ITC does not interfere in their resolution because it encourages sanchalaks to better serve their customer-base.

The Sanyojaks, or cooperating commission agents play a secondary, but still an important role. The Sanyojaks earn income from ITC by providing logistical services that substitute for the lack of rural infrastructure, by providing information and market signals on trading transactions to the e-Choupal system. In effect, ITC uses agents as providers of essential services, not as principals in a trading transaction. They play an especially important role in the initial stages of setting up the e-Choupals, because they know which farmers grow soy, what kind of families

Contd...

they have, what is their financial situation, and who is seen as "acceptable" in the villages and might thus make a good sanchalak. ITC is strongly committed for involving sanyojaks in the on-going operation of the e-Choupal system, allowing them revenue streams for providing services such as management of cash, bagging and labour in remote ITC procurement hubs, handling of mandi paperwork for ITC procurement, and as licensed principals for the retail transactions of the e-Choupal.

Since the e-Choupal system by-passes the agent-controlled mandis and has considerably reduced commission income, then the question arises, why do agents agree to cooperate with ITC? First, the company has made it clear that they will continue to buy produce through the mandis. Second, the company offers significant commissions for sanyojak services. Finally, the agents are fragmented and fear that if they do not agree to work with ITC, another agent will gain the promised e-Choupal revenues. One sanyojak reported, that he saw globalization as an irresistible trend, and although he saw loss of revenue in the short-term, his long-term interest lay in cooperating with an international company.

THE e-CHOUPAL SYSTEM

The re-engineered supply chain system looks very different from the existing system and has the following stages:

Pricing → Inbound logistics → Inspection & grading → Weighing & payment → Hub logistics

Pricing

The previous day's mandi closing price is used to determine the benchmark, Fair Average Quality (FAQ) price at the e-Choupal. The benchmark price is static for a given day. This information and the previous day mandi prices are communicated to the sanchalak through the e-Choupal portal. The commission agents at the mandi are responsible for entering daily mandi prices into the e-Choupal. If and when the Internet connection fails, the sanchalak calls an ITC field representative.

Inspection and Grading

To initiate a sale, the farmer brings a sample of his produce to the e-Choupal. The sanchalak inspects the produce and based on his assessment of the quality, makes appropriate deductions (if any) to the benchmark price and gives the farmer a conditional quote. The sanchalak performs the quality tests in the farmer's presence and justifies any deductions to the farmer. The benchmark price represents the upper limit of the price, a sanchalak can quote. These simple checks and balances ensure transparency in a process, where quality testing and pricing happen at multiple levels.

If the farmer chooses to sell his soy to ITC, the sanchalak gives him a note capturing his name, his village, particulars about the quality tests (foreign matter and moisture content), approximate quantity and conditional price.

Weighing and Payment

The farmer takes the note from the sanchalak and proceeds with his crop to the nearest ITC procurement hub, ITC's point for collection of produce and distribution of inputs sold into rural areas. Some procurement hubs are simply ITC's factories that also act as collection points. Others are purely warehousing operations. ITC's goal is to have a processing center within a 30 to 40

Contd...

kilometers radius of each farmer. There are currently 16 hubs, but there will eventually be 35 in the state of Madhya Pradesh.

At the ITC procurement hub, a sample of the farmer's produce is taken and set aside for laboratory tests. A chemist visually inspects the soybean and verifies the assessment of the sanchalak. It is important to note that this is the only test assessment before the sale. Laboratory testing of the sample for oil content is performed after the sale and does not alter the price. The reason for this is that farmers, having historically been exploited, are not immediately willing to trust a laboratory test. Therefore, pricing is based solely upon tests that can be understood by the farmer. The farmer accepts foreign matter deductions for the presence of stones or hay, based upon the visual comparison of his produce with his neighbours. He will accept moisture content deductions based upon the comparative softness of his produce when he bites it.

ITC is working to change farmer attitudes towards laboratory testing. It is developing an appreciation of better quality by using the subsequent lab tests to reward farmers with bonus points, if their quality exceeds the norm. At the end of the year, farmers can redeem their accumulated bonus points through the e-Choupal for farm inputs, or contributions towards insurance premiums.

After the inspection, the farmer's cart is weighed on an electronic weighbridge, first with the produce and then without. The difference is used to determine the weight of his produce.

Hub Logistics

After the inspection and weighing are complete, the farmer then collects his payment in full at the payment counter. The farmer is also reimbursed for transporting his crop to the procurement hub. Every stage of the process is accompanied by appropriate documentation. The farmer is given a copy of lab reports, agreed rates, and receipts for his records.

The samyojaks, who are adept at handling large amounts of cash, are entrusted with the responsibility of payment, except at procurement centres near large ITC operations where ITC looks after cash disbursement. Samyojaks also handle much of the procurement hub logistics, including labour management at the hub, bagging (if necessary), storage management, transportation from the hub to processing factories, and handling mandi paperwork for the crops procured at the hub. For his services in the procurement process, the samyojak is paid a 0.5% commission.

Farmer Gains

Prior to the introduction of e-Choupal, farmers' access to agricultural information was incomplete or inconsistent. The only sources of information, were word of mouth within the village and the commission agent. e-Choupal allows farmers daily access to prices at several nearby mandis. Some e-Choupal sanchalaks have taken this a level further by accessing external pricing sources such as prices on the Chicago Board of Trade, in order to track global trends and determine the optimum timing of sales. Moreover, through e-Choupal, farmers have access to prices and make the critical decision of when and where to sell his crop. Both factors work together to provide the farmers a better price for their crops.

Under the ITC's system, farmers no longer bear the cost of transporting their crops to the mandi and are instead reimbursed for transport to the procurement hub. The transaction at the ITC hub is also much faster than at the mandi, usually taking no more than two or three hours. Moreover,

Contd...

ITC's electronic weighing scales are accurate and not susceptible to sleight of hand like the manual weighing system at the mandi. The system also does not require produce to be bagged, which avoids the associated loss of produce by intentional spillage. Thus the e-Choupal system has logistical and transaction efficiencies. Finally, the ITC procurement centre is a professionally run operation, where the farmer is treated with respect and served as a customer. The dignity accorded to the farmers by the professional process of the e-Choupal cannot be understated. ITC's recognition that farmers are not simply agricultural producers, but integral partners in the supply process has elevated the level of respect paid to them. Simple provisions, such as a shaded seating area where farmers can sit while waiting for their paperwork, serve as indicators of ITC's respect for farmers and their produce. Though intangible, the self-confidence created by this professional treatment is affecting the way farmers conduct themselves. Sanchalaks and even commission agents have noted a change in their attitudes.

The incremental income from a more efficient marketing process is about US$6 per tonne, or an increase of about 2.5% over the mandi system. Farmers also can make use of the information available to them through e-Choupal to improve yields. Moreover, the seed, fertilizer, and consumer products offered to them through e-Choupal cost substantially less than through other local sources such as village traders. Thus, there are meaningful net economic benefits to the farmers, and it is having a measurable impact on what farmers choose to do: In areas covered by e-Choupals, the percentage of farmers planting soy has increased dramatically, from 50 to 90% in some regions, while the volume of soy marketed through mandis has dropped by as much as 50%.

ITC Gains

The commissions paid to the agents under the mandi system were not excessive, but because of the inefficiencies discussed earlier, the true cost of intermediation through the mandi system was between 2.5 and 3% of the procurement costs. While the retaining commissions paid for the sanchalaks' services, the 0.5% commission is significantly less than the costs associated with the mandi system. Direct reimbursement of transport costs to the farmer is estimated to be half of what ITC used to pay the commission agents for transport to their factory. Removal of intermediary manipulation of quality and the ability to directly educate and reward quality in the customer base, results in higher levels of quality in e-Choupal procurement. This results in higher oil yields, which, in turn, leads to higher profits for ITC.

e-Choupal also allows ITC to develop long-term supplier relationships with farmers and attains some degree of supply security over time. Risk is also managed in the e-Choupal system by a far stronger information infrastructure. Sanchalaks and samyojaks working on behalf of ITC, provide excellent bottom-up information on pricing, product quality, soil conditions, and expected yields. This allows ITC to better plan the future operations.

In the mandi system, there was a mark up of 7-8% on the price of soybean from the farm gate to the factory gate. Of this mark up, 2.5% was borne by the farmer while 5% was borne by ITC. With e-Choupal, ITC's costs are now down to 2.5 in absolute numbers, both the farmers and ITC save about US$6 (Rs. 270) per metric tonne.

Sustaining Commercial Volume

"Virtual vertical integration" can only work if there is a continuous flow of information between the e-Choupals and ITC. Because of the number and physical dispersion of the e-Choupals,

Contd...

this communication must be initiated by the sanchalaks. If their motivation to communicate with ITC diminishes, the channel will still function for procurement, but will lack the vitality to supply risk management, distribution, or product design. Maintaining continuous commercial flow keeps the sanchalak motivated to spend time and money, calling the ITC representative to ask about new products, convey village demand, and providing ITC with local updates. An example of the power of local information was seen early during the e-Choupal implementation period. A competitor attempted to divert the produce coming to the ITC factories by stationing representatives on the roads leading up to the plant. This person would stop the farmers on their way to the ITC hub and offer them a price higher than the ITC rate, at the competitor's plant. Farmers alerted the sanchalaks and they in turn provided ITC with the information necessary to address the situation. Sanchalaks thus, play an essential role in the chain of communication.

ITC maintains commercial volumes by sequencing procurement and sales year-round, thereby securing the continuous flow of commission checks through e-Choupals. Purchases and sales have been arranged so that kharif (the cropping season that coincides with India's monsoon, July through October) and rabi (winter cropping season in irrigated areas) inputs and procurement maintain a steady stream of revenue for sanchalaks.

Scaling the Model

Profitable re-engineering requires the unambiguous understanding of value provided, the circumstances in which they are applicable, and the revenues they are capable of generating. ITC's model identifies three sources of value for the company that can help scale the model:

- **Crop Specific Intervention**. ITC recognized that agrarian systems vary by crop. This means that the inefficiencies in the supply chain, the correction required from e-Choupal, and the magnitude and timing of the resulting revenues will differ by crop. For example, the systems, and consequently the e-Choupal models and payback streams, for coffee and shrimp are very different from those for soy. ITC's goals for soy intervention reflected this nuanced analysis and the project was targeted with recovering the entire cost of infrastructure from procurement savings. This is contrasted with the coffee and shrimp efforts, where the source of e-Choupal value is such, that the investment recovery horizon is much longer.
- **Low-Cost Last Mile.** The same system of physical and information exchange that brings produce from the village can be used to transfer goods to the villages. As infrastructure has already been paid for by procurement, it is available at marginal cost for distribution. This ties nicely with ITC's larger goal of transformation into a distribution super-highway. ITC's current channels reach areas with population of 5,000 and above. e-Choupals allow penetration into areas with population less than 5,000. Products such as herbicides, seeds, fertilizers, and insurance policies, as well as soil testing services are sold through e-Choupal. e-Choupal as a distribution channel begins in agriculture but extends well into consumer goods and services. In the traditional channel, comprising of mobile traders and cycle-based distributors, farmers lack the resources to make informed purchasing decisions. More often, than not, traders and distributors do not understand farmers' issues and end up selling them products and services that do not satisfy their needs. With many large companies hesitating to serve the rural market, farmers often do not have variety in their choice of products and services. This lack of choice means, not only are the farmers forced to buy whatever is available, but also very often, must pay a premium for those products.

Contd...

- **Intelligent First-Mile**. The global resources, best practices, and remunerations that the e-Choupal brings to the farmers have encouraged innovation and provided an avenue to see their ideas realized. This illustrates, ITC's vision of using e-Choupal as the "intelligent first mile." Farmers are now coming up with products and services that ITC could provide to further improve operations. Farmers are demanding that ITC certify and make available the "Samrat" variety of seeds that is preferred over the currently certified JS300 variety. Some farmers have urged ITC to bring its resources to bear on onion and potato crops. Responding to the fact, that the Indian onion crop is regarded as inferior to the Chinese crop in the world market, farmers recognize that this is due to the lack of availability of high quality seeds and information. They have approached ITC with a suggestion to create e-Choupals for these crops, pointing to the mutual profitability of such an effort.

ITC's objective is not to be a platform provider for sale of third-party products and services, but rather a network choreographer, who orchestrates bi-directional demand and supply of goods through a collaborative business model. ITC intends to differentiate itself by serving only those products and services to which it can add value. ITC's core asset is its knowledge of the customer. By transforming the value chain and setting up a platform for procuring commodities from them directly, they now have a foundation for forging a close relationship with the farmers. This relationship leads to a better understanding of the issues plaguing the farmers. Through e-Choupals, hubs, and processing centres, ITC has the ready infrastructure needed to implement an alternative channel for distribution of goods and services to rural India. e-Choupals can double as storefronts and hubs as centres for stocking inventory. In the long-term, ITC sees vast opportunities from its e-commerce platform and low-cost distribution system. Company officials have expressed the ambition to become "the Wal-Mart of India," and ITC chairman Y.C. Deveshwar told the media recently that "The e-Choupal network will serve area where nearly 70% of the country's population resides, (including) villages with populations of less than 5,000 people, where most businesses never venture."

In addition, the information infrastructure implemented by ITC can be used to enhance its business decision-making, better risk management, and identify opportunities for cross-selling and up-selling. The company can leverage detailed transactional data and transform it into actionable knowledge. Data mining and data warehousing will help the company executives to better understand the behaviour of their customers, identify unfulfilled needs and ways to serve them efficiently. The communication infrastructure compensates for the lack of physical infrastructure needed for marketing products and services in rural India. It enables rapid, low-cost information dissemination and a trusted brand for introducing new products, while minimizing the need for a travelling sales force. Online ordering and order management eliminate the need for physical storefronts. And the IT infrastructure and local sanchalak provide customer intelligence, thus maximizing customer satisfaction and profitability.

Additional Services: Credit and Insurance

Farmers' low income and difficulty in accessing credit severely limits their capacity to pursue opportunities within and outside the agriculture sector. Access to credit has long been considered a major poverty alleviation strategy in India. Demand for rural credit is estimated at US$31.6 billion (Rs. 1.43 trillion). The Indian government has implemented a number of subsidized credit-related programs. Among such programs, the Integrated Rural Development Program (IRDP), started in 1978, was a major national rural poverty alleviation program with a large credit component. Under the IRDP, nearly 53 million families were assisted with bank credit of

Contd...

US$684 million (Rs. 31 billion) and subsidy of US$231 million (Rs. 10.5 billion). But its impact had not matched the resources expended. The loans were not tailored to meet individual needs and it lacked the support systems necessary to help the farmers.

Many financial institutions are hesitant to serve rural India due to lack of credit history, high delivery, transaction and administration costs, and a perception of high risk that leads to high borrowing costs imposed on farmers.

ITC proposes to address these problems through e Choupals and through partnerships with financial institutions to capture the needed information and offer new products:

- **Capturing Credit History:** Farmers in rural India borrow money from local moneylenders, through government incentives, friends, relatives, or traders. Local moneylenders and intermediates are aware of farmers' creditworthiness and are therefore willing to loan money, albeit at a high interest rate. Through e-Choupal, ITC now has the capability to manage credit risk through its sanchalak network, which can be used not only to verify creditworthiness of individual farmers but also to continuously monitor credit risk. ITC will be able to create a consolidated farmers' database with information pertaining to their holdings and transactions that can be used as a source of credit report profiles.
- **Transaction and Administration Costs:** For major financial institutions, transaction costs involved in servicing the rural market have been high, because of the difficulty in reaching the market. e-Choupal can help overcome this problem by leveraging the IT infrastructure and the sanchalak network, thereby lowering the administrative costs.

ITC plans to partner with larger banks such as ICICI to design products for rural India. Some of the products being designed include:

- **Non-cash loans for farm inputs:** Instead of giving cash to the farmer directly, the financial institutions will purchase farm inputs on behalf of the farmer. Farmers are expected to pay back loans for the purchase price, to the financial institution.
- **Loans to sanchalaks:** Instead of giving loans directly to farmers, loans will be given to sanchalaks who, in turn, will loan money to farmers. Sanchalaks can manage credit risk better than a financial institution because they have better access to the farmer, and therefore, have more accurate information.
- **Direct loans to farmers based on sanchalak recommendations:** In this case, sanchalaks' commissions are based on the loan recovery and therefore, they have enough incentive to monitor the risk on a continuous basis.
- **Insurance and Risk Management Services:** Insurance products have been designed to deal with rural cash-cycles. There is recognition that in bad years, farmers may not be able to pay the insurance premium. Rather than penalize the farmer with his policy, ITC allows for catch-up payments in later years or, as an alternative, the reduction of the final payout. ITC uses the e-Choupal Web infrastructure to set up and issue electronic reminders for premium payments. This addresses a major weakness of the current insurance system. The agents currently selling insurance have little incentive to encourage renewals and the lapse rate among the policies is high. A system of interlocking instruments has been set up so that insurance premiums can be credited with quality bonus points from the farmer's soy sale. The sanchalak is assisted in making the sales pitch by informational Web-casts and video presentations.

Contd...

TECHNOLOGY

Characteristics of the Operating Environment

Understanding the constraints imposed by the physical and social environment in e-Choupals operate is necessary to provide the context for understanding the system design.

Overcoming Power Constraints

Power availability in rural India is unreliable and the quality of power is sub-standard. As power is usually available for only a few hours a day and at a sporadic schedule, the e-Choupal computer cannot always be accessed, when information is needed. Access to information in a timely manner is critical to the success of the business model. ITC has overcome the problem of local power supply by providing a battery-based UPS (Uninterrupted Power Supply) backup. With the reliability of a battery backup, the sanchalak can use the system at least twice a day—in the morning to check the prevailing mandi prices, and again in the evening to check the rate ITC is offering the next day. While the battery backup addresses the power supply issue, insufficient line power during the day poses the challenge of not having enough power to charge the backup battery. This has caused ITC to explore other power sources and ultimately ITC decided to use solar battery chargers. One full day of sunlight is enough to charge the battery for 70 to 80 minutes of computer usage.

The second problem with power is quality. Voltage fluctuations are endemic. The UPS unit is the most affected component. As a result of the erratic power supply, fuses are susceptible to being blown. To overcome this problem, ITC plans to install specially designed UPS units that remain effective between 90V and 300V. In order to control voltage spikes, they have introduced spike suppressors and filters. Phase imbalances, which lead to damage of equipment, have been addressed through the use of isolation transformers to correct neutral voltages.

Transportation

Most e-Choupal villages lack proper roads, limiting vehicle access. As such, public transportation access to many of the villages is infrequent. Some villages are served only once or twice a day by rural taxis. The population relies on two-wheeled bicycles and motorbikes and bullock carts as the main means of transportation. Moving equipment into and out of the villages is not an easy task. Providing system support and maintenance requires the technician to travel from outside areas to visit the e-Choupal. For these, and other reasons ITC initially placed e-Choupals in villages, that are within 10 to 15 kilometers radius of a city.

Telecom Infrastructure

The telecommunication infrastructure in villages is poor. Telephone exchanges are subject to sporadic power supply and have limited battery backup. When power is lost, phones cease to function. In addition, there is no local support staff to maintain or troubleshoot problems at telephone exchanges. The support team at the main exchange typically is responsible for eight to ten villages and is short-staffed. The turn-around time for fixing problems is often measured in days, not hours. Overhead telephone lines are exposed to the elements and run alongside high voltage power lines which can cause transmission quality problems. Currently, village telecommunication infrastructure is designed to carry voice traffic only and the transmission speed is so slow, that it renders Internet access impractical.

Contd...

Customer Base

Before the arrival of e-Choupal, most villagers had never seen a computer. ITC realized the importance of appropriate user interfaces. They organized meetings and focus, groups of farmers to gather information about potential user groups. The main focus of these meetings was to determine, what information farmers wanted to see? how the information would need to be presented (graphics or text)? And how often each page would need to be refreshed? The feedback that was collected from these focus groups was used in the design of the functionality and user interface of the application.

System Specification

The IT infrastructure can be comprehensively understood in the following four layers:

1. Organization Architecture – Training, support, planning, people, and processes
2. Information Architecture – Data gathered and managed
3. Application Architecture – Applications, goals, resources occupied, performance metrics
4. Technical Architecture – Servers, Clients, Network, System Software

The four layers are distinct but deeply interconnected and share goals and constrains.

Technical Architecture

From dial-up to VSAT: Connectivity Evolution in e-Choupals: ITC realized very early that the existing telecom infrastructure was not capable of supporting data traffic. Working with C-DoT (Center for Development of Telematics), they determined, that lack of synchronization between the village exchange and the main exchange was a major issue. C-DoT proposed the installation of RNS kits in the village exchanges. Even after the installation of RNS kits, however, the data throughput was a mere 12 Kbps. This is not sufficient to support their application requirements. With the help of C-DoT, ITC made modifications to the RNS kit, which helped them to achieve 40 Kbps throughput.

Despite achieving a significant improvement in the throughput rate, sporadic power supply in the village exchanges meant that the dial-up solution was not reliable. Even if the e-Choupal had power, the telephone exchange might not, thereby, rendering the system inoperable.

As the e-Choupal model progressed, ITC realized that dial-up connectivity is not sufficient to drive proposed future applications. In order to support transactional capabilities and multimedia applications, the company needed reliable connectivity with better throughput. They therefore, have decided to adopt a satellite-based technology (VSAT) which enables a throughput rate of upto 256 Kbps. This is, however, an expensive solution, costing about US$2,650 (Rs. 120,000) per installation.

Technical Equipment

Hardware:

Power: Solar battery charger, UPS (isolation transformer, spike suppressor)

Connectivity: Dial-up: Dial-up modem

VSAT: Solar battery charger, VSAT modem, antennae

Computer Hardware: PC with Intel Celeron processor, printer

Contd...

Software:

Operating System: Windows 98

Word processor: Ankur (Hindi word processor)

Other: Sunera Kal – Short movie on e-Choupal

Video Clips – Soil testing

Application Architecture

The application layer represents the logical muscle that rests atop the skeleton of technical infrastructure. Understanding the application architecture gives us a view of the functions enhanced by information technology and also illustrates, how business processes may be adapted to deal with constraints upon the IT infrastructure.

The Website www.soyachoupal.com is the gateway for the farmer. The Website is protected and requires a user ID and password to login. As of now, sanchalaks are the only registered users. Immediately after recruitment, an account is created for the sanchalak and he is given a user ID and password to access the system.

Features of the e-Choupal Website

Weather: Users can select their district of interest by clicking on the appropriate region of a map. Localized weather information is presented on regions within a 25-kilometer range. Typically 24- to 72-hour weather forecasts are available along with an advisory. Advisories are pieces of information directly related to the farmer-information, he can put to use. For instance, during the sowing season, a weather forecast for days following heavy rains may include an advisory that instructs the farmer to sow seeds while the soil is still wet.

Weather data is obtained from Indian Meteorological Department, which has a presence even in small towns and can provide forecasts for rural areas.

Pricing: The e-Choupal website displays both, the ITC procurement rate and the local mandi rates. ITC's next day rates are published every evening. The prices are displayed prominently on the top of the Web page on a scrolling ticker.

News: For the soy-choupal website, relevant news is presented from various sources. In addition to agriculture related news, this section also includes entertainment, sports, and local news.

Best Practices: Best farming practices are documented by crop. Here again, the information presented is action-based. For instance, this section not only highlights, what kind of fertilizers to use but also how and when to use them.

Q & A: This feature enables two-way communication. Here a farmer can post any agriculture related question he needs to be answered.

The sanchalaks and others who use the system have learned that, now there is a wide variety of information at their fingertips that they can access and benefit from. The following table lists just a few popular Internet destinations.

Other Internet Resources Accessed at the e-Choupal

News

Dainik Jagran, Web Dunia

Contd...

Market Prices

One sanchalak actually followed Chicago Board of Trade (CBOT) prices for a month and arrived at a correlation with the local market prices. He used this information and helped other farmers decide when to sell.

Entertainment

- Movie trivia
- Rent CDs to watch movies on the computer
- Music downloads from the Internet

Sports

Cricket related news

Education

Students use the Internet to check their exam results and grades online

Communication

E-mail

- The *sanchalaks* have e-mail accounts on Yahoo Chat.
- Some *sanchalaks* use chat rooms to chat with other *sanchalaks* and ITC managers.

General interests/Other

Information about cell phones

Information Architecture

The e-Choupal system is designed to gather customer information over time. The sources, structure, management, and use of this data are addressed within the information architecture. The technical details are routine, but the data itself and its potential uses are exciting. Data about the rural customer such as their location, creditworthiness, consumer preferences, financial position, and spending patterns represent the first link between this vast untapped market and urban commerce. Such information will eliminate the "unknowns" of rural engagement and enable planning, marketing, and the sales of a range of products.

The information gathering is currently semi-automated. Information on each sanchalak is gathered during user registration. The sanchalak also keeps a record of farmer visits, inquiries, purchases, etc. The Q & A section of the website allows for two-way transport of data that is stored in a database. The website does not currently process live transactions, but ITC has plans to do so in the future.

The Web database tracks the Internet usage patterns at e-Choupals. From this database, ITC has gathered information such as peak usage periods, preferred Internet destinations, information most sought after, information least sough after etc. ITC intends to leverage the information gathered to help better understanding the behaviour of their customers, identify unfulfilled needs, and develop ways to serve them efficiently.

Contd...

Organizational Architecture

The hardware and software infrastructure captured in the first three layers cannot exist in isolation. They need people, processes, and services to setup, maintain and run them. In the e-Choupal, training system support (repairing technical problems), and application support (usability query resolution) would provide the most unique information.

Training

Training the sanchalaks to use a computer effectively is deemed vital to the success of e-Choupal. The sanchalaks function as the human interface of the e-Choupals and therefore must be able to both, operate the computer and access the information requested by farmers.

The computer installed in the e-Choupals is usually the first computer in most villages. Immediately after sanchalaks are recruited, they are invited to the nearest ITC plant for a day-long training program. The majority of this training is centered around getting the sanchalaks comfortable with the equipment. This first phase of training comprises the following:

- **The fundamentals:** What is a computer? What is its purpose and practical applications?
- **Basic equipment training:** Turning the computer on and off, using the mouse, keyboard, printer etc.
- **Software training:**
  - (a) Word processing:
    - How to use Ankur (Hindi word processor)
    - How to type in Hindi
    - How to open, close, and save files
    - How to create and edit document
  - (b) Web Browsing: How to use a Web browser and find information on the Internet.
  - (c) e-Choupal Applications: How to use the soy-choupal website. What information is available on the website and how can it be accessed?

At the time of installation, a coordinator usually accompanies the vendor, who installs the system. The sanchalak is given some of the same basic training by the vendor. ITC then allows the sanchalak to experiment with the computer for about a week. During this time, typically the younger members of his family also get to use the computer. ITC has observed that children are quick learners and are eager to learn more.

After the first week, the sanchalaks are invited to the hub or the plant for the second phase of the training. In order to gauge their level of comfort, they are asked to operate the computer. Based on observation, customized training is then provided to raise each user's comfort and competency level. Sanchalaks may also bring their children or other members of the family, who are interested in learning about the computer. During this phase sanchalaks are trained to use the e-Choupal website and to access information from the site. Sanchalaks are given the opportunity to voice their concerns and ask questions during the training. Sanchalaks are generally enthusiastic about learning the computer skills required to carry out their work.

Contd...

After a month, trainees are brought in for a third and final phase of initial training. By this time, sanchalaks are usually fairly familiar with operating the computer and accessing information. The goal of this session is to learn to troubleshoot common problems. ITC hopes that improving the troubleshooting capacity of sanchalaks will significantly reduce the maintenance and system support costs. Sanchalaks are taught about the importance of other devices such as the UPS and the battery backup. They are given guidelines on what to look for when there is a problem. For instance, they are instructed regarding the significance of the display lights on the devices. When sanchalaks call for technical help, these details help the support staff identify and resolve problems, perhaps even over the phone, without the necessity of a site visit.

ITC considers training to be a continuous process, and one that requires a concerted effort from all field operatives, not just the support staff. All field operatives are encouraged to provide technology assistance, when they visit e-Choupals. When the local coordinator visits an e-Choupal, he may be required to help with usability issues, even though this is not his primary job.

System Support

ITC has about 15 engineers who provide field infrastructure support to the e-Choupals. Their average is about one or two calls a day. Each e-Choupal is visited about twice a month for infrastructure support. In order to overcome transportation problems, ITC purchased a fleet of approximately 25 motorcycles for its support staff. The support cost is estimated at US$6.60 (Rs. 300) per visit.

A majority of the issues reported are software-related. Users' lack of familiarity with the operating system has led to software issues. For instance, some users inadvertently delete desktop icons and then have to call for help. On other occasions, failures have occurred when users download and install untested or unapproved software.

Another issue encountered by the support staff has been the malfunctioning of the equipment due to voltage fluctuations. About 20-30% of the calls to support staff are related to a blown fuse in UPS units. Sanchalaks have now been provided with replacement fuses and have been trained to change fuses on their own. The vendor provides support for hardware failures.

In the future, ITC proposes to improve service and lower costs of infrastructure support through remote help desk tools and network automation.

THE SOCIAL IMPACT OF e-CHOUPAL

A major impact of the e-Choupal system comes from bridging the information and service gap of rural India. Agricultural research centres (such as the Indian Council for Agricultural Research), universities, and other agencies in India have developed several practices and technologies to improve productivity and crop quality. The impediment to implementation has been affordable, large-scale dissemination of this knowledge. The e-Choupal system leverages technology that can reach a wide audience literally at the click of a mouse. The constant presence of sanchalaks, who themselves are farmers and apply these techniques, ensures that the practices actually make their way from the website to the field. Some areas about which information and services are provided by the e-Choupal website and e-commerce system include:

- **Weather.** This is a very popular section on the website because it provides localized weather information at the district level. Other public sources generally provide only aggregated state-level weather information. e-Choupal's weather information is intelligently

Contd...

coupled with advice on the activities in the agricultural lifecycle. One farmer observed that prior to e-Choupal, unreliable weather information would result in prematurely planted seeds that would be washed out by early rains. The availability of accurate rain information has cut losses due to weather by more than half.

- **Agricultural Best Practices.** Scientific practices organized by crop type are available on the website. Additional questions are answered through FAQs and access to experts who respond to e-mails from the villages.
- **Customized Quality Solutions.** After the sale of a crop is completed, ITC performs laboratory testing of the sample collected. Based on these results, farmers are given customized feedback on how they can improve crop quality and the yield.
- **Intelligent Product Deployment.** Inputs such as fertilizers and pesticides are not generic in their application. The optimal application is relative to the soil and crop. Determining these parameters requires services such as soil testing. Past providers brought inputs but not the information and services required to make them effective. ITC's "full-service" approach corrects this by coupling the input sale to the information on the website and services such as soil testing.

The collective impact of better information and new services can be gauged by the fact that prior to e-Choupal, soy cultivation was on the decline. Productivity was stagnant and farmers saw no future in it. In Khasrod, soy production declined from a high of 100% to 50% of farmers planting soy and was expected to decline further. Since ITC's involvement, soy is seen as profitable again and nearly 90% of farmers are planting the crop.

A second major area of impact stems from the ability of the e-Choupal system to open a window to the world and thus impact the future of the villages in which they operate. Computers are bringing the same resources to villages as they brought to urban India, and their impact is no less dramatic. This, coupled with higher incomes and changes in farmers' attitudes, is causing several shifts in the social fabric of the village life.

Some accounts from villages include:

- Children are using computers for schoolwork and games. A particularly poignant story is that of Khasrod, where 2,000 local students used the local e-Choupal to print their grade sheets, saving them days of waiting and travel time.
- Sanchalaks use the Internet to chat extensively amongst themselves about the status of operations and agriculture in their villages.
- Villagers access global resources to learn about agriculture in other parts of the world and are taking action to compete in the world outside, not merely in the local mandi.
- Youngsters in the village use computers to research on the latest trends, movies, cell-phone models, and cricket news.

Winners and Losers

Not everyone has benefited from the introduction of e-Choupals. Indeed, lost income and jobs are directly connected to the overall increase in efficiency in the e-Choupal system. Some of the players in the mandi system have suffered loss of revenue. They include:

- **Commission agents:** Despite ITC's best efforts to maintain mandi volumes and compensate commission agents for lost income, there is little doubt that on the whole, they have lower incomes as a result of the introduction of e-Choupals.

Contd...

- **Mandi labourers:** The workers in the mandi who weighed and bagged produce have been severely impacted by the drop in volume. In the Sonkach mandi, for example, some 28 tulavatis and 300 labourers have been affected. ITC's long-term vision is to employ many of these people in the hubs in much the same functions as they perform in the mandi.
- **Bazaars near the mandi:** When farmers sold produce in the mandi, they would also make a variety of purchases at local bazaars. This revenue has now been diverted to shops near the ITC hubs. This, however, can be considered a diversion of revenue rather than its elimination.
- **Some mandi operations:** ITC still pays mandi tax for all the crops procured through e-Choupals but it now pays the tax to the mandi nearest to the procurement centre. As a result, taxes are being diverted from several mandis to the few mandis near procurement hubs. Hence, regional mandis have lost taxes that contribute to maintaining their infrastructure.
- **Competing processors:** Even before the advent of the e-Choupal, the soya crushing industry suffered from severe overcapacity (half of all capacity was excess). The efficiency pressures imposed by e-Choupal has spurred industry consolidation.

CHALLENGES

The e-Choupal system faces multiple continuing challenges. The first is the possibility that radical shifts in computing access could fundamentally alter community-based business models. That is one of the reasons, ITC seeks to build and control its own infrastructure. Second, as the number and power of the sanchalaks increase, there is a threat that they will unionize and extract "rents" – unwarranted additional payments based on their increasing influence on the system. Third, ITC's relationship with the samyojaks seems to be uneasy, and competitors with the financial muscle to invest for scale could conceivably use discontented sanyojaks as the base to obtain market share. Fourth, the scope of the e-Choupal operation, the diversity of activities required of every operative, and the speed of expansion create real threats to execution management.

ITC has awakened the aspirations of the farmers. If ITC fails to fulfil these aspirations, the farmers will look elsewhere for satisfaction. As an example, in our conversation with a sanchalak about the potential for Indian onions to succeed in the global market, he also understood what the key to success was – better seeds. He complained that he had told ITC, several times to begin selling better onion seeds, but to no avail. In a competitive environment, ITC would have to provide faster and more responsive customer service to maintain its distribution system.

The computer in the village is no doubt revolutionary, but there is also no doubt that the villages we saw were stratified to the point, where not everybody can walk up to the sanchalak and ask to be shown the computer. There are clearly some segments of the village society, including the entire adult female population that does not have access to the computer—although this may not be true in all regions. The presence of the computer by itself will not transcend this barrier unaided. This is not a reflection on ITC, but rather the nature of the society in rural Madhya Pradesh. The solution might lie in observing, where the system has driven social change. Village farmers belong to different social and economic strata. Yet the sanchalaks are servicing all of them equally. In this case, the potential for commerce has broken a barrier that society has built. Similarly, engagement with poorer segments of the society and women may be possible through the active distribution of products tailored

Contd...

specifically their needs.

STRATEGY FOR THE FUTURE

ITC recognizes the limitations of today's e-Choupals as a vehicle of procurement efficiency. Not every crop lends itself to such an intervention. In crops such as soy, where value can be maximized, followers will soon imitate ITC and eliminate the company's competitive advantage. ITC's vision for e-Choupal extends many generations, as e-Choupal evolves into a full-fledged orchestrator of a two-way exchange of goods and services between rural India and the world. The soy e-Choupal is "Wave I," with several more to follow.

- **Wave 2:** The source of value in this generation will be identity preservation through the chain. This is a significant source of value in crops such as wheat, where the grade of the grain determines its end use. The ability to separate different grades from field to consumer will command a price premium. e-Choupals in Uttar Pradesh have already started wheat procurement.
- **Wave 3:** This wave takes identity a step further by building the concept of traceability into the supply chain. This is vital for perishables, where traceability will allow ITC to address food safety concerns and once again provide a value that the customer is willing to pay for. Shrimp is a good example of a crop for which Wave 3 will be important. ITC's intervention in such products will occur at the production level. ITC will define standards that producers must adhere to and work with farmers to ensure product quality. Farmers in turn, will get the best price from ITC because ITC commands the traceability premium.
- **Wave 4:** The first three waves fill institutional voids while, Wave 4 creates institutions. The first three waves apply to environments in which ITC is the sole buyer in the e-Choupal channel. In commodities, where the underlying markets have reached a high degree of efficiency, such basic sources of value will not exist. In crops such as these, e-Choupal will serve as the market place, where multiple buyers and sellers execute a range of transactions. A good example of this is coffee. ITC's source of value will be the ruined cost of the IT infrastructure and the transaction fees.
- **Wave 5:** While the first four waves are related to sourcing from rural India, the fifth wave elaborates the rural marketing and distribution strategy. This is not the same as the rudimentary distribution of agri-inputs that is being done today. ITC plans to bring together knowledge of the customer, knowledge of the business, deployed infrastructure, its reputation, and experience gained over the first four waves, with an organization of people, processes, and partners. This base will allow ITC to bring value-added products and services to rural India.
- **Wave 6:** After the sourcing of goods from rural India, ITC's last wave has the ambitious vision of eventually sourcing IT-enabled services from rural India. Telemedicine, eco-tourism, traditional medicine, and traditional crafts are some of the services that can be sourced from rural India. While still a long way off, it is an agenda that inspires scale of the vision and potential impact on development in rural India.

SUMMARY

The e-Choupal model shows that a large corporation can combine a social mission and an ambitious commercial venture; that it can play a major role in rationalizing markets and increasing the efficiency of an agricultural system, and do so in ways that benefit the farmers and the rural communities as well as company shareholders. ITC's example also shows the key

Contd...

role of information technology—in this case provided and maintained by a corporation, but used by local farmers—in helping to bring about transparency, to increase access to information, and to catalyze rural transformation, while enabling efficiencies and low-cost distribution that make the system profitable and sustainable. Critical factors in the apparent success of this venture are ITC's extensive knowledge of agriculture, the effort ITC has made to retain many aspects of the existing production system, including the retaining of the integral importance of local partners, the company's commitment to transparency, and the respect and fairness with which both farmers and the local partners are treated.

QUESTION

1. Analyse various aspects of this case (e.g. What factors helped ITC in developing this concept?)

Case 8.8: Wall-Mart

In 1980s, Wall-Mart heavily invested in the IT Sector. Early in the year, the company began using Electronic Data Interchange (EDI) systems and linked stores and distribution centres through computers. This helped the company to keep track of goods movement in real-time and quickly replenish stocks at the stores. This also minimised incidence of out-of-stock situations and helped better management of the inventory. It eliminated the inconvenience to customers resulting from non-availability of products.

In 1987, Wal-Mart installed a satellite communication system that linked stores, distribution, and suppliers' systems and completely automated the entire distribution process of the company. The system also linked all the company stores to the General Office a two-way voice and data communication, and one-way video communication. It was in 1980s, that Wal-Mart management thought of using IT to get more customer-related information appreciating the rapid pace of the firm's expansion and the difficulties of keeping track of diverse needs of millions of customers. The buying habits, needs, and preferences differed in different areas. Products that were popular and high in demand in one outlet were not as hot in other stores. Wal-Mart started investing n-data warehousing systems located at its headquarters at Bentonville, Arkansas. The company gathered sales and customer-related information serviced by each store. To gain better insights into the needs, preferences, and purchase behaviour of consumers, the company used data mining tools that could be used to analyse gathered information related to products being sold at each store level, consumers' demographic and ethnic profiles in the store vicinity, and their frequency of purchases of each product and accordingly replenishment etc.

Experts at Wal-Mart used 3-D visualisation tools to make accurate estimates of products that were most likely to be bought by consumers depending on various aspects of their profiles, locations, events, weather conditions etc., considering around 10,000 parameters. This helped Wal-Mart replenish its 90% stocks every month.

To help customers and make their shopping experience pleasant, in 1996 the firm installed 2 to 5 information kiosks in each store, from where customers could access information. A customer could find out the price of any product, its brief description and locate availability of any item, which was not available in a particular store. Wal-Mart introduced a hand-held product locator device called 960. A store employee would assist the customer by entering the item number in 960. The 960 would indicate the nearest Wal-Mart store in a radius of 30 – 40 miles that had the product, store location, its telephone number, and the number of units available. If a customer needed something urgently, the employee would arrange that the product were brought to the store, where the customer was at that point of time. This service was highly admired by its customers.

Wal-Mart launched its website in 1996 – www.walmart.com- to make information accessible to the customers on all the products the company stocked and to enable its customers to make online purchases. The site had many user-friendly features, and for prompt delivery of the purchased items, Wal-Mart tied with Fingerhut, a US based direct marketing company.

Wal-Mart website had advanced features to ensure credit card security online. The site was also connected to a call centre, through which customers could place their queries and grievances. Customers registered at Wal-Mart site were kept informed of different in-store

Contd...

sales promotions and events in their nearest store. The website also has other customer service tools that enable customers to record a package lost in mail and then, Wal-Mart would send the required product to the customer.

In March 2003, Fortune magazine ranked Wal-Mart as the largest company in the world and America's most admired business house.

QUESTIONS

1. Explain how thc use of modern IT has helped Wal-Mart in delivering more in customer service.

2. Visit the Wal-Mart website and prepare a presentation highlighting different Internet aided services for the customers.

Index